THE
COMPLETE
BOOK OF
EMIGRANTS
IN
BONDAGE

1614-1775

Peter Wilson Coldham

GENEALOGICAL PUBLISHING CO., INC.
Baltimore 1988

The two previous editions of this work were published under
different titles, first, *English Convicts in Colonial America*, 2 vols.
[vol. 1, Middlesex; vol. 2, London] (New Orleans: Polyanthos,
Inc., 1974-76); second, *Bonded Passengers to America*, 9 vols. in 3
(Baltimore: Genealogical Publishing Co., Inc, 1983). The 1983
edition incorporated the two volumes of 1974 and 1976 for
Middlesex and London, added records from the Assize and
Palatinate courts for the rest of the counties of England, and was
introduced by a history of transportation. Omitting the history, this
present edition—in one volume—incorporates the previous
records, adds new records of the Courts of Quarter Session, and
integrates all the records into a single alphabetical sequence.

CONTENTS

INTRODUCTION

Between 1614 and 1775 some 50,000 Englishmen were sentenced by legal process to be transported to the American colonies. With notably few exceptions their names and the record of their trial have survived in public records together with much other information which enables us to plot the story of their unhappy and unwilling passage to America. These records are now combined and condensed in this volume to form the largest single collection of transatlantic passenger lists to be found during the earliest period of emigration.

The bitterness and controversy aroused amongst certain American scholars when the nature and scale of convict transportation to the colonies were first hinted at have been forced to yield to the weight of documentary evidence accumulated mainly during the post-war years. Marion and Jack Kaminkow were the first to publish extensive lists of transported felons taken from British Treasury records, and it was that work which encouraged me to undertake further research to determine the existence and location of other records in this area.[1] The scale on which transportation was regularly practised became clear as the annals of the Old Bailey were slowly unravelled and matched against the Treasury papers unearthed by the Kaminkows. The first fruits of this labour were published in *English Convicts in Colonial America*, Volume I (1974) covering Middlesex, and Volume II (1976) London.[2] In order to present a more comprehensive account, the records of the Assize and Palatinate courts covering all the counties of England were then studied one by one and a further series of volumes incorporating Vols. I and II of *English Convicts in Colonial America* was then published as *Bonded Passengers to America* (Baltimore: Genealogical Publishing Co., Inc., 1983). Bound in three volumes, it also included a history of transportation from 1615 to 1775. There remained to be examined, however, the scattered records of over fifty Courts of Quarter Session each having the power to impose sentences of transportation, and that work, which has now been largely accomplished, is included in this one comprehensive volume. To facilitate reference to what has grown into a publication of substantial proportions, the former arrangement by county has been dropped in favour of a completely alphabetical listing.

The notes and appendices which follow are intended to summarise the history of English criminal transportation and the nature and location of source material used in compiling this book. However, in view of the volume and diversity of the sources used, any who seek more detailed notes and references are advised to consult those which prefaced volumes in the original series of *Bonded Passengers to America*.

The idea of swelling the numbers of colonial labourers by emptying the gaols of England was almost as old as the founding of the colonies themselves and, indeed, Virginia was first recommended in 1606 as "a place where idle vagrants might be sent." [3] The first official record of such practice is found in 1618 in the archives of the London Bridewell (an institution set up for the care of vagrant and orphaned children) when several of its wards were set aside to be sent to Virginia. In 1611 Governor Dale of Virginia invited King James I "to banish hither all offenders condemned to die out of common gaoles," [4] and only three years later the Privy Council made the first order empowering themselves to reprieve prisoners from capital punishment in order "to yeald a profitable service . . . in partes abroad." [5] During the next few years not only were the gaols regularly cleared by the Virginia Company but the Bridewell was again pressed into service, being required to furnish 100 children for Virginia in 1619 and again in 1620 in order "to redeem so many poor souls from misery and ruin and putting them in a condition of use and service to the State." [6]

This forcible emigration system appears to have fallen into decline by the 1630s and was soon put out of mind with the onset of the English Civil War. The reforming Parliament, which took control of the nation's affairs in 1649, quickly found a use for the old methods, however. Having first disposed of several thousand defeated Royalists by sending them to New England, Virginia, and the sugar colonies, Parliament revived and reinforced the earlier provisions for disposing of unwanted felons. In 1655 a formal system was introduced for pardoning convicted felons on condition of their transportation; and in 1657 an Act was passed enabling Justices of the Peace to transport idle vagrants. These arrangements, in turn, were taken over and further developed after the restoration of the monarchy in 1660. Between then and 1717 pardons on condition of transportation were issued regularly each year (see Appendix I).

Such modest measures were perceived as inadequate by 1717. In the aftermath of the Scottish uprising of 1715 many of the "rebels" were crowded into inadequate prisons before being shipped off to the colonies, and this served only to throw into high relief the problem of increasing gaol populations at a time when over 200 offences were on the statute books which merited the death penalty. Early in 1718 a new Act was introduced which, for the first time, gave the Assize Courts the power to impose a sentence of transportation for a vast range of crimes ranging from petty larceny to bigamy. [7] This measure, and the continuation of pre-existing arrangements for the issue of Royal pardons, at least achieved one humanitarian result for, in proportion to the large number of death sentences actually handed down in the English courts, relatively few were ever carried out.

The scheme introduced in 1718 was, administratively, a great success. Justices in London and in each county were appointed to contract with merchants and ships' captains to arrange the shipment to Virginia or

Maryland of convicted felons and to guarantee their safe delivery. Most such contracts required the ship's captain to obtain a certificate of landing from the customs officer at the port of disembarcation, but the only surviving series covers the period from 1718 to 1736 in respect of London and the Home Counties only. London and Middlesex provided well over half of all transported felons, all of them housed in the infamous Newgate Prison before being embarked at St. Katherine's Dock in one or other of the ships which regularly plied this or the black slave trade to the southern colonies. Such ships were specially equipped to provide the maximum secure accommodation and attracted crews who were well drilled in dealing with potentially dangerous passengers.

Such a large and specialised business as convict transportation became the exclusive province of those who were equipped and organised to run it. From 1718 to 1742 the "Contractor for the Transports" for London, Middlesex, and much of the country beyond, was Jonathan Forward, a prosperous tobacco merchant and a man well connected in the criminal fraternity. He was succeeded by one of his associates, Andrew Reid, against whom it was alleged that "every species of complaint was made."[8] Reid held the post until 1763 when he was replaced by John Stewart who died in 1771. After that date no single contractor was appointed and merchants competed for contracts to transport felons at their own expense. There is little doubt that the business, though risky, could be immensely profitable, and accounts survive showing that a shipload of felons, if delivered "well-conditioned," could be auctioned for £10 to £20 each, or the equivalent in tobacco to be carried back to England in the same ships.

The outbreak of the Revolutionary War in 1775 brought to an end a trade in human cargoes which had been plied successfully and profitably for well over 150 years, and it was not until 1787 that the transportation of convicts from English gaols was re-started, this time to the Australian colonies.

The Organisation and Records of the Judicial System

To understand the way in which the English criminal courts were organised, and therefore the location and use of source documents, it is necessary to distinguish clearly between Courts of Quarter Session and Courts of Assize.

Each English county and each borough (usually a large city) convened Quarter Sessions whose business was divided between civil administration (e.g. taxes and licences) and its judicial function. These Sessions could try both civil cases (e.g. disputes over debts) and criminal prosecutions which were considered to be of relatively minor importance. More serious offences (usually those attracting the death penalty) were referred to the Assize Courts for trial. There is, however, no hard and fast distinction which can be made as to their jurisdiction.

The Assize Courts, responsible for trying the more important criminal cases arising outside the City of London and the County of Middlesex, were presided over by judges appointed by the Crown who, travelling in circuit, visited each part of the country regularly, usually twice a year. The circuits were divided as follows:

Home Circuit: Essex, Hertfordshire, Kent, Surrey, Sussex

Western Circuit: Cornwall, Devon, Dorset, Hampshire, Somerset, Wiltshire

Oxford Circuit: Berkshire, Gloucestershire, Herefordshire, Monmouthshire, Oxfordshire, Shropshire, Staffordshire, Worcestershire

Norfolk Circuit: Bedfordshire, Buckinghamshire, Cambridgeshire, Huntingdonshire, Norfolk, Suffolk

Northern Circuit: Cumberland, Northumberland, Westmorland, Yorkshire

Midland Circuit: Derbyshire, Leicestershire, Lincolnshire, Northamptonshire, Nottinghamshire, Rutland, Warwickshire

In addition, the Palatinate counties of Chester, Durham, and Lancaster, which had autonomous jurisdiction, each maintained records of criminal trials very similar in form and content to those of the Assize Courts.

All Assize and Palatinate Court records are held at the Public Record Office, Chancery Lane, London WC2A 1LR. Quarter Sessions records are invariably held at the County Record Office of the county concerned.

This leaves the City of London and the County of Middlesex unaccounted for. Each maintained its own courts of Quarter Session and, for more serious criminal cases, Sessions of Gaol Delivery. *The records for London will be found at the Corporation of London Records Office, Guildhall, London EC2P 2EJ; and those for Middlesex at the Greater London Records Office, 40 Northampton Row, London EC1 0AB.* Also included in this book, but without reference to county of origin which the original records fail to provide, are the names of those prisoners sentenced to transportation in 1685 after Monmouth's unsuccessful rebellion.

Complementary Records

The British Treasury, which financed the despatch to the New World of London, Middlesex, and Home Counties felons ordered for transportation, maintained meticulous records to justify its expenditures. Almost all of the 180 or so convict ships sent to America between 1716 and 1775 are listed in Treasury documents, many of them complete with the names of passengers (see Appendix II). A voluminous correspondence was conducted between Assize judges, clerks of Assize, and the central bureaucracy in London which often duplicated and amplified the Assize records themselves. Most of this correspondence is preserved in the State

Papers. In addition, many contracts for the transportation of felons, gaolers' accounts, bonds, and lists relating to transportation are to be found in County Record Offices. Further information about most of the felons sentenced to transportation in London and Middlesex may be found in the printed series of *Old Bailey Sessions Papers*, copies of which are held in the London Guildhall Library and in the British Library at Bloomsbury.

A summary list of references to Public Record Office documents used in the compilation of this volume will be found in Appendix I (pardons issued up to 1717), Appendix II (shipping and passenger lists), and Appendix III (Assize Court records).

Arrangement of this Book

It will be appreciated that the lists presented in this volume are very highly condensed from original records and are intended principally to show the researcher where to look for further information. Each entry is therefore constructed as follows:

a) Surname and Christian name(s) with aliases where given in original documents.

b) Parish of origin. (Where none is shown the original bills of indictment should be consulted.)

c) Occupation or status. (Most often shown as "labourer" in original documents and therefore not transcribed.)

d) Sentencing court, offence, and month and year of sentence.

e) Month, year, and ship (if known) on which transported.

f) Place, month, and year (if known) landed in America.

g) English county in which sentenced.

Additional detail has been given only when it appears to be of special interest.

An attempt has been made to arrange entries in alphabetical order of surname according to accepted modern spellings, with cross-references to original spellings where these may differ substantially.

Abbreviations used are:

als	=	alias
AT	=	Awaiting transportation
Bd	=	Bedfordshire
Be	=	Berkshire
Bu	=	Buckinghamshire
Ca	=	Cambridgeshire
Ch	=	Cheshire
City	=	Sentenced by City Borough Court
Co	=	Cornwall
Cu	=	Cumberland
Db	=	Derbyshire
De	=	Devon
Do	=	Dorset
Du	=	Durham
E	=	Essex
Fl	=	Flint
G	=	Gloucestershire
Ha	=	Hampshire
He	=	Herefordshire
HO	=	Home Office Papers
Ht	=	Hertfordshire
Hu	=	Huntingdonshire
K	=	Kent
L	=	London
La	=	Lancashire
LC	=	Landing Certificate
Le	=	Leicestershire
Li	=	Lincolnshire
M	=	Middlesex
Md	=	Maryland
Mo	=	Monmouthshire
NE	=	New England
Nf	=	Norfolk
Nl	=	Northumberland
No	=	Northamptonshire
Nt	=	Nottinghamshire
O	=	Oxfordshire
PC	=	Privy Council Papers
PT	=	Pleaded transportation
R	=	Reprieved for transportation
Ru	=	Rutlandshire
S	=	Sentenced to transportation
s	=	Stealing
SC	=	South Carolina
SEK	=	Sentenced to transportation at East Kent Quarter Sessions
SES	=	Sentenced to transportation at East Sussex Quarter Sessions
Sh	=	Shropshire

SL	=	Sentenced to transportation at Southwark
So	=	Somerset
SP	=	State Papers
SQS	=	Sentenced to transportation at Quarter Sessions
ST	=	Sentenced to transportation at Tower Liberty, London
St	=	Staffordshire
Su	=	Suffolk
SW	=	Sentenced to transportation at Westminster Sessions
SWK	=	Sentenced to transportation at West Kent Quarter Sessions
SWS	=	Sentenced to transportation at West Sussex Quarter Sessions
Sx	=	Sussex
Sy	=	Surrey
T	=	Transported
TB	=	Transportation Bond
Va	=	Virginia
Wa	=	Warwickshire
We	=	Westmorland
Wi	=	Wiltshire
Wo	=	Worcestershire
X	=	Stray records
Y	=	Yorkshire
*	=	found guilty of an offence for which transportation was a normal penalty

Peter Wilson Coldham
Purley, Surrey, England

Lent 1988
AMDG

Notes:

1. Marion and Jack Kaminkow, *Original Lists of Emigrants in Bondage from London to the American Colonies 1719-1744* (Baltimore: Magna Carta Book Company, 1967).

2. Published by Polyanthos, Inc., New Orleans.

3. Letter from Sir Walter Cope to Lord Salisbury in Salisbury MSS, Hatfield.

4. *Calendar of State Papers (Colonial),* 1611.

5. *Acts of the Privy Council,* 1619.

6. *Acts of the Privy Council,* 1620.

7. An Act (4 Geo.I Cap.XI) for the further preventing Robbery, Burglary and other Felonies and for the more effectual Transportation of Felons.

8. Memorial of John Stewart 30 December 1762: PRO T1/416.

THE COMPLETE BOOK OF
EMIGRANTS IN BONDAGE

1614-1775

A

Aaron, Moses. Died on passage in *Sukey* 1725. X.

Aaron als Claron, Thomas. S Lent T Summer 1725 *Supply* LC Md May 1726. Y.

Abbay, John. S Lent 1758. Y.

Abbey, John. T Apr 1770 *New Trial*. Ht.

Abey, Thomas. S Jun-Dec 1745. M.

Abby, William. SW & T Oct 1768 *Justitia*. M.

Abbis, Dorothy. PT & R May 1697 for Barbados or Jamaica. M.

Abbis, Edward. T Apr 1725 *Sukey* LC Md Sep 1725. Sy.

Abbotson, Margaret. AT Summer 1757. Y.

Abbot, Ann. S Apr 1773. M.

Abbott, Christopher. R 14 yrs Summer 1743. Y.

Abbott, Edward. Rebel T 1685.

Abbott, Edward. S s at St. Matthew, Ipswich, & R 14 yrs Summer 1774. Su.

Abbott als Hall als Harris, Elizabeth. R May T Jly 1722 *Alexander* to Nevis or Jamaica. M.

Abbott, George. S Lent R 14 yrs Summer 1736. Nt.

Abbott, George. S Jly T Nov 1759 *Phoenix*. M.

Abbott, George. S s sheep at Riseley & R Summer 1774. Bd.

Abbott, James. S Apr T Sep 1737 *Pretty Patsy* to Md. M.

Abbott, John. S Jly 1718 for T to Va. So.

Abbott, John. S Jan-May s wig T Jun 1738 *Forward* to Md or Va. M.

Abbott, John. S Sep T for life Oct 1768 *Justitia*. L

Abbott, Martha, of St. Luke, spinster. S s sheets & T Jan 1740 *York* to Md. M.

Abbott, Mary. R Dec 1716 T Jan 1717 *Queen Elizabeth*. M.

Abbot, Mary. S s handkerchiefs at Wem Lent R 14 yrs Summer 1762. Sh.

Abbott, Mary wife of John. S 14 yrs Apr 1773. M.

Abbott, Mary. S Oct 1773. M.

Abbott, Sarah. S for murder of her bastard child Lent R 14 yrs Summer 1751. Be.

Abbott, Thomas. T Apr 1742 *Bond*. K.

Abbott, William. R for Barbados Mar 1681. M.

Abbott, William. S Mar 1752. Do.

Abbott, William. R Dec 1765 T for life Jan 1766 *Tryal*. M.

Abell, Christopher. R Jan 1693 for Barbados or Jamaica. L.

Abel, Elizabeth. S s geese at Pembridge Lent 1767. He.

Abell, Henry. S Jly 1751 TB to Va. De.

Abel, Thomas. S Summer 1767. Le.

Abel, Susan. S s geese at Pembridge Lent 1767. He.

Abell als Milbourne, Thomas. S Lent R 14 yrs Summer 1750. Wo.

Abel, Thomas. S Jan-Feb T Apr 1771 *Thornton*. M.

Able, William. S s at Wokingham Summer 1737 R 14 yrs Lent 1738. Be.

Abell, William. S Mar 1772. Do.

Aberdeen, Nicholas. S Aug T Sep 1725 *Forward* to Md LC. M.

Ablet, John. S s horse Summer 1740 R 14 yrs Lent 1741. Su.
Ablet, John (1765). *See* Brigs. M.
Abraham, Anne (1683). *See* Slowe. L.
Abraham, Ann. S Feb T Apr 1741 *Speedwell*. L.
Abraham, Francis. R for Barbados or Jamaica Mar 1685. M.
Abraham, John of Lambeth. SQS & T Jan 1769 *Thornton*. Sy.
Abraham als Abrahams, John. R & T for life Apr 1770 *New Trial*. M.
Abraham, Judith wife of Solomon. S Sep-Oct T Dec 1771 *Justitia*. M.
Abraham, Mary wife of James. S & T Dec 1731 *Forward* to Md
  or Va. M.
Abraham, Meyer. S for receiving Dec 1765 T 14 yrs Jan 1766 *Tryal*. L.
Abraham, Moses. S Jan 1757. L.
Abraham als Scampey, Philip. S Feb T Mar 1764 *Tryal*. M.
Abraham als Browne, Sarah of Hunsdon. R for Barbados or Jamaica
  Mar 1694 & Feb 1696. Ht.
Abraham, Thomas. R Jun 1712. L.
Abraham, Thomas. S Sep 1733 T Jan 1734 *Caesar* LC Va Jly 1734. M.
Abraham, Thomas. R 14 yrs Apr 1747. De.
Abraham, William. S Summer 1742. We.
Abrahams, Alexander. S May T 14 yrs Jun 1756 *Lyon*. L.
Abrahams, Jacob. S Feb T Apr 1771 *Thornton*. L.
Abrahams, John. S s wheat at Cranfield Lent 1733. Bd.
Abrahams, John (1770). *See* Abraham. M.
Abrahams, Jonas. S Jan T Feb 1765 *Tryal*. L.
Abrahams als Solomons, Joseph. S Feb 1774. L.
Abrahams, Levy. S May-Jly 1773.
Abrahams, Lyon (1771). *See* Backarac. M.
Abrahams, Mordecai. S & T Dec 1734 *Caesar* LC Va Jly 1735. L.
Abrahams, Moses. S Jly 1774. L.
Abrahams, Samuel (1766). *See* Solomon. M.
Abrahams, Sarah. S Oct 1773. L.
Abrahams, Thomas. S s sheep at Stagsden & R Lent 1774. Bd.
Abrams, William. S & T Apr 1733 *Patapsco* LC Annapolis Nov 1733. M.
Abrey, Thomas. S Lent 1748. Sx.
Abthorpe, Thomas. S Apr T May 1719 *Margaret* LC Md Sep 1719 &
  sold to Peter Pinchton. L.
Acas als Acus, Thomas. R for Barbados Sep 1669. M.
Akister, Thomas. S s silver cup from Otton church Lent 1774. Y.
Acastle, Robert. Rebel T 1685.
Ackerett als Eccritt, Robert. R for life Mar 1774. De.
Ackfrill, Thomas (1727). *See* Johnson. Ca.
Ackron, Godfrey. T Sep 1766 *Justitia*. M.
Ackron, Lucretia of Bermondsey, spinster. SQS & T Jan 1769. Sy.
Ackroyd, Isaac. S s from tenters at Huddersfield Lent 1767. Y.
Acland, George. T May 1751 *Tryal*. K.
Acre als Acrey, Sarah. S Jun-Dec 1738. M.
Acres, Hannah (1725). *See* Daniel. M.
Acres als Fouracres, James. S Aug 1729. De.
Akers, Mary. S s at Old Windsor Summer 1757. Be.
Acres, Thomas. R Sep 1669 to 7 yrs Barbados. M.
Akres als Aires, Thomas. S Aug T Oct 1726 *Forward* to Va. M.

Acrey, Sarah (1738). *See* Acre. M.

Acton, John. T for life Apr 1769 *Tryal*. K.

Acton, Thomas. T for life Jly 1772 *Orange Bay*. Sy.

Acton, William. S Lent 1754. Bd.

Adam, John. S s horse Summer 1740 R Lent 1741. (SP). Be.

Adams, Alice (1719). *See* Thomas. L.

Adams als Haydon, Ann. S Jly T Sep 1767 *Justitia*. M.

Adams, Benjamin. T Oct 1750 *Rachael*. K.

Adams, Edward. Rebel T 1685.

Adams, Edward. LC from *Rappahannock*, Va Apr 1726. X.

Adams, Edward. S Dec 1766 T Jan 1767 *Tryal*. L.

Adams, Elianor. R for Barbados or Jamaica May 1684. M.

Adams, Eleanor. S Sep 1737 T Jan 1738 *Dorsetshire* to Va. M.

Adams, Elizabeth. S Sep T Nov 1762 *Prince William*. M.

Adams, Elizabeth. S & T Jly 1770 *Scarsdale*. M.

Adams, Francis. T 14 yrs Apr 1768 *Thornton*. Ht.

Adams, George of Cheshunt. R for Barbados or Jamaica Jly 1710. Ht.

Adams, George. S Sep T Dec 1736 *Dorsetshire* to Va. M.

Adams, George. S Oct 1737 T Jan 1738 *Dorsetshire* to Va. M.

Adams, Giles. S Mar 1754 TB to Va. De.

Adams, Hannah. S Jly T Nov 1762 *Prince William*. M.

Adams als Brackman, Henry. T Jly 1722 *Alexander*. Sy.

Adams, Henry. SQS & TB Apr 1769. So.

Adams, Isaac. S for cutting down trees at night Aug 1773. So.

Adams, Jacob. Rebel T 1685.

Adams, James. S Jan T Apr 1762 *Dolphin*. L.

Adams, James. S s clothing at St. Giles, Cripplegate Feb T Apr 1768 *Thornton*. L.

Adams, James. S Mar 1768. Ha.

Adams, Jane. S Jan T Feb 1733 *Smith*. L.

Adams, John (2). Rebels T 1685.

Addams, John of Ashdon. R for Barbados or Jamaica Jly 1705. E.

Addams, John. S Mar 1730. De.

Adams, John. S Mar 1732. Do.

Adams, John. S Lent R 14 yrs Summer 1736. Wa.

Adams, John. SQS Oct 1754. M.

Adams, John. S Jly 1755. Ha.

Adams, John. S Lent T Jun 1756 *Lyon*. K.

Addams, John. SQS Jly T Nov 1762 *Prince William*. M.

Adams, John. S for highway robbery at Bishopwearmouth & R for life Summer 1768. Du.

Adams, John. SQS & TB Apr 1769. So.

Adams, John of St. Saviour, Southwark. SQS Jan 1774. Sy.

Adams, Mary. S Mar 1720. De.

Adams, Mary. T Jly 1722 *Alexander*. Ht.

Adams, Mary. S Sep-Dec 1746. M.

Adams, Mary. S Feb-Apr T May 1751 *Tryal*. M.

Adams, Mary. S s at Richards Castle Summer 1756. Sh.

Adams, Peter. T Jan 1766 *Tryal*. M.

Adams, Philemon. R for Barbados or Jamaica Mar 1685. M.

Adams, Philip. S Dec 1753. M.

Adams, Richard. S Oct T Nov 1725 *Rappahannock* LC Rappahannock Apr 1726. L.

Adams als Bandy, Richard. T Apr 1770 *New Trial*. Sy.

Adams, Robert. R Oct TB Nov 1662. L.

Adams, Robert. S s mare Summer 1765 R 14 yrs Lent 1756. Li.

Adams, Roger. PT Jan R Mar 1685. M.

Adams, Samuel. Rebel T 1685.

Adams, Samuel. S Feb T Mar 1729 *Patapsco* but died on passage. M.

Adams, Samuel. S s at St. Nicholas, Abingdon, Summer 1729 Be.

Adams, Samuel. S s at Great Haseley Summer 1758. O.

Adams, Sarah. T 14 yrs Apr 1759 *Thetis*. Ht.

Adams, Thomas. Rebel T 1685.

Adams, Thomas. R for America Aug 1715. L.

Adams, Thomas. T Jun 1727 *Susanna*. Sx.

Adams, Thomas. S Dec-Jan T Mar 1750 *Tryal*. M.

Adams, Thomas. S Lent 1758. No.

Adams, Thomas of Basford, farrier. SQS s turkey Jly 1762. Nt.

Adams, Thomas. S Jly T Sep 1767 *Justitia*. M.

Adams als Stanley, Thomas. R & T 14 yrs Jly 1772 *Tayloe*. M.

Adams, William, a Quaker. R for plantations Jly 1665. Ht.

Adams, William of St. George, Southwark. SQS Jan 1752. Sy.

Adams, William. T 14 yrs Apr 1768 *Thornton*. K.

Adams, William. S Aug 1773. Do.

Adams, William. S for highway robbery & R Lent 1774. Be.

Adams, William. S s barley at St. Paul, Bedford, Lent 1774. Bd.

Adams, William. S s shoes at Stoke upon Trent Lent 1775. St.

Adamson, Isabell. R Jly 1730. Du.

Adamson, Joseph. S for highway robbery at Rotheram & R 14 yrs Lent 1769. Y.

Adamson, Margaret wife of Thomas. S Apr 1774. M.

Adamson, Mary. TB to Va from QS 1769. De.

Adamson, Susanna wife of George. S s at Monkwearmouth Summer 1772. Du.

Adamson, Walter. S Dec 1727. L.

Adcock, Richard. S Lent R 14 yrs Summer 1734. Nt.

Adcock, Thomas. S Jan-Jun T Jun 1728 *Elizabeth* LC Potomack Aug 1729. L.

Adcock, Thomas. S s from manor house of John Allcock & R Summer 1736. Su.

Adcock, Thomas. S & T Feb 1744 *Neptune* to Md. M.

Adcock, William. S Apr-May T Jly 1771 *Scarsdale*. M.

Adcroft, Thomas of Yatebank, Rossendale Forest, weaver. SQS Jan 1765. La.

Adcroft, Thomas of Manchester. SQS Apr 1775. La.

Adderly, Thomas. S Summer 1763. Wa.

Adderton, John of Oulton. R for America Mar 1697. St.

Addey, Sarah. S s at Longdon Summer 1764. St.

Addicott, John. SQS Jan 1733. So.

Addicott, William. SQS Jan 1733. So.

Addington, John of Bubbingworth. R for Barbados or Jamaica Jly 1702. E.

Addington, Laurence. R for Barbados Dec 1683. L.

Addes, Thomas. S Feb T Mar 1730 *Patapsco* LC Annapolis Sep 1730. M.

Addis, Thomas. T Dec 1752 *Greyhound*. M.

Addison, James (1716). *See* Allison. M.

Addison, James. R for life Lent 1775. K.

Addison, Joseph. T Oct 1732 *Caesar*. Sy.

Addison, Robert. S Apr 1763. L.

Addison, Simon. S Oct 1766. M.

Addison, Thomas. T Jun 1728 *Elizabeth* LC Va Aug 1729. Sy.

Addison, William. T Jun 1740 *Essex*. Sy.

Addleton, John. S Feb T Apr 1741 *Speedwell* or *Mediterranean* to Md. M.

Adjon, Peter. TB Aug 1718. L.

Adkins, James. S Lent 1737. Su.

Adkins, John. S Summer 1766. Wa.

Adkins, Joseph. S Lent 1737. Su.

Adkins, Sarah. S Dec 1774. L.

Adkins, Thomas. S for highway robbery Summer 1753 R 14 yrs Lent 1754. No.

Adkins, William. S Summer 1767. Bu.

Adley, Elizabeth, spinster. S s cloth at St. Mary Woolchurch Haw Dec 1768 T Jan 1769 *Thornton*. L.

Adley, Hannah wife of George, als Hannah Lane. S Apr T Jun *Bladon* to Md. M.

Adley, Mary (1753). *See* Hadley. M.

Adley, Thomas. S Jun 1733. M.

Adlington, George. TB Apr 1758. Db.

Adry, William. S Lent T *Lichfield* May 1750. Bu.

Adsett als Davenport, John. R Dec 1698 AT Jan 1699. M.

Adsey, Mary. R 14 yrs Aug T Sep 1718 *Eagle* LC Charles Town Mar 1719. L.

Adshed, John. R for Barbados or Jamaica Aug 1701. L.

Adwell, John, als Jack Above Ground. S Jly 1763. M.

Ady, Jonathan. R & T 14 yrs Sep 1737 *Pretty Patsy* to Md. M.

Agar, Frank. S Feb T Apr 1766 *Ann*. M.

Agar als Algar, George. S Lent 1765. Su.

Agar, James. S Lent 1753. Su.

Ager, William. S Sep-Oct 1773. M.

Agnis, John of St. Runwald, Colchester. SQS Apr 1754. E.

Ahock, Margaret. R Jly 1721 for Md or Va. M.

Ainsty, John. S Lent R 14 yrs Summer T Dec 1763 *Neptune*. Sy.

Ainsworth, Michael. S Apr T May 1752 *Lichfield*. L.

Aynsworth, Richard. S Lent R 14 yrs Summer 1765. O.

Ainsworth als Hains, Robert. T *Ann* Apr 1765. Bu.

Aires. *See* Ayres.

Airson als Arsom, Mary wife of William. S for shoplifting at Sedgefield Summer 1757. Du.

Aish, Thomas. S Aug 1726. Do.

Aishton, Daniel. SQS Jan TB to Md Feb 1743. So.

Aistrop, Robert. R Oct 1772 for 14 yrs. M.

Akerline, John. TB Mar 1770. Db.

Akerman, Ann. S Sep-Oct T Dec 1771 *Justitia*. M.

Akerman, Thomas. S Lent 1748. K.

Akister. *See* Acaster.

Akres. *See* Acres.

Alban, Daniel of Epping. R for Barbados or Jamaica Dec 1680. E.

Alban, Daniel of South Weald. R for Barbados or Jamaica Mar 1682 & Feb 1683. E.

Alberry, Thomas. S Lent T *Tryal* Sep 1755. Bu.

Albert, George. S May-Jly 1748. M.

Albert, Henry. S Summer 1740. Wo.

Albert, Henry. S Jan T Feb 1742 *Industry* to Md. M.

Albey, Joseph. S Feb 1752. L.

Albon, Daniel of Broxted. R for Barbados or Jamaica Mar 1678. E.

Alborough, Richard of Ilford. R (London) for Barbados or Jamaica Jly 1686. E.

Albrighton, William. S & T Apr 1733 *Patapsco* LC Annapolis Nov 1733. M.

Albrooke, Richard. S Lent R for Barbados May 1664. Sy.

Albutt, John of Bromsgrove. R for America Jly 1696. Wo.

Alchin, John (1757). *See* Kidder. K.

Alcock, Ann aged 16, fair. T Oct 1720 *Gilbert* LC Md May 1721. Ht.

Allcock, Ann. S Summer 1740. Wo.

Alcock, Anthony. S Lent TB Apr T Aug 1757 *Lux*. Db.

Alcock, Edward. R for America Aug 1715. L.

Alcock, George. S Aug 1732. Co.

Alcocke, John of Willaston. R for Barbados Sep 1671. Ch.

Alcock, John. S & T Jan 1722 *Gilbert* LC Annapolis Jly 1722. M.

Allcock als Hawkins, John. S s gelding Lent R Summer 1767. Bu.

Allcock, Lawrence. R 14 yrs Summer T Oct 1739 *Duke of Cumberland*. Sy.

Allcock, Margaret. LC from *Owners Goodwill* Annapolis Jly 1722. X.

Alcock als Taylor, Robert of Beerchurch. R Lent T 14 yrs Apr 1772 *Thornton*. E.

Alcock, Thomas. TB to Md Jly 1722. Db.

Alcock, Thomas. S & TB Apr 1746. G.

Alcon, Sarah. S Jan T Mar 1750 *Tryal*. L.

Alcraft, Francis of St. Saviour, Southwark. SQS Jun T Aug 1752 *Tryal*. Sy.

Alden, John (1665). *See* Holden. Nf.

Alder, Ann (1765). *See* Stanley. M.

Alder, George. S Jly T Oct 1741 *Sea Horse* to Va. M.

Alder, Jasper. S s sheep at Woodchester Lent 1729. G.

Alder, John. R & T May 1736 *Patapsco* to Md. M.

Alder, John. S Summer 1748 R 14 yrs Lent 1749. Be.

Alder, John. S Mar 1752. So.

Alder, John. S for demolishing a dwelling Lent R 14 yrs Summer 1768. G.

Alder, Thomas. S s sheep at Woodchester Lent 1729. G.

Alderkin, William of Braughing. R for Barbados or Jamaica Jly 1687. Ht.

Alderman, Richard. S & T Dec 1769 *Justitia*. M.

Alders, Anthony. T Jan 1736 *Dorsetshire*. Sy.

Alders, John. R Jly T for life Oct 1768 *Justitia*. M.
Aldersea, Stephen. S Aug T Oct 1724 *Forward* to Md. M.
Alderton, Samuel. R Feb AT May 1686. M.
Aldington, George. S Lent 1758. Db.
Aldis, William (1733). *See* Sickwell. M.
Aldred als Orrett, George of Atherton. SQS Jly 1766. La.
Aldred, Giles of Failsworth, weaver. SQS Oct 1771. La.
Aldridge, Anne. R Dec 1670 for 7 yrs Barbados. M.
Alldridge, Benjamin. R Jan T Feb 1724 *Anne* to Carolina. M.
Aldridge, Charles. S s at Waltham St. Lawrence Lent 1753 Be.
Aldridge, Deborah. R & T Dec 1716 *Lewis*. M.
Aldrich, Elizabeth. S Lent 1767. Su.
Aldridge, James. S Lent 1761. Nf.
Aldridge, John. R for Jamaica Jan 1663. M.
Aldridge, John als Anthony. T Oct 1720 *Gilbert*. Sy.
Alderidge, John (1721). *See* Fox. E.
Aldridge, John. S Mar 1730. Wi.
Aldridge, John. S & T Sep 1731 *Smith* to Va LC Va 1732. M.
Aldridge, John. R & T for life Sep 1766 *Justitia*. M.
Aldridge, Mary. S Jan T Sep 1737 *Pretty Patsy* to Md. M.
Aldridge, Mary. SQS Apr 1774. M.
Aldridge, Richard. S May T Jly 1771 *Scarsdale*. L.
Aldridge, Robert. S Jan-Jun 1747. M.
Aldridge, Susanna. S Feb-Apr T May 1751 *Tryal*. M.
Aldridge, Thomas. R 14 yrs Mar 1721. Wi.
Aldrige, William. R 14 yrs Aug T Sep 1718 *Eagle* LC Charles Town Mar 1719. L.
Aldridge, William. S Jly 1774. L.
Oldridge, William. SQS Dec 1774. M.
Aldsworth, Samuel. S & T Apr 1769 *Tryal*. L.
Aldworth, Mary (1748). *See* Alworth. Wi.
Aldwyn, William. S s mare Summer 1723 R 14 yrs Lent 1725. Sh.
Alett, John of Rotherhithe. SQS Jan T Apr 1762 *Neptune*. Sy.
Alewood. *See* Aylwood.
Alexander, Ann. S Jan T Feb 1744 *Neptune* to Md. M.
Alexander, Elizabeth. S Jly 1720. M.
Alexander, Elizabeth als Betty. S Jly TB to Va Sep 1756. Wi.
Alexander, James Jr. of Lambeth. SQS Apr T Sep 1751 *Greyhound*. Sy.
Alexander, James. S s fowls Lent 1753. Su.
Alexander, John. T Oct 1721 *William & John*. Sy.
Alexander, John (1733). *See* Hall. Cu.
Alexander als Clark, Joseph. T May 1719 *Margaret*; sold to Patrick Sympson Md May 1720. K.
Alexander, Margaret, als Brown, Elizabeth. S Feb T Mar 1730 *Patapsco* LC Md Sep 1730. L.
Alexander, Richard. S Mar 1721 T from Portsmouth 1723. Ha.
Alexander, Solomon. S May T Jly 1771 *Scarsdale*. L.
Alexander, Thomas (1672). *See* Smith. Ch.
Alexander, Thomas (1739). *See* Saunderson. M.
Alexander, Timothy. S s handkerchief at Tettenhall Summer 1738. St.
Alexander, William. R Dec 1667 for 7 yrs Barbados. M.

Alexander, William. S Apr-Jun 1739. M.

Alexander, William. S Apr T May 1750 *Lichfield*. M.

Alexander, William. S Jly T Sep 1767 *Justitia*. L.

Alexander, William. SWK Apr 1773. K.

Alford, James. S Lent R 14 yrs Summer 1742. Wo.

Alford, James the younger. S Mar 1752. Do.

Alford, John of Tisbury. R for Barbados Sep 1665. Wi.

Alford, Nathaniel of Ashton Gifford. SQS Warminster Jly TB to Va Sep 1772. Wi.

Algar, Arthur. S Ma 1731 TB to Va. De.

Algar, Daniel. S Mar 1742. De.

Algar, George (1765). *See* Agar. Su.

Algate, Mary. R 7 yrs Lent 1774. E.

Alinery, Robert. R Apr 1669 for 7 yrs Barbados. M.

Allam, Ann. S Sep-Oct 1773. M.

Allam, John. T Dec 1758 *The Brothers*. Ht.

Allam, Michael. S & T Apr 1733 *Patapsco* to Md. M.

Allambridge, John. Rebel T 1685.

Allanson als Leacock, David. S s horse at Filliskirk R 14 yrs Summer 1770 TB Aug 1771. Y.

Allard, Paul. S Feb 1757. M.

Allard, William. S s chain at Upton upon Severn Lent 1761; found at large in Severnstoke & R 14 yrs Summer 1765. Wo.

Allason. *See* Allison.

Allcott, Thomas. S Summer 1745 R 14 yrs Lent 1746. G.

Alcott, Thomas. S s sheep & R 7 yrs Summer TB to Md Sep 1772. Le.

Allcroft als Hawcroft als Hallcroft, John. S s wine measure at Sheffield Summer 1770. Y.

Allday, Thomas. SQS Feb 1757. M.

Allen, Ann. S & T Sep 1731 *Smith* LC Va 1732. L.

Allen, Ann. S Feb T Apr 1739 *Forward* to Va. M.

Allen, Ann. S Summer 1754. Ca.

Allen, Bartholomew of Milton by Sittingbourne. R for Barbados or Jamaica Jly 1674. K.

Allen, Bridget. R Oct TB Nov 1662. L.

Allan, David. SQS Apr 1756. Du.

Allen, David. S Jun T Jly 1771 *Scarsdale*. L.

Allen, David. SQS Dec 1774. M.

Allen, Dorothy. S Jan-Apr 1749. M.

Allen, Dorothy. S Jly T Oct 1768 *Justitia*. M.

Allen, Edward of Milton by Sittingbourne. R for Barbados or Jamaica Jly 1674. K.

Allen, Edward. S for life Feb 1754. M.

Allen, Edward. S Jan 1757. M.

Allen, Eleanor. S Oct 1733 T Jan 1734 *Caesar* LC Va Jly 1734. M.

Allen, Elizabeth. R for Barbados Jan 1679. L.

Allen, Elizabeth (1681). *See* Staines. M.

Allen, Elizabeth. S May T Jun 1727 *Susanna* to Va. M.

Allen, Elizabeth. S Dec 1754. L.

Allen, Elizabeth. R May T for life Sep 1758 *Tryal* to Annapolis. M.

Allen, Elizabeth. T Apr 1771 *Thornton*. K.

Allen, Elizabeth. SQS & T Jly 1771 *Scarsdale*. M.

Allen als Totty, Frances. S May T Jly 1723 *Alexander* LC Annapolis Sep 1723. M.

Allen, George. Rebel T 1685.

Allen, George. PT Jan 1700. M.

Allen, George. S Jly 1721 T from Southampton 1723. Ha.

Allen, George. S Sep 1735 T Jan 1736 *Dorsetshire* LC Va Sep 1736. M.

Allen, George. S Dec 1748 T Jan 1749 *Laura*. M.

Allen, George. S Feb T Mar 1750 *Tryal*. M.

Allen, George. T Sep 1766 *Justitia*. K.

Allen, George. SQS May T Jly 1773 *Tayloe* to Va. M.

Allen, Grace. S Jly T Sep 1764 *Justitia*. M.

Allen, Hanna wife of John. A Aug T Sep 1725 *Forward* LC Annapolis Dec 1725. M.

Allen, Henry. S Feb T Mar 1730 *Patapsco* LC Annapolis Sep 1730. M.

Allen, Herman John. T Apr 1753 *Thames*. K.

Allen, James, aged 21 dark. S & T Oct 1720 *Gilbert* LC Annapolis May 1721. M.

Allen, James. S Norwich Summer 1735. Nf.

Allen, James. S Mar TB to Va Apr 1742. Wi.

Allen, James. S & T Apr 1762 *Dolphin*. L.

Allen, James. S & T 14 yrs Mar 1763 *Neptune*. L.

Allen, James. S Summer TB to Va Sep 1767. Le.

Allan, James. S May T Jly 1770 *Scarsdale*. L.

Allen, James. S & T Dec 1770 *Justitia*. L.

Allen, Jeremiah. T Oct 1729 *Forward*. E.

Allen, John. R 7 yrs for Barbados May 1665. X.

Allen, John of Coventry. R for America Jly 1678. Wa.

Allen, John of Marchington. R for America Mar 1680. St.

Allen, John. R for America Jun 1684. No.

Allen, John. R for America Feb 1692. Le.

Allen, John. R May AT Jly 1697. M.

Allen, John of Rochford. R for Barbados or Jamaica Jly 1710. E.

Allen, John of Waltham Abbey. R for Barbados or Jamaica Jly 1712. E.

Allen, John. S Jan T Feb 1719 *Worcester* LC Annapolis Jun 1719. L.

Allen, John. T May 1737 *Forward*. K.

Allen, John. S Jun-Dec 1745. M.

Allen, John. S Lent R 14 yrs Summer 1746. O.

Allen, John. S May-Jly 1750. M.

Allen, John. S Dec 1750. L.

Allen, John. S Dec 1754. L.

Allen, John. S Nov T Dec 1763 *Neptune*. L.

Allen, John. S for ravishing 12 year old child at St. Giles, Cambridge, & R 14 yrs Summer 1770. Ca.

Allen, John. R Lent 1773. E.

Allen, John. SQS May T Jly 1773 *Tayloe* to Va. M.

Allen, John (Thomas in indictment). S s at Harborne Lent 1774. St.

Allen, John. S for highway robbery & R 14 yrs Lent 1775. No.

Allen, John. S Jan-Feb 1775. M.

Allen, Jonathan. T Apr 1731 *Bennet*. K.

Allen, Jonathan. S Lent R for life Summer 1763. Nf.

Allen als Biggs, Joseph. S May T Jly 1723 *Alexander*. M.
Allen, Joseph. S s horse Lent R 14 yrs Summer TB Aug 1736. Y.
Allen, Joseph. S Nov T Dec 1753 *Whiteing*. L.
Allen, Mary. S Feb T Mar 1729 *Patapsco* to Md. M.
Allen, Mary. S s silver spoons at Speen Lent 1757. Be.
Allen, Mary. S Apr T Sep 1757 *Thetis*. L.
Allen, Mary wife of Matterdell. S May T Sep 1766 *Justitia*. M.
Allen, Mary. S Summer T Sep 1770. Wa.
Allen, Mary, spinster. S s at Milton Ernest Summer 1771. Bd.
Allen als Blanchford, Mary. S 14 yrs for receiving Mar 1774. De.
Allen, Mathew. R for Va Jan 1620. M.
Allen, Nathaniel. T Jly 1722 *Alexander* LC Annapolis Sep 1723. Ht.
Allen, Nicholas. S Aug 1726. De.
Allen, Paul. R for America Feb 1683. No.
Allen, Phillip. S Sep-Dec 1746. M.
Allen, Phillipa. S May-Jun T Aug 1752 *Tryal*. M.
Allen, Richard. Rebel T 1685.
Allen, Richard of Gillingham. R for America Apr 1697. Nf.
Allen, Richard. S s at Kings Stanley Summer 1725. G.
Allen, Robert. R Oct s cloak TB Oct 1667. L.
Allen, Robert of Camberwell. R for Barbados or Jamaica Mar 1698. Sy.
Allen, Robert. S Mar 1732. So.
Allen, Roger (1738). *See* Douglass. M.
Allen, Roger. S May 1760. M.
Allen, Roger. S May 1763. M.
Allen, Samuel. SQS Jan TB to Md Feb 1743. So.
Allen, Samuel. R for pulling down mills Summer 1772. E.
Allen, Sarah. S Mar 1730. De.
Allen, Thomas. R for Jamaica Aug 1661. M.
Allen, Thomas. R (Home Circ) for Barbados Apr 1663. X.
Allen, Thomas (2). Rebels T 1685.
Allen, Thomas. R for Barbados or Jamaica Oct 1690. L.
Allen, Thomas. R for Barbados or Jamaica Oct 1694. L.
Allen, Thomas of Bristol. R for Barbados Feb 1697. G.
Allen, Thomas. TB Apr 1719. L.
Allen, Thomas. R Aug T Oct 1723 *Forward* to Va. M.
Allen, Thomas. S Feb T Mar 1729 *Patapsco* LC Annapolis Dec 1729. M.
Allen, Thomas. T Sep 1730 *Smith*. Sy.
Allen, Thomas. S Mar TB to Md Oct 1738. Le.
Allen, Thomas. S Mar 1742. Do.
Allen, Thomas. S Lent 1745. Nf.
Allen, Thomas. S (Norwich) Summer 1752. Nf.
Allan, Thomas of Guisborough, weaver. SQS Guisborough s yarn Jly
   TB Aug 1758. Y.
Allen, Thomas. S Summer 1760. G.
Allen, Thomas. S s at Tettenhall Summer 1774. St.
Allen, William. R s silver candlesticks & TB Oct 1667. L.
Allan, William. S Aug TB Sep 1723. Nt.
Allen, William of Winnington. S s 2 lambs Lent 1727. Bd.
Allen, William. SQS & TB Jly 1729. So.
Allen, William. SQS Jly 1736. So.

Allen, William. S Aug T Oct 1741 *Sea Horse* to Va. M.

Allen, William. S Mar 1742. Do.

Allen, William. S Aug 1757. Co.

Allen, William. R 14 yrs Jly 1765. Ha.

Allen, William. S s gold coin Summer 1766. Bd.

Allen, William. S Sep-Oct T Dec 1771 *Justitia*. M.

Allen, William. S for highway robbery at Hutton Moor R 14 yrs Lent 1774 TB Apr. Y.

Allen, William. S s barley at St. Paul, Bedford, Lent 1774. Bd.

Allender, Nathaniel. S s silver cup at Sheffield Summer 1739. Y.

Allener, John. S Mar 1754. Ha.

Allens, Richard. Rebel T 1685.

Allerton, Robert. S s sheep at Hampnell & R 14 yrs Lent 1770. Y.

Alleston, Bryan. S Aug 1736 TB Apr 1737. Le.

Allgood, John. R Dec 1693 AT Jan 1694 to Barbados. M.

Allgood, Richard. S Lent 1763. Ca.

Allibone, Benjamin. S s at Sarsden Lent 1748. O.

Allie. *See* Ally.

Allies, John. S May-Jly 1774. M.

Allifull, William. R for America Feb 1700. No.

Allington, Anne. R & T Apr 1725 *Sukey* to Md but died on passage. M.

Allis als Hall, Margaret. R & T Apr 1725 *Sukey* to Md. M.

Allison, Hester (1728). *See* Wheatley. M.

Allison als Addison, James. PT Oct R Dec 1716 T Jan 1717 *Queen Elizabeth* to Jamaica. M.

Allason, Joseph. S s sheep & R 14 yrs Summer 1753. Du.

Allison, Mary wife of Miles. R Oct T Dec 1724 *Rappahannock* to Va. M.

Allison als Cotsworth, Miles. R Aug T Oct 1724 *Forward* LC Md Jun 1725. M.

Allison, Robert. S Apr T May 1752 *Lichfield*. L.

Allison, Samuel. S Apr T May 1767 *Thornton*. M.

Allison, Thomas. S for highway robbery Lent R 14 yrs Summer 1765. Ca.

Allyson, William. S Summer 1766 R 14 yrs Lent 1767. Nf.

Alloway, Mary. R & T Jly 1770 *Scarsdale*. M.

Allum, Catherine. T Apr 1762 *Neptune*. K.

Allum, Thomas. R 14 yrs Mar 1772. Ha.

Alwood, James. S Mar TB 14 yrs to Va Aug 1768. Le.

Alwood, John. T May 1723 *Victory*. K.

Allwood, John. S s heifers & steers & R Lent 1768. Le.

Alwood, Richard. Rebel T 1685.

Allwood, William. TB May 1775. Nt.

Allwright, John. S Feb T Mar 1731 *Patapsco* LC Annapolis Jun 1731. L.

Allwright, Joseph. S Summer 1756 R 14 yrs Lent 1757. Wo.

Allwright, Richard. S Dec 1772. M.

Allie, Antonio. S & T Jly 1772 *Tayloe*. L.

Ally, Matthew. S s at St. Philip & Jacob Lent TB Mar 1748. G.

Almack, William of St. Olave, Southwark. SQS Feb T Jun 1764 *Dolphin*. Sy.

Alman, Samuel. T Oct 1721 *William & John*. Ht.

Almery, John. R Jun & Sep TB for Barbados Oct 1669. M.

Almond, John. S Jan-Feb T Apr 1772 *Thornton.* M.

Almon, Judith. S Jun T Nov 1743 *George William.* M.

Allmond, Richard. S Lent 1774. K.

Almond, Susan. R for Jamaica Aug 1661. L.

Alone, Mary. R for Barbados Aug 1668. M.

Alsom, William. S Oct 1774. L.

Alsopp, Anthony. SQS Mar TB Aug 1720 to be shipped to Md from Liverpool. Db.

Alsop, John. S Nov T Dec 1763 *Neptune.* L.

Alsop, John. T May 1767 *Thornton.* Sy.

Alsop, Joseph, als Taylor, George. S Lent R 14 yrs Summer TB Sep 1759. Db.

Alsop, Joseph. T May 1767 *Thornton.* Sy.

Alsop, Margaret. S Sep-Oct 1773. M.

Alsop, Robert. SQS Jly 1756. M.

Allsop, Sarah. S s at Hamstall Redware Summer 1764. St.

Allston als Allton, Butty als John. S Lent 1775. E.

Alston, John. Rebel T 1685.

Allstone, John. S & T Oct 1722 *Forward* LC Annapolis Jun 1723. L.

Alstone, Mary. R Aug T Oct 1723 *Forward* to Va. M.

Alston, Mary (1732). *See* Sharp. M.

Altop, Thomas. R Jan-Feb T 14 yrs Apr 1772 *Thornton.* M.

Alverstone, Thomas of Werrington. R for America Feb 1692. No.

Alway als Holway, William. S Mar 1730. So.

Always, Samuel. S Summer 1765. Wa.

Alwood. *See* Allwood.

Alworth als Aldworth, Mary. S Mar TB to Va Nov 1748. Wi.

Amber, William of Grafham. R for Barbados Feb 1664. Hu.

Ambery, John. S & T Mar 1760 *Friendship.* L.

Ambler, George. S Apr T Jun 1768 *Tryal.* M.

Ambler, Martha. S Jly T Aug 1721 *Prince Royal* LC Va Nov 1721. L.

Ambrose, Ann. S May T Jun 1726 *Loyal Margaret* LC Annapolis Oct 1726. M.

Ambrose, Ann. S Sep-Oct 1774. M.

Ambrose, Henry of Mortimore. R for America Jly 1700. Ha.

Ambrose, Robert (1715). *See* Andrews. M.

Ambrose, Thomas (1754). *See* Radborne. M.

Aymes, James. Rebel T 1685.

Ames, Mary. SQS & T July 1773 *Tayloe* to Va. M.

Amies, Edward. S Lent R 14 yrs Summer 1759. Mo.

Amis, Richard. T Oct 1726 *Forward.* Ht.

Amiss, Robert. T Jan 1738 *Dorsetshire.* E.

Amison als Emmerson als Emmerston, Charles. S s mare at Adbaston Summer 1734. St.

Amison, Jonathan. T Aug 1720 *Owners Goodwill.* K.

Amlett, Edward. S Summer 1757 R 14 yrs Lent 1758. St.

Amlett, John. S Summer 1757 R 14 yrs Lent 1758. St.

Amor, John. R 14 yrs Jly TB to Va Sep 1741. Wi.

Amor, Mary. R for Barbados or Jamaica Dec 1689. M.

Amor, William of Egham. SQS Jly 1760. Sy.

Amos, Ann. S & T Sep 1731 *Smith* LC Va 1732. M.

Amos, Josiah. S Jan-Jun T Jun 1728 *Elizabeth* LC Potomack Aug 1729. L.

Ancell. *See* Ansell.

Ancher, Sarah, spinster, als wife of John of St. Saviour, Southwark. R for Barbados or Jamaica Feb 1676. Sy.

Andersey, Alford. SQS & TB Oct 1749. So.

Andersey, Thomas. Rebel T 1685.

Anderson, Ann. T Dec 1731 *Forward.* Sy.

Anderson, Ann. S May T Sep 1737 *Pretty Patsy* to Md. M.

Anderson, Ann. S Jan 1745. L.

Anderson, Ann. AT City Summer 1759. Nl.

Anderson, Ann. S Apr-May 1775. M.

Anderson, Benjamin. S Jly T Sep 1766 *Justitia.* M.

Anderson, Charles. S Summer 1733 R Lent 1740 (SP). Sh.

Anderson, Christian. T Apr 1770 *New Trial.* Sy.

Anderson, David. SQS Apr 1719. Du.

Anderson, David. S Jan-Jun T Jun 1728 *Elizabeth* LC Va Aug 1729. M.

Anderson, Edward (1745). *See* Andrews. Su.

Anderson, Elizabeth. S Aug 1720 T Mar 1723. Bu.

Anderson als Fendeloe, Elizabeth. S Lent TB Apr 1756. Db.

Anderson, George. S s shirt Apr T Dec 1735 *John* LC Annapolis Sep 1736. M.

Anderson, George. S May 1760. M.

Anderson, Henry. T Apr 1766 *Ann.* K.

Anderson, Isabella (1760). *See* Paterson. M.

Anderson, James. R for Barbados Jly 1668. M.

Anderson, James, aged 16, fair. S Jan T Feb 1723 *Jonathan* LC Md Jly 1724. L.

Anderson, James (1736). *See* Henderson. Cu.

Anderson, James of St. Paul, Covent Garden, yeoman. S s plates & T Jan 1740 *York.* M.

Anderson, James. S Jly 1763. M.

Anderson, Jane. S & T Oct 1730 *Forward* LC Potomack Jan 1731. M.

Anderson, Jane. S May-Jly 1746. M.

Anderson, Jane. AT City Summer 1758. Nl.

Anderson, John (1688). *See* Barnes. L.

Anderson, John. R for Barbados or Jamaica May 1691.

Anderson, John. SQS Apr 1719. Du.

Anderson, John (1722). *See* Andrews. M.

Anderson, John. S Aug T Oct 1726 *Forward* to Va. M.

Anderson, John. S & T Oct 1730 *Forward* LC Potomack Jan 1731. M.

Anderson, John. S Mar 1740. De.

Anderson, John. S Mar TB Apr 1755. Le.

Anderson, Joseph of St. Giles in Fields. S s harness & T Dec 1740 *Vernon.* M.

Anderson, Joshua. S Jan-Feb T Apr 1753 *Thames.* M.

Anderson, Lionel. PT Jly 1680. M.

Anderson, Luke. S Jan-Jun 1747. M.

Anderson, Luke. S Oct T Dec 1771 *Justitia.* L.

Anderson, Margaret. AT City Summer 1758. Nl.

Anderson als Blacklock, Martha. R & T Oct 1722 *Forward* C Annapolis Jun 1723. M.

Anderson, Mary (1732). *See* Foster. Y.

Anderson als Strong, Mary of St. Clement Danes, widow. S s spoon Jly-Oct 1740 T Jan 1741 *Harpooner* to Va. M.

Anderson, Mary. S Apr T May 1750 *Lichfield*. L.

Anderson, Michael. S Feb T Mar 1727 *Rappahannock* to Md. M.

Anderson, Mildred. SQS at Faversham & R Jun 1720. K.

Anderson, Peter. R for Barbados Dec 1683. M.

Anderson als Davis, Peter. R for Barbados or Jamaica Dec 1699 & Aug 1700. L.

Anderson, Philip. S Summer 1740. Ch.

Anderson, Procter. S Jly T Oct 1741 *Sea Horse* to Va. M.

Anderson, Rachael. S Oct 1761 T Apr 1762 *Dolphin*. M.

Anderson, Richard. R & T Jan 1722 *Gilbert* LC Annapolis Jly 1722. M.

Anderson, Richard. R 14 yrs Mar 1750. Ha.

Anderson, Richard (1775). *See* Smith. Le.

Anderson als Petch, Robert. S s at Whitby Lent TB May 1772. Y.

Anderson, Sarah. S Jly T Sep 1755 *Tryal*. L.

Anderson, Sarah. R 14 yrs City Summer 1758. Nl.

Anderson, Thomas. AT from QS Summer 1725. St.

Anderson, Thomas. S May T Jun 1726 *Loyal Margaret* LC Annapolis Oct 1726. M.

Anderson, Thomas. S May-Jly 1746. M.

Anderson, Thomas (1759). *See* Heslop, John. Nl.

Anderson, William. T Apr 1733 *Patapsco* LC Md Nov 1733. Sy.

Anderson, William. S for coining Mar 1750 R Lent 1751
    T *Happy Jennett* LC Md Oct 1751. Db.

Anderson, William. S s malt at St. Oswald, Durham, Summer 1765. Du.

Anderton, Eleanor. S Lent 1745. Sy.

Anderton, Elizabeth. R for America Mar 1697. Le.

Anderton, George. R for Barbados & TB Oct 1667. L.

Anderton, Thomas. S Dec 1765 T Jan 1766 *Tryal*. L.

Anderton, William. S Jan T Mar 1764 *Tryal*. L.

Andley, Elizabeth. SQS Oct 1735 TB to Md Jan 1736. So.

Andre, Joseph. S s quilt & blankets Lent 1760. Be.

Andrew, Cullen. R 14 yrs Aug 1728. So.

Andrew, John of Crompsall. SQS Apr 1752. La.

Andrew, John of St. Saviour, Southwark. SQS Jly T Sep 1766 *Justitia*. Sy.

Andrew, Thomas. S Aug. 1767. Co.

Andrews, Aron. T Apr 1725 *Sukey* but died on passage. E.

Andrews, Amos. R 14 yrs Mar 1750. So.

Andrews, Anne, aged 27, black hair. S Jly T Oct 1720 *Gilbert* to Md. M.

Andrews, Charles. S Jun T Nov 1743 *George William*. M.

Andrews, Charles. S Feb 1749. Ha.

Andrews als Anderson, Edward. S Lent 1745. Su.

Andrews, Edward. T May 1751 *Tryal*. Sy.

Andrews, Edward (1765). *See* Andrews, Thomas. Ha.

Andrews, Elizabeth. AT Oct 1716 T Jan 1717 *Queen Elizabeth* to Jamaica. M.

Andrews, Elizabeth. S Norwich Summer 1764. Nf.

Andrews, George. S Apr-May T May 1744 *Justitia*. M.
Andrews, Hanna. R Dec 1679 AT Feb 1680. M.
Andrews, Ishmael of Calne. R for Barbados Jly 1688. Wi.
Andrews, James. S Lent 1763. K.
Andrews, James. S s linen from croft & R 14 yrs Summer 1775. Wo.
Andrews, Jasper. S Mar 1720 & T Jan 1722 *Gilbert* LC Annapolis Jly 1722. L.
Andrews, John. Rebel T 1685.
Andrews als Anderson, John. R May T Jly 1722 *Alexander* to Nevis or Jamaica. M.
Andrews, John. R 14 yrs Jly 1735. Wi.
Andrews, John (1738). *See* Sutton. So.
Andrews, John. S s horse Lent R Summer 1739. (SP). Wo.
Andrews, John. S Lent 1744. Su.
Andrews, John. S s at Westbury Summer TB Jly 1752. G.
Andrews, John. SQS & T Sep 1764 *Justitia*. M.
Andrews, John. S Apr 1769. De.
Andrews, Joseph. T Oct 1732 *Caesar*. Ht.
Andrews, Martha. SQS May 1754. M.
Andrews, Mary. R Oct 1724. M.
Andrews, Mary. S for buglary Summer 1729 R Summer 1730. Wo.
Andrews, Mary (1734). *See* Martin. M.
Andrews, Mary. S Mar 1771 TB to Va. De.
Andrews, Richard. T Jly 1722 *Alexander*. Sy.
Andrews, Richard. R 14 yrs Apr 1742. Ha.
Andrews, Richard (1766). *See* Richardson. Sh.
Andrews, Richard. S s at Bromyard Lent 1767. He.
Andrewes, Robert. R for Barbados or Jamaica Mar 1688. L.
Andrews als Ambrose, Robert. R for America Aug 1715. M.
Andrews, Robert of Bermondsey. SQS Jan T Apr 1765 *Ann*. Sy.
Andrewes, Susan. R for Jamaica Mar 1665.
Andrews, Thomas. T Nov 1725 *Rappahannock* LC Va Aug 1726. Sy.
Andrews, Thomas. R 14 yrs Aug 1742. So.
Andrews, Thomas als Edward. S Mar 1765. Ha.
Andrews, Thomas. S Mar 1765. Ha.
Andrews, Thomas. S & R 14 yrs Lent T Apr 1773. Wa.
Andrewes, William of Burnham, husbandman. R for Barbados Jly 1664. So.
Andrewes, William of Selscombe. R (Newgate) for Barbados Aug 1668. Sy.
Andrews, William. S & T Dec 1740 *Vernon*. L.
Andrews, William. T Sep 1757 *Thetis*. Sy.
Andrews, William T Apr 1762 *Neptune*. K.
Andrews, William. S s at St. Lawrence, Ludlow, & breaking out of gaol Lent 1764. Sh.
Andrews, William. S Oct 1768 T Jan 1769 *Thornton*. M.
Andrewsby, Jane. S Feb T Mar 1729 *Patapsco* LC Annapolis Dec 1729. M.
Andron, John. R for America Mar 1690. Le.
Angell, Isaac. S Feb 1754. L.
Angel, John. R & T Jan 1722 *Gilbert* LC Annapolis Jly 1722. M.

Angell, John. S & TB Aug 1739. G.

Angel, Nathaniel. S Lent 1766. Nf.

Anger, Elizabeth. R Aug T Oct 1723 *Forward* to Va. M.

Anger, Joseph. S Summer 1757. Nf.

Angess, William. S & T Sep 1766 *Justitia*. M.

Angle, Ann. S Jan-Feb T Apr 1772. *Thornton*. M.

Angus, Alexander. S Jly 1766. Ha.

Angus, Daniel. S Feb 1775. L.

Angus, Robert. R 14 yrs Summer 1729. Nl.

Angus, Robert. S Oct T Dec 1771 *Justitia*. L.

Angus, Robert. SQS May 1774. M.

Ankhorn, John. S Lent 1765. Wa.

Annable, Samuel. S Jly T Aug 1721 *Prince Royal* LC Va Nov 1721. L.

Annasant, Brillia of Newington. S Summer T Oct 1750 *Rachael*. Sy.

Annesley, William. R Apr TB for Barbados Jun 1669. M.

Annitts, Mary. S Dec 1733 T Jan 1734 *Caesar* but died on passage. M.

Ansees als Ansells, Hugh. S Dec 1727. M.

Ansell, George. S s heifers & R 14 yrs Lent T Sep 1768. Li.

Ansell, Henry. T Sep 1730 *Smith*. K.

Ancell, John. S s sheep Summer 1742 R 14 yrs Lent 1743. Li.

Ansell, John. SQS May 1764. Ha.

Ancell, Judith of Ayot. R for Barbados or Jamaica Feb 1676. Ht.

Ansell, William. S s at Cookham Lent 1752. Be.

Anslee, Jeremiah. SQS & TB Feb 1738. G.

Ansley, John. SQS Apr T May 1750 *Lichfield*. M.

Anslow, Jane. S s silver watch Jan T Apr 1735 *Patapsco* LC Md Oct 1735. L.

Anson, Benjamin. SQS Feb T Mar 1750 *Tryal*. M.

Anstead, Daniel. R for Barbados Jly 1675. L.

Anstis, Elizabeth. S Aug 1757. So.

Anstis, John. R 14 yrs Mar 1774. De.

Anteel, Susanna. S & T Dec 1736 *Dorsetshire*. L.

Anthony, Edward. R for Barbados or Jamaica Feb 1687. M.

Anthony, John. S Jly T Aug 1721 *Prince Royal* but died on passage. L.

Anthony als Jennings, Mary. S Mar 1754. L.

Anthony, Mary. S May T Jun 1768 *Tryal*. M.

Anthorp, Corbet. S & T Dec 1734 *Caesar* LC Va Jly 1735. L.

Antrobus, John. S Oct 1768 T Jan 1769 *Thornton*. M.

Apperley, John. S s at Kings Caple Lent 1751. He.

Apperton als Appleton, Ellen of Ashton. SQS Jly 1766. La.

Ap Phillips, Philip of Shrewsbury. R for America Nov 1694. Sh.

Appleby, Anne (1728). *See* Birch. X.

Appleby, Joan of St. George, Southwark. R for Barbados or Jamaica Feb 1696. Sy.

Appleby, Mary wife of George. S s silver spoon at Lent 1757. Sh.

Epelby, Mary. S Jan-Apr 1748. M.

Appleby, Richard. S s from ship in River Tees Summer 1754. Du.

Applebey, Robert. S Jan-Jun T Jun 1728 *Elizabeth* LC Potomack Aug 1729. M.

Appleby, Thomas. SQS Dec 1755 T Jan 1756 *Greyhound*. M.

Applethorpe or Abthorpe, John. T Jly 1724 *Robert* LC Md Jun 1725. Sy.

Appleton, Ellen (1766). *See* Apperton. La.
Appleton, Francis. S Summer 1740. Sh.
Appleton, Mary. S Feb T Mar 1731 *Patapsco* to Md. M.
Appleton, Mary. S Summer 1756. Sy.
Appleton, Thomas. S Jly 1738. Ha.
Appletree, Robert. R for Barbados May 1676. M.
Appleyard, Abraham. AT Lent & Summer 1765. Y.
Appleyard, Elizabeth. S Oct T Nov 1728 *Forward* LC Rappahannock
    Jun 1729. L.
Applin, Robert. S May T Jun 1764 *Dolphin*. M.
Aplyn, William. Rebel T 1685.
Apps, Thomas. S Oct 1772. L.
Apsly, Richard. PT May R Dec 1699. M.
Apted, Elizabeth. S Summer T Sep 1751 *Greyhound*. Sy.
Aram, Thomas. S s horse Lent R 14 yrs Summer 1731. Li.
Archdeacon, John. T May 1767 *Thornton*. K.
Archdeacon, William. S Feb T Apr 1741 *Speedwell* or *Mediterranean*. M.
Archer, Anne. R for Barbados Mar 1683. M.
Archer, Benjamin. S Lent 1763. Hu.
Archer, Daniel. R for America Aug 1715. L.
Archer, Daniel (1767). *See* Hudson. Nt.
Archer, Elizabeth wife of William. S Sep 1737 T Jan 1738 *Dorsetshire*. M.
Archer, Isaac. S May-Jly 1773. M.
Archer, John. R for plantations Jan 1665. L.
Archer, John. R (Midland Circ) for America Feb 1709. X.
Archer, John. T Oct 1720 *Gilbert*. Ht.
Archer, John. S s at Cirencester Summer 1758. G.
Archer, John. S May-Jly 1773. M.
Archer, Judith (1750). *See* Butler. M.
Archer, Mary (1728). *See* Lewent. M.
Archer, Mary (1758). *See* Hancock. St.
Archer, Matthew. S City Summer 1751. Nl.
Archer, Maurice. R for Barbados or Jamaica Jly 1686. L.
Archer, Peter. R for Va s horse Jly 1649. M.
Archer, William. S s 72 half pence at Rugeley Lent 1770. St.
Archer, William. S Jan-Feb 1774. M.
Archett als Orchard, Thomas. Rebel T 1685.
Ardern, Robert. S Feb T Mar 1758 *Dragon*. L.
Ardern, Robert. S Feb 1759. L.
Ardin, James. R Oct 1690. M.
Argent, Ann, of Wethersfield, spinster. SQS Apr T Sep 1767 *Justitia*. E.
Arkell, Mary. S s cloth at Cheltenham Summer 1729. G.
Arle, Elizabeth. LC from *Patapsco* Annapolis Nov 1733. X.
Arlett, Thomas. R for life Mar 1773. Ha.
Arlinge, Francis. S Dec 1772. M.
Arlington, Lidia (1682). *See* Garrington. L.
Arlise, John. S s cattle Lent R 14 yrs Summer 1759. Li.
Arlot, Francis. S Jly 1736. Ha.
Arlund, Thomas. SQS Jly 1732. So.
Arm, Elizabeth. S Feb T Apr 1741 *Speedwell*. L.
Arm, Thomas, als Hughes, John. R 14 yrs s sheep Summer 1769. Wa.

Armer, John. R Jly 1775 to be T 14 yrs. M.

Armory, Robert. R Apr TB for Barbados Jun 1669. M.

Armiger, James. S s at Painswick Summer 1775. G.

Armistead, Ann (1740). *See* Armstrong. L.

Armitage, Isaac of Gravely. R for Barbados or Jamaica Jly 1715. K.

Armitage, Mary. S Aug T Oct 1724 *Forward* to Md. M.

Armitage, Richard. S Summer R Aug 1665 for Barbados. Sy.

Armitage, Thomas. S Aug T Sep 1725 *Forward* LC Annapolis Dec 1725. L.

Armitage, William of Kimbolton, gent. R for America Mar 1682. He.

Armond, John. S Apr T Jly 1770 *Scarsdale*. L.

Armson, Thomas. R & T Dec 1734 *Caesar* LC Va Jly 1735. M.

Armstead, Hannah. S Oct T Nov 1759 *Phoenix*. L.

Armstrong als Armistead, Ann. S & T Dec 1740 *Vernon*. L.

Armstrong als Forster, Ann. AT City Summer 1759. Nl.

Armstrong, Charles. S Mar 1772 TB to Va. De.

Armstrong, Christopher. R 14 yrs s horse Sep 1768. Cu.

Armstrong, Elizabeth, als Little Bess. S & T Sep 1731 *Smith* LC Va 1732. L.

Armstrong, Frances (1773). See Stones, Rebecca.

Armestrong, Francis. R for America Jly 1687. Nt.

Armstrong, George. S Feb 1773. L.

Armstrong, James. AT Summer 1737. Cu.

Armstrong, James (1753). *See* Stothart. Nl.

Armstrong, John. TB Apr 1749. Db.

Armstrong, John. R 14 yrs Summer 1757. Cu.

Armstrong, John (1764). See Bell. Du.

Armstrong, John. T 14 yrs Dec 1771 *Justitia*. K.

Armstrong, Martha wife of John. S s at Stanton Lent 1770. Su.

Armstrong, Mary. SQS & T Sep 1751 *Greyhound*. M.

Armstrong, Mary. SQS Jan 1774. M.

Armstrong, Mary. S Feb 1774. L.

Armstrong, Obediah. S for perjury Summer 1755; to stand in pillory at Carlisle for 2 market days with a paper over his head denoting his crime before transportation. Cu.

Armstrong, Paul. T Sep 1751 *Greyhound*. M.

Armstrong, Robert. S Lent R 14 yrs Summer 1743. Su.

Armstrong, Robert. S Feb 1773. L.

Armstrong als Welchman, Samuel. R May T Jly 1722 *Alexander* to Nevis or Jamaica. M.

Armstrong, Solomon. S s at Windsor Lent 1725 T *Sukey* LC Md Sep 1725. Be.

Armstrong, Thomas. R Jly T Aug 1721 *Prince Royal* LC Va Nov 1721. M.

Armstrong, Thomas. S Summer 1721 R 14 yrs Summer 1724. Du.

Armstrong, Thomas. S & T Jan 1756 *Greyhound*. M.

Armstrong, Thomas (1758). *See* Best. Du.

Armstrong, Walter. S Summer 1729. Cu.

Armstrong, William. S s greatcoat at Cookham & frock at Bray Summer 1758. Be.

Armstrong, William. SQS Sep T Dec 1763 *Neptune*. M.

Armstrong, William. S for highway robbery at Kinver Lent R 14 yrs Summer 1774. St.

Arnaux, Jane. R for Barbados or Jamaica Mar 1685. M.

Arne, John of Shurdington. R fo America Jly 1683. G.

Arney, John (1699). *See* Barnicott. Co.

Arney, John. S Jly 1718 to be T to Va. So.

Arnoe, James. R May AT Jly 1697. M.

Arnold, Benjamin. S s at Hanney Lent 1744. Be.

Arnold als Onyon, Catherine. S Aug T Oct 1726 *Forward* to Va. M.

Arnold, Christian. S Aug T Oct 1726 *Forward*. L.

Arnold, Edward. TB Mar 1770. Db.

Arnold, George. S Mar 1740. De.

Arnold, George. T Sep 1767 *Justitia*. Ht.

Arnold, Henry Mitchell. S Feb T 14 yrs Mar 1730 *Patapsco* LC Md Sep 1730. L.

Arnold, James. S Feb T Mar 1730 *Patapsco* LC Annapolis Sep 1730. M.

Arnold, Jane. S for shoplifting & R 14 yrs Lent 1772. Be.

Arnold, John. Rebel T 1685.

Arnold, John. R for Barbados or Jamaica Dec 1698. L.

Arnold, John. T May 1744 *Justitia*. K.

Arnold, John of Christ Church. SQS & T Jan 1767 *Tryal*. Sy.

Arnold, Mary. R for America May 1704. L.

Arnold, Mary. S Mar 1732. Co.

Arnold, Mary. S Sep-Oct T Dec 1752 *Greyhound*. M.

Arnold, Mary. S Dec 1757 T Mar 1758 *Dragon*. M.

Arnold, Rebecca. S Jly T Sep 1766 *Justitia*. M.

Arnold, Richard. S Feb T Mar 1727 *Rappahannock* to Md. M.

Arnold, Richard. S Lent 1775. Sy.

Arnold, Robert of Manchester, tinplate worker. SQS Apr 1773. La.

Arnold, Rowland. S Sep T Dec 1767 *Neptune*. L.

Arnold, Ruth. S Jan T Feb 1724 *Anne*. L.

Arnold, Samuel. S Jan 1761. M.

Arnold, Sarah. S Jan T Mar 1750 *Tryal*. M.

Arnold, Susannah. S Apr T Nov 1759 *Phoenix*. M.

Arnold, Timothy. T Apr 1733 *Patapsco*. Ht.

Arnot, Mary. S Dec 1761 T Apr 1762 *Dolphin*. M.

Arons, Benie. S & T Jly 1771 *Scarsdale*. L.

Aronson, John. T Jun 1738 *Forward*. Sy.

Arpin, Robert. S Lent 1742. Sh.

Arrickson, Andrew. S at Ipswich Mar 1775. Su.

Arrington, Mary (1734). *See* Harrington. M.

Aris, Edward. S Jun-Dec 1738 T Jan 1739 *Dorsetshire* to Va. M.

Ariss, John. T 14 yrs Apr 1768 *Thornton*. Ht.

Aris, Samuel. R for Barbados or Jamaica Dec 1698. L.

Arris, Thomas. R (Midland Circ) for America Feb 1681. L.

Arrowsmith, Elizabeth. R 14 yrs for Carolina May 1719. L.

Arrowsmith, John. S Feb T Apr 1734 *Patapsco* to Md. M.

Arrowsmith, Martha. S May T Sep 1737 *Pretty Patsy* to Md. M.

Arrowsmith, Mary. S Sep T Nov 1762 *Prince William*. M.

Arrowsmith, William. R May AT Jun 1691. M.

Arscott, Grace. TB to Va from QS 1759. De.

Arscott, Mary wife of Richard. S 14 yrs Mar 1743. De.
Arscott, Richard the younger. R 14 yrs Jly 1743. De.
Arscott, William. S Mar 1725. De.
Arsom, Mary (1757). *See* Airson. Du.
Arson, Robert. S Summer 1774. Y.
Arter, John. S Summer 1761 R 14 yrs Lent 1762. Sy.
Artery, James. S Jly T Sep 1765 *Justitia*. M.
Arthur, Edward. R for Barbados Mar 1683. L.
Arthur, Hannah. T 14 yrs Nov 1762 *Prince William*. K.
Arthur, John. R for Barbados Aug 1676. Fl.
Arthur, John. S Mar 1734. Co.
Arthur, John. S City for highway robbery Lent R 14 yrs Summer
     1740. Y.
Arthur, Manners. S Mar 1765 TB to Va. De.
Arthur, Miriam als Magdalene of St. George, Southwark. R for
     Barbados or Jamaica Feb 1684. Sy.
Arthur, Richard. S Dec 1748 T Jan 1749 *Laura*. M.
Arthur, Robert of Bristol. R for Barbados Jun 1666. G.
Arthur, Thomas of Horsell. R for Barbados or Jamaica Jly 1696. Sy.
Arundell, Charity of Buckfontleigh. R for Barbados Jly 1683. De.
Arrundel, Israel of Lancaster. R for Barbados Jly 1681. La.
Arundell, John. S Mar 1730. Co.
Arundell, Richard. S Jly 1730. Co.
Arundell, Thomas. SQS Oct T Nov 1759 *Phoenix*. M.
Arwin, James of Rotherhithe. SQS Jan 1764. Sy.
Arwood, Mary. S & T Oct 1729 *Forward* but died on passage. M.
Asbury, John. S s sheep Summer 1750 R 14 yrs Lent 1751. Wa.
Ascock, Thomas aged 25, dark. LC from *Gilbert* Annapolis May 1721. X.
Ascot als Dann, John. S Mar 1740. De.
Ash, Ann of Stepney, spinster. S s spoon Apr T May 1740 *Essex* to Md
     or Va. M.
Ash, Elizabeth. S for murder of her bastard child Summer 1727 R
     14 yrs Summer 1728. St.
Ash, Charles. S Mar 1743. De.
Ash, Elizabeth. S Sep-Oct T Dec 1752 *Greyhound*. M.
Ash, Hannah. S Feb 1754. L.
Ash, John. S Jan-Apr 1748. M.
Ash, John. S Feb T Apr 1766 *Ann*. M.
Ash, John. S Apr T Jun 1768 *Tryal*. M.
Ash, Richard. S Sep T Dec 1735 *John* but LC from *Dorsetshire* Va Sep
     1736. M.
Ash, Richard. S Sep T Dec 1758 *The Brothers*. M.
Ashbolt, Thomas. S s mare Summer 1766 R 14 yrs Lent 1767. Hu.
Ashbrook, Hannah. S & T Dec 1758 *The Brothers*. L.
Ashburn, Joseph (1724). *See* Smith. L.
Ashburn, Mary. LC from *Supply* Md May 1726. X.
Ashburn, Mary (1748). *See* Aspinal. La.
Ashby, John. Died on passage in *Gilbert* 1721. X.
Ashby als Cromwell, John. S Lent 1752. Nf.
Ashby, John. T Sep 1755 *Tryal*. M.
Ashby, John. S Lent R 14 yrs Summer 1756. K.

Ashby als Ashley. Mary. S Dec 1735 T Jan 1736 *Dorsetshire* LC Va Sep 1736. M.

Ashby, Sarah. S Apr 1720. M.

Ashby, Thomas. S s horse Lent R 14 yrs Summer 1741 (SP). Be.

Ashby, Thomas. S Lent R 14 yrs Summer 1756. Le.

Ashcomb, John. S Feb T Mar 1727 *Rappahannock*. L.

Ashcraft als Ashcroft, Thomas. S s sheep & R Summer 1775. Wo.

Ashden, William. S Apr T 14 yrs May 1718 *Tryal* LC Charles Town Aug 1718. LM.

Ashden, William. S May T Jly 1722 *Alexander* to Nevis or Jamaica. M.

Ashenhurst, John. R Apr TB for Barbados Oct 1669. M.

Ashenore, John. R for Barbados Jly 1675. L.

Asher, Isaac. S Oct 1772. L.

Asher, James. S Mar TB to Va Apr 1767. Wi.

Asher, Levi. S May-Jly 1773. M.

Ashfield, Thomas. T Jun 1740 *Essex*. Sy.

Ashfield als Ashwell als Attaway, William of Northfield. R for America Feb 1690. Wo.

Ashford, Ambrose. Rebel T 1685.

Ashford, Elizabeth. S & T Sep 1767 *Justitia*. M.

Ashford, Elizabeth. SQS Feb T Apr 1769 *Tryal*. M.

Ashford, Ralph. SQS Jun T Sep 1766 *Justitia*. M.

Ashford, Samuel. T Jly 1770 *Scarsdale*. M.

Ashford, Thomas. TB to Va from QS 1740. De.

Ashford, Thomas. S Jly T Nov 1762 *Prince William*. M.

Ashford, William. S Summer 1749. K.

Ashford, William. S Jly 1774 to be T 14 yrs. L.

Ashkettle, John. S s wool at Nacton Summer 1772. Su.

Ashley, Ann. S Feb 1754. L.

Ashley, Ann. S Apr-Jun T Jly 1772 *Tayloe*. M.

Ashley, Charles Jr. of Stow on the Wold. R for America Feb 1700. G.

Ashly, Christopher. R for Barbados or Jamaica May 1684. L.

Ashley, Daniel. S Jan T Feb 1733 *Smith*. L.

Ashley als Ashby, Elizabeth. S Aug T Oct 1741 *Sea Horse* to Va. M.

Ashley, James. T Jan 1741 *Vernon*. E.

Ashley, Mary (1735). *See* Ashby. M.

Ashly, Sarah. S Dec 1719. M.

Ashley, Thomas. T Apr 1753 *Thames*. L.

Ashley, William. R Feb 1675. M.

Ashley, William of Woodstock. R for America Feb 1690. O.

Ashley, William. S Lent 1758. Su.

Ashman, Ann wife of Samuel. S s rum Oct T Dec 1736 *Dorsetshire* to Va. M.

Ashman, Charles. S Jan-Feb T Apr 1771 *Thornton*. M.

Ashman, Isaac. S Aug 1734. So.

Ashmore, Charles of St. Saviour, Southwark. SQS Jan T Apr 1768 *Thornton*. Sy.

Ashmore, Elizabeth. S Feb T Mar 1727 *Rappahannock* to Md. M.

Ashmore, Henry. S Summer 1743 R 14 yrs Lent 1774. St.

Ashmore, Robert. S s horse Lent R 14 yrs Summer TB Jly 1745. Db.

Ashton, Ann. S May 1770. M.

Ashton, Arthur. S Nov T Dec 1763 *Neptune*. L.

Ashton, James, clerk. S Jly T Sep 1757 *Thetis*. M.

Ashton, James. SQS Apr T Jly 1771 *Scarsdale*. M.

Ashton als Hamilton, John. S May T Jun 1727 *Susanna*. M.

Ashton, Joseph. S for highway robbery Lent R 14 yrs Summer 1728. G.

Ashton, Samuel of Manchester. SQS Apr 1741. La.

Ashton, William. R 14 yrs Mar 1767. Ha.

Ashwell, John. T Jun 1740 *Essex*. Sy.

Ashwell, Richard. S for highway robbery Summer 1758 R 14 yrs Lent 1759. Su.

Ashwell, Sarah. S for murder of her bastard child Lent R 14 yrs Summer 1742. Bd.

Ashwell, William (1690). *See* Ashfield. Wo.

Ashwood, John. R for America Aug 1713. L.

Ashworth, Ellis. S Summer 1772. La.

Ashworth, John of St. James, Westminster. SW Apr 1774. M.

Askeron, Thomas. S for highway robbery Summer 1744 R 14 yrs Lent TB May 1745. Y.

Askew, Anne. S Summer 1722 T Oct 1723 *Foward* to Va from London. Y.

Askew als Askiss, Catherine. S & T Apr 1759 *Thetis*. L.

Askew, Charles. S & T Dec 1731 *Forward*. L.

Askew, Jonathan. S s at Norton & Lenchwick Lent 1750. Wo.

Askew als King, Mary. S Feb T Mar 1731 *Patapsco* LC Annapolis Jun 1731. M.

Askew, Mary. S Apr-May 1754. M.

Askew, William. S Lent 1750. Hu.

Askin, John. S Lent T Apr 1768. Li.

Askins, Mary. S s at St. Martin, Worcester, Lent 1753. Wo.

Askiss, Catherine (1759). *See* Askew. L.

Aspenwell, William (Richard). SQS Apr T Jly 1753 *Tryal*. M.

Aspey, John. S s cow Lent R 14 yrs Summer 1748. He.

Aspinall, Alice of Manchester, spinster. SQS Apr 1742. La.

Aspinall, Katherine of St. George, Southwark. R for Barbados or Jamaica Jun 1675. Sy.

Aspinal, John. R 14 yrs Jly TB to Va Sep 1756. Wi.

Aspinall als Ashburn als Blackmall, Mary of Liverpool, spinster. SQS Jan 1748: lying-in charges and cost of burying her child paid by House of Correction in Manchester. La.

Aspinall, William of Haslingden, tailor. SQS Jan 1766. La.

Aspindale, Peter. S Lent T May 1755 *Rose*. E.

Aspiner, John. SWK Jly 1772. K.

Aspland, William. S Sep-Oct T Dec 1771 *Justitia*. M.

Aspley als Dalton, Jane. S & T Feb 1744 *Neptune* to Md. M.

Asplin, Minah (1775). *See* Rutter. Sh.

Asplyn, Samuel of Ashleworth. R for Jamaica, Barbados or Bermuda Feb 1686. G.

Asplin, William of Low Leyton, mariner. SQS Jan T May 1750 *Lichfield*. E.

Aspy, William. S s at Droitwich Lent 1724. Wo.

Assent, James. R for 14 yrs Oct 1772. M.

Asson, Samuel. S Summer R Aug 1663 for Barbados. Ht.
Astell, Mary. S Jan T Feb 1726 *Supply* LC Annapolis May 1726. M.
Astell, Thomas. S s horse Lent R 14 yrs Summer 1766. Nt.
Astley, Charles. R May 1684. M.
Astley, Esther. S & T Jan 1769 *Thornton*. M.
Astley, Peter of Bedford, weaver. SQS Jly 1763. La.
Astley, William. S s from corn mill Lent 1742. La.
Aston als Styck als Underwood, Dorothy. S s at Broseley Summer
    1768. Sh.
Aston, Jane wife of Walter. S & R Lent 1775. Sh.
Aston, John. S May-Jly 1750. M.
Aston, Thomas. S s at Aldridge Lent 1727. St.
Aston, Thomas (1750). *See* Smithiman. St.
Ater, John. S Feb 1727. L.
Ates, Joseph (1768). *See* Yates. L.
Atherley, Susannah. S May T Jun 1768 *Tryal*. M.
Atherton, James. R & T for life Jly 1770 *Scarsdale*. M.
Atherton, John. T Jly 1770 *Scarsdale*. M.
Atherton, Richard (1775). *See* Stot. Sh.
Atherton, Robert. T Sep 1730 *Smith*. Sy.
Atkey, William. S Aug 1732 TB to Va. De.
Atkins, Charles. S May T Jun 1726 *Loyal Margaret* LC Annapolis Oct
    1726. M.
Atkins, Edward. S Feb T Mar 1729 *Patapsco* LC Annapolis Dec 1729. M.
Atkins, Elizabeth. R for Jamaica Aug 1661. M.
Atkins, Elizabeth. T Jly 1722 *Alexander*. Sy.
Atkins, George. S Dec 1766 T Jan 1767 *Tryal*. M.
Atkins, Henry. S Jan 1724 for T to Carolina. M.
Atkins, Jeremy. Rebel T 1685.
Atkins, John. R for Barbados May 1676. L.
Atkins, John. S Jly 1737. Do.
Atkins, John (1759). *See* Ludkins. Nf.
Atkins, Joseph. S Jan T Sep 1737 *Pretty Patsy* to Md. M.
Atkins, Joseph. SQS May T Nov 1762 *Prince William*. M.
Atkins, Lydia of Whitechapel, widow. S s broom & T Dec 1740 *Vernon*
    to Md. M.
Atkins, Martha. S May-Jun T Jly 1753 *Tryal*. M.
Atkins, Mary. S Jly T Aug 1721 *Prince Royal* to Va. M.
Atkins, Mary. S & T Sep 1731 *Smith* LC Va 1732. L.
Atkins, Mary. S for shoplifting Lent R 14 yrs Summer 1737. Y.
Atkins, Richard of Clapham. SQS Jan T May 1767 *Thornton*. Sy.
Atkins, Sarah. S s at Bedwardine Lent 1772. Wo.
Atkins als Atkinson, Susannah. S May-Jly 1774. M.
Atkins, Thomas. PT Jan R Aug 1700. M.
Atkins, Thomas. S Dec 1765 T Jan 1766 *Tryal*. L.
Atkins, Thomas. S Dec 1766 T Jan 1767 *Tryal*. M.
Atkins, William. S Jan-Jun T Jun 1728 *Elizabeth* LC Potomack Aug
    1729. L.
Atkins, William. SQS Mar TB to Md Apr 1742. Le.
Atkins, William. S Summer 1750. Nf.
Atkinson, Barbara. R 14 yrs Summer 1755. Cu.

Atkinson, Christopher. S & T Apr 1733 *Patapsco* LC Annapolis Nov 1733. L.

Atkinson, Dorothy (1679). *See* Clarke. L.

Atkinson, Elizabeth. S & T Jan 1722 *Gilbert* LC Annapolis Jly 1722. M.

Atkinson, Frances (1656). *See* Jackson.

Atkinson, Henry. R May AT Jly 1697. M.

Atkinson, Jane (1700). *See* Biggs. M.

Atkinson, Jane. AT City Summer 1759. Nl.

Atkinson, John. S Oct T Dec 1724 *Rappahannock*. L.

Atkinson, John. SQS Wetherby Jan 1725 T *Supply* LC Md May 1726. Y.

Atkinson, John. S Apr T Jun 1742 *Bladon*. L.

Atkinson, John. S Jan-Apr 1749. M.

Atkinson, John. T 14 yrs Dec 1758 *The Brothers*. K.

Atkinson, John. S Lent TB Aug 1760. Y.

Atkinson, John. S s gelding at Topcliffe R 14 yrs Summer 1768 TB Apr 1769. Y.

Atkinson, John of St. Martin in Fields. SW Apr 1773. M.

Atkinson, John. S Summer 1774. E.

Atkinson, Joseph. S Aug 1727 T 14 yrs *Forward* LC Rappahannock May 1728. M.

Atkinson, Mary. S Summer 1740 R 14 yrs Lent 1743. Du.

Atkinson, Mary. SQS Apr T May 1750 *Lichfield*. M.

Atkinson, Miles of Asby. R for Barbados Feb 1673. We.

Atkinson, Richard (1753). *See* Bugg. Li.

Atkinson, Richard. S Sep-Oct T Dec 1753 *Whiteing*. M.

Atkinson, Richard. S s at Hovingham Summer TB Aug 1774. Y.

Atkinson, Robert. S May 1763. M.

Atkinson, Susannah (1774). *See* Atkins. M.

Atkinson, Thomas. S May T Jun 1726 *Loyal Margaret* LC Annapolis Oct 1726. M.

Atkinson, Thomas. S Oct 1774. L.

Atkinson, William. S s sheep Summer 1757 R 14 yrs Lent 1758. Li.

Atkinson, William. S Lent 1759. Y.

Atkinson, William, als Brown, John. AT Lent & Summer 1765. Y.

Atkinson, William. S May 1775. M.

Atley, Christopher of Newington. SQS Apr T May 1750 *Lichfield*. Sy.

Atsey, John. S May T Oct 1719 *Susannah & Sarah* LC Md Apr 1720. L.

Attaway, William (1690). *See* Ashfield. Wo.

Attenborough, Francis. TB Oct 1738. Db.

Atterbury, Henry. S Jan T Feb 1742 *Industry* to Md. M.

Atterbury, William. S & T Apr 1733 *Patapsco* LC Annapolis Nov 1733. M.

Attersley, John of Spalding. R for America Jly 1682. Li.

Attjoy, Peter. R 14 yrs Aug T Sep 1718 *Eagle* to Md or Va. M.

Atton, Geoffrey of Belton. R for America Jly 1716. Ru.

Attridge, William. T 14 yrs Apr 1770 *New Trial*. E.

Atwell, George. R for Barbados or Jamaica Feb 1686. M.

Attwell, Richard. S Summer 1758 R 14 yrs Lent 1759. Be.

Attwood, Francis. S s waggon wheel at Great Chawley Summer 1749. Be.

Atwood, Hannah. S & T Oct 1732 *Caesar* to Va. M.
Atwood, Hannah. S Oct 1772. L.
Attwood, Henry. S s horse Lent R 14 yrs Summer 1766. St.
Atwood, Jane. S Feb 1733. Ha.
Atwood, John. Rebel T 1685.
Atwood, Thomas. S Summer 1756 R 14 yrs Lent 1757. Wo.
Atwood, William. S Mar & Jly 1729. Ha.
Atwool, Thomas. S Mar 1772. So.
Auberry. *See* Awbury.
Auchinleck, Alexander. S s 12 handkerchiefs at New Woodstock Lent
    1769; wife Catherine acquitted. O.
Auckland, Edward, aged 33. R Feb 1664 (SP). L.
Audless, Margaret. S Apr 1746. L.
Ault, Sarah. AT from QS Lent 1773. Db.
Ausley, Adam of Landham. R (Midland Circ) for America Jly 1673. Y.
Ausley, Henry. S Summer 1756. Sy.
Ausley, William of Chiselhurst. R (Newgate) for Barbados Sep 1669. K.
Aust, Anthony. R 14 yrs Jly TB to Va Sep 1756. Wi.
Austin, Abraham. S Jly 1730. De.
Austin, Abraham. S s silver spoons & clogs Jly 1735 T Jan 1736
    Doresetshire LC Va Sep 1736. M.
Austin, Alice. S Oct T Dec 1771 *Justitia*. L.
Austin als Veil, Ann. S Oct 1773. L.
Austin, Bryant. SQS Oct 1774. M.
Austin, Dorothy. AT Feb 1673. M.
Austin als Furmentine, Elizabeth. S Jan T Feb 1733 *Smith*. L.
Austin als Thompson, Elizabeth. LC from *Caesar* Va Jly 1734. X.
Austyne, Gilbert of Christow, husbandman. R for Barbados Jly
    1667. De.
Austin, Henry. S Jan-Feb 1775. M.
Austin, Isaac. S Apr 1773. L.
Austin, Isaac. S Jly 1774. L.
Austin, John. R for Jamaica Feb 1665. M.
Austin, John (1666). *See* Scrugion. G.
Austin, John. S s cloth from tenters Lent 1719 R 14 yrs Summer 1721 T
    Oct 1723 *Forward* to Va. Y.
Austin, John. T May 1737 *Forward*. E.
Austin, John. S s horse Summer 1739 R 14 yrs Lent 1740. No.
Austin, John. S Mar 1755. So.
Austin, John. S Oct T Dec 1767 *Neptune*. L.
Austen, Martha of St. Saviour, Southwark. R for Barbados or Jamaica
    Jly 1677. Sy.
Austin, Mary. R 14 yrs Mar 1721. Wi.
Austin, Richard of Basingstoke. R for Barbados Jly 1677. Ha.
Austen, Richard. T Oct 1768 *Justitia*. K.
Austen, Thomas. R for Jamaica Aug 1661. M.
Austen, Thomas of St. Paul Covent Garden. R & TB for Barbados
    Oct 1667. M.
Austen, Thomas. Rebel T 1685.
Austen, Thomas. R for America Jly 1694. No.
Austin, Valentine, als Burridge, Henry. S Lent 1744. Nf.

Austin, William, als Hyde, Augustine. R for Barbados or Jamaica Feb 1687. M.

Autonreith, William. S for life Aug 1763. L.

Avenell, John. S Lent 1774. Sx.

Avenall, William. S Feb 1738. Ha.

Avergirl, Elizabeth of St. George, Southwark. SQS Apr T Sep 1751 *Greyhound*. Sy.

Averis, John. R for Barbados Mar 1681. M.

Avery, Elizabeth. TB to Va from QS 1738. De.

Avery als Weatherspun, Elizabeth. S Aug 1757. De.

Avery, James. LC from *Forward* Md Jun 1723. X.

Every, James. S s at Newbury Summer 1772. Be.

Avery, Jane. S Jan-Apr 1749. M.

Avery, John. R for Barbados or Jamaica Oct 1688. L.

Avery, John. S for ripping lead from house at St. Philip & Jacob Lent TB Mar 1748. G.

Avery, John. S Jly 1749. L.

Everee, John. S Jly T Sep 1767 *Justitia*. M.

Avery, John. S Mar 1768 TB to Va. De.

Every, Mary wife of John. S Jan-Feb 1773. M.

Avery, Mary. S 14 yrs Apr-May 1775. M.

Avery als MacDonald, Patrick. S Jly-Dec 1747. M.

Avery, Richard of Shipston on Stour. R for America Mar 1682. Wa.

Every, Robert of St. Martin in Fields. SW Jan 1775. M.

Avery als Smith, Smith. S s wheat at Aglingworth Lent TB Apr 1756. G.

Avery, Thomas. S Oct 1737 T Jan 1738 *Dorsetshire* to Va. M.

Avery, Thomas. R Mar 1774. Wi.

Avery, William. R Apr TB for Barbados Jun 1669. M.

Aviland, Richard (1664). *See* Smart. G.

Avill, Thomas. S Lent 1756. Ca.

Avis, James, als Mitchell, John. S Dec 1727 T Mar 1729 *Patapsco* LC Annapolis Dec 1729. L.

Aves, Matthew. S Lent 1763. Ca.

Avoake, John. Rebel T 1685.

Avon, William. S Aug 1750. So.

Aubery, John. S & T Dec 1752 *Greyhound*. M.

Awbury, Martha (1753). *See* Helliar, Mary. Ha.

Awbrey, William. S & T Dec 1758 *The Brothers*. L.

Auberry, William. S & R 14 yrs Summer 1768 T Jan 1769. No.

Awdrey, Jane (1747). *See* Wilkins. M.

Awtey, Joshua. S Summer 1740. Y.

Axeley, James. T Sep 1730 *Smith*. Sy.

Axleby, John S Lent s horse R 14 yrs Summer T Sep 1755 *Tryal*. K.

Axtell, Susanna. S Feb 1729. L.

Axton, Lawrence. PT May 1684. M.

Axton, Samuel als Slim John. S Jan 1726 T *Supply* LC Annapolis May 1726. M.

Ayanson, Susan of Egton cum Newland, spinster. R for Barbados Jly 1683. La.

Ayers. *See* Ayres.

Aylerd, Robert. S Jly 1753. Ha.

Aylett als Pallett, William of Watton at Stone. SQS s coat Apr 1774. Ht.

Ayliffe, Charles. S Mar TB Oct 1735. Wi.

Ayling als Pullin, John. S Lent R 14 yrs Summer T Sep 1757 *Thetis*. Sx.

Ayloffe als Ayliffe, Thomas of St. Margaret, Westminster. S s sheep Jly-Oct 1740 T Jan 1741 *Harpooner* to Rappahannock. M.

Aylsbury, Philip. R for America Mar 1697. Li.

Aylsbury, Thomas. S Jly T Sep 1767 *Justitia*. M.

Aylward, John of Bishops Waltham, miller. R for Barbados Feb 1714. Ha.

Aylward, Robert. S Mar 1741. Ha.

Alewood, William. S Mar TB Apr 1775. Nt.

Aymer, Thomas. S Jly 1745. Ha.

Aymes. *See* Ames.

Aires, Aaron. SWK July T Dec 1771 *Justitia*. K.

Ayers, Ann. S Jly-Dec 1747. M.

Ayres, Deborah wife of Robert. S & T Oct 1730 *Forward* LC Potomack Jan 1731. M.

Ayres, Edward of Newington. R for Barbados or Jamaica Jly 1678. Sy.

Eyres, Edward of Venge. R for Barbados or Jamaica Mar 1707. E.

Ayres, Elizabeth. S Aug T Oct 1726 *Forward*. L.

Ares, Garrard. LC from *Robert* Md Jun 1725. X.

Aires, James. T Apr 1759 *Thetis*. Sy.

Ayres, James. S s 8 iron bars at St. Peter in East, Oxford, Summer 1766. O.

Ayres, James. R 14 yrs Aug 1767. So.

Eyres, Jane. S Mar 1766. So.

Ayres, Jeremy. S May T Jun 1726 *Loyal Margaret* to Md. M.

Ayres, John. S Feb T Mar 1729 *Patapsco* LC Annapolis Dec 1729. L.

Ayres, John. T Oct 1738 *Genoa*. K.

Ayers, John. S May T Jun 1756 *Lyon*. L.

Ayres, John (1769). *See* Heirs. Be.

Ayres, John. S Oct 1774. L.

Eyres, Joseph. S Feb T Mar 1727 *Rappahannock* to Md. M.

Ayres, Leonard. S May T Jun 1738 *Forward*. L.

Ayres, Mary. S Jly T 14 yrs Sep 1766 *Justitia*. M.

Ayers, Mary Lhuillier. S Apr T May 1743 *Indian Queen* to Md. M.

Eyres, Robert. S Dec 1737 T Jan 1738 *Dorsetshire*. L.

Ayres, Robert. S Apr-Jun T Jly 1772 *Tayloe*. M.

Aires, Samuel. SWK Jly T Dec 1771 *Justitia*. K.

Aires, Thomas (1726). *See* Acres. M.

Eyres, William. Rebel T 1685.

Eyres, William (1737). *See* Wheeler. So.

Eyres, William. S s heifer & R 14 yrs Summer T Sep 1773. No.

Ayris, Charles. S s sheets at St. Michael, Oxford, Lent 1765; S Berkshire for being at large Lent 1767 & R for life Summer 1767. O.

Ayris, William. SQS Feb 1773. M.

Ayton, Robert. S s at Calverley Lent 1773. Y.

B

Babb, Thomas. S Mar 1746. De.
Babb, Thomas. S Oct T Dec 1769 *Justitia*. L.
Babbington, John. S & R Lent 1731. Sh.
Babington, Joseph. S Summer 1738 R 14 yrs Lent 1739. He.
Babington, Randall. Rebel T 1685.
Babington, William (1694). *See* Smith. M.
Babbs, James. T May 1736 *Patapsco*. K.
Bable, Ann (1726). *See* Elwood. M.
Bacchus, Philip. S s mare at Tunstead Summer 1767 R 14 yrs Lent
    1768. Nf.
Baccus, Thomas. S May T Jun 1727 *Susanna* to Va. M.
Bacealake, Elizabeth. R 14 yrs Jly 1724. De.
Bache, Edward of Ledbury. R 7 yrs for Barbados Feb 1665. He.
Bach, John. R for Barbados Aug 1668. M.
Bache als Batch, John. S Summer 1742 R 14 yrs Lent 1743. Wo.
Bach, Samuel. S s at Sutton Maddock Lent 1763. Sh.
Back, Francis. TB Jly 1766. Db.
Backarac als Abrahams als Isaacs, Lyon. S & T Dec 1771 *Justitia*. M.
Backham, Richard. Rebel T 1685.
Backhouse, Joseph. S Summer 1772. Li.
Backhouse, Margery of Lytham, spinster. SQS Apr 1745. La.
Backway, William. S Mar 1753. Co.
Bacon, George. S s ewes & R 7 yrs Lent 1775. Le.
Bacon, John. S 14 yrs for receiving goods at Wortwell stolen by James
    Rant *(qv)* Summer 1771. Nf.
Bacon, John. S & R Norwich for highway robbery at Heigham Summer
    1772. Nf.
Bacon, Martin. S Lent T *Patapsco* May 1736. Bu.
Bacon, Mary. R & T Apr 1725 *Sukey* LC Annapolis Sep 1725. M.
Bacon, Samuel. R for life Oct 1751-Jan 1752. M.
Bacon, Thomas. S Lent TB Apr 1741. Y.
Bacy. *See* Baisy.
Badal, Anthony (1728). *See* Beadle. L.
Badcock, John. S Aug T Oct 1724 *Forward* LC Annapolis Jun 1725. M.
Badcock, William. TB to Va from QS 1767. De.
Baddely, Thomas. S Lent R 14 yrs Summer 1751. St.
Badenham, John of Tunbridge. R for Barbados or Jamaica Jly 1687. K.
Badge, Sarah. S Sep T Oct 1750 *Rachael*. M.
Badge, Thomas. R Dec 1699 AT Jan 1700. M.
Badger, Alexander of Worcester. S Lent 1720. Wo.
Badger, Charles. S Aug T Sep 1725 *Forward* LC Annapolis Dec 1725. L.
Badger als Brookes, Richard. S 14 yrs for receiving goods stolen at
    Walsall Lent 1771. St.
Badger, Mary (1730). *See* Harwood. M.
Badger, Samuel. S s at Fladbury Lent 1735 R 14 yrs Lent 1736. Wo.
Badger, Thomas. S s at Stoughton Lent 1751. Wo.

Badham, John of Stoke Lacy. R (Western Circ) for America Jly 1700. He.

Badminton, Henry. S Mar 1759. Wi.

Badmington, John. SQS Devizes & TB to Va Apr 1766. Wi.

Badnedge, Edward Jr. S Dec 1753 TB with Edward Badnedge Sr. L.

Badsey, John Jr. S & R 14 yrs Summer 1732. Sh.

Bagdurf, Christopher. S Jan T Mar 1758 *Dragon*. M.

Badgint, Thomas. S Mar 1770. Ha.

Bagent, John. R 14 yrs Jly 1743. Ha.

Bagguley, Ann. R for America Jly 1707. Li.

Bagerley, Anthony (1730). *See* Bagley. M.

Bagford, John. S Aug T Sep 1725 *Forward* LC Annapolis Dec 1725. L.

Bagg, Elizabeth. S Jly T Sep 1755 *Tryal*. L.

Bagg, Thomas of Gregory Stoke. R for Barbados Jly 1688. So.

Bagger, Charles (1725). *See* Badger. L.

Baggott, John. S Apr T May 1750 *Lichfield*. M.

Bagley als Bagerley, Anthony. S & T Oct 1730 *Forward* LC Potomack Jan 1731. M.

Bagley, Edward of Rotherhithe, broker. SQS Jan T Apr 1765 *Ann*. Sy.

Bagley, Thomas. Rebel T 1685.

Baglin, Richard. S Lent R 14 yrs Summer 1724. G.

Bagnall, James. S s sheep Lent R 14 yrs Summer TB Jly 1763. Db.

Bagnall, John. S Summer TB Aug 1771. Nt.

Bagnall, John. R 14 yrs Apr 1773. M.

Bagnell, William. S Oct T Dec 1769 *Justitia*. L.

Bagnon als Berville als Lewis, Philip. S & T Jan 1766 *Tryal*. M.

Bagot, Ann. S Summer 1772. Wa.

Bagot, Stephen. S Apr T May 1752 *Lichfield*. L.

Bagott, William. R for America Feb 1700. Li.

Bagshaw, Henry. S May-Jly T Sep 1751 *Greyhound*. M.

Bagwell, Francis. Rebel T 1685.

Bagwell, John. Rebel T 1685.

Bagwell, Margaret. S Dec 1747. L.

Bagwell, Mary. R Mar 1773. Ha.

Bagwell, Peter. Rebel T 1685.

Baildon, Thomas. R 14 yrs Summer 1730. Y.

Baily, Abraham. S May-Jly 1750. M.

Bailey, Adam. S Lent 1761. No.

Bayly, Alice, spinster, als wife of Henry, aged 63. R for Barbados Feb 1664. L.

Bailey, Alice of Croston, widow. SQS Jly 1753. La.

Bailey, Andrew. R 14 yrs Jly TB to Va Aug 1749. Wi.

Bailey, Ann. S Lent 1752. Bd.

Bayley, Ann. S May 1758. M.

Bayley, Ann. S May T Nov 1759 *Phoenix*. M.

Bailey, Ann, spinster. S s clothing at Blackfriars Dec 1768 T Jan 1769 *Thornton*. L.

Bailey, Cecily (1700). *See* Labree. L. or M.

Bayley, Charles of Wells, husbandman. R for Barbados Feb 1673. So.

Bailey, Charles. TB to Va from QS 1735. De.

Bayley, Charles. SQS Warminster Jly TB to Va Aug 1758. Wi.

Bailey, Charles of East Retford, butcher. SQS s sack Jan 1765. Nt.

Baily, David. SQS May 1764. Ha.

Bailey, Edward. S Sep T Oct 1744 *Susannah*. M.

Baily, Elias. R for life Mar 1775. Ha.

Bayley, Elizabeth. R for plantations Jan 1665. L.

Baily, Elizabeth. R for Jamaica Feb 1666. M.

Baily als Dozzington, Elizabeth. R & T Jan 1722 *Gilbert* LC Md Jly 1722. M.

Bailey als Fry, Elizabeth. S Feb 1770. M.

Bailey, Elizabeth. S Lent 1770. Le.

Bayly, Francis of Horseheath. R (Norf Circ) Feb 1664. K.

Bayley, Francis, aged 25, dark. LC Annapolis May 1721 from *Gilbert*. X.

Bailey, Francis. S Jan-Feb 1775 but marked "stopt". M.

Bailey, Henry. R Jan 1663 to be T 12 yrs. L.

Baily, Henry. R Jly T Aug 1721 *Prince Royal* to Va. M.

Baily, Henry. S Aug 1727. M.

Bailey, Henry. S s shoes at Burford Summer 1738. O.

Bailey, Henry. R City 14 yrs Summer 1754. Nl.

Bayley, Henry. S & R 14 yrs Summer 1758. St.

Bailey, Isaac. S Feb T Sep 1737 *Pretty Patsy* to Md. M.

Bayly, James. S Lent R 14 yrs Summer 1744. Li.

Bailey, James. S Summer T Sep 1751 *Greyhound*. K.

Bayley, James. S s at Berkeley Summer TB Jly 1752. G.

Bailey, James. S Feb T Apr 1768 *Thornton*. M.

Bayley, James of Manchester, shopkeeper. SQS Jan 1772. La.

Bayly, Jane. R Summer 1731. O.

Bailey, Jane. T from Bristol by *Maryland Packet* 1761 but intercepted by French; T Apr 1763 *Neptune*. Wo.

Bayley, John. R for Barbados Mar 1681. M.

Bayley, John (1726). *See* Shales. L.

Bailey, John. S & T Oct 1732 *Caesar* to Va. M.

Bailey, John. S & T Dec 1734 *Caesar* LC Va Jly 1735. L.

Bailey, John. S Jun T Dec 1736 *Dorsetshire* to Va. M.

Bailey, John. S Jan-May T Jun 1738 *Forward* to Md or Va. M.

Baily, John. S Mar 1742. De.

Bailey, John. T Apr 1743 *Justitia*. K.

Bailey, John. S s deer traps at Stow Lent 1745. St.

Bailey, John. S May-Jly 1750. M.

Bailey, John. S City Summer 1753. Nl.

Bailey, John. R 14 yrs Mar 1762. So.

Bailey, John. R for life Lent 1773. Sy.

Bailey, John. S May-Jly 1773. M.

Bailey, John. S May 1775. L.

Bailey, Joseph. S s at Chipping Sodbury Summer 1732. G.

Bailey, Joseph. TB to Va from QS 1741. De.

Bailey, Mark. S s at Whittington Summer 1769. Sh.

Bayly, Martha. PT Oct 1700 R Aug 1701. M.

Bailey, Mary (1725). *See* Savage. L.

Bailey, Mary. TB to Va from QS 1741. De.

Bailey, Mary. S Mar 1766. So.

Bailey, Mary (1774). *See* Bandy. Le.

Bailey, Matthew. SQS Mar TB Apr 1727. Nt.
Bailey, Matthew. S for killing lambs R for life Lent TB Apr 1774. Nt.
Bayley als Bayless, Nathaniel. S Apr-May T Jly 1771 *Scarsdale*. M.
Bailey, Peter. S Summer 1738 R 14 yrs Summer 1739. Cu.
Bayley, Rachael. S Feb-Apr T May 1751 *Tryal*. M.
Bayly als Densloe, Richard of Netherbury. R for Barbados Jly 1681. Do.
Bayly, Richard. S s horse Summer 1731 R 14 yrs Lent 1732. He.
Bailey, Richard. S Feb 1754. L.
Bayley als Beoly, Richard. S for highway robbery Summer 1755 R
    14 yrs Lent TB Apr 1756. Db.
Bailey, Richard of St. Saviour, Southwark, basket maker. SQS Jan
    1775. Sy.
Bailey, Robert. S Oct 1740. L.
Bailey, Robert (1751). *See* Gosling. Nf.
Bailey, Robert. AT Summer 1753. Y.
Bayley, Robert. S for killing cow Lent R 14 yrs Summer 1768. St.
Baily, Robert. T Apr 1771 *Thornton*. Sx.
Bailey, Samuel. S Oct T Dec 1769 *Justitia*. L.
Bailey, Samuel. S s at Hurst Lent 1770. Be.
Baily, Sara. R for Barbados Jly 1674. M.
Bailey als Satchwell, Sarah. S s breeches & T Jan 1736 *Dorsetshire* LC
    Va Sep 1736. M.
Bailey, Sarah. S Jun 1754. L.
Baily, Simon. R 14 yrs Aug 1742. De.
Bailey, Simon. T May 1744 *Justitia*. E.
Bailey, Susannah. S Dec 1743 T Feb 1744 *Neptune* to Md. M.
Bailey, Susannah. S Sep T Oct 1750 *Rachael*. M.
Bailey als Bowden, Susannah. S Sep-Oct 1774. M.
Bayly, Thomas of Sutton Pointz, tailor. R for Barbados Apr 1668. Do.
Bayly, Thomas of Puddletrenthide, husbandman. R for Barbados Feb
    1672. Do.
Bayley, Thomas. S Feb T May 1719 *Margaret* but died on passage. L.
Bayly, Thomas. S Jan T Feb 1724 *Anne*. L.
Bayly, Thomas. T Oct 1726 *Forward*. Sx.
Bailey, Thomas. S s coalpit ropes at Stapleton Lent TB Mar 1749. G.
Bailey, Thomas. T 14 yrs Aug 1752 *Tryal*. K.
Bailey, Thomas. T Apr 1766 *Ann*. K.
Bailey als Bailiffe, Thomas. S s at Chipping Norton & for being at large
    after sentence of transportation given at Gloucester & R Lent 1774. O.
Bailey, Walter. R for Barbados Mar 1677 & May 1678. L.
Bailey, Walter. S Feb T Mar 1730 *Patapsco*. L.
Bayley, Walter. T Sep 1730 *Smith*. E.
Bayly, William. Rebel T 1685.
Bayley, William of Halling. R for Barbados or Jamaica Feb 1690. K.
Bailey, William. S Jan-Jun 1728 LC from *Elizabeth* Potomack Aug
    1729. M.
Bailey, William. S s shoes at Burford Summer 1738; wife Rosomund
    acquitted. O.
Bayley, William. R 14 yrs Apr 1742. Ha.
Bailey, William. S Apr 1753 R 14 yrs Aug 1753. So.
Bailey, William. S s sheep Summer 1762 R 14 yrs Lent 1763. He.

Baily, William. S for highway robbery Summer 1766 R 14 yrs Lent T May 1767 *Thornton*. Bu.

Bayly, William. SQS Warminster or New Sarum & TB to Va Oct 1768. Wi.

Bailiffe, Thomas (1774). *See* Bailey. O.

Bailiss. *See* Bayliss.

Bailson, John of Over Wyersdale. S Summer 1754. La.

Bayne, James. S Dec 1727. L.

Bainard. *See* Baynard.

Bainbridge, Bridget. S Lent 1763. Y.

Bainbridge, James of Halton. SQS Jly 1761. La.

Baines, Andrew. R for America Nov 1710. M.

Baines, George (1734). *See* Cotterell. M.

Baines, Henry (1751). *See* Charity, John. Y.

Banes, John. T Jan 1736 *Dorsetshire*. Sy.

Baines, Joshua. S Summer 1740 R 14 yrs Lent 1741. Li.

Baines, Richard. S & T Mar 1763 *Neptune*. L.

Bainting, Timothy. SQS Jan 1751. M.

Bainton. *See* Baynton.

Bake, Henry. S Oct 1766. M.

Baker, Anne. R for Barbados Jly 1674. M.

Baker, Anne. R Aug T Oct 1723 *Forward* to Va. M.

Baker, Ann wife of James. S Feb T Mar 1729 *Patapsco* LC Annapolis Dec 1729. M.

Baker als Black, Ann. S Oct T Nov 1762 *Prince William*. M.

Baker, Arthur. SQS & TB Oct 1749. So.

Baker, Benjamin. S for highway robbery Lent R 14 yrs Summer T Oct 1750 *Rachael*. K.

Baker, Benjamin. S s horse Lent R 14 yrs Summer 1751. Nt.

Baker, Benjamin. S Jun T Sep 1764 *Justitia*. M.

Baker, Charles. Rebel T 1685.

Baker, Charles. S & T for life Jly 1771 *Scarsdale*. M.

Baker, Daniel. S Jun T Nov 1743 *George William*. M.

Baker, Daniel. S s at English Bicknor Summer TB Aug 1751. G.

Baker, Dorothy, widow. S Apr T Jly 1770 *Scarsdale*. L.

Baker, Edmund. SQS & TB Oct 1733. G.

Baker, Edward of Chard, husbandman. R for Barbados Feb 1673. So.

Baker, Edward. S Oct T Nov 1728 *Forward* but died on passage. L.

Baker, Edward. S Jly 1729. Ha.

Baker, Eleanor als Jane, spinster, als wife of Fortunate of Woolaston. R for America Jly 1677. G.

Baker, Elizabeth, spinster of Aylesford. R for Barbados or Jamaica Jly 1715. K.

Baker, Elizabeth. S Dec 1719. M.

Baker, Elizabeth. S & T Oct 1722 *Forward* LC Annapolis Jun 1723. L.

Baker, Elizabeth wife of Thomas. S Feb T Apr 1732 *Patapsco* LC Md Oct 1732. M.

Baker, Elizabeth. S Dec 1733 T Jan 1734 *Caesar* LC Va Jly 1734. M.

Baker als Moore, Elizabeth. S Jly-Sep 1754. M.

Baker, Elizabeth (1760). *See* Bromage, Phebe. He.

Baker, Francis of Bow Brickhill. R for America Feb 1664. Bu.

Baker, Francis. T Apr 1762 *Neptune*. Ht.
Baker, George. T Oct 1721 *William & John*. Sy.
Baker, George. R Lent 1775. K.
Baker, Giles. S & R Summer 1768. Nf.
Baker, Henry. S Jan 1656 to be whipped & to House of Correction unless he consents to be T. M.
Baker, Henry. R Jly 1702 (SP). L.
Baker, Henry. S Sep-Oct T Dec 1752 *Greyhound*. M.
Baker, Isaac. R 14 yrs Jly 1725. Wi.
Baker, James. PT Jly 1680. M.
Baker, James. Rebel T 1685.
Baker, James of Halwell. R for Barbados Mar 1686. De.
Baker, James. T Apr 1732 *Patapsco*. Sy.
Baker, James. T Oct 1738 *Genoa*. K.
Baker, James. T Apr 1759 *Thetis*. Sy.
Baker als Lutterell, James. S Jly T Nov 1759 *Phoenix*. M.
Baker, James. S s Cheshire cheese Summer 1767. Bd.
Baker, Joan. S Mar 1749. So.
Baker als Frohen, Johanna. S Sep 1740. L.
Baker, John. PT Dec 1675. M.
Baker, John (4). Rebels T 1685.
Baker, John of Pluckley. R for Barbados or Jamaica Jly 1688. K.
Baker, John. T 14 yrs May 1719 *Margaret*; sold to Patrick Sympson Md May 1720. K.
Baker, John. S Jly 1722. De.
Baker, John. S for stealing & breaking Pontefract Gaol Lent 1724 T Summer 1725 LC from *Supply* Annapolis May 1726. Y.
Baker, John. S Dec 1727. M.
Baker, John. TB to Va from QS 1729. De.
Baker als Beezley, John. S Jan T Feb 1733 *Smith* to Md or Va. M.
Baker, John Jr. S Mar 1736. So.
Baker, John. S Feb T Apr 1742 *Bond* to Potomack, Md. M.
Baker, John. S Summer 1757 s oatmeal at Whitchurch. Sh.
Baker, John. S 14 yrs for receiving Mar 1759. Ha.
Baker, John. S & T Mar 1760 *Friendship*. L.
Baker, John. S Summer 1760. K.
Baker, John. S Mar 1767. Co.
Baker, John. S 14 yrs for receiving goods stolen in Essex May T Aug 1769 *Douglas*. M.
Baker, John. SQS Sep T Dec 1769 *Justitia*. M.
Baker, John. T Apr 1770 *New Trial*. Sy.
Baker, John. S Jan-Feb 1773. M.
Baker, Joseph of Norborne. R for Barbados or Jamaica Jly 1677 & 1678. K.
Baker, Joseph. S Lent 1746. E.
Baker, Joseph. S Lent T May 1770. Wa.
Baker, Leonard. S Apr T May 1755 *Rose*. L.
Baker, Margaret of Cambridge, spinster. R for America Mar 1709. Ca.
Baker, Margaret wife of Richard. S & T Dec 1734 *Caesar* LC Va Jly 1735. M.
Baker, Margaret. S Jan T Apr 1743 *Justitia*. M.

Baker, Mary wife of Benjamin. S & T Sep 1731 *Smith* LC Va 1732. M.
Baker, Mary. TB from QS 1735. De.
Baker, Mary wife of James. S Feb T Sep 1737 *Pretty Patsy* to Md. M.
Baker, Mary (1744). *See* Deal. L.
Baker, Mary. S Jly-Dec 1747. M.
Baker, Mary. S Oct 1756. M.
Baker, Mary. S Mar 1768 TB to Va. De.
Baker, Nathaniel of Shute. R for Barbados Mar 1686. De.
Baker, Richard. T Aug 1720 *Owners Goodwill*. K.
Baker, Richard. R Oct 1741 T for life Feb 1742 *Industry* to Md. M.
Baker, Richard. R 14 yrs Mar 1764. Ha.
Baker, Richard. S s man's hat at St. Nicholas, Cole Abbey, Feb T Apr
    1768 *Thornton*. L.
Baker, Robert. TB to Va from QS 1740. De.
Baker, Robert (1772). *See* Linnick. M.
Baker, Robert. S for killing lambs & R Summer 1775. Le.
Baker, Roger. SQS Jly TB to Md Oct 1737. So.
Baker, Rose of St. Olave, Southwark. R for Barbados Apr 1668. Sy.
Baker, Rowland (1775). *See* Meed. E.
Baker, Samuel. S Feb 1758. Ha.
Baker, Sarah. R Jan T Feb 1724 *Anne* to Carolina. M.
Baker, Sarah. S s at Bridgenorth Lent 1724. Sh.
Baker, Susanna. R & T Apr 1725 *Sukey* LC Annapolis Sep 1725. M.
Baker, Susanna. S Jun 1733 T Jan 1734 *Caesar* LC Va Jly 1734. M.
Baker, Susannah. S & T Sep 1764 *Justitia*. M.
Baker, Susanna. S Aug 1770. Co.
Baker, Thomas. T *Robert* Jly 1724 LC Md Jun 1725. Bu.
Baker, Thomas. SQS Jan T Mar 1750 *Tryal*. M.
Baker als Haywood, Thomas. S s horse Lent R 14 yrs Summer
    1756. No.
Baker, Thomas. R 14 yrs Mar 1761 TB to Va. De.
Baker, Thomas. S Dec 1761 T Apr 1762 *Dolphin*. M.
Baker, Thomas. R 14 yrs Aug 1764. De.
Baker, Thomas. SW & T Apr 1770 *New Trial*. M.
Baker, Thomas (1772). *See* Bennett. De.
Baker, Thomas. S Lent 1774. G.
Baker, William of Clapham. R for Barbados Aug 1662. Sy.
Baker, William. R (Home Circ) for Barbados Apr 1663. X.
Baker, William. Rebel T 1685.
Baker, William of Glympton. R for America Jly 1698. O.
Baker, William of Messing. R for Barbados or Jamaica Feb 1696. E.
Baker als Clarke, William of Witham. R for Barbados or Jamaica Jly
    1710. E.
Baker, William. S & T Oct 1730 *Forward* LC Potomack Jan 1731. M.
Baker, William. S Lent 1740. Wo.
Baker, William. S & TB Apr 1740. G.
Baker, William. S Lent 1748. K.
Baker, William. S May-Jly 1750. M.
Baker, William. S Lent 1754. Sx.
Baker, William (1754). *See* Barker. M.
Baker, William. SQS Sep T Dec 1769 *Justitia*. M.

Baker, William. S s at Chesham Lent T Apr 1770 *New Trial*. Bu.

Baker als Sawcer, William. R 14 yrs Mar 1771 TB to Va. De.

Baker, William. S s at Ross Lent 1773. He.

Bakewell, Thomas. S Dec 1749-Jan 1750 T Mar 1750 *Tryal*. M.

Bala, Thomas. LC Dec 1725 Annapolis Md from *Forward*. X.

Balch, Roger. S Apr 1753. So.

Balcombe, Edward. T Apr 1742 *Bond*. Sy.

Balcombe, Elizabeth. T Apr 1742 *Bond*. Sy.

Balderson, Thomas. S s silver chalice from church Summer 1746. Y.

Balding, Judith. R & T 14 yrs Apr 1770 *New Trial*. M.

Balding, Thomas. R for Jamaica Aug 1661. M.

Baldock, Richard of Edmonton. S s cow Sep 1740 T Jan 1741 *Harpooner*. M.

Balldock, William (1764). *See* Pauldock. M.

Baldwin, Ann of Ormskirk, spinster. SQS Oct 1756. La.

Baldwin, Charlotte. S & T Jly 1772 *Tayloe*. M.

Baldwyn, Edward of All Saints, Worcester. R for America Mar 1710. Wo.

Baldwin, Edward. S for attempted robbery at Chesham Bois & R Summer 1775. Bu.

Baldwin, Elizabeth (1669). *See* More. M.

Baldwyn, Francis. S Lent R for Barbados May 1664. Sy.

Baldwyn, John of Toersey. R for America July 1699. O.

Baldwin, John of St. Margaret, Westminster. SW Jan 1773. M.

Baldwin, Matthew. S Summer 1741. Sh.

Baldwyn, Nicholas. S & T 14 yrs Dec 1734 *Caesar* LC Va Jly 1735. L.

Baldwin, Richard. S Jan T Jun 1738 *Forward* to Md or Va. M.

Baldwin, Samuel. SQS 1774. Ht.

Baldwin, Thomas. R for Jamaica Aug 1661. L.

Baldwin, Thomas. S Lent R 14 yrs Summer 1760; to enlist in Regiment for Jamaica. Sy.

Baldwin, Thomas. S Feb T Apr 1769 *Tryal*. M.

Baldwin, Thomas. S May-Jly 1774. M.

Baldwyn, William of Caleston. R for Barbados Jly 1685. La.

Baldwin, William. S Jan T Feb 1724 *Anne*. L.

Bale, George. S Sep-Oct T Dec 1771 *Justitia*. M.

Bale, John (1766). *See* Chambers. Wa.

Bale, Richard. S s silver teaspoons at Doddington Lent 1774. G.

Bale, Robert. R 14 yrs Aug 1750 TB to Va. De.

Bale, Sarah. S Lent 1768. Nf.

Bales als Brown als Gough, Eleanor. S Feb T Apr 1766 *Ann*. M.

Belfour als Belford, John. T Oct 1768 *Justitia*. Sy.

Ball, Albanus. S Mar 1758. Do.

Ball, Benjamin. S Dec 1754. L.

Ball, Edward. S s cider at Almondsbury Summer 1729. G.

Ball, Eleanor. S s at St. Helen, Worcester, Lent 1775. Wo.

Ball, Elizabeth. R for Barbados Jly 1674. M.

Ball, Elizabeth. R 14 yrs for murder Lent 1721. St.

Ball als Brawden als Swift, Elizabeth. S May T Jun 1727 *Susanna*. L.

Ball, Elizabeth. S Jly 1747. L.

Ball, James. R 14 yrs Jly TB to Va Sep 1750. Wi.

Ball, John. R for America Jly 1686. Db.

Ball, John. R Aug T Oct 1724 *Forward* to Md. M.

Ball, John. S & T Oct 1732 *Caesar* to Va. M.

Ball, John. S s sheep Lent R 14 yrs Summer 1752. Nf.

Ball, John of Bermondsey. SQS Feb T Mar 1758 *Dragon*. Sy.

Ball, John. S & T Dec 1767 *Neptune*. M.

Ball, John Sr. S Mar 1773. Do.

Ball, Jonathan. R Jly 1686. M.

Ball, Philip. T Apr 1742 *Bond*. Sy.

Ball, Richard. S s horse Lent 1733. Wo.

Ball, Sarah. S Apr-May T May 1744 *Justitia*. M.

Ball, Susannah. S Sep-Oct 1773. M.

Ball, William of Carle Stoke, husbandman. R for Barbados Jly 1667. Wi.

Ball, William of Leicester. R for America Jly 1674. Le.

Ball, William. S Lent 1766. No.

Ballam, Mary. LC Nov 1733 Annapolis Md from *Patapsco*. X.

Ballance, Edward. S & T Dec 1734 *Caesar* LC Va Jly 1735. L.

Ballance, James. R for Barbados or Jamaica Aug 1700. L.

Ballance, James (1725). *See* Barrance. L.

Ballantine, William. S Lent T Sep 1757 *Thetis*. E.

Ballard, Ann wife of Isaac. S Summer 1767. Sh.

Ballard, John. S & T Dec 1731 *Forward*; committed in Jan 1734 on suspicion of returning from transportation. M.

Ballard, John. S & T Jan 1736 *Dorsetshire* LC Va Sep 1736. L.

Ballard, John. S Lent 1754. Sx.

Ballard, John. S Sep T Dec 1767 *Neptune*. L.

Ballard, Maximilian. S s sheep at Cwmyoy & R Summer 1761. Mo.

Ballard, Richard of Pershore. R for America Jun 1692. Wo.

Ballard, Richard. S Lent 1750. Sx.

Ballard, Thomas. S s sheep Lent R 14 yrs Summer 1762. Nf.

Ballinger, Daniel of Southall. S s 2 shirts Jly 1740. M.

Ballinger, Thomas. S for highway robbery Lent R 14 yrs Summer 1744. Bu.

Ballmore, John. S Lent 1764. No.

Balls, Edward. S s sheep. Lent R 14 yrs Summer 1763 Nf.

Balls, Susannah. S s at Houghton Regis Summer 1773. Bd.

Balm, John. T 14 yrs Sep 1765 *Justitia*. Ht.

Balson, Susannah wife of John Sr. S Mar 1743. De.

Balster. *See* Bolster.

Bamber, James. S for maiming mare Summer 1758 R 14 yrs Lent 1759. La.

Bamber, Robert. S May 1733 T Jan 1734 *Caesar* LC Va Jly 1734. M.

Bambrick, Richard. S Apr T May 1750 *Lichfield*. M.

Bamfield als Bamford, Benjamin. S for highway robbery Lent & R for life because of ill health Summer 1774. Le.

Bamfield, John (1774). *See* Bamford. Le.

Bampfield, Hannah. TB to Va from QS 1771. De.

Banfield, James. S Lent R 14 yrs Summer 1765. G.

Bampfield, Joan of Sandford, singlewoman. R for Barbados Feb 1673. De.

Bamfield, John. R for Barbados Jun 1666. Y.

Bamford als Bamfield, John. S Jly TB for life to Va Aug 1774. Le.

Bampfield, Richard. R Mar 1772. So.

Banfield, Richard. S Jan-Feb 1775. M.

Bampsfield, Elianor wife of Robert of St. Saviour, Southwark. R for Barbados or Jamaica Feb 1684. Sy.

Bampton, George. S Lent R 14 yrs Summer T Sep 1751 *Greyhound*. Ht.

Banbrook, Sarah wife of Thomas. S 14 yrs for receiving Summer 1775. Wa.

Banbury, Edmund of Thorney, Isle of Ely. R (Midland Circ) for America Jly 1677. Ca.

Bambury, Thomas. Rebel T 1685.

Band, James of Ausley. R for America Jly 1673. Wa.

Bandy, John of Pulloxhill. R for America Feb 1688. Bd.

Bandy als Bailey als Richards, Mary. S s mare & R 7 yrs Lent TB to Va Apr 1774. Le.

Bandy, Richard (1770). *See* Adams. Sy.

Banes. *See* Baines.

Banfield. *See* Bampfield.

Banford als Bradford, Isaac. R for Barbados or Jamaica Jly 1688. K.

Banford, James. R 14 yrs Jly 1744. Ha.

Bamford, John. SQS Dec 1753. M.

Banham als Greenwood, Carolina. S Sep T Oct 1744 *Susannah*. M.

Banion. *See* Banyon.

Banister. *See* Bannister.

Banks, Andrew. SQS Jun T Sep 1758 *Tryal* to Annapolis. M.

Banks, Ann. S Apr-May T Jly 1771 *Scarsdale*. M.

Bankes, Arthur. S & T Oct 1729 *Forward* but died on passage. M.

Banks, Charles. S May T Jun 1764 *Dolphin*. M.

Banks, David. S Jan-Feb T Apr 1772 *Thornton*. M.

Banks, Edward (1768). *See* Genders, John. Wa.

Banks, Elizabeth. S Jan T Feb 1724 *Anne*. L.

Banks, Francis. S Mar 1730. De.

Banks, Henry of Tarleton. S s horse Summer 1757 R 14 yrs Lent 1758. La.

Banks, John. S Feb T Sep 1731 *Smith* LC Va 1732. M.

Banks, John. T May 1736 *Patapsco*. K.

Banks, Joseph. S & T Apr 1753 *Thames*. L.

Banks, Joseph. T Mar 1758 *Dragon*. L.

Banks, Joseph. T 14 yrs Apr 1768 *Thornton*. K.

Banks, Randall. S & T Jan 1756 *Greyhound*. M.

Banks, Rebecca (1748). *See* Coseret. M.

Bankes, Richard of Salwarpe. R for America Nov 1694. Wo.

Banks, Thomas. T Oct 1721 *William & John*. K.

Bankes, William. S Summer R for Barbados Aug 1664. K.

Banks, William. R 14 yrs Lent 1721 T *Owners Goodwill* LC Md Jly 1722. Be.

Banks, William. S & T Dec 1734 *Caesar* LC Va Jly 1735. L.

Banks, William. S Feb-Apr T May 1755 *Rose*. M.

Banks, William. T 14 yrs Dec 1771 *Justitia*. Ht.

Banne, John of Glovers Stone. R for Barbados Feb 1679. Ch.

Bannell als Bland, Hannah. S Feb-Apr T May 1752 *Lichfield*. M.

Banner, Joseph. S s lead pipe from Earl of Shrewsbury at Manor of Grafton Summer 1765. Wo.

Bannerman, John. T Apr 1766 *Ann*. M.

Banning, James. R Jly 1774. M.

Bannin, William. R 11 yrs Jly TB Aug 1754. Wi.

Bannister, Cornelia. R for Barbados Apr 1669. M.

Banister, Edward of Callow. R Feb 1716. He.

Bannister, Edward (1744). *See* Wandon. M.

Bannister, George. S Jan 1746. L.

Banister, George. S Lent T May 1750 *Lichfield*. E.

Bannister, George. S Jan 1761. M.

Bannister, Henry. R 14 yrs for Carolina May 1719. L.

Bannister als Jones, Isabella. S Sep 1733 T Jan 1734 *Caesar* LC Va Jly 1734. M.

Banister, John. R for Barbados or Jamaica Jly 1696. X.

Bannister, Mark. S Jly T Sep 1766 *Justitia*. L.

Bannister, Mary. S Dec 1745. L.

Bannister, Mary. S Jly 1773. L.

Bannister, Richard. S Oct T Dec 1716 *Lewis* to Jamaica. M.

Bannister, Richard. S Feb T Apr 1765 *Ann*. M.

Banister, William. R for Barbados or Jamaica Oct 1690. L.

Bannister, William. S Jan-Jun T Jun 1728 *Elizabeth* LC Potomack Aug 1729. L.

Banser als Gibson als Greene, Susan. R for Barbados May 1678 & Jan 1679. L.

Banshaw, Joseph. R Oct 1724. M.

Bansom, Richard of Hawkesbury. R for America Jly 1696. G.

Banstead, Jane. SQS Feb T May 1752 *Lichfield*. M.

Bant, Mathias. R 14 yrs Mar 1738. Co.

Banton, Hugh. Rebel T 1685.

Banton, John of Martock. R for Barbados Jun 1702. So.

Banion, William. S Dec 1727. M.

Banyon, William of St. George, Southwark. SQS Apr T Sep 1751 *Greyhound*. Sy.

Barbadoes, Robert. R for Barbados May AT Sep 1684. M.

Barben, Mary. S Jly-Dec 1747. M.

Barber, Ann. S Jan 1745. L.

Barber, Charles of St. Catherine. S s watch Jly-Oct 1740 T Jan 1741 *Harpooner*. M.

Barber, Charles. S Norwich Summer 1759. Nf.

Barber, Daniel. S Summer 1756. Su.

Barber, Edward. S s at Wellington Lent 1727. He.

Barber, Elizabeth. S & T Jun 1742 *Bladon* to Md. M.

Barber, Elizabeth. S Mar 1749. So.

Barber, Elizabeth. S & T 14 yrs Nov 1762 *Prince William*. L.

Barber, George. R for Barbados Jun 1671. M.

Barber, George. S Aug 1754 TB 14 yrs Apr 1755. Le.

Barber, James. S City for assault with intent to rob Summer 1759. Nl.

Barber, James. S Lent 1770. Nt.

Barber, James. SQS New Sarum or Marlborough & TB to Va Jan 1774. Wi.
Barber, Jane. S Dec 1742 T Mar 1743 *Justitia*. L.
Barber, Jane. S Feb-Apr T May 1751 *Tryal*. M.
Barber, John. S Lent 1722 T Oct 1723 *Forward* to Va from London. Y.
Barber, John. S s horse Summer 1730 R 14 yrs Lent 1731. Wa.
Barber, John. T Sep 1742 *Forward*. K.
Barber, John (1757). *See* Rogers. So.
Barber, John. S Oct T Nov 1759 *Phoenix*. M.
Barber, Mary. S Nov T Dec 1770 *Justitia*. L.
Barber, Peter of Hodden. R for Barbados Jly 1677. Y.
Barber, Robert. S Jly 1724. De.
Barber, Robert. S Sep T Dec 1734 *Caesar* LC Va Jly 1735. M.
Barber, Robert. S for burglary Summer 1736; found at large & ordered for transportation Winter 1738. Su.
Barber, Robert. S Dec 1753-Jan 1754. M.
Barber, Samuel. PT Oct 1701. M.
Barber, Samuel. S s fowls at Tamworth Summer 1742. St.
Barber, Samuel (1761). *See* Gill, William. Le.
Barber, Susanna. S Sep T Dec 1752 *Greyhound*. M.
Barber als Lane, Thomas. S & T Jan 1736 *Dorsetshire* LC Va Sep 1736. L.
Barber, Thomas. SQS Jly TB Aug 1758. So.
Barber, Thomas. S Feb T Apr 1770 *New Trial*. L.
Barber, Thomas Sr. S s firewood at Drayton Lent T Apr 1771 *Thornton*. Bu.
Barber, Thomas Jr. S s firewood at Drayton Lent T Apr 1771 *Thornton*. Bu.
Barber, William. S Mar TB to Va Apr 1768. Le.
Barkley, Anne. S Oct T Nov 1728 *Forward* but died on passage. M.
Barkley, Edward. SQS Dec 1664 for attending a conventicle. M.
Berkley, Elizabeth. S & T Jan 1736 *Dorsetshire* LC Va Sep 1736. L.
Barclay, David. T Jly 1753 *Tryal*. M.
Barclay, Henry. S Jun T Jly 1772 *Tayloe*. L.
Berkley, Jane. S & T Oct 1722 *Forward* to Md. M.
Barclay, John. S Sep-Oct 1749. M.
Berkley, William (1769). *See* Forsith, John. Sy.
Barden, John. S Jly T Sep 1764 *Justitia*. M.
Bare. *See* Bear.
Barefoot, Charles. S Feb T Mar 1750 *Tryal*. M.
Barefoot, Elizabeth (1743). *See* Miller. M.
Barfoot, John. S Feb T Apr 1769 *Tryal*. M.
Barew. *See* Baruh.
Barfield als Bradfield, Ann. S Jan-Feb T Apr 1771 *Thornton*. M.
Barfield als Warfield als Wastfield, John of Balconsbury. R for Barbados Jly 1677. So.
Barford, Elizabeth. T Apr 1742 *Bond*. Ht.
Barford, William. S Mar TB to Va Apr 1764. Wi.
Barford, William. S s at Warham Lent 1773. Nf.
Barge, Bartholomew. Rebel T 1685.
Barge, Robert. Rebel T 1685.

Barge, William. S Lent R 14 yrs Summer TB Jly 1743. G.
Bargess als Vargess als Porter, Elizabeth of Woodplumpton, spinster. SQS Oct 1747. La.
Bargier, Abigael. R for Barbados or Jamaica Dec 1689. M.
Bargier, John. R for Barbados or Jamaica Dec 1689. M.
Bargier, Paul. S & T Jun 1756 *Lyon*. M.
Bargo, Sarah wife of Peter. S Sep-Oct 1775. M.
Barham, Joseph. S s sheep Summer 1742 R 14 yrs Lent 1743. Su.
Barham, Thomas. S & T for life Oct 1720 *Gilbert*. M.
Bark, Francis. S Lent R 14 yrs Summer 1766. Db.
Barker, Abraham. S s boards at Stradbrook Lent 1772. Su.
Barker, Charles. S Mar 1754. L.
Barker, Christian wife of John. S Jun T 14 yrs Sep 1758 *Tryal* to Md. M.
Barker, Christopher. S s at Scarborough Summer TB Aug 1770. Y.
Barker, Daniel. Rebel T 1685.
Barker, Edmund. S City s silk ribbon in Liberty of St. Peter Summer 1772. Y.
Barker, Elizabeth. R Apr TB for Barbados Jun 1669. M.
Barker, Elizabeth of Newport. R (Newgate) for Barbados Sep 1669. E.
Barker, Elizabeth. S Aug 1763. L.
Barker, Frances. R & T Jan 1722 *Gilbert* to Md. M.
Barker, Hannah. S Mar 1755. De.
Barker, Henry. T Oct 1726 *Forward*. Ht.
Barker, Henry. S Lent 1752. Bd.
Barker, Isaac of Cold Norton. S Lent R 14 yrs Summer 1760. E.
Barker, James. S Summer TB Aug 1771. Nt.
Barker, John of Stow Bardolph. R for Barbados Mar 1679. Nf.
Barker, John. AT to Barbados Jan 1694. M.
Barker, John of Bristol. R for Barbados Feb 1697. G.
Barker, John of Southampton. R for Barbados Jly 1698. Ha.
Barker, John. T May 1719 *Margaret* LC Md May 1720 & sold to Richard Snowden. Sy.
Barker, John. SQS s handkerchiefs at Clarborough Jan 1744. Nt.
Barker, John. S s sheep Summer 1753 R 14 yrs Lent 1754. Li.
Barker, John. S s sheep & R 14 yrs Lent 1754. Bd.
Barker, John. S & R 14 yrs Norwich Summer 1757. Nf.
Barker, John. S & T Apr 1765 *Ann*. L.
Barker, John. S s cloth at Knaresborough Lent TB Aug 1773. Y.
Barker, Joseph. S s mare & R 7 yrs Lent TB May 1772. Db.
Barker, Joseph. S Jly 1773. L.
Barker, Martha. S Apr T May 1719 *Margaret*; sold to Daniel Carter Md Aug 1719. L.
Barker, Mary. R Aug AT Dec 1679. M.
Barker, Mary. S Apr T May 1751 *Tryal*. L.
Barker, Samuel. S Lent R 14 yrs Summer 1757. Sh.
Barker, Samuel. T 14 yrs Sep 1765 *Justitia*. K.
Barker, Samuel. S for highway robbery & R Lent 1775. Wa.
Barker, Susanna. S Feb 1752. L.
Barker, Thomas of St. Michael, Oxford, carpenter. R for Barbados Oct 1663. O.
Barker, Thomas. R for America Feb 1700. Db.

Barker, Thomas. S Jan 1745. L.
Barker, Thomas. S Feb-Apr T May 1751 *Tryal*. M.
Barker, Thomas. S Lent R 14 yrs Summer 1751. Sh.
Barker, William. S & R 14 yrs Summer 1729 T Summer 1730. Y.
Barker, William. S & T Oct 1730 *Forward* LC Potomack Jan 1731. M.
Barker, William. S s sheep Summer 1742 R 14 yrs Lent 1743. Y.
Barker, William. S Feb 1744. Ha.
Barker als Baker, William. S May-Jly 1750. M.
Barker, William. S s flour at Caversham Lent 1769. O.
Barkley. *See* Barclay.
Barkwell, Hugh als William. S Apr 1769. De.
Barlat, Thomas. SQS Apr T May 1750 *Lichfield*. M.
Barley, James, als Barney, Charles. R 14 yrs Aug 1764. Co.
Barloe, Benjamin. S Lent 1749. Ca.
Barlow, Elizabeth. LC Dec 1725 Annapolis Md from *Forward*. X.
Barlow, Jane. S s lambs Summer 1742 R 14 yrs Lent 1743. Nt.
Barlow, John (1738). *See* Goodwin. Y.
Barlow, John. S Lent R 14 yrs Summer 1761. E.
Barlow, Margaret. S & T Jan 1736 *Dorsetshire* LC Va Sep 1736. L.
Barlow, Rachel. R for Jamaica Mar 1665. L.
Barlow, Ralph. S May T Jly 1723 *Alexander* LC Annapolis Sep 1723. M.
Barlow, Samuel. S s at Claines Summer 1755. Wo.
Barlow, Samuel. S Dec 1764 T Jan 1765 *Tryal*. M.
Barlow, Sarah. R for Barbados Jly 1675. L.
Barlow, Sarah. SQS Dec 1765 T Jan 1766 *Tryal*. M.
Barlow, Solomon. S May T Jly 1723 *Alexander* LC Annapolis Sep 1723. M.
Barlow, Thomas. R for Barbados or Jamaica Dec 1689. M.
Barlow, Thomas. R May T Jun 1691. M.
Barlow, Thomas. SQS & T Jan 1767 *Tryal*. Ht.
Barlow, William. R for America Mar 1697. Ru.
Barlow, William (1755). *See* Darlow. M.
Barnaby, Edward. S s horse Mar R 14 yrs Summer TB to Md Oct 1738. Le.
Barnard. *See* Bernard.
Barnefield, Thomas. S s at Whitchurch Lent 1749. Sh.
Barner, Henry. T 14 yrs Apr 1772 *Thornton*. K.
Barnes, Anne. R for Barbados Jun 1670. M.
Barns, Ann. S Apr-May T Jly 1771 *Scarsdale*. M.
Barnes, Benjamin. SWK Jan 1775. K.
Barns, Christian. PT Oct 1700. M.
Barns, Due. R 14 yrs Mar 1773. Ha.
Barnes, Elizabeth. R for Barbados or Jamaica Aug 1700. L.
Barnes, Elizabeth. SQS Oct 1754. M.
Barnes, Elizabeth. S May T Jun 1764 *Dolphin*. M.
Barnes, Ezekiel. S May-Jun T Aug 1752 *Tryal*. M.
Barnes, Frances (1671). *See* Jobson. M.
Barnes, George. S s lambs Summer 1769 R 14 yrs Lent 1770. G.
Barnes, Giles. S Summer 1725 R 14 yrs Lent 1726. Wo.
Barnes, Hannah wife of John of Manchester. SQS Aug 1759. La.
Barnes, Henry of St. Luke. S s stewpan etc. Jly 1740 M.

Barnes, Henry of Blackburn. SQS Apr 1772. La.
Barnes, James. T Jly 1724 *Robert* LC Md Jun 1725. Sx.
Barnes, James. S Jan-Jun T Jun 1728 *Elizabeth* LC Potomack Aug 1729. M.
Barnes, Jane. S Feb T Apr 1732 *Patapsco* LC Annapolis Oct 1732. M.
Barnes als Anderson, John. R for Barbados or Jamaica Oct 1688. L.
Barnes, John. R 14 yrs for Carolina May 1719. L.
Barnes, John. S Jan-Apr 1748. M.
Barnes, John. S Jan T Feb 1765 *Tryal*. L.
Barnes, John. SQS for perjury Apr 1774. M.
Barnes, Joseph. S s at Cleobury Mortimer Summer 1726. Sh.
Barnes, Joseph. S s ribbon at Birstal & R 14 yrs Lent 1772. Y.
Barnes, Josiah. S May-Jun T Jly 1753 *Tryal*. M.
Barnes, Martha (1732). *See* Hobbs. G.
Barnes, Mary. T Aug 1720 *Owners Goodwill*. K.
Barnes, Mary. S & T May 1736 *Patapsco*. L.
Barns, Mary. S & T Jly 1771 *Scarsdale*. M.
Barnes, Nicholas. S Lent 1736. Su.
Barnes, Ruth of Offenham. R for America Jly 1682. Wo.
Barns, Samuel of Manchester, husbandman. SQS Oct 1745. La.
Barnes, Samuel. S Oct T Dec 1771 *Justitia*. L.
Barnes, Sarah. S & T Jly 1770 *Scarsdale*. M.
Barnes, Stephen. S for life Feb 1754. M.
Barnes, Storme. S Feb T Sep 1737 *Pretty Patsy* to Md. M.
Barnes, Thomas. S Feb-Apr T May 1752 *Lichfield*. M.
Barnes, Thomas. S Dec 1755 T Jan 1756 *Greyhound*. L.
Barnes, Thomas (1770). *See* Wakeling. Be.
Barnes, William of St. George, Southwark. R for Barbados or Jamaica Jun 1675. Sy.
Barnes als Price als Carne, William. S for burglary at Trelleck Grange Summer 1724. Mo.
Barnes, William. S s a greatcoat Lent 1741. O.
Barnes, William. R for sacrilege Oct T 14 yrs Nov 1762 *Prince William*. L.
Barnes als Burn, William of Bradmore. SQS for obtaining money by pretending to have a lame arm Oct 1765. Nt.
Barnes, William of Bishops Stortford. R 14 yrs Lent T Apr 1772 *Thornton*. Ht.
Barnes, William. S Feb T Apr 1772 *Thornton*. L.
Barnesfield, Richard of Gloucester. R for America Feb 1690. G.
Barnet, Abraham. S Sep T Dec 1769 *Justitia*. M.
Barnett, Ann. S Apr-May T May 1744 *Justitia*. M.
Barnett, Betty wife of William. SQS 14 yrs for receiving Apr TB Sep 1772. So.
Barnett, Henry. S Lent 1772. K.
Barnett, Hester. S Lent R 14 yrs Summer 1753. Bu.
Barnett, James. S s at St. Peter, Worcester, Lent 1774. Wo.
Barnett, John (1740). *See* Mounslow. M.
Barnett, John. S Mar 1746. Ha.
Barnett, John. S s wheat from a barge at Bridstow Lent 1757. He.
Barnett, John. S Mar 1765. Ha.

Barnet, John. S Sep T Oct 1768 *Justitia*. M.

Barnet, Joseph. S & T Aug 1752 *Tryal*. L.

Barnet, Joseph. S Lent 1763. Ht.

Barnett, Levy. S Jly TB to Va Aug 1765. Wi.

Barnett, Robert. S Jly R 14 yrs & T Aug 1718 *Eagle* LC Charles Town Mar 1719. L.

Barnett, Robert, als Lawrence, John. S Oct T Dec 1724 *Rappahannock*. L.

Barnett, Sarah. S s at Cheltenham Lent TB Mar 1752. G.

Barnett, Sarah. S Dec 1755 T Jan 1756 *Greyhound*. L.

Barnet, Stair. S Apr 1763. M.

Barnet, Susanna. SQS Feb T Mar 1763 *Neptune*. M.

Barnett, William. S Feb 1757. M.

Barney, Charles (1764). *See* Barley, James. Co.

Barney, Thomas. S s at Ludlow Summer 1751. Sh.

Barnfather, Samuel. S & T Jly 1753 *Tryal*. M.

Barnfield, Isaac. S Dec 1765 T Jan 1766 *Tryal*. M.

Barnfield, John. S s cowhide at Harthbury Lent 1766. Wo.

Barnfield, William. S Apr 1767. So.

Barnicott als Arney, John of Bodmin, miller. R for Barbados Jun 1699. Co.

Barns. *See* Barnes.

Barnsides als Downing, Michael. S Sep-Oct 1749. M.

Barnsley, Thomas. S Aug 1727. So.

Barnstaple, Edward. SQS Oct 1735 TB to Md Jan 1736. So.

Barnwell, Elizabeth. S Jly T Dec 1736 *Dorsetshire* to Va. M.

Barnwell, Mary Falicia, aged 21, fair. T Oct 1720 *Gilbert* LC Md May 1721. Sy.

Baron. *See* Barron.

Barraclough, Abraham. R 14 yrs Summer 1750. Y.

Barrale/Barrell. *See* Burrell.

Barrance, James. S Aug T Sep 1725 *Forward* LC Annapolis Dec 1725. L.

Barranclaugh als Reeves als Grant, Elizabeth. R Dec 1698 AT Jan 1699. M.

Burras, Joshua, clog maker aged 21, dark. S & T 14 yrs Oct 1720 *Gilbert* LC Annapolis May 1721. L.

Barratt. *See* Barrett.

Barrell. *See* Burrell.

Barrett, Abraham. R 14 yrs Mar TB to Va Apr 1765. Wi.

Barrett, Ann. S Aug T Sep 1727 *Forward* LC Rappahannock May 1728. L.

Barrett, Ann. S Apr 1748. L.

Barrett, Anne. S Dec 1767. M.

Barrett, Ann. S Sep T Dec 1769 *Justitia*. M.

Barret, Benjamin. S Summer 1755. Y.

Barrett, Daniel of St. George, Southwark, victualler. SQS Jan 1757. Sy.

Barrett, Edmund. S Oct T Dec 1758 *The Brothers*. L.

Barrett, Edward. S Jan T Feb 1724 *Anne*. L.

Barrett, Edward. SQS Feb T Apr 1772 *Thornton*. M.

Barrett, Elizabeth. S Apr 1760. M.

Barret, Frances wife of John. S May T Nov 1743 *George William*. M.

Barrett, Francis. S s at Binham Summer 1774. Nf.

Barrett, George. R 14 yrs Summer 1736. O.

Barrett, Henry. S Oct T 14 yrs Oct 1732 *Caesar* to Va. M.

Barrett, Hester. LC Va Sep 1736 from *Dorsetshire*. X.

Barrett, James. S Jly 1718 to be T to Boston, NE. Wi.

Barrett, James. S Jan T Feb 1742 *Industry*. L.

Barrett, James. S Jun T Jly 1772 *Tayloe*. L.

Barrett, James. S Jan-Feb 1774. M.

Barrett, John. S for highway robbery Summer R 14 yrs Nov 1741. No.

Barrett, John. S s at Siston Lent 1763. G.

Barrett, John. R & T for life Mar 1764 *Tryal*. M.

Barratt, Joseph. T Apr 1732 *Patapsco*. Sy.

Barrett als Barrell, Lancelot. S Dec 1748 T Jan 1749 *Laura*. M.

Barrett als Massey, Margaret. S Apr T Jun 1742 *Bladon* to Md. M.

Barrett, Mary (1754). *See* Riley. M.

Barret, Mary. SQS Apr T Sep 1758 *Tryal* to Md. M.

Barrett, Mary. S & R 14 yrs Summer 1773. Mo.

Barrett, Mathew. R 14 yrs Aug 1746. Ha.

Barrett, Nathaniel. T Lent R 14 yrs Summer 1760. Sy.

Barrett, Peter. S May 1775. L.

Barrett, Ralph of Topcroft. R for Barbados Aug 1671. Nf.

Barrett, Richard. S Nov T Dec 1763 *Neptune*. L.

Barrett, Sampson of Sheffield. R for Barbados Jly 1705. Y.

Barrett, Sarah. S Jan T Feb 1733 *Smith* to Md or Va. M.

Barratt, Sarah. T May 1767 *Thornton*. K.

Barrett, Stephen. AT Lent 1766. Y.

Barrett, Susannah. T May 1752 *Lichfield*. L.

Barrett, Thomas. PT August R Dec 1683. M.

Barritt, Thomas. Died on passage in *Rappahannock* 1726. Li.

Barrett, Thomas. SQS Apr 1728. So.

Barrett, Thomas. S Summer 1749. K.

Barrett, Thomas. R 14 yrs Mar 1768. Co.

Barrett, Thomas (1770). *See* Newby, Godfrey. Be.

Barrett, William. S Jan-Jun T Jun 1728 *Elizabeth* LC Potomack Aug 1729. L.

Barrett, William (1731), *See* Taylor. Wi.

Barrett, William. S Jan-Apr 1749. M.

Barrett, William. S s sheep Lent R 14 yrs Summer 1767. Be.

Barrett, William. S May-Jly 1773. M.

Barratt, William. S 14 yrs for receiving Lent 1774. Li.

Barrett, William. R 14 yrs Jly 1775. M.

Barridge, John. S Summer 1730. Y.

Barrington, Abigail, spinster, als wife of John, aged 20. R for Barbados Feb 1664. L.

Barrington, Mary. S Lent R 14 yrs Summer 1760. K.

Barrington, Thomas. R 14 yrs Jly TB to Va Sep 1759. Wi.

Barrington, Thomas. S Apr 1775. So.

Baron, Anne. S Jan T Feb 1726 *Supply* LC Annapolis May 1726. M.

Baron, John. S Mar 1727 TB to Md. De.

Barron, John. S & T Sep 1755 *Tryal*. L.

Barron, Peter of Thornbury. R for America Feb 1681. G.

Barrow, Christian (1763). *See* Read. M.
Barrow, Henry. SQS & TB Oct 1733. G.
Barrow, Honour. S Feb T Mar 1743 *Justitia*. L.
Barrow, James. PT Sep 1691. M.
Barrow, John. S & T Oct 1729 *Forward* but died on passage. M.
Barrow, John. S s wheat Lent 1734. Sh.
Barrow, John. S Jly 1734. Wi.
Barrow als Rennet, Joseph. R 14 yrs Aug 1739. De.
Barrow, Mary. S s coral set in silver Jun T Dec 1736 *Dorsetshire*
    to Va. M.
Barrow als Godfrey, Mary. S Apr-May 1741. M.
Barrowe, William. R for Barbados or Jamaica Aug 1700. L.
Barrows, Richard. T May 1737 *Forward*. K.
Barrs, James. S s sheep Summer 1767 R 14 yrs Lent 1768. Wa.
Barry, Ann. S Jan-Feb 1774. M.
Barry, Barnard. S Apr T May 1752 *Lichfield*. L.
Barry, Edward. S Jly T Sep 1764 *Justitia*. M.
Barry, Edward. R & T 14 yrs Jly 1772 *Tayloe*. M.
Barry, Elizabeth. R for America Mar 1690. Wa.
Barry, Frances. S Oct T Dec 1758 *The Brothers*. L.
Barry, John. S Aug 1732 TB to Va. De.
Barry, John. S Jly T Sep 1755 *Tryal*. L.
Barson, Robert of Kingston on Thames. R for Barbados Apr 1668. Sy.
Barson, Temple. S Summer 1759 T from Whitehaven Sep 1760. We.
Bart, Henry (1726). *See* Burt. M.
Bartelott, George (1773). *See* Ridgely. Wi.
Bartelott, John. R for life Mar 1773. Ha.
Bartelott, Robert (1773). *See* Long. Wi.
Barter, Mark. TB to Va 1768. De.
Barter, William. R Jan T Feb 1724 to Carolina. M.
Barter, William. SQS Jan 1754. M.
Barthelemi, James. S Sep T Dec 1735 *John* to Md. M.
Bartholomew, Edmund. T 14 yrs Apr 1768 *Thornton*. Sx.
Bartholomew, John of Cuckfield. R for Barbados or Jamaica Feb
    1676. Sx.
Bartholomew, Robert. TB to Md Aug 1729. Db.
Bartington, Enock of Somerford Booths. R for Barbados or Jamaica
    Mar 1694. Ch.
Bartlem, George. S s at Codsall & R 14 yrs Summer 1769. St.
Bartlam, John of Strelley, coalminer. SQS s vegetables Oct 1771 TB
    May 1772. Nt.
Bartle, James of Great Cressingham. S Summer 1728. *Nf.
Bartlemer, Anne of Kintbury. R for America Jly 1678. Be.
Bartlett, Ambrose. R for Barbados Sep 1670. L.
Bartlett, Ann. SQS Devizes & TB to Va Apr 1765. Wi.
Bartlett, Hannah wife of George of Clavill, husbandman. SQS in Sussex
    s gamecock at Elsted Jan T Apr 1772 *Thornton*. Ha.
Bartlett, James of Christ Church. SQS Oct 1765 T Jan 1766 *Tryal*. Sy.
Bartlett, James. S Aug 1765. So.
Bartlett, John (2). Rebels T 1685.
Bartlett, John of Buckland. S s wheat Summer 1741 TB Jly 1742. G.

Bartlet, John. S Mar 1744. De.
Bartlet, John. AT Summer 1753. Y.
Bartlett, John. SQS Apr TB May 1767. So.
Bartlett, Mary. R Mar 1758. De.
Bartlett, Mary. S Apr T May 1767 *Thornton*. M.
Bartlet, Nicholas. S Mar 1744. De.
Bartlett, Samuel. S Mar 1763. So.
Bartlet, Sarah. S Jun T Nov 1743 *George William*. L.
Bartlett, Thomas, als Wheatley, Henry. S Jan-Jun T Jun 1728 *Elizabeth*
    LC Potomack Aug 1729. M.
Bartlett, William. S Jly 1721. Wi.
Bartlett, William. S Jan-Feb T Apr 1753 *Thames*. M.
Bartlett, William. S Apr 1765. So.
Bartlett, William, als James, John. S Mar TB to Va Apr 1766. Wi.
Bartley, David. R & T for life Jly 1753 *Tryal*. M.
Bartley, James. S & T Feb 1740 *York*. L.
Bartley, Robert (1698). *See* Richards. Co.
Bartlom, Edward. S Jan T Apr 1762 *Dolphin*. L.
Barto, Samuel. R for life Apr 1747. De.
Barton, David. R for Barbados or Jamaica Feb 1686. M.
Barton, Edward of Tamworth. R (Midland Circ) for America Jly
    1677. St.
Barton, Elizabeth. S Feb T Mar 1727 *Rappahannock* to Md. M.
Barton, Elizabeth. S s sheep Summer 1764 R 14 yrs Lent T Oct
    1765. Bd.
Barton, Henry. SQS Dec 1758. M.
Barton, Henry. S & T Dec 1758 *The Brothers*. L.
Barton, James of Liscoe St. Michael. R for Barbados Jly 1685. La.
Barton, John. S Jun-Dec 1745. M.
Barton, John. S Summer 1749. Hu.
Barton, John. T Oct 1750 *Rachael*. K.
Barton, John of St. George, Southwark. SQS Mar T Apr 1753
    Thames. Sy.
Barton, John. S Lent R 14 yrs Summer 1761. Bu.
Barton, Leonard. S & T Sep 1731 *Smith* but died on passage. M.
Barton, Martha. S Sep T Nov 1743 *George William*. M.
Barton, Richard. S May-Jun T Jly 1753 *Tryal*. M.
Barton, Thomas. S & T Apr 1741 *Mediterranean*. L.
Barton, Thomas. S & R Norwich for highway robbery at Heigham
    Summer 1772. Nf.
Barton, William. R Dec 1716 T Jan 1717 *Queen Elizabeth*. M.
Barton, William. S Jan T Feb 1719 *Worcester* LC Annapolis Jun 1719. L.
Barton, William. S Dec 1745. L.
Bartram, Anthony. SQS Dec 1772. M.
Bartram, Mary. S & T Jan 1769 *Thornton*. M.
Baruh, Abraham. S Oct 1757 T Mar 1758 *Dragon*. L.
Baruh, Abraham. S Jan 1759. L.
Barew, Abraham. S May T Jly 1771 *Scarsdale*. M.
Barew, Moses. S Jun T Sep 1767 *Justitia*. L.
Barew, Solomon. S s silver watch at St. Vedast Dec 1768 T Jan 1769
    Thornton. L.

Barwell, Mary of Lancaster. R for Barbados Jly 1699. La.

Barwell, Robert of Sandon. R (Newgate) for Barbados Apr TB Oct 1669. E.

Barwick, Benjamin. R 14 yrs Summer 1744. Nf.

Barwis, John of Dovenby. R for Barbados Jly 1684. Cu.

Base, Philip of Stapleford. R for America Jly 1702. Ca.

Basley, Ann wife of Argenton. R 14 yrs Mar 1740. De.

Basely, Thomas. R 14 yrs Aug 1724. Co.

Basely, William. R Aug 1738. Co.

Basey, Ann. S Sep 1760. M.

Baisy, John Baptist Robert Fountain. S for wounding Customs officers Summer 1742. Y & Nl.

Bazil als Basil, Susannah. S Jly T Oct 1741 *Sea Horse*. L.

Basil als Boswell, Timothy. S s shoes at Shipston on Stour Lent 1773. Wo.

Baskerville, Mary (1656). *See* Deane. M.

Baskerville, Richard. S s mare Aug 1654 R Feb 1656. M.

Baskett, Richard. T May 1736 *Patapsco*. E.

Basnett, John. TB May 1734 T *Squire* LC Md Aug 1735. Db.

Bason, John. Rebel T 1685.

Bason, Rockingham of Haddon. R for Barbados Apr 1668. Ht.

Bason, Thomas of Swanswick, Titchfield, husbandman. R for Barbados Jun 1669 Ha.

Bass, George. S s at Wickhambrooke Summer 1771. Su.

Bass, Jane (1746). *See* Ross. L.

Basse, John. LC Annapolis Md Sep 1725 from *Sukey*. X.

Bass, John of Thaxted, blacksmith. SQS Jly T Sep 1751. E.

Basse, Michael of Crediton, husbandman. R for Barbados Jly 1667. De.

Bass, Robert. S Mar 1750. So.

Bass, William (1761). *See* Gill. Le.

Bassage, William. S s at Halesowen Summer 1759. Wo.

Bassett, Alexander of Limpsfield. SQS Jly T Sep 1765 *Justitia*. Sy.

Bassett, Andrew of Bermondsey. SQS Jan T Mar 1764 *Tryal*. Sy.

Bassett, Benjamin. S Lent R for life Summer 1767. Bd.

Bassett, Catherine wife of Richard. S for shoplifting at Walsall Lent 1774. St.

Bassett, Elisha. S Sep-Oct 1775. M.

Bassett, Elizabeth. S Sep-Dec 1746. M.

Bassett, Henry. R 14 yrs Apr 1770. So.

Bassett, James of Biddenden. R for plantations Feb 1656. K.

Bassett, Jane wife of Basil, als Hill als Graves, of St. Saviour, Southwark. R for Barbados or Jamaica Mar 1680. Sy.

Bassett, John of Waltham Abbey. R for Barbados or Jamaica Feb 1686. E.

Bassett, Joseph. T May 1751 *Tryal*. Ht.

Bassett, Philip. S Lent R for life Summer 1767. Bd.

Bassett, Richard. S Feb 1663 to House of Correction unless he agrees to be transported. M.

Bassock, Thomas. T Oct 1721 *William & John*. K.

Bastard, John. S Jly 1765 TB to Va 1766. De.

Bastin, William. SQS & T May 1750 *Lichfield*. Ht.

Bastings, Isaac (1696). *See* Baston. G.

Baston als Bastings, Isaac of Bitton. R for America Jly 1696. G.

Baston, James. S Dec 1749-Jan 1750 T Mar 1750 *Tryal*. M.

Basten, John. T May 1737 *Forward*. Ht.

Baswell als Bazwell, Jonathan. S s lead from Lady Beauclerk at
  Somerset House Jan T Mar 1764 *Tryal*. M.

Baswicke, George of St. George, Southwark. SQS Apr T Sep 1751
  Greyhound. Sy.

Batch, John (1742). *See* Bache. Wo.

Batchelor, Ambrose. R 14 yrs Jly 1757. Ha.

Batchelor, Edward of Horsham. R for Barbados Jly 1679. Sx.

Batchelor, James. T Jun 1764 *Dolphin*. K.

Batchelor, Jane. S Jan-Feb T Apr 1753 *Thames*. M.

Batchelor, Margaret. R May T Jun 1691. M.

Batchelor, Peter. S Apr T Jly 1770 *Scarsdale*. M.

Batchelor, Richard. T Oct 1732 *Caesar*. Sy.

Batchelor, Robert (1661). *See* Wood. L.

Bate, Benjamin. S Lent T Apr 1773. Wa.

Bate, Edward. S for highway robbery at Stapleton Summer TB Aug
  1748. G.

Bate, Henry of Bolton in the Moors and Manchester. SQS Oct 1748. La.

Bate, James. S Mar 1749. Co.

Bate, John. S s mare at Morningthorpe & R Summer 1770. Nf.

Bate, Thomas (1767). *See* Chambers. Wa.

Bateman, Elizabeth of Westerham. R for Barbados or Jamaica Mar
  1680. K.

Bateman, Elizabeth (1759). *See* Jenkins. L.

Bateman als Batson, George of Kingston on Thames. SQS Jan 1772. Sy.

Bateman, Harriot. S Apr-May T Jly 1771 *Scarsdale*. M.

Bateman, Joseph. S City Summer 1729. Nl.

Bateman, Mary. S Summer 1750. Y.

Bateman, Peter. S Sep T Oct 1750 *Rachael*. M.

Bateman, Samuel. S Feb T Apr 1770 *New Trial*. L.

Bateman, Thomas. S 14 yrs for receiving goods stolen at Huntingdon
  Feb T Apr 1735 *Patapsco* LC Annapolis Oct 1735. M.

Bateman, Thomas. S Summer 1740. Wo.

Bateman, Thomas. TB Oct 1752. Db.

Bateman als Bater, Thomas. SQS Oct 1772. M.

Bateman, William of Dunkswick. R for Barbados Jly 1690. Y.

Bateman, William. S Lent R 14 yrs Summer 1727. G.

Bateman, William. S s at Rocester Lent 1745. St.

Bates, Edward aged 20, dark. LC Annapolis Md May 1721 from
  Gilbert. X.

Bates, George. SQS Mar TB to Md Apr 1753. Le.

Bates, Hannah wife of William, soldier of Ross. S Lent 1720. He.

Bates als Clerke, Joanna, als Lambeth, Elizabeth. R Dec 1695 & May
  1697 AT Jly 1697. M.

Bates, John (1676). *See* Prince. M.

Bates, John. T Oct 1726 *Forward*. Sx.

Bates, John. S Oct T Nov 1728 *Forward* LC Rappahannock Jun 1729. M.

Bates, John. S s gelding at Midgham Lent R 14 yrs Summer 1737. Be.

Bates, John. S Summer T May 1755 *Rose*. K.
Bates, John. T Sep 1764 *Justitia*. Sy.
Bates, John of Coleshill. SQS Jan T May 1767 *Thornton*. Ht.
Bates, John. S s ducks at Biggleswade Lent 1770. Bd.
Bates, John (1775). *See* Gibbons, William. Ha.
Bates, Jonathan. R for Barbados Feb 1675. L.
Bates, Joseph. S Lent R Summer 1726. No.
Bates, Joseph. S Lent 1770. Nt.
Bates, Margaret. S & T Dct 1730 *Forward* LC Potomack Jan 1731. L.
Bates, Richard. S & T Oct 1732 *Caesar* to Va. M.
Bates, Robert. R Apr TB for Barbados Jun 1669. M.
Bates, Roger. R for Barbados Apr 1669: sentenced with Robert Bates
    (qv) for wandering the country as vagabonds with other lewd persons
    calling themselves Egyptians and pretending to tell fortunes. M.
Bates, Rowland. S s at Kinnersley Summer 1761. Sh.
Bates, Susannah. S Jun 1761. M.
Bates, Thomas. R for Barbados Mar 1681. L.
Bates, Thomas. S Oct T Nov 1759 *Phoenix*. L.
Bates, Thomas of Nottingham, framework knitter. SQS s stockings Oct
    1765. Nt.
Bates, William. S & T Apr 1733 *Patapsco* LC Annapolis Nov 1733. M.
Bates, William. S Dec 1733 T Jan 1734 *Caesar* LC Va Jly 1734. M.
Bates, William. S May-Jly 1749. M.
Bates, William. S Feb T 14 yrs Apr 1772 *Thornton*. L.
Bates, William. R Summer 1773. Ht.
Bateson, John. S Summer 1754. La.
Bath, Edward of Stroud, butcher. S s breeches Lent 1719. G.
Bath, Malachi. R 7 yrs Mar 1755. Co.
Bath, William. S & T Sep 1751 *Greyhound*. M.
Bathaw, John. S Sep 1744. L.
Bather als Batho, Francis of Leek, baker. R for America Feb 1700. St.
Bathoe, Francis of White Ladies Aston. R for America Jly 1691. Wo.
Batho, Francis (1700). *See* Bather. St.
Batho, Thomas. S s from warehouse Lent 1737. Nf.
Bathurst, Mary. R for Barbados or Jamaica Oct 1688. L.
Batley, Joseph. S Lent 1749. Y.
Batson, George (1772). *See* Bateman. Sy.
Batson, James. S s at Wymondham Lent 1774. Nf.
Batson, Mordecai. S Apr-Jun 1739. M.
Batt, Benjamin. S Mar 1775. Do.
Batt, Esther. S & T Oct 1729 *Forward* LC Va Jun 1730. L.
Batt, George. R 14 yrs Aug 1731. Do.
Batt, Henry of Deptford. R for Barbados or Jamaica Jly 1702. K.
Batt, John. S for counterfeiting at St. Mary, Reading, Lent 1759 R 14 yrs
    Lent 1760. Be.
Batt, Jonathan. S Dec 1733 T Jan 1734 *Caesar* LC Va Jly 1734. M.
Batt, Philip (1752). *See* Egerton. M.
Batt, Robert. Rebel T 1685.
Batt, Samuel. T Apr 1765 *Ann*. K.
Batt, Susan wife of Henry *(qv)* of Deptford. R for Barbados or Jamaica
    Jly 1702. K.

Batt, Thomas. S Apr T May 1719 *Margaret*: sold to Patrick Sympson & William Black Md Sep 1719. L.

Batten, Edward. S & T Apr 1753 *Thames*. L.

Batten, Hanna of East Coulston, singlewoman. R for Barbados Jly 1693. Wi.

Batten, John. SQS Jan TB Sep 1728. So.

Batten, William. T 14 yrs Apr 1768 *Thornton*. K.

Batterby, Benjamin. S s cloth at Palgrave Lent 1770. Su.

Batterele, John. S Mar 1740. Co.

Battersby, John. S s sheep at Ormsby Lent R 14 yrs Summer TB Aug 1767. Y.

Batterson, John. S s at Newport Pagnell Lent 1775. Bu.

Batton, Francis of St. Saviour, Southwark. SQS May 1754. Sy.

Battin, John. S for highway robbery Lent 1741 R 14 yrs Lent 1743. O.

Battin, John. R Aug 1770 TB to Va 1771. De.

Battin, Joseph. S Lent R 14 yrs Summer 1760; to enlist in Regiment for Jamaica. Sy.

Batton, Mary. S Apr 1749. L.

Baton, Thomas als John. S Sep-Oct 1748 T Jan 1749 *Laura*. M.

Battin, William. PT Aug R Dec 1689. M.

Battishill, Thomas. TB to Md 1728. De.

Battle, James. S Sep T Dec 1758 *The Brothers*. M.

Battye als Bettice, James. S Lent 1750. La.

Batty, James. S Feb 1773. L.

Batty als Battie, Margaret. AT Lent 1766. Y.

Batty, William. S Feb T Apr 1765 *Ann*. L.

Baugh, Alexander. S Mar TB May 1756. Wi.

Baugh, John of Worcester. S Lent 1720. Wo.

Baugh, Jonathan. S Oct T Nov 1728 *Forward* LC Rappahannock Jun 1729. M.

Baughurst, Richard. S s at Shinfield Lent 1769. Be.

Baumer, William. T 14 yrs Dec 1758 *The Brothers*. K.

Baulfield, Elizabeth, als Carter als Howard als Smith, Katherine. R for Barbados or Jamaica Feb 1687. M.

Bauskin als Winter, John. S Mar TB to Va Apr 1751. Wi.

Bavin, Thomas. S Dec-Jan T Mar 1750 *Tryal*. M.

Bawcock, John. T Apr 1742 *Bond*. Ht.

Bawcock, John. T May 1751 *Tryal*. E.

Baucot, Samuel. S Lent R 14 yrs Summer 1762. Bd.

Bawcutt, William of Epsom. S Lent T Apr 1772 *Thornton*. Sy.

Bawd, Richard. S Aug 1751. Co.

Bawden, Ann. TB from QS 1770. De.

Bawden, Henry. R 14 yrs Aug 1738. Co.

Bawden als Mercer, Sarah wife of Richard of Sefton, husbandman. SQS Apr 1766. La.

Bawin, Thomas. S May-Jly 1749. M.

Bawler, Philip. SQS Apr 1730. So.

Bax, Jeremmah. S Lent 1754. K.

Baxall, William (1774). *See* Boxwell. Ha.

Baxforth, Richard of Lancaster. R for Barbados Jly 1699. La.

Baxson, Mordecai. S Jun 1747. L.

Baxon, Powell. S Apr 1718. M.

Baxter, Anne. R & T Oct 1722 *Forward* LC Annapolis Jun 1723. M.

Baxter, Ann wife of Robert. S s silver spoon at St. Giles, Norwich, Summer 1769. Nf.

Baxter, Edward. R for America Aug 1715. M.

Baxter, Elizabeth of Manchester, spinster. SQS Apr 1741. La.

Baxter, Elizabeth. S Jly 1745 TB to Va Apr 1746. Wi.

Baxter, Esther. S for shoplifting Lent 1753. Hu.

Baxter, George. R for America Jly 1686. Li.

Baxter, George. R for life for highway robbery Lent TB Apr 1763. Db.

Baxter, George. S May 1768. M.

Baxter, Henry. S Dec 1743 T Feb 1744 *Neptune* to Md. M.

Baxter, Hester. S Feb-Apr T May 1755 *Rose.* M.

Baxter, James. SQS Sep 1772. M.

Baxter, John. S Lent R 14 yrs Summer 1750. Nf.

Baxter, John. S Nov T Dec 1753 *Whiteing.* L.

Baxter, John. S Summer 1757 R 14 yrs Lent T Apr 1758. Bd.

Bexter, John. S Lent R 14 yrs Summer 1760. K.

Baxter als Jones, Mary, als Black Moll. R 14 yrs Mar 1753 De.

Baxter als Jones, Mary, als Black Moll. R for being at large before expiry of her term May T for life Sep 1758 *Tryal.* Md.

Baxter, Richard. S Jun 1736 s cloth. M.

Baxter, Sarah. S Sep T Dec 1769 *Justitia.* M.

Baxter, William of St. John's. SQS Jan T Mar 1763 *Neptune.* Sy.

Bayes, Elizabeth. S Norwich as pickpocket Summer 1749. Nf.

Bayes, John. S s clothing Apr T Dec 1735 *John* LC Annapolis Sep 1736. M.

Bayes, Stephen. S s horse Summer 1753 R 14 yrs Lent 1754. Li.

Bayes, William. S Feb T Mar 1727 *Rappahannock* to Md. M.

Bayham, Simon (1741). *See* Bockin. Wi.

Bayley. *See* Bailey.

Baylin, John (1764). *See* Boyland. M.

Baylis, Abraham. S s at Kidderminster Summer 1770. Wo.

Bayliss, James. R & T Sep 1737 *Pretty Patsy* to Md. M.

Bayliss, James. S s at All Saints, Worcester, Summer 1748. Wo.

Bayliss, Jane. S for murder of her bastard child Lent R 14 yrs Summer 1725. St.

Baylis, Jane. S s at Clifton upon Teme Lent 1761. Wo.

Baylis, John. LC Annapolis Md Nov 1733 from *Patapsco.* X.

Baylis, John. S & T Jly 1771 *Scarsdale.* L.

Bailiss, John of Tooting. SQS Jan 1774. Sy.

Baylis, Joseph. S May 1763. M.

Bayless, Nathaniel (1771). *See* Bayley. M.

Bayliss, Richard. S s sheep & R Lent T Apr 1771. Wa.

Baylis, William. R 14 yrs Jly 1744. So.

Baylis, William, son of Robert. S Lent R 14 yrs Summer TB Aug 1751. G.

Baylis, William. S Lent R 14 yrs Summer 1757. O.

Bayliss, William. S & T Dec 1771 *Justitia.* M.

Bainard, John (1764). *See* Barnard. Co.

Bayne. *See* Bain.

Baynham, Henry. S Apr 1763. L.

Baynam, John. S Lent R 14 yrs Summer 1730. G.

Baynham, William. S & T 14 yrs Apr 1718 *Tryal* LC Charles Town Aug 1718. L.

Bainton, Esther (1725). *See* James. M.

Baynton, John. R 14 yrs Apr 1756. So.

Beinton, Thomas. T Sep 1730 *Smith*. E.

Baythorne, James. R May T for life Sep 1757 *Thetis*. M.

Baythorn, William. S & T Aug 1752 *Tryal*. L.

Bazeley, William. R 14 yrs May 1774 (SP). O.

Bazil. *See* Basil.

Bazor als Lewis, John. R 14 yrs Mar TB to Va Apr 1758. Wi.

Beach. *See* Beech.

Beacham, George. R 14 yrs Mar 1772 TB to Va. De.

Beacham, John (1697). *See* James. M.

Beacham, John. S Aug T Sep 1725 *Forward* LC Annapolis Dec 1725. M.

Beauchamp, John. T May 1744 *Justitia*. Sy.

Beacham, Rebecca. S May T Jun 1768 *Tryal*. L.

Beecham, William. S Lent R 14 yrs Summer 1765. Nt.

Bead. *See* Bede.

Beadle, Anthony. S Jan-Jun T 14 yrs Jun 1728 *Elizabeth* LC Potomack Aug 1729. L.

Beadle, John (1725). *See* Gold. M.

Beedle, Laurence. R for Barbados Feb 1672. M.

Beadle, Mary. S May-Jly 1748. M.

Beadle, Richard of Newington. SQS Jan T Apr 1768 *Thornton*. Sy.

Beadle, William. S Feb-Apr T May 1752 *Lichfield*. M.

Beadon, John. S Aug T Sep 1764 *Justitia*. L.

Beadon, Richard of Taunton, woolcomber. R for Barbados Jly 1693. So.

Beaden, Thomas. SQS Dec 1764 T Jan 1765 *Tryal*. M.

Beak, John. S Apr T Sep 1758 *Tryal* to Md. M.

Beake, William. S s horse Summer 1729 R Lent 1730. St.

Beake, William. S & T Oct 1732 *Caesar* to Va. M.

Beakley, Magdalene (1745). *See* Swawbrook. M.

Beale, Bridget wife of John. S Feb T Apr 1741 *Speedwell* or *Mediterranean*. M.

Beale, George. S Feb T Mar 1731 *Patapsco* LC Annapolis Jun 1731. M.

Beale, John. S Jan-Jun T Jun 1728 *Elizabeth* LC Potomack Aug 1729. M.

Beale, John of St. James, Westminster. S s coat Oct 1740 T Jan 1741 *Harpooner*. M.

Beale, John. S Feb T Apr 1741 *Speedwell* or *Mediterranean*. M.

Beale, John. S Oct T Dec 1767 *Neptune*. M.

Beele, Mary. TB 14 yrs Oct 1719 T *Susannah & Sarah* LC Annapolis Md Apr 1720. L.

Beale, Philip. S Summer 1756 R 14 yrs Lent 1757; but then acquitted. Nf.

Beale, Robert. Rebel T 1685.

Beal, Samuel of Wethersfield. SQS Oct 1773 to be T 5 yrs for running away from his family after being judged an incorrigible rogue. E.

Beale, Thomas. S Aug T Sep 1725 *Forward* to Md. M.

Beales, Jane wife of John. S Jan T Mar 1764 *Tryal*. M.

Beels, William of Wigtoft. R for America Jly 1678. Li.

Beales, William. R Aug T Sep 1725 *Forward* LC Annapolis Dec 1725. M.

Beales, William. S Norwich Summer 1756 R 14 yrs Summer 1757. Nf.

Bealey, John of South Croxton. R for America Jly 1670. Le.

Beeley, Thomas, als Walker, John. S s sheep at Wooley & R Lent 1774. Y.

Beaman. *See* Beaumont.

Beames, Peter. S Mar 1721. Wi.

Beames, Robert (1688). *See* Browne. M.

Beamhouse, Edward. R for Barbados May 1665. X.

Beamsley, Thomas. S s at Thame Lent 1728. O.

Bean, Daniel. S Jan-Feb 1774. M.

Bean als Macoppy, Jane. R May T 14 yrs Jly 1722 *Alexander* to Nevis or Jamaica. M.

Bean, Mary wife of William. S Jan T 14 yrs Feb 1744 *Neptune* to Md. M.

Bean, Mary wife of John. S Sep-Oct T Dec 1771 *Justitia*. M.

Beane, Peter of Westminster. R Aug 1663 (PC). M.

Beane, Robert. T Apr 1753 *Thames*. K.

Bean, Susannah. S & T May 1736 *Patapsco*. L.

Bean, Thomas. S & T Sep 1731 *Smith* LC Va 1732. L.

Been, Timothy. S May-Jly 1749. M.

Bean, William. S for highway robbery & R 14 yrs Summer 1772. Be.

Beancott, Ann (1730). *See* Wheeler. M.

Bare, Elizabeth. R Sep 1671 AT Oct 1673. M.

Bear, Elizabeth. TB Aug 1740. Db.

Bear als Lacy, Elizabeth. S Feb-Apr T May 1755 *Rose*. M.

Beare, George. R 14 yrs Aug 1747. De.

Bear, Hervey. R 14 yrs Aug 1720. De.

Beare, Humphrey. R for Jamaica Aug 1661. M.

Bare, John. S Jly 1732. Ha.

Bear, John. S s sheep Lent R 14 yrs Summer 1742. Be.

Beare, Peter of Banbury. R for America Mar 1688. O.

Bear, Richard. T Apr 1771 *Thornton*. Sy.

Beare, William. R for Va May 1622 (SP). Sy.

Bear, William. S Jan T Apr 1735 *Patapsco* LC Annapolis Oct 1735. L.

Beard, Ann (1735). *See* Tyers. M.

Beard als Butcher, Charlotte. S May-Jly 1773. M.

Beard, Daniel. S Feb T Mar 1730 *Patapsco* LC Annapolis Sep 1730. M.

Beard, Gilbert aged 37, dark. S & T Oct 1720 *Gilbert* LC Md May 1721. M.

Beard, Henry. AT from QS Lent 1769. G.

Beard, John (1713). *See* Davis. M.

Beard, John. T Apr 1735 *Patapsco*. K.

Beard, John. SQS Oct 1761 T Apr 1762 *Dolphin*. M.

Beard, John. S s at Scalby Lent TB Aug 1767. Y.

Beard, Joseph. S s canvas at Bridegnorth Lent 1724. Sh.

Beard, Margaret. R for Barbados or Jamaica Jan 1692. L.

Beard, Nicholas. S for highway robbery & R 21 yrs Lent 1765. Ch.

Beard, Richard. S May-Jly T Sep 1751 *Greyhound*. M.

Beard, Samuel. S s sheep at Stroud Lent 1736. G.

Beard, Samuel. S s sheep & R Summer 1772. G.

Beard, Sarah. S Jan-May T Jun 1738 *Forward* to Md or Va. M.
Beard, Stephen of Randwicke. R for America Nov 1694. G.
Beards, Joseph. S Lent T Apr 1771. Wa.
Beardsall, John. S Summer 1753. Y.
Beardsley, John. TB May 1734 T *Squire* LC Md Aug 1735. Db.
Beardson, Mary wife of John. S Lent 1756. Y.
Bearman, Elizabeth. S Summer 1748 T Jan 1749 *Laura*. E.
Bearman, William. S Summer 1754 R 14 yrs Lent T May 1755 *Rose*. E.
Beesly, Ann. S Jun-Dec 1738 T Jan 1739 *Dorsetshire* to Va. M.
Beezley, Ann. S Feb 1754. L.
Beaseley, Edward. R Jly 1771. Ha.
Beasley, Isaac. R 14 yrs s horse Summer 1721 T *Robert* LC Md Jun
   1725. Le.
Beazely, John (1697). *See* Browne. Bu.
Beezley, John (1735). *See* Baker. M.
Beesly, John. S s coat at Newbury Lent 1749. Be.
Beasley, John. S Apr T May 1751 *Tryal*. L.
Bezely, John of Bermondsey. SQS Oct 1754. Sy.
Beazley, John. S & R 14 yrs Lent 1775. Wo.
Beazley, Richard. S & T Dec 1752 *Greyhound*. M.
Beesly, Thomas, brickmaker aged 21, fair. R Jan T Feb 1723 *Jonathan*
   LC Md Jly 1724. M.
Beasly, William. R Dec 1698 AT Jan 1699. M.
Beesley, William. S s 2 shillings Dec 1735 T Jan 1736 *Dorsetshire* LC Va
   Sep 1736. M.
Beaseley, William. S Aug 1759. De.
Beason. *See* Beeson.
Beate, Leonard. R for Barbados or Jamaica Feb 1686. M.
Beatley, Thomas. SQS May T Aug 1769 *Dragon*. M.
Beaton, James. S & T Sep 1731 *Smith* LC Va 1732. M.
Beaton, James. S Apr T May 1751 *Tryal*. L.
Beaton, John. S & T Jan 1722 *Gilbert* LC Annapolis Jly 1722. L.
Beeton, Margaret. S Apr 1773. M.
Beaton, Nathaniel. Rebel T 1685.
Beaton, Robert. Rebel T 1685.
Beaton, Robert. S Aug T Sep 1727 *Forward* LC Rappahannock May
   1728. L.
Beaton, Timothy. R for Barbados or Jamaica Jly 1687. M.
Beauchamp. *See* Beacham.
Beaucline, Elizabeth. S & T Mar 1760 *Friendship*. L.
Beaule als Handy, John. R Jly 1721 T *Prince Royal* LC Va
   Nov 1721. M.
Buley, John. S Sep-Oct 1749. M.
Bewley, Mary. S & T Aug 1752 *Tryal*. L.
Booley, Thomas. T Sep 1730 *Smith*. Sy.
Beaumont als Harridge, Abraham of Dalton. R (Midland Circ) for
   America Jly 1673. Y.
Beamont, Elizabeth wife of Thomas. S Sep 1761. M.
Beaman, Henry of Chippenham. R for Barbados Dec 1686. Wi.
Beaumont, James. S Summer 1775. K.
Beaumont, John. SQS Jan 1665 as idle & disorderly. M.

Beauman, Sarah (1770). *See* Williams. K.

Beamont, Thomas. R & T Apr 1735 *Patapsco* LC Annapolis Oct 1735. M.

Beuman als Beaumont, Thomas. S s at Wolverhampton Lent 1764. St.

Beaumont, William. R 14 yrs Summer 1756. Y.

Beaumont, William. S Summer 1756. K.

Beaumont, William of St. Olave, Southwark. SQS Feb T Apr 1771 *Thornton*. Sy.

Beaver, Ann. S Apr-May T Jly 1771 *Scarsdale*. M.

Beaver, John. S s at Woburn & R 14 yrs Lent 1774. Bu.

Beavor, Sarah. S Feb T Mar 1730 *Patapsco* LC Annapolis Sep 1730. M.

Beavers als Hopkins, Bridget. S Feb T Mar 1730 *Patapsco* LC Md Sep 1730. L.

Beavis, Ann. TB to Va from QS 1740. De.

Beavis, Eleanor. S Aug 1755. So.

Beavis, Elizabeth (1756). *See* Hall. Do.

Beavis, William. S Jly 1741. De.

Beazley. *See* Beasley.

Beazor, John. R Apr 1773. M.

Beazor, Richard. R Apr 1773. M.

Beck, John. R for highway robbery Summer 1728 (SP). Nf.

Beck, Mary. S Jan 1746. L.

Beck, Matthew. S s earrings at St. Dunstan in West Apr T Jun 1768 *Tryal*. L.

Becke, Robert. R for Barbados or Jamaica Oct 1694. L.

Beckett, George. S s mare at Shenstone Lent R 14 yrs Summer 1737. St.

Beckett, George. SWK Apr T Oct 1768 *Justitia*. K.

Beckett, Humphrey. R for Barbados Jly 1675. M.

Becket, James. R 14 yrs Summer 1754. Su.

Beckett, John. SQS Apr T May 1755 *Rose*. M.

Becket, John. S s horse Lent R 14 yrs Summer 1767. St.

Beckett, Richard. S s sheep at Darrington & R Lent 1774. Y.

Beckett, Robert. R May T Jly 1723 *Alexander*. M.

Beckett, Rose. S s at Stoke Church Summer 1752. O.

Beckford, Edward. R for Jamaica Aug 1661. L.

Beckham, Benjamin. S Lent 1752. Nf.

Becods, Joseph. R for life for being found at large after sentence of transportation Lent 1775. K.

Beddily, Edward. PT Jan 1699. M.

Bedding, John. R for America Jly 1693. Wa.

Beddington, Edward. S Jan-Feb T Apr 1771 *Thornton*. M.

Beddow, Thomas. S Apr 1718 T *Eagle* LC Charles Town Mar 1719. M.

Beddo, William. S May T Jun 1727 *Susanna* to Va. M.

Bedoe, William. R 14 yrs Mar 1756. Ha.

Bead, John. R for Barbados Aug 1668. M.

Bede, Thomas. S & T Dec 1770 *Justitia*. L.

Bedford, Catherine. S Sep T Oct 1768 *Justitia*. M.

Bedford, Christian. SL Jly 1755 T Jan 1756 *Greyhound*. Sy.

Bedford, John of Manchester, weaver. SQS Jly 1774. La.

Bedford, Mary. S Lent 1761. Wa.

Bedford, Samuel. S & R Lent 1768. Wa.

Bedford, Walter. S Dee 1753-Jan 1754. M.
Bedford, William. S Jun T Jly 1772 *Tayloe*. L.
Bedgood, Nicholas. S Lent R 14 yrs Summer TB Aug 1751. G.
Bedkin, Henry. S Sep-Oct T Dec 1771 *Justitia*. M.
Bedleston, George. T Apr 1766 *Ann*. K.
Bedoe. *See* Beddow.
Bedwell, James. S Jly T Sep 1757 *Thetis*. L.
Bedwell, Martha wife of John of St. George, Southwark. SQS Jan
    1754. Sy.
Bee, Elizabeth wife of John. S Summer 1774. Li.
Beeby, George. PT Summer 1719. St.
Beeby, Richard. PT Summer 1719. St.
Beeby, Richard. T Oct 1723 *Forward*. Sy.
Beech, James of Wisborough Green. R for Barbados or Jamaica Mar
    1682 & Feb 1684. Sx.
Beach, John. S Jan-Feb T Apr 1771 *Thornton*. M.
Beech, Joseph. S Sep-Dec 1746. M.
Beech, Richard. S Lent 1741. Wo.
Beech, Sarah. S Aug T Oct 1724 *Forward* LC Annapolis Jun 1725. L.
Beecham. *See* Beacham.
Beechin, Richard. T Apr 1732 *Patapsco*. Sx.
Beeching, Thomas. T Sep 1765 *Justitia*. K.
Beechley, Grace. R for Jamaica for housebreaking Feb 1665. M.
Beechy als Petchy, Elizabeth. T Oct 1723 *Forward*. E.
Beecroft, George of Yarm, cooper. SQS New Malton s butter Jan AT
    Lent 1766. Y.
Beeding, Bridget. S May 1733 T Jan 1734 *Caesar* LC Va Jly 1734. M.
Beedle. *See* Beadle.
Beefey (Beesley) als Duggan, John. S Mar 1754. L.
Beeks, Christopher. S for assault on highway Lent 1770. La.
Beeks, Sarah. R Jan-Feb T 14 yrs Apr 1772 *Thornton*. M.
Beeley. *See* Bealey.
Beels. *See* Beales.
Beem, William. S Oct 1774. L.
Beer, Hugh, als Thomas, William. R 14 yrs Aug 1736. So.
Beere, Jane wife of John. S Mar 1740. So.
Bere, John. S Mar 1752. De.
Beer, Josias. R 14 yrs Aug 1735. De.
Beere, William of Braughin. R for Barbados or Jamaica Jun 1699. Ht.
Bees, Robert. SQS & TB Jan 1773. So.
Beeseh, Moses. S Oct-Dec 1739. M.
Beesly. *See* Beasley.
Beesmore, Elizabeth. SQS Feb T May 1767 *Thornton*. M.
Beeson, James. S Oct 1774. L.
Beason, William. S Jun-Dec 1745. M.
Beetle, Frances, aged 29. R for Barbados Feb 1664. L.
Beetle, James. S Norwich Summer 1764. Nf.
Beezley. *See* Beasley.
Beford, Thomas of Buckingham. R for Barbados Feb 1664. Bu.
Behoe, Moses. S s wigs & hair at Reading Summer 1722 LC Md Jun
    1723. Be.

Beinton. *See* Baynton.

Bekindtome, John of Liverpool. SQS Jan 1759. La.

Belbin, Anne of New Sarum, singlewoman. R for Barbados Jly 1693. Wi.

Belcham, James (1699). *See* Bycham. E.

Belcheire, Anne, spinster. R for Barbados Dec 1667. M.

Belcher, George. S Aug T Sep 1725 *Forward* LC Annapolis Dec 1725. L.

Belcher, Henry of Shelton. S s linen bag Summer 1724. Bd.

Belcher, John. R for Barbados Sep 1682. L.

Belcher, Martyr. S & T Apr 1753 *Thames.* L.

Belcher, Sarah. S Jun T Aug 1769 *Douglas.* L.

Belchier als Kempster als Fowell, Susanna. S Aug T 14 yrs Sep 1725 *Forward.* M.

Belcher, Thomas of Bromsgrove. R for Barbados Jly 1664. Wo.

Belfield, Simon. TB Apr 1765. Db.

Belford, Elizabeth (1753). *See* Owen. Sy.

Belfour. *See* Balfour.

Bellam, Elizabeth. R Aug T Oct 1724 *Forward* LC Annapolis Jun 1725. M.

Belham, Mary. AT Lent 1749. Be.

Bell als Webster, Alison. R for Barbados Jun 1670. M.

Bell, Anne. R for Jamaica Jan 1633 M.

Bell, Ann. S Sep T Dec 1758 *The Brothers.* M.

Bell, Catherine. LC Annapolis Md Sep 1736 from *John.* X.

Bell, Cuthbert. S s lead Summer 1756. Du.

Bell, David. R 14 yrs Summer 1729. Nl.

Bell, Dorothy. S s sheep & R 14 yrs Summer 1757; then given free pardon. Du.

Bell, Edward. S s horse Summer 1720 R 14 yrs Summer 1721. Nt.

Bell, Elizabeth. TB Aug 1740. Db.

Bell, Hannah. S Oct 1774. L.

Bell, James, tailor aged 20, dark. S Jan T Feb 1723 *Jonathan* LC Md Jly 1724. L.

Bell, James. S Jan 1745. L.

Bell, James. S Jly 1761. L.

Bell, James. T for life Oct 1768 *Justitia.* Sy.

Bell, John. T Aug 1721 *Owners Goodwill.* E.

Bell, John. S s horse Lent R 14 yrs Summer 1731. Li.

Bell, John. S Lent 1748. E.

Bell, John. S Dec 1753-Jan 1754. M.

Bell, John. S City s silver mug Lent 1764; S Lent 1766 for being at large at New Malton & R for life Summer TB Aug 1766. Y.

Bell als Armstrong, John. SQS s silver gill Easter 1764. Du.

Bell, John (1770). *See* Day. Su.

Bell, Joseph. S Summer 1760. Wa.

Bell, Mary. T Jun 1727 *Susanna.* K.

Bell, Mary. S 14 yrs Feb-Apr 1746. M.

Bell, Mary. SL Jly T Sep 1755 *Tryal.* Sy.

Bell, Mary. S s sheep & R 14 yrs Summer 1757; then given free pardon. Du.

Bell, Robert. S s sheep & R 14 yrs Summer 1757; then given free pardon. Du.

Bell, Robert. S Oct T Dec 1769 *Justitia*. L.

Bell, Samuel. S Sep-Oct T Dec 1752 *Greyhound*. M.

Bell, Sarah. R for Barbados or Jamaica Jly 1685. M.

Bell, Thomas of Cawston. R for Barbados Jan 1665. Nf.

Bell, Thomas (1702). *See* Williams. Sy.

Bell, Thomas. S for issuing false coinage Summer 1729 AT Summer 1732. Nl.

Bell, Thomas. S Summer 1762 R 14 yrs Lent 1763. K.

Bell, Thomas. SQS Dec 1766 T Jan 1767 *Tryal*. M.

Bell, Thomas. S s shoes at St. Bartholomew the Great Apr T Jun 1768 *Tryal*. L.

Bell als Tessimond, William. S s horse Summer 1726 R 14 yrs Lent 1729. Y.

Bell, William. S s horse Summer 1731 R 14 yrs Summer 1732. Li.

Bell, William (1747). *See* Forster, Robert. Nl.

Bell, William of Clapham. SQS Apr T Sep 1751 *Greyhound*. Sy.

Bell, William. S Feb T Apr 1759 *Thetis*. M.

Bellam. *See* Belham.

Bellamy, Edward. Rebel T 1685.

Bellamy, Elizabeth. S & T Apr 1733 *Patapsco* LC Md Nov 1733. L.

Bellamy, John. SW & T Apr 1770 *New Trial*. M.

Bellamy, John. S Mar 1771. So.

Bellamy, William. S & T Sep 1731 *Smith* LC Va 1732. M.

Bellass, Anne. S Feb T Mar 1730 *Patapsco* LC Annapolis Sep 1730. M.

Bellchamber, Elizabeth. T 14 yrs Dec 1758 *The Brothers*. Sx.

Bellenger, Henry. S Jly T Sep 1751 *Greyhound*. L.

Bellgrove, Benjamin of Harrow. S s ducks Feb 1740. M.

Belling, Thomas of Brampton. S Summer 1726. *Hu.

Bellis, Henry. S Sep 1764. M.

Bellis, John. R 7 yrs Lent 1774. Ht.

Bellisford, William. S Jun T Sep 1751 *Greyhound*. L.

Bellsford als Bottsford, John of Essondon. T Apr 1753 *Thames*. Ht.

Bellybone, George. S Summer 1751. Nf.

Belman, Peter of Disforth. R for Barbados Jly 1671. Y.

Belmasset, Humphrey. S Feb T 14 yrs Mar 1731 *Patapsco* LC Md Jun 1731. L.

Belmorshed, Humphrey. S s gowns Oct 1735 T Jan 1736 *Dorsetshire* LC Va Sep 1736. M.

Belot, Daniel. S Dec 1742 T Apr 1743 *Justitia*. M.

Belt, Elias. R for Barbados Jun 1671. L.

Benbow, Francis. R for Jamaica Feb 1665. M.

Benbowe, John. R for America Feb 1700. Nt.

Benbow, Thomas. S s corn Lent 1742. Sh.

Benbow, Thomas. T Apr 1770 *New Trial*. Bu.

Benbrook, Abraham. S & T Jan 1739 *Dorsetshire*. L.

Bence, James. SQS & TB Apr 1774. So.

Bencoe, Thomas. SQS Jan-Mar TB to Va Apr 1741. Wi.

Bendall, Christopher. S Mar TB Oct 1735. Wi.

Bendall, Christopher. S Jly 1736. Wi.

Bendle, James. SQS Jan TB Apr 1729. So.

Bendall, Joseph. S & TB Aug 1740. G.

Bendall, Thomas. R 14 yrs Mar 1750. So.

Bendall, Thomas. S Aug T Sep 1764 *Justitia*. L.

Bending, Gilbert. R 14 yrs Aug 1720. De.

Bendley, Jonathan. T May 1719 *Margaret* LC Md Sep 1719; sold to
  Patrick Sympson & William Black. Sy.

Bends, James. R Oct 1694 AT Jan 1695. M.

Bendyfield, Sarah. S s handkerchief etc Sep 1735 T Jan 1736 *Dorsetshire*
  LC Va Sep 1736. M.

Benfield, Thomas. S Jly T Aug 1721 *Prince Royal* LC Va Nov 1721. L.

Benfield, William. T Apr 1742 *Bond*. K.

Benford, Alice. R for Barbados Dec 1671. M.

Benham als Smith, Hester. S Mar 1740. Ha.

Benham, John. S Mar 1764. Ha.

Benham, John. T Sep 1767 *Justitia*. M.

Benham, Mary (1750). *See* Bramstone. K.

Benham, Richard. R May T for life Sep 1758 *Tryal* to Annapolis. M.

Benham, Samuel. S Mar 1775. Ha.

Benham, William of Crediton. R for Barbados Jly 1677. De.

Benioge, Richard (1671). *See* Benjon. M.

Benion, Peter. S Apr T Sep 1737 *Pretty Patsy* to Md. M.

Benjon als Benioge, Richard. R for Barbados Dec 1671. M.

Benison, Joseph. R 14 yrs Aug 1731. So.

Benjamin, Abraham. S Apr T May 1752 *Lichfield*. L.

Benjamin, Benjamin. SW & T Apr 1770 *New Trial*. M.

Benjamin, Joseph. SQS Sep T Oct 1768 *Justitia*. M.

Benjamin, Samuel. S May-Jly 1773. M.

Benjamin, Simon. S Feb T Apr 1771 *Thornton*. L.

Benly, William. S s sheep Summer 1765 R 14 yrs Summer 1766. Nl.

Benmead, Sarah. S Jly 1740. Wi.

Benn, John. S Lent 1760. Hu.

Benn, William. S Jan-Feb 1773. M.

Bennell, Ann (1736). *See* Bennett. Sy.

Bennett, Alexander. R 14 yrs Mar 1771 TB to Va. De.

Bennett als Bennell, Ann. T Dec 1736 *Dorsetshire*. Sy.

Bennett, Ann. S Oct T Nov 1759 *Phoenix*. L.

Bennet, Ann. S Jan-Feb 1774. M.

Bennett, Bartholomew of West Malling. R for America Jly 1700. K.

Bennet, Catherine. S Aug T Sep 1725 *Forward* LC Annapolis Dec
  1725. L.

Bennet, Catherine. S & T Oct 1732 *Caesar*. L.

Bennett, Charles. Rebel T 1685.

Bennett, Charles of Mangotsfield. S as dangerous idle person &
  threatening the King's officers and witnesses Lent 1718. G.

Bennett, Charles of Frampton Cotterell. S Lent 1721. G.

Bennett, Charlotte. T Sep 1765 *Justitia*. K.

Bennett, Edward. T for life Apr 1770 *New Trial*. Sy.

Bennet, Eleanor. S Feb-Apr 1746. M.

Bennett, Elizabeth. S & T Oct 1729 *Forward* to Va but died on
  passage. M.

Bennett, Elizabeth wife of Mark of St. George. S s bed linen Jly 1740 T Jan 1741 *Harpooner*. M.

Bennett, Elizabeth. S Oct 1741 T for life Feb 1742 *Industry* to Md. M.

Bennett, Elizabeth. S Dec 1747. L.

Bennett, Elizabeth. S Jan T Mar 1750 *Tryal*. L.

Bennett, Elizabeth. S May-Jly T Sep 1751 *Greyhound*. M.

Bennett, Gabriel. S Lent 1774. G.

Bennett, George of Harborne, blacksmith. R for America Jly 1681. St.

Bennett, George. S Jly 1718 to be T to Va. De.

Bennett, George. S Jun T Nov 1743 *George William*. M.

Bennett, George als Joseph. S s at Undy Summer 1766. Mo.

Bennett, George. S s sheep at Chelmarsh & R 14 yrs Summer 1771. Sh.

Bennett, Giles. S s at Sapperton Lent 1774. G.

Bennet, Hannah. S Apr 1756. So.

Bennett, Henry. S Mar 1772. So.

Bennett als Burdett, Hester. S Jly T Aug 1721 *Prince Royal* LC Va Nov 1721. L.

Bennett, Hooper. S & T Jan 1769 *Thornton*. M.

Bennett als Benne, James of Ilford. R for Barbados or Jamaica Jly 1696. E.

Bennett, James (1732). *See* Ireman. M.

Bennett, James. S Jly T Oct 1741 *Sea Horse*. L.

Bennett, James. S s at St. Peter, Cambridge, Lent 1769. Ca.

Bennett, Jasper of Crewkerne, husbandman. R for Barbados Apr 1668. So.

Bennet, John of Thorndon Garnon. R (Newgate) for Barbados Aug 1668. E.

Bennett, John. R for Barbados Sep 1672. L.

Bennett, John (2). Rebels T 1685.

Bennett, John. R Jan T Feb 1724 *Anne* to Carolina. M.

Bennett, John. T Nov 1728 *Forward*. Sx.

Bennet, John. R 14 yrs Mar 1736. So.

Bennett, John. S s gelding Summer R 14 yrs Nov 1736. Bd.

Bennett, John of St. Marylebone. S s waistcoat Apr T May 1740 *Essex*. M.

Bennett, John. S Jly 1741. Co.

Bennett, John. S Jan T Apr 1743 *Justitia*. M.

Bennett, John. S Sep 1747. L.

Bennett, John (1750). *See* Dale. Nt.

Bennett, John. S s sheep Lent R 14 yrs Summer 1750. Wa.

Bennett, John. S Oct 1751-Jan 1752. M.

Bennett, John. S Lent 1752. Y.

Bennet, John. S Aug 1758. So.

Bennett, John. S & T Apr 1759 *Thetis*. L.

Bennett, John (1761). *See* Cade. L.

Bennet, John (1764). *See* Ingram. G.

Bennet, John. S Summer 1765. Wa.

Bennett, John (1768). *See* Benny. M.

Bennett, John. S Apr T Jly 1770 *Scarsdale*. M.

Bennett, John of Bushey. R 14 yrs Lent T Apr 1772 *Thornton*. Ht.

Bennet, Joseph. S Lent 1766. Wa.

Bennett, Lucy wife of Tobias. S s from Worcester College Lent 1769. O.
Bennett, Mary. R for Barbados or Jamaica Dec 1695. L.
Bennett, Mary (1700). *See* Benny. Nf.
Bennett als Tipping, Mary. S Aug T Sep 1725 *Forward* LC Md Dec 1725. M.
Bennett, Mary. S Jan T Feb 1726 *Supply* LC Annapolis May 1726. L.
Bennett, Mary (1734). *See* Kerril. So.
Bennett, Mary. T Oct 1750 *Rachael*. M.
Bennet, Mary. S Jan 1757. M.
Bennet, Michael. S Mar 1775. Ha.
Bennett, Nathaniel. S s at Wootton under Edge Lent 1745. G.
Bennett, Nicholas of Bromfield. R for Barbados Mar 1686. So.
Bennet, Nicholas. S Mar 1720 T Mar 1723. Bu.
Bennett, Nicholas. S & T Oct 1730 *Forward* LC Potomack Jan 1731. M.
Bennitt, Richard. R for Barbados or Jamaica Aug 1700. M.
Bennett, Richard. T Apr 1731 *Bennett*. Ht.
Bennett, Richard. S & T Sep 1731 *Smith* but died on passage. L.
Bennett, Richard. S Summer 1732. Y.
Bennett, Richard. TB to Va from QS 1741. De.
Bennett, Richard. S Mar 1767 TB to Va. De.
Bennett, Richard. S s at Great Tew Summer 1773. O.
Bennett, Robert of Horton. R for Barbados Jly 1664. So.
Bennett, Robert. S & R 14 yrs Summer 1747. Mo.
Bennett, Samuel. S Jly 1718 to be T to Va. Co.
Bennet, Samuel, husbandman aged 57, black complexion. S Sep T Oct 1720 *Gilbert* LC Md May 1721. L.
Bennet, Samuel. Died on passage in *Alexander* 1723. X.
Bennett, Sarah. S Feb T Apr 1734 *Patapsco* to Md. M.
Bennett, Sarah. S Jan T Mar 1750 *Tryal*. L.
Bennet als Williams, Thomas. S for robbery Mar 1654 R 10 yrs in plantations Aug 1655 AT Lent 1758. Sy.
Bennett, Thomas. Rebel T 1685.
Bennett, Thomas. S Dec 1733 T Jan 1734 *Caesar* LC Va Jly 1734. M.
Bennett, Thomas. S Sep-Oct 1749. M.
Bennett, Thomas. S Lent 1756 R 14 yrs Summer 1757. Ch.
Bennett, Thomas. S Mar 1764. Ha.
Bennett als Baker, Thomas. S Mar 1772. De.
Bennett, Thomas. S s at St. Chad, Shrewsbury, Lent 1772. Sh.
Bennett, Thomas. S s horse & R 14 yrs Lent 1773. G.
Bennett, Walter. S Mar 1772. Do.
Bennett, William. Rebel T 1685.
Bennett, William. R Aug 1700. M.
Bennet, William. S Jan T Feb 1726 *Supply* LC Annapolis May 1726. L.
Bennet, William. S Feb T Mar 1730 *Patapsco* to Md but died on passage. M.
Bennet, William. S Mar 1741. De.
Bennet, William. R 14 yrs Lent 1757. Ch.
Bennett, William. S Mar 1772. Do.
Bennett, William of Oving. S Lent T Apr 1772 *Thornton*. Sx.
Bennett, William. S Mar 1774. Ha.
Bennison, Robert. R for Barbados or Jamaica Jan 1692. L.

Benny, Alexander. R for Barbados Jun 1670. M.
Benny als Bennett, John. SQS May T Oct 1768 *Justitia*. M.
Benny als Bennett, Mary of Littlebrough. R for America Jly 1700. Nf.
Benny, Susan. S Dec 1741 T 14 yrs Feb 1742 *Industry* to Md. M.
Benoit, Joseph. S Apr-May 1775. M.
Bensly, William. S Norwich s guinea Summer 1751. Nf.
Benson, Ann of Swillington, widow. R for Barbados Jly 1686. Y.
Benson, Benjamin. S Summer 1753 R 14 yrs Lent 1754. E.
Benson, Francis. S Sep T Nov 1762 *Prince William*. M.
Benson, George. S Lent R 14 yrs Summer 1766. St.
Benson, Henry of Leighton Buzzard. R for America Feb 1664. Bd.
Benson, Henry of New Sarum. R for Barbados Feb 1714. Wi.
Benson, Isaac. S Mar 1721. Wi.
Benson, James of St. Andrew Undershaft. S s sugar Jan T Jun 1738
    Forward. L.
Benson, James. S Mar 1759. Ha.
Benson, James. S May T Jly 1770 *Scarsdale*. M.
Benson, John of Rowley Regis, nailer. R for America Jly 1693. St.
Benson als Fudges, John, aged 37, black hair. T Oct 1720 *Gilbert* LC Md
    May 1721. Sy.
Benson, John. S for killing deer at Great Tew Summer 1751. O.
Benson, Peter. R s gelding Jly 1730. Du.
Benson, Thomas. S s sheep Lent R 14 yrs Summer 1744. Y.
Benson, Thomas. S & T Jun 1756 *Lyon*. M.
Benson, Zachary of Rowley Regis, nailer. R for America Jly 1693. St.
Bent, Daniel. S & T Sep 1766 *Justitia*. L.
Bentley, Katherine. R for Barbados Feb 1664. M.
Bentley, John of Walton on Thames. R for Barbados or Jamaica Feb
    1676 & Jly 1677. Sy.
Bentley, John. S & T 14 yrs Sep 1731 *Smith* LC Va 1732. L.
Bentley, John. AT Summer 1750. Y.
Bently, John. S s at Stotfold & R 14 yrs Summer 1769. Bd.
Bentley, Martha. S Oct T Nov 1728 *Forward* LC Rappahannock Jun
    1729. L.
Bentley, Mathew. S Jan T Feb 1742 *Industry*. L.
Bentley, Peter. T Apr 1753 *Thames*. Sx.
Bentley, Samuel. S Dec 1755 T Jan 1756 *Greyhound*. L.
Bentley, Thomas. S s wheat Lent T Oct 1765. Bd.
Bentley, William of Rochford. R for Barbados or Jamaica Jly 1710. E.
Bentley, William. T Apr 1732 *Patapsco*. Ht.
Bentley, William. S Feb T Apr 1735 *Patapsco* LC Annapolis Oct
    1735. M.
Bentley, Zachariah. S s from tenters at Alverthorp Summer 1765. Y.
Benton, Ann. S May T Sep 1766 *Justitia*. M.
Benton, George. R for Barbados Sep TB Oct 1669. L.
Benton, John. S Feb-Apr T Jun 1756 *Lyon*. M.
Benton, Philip. S Mar 1774. Ha.
Beoly, Richard (1755). *See* Bayley. Db.
Bergenhow, Peter. S Oct 1774. L.
Bergum, William (1727). *See* Vergoe. G.
Berk. *See* Burk.

Berkins, Elizabeth wife of William. R for Barbados Jun 1702. So.

Berkley. *See* Barclay.

Berklise, Rachael, spinster. S s household goods at St. Botolph Aldersgate Apr T Jun 1768 *Tryal*. L.

Berks, Sarah wife of Thomas. S Lent R 14 yrs Summer 1751. St.

Berks, William of Mansfield. SQS s fowl Jan 1775. Nt.

Berkshire, John. R & T Apr 1735 *Patapsco* LC. M.

Berlow, John. S Mar 1741. Ha.

Bern. *See* Burn.

Bernard, Anne. R for America Jly 1683. Li.

Barnard, Ann of Rotherhithe. SQS Mar T Apr 1753 *Thames*. Sy.

Barnard, Daniel. R 14 yrs Mar 1731. Co.

Barnard, Edward. T 14 yrs Sep 1765 *Justitia*. E.

Barnard, Ezechiel. R Summer 1774. E.

Bernard, Henry. S & T Oct 1729 *Forward* LC Va Jun 1730. M.

Burnard, John of Sance, miller. R for Barbados Feb 1668. De.

Bernard, John. R for Barbados or Jamaica May 1684. L.

Bernard, John. R 14 yrs Jly 1753. Ha.

Barnard als Bainard, John. S Mar 1764. Co.

Barnard, John. S s wheat at Bishops Cleave Lent 1768. G.

Barnard, Joseph. S Nov T Dec 1763 *Neptune*. L.

Burnard, Mary (1760). *See* Burnell. De.

Barnard, Thomas. S Sep 1761. M.

Bernard, William. Rebel T 1685.

Bernett. *See* Burnett.

Berridge, Benjamin. R for America Aug 1715. L.

Berridge, Edward. S s sheep at Great Gidding & R Lent 1775. Hu.

Berridge, Patrick. S s sheep at Thurning & R Lent 1775. Hu.

Berriford, Thomas of Blithfield. R for America Feb 1716. St.

Berrington, Samuel of Monmouth, gunsmith. R for America Mar 1688. Mo.

Berrisford, Mary. S Dec 1768 T Jan 1769 *Thornton*. M.

Berrisford, William of Alstonfield. R for America Jly 1693. St.

Berritt, Ann. S s silk ribbon Apr T Jun 1742 *Bladon* to Md. M.

Berrow, Joseph. S Summer 1756 R 14 yrs Lent 1757. Wo.

Berry, Alice. S May 1775. L.

Berry, Anne. S & T Oct 1729 *Forward* to Va but died on passage. M.

Berry, Ann. S Feb 1761. L.

Berry, Ann. S Feb T Apr 1768 *Thornton*. M.

Berry, Catherine. S & T May 1736 *Patapsco*. L.

Berry als Cole, Diana. S Apr T Aug 1719 *Savoy*. M.

Berry, Edward. SQS & T Sep 1765 *Justitia*. M.

Berry, Edward. S Apr T Jly 1770 *Scarsdale*. M.

Berry, Elizabeth wife of Ambrose. S s at St. Aldate, Oxford, Lent 1739. O.

Berry, Elizabeth. S Dec 1764 T Jan 1765 *Tryal*. M.

Berry, Elizabeth wife of Richard, als Elizabeth Wade of Manchester. SQS Apr 1768. La.

Berry, Elizabeth wife of William. S s Shipton upon Charwell Summer 1768; husband & daughter Elizabeth acquitted. O.

Berry, Grace. R for Barbados Sep 1669. M.

Berry, Harry. LC Annapolis Md Jly 1722 from *Gilbert*. X.

Berry, Hester. S Dec 1762 T Mar 1763 *Neptune*. M.

Bury, Isaac. R Oct T Dec 1724 *Rapppahannock* to Va. M.

Berry, James. S Dec 1754. L.

Berry, James. S Mar 1755. De.

Berry, James. SL & T Jan 1767 *Tryal*. Sy.

Berry, James. SQS Oct 1767. Ha.

Bury, James. T Apr 1771 *Thornton*. K.

Berry, James. SW & T Jly 1771 *Scarsdale*. M.

Berry, John of Rotherhithe. S Summer 1746. Sy.

Bury, John. S s mare Lent R 14 yrs Summer 1766. Sh.

Burry, John. S Mar 1774. Ha.

Berry, Jonathan. S Sep T Nov 1743 *George William*. M.

Berry, Joseph. R & T Oct 1722 *Forward* LC Annapolis Jun 1723. M.

Berry als Houseley, Marella. S Summer 1772. Db.

Berry, Margaret. R & T Apr 1734 *Patapsco* to Md. M.

Berry, Margaret. S Apr-May 1775. M.

Bury, Mary. S Lent T May 1755 *Rose*. Sy.

Berry, Mathias. S Feb T Apr 1739 *Forward* to Va. M.

Berry, Matthew. T Aug 1721 *Owners Goodwill*. E.

Berry, Mathew. LC Md Jly 1722 from *Gilbert*. Sy.

Berry, Michael. S Apr-Jun 1739. M.

Berry, Richard. SQS Jan 1731. So.

Berry, Richard. S Oct T Nov 1759 *Phoenix*. M.

Berry, Robert. R 14 yrs Mar 1744. De.

Berry als Houseley, Samuel. S s at Staveley Summer TB Oct 1764. Db.

Berry, Thomas. S Aug T Sep 1727 *Forward* LC Rappahannock May 1728. L.

Berry, Thomas of Warrington. SQS Jan 1743. La.

Bury, Thomas of Great Bolton, whitster. SQS Jly 1753. La.

Berry, Thomas. S Apr T Jun 1768 *Tryal*. M.

Berry, Timothy. T Oct 1738 *Genoa*. Sy.

Berry, William of Great Catworth. R for Barbados or Jamaica Mar 1697. Hu.

Berry, William of St. John Evangelist. S s teaspoons Dec 1739 T Jan 1740 *York*. M.

Bury, William. S Lent R 14 yrs Summer 1761 E.

Berry, William. S Apr T Jly 1770 *Scarsdale*. L.

Berryball, Pasch. S Mar 1737. Co.

Berryman, John. S Aug 1757. Co.

Berryman, Robert. S Apr T Aug 1718 *Eagle* to Md or Va. L.

Berryman, William. R 14 yrs Jly 1721. De.

Berryman, William. R 14 yrs Aug 1729. De.

Bertie, Elizabeth (1750). *See* Bush. L.

Bertie, George. S Apr T May 1751 *Tryal*. L.

Berville, Philip (1766). *See* Bagnon. M.

Berwick, William. R for life Lent 1774. Sy.

Besford, Sarah. S s at Newland Summer 1766. Wo.

Beshaw, Josiah. Died on passage in *Dorsetshire* 1736. X.

Bess, Edward of Bristol. R 14 yrs s sheep Sep 1768. G.

Bess als Best, James. S & T Dec 1767 *Neptune*. M.

Bessicke als Smith, James of St. Nicholas, Guildford. R for Barbados or Jamaica Jly 1702. Sy.

Bessom als Norrington, Thomas. S & R 14 yrs Lent 1769. G.

Best, Andrew. S Feb T Mar 1727 *Rappahannock*. L.

Best, Edward. S s at Hartlebury Lent 1739. Wo.

Best, Elizabeth. SQS & T Jly 1753 *Tryal*. M.

Best, George. R 14 yrs Aug 1772. So.

Best, James. Rebel T 1685.

Best, James (1767). *See* Bess. M.

Best, Jane. S Apr T May 1720 *Honor* to Yor'· River Va. L.

Best, John of Fulbrook. R for Barbados Oct 1663. O.

Best, John of Yarm. R for Barbados Jly 1671. Y.

Best, John. S Aug T Sep 1725 *Forward* LC Annapolis Dec 1725. L.

Best, John. T Apr 1753 *Thames*. Sy.

Best, John of St. Margaret, Westminster. SW Jan 1775. M.

Best, John. S s sheep & R 14 yrs Summer 1775. G.

Best, Paul. S Lent 1770. Wo.

Best, Richard. S s horse Lent R 14 yrs Summer 1748. Wa.

Best, Richard. S Dec 1772.

Best, Robert. Rebel T 1685.

Best, Thomas. Rebel T 1685.

Best, Thomas. S Lent R 14 yrs Summer 1720 T Oct 1723 *Forward* to Va from London. Y.

Best als Armstrong, Thomas. S s chickens Summer 1758. Du.

Best, Thomas. SWK Jan T Jun 1764 *Dolphin*. K.

Best, William. Rebel T 1685.

Best, William (1747). *See* West. O.

Best, William. T Sep 1758 *Tryal*. Sy.

Bestow, Jane. R for Barbados or Jamaica Aug 1700. M.

Bethell als Bethwin als Barwin, Arthur. S & T 14 yrs Dec 1740 *Vernon* to Md. M.

Bethell, James. S Mar 1748. So.

Bethell, James. S Mar 1751. De.

Bethell, Thomas. S for highway robbery at Hutton Moor R 14 yrs Lent TB Apr 1774. Y.

Bethel, William. SQS Canterbury Lent R Summer 1756. K.

Betson, Thomas. S s gelding Summer 1765 R 14 yrs Lent 1766. Ca.

Betteris, Dorothy. R for Jamaica Mar 1665. L.

Bettesworth, Thomas. S Mar TB to Va Apr 1742. Wi.

Bettice, James (1750). *See* Battye. La.

Betts, Abraham. S & T Oct 1732 *Caesar*. L.

Betts, Elizabeth. R for Barbados Dec 1668. Order made May 1669 for custody of her bastard child delivered in Newgate. M.

Bets, John. LC Rappahannock Va May 1728 from *Forward*. X.

Betts, John of Rotherhithe. SQS Oct 1752 T Jly 1753 *Tryal*. Sy.

Betts, Joseph. S Lent 1753 s at Bromsgrove. Wo.

Betts, Lowry. S Sep T Oct 1744 *Susannah*. L.

Betts, Margaret. S Dec 1739 T Jan 1740 *York* to Md. M.

Betts, Mary. R 14 yrs for Carolina May 1719. L.

Betts, Thomas. S & T Sep 1731 *Smith* LC Va 1732. M.

Betts, William. T 14 yrs Apr 1768 *Thornton*. Ht.

Betts, William. S for highway robbery & R Summer 1774. Wa.

Betty, Robert (1688). *See* Browne. M.

Betty, Robert. S Aug T Oct 1724 *Forward* LC Annapolis Jun 1725. L.

Beuce, Thomas. S Mar 1741. Wi.

Beuman. *See* Beaumont.

Bevan, George. S & TB Jly 1742. G.

Bevan, Isaac (1700). *See* Jones. He.

Bevan, John. R & T 14 yrs Sep 1766 *Justitia* M.

Bevan, Matthew. S Apr 1773. M.

Bevan, Philip. S Aug T Sep 1725 *Forward* LC Annapolis Dec 1725. M.

Bevan, Rice. S Feb T Mar 1729 *Patapsco* but died on passage. L.

Bevan, Thomas. S Jun-Dec 1738 T Jan 1739 *Dorsetshire* to Va. M.

Bevan, Thomas of Bristol. R 14 yrs Sep 1768 (SP). G.

Bevan, Thomas. R & T for life Jly 1770 *Scarsdale*. M.

Bevan, William. S s sheep Lent R 14 yrs Summer 1774. He.

Bever, John (1768). *See* Vevers. L.

Beverley, John. T Jan 1736 *Dorsetshire*. K.

Beverley, John. S & T Jly 1753 *Tryal*. M.

Beverley, Joseph. S Lent R 14 yrs Summer 1750. Wo.

Beverley, William. S Apr T May 1750 *Lichfield*. L.

Bevers als Nevers, Thomas. S s silver watches at Doncaster Lent 1772. Y.

Beverton, Simon. S Lent T May 1750 *Lichfield*. K.

Beverton, Simon. SEK & T Nov 1762 *Prince William* & Sep 1764 *Justitia*. K.

Bevill, Mary of St. Saviour, Southwark. R for Barbados or Jamaica Mar 1698. Sy.

Bevin, Elizabeth. S Lent 1749. Ca.

Bevin, John. S Lent 1749; Jane Bevin acquitted. Ca.

Bevington, Francis. SQS Oct T Dec 1771 *Scarsdale*. M.

Bevis, George. S Feb T 14 yrs Mar 1731 *Patapsco* LC Annapolis Jun 1731. L.

Bevis, John. SQS Jun TB Aug 1769. So.

Bevas, Richard. T Sep 1764 *Justitia*. M.

Bevis, Simon. T 14 yrs Dec 1753 *Whiteing*. K.

Bew als Edwards, John. S Sep-Oct 1748 T Jan 1749 *Laura*. M.

Bue, Thomas of Oxford. R for America Feb 1690. O.

Bew, William of Great Amwell. R for Barbados or Jamaica Feb 1690. Ht.

Bewley. *See* Beaulieu.

Bexter. *See* Baxter.

Bezant, Randolph. S Jly 1764. Ha.

Bibb, Michael. SQS Apr T May 1767 *Thornton*. M.

Bibben, Ann, spinster of St. Saviour, Southwark. SQS Jan T Mar 1763 *Neptune*. Sy.

Bibby, Elizabeth. R Aug T Oct 1723 *Forward* to Va. M.

Bibey, Mary (1773). *See* Worth. M.

Bibby, Matthew of Wigan. S for breaking into yarn croft Summer 1741. La.

Bibby, Peter of Chorley. SQS Jly 1753. La.

Bibby, Sarah. S Dec 1745. L.

Bibby, Thomas. S Feb T Mar 1730 *Patapsco*. M.
Bibby, William, tripeman of Bishops Hatfield. SQS Sep T Oct 1768
  Justitia. Ht.
Bickers, Anne of Bury St. Edmunds. R for Barbados Feb 1664. Su.
Bickerster, Edward. S Summer R for Barbados Aug 1663. Ht.
Bickerstaff, Henry. S Summer 1745 R 14 yrs Summer 1746. Cu.
Biccarstaffe, John of Macclesfield. R for Barbados Jly 1683. Ch.
Biggerton, Ann (1664). *See* Purse. L.
Bickerton, George. S s sheep & R 14 yrs Summer 1774. He.
Bickerton, Joan. R for Barbados Feb 1675. L.
Bickerton, John. R & T 14 yrs Jan 1722 *Gilbert* LC Annapolis Jly
  1722. M.
Bickerton, John. S Oct 1751-Jan 1752. M.
Bickley, James. Rebel T 1685.
Bickley, Sarah (1740). *See* Ranson. M.
Bickley, William. R 14 yrs Mar 1758. De.
Bicklin, Thomas. S Mar 1768. So.
Bicknell, William. S Mar 1740. So.
Biddesford, Thomas. S s at Wolverhampton Lent 1773. St.
Biddis, Jane. S Sep T Dec 1769 *Justitia*. M.
Biddle, Benjamin als Benijah. S s at Stonehouse Lent TB May 1736. G.
Biddle, John of Norton Regis. R for America Feb 1690. Wo.
Biddle, John. S s sheep & R Summer 1772. Wa.
Biddleston, Jonathan. S & T Dec 1770 *Justitia*. M.
Biddulph, Anthony of Ediall. R for America Jly 1696. St.
Bide als Bine, Mary. S Apr T Jun 1742 *Bladon* to Md. M.
Byde, Mary. S Feb 1754. L.
Bidgood, Ann. S Mar 1738. So.
Bidgood, Philip. R 14 yrs Mar 1773. De.
Bidgood, Thomas. TB to Va from QS 1751. De.
Bidwell, John. R Aug 1775. De.
Bigge, Thomas (1681). *See* Granwell. M.
Bigg, Thomas. T May 1723 *Victory*. K.
Biggen, Moses. SQS Jan 1665 as idle & disorderly. M.
Biggerton. *See* Bickerton.
Bigglestone, Richard. S Sep-Oct T Dec 1771 *Justitia*. M.
Biggs als Deverall als Atkinson, Jane. R for Barbados or Jamaica Aug
  1700. M.
Biggs, Jane (1764). *See* Newman. E.
Biggs, John. S s sheep Lent R 14 yrs Summer 1756. Bu.
Biggs, Joseph (1723). *See* Allen. M.
Biggs als Grove, Margaret. R for Barbados Jly 1675. L.
Biggs, Mary. S Feb T Apr 1742 *Bond*. L.
Biggs, Reuben. S Sep T for life Dec 1769 *Justitia*. M.
Biggs als Bricks, Richard. S s gelding Mar 1653 R for plantations Aug
  1655. Sy.
Biggs, Richard. R 14 yrs & TB to Va Mar 1761. Wi.
Biggs, Robert Jr. S Lent T *Dolphin* Jun 1764. Bu.
Biggs, Sarah. T Jly 1724 *Robert* LC Md Jun 1725. E.
Biggs, Stephen. S for highway robbery at Hardwick & R Summer
  1777. Bu.

Biggs, Thomas. S & T Aug 1752 *Tryal*. L.
Biggs, Thomas. S Apr-May 1754. M.
Biggs, Thomas. SQS Dec 1757 T Mar 1758 *Dragon*. M.
Biggs, Thomas, als Chatting, John. S Lent 1774. Wa.
Biggs, William. Rebel T 1685.
Bignall, George. S Jly T Oct 1768 *Justitia*. M.
Bignell, Gibson. S Apr T Jun 1768 *Tryal*. M.
Bignall, James. S Sep T Oct 1739 *Duke of Cumberland*. L.
Bignall, James. S Sep-Oct T Dec 1753 *Whiteing*. M.
Bignell als Brown, John. T Jan 1766 *Tryal*. M.
Bignell, Joseph. S s mare at Emberton & R Lent 1773. Bu.
Bignoll, Marmaduke of St. James, Westminster. S s money & T Feb
    1740 *York* M.
Bignall als Ward, Mary of Bermondsey. R for Barbados or Jamaica Jun
    1699. Sy.
Bignall, Rebecca. S May T Jun 1726 *Loyal Margaret* LC Annapolis Oct
    1726. M.
Bignell, Rose (1740). *See* Mahone. M.
Bignall, Sara. S Jan T Feb 1719 *Worcester* LC Annapolis Jun 1719. L.
Bigsby, Joseph. S Summer 1745. Su.
Bilby, Richard. R Apr 1773. M.
Bilby, William. S Oct 1747. L.
Bilby, William. S Summer 1748 T Jan 1749 *Laura*. E.
Bilding, John. S Lent 1734. *Hu.
Billcox, Thomas. S May T Jun 1727 *Susanna*. L.
Billemore, Hugh of Ufton. R for America Jly 1681. Be.
Billens, William. R for life Lent 1775. Sy.
Billet, William. T Sep 1764 *Justitia*. M.
Billials, John. S Summer 1761. Nl & Nt.
Billian, James. S Sep-Dec 1755 T for life Jan 1756 *Greyhound*. M.
Billing, John (1682). *See* Stephens. Sy.
Billing, John. S Nov T Dec 1770 *Justitia*. L.
Billinge, William. SQS Mar 1719, escaped & recaptured, TB to Md Aug
    1720. Db.
Billing, William. TB to Md Aug 1728. Db.
Billingham, Edward. SQS 1766. Du.
Billingham, Mary. S Jan T 14 yrs Apr 1741 *Speedwell*. L.
Billingham, Thomas. S s iron at Kingswinford Summer 1772. St.
Billingham, William of Rothwell. R for America Feb 1713. No.
Billings, Christopher. S Feb T Mar 1731 *Patapsco* LC Annapolis Jun
    1731. L.
Billings, John. T Sep 1764 *Justitia*. Sy.
Billings, John. S Apr 1774. M.
Billings, William. SQS Mar 1720 to be shipped to Md from
    ' Liverpool. Db.
Billings, William. TB Aug 1733. Nt.
Billingsgate, William. SL Oct 1754. Sy.
Billingsley, Bold. R for Barbados or Jamaica Dec 1698. M.
Billingsley, Charles. S Sep T Oct 1744 *Susannah*. L.
Billingsley, Francis of Rathbury. S s snuff box Lent T Oct 1726
    Forward. Bu.

Billingsly als Low, Jane. S Jun-Dec 1738 T Jan 1739 *Dorsetshire* to Va. M.

Billington, John. S Summer 1757 R 14 yrs Lent T Apr 1758. Bd.

Bills, William. S Lent R 14 yrs Summer 1754. K.

Bills, William. S & T Jan 1756 *Greyhound*. L.

Bilson, Benjamin. T Apr 1766 *Ann*. E.

Bilson, George. SQS Mar TB Apr 1737. Le.

Bilson, John. S Lent 1760. Le.

Bilson, William. S Feb 1752. L.

Bilth, James. SQS Feb 1773. M.

Bilton, Mathew. R for life for high treason Summer 1758. Y.

Bilton, Robert. S & R for life s horse Aug 1767. Nl.

Bindon, Thomas. S Mar 1738. So.

Bine, Mary (1742). *See* Bide. M.

Bine, Stephen. S & T Apr 1769 *Tryal*. M.

Binfield, Elinor of Basingstoke, singlewoman. R for Barbados Feb 1668. Ha.

Bing. *See* Byng.

Binham, Benjamin. S Feb T Mar 1730 *Patapsco* LC Annapolis Sep 1730. M.

Bingham, Elizabeth. S Lent T Apr 1772 *Thornton*. K.

Bingham, John of Folshill, Coventry. R for America Jly 1674. Wa.

Bingham, Joseph. S & T Dec 1734 *Caesar* but died on passage. L.

Bingham, Thomas. PT Jun R Oct 1673. M.

Bingley, John. S Jly T Sep 1765 *Justitia*. M.

Binke, William. PT Jly 1680. M.

Binks, Jacob of Ash. S Lent T May 1719 *Margaret* LC Md May 1720; sold to William Pinkstone. Sy.

Binmore, William. S Aug 1756 TB to Va. De.

Binn, Mary. S Aug 1772. De.

Binnell, Alice. S Oct 1733 T Jan 1734 *Caesar* LC Va Jly 1734. M.

Binney, Alice. R for Barbados Jun 1663. M.

Binney, James. R 14 yrs Jly 1738. De.

Binney, William. S Mar 1756. Co.

Binnick, Grace. TB to Va from QS 1765. De.

Binnifield, John of St. George, Southwark. SQS for making rope ladder for escape from prison Mar T Apr 1768 *Thornton*. Sy.

Binns, Mary. S Sep-Oct 1775. M.

Binnyon, Charles. S s at Clifton Summer 1765. G.

Binsted, John. T Apr 1753 *Thames*. Sx.

Binsted, Mary. S & T Jan 1756 *Greyhound*. L.

Binstead, Thomas. S & T Oct 1730 *Forward* LC Potomack Jan 1731. M.

Birch als Appleby als Minsall, Anne. LC Va May 1728 from *Forward*. X.

Birch, Ann. S & T Apr 1769 *Tryal*. L.

Birch, Edward. SQS Jun T Sep 1766 *Justitia*. M.

Burch, Elizabeth. R for Barbados Feb 1673. L.

Birch, Esther. S & T Sep 1757 *Thetis*. M.

Birtch, George. S s pig at Stone Lent 1772. Wo.

Birch, Hannah. S Lent R 14 yrs Summer 1757. Wa.

Burch, James. S & T Oct 1732 *Caesar* to Va. M.

Birch, John. S Sep T Oct 1719 *Susannah & Sarah* LC Md Apr 1720. L.

Birch, John. S Oct 1749. L.

Burch, John. S Jan T Mar 1760 *Friendship*. M.

Birch, John of Blakeley. SQS Oct 1764. La.

Birch, John. S & T Sep 1765 *Justitia*. L.

Birch, John. R Jly 1773. M.

Birch, Joseph. S Sep T Oct 1720 *Gilbert*. L.

Birch, Joseph. S Apr T May 1743 *Indian Queen* to Potomack. M.

Birch, Joseph. S Summer 1745. K.

Birch, Lucy. S Lent 1765. St.

Birch, Mary. S Apr-Jun 1739. M.

Birch, Mary. S Oct T Dec 1763 *Neptune*. M.

Birch, Moses. S Jly 1760. M.

Birch, Richard. S Feb T Mar 1730 *Patapsco* LC Annapolis Sep 1730. L.

Birch, Richard. S Summer 1740. He.

Birch, Richard. R for life for a shooting Lent 1773. Wa.

Birch, Samuel. S s horse Summer 1725 R 14 yrs Lent 1726. St.

Birch, Thomas of Wokingham. R for America Mar 1680. Be.

Byrch als Evans, Thomas of Stretford. S Summer 1718. He.

Burch, Thomas. SQS Apr T May 1751 *Tryal*. M.

Birch, Thomas of Bolton. SQS Jan 1768. La.

Birch, William. R for Barbados Jly 1674. M.

Burch, William. R 14 yrs Aug 1720. De.

Birch, William. S & T Jan 1739 *Dorsetshire*. L.

Birch als Birchman als Burchmore, William. S Dec 1739 T Jan 1740 *York*. M.

Birch, William of Spotland, fuller. SQS s cloth Aug 1748. La.

Burche, William. S Lent R 14 yrs Summer 1766. St.

Burch, William. T Sep 1766 *Justitia*. Sy.

Birch, William. R Aug 1774. Y.

Birchall, Michael of Winwick. S s fustian Lent 1737. La.

Birchinald, Elizabeth. TB Sep 1760. Db.

Bird, Anthony. S s at St. Peter, Hereford, Lent 1772. He.

Bird, Bertram als Bartholomew. S Apr-Jun 1739. M.

Bird, Charles. S Apr-May T May 1741 *Catherine & Elizabeth* to Md. M.

Bird, Eleanor. S Apr 1760. M.

Bird, Elizabeth. R for Barbados Dec 1683. M.

Bird, Elizabeth. R for Barbados or Jamaica Oct 1694. M.

Bird, Elizabeth. S Summer 1765 R 14 yrs Lent 1766. Wo.

Bird, Elizabeth. S May 1770. M.

Bird, Francis. S Aug T Oct 1726 *Forward*. L.

Bird, George. R & T May 1736 *Patapsco* to Md. M.

Bird, George. S 14 yrs Apr-Jun 1739. M.

Bird, George. S Lent 1758. Su.

Bird, James. S Summer 1742. Su.

Burde, James. S Jly 1775. M.

Bird, John. R for Barbados May 1664. M.

Bird als Budd, John. PT Oct 1700 R Aug 1701. M.

Bird, John. T Jun 1738 *Forward*. Sx.

Bird, John. S Summer 1738 R 14 yrs Lent 1739. La.

Bird, John. S & TB Apr 1742. G.
Bird als Brand, John. S s mare Lent R 14 yrs Summer 1755. Su.
Bird, John. S Dec 1763 T Mar 1764 *Tryal*. M.
Burd, John, als Eavans, Thomas. AT City Lent 1764. Y.
Bird, John. SQS Jly T Oct 1768 *Justitia*. M.
Bird, John. S Jun T Aug 1769 *Douglas*. M.
Bird, John. S May T Jly 1770 *Scarsdale*. M.
Birde, John. S Jly 1773. L.
Bird, John, als Holton, Griffith. SWK Jan 1774. K.
Bird, John. S s blankets at Ludlow Summer 1774. Sh.
Bird, John. S Feb 1775. L.
Bird, Jonathan (1760). *See* Mason. Ca.
Bird, Joseph. S Feb T Mar 1729 *Patapsco* LC Annapolis Dec 1729. L.
Bird, Lydia. S & T Feb 1744 *Neptune* to Md. M.
Bird, Matthew. S Lent 1754. Sy.
Bird, Michael. R for Barbados Jly 1674. L.
Burd als Bird, Nicholas of Shaston. R for Barbados Mar 1686. Do.
Bird, Peter. Rebel T 1685.
Bird, Richard. S s at St. Mary le Crypt, Gloucester, Summer 1751, G.
Bird, Robert. Died on passage in *Margaret* 1720. X.
Bird, Robert. S Summer 1734. Su.
Bird als Boyle, Samuel. S Nov T Dec 1770 *Justitia*. L.
Bird als Holt, Simon, mariner. S s at Sprowston Lent 1771. Nf.
Bird, Stephen of St. Saviour, Southwark. R for Barbados or Jamaica
    Mar 1698. Sy.
Bird, Susanna. S Jly T Sep 1755 *Tryal*. L.
Bird als Budd, Thomas. R Oct 1700. M.
Bird, Thomas. S Aug T Oct 1726 *Forward*. L.
Bird, Thomas. S Aug T Oct 1742 *Bond*. L.
Bird, Thomas. S s harness at Yoxall Lent 1746. St.
Bird, Thomas. R 14 yrs Lent 1761. Li.
Bird, Thomas. S Oct 1765 T Jan 1766 *Tryal*. M.
Bird, Thomas. S Sep T Dec 1767 *Neptune*. M.
Bird, Thomas. S Apr T Jly 1770 *Scarsdale*. L.
Bird, Thomas. S for setting fire to corn stack & R Summer 1772. Wa.
Bird, Thomas. S Jan-Feb 1773. M.
Bird, Thomas. R 14 yrs Aug 1773. So.
Bird, William of White Ladies Aston. R for America Jly 1691. Wo.
Bird, William. S Jan T for life Apr 1743 *Justitia*. M.
Bird, William. S s mare Lent R 14 yrs Summer 1769. Li.
Bird, William. S s coat at Bisley Summer 1772. G.
Bird, William Reynolds. S Dec 1765 T Jan 1766 *Tryal*. L.
Birdwood, Francis of Marshfield. R for America Mar 1710. G.
Birdworth, Mary. S Summer T Sep 1751 *Greyhound*. Sy.
Birk. *See* Burk.
Birkenshaw, Joyce wife of Nicholas. SQS Rotherham Aug 1724 T *Supply*
    LC Md May 1726. Y.
Birkett. *See* Burkett.
Birstall, Phillip. S Mar TB to Va Apr 1765. Le.
Birt. *See* Burt.
Birthwhistle, James. AT Lent 1766. Y.

Birtles als Bryant, William. S Mar 1721. So.
Bisbee, James. S Apr T May 1751 *Tryal.* L.
Bisby, William. S Summer 1742. Y.
Biscoe, Florenz. R for Barbados Jun 1665. M.
Bishop, Charles of Griston. S Lent R 14 yrs Summer 1745. K.
Bishopp, Dorothy. R for Barbados Sep 1682. L.
Bishop, Edward. S Jly 1721 T Mar 1723. Bu.
Bishop, Eliza. S Aug T Oct 1726 *Forward.* L.
Bishop, Elizabeth. R Mar AT Apr 1677. M.
Bishopp, Emanuel of Otford. R for Barbados or Jamaica Jly 1696. K.
Bishop, Gamaliel. S & T Oct 1730 *Forward* LC Potomack Jan 1731. M.
Bishop, George. S May T 14 yrs Jly 1722 *Alexander.* L.
Bishop, George. S Lent 1775. Sy.
Bishop, Giles. S Jan T Mar 1764 *Tryal.* L.
Bishop, Henry. S Mar 1775. Ha.
Bishopp, James of Trent. R for Barbados Jan 1675. So.
Bishop, John. Rebel T 1685.
Bishopp, John of Leominster. R for America Jly 1696. He.
Bishop, John. S Jan-Feb T Apr 1722 *Thornton.* M.
Bishop, John. S Jan T Jun 1738 *Forward* to Md or Va. M.
Bishop, John. R 14 yrs Apr 1741. So.
Bishop, John. S s food at Bayton Summer 1742. Wo.
Bishop, John. S 14 yrs for receiving Jly 1765. Do.
Bishop, Jonathan. S s mare & R Summer 1754. Nf.
Bishopp, Joseph. R for America Jly 1693. Db.
Bishop, Joseph. S s cloth at Painswick Lent 1769. G.
Bishop, Lucas. T Dec 1767 *Neptune.* L.
Bishop als Castle, Martha. T Dec 1731 *Forward.* Sy.
Bishop als Cane, Mary. S Jan T Feb 1719 *Worcester* LC Annapolis Jun
   1719. L.
Bishop, Mary. R 14 yrs Jly 1744 TB to Va 1745. De.
Bishop, Mary. SQS Oct 1774 TB Apr 1775. So.
Bishop, Mary. SQS Dec 1774. M.
Bishop, Roger of Great Maplestead, husbandman. SQS Jly 1773. E.
Bishop, Samuel. S s at Kinlet Summer 1726. Sh.
Bishop, Solomon. R 14 yrs Mar 1745. Ha.
Bishop, Thomas. R Aug T Oct 1724 *Forward* LC Annapolis Jun 1725. M.
Bishop, Thomas. S s at High Ercall & Wellington Summer 1749. Sh.
Bishopp, William of St. George, Southwark. R for Barbados or Jamaica
   Mar 1682 & Feb 1683. Sy.
Bishop, William. R Dec 1698 AT Jan 1689. M.
Bishop, William. T Apr 1735 *Patapsco.* K.
Bishop, William. T Apr 1742 *Bond.* E.
Bishop, William. S Summer 1745 R 14 yrs Lent TB Apr 1746. G.
Bishop, William. S Feb-Apr T May 1751 *Tryal.* M.
Bisrow, Charles of Slinfold. R for Barbados or Jamaica Jly 1688. Sx.
Bisse, John. Rebel T 1685.
Bisse, Mary (1742). *See* Robinson. M.
Bissell, Mary. S s cloth at Ribbesford Lent 1738. Wo.
Bisset, Alexander. S Nov T Dec 1753 *Whiteing.* L.
Bissett, James. S Oct 1751-Jan 1752. M.

Bissett, Mary. R May T Jly 1723 *Alexander* LC Annapolis Sep 1723. M.
Bisset, Robert. S May T Jly 1770 *Scarsdale*. M.
Bisshe, William. PT Apr 1691. M.
Bitman, Samuel. S & R Summer 1735. Su.
Black Andrew (1729). *See* Hetherington, Andrew. Y.
Black Bess (1719). *See* Burton, Elizabeth. L.
Black Bess (1727). *See* Hughes, Elizabeth. O.
Black Dick (1701). *See* Noyes, Richard. Wi.
Black George (1772). *See* Burrell, George. Wi.
Black Jack (1734). *See* Fletcher, Nathaniel. Ca.
Black Jack (1741). *See* Wallis, John. M.
Black Jack (1753). *See* Jarvis, John. L.
Black Jack (1773). *See* Blundell, John. O.
Black Jenny (1723). *See* Thornton, Jane. L.
Black Moll (1753). *See* Baxter, Mary. De.
Black, Ann (1762). *See* Baker. M.
Black, Barbara. S & T Apr 1733 *Patapsco* LC Annapolis Nov 1733. M.
Black als Blackham, Daniel. S for murder of bastard child Summer
    1741 R 14 yrs Lent 1742. Wa.
Black, Eleanor wife of William. S Sep-Oct 1775. M.
Black, Henry. S Apr T May 1767 *Thornton*. M.
Black, Jane. T Oct 1722 *Forward* LC Md Jun 1723. Sy.
Black, Joseph. S Jan-Apr 1748. M.
Black, Mary wife of John. S s brass knobs at Wolverhampton Lent
    1757. St.
Black, Robert. S Jun 1733 T Jan 1734 *Caesar* LC Va Jly 1734. M.
Black, Robert (1763). *See* Bleak. La.
Blackall, John. S s sheet at Henley on Thames Lent 1770. O.
Blackburn, Benjamin. S 14 yrs Sep-Oct 1772. M.
Blackburne, Catherine. S Sep-Oct T Dec 1753 *Whiteing*. M.
Blackbourn, Catherine wife of John. R Oct 1775. M.
Blackbourn, Elizabeth. S May 1745. M.
Blackborn, Herbert. S & T Dec 1740 *Vernon*. L.
Blackbourne, John. T Jun 1740 *Essex*. Sy.
Blackbourne, John of Camberwell. SQS Jan 1751. Sy.
Blackbourne, John. T 14 yrs Sep 1766 *Justitia*. E.
Blackbourne, Lydia, spinster of St. George, Southwark. SQS Apr T May
    1752 *Lichfield*. Sy.
Blackbourne als Young, Margaret. T Apr 1731 *Bennett*. Sy.
Blackburn, Matthew. TB to Md Aug 1727. Db.
Blackbourne, Richard. S Lent 1745 R 14 yrs Lent 1747; found at large &
    S to hang Lent but R 14 yrs Summer 1750. He.
Blackbourn, Richard. S s clock Lent 1754. He.
Blackburne, Thomas of Altrincham. S Lent 1764. Ch.
Blackburne, William. R for Barbados May 1665. X.
Blackburne, William. S Lent 1723. Y.
Blackburn, William. S s gelding Summer 1763 R 14 yrs Lent 1764. Nf.
Blackburn, William of Mortlake. SQS & T Jan 1766 *Tryal*. Sy.
Blackden, Joseph. TB Apr 1763. Db.
Blackdon, William. S Aug 1750 TB to Va. De.

Blackerby, Ann. S Jly T Dec 1735 *John* to Md; when sentenced she cursed the court: "My curse and God's curse go with ye, and the prayers of my children fall upon ye." M.

Blackett, Joshua. S Dec 1739 T Jan 1740 *York* to Md. M.

Blackett, Robert. S Summer 1741 R 14 yrs Lent 1743. Du.

Blackett, Thomas of Royston. R for Barbados Apr 1668. Ht.

Blackford, Henry. S for ripping lead from house at St. Philip & Jacob Lent TB Mar 1748. G.

Blackgrove, John. S Apr-Jun T Jly 1772 *Tayloe*. M.

Blackguard Jack (1698). *See* Thomas, John. M.

Blackham, Benjamin. S s at Wolverhampton Lent R 14 yrs Summer 1737. St.

Blackhead, William (1734). *See* Newell. M.

Blackhood, John. S Jan-Jun 1747. M.

Blackler, John. S Jly 1730. De.

Blackler, Mary wife of Francis. S Mar 1729 TB to Va. De.

Blacklock, Martha (1722). *See* Anderson. M.

Blackmall, Mary (1748). *See* Aspinal. La.

Blackman, John. S Jly 1718 to be T to Boston, NE. Wi.

Blackman, Robert. R Aug T Sep 1725 *Forward* to Md. M.

Blackman, Thomas of Westerham. R for Barbados or Jamaica Mar 1680. K.

Blackmore, Daniel. SQS & TB Mar 1736. G.

Blackmore, Edmond. R Jly 1775. M.

Blackmore, Grace. S s at High Ercall Lent 1727. Sh.

Blackmore, James. R 14 yrs Jly 1737. Ha.

Blackmore, James. S & T Mar 1760 *Friendship*. L.

Blackmoor, Jonas. S Mar 1758. So.

Blackmore, Mary. S Mar 1725. De.

Blackmore, Richard. TB to Va from QS 1749. De.

Blackmore, Robert. S Mar 1773. Ha.

Blackmore, Samuel. Rebel T 1685.

Blackmore, Samuel. R 14 yrs Lent 1721. St.

Blackmore, Thomas. TB to Va from QS 1741. De.

Blackmore als Blakeman, William. S s at Walsall Lent 1773. St.

Blacknell, Henry. T Oct 1720 *Gilbert* but died on passage. Ht.

Blackow als Blackurst, Henry of Down Holland. SQS Oct 1770; S & R 14 yrs Lent 1771 for being at large after sentence of transportation. La.

Blacksby, Edward. S & T Oct 1720 *Gilbert* to Md. M.

Blackshaw, Thomas of Manchester. SQS Apr 1768. La.

Blackston, Elias of Anstey. R for America Jly 1678. Le.

Blackstone, John. S Apr T May 1720 *Honor* to York River. L.

Blackston, John. S Dec 1749-Jan 1750 T Mar 1750 *Tryal*. M.

Blackstone, Richard. R 14 yrs Apr 1770. De.

Blackstone, Zebulon Thrift. S & T Sep 1755 *Tryal*. L.

Blackurst, Henry (1771). *See* Blackow. La.

Blackwell, Barnaby. S Lent TB Mar 1737. G.

Blackwell, Charles. S Jly T Oct 1741 *Sea Horse*. L.

Blackwell, Deborah. S Sep-Oct T Dec 1771 *Justitia*. M.

Blackwell, Elizabeth. S s at Tewkesbury Summer 1723. G.

Blackwell, Elizabeth (1727). *See* Cope. Sh.
Blackwell als Connor, Elizabeth. S May-Jun T Jly 1753 *Tryal*. M.
Blackwell, Joan. R for Barbados Dec 1679. L.
Blackwell, John. S Jan-May T Jun 1738 *Forward* to Md or Va. M.
Blackwell, Josiah. S s at St. Michael, Oxford, Summer 1760. O.
Blackwell als Ridgway, Sara. TB 14 yrs Oct 1719 T *Susannah & Sarah*
LC Annapolis Apr 1720. L.
Blackwell, William. S Lent s horse R 14 yrs Summer 1756. Sy.
Blackwood, Hamilton. S Summer 1751 R 14 yrs Lent T May 1752
Lichfield. K.
Blades, Henry of St. Saviour, Southwark. S Summer 1748 T Jan 1749
Laura. Sy.
Bladon, Charles. S for perjury at St. Mary, Stafford, Lent 1774. St.
Bladen, Thomas. S Summer 1729 R Lent 1730 (SP). Sh.
Blaydon, Thomas. S 14 yrs for receiving goods stolen by Thomas Orage
(qv) Summer 1773. Su.
Bladwell, Symon of Barton. R for America Mar 1680. Su.
Blaesdale, Thomas. S for sodomy Summer 1744 R 14 yrs Lent 1745. Nt.
Blagdon, George. S Jly TB to Va Aug 1751. Wi.
Blair, Andrew. S Sep-Oct 1775. M.
Blaire, David. R Dec 1716 T Jan 1717 *Queen Elizabeth*. M.
Blair, Margaret. S Feb T Mar 1729 *Patapsco* LC Annapolis Dec 1729. L.
Blair, Mary. S May T Jun 1764 *Dolphin*. M.
Blair, Mary. S Lent 1775. Wa.
Blair, Richard (1738). *See* Graham, John. Cu.
Blair, Robert of St. Paul, Covent Garden. SW Jun 1774. M.
Blake, Alexander. S Aug 1726. Wi.
Blake als Groves, Ann. SQS Feb T May 1767 *Thornton*. M.
Blake, Arthur. S Jun 1733. M.
Blake, Charles. S Lent T May 1755 *Rose*. Sy.
Blake, Daniel. S Jly 1748. L.
Blake, Edith. R 14 yrs Aug 1749. So.
Blake, Edward (1689). *See* Thompson. M.
Blake, Edward. S & T Sep 1764 *Justitia*. M.
Blake, Frederick. S Jly T Aug 1721 *Prince Royal* LC Va Nov 1721. L.
Blake, Henry. S Aug 1732 TB to Va. De.
Blake, Jane. S Aug T Sep 1725 *Forward* LC Annapolis Dec 1725. L.
Blake als Buckley, Jane. S Dec 1763 T Mar 1764 *Tryal*. M.
Blake, Jane. S Oct 1772. L.
Blake, Joane. R 14 yrs Aug 1721. So.
Blake, John. S & T Feb 1740 *York* to Md. M.
Blake, John. Noted Summer 1748 "to go with next transports at his own
request." Nf.
Blake, John. S s at Thwaite & R Lent 1773. Su.
Blake, John. S Apr 1774. L.
Blake, John. S Dec 1775. M.
Blake, Mary wife of John of Hamptworth Downton. R for Barbados Jly
1717. Wi.
Blake, Mary. S Oct T Nov 1762 *Prince William*. M.
Blake, Penelope. S Aug T Sep 1725 *Forward*. L.
Blake, Philip. S Feb-Apr T May 1751 *Tryal*. M.

Blake, Philip. S Feb 1768. M.
Blake, Richard. S Apr T Aug 1718 *Eagle* LC Charles Town Mar 1719. L.
Blake, Sarah. S Mar TB to Va Sep 1744. Wi.
Blake, Thomas. S s silver spurs at St. Giles, Reading, Lent 1749 Be.
Blake, Thomas. S Mar TB to Va Apr 1751. Wi.
Blake, Tuthill of Mundham. S s sheep Summer 1738. Nf.
Blake, William. R for Barbados Feb 1680. M.
Blake, William. LC Annapolis Md May 1726 from *Loyal Margaret*. X.
Blake als Clarke, William. S s mare Lent R 14 yrs Summer 1765. Su.
Blakely, George. R 14 yrs Aug 1766. So.
Blakeley, Isabel. S Summer 1741. Cu.
Blakeley, Jane. R for America Jun 1684. Li.
Blakeman, Thomas of Hurst. R for Barbados or Jamaica Feb 1683. Sx.
Blakeman, William (1773). *See* Blackmore. St.
Blakemore, Samuel. S s at Wolverhampton Summer 1768. St.
Blakeney, William (1771). *See* Cain, John. M.
Blaker als Parker, William. S Summer 1774. Sx.
Blakes als Colhoun, John. S May T Jun 1727 *Susanna* to Va. M.
Blakeway, John. S s at Halesowen Lent 1767. Sh.
Blakey, Ralph of York Castle. SQS Thirsk s sheep Apr 1731. Y.
Blakey, William. LC Annapolis Md May 1726 from *Supply*. X.
Blakey, William of York Castle. SQS Thirsk s sheep Apr 1731. Y.
Blamey, Daniel. S Aug 1759. De.
Blammire, Stephen. S Feb 1764, sent to Essex to be tried on capital
    offence but acquitted, T Jun 1764 *Dolphin*. M.
Blanch als Branch, John. T Jly 1724 *Robert*. K.
Blanch, John. S s handkerchief at St. Brides's Dec 1768 T Jan 1769
    Thornton. L.
Blanchard, James. S Mar 1772. Ha.
Blanchett, James. S & T Oct 1730 *Forward* LC. M.
Blanchfield, John. SQS Sep T Dec 1769 *Justitia*. M.
Blanchflour, Elizabeth. S & T Oct 1719 *Susannah & Sarah* but died
    on passage. M.
Blanchford, Amos (1774). *See* Allen. De.
Blanchford, Elizabeth. TB Oct 1719. L.
Blanchford, John. TB to Va from QS 1769. De.
Blanchford, John Jr. TB to Va from QS 1769. De.
Blanchford, Mary (1774). *See* Allen. De.
Bland, Ambrose. SQS May T Sep 1755 *Tryal*. M.
Bland, Anne. R for Barbados Sep 1682. L.
Bland, Arthur. S Lent 1771. No.
Bland, Francis. S for housebreaking Lent R 14 yrs Dec 1731 T Apr 1733
    Patapsco LC Md Nov 1733. Bu.
Bland, Hannah (1752). *See* Bannell. M.
Bland, John of Maulden. R for Barbados Mar 1679. Bd.
Bland, John. S Summer 1741. We.
Bland, John. S Oct 1764 T Jan 1765 *Tryal*. M.
Bland, Sarah. T Jly 1724 *Robert* LC Md Jun 1725. Sy.
Bland, Thomas. S Lent 1763. E.
Bland, Thomas. SQS Oct T Dec 1770 *Justitia*. M.
Bland, William. SQS Apr T Jly 1771 *Scarsdale*. M.

Bland, William. S Feb T Apr 1772 *Thornton*. L.

Blandell, Eleanor. S Jan-Feb 1775. M.

Blanford, Giles of Devizes. R for Barbados Jly 1681. Wi.

Blandford, John. S for poaching deer & assaulting keeper Jly 1758. Do.

Blandford, Joshua. S Mar 1756. Ha.

Blandford, William. R for life Lent 1775. Sy.

Blane, Joseph. SQS Jly T Sep 1765 *Justitia*. M.

Blaney als Evans, William. S May-Jly 1773. M.

Blank, James. S Oct 1743 T Feb 1744 *Neptune*. L.

Blankard, John. PT Jan 1675. M.

Blanket, Christopher. R 14 yrs Mar 1764. De.

Blankill, William. S & T Jly 1772 *Tayloe*. M.

Blanthorn, James. S Apr T May 1750 *Lichfield*. M.

Blachford, Thomas als William. T Apr 1766 *Ann*. Sx.

Blatchford, Thomas. R 7 yrs Apr 1775. Co.

Blatchley, John of Wedmore. R for Barbados Jan 1676. So.

Blathwaite als Yawdell, Mabel of Warchott. R for Barbados Jly 1683. Cu.

Blaxland, William. T for life Dec 1770 *Justitia*. K.

Blay, Richard. S & T Feb 1744 *Neptune*. L.

Blaydon. *See* Bladon.

Blaze, Joseph. S Jan T Apr 1759 *Thetis*. M.

Bleake, John. S for highway robbery Lent R 14 yrs Summer 1741. Nf.

Bleak als Black, Robert of Fazakerley. SQS Jly 1763. La.

Blease, Isaac. S & R Lent 1768. Ch.

Bleaze, Peter of Manchester. SQS May 1757. La.

Bledall, William. S May T Jun 1726 *Loyal Margaret* to Md. M.

Blee, John. S Feb 1752. L.

Blenheim, Francis. S Feb T Apr 1741 *Speedwell* or *Mediterranean*. M.

Bleson, William. S Jan-Apr 1749. M.

Bletsley, William. R & T Sep 1766 *Justitia*. M.

Blew, Walter. Rebel T 1685.

Blewit, Charles. S s at Wolverhampton Lent 1750. St.

Blewett, Jane of Madderne, singlewoman. R for Barbados Jun 1687. Co.

Blewitt, Jane. R for Barbados or Jamaica Dec 1695 & May 1697. L.

Blewitt als Johnson, Johanna of St. Olave, Southwark. R for Barbados Aug 1668. Sy.

Blewett als Bowler als Dixon, Mary. S Aug T Oct 1726 *Forward*. L.

Blewit, William. S May T Jly 1722 *Alexander*. L.

Blewitt, William. R Oct T 14 yrs Dec 1724 *Rappahannock* to Va. M.

Blick, William. S Aug 1726. L.

Blight, John. R 14 yrs Mar 1773. De.

Blight, Roger. R 14 yrs Mar 1742. De.

Blimstone, Robert (1770). *See* Bold. Ch.

Blinco, Clinch. S s pig at Leiston Lent 1772. Su.

Blind Isaac (1750). *See* Solomon, Robert. L.

Blind Jack the Kidnapper (1772). *See* Talmy, John. L.

Blindman, Anna (1739). *See* Bluyman, Hannah. M.

Blinckhorn, Ann of Manchester, spinster. SQS Jan 1742. La.

Blinkhorne, John (1749). *See* Low. L.

Blinkin, Thomas. S Apr 1748. L.

Blinston, Catherine of Astmore, Chesh, spinster. SQS May 1764. La.
Bliss, Argent. S Mar 1738. Co.
Bliss, Elizabeth. TB to Va 1728. De.
Bliss, John. S Mar 1721. De.
Blisse, William. R 10 yrs Lent 1655 to be T by Thomas Vincent & Samuel Highland. Sy.
Bliss, William. S & T Dec 1767 *Neptune*. L.
Blissed, Guido. S Jan-Feb 1774. M.
Blissett, George. S Feb T Apr 1761 *Thornton*. M.
Blister, William. S Summer 1756 R 14 yrs Lent 1757. K.
Blizerd, Joseph. S Jan-Apr 1749. M.
Blizard, Joseph of St. Saviour, Southwark. SQS & T Jan 1767 *Tryal*. Sy.
Blizard, William. S s sheep Lent R 14 yrs Summer 1769. Wa.
Block, John. S Summer 1752. Bd.
Blofield, Robert. S s naval stores Summer 1746; noted as "dangerous man." Nf.
Blomily, Thomas of Turton. SQS Apr 1773. La.
Blood, Catherine (1723). *See* White. M.
Blood, Richard. S s cow Lent R 14 yrs Summer 1744. Le.
Bloom, David. S & T Sep 1751 *Greyhound*. M.
Bloome, John of East Dereham. R for Barbados Aug 1671. Nf.
Bloomer, William. S Apr T Sep 1758 *Tryal* to Annapolis. M.
Bloomley, John. S Summer 1749. K.
Bloor, James. S Feb T Apr 1762 *Dolphin*. M.
Bloor, James. TB May 1772. Db.
Bloor, John. TB May 1772. Db.
Bloss, Sarah. S Sep 1754. L.
Blott, Mary. S May T Sep 1766 *Justitia*. M.
Blount, Charles. S s silver watch at Bewdley Lent 1739. Wo.
Blount, Edward. S s at St. Owen Lent 1764. He.
Blount, John of Mindtown, gent. R for Barbados Mar 1663. Sh.
Blount, Mary. SQS Sep 1750. M.
Blower, John (1719). *See* Dobson. E.
Blower, John. S s handkerchief at Alberbury Lent 1764. Sh.
Blower, Joseph. S & TB to Va Apr 1764. Le.
Blower, Martha. LC Annapolis Md Jun 1725 from *Robert*. X.
Blower, Thomas. S s at Westbury Lent 1726. Sh.
Bloxam, John. S Jly-Sep T Sep 1742 *Forward*. M.
Bloxham, Joseph. S Jan-Jun T Jun 1728 *Elizabeth* LC Potomack Aug 1729. L.
Bloxham, Samuel. R for life Jly TB to Va Oct 1742. Wi.
Bloxon, Walter. S Jan 1757. M.
Bluck, Francis. R for Barbados or Jamaica Jan 1692. M.
Bluck, John. S Feb T Apr 1744 *Justitia*. M.
Bluck, Mary. S & T Oct 1732 *Caesar*. L.
Bluck, William. T Dec 1753 *Whiteing*. K.
Bluck, William. S Lent T Apr 1772 *Thornton*. K.
Bluckfield, Joseph. S Jun T Aug 1769 *Douglas*. L.
Blundell, Ann. S & T Apr 1753 *Thames*. L.
Blundell, Charles of Rotherhithe. SQS Jan T Mar 1764 *Tryal*. Sy.
Blundell, George. S Jan-Feb T Apr 1753 *Thames*. M.

Blundell, James. S & T Apr 1753 *Thames*. L.
Blundell, James. S Oct T Dec 1767 *Neptune*. L.
Blundell, John, a Quaker. S Summer 1664 for attending conventicle. Ht.
Blundell, John. S Lent R 14 yrs Summer 1761. Sy.
Blundell, John, als Black Jack. S s at Henley Lent 1773. O.
Blundall, Peter. S Lent 1730. Sh.
Blundall, Peter. S s sheep at Quatford Lent 1739. Sh.
Blunder, Sarah. S Feb T Apr 1770 *New Trial*. L.
Blunderfield, Thomas. R May AT Jly 1697. M.
Blundy, Charles. SQS Oct T Dec 1771 *Justitia*. M.
Blunt, Charles. R for Barbados May TB Jun 1668. M.
Blunt, David. S Lent T May 1755 *Rose*. Ht.
Blunt, Isaac. R for Barbados Jan 1694. M.
Blunt als Butler, James. S Sep-Dec 1755 T Jan 1756 *Greyhound*. M.
Blunt, Jane wife of William. S & T Jly 1772 *Tayloe*. M.
Blunt, John. S Aug T 14 yrs Sep 1718 *Eagle* LC Charles Town Mar
    1719. L.
Blunt, John. LC Rappahannock Va May 1728 from *Forward*. X.
Blunt, Richard. S Apr T Sep 1737 *Pretty Patsy* to Md. M.
Blunt, Sarah. Died on passage in *Susannah & Sarah* 1720. X.
Bluyman, Hannah wife of John, als Blindman, Anna. S Apr-Jun
    1739. M.
Bly, Thomas. S Jly 1745. Ha.
Blynn als Stevens, Jane. S for perjury Jan 1755. L.
Blyth, John (1755). *See* Longden. Nf.
Blith, Robert. S s horse Summer 1724 R 14 yrs Lent 1725. Su.
Blyth, Robert. S Summer 1732. Nl.
Blyth, Robert of St. Olave, Southwark. SQS Feb 1757. Sy.
Blythe, Sarah (1772). *See* Jordan. M.
Blyth, Thomas (1699). *See* Sherley. M.
Boacock. *See* Bowcock.
Boam, Mary. S Summer TB Sep 1759. Db.
Boar als Bourman, Robert, als Norfolk Bob. T Apr 1753 *Thames*. E.
Board, Thomas. S Mar 1774. So.
Boardman, Charles. S s at Stoke upon Trent Lent 1750. St.
Boardman, Israel of Wavertree. SQS May 1770. La.
Boardman, John of Farnworth. SQS Jan 1775. La.
Boardrey, Paul. S Jan-Jun T Jun 1728 *Elizabeth* to Md or Va. M.
Boast, Sarah wife of John, als Siddell, Sarah, spinster. S Apr T May
    1767 *Thornton*. M.
Boat, John. R & T Oct 1722 *Forward* to Md. M.
Boatman, George. T May 1736 *Patapsco*. E.
Boatson, Michael. S Summer T Sep 1751 *Greyhound*. Sy.
Bockin als Bayham, Simon. S Jly 1741. Wi.
Bocking, William. R for America Mar 1690. Db.
Bockumb, Peter. S Jan-Feb T Apr 1753 *Thames*. M.
Boden, John. S s cloth at Newcastle under Lyme Lent 1763. St.
Boden als Boardman, John of Liverpool, joiner. S Summer 1770; found
    at large & R 14 yrs Lent 1771. La.
Boden, Richard of Walsall. R (Western Circ) for America Jly 1700. St.
Bodden, Samuel. S Jan-Feb 1774. M.

Bodden, Thomas. TB Aug 1718. L.

Boddenham, Edward. LC Va Jly 1734 from *Caesar*. X.

Bodenham, George. S Mar TB to Va Apr 1746. Wi.

Boddington, Martha. R for Barbados Apr 1669. M.

Boddoe, John. S Oct T Nov 1728 *Forward* LC Rappahannock Jun 1729. L.

Bodeymyer, Daniel. S Sep-Dec 1746. M.

Bodger, Thomas. S Dec 1763 T Mar 1764 *Tryal*. M.

Boddily, Edward. R for Barbados or Jamaica Dec 1698. M.

Boddily, John. S Summer 1745. Db.

Bodily, John Parfett. S Lent R 14 yrs Summer 1766. St.

Bodily, Thomas. R 14 yrs Aug 1759. So.

Bodle, Dorothy wife of William. R 14 yrs Summer 1759. Cu.

Bodman, Hugh. S & TB Aug 1739. G.

Bodman, James. S Lent T May 1770. Wa.

Bodray, Paul. LC Potomack Va Aug 1729 from *Elizabeth*. X.

Body, Thomas. Rebel T 1685.

Boddy als Walmsley als Skipton, William. S & R 14 yrs Summer 1729 T Summer 1730. Y.

Body als Bodway, William. S Mar 1737. Co.

Bodnam, Thomas. S & TB May 1736. G.

Boff, John. S Summer 1772. Wa.

Bogg, Daniel (1700). *See* Johnson. M.

Boggs, Robert. SWK Jan 1754. K.

Bohannan, James. R Jly T for life Oct 1768 *Justitia*. M.

Boiling, Richard. SQS Wisbech s sheep & R 14 yrs Sep 1773 Ca.

Boland, James. S Jan T Mar 1764 *Tryal*. L.

Bolus, Elizabeth. S & T Apr 1766 *Ann*. M.

Bolas, Francis. S s iron chain at Buildwas Summer 1723. Sh.

Bould, John. S s horse & R 14 yrs Summer 1766. St.

Bold als Blimstone, Robert. S s heifer Summer 1770 R Lent 1771. Ch.

Bolderson, Thomas. AT Lent 1747. Y.

Bole. *See* Bowl.

Boles. *See* Bowles.

Boley. *See* Bowley

Bolingbroke, Mary, als wife of James Deal. S 14 yrs Apr-Jun 1739. M.

Bollard, Richard. T May 1750 *Lichfield*. Sx.

Bollis, Henry. T Sep 1764 *Justitia*. M.

Bolster, Isaac. Rebel T 1685.

Bolt, James. S Feb 1752. L.

Bolt, Robert. S & T Dec 1736 *Dorsetshire*. L.

Bult, Robert. R s cloth from a rack Mar 1750. So.

Bult, William. R 14 yrs Aug 1757. So.

Bolton, Catherine (1765). *See* Wilkes. L.

Bolton, Elianor of St. Giles in Fields, widow. S s stockings & T Jan 1740 *York* to Md. M.

Bolton, Elizabeth. S City s at St. Sampson Lent 1765. Y.

Bolton, Francis. R 14 yrs s sheep Summer 1766. Li.

Bolton, Hannah. S & T Sep 1765 *Justitia*. M.

Bolton, John. R (Home Circ) for Barbados May 1664. X.

Boulton, John. R for America Jly 1687. Db.

Bolton, John. LC Annapolis Md Jun 1723 from *Forward.* X.
Bolton, John. S & T Dec 1734 *Caesar* but died on passage. M.
Bolton, John. S Feb 1752. L.
Bolton, John. AT Lent & Summer 1765. Y.
Bolton, John. S s sheep at Bolton upon Swale R Lent TB Apr 1773. Y.
Bolton als Duck, John Joseph. S & R 14 yrs Lent 1774. Wo.
Bolton, Joseph of St. Luke. S s lead & T May 1740 *Essex* to Md or Va. M.
Bolton, Joseph. S for aiding escape of prisoners in Stafford Gaol Lent 1758. St.
Bolton, Martha. S Feb T Mar 1730 *Patapsco* LC Annapolis Sep 1730. L.
Bolton, Mary. R 10 yrs in plantations Oct 1662. M.
Boulton als Gatley, Mary. S Oct T Nov 1728 *Forward* LC Rappahannock Jun 1729. M.
Bolton, Nathaniel. S Summer 1750. Ch.
Boulton, Richard. S Jan T Feb 1719 *Worcester* LC Annapolis Jun 1719. L.
Bowlton, Richard. S Lent 1754. E.
Boulton, Robert. S s at Leek Summer 1774. St.
Bolton, Sarah. SQS & T Dec 1771 *Justitia*. M.
Bolton als Demarry, Thomas. R for Barbados Mar 1681. L.
Boulton als Bolton, Thomas. S for false pretences Summer 1761. O.
Bolton, Thomas of Chipping. S Lent R 14 yrs Summer 1767. La.
Bolton, Timothy. R for Barbados Mar 1683. L.
Bonady, John (1698). *See* Thomas. De.
Bonaretta, Anthony. T May 1744 *Justitia*. Sy.
Bonas, Abraham. S Lent AT Summer 1720. Y.
Boncer. *See* Bonser.
Bond, Ambrose. S Mar 1723. Co.
Bond, Charles of St. George, Southwark. SQS & T Jan 1769 *Thornton*. Sy.
Bond, Edward. SQS Oct 1726 TB Sep 1728. Wi.
Bond, Elisha. TB to Va from QS 1746. De.
Bond, Elizabeth. R for Barbados Oct TB Oct 1667. L.
Bond, Elizabeth. S Mar 1768. So.
Bond, Francis. R for America Jly 1688. Li.
Bond, Hannah (1729). *See* Fox. M.
Bond, Hester (1748). *See* Lynn. M.
Bond, John of Halberton. R for Barbados Jly 1681. De.
Bond, John. S Dec 1748 T Jan 1749 *Laura*. M.
Bond, John. SQS Apr TB Aug 1749. So.
Bond, John. R 14 yrs Apr 1756. So.
Bond, John. S Mar 1768. Co.
Bond, Joseph of Bermondsey. S Summer T Oct 1750 *Rachael*. Sy.
Bond, Martha. SQS Jly TB to Md Nov 1740. So.
Bond, Mary. S Mar 1768. Do.
Bond, Nicholas. S Dec 1749-Jan 1750 T Mar 1750 *Tryal*. M.
Bond, Peter. S Apr 1728. De.
Bond, Phillip. S Feb T Mar 1727 *Rappahannock*. L.
Bond, Richard. TB to Va from QS 1738. De.
Bond, Richard. R 14 yrs Jly 1749. Ha.

Bond als Clark, Richard. S & T Sep 1764 *Justitia*. L.
Bond, Robert. S Apr 1745. So.
Bond, Samuel (Emanuel). Rebel T 1685.
Bond, Thomas. S Mar 1749. Co.
Bond, Thomas. R Apr 1773. M.
Bond, Thomas of Warrington. SQS Apr 1773. La.
Bond, Uriah. S & R Lent T *Genoa* Oct 1738. Bu.
Bond, William. S Apr T May 1720 *Honor*; escaped in Vigo, Spain. L.
Bond, William. R 14 yrs Aug 1756
Bonder, John. AT from QS Summer 1728. St.
Bone, Ann. S Jan T 14 yrs Feb 1744 *Neptune* to Md. M.
Bone, Anne. S Jly 1745. Ha.
Bone, Edward. T Apr 1753 *Thames*. K.
Bone, Elizabeth. S & T Oct 1730 *Forward* to Va. M.
Bone, John. R for America Jly 1693. Le.
Bone, John (1737). *See* Bourne. M.
Bone, John. S Feb 1738. Ha.
Bone, John. S & T Jly 1753 *Tryal*. L.
Bone, Mary. SQS Apr 1752. M.
Bone, Nicholas Jr. S Mar 1739. Co.
Bone, William. S May T Sep 1737 *Pretty Patsy* to Md. M.
Bones, Elizabeth. S Dec 1749-Jan 1750 T Mar 1750 *Tryal*. M.
Bones, Robert. T Apr 1759 *Thetis*. E.
Bonfield, Richard. S for burglary Summer 1739 R 14 yrs Lent 1740. Nf.
Bonner, Ann. SQS Sep 1773. M.
Bonner, Hannah. R 14 yrs Jly 1758. De.
Bonner, James. R for America Aug 1715. M.
Bonner, John. R Oct T 14 yrs Dec 1724 *Rappahannock* to Va. M.
Bonner, Ralph. S City Summer 1735. Nl.
Bonner, Robert. S s calf Summer 1759 R 14 yrs Lent 1760. Le.
Boner, Thomas. R 14 yrs Apr 1775 (HO). De.
Bonner, William. R for Barbados Jly 1675. L.
Bonner, William. S Jly R 14 yrs TB Dec 1734. Bd.
Bonner, William. T Sep 1757 *Thetis*. K.
Bonnevan, John (1749). *See* Pyke. De.
Bonney, Joseph. SQS May T Jly 1773 *Tayloe* to Va. M.
Boney, Julia of St. Margaret, Westminster, spinster. M.
Bonney, Thomas. S Lent 1772 s horse. Be.
Bonney, Thomas. S s at Benson Lent 1773. O.
Bonniface, William. S Sep-Oct 1772. M.
Bonsall als Bonsor, Joseph. TB Apr 1742. Db.
Bonse, Sarah (1719). *See* Bowge. M.
Bonsellers, Dennis. R for Barbados or Jamaica Aug 1700. L.
Bonser, Catherine. SQS Aug TB to Va Sep 1751. Le.
Bonsor, Joseph (1742). *See* Bonsall. Db.
Bonsor, Thomas. S Mar R 14 yrs Summer TB to Va Sep 1742. Le.
Boncer, William. S & R 7 yrs Lent TB May 1772. Nt.
Bonten, James als Rip (1770). *See* Mack. Hu.
Bonython als Saundry, Alexander. R 14 yrs Aug 1745. Co.
Booby, John. R 14 yrs Mar 1740. So.

Booden, Agnes. SQS & T Sep 1755 *Tryal* but also noted as T Jan 1756 *Greyhound*. M.

Book, John. SQS & TB Jan 1733. G.

Bookham, Jacob. R Apr TB for Barbados Jun 1669. M.

Bookeham, James of Shoreham. R (Newgate) for Barbados Sep 1669. K.

Booker als Kennard, George of Beeding. R for Barbados or Jamaica Jly 1710. Sx.

Booker, John. S Jan T 14 yrs Feb 1733 *Smith* to Md or Va. M.

Booker, John of Waddington, Yorks. SQS Jan 1770. La.

Booker als Fagg, Mary. R for Barbados or Jamaica May 1697. L.

Booker, Richard. S Feb T Mar 1758 *Dragon*. L.

Booker, Samuel. S Dec 1742 T Apr 1743 *Justitia*. M.

Booker, Thomas of St. Saviour, Southwark. SQS 14 yrs Jan T Mar 1763 *Neptune*. Sy.

Bool, William. S s horse Lent R 14 yrs Summer 1731. Nt.

Booley. *See* Beaulieu.

Boone, Jeremiah of Pebmarsh. SQS for second offence as rogue & vagabond Jan T Jun 1756 *Lyon*. E.

Boon, Joseph. T Apr 1769 *Tryal*. E.

Boone, Mary. SQS Jly TB Oct 1728. So.

Boon, Mary. R 14 yrs Mar 1766 TB to Va. De.

Boon, Moses of St. Saviour, Southwark. SQS Feb T Apr 1770 *New Trial*. Sy.

Boone, Samuel. Rebel T 1685.

Boone, Samuel. T Oct 1729 *Forward*. Sy.

Boone als Booth, Thomas. R May AT Jly 1697. M.

Boon, Thomas. S s wheat at Stoke on Trent Summer 1762. St.

Boone, William (1664). *See* Boorne. Su.

Boot, Daniel. S Mar 1761. Ha.

Boot, Daniel. S s at Hodnet Lent 1772. Sh.

Boote, Henry of Belaugh. R for America Feb 1664. Nf.

Booth, Anne. S Lent 1739. Ch.

Booth, Ann (1743). *See* Stone. M.

Booth, Ann. S Jan-Feb T Apr 1771 *Thornton*. M.

Booth, Benjamin of Eaton. SQS s wheat Apr 1749. Nt.

Booth, Elizabeth of Bermondsey. R for Barbados or Jamaica Feb 1683. Sy.

Booth, Elizabeth. S Feb T Apr 1739 *Forward* to Va. M.

Booth, Elizabeth. S Dec 1774. M.

Booth, George. S Jly T Sep 1725 *Forward* LC Annapolis Md Dec 1725. Nt.

Booth, Hannah. S Feb-Apr 1745. M.

Booth, Henry. S for perjury Summer 1764. La.

Booth, Henry. S Feb T Apr 1765 *Ann*. M.

Booth, John. S s lamb at St. Mary, Reading, Lent 1728. Be.

Booth, John. S Summer 1746. K.

Booth, John. S s sheep Lent R 14 yrs Summer 1751. Nt.

Booth, John. AT Lent 1766. Y.

Boothe, John. S Lent R 14 yrs Summer 1768. G.

Booth, John. S for highway robbery & R 14 yrs Lent 1775. Y.

Booth, Joseph. R for Barbados or Jamaica Mar 1688. M.

Booth, Joseph. S & T Oct 1722 *Forward* LC Annapolis Jun 1723. M.

Booth, Langham. S Lent 1748. Ch.

Booth, Lucy. S Feb 1752. L.

Booth, Lydia. S Apr-May T May 1744 *Justitia*. M.

Booth, Margaret (1721). *See* Yeomans. L.

Booth, Thomas (1697). *See* Boone. M.

Booth, Thomas. S & T Aug 1718 *Eagle* LC Charles Town Mar 1719. L.

Booth, Thomas. S Lent 1730. Wo.

Booth, William. S Apr T May 1718 *Tryal* LC Charles Town Aug 1718. M.

Booth, William. R 14 yrs Summer 1731. Y.

Booth, William. R 14 yrs Summer 1750. Nl.

Booth, William. SW & T Dec 1771 *Justitia*. M.

Booth, William. R 14 yrs Apr 1773. M.

Booth, William Edmund. S & T Sep 1731 *Smith* LC Va 1732. L.

Boothby, Marmaduke. S for housebreaking Lent R 14 yrs & T Summer 1736. Y.

Boothman, Jonathan. S May-Jly 1773. M.

Bootman, Stephen. S s at Kessingland & R Lent 1773. Su.

Boythroyd, Jeremiah. S Lent 1772 s at Leeds. Y.

Bootts, Richard. T Jly 1724 *Robert*. K.

Boraston, Edward. S Sep T Oct 1744 *Susannah*. L.

Borcham, George of Writtle. SQS Oct 1751 T May 1752 *Lichfield*. E.

Boram, Mary. T Nov 1725 *Rappahannock* but died on passage. Sy.

Boreham, Thomas of Blackmore. R (Newgate) for Barbados Aug 1668. E.

Boreham, Thomas. S & T Jan 1766 *Tryal*. M.

Boreman, Elizabeth. S Lent T Jun 1756 *Lyon*. Sy.

Borer, Wiiliam of Sharley, Milbrooke. R for Barbados Jun 1687. Ha.

Borges, Sarah (1764). *See* Burgess. Y.

Borlase als May, Richard. S Jly 1725. Co.

Borne. *See* Bourne.

Borras, James. S s sheep & R 14 yrs Lent 1770. G.

Borrill, Francis. S Lent R 14 yrs Summer 1733. Y.

Borthwick, James. S & T 14 yrs Oct 1732 *Caesar*. L.

Burthwick, Thomas, aged 36. R for Barbados Feb 1664. M.

Bosantine, Charles. S Jan T Feb 1733 *Smith* to Md or Va. M.

Boscowe, James. S Feb T Mar 1730 *Patapsco* LC Annapolis Sep 1730. L.

Boseden, John (1766). *See* Strutt, Elizabeth (*sic*). M.

Bozeley, Mary. S Jly T Oct 1741 *Sea Horse* to Va. M.

Bosely, Thomas. S Oct-Dec 1750. M.

Bosley, William. S May 1727. M.

Bosman, Edward. S Feb T Apr 1741 *Speedwell* or *Mediterranean* to Md. M.

Boss, Anthony. S s sheep Lent R 14 yrs Summer 1742. Y.

Bossom, Charles. S s at St. Giles, Reading, Lent 1748. Be.

Bossom, William. S s at St. Peter in the East, Oxford, Summer 1768. O.

Bosson, Samuel. S s horse & R 14 yrs Summer 1763. Ch.

Bostock, Henry. S Feb T Mar 1729 *Patapsco* LC Annapolis Dec 1729. L.

Bostock, Nathaniel. S & T Dec 1734 *Caesar* LC Va Jly 1735. L.

Bostock, Thomas (1720). *See* Bostwick. L.

Bostock, William. S for burglary Summer 1763 R 14 yrs Lent 1764. Sh.
Boston, Beverly. S Feb T Mar 1758 *Dragon*. M.
Boston, Joseph. S Jan-Jun T Jun 1728 *Elizabeth* LC Potomack Aug 1729. M.
Boston, Mary wife of David. S Oct T Nov 1759 *Phoenix*. M.
Boston, Mary. S Apr-May T Jly 1771 *Scarsdale*. M.
Boston als Wilmott, Thomas. S Feb T Mar 1731 *Patapsco* LC Md Jun 1731. L.
Bostwick als Bostock, Thomas. S & T Oct 1720 *Gilbert* but died on passage. L.
Boswell, Ann (1745). *See* Davis. L.
Boswell, Ann. S Jly-Dec 1747 to be T 14 yrs. M.
Boswell, Anthony. R for Barbados Aug 1679. L.
Boswell, Charles Sr. T Jun 1740 *Essex*. Ht.
Boswell, Charles Jr. T Jun 1740 *Essex*. Ht.
Boswell, Custelow. S s from stable Lent 1751. Nf.
Boswell, Edward. S Aug T 14 yrs Oct 1726 *Forward* to Va. M.
Boswell, Edward. S s brass & pewter at Garsington Lent 1750. O.
Boswell, Elizabeth (1685). *See* Browne. Li.
Boswell als Mason, Elizabeth. S & R 14 yrs Summer 1775. O.
Boswell, Henry. S City Summer 1752. Y.
Boswell, Henry (1773). *See* Basil. Wo.
Boswell, Jane, spinster of St. Saviour, Southwark. SQS Mar T Apr 1768 *Thornton*. Sy.
Boswell, John, butcher aged 25, fair. S Jly T Oct 1720 *Gilbert* LC Md May 1721. M.
Boswell, John. S May T Jun 1726 *Loyal Margaret* LC Annapolis Oct 1726. M.
Boswell, John (1760). *See* Finnamore. O.
Boswell, John of Bristol. R 14 yrs Mar 1764 (SP). G.
Boswell, Joseph. S s at Denchworth Lent 1765. Be.
Boswell, Letitia. T Jun 1740 *Essex*. Ht.
Boswell als Ward, Mary. S Jan T Feb 1726 *Supply* LC Annapolis May 1726. M.
Boswell, Ruth. T Jun 1740 *Essex*. Ht.
Boswell, Samuel. S Apr 1773. L.
Boswell, Sarah. S Summer TB Oct 1764. Db.
Boswell, Thomas. S Lent T *Tryal* Sep 1755. Bu.
Boswell, Timothy (1773). *See* Basil. Wo.
Boswell, William. S Jly T Oct 1720 *Gilbert* but died on passage. M.
Boswell, William. S Lent T *Tryal* Sep 1755. Bu.
Bosworth, John. S for highway robbery Summer 1737 R 14 yrs Lent 1738. No.
Bosworth, John. S Feb T Apr 1739 *Forward* to Va. M.
Botfield, Elizabeth of St. John, Worcester. R for America Feb 1681. Wo.
Botham, Joseph. TB to Md Jly 1722. Db.
Bothams, John. TB to Md Aug 1727. Db.
Bothomley. *See* Bottomley.
Botman, Thomas (1748). *See* Ellis. Y.
Botsell, William. LC Annapolis Md Dec 1729 from *Patapsco*. X.
Botsford, John. S s hog Lent 1747. *Bd.

Bott, Edward of Wolverhampton. R for Barbados Feb 1665. St.

Bottens, Robert. S Jun T Aug 1769 *Douglas*. M.

Bottin, John. S Feb T May 1767 *Thornton*. L.

Bottles, Sarah. S Jly-Dec 1747. M.

Bottomley, John. S Lent 1758. La.

Bothomly, Joseph. R for America Jly 1694. Li.

Bothomley, Michael. S s cloth from tenters Lent R 14 yrs Summer 1721. Y.

Bottsford, John (1753). *See* Bellsford. Ht.

Bouch, John. SW & T Jly 1772 *Tayloe*. M.

Bowcher als Davis als Smith, Ann. R Oct 1694 AT Jan 1695. M.

Boucher, Elizabeth (1727). *See* Wade. L.

Boucher, Elizabeth. S Sep T Dec 1734 *Caesar* LC Va Jly 1735. M.

Boucher, John. S May T 14 yrs Jun 1727 *Susanna*. L.

Boucher, Margaret (1744). *See* Stansbury, Mary. L.

Boucher, Mary. SQS Oct 1751. M.

Boucher, Stephen. S & T Sep 1765 *Justitia*. M.

Boucher, Thomas. SQS Oct 1754. M.

Bouchier, Mary (1772). *See* Walker. M.

Bould. *See* Bold.

Boulin, Honor. S Apr-Jun 1739. M.

Boulter, Sarah. T May 1751 *Tryal*. E.

Boulter, William. S May-Jly 1748. M.

Boulton. *See* Bolton.

Bounce, Sarah. S Sep-Oct 1773. M.

Bound, John. S s nails at Churchill Summer 1752. Wo.

Bounds, George. S Mar 1750. Ha.

Bounds, Joseph of West Derby, cooper. S for highway robbery & R 14 yrs Lent 1773. La.

Bounds, Thomas. S Feb T Mar 1763 *Neptune*. M.

Bourand, Francis. T Apr 1742 *Bond*. K.

Bourke. *See* Burk.

Bourman, Robert (1753). *See* Boar. E.

Bourne, Catherine. S May-Jly 1748. M.

Bourne als Knowland, Catherine. S Apr T Sep 1757 *Thetis*. L.

Bourne, Charles. T from Bristol by *Maryland Packet* 1761 but intercepted by French; T Apr 1763 *Neptune*. So.

Bourne, Dorothy (1697). *See* Cozin. L.

Bourne, Henry of Edgware, yeoman. R for Bermuda s sheep Jun 1614. M.

Bourne, Henry. S Sep T Oct 1719 *Susannah & Sarah* but died on passage. L.

Bourn, James. S Dec 1727. M.

Bourne, Jane. R for Barbados or Jamaica Mar 1685. M.

Borne, Jane. R 14 yrs Jly 1721 T from Southampton 1723. Ha.

Bourne als Bone als Byre, John. S Jan T Sep 1737 *Pretty Patsy* to Md. M.

Bourne, John. S Norwich Summer 1756. Nf.

Borne, Joseph. S & T Apr 1766 *Ann*. M.

Bourn, Leonard. R 14 yrs Mar 1752. De.

Bourne, Richard. R for Barbados or Jamaica Oct 1690. M.

Bourne, Thomas of Norwich. R for America Jly 1703. Nf.
Boorne als Boone, William of Mutford. R for Barbados Feb 1664. Su.
Bourne, William. T May 1737 *Forward*. Sy.
Bousden, John. T 14 yrs Sep 1766 *Justitia*. K.
Bousfield, Thomas. R Jly 1730. Du.
Bovett, Edmund. Rebel T 1685.
Bovett, John. Rebel T 1685.
Bovett, Thomas. Rebel T 1685.
Bovet, William. R 14 yrs Aug 1736. De.
Bow, John. S Aug 1727. M.
Bowe, John. S Summer 1732 R 14 yrs Summer 1733. Cu.
Bow, John. S May T Sep 1766 *Justitia*. L.
Bow, Thomas. S & T Oct 1730 *Forward* LC Potomack Jan 1731. M.
Bowater, William of Dudley. R for Jamaica, Barbados or Bermuda Feb
    1686. Wo.
Bowcher. *See* Boucher.
Boacock, John. S s sheep Summer 1742 R 14 yrs Lent 1743. Li.
Bowcock, John. S s cloth from tenters at Heptonstall & R Summer
    1774. Y.
Bowdell, William (1764). *See* Bowden. Li.
Bowden, Dorothy, aged 28. R for Barbados for uttering false money
    May 1664. M.
Bowden, Edward. TB Aug 1735 T *Squire* LC Md Apr 1736. Db.
Bowden, Elizabeth. R for Barbados Jun 1671. L.
Bowden, Henry. R 14 yrs Mar 1746. Co.
Bowden, John. R for Jamaica Aug 1661. M.
Bowden, John. T May 1751 *Tryal*. K.
Bowden, Mary. S & T Apr 1759 *Thetis*. L.
Bowdon, Robert. S Feb T Mar 1731 *Patapsco* LC Annapolis Jun
    1731. M.
Bowden, Roger of Waltham Abbey. R for Barbados or Jamaica Mar
    1682. E.
Bowden, Samuel. SQS Warminster Jly TB to Va Sep 1741. Wi.
Bowden, Samuel. S Aug 1752. So.
Bowden, Susannah (1774). *See* Bailey. M.
Bowden, Thomas. SQS Oct 1766 T Jan 1767 *Tryal*. M.
Bowden, William of Caton. SQS Apr 1756. La.
Bowden als Bowdell, William. S Lent 1764. Li.
Bowden, William, als Hill, John. R 14 yrs Mar 1772 TB to Va. De.
Bowdler, Henry of Bridgnorth. R for America Jly 1675. Sh.
Bowdler, John (1754). *See* Green. He.
Bowdler, Zachariah. S Summer 1751. Sh.
Bowdley, Elizabeth. R Sep 1671 AT Jly 1672 & Oct 1673. M.
Bowdry, George of St. Saviour, Southwark. R for Barbados Jly 1679. Sy.
Bowen, Ann. S Feb T Mar 1758 *Dragon*. M.
Bowen, Charles. S Apr T May 1751 *Tryal*. L.
Bowen, Charles. S Aug 1760. So.
Bowen als Preece, Edward. S s sheep & R Lent 1774. Sh.
Bowen, Elizabeth (1756). *See* Holl. M.
Bowen, Elizabeth. S Sep T Oct 1768 *Justitia*. M.
Bowen, James. S & T Dec 1752 *Greyhound*. L.

Bowen, John. R for America May 1709. M.
Bowen, John. S & T Oct 1732 *Caesar* to Va. M.
Bowen, John. S s at Ombersley Lent 1763. Wo.
Bowen, John. S Summer 1774. Sy.
Bowon, Oliver (1773). *See* Bower. Ha.
Bowen, Rachael. S Mar 1746. So.
Bowen, Richard. R for Barbados Feb 1675. L.
Bowen als Smith, Sarah. R for Barbados Mar 1677. M.
Bowen als Browne, Sarah. R for Barbados Mar 1683. M.
Bowen, Sarah (1727). *See* Newington. Be.
Bown, Sarah. R 14 yrs Mar 1771. Do.
Bowen, William. S Aug T Oct 1723 *Forward* to Va. M.
Bowen, William. S Oct-Dec 1754. M.
Bowen, William. S Aug 1760. L.
Bower, John. T Jly 1770 *Scarsdale*. M.
Bower als Bowon, Oliver. S Mar 1773. Ha.
Bower, William. S 14 yrs for receiving goods stolen at York Castle
    Summer TB Aug 1773. Y.
Bowerman, John. SQS Jly 1741 TB to Md May 1742. So.
Bowers, Ann. S Jan T Feb 1726 *Supply* LC Annapolis May 1726. L.
Bowers, Gwenllyan als Winifred of Clytha. R for America Mar
    1710. Mo.
Bowers, James (1752). *See* Bowen. L.
Bowers, John, als Power, Edward. R 14 yrs Jly 1767. Ha.
Bowers, John. R & T 14 yrs Jly 1772 *Tayloe*. M.
Bowers, Robert. S Apr-May 1775. M.
Bowers, Sarah. S Summer T Sep 1751 *Greyhound*. Sy.
Bowers, Thomas, als Horton, John. S Lent R 14 yrs Summer 1760. Wo.
Bowers, Thomas. S Sep T Dec 1767 *Neptune*. L.
Bowers, William. S Apr-May T May 1741 *Catherine & Elizabeth* to
    Md. M.
Bowes, Joshua. R for Barbados Mar 1683. L.
Bowes, Margaret. S May T Jly 1723 *Alexander* LC Annapolis Sep
    1723. M.
Bowes, Richard. S Summer 1741. We.
Bowes, Thomas. S s horse Jly 1741 R 14 yrs Lent TB to Md Apr
    1742. Le.
Bowhay, Elizabeth (1743). *See* Guard. Co.
Bowie, David. S Summer 1754. Du.
Bowie, George. T Sep 1764 *Justitia*. E.
Bowing, William. S s pigs Lent 1750. Nf.
Bowker, Abraham of Salford. SQS Jan 1741. La.
Bowker, John of St. Saviour, Southwark. SQS Jan 1775. Sy.
Bole, Edward. S Lent 1743. *Su.
Bowle, John. S & T Sep 1751 *Greyhound*. M.
Bowell, John. S Feb T Apr 1770 *New Trial*. L.
Bowle, William. S & T Oct 1722 *Forward* LC Annapolis Jun 1723. L.
Bowler, Hannah. S s at Wolstanton Summer 1750. St.
Bowler, John. R & T Apr 1725 *Sukey* LC Annapolis Sep 1725. M.
Bowler, John. S Oct T Dec 1771 *Justitia*. L.
Bowler, Jonathan. SWK Oct 1768 T Jan 1769 *Thornton*. K.

Bowler, Mary (1726). *See* Blewett. L.
Bowler, Robert. S s at Merrington Summer 1773. Du.
Bowler, William of Sillington. R for Barbados or Jamaica Mar 1698. Sx.
Bowles, Elizabeth. S Apr 1774. M.
Boles, James. R (Home Circ) for Barbados Apr 1663. X.
Bowles, James. T Apr 1771 *Thornton*. Ht.
Bowles, Mary. S Jly 1757. Ha.
Bowles, Richard. S Summer 1744. Y.
Bowles, Samuel. S Feb 1752. L.
Bowles, Thomas. S Feb 1729. M.
Bowles, Thomas. S May T Jun 1764 *Dolphin*. M.
Boley, James, mariner. S s at St. Peter, Ipswich, Lent 1771. Su.
Bowley, Mary (1752). *See* Beaulieu. L.
Bolley, Polyna (1736). *See* Peel. L.
Bowley, Robert. SQS Jan 1665 as idle & disorderly. M.
Bowling, Rachel. S & T May 1740 *Essex*. L.
Bowlton. *See* Bolton.
Bowman, Daniel. S Summer 1728 R 14 yrs Lent 1729. G.
Bowman, Elizabeth. R for America Aug 1715. L.
Bowman, Elizabeth. R May T Jly 1723 *Alexander* to Md. M.
Bowman, James (1772). *See* Bowman, Joseph. M.
Bowman, John. S & TB Mar 1732. G.
Bowman, John. S Sep-Oct T Dec 1752 *Greyhound*. M.
Bowman, John. T Sep 1758 *Tryal*. Ht.
Bowman, Joseph als James. R & T 14 yrs Jly 1772 *Tayloe*. M.
Bowman, Samuel. S Oct 1774. L.
Bomen, Thomas. R 14 yrs Jly 1725. Wi.
Bowman, Thomas. S Jly TB to Va Sep 1756. Wi.
Bowring, Mary. S & T Oct 1720 *Gilbert* to Md. M.
Bowse, Sarah (1719). *See* Bowye. L.
Bowshott, Jane. SQS Jan TB to Jamaica Sep 1727. So.
Bowye als Bowse, Sarah. S Jan T Feb 1719 *Worcester* to Md. L.
Bowyer, Charles (1676). *See* Mortall. M.
Bowyer, Francis of St. Clement Danes. SW Oct 1766 T Jan 1767
    Tryal. M.
Bowyer, John. S Lent R 14 yrs Summer 1743. Wo.
Bowyer, Mary. R for America Mar 1690. Wa.
Bowyer, Peter, als Peter Boy. S Mar 1765. Do.
Bowyer, Thomas. S & T Jly 1772 *Tayloe*. M.
Bowyer als Scampey, William. S Jly T for life Sep 1755
    Tryal. L.
Bowyers, Catherine. S Apr 1745. L.
Box, John. SQS Warminster Jly TB to Va Oct 1742. Wi.
Box, Leonard. S Mar TB to Va Apr 1751. Wi.
Box, Mary wife of Edward. S & T Oct 1730 *Forward* LC Potomack Jan
    1731. M.
Boxall, Henry. T Sep 1757 *Thetis*. Sx.
Boxall, James. S Lent s sheep R 14 yrs Summer 1749. Sx.
Boxall, Robert. S Lent 1779. Sy.
Boxer, Benjamin (1774). *See* Seager. St.

Boxer, William of South Weald. R for Barbados or Jamaica Mar 1688. E.
Boxteed, Thomas. T Apr 1741 *Speedwell* or *Mediterranean*. E.
Boxwell alias Baxall, William. S Jly 1774. Ha.
Boy, John. R 14 yrs Mar 1768. Co.
Boyce, Andrew. Rebel T 1685.
Boyce, Elizabeth. S & T Sep 1767 *Justitia*. M.
Boyce, James. SQS New Sarum Jan TB to Va Apr 1742. Wi.
Boyce, James. R 14 yrs Mar 1765. Ha.
Boys, John (1673). *See* Briggs. L.
Boyce, John. T Oct 1726 *Forward*. E.
Boyce, Mary. S Oct 1743 T Feb 1744 *Neptune*. L.
Boys, Mary. S May-Jly 1750. M.
Boyce, Mary. S Mar 1766. So.
Boys, Richard. S for highway robbery at Halifax Summer 1767. Y.
Boyce, Robert. S s at St. Chad, Shrewsbury, Summer 1734. Sh.
Boyce, Samuel. S Jly T Aug 1721 *Prince Royal* to Va. M.
Boys, Thomas. S for highway robbery at Halifax Summer 1767. Y.
Boyce, Thomas. S Apr-May T Jly 1771 *Scarsdale*. M.
Boyce, William. T Jan 1738 *Dorsetshire*. K.
Boyce, William. S Aug 1759. Co.
Boyd, Elizabeth wife of Terence. S May T Nov 1743 *George William*. M.
Boyd, Hugh. R 14 yrs Summer TB Sep 1750. Y.
Boyde, James. S Jan-Feb 1773. M.
Boyd, Patrick. S Lent 14 yrs Summer 1752. Ch.
Boyd, Robert. S & T Sep 1757 *Thetis*. L.
Boyden, Elizabeth. LC Potomack Va Aug 1729 from *Elizabeth*. X.
Boyer, John (1756). *See* Wray. Y.
Boyer, Mary. R 14 yrs Jly 1758. De.
Boyer, William. S Nov T Dec 1770 *Justitia*. L.
Boyland als Baylin, John. T Sep 1764 *Justitia*. M.
Boylan, William of St. Saviour, Southwark. SQS Apr T Sep 1751 *Greyhound*. Sy.
Boyle, Alice. S Dec 1772. M.
Boyle, Christopher. S & T Apr 1733 *Patapsco* LC Annapolis Nov 1733. M.
Boyle, Elizabeth. R for Barbados or Jamaica Dec 1689. M.
Boyle, Elizabeth wife of Dennis. S May T Sep 1737 *Pretty Patsy* to Md. M.
Boyle, James. T May 1751 *Tryal*. K.
Boyle, James. S Mar 1752. Co.
Boyle, John. S s at St. Philip & Jacob Lent 1764. G.
Boyle, Margaret. S & T Aug 1718 *Eagle* to Md or Va. L.
Boyle, Mary. S Nov T Dec 1752 *Greyhound*. L.
Boyle, Samuel (1770). *See* Bird. L.
Boys. *See* Boyce.
Boyston, Edward. S Summer R for Barbados Aug 1663. Sy.
Boyton, Elizabeth. S Jan-Jun T Jun 1728 *Elizabeth* to Md or Va. M.
Bozeley. *See* Bosley.
Bozey als Bland, Golden. S Sep T Dec 1769 *Justitia*. M.

Brabazon, Barnabas. R for Barbados of Jamaica Dec 1699 & Aug 1700. L.

Brace, Daniel. S s geese at Pencoyd Lent 1771. He.

Brace, George. S Apr-May T Jly 1771 *Scarsdale*. M.

Brace, John. S s at Great Witley Lent 1726. Wo.

Brace, John. S Sep-Oct T Dec 1771 *Justitia*. M.

Brace, Mary wife of John. R Aug T Sep 1725 *Forward* LC Annapolis Dec 1725. M.

Brace, Richard. S s geese & ducks at Hentland Lent 1771. He.

Brace als Braca, Samuel of Newington. SQS Jan T Apr 1770 *New Trial*. Sy.

Bracey, John. S Sep T Dec 1770 *Justitia*. M.

Brack, Alice. AT City Summer 1755. Nl.

Brackett, Daniel. S Dec 1748 T Jan 1749 *Laura*. L.

Brackett, Mary. S Oct T Dec 1767 *Neptune*. M.

Brackien, Lancelot (1765). *See* Johnson, Robert. Y.

Brackman, Henry (1722). *See* Adams. Sy.

Brackstone, Thomas. T Sep 1764 *Justitia*. L.

Bracley,*Mary. S Feb T Mar 1727 *Rappahannock* to Md. M.

Bradborne, Thomas. S & T Sep 1731 *Smith* LC Va 1732. L.

Bradburne, William. S Lent 1753. Bd.

Bradburn, William. S Mar 1765. Ha.

Bradbury, George. S Lent R 14 yrs Summer 1736. Wa.

Bradbury, John. S s mare & R Lent 1763. Bu.

Braddock, Henry. S s at Tettenhall Lent 1739. St.

Braddon, Nicholas. Rebel T 1685.

Brade, James. S Jly 1763. M.

Bradey. *See* Brady.

Bradfield, Ann (1771). *See* Barfield. M.

Bradfield, Thomas of Yatesbury. R for Barbados Mar 1694. Wi.

Bradfield, Thomas of Maston, Potterne. R for Barbados Feb 1698. Wi.

Bradford, Constantine. S s at Withersfield Lent 1769. Su.

Bradford, Elizabeth (1736). *See* Broadfield. M.

Bradford, Elizabeth. S & T Mar 1763 *Neptune*. L.

Bradford, Isaac (1688). *See* Banford. K.

Bradford, John of Barton, Temple Guiting. R for Jamaica, Barbados or Bermuda Mar 1688. G.

Bradford, John. SQS & T Sep 1766 *Justitia*. M.

Bradford, Richard. S Jan 1775. M.

Bradford, Thomas. T Apr 1743 *Justitia*. Sy.

Bradford, William. S City s shirt at St. Maurice Lent 1774. Y.

Bradham, Thomas. SQS Dec 1774. M.

Bradin, John (1702). *See* Bradney. Bu.

Brading, John. S Lent T *Thornton* May 1767. Bu.

Bradley, Andrew. T Dec 1771 *Justitia*. Sy.

Bradley, Charles. S Mar 1773. Ha.

Bradley, Edward. T Sep 1730 *Smith*. Ht.

Bradley, Edward. S s mare & R Summer 1774. Li.

Bradley, Elizabeth. S for shoplifting & R 7 yrs Lent 1774. Wa.

Bradley, Francis. T Jun 1764 *Dolphin*. K.

Bradley, Hannah. S May-Jly 1749. M.

Bradely, Humphry. S s at Bromsgrove Lent 1747. Wo.
Bradley, James. S & T Jan 1769 *Thornton*. L.
Bradley, John. R for Barbados Sep 1677. L.
Bradley, John. S Jan s sheets T Apr 1735 *Patapsco* Annapolis Oct 1735. M.
Bradley, John. S Lent 1738. Su.
Bradley, John. S s naval stores Summer 1749. K.
Bradley, Joseph. S Jun-Dec 1738 T Jan 1739 *Dorsetshire* to Va. M.
Bradley, Joseph. T Oct 1750 *Rachael*. M.
Bradley, Mary. S & T Oct 1732 *Caesar* to Va. M.
Bradley, Richard (1727). *See* Winston. O.
Bradley, Richard. R Dec 1773. M.
Bradley, Robert of Bermondsey. R 10 yrs in plantations Feb 1656. Sy.
Bradley, Susannah of Manchester, singlewoman. SQS Apr 1756. La.
Bradley, Thomas. T Apr *Sukey* LC Md Sep 1725. Sx.
Bradley, Thomas. Died on *Rappahannock* on passage to America 1726. Li.
Bradley, Thomas of Hornchurch. S Lent 1745. E.
Bradley, Thomas. S Dec 1766 T Jan 1767 *Tryal*. L.
Bradley, Thomas. S s gelding at Beaconsfield R 14 yrs Lent T Apr 1771 *Thornton*. Bu.
Bradley, Thomas. R for life Summer 1772 for being at large after sentence of T. Ht.
Bradley, William. T *Bond* Apr 1742. Bu.
Bradley, William. S s at Westcot Barton Lent 1749. O.
Bradley, William. T Dec 1758 *The Brothers*. K.
Bradney als Bradin als Ross, John of Linslade. R for America Jly 1702. Bu.
Bradrilk, Christopher. T Dec 1731 *Forward*. Sy.
Bradshaw, Andrew. SQS Jly T Nov 1762 *Prince William*. M.
Bradshaw, Ann (1726). *See* Briton. M.
Bradshaw, Benjamin. S s horse Summer 1729 R Lent 1730 (SP). St.
Bradshaw, Edward. SQS Jan 1756. La.
Bradshaw, Elizabeth. S Oct T Dec 1769 *Justitia*. L.
Bradshaw, Henry (1752). *See* Whiteside, Thomas. La.
Bradshawe, John of Oxford. R for America Jly 1678. O.
Bradshawe, John Jr. of Calsett, clothmaker. R for Barbados Jly 1688. Y.
Bradshaw, John of St. George, Southwark. SQS Jan 1772. Sy.
Bradshaw, Joseph. T May 1736 *Patapsco*. Sy.
Bradshaw, Richard. SQS Coventry Apr 1765. Wa.
Bradshaw als Smith, Robert. S & T Sep 1766 *Justitia*. M.
Bradshaw als Bradyer, Rose. S May T Jun 1727 *Susanna* to Md. M.
Bradshawe als Brashaw, Thomas. S s sheep at Kildurck Lent R 14 yrs Summer 1767. Y.
Bradshaw, William. S Aug T Oct 1724 *Forward* to Md LC Annapolis Jun 1725. M.
Bradshaw, William. S Apr T May 1767 *Thornton*. L.
Bradshaw, William. S Jan-Feb 1775. M.
Bradstreet, Francis. S Jun-Dec 1738 T Jan 1739 *Dorsetshire* to Va. M.
Bradway, George. S s sheep Lent R 14 yrs Summer TB Sep 1754. Db.
Brady, Ann. S 14 yrs for receiving Jun T 14 yrs Jly 1772 *Tayloe*. L.

Bradey, Benjamin. S Oct T Nov 1728 *Forward* LC Rappahannock Jun 1729. L.
Brady, Catherine. SQS & T Jan 1756 *Greyhound*. M.
Bradey, Farrell. S & T Oct 1732 *Caesar* to Md. M.
Brady, Henry of Necton. R for Barbados Aug 1671. Nf.
Brady, Mary. T Jly 1724 *Robert* LC Annapolis Md Jun 1725. Sy.
Brady, Mary. S Jan T Apr 1762 *Dolphin*. L.
Brady, Terence. T Apr 1732 *Patapsco*. K.
Bradey, Thomas. S & T Oct 1729 *Forward* but died on passage. M.
Brady, Timothy. S s watch at St. Peter Mountergate, Norwich, & R Summer 1773. Nf.
Bradyer, Rose (1727). *See* Bradshaw. M.
Braechan, Thomas. T May 1719 *Margaret*. E.
Braffitt, William. S Lent 1755. Ca.
Brage, William of Halstead. SQS Jan T May 1755 *Rose*. E.
Bragg, Andrew of Shebbear, husbandman. R for Barbados Apr 1668. De.
Bragg, Ann. SQS s coal from Sir James Lowther Easter 1774. Du.
Bragg, Edward of Dolton. R for Barbados Jly 1695. De.
Bragg, George. S Mar 1736. De.
Bragge, John. Rebel T 1685.
Bragg, John. T Apr 1741 *Speedwell* or *Mediterranean*. E.
Bragg, John. S for perjury Summer 1762; to be imprisoned one month and fined a shilling before T. Cu.
Bragg, Mary. SQS s coal from Sir James Lowther Easter 1774. Du.
Bragg, William. S Jly 1743. De.
Bragg, William. S Apr 1751. So.
Brailsford, John. T Jun 1740 *Essex*. K.
Braily, Joseph. S & TB Sep 1732. G.
Brain. *See* Brayne.
Brathwaite, Martha. R Aug T Sep 1775 *Forward* to Md. M.
Brathwaite, Matthew. S Jly 1760 & R for fleet (HO). Ha.
Braithwaite, Thomas. S Summer 1741. Y.
Bramald als Bramall, Francis. AT Lent & Summer 1765. Y.
Bramble, James. Rebel T 1685.
Bramble, John. Rebel T 1685.
Bramble, Thomas (1740). *See* Mill. De.
Brambleby, William Henry. T 14 yrs Sep 1767 *Justitia*. K.
Brame, James. S s hog at Swilland Lent 1769. Su.
Bramhall, Jonas. S Lent R 14 yrs Summer 1768. Y.
Bramhall, Martha. R for life Summer 1768. We.
Bramingham, Elizabeth. S Jun-Dec 1745. M.
Bremingham, George. SQS Oct 1766 T Jan 1767 *Tryal*. M.
Bramley, William. S s at Knaresborough Lent 1773. Y.
Brammer, George. S Feb T Sep 1737 *Pretty Patsy* to Md. M.
Brammah, Susanna of St. George Hanover Square. S s clothing Jly T Dec 1740 *Vernon* to Md. M.
Brampton, John. T Nov 1728 *Forward*. Sy.
Brampton, John. S s axe at Wendover Summer T Oct 1768 *Justitia*. Bu.
Bramsby als Bramsey, Thomas. S s clothing Apr T Dec 1735 *John* LC Md Sep 1736. M.

Bramsby, William. T Apr 1768 *Thornton*. Sy.

Bramsey, John. R Dec 1699 AT Jan & Aug 1700. M.

Bramston, John. S Feb-Apr 1746. M.

Bramstone als Benham, Mary, spinster of Maidstone. S Lent T May 1750 *Lichfield*. K.

Branbery, Ann. S & T 14 yrs Oct 1730 *Forward* LC Potomack Jan 1731. L.

Branch, Ann. S Oct T Dec 1724 *Rappahannock*. L.

Branch, Elizabeth. S Dec 1766 T Jan 1767 *Tryal*. M.

Branch, John (1724). *See* Blanch. K.

Branch, Mary (1746). *See* Lee. De.

Branchin, Thomas. T May *Margaret* LC Md Sep 1719; sold to William Orrick. Sy.

Brand, Benjamin. S Aug T Sep 1718 *Eagle* LC Charles Town Mar 1719. L.

Brand, John of Bildeston. R for America Feb 1681. Su.

Brand, John (1755). *See* Bird. Su.

Brand, Mary, spinster of Felsted. R for Barbados or Jamaica Mar 1694 & Feb 1696. E.

Brand, Zachariah. S Oct T Nov 1762 *Prince William*. M.

Brandett, Eleanor. S Jun T Jly 1772 *Tayloe*. L.

Brandon, William. SQS Summer 1774. Ht.

Branklyn, James. S Summer 1754. Bu.

Brannon, John of St. Paul Covent Garden. SW Apr T May 1767 *Thornton*. M.

Brannon, Michael. R for life Dec 1774. M.

Brannon, Nicholas. SW & T Oct 1768 *Justitia*. M.

Brannon, Thomas of St. Botolph Aldgate. S s shoes Jly T Sep 1742 *Forward*. L.

Brannum, Elizabeth of St. Martin in Fields. S s linen Feb T May 1736 *Patapsco*. M.

Bransbury, Daniel. R for Barbados or Jamaica Jan 1692. M.

Branscombe, Andrew of Cullompton, husbandman. R for Barbados Jun 1669. De.

Bransgrove, Edward. R & T 14 yrs Jly 1772 *Tayloe*. M.

Branston, John. SQS Feb 1773. M.

Branvile, Jane. SQS Jun T Jly 1753 *Tryal*. M.

Brashaw. *See* Bradshaw.

Brasie, Mary (1735). *See* Johnson. M.

Brasier, Bartholomew of Reading. R for America Feb 1690. Be.

Brasier, Bartholomew of Watford. R (London) for Barbados or Jamaica Dec 1695. Ht.

Brasier, John. R Summer 1755 T 14 yrs Jun 1756 *Lyon*. Sy.

Brasier, John. S s yarn at Little Whitley Lent 1762. Wo.

Brazier, Richard. S s sheep Summer 1769 R for life Lent 1770. He.

Brazier, Susannah. SQS May T Jly 1771 *Scarsdale*. M.

Brasyer, William of St. George, Southwark. R for Barbados or Jamaica Feb 1684. Sy.

Brassell, Daniel. S May T Jun 1756 *Lyon*. L.

Brassington, Samuel. S Jan-Apr 1749. M.

Brathwaite. *See* Braithwaite.

Bratt, Thomas. S s at Rugeley Lent 1763. St.
Bratton, Richard. R Jly T Sep 1767 *Justitia*. M.
Braugham, Mary. S & T Jun 1756 *Lyon*. L.
Brawden, Elizabeth (1727). *See* Ball. L.
Braxton, John. LC Port York Va Jan 1721 from *Honor*. X.
Bray, Ann. TB to Va from QS 1762. De.
Bray, Benjamin. S Feb 1754. L.
Bray, Eleanor. R 14 yrs Jly 1749. De.
Bray, Hester. S Dec 1733 T Jan 1734 *Caesar* LC Va Jly 1734. M.
Bray, Humphrey. S s cloth at Penniston Lent 1769. Y.
Bray, James. R Apr 1773. M.
Bray, John. Rebel T 1685.
Bray, John. T Oct 1738 *Genoa*. Sy.
Bray, John. S Jly 1771. Ha.
Bray, John. S Lent 1775. Li.
Bray, Judith. S Dec 1727 T Jun 1728 *Elizabeth* LC Potomack Aug
    1729. M.
Bray, Robert of Claines. R for America Sep 1671. Wo.
Bray, Robert. S Apr T Sep 1758 *Tryal* to Annapolis, Md. M.
Bray, Thomas. Rebel T 1685.
Bray, Thomas, als Price, Edward. S s at St. Maughan Lent 1723 Mo.
Bray, Thomas. S Mar 1730. De.
Bray, Thomas. S Lent R 14 yrs Summer 1736. He.
Bray, Thomas. S Dec 1748 T Jan 1749 *Laura*. L.
Bray, Timothy. S Oct 1773. L.
Bray, William. T May 1719 *Margaret* LC Md May 1720; sold to Thomas
    Rouls. Sy.
Bray, William. T Jun 1740 *Essex*. Sy.
Braybrooke als Bush, Edward of Little Leighs. R for America Jly
    1700. E.
Brayley, Nicholas. S Aug 1735. De.
Brain, Elizabeth. S Feb 1754. M.
Braine, Joseph. S & T Apr 1766 *Ann*. L.
Brayne, Mary. R & T 14 yrs Jly 1772 *Tayloe*. M.
Brain, Samuel. S s at St. Philip & Jacob Lent 1768. G.
Brayne, William. S & TB Aug 1740. G.
Brayner, Mary. S Oct T Nov 1759 *Phoenix*. L.
Breadcott, Hannah. S & T Jan 1736 *Dorsetshire* but died on passage. L.
Breadstreet, John. S Aug T Sep 1725 *Forward* LC Annapolis Dec
    1725. L.
Breadway, Edward. S Apr 1748. L.
Breakspear, Jane wife of John. S Apr 1773. M.
Brearley, Ann wife of John of Heap, woollen weaver. SQS Aug 1765. La.
Brearly, William. R for America Jly 1686. Nt.
Breasly, Sarah of Lancaster. R for Barbados Jly 1699. La.
Brechley, Grace. R for plantations Jan 1665. M.
Breed, Thomas, als Buckingham, Richard. R Oct 1694 AT Jan 1695. M.
Breeden, Edward of St. Olave, Southwark. SQS Nov T Dec 1753
    Whiteing. Sy.
Breedon, Beatrice. R Jan AT Feb 1679. M.
Breedon, Elizabeth. S Oct T 14 yrs Dec 1724 *Rappahannock*. L.

Breadon, Thomas. S s horse Lent R 14 yrs Summer 1726. St.

Breen als Brend, William. SQS Dec 1664 for attending a conventicle. M.

Breeze, Jonathan. S for perjury Lent 1765: to stand in pillory at East Dereham for an hour before transportation. Nf.

Breese, Thomas of Drayton. R for America Aug 1691. Nf.

Brees, William. S Summer 1742 R 14 yrs Lent 1743. Du.

Breffett (Bressett), John. Rebel T 1685.

Bremer, Christopher. S & T Dec 1731 *Forward*. L.

Bremer, Jacob. T May 1751 *Tryal*. K.

Bremingham. *See* Bramingham.

Brenable, Giles. S Mar 1729. So.

Brennan, James. S & T Oct 1730 *Forward* LC Potomack Jan 1731. L.

Brenan, Martha. S & T Sep 1731 *Smith* LC Va 1732. M.

Breno, Andrew of Maidstone. R for Barbados Apr 1668. K.

Brent, Samuel. T Apr 1766 *Ann*. Sy.

Brentnall, William. S s heifers Lent R 14 yrs Summer 1760. Nf.

Brenton, John. S Jly 1718 to be T to Va. Co.

Brestbone, John, a Quaker. R for plantations Jly 1665. (SP). Ht.

Brestboone, John. R May AT Jly 1697. M.

Bretherton, John of Preston, skinner. SQS Oct 1744. La.

Breton, Robert. R 14 yrs for highway robbery Feb 1764. Li.

Brett, Anne. S Apr T May 1720 *Honor* LC Port York Jan 1721. L.

Brett, James. T May 1751 *Tryal*. E.

Brett, John. S May T Jly 1771 *Scarsdale*. L.

Brett, John. S Mar 1772. Ha.

Brett, Richard of Drayton. R for America Aug 1691. Nf.

Brett, William. T Oct 1738 *Genoa*. Ht.

Brett, William. S Lent R 14 yrs Summer T Sep 1767 *Thetis*. Bu.

Brevitt, John. S s iron vices at Wolverhampton Summer 1765. St.

Brewell, Eleanor. AT City Summer 1758. Nl.

Bruel, Frances. S Sep-Oct T Dec 1753 *Whiteing*. M.

Brewell, Susan. S Feb T Mar 1727 *Rappahannock* to Md. M.

Brewer, Ann. S & T May 1736 *Patapsco*. L.

Brewer, Ann. S Jly T Sep 1767 *Justitia*. L.

Brewer, Edward. S Apr 1734. So.

Brewer, George. LC Annapolis Md Nov 1733 from *Patapsco*. X.

Brewer, Henry. S Aug T Oct 1726 *Forward*. L.

Brewer, Henry. SQS Feb T Apr 1772 *Thornton*. M.

Brewer, Henry. S Aug 1773. So.

Brewer, John. R May AT Jly 1697. M.

Brewer, John. T Apr *Sukey* LC Md Sep 1725. K.

Brewer, John. S Mar 1730. Do.

Brewer, Mary. T Oct 1722 *Forward* LC Md Jun 1723. E.

Brewer, Patrick. S Aug T Sep 1764 *Justitia*. L.

Brewer, Richard of Great Leighs. SQS Jan 1763. E.

Brewer, Sarah wife of John of St. Giles in Fields. S s lead pipe & T Dec 1740 *Vernon*. M.

Brewer, Sarah. SQS Dec 1774. M.

Brewer, William. R for Barbados or Jamaica Oct 1694. L.

Brewett, William. PT Oct 1672 R Oct 1673. M.

Brewin, Benjamin, aged 25, dark. S Summer 1721 R 14 yrs Summer
  1722 T *Jonathan* LC Md Jly 1724. No.
Brewin, William. S Jun-Dec 1745. M.
Brewster, Anne. S Summer 1720 R 14 yrs Summer 1721. Li.
Brewster, John. R for Barbados or Jamaica Aug 1700. M.
Brewster, John. S s mare & R Lent 1737. Su.
Brewster, Robert. S s clothing Christmas 1771 LC from
  Lowther & Senhouse Va May 1772. Nl.
Broster, Susan. S Jan-Jun T Jun 1728 *Elizabeth* LC Potomack Aug
  1729. L.
Brewton, Matthew. S s at Torrington Summer 1768 R 14 yrs Lent
  1769. He.
Brooton, Sarah. S Lent T Apr 1768. Li.
Brewton, Thomas. S & R 14 yrs Summer 1772. Wo.
Brian. *See* Bryan.
Briant. *See* Bryant.
Brice, Katherine of Winchester. R for Barbados Jun 1702. Ha.
Brice, Christopher of Walpole St. Andrew. R for America Feb 1695. Nf.
Brice, Edward (1753). *See* Price. So.
Brice, Elizabeth. S Feb T Apr 1768 *Thornton*. M.
Brice, John. Rebel T 1685.
Brice, Mary. S Mar 1759 TB to Va. De.
Brice, Robert. R 14 yrs Mar 1741. Ha.
Brick, William. S May T Jly 1723 *Alexander* LC Annapolis Sep 1723. L.
Bricken, Robert. S Feb s sheets T Jun 1738 *Forward* to Md or Va. M.
Brickland, Mary of St. Saviour, Southwark. R for Barbados or Jamaica
  Jly 1702. Sy.
Brickland, Richard. R for America Aug 1715. M.
Bricklebank als Quin, Mary. S Jun T Sep 1758 *Tryal*. L.
Bricks, Richard (1653). *See* Biggs. Sy.
Bride, Ann. S Dec 1735 T Jan 1736 *Dorsetshire* LC Va Sep 1736. M.
Bryde, Eleanor. T Jan 1766 *Tryal*. M.
Bride, Jane. R for Barbados Oct 1673. M.
Bride, Thomas. S Jun-Dec 1745. M.
Bridford, George. R for Barbados Jly 1681. De.
Bridgeford, Elizabeth. S Apr T Jun 1768 *Tryal*. M.
Bridger, James. S Nov T Dec 1753 *Whiteing*. L.
Bridger, John. S Lent 1775. Sx.
Bridges, Elinor. TB 14 yrs Oct 1719 T *Susannah & Sarah* LC
  Annapolis Apr 1720. L.
Bridges, Israel. R Dec 1698 AT Jan 1699. M.
Bridges, James. S Mar 1768. So.
Bridges, John. TB Oct 1719 T *Susannah & Sarah* LC Annapolis Apr
  1720. L.
Bridges, John. S Oct T Nov 1728 *Forward* LC Rappahannock Jun
  1729. L.
Bridges, John of Baldock. S Summer T Oct 1739 *Duke of
  Cumberland*. Ht.
Bridges, Thomas. R 14 yrs Aug 1751. So.
Bridgman, Ann. S & T Sep 1766 *Justitia*. M.
Bridgman, Francis of St. George, Southwark. SQS 14 yrs Jan 1772. Sy.

Bridgman, Jane. S Jly TB to Va Aug 1751. Wi.

Bridgman, John. S May-Jun T Aug 1752 *Tryal*. M.

Bridgman, Philip of Chipping Wycombe. R for America Jly 1700. Bu.

Bridgeman, Roger. SQS New Sarum Jan TB to Va Jun 1747. Wi.

Bridgman, Susannah. S May-Jly 1774. M.

Bridgman, William. S Jly T Aug 1721 *Prince Royal* to Va. M.

Bridgewater, Elizabeth (1730). *See* Scott. M.

Bridgwater, Elizabeth (1746). *See* Gardner. M.

Bridgwood, Thomas. Rebel T 1685.

Bridle, Henry Jr. S Mar 1756. Do.

Bridle, John. Rebel T 1685.

Brierly, Ann (1768). *See* Greaves. La.

Brierly, Mary (1768). *See* Greaves. La.

Briers, William. S Apr s peruke T Jun 1742 *Bladon*. L.

Brigg, William. SQS Feb T Apr 1753 *Thames*. M.

Briggs, Jane. S Oct T Nov 1728 *Forward* LC Rappahannock Jun 1729. M.

Briggs als Boys, John. R for Barbados Oct 1673. L.

Briggs, John of Northampton. R for America Jly 1679. No.

Briggs, John. T Apr 1743 *Justitia*. Sy.

Briggs, John. TB Sep 1745. Db.

Brigs als Ablet, John. S Dec 1765 T Jan 1766 *Tryal*. M.

Briggs, Mary. S Sep 1756. M.

Briggs, Sarah. S & T Oct 1732 *Caesar* to Va. M.

Briggs, Sarah. S May-Jly 1749. M.

Briggs, Thomas. S May 1760. M.

Bright, Edward. S Summer 1736. *Bd.

Bright, John. Rebel T 1685.

Bright, John. S s horse Summer 1742 R 14 yrs Lent TB Mar 1743. G.

Bright, Oliver. R Dec 1698 AT Jan 1699. M.

Bright, Richard, als John of Bow or Nuntracy. R for Barbados Jly 1698. De.

Bright, Stephen. S Jun-Dec 1738 T Jan 1739 *Dorsetshire* to Va. M.

Bright, Thomas. S Jan-Feb 1774. M.

Bright, William. S Jan-Jun 1747. M.

Bright, William. S May T Sep 1765 *Justitia*. M.

Brightman, William. S Feb-Apr T May 1751 *Tryal*. M.

Brighton, Daniel. S Dec 1742 T Mar 1743 *Justitia*. L.

Brightwell, Elizabeth. S Nov T Dec 1752 *Greyhound*. L.

Brightwell, Mary. S Jly 1750. L.

Brightwell, William. R 14 yrs Jly 1745. Ha.

Brighty, Thomas of Prestbury. R for America Jly 1693. G.

Brigland, James. SQS May T Sep 1766 *Justitia*. M.

Brim, Ann. TB from Qs 1770. De.

Brimble, Henry of South Petherton. R for Barbados Jly 1698. So.

Brimington, Mary. T Jly 1724 *Robert* LC Md Jun 1725. Sy.

Brimley, John Jr. S Lent 1747. Bu.

Brin, Anthony. S Mar 1728. Ha.

Brindley, Elizabeth. S Sep-Oct 1773. M.

Brindley, Jonathan. T May 1719 *Margaret* LC Md May 1720; sold to Patrick Sympson. Sy.

Brindley, Michael. S s at Wolverhampton & R 14 yrs Summer 1768. St.
Brindley, Michael. R 14 yrs s horse Summer 1768. La.
Brining, Thomas (1760). *See* Browning. De.
Brinkinshire, Richard. S Feb-Apr T May 1755 *Rose*. M.
Brinkley, James. S Feb-Apr T May 1755 *Rose*. M.
Brinkley, John of St. Ann Westminster. S Jly 1773. M.
Brinklow, John. S Aug 1763. L.
Brinklow, Sarah, spinster. S Lent 1760. Bu.
Brinkworth, Thomas. S & TB Apr 1740. G.
Brinley, Jonathan. S & T Jan 1722 *Gilbert* LC Annapolis Jly 1722. L.
Brinnam, Eleanor wife of Richard. S as pickpocket Lent R 14 yrs
  Summer 1752. Sh.
Brinsford, Thomas. S & R 14 yrs Lent 1773. Sh.
Brinton, Benjamin. T Oct 1726 *Forward*. K.
Brinton, Thomas. AT Summer 1733. Wo.
Brisbin, James. S Summer 1743. Y.
Briscoe, Elizabeth of St. Saviour, Southwark. R for Barbados or Jamaica
  Feb 1684. Sy.
Briscoe, William. R for Jamaica Jan 1663. M.
Brisley, Daniel. R for Barbados May 1664. M.
Brissenden, Isaac of Kennington. R for Barbados or Jamaica Mar
  1682. K.
Bristol Jack (1698). *See* Hitchcock, William. M.
Bristol, John. S Jun T Jly 1772 *Tayloe*. L.
Bristow, James. S Jan T Feb 1724 *Anne* to Carolina. M.
Bristow, James. S Norwich Summer 1764. Nf.
Bristow, John of St. James Westminster. S s coat Oct 1740 T Jan
  1741 *Rappahannock*. M.
Bristowe, John. S Summer 1749 R 14 yrs Lent 1750. Nt.
Bristow, Margaret. S Oct T Nov 1728 *Forward* LC Rappahannock Jun
  1729. L.
Bristow, Sarah. SQS Oct 1766. M.
Bristow, Susannah. S s household goods Feb T Jun 1738 *Forward*. L.
Bristue, William. R for Barbados or Jamaica Oct 1690. M.
Bristow, William. S & T Oct 1722 *Forward* LC Annapolis Jun 1723. M.
Britchford, John. S May 1727. M.
Britt, John. S Jly-Sep T Oct 1739 *Duke of Cumberland* to Va. M.
Brittle, John. S Mar 1744. So.
Brittain als Bradshaw, Ann. S Aug T 14 yrs Oct 1726 *Forward*. M.
Britton, Christopher. S Summer 1760. Y.
Brittain, James. T Sep 1758 *Tryal*. K.
Britton, John. PT Jun 1673. M.
Britten, John (1697). *See* Lagdell, George. Su.
Britton, John. S Summer 1718 R 14 yrs Summer 1721 T Oct 1723
  Forward from London. Y.
Brittain, John. S Oct T Dec 1724 *Rappahannock*. L.
Briton, John of St. Saviour, Southwark. SQS Mar T Apr 1768
  Thornton. Sy.
Britain, Jonas. S s iron chain at Bloxwich Summer 1769. St.
Britton, Samuel. T Apr 1765 *Ann*. M.
Britton, Samuel. SQS Dec 1766 T Jan 1767 *Tryal*. M.

Britain, Susannah wife of Jonas. S s at Newcastle under Lyme Summer 1765. St.
Britton, Thomas. S & R Lent 1738. Su.
Britain, Thomas. S s cock at Bredon Lent 1750. Wo.
Brittaine, William. R for Barbados Jly 1668. L.
Britnall, Samuel. S for highway robbery Lent R 14 yrs Summer 1764. Bd.
Broach, Thomas (1751). *See* Smith. M.
Broad, Elizabeth. SQS Jan TB Apr 1753. So.
Broad, John of Abbots Langley. R for Barbados Apr 1668. Ht.
Broad, John. S s beans Summer 1754. Wo.
Broad, John. S 14 yrs for receiving goods stolen at Hartlebury Summer 1773. Wo.
Broad, Mary. S Dec 1737 T Jan 1738 *Dorsetshire*. L.
Broad, Robert. S Sep-Oct 1773. M.
Broadas, Joseph. S Oct 1773. L.
Broadbent, John. S Lent TB Mar 1761. Db.
Broadbent, Joseph. S s at Sowerby Lent 1772. Y.
Broadbent, Richard. SQS Sep 1774. M.
Broadbent, William. S Apr T 14 yrs May 1718 *Tryal* LC Charles Town Aug 1718. M.
Broadbridge, Elizabeth. T Apr 1769 *Tryal*. Sy.
Broadfield als Bradford, Elizabeth wife of William. S s cotton & T May 1736 *Patapsco*. M.
Brodfield, William. S s watch at Bridgenorth Summer 1774. Sh.
Broadhead, Caleb. S Sep T Dec 1767 *Neptune*. M.
Broadhead, Joshua of Manchester. R for Barbados Jly 1683. La.
Broadhead, Thomas. S & T Apr 1759 *Thetis*. L.
Broadhurst, John. S Summer 1733 AT Lent 1734. Wo.
Broadley, Ann. S Lent 1771. Li.
Broadrip, William. SQS Jan TB Feb 1757. So.
Broadwater, John of Tonge. R for America Sep 1671. Sh.
Broadway, John. T Nov 1741 *Sea Horse*. Ht.
Broadway, John. S s at Inglefield Summer 1742. Be.
Broadway, Robert (1724). *See* Wright, Joseph. Sh.
Broadwood, James. S Jan-Feb T Apr 1772 *Thornton*. M.
Brocas, Thomas. S s gown Jan T Apr 1735 *Patapsco* LC Annapolis Oct 1735. L.
Brock, Elizabeth. S s at Finningham Lent R 14 yrs Summer 1767. Su.
Brock, Mary (1771). *See* Lockitt. L.
Brock, Samuel. Died on passage in *Loyal Margaret* 1726. X.
Brock, Thomas. Rebel T 1685
Brock, William. S 14 yrs for receiving Aug 1754. So.
Brockden, William. TB to Va from QS 1741. De.
Brocker, John. S & T Mar 1763 *Neptune*. L.
Brockett, Theophilus. TB Sep 1737. Db.
Brockett, Thomas. S Feb 1731. M.
Brockhouse, Anne of Bermondsey. R for Barbados Jly 1679. Sy.
Brockington, Philip. TB to Va from QS 1743. De.
Brocklebank, Jonathan. S & T Jan 1756 *Greyhound*. M.
Brocklehurst, William. S May T Nov 1762 *Prince William*. M.

Brockley, Catherine. S Feb T Apr 1743 *Justitia*. M.
Brockley, Thomas. S Apr T May 1752 *Lichfield*. L.
Brockman, James. S Summer 1746. K.
Brockman, John. S Summer 1749. K.
Brockwell, James. S Dec 1739 T Jan 1740 *York* to Md. M.
Brockwell, Thomas. S Lent 1763. E.
Broctin, George. S s at Briskay Rigg Lent 1719 AT Summer 1720. Y.
Brodbeare, Robert. Rebel T 1685.
Brodbeare, William. Rebel T 1685.
Brodd, James. T 14 yrs Aug 1769 *Douglas*. E.
Broderick, David of Islip. S Summer 1720. O.
Broderick, Joseph. SQS & T Jan 1766 *Tryal*. M.
Broffit, Mary. Died on passage in *Alexander* 1723. X.
Brogden, Ann (1741). *See* Hickman. M.
Bromage, Percy. S & TB Aug 1740. G.
Bromall. *See* Broomhall.
Broman, John of Guildford. R for Barbados or Jamaica Jun 1684. Sy.
Brome. *See* Broom.
Bromfield. *See* Broomfield.
Bromhill. *See* Broomhill.
Bromley, Catherine. S May T Dec 1734 *Caesar* to Va but died on
    passage. M.
Bromley, John. S Dec 1733 T 14 yrs Jan 1734 *Caesar* LC Va Jly 1734. L.
Bromley als Griffith, Mary. PT Apr R Oct 1673. M.
Brumley, Mary. S May-Jly 1746. M.
Bromley, William. S Oct 1744-Jan 1745. M.
Brompton, Richard. LC Annapolis Md Jun 1723 from *Forward*. X.
Brommedge, Edward of Christ Church. R for Barbados or Jamaica Mar
    1698. Sy.
Bromwich, Elizabeth. S Summer 1760. Wa.
Bromidge, James. S Summer T Sep 1770. Wa.
Bromwich, John. S Lent 1763. Wa.
Bromage, Phebe, als Baker, Elizabeth. S s at Richards Castle Lent
    1760. He.
Bromwich, Samuel. T Mar 1763 *Neptune*. L.
Bronkee als Bunker, Abraham. S Feb 1754. M.
Brookbank, Edward. S City s from warehouse at St. Sampson Summer
    1771. Y.
Brooke, Francis Jr. of Minehead. R for Barbados Feb 1688. So.
Brooke, James. S & T Lent 1729. Y.
Brooke, John. R for Barbados May 1665. X.
Brooke, John (1667). *See* Ediver. De.
Brooke, Joseph. S Lent 1740. Y.
Brook, Joseph of Manchester. SQS Oct 1756. La.
Brooke, Mary. S Summer 1768. Y.
Brooke, Nathaniel Jr. R 14 yrs Aug 1767. Do.
Brook, William. R 14 yrs Apr 1742. So.
Brooken, Joseph. S & T Oct 1729 *Forward* to Va but died on passage. M.
Brooker, Edward. T Apr 1753 *Thames*. Sx.
Brooker, Jane. S Feb T Mar 1758 *Dragon*. L.
Brooker, John of Edenbridge. R for Barbados or Jamaica Mar 1682. K.

Brooker, John. T Jun 1727 *Susanna*. K.
Brooker, Penelope. T Apr 1743 *Justitia*. E.
Brooker, Richard. T for life Jly 1771 *Scarsdale*. Sy.
Brooker, Robert. S & T Apr 1733 *Patapsco* to Md. M.
Brooker, Susanna (1772). *See* Brookes. He.
Brookes als Taylor, Agnes. S Sep T Nov 1762 *Prince William*. M.
Brookes, Ann, spinster, als wife of Richard of Chelmsford. R for
    Barbados or Jamaica Feb 1686. E.
Brookes, Ann. S Sep-Oct 1749. M.
Brooks als Sharpless, Catherine. S May-Jly 1748. M.
Brookes, Charles. S for forgery Lent R 14 yrs Summer 1767. Sh.
Brookes als Penn, Daniel. R for Barbados or Jamaica Jly 1687. L.
Brookes, Daniel. R Dec 1698 AT Jan 1699. M.
Brookes, Edward. PT May R Jly 1687. M.
Brookes, Edward. S Lent R 14 yrs Summer 1721. St.
Brooks, Edward. T Oct 1738 *Genoa*. Ht.
Brooks, Edward. R for life Oct 1751-Jan 1752. M.
Brookes, Edward. S Summer 1754. Ca.
Brooks, Elizabeth. S May T Jun 1727 *Susanna*. L.
Brooks als Smith, Francis. S & T Oct 1739 *York* to Md. M.
Brooks, George. R Mar TB to Va Apr 1772. Wi.
Brooks, James. S Oct T Nov 1728 *Forward* but died on passage. M.
Brooks, James. S Lent R 14 yrs Summer 1742. La.
Brooks, James. S & T 14 yrs Sep 1764 *Justitia*. L.
Brookes, James. S Norwich Summer 1766. Nf.
Brooks, Jane. S Dec 1727. L.
Brookes, Jane. S May-Jun T Jly 1753 *Tryal*. M.
Brooks, John. R for America Jly 1688. Wa.
Brookes, John. S Feb T Mar 1731 *Patapsco* LC Annapolis Jun 1731. M.
Brooks, John. S Feb T Apr 1742 *Bond* to Potomack. M.
Brooks, John. R 14 yrs Jun 1761. Ha.
Brooks, John. TB to Va from QS 1764. De.
Brookes, Josiah. S & T Oct 1729 *Forward* LC Va Jun 1730. M.
Brookes, Mary. S & T Dec 1731 *Forward*. L.
Brooks als Delany, Mary. S Sep 1760. M.
Brooks, Matthew. S & T Oct 1730 *Forward* LC Potomack Jan 1731. L.
Brookes, Richard. T Apr 1757. Db.
Brookes, Richard. S Lent 1757. Le.
Brookes, Richard. S Nov T Dec 1763 *Neptune*. L.
Brookes, Richard (1771). *See* Badger. St.
Brookes, Robert. Rebel T 1685.
Brookes, Robert. R for Barbados or Jamaica Feb 1686. L.
Brooks, Robert. R Aug AT Oct 1700. M.
Brooks, Robert. S Aug 1727 T *Forward* LC Rappahannock May 1728. M.
Brooks, Robert. S s cloth at Stroud & Tedbury Lent TB Mar 1737. G.
Brookes, Samuel. R & T Apr 1725 *Sukey* to Md. M.
Brookes, Samuel. T Summer T Oct 1739 *Duke of Cumberland*. Sy.
Brooks, Sarah, spinster of St. Peter, Colchester. R for Barbados or
    Jamaica Jly 1687. E.
Brooks, Sarah (1765). *See* Murrell. L.
Brookes als Brooker, Susanna. S s at Bromyard Lent 1772. He.

Brookes, Thomas of Pontesbury. R for America Jly 1693. Sh.
Brooks, Thomas. S s at St. Philip & Jacob Summer TB Aug 1738; wife Hester discharged. G.
Brookes, Thomas. S Summer T *Forward* Sep 1742. Bu.
Brooks, Thomas. R Lent R 14 yrs Summer T Sep 1751 *Greyhound*. K.
Brooks, Thomas. S Sep-Oct T Dec 1753 *Whiteing*. M.
Brooks, Thomas. S Lent T May 1755 *Rose*. K.
Brooks, Thomas. T Apr 1762 *Neptune*. Sx.
Brooks, Thomas. S Apr T Jun 1768 *Tryal*. M.
Brooks, William. S Jan T Feb 1726 *Supply* LC Annapolis May 1726. L.
Brookes, William. S Feb 1752. L.
Brooks, William of Ainsworth, carpenter. SQS Aug 1759. La.
Brookes, William. S s cheese & bacon at Newcastle under Lyme Summer 1762. St.
Brooks, William. S s gelding & R 14 yrs Summer 1770. No.
Brooks, William. S for bestiality & R for life Summer 1772. Be.
Brookfield, Joseph. S Nov T Dec 1770 *Justitia*. L.
Brooking, Alphonso. S Jly 1719 to be T to Va. De.
Brooking, Samuel. S Nov T Dec 1752 *Greyhound*. L.
Brookland, John. S s at Cookham Lent 1769. Be.
Brookman, James. T Apr 1731 *Bennett*. Sy.
Brookman, Thomas. S Mar 1730. Wi.
Brooksbank, Epaphroditus. S Lent 1755. Y.
Brooksby, Samuel. S Jan T Apr 1762 *Dolphin*. L.
Brookshead, James. SQS Jan 1751. M.
Broom, Edward. S Summer 1755 s shoes at Witney. O.
Brome, Elizabeth. S Feb-Apr T May 1752 *Lichfield*. M.
Broom, James. S Apr T May 1743 *Indian Queen* to Potomack. M.
Broom, John. R May T Jly 1722 *Alexander* to Nevis or Jamaica. M.
Broom als Brown, John. S Feb T Jun 1727 *Susanna*. L.
Broom, Robert. S Lent 1758. No.
Broome, Samuel. R 14 yrs Mar 1758. So.
Broom, William. S Lent R 14 yrs Summer 1746. St.
Brooman, William of Hatfield Broadoak. R for Barbados or Jamaica Mar 1694. E.
Bromfield als Jorden als Christian, Christian. R for Barbados or Jamaica Mar 1685. L.
Bromfield, James. S Jan T Mar 1758 *Dragon*. L.
Bromfield, Robert. TB Oct 1719 T *Susannah & Sarah* LC Annapolis Apr 1720. L.
Broomfield, Thomas. S & R 14 yrs Summer 1774. O.
Broomhall, Mary of St. Andrew Holborn. S Jly T Sep 1742. S Jly T Sep 1742 *Forward*. L.
Broomhall, Sarah. S & T Oct 1730 *Forward* LC Potomack Jan 1731. L.
Bromhill, Elizabeth, spinster, als wife of John. R for plantations Jan 1665. L.
Bromall, Thomas. S 14 yrs for receiving goods stolen by John Serjeant *(qv)* Lent 1769. St.
Broster. *See* Brewster.
Brothericke, Edward of Leeds. R for Barbados Jly 1683. Y.

Brothers, John. S 14 yrs for receiving coal from Thomas Pearce *(qv)* Lent 1774. G.

Brothers, Samuel. S Summer 1750. Nf.

Brotherton, Edward. S s sheep Summer 1757 R 14 yrs Lent T Apr 1758. Bd.

Bruff, John. S Feb-Apr T May 1775 *Rose.* M.

Bruffe als Browse, Thomas. S Oct T 14 yrs Dec 1724 *Rappahannock* to Va. M.

Broughton, Charles. Rebel T 1685.

Broughton, Elizabeth wife of Thomas. S Jly T Sep 1757 *Thetis.* M.

Broughton, Eunice. S & T Sep 1731 *Smith* LC Va 1732. L.

Broughton, James. Rebel T 1685.

Broughton, James. S for highway robbery Summer 1761 R 14 yrs Lent 1762. Nf.

Broughton, John. S Lent 1734. *Nf.

Broughton, William. S May-Jly 1746. M.

Browington, John, aged 18, fair. S & T Oct 1720 *Gilbert* LC Md May 1721. M.

Brown, Aaron. S s at Clee St. Margaret & R 14 yrs Summer 1768. Sh.

Brown, Abraham. S Mar 1741. Co.

Brown, Alice. S Sep-Oct 1748 T Jan 1749 *Laura.* M.

Browne, Andrew. R for Barbados or Jamaica Oct 1690. M.

Brown, Andrew. S Sep-Oct 1773. M.

Browne, Anne, spinster. R (Home Circ) for Barbados Apr 1663. X.

Browne, Anne. R for Barbados Jun 1670. M.

Brown, Ann. S & T May 1736 *Patapsco.* L.

Brown als Eler, Ann. S Dec 1753-Jan 1754. M.

Brown, Ann. S Summer 1756. K.

Brown, Ann wife of George of Eddingley, blacksmith. SQS s fowls Jly TB Aug 1771. Nt.

Brown, Ann. S Feb T Apr 1772 *Thornton.* L.

Brown, Ann. S Jan-Feb T Apr 1772 *Thornton.* M.

Brown, Ann. S Sep-Oct 1773. M.

Brown, Anthony. S s horse Summer 1733 R 14 yrs Summer 1734. Nl.

Brown, Bartholomew. S Sep T Dec 1770 *Justitia.* M.

Brown, Benjamin. SL Feb 1754. Sy.

Brown, Catherine. S Jan T Feb 1719 *Worcester* LC Annapolis Jun 1719. L.

Browne, Katherine. S & T Oct 1729 *Forward* LC Va Jun 1730. M.

Brown, Catherine (1745). *See* Herring. M.

Brown, Catherine. S Dec 1753-Jan 1754. M.

Browne, Charles. R Sep 1671 AT Jly 1672. M.

Browne, Charles of Morton. R for America Jly 1677. Li.

Brown, Charles. S & T Oct 1730 *Forward* LC Potomack Jan 1731. L.

Brown, Charles. T May 1751 *Tryal.* K.

Brown, Charles. S Feb T Apr 1768 *Thornton.* M.

Brown, Charles. S s at Belford Summer 1769. Nl.

Brown als Campbell, Charles. S s cloth at Brampton Summer 1773. Cu.

Brown, Christian. S Jun T Nov 1743 *George William.* M.

Brown, Christian. S Summer 1754. Sy.

Browne, Christopher of Greenwich. R for America Jly 1700. K.

Brown, Daniel. SQS & T Apr 1769 *Tryal*. M.
Browne, Edward. R for America Jun 1684. Db.
Brown, Edward (1712). *See* Buss. Sx.
Brown, Edward. S s horse Lent R 14 yrs Summer 1734. Wo.
Browne, Edward. TB to Va from QS 1738. De.
Browne, Edward. S Feb T Apr 1741 *Speedwell* or *Mediterranean*. M.
Brown, Edward. S Dec 1742 T Apr 1743 *Justitia*. M.
Brown, Edward. SW & T Jun 1768 *Tryal*. M.
Brown, Edward. S Mar 1772. Do.
Browne, Eleanor. S & T Dec 1731 *Forward* to Md or Va. M.
Brown, Eleanor. S Summer 1754. Nl.
Browne als Boswell, Elizabeth. R for America Aug 1685. Li.
Browne als Latham, Elizabeth. R for Barbados or Jamaica Dec 1689. L.
Brown, Elizabeth of St. George, Southwark. R for Barbados or Jamaica
  Jly 1715. Sy.
Brown als Wright, Elizabeth. S & T Jan 1722 *Gilbert* LC Md Jly
  1722. M.
Brown, Elizabeth (1725). *See* Russell. L.
Brown, Elizabeth (1730). *See* Alexander, Margaret. L.
Brown, Elizabeth. S Feb T Apr 1734 *Patapsco* to Md. M.
Brown, Elizabeth. S Feb-Apr 1745. M.
Brown, Elizabeth. S Feb-Apr 1751 T May 1751 *Tryal*. M.
Brown, Elizabeth. S 14 yrs Feb 1754. M.
Brown, Elizabeth. S Feb-Apr T Jun 1756 *Lyon*. M.
Brown, Elizabeth. S Summer 1757. Nf.
Brown, Elizabeth (1758). *See* Cale. M.
Brown, Elizabeth. S Feb T Apr 1759 *Thetis*. M.
Brown, Elizabeth. S Sep 1761. M.
Brown als Hillman, Elizabeth. S Dec 1765 T Jan 1766 *Tryal*. M.
Brown, Elizabeth. S Jly 1766. Do.
Brown, Elizabeth. S Apr T Jun 1768 *Tryal*. M.
Brown, Elizabeth. S Sep T Dec 1769 *Justitia*. M.
Brown, Elizabeth wife of William. S & T Dec 1770 *Justitia*. M.
Brown, Elizabeth. SQS Jun T Jly 1772 *Tayloe*. M.
Brown, Elizabeth (1774). *See* Holton. Sy.
Brown, Elizabeth (1775). *See* Hoare. M.
Brown, Frances. S Jly T Sep 1766 *Justitia*. M.
Browne, Francis of Lenton. R for America Jly 1679. Nt.
Browne, Francis of Walsoken. R for America Feb 1681. Nf.
Browne, Francis of Soham. R for America Mar 1686. Ca.
Brown, Francis. S s horses Lent R 14 yrs Summer 1756. Sy.
Brown, Francis. S Jun T Sep 1767 *Justitia*. M.
Brown, George. S & T Oct 1730 *Forward* LC Potomack Jan 1731. M.
Browne, George. TB to Va from QS 1740. De.
Brown, George. S Feb T Apr 1743 *Justitia*. M.
Brown, George. SQS & TB Apr 1750. So.
Brown, George. S & R 14 yrs Summer 1767. Nl.
Brown, George. R 14 yrs Summer 1768 s sheep. We.
Brown, George. R Dec 1773. M.
Browne, Grace. R for America Feb 1692. Db.
Browne, Grace. S 14 yrs Dec 1727. M.

Brown als Scott, Hannah. S Feb 1774. L.
Browne, Helen. R for Barbados Dec 1681. L.
Browne, Henry of Walpole. R for America Jly 1702. Su.
Brown, Henry (1737). *See* Browny. Y.
Brown, Henry. SQS Apr T May 1750 *Lichfield*. M.
Brown, Henry. S Summer 1753. Nl.
Brown, Henry (1755). *See* Brown, John. M.
Brown, Henry. S s at Bray Lent 1765. Be.
Browne, Hugh. R for Jamaica Aug 1661. L.
Browne, Hugh of Chorley, hatmaker. R for Barbados Jly 1683. La.
Brown, Hugh (1741). *See* King. Cu.
Brown, Hugh. R for life Mar 1765 TB to Va. De.
Brown, Isabella. S Oct 1742 T 14 yrs Apr 1743 *Justitia*. M.
Brown, James. S Jan T 14 yrs Feb 1719 *Worcester* to Md but died on
    passage. L.
Brown, James. R 14 yrs Jly 1735. Ha.
Brown als Butler, James. S Jly 1737. Wi.
Brown, James. S Aug T Oct 1741 *Sea Horse* to Va. M.
Brown, James. S s sheep Lent R 14 yrs Summer 1742. O.
Brown, James. T Apr 1743 *Justitia*. K.
Brown, James. S Sep-Oct 1748 T Jan 1749 *Laura*. M.
Browne, James. S Jan-Apr 1749. M.
Brown als Thompson, James. S May-Jly 1749. M.
Brown, James. T May 1751 *Tryal*. E.
Brown, James. T May 1751 *Tryal*. Sy.
Brown, James. S Lent 1754. Y.
Brown, James. S s silver tumbler at St. Mary, Stafford, Lent 1761 T *Atlas*
    from Bristol. St.
Brown, James. R for life Jly 1763. M.
Brown, James. S s from bleaching ground at Pickering Lent TB Oct
    1764. Y.
Brown, James. S Oct 1766 T Jan 1767 *Tryal*. L.
Brown, James. S s at Sheffield Summer 1768. Y.
Brown, James. T 14 yrs Apr 1769 *Forward*. K.
Brown, James. S s at St. Nicholas Lent 1771. G.
Brown als MacDonald, James. S & T Jly 1772 *Tayloe*. L.
Brown, James. S Summer 1773. Ht.
Brown, James. S Lent 1774. G.
Brown, James. S Lent 1774. Sx.
Browne, Jane (1697). *See* Jenkins. L.
Browne, Jane (1697). *See* Pretious. L.
Browne, Jane. R for Barbados or Jamaica Dec 1698. L.
Brown, Jane. S & T Feb 1719 *Worcester* LC Annapolis Jun 1719. M.
Brown, Jane. T Oct 1723 *Forward*. K.
Browne, Jane. S & T Oct 1729 *Forward* LC Va Jun 1730. M.
Brown, Jane. S Feb T Mar 1750 *Tryal*. M.
Brown, Jane wife of William. S s at Bettws Lent 1751. Mo.
Brown als Delapp, Jane. S Jly T Sep 1767 *Justitia*. M.
Brown, Jane. S Apr T Jly 1770 *Scarsdale*. M.
Browne, Jervase. R Jly 1679. Db.
Browne, Joane. AT Oct 1697. M.

Browne, Joanna. R Oct 1694 AT Jan 1695. M.
Brown, Jocelyn. SQS Sep T Dec 1763 *Neptune*. M.
Browne, John. R for Va Mar 1618 (SP). K.
Browne, John. S Lent R for Barbados May 1664. E.
Browne, John of Plucknett, husbandman. R for Barbados Feb 1665. So.
Browne, John of Ingrave. R (Newgate) for Barbados Apr TB Oct 1669. E.
Browne, John of Bermondsey. R for Barbados or Jamaica Feb 1684. Sy.
Browne, John (3). Rebels T 1685.
Browne, John of Great Hoole. R for Barbados Jly 1685. La.
Browne, John. R for America Jly 1694. No.
Browne als Beazely, John of West Wycombe. R for Barbados or Jamaica Mar 1697. Bu.
Brown als Smith, John of St. Nicholas, Rochester. S Lent T May 1719 *Margaret* but died on passage. K.
Brown, John. S Mar 1724. So.
Brown, John. S Aug T Oct 1724 *Forward* LC Annapolis Jun 1725. M.
Brown, John (1727). *See* Broom. L.
Brown, John. S s at Wolverhampton Lent 1729. St.
Brown, John. S & R 14 yrs Summer 1729 T Summer 1730. Y.
Browne, John. S & T Sep 1731 *Smith* to Va. M.
Brown, John. S Sep T Dec 1734 *Caesar* to Va but died on passage. M.
Brown, John. S Lent 1735. Y.
Brown, John. S Jly 1735. M.
Brown, John. S Jan-May T Jun 1738 *Forward* to Md or Va. M.
Brown, John. T Apr 1741 *Speedwell* or *Mediterranean*. E.
Brown, John. S Sep T Nov 1743 *George William*. L.
Brown, John. S Dec 1743 T Feb 1744 *Neptune* to Md. M.
Brown, John. S Lent 1746. Nf.
Brown, John (1747). *See* Stanley. M.
Brown, John. S May-Jly 1748. M.
Brown, John. S Jan-Apr 1749. M.
Brown, John. S Jly 1749. L.
Brown, John (1750). *See* Kingston. L.
Brown, John. S Oct-Dec 1750. M.
Brown, John. SQS Jly T Sep 1751 *Greyhound*. M.
Brown, John. S Mar 1752. Ha.
Brown, John. T Apr 1753 *Thames*. K.
Brown, John. T 14 yrs Dec 1753 *Whiteing*. Sy.
Brown, John. T 14 yrs Dec 1753 *Whiteing*. K.
Brown, John als Henry. S Jan 1755. M.
Browne, John. TB Oct 1756. Nf.
Brown, John. S May T Sep 1757 *Thetis*. M.
Brown, John. S Lent 1758. Hu.
Brown, John. S Oct T Dec 1758 *The Brothers*. L.
Brown, John of Rotherhithe. SQS Jan T Apr 1759 *Thetis*. Sy.
Brown, John. SQS Jan T Mar 1760 *Friendship*. M.
Brown, John. S s fowls at St. Mary, Oxford, Lent 1760. O.
Brown, John. R 14 yrs s sheep Summer 1762. Li.
Brown, John. S Dec 1762 T Mar 1763 *Neptune*. M.
Brown, John. S Lent 1763. Li.

Brown, John. S Sep T Dec 1763 *Neptune*. M.
Brown, John. S Jan R Feb T for life Mar 1764 *Tryal*. M.
Brown, John. T Jun 1764 *Dolphin*. M.
Brown, John. S & T Sep 1764 *Justitia*. L.
Brown, John (1765). *See* Atkinsdon, William. Y.
Brown, John. T Sep 1765 *Justitia*. Sy.
Brown, John (1767). *See* Willington. Sh.
Brown als Mayer als Major, John. S s at Streatley Summer 1767. Bd.
Brown, John. S s razors & scissors at St. Dunstan in East Jan T Apr
    1768 *Thornton*. L.
Brown, John. SQS Mar T Apr 1768 *Thornton*. Sy.
Brown, John. T 14 yrs Apr 1770 *New Trial*. Sy.
Brown, John. S Apr T Jly 1770 *Scarsdale*. M.
Brown, John. S s at Somersham Summer 1770. Hu.
Brown, John. R Aug 1770. Wi.
Brown, John. T Dec 1770 *Justitia*. Sy.
Brown, John. S s at Wolstanton Lent 1772. St.
Browne, John. R 14 yrs Aug 1772. So.
Browne, John. SQS Ipswich Feb 1773. Su.
Brown, John. S Summer 1773. E.
Brown, John. S Apr 1774. L.
Browne, Jonas. Rebel T 1685.
Browne, Joseph, apprentice carpenter. R for America Feb 1700. No.
Brown, Joseph of Harborne. R for America Feb 1714. St.
Browne, Joseph. S Feb T Mar 1730 *Patapsco* to Md but died on
    passage. M.
Brown, Joseph. S Norwich Summer 1756 R 14 yrs Summer 1757. Nf.
Brown, Joseph. S Oct T Dec 1767 *Neptune*. L.
Brown, Joseph. T 14 yrs Apr 1769 *Tryal*. K.
Brown, Joseph. S Oct 1772. L.
Browne, Margaret, spinster, als wife of John. R for Barbados Jly 1663. L.
Browne als Jones, Margaret. S & T Oct 1729 *Forward* but died on
    passage. M.
Browne, Margaret. S & T Oct 1730 *Forward* LC Potomack Jan 1731. M.
Browne, Margaret wife of Edward. S Jan-May 1738. M.
Browne, Marina. R for Barbados Dec 1693 AT Jan 1694. M.
Brown, Mark. S Jan-Feb 1774. M.
Browne, Martha. R for Barbados Jun 1665. L.
Browne, Martha. S Aug T Oct 1724 *Forward* LC Annapolis Jun 1725. M.
Browne, Martin of St. Saviour, Southwark. SQS Oct 1774. Sy.
Browne, Mary (1688). *See* Spencer, Ann. Sy.
Brown, Mary. R 14 yrs Mar 1721 T *Gilbert* but died on passage. Co.
Brown, Mary (1726). *See* Phillips. M.
Browne, Mary. S May T Jun 1727 *Susanna* to Va. M.
Brown, Mary. S & T Oct 1730 *Forward* LC Potomack Jan 1731. M.
Brown, Mary wife of Sexton. S Jly T Dec 1734 *Caesar* LC Va Jly
    1735. M.
Browne, Mary. S Jly T 14 yrs Sep 1737 *Pretty Patsy*. L.
Brown, Mary of St. James Clerkenwell, spinster. S s gown Oct 1740 T
    Jan 1741 *Harpooner* to Rappahannock. M.
Brown, Mary (1743). *See* White. Nl.

Brown, Mary. S Jun T Oct 1744 *Susannah*. M.
Brown, Mary wife of Daniel. R 14 yrs Aug 1746 TB to Va Jun 1747. Wi.
Browne, Mary. TB to Va from QS 1748. De.
Brown, Mary. S Dec 1748 T Jan 1749 *Laura*. M.
Brown als Morley, Mary. S Jan-Apr 1749. M.
Brown, Mary. S Oct-Dec 1750. M.
Brown, Mary (1751). *See* Smith. M.
Brown, Mary. S Oct 1751-Jan 1752. M.
Brown, Mary. S Feb-Apr T May 1752 *Lichfield*. M.
Brown, Mary. SQS Feb T Apr 1753 *Thames*. M.
Brown, Mary (1753). *See* Smith. M.
Brown, Mary. S May-Jun T Jly 1753 *Tryal*. M.
Brown, Mary. SQS Jly T Nov 1759 *Phoenix*. M.
Brown, Mary (1762). *See* Thomson. M.
Brown, Mary. S Dec 1763 T Mar 1764 *Tryal*. M.
Brown, Mary (1766). *See* Wright. M.
Brown, Mary. S Feb T 14 yrs Apr 1766 *Ann*. M.
Brown, Mary wife of Benjamin. S Oct T Dec 1767 *Neptune*. L.
Brown, Mary wife of Henry. S Jly 1771 TB to Va Apr 1772. Wi.
Brown, Mary. S Apr 1775. M.
Browne, Michael. S Summer R for Barbados Aug 1663. Sy.
Brown, Moses. S s pigs at Caversham Summer 1773. O.
Brown, Peter. S s at Eland Lodge, Forest of Needwood, Lent 1733. St.
Brown, Peter. S as pickpocket Summer 1742 R 14 yrs Lent 1743. Li.
Brown, Peter. S Oct 1749. L.
Brown, Philip of Capley. R for America Feb 1713. St.
Brown, Philip. S Jan T Jun 1738 *Forward* to Md or Va. M.
Browne, Phillis. S Jan T Feb 1733 *Smith* to Md or Va. M.
Browne, Richard. R for America Jly 1686. Nt.
Browne, Richard (1700). *See* Howlin. L.
Browne, Richard. PT Oct 1699 R Aug 1700. M.
Browne, Richard. S Jly T Aug 1721 *Prince Royal* LC Va Nov 1721. L.
Brown, Richard. S Apr 1742. Ha.
Brown, Richard. S Lent 1750. La.
Brown, Richard. S Aug 1758. So.
Brown, Richard. S Summer 1759 R 14 yrs Lent T Apr 1760 *Thetis*. K.
Brown, Richard. S Apr 1773. L.
Browne, Robert (1669). *See* Miller. De.
Browne, Robert. R Jly 1679. Db.
Browne, Robert of Allington. R for Barbados Jly 1683. Nl.
Browne, Robert. R for America Jly 1683. Nt.
Browne als Beames als Betty, Robert. R for Barbados or Jamaica Mar
    1688. M.
Brown, Robert. S s cloth from tenters Lent 1719 R 14 yrs Summer 1721
    T Oct 1723 *Forward* from London. Y.
Brown, Robert, als Glenton, John. S s horse Lent 1720 R 14 yrs Summer
    1721 T Oct 1723 *Forward* from London. Y.
Brown, Robert. T Oct 1720 *Gilbert*. Ht.
Brown, Robert. S Jly 1766. Ha.
Brown, Robert. S Mar 1771 TB to Va. De.
Brown, Robert. S s horse & R 7 yrs Summer 1772. Nl.

Browne als Hamlet, Robert. S s horse & R 14 yrs Lent 1774. G.

Brown, Rose. T Nov 1741 *Sea Horse*. E.

Browne, Samuel of Wymondham. R for Barbados Aug 1671. Nf.

Brown, Samuel. S Lent 1746. Hu.

Browne, Samuel Jr. SQS Ipswich Jly 1773. Su.

Browne, Sarah (1683). *See* Bowen. M.

Browne, Sarah (1694). *See* Abraham. Ht.

Browne als Burroughes, Sarah. R for America Aug 1702; to be transported at her own charge or else executed. L.

Brown, Sarah. S Jly TB Oct 1735. Wi.

Brown, Sarah. S Sep 1740. L.

Brown, Sarah. S & T Apr 1741 *Speedwell* or *Mediterranean* to Md. M.

Brown, Sarah (1743). *See* Taylor. M.

Brown, Simon. T Apr 1766 *Ann*. Sy.

Brown, Susanna. S Jan T Apr 1734 *Patapsco* to Md. M.

Browne, Thomas. R for Barbados Jly 1674. L.

Browne, Thomas of St. Olave, Southwark. R for Barbados or Jamaica Jly 1674. Sy.

Browne, Thomas. PT Sep 1684 R Jly 1685. M.

Browne, Thomas. Rebel T 1685.

Brown, Thomas (1720). *See* Salter. K.

Brown als Cassill, Thomas. S Apr T May 1720 *Honor* LC Port York Jan 1721. L.

Brown, Thomas. T Oct 1723 *Forward*. Sy.

Brown, Thomas. S Jan T Feb 1726 *Supply* LC AAnapolis May 1726. M.

Brown, Thomas. T Oct 1726 *Forward*. E.

Brown, Thomas. S s sheep at Christchurch Summer 1729. Mo.

Brown, Thomas. S Lent R 14 yrs Summer 1731. No.

Brown, Thomas. S s at Wantage Lent 1735. Be.

Brown als Elkington, Thomas. S s gelding at Tilehurst Lent R Summer 1736. Be.

Brown, Thomas. S & T Dec 1736 *Dorsetshire*. L.

Browne, Thomas (1738). *See* Jones. M.

Brown, Thomas. S s tobacco Summer 1738. Be.

Brown, Thomas. S s heifers Summer 1739. St.

Brown, Thomas. S & T Feb 1744 *Neptune* to Md. M.

Browne, Thomas. S Lent R 14 yrs Summer T Oct 1744 *Susannah*. Sy.

Brown, Thomas. S Jly-Dec 1747. M.

Brown, Thomas. S s at Great Westbury Summer TB Aug 1749. G.

Brown, Thomas. S s sheep Lent R 14 yrs Summer 1753. Bu.

Brown, Thomas (1755). *See* Londen, John. Nf.

Brown, Thomas, als Lanham, Henry. S Jun T Sep 1758 *Tryal* to Annapolis. M.

Brown, Thomas. S Lent R 14 yrs Summer 1760. St.

Brown, Thomas. S Dec 1763 T Mar 1764 *Tryal*; found at large & ordered for transportation Sep 1765. L.

Brown, Thomas. S Feb T Mar 1764 *Tryal*. M.

Brown, Thomas (1765). *See* Savell, Ann (*sic*). M.

Brown, Thomas. S & T Apr 1765 *Ann*. L.

Brown, Thomas. T May 1767 *Thornton*. K.

Brown, Thomas. S Apr-May T Jly 1771 *Scarsdale*. M.

Brown, Thomas. S Summer 1772. Sy.

Brown, Thomas. S s malt at St. Helen, Abingdon, Summer 1773 Be.

Brown, Thomas. S Oct 1774. L.

Brown, Thomas. S May 1775. M.

Browne, Timothy, als Ferryman, Stephen of Prescott. SQS Jan 1770. La.

Browne, William. R (Home Circ) for Barbados Apr 1663. X.

Browne, William of Norton Folgate. R for Barbados Apr 1669. M.

Browne, William. R for Barbados Jly 1674. L.

Browne, William of Ongar. R for Barbados Jly 1678 & 1679. E.

Browne, William of Blackmore. R for Barbados or Jamaica Mar 1682 &
Feb 1683. E.

Browne, William. Rebel T 1685.

Browne, William of Wolverhampton. R for America Jun 1692. St.

Browne, William. R for Barbados or Jamaica Oct 1694. L.

Brown, William. R Dec 1699 & Aug 1700. M.

Browne, William of Selling. R for America Jly 1700. K.

Browne, William of Blyth, weaver. R for America Feb 1713. Nt.

Brown, William. S Jan 1723. M.

Brown, William. S Oct T Dec 1724 *Rappahannock* to Va. M.

Browne, William. S Mar 1727 & Mar 1728. Co.

Browne, William. S Oct T Dec 1735 *John*. L.

Brown, William of St. Giles in Fields. S s brass nails & T Jan 1740
York. M.

Brown, William. TB to Va from QS 1741. De.

Brown, William. S Jan T Feb 1742 *Industry* to Md. M.

Brown, William. S to hang Summer 1743 for being at large after
sentence of transportation. Nl.

Brown, William. S & T Feb 1744 *Neptune*. L.

Brown, William. S Jan T 14 yrs Feb 1744 *Neptune* to Md. M.

Brown, William (1751). *See* Davis. Be.

Brown, William. T May 1751 *Tryal*. M.

Brown, William. S Jly-Sep 1754. M.

Brown, William. R 14 yrs Mar 1756. Do.

Browne, William. S s wheat at Hereford Summer 1757. He.

Brown, William of Halstead. SQS Oct 1761 T Apr 1762 *Neptune*. E.

Brown, William. S Lent 1763. Wa.

Brown, William. S Oct T Dec 1763 *Neptune*. M.

Brown, William. S Aug T for life Sep 1764 *Justitia*. L.

Brown, William of Berkhampstead St. Peter. SQS & T Apr 1766
Ann. Ht.

Brown, William of Lancaster. SQS Jan 1767. La.

Brown, William of Wood Ditton. S s bullocks Lent R 14 yrs Summer
1767. Ca.

Brown, William. T 14 yrs Aug 1769 *Douglas*. Sy.

Brown, William. S s horse & R 7 yrs Summer 1772. Nl.

Brown, William. S Summer T Sep 1773. Wa.

Browne, William. S Feb 1774. L.

Brown, William Trueman. S Jan-Feb T Apr 1772 *Thornton*. M.

Brownfield, Elizabeth. T 14 yrs Apr 1768 *Thornton*. K.

Browning, Charles of St. Saviour, Southwark. R for Barbados or
Jamaica Jly 1687. Sy.

Browning, Elizabeth. S Summer 1731. Sh.

Browning, George Jr. of Bristol. R for life for murder Apr 1774. G.

Browning, James. S Jly T Aug 1721 *Prince Royal* LC Va Nov 1721. M.

Browning, John. S Jly 1722. Ha.

Browning, John. T May 1744 *Justitia*. Sx.

Browning, John. S May T Jly 1770 *Scarsdale*. M.

Browning, Joseph. S s mare & R Lent 1766. Su.

Browning, Joseph. S Jan-Feb 1775. M.

Browning als Brinning, Thomas. R 14 yrs Mar 1760 TB to Va. De.

Browning, William. S Lent 1748. Nf.

Browning, William. S Aug 1765. So.

Brownsmith, Digby. S s sheep Lent R 14 yrs Summer 1751. Su.

Brownsword, William of Northampton, baker. R for America Feb 1700. No.

Browny als Brown, Henry. S s horse Lent 1737 R 14 yrs Summer 1738. Y.

Browse, Thomas (1724). *See* Bruffe. M.

Broxham, Jane. S Summer 1765. Li.

Broxton, Thomas. S Jan T Apr 1743 *Justitia*. M.

Brozon, Jane. S Jly-Dec 1747. M.

Bruce, Charles. S Feb-Apr T May 1751 *Tryal*. M.

Bruce, George of St. George Hanover Square. SW Oct 1766 T Jan 1767 *Tryal*. M.

Bruce, Henry. S Mar 1751. Ha.

Bruce, John. S 14 yrs Jly-Dec 1747. M.

Bruce, Robert. S City Summer 1739. Nl.

Bruce, Rosamond. S Dec 1727. M.

Bruce, Samuel. S s at Sheffield Summer 1768. Y.

Bruce, William. S Mar 1772. So.

Brudenell, Charlot. TB 14 yrs Oct 1719 T *Susannah & Sarah* LC Annapolis Apr 1720. L.

Bruel. *See* Brewell.

Bruenna, Margaret. S Jun T Sep 1758 *Tryal*. L.

Bruff. *See* Brough.

Brugmore, Lucy. S Aug 1763. L.

Brunt, George. S for shooting with intent to rob Lent R 14 yrs Summer 1765. St.

Brunt, Sara. TB 14 yrs Oct 1719. L.

Brunton, William. S s sow at Honingham Summer 1772. Nf.

Bryan, Anne (1729). *See* Smith. M.

Bryan, Ann (1765). *See* Turner, Sarah. M.

Bryan, Catharine. S Jan-Jun T Jun 1728 *Elizabeth* LC Potomack Aug 1729. L.

Bryan, Catherine. S 14 yrs Apr 1773. M.

Bryan, Darby. S Sep T Oct 1719 *Susannah & Sarah* LC Annapolis Apr 1720. L.

Bryan, Eleanor wife of Thomas. S & T Sep 1731 *Smith* but died on passage. M.

Bryan, Elizabeth. R for Barbados or Jamaica May AT Jly 1697. M.

Bryan, Elizabeth. T Oct 1726 *Forward*. Sy.

Bryan, Elizabeth. S Apr T Nov 1759 *Phoenix*. M.

Bryan, George. S Jan T Apr 1735 *Patapsco* LC Annapolis Oct 1735. M.
Bryan, Hugh, ship carpenter. R (Western Circ) for Barbados Jly 1688. L.
Bryan, James. S Sep-Dec 1755 T Jan 1756 *Greyhound*. M.
Bryan, James. S Apr 1763; wife Sarah acquitted. M.
Bryan, James. S Oct T Dec 1767 *Neptune*. L.
Bryan, James. S 14 yrs for receiving goods stolen by Rachel Bryan *(qv)*
    Lent 1772. Y.
Bryan, John. S Summer 1736 R 14 yrs Summer 1737. Y.
Bryan, John. S Feb-Apr T May 1752 *Lichfield*. M.
Bryan, John. S Mar 1761. Ha.
Bryan, John. S Summer 1763. La.
Bryan, John. S May T Sep 1765 *Justitia*. M.
Bryan, John. T 3 yrs Apr 1770 *New Trial*. Sy.
Bryan, Joseph. S Apr T May 1720 *Honor*. L.
Bryan, Lawrence. S Jan 1757. M.
Bryan, Lowry. R for America Aug 1715. M.
Bryan, Martha. S s at All Saints, Worcester, Lent 1751. Wo.
Bryan, Mary. S s at Eaton Lent 1744. Sh.
Brien, Patrick of St. Martin in Fields. SW Jan 1774. M.
Bryan, Rachel wife of James *(qv)*. S s at Leeds Lent 1772. Y.
Bryan, Stephen als Thomas. S Summer 1772. Wa.
Bryan, Thomas. R for America Jly 1694. No.
Bryan, Thomas. S Jun T Aug 1769 *Douglas*. M.
Bryan, William. R for America Jly 1694. No.
Brian, William. T May 1737 *Forward*. E.
Bryan, William. S Mar 1761. So.
Bryan, William. R 14 yrs Aug 1766. So.
Bryant, Ann. S Lent 1775. K.
Bryant, Bernard. Rebel T 1685.
Bryant, Daniel. SQS Dec 1774. M.
Bryant, Hugh of North Mimms. R for Barbados or Jamaica Jly
    1687. Ht.
Bryant, James (1721). *See* Waters. So.
Bryant, Jane wife of John. SQS Oct 1742 TB to Md Feb 1743. So.
Bryant, Joan. S Mar 1744. So.
Briant, John (1742). *See* Joyner. Do.
Bryant, John. S Dec 1753-Jan 1754. M.
Bryant, John. SQS New Sarum Jan TB to Va Apr 1765. Wi.
Bryant, Martha (1759). *See* Eacot. Wi.
Bryant, Mary (1683). *See* Marshall. M.
Bryant, Mary. TB to Va from QS 1768. De.
Bryant, Michael. S Sep-Oct 1773. M.
Bryant, Patrick. SQS Sep 1771. M.
Bryant, Richard. S Feb T Mar 1727 *Rappahannock* to Md. M.
Bryant, Richard. S Summer 1757 R 14 yrs Lent 1758. Be.
Bryant, Richard. S Jan T Apr 1762 *Dolphin*. L.
Bryant als Hooper, Roger. Rebel T 1685.
Bryand als Bryant als Bryan, Rowland of St. Clement Danes. SW Apr
    1777. M.
Bryant, Samuel. SQS Jly 1774. M.
Bryant, Samuel. S May 1775. L.

Bryant, Thomas. S s at Stapleton Lent TB Mar 1752. G.

Bryant, Thomas. T Jun 1764 *Dolphin*. K.

Bryant, William (1721). *See* Birtles. So.

Bryant, William. SQS Jly 1741 TB to Md May 1742. So.

Bryant, William. TB to Va from QS 1745. De.

Bryar, Henry of Culmstock, husbandman. R for Barbados Apr 1668. De.

Bryer, John. Rebel T 1685.

Bryde. *See* Bride.

Bryden, Robert. R 14 yrs Summer 1774. We.

Buchanon, Alexander. SWK Apr 1772. K.

Buck, Benjamin. S Lent R 14 yrs Summer 1760. Su.

Bucke, Elizabeth. S s hemp yarn at Berrington Summer 1768. Sh.

Buck, Esther. S Jun T Oct 1774 *Susannah*. M.

Buck, George. T May 1751 *Tryal*. Sy.

Buck als Churches, Jeremiah of Frocester. R for America Jly 1698. G.

Buck, John. S Lent 1775. K.

Buck, Mary. SW & T Jan 1769 *Thornton*. M.

Buck, Peter. S Jan T Apr 1734 *Patapsco* to Md. M.

Buck, Thomas. S Lent R 14 yrs Summer 1760. Su.

Buckeridge, James of Bermondsey. SQS Apr T May 1750 *Lichfield*. Sy.

Buckeridge, Ruth. S Jly 1756. M.

Buckhurst, Elizabeth. S & T Jun 1756 *Lyon*. L.

Buckingham, Ann. S Aug T Oct 1726 *Forward*. L.

Buckingham, John. S s poultry at Appleton Lent 1743. Be.

Buckingham, Joseph. S s sheep at Dinton & R Lent 1775. Bu.

Buckingham, Mary. S & T Oct 1732 *Caesar* to Va. M.

Buckingham, Richard (1694). *See* Breed, Thomas. M.

Buckingham, Thomas. S s fowls Lent 1755. Be.

Buckingham, Thomas. S s sheep at Dinton & R Lent 1775. Bu.

Buckingham, William. S s sheep at Haresfield Lent R 14 yrs Summer 1762. G.

Buckland, John. S Jun T Sep 1758 *Tryal*. L.

Buckland, Thomas, als Buckley, Humphrey. S Jly-Sep 1754. M.

Buckland, Walter. S Oct T 14 yrs Dec 1758 *The Brothers*. L.

Buckland, William (1735). *See* Butler. M.

Buckle, Benjamin. S Jan-Jun 1747. M.

Buckle, Constance. S 14 yrs Feb T Mar 1731 *Patapsco* LC Annapolis Jun 1731. M.

Buckle, Daniel of Broxbourne. S for infanticide Summer 1745 R 14 yrs Lent 1746. Ht.

Buckle, Elizabeth. S Aug T Oct 1723 *Forward* to Va. M.

Buckle, Elizabeth. S Mar 1763. Ha.

Buckle, Henry. S Jly 1773. Ha.

Buckle, John. S Lent R 14 yrs Summer 1750. Ru.

Buckle, Robert. S s wheat at Thwaite Lent 1769. Su.

Buckle, Samuel of Weely. R for Barbados or Jamaica Jly 1704. E.

Buckle, William of Catterick, tinker. SQS Thirsk Apr TB Aug 1758. Y.

Buckler, Charles of Friern Barnet R Mar AT Apr 1685. M.

Buckles, Dorothy. S Feb-Apr 1745. M.

Buckley, Abraham of Crompton. SQS Jun 1767. La.

Buckley, Butler. T Jan 1736 *Dorsetshire.* Sy.
Buckley, Cornelius of Whitechapel. S s looking glass & T May 1740
    Essex. M.
Buckley, Daniel. S Dec 1750. L.
Buckley, Edward. T Jun 1738 *Forward.* Sy.
Buckley, Elizabeth. S Lent T Apr 1771. Wa.
Buckley, Francis. R for Barbados or Jamaica Dec 1695 & Jan 1697. M.
Buckley, Francis. S May-Jly 1748. M.
Buckley, Humphrey (1754). *See* Buckland, Thomas. M.
Buckley, James. S Oct 1740. L.
Buckley, Jane (1763). *See* Blake. M.
Buckley, John. T Dec 1752 *Greyhound.* M.
Buckley, Jonas. S Summer 1758 R 14 yrs Lent 1759. Be.
Buckley, Joseph. S s horse Lent R Summer 1739 (SP). Sh.
Buckley, Mary. S s coffee pot Jun T Dec 1736 *Dorsetshire* to Va. M.
Buckley, Mary. S Oct T Dec 1758 *The Brothers.* L.
Buckley, Thomas. S Lent 1758. No.
Buckley, Timothy. R Jly TB to Va Sep 1774. Wi.
Bucklinghorn, Sarah. S & T Sep 1765 *Justitia.* M.
Buckmaster, John of R—-bury. R for Barbados Jly 1664. Be.
Bucknall, Humphrey of Birmingham. R for America Feb 1681. Wa.
Bucknell, John. S Lent R 14 yrs Summer 1752. Li.
Bucknole, Joseph. TB to America from QS 1751. De.
Bucknell als Foot, Magdalen. S Feb T Mar 1731 *Patapsco* LC Md Jun
    1731. L.
Bucknell, William. S Oct T Dec 1724 *Rappahannock.* L.
Bucktrout, Martha. T Dec 1752 *Greyhound.* M.
Buckworth, Thomas. S s cheese Lent 1740. Wo.
Budbrook, John (1744). *See* Preston. De.
Budd, Ann. S Apr-May T May 1744 *Justitia.* M.
Budd, Elizabeth. R for Barbados Jun 1663. M.
Budd, Elizabeth wife of Thomas of Gravesend. R for Barbados or
    Jamaica Jly 1715. K.
Budd, Henry. S Feb T Mar 1730 *Patapsco* LC Annapolis Sep 1730. L.
Budd, John (1700). *See* Bird. M.
Budd, John. S Aug 1756. So.
Budd, Josias. R 14 yrs MAr 1758. De.
Budd, Mary. S & T Oct 1729 *Forward* LC Va Jun 1730. L.
Budd, Robert. S & T Dec 1734 *Caesar* LC Va Jly 1735. L.
Budd, Robert. S Dec 1742 T 14 yrs Mar 1743 *Justitia.* L.
Budd, Thomas (1700). *See* Bird. M.
Budd, Thomas. S May T Jly 1722 *Alexander.* L.
Budd, Thomas. R 14 yrs Jly 1724. De.
Budding, Thomas of Berkeley. R for America Jly 1687. G.
Buddington, Cain. S s cloth Lent R 14 yrs Summer 1768. St.
Budds, Elizabeth. SQS Ipswich Jly 1774. Su.
Budge, John. Rebel T 1685.
Budwell, John of Ampthill. R for America Apr 1697. Bd.
Bue. *See* Bew.
Buff, Henry. S s mare Lent R 14 yrs Summer 1758. Nf.
Bugby, Samuel of Ware. R (Newgate) for Barbados Aug 1668. Ht.

Bugden, Jane of Tarrant Kingston. R for Barbados Jly 1681. Do.
Bugdon, John als Samuel. S May T 14 yrs Jun 1738 *Forward*. L.
Bugden, Tobias. S Feb T Apr 1734 *Patapsco*. L.
Bugg, John. S Lent 1748. Su.
Bugg als Atkinson als Parker, Richard. S s horse Summer 1753 R 14 yrs
    Lent 1754. Li.
Buggs, Phoebe. S Summer 1745. K.
Buglar, Thomas. Rebel T 1685.
Bulbeck, Thomas. S for assault on Customs officer Summer 1773. Sx.
Bulbrooke, William. S Jan T Sep 1737 *Pretty Patsy* to Md. M.
Buley. *See* Beaulieu.
Bulger, John. SW & T Oct 1768 *Justitia*. M.
Bulger, Judith wife of James of St. Saviour, Southwark. SQS & T Jan
    1767 *Tryal*. Sy.
Bulger, Mary (1749). *See* Quin. M.
Bulger, Mary (1752). *See* Ryley. M.
Bulger, Mary. S Jan T for life Apr 1762 *Dolphin*. L.
Bull, Edward (1770). *See* Pope. Do.
Bull, Henry. T May 1737 *Forward*. Sy.
Bull, James. S Feb T Mar 1730 *Patapsco* to Md. M.
Bull, Jane. T Jan 1766 *Tryal*. M.
Bull, John. LC Annapolis Md Jun 1725 from *Forward*. X.
Bull, John. S & R Lent T *Patapsco* May 1736. Bu.
Bull, John. S & T Jan 1739 *Dorsetshire*. L.
Bull, John. S Summer 1773. Sy.
Bull, Joseph. S Jly 1766. Ha.
Bull, Joseph. R Mar 1774. So.
Bull, Mary wife of John of St. Paul Shadwell. S s clothing & T Dec 1740
    Vernon. M.
Bull, Mathew. T Oct 1720 *Gilbert* but died on passage. E.
Bull, Samuel. S Summer 1760. Wa.
Bull, Stephen of Bisley. R for America Jly 1699. G.
Bull, Thomas (1720). *See* Butler. L.
Bull, Thomas. AT Summer 1742. Wo.
Bull, William. Rebel T 1685.
Bull, William. S Apr-Jun 1739. M.
Bull, William Sr. S Mar 1757. So.
Bullard, William. S Lent 1745. *Su.
Bullen, Elizabeth. S & T Dec 1734 *Caesar* LC Va Jly 1735. L.
Bullen, James. T 14 yrs Oct 1768 *Justitia*. Sy.
Bullen, James. T 14 yrs Apr 1771 *Thornton*. Sy.
Bullen, John of Walton on Thames. R for Barbados or Jamaica Jly
    1674. Sy.
Bullen, Joseph. T Aug *Owners Goodwill* LC Md Nov 1721. Sy.
Bullen, Joseph. S May T Jly 1723 *Alexander* LC Annapolis Sep 1723. L.
Bullen, Richard. S Feb-Apr T May 1752 *Lichfield*. M.
Buller, James. S s silver knee buckles at Cripplegate Feb T Apr 1768
    Thornton. L.
Bulling, Richard. T Jan 1738 *Dorsetshire*. E.
Bullivant, John. S Mar R 14 yrs & TB Sep 1727. Nt.
Bullivant, Joseph. S Jun T Dec 1736 *Dorsetshire* to Va. M.

Bullivant, Robert. S s horse Lent R 14 yrs Summer TB Aug 1730. Nt.
Bullivant, Thomas. S s mare Summer 1741 R 14 yrs Lent 1742. No.
Bullman, John. S & T Oct 1722 *Forward* LC Annapolis Jun 1723. M.
Bullman, Samuel. S Lent 1738. Nf.
Bullock, Abraham. S for burglary Lent R Summer 1721 (SP). Sh.
Bullock, Benjamin. S for assault with intent to rob Lent 1749. Nf.
Bullocke, Katherine (1662). *See* Ward. L.
Bullock, Catherine. S Feb 1754. L.
Bullock, Edmund. S s brass at Barrow Summer 1763. Sh.
Bullock, Edward of Kensington. S s lambs Jly 1740 T Jan 1741
    Harpooner to Rappahannock. M.
Bullock, Henry. S s clothing Sep 1736. M.
Bullock, James. T Oct 1738 *Genoa*. Sx.
Bullock, James. S Feb-Apr 1746. M.
Bullock, James. S s saddle at Adderbury Lent 1747. O.
Bullocke, John. R for Jamaica Mar 1665. L.
Bullock, John. S Apr T May 1718 *Tryal* LC Charles Town Aug 1718. L.
Bullock, John. S s barley at Besselsleigh Lent 1738. Be.
Bullock, John. S s at Wellington Summer 1751. He.
Bullock, John (1752). *See* Jones, William. G.
Bullock, Mary. R 14 yrs Summer T Oct 1739 *Duke of Cumberland*. Sy.
Bullock, Mary. S Lent 1746 R 14 yrs Lent 1747. He.
Bullock, Robert. S Jly TB to Va Oct 1742. Wi.
Bullock, Sarah. S s at Cwmcarvan Summer 1765. Mo.
Bullocke, Thomas. R for Jamaica Aug 1661. M.
Bullock, William. S Aug T Sep 1718 *Eagle* LC Charles Town Mar
    1719. L.
Bullock, William. S Feb T Apr 1734 *Patapsco* to Md. M.
Bullock, William. S & R Lent 1769. St.
Bullock, William. S May T Jly 1771 *Scarsdale*. L.
Bullowes, Alice of Stourbridge, widow. R for America Jly 1687. Wo.
Bullows, Joseph. S Lent 1774. St.
Bully, George (1740). *See* Rice. M.
Bully, Susanna. SQS Oct T Dec 1767 *Neptune*. M.
Bulmer, John of Whittlesey. R for Barbados or Jamaica Mar 1697. Hu.
Bulmer, Roger. S s sheep at North Frodingham & R 14 yrs Lent
    1772. Y.
Bulney, John. T Apr 1735 *Patapsco*. Sy.
Bult. *See* Bolt.
Bulwinkle, Thomas. S Nov T Dec 1752 *Greyhound*. L.
Bumstead, Harper John als Half a John. S tea at St. Matthew, Ipswich,
    Lent 1775. Su.
Bumpstead, Stephen. R for Barbados or Jamaica May 1684. L.
Bunce, James. S & T Dec 1770 *Justitia*. L.
Bunce, Margery. S Jly T 14 yrs Oct 1741 *Sea Horse*. L.
Bunce, Richard. S May T Jun 1764 *Dolphin*. M.
Bunch, Robert. S Apr T Jun 1742 *Bladon*. L.
Bundy, Elizabeth (1730). *See* Richardson. M.
Bunfield, John. S s sheep Lent R 14 yrs Summer 1767. Nf.
Bunfield, Thomas. S Lent 1767. Nf.
Bunker, Abraham (1754). *See* Bronkee. M.

Bunker, Henry Jr. R 14 yrs Aug 1739. De.
Bunker, Martha. SQS Jan T Mar 1764 *Tryal*. M.
Bunn, Durance. S Aug T Oct 1724 *Forward* LC Annapolis Jun 1725. M.
Bunn, Francis. S s hogs at Merton Lent 1771. Nf.
Bunn, John. S & R 14 yrs Lent 1735. Nf.
Bunn, John. S Jan T 14 yrs Feb 1744 *Neptune* to Md. M.
Bunn, Joseph of North Hall. R for Barbados or Jamaica Jly 1696. Ht.
Bunn, Thomas of Stoke Newington. S s fowls Jly-Sep T Sep 1742
    Forward. M.
Bunnell, Mary. S Feb T Apr 1765 *Ann*. L.
Bunnett, William. S Summer 1747. K.
Bunney, Bartholomew. S s guinea & T Dec 1758 *The Brothers*; wife
    Mary Ann to hang for receiving it. M.
Bunney als Stowe, Mary Anne. R Feb T for life Apr 1762 *Dolphin*. M.
Bunney, Ursula. R for Barbados Aug 1664. L.
Bunning, Elizabeth. S Lent 1759. Ca.
Bunton, John (1673). *See* Burton. M.
Bunworth, John. S Jan T Feb 1724 *Anne* to Carolina. M.
Bunyan, Ann. S Sep-Oct T Dec 1753 *Whiteing*. M.
Bunyan, John. S Lent 1756. Bd.
Bunyard, James. S & T Mar 1764 *Tryal*. L.
Buquoise, Daniel of Willindale. R for Barbados or Jamaica Jly 1715. E.
Burason, Sarah. S s at Elmbridge Lent 1729. Wo.
Burbage als Chapple, John, als Hutchins, Stephen of Almsea. R for
    Barbados Mar 1694. So.
Burbidge, Michael. S s horse Lent R 14 yrs Summer 1751. No.
Burbridge, Elizabeth. S Dec 1774. M.
Burbridge, John. SQS Mar 1752. Ha.
Burbridge, Thomas. S Jan T Apr 1772 *Thornton*. M.
Burbridge, William. SWK Jly T Dec 1700 *Justitia*. K.
Burch. *See* Birch.
Burchall, Earle. SQS Warminster Jly TB to Va Sep 1741. Wi.
Burcher, Margaret (1744). *See* Stansbury, Margaret. L.
Burcher, William. R 14 yrs Mar 1767. Ha.
Burchett, John of Mitcham. SQS Oct 1773. Sy.
Burchett, Mary. S Sep 1740. L.
Burchett, Thomas of Camberwell. SQS Jan T Mar 1764 *Tryal*. Sy.
Burchinough, Sarah wife of John. S Oct 1730 T 14 yrs Mar 1731
    Patapsco LC Annapolis Jun 1731. M.
Burchmore, William (1739). *See* Birch. M.
Burclare, James. S s at Cookham Summer 1769. Be.
Burd. *See* Bird.
Burdell, James. S Jan-Feb 1774. M.
Burden, Elizabeth. S & T Oct 1722 *Forward* to Md. M.
Burden, Elizabeth. S Oct 1727-Jun 1728 T 14 yrs Jun 1728 *Forward*. M.
Burden, James. S Apr 1742. Ha.
Burden, John. T Jun 1740 *Essex*. Ht.
Burdon, Joseph. S Mar 1741. Do.
Burden, Mary. S Lent 1738 R 14 yrs Summer 1739. Y.
Burdon, Mary. R 14 yrs Mar 1774. De.
Burden, Thomas. S Dec 1733 T Jan 1734 *Caesar* LC Va Jly 1734. M.

Burdett, Benjamin. S & T Apr 1733 *Patapsco* LC Annapolis Nov 1733. L.
Burditt, Benjamin. S Lent 1775. No.
Burditt, John. S Jan-Jun T Jun 1728 *Elizabeth* LC. M.
Burdett, Hester (1721). *See* Bennett. L.
Burdett, John. S Jly 1761. L.
Burdet, Robert. T Oct 1732 *Caesar*. K.
Burdett, Robert. S & R 14 yrs Lent 1738. Nf.
Burdus, John. S Feb T Apr 1741 *Speedwell* or *Mediterranean*. M.
Burford, Ann (1738). *See* Hicks. M.
Burford, Joseph (George). S Jan T Apr 1768 *Thornton*. M.
Burford, Martha. S Summer 1740. Wo.
Burford, Samuel. S & T Sep 1766 *Justitia*. M.
Burford, Thomas. S Mar 1774. Wi.
Burford, William. S s sheep Lent R 14 yrs Summer 1742. He.
Burgan, Elizabeth of St. George, Southwark. R for Barbados or Jamaica Jly 1715. Sy.
Burgan, Mary of Stanley, spinster. R for America Mar 1710. Y.
Burge, James of Cirencester. S s flour Summer TB Jly 1742. G.
Burge, John of Durley, husbandman. R for Barbados Jly 1664. So.
Burge, John. S Mar 1758. So.
Burge als Shelton, Mary. S Summer T Sep 1751 *Greyhound*. Sy.
Burge, Thomas. S & T Apr 1725 *Sukey* LC Annapolis Sep 1725. M.
Burge, Thomas Sr. S Aug 1773. So.
Burge, Thomas Jr. R Mar 1773. So.
Burgeman, John. S Mar TB to Va Apr 1741. Wi.
Burges, Charles. S & R 14 yrs Lent 1770. He.
Burgess, Edward. S & T Aug 1752 *Tryal*. L.
Burges, Elizabeth. S Summer R for Barbados Aug 1663. K.
Burgess, Elizabeth wife of Samuel. S Sep-Dec 1746. M.
Burgess, Elizabeth. S & T Apr 1769 *Tryal*. M.
Burgess, Frances wife of Thomas. S s household goods Sep T Dec 1736 *Dorsetshire*. M.
Burgess, Hannah. S Apr 1747. So.
Burgess, Henry. S s saddle at Bray Lent 1773. Be.
Burgess, Jane. S Feb T Mar 1729 *Patapsco* to Md but died on passage. M.
Burges, John. Rebel T 1685.
Burgess, John. S Feb T Mar 1730 *Patapsco* LC Annapolis Sep 1730. M.
Burgess, John. T Oct 1738 *Genoa*. K.
Burgis, John. S Jun-Dec 1738 T Jan 1739 *Dorsetshire*. M.
Burgess, John. S Lent 1745. Sy.
Burgess als Platt, John of Worsley and Manchester. SQS May 1751. La.
Burgess, John. S s gelding Lent R 14 yrs Summer 1765. La.
Burgess, John. S Mar 1768. Ha.
Burgess, John. S s at St. Michael Coslany, Norwich, Summer 1769. Nf.
Burges, John (1773). *See* Evans. St.
Burgesse, Jonas. T Oct 1721 *William & John*. K.
Burgiss, Joseph. S Feb-Apr T May 1752 *Lichfield*. M.
Burgess, Nathaniel of St. Thomas. SQS Jan T Apr 1753 *Thames*. Sy.
Burgess, Peter. S Oct T Dec 1724 *Rappahannock* to Va. M.
Burgess, Richard. S Jan T 14 yrs Feb 1742 *Industry* to Md. M.

Burges, Robert. R for America Feb 1683. Le.

Burgess, Samuel of Salford. SQS Feb 1755. La.

Burgess als Borges, Sarah wife of Philip. S at Hull for shoplifting Summer 1764. Y.

Burges, Thomas of Walton. R for America Jly 1678. No.

Burgis, Thomas of Fenny Stratford. R for Barbados or Jamaica Mar 1697. Bu.

Burgess, Thomas. S & T Mar 1763 *Neptune*. L.

Burges, Thomas. S Sep-Oct T Dec 1771 *Justitia*. M.

Burgess, Thomas. T Jly 1772 *Orange Bay*. Ht.

Burges, William. Died on passage in *Sukey* 1725. X.

Burgess, William. T Nov 1741 *Sea Horse*. Sx.

Burgess, William. S s wheat at Oddington Lent 1760. O.

Burgis, William. S & T Sep 1766 *Justitia*. L.

Burges, William. SQS May T Aug 1769 *Douglas*. M.

Burgin, John. S Feb T Apr 1765 *Ann*. L.

Burgis. *See* Burgess.

Burke, Alexander. S Jly T Sep 1766 *Justitia*. M.

Burk, Alice. S Apr T May 1743 *Indian Queen*. L.

Burk, Andrew. S May T Aug 1769 *Douglas*. M.

Burk, Ann. S May-Jun T Aug 1752 *Tryal*. M.

Burk, Catherine. S Feb-Apr 1746. M.

Birk, Eleanor. S & T Apr 1762 *Neptune*. M.

Burk, Frances wife of Edward. S Feb T Apr 1765 *Ann*. M.

Burk als Wellum, Jane. S May T Jly 1723 *Alexander* LC Md Sep 1723. M.

Burk, John. S Jan-Jun T Jun 1728 *Elizabeth* LC Potomack Aug 1729. M.

Burk, John. S Feb 1736. M.

Burk, John. S Feb T Apr 1765 *Ann*. L.

Burk, John of St. James Westminster. SW Oct 1774. M.

Burk, Leonard. S Aug T Oct 1724 *Forward* LC Annapolis Jun 1725. M.

Burk, Margaret. S Sep T Dec 1758 *The Brothers*. M.

Burke, Mary Ann. S Oct 1768. M.

Birk, Peter. S Sep T Dec 1770 *Justitia*. M.

Birk, Richard. S Dec 1742 T Mar 1743 *Justitia*. L.

Burk, Sarah. S s peruke Apr T Jun 1742 *Bladon*. L.

Burk, Thomas. S Jun T Nov 1743 *George William*. M.

Bourke als Carr, Thomas. S & T Jan 1767 *Tryal*. M.

Berk, Thomas (1772). *See* Hollis, William. M.

Burk, William. S Lent T May 1750 *Lichfield*. K.

Burke als Johnson, William. S Mar 1773. Ha.

Birkett, Samuel. SQS Feb T Mar 1750 *Tryal*. M.

Birkett, Samuel. S s mare & R 14 yrs Lent T Sep 1768. Li.

Burkett, Thomas. S Summer s wheat T *Neptune* Dec 1763. Bu.

Burkin, Elizabeth. R for Barbados or Jamaica Dec 1693. L.

Birks, John. S Sep-Oct 1772. M.

Burland, Richard. S Apr 1767. So.

Burle, Jane. S Jan 1746. M.

Burley, Elizabeth. R 14 yrs Aug 1750 TB to Va. De.

Burleigh, George of Woodham Walter. R for America Jly 1700. E.

Burley, John. S s at Kersall Summer 1737 R 14 yrs Lent 1738. St.

Burley, Robert. R 14 yrs Summer 1754. Y.
Burleigh, William (1729). *See* Taylor. L.
Burling, Michael. S Feb-Apr T May 1751 *Tryal*. M.
Burling, Thomas. S Sep-Oct 1772. M.
Burling, William. T Apr 1741 *Speedwell* or *Mediterranean*. Ht.
Burman als Moggridge, Richard. S Aug 1728. So.
Burman als Moggridge, Samuel. S Mar 1729. So.
Burn, Ann. S May-Jly 1746. M.
Burn, Ann. S May T Jun 1768 *Tryal*. M.
Burn, Ann. S s cloth Lent 1770. Nl.
Byrne, Anthony. R & T Apr 1735 *Patapsco* LC Annapolis Oct 1735. M.
Byrne, Arthur. R Oct 1772. M.
Burne, Charles. S Apr T Sep 1737 *Pretty Patsy* to Md. M.
Byrne, Garrett. S Feb T Apr 1766 *Ann*. M.
Burne, George. S Feb-Apr 1746. M.
Burn, Henry of Manchester. SQS Oct 1748. La.
Byrne, James of Charing. R for Barbados or Jamaica Jly 1710. K.
Byrne, James. S Mar 1763. Ha.
Byrne, James. SQS Jly T Sep 1764 *Justitia*. M.
Burn, James. S s copper halfpennies at St. Dionis Backchurch Jan T
    Apr 1768 *Thornton*. L.
Burn, Jeremiah. S May-Jly 1774. M.
Byrne, John. S May T Jun 1764 *Dolphin*. L.
Burne, John. S Feb T Apr 1765 *Ann*. L.
Byrne, John. SW & T Oct 1768 *Justitia*. M.
Burn, John. S Lent 1769 s at Sheffield. Y.
Burn, Judith. S Jly T Sep 1764 *Justitia*. M.
Burn, Luke. S s watch at All Saints, Newmarket, Summer 1774. Ca.
Burn, Mary, widow. S Summer 1720. Nl.
Burn, Mary. S Oct 1760. M.
Burn, Patrick. S Dec 1749-Jan 1750 T Mar 1750 *Tryal*. M.
Burn, Patrick. S Aug 1763. L.
Burne, Patrick. SQS Jun T Sep 1767 *Justitia*. M.
Burn, Patrick. S Mar 1768. Ha.
Burn, Patrick. R Jun T 14 yrs Aug 1769 *Douglas*. M.
Burn, Patrick. S Mar 1773. De.
Byrne, Peter. S Aug 1749. So.
Burn, Tanglis. S Summer 1756. Ht.
Burn, Thomas. R Jly 1773. M.
Burn, Timothy. S & T Apr 1741 *Mediterranean*. L.
Burn, Timothy. S Jan-Feb 1773. M.
Burne, Tobias. S Dec 1745. L.
Burn als Bern, William. S Sep 1743. M.
Burn, William. S May-Jly 1746. M.
Burn, William (1765). *See* Barnes.
Burn, William. S Oct 1765 T Jan 1766 *Tryal*. M.
Burnaby, Carew. S Sep T Dec 1758 *The Brothers*. M.
Burnall. *See* Burnell.
Burnard. *See* Bernard.
Burnby, Thomas. S s sheep Summer 1755 R 14 yrs Lent 1756. No.
Burnall, Elizabeth. S Aug 1757. So.

Burnell als Burnard, Mary. R 14 yrs Mar 1760 TB to Va 1761. De.

Burnell, Robert. R 14 yrs Aug 1754. So.

Burnell, Thomas. S Jan 1751. L.

Burnett, Alexander. AT Feb 1675. M.

Burnett, Edward. SQS Jly TB to Md Nov 1740. So.

Burnett, Elizabeth. S Jan-Apr 1749. M.

Burnett, James. S Feb T Jun 1738 *Forward*. L.

Burnett, John of Biskerthorpe. R for America Jly 1678. Li.

Burnett, John. S Jly 1727. Wi.

Burnett, Sir John. S for counterfeiting marriage indenture of 1697 between William Cotton & Elizabeth Wise, daughter of William Birkin & Walter Bridley of Coton Summer 1738 R 14 yrs Lent 1739. St.

Burnett, John. S Jly T Sep 1755 *Tryal*. L.

Burnett, John. S May T Aug 1769 *Douglas*. M.

Burnett, Joseph. S Mar TB to Va Apr 1767. Wi.

Burnett, Mary. SQS Jly TB Aug 1758. So.

Burnett, Richard. S 14 yrs Jly 1774. L.

Burnet, Robert. S Summer 1722 T Oct 1723. Y.

Burnett, Thomas. S Lent 1742. Sh.

Burnett, Thomas. S May T Jun 1764 *Dolphin*. L.

Burnett, Thomas Jr. S s horse & R Lent 1775. Y.

Bernett, William. S Mar 1725. Wi.

Burnett als Cole, William. S for highway robbery Summer 1736 R Lent 1737. Be.

Burnet, William. R 14 yrs Summer 1757. Y.

Burnham, Esther. S Jly-Sep T 14 yrs Sep 1742 *Forward*. M.

Burnham, James. S Feb T Apr 1766 *Ann*. M.

Burnham, John. S & T Oct 1730 *Forward* LC Potomak Jan 1731. L.

Burnham, John. S Dec 1750. L.

Burnham, John. S s lace at Turvey Lent 1770. Bd.

Burnham, John. SQS Feb 1773. M.

Burnham, John. S Jan 1775. M.

Burnham, Mary. S Sep-Oct 1773. M.

Burnam, Samuel. S Lent R Summer 1725 died on *Rappahannock*. No.

Burnham, Solomon. S Lent 1774. Sy.

Burneham, William. R for America Jly 1686. Li.

Burnham, William. SQS & TB Jan 1771. Db.

Burnish, Jane. S Feb T Mar 1760 *Friendship*. M.

Byrns, Matthew. S Summer 1742 R 14 yrs Summer 1743. St.

Burnstone, Samuel. S Aug T Oct 1724 *Forward* LC Annapolis Jun 1725. L.

Burr, William, a Quaker. R for plantations Jly 1665. (SP). Ht.

Burrard als Johnson, Samuel. S Feb T Mar 1730 *Patapsco* LC Md Sep 1730. M.

Burraway, Thomas. S Summer 1766 R 14 yrs Lent 1767.

Burrill, Anne, aged 18, fair. S & T Oct 1720 *Gilbert* LC Md May 1721. M.

Burrell, Benjamin. S s sheep Lent 1722. O.

Burrell, Elizabeth. S & T Dec 1759 *Phoenix*. M.

Burrell, George, als Black George, als Othello. S Mar TB to Va Apr 1772. Wi.

Barrale, John. S Aug T Oct 1723 *Forward* to Va. M.

Barrell, John. S s gun at Foy Lent 1738. He.

Barrell, John. S s bread & cheese Summer 1753. He.

Barrell, Lancelot (1748). *See* Barrett. M.

Barrel, Susanna. S Lent 1748. He.

Barrell, Thomas. S Oct 1766 T Jan 1767 *Tryal*. L.

Burrell, Thomas. S Jan-Feb 1773. M.

Burrell, Thomas. S for highway robbery at Hardwick & R for life Summer 1773. Bu.

Barrell, William. S for highway robbery Lent R 14 yrs Summer 1752. He.

Burrell, William. S & R 14 yrs Summer 1755; then R for 49th Regiment. Du.

Barrel, William. S s at Hampton Bishop Lent 1766. He.

Burridge, Charles. Rebel T 1685.

Burridge, Charles. S Oct T Dec 1769 *Justitia*. L.

Burridge, Hannah. S Feb T Mar 1730 *Patapsco* LC Annapolis Sep 1730. M.

Burridge, Henry (1744). *See* Austin, Valentine. Nf.

Burridge, John. T Jly 1724 *Robert*. E.

Burridge, John. S for obstructing Customs officer Summer 1737. Nf.

Burridge, Joseph. S Aug 1735. De.

Burridge, Matthew. R for Barbados Aug 1664. L.

Burrage, Richard. LC Annapolis Md Dec 1725 from *Forward*. X.

Burridge, Robert (2). Rebels T 1685.

Burridge, Robert. S for life Oct-Dec 1750. M.

Burridge, Thomas. Rebel T 1685.

Burridge, Thomas. S Mar 1735. So.

Burridge, Thomas. S Apr T May 1743 *Indian Queen*. M.8

Burrage, William. S Aug T 14 yrs Sep 1718 *Eagle* LC Charles Town Mar 1719. L.

Burridge, William. SQS Dec 1768 T Jan 1769 *Thornton*. M.

Burrill. *See* Burrell.

Burrin, Thomas of Uxbridge. S s sheet etc. Sep 1740 M.

Burrold, Thomas. S for assault with intent to rob Summer T *Neptune* Dec 1763 for. Bu.

Burrough. *See* Burrow.

Burroughs, Amy. S & T Dec 1724 *Rappahannock*. L.

Burrows, Benjamin. S for highway robbery & R Lent 1775. Wa.

Burrows, Charles. T Sep 1742 *Forward*. Sy.

Burrows, George. S Lent R 14 yrs Summer 1748 T Jan 1749 *Laura*. Ht.

Burrows, James of Manchester. SQS Apr 1749. La.

Burrows, John. S Aug T Oct 1726 *Forward*. L.

Burroughs, John. T Apr 1753 *Thames*. E.

Burroughs, John. R Jun T Sep 1758 *Tryal* to Annapolis Md. M.

Burroughs, John. S s poultry at Redenhall Summer 1767. Nf.

Burras. *See* Barrass.

Burrows, Margaret, widow, als wife of John. S Oct T Dec 1770 *Justitia*. M.

Burroughs, Mary, aged 22, black hair. R Jan T 14 yrs Feb 1723 *Jonathan* LC Annapolis Jly 1724. M.

Burroughs, Mary. T *Caesar* Dec 1734. Bu.

Burroughs, Mary (1735). *See* Collins. L.

Burroughs, Michael. R for Barbados Jly 1675. M.

Burroughs, Richard (1718). *See* Burwas. Sh.

Burrows, Richard. S & R 14 yrs Lent 1773. St.

Burroughes, Sarah. R for Barbados or Jamaica Dec 1689. M.

Borroughs als Hill, Sarah. R for Barbados or Jamaica May 1697. L.

Burroughs, Sarah (1702). *See* Browne. L.

Burroughs als Burrus, Sarah. S & T Apr 1725 *Sukey* LC Annapolis Sep 1725. M.

Burroughs, Thomas. T *Susanna* Jun 1727. Bu.

Burroughs, William. Rebel T 1685.

Burroughs, William. S Jly T 14 yrs Aug 1721 *Prince Royal* LC Va Nov 1721. M.

Burroughs, William. SQS & T Apr 1766 *Ann.* M.

Burroughs, William (1774). *See* Turner. St.

Burrough, Anthony. S for breaking & entering at Ilkley Lent 1725 T *Supply* LC Md May 1726. Y.

Burrough, Edward. S Mar TB to Va Apr 1740. Wi.

Burrow, Joseph. R 14 yrs Aug 1757. So.

Burrough, Samuel. S Dec 1754. L.

Burrough, Thomas. R for America Jly 1694. No.

Burrow, Thomas. TB to Va from QS 1741. De.

Burrow, William. S s sheep Summer 1752 R 14 yrs Lent 1753. Wo.

Burrows. *See* Burroughs.

Burrus, Sarah (1725). *See* Burroughs. M.

Bursy, Catherine. SQS Jan 1752. M.

Bursey, Richard. S Oct 1741 T Feb 1742 *Industry* to Md. M.

Bursfield, Thomas. T May 1719 *Margaret* LC Md May 1720; sold to Caesar Ghiselin. Sy.

Burshal, Daniel (1775). *See* Butcher. Sy.

Burshall, Earl. S Jly 1741. Wi.

Burskerl, John. S Lent 1751. Nf.

Burt, Aaron. S & R Summer 1737 T *Dorsetshire* Jan 1738. Bu.

Burt, Ann. S Jly 1745 TB to Va Apr 1746. Wi.

Burt als Bart, Henry. S Jan 1726. M.

Burt, Jonathan of Clerkenwell. S s silk & T Dec 1740 *Vernon* to Md. M.

Burt, Jonathan. S Aug 1757. So.

Burt, Joseph. S Mar 1730. Do.

Burt, Robert. S Mar 1746. Do.

Birt, Robert. S May-Jun T Jly 1753 *Tryal.* M.

Burt, Robert (Richard in sentence). S s gelding Lent R 14 yrs Summer 1754. Su.

Burt, Thomas. S Apr-May T Jly 1771 *Scarsdale.* M.

Burt, William. S Oct T Nov 1728 *Forward* LC. M.

Burton, Abraham. LC Annapolis Md Sep 1725 from *Sukey.* X.

Burton, Abraham. T Apr 1732 *Patapsco.* K.

Burton, Abraham. S Feb 1761. L.

Burton, Ann. S s at Bishops Cleve Summer 1758. G.

Burton, Anthony. S s gelding at St. Clement, Oxford, & R for life Summer 1770. O.

Burton, Benjamin. S Lent R 14 yrs Summer 1747. O.

Burton, Benjamin. S Dec 1768 T Jan 1769 *Thornton*. M.

Burton, Catherine. S May 1763. M.

Burton, Edmund. R 14 yrs Oct 1772. M.

Burton, Elizabeth, widow. R for Barbados Nov 1668. L.

Burton, Elizabeth, als Black Bess. S Jan T Feb 1719 *Worcester* to Md. L.

Burton, Elizabeth, aged 22, black hair. LC Annapolis from *Gilbert* May 1721. X.

Burton, Elizabeth. LC Annapolis Md Jun 1723 from *Forward*. X.

Burton, Elizabeth. LC Potomack Va Aug 1729 from *Elizabeth*. X.

Burton, Elizabeth. SWK Jan T Sep 1758 *Tryal*. K.

Burton, Francis. S Sep-Dec 1755 T Jan 1756 *Greyhound*. M.

Burton, George. S & T Jly 1772 *Tayloe*. M.

Burton, Humphrey. R for Barbados or Jamaica Oct 1694, Dec 1695 & Jan 1697. L.

Burton, Isaac. S Lent 1766. Nf.

Burton, James. S Aug T Sep 1725 *Forward* LC Annapolis Dec 1725. M.

Burton, Jane. S Oct T Nov 1759 *Phoennx*. L.

Burton als Bunton, John. PT Feb R Oct 1673. M.

Burton, John. R for America Jly 1694. Li.

Burton, John. S Mar 1729. So.

Burton, John of St. Saviour, Southwark. SQS Nov T Dec 1753 *Whiteing*. Sy.

Burton, John. S & T Sep 1766 *Justitia*. M.

Burton, John. T Jan 1767 *Tryal*. M.

Burton, John. S City s gold coins at Bishopthorpe Summer 1767. Y.

Burton, Joseph. T Jly 1770 *Scarsdale*. M.

Burton, Leonard. S & T Oct 1730 *Forward* LC Potomack Jan 1731. M.

Burton, Mary. R for Barbados or Jamaica Mar 1688. M.

Burton, Mary (1748). *See* Sanders. La.

Burton, Mary. T Apr 1753 *Thames*. Ht.

Burton, Richard of St. Saviour, Southwark. S Summer 1748 T Jan 1749 *Laura*. Sy.

Burton, Richard. SQS Dec 1764 T Jan 1765 *Tryal*. M.

Burton, Richard. S s silver tablespoon at Pyrton Lent 1768. O.

Burton, Robert. R 14 yrs Jly 1719 to be T to Va. So.

Burton, Sarah. S Jan-Jun T Jun 1728 *Elizabeth* LC Potomack Aug 1729. L.

Burton, Thomas. S Summer 1751. Y.

Burton, Thomas. R Mar 1774. So.

Burton, William Sr. of Misson. SQS East Retford s from boat Jan TB May 1723. Nt.

Burton, William of Epping. SQS Jan T Apr 1741 *Speedwell* or *Mediterranean*. E.

Burton, William. S s sheep Summer 1748 R 14 yrs Lent 1749. Li.

Burton, William. S Lent TB Apr 1758. Db.

Burvill als Nash, Richard als John. S Lent 1773. K.

Burwas als Burroughs, Richard of St. Mary's. S Summer 1718. Sh.

Bury. *See* Berry.

Busan, Philip. T Jan 1741 *Vernon*. K.

Busan, William. T Jan 1741 *Vernon*. K.

Busby, Christian. S Aug T Oct 1724 *Forward* LC Annapolis Jun 1725. L.

Busby, Christopher. R & T for life Apr 1770 *New Trial*. M.

Busby, Edward. S Apr T May 1720 *Honor* but escaped in Vigo, Spain. L.

Busby als Noble, Elizabeth. R for Barbados or Jamaica May 1691. L.

Busby, Elizabeth, spinster of St. George, Southwark. SQS Apr T Sep 1751 *Greyhound*. Sy.

Busbey, Henry. R for Barbados Jly 1674. L.

Busby, John. S s sheep Lent 1738. O.

Busby, John. T *Speedwell* or *Mediterranean* Apr 1741. Bu.

Busby, John. SQS Feb T Mar 1750 *Tryal*. M.

Busby, Joseph. T *Alexander* Jly 1723 but died on passage. Bu.

Busby, Richard of Bletchley. R for America May 1693. Bu.

Busby, Thomas. S s lead at Witney Lent 1758. O.

Buscall, John. S s sheep Summer 1743. Nf.

Busco, Elizabeth. S Jun-Dec 1738 T Jan 1739 *Dorsetshire* to Va. M.

Busco, Mary (1736). *See* Smith. M.

Busfield, Isaac. R for Barbados or Jamaica Mar 1688. L.

Busfield, John (1757). *See* Carr. Y.

Bush, Ann, spinster of All Hallows. S for murder of her infant bastard Lent R 14 yrs Summer 1745. K.

Bush, Ann. S Jan 1761. M.

Bush, Edward (1700). *See* Braybrooke. E.

Bush als Bertie, Elizabeth. S & T 14 yrs Aug 1752 *Tryal*. L.

Bush, Francis. S May T Aug 1769 *Douglas*. M.

Bush, James. Died on passage in *Rappahannock* 1726. X.

Bush, James (1730). *See* Reynolds. M.

Bush, John of Carshalton. R for Barbados or Jamaica Jly 1702. Sy.

Bush, John. S Summer 1757. Nf.

Bush, Margaret. S & T 14 yrs Aug 1752 *Tryal*. L.

Bush, Martha. S & T Aug 1752 *Tryal*. L.

Bush, Mary (1736). *See* Clark. X.

Bush, Nathaniel. S Jan T Feb 1719 *Worcester* but died on passage. L.

Bush, Thomas. T Nov 1728 *Forward*. E.

Bush, Thorny. S Lent 1736. Su.

Bush, William. Rebel T 1685.

Bushby, John. S & T Oct 1730 *Forward* to Va. M.

Bushby, Mary. S Dec 1745. L.

Bushby, William. S Mar 1755. So.

Bushell, Elizabeth. S Jan T Feb 1724 *Anne* to Carolina. M.

Bushell, Hugh. S Jly 1727. Ha.

Bushell, Richard of St. Giles in Fields. R for America Aug 1713. M.

Bushell, William. S Oct 1748 T Jan 1749 *Laura*. L.

Bushell, William. S Jly 1758. Ha.

Buskin, Thomas. T Oct 1729 *Forward*. Sy.

Buskley, John (1730). *See* Buttler. L.

Buss als Brown, Edward of Ticehurst. R for Barbados or Jamaica Jly 1712. Sx.

Bussell, George. R 14 yrs Jly 1719 to be T to Va. De.

Bussell, William T 14 yrs May 1767 *Thornton*. E.

Bussett, Richard. S Mar 1729 TB to Va. De.
Bussett als Drew, William Jr. R 14 yrs Mar 1775. De.
Busson, John (1685). *See* Bason.
Busting, Robert. R for life for highway robbery Lent 1758. Nf.
Buswell, Stephen. S Oct T Nov 1759 *Phoenix*. L.
Buswell, Thomas. S Feb T 14 yrs Apr 1741 *Speedwell* or
  Mediterranean. M.
Butcher, Andrew. S s sheep at Hopton Wafers Lent 1722. Sh.
Butcher, Ann. S Apr T May 1743 *Indian Queen*. L.
Butcher, Charles. LC Port York Va Jun 1721 from *Mary*. X.
Butcher, Charlotte (1773). *See* Beard. M.
Butcher als Burshal, Daniel of Croydon. SQS Apr 1775. Sy.
Butcher, Edward. S s sheep & R 14 yrs Summer 1773. Wo.
Butcher, George. Rebel T 1685.
Butcher, George (1772). *See* Kem. M.
Butcher, Henry. S Summer 1774. E.
Butcher, Isaac. T Apr 1768 *Thornton*. E.
Butcher, James. LC Annapolis Md Jun 1725 from *Forward*. X.
Butcher, James. S Feb T Mar 1763 *Neptune*. M.
Butcher, James. T Apr 1766 *Ann*. E.
Butcher, John. Rebel T 1685.
Butcher, John. S Mar 1724. De.
Butcher, John. S s cloth at Old Swinford Summer 1727. Wo.
Butcher, John. S Feb T Mar 1731 *Patapsco* LC. M.
Butcher, John. T Dec 1731 *Forward*. E.
Butcher, John. S s gelding Lent R 14 yrs Summer 1770. Wo.
Butcher, John. S Jan-Feb 1774. M.
Butcher, John (1774). *See* Pike. G.
Butcher, Judith. S Jan T Mar 1750 *Tryal*. L.
Butcher, Mary. S Lent 1745. *Su.
Butcher, Matthew of Alvington. S s raincoats Summer 1720. G.
Butcher, Richard of Lambeth. SQS Jan 1751. Sy.
Butcher, Richard. S & T for life Jly 1771 *Scarsdale*. M.
Butcher, Samuel. S s at Hopton Wafers Lent 1758. Sh.
Butcher, Sarah. T May 1737 *Forward*. E.
Butcher, Susanna. S Feb 1752. L.
Butcher, Thomas. R for Barbados or Jamaica Dec 1695 & Jan 1697. M.
Butcher, Thomas. S Jly T Aug 1721 *Prince Royal* LC Va Nov 1721. M.
Butcher, Thomas. S Dec 1772. M.
Butcher, William of Blackbourton. R for America Feb 1713. O.
Butcher, William. S & T Jan 1736 *Dorsetshire* but died on passage. L.
Butcher, William. T Sep 1758 *Tryal*. E.
Butfield, John. Rebel T 1685.
Butfield, William. R 14 yrs Mar 1750. Ha.
Butland, Joseph. TB to Va from QS 1736. De.
Buttland, Thomas of Tregony. R for Barbados Feb 1688. Co.
Butlas als Neale, Rebecca. S Jly T 14 yrs Aug 1721 *Prince Royal* LC Va
  Nov 1721. L.
Butler, Abigail. S Apr 1749. L.
Butler, Alice wife of William. S May-Jly 1746. M.
Butler, Ann. T Oct 1723 *Forward*. K.

Butler, Ann, als Jones, Margaret. S Jan T Jun 1726 *Loyal Margaret* LC Md Oct 1726. M.
Butler, Ann. S Jly 1775. M.
Butler, Carolina. S Dec 1754. L.
Butler, Charles. S Lent R 14 yrs Summer 1727. G.
Butler, Charles. S s horse Summer 1737 R 14 yrs Summer 1738. Wa.
Butler, Charles. S Jan 1757. L.
Butler, Edward. R for Barbados or Jamaica Aug 1700. M.
Butler, Edward. S May-Jly 1773. M.
Butler, Eleanor. SQS Jun T Jly 1753 *Tryal*. M.
Butler, Elizabeth. S Feb T Apr 1734 *Patapsco* to Md. M.
Butler, Elizabeth (1738). *See* Ward. M.
Butler, Elizabeth of St. Saviour, Southwark. SQS Jan 1752. Sy.
Butler, Elizabeth. T Sep 1755 *Tryal*. M.
Butler als Buttles, George of York. R for Barbados s mare Jly 1691. Y.
Butler, George. S Feb 1754. L.
Butler, George. S s linen yarn at Longdon Summer 1761. St.
Butler, Grace. PT Jan 1695. M.
Butler, Hanna. S Oct 1718 T Feb 1719 *Worcester* to Md. M.
Butler, Henry. S s sheep Lent R 14 yrs Summer 1766. St.
Butler, Isabella wife of Thomas. S Sep T Dec 1758 *The Brothers*. M.
Butler, James. S & T Oct 1729 *Forward* LC Va Jun 1730. M.
Butler, James. S May T Sep 1737 *Pretty Patsy* to Md. M.
Butler, James (1737). *See* Brown. Wi.
Butler, James. S Lent R 14 yrs Summer T Oct 1744 *Savannah*. E.
Butler, James (1755). *See* Blunt. M.
Butler, Jane. S Jan T Feb 1726 *Supply* LC Annapolis May 1726. M.
Butler, John. R for Barbados Dec 1683. L.
Butler, John. R for America Feb 1700. No.
Butler, John. S Jan-Jun T Jun 1728 *Elizabeth* LC Potomack Aug 1729. M.
Butler, John. S Mar 1730. Ha.
Buttler, John. S & T Oct 1730 *Forward* LC Potomack Jan 1731. L.
Butler, John of Warrington. SQS Apr 1743. La.
Butler, John. AT Summer 1756. Y.
Butler, John. T Sep 1766 *Justitia*. K.
Butler, John. S Apr T May 1767 *Thornton*. L.
Butler, John. SQS Jly T Sep 1767 *Justitia*. M.
Butler, John. S May T Aug 1769 *Douglas*. M.
Butler, John. R for life Lent 1773. Sy.
Butler als Archer als Ogden, Judith. S 14 yrs May-Jly 1750. M.
Butler, Margaret (1741). *See* Lawler. M.
Butler, Mary of Deptford. R for Barbados or Jamaica Mar 1688. K.
Butler, Mary. S Dec 1733 T Jan 1734 *Caesar* LC Va Jly 1734. M.
Butler, Michael. S Mar 1759 TB to Va. De.
Butler, Richard of Chart. R for Barbados or Jamaica Feb 1686. K.
Butler, Richard. T *Bond* Apr 1742. Bu.
Butler, Richard. SQS & T Jly 1753 *Tryal*. M.
Butler, Samuel of Tewkesbury. S s cloth Lent 1720. G.
Buttler, Thomas. T May 1719 *Margaret* LC Md Sep 1719; sold to Andrew David. E or Sy.

Butler als Clarke als Smith als Bull, Thomas, aged 35, dark, husbandman. S & T Oct 1720 *Gilbert* LC Annapolis May 1721. L.
Butler, Thomas. S & T Apr 1725 *Sukey* LC Annapolis Sep 1725. M.
Butler, Thomas (1730). *See* Griffis. M.
Butler, Thomas. S Mar 1730. Do.
Butler, Thomas. S Jly-Sep T Oct 1739 *Duke of Cumberland* to Va. M.
Butler, Thomas. S Jan-Jun 1747. M.
Butler, Thomas. S Summer 1754. Be.
Butler, Thomas. R 14 yrs Mar 1775. De.
Butler, Tobias. PT Jly 1680. M.
Butler, William. PT Oct 1684 R Mar 1685. M.
Butler, William. S Jan T Feb 1719 *Worcester* LC Annapolis Jun 1719. L.
Butler, William. S & T Apr 1725 *Sukey* LC Annapolis Sep 1725. M.
Butler als Buckland als Simmonds, William. S Jly 1735 s watch from prosecutor's wife while on trial for s gelding. M.
Butler, William. S Lent R 14 yrs Summer 1755. O.
Butler, Willalm. S Feb T Apr 1770 *New Trial*. M.
Butler, William. S Apr T Jly 1770 *Scarsdale*. M.
Butlin, John. R for Barbados Jly 1668. L.
Butsell, William. S Feb T Mar 1729 *Patapsco* to Md. M.
Butt, John. R 14 yrs Mar 1752. So.
Butt, William. S s gelding at Bisley & R 14 yrs Summer 1771. G.
Buttenshaw, Thomas. S Lent T May 1750 *Lichfield*. E.
Butterfield, Abraham. S Dec 1774. L.
Butterfield, Ann wife of William. S & T Dec 1771 *Justitia*. M.
Butterfield, George. S & T Dec 1731 *Forward* to Md or Va. M.
Butterfield, John. S Lent 1719. Y.
Butterfield, John. S Feb T Mar 1729 *Patapsco* LC Annapolis Dec 1729. M.
Butterfield, Mary. S & T Dec 1759 *Phoenix*. M.
Butterfield, Thomas. S Feb T Mar 1764 *Tryal*. M.
Butteriss, Robert. S Sep T Oct 1739 *Duke of Cumberland*. L.
Butteris, Thomas. S Oct T Nov 1728 *Forward* LC Rappahannock Jun 1729. L.
Butterom, Elizabeth. S & T Dec 1770 *Justitia*. M.
Butters, William. S Summer T Oct 1750 *Rachael*. K.
Buttersfield, William. S Jan-Feb T Apr 1753 *Thames*. M.
Butterwicke, John. S s gold coin at Strensall Lent TB Aug 1773. Y.
Butterworth, Edward (1698). *See* Ratcliffe. St.
Butterworth, James of Haslingden, woollen weaver. SQS Apr 1775. La.
Butterworth, Joseph. S Feb-Apr T May 1752 *Lichfield*. M.
Butterworth, Mary. S s at Hanley Castle Summer 1766. Wo.
Butterworth, Robert of Newbold within Castleton, woollen weaver. SQS Feb 1759. La.
Butterworth, Robert of Butterworth, woollen weaver. SQS Jly 1761. La.
Butterworth, William of Manchester, checkweaver of Manchester. S for murder & R 14 yrs Summer 1771. La.
Buttles, George (1691). *See* Butler. Y.
Button, David of Walthamstow. SQS Jan 1767 T Apr 1768 *Thornton*. E.
Button, Mary. S 14 yrs for receiving Lent 1775. Wa.
Button, Thomas. R for 10 yrs in plantations Oct 1662. M.

Butts, William. S Feb 1775. L.

Buxey, John. S Jly 1755. Ha.

Buxton, Anthony. R 14 yrs Jly TB to Va Nov 1748. Wi.

Buxton, Elizabeth. S Jan-Jun T Jun 1728 *Elizabeth* LC Potomack Aug 1729. L.

Buxton, James of St. Cuthbert, Wells. R for Barbados Jan 1676. So.

Buxton, John. S Lent 1761. Db.

Buzell, Ann. S Jly T Dec 1736 *Dorsetshire* to Va. M.

Byall, John. S Dec 1750. L.

Byass, Daniel. S Summer T Sep 1755 *Tryal*. Sy.

Biass, James. T Apr 1770 *New Trial*. E.

Byas, Stephen. S s cow R 14 yrs Summer TB Sep 1759. Y.

Byatt, Elizabeth. S Lent 1754. Ht.

Bycham als Belcham, James of High Ongar. R for Barbados or Jamaica Jun 1699. E.

Bye, John. S s at Bessesleigh Summer 1751. Be.

Bye, Sarah. S & T Sep 1731 *Smith* LC Va 1732. M.

Byre, John (1737). *See* Bourne. M.

Byers, Elizabeth, spinster of St. George, Southwark. SQS Oct 1751. Sy.

Byfield, Robert. S Oct 1765 T Jan 1766 *Tryal*. M.

Byfill, John of Hornchurch. R for Barbados or Jamaica Mar 1694. E.

Byham, Ann. T Oct 1726 *Forward*. Sy.

Byles, Elizabeth. S Mar 1733. Wi.

Byles, John. S for highway robbery Lent R 14 yrs Summer 1753. No.

Byles, William. S s at Pyrton Lent 1752. O.

Bing, Deborah. SQS & TB Oct 1737. G.

Bynion, Thomas. SQS Apr T Sep 1757 *Thetis*. M.

Byram, Henry. S Summer 1759. Su.

Byram, Richard. R 14 yrs Summer 1757. We.

Byrne. *See* Burn.

Byrom, James. S s at Ashton in Mackerfield Lent R 14 yrs Summer 1765. La.

Byrom, John Sr. S 14 yrs for receiving Lent 1765. La.

Byrom als Byron, William. S s stockings Jly 1735 T Jan 1736 *Dorsetshire* LC Va Sep 1736. M.

Byron, Elizabeth aged 40. R for 7 yrs in Barbados Feb 1664. M.

Byron, John. S for ripping lead from a building Jun T Sep 1767 *Justitia*. L.

Bywell, Robert. SQS Richmond Jan 1744. Y.

C

Cabbidge, Samuel (1726). *See* Johnson. M.

Cabitch, William (1728). *See* Cobitch. L.

Cable, Benjamin. Rebel T 1685.

Cable, Charles. S s gelding Lent R 14 yrs Summer 1767. Su.

Cable, Elizabeth. S Summer 1758. Su.

Cable, Isabella. S Feb-Apr 1745. M.

Cable, John of St. Luke. S s shirt Jly 1740 T Jan 1741 *Harpooner*. M.

Caborell, Alice. R for America Aug 1715. L.

Caddell, Elizabeth (1767). *See* Sprigmore. M.

Caddy, Samuel. TB to Va from QS 1756. De.

Cade, Ann (1664). *See* Pettis. L.

Cade, John. R for America Jly 1694. Li.

Cade als Bennett, John. S Oct 1761. L.

Cade, Rebecca. S Feb T Mar 1727 *Patapsco* but died on passage. L.

Cadman, James. S s fowls at Wolverhampton Summer 1752. St.

Cadman, James. S Lent 1775. Wa.

Cadman, Joshua. T May 1736 *Patapsco*. Ht.

Cadman, Warner. T Jun 1764 *Dolphin*. M.

Cadman, William. S Lent R 14 yrs Summer 1757. Sh.

Cadogan, George. S Summer 1739 R Lent 1740 (SP). Mo.

Caduggan, Phillip. TB to Va from QS 1773. De.

Cadogan, William (1675). *See* Pritchard. Mo.

Cadwalader, Mark. S Apr 1740. Fl.

Cadward, Thomas. S Lent R 14 yrs Summer 1748. G.

Kaghill, John. S & T Sep 1731 LC Va 1732. L.

Cahill als Porter, Elizabeth. R 14 yrs Summer 1735. Y.

Cain. *See* Cane.

Caines. *See* Canes.

Caistor, Elizabeth. R for America Jly 1707. Li.

Calaspine, Thomas. R May AT Oct 1678. M.

Calcott als Cancott, William. S Summer 1742 R 14 yrs Lent T Apr 1743 *Justitia*. Bu.

Cauldecord, Edward. S Summer 1768. Wa.

Caldicott, John. S s iron Summer 1741. Wo.

Caldwell, John. R for America Jly 1693. Nt.

Caldwell, William. S Apr T Sep 1757 *Thetis*. L.

Cale, Elizabeth of St. George, Southwark. SQS Jan 1755. Sy.

Cale als Brown, Elizabeth. S Sep T Nov 1759 *Phoenix*. M.

Cale, Mary. R for Barbados or Jamaica Jly 1686. M.

Calebna, Jane (1723). *See* Uren. Co.

Calendar, Phillip. SQS Jly TB Aug 1765. So.

Calfe, James. S & T Jan 1722 *Gilbert* to Md. M.

Calkin, Timothy. S Apr T Dec 1735 *John* LC Annapolis Sep 1736. M.

Call, Robert. S Dec 1737 T Jan 1738 *Dorsetshire*. L.

Callagan als Gallagher, Charles. R Jly T for life Jly 1771 *Scarsdale*. M.

Callaghan, Gerhard. S Sep T Dec 1763 *Neptune*. M.

Callagan, James. S Feb s silk handkerchief at St. George, Botolph Lane, Feb T Apr 1768 *Thornton*. L.

Calyhan, John. S Jun 1761. M.

Callihan, John. SWK Oct 1772. K.

Callaghan, Thomas of St. Saviour, Southwark. SQS Oct T Dec 1771. Sy.

Kallagham, William. S Dec 1756. M.

Callander, Robert. R 14 yrs Jly 1761 TB to Va. De.

Callaway, John of Berriton. R for Barbados Feb 1699. Ha.

Callaway, William. S Jly 1722. De.

Callden, Robert. S May-Jun T Aug 1752 *Tryal*. M.

Callen, Eleanor. S Apr-May 1744. M.

Callys, Augustine. R for Bermuda Oct 1614. M.

Calles als Careless, Robert. S Summer 1771 R 14 yrs Lent & T Apr 1772 *Thornton*. K.

Callow, Agatha. S Lent 1724 R 14 yrs Lent 1725 (SP). Su.

Callow, Christian. PT Oct 1697 AT Jly R Dec 1698. M.

Callow, Henry. S Aug 1741. So.

Callow, Richard. S s horse hair at Holt Summer 1768. Wo.

Calloway, John (1723). *See* Carne. Co.

Callwell, Charles. SQS Dec 1764 T Jan 1765 *Tryal*. M.

Calwell, William of Liverpool. S for highway robbery Lent R 14 yrs Summer 1763. La.

Calvert, Mary. SQS & T Jan 1766 *Tryal*. M.

Calvert, Sarah (1750). *See* Knocky. Cu.

Calvert, William. T Apr 1770 *New Trial*. K.

Cam, William. S for highway robbery Summer 1739 R 14 yrs Lent 1740. Li.

Camber, James. S Oct 1773. L.

Camber, William. SW & T Jly 1770 *Scarsdale*. M.

Cambourn, Robert. R for Barbados or Jamaica Oct 1688. M.

Cambridge Moll (1694). *See* Morrell, Mary. L.

Cambridge, Martha. S at Bristol Lent 1772. G.

Cambridge, Nicholas, aged 21. R Feb 1664 (SP). M.

Came, Francis. Rebel T 1685.

Camell, Anne. S Jly T Aug 1721 *Prince Royal* to Va. M.

Cammell, Daniel. T Jun 1740 *Essex*. K.

Cammell, George. S Jan T Mar 1750 *Tryal*. L.

Cammill, John. S Summer 1742 R 14 yrs Lent 1743. Wo.

Camell als Scamell als Fielder, Sarah. T Jun 1742 *Bladon*. Sx.

Camell, Thomas. S Feb-Apr 1746 to be T 14 yrs. M.

Cammele, William. S Dec 1733 T Jan 1734 *Caesar* LC Va Jly 1734. L.

Camell als Macoy, William. S 14 yrs Mar 1746. So.

Cameron, Duncan. S Feb T Apr 1742 *Bond* to Potomack Md. M.

Cameron, John. S Lent T 14 yrs Summer 1747. Sy.

Cameron, Margaret. S Apr T Sep 1758 *Tryal* to Annapolis Md. M.

Camfield als Campbell, Elizabeth. S & T Sep 1731 *Smith* but died on passage. M.

Camock, John. SQS & TB Jan 1733. G.

Camp, Agnes. S Mar 1766 TB to Va. De.

Camp, Thomas. R 14 yrs Jly 1721. De.

Camp, William. R 14 yrs Mar 1721. De.

Campbell, Alexander. S Dec 1742 T Apr 1743 *Justitia*. M.
Cambell, Archibald. S Apr-May T May 1744 *Justitia*. M.
Campbell, Catherine. S May-Jly 1748. M.
Gambell, Catherine. SQS Apr 1752. M.
Campbell, Catherine of Manchester. SQS Jan 1773. La.
Campbell, Charles. S & T Feb 1719 *Worcester* LC Annapolis Jun
   1719. M.
Campbell, Charles. T for life Aug 1752 *Tryal*. Sy.
Campbell, Charles. S & R 7 yrs s horse Mar 1766. Fl.
Campbell, Charles (1773). *See* Brown. Cu.
Campbell als Toms, Christiana. S May T Jun 1726 *Loyal Margaret* LC
   Md Oct 1726. M.
Campbell, Duncan. S Dec 1763 T Mar 1764 *Tryal*. M.
Campbell, Duncan, als Douglas, John Hunter. SQS & T Jly 1771
   Scarsdale. M.
Campbell, Edward. S Apr-Jun 1739 to be T 14 yrs. M.
Campbell, Eleanor. SQS Stokesley s cloth Jly TB Aug 1766. Y.
Campbell, Eleanor. SQS Summer 1773. Du.
Campbell, Elizabeth. PT Oct R Dec 1716 T Jan 1717 *Queen Elizabeth*
   to Jamaica. M.
Campbell, Elizabeth wife of William. S Sep 1737 T Jan 1738
   Dorsetshire. M.
Campbell, Elizabeth. S Dec 1757 T Mar 1758 *Dragon*. L.
Campbell, Elizabeth. S Jan 1759. L.
Cambell, Elizabeth. S Lent 1766. Bd.
Campbell, Elizabeth (1771). *See* Camfield. M.
Campbell, George. S Dec 1742 T Apr 1743 *Justitia*. M.
Cambell, Hugh. S & T Sep 1731 *Smith* LC Va 1732. M.
Cambell, Hugh. S Jan-Apr 1748. M.
Campbell als Mitchell, James. S s horse Summer 1736 R 14 yrs Summer
   1737. Cu.
Gambell, James of St. Olave, Southwark. S Lent T May 1750
   Lichfield. Sy.
Campbell, James. T Dec 1763 *Neptune*. K.
Campbell, Jane. S City Summer 1756. Nl.
Campbell, John. R 14 yrs Summer 1721. Y.
Gambell, John. T Aug 1721 *Owners Goodwill* LC Md Jly 1722. Sy.
Campbell, John. S Dec 1748 T Jan 1749 *Laura*. M.
Cambell, Mary. S Feb T Apr 1766 *Ann*. M.
Campbell, Peter. S & T Mar 1750 *Tryal*. L.
Campbell, Robert. S Apr 1774. M.
Campbell, Sarah wife of Duncombe. S Sep T Nov 1759 *Phoenix*. M.
Cambell, William (1692). *See* Wisdom. Li.
Gambell, William. TB 14 yrs Oct 1719 T *Susannah & Sarah* LC
   Annapolis Apr 1720. L.
Campbell, William. R 14 yrs Summer TB Aug 1741. Y.
Campbell, William. S Summer 1774. K.
Campden, John. S Lent R 14 yrs Summer 1749. O.
Campen, William. T Dec 1753 *Whiteing*. E.
Campion, Hyder. S Sep-Oct 1775. M.
Campion, Robert. S Feb 1761. L.

Cancott, William (1742). *See* Calcott. Bu.

Candiland als Halmark, George. S s at Whitchurch Lent 1766. Sh.

Candler, Frances (1671). *See* Jobson. M.

Candler, John. S Summer 1754. Su.

Candy, Christopher. Rebel T 1685.

Candy als Powell, Elizabeth. S Aug T Oct 1722 *Forward* LC Md Jun 1725. M.

Candy, Mary of St James Westminster, spinster. S s clothing Apr T May 1740 *Essex*. M.

Cane, Abraham. S & T Dec 1767 *Neptune*. M.

Cane, Anne. T Oct 1722 *Forward* LC Md Jun 1723. Sy.

Kane, Arthur. S Jly T Sep 1764 *Justitia*. M.

Cane als Cain, Edward. S Dec 1768 T Jan 1769 *Thornton*. L.

Cane als Lawrence, Elizabeth. S Oct 1744-Jan 1745 to be T 14 yrs. M.

Cane, James. S Lent 1749. K.

Kane, Jane wife of Edward. S Sep 1761. M.

Cain, Job of St. Martin in Fields. SW Apr T Jly 1772 *Tayloe*. M.

Cane, John. R for America Aug 1715. M.

Cane als Dixon, John. S & T Sep 1731 *Smith* LC Va 1732. M.

Cane, John. S & T Oct 1732 *Caesar*. L.

Cane, John of St. Martin in Fields. S s linen Apr T May 1740 *Essex*. M.

Cain, John (1745). *See* Keen. Ha.

Cain, John, als Blakeney, William. S Sep-Oct T Dec 1771 *Justitia*. M.

Cane, Lewis. SQS Jly TB Sep 1767. So.

Cane, Margaret. S Lent 1760. Bu.

Cane, Mary (1719). *See* Bishop. L.

Cane, Mary (1731). *See* Rowe. M.

Cain, Morris. S Lent T May 1755 *Rose*. Sy.

Cain, Nathaniel. S & T Jly 1772 *Tayloe*. M.

Cain als Kayne, Patrick. S Apr T May 1751 *Tryal*. L.

Caen, Patrick. S Oct T Dec 1763 *Neptune*. M.

Cain, Richard. SW & T Jly 1771 *Scarsdale*. M.

Kaine, Robert. S Jan-Apr 1749. M.

Cane, Robert of St. Margaret Westminster. SW Jan 1775. M.

Cane, Thomas. TB Oct 1719 T *Susannah & Sarah* LC Annapolis Apr 1720. L.

Cane, Thomas. S Sep 1740. L.

Cane, Thomas. SW & T Jan 1769 *Thornton*. M.

Cane, Thomas. S May T Jly 1770 *Scarsdale*. M.

Cain, Thomas. SQS Wisbech & R 14 yrs Sep 1773 (SP). Ca.

Cane, William. S Jly T Aug 1721 *Prince Royal* LC Va Nov 1721. M.

Cane, William. S Jan-Apr 1749. M.

Cane als Wayne, William. S & T Dec 1767 *Neptune*. M.

Caines, George. S Mar TB Apr 1734. Wi.

Caines, William. R 14 yrs Jly 1719 to be T to Va. So.

Kaines, William. S Jly 1759. Wi.

Canfield als Corps, John. S s at St. Botolph, Cambridge, Summer 1773. Ca.

Canfield, Thomas of St. Saviour, Southwark. SQS Jan 1773. Sy.

Cann, Elizabeth. S Mar 1752. De.

Cann, John. S May T Jun 1738 *Forward*. L.

Cann, Richard. S Mar 1730. De.
Cann, Richard. S Aug 1754. De.
Can, William. S Summer 1749. Y.
Cannabe, Robert. T Nov 1725 *Rappahannock* but died on passage. K.
Cannam, John. S Lent 1765. No.
Cannam, William (1769). *See* Channam. K.
Canner, John (1722). *See* Conner. M.
Canner, Thomas. S Summer 1762. Nt.
Cannew, James. S Sep-Dec 1746. M.
Canning, Elizabeth. S Jly 1754. L.
Canning, William of Stratford on Avon. R for America Jly 1678. Wa.
Cannon, Ann. S Jly T Nov 1759 *Phoenix*. M.
Cannon, Bridget. SQS Sep 1774. M.
Cannon, Catherine. S & T Oct 1730 *Forward* LC Potomack Jan 1731. M.
Cannon, Edward. S s silver watch at Elkstone Lent 1764. G.
Cannon, Elizabeth. S Mar 1748. De.
Cannon, John. T Apr 1739 *Forward*. Sy.
Cannon, Michael. SW & T Dec 1771 *Justitia*. M.
Cannon, Susannah. S Sep T Nov 1743 *George William*. L.
Cannon, Thomas. S & T Sep 1757 *Thetis*. L.
Cannons, Charles. S & R 14 yrs Summer 1760. Be.
Cansdell, Thomas. R Summer 1774. E.
Cant, Robert. R for Barbados Aug 1679. M.
Cantlebury, John. Rebel T 1685.
Cantrill, Benjamin of Dunham. SQS s iron bars Jly 1765. Nt.
Cantrell, James. T Apr 1741 *Speedwell* or *Mediterranean*. E.
Canterell, John. S & T Oct 1732 *Caesar* to Va. M.
Cantrell, John. S Mar 1756 TB to Va. De.
Cantrell, Joseph. S Summer 1772. Db.
Cantrell, Thomas. R 14 yrs Aug 1729. De.
Cape, Ann. S & T Dec 1740 *Vernon*. L.
Cape, John. S Feb T May 1767 *Thornton*. M.
Cape, Joseph. S Jun 1747. L.
Cape, Mary wife of Thomas of Kingston on Thames. R for Barbados or Jamaica Mar 1707. Sy.
Cape, Robert. R 14 yrs Aug 1727. So.
Cape, William. SQS Oct 1755 TB May 1756. So.
Capell, Mary. S Jan-Jun 1747. M.
Capell, Richard. SWK Oct 1774. K.
Capell, Sarah. S Jun T Nov 1743 *George William*. M.
Capell, William of Woburn. R for America Apr 1697. Bd.
Capells, Thomas (1720). ee Brown. L.
Caper, William. S May T Jun 1727 *Susanna* to Md. M.
Capes, William. S Lent 1763. Li.
Caplin, William. S Mar 1751. Ha.
Capon, Edward Sr. of Pettick, Childrey. R for Barbados Oct 1663. Be.
Capon, Edward Jr. of Pettick, Childrey. R for Barbados Oct 1663. Be.
Capon, Rowland. S s game cock at Ridgmont Summer 1769. Bd.
Capp, George. TB 14 yrs Oct 1719 T *Susannah & Sarah* but died on passage. L.
Capp, John. T Sep 1767 *Justitia*. E.

Cap, Thomas. S Apr T May 1767 *Thornton*. L.
Capper, Richard. R for Jamaica Aug 1661. M.
Cappock, John. S Lent 1749. Ht.
Capps, James of Newington. SQS Jan T Apr 1768 *Thornton*. Sy.
Capron, Richard. S Mar 1740. De.
Capron, Robert. SQS Jan TB Feb 1749. So.
Capstick, Daniel (1719). *See* Richardson. L.
Capstick, Richard. S Jly T 14 yrs Aug 1718 *Eagle* LC Charles Town Mar 1719. L.
Carballo, Jacob. S Aug 1727 T *Forward* LC Rappahannock May 1728. M.
Card, Charles. S s lead weight at Newbury Lent 1727. Be.
Card, Peter. T for life May 1767 *Thornton*. Sx.
Cardell, William. R & T 14 yrs Feb 1740 *York*. L.
Carden, Richard of Dorrington. R for America Nov 1694. Sh.
Carden, Thomas. Rebel T 1685.
Carder, Amos. R Jly 1719 to be T to Va. De.
Cardiff, Thomas of St. Martin in Fields. SW Apr 1773. M.
Cardigan, Mary. S May T Sep 1766 *Justitia*. M.
Cardinall, Thomas. S Apr-May 1754. M.
Cardon, Richard. S Dec 1748 T Jan 1749 *Laura*. L.
Care, Anthony of Wantage. R for America Jly 1698. Be.
Care, William. R 14 yrs Mar 1731. Wi.
Careless. *See* Carless.
Caren, Philip. R for Barbados or Jamaica Dec 1698. M.
Carew, Bampfield Moore. TB to Va from QS 1738. De.
Carey, Eleanor. S Jly 1736. M.
Carey, George. SWK Oct T Dec 1770 *Justitia*. K.
Carey, George. S Apr-May T Jly 1771 *Scarsdale*. M.
Cary, Henry. S Apr-Jun 1739. M.
Carey, Henry. S Oct T Dec 1770 *Justitia*. M.
Carey, James. R for Barbados Dec 1693 AT Jan 1694. M.
Carey (Carry), James. S s at Week & Abston Lent TB Mar 1750. G.
Carey, James. T Aug 1752 *Tryal*. M.
Carey, James of Warrington, weaver. SQS Jly 1757. La.
Carey als Carus, John. R for Barbados or Jamaica May 1684. L.
Carey, John. T Apr 1766 *Ann*. Bu.
Carey, Margaret. S Oct 1774. L.
Cary als Davis, Mary. R for Barbados or Jamaica Jly 1685. M.
Carrey, Phillip. PT Jan 1699. M.
Cary als Rooke, Susannah. S Feb T Apr 1770 *New Trial*. M.
Carey, Thomas. S s horse & R 14 yrs Summer 1773. Wo.
Cary, William. S Jly T Nov 1762 *Prince William*. M.
Carey, William. SQS May T Sep 1764 *Justitia*. M.
Carey, William. S Oct 1764 T Jan 1765 *Tryal*. M.
Carfoot, Eleanor. TB Feb 1747. Db.
Cariffe, Thomas. R for Barbados Dec 1683. M.
Carle, Elizabeth. R Apr TB to Barbados Jun 1669. L.
Carle, Thomas. S Aug 1760. L.
Carless, John. T May 1737 *Forward*. Sy.

Carless, Joseph of Cardington. S s barley Summer 1727. *Bd.
Careless, Robert (1771). *See* Calles. K.
Careless, Thomas. S Jun s iron bars T Dec 1736 *Dorsetshire* to Va. M.
Carlisle, John. S & R Summer 1718. Cu.
Carlile, Richard, aged 48, dark. T Oct 1720 *Gilbert* LC Md May 1721. Sy.
Carlisle, William. S Feb T Mar 1730 *Patapsco* LC Annapolis Sep 1730. L.
Carlow, Isaac. S City Lent 1743. Y.
Carlow, John (1765). *See* Carrol. M.
Carleton, Anne. S Summer 1741. We.
Carlton, Judith. SQS Jan 1752. M.
Carleton, Mary (1671). *See* Lyon. M.
Carmalt, Henry. R 14 yrs Summer 1738. Cu.
Carman, John. S s sheep Summer 1758 R 14 yrs Lent 1759. Nf.
Carman, Richard. S s sheep Summer 1758 R 14 yrs Lent 1759. Nf.
Carman, Robert. S Summer R for Barbados Aug 1665. Ht.
Carman, Robert. S Lent 1736. Su.
Carmichael, James. S Lent AT Summer 1730. Y.
Caermichael, Mary. S Sep-Oct 1749. M.
Carmody, Michael. S Sep 1772. M.
Carmuck, Patrick. T May 1744 *Justitia*. K.
Carnaby, Elizabeth (1741). *See* Jones. M.
Carnal, Thomas. S Mar 1763 TB to Va. De.
Carnall, William. TB Sep 1750. Db.
Carne, Elizabeth. S May-Jly 1748. M.
Carne als Calloway, John. S Mar 1723. Co.
Carne, Peter. S Apr T Jly 1770 *Scarsdale*. L.
Carne, William (1724). *See* Barnes. Mo.
Carnegie, John. S Aug 1746. Ha.
Carnes, Amos. S Lent 1749. Sy.
Carnes, Arundell. SQS Dec 1765 T Jan 1766 *Tryal*. M.
Carnes, Mary. S Jly-Dec 1747. M.
Carney, John. S Dec 1772. M.
Carney, Margaret. S Dec 1766 T Jan 1767 *Tryal*. M.
Carney, Mary. R May T for life Sep 1758 *Tryal* to Annapolis Md. M.
Carney, Michael. S Feb 1754. M.
Carod, Henry. SWK Jan T Jun 1764 *Dolphin*. K.
Carpenter, Elizabeth. S & T Oct 1729 *Forward* LC Va Jun 1730. M.
Carpenter, James. S Mar 1754. Ha.
Carpenter, Jeremiah. S s at Clifton Summer 1729. Wo.
Carpenter, John. R Sep 1669 to be T 7 yrs to Barbados. M.
Carpenter, John. R for Barbados or Jamaica Jly 1687. L.
Carpenter, John. S May T Jun 1726 *Loyal Margaret* LC Md Oct 1726. M.
Carpenter als Huckle, John. S Feb T Mar 1764 *Tryal*. M.
Carpenter, Joseph. S s sheep Summer 1772. K.
Carpenter, Martha. S Feb 1775. L.
Carpenter, Susanna. T Oct 1723 *Forward*. Sy.
Carpender, Thomas. T Jan *Caesar* LC Va Jly 1734. Sy.
Carpenter, Timothy. S Lant R 14 yrs Summer 1756. Be.
Carpenter, William. S killing deer at Great Tew Summer 1751. O.

Carpenter, William. S s sheep Summer 1765 R 14 yrs Lent 1766. Hu.
Carr, Abraham. S Aug 1727 T *Forward* LC Rappahannock May
    1728. M.
Carr, Ann. S Apr-May 1754. M.
Carr, Elizabeth. S Dec 1745. L.
Carr, Elizabeth. S Oct 1760. M.
Carr, Elizabeth. T Aug 1769 *Douglas*. Sy.
Carr, George. S City Summer 1756. Nl.
Carr, George. S & R 14 yrs s cow at Tickhill Lent 1770. Y.
Carr, Henry. SWK Jly 1774. K.
Carr, James. S City Summer 1734. Nl.
Carr, James. S s watch at Malton Lent TB Aug 1758. Y.
Carr, James. S Lent R Apr 1768. Li.
Carr, Jane. R for Barbados or Jamaica May 1691. L.
Carr, John. S s heifer Summer 1739. Nl.
Carr, John. T Apr 1741 *Speedwell* or *Mediterranean*. Sy.
Carr, John. S s horse Summer 1743 R 14 yrs Lent 1744. Du.
Carr, John. S Apr T May 1752 *Lichfield*. L.
Carr als Busfield, John. S s from bleaching yard Lent TB Aug 1757. Y.
Carr, John of St. Mary le Strand. SW Jly T Sep 1767 *Justitia*. M.
Carr, Lewis. S Jan-Feb 1775. M.
Carr, Mary als Sarah. S for highway robbery Summer 1750 R 14 yrs
    Lent 1752. Du.
Carr, Mary. S Sep-Dec 1755 T Jan 1756 *Greyhound*. M.
Carr, Michael. R 14 yrs Mar 1764. Ha.
Car, Peras (1772). *See* Mascada, Francis. M.
Carr, Priscilla. S Oct-Dec 1750. M.
Carr, Robert. S Feb T Mar 1730 *Patapsco* LC Annapolis Sep 1730. M.
Carr, Sarah. SQS Dec 1768 T Jan 1769 *Thornton*. M.
Carr, Thomas (1767). *See* Bourke. M.
Carr, William. S Lent 1736. Nf.
Carr, William. S & TB to Va Mar 1738. Wi.
Carr, William. S Summer 1748. Y.
Carr, William of St. Olave, Southwark. SQS Oct 1750. Sy.
Carr, William. T for life Dec 1770 *Justitia*. K.
Carrades, William. S City s silk ribbon in Liberty of St. Peter Summer
    1772. Y.
Carragan, James. S Apr 1773. L.
Carrawin, William. R for America Feb 1700. Le.
Carrell. *See* Carroll.
Carrick, Christian. S s cloth from shop Summer 1758. Du.
Carrington, Alice. T Jun *Loyal Margaret* LC Md Dec 1726. K.
Carrington, Daniel. S Oct 1761. L.
Carrivan als Kerrivan, Edward. S Feb T Apr 1766 *Ann*. M.
Carrowdice, John. TB Feb 1747. Db.
Carrodice, Mary (1749). *See* Hetherington. Db.
Carrodus, Margaret. S s linen shirt Dec 1771 LC from
    Lowther & Senhouse Va May 1772. Nl.
Carroll als Dutton, Andrew. S Sep-Oct T Dec 1752 *Greyhound*. M.
Carroll, Ann. S Feb-Apr T May 1752 *Lichfield*. M.
Carroll, Ann. S Jly 1760. M.

Carroll als Kaurhill, Daniel. R Feb 1675. M.
Carroll, Eleanor wife of Owen. S s from Sir Thomas Newcombe Oct 1764 T Jan 1765 *Tryal*. M.
Carroll, Hugh. S Feb T Apr 1770 *New Trial*. M.
Carroll, Jane. S Jan 1757. L.
Carroll, Jane wife of Peter. S & T Dec 1771 *Justitia*. M.
Carroll, John. S Apr R 14 yrs for Carolina May 1718. L.
Carrill, John. S Feb T Mar 1731 *Patapsco* LC Annapolis Jun 1731. M.
Carroll, John. R Sep T for life Oct 1750 *Rachael*. M.
Carroll, John. S Jan 1751. M.
Carroll, John. S Dec 1755 T 14 yrs Jan 1756 *Greyhound*. L.
Carrol als Carlow, John. S Feb T Apr 1765 *Ann*: his wife Mary Carrol als MacGee *(qv)* acquitted. M.
Carroll, John. S Apr T May 1767 *Thornton*. M.
Carroll, John. S & T Dec 1769 *Justitia*. L.
Carroll, John. S Nov T Dec 1770 *Justitia*. L.
Carryl, John. SW & T Jly 1772 *Tayloe*. M.
Karrell, Joseph. S Feb 1752. L.
Carroll als Macgee, Mary. S Feb T Apr 1765 *Ann*. M.
Carroll, Patrick. S Feb T Mar 1763 *Neptune*. M.
Carroll, Patrick. S Dec 1766 T Jan 1767 *Tryal*. L.
Carroll, Thomas. S May-Jun T Jly 1753 *Tryal*. M.
Carroll, Timothy. S Apr-May 1754. M.
Carrell, William. T Jun 1727 *Susanna*. Sy.
Carryl, Winifred. S May T Aug 1769 *Douglas*. M.
Carrott, John (1697). *See* Smith, William. M.
Carrow, George. Rebel T 1685.
Carrow, Mary. T Dec 1753 *Whiteing*. K.
Carrow als Crow, Thomas of Grimston. R for America Feb 1684. Nf.
Carryer, Thomas. R for Jamaica Mar 1665. L.
Carryl. *See* Carroll.
Carsey, Jeremiah. S Jan-Apr 1749. M.
Cart, Mary wife of James. S Aug T Oct 1741 *Sea Horse* to Va. M.
Carteen, Charles. S Feb T Mar 1727 *Rappahannock* to Md. M.
Carter, Ann. S Mar 1741. Ha.
Carter, Ann. S Feb-Apr T May 1752 *Lichfield*. M.
Carter, Ann. T Jly 1770 *Scarsdale*. M.
Carter, Anthony. SL & T Jly 1770 *Scarsdale*. Sy.
Carter, Arthur of Burton on Trent. R for America Feb 1714. St.
Carter, Katherine (1687). *See* Baulfield, Elizabeth. M.
Carter, Christian. R for Barbados or Jamaica Dec 1695 & May 1697 AT Jly 1697. M.
Carter, Daniel of Low Layton. R for Barbados or Jamaica Jly 1688 & Feb 1690. E.
Carter, Daniel. S Aug 1767. So.
Carter, Dennis. T May 1767 *Thornton*. Sy.
Carter, Dorothy. S Oct 1733 T Jan 1734 *Caesar* LC Va Jly 1734. M.
Carter, Edward. S Summer 1726. Sh.
Carter, Elizabeth (1748). *See* Fowler. M.
Carter, Elizabeth. S Jun 1754. L.
Carter, Elizabeth (1767). *See* Hart. L.

Carter, Elizabeth wife of John. S s books at St. Sepulchre Feb T Apr 1768 *Thornton*. L.
Carter, Francis. Rebel T 1685.
Carter, Francis. R 14 yrs Lent 1721. Be.
Carter, Francis. S at Bristol 14 yrs for receiving Lent 1772. G.
Carter, George. R 14 yrs Jly 1732. Do.
Carter, Henry. S Mar 1724. Wi.
Carter, Henry. S s coals at Henley Lent 1773. O.
Carter, Isaac. S Jly 1737. Wi.
Carter, James. S Jly 1746. L.
Carter, James. S s wheat at St. Aldates Summer 1757. Be.
Carter, James. S Feb 1773. L.
Carter, Jane. S Feb-Apr 1746. M.
Carter, Jane. S Mar 1756. Ha.
Carter, John. S s horse Sep R for Va or Bermuda Nov 1622. L.
Carter, John of Radley. R 7 yrs for Barbados Feb 1665. Be.
Carter, John of Shipton, miller. R for America Mar 1688. O.
Carter, John. R for Barbados or Jamaica Oct 1690. M.
Carter, John. S Jan T Feb 1726 *Supply* LC Annapolis May 1726. M.
Carter, John. S & T Oct 1729 *Forward* but died on passage. M.
Carter, John. S & T Oct 1730 *Forward* but died on passage. M.
Carter, John. S Summer 1731. G.
Carter, John. S Lent 1736.
Carter, John. S s pigs at South Cerney Lent TB Mar 1743. G.
Carter, John. S Mar 1749. Wi.
Carter, John. T May 1767 *Thornton*. Sx.
Carter, John (Thomas in calendar). S s sheep in Tillbrook Summer 1767 R 14 yrs Lent 1768. Bd.
Carter, John. S Sep-Oct T Dec 1771 *Justitia*. M.
Carter, John. R Lent 1775. E.
Carter, Joseph. T 14 yrs Dec 1753 *Whiteing*. K.
Carter, Joseph. S s at Skenfrith Lent 1772. Mo.
Carter, Joyce (1764). *See* Massey. Sh.
Carter, Martha. S Lent 1749. Sy.
Carter, Mary. S s at St. Mary's Lent 1762. Sh.
Carter, Mary. SQS Oct 1768 T Jan 1769 *Thornton*. M.
Carter, Mary. S Jly 1773. L.
Carter, Nathaniel. S for grand larceny Lent T May 1750 *Lichfield*. Ht.
Carter, Phillip. R Lent 1775. E.
Carter, Rebecca. S Feb T Apr 1734 *Patapsco*. L.
Carter, Richard. T May 1767 *Thornton*. K.
Carter, Richard. T Sep 1767 *Justitia*. Sy.
Carter, Richard. R & T 14 yrs Apr 1770 *New Trial*. M.
Carter, Robert. Rebel T 1685.
Carter, Robert. S Jan 1745 to be T 14 yrs. L.
Carter, Robert. S Lent T May 1755 *Rose*. E.
Carter, Robert. T for life Apr 1768 *Thornton*. K.
Carter, Robert. T 14 yrs Dec 1771 *Justitia*. Sy.
Carter, Samuel. T Apr *Patapsco* LC Md Nov 1733. E.
Carter, Samuel. R 14 yrs Apr 1770. So.
Carter als Gasford, Samuel. R Jan-Feb T for life Apr 1772 *Thornton*. M.

Carter als Eden, Sarah. R for Barbados or Jamaica Mar 1685. L.
Carter, Sarah. SQS Coventry Mar 1751. Wa.
Carter, Thomas. S Jun-Dec 1738 T Jan 1739 *Dorsetshire* to Va. M.
Carter, Thomas. S Feb-Apr T May 1751 *Tryal*. M.
Carter, Thomas. S s hogs Summer 1768. Nf.
Carter, Timothy. S Oct T Nov 1728 *Forward* but died on passage. L.
Carter, Timothy. S May s pewter plates T May 1736 *Patapsco* to Md. M.
Carter, William. R for Barbados or Jamaica Jan 1693. L.
Carter, William. R Oct 1694 AT Jan 1695. M.
Carter, William of Chislett. R for Barbados or Jamaica Mar 1698. K.
Carter, William. T Oct 1723 *Forward*. Ht.
Carter, William. S May 1745. M.
Carter, William. SQS Feb T Jun 1756 *Lyon*. M.
Carter, William. S s sheep Lent R 14 yrs Summer 1759. Nf.
Carter, William. SWK Jan T Apr 1771 *Thornton*. K.
Cartledge, Joseph. R 14 yrs Summer 1755. Y.
Cartmore, Charles. PT Sep 1684. M.
Cartridge, John. T Sep 1764 *Justitia*. Sy.
Cartwright, Ann. S Apr-May 1754. M.
Cartwright, Dicken. S Feb T Apr 1743 *Justitia*. M.
Cartwright, Elizabeth. T Apr *Sukey* LC Md Sep 1725. K.
Cartwright, Elizabeth. S July-Sep T Oct 1739 *Duke of Cumberland*. M.
Cartwright, George. S & T Sep 1757 *Thetis*. M.
Cartwrite, Hannah. S Jan-Jun T June 1728 *Elizabeth* LC Potomack Aug
    1729. M.
Cartwright, James. Died on passage 1726 in *Loyal Margaret*. X.
Cartwright, James. S & T Jly 1772 *Tayloe*. M.
Cartwright, John. S & T Apr 1766 *Ann*. L.
Cartwright, Joseph. S & T Jan 1756 *Greyhound*. M.
Cartwright, Joseph. S s glasses at Old Swinford Lent 1767. Wo.
Cartwright, Joshua. S s mare Lent R 14 yrs Summer 1755. Li.
Cartwright, Lucretia. S & T Dec 1752 *Greyhound*. M.
Cartwright, Matthew. S & T Aug 1752 *Tryal*. L.
Cartwright, Peter. S Aug T Sep 1725 *Forward* LC Annapolis Dec 1725. L.
Cartwright, Ralph (1758). *See* Sadler. M.
Cartwright, Richard. S Sep T Nov 1743 *George William*. M.
Cartwright, Robert. SQS Dec 1750. M.
Cartwright, Samuel. S s at Frampton Cotterell Summer 1750. G.
Cartwright, Thomas. S May T Jun 1726 *Loyal Margaret* to Md. M.
Cartwright, Thomas. T Sep 1758 *Tryal*. Sy.
Cartwright, Thomas. S s hay at Tewkesbury Lent 1774. G.
Carty, Peter. T Apr 1772 *Thornton*. Sy.
Carty, Timothy. SQS Oct T Dec 1767 *Neptune*. M.
Carus, John (1684). *See* Carey. L.
Carver, Ann. S May 1763. M.
Carver, Hannah als Susannah, wife of Mathew Carver of Blackburn.
    SQS Oct 1771. La.
Carver, John. R for life Feb 1758. Ha.
Carver, Margaret. S Summer 1749. Nf.
Carver, Richard. T Apr 1753 *Thames*. E.
Carwardine, William. S & TB Apr 1742. G.

Carway, John. SQS Dec 1752. M.

Carwithen, Mary. S Aug 1731 TB to Va. De.

Carwithen, Susannah. R for life Apr 1747. De.

Cary. *See* Carey.

Caseing als Cason, Ann. S Jun s handkerchiefs T Dec 1736 *Dorsetshire*. M.

Caseley, Samuel. S Apr s iron bars T Dec 1735 *John* LC Annapolis Sep 1736. L.

Casewell. *See* Caswell.

Casey, Alexander (1749). *See* Fisher. M.

Casey, Elizabeth (1725). SSe Edwards. M.

Casey, Isabella. S & T Jun 1756 *Lyon*. M.

Casey, John. S Oct 1749. L.

Casey, John. S Feb T Apr 1759 *Thetis*. M.

Casey, John. S Jly 1763. M.

Casey als Clarke, John. S Jan T Apr 1768 *Thornton*. M.

Casey, John. S Feb 1775. M.

Casey, Lawrence. SQS Oct 1750. M.

Casey, Mary. T 14 yrs May *Margaret*; sold to Mrs. Rosenquist Md Sep 1719. E.

Cassey, Mary (Elizabeth). S & T Apr 1733 *Patapsco* LC Annapolis Nov 1733. L.

Casey, Mary. S Jan-Feb 1773. M.

Casey, Patrick. S & T Jan 1739 *Dorsetshire*. L.

Casey als Gaffney, Patrick. S Jan T Feb 1744 *Neptune* to Md. M.

Casey, Richard. T May 1737 *Forward*. Sy.

Kasey, Thomas. S Sep-Dec 1746. M.

Cash, Edward of Atherton, collier. SQS Jan 1774. La.

Cash, Paul. S s at Cheadle Lent 1767. St.

Cashbolt, John. S Jan 1755. M.

Cashell, Mary (1746). *See* Hughes. G.

Cashall, Thomas. R Aug 1700. M.

Cashleake als Hough, James. S s at Shrewsbury Lent 1750. He.

Cashmore, Edward. S Summer 1772. Wa.

Cason. *See* Casson.

Caspen, William. SWK & T Apr 1769 *Tryal*. K.

Cass, John of Birch. SQS Apr 1775. E.

Cass, Mary (1718). *See* White. L.

Cass, Thomas. S Mar 1724. Do.

Cass, Thomas. S Lent R 14 yrs Summer 1747. G.

Cassander, William. S Oct-Dec 1754. M.

Cassell, Henry. SQS & TB Jan 1733. G.

Cassell, James. S & T Sep 1764 *Justitia*. M.

Cassell, Mary. S May T Jly 1723 *Alexander* LC Annapolis Sep 1723. L.

Cassells, Thomas. SQS Mar R 14 yrs & TB Sep 1727. Nt.

Casselty, Owen. S Jan 1766. M.

Cassody, Elizabeth (1754). *See* Mills. M.

Cassody, Laurence. SQS Jly T Sep 1764 *Justitia*. M.

Cassill, Thomas (1720). *See* Brown. L.

Cason, Ann (1736). *See* Caseing. M.

Cason, Barnard. S Dec 1745. L.

Casson, Thomas. S Jan T Feb 1719 *Worcester* LC Annapolis Jun 1719. L.
Cassy, Elizabeth of Walsall. R for America Jly 1677. St.
Castaign, Elie. S Oct 1744-Jan 1745. M.
Casteles, William. LC Rappahannock May 1728 from *Forward*. X.
Castelow. *See* Costello.
Caster als Harman, Anne. R Mar & Dec 1681 AT Jan 1682. M.
Castilion, Thomas. R for Barbados Jly 1680. M.
Castle, Ann. S Aug T Oct 1741 *Sea Horse* to Va. M.
Castle, Ann. S Dec 1766 T Jan 1767 *Tryal*. M.
Castle, Eleanor. S Sep-Oct T Dec 1752 *Greyhound*. M.
Castle, Elizabeth wife of Richard. S Oct T Dec 1770 *Justitia*. M.
Castle, Francis. S & R for life Summer 1775 for being at large after
    sentence of T. Li.
Castle, John. S Sep-Oct T Dec 1771 *Justitia*. M.
Castle, John. S May 1775. L.
Castle, Joseph. S Sep 1719. M.
Castle, Martha (1731). *See* Bishop. Sy.
Castle, Mary. S & T Oct 1739 *York* to Md. M.
Castle, Richard (1698). *See* Harris. Be.
Castle, Richard. S s sheep at Charlbury Lent 1738. O.
Castle, Sarah. S Feb T Mar 1727 *Rappahannock* to Md. M.
Castle, Susanna. SQS Sep T Dec 1769 *Justitia*. M.
Castle, William of Berkhampstead St. Peter. SQS Aug T Sep 1767
    Justitia. Ht.
Castleden, William of Fant. R for Barbados or Jamaica Jly 1688. Sx.
Castleton, George of Ingatestone. R for Barbados Apr TB Oct 1669. E.
Castleton, Mary. S Mar 1763 TB to Va. De.
Castleton, Robert. R for Barbados Sep 1672. L.
Caston, Mary. S Feb T Apr 1762 *Dolphin*. M.
Caston als Easter, Robert. S Lent R 14 yrs Summer 1738. Le.
Caston, Robert. S Summer 1745. Su.
Castrey, Edward. S s cheese Lent 1742. Sh.
Caswell, John. S Apr 1749. L.
Caswell, Lawrence. Rebel T 1685.
Casewell, Roger. Rebel T 1685.
Casswell, William. S Lent R 14 yrs Summer 1765. Wo.
Casworth, Thomas. S for highway robbery Summer 1729 R 14 yrs Lent
    1730. G.
Catch als Clarke, Edward. R for Barbados or Jamaica Aug 1701. L.
Catchfield, John. S Lent 1763. Nf.
Catchman, George of St. George, Southwark. R for Barbados Apr
    1668. Sy.
Catchmay, William. S Aug 1765. So.
Catchmoore, Thomas. S Aug 1750. So.
Catenach, William. S Lent R for life Summer 1774. G.
Cater, Edward. TB to Va from QS 1756. De.
Cater, Hannah. TB Jun 1738. Db.
Cater, Henry. S Mar 1736. Wi.
Cater, John. R for America Jly 1708. Li.
Cator, Joseph of Shibhorne. R for Barbados or Jamaica Jly 1710. K.
Cater, Mary. S Aug T Oct 1726 *Forward* L.

Cater, Richard. S Summer R for Barbados Aug 1663. Sy.
Cater, Richard of Whaddon. R for Barbados Jun 1687. Wi.
Cater, Sarah wife of Solomon. S Sep T Nov 1759 *Phoenix.* M.
Cater, Thomas. T Apr 1741 *Speedwell* or *Mediterranean.* Bu.
Catheral, William. S Lent 1764. Ch.
Catherine, Christian als Kitty (1752). *See* Ralph. Co.
Cathorne, Jane (1745). *See* Caton. M.
Catling, James. S Jun T Aug 1769 *Douglas.* L.
Catlin, Mary, spinster, als wife of Nathaniel of Ovington. R for
    Barbados or Jamaica Jly 1674. E.
Catlin, Thomas. S Apr s saddle & coat T Jun 1742 *Bladon* to Md. M.
Cato, John. S s at Oakley Lent T Apr 1770 *New Trial.* Bu.
Cato, William. SQS Apr 1773. M.
Catt, Curtis. T 14 yrs May 1767 *Thornton.* Sx.
Catt, John. T May 1737 *Forward.* Sx.
Catt, Nicholas. T Apr 1743 *Justitia* but died on passage. K.
Catt, William. T Apr 1771 *Thornton.* Sx.
Caton, Ann. S & T Jly 1771 *Scarsdale.* L.
Caton als Cathorne, Jane. S Jun-Dec 1745. M.
Catton, John. R Sep 1671 AT May 1672 & Oct 1673. M.
Catton, John. S Sep T Dec 1769 *Justitia.* M.
Catton, Nicholas of St. Martin in Fields. SW Apr 1773. M.
Catton, Samuel. S Lent 1758. Su.
Cayton, William. S Jan-Feb 1773. M.
Cauldecord. *See* Caldecott.
Caulfield, William. S Aug TB to Va Oct 1739. Wi.
Caustin, Paul. S Sep T Dec 1769 *Justitia.* M.
Caustin, William. S Sep 1769. M.
Cautrell, John (1656). *See* Cotterell. L.
Cave, Felix. SQS Jun T Jly 1753 *Tryal.* M.
Cave, George. S Dec 1733 T Jan 1734 *Caesar* LC Va 1734. L.
Cave, James. LC Annapolis Jly 1722 from *Gilbert.* X.
Cave, James. S Oct 1741. M.
Cave, John. S Oct T Dec 1769 *Justitia.* L.
Cave, John. S Aug 1773. Do.
Cave, Joseph. S & R 14 yrs Lent 1738. No.
Cave, Patrick. S Jan 1746 to be T 14 yrs. M.
Cave, Richard. S s pocket book at St. Michael Cornhill Apr T Jun 1768
    Tryal. L.
Cave, Thomas. S Lent T Oct 1765. Bd.
Cave, Thomas. S & T Dec 1769 *Justitia.* L.
Cave, William. S Summer 1751. Cu.
Cavenagh, Hannah. S Feb T Apr 1771 *Thornton.* L.
Cavenagh, Honor. R Apr T for life May 1743 *Indian Queen* to
    Potomack. M.
Cavaner, Jane. S Oct 1728 T *Forward* LC Rappahannock Jun 1729. M.
Cavenaugh, Thomas. S Jan-Feb T Apr 1772 *Thornton.* M.
Cavendish, Margaret. S Apr T May 1752 *Lichfield.* L.
Caver, John. R for Barbados Feb 1664. M.
Caverley, Richard. S Jly 1721 T Mar 1723. Bu.
Cavery als Goathorne, Richard. S s sheep at Adderbury Lent 1722. O.

Cavey, Elizabeth. R Apr TB to Barbados Jun 1669. L.
Cavill, Sarah. SQS Oct 1759 TB Apr 1760. So.
Cavill, Sarah. SQS & TB Oct 1764. So.
Cavill, William. SQS Jan TB Apr 1764. So.
Cavill, William. S Apr 1747. So.
Caudell, James. S s gelding at Fressingfield Lent R Summer 1775. Su.
Cawdell, John. S & T Dec 1740 *Vernon*. L.
Cawdell, Mary. S Jan T Feb 1744 *Neptune*. L.
Cawger, Ann, spinster. R for America Mar 1697. Li.
Cawkin, Alice. S Jly-Sep T Oct 1739 *Duke of Cumberland* to Va. M.
Cawley, John of St. John's, waterman. SQS & T Jan 1769 *Thornton*. Sy.
Cawley, Mary. S Mar 1757. Do.
Cawthorne, Adey. S Summer 1759. Hu.
Cauthorn, Ann. S Lent 1769. Nt.
Cawthorne, Charles. S Jun T Oct 1720 *Gilbert*. L.
Cawthrey, Isaac. AT Lent & Summer 1750. Y.
Cayley, William. R Jly T for life Oct 1768 *Justitia*. M.
Cedar, William. S Jan T Feb 1724 *Anne* to Carolina. M.
Cerda, Domingo. R for Barbados or Jamaica Jly 1687. M.
Certain, Jacob. PT Aug 1676. M.
Chad, William. S & T Jun 1742 *Bladon*. L.
Chadburn, Joseph. S Lent TB Apr 1766. Db.
Chadburne, Joseph. S s mare at Darfield & R 14 yrs Summer 1768. Y.
Chadwick, Elizabeth (1728). *See* Currant. L.
Chadwick, Hannah. T Apr *Patapsco* LC Md Nov 1733. K.
Chadwick, John. S Apr 1748. L.
Chadwick, Jonathan of Hollinwood, woollen weaver. SQS Apr 1758. La.
Chadwick, Michael of Huntslett. R for Barbados Jly 1685. Y.
Chadwick, Moses. TB Sep 1737. Db.
Chadwick, Richard (1773). *See* Illingworth. Y.
Chadwick, Susannah of Manchester, singlewoman. SQS Apr 1756. La.
Chadwick, Thomas. S Lent R 14 yrs Summer 1752. La.
Chadwick, Thomas. S Summer 1763. Li.
Chaff, Patrick. S Apr T May 1767 *Thornton*. L.
Chaffey, James. S Jan T Apr 1762 *Dolphin*. L.
Chaffey, John. R 14 yrs Apr 1770. So.
Chaire, Henry of Tiverton. R for Barbados Mar 1691. De.
Chaires, James. S May T Jly 1722 *Alexander* to Nevis or Jamaica. M.
Chaires, John. S May T Jly 1722 *Alexander* to Nevis or Jamaica. M.
Chaldecott, Christian wife of Benjamin. S Mar 1738. Do.
Chalder, James. S Mar 1757. So.
Challice, Brian of Royston. R Oct 1620. Ht.
Challis, John. S s malt at Newbury Lent 1758. Be.
Chalice, Robert of Broadhembury, husbandman. R for Barbados Dec 1673. De.
Chaulke, Henry of Hillingdon. R Nov 1690 & May 1691 T Jun 1691. M.
Chalker, Richard of South Weald. R for Barbados or Jamaica Mar 1688. E.
Chalkley, Ann of Chelmsford, spinster. SQS Oct 1758 T Apr 1759 *Thetis*. E.
Chalkley, John. S & T Oct 1732 *Caesar*. L.

Chalkley, Thomas. S for perjury May 1775. L.
Challenge, Mary. R 14 yrs Jly 1744. So.
Challenge, Samuel. R for America Feb 1692. No.
Challingsworth, Sarah. S Summer T Sep 1773. Wa.
Challener, George. S Apr-May T May 1744 *Justitia*. M.
Chaloner, Nathaniel of Prescott, husbandman. SQS Oct 1764. La.
Challoner, Thomas of Leek. R for America Feb 1687. St.
Challener, William. S s oatmeal at Whitchurch Summer 1757. Sh.
Chalmer, Alexander. S Jan T Feb 1733 *Smith* to Md or Va. M.
Chamers, John. S Summer 1733 R Lent 1734. Mo.
Chalmers, Margaret. S May T Sep 1757 *Thetis*. M.
Chamber, Ann (1748). *See* Silcock. M.
Chamber, Mary. S Jan T Apr 1762 *Dolphin*. M.
Chamberlain, Ann wife of William. S & T Apr 1741 *Speedwell* or
    Mediterranean. M.
Chamberlayne, Daniel. S Mar 1736. De.
Chamberleine, Elizabeth. R for Barbados Jly 1675. L.
Chamberlaine, Elizabeth. R Jan T Feb 1733 *Smith*. L.
Chamberlain, George. S Jun-Dec 1738 T Jan 1739 *Dorsetshire* to Va. M.
Chamberlain, Henry of Mundham. S Summer 1731. *Nf.
Chamberlain, Mary. S Sep T Dec 1763 *Neptune*. L.
Chamberlain, Richard. S Feb T May 1719 *Margaret*: sold to John Straw
    Md Sep 1719. L.
Chamberlain, Richard. R 14 yrs Jly 1746 TB to Va Jan 1747. Wi.
Chamberlain, Richard. S s at Ashbourne Summer TB Jly 1763. Db.
Chamberlain, Samuel. S s silver cup at Tetbury Lent 1768. G.
Chamberlain, Samuel. S Mar 1772. So.
Chamberlyn, Thomas (John). Rebel T 1685.
Chamberlain, Thomas. TB to Va from QS 1738. De.
Chamberlaine, William. R for America Feb 1700. Nt.
Chamberlain, William. S Jun T Sep 1758 *Tryal*. L.
Chambers, Ann. S Dec 1741 T Feb 1742 *Industry* to Md. M.
Chambers, Ann. S s at Caversham Lent 1748. .
Chambers, Arthur. R for Barbados or Jamaica Aug 1700. L.
Chambers, Charles. R Jly AT Sep 1675. M.
Chambers, Edward. S Lent R 14 yrs Summer TB to Md Oct 1738. Le.
Chambers, Henry. Rebel T 1685.
Chambers, James. S Lent R for Barbados May 1664. Ht.
Chambers, John (1681). *See* Ireland. St.
Chambers, John. S & R Summer 1739 (SP). Ca.
Chambers, John. T Oct 1750 *Rachael*. M.
Chambers, John. S for highway robbery Lent R 14 yrs Summer
    1764. Wa.
Chambers, John. S May T Jun 1764 *Dolphin*. M.
Chambers, John. S Mar 1765. Ha.
Chambers als Bale, John. S s mare Summer 1766 R 14 yrs Lent
    1767. Wa.
Chambers, Margaret. S Sep 1756. M.
Chambers, Mary. R for Barbados or Jamaica May AT Jly 1697. M.
Chambers, Mary. S Jly 1761. L.

Chambers, Robert of Low Worsall. SQS Richmond Jan AT Lent 1747. Y.

Chambers, Stephen. S Aug T Oct 1726 *Forward* to Va. M.

Chambers, Thomas. S Feb 1732. M.

Chambers, Thomas. S Jun 1733 s silver watch T Dec 1734 *Caesar* to Va. M.

Chambers, Thomas. S & T Dec 1734 *Caesar* LC Va Jly 1735. L.

Chambers, Thomas. T Apr 1741 *Speedwell* or *Mediterranean*. Bu.

Chambers, Thomas. T Sep 1742 *Forward*. Ht.

Chambers, Thomas. SQS Sep 1754. M.

Chambers, Thomas. S 14 yrs for receiving Lent T Apr 1773. No.

Chambers, William of Horsham. R for Barbados or Jamaica Apr 1668. Sx.

Chambers, William. S s sheep at Bradwell Abbey & R 14 yrs Lent 1744. Bu.

Chambers, William. S for highway robbery Lent R 14 yrs Summer 1764. Wa.

Chame, Jeremiah. S for counterfeiting Summer 1742 R 14 yrs Lent 1743. Bd.

Chameron, Mary Catherine. S Jan-Feb 1773. M.

Chamers. *See* Chalmers.

Chamneys, John. T Oct 1738 *Genoa*. Sx.

Champaigne, Nicholas. S Aug T Sep 1725 *Forward* LC Md Dec 1725. M.

Champion, John. S s mare at Marshfield Summer 1736 R 14 yrs & TB Mar 1737. G.

Chance, Francis.S for obtaining goods at Ledbury by false pretences Lent 1768. He.

Chance, Thomas. S for sodomy Summer 1729 R Summer 1730. Wo.

Chandler, Edward. S Lent 1757. K.

Chandler, Elizabeth. S Jan T Feb 1726 *Supply* LC Annapolis May 1726. M.

Chandler, Hester. S Summer 1748 T Jan 1749 *Laura*. Ht.

Chandler, John. S Mar 1750. Ha.

Chandler, John. SQS & T Dec 1758 *The Brothers*. Ht.

Chandler, Joseph. T Apr 1732 *Patapsco*. E.

Chandler, Joseph. SQS Oct 1772. M.

Chandler, Luke (1740). *See* Mortimor. Bd.

Chandler, Mary. S May T 14 yrs Jly 1723 *Alexander* LC Md Sep 1723. L.

Chandler, Mary. S & R Lent 1735 T Jan 1736 *Dorsetshire*. Bu.

Chandler, Mary wife of William. S Mar 1764. Ha.

Chandler, Sarah. R for Barbados or Jamaica Jan 1693. M.

Chaundler, Thomas of Hampton Lovett. R for America Jly 1678. Wo.

Chandler, Thomas. S for taking false oath at Bray Lent 1751; to be imprisoned for 3 months before transportation. Be.

Chandler, William. S & TB Mar 1754. G.

Chandler, William. S s bags at Bushbury Lent 1763. St.

Chandler, William (1769). *See* Chantler, Nathaniel. Sx.

Chandler, William. S & R s gelding at Bures St. Mary Lent 1770. Su.

Chaney. *See* Cheney.

Channam als Cannam, William. T Aug 1769 *Douglas*. K.

Channell, Edmund. T Apr 1741 *Speedwell* or *Mediterranean*. Sy.

Channing, Roger. Rebel T 1685.

Channing, Thomas. Rebel T 1685.

Chanings, John of Symondsbury, husbandman. R for Barbados Jly 1667. Do.

Channon als How, John. R 14 yrs Aug 1774. De.

Chant, Robert. S Mar 1761. So.

Chantler, Joseph (1765). *See* Newton. Ch.

Chantler, Nathaniel, als Chandler, William. T 14 yrs Apr 1769 *Tryal*. Sx.

Chantrill, Thomas. S s sheep Aug TB 14 yrs to Va Sep 1773. Le.

Chapbell, Charles. S Jan R 14 yrs for Md or Va Feb 1719. L.

Chaplin, Catherine. S Jun T Nov 1743 *George William*. M.

Chaplain, George. R 14 yrs Summer 1756. Y.

Chaplin, Mary. R for Barbados Jun 1670. M.

Chaplin, Nicholas (1695). *See* Cappell. M.

Chaplin, Richard. Rebel T 1685.

Chaplin, Samuel. R for Barbados or Jamaica May 1691. M.

Chaplin, Samuel. S Aug 1731. So.

Chaplain als Turner, Susan. S s at Walsall Lent 1727. St.

Chaplin, Thomas. S Summer T Dec 1736 *Dorsetshire*. Bu.

Chaplin, William. T May 1767 *Thornton*. E.

Chaplow, James. S Lent T May 1750 *Lichfield*. K.

Chapman, Anne. S Mar T May 1720 *Honor* LC Port York Jan 1721. L.

Chapman, Benjamin. S s horse Lent R 14 yrs Summer 1727. Be.

Chapman, Charles. T May 1752 *Lichfield*. Ht.

Chapman, Edward of Isle of Ely. R for Barbados or Jamaica Oct 1664. Ca.

Chapman, Edward. S Lent R 14 yrs Summer 1750. Be.

Chapman, Elizabeth. S s cloth at Broad Campden Lent TB Apr 1747. G.

Chapman, George. S Summer 1761. Nl.

Chapman, George. S Summer 1761. Nt.

Chapman, Giles. S Lent R 14 yrs Summer T Sep 1761 *Greyhound*. K.

Chapman, Henry. R Dec 1699 & Aug 1700. M.

Chapman, Henry. S & T Oct 1739 *York* to Md. M.

Chapman, Henry. S s mare Lent R 14 yrs Summer 1754. Nf.

Chapman, Henry. S Aug 1756. So.

Chapman, Isabella. Died 1721 on passage in *Gilbert*. X.

Chapman, Jacob. S Sep T Nov 1743 *George William*. M.

Chapman, Jacob. S Lent T May 1752 *Lichfield*. Sy.

Chapman, James. T 14 yrs Apr 1769 *Tryal*. K.

Chapman, Jane. S Summer 1762. Nf.

Chapman, John. T Oct 1724 *Forward*. Ht.

Chapman, John. LC Annapolis Jun 1725 from *Robert*. Be.

Chapman, John. S Apr 1749. L.

Chapman, John. S Lent T May 1752 *Lichfield*. Sy.

Chapman, John. S s cloth from tenter & R 14 yrs Summer 1775. G.

Chapman, Joseph of Warsop. R for America Jly 1716. Nt.

Chapman, Joseph (John). S May 1723 T 14 yrs *Alexander* LC Md Sep 1723. M.

Chapman, Joseph. R 14 yrs Aug 1750. So.

Chapman, Joseph. S s horse Lent R 14 yrs Summer TB to Va Sep 1754. Le.

Chapman, Joseph. SQS Apr T May 1767 *Thornton*. M.

Chapman, Joseph als Richard. SW & T Jly 1770 *Scarsdale*. M.

Chapman, Joseph. S Nov T Dec 1770 *Justitia*. L.

Chapman, Margaret. TB 14 yrs Oct 1719 T *Susannah & Sarah* LC Annapolis Apr 1720. L.

Chapman, Martha. R for Barbados Dec 1670. M.

Chapman, Mary wife of Thomas. S Lent 1745. Y.

Chapman, Nathaniel. S Apr-May 1775. M.

Chapman, Peter. S Feb-Apr 1745. M.

Chapman, Richard (1713). *See* Hope, Robert. M.

Chapman, Richard. S for highway robbery Summer 1744 R 14 yrs Summer 1745. Nl.

Chapman, Richard (1770). *See* Chapman, Joseph. M.

Chapman, Robert. R 12 yrs Jan 1663 (SP). L.

Chapman, Robert. R for Barbados Jan 1664. M.

Chapman, Robert. R 14 yrs Summer 1738. O.

Chapman, Samuel. S Feb 1774. L.

Chapman als Good, Sarah. R for Barbados Dec 1681. L.

Chapman, Sarah. S Jan T Feb 1724 *Anne*. L.

Chapman, Sarah. S Summer 1741. St.

Chapman, Stephen. S Jan-Feb 1775. M.

Chapman, Susan. S Aug T Sep 1718 *Eagle* LC Charles Town Mar 1719. L.

Chapman, Thomas. S Aug T Oct 1724 *Forward* LC Annapolis Jun 1725. M.

Chapman, Thomas. Died 1726 on passage in *Rappahannock*. Li.

Chapman, Thomas. S Nov T Dec 1753 *Whiteing*. L.

Chapman, Thomas. S Lent R 14 yrs Summer 1756. Nf.

Chapman, Thomas. S Feb T Apr 1765 *Ann*. M.

Chapman, Thomas. T 14 yrs Apr 1772 *Thornton*. Sy.

Chapman, William. LC Annapolis Jun 1725 from *Forward*. X.

Chapman, William of West Ham. S Lent R Summer 1745. E.

Chapman, William. T May 1751 *Tryal*. K.

Chapman als Fitch, William. T 14 yrs Dec 1753 *Whiteing*. E.

Chapman, William. S 14 yrs for receiving Summer 1762. No.

Chapman, William. S Lent R 14 yrs Summer T Dec 1763 *Neptune*. K.

Chapman, William. S Summer 1763. Li.

Chapman, William. S & R 14 yrs for highway robbery at Hemingford Abbots Lent 1772. Hu.

Chapel, Alice. S Feb T Apr 1766 *Ann*. M.

Chapple, Ambrose. R 14 yrs Aug 1731. So.

Chappell, Benjamin. T Dec 1763 *Neptune*. Sy.

Chapele, Francis. R 14 yrs Jly 1740. Ha.

Chappell, George. R for America Feb 1692. Li.

Chappell, Grace. SQS Warminster Jly TB to Va Sep 1741. Wi.

Chappell, Henry. S Mar 1720. Do.

Chaple, Henry. T Apr 1735 *Patapsco*. E.

Chappell, John. Rebel T 1685.

Chapple, John (1694). *See* Burbage. So.

Chappell, John. S s at Great Witcombe Summer 1750. G.

Chapple, John. S s lead at Wotton under Edge Summer 1761. G.

Chapple, Joseph. S Mar 1737. De.

Chappell, Mary. S Apr T May 1743 *Indian Queen* to Potomack. M.

Chappell als Chaplin, Nicholas. R Oct 1694 AT Jan 1695. M.

Chappel, William of Meesden. SQS Apr T Jun 1764 *Dolphin*. Ht.

Chapperlin, Mary. S & T Jly 1772 *Tayloe*. M.

Charbilies, Maria Louisa. S Jly T Sep 1766. M.

Chard, Cornelius. S Jly 1766. De.

Chard, George. R 14 yrs Aug 1758. So.

Chard, James. SQS Jan TB Apr 1764. So.

Chard als Charter, John of Blackford. R for Barbados Feb 1688. So.

Chard, John. R 14 yrs Aug 1765. So.

Chard, John. SQS Jly TB Sep 1767. So.

Chard, Nicholas. S Jly 1761. So.

Chard, William. S Aug 1740. So.

Chariot, George. PT Apr 1684. M.

Charity, John, als Baines, Henry. R City Summer 1751. Y.

Charles, Elizabeth. S s at Alveston Summer 1759. G.

Charles, George. PT Jly 1684. M.

Charles, John of Pockington. R for America Jly 1678. Sh.

Charles, John (1751). *See* Williams. So.

Charles, John. S Summer 1769. No.

Charles, John. R 14 yrs Jly 1774. M.

Charles, Thomas (1719). *See* James. Be.

Charles, Thomas (1720). *See* James. Mo.

Charles, William of Powick. R for America Mar 1701. Wo.

Charlesworth, John. TB Aug 1741 T *Shaw* LC Antigua Jun 1742. Db.

Charley, William of Coventry. R for America Jly 1678. Wa.

Charlock, William. S s from slaughter house at Newbury Summer 1724. Be.

Charleton, Elizabeth. S & T Dec 1736 *Dorsetshire*. L.

Charlton, George (1757). *See* Cheaton. St.

Charlton, James. R Summer 1775. Sy.

Charlton, Jane. S & T Dec 1759 *Phoenix*. M.

Charlton, John. S Apr s coats T Jun 1742 *Bladon* to Md. M.

Charlton, Josiah. S May T Jun 1726 *Loyal Margaret* LC Md Oct 1726. M.

Charleton, Thomas. S & T Apr 1725 *Sukey* LC Md Sep 1725. M.

Charlton, Thomas. S for picking pockets at Steelhill, Annandale, Scotland, Summer 1758. Nl.

Charnock, James. S Jan T Feb 1724 *Anne*. L.

Charter, Frances. S Summer 1733 AT Summer 1734. Nl.

Charter, John (1688). *See* Chard. So.

Charter, John. S & T Apr 1769 *Tryal*. L.

Chase, Elizabeth. S Lent 1762. Su.

Chasemore, Joseph. T Dec 1753 *Whiteing*. Sx.

Chason, Elizabeth (1727). *See* Cope. Sh.

Chassereau, Pearce John Anthony. S & T Sep 1766 *Justitia*. M.

Chatfield, Robert. R for Barbados or Jamaica Jan 1692. M.

Chatham, Ann. S Dec 1773. M.

Chettum, William als Samuel. S May-Jly 1748. M.
Chattell, Thomas. SW & T Jan 1769 *Thornton*. M.
Chattenau, Anthony. S & T Dec 1771 *Justitia*. M.
Chatterley, Charles. R & T for life Jly 1770 *Scarsdale*. M.
Chatting, John (1774). *See* Biggs, Thomas. Wa.
Chauncer, Henry. T Sep 1730 *Smith*. E.
Chaunter, John. R 14 yrs Aug 1736. De.
Chaunter, Nicholas of Soake near Winchester. R for Barbados Mar
    1686. Ha.
Chaunter, Thomas. SQS Jly TB Aug 1749. So.
Chavin, Elizabeth. SL Oct T Nov 1759 *Phoenix*. Sy.
Cheaton als Charlton, George. S s nails at Darlaston Lent 1757. St.
Checkley, John (1755). *See* Clark. No.
Chedzoy, Edward. Rebel T 1685.
Cheek, Edward. R 14 yrs Mar 1750 TB to Va. De.
Cheek, George. S Feb T Apr 1742 *Bond* to Potomack. M.
Cheeke, Philip. Rebel T 1685.
Cheek, William. S Mar 1747. Ha.
Cheeke, William. S Lent 1754. Sy.
Cheese, Edward. S s at Malvern Summer 1755. Wo.
Cheese, James. S Summer 1743. *Su.
Cheese, John. S Dec 1766 R for life Lent 1767. Be.
Cheese, Richard. S Summer 1755 R 14 yrs Lent 1756. He.
Cheese, Robert of Quainton. R for America Feb 1664. Bu.
Cheeselett, John. S s brass wire at St. Michael, Gloucester, Lent 1764. G.
Cheesman, John of Linstead. R for Barbados Aug 1662. K.
Cheesman, John of Windlesham. R for Barbados or Jamaica Jly
    1710. Sy.
Cheeseman, Richard. S Lent R 14 yrs Summer 1748 T Jan 1749
    Laura. K.
Cheesman, Robert. S Oct T Dec 1724 *Rappahannock*. L.
Chiesman, Thomas. R s mare Lent 1772. Sy.
Cheeseman, William. T Jun 1738 *Forward*. Sx.
Chesman, William S Mar 1741. Ha.
Cheetham, James. SQS Oct 1762. La.
Cheevers. *See* Chivers.
Chelcote. *See* Chilcott.
Cheldron, Robert. AT City Summer 1761. Y.
Chelew, Nicholas. S for perjury Mar 1734. Co.
Chellingworth, Isabella wife of Roger. S s at Bromsgrove Lent 1763;
    Catherine Chellingworth burned in the hand. Wo.
Cheney, Charles. S Feb T Mar 1729 *Patapsco* LC Md Dec 1729. L.
Cheyney, John. S Jun T Aug 1769 *Douglas*. L.
Cheney, Elizabeth. S & T Oct 1732 *Caesar* to Va. M.
Cheney, John. T Dec 1731 *Forward*. Sy.
Chaney, John. S s gelding Summer 1763 R 14 yrs Lent 1764. Nf.
Chiney, William. SQS Feb T Apr 1753 *Thames*. M.
Cheney, William. S Lent 1774. E.
Chequer, William. R 14 yrs Mar TB to Va Apr 1766. Wi.
Cheriton, Elizabeth. S Dec 1757 T Mar 1758 *Dragon*. M.
Cheriton, George. S Mar 1742. De.

Cherrington, John. S Lent 1767. Wa.

Cherriton, John. S at Bristol Lent 1772. G.

Cherrington, Richard. S s wheat & bacon at Norton Summer 1762. Wo.

Cherry, Elias. S May-Jly 1773. M.

Cherry, Henry. S Dec 1748 T Jan 1749 *Laura*. M.

Cherry, William. S Jly 1773. L.

Cherryholme, William. S Lent 1749. Y.

Cheshire, Anne. T Apr 1765 *Ann*. E.

Cheshire, John. S Feb T Mar 1731 *Patapsco* LC Annapolis Jun 1731. M.

Cheshire, John. T May 1755 *Rose*. M.

Cheshire, John. S Summer T Sep 1755 *Tryal*. Sy.

Cheshire, John. S s at Bratby Summer TB Jly 1763. Db.

Cheshire, John. S Lent 1765. Wa.

Cheshire, Thomas. PT Jan 1700. M.

Cheslin, Samuel. T Jun 1740 *Essex*. E.

Chesman. *See* Cheesman.

Chessam, Thomas. S Dec 1749-Jan 1750 T Mar 1750 *Tryal*. M.

Chessells, William. S Lent R 14 yrs Summer 1738. G.

Chesson, Anthony of High Halden. R for Barbados or Jamaica Feb 1676. K.

Chest, John. S Jan T Jun 1738 *Forward* to Md or Va. M.

Chester, Christopher. T Oct 1729 *Forward*. Sy.

Chester als Lewis, Elizabeth. S Lent T Sep 1757 *Thetis*. Bu.

Chester, John of Grantham. R for America Jly 1678. Li.

Chester, Mary. S Jan 1751. M.

Chester, Mary, widow. S Apr T Sep 1757 *Thetis*. M.

Chester, Richard. S Oct T Dec 1758 *The Brothers*. L.

Chester, Thomas. S for cutting down oak trees Lent R 14 yrs Summer 1731. No.

Chesterman, Thomas of Wivenhoe. R Lent T 14 yrs Apr 1772 *Thornton*. E.

Chesteny, Robert of Brinton. S Lent 1734. *Nf.

Chestney, Robert. S s mare Lent R 14 yrs Summer 1745. Nf.

Cheswell, William. S & TB Aug 1738. G.

Chettoe, John. S s cloth at St. Chad Lent 1762. Sh.

Chetts, Mahatabell. LC Annapolis Jun 1725 from *Forward*. X.

Chettum. *See* Chatham.

Chevening, James, als Reynolds, Richard of Limpsfield, butcher. SQS & T Jan 1767 *Tryal*. Sy.

Cheventum, Thomas of Low Leyton. S Lent 1745. E.

Chevys, George. S May-Jly 1774. M.

Chevis, William S for assault with intent to rob Lent 1747. Ca.

Chew, Hannah aged 31, fair. S & T Oct 1720 *Gilbert* LC Md May 1721. M.

Chew, Matthew. S s at St. Philip & Jacob Lent TB Mar 1747. G.

Chew, Samuel. S s at St. Philip & Jacob Lent TB Mar 1747. G.

Chew, William. S s cloth at Rodborough Lent 1773. G.

Chibbett, George of Cullompton, fuller. R for Barbados Jun 1669. De.

Chick, John. T Oct 1732 *Caesar*. Sy.

Chick, Robert. R 14 yrs Jly 1729. Ha.

Chicken, William (1752). *See* Jackson. Nf.

Chickley, Sarah (1740). *See* Ranson. M.
Chickley, William. S Dec 1733 T Jan 1734 *Caesar* LC Va Jly 1734. L.
Chidley, John. S & T Dec 1736 *Dorsetshire*. L.
Chiesman. *See* Cheesman.
Chilcott, Alexander (1744). *See* David, Thomas. So.
Chilcott, James. S Oct T Dec 1767 *Neptune*. M.
Chelcote, Joane. S & TB Aug 1739. G.
Chilcott, Joan. S Aug 1753. So.
Chilcot, John. Rebel T 1685.
Chilcott, John. S for highway robbery Summer 1724 R 14 yrs Lent T
    Apr 1725 *Sukey* LC Md Sep 1725. Bu.
Chelcote, John. S Lent R 14 yrs Summer 1739 (SP). G.
Chilcott, John. S Jan T 14 yrs Apr 1741 *Speedwell*. L.
Chilcott, John. S Mar 1750. So.
Chilcott, Samuel. S Aug 1749. So.
Chilcott, William. Rebel T 1685.
Chilcott, William. R 14 yrs Mar 1774. De.
Child, Andrew. S as pickpocket Lent R 14 yrs Summer 1765. Sh.
Child, Ann. R for Barbados or Jamaica Mar 1688. M.
Child, Edward. S Feb-Apr T May 1752 *Lichfield*. M.
Child, Edward (1758). *See* Thirchild. Sh.
Child, Henry. S May-Jun T Aug 1752 *Tryal*. M.
Childe, John. R for Barbados Jan 1693. M.
Child, John. S May-Jun T Aug 1752 *Tryal*. M.
Child, John. S s horse Summer 1755 R 14 yrs Lent 1760. Wa.
Child, John. S Summer 1762 R 14 yrs Lent 1763. Wo.
Child, John. S & T Sep 1766 *Justitia*. M.
Childe, Mary. R for Barbados Dec 1693 AT Jan 1694. M.
Child, Mary. AT Summer 1749. Y.
Child, Sarah. T Jly 1770 *Scarsdale*. M.
Child, Thomas. S s silver spoon at Newcastle under Lyme Lent 1756. St.
Childerley, Joan. R Feb 1675. M.
Childerton, Benjamin. R for Jamaica Aug 1661. L.
Childs, Elizabeth. S Aug T Sep 1725 *Forward* LC Annapolis Dec
    1725. L.
Childs, William. S Jan-Feb 1774. M.
Chilman, George. SWK & T Apr 1771 *Thornton*. K.
Chilson, Brown. T Jun 1764 *Dolphin*. E.
Chilton, Alice. PT Jan R May 1678. M.
Chilton, John. S for perjury Dec 1773. L.
Chilver, John. R (Norfolk Circ) Jly 1663. X.
Chiman, Philip. S Jly 1773. Ha.
Chinnery, Rebecca. S Sep-Dec 1755 T Jan 1756 *Greyhound*. M.
Chinery, Robert. S for killing sheep Summer 1742 R 14 yrs Lent
    1743. Su.
Chinery, William. S s horse Summer 1728. Su.
Chippendale, George. R for life Jly 1763. M.
Chipper, Edward. S Summer 1775. Sy.
Chipperfield, James. T 14 yrs Apr 1759 *Thetis*. E.
Chippett als Sansome, George of Henstridge, husbandman. R for
    Barbados Feb 1665. So.

Chizley, Owen. S & T Apr 1766 *Ann.* M.
Chisley, Tabitha. T May 1744 *Justitia.* K.
Chisnall, Johanna of Dalton, singlewoman. SQS Jan 1765. La.
Chisnell, Martha (1758). *See* Osborne. E.
Chisnall, Peter of West Derby, blacksmith. SQS Jan 1770. La.
Chisselden, Edward of St. Saviour, Southwark. SQS Jan T Apr 1759
 Thetis. Sy.
Chissers, Abraham. R for Barbados Aug 1679. L.
Chiswell, John (1734). *See* Holt. St.
Chitley, Simon (1752). *See* Chittey. L.
Chittenden, Mary. S for setting fire to barns Lent R 14 yrs Summer T
 Sep 1755 *Tryal.* K.
Chittenden, William. S for highway robbery Lent R Summer 1746. K.
Chittmey, William of Merton. SQS Jan 1772. Sy.
Chitty, George. R 14 yrs Mar 1762. Ha.
Chittey, Simon. S Apr T May 1752 *Lichfield.* L.
Chitwood, John. R for Barbados Dec 1693 AT Jan 1694. M.
Cheevers, Richard. R for Barbados or Jamaica Jly 1696. X.
Chivers, Thomas. T Sep 1730 *Smith.* Sy.
Chivers, William of Batchford, weaver. R for Barbados Jun 1666. So.
Chorey, John of St. George, Southwark. SQS Apr T Sep 1751
 Greyhound. Sy.
Chorley, Joseph. S & T 14 yrs Oct 1732 *Caesar* to Va. M.
Chosling, William. S Summer 1745. E.
Christian, Catherine. SQS May T Jun 1768 *Tryal.* M.
Christian, Christian (1685). *See* Bromfield. L.
Christian, Daniel. SQS Jan 1752. M.
Christian, Hannah. S Apr 1749. L.
Christian, Mary of St. Olave, Southwark. R for Barbados or Jamaica Jly
 1696. Sy.
Christian, Nicholas. S Lent 1752. Su.
Christie als Ware, Agnes. S Jly s silver spoon T Dec 1735 *John* LC Md
 Sep 1736. M.
Christy, Elizabeth. S Lent R 14 yrs Summer 1760. Sy.
Chresty, James. S May-Jly 1773. M.
Christopher, John. S s sheep at Usk Summer 1718. Mo.
Christopher, John. S Jan 1755. M.
Christopher, John. S Apr 1773. M.
Christofer, Thomas. R for Barbados Feb 1675. M.
Christofers, Francis. S Aug 1720. De.
Chrole, George. SQS Jan & Apr 1725. So.
Chubb, Honor. S Aug 1731 TB to Va. De.
Chubb, John. S Mar 1733. Co.
Chudley, William of Buckland Brewer. R for Barbados Jly 1667. De.
Chum, Francis. R 14 yrs Aug 1724. So.
Chumley, George (1766). *See* Harrison. Wa.
Church, Abraham. S & T Apr 1769 *Tryal.* M.
Church, Benjamin. S Jan T Apr 1770 *New Trial.* M.
Church, Elizabeth. S May-Jly 1746. M.
Church, Henry. R for Barbados Aug 1664. M.

Church, Henry. S s at Newbury Lent 1725 & died on passage in *Sukey*. Be.

Church, James. T Oct 1732 *Caesar*. Ht.

Church, James. S Summer 1757 R 14 yrs Lent 1758. G.

Church, John. S Summer R for Barbados Aug 1665. Sy.

Church, John. S & R 7 yrs s sheep Summer T Sep 1773. No.

Church, Peter (1767). *See* Price. M.

Church, Robert. Died 1726 on passage in *Rappahannock*. X.

Church, Thomas. T Dec 1734 *Caesar*. E.

Church, Thomas Price. S s horse Lent R 14 yrs Summer 1770. Sh.

Churches, Jeremiah (1698). *See* Buck. G.

Churches, John. S for riot Lent R 14 yrs Summer 1768. G.

Churches, Robert. S s cloth at Stanley St. Leonards Lent 1774. G.

Churchhouse, Thomas. Rebel T 1685.

Churchhouse, William. R 14 yrs Mar 1774. Do.

Churchill, Jane wife of William. S Jly 1732. Do.

Churchill, John. S Mar 1739. Do.

Churchill, John. SQS Apr T May 1767 *Thornton*. M.

Churchill, John. SW & T Jan 1769 *Thornton*. M.

Churchill, Jonathan. S Mar 1730. Do.

Churchill, Mary. S Jan T Feb 1733 *Smith* to Md or Va. M.

Churchill, Sarah. S & T Oct 1722 *Forward* LC Annapolis Jun 1723. M.

Churchill, William. S Oct T Nov 1728 *Forward* LC Rappahannock Jun 1729. L.

Churchman, Ann (1725). *See* Harwood. L.

Churchman, Edward. S & T Dec 1736 *Dorsetshire*. L.

Churchman, Margaret of Bath. R for Barbados Mar 1679. So.

Churchman, Walter of St. Margaret Westminster. SW Jun 1775. M.

Churchman, William. SQS Jan 1757. Ha.

Churne, George. S s wheat at Broad Rissington Lent TB Apr 1751. G.

Chynn, Simon. Rebel T 1685.

Chynn, Thomas. Rebel T 1685.

Chynne, William. Rebel T 1685.

Cisson, Francis of Cookham. R for America Jly 1687. Be.

Cisty, John. S Jly s pocket book & handkerchief T Dec 1736 *Dorsetshire*. M.

Civility, Sarah (1731). *See* Cross. M.

Clackson, Ann (1770). *See* Claxton. M.

Claiter, Edward. S s heifer Summer 1743 R 14 yrs Lent 1744. Le.

Clancey, Daniel. S Jan T Mar 1764 *Tryal*. L.

Clancey als Clarke, William. S Aug T Sep 1725 *Forward* LC Md Dec 1725. M.

Clapham, William. T Dec 1736 *Dorsetshire*. Ht.

Clapp, James. S Mar 1757. So.

Clapp, Thomas. R 14 yrs Mar 1749 TB to Va. De.

Clapshaw, George. S Mar 1765. Ha.

Clapton, John. S Apr T Sep 1737 *Pretty Patsy* to Md. M.

Clapton, Joseph. S Apr T Sep 1737 *Pretty Patsy* to Md. M.

Clare, Benjamin. S Oct T Dec 1771 *Justitia*. L.

Clare, George. SW & T Oct 1768 *Justitia*. M.

Clare, John, weaver aged 21, fair. S & T Oct 1720 *Gilbert* LC Md May 1721. M.

Clare, William. S Dec 1765. M.

Clareborough, Richard. S s sheep Summer 1743 R 14 yrs Lent 1744. Y.

Clarey, Margaret. SQS Jun T Jly 1753 *Tryal*. M.

Clargoe, Thomas of Swindon. R for Barbados Mar 1691. Wi.

Claridge, James. S s horse 1720 Summer 1753 R 14 yrs Lent 1754. Wa.

Clarke, Abraham. SQS Aug TB Sep 1774. Nf.

Clarke, Alice wife of John of Bury St. Edmunds, yeoman. R for Barbados Feb 1664. Su.

Clark, Alice. S Feb T Mar 1760 *Friendship*. M.

Clark, Alice. S Feb 1761. L.

Clarke, Allanson of Waltham. R for Barbados or Jamaica Jun 1684. E.

Clarke, Andrew. S Jan-Apr 1749. M.

Clarke, Anne (1688). *See* Yates. L.

Clarke, Ann. S & T Oct 1732 *Caesar* to Va. M.

Clark, Ann. S s clothing Summer 1737. Nl.

Clarke, Ann. S & T Feb 1744 *Neptune* to Va. M.

Clarke, Ann. S Feb 1754. M.

Clarke, Ann. S Feb-Apr T May 1755 *Rose*. M.

Clarke, Ann (1761). *See* Collins. M.

Clark als Lenorchan, Ann. S Dec 1762 T Mar 1763 *Neptune*; sentenced with George Watson als Clark *(qv)*. M.

Clark, Ann. S City s at All Saints Pavement Lent 1766. Y.

Clarke, Ann. S Jun T Sep 1767 *Justitia*. L.

Clark, Ann. SQS & T Sep 1767 *Justitia*. M.

Clarke als Green, Ann. S May-Jly 1774. M.

Clarke, Arabella. S Dec 1735 s gown T Jan 1736 *Dorsetshire* LC Va Sep 1736. M.

Clarke, Arthur. S Sep, detained for examination as bankrupt, T 14 yrs Nov 1762 *Prince William*. M.

Clarke, Arthur. S for highway robbery Lent 1766. Su.

Clarke als Hamilton, Barbara. S & T Apr 1766 *Ann*. L.

Clark, Benjamin. S & T Oct 1730 *Forward* LC Potomack Jan 1731. L.

Clarke, Benjamin (1750). *See* McMahon. M.

Clarke, Benjamin. S Mar 1757. De.

Clarke, Burton. S & T Mar 1763 *Neptune*. L.

Clarke, Caleb of Great Braxted. R for Barbados or Jamaica Jun 1692. E.

Clark, Catherine. SQS as rogue, vagabond and beggar Jly 1756. Ha.

Clark, Catherine. S & T Jan 1765 *Tryal*. M.

Clarke, Catherine. S & T Jan 1769 *Thornton*. M.

Clarke, Charles. S s geese at Defford Lent 1769. Wo.

Clarke, Charlotte, spinster. S & T Dec 1767 *Neptune*. L.

Clark, David. S Lent 1749. Sy.

Clarke als Atkinson, Dorothy. R for Barbados Jan 1679. L.

Clarke, Daniel. R for Barbados Feb 1675. L.

Clarke, Edmund. R for life Lent 1773. K.

Clarke, Edward (1701). *See* Catch. L.

Clark, Edward. T Oct 1738 *Genoa*. Ht.

Clarke, Eleanor wife of William. S Sep 1737 T Jan 1738 *Dorsetshire*. M.

Clark, Elijah. S Apr 1774. L.

Clarke, Elizabeth wife of John of St. George, Southwark. R for Barbados or Jamaica Feb 1690. Sy.

Clarke, Elizabeth. PT Dec 1699 R Aug 1700 AT Feb 1702. M.

Clarke, Elizabeth aged 30, ruddy. LC Annapolis May 1721 from *Gilbert*. X.

Clarke, Elizabeth. S Aug T Oct 1726 *Forward* to Va. M.

Clarke, Elizabeth. AT City Summer 1759. Nl.

Clarke, Elizabeth. SQS Jly T Sep 1764 *Justitia*. M.

Clarke, Emanuel. S Oct 1751-Jan 1752 to be T for life. M.

Clarke als Waines, Frances. S Oct 1744-Jan 1745. M.

Clarke, George. R for Barbados or Jamaica Mar 1685. M.

Clarke, George. PT Dec 1687 R Mar 1688. M.

Clark, George. S s horse Summer 1737 R 14 yrs Summer 1738. Y.

Clarke, George. S Feb 1754. L.

Clarke, George. S Mar 1762. Do.

Clarke, Gilbert. R for Barbados Jun 1663. M.

Clarke, Henry. R for Barbados or Jamaica Jly 1686. M.

Clarke als Potter, Henry. S s at St. Giles, Reading, Lent 1750. Be.

Clarke, Isaac of Hermitage. R for Barbados Jly 1688. Do.

Clerk, Isaac. S Oct T Dec 1724 *Rappahannock* to Va. M.

Clerke, Isabel (1694). *See* Harris. L.

Clark, James (1719). *See* Taylor. Y.

Clarke, James. S Mar 1719 to be T to Va. Wi.

Clarke, James. S Aug T Sep 1725 *Forward* LC Annapolis Dec 1725. M.

Clarke, James. T Apr 1742 *Bond*. Ht.

Clarke, James. R 14 yrs Jly 1746 TB to Va Jan 1747. Wi.

Clarke, James. SQS & T May 1750 *Lichfield*. Ht.

Clarke, James. S s wheat at Leigh Lent 1751. Wo.

Clarke, James (1751). *See* Dikes, Henry. M.

Clark, Jane. SQS Jan 1752. M.

Clark, James. T Mar 1742. Ht.

Clarke, James. S & T Sep 1755 *Tryal*. L.

Clark, James. S Apr T May 1767 *Thornton*. M.

Clark, James. T Sep 1767 *Justitia*. Sy.

Clark, James. S Jan-Feb T Apr 1772 *Thornton*. M.

Clark, James. R 14 yrs Jun 1772 (SP). G.

Clarke, James. S & R s at Polstead Summer 1772. Su.

Clark, James. SQS Apr 1774. M.

Clerke, Joanna (1695). *See* Bates. M.

Clark, John. AT Winter 1667 & Winter 1668. Bd.

Clarke, John of Isle of Ely. R for Barbados Jly 1672. Ca.

Clarke, John of Ledbury. R for America Feb 1681. He.

Clarke, John. Rebel T 1685.

Clarke, John. R for Barbados or Jamaica Feb 1687. M.

Clarke, John of Gloucester. R for America Jly 1691. G.

Clarke, John of Caleshall. R for Barbados Feb 1697. Y.

Clarke, John. R for Barbados or Jamaica Dec 1698. L.

Clerk als Hall, John. S Jly T 14 yrs Aug 1718 *Eagle* LC Charles Town Mar 1719. L.

Clarke, John. S Lent 1733 T *Patapsco* LC Annapolis Nov 1733. Be.

Clarke, John. S 14 yrs for receiving goods stolen at Huntingdon Feb T Apr 1735 *Patapsco* LC Md Oct 1735. M.

Clerke John. S s at Burford Summer 1738. O.

Clarke, John. T Oct 1738 *Genoa*. K.

Clarke, John. S Oct 1740. L.

Clarke, John. S s geese Lent 1742. St.

Clarke, John. S Lent R 14 yrs Summer 1742 (SP). Nf.

Clark, John. T Nov 1743 *George William*. E.

Clarke, John. S Lent R 14 yrs Summer 1744. Su.

Clarke, John. S & TB Oct 1745. G.

Clarke, John (2). S Sep-Oct 1748 T Jan 1749 *Laura*. M.

Clark, John of St. Olave, Southwark. S Summer T Oct 1750 *Rachael*. Sy.

Clarke, John. TB to America from QS 1751. De.

Clark, John. T May 1751 *Tryal*. Sx.

Clark, John. S s sheep Lent R 14 yrs Summer 1752. Li.

Clarke, John. S & T Dec 1752 *Greyhound*. M.

Clarke, John. S s at Stone Lent 1753. St.

Clarke, John. SQS Kings Lynn & R 14 yrs for burglary Summer 1754. Nf.

Clarke, John. S for highway robbery Lent R 14 yrs Summer 1755. Nt.

Clark als Checkley, John. S s mare Lent R 14 yrs Summer 1755. No.

Clarke, John. S s horse Summer 1755 R 14 yrs Lent 1756. No.

Clark, John, als Pickering, Benjamin. S s horse Lent R 14 yrs Summer 1756. Wa.

Clarke, John. S Lent 1757. K.

Clarke, John. S Apr 1760. M.

Clarke, John. S Summer 1762. No.

Clark, John. S s chains Lent 1763. Bd.

Clerke, John. S for assault with intent to rob at Henbury Summer 1763. G.

Clarke, John. S Nov T Dec 1763 *Neptune*. L.

Clark, John. S s lambs at Otley Summer 1764 AT Lent & Summer 1765. Y.

Clarke, John. T Jun 1764 *Dolphin*. K.

Clarke, John. SQS Feb T Apr 1766 *Ann*. M.

Clark, John of Low Layton. SQS Jly T Sep 1766 *Justitia*. E.

Clark, John Jr. S Norwich Summer 1766. Nf.

Clark, John of St. Paul Covent Garden. SW & T Jan 1767 *Tryal*. M.

Clarke, John of Beaumont, carpenter. SQS Apr T Sep 1767 *Justitia*. E.

Clarke, John. S s sheep Lent R 14 yrs Summer 1767. Bu.

Clarke, John (1768). *See* Casey. M.

Clarke, John. S & T Jan 1769 *Thornton*. M.

Clarke, John. S & T Dec 1769 *Justitia*. M.

Clark, John of St. George, Southwark. SQS Apr T Jly 1770 *Scarsdale*. Sy.

Clarke als Farrell, John. S Apr-May T 14 yrs Jly 1771 *Scarsdale*. M.

Clark, John. S Oct T Dec 1771 *Justitia*. L.

Clarke, John. S Jan-Feb 1774. M.

Clark, John. S Lent 1775. Sx.

Clarke, Joseph. S Mar 1732 TB to Va. De.

Clarke, Joseph. S Lent R 14 yrs Summer 1742 (SP). Nf.

Clarke, Joseph. S Mar 1753. Ha.

Clerk, Joseph. S s at Claines Summer 1763 R 14 yrs Lent 1764. Wo.
Clarke, Joseph. S Mar 1768. Ha.
Clark, Joseph. T Dec 1771 *Justitia*. Sy.
Clarke, Leonard. S Feb 1757 for assault in St. James Park. M.
Clarke, Lewis. S Aug 1764. De.
Clerke, Margaret. S Jly T Aug 1721 *Owners Goodwill* LC Md Jly
   1722. M.
Clarke als Grigge, Margaret. S Jly-Sep 1754 to be T 14 yrs. M.
Clarke, Mary. PT Apr 1692. M.
Clark, Mary. S Aug T Oct 1724 *Forward* LC Annapolis Jun 1725. M.
Clark, Mary. S Feb T Mar 1727 *Rappahannock* to Md. M.
Clark als Forton, Mary. S May T Jun 1727 *Susanna* to Va. M.
Clarke, Mary. S & T Oct 1730 *Forward* LC Potomack Jan 1731. M.
Clark als Bush, Mary. LC Va Sep 1736 from *Dorsetshire*. X.
Clark, Mary. S Jan-May s clothing T Jun 1738 *Forward* to Md or Va. M.
Clarke, Mary wife of Jonas. S Jly T Oct 1741 *Sea Horse* to Va. M.
Clarke, Mary of St. Nicholas, Colchester, widow. SQS Jly 1747. E.
Clarke, Mary. S Jan-Apr 1748. M.
Clarke, Mary. S Jan-Apr 1749. M
Clarke, Mary. S Apr-May 1754: one of this name arrested in 1758 for
   returning from transportation. M.
Clark, Mary, spinster of Clapham. SQS Jan T Apr 1765 *Ann*. Sy.
Clarke, Michael. PT Jan 1675. M.
Clarke, Peter of Newington. R for Barbados Aug 1662. Sy.
Clarke, Peter of Edworth. R for America Feb 1681. Bd.
Clarke, Peter. S Lent 1765. Wa.
Clarke, Philip. S Mar 1760. Ha.
Clarke, Philip. R Jly T 14 yrs Oct 1768 *Justitia*. M.
Clarke, Phillis. S Mar 1771 TB to Va. De.
Clark, Ralph. S s mare Lent R 14 yrs Summer 1742. Li.
Clarke, Rebecca. R for Barbados Jun 1665. M.
Clarke, Richard. S Feb 1663 to House of Correction unless he agrees to
   be transported. M.
Clarke, Richard. R for Barbados Jun 1665. M.
Clarke, Richard. T Oct 1729 *Forward*. K.
Clark, Richard. S for demanding money with menaces in York Lent TB
   Sep 1759; suspected deserter from 66th Regiment. Y.
Clark, Richard (1764). *See* Bond. L.
Clark, Richard. S Summer 1765. Cu.
Clark, Richard. S Jly T Sep 1767 *Justitia*. L.
Clarke, Richard. ST & T Apr 1770 *New Trial*. L.
Clarke, Robert of Caston. R for America Feb 1664. Nf.
Clarke, Robert (3). Rebels T 1685.
Clark, Robert. S s horse Summer 1741 R 14 yrs Lent 1742. Li.
Clarke, Robert. S Jly T Sep 1765 *Justitia*. M.
Clarke, Samuel. Rebel T 1685.
Clerk, Samuel. S Jly T Aug 1721 *Prince Royal* LC Va Nov 1721. M.
Clarke, Samuel. S Jun-Dec 1738 T Jan 1739 *Dorsetshire* to Va. M.
Clarke, Samuel. S Apr 1754. So.
Clark, Samuel. SQS May T Jly 1773 *Tayloe* to Va. M.
Clark, Sarah. TB to Va from QS 1757. De.

Clarke, Sarah. S & T Apr 1762 *Neptune*. M.
Clarke, Sarah. S Sep T Dec 1763 *Neptune*. M.
Clarke, Sarah. S s at Salwarpe Lent 1764. Wo.
Clarke, Sarah. S Sep-Oct 1775. M.
Clerke, Stephen. S Apr T Oct 1719 *Susannah & Sarah* LC Md Apr 1720. L.
Clarke, Steptow. S s sheep at Witney Lent 1729. O.
Clarke, Susanna. S & T Oct 1719 *Susannah & Sarah* LC Md Apr 1720. L.
Clarke, Thomas. Rebel T 1685.
Clarke, Thomas of Stourbridge. R for America Mar 1710. Wo.
Clerk, Thomas (1720). *See* Butler. L.
Clark, Thomas. S May T Jun 1726 *Loyal Margaret* LC Md Oct 1726. M.
Clark, Thomas. T Apr 1741 *Speedwell* or *Mediterranean*. Sy.
Clarke, Thomas. S s corn Lent 1742. St.
Clark, Thomas. T Apr 1742 *Bond*. K.
Clarke, Thomas, als Sanderson, John. S Lent 1747. Y.
Clarke, Thomas. S Jly 1750. L.
Clarke, Thomas. S May-Jly T Sep 1755 *Tryal*. M.
Clark, Thomas. S Jan T Mar 1758 *Dragon*. M.
Clarke, Thomas, als Patience, William. S Jly 1758. Wi.
Clarke als Williams, Thomas. SQS Warminster Jly TB to Va Aug 1758. Wi.
Clarke, Thomas. T Sep 1766 *Justitia*. K.
Clark, Thomas. SQS Oct 1774. M.
Clark, Valentine. R 14 yrs Summer 1747. Cu.
Clarke, Walter. S Lent 1742. St.
Clarke, William of Edgware. R for Bermuda s sheep Jun 1614. M.
Clarke, William. R 7 yrs for Barbados May 1664 & May 1665. X.
Clarke, William of Newtown. R for Barbados Feb 1673. Nl.
Clarke, William of Tamerton Foliot. R for Barbados Jly 1678. De.
Clarke, William. R for Barbados or Jamaica Mar 1685. M.
Clarke, William (2). Rebels T 1685.
Clarke, William (1710). *See* Baker. E.
Clarke, William (1725). *See* Clancey. M.
Clark, William. LC Annapolis Oct 1726 from *Loyal Margaret*. X.
Clarke, William, "a little boy", S s sheet Jun T Dec 1736 *Dorsetshire*. M.
Clarke, William (1737). *See* Piggett. Nf.
Clarke, William. S Jan-May 1738 to be T 14 yrs. M.
Clarke, William. R 14 yrs Mar TB to Va Apr 1741. Wi.
Clark, William. SQS & T Jly 1741. Bd.
Clarke, William Jr. S s sheets Lent 1742. St.
Clarke, William. S Dec 1747. L.
Clarke, William. S Jan T Mar 1750 *Tryal*. L.
Clarke, William. S Jly 1750. L.
Clarke, William. S s horse Summer 1750 R 14 yrs Lent 1751. Ru.
Clarke, William. S May-Jun T Aug 1752 *Tryal*. M.
Clarke, William. S Nov T Dec 1752 *Greyhound*. L.
Clark, William. S s frock Summer 1753. Sh.
Clarke, William. SQS Feb 1754. M.

Clarke, William. S Lent 1754. K.
Clarke, William. S Norwich Summer 1754 R 14 yrs Summer 1755. Nf.
Clark, William (1762). *See* Watson, George. M.
Clark, William. S s hogs at St. Mary Magdalen, Oxford, Lent 1764. O.
Clarke, William (1765). *See* Blake. Su.
Clarke, William. S May T Sep 1766 *Justitia*. L.
Clarke, William. S & T Jan 1769 *Thornton*. L.
Clarke, William. S s silver tablespoon at Oswestry Lent 1769. Sh.
Clark, William. R & T 14 yrs Apr 1770 *New Trial*. M.
Clark, William of Salford, peruke maker. SQS Oct 1768. La.
Clarke, William. S Oct T Dec 1770 *Justitia*. M.
Clarke, William. S Apr-May T Jly 1771 *Scarsdale*. M.
Clarke, William. S & R 14 yrs Lent 1774. Be.
Clark, William. S Aug 1774. Co.
Clark, William. S Lent 1775. K.
Clarkin als Larkin, John. T Jly *Alexander* LC Md Sep 1723. E.
Clarkland, Mary. S s silk gowns Apr 1735. M.
Clarkson, Richard. R Summer 1773. Sy.
Clarkson als Clarson, Sarah. S s casks Summer 1755. Du.
Clarkson, Sarah wife of John of Stockport, Chesh. SQS Aug 1762. La.
Clarkson, Thomas. Summer 1756 R 14 yrs Lent 1757. K.
Clarkson, William of Scarisbrick. SQS Jly 1757. La.
Clarson, Sarah (1755). *See* Clarkson. Du.
Class, John Christopher. S Summr 1764. Wa.
Classey, John. Rebel T 1685.
Clatworthy, William. Rebel T 1685.
Claver, William. R for Barbados Jun 1663. M.
Claverley. *See* Cleverley.
Clavey, Joseph. S Mar 1768. So.
Claxton als Darling als Underwood, Ann. R & T for life Apr 1770
    New Trial. M.
Claxton, Edward. S May T 14 yrs Jly 1722 *Alexander*. L.
Claxton, George. S Apr T May 1767 *Thornton*. L.
Claxton, John of Camberwell. R for Barbados or Jamaica Feb 1696. Sy.
Claxton, John. S Aug T Sep 1725 *Forward*. L.
Claxton, John of St. Sepulchre. S s linen sheet & T Jan 1740 *York* to
    Md. M.
Claxton, William. T May 1751 *Tryal*. K.
Clay, Anne. S Aug T Oct 1724 *Forward* to Md. M.
Clay als Johnson, Elizabeth. S & T Apr 1741 *Mediterranean*. L.
Clay, Elizabeth. S May 1761 to be T 14 yrs. M.
Clay, Ellen wife of Samuel of Manchester, weaver. SQS Apr 1745. La.
Clay, Granger. T May 1751 *Tryal*. Sx.
Clay, James. S s horse Summer 1729 R 14 yrs Summer TB Aug
    1730. Nt.
Clay, John. SQS Mar TB to Md Apr 1753. Le.
Clay, John. S Summer 1756. E.
Clay, John. S & R s mare Lent T May 1770. Wa.
Clay, Joseph. TB May 1734 T *Squire* LC Md Aug 1735. Db.
Clay, Matthew. R s sheep Summer 1771. Li.
Clay, Percival. S at Hull s at Kirk Ella Summer 1745. Y.

Clay, Samuel. S Mar 1720 T *Honor* but escaped in Vigo, Spain. L.
Clay, William. ST & T Aug 1769 *Douglas*. L.
Claydon, William of Hawstead. R for America Feb 1695. Su.
Claymore als Clymer, Margaret. S Dec 1735 T Jan 1736 *Dorsetshire* LC Va Sep 1736. M.
Clayton, Ann wife of William. S & T Feb 1744 *Neptune* to Md. M.
Clayton, Daniel. R for America Feb 1700. Le.
Clayton, James. S Apr-Jun T Jly 1772 *Tayloe*. M.
Clayton, James, als Rhodes, John. S Lent 1775. Y.
Clayton, John of Newington. SQS Apr T May 1752 *Lichfield*. Sy.
Clayton, John. S Dec 1755 T Jan 1756 *Greyhound*. L.
Clayton, John (1767). *See* Potter. Wi.
Clayton, John. SQS Apr T Jly 1772 *Tayloe*. M.
Clayton, Joseph. S s at Huddersfield Lent 1766. Y.
Clayton, Joseph. SW & T Jly 1771 *Scarsdale*. M.
Clayton, Samuel. S Nov T Dec 1752 *Greyhound*. L.
Clayton, Sarah, spinster, als wife of John Hughes. S s shirt & T Dec 1740 *York* to Md. M.
Clayton, Sarah. S Lent 1763. Nt.
Clayton, Susan. R for Barbados or Jamaica Dec 1695 & May 1697 AT Jly 1697. M.
Clayton, Susannah (1767). *See* Sherman. M.
Clayton, Thomas. S Oct 1749. L.
Clayton, Thomas of St. Saviour, Southwark. SQS Jly T Sep 1766 *Justitia*. Sy.
Clayton, William of All Hallows Barking. S s tobacco Jly T Sep 1742 *Forward*. L.
Clayton, William. S Jan-Feb 1775. M.
Clean, William. S Dec 1765 T Jan 1766 *Tryal*. M.
Cleaver, Charles. S Sep T Oct 1744 *Susannah*. M.
Cleaver, Edward. S Jan T Apr 1759 *Thetis*. M.
Clever, James. S Jan T Apr 1734 *Patapsco* to Md. M.
Clever, Mary. S Summer 1766. Wa.
Cleever, Robert. S s horse Summer 1738 R 14 yrs Lent 1739. Wa.
Cleaver, William. S s horse Summer 1740 R 14 yrs Lent 1741. Su.
Clever, William. T Apr 1741 *Speedwell* or *Mediterranean*. Bu.
Cleeve, Edward, als Wild, Stephen, als Little Ned. S Jly 1756. Ha.
Cleave als White, John. R 14 yrs Apr 1754. So.
Cleeve als Hammett, Joseph. R 14 yrs Aug 1745. De.
Cleaves, Edward (1697). *See* Gleaves. Y.
Cleford, Thomas. S Summer T Oct 1750 *Rachael*. K.
Clefts, Philip (1742). See Stone. Wi.
Clegg, John of Rochdale. SQS Jly 1775. La.
Clegg, Joseph of Spotland. SQS May 1757. La.
Clegg, William. R Summer 1732. Y.
Cleghorn, John (1738). *See* Gladstones. Nl.
Cleghorn, Robert. S May T Jly 1771 *Scarsdale*. L.
Clement, Edward. TB to Va from QS 1740. De.
Clement, Eleanor. TB to Va from QS 1740. De.
Clement, John. S Mar 1729 R 14 yrs Aug 1730. So.
Clement, Lewis. S Mar 1737. So.

Clement, Mary. TB to Va from QS 1740. De.
Clement, Nathaniel. R 14 yrs Jly 1733. Ha.
Clement, Robert. T Oct 1720 *Gilbert* but died on passage. E.
Clements, Ann. S Feb T Mar 1763 *Neptune*. M.
Clements, Edward. R 14 yrs Jly 1725. Wi.
Clements, Edward. SQS Jan TB Apr 1775. So.
Clements, Elizabeth. R for Barbados Dec 1681. L.
Clements, Elizabeth (1748). *See* Fowler. M.
Clements als Smith, Elizabeth. R Feb R for life Apr 1762 *Dolphin*. M.
Clements, Harris. R 14 yrs Feb 1765. Ru.
Clements, James. S Jun T Sep 1767 *Justitia*. L.
Clements, John. T Apr 1759 *Thetis*. E.
Clements, Jonathan. S & R Summer 1737. Su.
Clements, Margaret. S Jan T Mar 1743 *Justitia*. L.
Clements, Mark. R Lent 1773. Ht.
Clements, Mary. R for Barbados or Jamaica May 1697. L.
Clements, Mary (1715). *See* Godson. L.
Clements, Mary. SQS Jan 1752. M.
Clements, Richard. R for Barbados or Jamaica Oct 1694. L.
Clements, Richard. S s fishing net at Sonning Summer 1758. Be.
Clements, Richard. S Oct T Dec 1769 *Justitia*. L.
Clemens, Samuel als Felix. R 7 yrs Mar 1773. Co.
Clements, Thomas of Lambeth. SQS & T Jan 1767 *Tryal*. Sy.
Clements, William. S Summer 1762. Nf.
Clementson, Ambrose. TB Apr 1769. Y.
Clemmenshaw, Elizabeth wife of Thomas. S & T Jly 1771 *Scarsdale*. M.
Clempson, Thomas of Milwich. R for Barbados Oct 1663. St.
Clemson, William. S Jly T Sep 1737 *Pretty Patsy* to Md. M.
Clendon, Charles. S Sep-Oct T Dec 1753 *Whiteing*. M.
Clenian, Robert of St. Martin in Fields. SW Apr 1773. M.
Clennell, Mary (1759). *See* Jobson, Margaret. Nl.
Clerk/Clerke. *See* Clarke.
Cleveland, John. S Summer 1773. K.
Cleveland, Thomas. S s at St. Clement, Worcester, Lent 1767. Wo.
Clever. *See* Cleaver.
Cleverley, Daniel of Waltham. R for Barbados Mar 1694. Ha.
Cleverly, John. T Jun 1764 *Dolphin*. Ht.
Claverley, Robert. S Mar 1765. Ha.
Cleverley, Thomas. S Mar 1766. Ha.
Cleverton, Ann. S & T Jan 1756 *Greyhound*. L.
Clewer, William. R for life for highway robbery Summer 1775. Wa.
Clewes, Mary. S Oct 1760. M.
Clewit, Richard (1766). *See* Richardson. Sh.
Clewley, John. S Lent R 14 yrs Summer 1755. St.
Clewley, Joseph. S Apr 1774. M.
Clews, Richard. S Lent T Apr 1771. Wa.
Clews, Samuel. S s malt at Audley Lent 1767. St.
Cliff, Mathew. T Apr *Sukey* LC Md Sep 1725. Sy.
Cliffe, Robert of Bermondsey. R for Barbados or Jamaica Feb 1690. Sy.
Cliffe, Thomas. S Summer R for Barbados Aug 1664. K.
Clifford, Ann. S Dec 1765 T Jan 1766 *Tryal*. M.

Clifford, Ann. S Feb T Apr 1768 *Thornton*: sentenced with Mary Clifford *(qv)*. M.

Clifford, Benedict. S Oct 1718. M.

Clifford, Edward. T for life Apr 1769 *Tryal*. K.

Clifford, Elizabeth. S Lent TB Aug 1758. Y.

Clifford, John of Inkpen. R for Barbados Jly 1664. Be.

Clifford, John. S Apr 1727. So.

Clifford, John. T Jun 1727 *Susanna*. E.

Clifford, Mary. S Feb 1768 with Ann Clifford *(qv)*. M.

Clifford, Thomas. S s saw at Wellington Summer 1756. Sh.

Clifford, William. S Apr T May 1767 *Thornton*. L.

Clift, James. Rebel T 1685.

Clift, Jonathan. SQS Jan 1767. Ha.

Clift, Thomas. S May 1775. L.

Clifton, Francis. R for America Feb 1700. Li.

Clifton als Clipps, Henry of Thornecutt, Morhill. R for America Feb 1681. Bd.

Clifton, John. T Jly 1722 *Alexander*. Sy.

Clifton, John. S s at Rowley Summer 1728. St.

Clifton, John. S Apr 1747. Co.

Clifton, Thomas. S Apr 1761. L.

Clifton, William. R 14 yrs Jly 1775. M.

Clinch, Elizabeth. S Oct T Dec 1770 *Justitia*. M.

Clinch, William. S & T Nov 1762 *Prince William*. L.

Clinchmate, Lawrence. LC from *Elizabeth* Potomack Aug 1729. X.

Clyncke, William of St. Mary Magdalene, Southwark. R (Newgate) for Barbados Apr TB Oct 1669. Sy.

Clinker, John. S Lent 1767. Bu.

Clinton, John. S Jan-Feb T Apr 1753 *Thames*. M.

Clinton, Susan. Died on passage in *Patapsco* 1729. X.

Clinton, Valentine. S Aug T Oct 1724 *Forward* LC Md Jun 1725. M.

Clippingdale, George of Bristol. R for life for murder May 1763. G.

Clipps, Henry (1681). *See* Clifton. Bd.

Clisby, Joseph. S s sheets at Watlington Lent 1761. O.

Clisby, William. S & T Dec 1767 *Neptune*. M.

Clissold, Samuel. SQS & TB Aug 1738. G.

Clissold, William. S s hats at St. Mary Lode, Gloucester, Lent TB Apr 1757. G.

Clitheroe, John. S & T Sep 1731 *Smith* LC Va 1732. M.

Cloak, John. S Aug 1736. De.

Cloake, Mary. TB to Va from QS 1736. De.

Clode, John. Rebel T 1685.

Clodd als Theobald, Robert. S s mare Lent R 14 yrs Summer 1765. Su.

Clod, Robert. SQS Jly T Sep 1767 *Justitia*. M.

Cloden, Garrett of Stebbing, cordwainer. SQS Jly 1754. E.

Clogg, Robert Jr. S Mar 1741. De.

Clogg, William. S Jly 1741. De.

Clopper, Mary. S & T Jan 1722 *Gilbert* LC Annapolis Jly 1722. L.

Close, John. S s harness at Dean Summer 1737. Cu.

Close, Richard, aged 24, dark. LC from *Gilbert* Annapolis May 1721. X.

Clossen, Peter. SQS Jly 1763. M.

Cloathier, William. S Summer 1742 R 14 yrs Lent T Nov 1743
George William. Bu.
Cluff, Hannah. S May T Jun 1726 *Loyal Margaret* LC Md Oct 1726. M.
Clough, James. S Lent 1758. Y.
Clough, John. R for America Jly 1707. Le.
Clough, John. S Dec 1743 T Jan 1744 *Neptune* to Md. M.
Clough, John of Bristol. R 14 yrs Jun 1772 (SP). G.
Clover, William. R s gelding Summer 1748. E.
Clowds, Millicent. S Jly T Aug 1721 *Prince Royal* LC Va Nov 1721. M.
Clowdy, John. S Mar 1759 TB to Va. De.
Clowes, Elizabeth. S Jan T Mar 1750 *Tryal*. L.
Cloyes, Nicholas. R for Barbados Jly 1674. L.
Clubb, Alexander. R for life Lent T Apr 1772 *Thornton*. K.
Cluff. *See* Clough.
Clunis, Robert of St. Ann, Westminster. SW Jan 1775. M.
Clutterbuck, John. S s at Stroud Lent 1765. G.
Clitterbuck, Joseph. S Feb T Mar 1729 *Patapsco* LC Md Dec 1729. M.
Clutterbuck, Samuel. R (Western Circ) for Barbados Mar 1686. L.
Clutterbuck, William. S s gelding at Stonehouse & R 14 yrs Summer
1770. G.
Clutton, John. R for Barbados or Jamaica Mar 1685. M.
Cly, Henry. T Jly 1770 *Scarsdale*. M.
Clymer, Margaret (1735). *See* Claymore. M.
Clymer, Sarah wife of John. S for shoplifting R 14 yrs Lent 1773. Wo.
Coachman, James. R for Barbados Feb 1664 (SP). M.
Coachman, Thomas of Great Chart. R for Barbados or Jamaica Mar
1688. K.
Coale. *See* Cole.
Coaly, John. S & T Jly 1770 *Scarsdale*. M.
Coant, John. S Jly T Sep 1767 *Justitia*. L.
Coars, Isaac. S Feb T Mar 1743 *Justitia*. L.
Coate, Leonard of North Petherton, tailor. R for Barbados Jly 1672. So.
Coate, Richard. S Mar 1757. So.
Coates, Anthony of Rotherhithe. SQS Jan 1755. Sy.
Coates, Benjamin. SL May T Jun 1756 *Lyon*. Sy.
Cotes, Eleanor. S Jan T Mar 1764 *Tryal*. L.
Coates, Elizabeth. S Lent 1719. Y.
Coates, Elizabeth. AT City Summer 1758. Nl.
Coates, George (1663). *See* Jackson. O.
Coates, George of St. James Westminster, yeoman. S s clothing Oct 1740
T Jan 1741 *Harpooner*. M.
Coats, James. SQS Sep T Oct 1750 *Rachael*. M.
Coates, Jeremy of Kingscleere. R for Barbados Jly 1681. Ha.
Coates, John. S Jly-Sep T 14 yrs Oct 1739 *Duke of Cumberland*. M.
Coates, John. T Nov 1741 *Sea Horse*. E.
Coates, John of Bermondsey. SQS Jly T Sep 1764 *Justitia*. Sy.
Coats, Lydia wife of William. S Lent 1751. Su.
Coates, Mary (1722). *See* Harvey. L.
Coates, Mary. S May T 14 yrs Jly 1722. L.
Cotes, Mary wife of George. S Aug T Oct 1726 *Forward* to Va. M.

Coates, Sara. S Aug T 14 yrs Sep 1718 *Eagle* LC Charles Town Mar 1719. L.

Cobane, Rachael wife of Joseph. S May T Jun 1764 *Dolphin*. M.

Cobb, Anne wife of Walter. S Jly 1759. Ha.

Cobb, Daniel. S & T Apr 1733 *Patapsco* LC Annapolis Nov 1733. L.

Cobb, James. S s at Redenhall cum Harleston & R 14 yrs Summer 1775. Nf.

Cobb, John of Birdsall. R for Barbados Jly 1690. Y.

Cobb, Samuel of Wheatenhurst. S Lent 1721. G.

Cobb, Samuel. S Jan-Jun 1747. M.

Cobb, Thomas. S s horse Lent R 14 yrs Summer 1727. Be.

Cobb, William of Wheatenhurst. S Lent 1721. G.

Cobble, Priscilla of Ardleigh, spinster. SQS Oct 1755 T Jun 1756 *Lyon*. E.

Cobbs, Richard. T Nov 1741 *Sea Horse*. E.

Cobby, Anthony (1755). *See* Cubberd. E.

Cobey, Sarah. S Sep T Dec 1763 *Neptune*. L.

Cobbey, Walter. T Jun 1728 *Elizabeth* LC Va Aug 1729. Sy.

Cobby, William (1755). *See* Cubberd. E.

Cobbyn, William. S s sheep & R 14 yrs Lent 1770. He.

Cobert, John. S Jan T Mar 1764 *Tryal*. L.

Cobham, James. S Sep-Oct T Dec 1771 *Justitia*. M.

Cobitch, William. S Jan-Jun T Jun 1728 *Elizabeth* LC Potomack Aug 1729. L.

Cobley, Robert. SQS & TB Oct 1749. So.

Cobley, Samuel. R 14 yrs MAr 1774. De.

Coblin, William. SQS & T Dec 1771 *Justitia*. M.

Cobridge, John. S Jun-Dec 1738 T Jan 1739 *Dorsetshire* to Va. M.

Cock Her Plump, Sarah (1726). *See* Price. Sy.

Cock, Ann. T Jun 1727 *Susannah*. Sy.

Cock, Edward. S s hens Summer 1740. O.

Cock, Eleanor. S Nov T Dec 1770 *Justitia*. L.

Cock als Thrustlecock, John. S Lent R 14 yrs Summer 1757. Sh.

Cock, Mary. S Norwich Summer 1748. Nf.

Cock, Nicholas. TB 5 yrs to Va Nov ?1661. L.

Cocke, Nicholas. R for Jamaica Jan 1663. M.

Cock, Richard of Great Bookham. R for Barbados or Jamaica Jly 1715. Sy.

Cock, Richard. R 14 yrs Jly 1734. Ha.

Cock, Richard. S s gelding Summer 1763 R 14 yrs Lent T Jun 1764 *Dolphin*. Bu.

Cock, Thomas. S Feb T Apr 1739 *Forward*. L.

Cock, Thomas. R 14 yrs Summer T Sep 1742 *Forward*. Bu.

Cockbill, Joseph. S s horse Summer 1720 R 14 yrs Summer 1721. Wa.

Cockburn, Eleanor. AT City Summer 1758. Nl.

Cockburn, Margaret. R 14 yrs for forgery Summer 1767. Nl.

Cockburn, Mary wife of James. S City s lead Summer 1732. Nl.

Cockdale, Henry. R for Barbados Dec 1671. M.

Cocker, Thomas. T Jun 1740 *Essex*. E.

Cockerill, Henry of Offham. R for Barbados or Jamaica Feb 1684. K.

Cockerell, Nicholas. R for Barbados Mar 1677 & May 1678. L.

Cockerill, William of St. George, Southwark. R for Barbados or Jamaica Jly 1696. Sy.

Cockerton, John. S Lent T Oct 1765. Bd.

Cockett, Francis. S Oct 1733 T Jan 1734 *Caesar* to Va. M.

Cockett, John. S & T Sep 1731 *Smith* LC Va 1732. M.

Cockham, Mary (1726). *See* Cornwell. Sx.

Cockhead, Joseph. S s shoes at Burford Lent 1758. O.

Cocking als Noddy, Francis. S Mar 1740. Co.

Cockle, Clement. S Summer 1775. K.

Cockle, John. S Jun T Sep 1767 *Justitia*. L.

Cockley, William. T 14 yrs Apr 1759 *Thetis*. E.

Cocklin, Jane. S Apr-May T Jly 1771 *Scarsdale*. M.

Cockney, John (1738). *See* Parsley. G.

Cockram, George. R 14 yrs Aug 1742. De.

Cockram, George of Brewhouse Yard, framework knitter. SQS s watch Oct 1767. Nt.

Cockram, John. S Jly 1751 TB to Va. De.

Cockran, Francis. T Dec 1736 *Dorsetshire*. Sy.

Cockran, James. Rebel T 1685.

Cockran, James (1759). *See* Ray, William. M.

Cockran, John. Rebel T 1685.

Cockran, Mary. S Sep T Nov 1762 *Prince William*. M.

Cockran, Nathaniel. S Jan-May T Jun 1738 *Forward* to Md or Va. M.

Cockran, William. S Jun-Dec 1738 T Jan 1739 *Dorsetshire* to Va. M.

Cocks. *See* Cox.

Codd, Henry of Wiveliscombe. R for Barbados Feb 1684. So.

Codd, John. R for Barbados May 1684. M.

Codey, Richard. S Jan T Mar 1764 *Tryal*. L.

Codner, James. S special court Norwich for rioting Dec 1766 R for life Summer 1767. Nf.

Codry, William. S s horse Lent R Summer 1730 (SP). Be.

Coe, Anthony. S Feb 1761. L.

Coe, Catherine. S Apr T Dec 1734 *Caesar* LC Va 1735. M.

Coe, John. T Oct 1720 *Gilbert* but died on passage. E.

Coe, Mark. S s at Tattersall & R for life Lent 1774. Nf.

Cooe, Rachael. S Oct T Nov 1725 *Rappahannock* but died on passage. M.

Coe, Richard of Manchester, butcher. SQS Oct 1773. La.

Coemack, Ann. S Jly-Dec 1747. M.

Coffee als Coffield, Ann. SW & T Apr 1769 *Tryal*. M.

Coffee, James. SQS Northallerton Jly 1746 AT Lent 1747. Y.

Coffee, Peter. S & T 14 yrs Oct 1730 *Forward* LC Potomack Jan 1731. L.

Coffee, William (1700). *See* Dickate. L.

Coffery, Thomas (1771). *See* Smith. M.

Coffield, Ann (1769). *See* Coffee. M.

Cofield, Elizabeth (1734). *See* Hook. L.

Coffield, William. S Jun T Sep 1758 *Tryal*. L.

Coffin, George of St. George, Southwark. R for Barbados or Jamaica Jly 1702. Sy.

Coffin, John. S Mar 1752. Do.

Coffley, William. S Jly-Sep T Oct 1739 *Duke of Cumberland* to Va. M.

Coffton, John. S Lent 1751. Su.

Coggin, John. S Jan-May T Jun *Forward* to Md or Va. M.

Coggen, Thomas. S for highway robbery Lent R 14 yrs Summer 1750. Wa.

Cogswell, Valentine of Deptford. R for Barbados or Jamaica Jun 1684. K.

Cogswell, Valentine. R Oct AT Dec 1688. M.

Cohen, Abraham. S & T Jan 1767 *Tryal*. L.

Cohen, Henry. SW & T Jly 1771 *Scarsdale*. M.

Cohen, Isaac. S & T Apr 1762 *Neptune*. L.

Cohen, Jacob. S & T Mar 1764 *Tryal*. L.

Cohan, Joseph. SQS Oct 1764 T Jan 1765 *Tryal*. M.

Coen, Sarah. S Jun T Sep 1764 *Justitia*. M.

Cohogh, Thomas of Rotherhithe. SQS & T Apr 1765 *Ann*. Sy.

Coker, James. S s at Tittleshall Lent 1769. Nf.

Coker als Cowen, Jane. S Aug T Oct 1726 *Forward* to Va. M.

Coker, John of Great Canford. R for Barbados Feb 1668. Do.

Coker, John. S Jan 1775. M.

Colebourne, John. Rebel T 1685.

Colborn, Thomas. S s iron spade at Wolverhampton Summer 1763. St.

Colbrath, John. S Lent 1775. E.

Colchin, John. T Nov 1762 *Prince William*. K.

Colder, Elizabeth. S & TB Aug 1740. G.

Coldgate, Edward of Speldhurst. R for Barbados or. Aug 1662. K.

Coldgrave, Elizabeth. S May T Jly 1722 *Alexander*. L.

Cole, Ann. S & T Dec 1734 *Caesar* LC Va Jly 1735. L.

Cole, Ann (1758). *See* Matthews. M.

Cole, Benjamin of Christchurch. SQS Jan 1774. Sy.

Cole, Charles. S May T Nov 1743 *George William*. M.

Cole, Diana. S May T Jly 1719 to Md or NE. L.

Cole, Diana (1719). *See* Berry. M.

Cole, Diana. S Oct-Dec 1739 T Jan 1740 *York* to Md. M.

Cole, Edward. S Aug 1767. So.

Cole, Elizabeth. S Feb T Mar 1729 *Patapsco* LC Annapolis Dec 1729. L.

Cole, Elizabeth. S & T Sep 1731 *Smith* LC Va 1732. M.

Cole, Elizabeth. S Jan-Apr 1749. M.

Cole, Elizabeth wife of Zachariah. S Jly 1760 TB to Va 1761. De.

Cole, Francis. R for Jamaica Aug 1661. M.

Cole, Francis. TB to Va 1770. De.

Cole, George. LC Potomack Va Aug 1729 from *Elizabeth*. No.

Cole, George. S Jan 1754 & May 1758 T Sep 1758 *Tryal* to Annapolis. M.

Cole, George. S Lent T 14 yrs Apr 1772 *Thornton*. K.

Cole, Henry. R for Barbados Jun 1665. M.

Cole, Henry of Bletchley. R for America May 1693. Bu.

Cole, Henry. T Apr 1739 *Forward*. Sy.

Cole, James. R 14 yrs Summer 1744. Nf.

Cole, James. S Lent 1746. K.

Cole, James. T May 1751 *Tryal*. E.

Cole, James. SQS Oct 1754. M.

Cole, James. S Sep T Dec 1770 *Justitia*. M.

Cole, James. SW & T Jly 1772 *Tayloe*. M.
Cole, John of Whatley. R 7 yrs for Barbados Feb 1665. So.
Cole, John of Taunton, husbandman. R for Barbados Sep 1665. So.
Cole, John, als Crawford, William. S Jan T 14 yrs Feb 1719 *Worcester*
    LC Md Jun 1719. L.
Cole, John of Clent. S Lent 1720. St.
Cole, John. Died 1725 on passage in *Sukey*. X.
Cole, John. SQS Jan TB Apr 1729. So.
Cole, John. S s at Trentham Summer 1734. St.
Cole, John (1749). *See* Poker. M.
Cole, John. S Feb-Apr T May 1751 *Tryal*. M.
Cole, John. S Apr T May 1767 *Thornton*. M.
Cole, John. S Jly 1767. Ha.
Cole, John. T 14 yrs Apr 1768 *Thornton*. Sy.
Cole, John. SQS Feb 1773. M.
Cole, John. S Lent 1774. G.
Cole, John. S Lent 1775. Ht.
Coale, Joseph. S & T Apr 1741 *Mediterranean*. L.
Cole, Judith. S Sep-Dec 1746. M.
Coal, Mary. Died 1726 on passage in *Loyal Margaret*. X.
Cole, Mary. T Apr 1739 *Forward*. Sy.
Cole als Johnson, Mary. SQS May T Sep 1751 *Greyhound*. M.
Cole, Philip of Kilton, worsted comber. R for Barbados Jly 1667. So.
Cole, Rebecca. T Nov 1728 *Forward*. K.
Cole, Richard of Greenwich. R for Barbados or Jamaica Jly 1688 & Feb
    1690. K.
Cole, Richard. S Sep 1733 T Jan 1734 *Caesar* LC Va Jly 1734. M.
Cole, Richard. T Oct 1738 *Genoa*. Sy.
Cole, Richard. S Mar 1743. De.
Cole, Richard. S Sep T Oct 1750 *Rachael*. M.
Cole, Richard of Marks Tey, blacksmith. SQS Jan T Sep 1757 *Thetis*. E.
Cole, Richard. R Oct 1772 to be T 14 yrs. M.
Cole, Robert. S & T Apr 1725 *Sukey* to Md. M.
Cole, Robert. S Lent 1754. Ht.
Cole, Roger. Rebel T 1685.
Cole, Samuel, aged 27, dark. S Jan T Feb 1723 *Jonathan* LC Md Jly
    1724. L.
Cole, Samuel. S Aug 1724. Co.
Cole, Sarah of Peldon, spinster. SQS Jan T Sep 1758 *Tryal*. E.
Cole, Thomas. T Sep 1730 *Smith*. Sy.
Cole, Thomas. S & T Sep 1755 *Tryal*. L.
Cole, Thomas. T from Bristol by *Maryland Packet* 1761 but intercepted
    by French; T Apr 1763 *Neptune*. So.
Cole, Thomas. S Nov T Dec 1763 *Neptune*. L.
Cole, Thomas. S Summer 1765. Ca.
Cole, Ulalia. R Mar 1737. De.
Cole, William. R for Barbados Mar 1677. L.
Cole, William. R for Barbados or Jamaica Jly 1686. L.
Cole, William. R May T Jun 1691. M.
Cole, William. S Aug T Sep 1725 *Forward* LC Annapolis Dec 1725. L.
Cole, William (1736). *See* Burnett. Be.

Cole, William. S Feb T Apr 1741 *Speedwell* or *Mediterranean*. M.

Cole, William. S & T Jly 1770 *Scarsdale*. L.

Colebarrow, Richard of Camberwell. SQS Jan 1757. Sy.

Colebeck, Lucas. R for America Jly 1707. Nt.

Collebeck, Thomas. S Lent R 14 yrs Summer 1756. Nt.

Coleberd, James. S Mar 1755. So.

Coleberd, Mary. S 14 yrs for receiving Mar 1755. So.

Colebrooke, Samuel. T Jun 1726 *Loyal Margaret* but died on
   passage. K.

Colefoot, John. SWK Apr T Jly 1772 *Orange Bay*. K.

Coleman, Daniel. S Dec 1766 T Jan 1767 *Tryal*. M.

Coleman, Edward. R for Barbados Jun 1670. M.

Coleman, Edward (1679). *See* Swaine. M.

Coleman, Edward. S Dec 1773. L.

Coleman, Eleanor. S Jan T Sep 1737 *Pretty Patsy* to Md. M.

Coleman, Elizabeth. S killing sheep Lent R 14 yrs Summer 1742. O.

Coleman, Elizabeth. S Mar 1756 TB to Va. De.

Coleman, Esther. S Dec 1765 T Jan 1766 *Tryal*. M.

Coleman, George. S & T Oct 1729 *Forward* LC Va Jun 1730. M.

Coleman, Henry. S Sep-Oct 1772. M.

Coleman, Isaac of Faversham. S Lent T May 1750 *Lichfield*. K.

Coleman, James. S Mar 1742. De.

Coleman, John. Rebel T 1685.

Coleman, John of Frampton Cotterrell, yeoman. R for America Feb
   1714. G.

Coleman, John. T May 1737 *Forward*. Sy.

Coleman, John. R 14 yrs Jly 1747. Wi.

Coleman, John. S s mare Lent R 14 yrs Summer 1756. No.

Coleman, John. T Sep 1764 *Justitia*. K.

Coleman, John. S Lent R 14 yrs Summer 1767. No.

Coleman, John. S Feb T Apr 1772 *Thornton*. L.

Coleman, John. S Apr 1773. M.

Coleman, Joseph. S Apr-Jun 1739. M.

Coleman, Mary Ann. S & T Sep 1757 *Thetis*. M.

Coleman, Nicholas. S Jly 1721. De.

Coleman, Penelope. S & T Apr 1741 *Mediterranean*. L.

Coleman, Richard. S & T Dec 1771 *Justitia*. M.

Colman, Robert. S & R s sheep at Ludham Summer 1772. Nf.

Coleman, Roger. SQS Apr 1730. So.

Coleman, Rose. S & T Dec 1770 *Justitia*. L.

Coleman, Samuel. S for highway robbery Lent R 14 yrs Summer T Oct
   1744 *Savannah*. Bu.

Coleman, Stephen. R for life Aug 1771. Co.

Coleman, Thomas, Rebel T 1685. *See* Doleman.

Coleman, Thomas. S Apr-Jun 1739. M.

Coleman, Thomas. S s sheep & R 14 yrs Lent 1747. Bu.

Coleman, William. S s horse Lent R 14 yrs Summer 1727 T *Elizabeth*
   LC Potomack Aug 1729. Be.

Coles, Elizabeth. S Mar 1737. Ha.

Coles, John. S Aug 1729. De.

Coles als Digle, John. SQS Jan TB to Md Nov 1731. So.

Coles, Jonathan. R 14 yrs Mar 1771. So.
Coles, Richard of Godshill, Isle of Wight. R for Barbados Feb 1692. Ha.
Coles als Digle, Richard. SQS Jan TB to Md Nov 1731.
Coles, Samuel. AT from QS Lent 1726. St.
Coales, Sara (1718). *See* Coates. M.
Coles, Thomas. SQS Jan TB Mar 1761. So.
Coles, William of Crediton. R for Barbados Jly 1681. De.
Coles, William. Rebel T 1685.
Coleson. *See* Coulson.
Colesworthy, Abel. SQS Jly TB Oct 1728. So.
Colesworthy, Roger. S Mar 1745 TB to Va. De.
Colethorpe, Robert. S Oct T Dec 1724 *Rappahannock* to Va. M.
Coley. *See* Colley.
Colhoun, John (1727). *See* Blakes. M.
Colick, William. SQS & TB Jan 1758. So.
Collard, Mary. R for Barbados or Jamaica Feb 1686. M.
Collard, Stephen. S Jly T 14 yrs Sep 1737 *Pretty Patsy*. L.
Collard, Thomas. S Aug 1764. So.
Collech, Edward. S s wheat at Witham Lent 1757. Be.
Colleprie, John. R 14 yrs Mar 1737. So.
Colless, James. R 14 yrs Mar 1767. Do.
Collett, Edith. R Feb 1675. M.
Collett, Elizabeth. S Mar 1747. Ha.
Collett, John of Luton. R for America Jly 1682. Bd.
Collett, John. R Oct AT Dec 1688. M.
Collett, John. T Oct 1723 *Forward*. Sy.
Collett, John. S Feb T Apr 1772 *Thornton*. L.
Collett, Joseph. S Summer 1768. Wa.
Collet, Lydia. S & T Feb 1744 *Neptune*. L.
Collett, Mary (1732). *See* Edwards. G.
Collet, Mary wife of William. S s at Witney Lent 1767. O.
Collett, Sarah. S Sep T Oct 1744 *Susannah*. M.
Collett, Stephen. S Apr 1749. L.
Collett, Thomas. S Lent 1724 R 14 yrs Lent 1729. Y.
Collett, William. T Oct 1729 *Forward*. Bu.
Collett, William. S s at Enstone Lent 1768. O.
Colley als Farmer, Ann. S Feb-Apr T May 1751 *Tryal*. M.
Colley, James. S Jan T Feb 1765 *Tryal*. L.
Colley, John. S s timber at Frankley Summer 1755. Wo.
Colley, Joseph. S & R 14 yrs Lent 1773. St.
Colley, Richard. S Lent 1755. Sh.
Collicutt, John. S Aug 1736. De.
Collier, Ann. S & T Oct 1732 *Caesar*. L.
Collier, Benjamin. T May 1752 *Lichfield*. K.
Collier, Caesar. S s fowls at Witney Summer 1748. O.
Collyer, Catherine. T Nov 1728 *Forward*. Sy.
Collyer, Elizabeth. S Jun-Dec 1738 T Jan 1739 *Dorsetshire* to Va. M.
Collyer, Elizabeth. S Jan-Apr 1749. M.
Collier, John. S Jly-Sep 1754. M.
Collyer, John. T Apr 1771 *Thornton*. E.
Collyer, Martin (1741). *See* Collins. L.

Collyer, Mary. S Aug T Oct 1723 *Forward*. L.
Collyer, Mary. S Aug T Oct 1724 *Forward* LC Annapolis Jun 1725. M.
Collyer, Mary (1761). *See* Green. M.
Collier, Richard. R Aug AT Oct 1701. M.
Collyer, Richard. T Apr *Patapsco* LC Md Nov 1733. Sy.
Collyer, Samuel. S s deer from enclosed park Summer 1739 R 14 yrs
    Lent 1740. No.
Collier, Sarah wife of John. S May-Jly 1774. M.
Collyer, Thomas. S Oct T Nov 1728 *Forward* LC Rappahannock Jun
    1729. L.
Collier, William. Rebel T 1685.
Collier, William. LC Annapolis Sep 1721 from *Sukey*. X.
Collier, William of Lancaster. SQS Jan 1762. La.
Collier, William. R Dec 1774 to be T 14 yrs. M.
Collier, Zachary. S Jly T Aug 1721 *Prince Royal* LC Va Nov 1721. L.
Collin, Samuel. S Sep T Nov 1743 *George William*. L.
Collins, Alice. S Dec 1773. M.
Collins, Ann. S Dec 1749-Jan 1750 T Mar 1750 *Tryal*. M.
Collins, Ann. S Apr-May 1754. M.
Collins als Clarke, Ann. S Oct 1761 T Apr 1762 *Dolphin*. M.
Collings, Ann. S Summer 1766. Wa.
Collins, Benjamin. S May T Jun 1764 *Dolphin*. L.
Collins, Bernard. R 14 yrs Aug 1736. De.
Collins, Charles. S Sep 1737. M.
Collings, Christian. SQS Apr 1754. M.
Collins, Edmund of St. Paul Covent Garden. SW Oct T Dec 1763
    Neptune. M.
Collins, Edward. S Lent 1730. G.
Collins, Edward. S s at Wentnor Lent 1757. Sh.
Collins, Elizabeth. S & T Jan 1756 *Greyhound*. L.
Collins, Elizabeth wife of Richard, als Elizabeth Smith, of Papplewick.
    SQS s cloth Jly 1757. Nt.
Collins, Emanuel. Rebel T 1685.
Collins, Faith. S Aug T Oct 1724 *Forward* LC Annapolis Jun 1725. M.
Collins, George. S s shirts Lent 1755. Be.
Collins, Henry. Rebel T 1685.
Collins, Henry. S s at St. Helen, Abingdon, Lent 1735. Be.
Collins, Honor, aged 18. R for Barbados Feb 1664. M.
Collins, Hugh. S Sep 1760. M.
Collins, Hugh. S Jly 1763. M.
Collings, Isabella. S & T Oct 1729 *Patapsco* LC Va Jun 1730. M.
Collins, James. S Oct T Dec 1724 *Rappahannock* to Va. M.
Collins, James. S May-Jun T Jly 1753 *Tryal*. M.
Collins, Jane. S & TB Aug 1734. G.
Collings, Jane. SQS Jly TB Nov 1746. So.
Collins, John of North Cray. R for Barbados or Jamaica Mar 1682. K.
Collins, John (2). Rebels T 1685.
Collins, John. S & T Oct 1730 *Forward* LC Potomack Jan 1731. M.
Collings, John. TB to Va from QS 1734. De.
Collins, John. S & T Jan 1739 *Dorsetshire*. L.
Collins, John. S Jan T Apr 1741 *Speedwell* or *Mediterranean*. M.

Collings, John. S Jan-Jun 1747. M.
Collins, John. R 14 yrs Jly 1747. Ha.
Collins, John. S s sheep Lent R 14 yrs Summer 1754. Bu.
Collins, John. S s gelding Lent R 14 yrs Summer T Sep 1755 *Tryal*. E.
Collins, John. S Mar 1758. Do.
Collins, John. S Jly T Oct 1768 *Justitia*. M.
Collins, John. S Apr T Jly 1770 *Scarsdale*. M.
Collins, John, als Jones, Thomas. S Apr-Jun T Jly 1772 *Tayloe*. M.
Collins, John. S Sep-Oct 1772. M.
Collins, John. R Mar 1773. So.
Collins, John als Tom. S s at Grimley Summer 1775. Wo.
Collins, Joseph. S Sep T Dec 1767 *Neptune*. L.
Collins als Collyer, Martin. S Jly T Oct 1741 *Sea Horse*. L.
Collins, Mary (1715). *See* Godson. L.
Collins, Mary. S Jan-Jun T Jun 1728 *Elizabeth* to Md or Va. M.
Collins, Mary. S & T Oct 1730 *Forward* LC Potomack Jan 1731. M.
Collins, Mary. S & T Dec 1734 *Caesar* LC Va Jly 1735. L.
Collins als Tilly als Burroughs, Mary. S Jan T Apr 1735 *Patapsco* LC
  Md Oct 1735. L.
Collins, Mary. S Aug 1756. Co.
Collins, Michael. S Sep-Oct 1748 T Jan 1749 *Laura*. M.
Collins, Nicholas. R 7 yrs for Barbados May 1665. X.
Collins, Nicholas Jr. Rebel T 1685.
Collins, Richard. S s sows Summer T Sep 1764 *Justitia*. Bu.
Collins, Richard. S Dec 1772. M.
Collins, Robert. PT Oct 1700. M.
Collins, Robert. R for America Feb 1709. No.
Collins, Robert. S Jan T Feb 1726 *Supply* LC Annapolis May 1726. M.
Collins, Robert. S & R Summer T Sep 1772 *Trimley* from London. Ru.
Collins, Robert. R 14 yrs Aug 1773. So.
Collins, Samuel. Rebel T 1685.
Colings, Samuel. S Aug T Sep 1725 *Forward* LC Annapolis Dec
  1725. M.
Collins, Samuel. S Aug 1750. Do.
Collins, Samuel. R Jly T for life Sep 1767 *Justitia*. M.
Collins, Stephen. R 7 yrs for Barbados May 1665. X.
Collins, Susanna wife of John. S & T Oct 1730 *Forward* LC Potomack
  Jan 1731. M.
Collins, Susanna. S 14 yrs for receiving Aug 1756. Co.
Collins, Thomas. R for Barbados Feb 1675. L.
Collins, Thomas of Northampton, shoemaker. R for America Jly
  1678. No.
Collins, Thomas. T Apr 1733 *Patapsco* LC Annapolis Nov 1733. Bu.
Collins, Thomas. S Mar 1752. Ha.
Collins, Thomas. S s sheep Lent R 14 yrs Summer T Sep 1755 *Tryal*. E.
Collins, Thomas. S Oct 1772. L.
Collins, Timothy. S Feb 1773. L.
Collins, William. R 14 yrs for Carolina May 1719. L.
Collins, William. S Aug 1728. So.
Collins, William. S s sheep Summer 1741. Wo.
Collins, William. S s sheep Summer 1741. Sh.

Collins, William. S Jan-Apr 1748. M.
Collins, William. S May-Jly 1748. M.
Collins, William. S Jly 1763. M.
Collins, William. R Jly T 14 yrs Sep 1767 *Justitia*. M.
Collins, William S & R 14 yrs Summer 1769. Be.
Collins, William. S Aug 1772. So.
Collinson, Richard of Wensley, tailor. SQS Thirsk s barley Oct 1733. Y.
Collis, Abraham. T May 1741 *Miller*. K.
Collis, Jane. S Jun-Dec 1738. M.
Collis, Thomas. S Sep 1754. L.
Collis, William (1762). *See* Collison. E.
Collison als Collis, William. T Apr 1762 *Neptune*. E.
Collop, George. S Dec 1774. M.
Collop, Thomas. S Feb T Apr 1768 *Thornton*. M.
Collyer. *See* Collier.
Colmer, James. SQS Jly TB Sep 1763. So.
Colnet, Isaac. S Jly 1763. M.
Colpitts, Thomas. S Summer 1736. We.
Colson. *See* Coulson.
Colston/Coleston. *See* Coulston.
Colter. *See* Coulter.
Colthropp, Mary (1697). *See* Newman. L.
Colthurst. *See* Coulthurst.
Coltman, Judith. S Sep-Dec 1755 T Jan 1756 *Greyhound*. M.
Colvell. *See* Colvill.
Colvill, John. S & T Jan 1769 *Thornton*. L.
Colvill, Thomas. R (Home Circ) for Barbados May 1664. X.
Colvall, Thomas. S Dec 1763 T Mar 1764 *Tryal*. M.
Colvell, William. T Sep 1757 *Thetis*. Sy.
Colway als Colwell, David of Morchard Bishop, shoemaker. R for
    Barbados Feb 1699. De.
Colwill, Anne. R 14 yrs Aug 1726. De.
Colwell, David (1699). *See* Colway. De.
Colwell, John. R 14 yrs Mar 1758. Co.
Colwell, Thomas. S Mar 1738. De.
Colwell, Ufan. S Oct-Dec 1750. M.
Colwell, William. S s at Chipping Norton Lent 1764. O.
Coman, William. S & R s at South Repps Summer 1772. Nf.
Combden, William. Rebel T 1685.
Comber, Richard. S Lent R 14 yrs Summer 1745. Sx.
Comberlidge, Thomas. S s at Leek Lent 1750. St.
Combes. *See* Coombes.
Combot, Elizabeth (1726). *See* Hudson. M.
Come, Richard. S Aug T Oct 1723 *Alexander* to Md. M.
Comer, George. SQS Jan TB Feb 1757. So.
Comer, Richard of Huntspill. R for Barbados Jly 1698. So.
Comer, Richard. S Apr 1773. M.
Comerford, James. S Jly T Sep 1764 *Justitia*. M.
Comford, Francis (1770). *See* Comfort. M.
Comford, Sarah. R for Barbados Mar 1677. L.
Comfort als Comford, Francis. S Apr T Jly 1770 *Scarsdale*. M.

Comins. *See* Cummins.

Comly, Thomas R Mar 1774. Wi.

Commings. *See* Cummins.

Commons, Thomas. R 14 yrs Aug 1738. So.

Comondale, William. S Summer 1730. Y.

Compton als Nawnton, James. R for America Aug 1715. M.

Compton, James. S s at Minety Lent 1758. G.

Compton, James. S Apr 1773. L.

Compton, John. SQS Marlborough Oct 1749 TB to Va Apr 1750. Wi.

Compton, Margaret. S Apr-May T May 1744 *Justitia*. M.

Compton, Mary wife of Robert of St. Olave, Southwark. R for Barbados
    or Jamaica Mar 1698. Sy.

Compton, Thomas. S Feb T Apr 1739 *Forward*. L.

Compton, Walter. S Feb-Apr T May 1752 *Lichfield*. M.

Comyns. *See* Cummins.

Conant, John. Rebel T 1685.

Concklyn, Charles (1699). *See* Congill. M.

Condron, James. S Feb T Mar 1727 *Rappahannock* to Md. M.

Condren, Thomas. S May-Jly 1748 to be T 14 yrs. M.

Conduit, John. S Jly 1749. L.

Conduit, Mary. S & T Sep 1757 *Thetis*. M.

Coney, Elizabeth. S & T Apr 1733 *Patapsco* LC Annapolis Nov 1733. M.

Coney, George. S Oct-Dec 1754. M.

Coney, Mark. S Lent R 14 yrs Summer T Oct 1744 *Savannah*. E.

Coney, Richard. R for Jamaica Feb 1665. M.

Congdon, Elizabeth wife of Faithful. R 7 yrs Aug 1772. Co.

Congden, John of Lower St. Cullumb. R for Barbados Apr 1668. Co.

Congdon, Richard. S Mar 1730. Co.

Congill als Concklyn, Charles. R Dec 1699 AT Jan 1700. M.

Conybeare, Ann. SQS 14 yrs for receiving Oct 1772 TB Jan 1773. So.

Conibeer, Anthony. TB to Md from QS 1737. De.

Conybear, John (1759). *See* Hill. De.

Conibear, Thomas. S Apr 1747. So.

Conibeer, William. S Mar 1774. So.

Conings, Thomas of Tiverton, husbandman. R for Barbados Apr
    1668. De.

Conkin, George. S Jun T Sep 1764 *Justitia*. M.

Conley, William. S Summer R for Barbados Aug 1664. Sy.

Conn, John of High Ongar. S Lent R 14 yrs Summer 1760. E.

Connell, Alexander. S May 1745. M.

Connell, Alexander. S & T Jan 1765 *Tryal*. M.

Connell, Ann. S Apr T Nov 1759 *Phoenix*. M.

Connell, Ann. S Dec 1765 T Jan 1766 *Tryal*. L.

Connell, Catherine. S Oct T Nov 1759 *Phoenix*. M.

Connell, Collumb. S Sep 1740. L.

Connell, John of Reading. R for America Feb 1690. Be.

Connell, Robert. S s at Whitby Lent TB Aug 1767. Y.

Connell, Teague. R 7 yrs for Barbados May 1665. X.

Connell, Thomas. S Oct 1733 T Jan 1734 *Caesar* LC Va Jly 1734. M.

Connell, William of Newington. R for Barbados Apr 1668. Sy.

Connell, William. LC Rappahannock May 1728 from *Forward*. X.

Connell, William. S Feb T Apr 1739 *Forward* to Va. M.

Connolly als O'Hara, Ann of St. Martin in Fields, spinster. S s watch Oct 1740 T Jan 1741 *Harpooner*. M.

Conolly, Arthur. R 14 yrs Mar 1763. Ha.

Connolly, Cornelius. S Dec 1768 T Jan 1769. M.

Connolly, Dennis. S Apr 1773. L.

Connelly, Edward. S Jan T Mar 1764 *Tryal*. M.

Connelly, Edward. S Sep 1775. M.

Connerly, Eleanor. S May-Jly 1774. M.

Conolly, James. S Mar 1763. Ha.

Connolly, James. S Nov T Dec 1770 *Justitia*. L.

Connerly als Connolly, John. S Jan 1751. M.

Connolly, John. S s at Stow on the Wold Lent 1768. G.

Conolley, Margaret. S Jan-Jun T Jun 1728 *Elizabeth* LC Potomack Aug 1729. M.

Connelly, Margaret. S Sep s clothing T Dec 1736 *Dorsetshire* to Va. M.

Connolly, Margaret. S Nov T Dec 1770 *Justitia*. L.

Connelly, Michael. S Feb T Mar 1729 *Patapsco* LC Md Dec 1729. M.

Connelly, Patrick. S for highway robbery Lent R 14 yrs Summer 1721. G.

Connelly, Patrick. S Jan-Jun 1747. M.

Connelly, Thomas (1721). *See* Conway. G.

Conney, Elizabeth. S for murder of her bastard child Summer 1744 R 14 yrs Lent TB May 1745. Y.

Connick, Isabel als Isabella, wife of Anthony of Liverpool, mariner. S for forging seaman's will Lent R for life Summer 1767. La.

Connington, Lewis. S & T Sep 1757 *Thetis*. M.

Connolly. *See* Connelly.

Connor, Daniel. S & T Sep 1765 *Justitia*. M.

Connor, David. SQS Feb T May 1752 *Lichfield*. M.

Connor, Elizabeth (1753). *See* Blackwell. M.

Connor, Francis. S Jun 1754. L.

Conner, Gamble. S & T Jan 1739 *Dorsetshire*. L.

Connor, Hugh. S Jan 1746 to be T 14 yrs. M.

Connor, James. SW & T Jun 1768 *Tryal*. M.

Connor, Jane wife of John. S Feb T Mar 1731 *Patapsco* LC Md Jun 1731. M.

Conner, John. R for Barbados Sep 1669. M.

Conner als Canner, John. S & T Jan 1722 *Gilbert* LC Md Jly 1722. M.

Conner, John. S May T Jly 1722 *Alexander*. M.

Conner, John. S Jly 1749. Ha.

Conner als Doyle, Margaret. S Feb T Apr 1735 T *Patapsco* LC Md Oct 1735. M.

Connor, Mary. S Feb 1754. M.

Conner, Mary. S Jly-Sep 1754. M.

Conner, Mary. SQS Jly T Sep 1767 *Justitia*. M.

Conner, Mary. SQS Summer 1775. Ht.

Connor, Patrick. S Apr T May 1767 *Thornton*. M.

Conner, Sarah (1757). *See* Gascoyne. L.

Conner, Temperance. R 14 yrs Jly 1734. Co.

Connor, Terence. S Feb-Apr T May 1755 *Rose*. M.

Conner, Thomas of Snenton, boatman. SQS s wine Oct 1762. Nt.
Connor, Thomas. S Jun T Sep 1767 *Justitia*. M.
Connor, Thomas. SQS Sep T Oct 1768 *Justitia*. M.
Conner, William. S Jan TB to Md or Va Feb 1719. L.
Conner, William. S Jly T Oct 1741 *Sea Horse* to Va. M.
Conquest, John. S May-Jly T Sep 1755 *Tryal*. M.
Conroy, James. S Oct T Dec 1770 *Justitia*. M.
Conscollen, MAry. S Jly T Oct 1768 *Justitia*. M.
Conson, Ann. S Oct 1751-Jan 1752. M.
Constable, Elizabeth wife of Samuel. S May-Jly 1774. M.
Constable, John of Clapham. R Feb 1719. Sy.
Constable, John. S Summer 1754 T May 1755 *Rose*. K.
Constable, Philip. R Oct 1694 AT Jan 1695. M.
Constable, Robert of Swaffham. R for America Feb 1664. Nf.
Constable, Robert. S Feb T Mar 1729 *Patapsco* LC Md Dec 1729. M.
Constable, Sarah. T May 1767 *Thornton*. K.
Constable, Sarah. SWK Jly 1772. K.
Constable, Thomas of Middleton. SQS Apr T Sep 1758 *Tryal*. E.
Constantine, Charles. R Mar AT Apr 1677. M.
Contrill. *See* Cantrell.
Conwall. *See* Cornwall.
Conway, Ann wife of John. S Sep 1756. M.
Conway, Cornelius of St. Decomans. R for Barbados Feb 1669. So.
Conway als Connoway, Edward. R for Barbados Mar 1681. M.
Conway, John. S Feb T Apr 1741 *Speedwell*. L.
Conway, John. SQS Apr T Jly 1772 *Tayloe*. M.
Conway, Jonathan. S May T Jly 1722 *Alexander* to Nevis or Jamaica. M.
Conoway, Mathew. S Jan T Feb 1744 *Neptune*. L.
Conway, Roger. R for America Aug 1715. L.
Conway, Rose (1721). *See* Conwall. He.
Connaway, Solomon. LC Annapolis Jun 1725 from *Forward*. X.
Connaway, Terrence. S & T Dec 1731 *Forward* to Md or Va. M.
Connaway als Connelly, Thomas. S for highway robbery Lent R 14 yrs Summer 1721. G.
Conaway, Thomas. R 14 yrs Jly TB Aug 1755. Wi.
Conway, Thomas. SQS & T Apr 1769 *Tryal*. M.
Connaway, William. S & T Mar 1764 *Tryal*. L.
Conyers, Eleanor. S & T Apr 1733 *Patapsco* LC Annapolis Nov 1733. M.
Conyers, Grace. S & T Oct 1729 *Forward* LC Va Jun 1730. M.
Coniers, Lewis. S Feb T Apr 1732 *Patapsco* LC Annapolis Oct 1732. M.
Conyers, Mary. R 14 yrs for Carolina May 1719. L.
Conyers, Sarah. S Dec 1753-Jan 1754. M.
Coobidge, Walter. LC Va Aug 1729. Sy.
Cooe. *See* Coe.
Cook, Adam of St. George, Southwark. SQS Jan 1754. Sy.
Cook, Alexander. S Dec 1774. L.
Cook, Ann (1734). *See* Elwood. M.
Cooke, Ann. T Sep 1755 *Tryal*. M.
Cook, Ann. S Dec 1760. M.
Cook, Archibald. SL May T Jun 1764 *Dolphin*. Sy.
Cook, Benjamin, als Smith, Richard. S Mar 1720. L.

Cook, Bridget. S & T Jly 1772 *Tayloe*. M.
Cook, Charles. S Mar 1752. De.
Cook, Charles. S & T Jly 1753 *Tryal*. L.
Cooke, Charles. S Aug TB to Va Sep 1765. Le.
Cook, Charles, als Holm, George, als Pool, James. S s at Colwich Summer 1771. St.
Cooke, Charles. S Jan-Feb 1775. M.
Cook, Christopher of Witton, baker. R for America Jly 1686. So.
Cook, Daniel. S Apr 1734. M.
Cooke, David. R & T Dec 1716 *Lewis* to Jamaica. L.
Cooke, Edward of Birmingham. R for America Jly 1682 & Feb 1683. Wa.
Cooke, Edward. S & T Sep 1764 *Justitia*. L.
Cook, Elizabeth. S & T Dec 1734 *Caesar* but died on passage. L.
Cook, Elizabeth. SQS Dec 1751. M.
Cook, Elizabeth. SEK & T Apr 1771 *Thornton*. K.
Cook, Elizabeth, widow. S s at St. Peter, Sudbury, Lent 1772. Su.
Cook, Farmer. S Feb T Mar 1727 *Rappahannock*. L.
Cook, George (1663). *See* Jackson. O.
Cooke, George. R 14 yrs Aug 1726. De.
Cooke, George. S Feb 1757. M.
Cook, George. S s horse Lent R 14 yrs Summer 1762. Nt.
Cooke, George. S Sep-Oct 1772. M.
Cooke, Giles (1721). *See* Dowden. Do.
Cooke, Grace wife of Matthew of Kingston on Thames. R for Barbados or Jamaica Mar 1707. Sy.
Cooke, Henry. Rebel T 1685.
Cooke, Henry. S Lent 1745. E.
Cook, Henry. S s silk handkerchief at St. Michael, Cornhill, Feb T Apr 1768 *Thornton*. L.
Cooke, Ingram of Eastry. R for Barbados or Jamaica Jly 1710. K.
Cook, James. S City s horse Lent R 14 yrs Summer 1736. Y.
Cook, James. S Lent R 14 yrs Summer T Sep 1751 *Greyhound*. E.
Cooke, James. S & T Apr 1753 *Thames*. L.
Cook, James. S Mar 1763. Ha.
Cooke, Jane wife of James. S s at St. Philip & Jacob Summer 1750. G.
Cooke, Joane. R Jly 1686. M.
Cooke, John. S Summer R for Barbados Aug 1663. E.
Cooke, John. R for Barbados Dec 1668. M.
Cooke, John. R for Barbados Jun 1671. M.
Cooke, John of Dulleland. R for Barbados or Jamaica Jly 1681. E.
Cooke, John (2). Rebels T 1685.
Cooke, John. R for Barbados or Jamaica Oct 1694. L.
Cooke, John. S Jan 1724 & T by bond with Samuel Timson & Walter Rowbotham. M.
Cook, John. S Sep 1733 T Jan 1734 *Caesar* LC Va Jly 1734. M.
Cook, John (1737). *See* Cook, Samuel. L.
Cook, John. S Summer 1739 R 14 yrs Lent 1740. O.
Cook, John. S & TB Aug 1740. G.
Cooke, John (1742). *See* Meredith. He.
Cook, John. SQS Apr TB to Md May 1742. So.

Cooke, John. S Apr T May 1743 *Indian Queen* to Potomack. M.
Cook, John. S Jan-Apr 1748 to be T 14 yrs. M.
Cook, John. S Jan 1751. L.
Cook, John. T Dec 1752 *Greyhound*. Bu.
Cook, John. S May-Jun T Jly 1753 *Tryal*. M.
Cook, John. SQS & TB Oct 1756. So.
Cooke, John. S 14 yrs for receiving Mar 1759. Ha.
Cooke, John. S & T Apr 1765 *Ann*. L.
Cook, John. S Oct T Dec 1769 *Justitia*. M.
Cook, John. S May T Jly 1770 *Scarsdale*. M.
Cook, John. S Apr-Jun T Jly 1772 *Tayloe*. M.
Cook, John. S & T Jly 1772 *Tayloe*. M.
Cook, John. R 7 yrs Jly 1773. M.
Cook, John. S Jan-Feb 1774. M.
Cooke, Jonathan of Theydon Garnon. R for America Jly 1700. E.
Cook, Joseph. R Mar TB to Va Apr 1773. Wi.
Cooke, Judith. LC Annapolis Oct 1726 from *Loyal Margaret*. X.
Cooke, Marmaduke. R May AT Jly 1697. M.
Cooke, Martha. PT Jly 1680 R Mar 1681. M.
Cooke, Mary of Lambeth. R for Barbados or Jamaica Jly 1702. Sy.
Cooke, Mary als Sarah. S for burglary Lent R Summer 1721 (SP). Sh.
Cook, Mary. S & T 14 yrs May 1738 *Forward*. L.
Cooke, Mary. S Jan-Jun 1747. M.
Cooke, Mary. S Sep 1754. L.
Cooke, Mary of Epsom, spinster. SQS Jan T Mar 1758 *Dragon*. Sy.
Cooke, Mathew. Rebel T 1685.
Cooke, Matthew. S Lent TB Aug 1753. Y.
Cooke, Miles. S Apr 1763. M.
Cook, Nathaniel. S Summer 1747. K.
Cooke, Nicholas of Dodbrooke, miller. R for Barbados Feb 1683. De.
Cook, Palgrave. S for shoplifting Summer 1734; to be burnt in hand before transportation. Nf.
Cook, Pendell, als Smith, Richard. S Apr T May 1720 *Honor* LC Port York Jan 1721. L.
Cooke, Peter. S Feb T Apr 1772 *Thornton*. L.
Cook, Ralph. S 14 yrs s linen from bleaching croft at Osmotherly Summer TB Aug 1773. Y.
Cooke, Richard of Upton St. Leonard. R for America Feb 1673. G.
Cook, Richard. S Oct 1733 T Jan 1734 *Caesar* LC Va Jly 1734. M.
Cook, Richard. S Apr T Sep 1737 *Pretty Patsy* to Md. M.
Cook, Richard. S Jan-Apr 1749. M.
Cooke, Robert. S Aug 1735. So.
Cooke, Robert. S Summer 1746. Su.
Cook, Robert of Merstham. SQS Oct 1750. Sy.
Cook, Samuel (John). S Dec 1737 T Jan 1738 *Dorsetshire*. L.
Cooke, Sarah. S Apr T 14 yrs May 1718 *Tryal* LC Charles Town Aug 1718. L.
Cooke, Sarah. S s at Burford Lent 1722. O.
Cook, Sarah. S Oct 1733 T Jan 1734 *Caesar* LC Va Jly 1734. M.
Cooke, Sarah. S Lent R 14 yrs Summer 1754. Sy.

Cook, Sarah wife of John. S Summer 1759 for perjury at Newbury in accusing Francis Page of fathering her bastard child; to stand in pillory at Newbury for an hour before transportation. Be.

Cooke, Stephen. S Oct T Dec 1771 *Justitia*. L.

Cook, Stephen. S for highway robbery at Granborough & R Lent 1775. Bu.

Cooke, Susanna. S Sep T Oct 1719 *Susannah & Sarah* to Md. L.

Cooke, Susannah (1741). *See* Saunders. M.

Cooke, Susan. S 14 yrs Summer 1746 for receiving stolen goods from Robert Cooke *(qv)*. Su.

Cooke, Susanna. T Sep 1751 *Greyhound*. Sx.

Cooke, Thomas. R for Jamaica Aug 1661. M.

Cooke, Thomas of Wells. R for Barbados Jan 1675. So.

Cooke, Thomas of Cumnor. R for America Mar 1697. Be.

Cooke, Thomas. R for America Mar 1697. Nt.

Cooke, Thomas. R for America Feb 1700. Nt.

Cook, Thomas. T from London Oct 1723 *Forward*. Y.

Cook, Thomas of Aylsham. S s gun Summer 1728. *Nf.

Cooke, Thomas. T Oct 1729 *Forward*. Bu.

Cooke, Thomas. SQS Mar TB Apr 1731. Nt.

Cook, Thomas. S & T Apr 1733 *Patapsco* LC Annapolis Nov 1733. L.

Cook, Thomas. S s at Hinton on the Green (Worcs) Lent AT Summer 1736. G.

Cook, Thomas (1739). *See* Cock. L.

Cooke, Thomas. S s at Oxenden Lent TB May 1744. G.

Cooke, Thomas. S as pickpocket Summer 1744 R 14 yrs Lent 1745. Y.

Cook, Thomas. S Jly-Dec 1747. M.

Cook, Thomas. TB to Va from QS 1749. De.

Cook, Thomas. S s at Wargrave Summer 1750. Be.

Cook, Thomas. S Summer 1750. Bu.

Cooke, Thomas. S Dec 1753-Jan 1754. M.

Cooke, Thomas. S Mar TB Apr 1755. Wi.

Cooke, Thomas. S Summer 1758 R 14 yrs Lent 1759. Le.

Cooke, Thomas. S Jan T Mar 1764 *Tryal*. L.

Cook, Thomas of St. George, Southwark, packer. SQS May 1764. Sy.

Cook, Thomas (1765). *See* Dean. L.

Cook, Thomas. S Mar TB to Va Apr 1768. Le.

Cooke, Thomas. S May T Jly 1770 *Scarsdale*. M.

Cook, Thomas. S Apr-Jun T Jly 1772 *Tayloe*. M.

Cooke, Thomas. S s sheep & R 14 yrs Lent 1773. G.

Cook, Thomas. S Summer 1774. Sy.

Cook, Thomas. S Sep-Oct 1775. M.

Cooke, William of Ivinghoe. R for Barbados Feb 1664. Bu.

Cooke, William. R for Barbados May 1664. M.

Cooke, William. R for Barbados Dec 1670. M.

Cook, William. T Jun 1728 *Elizabeth* LC Va Aug 1729. Sx.

Cook, William. S Oct T Nov 1728 *Forward* LC Rappahannock Jun 1729. M.

Cook, William. S Lent R 14 yrs Summer 1734. Li.

Cooke, William. S s linen at Comderton Summer 1752. Wo.

Cooke, William. S Summer 1753. Nl.

Cook, William. S Oct 1756. L.

Cook, William. S Summer 1762 R 14 yrs Lent 1763. E.

Cook, William. S s wheat Summer TB Oct 1764. Db.

Cook, William. S s calf skins Lent 1765. Su.

Cooke, William. S s sheep Lent R 14 yrs Summer 1765. He.

Cooke, William. S Jly T Sep 1765 *Justitia*. L.

Cooke, William. R Apr 1770. Do.

Cook, William. S Mar 1773. Ha.

Cook, William. S Jly 1774. Ha.

Cooke, William. T Sep 1755 *Tryal*. M.

Cookman, James. S Mar 1772. Ha.

Cooksey, John of St. Paul Covent Garden. SW Jly T Sep 1767
  Justitia. M.

Cooksey als Coxey, William. S for highway robbery Lent TB for life to
  Va Apr 1774. Le.

Cooksley, Mary (1686). *See* Sealey. So.

Cookson, Lancelot. S s at St. Leonard Summer 1743. Sh.

Cookson als Howarth, William. S Lent 1758. Y.

Coolet, Mary. S Jan T Apr 1762 *Dolphin*. L.

Cooley, James. SQS Jan 1755. M.

Cooley, John. S Aug T Oct 1723 *Forward* to Va. M.

Cooley, John. S Feb-Apr 1746. M.

Cooley, John. S Jan-Feb 1774. M.

Cooley, Margaret. S Dec 1755 T Jan 1756 *Greyhound*. L.

Cooley, Richard. S Dec 1742 T 14 yrs Mar 1743 *Justitia*. L.

Cooley, Robert. S for highway robbery Lent R 14 yrs Summer 1742. Nt.

Cooley, Robert. S Summer T Sep 1751 *Greyhound*. K.

Cooley, Thomas (John). S & T Jly 1753 *Tryal*. M.

Coolley, Thomas of St. Saviour, Southwark. SQS Oct 1764 T Feb 1765
  Tryal. Sy.

Cooling, Thomas. T May 1751 *Tryal*. Sy.

Combe, James. Rebel T 1685.

Combe, John. S May T Jun 1727 *Susannah*. L.

Combe, Thomas. R 14 yrs Jly 1719 to be T to Va. De.

Combe, William. Rebel T 1685.

Combe, William of East Moulsey. R for Barbados or Jamaica Jly
  1696. Sy.

Combe, William. S Mar 1734. De.

Combe, William. R 14 yrs Aug 1750. So.

Coombes, Catherine. S s clothing & T Dec 1734 *Caesar* LC Va Jly
  1735. M.

Combes, Charles. S Feb T Apr 1765 *Ann*. M.

Coombs, Elizabeth. S s ribbon & T May 1736 *Patapsco* to Md. M.

Combes, James of Bermondsey. SQS Jan 1774. Sy.

Coombs, John Sr. S Mar 1774. So.

Coomes, Mary. S Sep 1747 but died in gaol. L.

Coombes, Richard. SQS & TB Jly 1729. So.

Combes, Robert of Hilperton. R for Barbados Jan 1676. Wi.

Combes, Thomas of Belchwell, carpenter. R for Barbados Feb 1710. Do.

Coombs, Thomas. T Apr 1743 *Justitia*. Sy.

Combs, William. R 14 yrs Aug 1721. So.

Cooms, William. S Apr T May 1743 *Indian Queen* to Potomack. M.

Coombes, William. S Summer T Sep 1755 *Tryal*. Sy.

Coomer, Richard of St. George, Southwark. SQS Jan 1754. Sy.

Coomley, Henry. S Dec 1742 T Mar 1743 *Justitia*. L.

Cooper, Ann. S Lent 1768. Ca.

Coop(er), Arthur. LC Rappahannock May 1728 from *Forward*. X.

Cooper, Charles. R Aug 1700. M.

Cooper, Charles. R Jly 1702 (SP). L.

Cooper, Charles. S s horse Lent R 14 yrs Summer 1727. Be.

Cooper, Charles. S Feb 1738. Ha.

Cooper, Charles. S Apr-May 1775. M.

Cooper, Christopher. Rebel T 1685.

Cooper, Daniel. S & R 14 yrs s mare Lent T Sep 1768. Li.

Cooper, Edmund of Middleton, weaver. SQS Mar 1767; S Summer 1768 for returning from transportation; for lack of evidence to await T. La.

Cooper, Edward. R 14 yrs Mar 1763. So.

Cooper, Edward. S s shoe buckles at Bures St. Mary Lent 1775. Su.

Cooper, Eleanor. SQS Oct 1768 T Jan 1769 *Thornton*. M.

Cooper, Elizabeth of St. Olave, Southwark. R for Barbados Apr 1668. Sy.

Cooper, Elizabeth. S & T Oct 1719 *Susannah & Sarah* LC Md Apr 1720. L.

Cooper, Elizabeth. S Sep T Dec 1734 *Caesar* but died on passage. M.

Cooper, Elizabeth. S Apr 1749. L.

Cooper, Elizabeth. S Oct-Dec 1754. M.

Cooper, Elizabeth. S Aug T Sep 1764 *Justitia*. L.

Cooper, George. T May 1767 *Thornton*. M.

Cooper, George. SQS Jan TB May 1770. So.

Cooper, Grace, aged 28, dark. S Jly T Oct 1720 *Gilbert* LC Md May 1721. M.

Cooper, Henry. R Apr TB for Barbados Jun 1668. L.

Cooper, Henry. S Mar TB Sep 1728. Wi.

Cooper, James of Winchester. R for Barbados Jly 1677. Ha.

Cooper, James. T Jly 1722 *Alexander*. Sy.

Cooper, James. S & R 14 yrs s horse Lent 1735. Nf.

Cooper, James. S & T Sep 1757 *Thetis*. M.

Cooper, James. S for receiving goods stolen from Earl of Harrington Dec 1764 T 14 yrs Jan 1765 *Tryal*. M.

Cooper, James (1765). *See* Knott. La.

Cooper, James. R Jun T 14 yrs Aug 1769 *Douglas*. M.

Cooper, Joan. R for Barbados Apr 1669. M.

Cooper, John of Isle of Ely. R for Barbados Jly 1672. Ca.

Cooper, John. R Mar AT May 1688. M.

Cooper, John. T Oct 1723 *Forward*. E.

Cooper, John. S & R for highway robbery Lent 1738. Su.

Cooper, John of Falmer. S Summer T Oct 1739 *Duke of Cumberland*. Sx.

Cooper, John. T Jun 1740 *Essex*. E.

Cooper, John. T Apr 1741 *Speedwell* or *Mediterranean*. E.

Cooper, John. S s mare Summer 1747 R 14 yrs Lent 1748. Le.

Cooper, John. S Lent 1748. K.

Cooper, John. S May-Jly 1749. M.
Cooper, John. S Mar 1752. Ha.
Cooper, John. T Aug 1752 *Tryal*. K.
Cooper, John. S Lent 1754. Ht.
Cooper, John (1755). *See* Piercy. L.
Cooper, John of Manchester. SQS Jan 1757. La.
Cooper, John. S s ox & cow Lent R 14 yrs Summer 1761. No.
Cooper, John. S Oct 1766 T Jan 1767 *Tryal*. M.
Cooper, John (George). S Apr T May 1767 *Thornton*. M.
Cooper, John. R Lent 1773. E.
Cooper, John. S Sep-Oct 1774. M.
Cooper, Jordan. S Sep-Oct T Dec 1752 *Greyhound*. M.
Cooper, Joseph. Rebel T 1685.
Cooper, Joseph. SQS Mar TB Aug 1720 to be shipped to Md from
    Liverpool. Db.
Cooper, Joseph. T Jun 1740 *Essex*. Sy.
Cooper, Joseph. S Feb T Mar 1750 *Tryal*. M.
Cooper, Joseph. S Nov T Dec 1753 *Whiteing*. L.
Cooper, Joshua. S Jly 1764. Ha.
Cooper, Mark. S & R Lent 1738. Su.
Cooper, Mary. S Jly T Sep 1718 *Eagle* LC Charles Town Mar 1719. L.
Cooper, Mary. S & T Oct 1730 *Forward* LC Potomack Jan 1731. M.
Cooper, Mary. S Feb T Apr 1732 *Patapsco* LC Annapolis Oct 1732. M.
Cooper, Mary of Weston Underwood, spinster. S Lent T Apr 1739
    Forward. Bu.
Cooper, Mary. S Sep T Nov 1759 *Phoenix*. M.
Cooper, Mary. S City Summer 1763. Nl.
Cooper, Mary. S Lent 1768. Ca.
Cooper, Matthew of Northampton. R for America Feb 1681. No.
Cooper, Matthew of Worcester. R for America Jly 1698. Wo.
Cooper, Richard. S for burglary Lent R 14 yrs Summer 1722. O.
Cooper, Richard. S s cheese at Leamington Lent 1745. G.
Cooper, Richard. SQS Mar TB Apr 1754. Le.
Cooper, Robert of Prescott. SQS Jan 1741. La.
Cooper, Robert. S s at Tetbury Summer TB Aug 1749. G.
Cooper, Samuel. S Lent 1766. Wa.
Cooper, Samuel Joseph. S & T Dec 1769 *Justitia*. M.
Cooper, Sarah. S & T May 1744 *Justitia*. L.
Cooper, Sarah. S s at Walsall Lent R 14 yrs Summer 1761. St.
Cooper als Foster, Sarah. S Sep-Oct T Dec 1771 *Justitia*. M.
Cooper, Shadrack. S Mar 1752. So.
Cooper, Stephen. S for rape Summer 1738 R 14 yrs Lent 1739. Li.
Cooper, Thomas of Ruddington. R for America Jly 1678. Nt.
Cooper, Thomas of Leek. R for America Feb 1681. St.
Cooper, Thomas. R Oct 1694 AT Jan 1695. M.
Cooper, Thomas of Isley, Brancepath, yeoman. S s sheep Summer
    1729. Du.
Cooper, Thomas. S & T Oct 1730 *Forward* LC Potomack Jan 1731. L.
Cooper, Thomas. S Lent 1736. Wo.
Cooper, Thomas. S Jan T Feb 1742 *Industry*. L.
Cooper, Thomas. S Dec 1748 T Jan 1749 *Laura*. L.

Cooper, Thomas. S & T Mar 1750 *Tryal*. L.
Cooper, Thomas. S Mar 1751. Ha.
Cooper, Thomas. SQS Aug TB to Va Sep 1751. Le.
Cooper, Thomas, als Cope, James. SQS Feb T Apr 1753 *Thames*. M.
Cooper, Thomas. R 14 yrs Mar 1753. Do.
Cooper, Thomas. S Oct-Dec 1754. M.
Cooper, Thomas. S Lent T Jun 1756 *Lyon*. E.
Cooper, Thomas. S s at Britwell Lent 1759. O.
Cooper, Thomas. S Lent 1761. No.
Cooper, Thomas. S s at Woolhampston Lent 1768. Be.
Cooper, Thomas. S Lent 1775. K.
Cooper, William aged 30. R for Barbados Feb 1664. M.
Cooper, William. LC Annapolis Jly 1722 from *Gilbert*. X.
Cooper, William (1746). *See* Davis. G.
Cooper, William. R Summer 1755. Ht.
Cooper, William. S s sheep Summer 1757 R 14 yrs Summer 1758. Ca.
Cooper, William. S s sheep Lent R 14 yrs Summer 1758. Wa.
Cooper, William. S s mare Lent R 14 yrs Summer 1760. Nf.
Cooper, William. T Sep 1765 *Justitia*. Sy.
Cooper, William. S s shirt at Nettlebed Summer 1769. O.
Coopes, Edward of Bishops Stortford. R for Barbados or Jamaica Feb
    1686. Ht.
Coopey, Joseph. S Feb T Apr 1742 *Bond* to Potomack. M.
Coose, John (1720). *See* Williams. Sy.
Coote, Samuel. S Lent 1759. Nf.
Cooter, John. T May 1751 *Tryal*. K.
Cooton. *See* Cotton.
Cope, Anthony. S & T Jan 1722 for Jamaica in *Christabella*. L.
Cope, Eleanor. S Apr-Jun 1739. M.
Cope als Chason als Blackwell, Elizabeth. S s at Meole Brace Summer
    1727. Sh.
Cope, Hugh of Westerham. R for Barbados or Jamaica Mar 1680. K.
Cope, James. S May T 14 yrs Jun 1738 *Forward*. L.
Cope, James (1753). *See* Cooper. M.
Cope, John. T Jly *Alexander* LC Md Sep 1723. Ht.
Cope, John. S Apr-Jun 1739. M.
Cope, John. R 14 yrs Aug 1746. Ha.
Cope, John. S s from warehouse at St. Chad Lent 1766. St.
Cope, John. S s at Wolverhampton Lent 1771. St.
Cope, Robert. S Feb T Mar 1727 *Rappahannock*. L.
Cope, William. SQS 14 yrs Mar TB to Va Oct 1729. Le.
Cope, William. TB Aug 1733. Db.
Copeg, Henry. T Sep 1730 *Smith*. Sy.
Copeland, John. R for Barbados Jun 1665. L.
Copeland, John. S Mar TB to Va Apr 1765. Le.
Copeland, Margaret. S Feb T Apr 1741 *Speedwell* or *Mediterranean*. M.
Cowpland, Thomas. S s horse Lent 1729 R 14 yrs Lent 1730. Y.
Coupland, William. S Feb T Mar 1758 *Dragon*. M.
Copeman, George of North Creake. R for Barbados Jan 1665. Nf.
Copes, John. R Apr 1773 to be T 14 yrs. M.
Copestaff, Thomas. S s at Milson & Hopton Wafers Summer 1742. Sh.

Copestakes, Hannah. S Sep T Nov 1743 *George William*. M.
Copp, Sarah. TB to Md from QS 1727. De.
Copping, Thomas. S & R 14 yrs s gelding Lent 1738. Nf.
Coping, Thomas. T Apr 1743 *Justitia* but died on passage. E.
Copping, William of Tharston. R for America Feb 1664. Nf.
Coppinger, Matthew. R Feb 1675. M.
Copps, James. T Oct 1726 *Forward*. Ht.
Copps, Nathaniel of Hunstanton. R for America Apr 1697. Nf.
Copsey, Thomas. S s at Little Waldingfield Lent 1774. Su.
Copsey, William. S Lent 1737. Su.
Copus, John. T Apr 1769 *Tryal*. K.
Coram, John. S Feb-Apr T 14 yrs Jun 1756 *Lyon*. M.
Coram, Stephen of St. Ives. R for Barbados Feb 1700. Co.
Coram, William. S Feb T Mar 1727 *Rappahannock* to Md. M.
Corbett, Benjamin. S s at Lower Bullingham Lent 1778. He.
Corbett, Charles. S s mortar & pestle at Walsall Lent 1761 T *Atlas* from Bristol. St.
Corbett, Edward of Warwick. R for America Jly 1678. Wa.
Corbett, Francis of St. Saviour, Southwark. R for Barbados or Jamaica Jly 1674. Sy.
Corbet, George. PT May 1684. M.
Corbet, Henry. S killing deer at Uttoxeter Lent 1762. St.
Corbet, Henry. S Feb T Apr 1766 *Ann*. M.
Corbet, James. S Feb 1775. M.
Corbett, John. R for Barbados Feb 1675. L.
Corbett, John. S Oct T Dec 1763 *Neptune*. M.
Corbett, Richard. R for Barbados Jun 1670. M.
Corbett, Richard. S s in Worcester Lent 1737 R 14 yrs Lent 1740. Wo.
Corbet, Richard. S Lent R 14 yrs Summer 1757. Sh.
Corbett, William. S Summer 1731. Sh.
Corbett, William. S s horse Lent R 14 yrs Summer 1736. No.
Corbett, William. S Mar 1750. Ha.
Corbin, Robert. S at Dover & T Dec 1770 *Justitia*. K.
Corbin, William. R 14 yrs Jly 1761. Do.
Corbold, John. S Summer 1746. Su.
Courby, Peter of St. George, Hanover Square. S s handkerchief Sep 1740. M.
Cordelion, Peter. Rebel T 1685.
Cordall, Mary. S Jan T Mar 1760 *Friendship*. M.
Cordall als Cowdell, Richard. S & T Dec 1767 *Neptune*. M.
Cordell, Sarah. S Jan T Feb 1719 *Worcester* LC Annapolis Jun 1719. L.
Corder, Edward. S & T Jan 1722 *Gilbert* LC Annapolis Jly 1722. L.
Corder, John of Waltham Abbey. R for Barbados or Jamaica Mar 1682. E.
Corder, Thomas. T 14 yrs Apr 1768 *Thornton*. E.
Corderoy, John. S s wheat at Stokenchurch Lent 1775. O.
Corderoy, Philip. S s at Inglefield Summer 1766. Be.
Corderoy, Robert. S Jly 1774. L.
Cordin, Robert (1741). *See* Wills. Le.
Cordoza, Aaron. S Apr T 14 yrs May 1752 *Lichfield*. L.
Cordosa, Jacob. S May 1743 to be T for life. M.

Cordosa, Jacob. SQS Dec 1770 T Apr 1771 *Thornton*. M.
Cordoza, Samuel. S Sep T Oct 1750 *Rachael*. L.
Cordwell, James. S Jun T Nov 1743 *George William*. L.
Core, Mary. S Oct T Nov 1728 *Forward* LC Rappahannock Jun 1729. L.
Corey, Dorothy. R for Barbados or Jamaica Aug 1700. L.
Corey, Richard. T Apr 1731 *Bennett*. Sy.
Corke, Arthur. T 14 yrs Apr 1765 *Ann*. Sx.
Corke, Ralph. S s at Wolverhampton Lent 1770. St.
Cork, Richard. SQS Jly TB to Md Nov 1731. So.
Corker, James. PT Jly 1680. M.
Corker, Mary. S Dec 1743 T Feb 1744 *Neptune* to Md. M.
Corkup, Mary. S & T Jun 1756 *Lyon*. M.
Cormack, Benjamin. T Jun 1728 *Elizabeth* LC Va Aug 1729. Sy.
Cormack, Christopher (1731). *See* Corneck. L.
Cormack, Christopher. S Dec 1763 T Mar 1764 *Tryal*. M.
Cormick, Dennis. S & T Oct 1730 *Forward* LC Potomack Jan 1731. L.
Cormick, Michael. S Jun T Sep 1767 *Justitia*. L.
Cormer, William. LC Annapolis Jun 1719 from *Worcester*. X.
Cornbury, Richard. S Sep-Dec 1755 T Jan 1756 *Greyhound*. M.
Corne, Richard. S May T Jly 1722 *Alexander* to Nevis or Jamaica. M.
Corneck als Cormack, Christopher. S Feb T Mar 1731 *Patapsco* LC Md
    Jun 1731. L.
Cornelius, Andrew. R Apr 1770. Do.
Cornelius als Useley, Barbara. S Jan T Feb 1733 *Smith* to Md or Va. M.
Cornelius, James. S Jly 1773. L.
Cornelius, John of Stoke Damerell. R for Barbados Feb 1701. De.
Cornelius, Joseph. S & T Dec 1731 *Forward* to Md or Va. M.
Cornelius, Peter, weaver aged 20, dark. S & T Oct 1720 *Gilbert* LC Md
    May 1721. M.
Cornelius, Thomas. Rebel T 1685.
Cornell, John (1760). *See* Cornhill. St.
Cornell, William. S Aug 1727. M.
Cornew, Thomas. S s naval stores Summer 1748 T Jan 1749 *Laura*. K.
Cornew, William. S & T Apr 1759 *Thetis*. L.
Cornhill, John. S & T Jly 1753 *Tryal*. L.
Cornhill als Cornell, John. S Summer 1760 R 14 yrs Lent 1761 T *Atlas*
    from Bristol. St.
Cornish als Pedrick als Johnson, Charles of Fremington. R for
    Barbados Feb 1688. De.
Cornish, Charles. S & T Oct 1730 *Forward* LC Potomack Jan 1731. M.
Cornish, Edward of Peters Morlynge, husbandman. R for Barbados Jly
    1667. De.
Cornish, Henry. R 14 yrs Mar 1752. De.
Cornish, John of St. Ives. R for Barbados Jly 1667. Co.
Cornish, Samuel. S Feb T Apr 1741 *Speedwell* or *Mediterranean*. M.
Cornish, Thomas. Rebel T 1685.
Cornish, William. S Apr T May 1750 *Lichfield*. L.
Cornish, William. T Apr 1766 *Ann*. E.
Cornoe, John. T Dec 1734 *Caesar*. Sy.
Cornewall, Anne. R for Barbados Sep 1672. L.
Cornwall, Elizabeth. S Jan 1755. L.

Cornwell, James. S & T Sep 1731 *Smith* LC Va 1732. L.
Cornwell als Cockham, Mary. T Jun 1726 *Susanna*. Sx.
Cornwell, Mary. S & T Oct 1730 *Forward* LC Potomack Jan 1731. L.
Cornwall, Mary. S 14 yrs Lent T May 1755 *Rose*. Sy.
Cornwell, Richard of Geaton. S s bacon & cheese Summer 1719. St.
Cornwall, Richard. T Aug 1769 *Douglas*. K.
Conwall als Conway, Rose of Ledbury. S Lent 1721. He.
Corp, Edward. S Dec 1746. L.
Corpe, Richard. S Jan-Feb 1773. M.
Corp, Thomas. S Mar 1721. So.
Corp, Thomas. S Feb T Apr 1766 *Ann*. L.
Corps, John (1773). *See* Canfield. Ca.
Corrand, John (1769). *See* Currant. M.
Corrigan, Hugh. S Oct-Dec 1750. M.
Corrigan, James. SQS May T Sep 1764 *Justitia*. M.
Corrington, Hannah. S Mar 1739. Wi.
Coryton, John (1767). *See* Hele. Co.
Cosby, John. S & R for highway robbery Lent T Oct 1768 *Justitia*. Bu.
Coseret als Banks, Rebecca. S Sep-Oct 1748 T Jan 1749 *Laura*. M.
Cosgrove, James (1774). *See* Kennedy. La.
Cosley, Richard. PT Apr 1673. M.
Cossett, John. S Oct 1744-Jan 1745. M.
Cosson, John. S Dec 1750. L.
Costard, William. S s at Winkfield Summer 1769. Be.
Costello, Honor. S Feb-Apr T Jun 1755 *Lyon*. M.
Costello, James of Manchester, check weaver. SQS Oct 1743. La.
Costello, Robert. S Aug 1763. L.
Castelow, Thomas. S Jan 1746. L.
Coster, Anne of St. George, Southwark, spinster. R for Barbados or
    Jamaica Jly 1674. Sy.
Coster, James. R for life Lent 1775. Sy.
Coster, Joshua. R Jly 1774 to be T 14 yrs. M.
Coster, Richard. T Sep 1758 *Tryal*. Sy.
Coster, William. S Dec 1772. M.
Costin, Elizabeth. R for Barbados Aug 1679. M.
Costin, Mary wife of John of St. Saviour, Southwark. R for Barbados or
    Jamaica Jly 1715. Sy.
Costin, Mary. S & T Sep 1731 *Smith* LC Va 1732. M.
Coston, Hannah wife of John. S Jan T Feb 1726 *Supply* LC Md May
    1726. M.
Coston, William of Winstanstow. R for America Jly 1678. Sh.
Cotes. *See* Coates.
Cotsworth, Miles (1724). *See* Allison. M.
Cott, Daniel. S Lent 1748. *Nf.
Cottam, William. S Lent TB Apr 1771. Nt.
Cottell. *See* Cottle.
Cotter, Eleanor. S Jan-Feb T Apr 1772 *Thornton*. M.
Cotterell, Barbara. S Apr T Dec 1734 *Caesar* LC Va Jly 1735. M.
Cotterell als Irish als Jones, Katherine. R for Barbados or Jamaica Mar
    1685. M.
Cotterell, Edward. S Jly T Aug 1721 *Prince Royal* LC Va Nov 1721. M.

Cotterell, Elizabeth. SQS & T Dec 1758 *The Brothers*. M.
Cottrell, George. R s horses 14 yrs Jly 1724. Ha.
Cotterell als Baines, George. S & T Apr 1734 *Patapsco* to Md. M.
Cotterell, George. T Apr 1739 *Forward*. Sy.
Cotterell, James. S & T Apr 1766 *Ann*. L.
Cotteral, James. S Feb T Apr 1770 *New Trial*. M.
Cotterell als Cautrell, John. R for plantations Feb 1655. L.
Cotterall, John. TB to Va from QS 1740. De.
Cotterell, John. S s cow Lent R 14 yrs Summer 1759. Wo.
Cotterell, Joseph. R 14 yrs Jly 1737. Wi.
Cotterell, Nicholas of Lambeth. SQS Feb 1757. Sy.
Cotterel, Sarah wife of John. S Sep T Nov 1759 *Phoenix*. M.
Cotterell, Sarah. S s clothing at Ledbury Summer 1764. He.
Cotterell, Stephen. SQS Devizes & TB to Va Apr 1766. Wi.
Cotteril, William. T Aug 1752 *Tryal*. Sy.
Cotterell, William. S Feb 1773. L.
Cottle, Ann of Bristol. S confirmed May 1772 (SP). G.
Cottle, Dinah. S 14 yrs for receiving stolen goods from Thomas Cottle
    (qv) Summer TB Aug 1757. G.
Cottle, Grant of Bristol. R for life May 1771 (SP). G.
Cottle, Hannah of Frome Selwood, spinster. R for Barbados Feb
    1710. So.
Cottell, Thomas. S Aug T Oct 1741 *Sea Horse* to Va. M.
Cottle, Thomas. S s at Bitton Summer TB Aug 1757. G.
Cottle, Uriah. S Mar 1752. So.
Cotton, Betty. S & TB to Va Mar 1761. Wi.
Cotton, Edward. S Lent TB Apr T Aug 1757 *Lux*. Db.
Cooton, John. R for Barbados Dec 1667. M.
Cotton als Jarvis, John of Stanground. R for Barbados Mar 1679. Hu.
Cotton, John. R for Barbados Mar 1683. L.
Cotton, John. S s horse Lent R 14 yrs Summer 1753. Wa.
Cotton, Joseph Winter. LC Port York, Va, Jan 1721 from *Honor*. X.
Cotton, Joshua. S s sheep Lent R 14 yrs Summer 1754. La.
Cotton, Joshua. S Oct 1774. L.
Cotton, Margaret. S Oct T Nov 1725 *Rappahannock* LC Rappahannock
    Apr 1726. M.
Cotton, Mary. SQS May T Jly 1773 *Tayloe* to Va. M.
Cotten, Matthew. R for Barbados Dec 1667.
Cotton, Oliver. R for Barbados Jun 1665. M.
Cotton, William of Epsom. R for Barbados or Jamaica Jly 1687. Sy.
Cotton, William of St. Saviour, Southwark. SQS Jun T Aug 1752
    Tryal. Sy.
Cotton, William. SQS Apr 1774. M.
Cottoway, Thomas. T Apr *Sukey* LC Md Sep 1725. Bu.
Couch, Elianore. S May 1760. M.
Couch, George (1770). *See* Parsons. Co.
Couch, John. R 14 yrs Mar 1750 TB to Va. De.
Couch, William. S Aug 1752. Co.
Coughlin, William (1746). *See* Cowlin. Y.
Coulscot, John. S Mar 1740. De.
Coulsey, Thomas. S Oct 1751-Jan 1752. M.

Coulson, Chester. S Aug T Oct 1724 *Forward* LC Annapolis Jun 1725. M.

Coulson, John, aged 21, ruddy, miller. LC Annapolis May 1721 from *Gilbert*. X.

Coulson als Lister, John. S Lent 1728 R 14 yrs Lent 1729. Y.

Colson, Robert. T 14 yrs Apr 1766 *Ann*. Sy.

Colson, Thomas. R for America Jly 1694. No.

Coulson, William. S Apr T 14 yrs May 1718 *Tryal* LC Charles Town Aug 1718. L.

Coleson, William. Died 1721 on passage in *Gilbert*. X.

Colson, William. S Lent 1744. Db.

Colston, John. T Sep 1765 *Justitia*. M.

Coulston, Thomas. S Jly T Sep 1755 *Tryal*. L.

Coleston, William. S City Lent 1754. Y.

Coulter, Mary of Mitcham, spinster. SQS & T Jan 1767 *Tryal*. Sy.

Colter, Richard als John. R Aug 1770. Wi.

Coulter, William. S Mar TB Apr 1755. Wi.

Coulthurst, Joseph. S Summer 1737 R 14 yrs Summer 1738. We.

Colthurst, Mary. S Feb T Mar 1730 *Patapsco* LC Annapolis Sep 1730. L.

Coultis, Thomas. SQS Oct T Dec 1753 *Whiteing*. M.

Coulton, Gervase. SQS Mar TB Apr 1730. Nt.

Councell, Edward. Rebel T 1685.

Counsellor, Jacob. SQS Feb 1774. M.

Councellor, Thomas. SQS 1766. Du.

Count, William. T Sep 1730 *Smith*. Sy.

Counter, Bartholomew. S Mar 1738. De.

Coupland. *See* Copeland.

Courby. *See* Corby.

Court, Bridget of Worcester. R for America Mar 1688. Wo.

Court, Clement. S Sep-Oct 1775. M.

Court, Elizabeth. SQS Jan TB Apr 1746. So.

Court, James. T Dec 1763 *Neptune*. K.

Court als Smith, John of Killingworth. R for America Jly 1678. Wa.

Court, John. S s lead weights at Inkberrow Summer 1758. Wo.

Court, Joseph. R 14 yrs Aug 1727. So.

Court, Robert. Rebel T 1685.

Court, Salathiel. S 14 yrs for clandestine marriage Summer 1760. Cu.

Courtney, Elizabeth. R Jan AT Feb 1679. M.

Courtney, Elizabeth wife of William. S & T Sep 1757 *Thetis*. M.

Courtney als Oliver, Hannah. S Feb T Apr 1741 *Speedwell* or *Mediterranean*. M.

Courtney, James. S Jly 1747. L.

Courtney, John. S s bill of exchange at Downing Summer TB Aug 1756. G.

Courtney, John. SW & T Dec 1767 *Neptune*. M.

Coutney, Patrick. S Feb T 14 yrs Apr 1765 *Ann*. M.

Courtney, Sarah. S Jun 1747. L.

Courtney, William. S Mar 1756. Do.

Cozin als Bourne, Dorothy. R for Barbados or Jamaica May 1697. L.

Cousen, Eleanor. S Jun for receiving T 14 yrs Dec 1736 *Dorsetshire*. M.

Cousins, George. S Mar 1758. So.

Cosins, John. T 14 yrs Sep 1767 *Justitia*. E.

Cozens, John. R 14 yrs Aug 1773. So.

Cousins, Mary of St. Giles Colchester, spinster. SQS Oct 1748 T Jan 1749 *Laura*. E.

Cousins, Robert. S Lent 1752. Nf.

Cousins, Samuel of North Petherton. R for Barbados Sep 1665. So.

Cousins, Thomas of York Castle. R for Barbados Jly 1679. Y.

Couzens, Thomas. PT May 1687. M.

Cossens, William. Rebel T 1685.

Cove, Edward. S Summer 1729 R 14 yrs Summer 1730. No.

Coventry, Charles. SQS Dec 1768 T Jan 1769 *Thornton*. M.

Coventry, Elizabeth. S May-Jly 1750. M.

Coventry, Thomas. S & T Dec 1731 *Forward*. L.

Coverley, Thomas. S Feb T Mar 1730 *Patapsco* LC Annapolis Sep 1730. L.

Covey, John. R Dec 1699 AT Jan 1700. M.

Covill, John. T Oct 1723 *Forward*. Sy.

Covington, Peter. S Aug T Sep 1725 *Forward* LC Annapolis Dec 1725. M.

Covington, Richard. T 14 yrs Oct 1768 *Justitia*. Ht.

Covnett, John. S Jly 1773. L.

Coward, James. S May T Jly 1771 *Scarsdale*. L.

Coward, Sarah. R for America Aug 1702. L.

Coward, William of Whitchurch. R for America Mar 1680. Sh.

Cowcraft, John. SQS Apr T Sep 1758 *Tryal* to Annapolis. M.

Cowdall, Ann wife of Saul of Frome Selwood. R for Barbados Jly 1698. So.

Cowdell, Richard (1767). *See* Cordall. M.

Cowdell, Thomas. S Feb-Apr T May 1751 *Tryal*. M.

Cowden, Susanna. S Lent 1761. O.

Cowdrey, Ann wife of Richard. S Feb T Mar 1760 *Friendship*. M.

Cowell, Caleb. S Lent 1754. K.

Cowell, Francis. S s horse & R 14 yrs Lent 1769. Wo.

Cowell, John. S Summer 1752. Nf.

Cowell, Joseph of Eckington. R for America Jly 1677. Wo.

Cowell, Joseph. S s sheep Lent R 14 yrs Summer T Oct 1750 *Rachael*. E.

Cowell, Mary. S & T Oct 1729 *Forward* LC Va Jun 1730. L.

Cowell, Robert Jr. S Lent 1752. Nf.

Cowen, Aaron. S Nov T Dec 1770 *Justitia*. L.

Cowen, Eleanor. SQS Oct 1768 T Jan 1769 *Thornton*. M.

Cowen, Israel. S for receiving Jun T 14 yrs Sep 1767 *Justitia*. L.

Cowen, Jacob. SQS Apr 1763. M.

Cowne, James. S Aug 1746. De.

Cowen, Jane (1726). *See* Coker. M.

Cowen, John. S Apr T Nov 1759 *Phoenix*. M.

Cowes, Joseph. Rebel T 1685.

Cowlan, Thomas. S s horse Summer 1725 R 14 yrs Lent 1729. Y.

Cowland, James of Little Baddow. SQS Jan 1744. E.

Cowlen. *See* Cowling.

Cowles, Anne. S s at Doddington Summer 1729. G.

Cowley, Alice (1661). *See* Stewkley. M.

Cowley, Henry. S Mar 1742. De.
Cowley, John. S Apr T 14 yrs May 1755 *Rose*. L.
Cowley, John (1767). *See* Cowling. De.
Cowley als Curtis, Mary. S Aug T Oct 1724 *Forward* LC Md Jun
    1725. M.
Cowley, Mary wife of George. S Jly T Sep 1765 *Justitia*. M.
Cowley, Richard. R for Barbados Oct 1673. M.
Cowley, Thomas of Putney. R for Barbados or Jamaica Jly 1677. Sy.
Cowley, Thomas Jr. S Jly TB to Va Aug 1751. Wi.
Cowling als Cowley, John. R 14 yrs Aug 1767 TB to Va. De.
Cowlen, Thomas. R 14 yrs Aug 1775. De.
Cowlin als Coughlin, William. S s at Leeds Lent 1746. Y.
Cowne. *See* Cowen.
Cowpe, Alice. S Lent 1768. Nt.
Cowper, James. S Jly T Sep 1765 *Justitia*. M.
Cowper, John. S Summer 1728. Y.
Cowper, John. T Apr 1732 *Patapsco*. Sy.
Cowper, John (1758). *See* Steward. Y.
Cowper, Thomas of Reed. R for Barbados or Jamaica Mar 1680. Ht.
Cowper, William. S Lent 1734. Sh.
Cowsell, William. S & T Oct 1729 *Forward* LC Va Jun 1730. M.
Cox, Alice. S & T Dec 1731 *Forward* to Md or Va. M.
Cox, Ann. S Oct 1737 T Jan 1738 *Dorsetshire* to Va. M.
Cox, Ann. S s at Dudley Summer 1757. Wo.
Cox, Ann. R 14 yrs Aug 1771. So.
Cox, Benjamin. S 14 yrs for receiving Lent 1742. Sh.
Cox, Benjamin. SQS New Sarum Jan TB to Va Mar 1760. Wi.
Cox, Benjamin. S Apr-Jun T Jly 1772 *Tayloe*. M.
Cox, Charles. S Jan T Feb 1719 *Worcester* LC Annapolis Jun 1719. M.
Cox, Charles. S Lent 1774. K.
Cox, Edmund (1701). *See* Diston. De.
Cox, Edward. S s silver shoe buckles at St. Lawrence Jewry Oct 1768 T
    Jan 1769 *Thornton*. L.
Cox, Elizabeth. S Feb T Apr 1734 *Patapsco*. L.
Cox, Elizabeth wife of John. SQS Apr 1743. So.
Cox, Elizabeth. S Jan 1757. L.
Cox, Elizabeth. SW & T Apr 1769 *Tryal*. M.
Cox, George. R 14 yrs Jly 1721. Do.
Cox, George. T Oct 1741 *Kitty*. K.
Cox, Grace. S & T Oct 1729 *Forward* but died on passage. L.
Cox, Hannah. T Sep 1758 *Tryal*. E.
Cox, James. S Sep T Oct 1768 *Justitia*. M.
Cocks, James of Bishops Hatfield. SQS s shirts Apr T Jly 1772
    Orange Bay. Ht.
Cox, James. R 14 yrs Aug 1772. So.
Cox, Jane. S Dec 1748 T Jan 1749 *Laura*. L.
Cox, Jeremiah. S s linen handkerchief at St. Sepulchre Sep T Oct 1768
    Justitia. L.
Coxe, John (1673). *See* Jackson. L.
Cox, John (1677). *See* Wilson. L.
Cox, John. Rebel T 1685.

Cox, John of Abingdon. R for America Mar 1701. Be.
Cox, John. R 14 yrs Summer 1721 T Oct 1723 *Forward* from London. Y.
Cox, John. S s shoes at Kings Norton Lent 1724. Wo.
Cox, John. S Dec 1733 T Jan 1734 *Caesar* but died on passage. M.
Cox, John. S s horse Summer 1737 R 14 yrs Lent 1738. O.
Cox, John. TB to Va from QS 1740. De.
Cox, John. S Jan 1751. M.
Cox, John. SQS Oct 1751. M.
Cox, John. S s linen at Bromsgrove Summer 1752. Wo.
Cox, John. S s sheep Lent R 14 yrs Summer 1754. Bu.
Cox, John. S s at Fringford Summer 1767. O.
Cox, John. S Jan T Apr 1770 *New Trial.* M.
Cox, John. S & T Dec 1771 *Justitia.* L.
Cox, John. S s clothing at Lambourn Lent 1773. Be.
Cox, John. R Mar 1773. So.
Cox, John. S Sep-Oct 1775. M.
Cox, Joseph. S Mar TB to Va Apr 1766. Wi.
Cox, Joseph. R & T Jly 1770 *Scarsdale.* M.
Cox, Margaret. S Aug T 14 yrs Sep 1718 *Eagle* LC Charles Town Mar 1719. L.
Cox, Mary. R for Barbados Aug 1668. M.
Cox als Shears, Mary. S Feb T 14 yrs Mar 1730 *Patapsco* LC Md Sep 1730. L.
Cox, Mary (1753). *See* Smith. M.
Cox, Peter. SQS Sep 1772. M.
Cox, Peter. S Feb 1775. M.
Coxe, Philip. Rebel T 1685.
Cox, Philip. R 14 yrs Mar 1766. So.
Cox, Richard. R 14 yrs Aug 1764. So.
Cox, Samuel. S Feb T Apr 1742 *Bond* to Potomack. M.
Cox, Samuel. S s cloth at Broughton Summer 1750. O.
Cox, Sarah. S Sep-Oct T Dec 1771 *Justitia.* M.
Cox, Susanna. S Dec 1727. M.
Cox, Thomas. S Jly T Aug 1721 *Prince Royal* LC Va Nov 1721. M.
Cox, Thomas. S Jun-Dec 1738 T Jan 1739 *Dorsetshire* to Va. M.
Cox, Thomas. AT from QS Lent 1739. St.
Cox, Thomas. S s at St. Mary Virgin, Oxford, Summer 1750. O.
Cox, Thomas. S Lent T Sep 1755 *Tryal.* Bu.
Cox, Thomas (1765). *See* Wilcox. M.
Cox, Thomas. R 14 yrs Jly TB to Va Sep 1774. Wi.
Cox, William. R for Barbados Feb 1675. L.
Cox, William. S Aug T Oct 1741 *Sea Horse* to Va. M.
Cox, William. S Jly 1744. So.
Cox, William. S Lent R 14 yrs Summer 1756. Le.
Cox, William. S Lent 1763. Sy.
Cox, William. S Jly T Sep 1767 *Justitia.* M.
Cox, William. S s at Evesham Summer 1772. Wo.
Cox, William of St. Martin in Fields. SW Oct 1773. M.
Cox, Winifred. S Feb T Apr 1759 *Thetis.* M.
Coxey, William (1774). *See* Cooksey. Le.

Coxhead, Mary. S May T Jun 1726 *Loyal Margaret* LC Md Oct 1726. M.

Coxhill, Henry Joseph. S Lent 1775. Sy.

Coxill, John. S s sheep at Mixbury Lent R 14 yrs Summer 1763. O.

Coxon, Edward. LC Va May 1728 from *Forward*. X.

Coxon, Thomas. R for America Aug 1685. Li.

Coy, Edward. R Feb 1695. M.

Coy, Richard. R for Barbados or Jamaica Feb 1686. M.

Coyle, James. S Jan-Apr 1748. M.

Coyle, Michael. S Jan-Apr 1748. M.

Coyn, James. T Jly 1770 *Scarsdale*. M.

Coyne, William. R 14 yrs Aug 1730. So.

Coyta, John. R 14 yrs Jly 1761 TB to Va. De.

Cozens. *See* Cousins.

Cozin. *See* Cousin.

Crab, James. S Apr T May 1743 *Indian Queen*. L.

Crabb, John of Luckinhorne. R for Barbados Jly 1715. Co.

Crab als Masterman, John. S Jun 1733 T Jan 1734 *Caesar* LC Va Jly 1734. M.

Crabb, Joseph. R 14 yrs Jly 1738. De.

Crabb, Mary. S & T Dec 1731 *Forward*. L.

Crabb, Moses. R 14 yrs Lent 1756. Ca.

Craball, William. S s cow at Whitchurch Lent 1738. Sh.

Crabtree, Samuel of Huddersfield. SQS Aug 1754. La.

Crackles, Thomas. S Aug 1760. L.

Cracknell, John. S Lent 1757. Nf.

Cracknal, William. T 14 yrs Apr 1768 *Thornton*. E.

Craddock, Anthony. S s at Rock Lent 1743. Wo.

Craddock, Elizabeth. S 14 yrs Summer 1770 for receiving coins stolen at Stoke Bliss by her husband who was burnt in the hand and discharged. He.

Craddock, James (1773). *See* Town. St.

Cradock, Mary. S Dec 1753-Jan 1754. M.

Craddock, Samuel. S s at Stoke Summer 1756. Wo.

Craddocke, Tobias. R for Barbados or Jamaica Dec 1693. L.

Craddock, William. T Dec 1770 *Justitia*. K.

Crady, John, aged 22, fair. S Jan T Feb 1723 *Jonathan* LC Md Jly 1724. M.

Craford als Crawford, Edward. S Feb 1732. M.

Craford, George. R for Barbados or Jamaica Oct 1690. M.

Craft, Ann. S Jly s stockings T Dec 1735 *John* LC Annapolis Sep 1736. M.

Craft, John. S May T Jly 1770 *Scarsdale*. L.

Craft, John. S & R s gelding Summer 1772. Wa.

Craft, Mary. S Summer 1763. Li.

Craft, Matthew Jr. Rebel T 1685.

Crafter, John. T Apr 1766 *Ann*. M.

Crafter, William. S May T Jun 1727 *Susanna* to Va. M.

Crafts, Francis. S May-Jly T Sep 1751 *Greyhound*. M.

Crafts, Hester (1734). *See* Howard. L.

Crafts, Ralph. S Aug T Oct 1724 *Forward* LC Annapolis Jun 1725. M.

Crafts, Thomas. S Apr 1748. L.

Cragg, Robert. R Jly 1686. M.

Craggs, Henry. S Summer TB Oct 1748. Y.

Craggs, Robert. S & R s sheep at Easby Lent TB Apr 1774; Margaret Craggs acquitted. Y.

Crags als Shaw, Thomas. S Apr T May 1750 *Lichfield*. L.

Craggs, Walter. S Summer 1773. Nl.

Cragy, Charles. S Dec 1750. L.

Craig, Charles. SW & T Apr 1770 *New Trial*. M.

Craig, George. SQS Feb 1761. M.

Creg, Thomas. S s teaspoons at Stanlake Lent 1775. O.

Crain. *See* Crane.

Craith, Bridget. S Dec 1747. L.

Cram, Ann. T 14 yrs Apr 1768 *Thornton*. K.

Cramford, Mary. T Jly *Alexander* LC Md Sep 1723. Sy.

Crammock, Edward. S Jan 1744. M.

Cramp, East. S Jly T Oct 1741 *Sea Horse*. L.

Cramp, Stephen. S & T Dec 1736 *Dorsetshire*. L.

Cramp, William. T Sep 1758 *Tryal*. Sx.

Cramphorne, William of Bishops Stortford. SQS s oats Jan 1775. Ht.

Crampton als Thompson, Robert. S Lent 1761. La.

Cran, Mary wife of William. S s at Lydbury North Lent 1756. Sh.

Cran, William. S s at Church Stretton Lent 1756. Sh.

Cranaway, John (1760). *See* Cranwell. Bu.

Crandon, Abraham. R 14 yrs Jly 1724. Do.

Crane, Francis. S s at Kidderminster Lent 1751. Wo.

Crane, Giles. Rebel T 1685.

Crain, Jasper. T Apr 1741 *Speedwell* or *Mediterranean*. Ht.

Crane, John. Rebel T 1685.

Crane, John. R for America Feb 1700. Le.

Crane, John. S Mar 1768. Ha.

Crane, Lucy (1764). *See* Gregory. M.

Crane, Nathan (1736). *See* Crean. E.

Crane, Thomas. T Oct 1719 *Susannah & Sarah*. L. or M.

Crane, Thomas (1771). *See* Smith. Ca.

Crane, William. S & T Sep 1764 *Justitia*. L.

Cranfield, Alice. R for Barbados May AT Sep 1684. M.

Cranfield, Henry. S Jly T Aug 1721 *Prince Royal* LC Va Nov 1721. L.

Crank, Sarah wife of John. S Jan T Apr 1743 *Justitia*. M.

Crank, Thomas (1757). *See* Jones. Sh.

Crank, William. S Dec 1733 T Jan 1734 *Caesar* LC Va Jly 1734. L.

Cranley, Joseph of Lambeth. SQS Oct T Dec 1763 *Neptune*. Sy.

Crannum, William. S s at St. Philip & Jacob Lent 1723. G.

Cranston, Elizabeth. S 14 yrs Summer 1728. Y.

Cranwell als Cranaway, John. S for highway robbery Lent R 14 yrs Summer 1760. Bu.

Crapp, John. R 14 yrs Mar TB to Va Apr 1745. Wi.

Crapp, Mary. S Jly 1718 to be T to Va. Co.

Craske, William of Besthorpe. R for Barbados or Jamaica Mar 1697. Nf.

Crate, Charles. R 14 yrs Jly 1752. Ha.

Crate, Jack (1770). *See* Morgan, John. He.

Crateman, Jane. S Jly-Sep T Sep 1742 *Forward*. M.
Craten, James. S Mar 1764. Ha.
Crater, Thomas. T Apr 1741 *Speedwell* or *Mediterranean*. Bu.
Craven, Edward. S May-Jly 1773. M.
Craven, Francis. S Sep-Oct T Dec 1771 *Justitia*. M.
Craven, John. S Jan T Mar 1758 *Dragon*. M.
Craven, Richard of Chelmsford. R for Barbados or Barbados Jly
    1677. E.
Craven, Richard. S & R 14 yrs s sheep at Bentham Lent 1769. Y.
Crawford, Daniel. S Feb T Mar 1729 *Patapsco* LC Annapolis Dec
    1729. M.
Crawford, Daniel of St. Olave, Southwark. SQS Oct 1749. Sy.
Crawford, Edward (1732). *See* Craford. M.
Crawford, John. S Apr T May 1719 *Margaret*; sold to Mr. Polea,
    Annapolis, Sep 1719. L.
Crawford, Mary. S Oct T Nov 1759 *Phoenix*. M.
Crawford, Susanna. S Jly-Dec 1747. M.
Crawford, Thomas. S Lent 1733 T *Patapsco* LC Annapolis Nov 1733. Be.
Crawford, Thomas. S Feb T Apr 1741 *Speedwell*. L.
Crawford, Thomas. S Dec 1748 T Jan 1749 *Laura*. M.
Crawford, Thomas. S Feb T 14 yrs Mar 1750 *Tryal*. M.
Crawford, Thomas of St. Martin in Fields. SW Oct 1766 T Jan 1767
    Tryal. M.
Crawford, William (1719). *See* Cole, John. L.
Crawford, William. S Feb T Apr 1766 *Ann*. L.
Crawley, Daniel. S & T Nov 1762 *Prince William*. L.
Crawley, Edward. S & T Oct 1732 *Caesar* to Va. M.
Crawley, Jacob. S Summer 1762. Bd.
Crawley, Jacob. S Lent 1773. Ht.
Crawley, James. S Jly T Sep 1765 *Justitia*. M.
Crawley, John. S Feb T Mar 1729 *Patapsco* LC Annapolis Dec 1729. M.
Crawley, John. S s sheep Summer 1758 R 14 yrs Lent T Apr 1759
    Thetis. Bu.
Crawley, Joseph. T Apr 1765 *Ann*. Ht.
Crawley, Richard. S s sheep Summer 1758 R 14 yrs Lent T Apr 1759
    Thetis. Bu.
Crawley, Thomas, a Quaker. R for plantations Jly 1665 (SP). Ht.
Cray, Anne. SQS Oct TB Nov 1746. So.
Cray, Paul. S & T Oct 1732 *Caesar* to Va. M.
Craycraft, Samuel. R Jun T 14 yrs Aug 1769 *Douglas*. M.
Craydon, Elizabeth. S & T Sep 1767 *Justitia*. M.
Craydon, Richard of Marlow. S Summer T Oct 1729 *Forward*. Bu.
Craythorn, Richard Jr. S Lent 1775. Y.
Cremer, John of St. Olave, Southwark. SQS Jan 1752. Sy.
Creamer, John. R & T 14 yrs Apr 1770 *New Trial*. M.
Creamer als McCarty, Michael. S Sep-Oct T Dec 1771 *Justitia*. M.
Cremer, Susanna. S Jly T Aug 1721 *Prince Royal* LC Va Nov 1721. M.
Crean als Crane, Nathan. T May 1736 *Patapsco*. E.
Creebar, John of Meavy, blacksmith. R for Barbados Feb 1698. De.
Creech, Sarah. S Dec 1742 T Mar 1743 *Justitia*. L.
Creed, Henry. S Apr-May T May 1744 *Justitia*. M.

Creed, James. T 14 yrs Apr 1768 *Thornton*. Sy.
Creg. *See* Craig.
Creighton, John. S Dec 1742 T Apr 1743 *Justitia*. M.
Cressey, Thomas. S at Hull s sheep at Holy Trinity Summer 1764. Y.
Creswell, Ann. S Summer 1753. Du.
Creswell, Catherine (1749). *See* Criswell. La.
Creswell, Isaac of Wolverhampton. R for Barbados Feb 1665. St.
Cresswell, Richard. S s at Aldridge Summer 1738. St.
Creswell, Richard of Manchester, weaver. SQS Oct 1771. La.
Creswell, Robert. S & R 14 yrs s handkerchiefs at Groton Lent 1775. Su.
Cresswell, Thomas of Manchester, linen weaver. S Lent R 14 yrs
    Summer 1757. La.
Crew, Ann. S Jun-Dec 1745. M.
Crew, Charles. R Jun T Aug 1769 *Douglas*. M.
Crew, Daniel. S & TB Jly 1742. G.
Crew, John of St. George, Southwark. SQS Jan 1752. Sy.
Crew, John of St. Saviour, Southwark. SQS Jan 1754. Sy.
Crew, John. S Oct 1765 T Jan 1766 *Tryal*. M.
Crew, Mary wife of Joseph. S Aug 1758. So.
Crew, Robert. S Summer TB Aug 1740; found at large & S to hang
    Summer 1742 R 14 yrs Lent TB Mar 1743. G.
Crew, Simon (1749). *See* Thompson. M.
Crew, Thomas. S Summer TB Aug 1740. G.
Crew, William. S & TB Jly 1752. G.
Crew, William. T Apr 1765 *Ann*. Sy.
Crew, William. S s at Boxwell Summer 1775. G.
Cruise, Peter. S Dec 1749-Jan 1750 T Mar 1750 *Tryal*. M.
Crews, Timothy. R 14 yrs Mar 1730. So.
Crewis, William. S Mar 1764. So.
Crickmore, Francis. S & R Lent 1764. Nf.
Cridon, George of Leatherhead. R for Barbados or Jamaica Mar
    1698. Sy.
Cringin, James. S Feb T May 1719 *Margaret*; sold to Patrick Sympson &
    William Black Md Sep 1719. M.
Crippen, Mary. T Nov 1728 *Forward*. K.
Cripps als Moore, Diana. S s silver spoon at St. Mary Virgin, Oxford,
    Summer 1774. O.
Cripps, Edward. S s watch Summer 1765. Be.
Cripps, John. S Jly-Dec 1747 to be T 14 yrs. M.
Cripps als Peeke, John. R 14 yrs Aug 1760. So.
Cripps, Michael. S Summer 1754. Bu.
Cripps, Nathaniel. S & R Summer 1764 T Sep 1765 *Justitia*. Bu.
Cripps, Philip. S Sep-Oct 1748 T Jan 1749 *Laura*. M.
Crisp, Edward. S Feb T Mar 1727 *Rappahannock*. L.
Crispe, George. S s mare Summer 1742 R 14 yrs Lent 1743. Su.
Crisp, George (1745). *See* Dawkins, John. E.
Crispe, John. S & R for highway robbery Lent 1737. Su.
Crisp, John. S Summer 1742. Nf.
Crispe, Richard. R for Barbados Nov 1668. L.
Crisp, Robert. R 14 yrs Summer 1745 AT Lent 1746. Sy.
Crispe, Sarah als Ridge. S Jly-Dec 1747. M.

Crisp, Thomas. S Apr T May 1751 *Tryal*. L.
Crisp, William. LC Port York, Va, Jun 1721 from *Mary*. X.
Crispin, Alexander. TB to Va 1770. De.
Crispin, Ann. S Dec 1766 T Jan 1767 *Tryal*. M.
Crispin, Robert. S Nov T Dec 1763 *Neptune*. L.
Crissell, Edward. S Summer 1752. Su.
Crissell, William. S Summer 1752. Su.
Criswell als Creswell, Catherine of Manchester, widow. SQS Jan
    1749. La.
Critchett, Mary. S Oct T Nov 1728 *Forward* LC Rappahannock Jun
    1729. M.
Critchley, Henry of Wigan. S & R 14 yrs for highway robbery near
    Wigan Summer 1770. La.
Crittenden, Thomas. T Oct 1768 *Justitia*. K.
Critton, John. S Summer 1745. Su.
Croam, Jonathan. S Sep s cocks T Nov 1757 *Phoenix*. M.
Crochifer, Robert. T Apr 1739 *Forward*. Sy.
Crocker, Benjamin of Crediton. R for Barbados Feb 1697. De.
Crocker, Isaac. S Aug 1740 TB to Va. De.
Crocker, John. S Aug 1740 TB to Va. De.
Croker, John. SQS Feb T Mar 1764 *Tryal*. M.
Crocker, Thomas. S & T Apr 1769 *Tryal*. M.
Crocker, William. TB to Va from QS 1738. De.
Crockett, Francis. LC Va Jly 1734 from *Caesar*. X.
Crockett als Rockett, John. S May T Sep 1737 *Pretty Patsy* to Md. M.
Crockett, John. S Feb T Apr 1739 *Forward* to Va. M.
Crockatt, William. S Dec 1746. L.
Crockford, John. S Oct T Nov 1759 *Phoenix*. M.
Crockford, William. S Jly 1720 T from Portsmouth 1723. Ha.
Crockstone, John (1767). *See* Miller. M.
Croft, John. S Lent R 14 yrs Summer T Sep 1751 *Greyhound*. Ht.
Croft, Matthew. S Oct T Dec 1769 *Justitia*. L.
Croft, Robert. S & T Oct 1722 *Forward* LC Annapolis Jun 1723. M.
Croft, Robert. S & T Dec 1736 *Dorsetshire*. L.
Crofte, William. Rebel T 1685.
Crofts, Alice. S Oct T Dec 1724 *Rappahannock*. L.
Crofts, Edward. S s sheep Summer 1764 R 14 yrs Lent 1765. Wa.
Crofts, Elizabeth. R for Barbados Oct 1673. L.
Crofts, John. R for Barbados or Jamaica Jly 1686. M.
Crofts, Ralph (1724). *See* Crafts. M.
Crofts, Sarah of Beckenham. R for Barbados or Jamaica Mar 1680. K.
Crofts, Thomas. R & T 14 yrs Jly 1772 *Tayloe*. M.
Crofts, William. S & T Dec 1752 *Greyhound*. M.
Cromb, Ann. S Apr 1761. M.
Cromby, Andrew. R 14 yrs Summer TB Sep 1754. Y.
Cromer, Charles. S Aug 1756. Ha.
Cromer, Jeremiah. S Mar 1757. De.
Cromey, Jane. S Aug T 14 yrs Sep 1727 *Forward* LC Rappahannock
    May 1728. L.
Crompton, Ann. S Jly T Sep 1766 *Justitia*. L.

Crumpton, Catherine, aged 40, dark. S & T Oct 1720 *Gilbert* LC Annapolis May 1721. M.

Crompton, Charles. S s at Bromyard Summer 1751. He.

Crompton, Elizabeth wife of William of Henley on Thames. R for Barbados Oct 1663. O.

Crompton, Fitzallan. R for Barbados Sep 1672. L.

Crompton, James. S Jan-Feb 1775. M.

Crompton, John Sr. of Little Lever, weaver. S s fustian Lent 1737. La.

Crompton, John Jr. of Little Lever. S s fustian Lent 1737. La.

Crompton, Thomas. S & T Jan 1739 *Dorsetshire*. L.

Crompton, William. S Lent 1752. La.

Cromwell, James. S Mar 1772; dead by Apr 1772. Wi.

Cromwell, John (1752). *See* Ashby. Nf.

Cromwell, William. SQS New Sarum Jan TB to Va Mar 1760. Wi.

Crondall, Samuel. S s mare Summer 1767 R 14 yrs Lent 1768. O.

Crone, Fergus. S May-Jly 1748. M.

Crone, William. S & T 14 yrs Apr 1733 *Patapsco* LC Annapolis Nov 1733. L.

Cronidge, Mary. S s horse Summer 1762 R 14 yrs Lent 1763. Nt.

Cronyn, John. S Mar TB to Va Jun 1747. Wi.

Crooke, Benjamin. R Jly AT Aug 1685. M.

Crook, Charles. TB to Va from QS 1729. De.

Crook, Francis. S Aug T Sep 1764 *Justitia*. L.

Crook, Henry. SQS Warminster Jly TB to Va Sep 1773. Wi.

Crooke, John Jr. S s at Watlington Summer 1757. O.

Crook, John. R 14 yrs Mar TB to Va Oct 1768. Wi.

Crooke, Jonathan. S s at Watlington Summer 1757. O.

Crook, Mary. R 14 yrs Jly 1766. De.

Crook, Mary. S for murder of her bastard child Summer 1740 R 14 yrs Lent 1741. Wa.

Crooke, Robert, a Quaker. R for plantations Jly 1665 (SP). Ht.

Crook, Samuel. S 14 yrs s linen from bleaching yard Lent 1762. Nf.

Crook, Samuel. S Mar 1767. De.

Crook, William. S Jly 1718 to be T to Va. De.

Crook, William. S Feb T Apr 1771 *Thornton*. L.

Crookhorne, Thomas. S s sheep Lent R 14 yrs Summer 1766. Ru.

Crookshanks, William. S Jan T Feb 1719 *Worcester* LC Annapolis Jun 1719. L.

Croom, John. Rebel T 1685.

Croot, Bartholomew. S Aug 1740 TB to Va; R 14 yrs Aug 1742. De.

Crop, Sarah (1733). *See* Simper. Wi.

Cropper, Robert. S Mar TB to Va Apr 1740. Wi.

Cropper, William. S & T Jan 1722 *Gilbert* to Md. M.

Cropwell, John. T May 1737 *Forward*. E.

Crossby, Elizabeth wife of John. S s at Newbury Lent 1734. Be.

Crosby, James. SW & T Apr 1768 *Thornton*. M.

Crosby, John. S Sep-Oct 1749. M.

Crosby, John. S City s silver at St. Martin, Coney Street, Summer 1767. Y.

Crosby, Mary. LC Rappahannock May 1728 from *Forward*. X.

Crosby, Richard. S Summer 1753 R Lent TB Apr 1754. Db.

Crosby, Thomas. SQS Dec 1761 T Apr 1762 *Dolphin*. M.
Crosgell, John. S Jan T Feb 1765 *Tryal*. L.
Croshaw, Elizabeth. S Apr-May 1754. M.
Croskin, Mary. S Norwich 14 yrs Summer 1754 for receiving goods
    stolen by John Mickleburgh *(qv)* Summer 1754. Nf.
Croskin, Mary. S Aug TB Sep 1774. Nf.
Cross, Arthur. S Aug 1727. M.
Cross, Bartholomew. S Mar 1759. Ha.
Cross, Charles, aged 24, dark. LC Annapolis May 1721 from *Gilbert*. X.
Cross, Charles. S Jun 1739. L.
Cross, Charles. S May-Jly 1750. M.
Cross, Edward. S Lent 1738. Su.
Cross, Elizabeth. S & T Sep 1751 *Greyhound*. L.
Cross, Elizabeth. S Jan-Feb T Apr 1772 *Thornton*. M.
Cross, Francis. S Lent R 14 yrs Summer 1752. Nf.
Cross, George. T May 1751 *Tryal*. K.
Cross, Hannah. S & T Dec 1736 *Dorsetshire*. L.
Cross, Hannah. TB to Va from QS 1758. De.
Cross, James. S Apr T May 1750 *Lichfield*. L.
Crosse, John. R for Bermuda Oct 1614. M.
Crosse, John. Rebel T 1685.
Cross, John of Lustleigh, tanner. R for Barbados Jun 1699. De.
Cross, John. S Jan T Feb 1719 *Worcester* LC Annapolis Jun 1719. L.
Cross, John. S & T Sep 1731 *Smith* LC Va 1732. M.
Cross, John. S for highway robbery Lent R 14 yrs Summer 1759. Nf.
Cross, John (1765). *See* Cross, Thomas. M.
Crosse, Jonas. Rebel T 1685.
Crosse, Mary. R for Barbados or Jamaica Dec 1689. M.
Cross, Mary. S & T Oct 1730 *Forward* LC Potomack Jan 1731. M.
Cross, Mary (1748). *See* May. M.
Crosse, Peter of Scitvole, Exeter, woolcomber. R for Barbados Feb
    1673. De.
Cross, Richard of Marke, tinker. R for Barbados Jun 1699. So.
Cross, Richard. S Lent R 14 yrs Summer 1734 AT Lent 1735. Be.
Cross, Richard. S Apr T Dec 1734 *Caesar* LC Va Jly 1735. M.
Cross, Richard. R 14 yrs Jly TB to Va Aug 1751. Wi.
Cross, Robert. T Apr 1732 *Patapsco*. Sy.
Cross, Robert. S Norwich for destroying satin warp on loom Summer
    1739 R 14 yrs Lent 1740 (SP). Nf.
Cross, Robert (1765). *See* Cross, Thomas. M.
Crosse als Jiggam, Samuel of Preston upon Stour. S Summer 1720. G.
Cross, Samuel. R 14 yrs Jly 1775. M.
Cross als Civility, Sarah. S Feb T Mar 1731 *Patapsco* LC Md Jun
    1731. M.
Crosse, Thomas of Sevenhampton. R for America Jly 1675. G.
Cross, Thomas. Rebel T 1685.
Cross, Thomas. S Jly 1718 to be T to Boston NE. Wi.
Cross, Thomas. S May T 14 yrs Jly 1722 *Alexander*. L.
Cross, Thomas als John als Robert. S & T Sep 1765 *Justitia*. M.
Cross, Thomas. S s at Stow on the Wold Lent 1770. G.
Crosse, William. Rebel T 1685.

Cross, William. S Mar TB to Va Apr 1768. Wi.
Cross, William. S Summer T Aug 1771. Wa.
Crossing, William. S for perjury Mar 1744. De.
Crosland, George of Basford. SQS s geese Jan TB Apr 1773. Nt.
Crossley, David. S Summer 1751 R 14 yrs Lent 1752. St.
Crossley, Elizabeth of Colne, spinster. S Lent 1741. La.
Crossley, John. S s sheep at Halifax Summer 1767 R 14 yrs Summer 1768. Y.
Crossley, Mary of Colne, spinster. S Lent 1741. La.
Crost als Crowhurst, John. S Summer 1751 R 14 yrs Lent T May 1752 *Lichfield*. E.
Crosthwaite, Edward. S Lent 1764. La.
Croston, James of Atherton, collier. SQS Apr 1752. La.
Crotch als Yarmouth, John. S & T Oct 1732 *Caesar*. L.
Crouch, Absalom. S & T Oct 1729 *Forward* LC Va Jun 1730. M.
Crouch, Cornelius. SQS Sep 1677 & at his own consent to be T to Jamaica by *Duke of York*. M.
Crouch, Honora. S Norwich s gown Summer 1761. Nf.
Crouch, John. SQS & T Jan 1766 *Tryal*. Ht.
Crouch als Crouchefer, Mary. S Jan T Apr 1762 *Dolphin*. L.
Crouch, Richard. R for life Mar TB to Va Apr 1769. Wi.
Crouch, Sarah. S May T Jun 1727 *Susanna* to Va. M.
Croutch, Thomas. S Jan-Apr 1749. M.
Croucher, George. S Oct T Dec 1769 *Justitia*. M.
Crouchley, John. R for Barbados Jun 1671. M.
Crouchley, Thomas. R for Va Jly 1618. O.
Crouchley, Thomas of Bedford, weaver. SQS Jly 1763. La.
Crow, Alice. S Oct T Dec 1770 *Justitia*. M.
Crow, Ann. S for shoplifting Lent 1767. Su.
Crowe, Benjamin. Rebel T 1685.
Crowe, Daniel. S & T Dec 1767 *Neptune*. M.
Crow, John (1722). *See* Scoon. L.
Crow, John. S Apr-Jun T Jly 1772 *Tayloe*. M.
Crow als Farrell, Margaret. S Apr T Jun 1768 *Tryal*. M.
Crow, Peter. S s at Bitton Summer TB Aug 1756. G.
Crow, Richard. S Summer R for Barbados Aug 1664. K.
Crow, Thomas of Spalding. R for America Jly 1679. Li.
Crow, Thomas (1684). *See* Carrow. Nf.
Crow, Thomas of Ealing. S s wine & T Dec 1740 *Vernon* to Md. M.
Crow, Thomas. S Apr-May T Jly 1771 *Scarsdale*. M.
Crowder, Charles. S & R 7 yrs Summer T Sep 1773. Wa.
Crowder, Eleanor. S Sep s sheets T Dec 1736 *Dorsetshire* to Va. M.
Crowder, George. R & T 14 yrs Apr 1770 *New Trial*. M.
Crowder, John. Rebel T 1685.
Crowder als Strowder, John of Longdon. R for America Jly 1686. St.
Crowder, John of Levenshulme, crofter. SQS Jly 1773. La.
Crowder, Joseph. S Lent 1775. Wa.
Crowder, Thomas. S Apr-May 1775. M.
Crowdson als Mazey, Thomas. S Lent 1766. La.
Crowhurst, John (1752). *See* Crost. E.
Crowhurst, John. T Sep 1764 *Justitia*. K.

Crowley, Alice (1661). *See* Stewkley. M.

Croley, Simon of Dudley, nailer. R for America Jly 1693. Wo.

Crowney, Paul. S Feb T Mar 1730 *Patapsco* LC Annapolis Sep 1730. L.

Crowther, Edward. S Apr 1746. L.

Crowther, Edward. S s at Ribbesford Lent 1767. Wo.

Crowther, Eli. S s watch at Halifax Lent 1769. Y.

Crowther, Elizabeth wife of John. S Summer 1744. Y.

Crowther, John. S & T Dec 1759 *Phoenix*. L.

Crowther, Percival. S s pewter pot & T Dec 1734 *Caesar* LC Va Jly 1735. M.

Croxall, George. TB Jun 1738. Db.

Croxall, William. S Lent 1764. Wa.

Crozier, Thomas. S s at Holy Well als St. Cross Summer 1746. O.

Cruckland, John. S & R 14 yrs Summer 1742. Nf.

Cruckson, John of Worthen. R for America Mar 1697. Sh.

Cruddess, William (1754). *See* Thompson, Richard. Du.

Cruise. *See* Crews.

Crump, Elizabeth. S for receiving goods stolen at St. Nicholas, Worcester, Lent 1736. Wo.

Crump, Francis. S Oct 1760. M.

Crumpe, James of Rushberry. R for America Feb 1700. Sh.

Crumpe, Thomas. R for Barbados Aug 1664. L.

Crumpton. *See* Crompton.

Crupper, Peter. S for highway robbery Lent R 14 yrs Summer 1742. Nt.

Crust, Charles. R (Home Circ) for Barbados May 1664. X.

Cruttenden, Thomas. S Summer 1748 R 14 yrs Lent 1749. Sx.

Cryer, Edward. R 14 yrs Aug TB to Va Oct 1739. Wi.

Cryer, Edward. S Mar 1745. Ha.

Cryer, Jane (1755). *See* Nicholls. L.

Cryer, Richard. S Summer 1755 R 14 yrs Lent T Jun 1756 *Lyon*. K.

Cryer, William. S & T 14 yrs Jan 1722 *Gilbert* LC Annapolis Jly 1722. M.

Cryer, William. S Jan T Feb 1724 *Anne* to Carolina. M.

Cryer, William. S Jun s lead T Dec 1736 *Dorsetshire* to Va. M.

Cubberd als Cobby als Kirbee, Anthony of Basildon. SQS Oct 1755 T Jun 1756 *Lyon*. E.

Cubberd als Cobby als Kirbee, William of Basildon. SQS Oct 1755 T Jun 1756 *Lyon*. E.

Cubbidge, John. T Apr 1739 *Forward*. Bu.

Cuckeele als Gater, Mary. R for Barbados Jun 1671. M.

Cuddy, Sophia. S Jly-Dec 1747. M.

Cudmore, William. R Mar 1750 TB to Va. De.

Cue, Edward. S Lent R 14 yrs Summer TB Aug 1740. G.

Cue, Edward. S & TB Jly 1742. G.

Cuff, Thomas. S Mar 1755. So.

Cuff, William. R 14 yrs Jly 1765 TB to Va 1766. De.

Culberson, James. SQS May T Jly 1773 *Tayloe* to Va. M.

Culham, John. S s mare Lent R 14 yrs Summer 1756. Nf.

Cullen, John. SQS Feb T Apr 1772 *Thornton*. M.

Culley, Charles. S Dec 1748 T Jan 1749 *Laura*. M.

Cully, Luke. S Mar 1726. Ha.

Culliford, John. R Apr AT Jun 1690. M.

Culliford, John. S Jly 1752. Do.
Cullimore, James. S Dec 1741 T Feb 1742 *Industry* to Md. M.
Cullimore, William. S Aug 1764. So.
Cullum, Elizabeth, aged 16, dark. S Jly T Oct 1720 *Gilbert* LC Md May 1721. M.
Cullum, Robert. S s horse Lent R 14 yrs Summer 1741 (SP). Su.
Cullam, Thomas. S Oct 1741 T Feb 1742 *Industry* to Md. M.
Cullum, William. S s gelding Summer 1750 R 14 yrs Lent 1751. Su.
Culmore, Joseph of Rotherhithe. SQS Jan T Apr 1765 *Ann.* Sy.
Culpepper, Margaret. S & T Sep 1751 *Greyhound.* M.
Culpin, Henry of Great Warley. R for Barbados or Jamaica Jly 1704. E.
Culshaw, Hester. S s at Avening Lent 1763. G.
Culverhowse, William of Heanton. R for Barbados Jly 1672. So.
Culverwell, James. R 14 yrs Apr 1756. So.
Culverwell, John. Rebel T 1685.
Culverwell, John. R for Barbados or Jamaica Feb 1687. L.
Culverwell, Richard. SQS 14 yrs Oct 1758 TB May 1759. So.
Culverwell, William. S Aug 1727. So.
Cumber, John of Milton, joiner. R for Barbados Feb 1665. O.
Cumber, William of Bermondsey. R for Barbados or Jamaica Feb 1690. Sy.
Cumberbatch, Francis. S Summer 1758. Le.
Cumberford, John. S Feb T Apr 1743 *Justitia.* M.
Cumberland, John. R for Barbados or Jamaica May 1697. L.
Cumbershall, Thomas of Forcehill, West Chaldon. R for Barbados Feb 1699. Do.
Cumby, Judith. R for Barbados or Jamaica Aug 1700. M.
Cumming, John of Mehemnet. R for Barbados Jly 1715. Co.
Cummins, Edward. S Aug T Oct 1741 *Sea Horse* to Va. M.
Cummins, Elizabeth. S Apr 1749. L.
Cummins, George. SQS May 1763. M.
Comyns, James. S Feb T Apr 1766 *Ann.* L.
Cummings, John. S Feb T Mar 1729 *Patapsco* LC Annapolis Dec 1729. L.
Commings, John. S for perjury Jun T Jly 1772 *Tayloe.* L.
Cummings, Joseph. S Apr-May 1754. M.
Comyns, Lawrence. S Feb T Mar 1764 *Tryal.* M.
Cummins, Nicholas. Rebel T 1685.
Cummins, Patrick. S Jly-Sep T Oct 1739 *Duke of Cumberland.* M.
Kummings, Thomas. S Nov T Dec 1753 *Whiteing.* L.
Comins, Thomas. S Lent 1757. K.
Cummins, William. S Feb T Apr 1735 *Patapsco* LC Annapolis Oct 1735. L.
Cundell, Edward. S Jan T Jun 1738 *Forward* to Md or Va. M.
Cundale, John. S Lent 1731. Y.
Cundell, Robert. S Feb T Sep 1737 *Pretty Patsy* to Md. M.
Cundit, John. SQS New Sarum Jan TB to Va Apr 1773. Wi.
Cunningham, Ann. S Feb-Apr T May 1752 *Lichfield.* M.
Cunningham, Edward of York City. R for Barbados Jly 1699. Y.
Cunningham, Hugh. S Apr-Jun 1739. M.
Cunningham, James. R Sep 1671 AT Oct 1673. M.

Cunningham, James. S Feb T Apr 1742 *Bond*. L.

Cunningham, James. S Sep T Dec 1767 *Neptune*. L.

Cunningham, James. S Oct T Dec 1767 *Neptune*. L.

Cunningham, Jane. S Feb T Apr 1770 *New Trial*. M.

Cunningham, John. S May T Jun 1764 *Dolphin*. M.

Cunningham, John. S May 1770. M.

Cunningham, Joseph. S Nov T Dec 1753 *Whiteing*. L.

Cunningham, Joseph. S for s plants from nursery May T Jun 1768 *Tryal*. M.

Cunningham, Thomas. S Jan 1751. L.

Cunningham, Thomas of St. Saviour, Southwark. SQS Jan 1755. Sy.

Cunningham, William (1773). *See* Orr. Nl.

Cunnington, Alice. S Jan 1746. M.

Cunnington, James of Burton Latimer. R for America Feb 1713. No.

Cunnycut, Nicholas. S Feb T Apr 1732 *Patapsco* LC Md Oct 1732. M.

Cunold, William. S s from warehouse Summer 1756; wife Elizabeth acquitted. Su.

Cupit, Judith. S Sep T Dec 1734 *Caesar* but died on passage. M.

Curby. *See* Kirby.

Curd, Christopher. S Sep-Oct 1772. M.

Curd, James. S May-Jly 1750. M.

Curd, Sarah. T Sep 1730 *Smith*. K.

Cure, William. R 14 yrs Apr 1759. So.

Curgis, James. PT Summer 1719. G.

Curle, William. SQS Jan TB Mar 1768. So.

Curley, Henry. PT Sep 1684 R Mar 1685. M.

Curmick, Jane. SQS New Sarum or Marlborough & TB to Va Jan 1774. Wi.

Curram, William. R 14 yrs Mar 1775. De.

Currance, William of St. Luke. S Jan-May s apron T Jun 1738 *Forward*. M.

Currant als Chadwick, Elizabeth. S Jan-Jun T Jun 1728 *Elizabeth* LC Potomack Aug 1729. L.

Currant als Corrand, John. S Feb T Apr 1769 *Tryal*. M.

Currell, Elizabeth, als wife of Thomas Keithly. S Jly T Sep 1766 *Justitia*. M.

Currall, James. S Oct-Dec 1750. M.

Currin, James. S Apr T Jun 1768 *Tryal*. M.

Curry, Ann. S Sep T Oct 1739 *Duke of Cumberland*. L.

Curree, Elizabeth. S Sep T Oct 1719 *Susannah & Sarah* LC Md Apr 1720. L.

Curry, Elizabeth (1732). *See* Giles. L.

Curray als McGrath, Elizabeth. S Jun T Sep 1767 *Justitia*. M.

Curry, Henry. S Mar 1765. Ha.

Curry, John. R 14 yrs Jly 1738. Do.

Currey, Mary. AT City Summer 1755. Nl.

Curry, Michael. S & T Sep 1757 *Thetis*. L.

Curry, Rose. S Feb T Apr 1732 *Patapsco* LC Annapolis Oct 1732. L.

Curry, Thomas of York City. R for America Mar 1710. Y.

Curry, Thomas. S Aug 1741. So.

Curry, William of Charlinch. R for Barbados Feb 1692. So.

Curryer, William. S Nov T Dec 1752 *Greyhound*. L.

Curson, John. S Lent 1758. Nf.

Curson, Richard, "an old convict". S for fraud Summer 1762 R Lent 1763. Nf.

Cursworth, Jeremiah. SQS Mar TB to Md Apr 1741. Le.

Curtain, James. R for life Jan 1775 (SP). O.

Curtess, Richard. *See* Curtis. Nl.

Curtis, Katherine. S Aug T Oct 1723 *Forward* to Va. M.

Curtis, Catherine. S & T Sep 1755 *Tryal*. L.

Curtis als Richardson, Daniel. S Oct-Dec 1750. M.

Curtis, Deborah. R & T Sep 1766 *Justitia*. M.

Curtis, Edward. R 14 yrs Mar 1755. Ha.

Curtis, Edward. SQS Jan TB Apr 1764. So.

Cortis als Hutchinson, George. R 14 yrs Aug 1767 TB to Va. De.

Curtis, Henry. S s pigs at Cirencester Lent TB Mar 1750. G.

Curtis, Isaac. S Jly 1753. Ha.

Curtis, James. T Jun 1764 *Dolphin*. Ht.

Curtis, James. S Oct 1768 T Jan 1769 *Thornton*. M.

Curtis, John of St. Winnow. R for Barbados Feb 1714. Co.

Curtis, John. S Feb T Mar 1729 *Patapsco* LC Annapolis Dec 1729. M.

Curtis, John. S s at Leckhampton Lent TB Oct 1737. G.

Curtis, John. S s horse Lent R Summer 1737. G.

Curtis, John. S & T Sep 1765 *Justitia*. L.

Curtis, Joseph. R for Barbados or Jamaica Dec 1683 & May 1684. L.

Curtis, Mark. S Mar 1737. Co.

Curtis, Martha (1728). *See* Pagett. L.

Curtis, Mary (1724). *See* Cowley. M.

Curtis, Mary wife of Thomas. S Jly-Sep T Oct 1739 *Duke of Cumberland*. M.

Curtis, Mary. T Apr 1741 *Speedwell* or *Mediterranean*. E.

Curtis, Prudence. S Lent R 14 yrs Summer TB Aug 1739. G.

Curtis, Richard. TB to Va from QS 1736. De.

Curtis als Curtess, Richard. R City for life Summer 1758. Nl.

Curtis, Samuel. S Aug T Sep 1764 *Justitia*. L.

Curtis, Sarah. S & T Jly 1753 *Tryal*. L.

Curtis, Simon. R Mar 1774. So.

Curtis, Susannah. T Apr 1769 *Tryal*. E.

Curtis, Thomas. Rebel T 1685.

Curtis, Thomas. S & T Jan 1739 *Dorsetshire*. L.

Curtis, Thomas. S Dec 1749-Jan 1750 T Mar 1750 *Tryal*. M.

Curtis, William. S Mar 1730. Wi.

Curtis, William. S Mar TB to Va Apr 1732. Wi.

Courtis, William. R 14 yrs Mar 1739. Co.

Curtis, William. S Lent R 14 yrs Summer TB Aug 1740. G.

Curtis, William. S s silver spoons at Gorleston Lent 1772. Su.

Cushing als Cushin als Cushon, Richard. S & R s lambs at Cley Summer 1770. Nf.

Cuss, Richard. R for Barbados or Jamaica May 1684. M.

Cuss, Thomas. S & TB Aug 1747. G.

Cussens, Peter. R & TB Oct 1662. L.

Cust, Christopher. S Jan 1746. M.

Cut and Slash (1774). *See* Vallett, James. M.

Cutforth, Alexander. R for America Jly 1688. Li.

Cuthbert, Ann. S Jan-Apr 1748. M.

Cuthbert, George. S Sep-Oct 1775. M.

Cuthbert, James. S Sep-Oct 1773 to be T 14 yrs. M.

Cuthbert, Samuel. S 14 yrs Lent T May 1755 *Rose*. Sy.

Cuthbert, William. S Sep T Dec 1767 *Neptune*. L.

Cuthbertson, John. S Apr 1761. M.

Cuthbertson, Robert. S City Summer 1756. Nl.

Cutler, Edmund. S May T Jun 1764 *Dolphin*. M.

Cutler, Edward of Tewkesbury. R for America Jly 1678. G.

Cutler als Longman, Elizabeth. R for Barbados Oct 1673. L.

Cutler, Elizabeth. AT from QS Summer 1728. St.

Cutler, Francis. SQS Jan TB Jly 1735. So.

Cutler, Grace. R for Barbados or Jamaica Oct 1694. M.

Cutler, Henry. S Apr 1745.

Cutler, Thomas. Rebel T 1685.

Cutler als Weedon, Thomas. R Lent 1773. Ht.

Cutler, William. S Jly T Sep 1718 *Eagle* LC Charles Town Mar 1719. L.

Cutmore, Joshua. T Jun 1764 *Dolphin*. Ht.

Cutmore, William. T Jun 1764 *Dolphin*. Ht.

Cutting, Edward. LC Va Sep 1736 from *Dorsetshire*. X.

Cuttridge, Thomas. S Summer 1749. E.

Cutts, Charles. SQS Devizes Apr TB to Va Aug 1752. Wi.

Cutts, Francis. S s horse Summer 1738 R 14 yrs Lent 1739. Li.

Cuzee als McKecky, Joseph. S Oct T Nov 1725 *Rappahannock* LC
    Rappahannock Apr 1726. M.

D

Dabbs, John. S s fowls at Wellington Lent 1764. Sh.
Dabbs, John. S s at Wolverhampton Summer 1764. St.
Dabbs, William. R 7 yrs Lent 1774. Sx.
Dabey, William. S Oct T Dec 1758 *The Brothers*. L.
Dabney, Robert of Whittington. S Lent 1721. G.
Dabney, William. R 14 yrs Jly 1737. Wi.
Dace, Daniel. S May T Sep 1737 *Pretty Patsy* to Md. M.
Dacey, Mary. SQS Sep T Dec 1770 *Justitia*. M.
Dacock, Thomas. T May 1752 *Lichfield*. Sy.
Da Costa, Antonio. S Feb T Mar 1750 *Tryal*. M.
Da Costa, Isaac Alvarez. S Sep-Oct 1748 T Jan 1749 *Laura*. M.
Dadd, Edward. S Aug 1727 TB to Md. De.
Dadds, John. S Apr 1747. De.
Dadsley, William. S Jun T Sep 1767 *Justitia*. L.
Daffy, Isabella. S May 1761. M.
Dagenhart, John. S Feb T Apr 1765 *Ann*. M.
Dagger, Mary. T May 1744 *Justitia*. Sy.
Dagmore, Isabel (1773). See Dugmore. Du.
Dagnell, Elizabeth. SQS Sep T Oct 1768 *Justitia*. M.
Daikins, Anna Maria. S Sep-Oct 1774. M.
Daily/Dailey. See Daley.
Daines, Edward. S Dec 1750. L.
Dains, Jacob. S Norwich Summer 1765. Nf.
Daintry, William. R Oct 1694 AT Jan 1695. M.
Daland, Eleanor wife of Lawrence. S Jan T Apr 1759 *Thetis*. M.
Dalby, Daniel. T Apr 1769 *Tryal*. Sy.
Dalby, Mary. S Jan 1745. L.
Dalby, Susan. S s linen Jly T Dec 1735 *John* LC Annapolis Sep 1736. M.
Dalby, William. S s horse at Birstall & R 14 yrs Lent 1770. Y.
Dale, Ann. S s at Drayton Lent 1768. Sh.
Dale als Dell, Edward. S Feb T 14 yrs Apr 1732 *Patapsco* LC Md Oct 1732. M.
Dale, Edward. S s horse Summer 1742 R 14 yrs Lent 1743. Y.
Dale, Henry. R 14 yrs Lent 1721. St.
Dale, James. S s handkerchiefs at Cookham Lent 1752. Be.
Dale, John of Pirton. R for Jamaica, Barbados or Bermuda Feb 1686. Wo.
Dale als Bennett, John, als Husson, Edward. S s sheep Summer 1750 R 14 yrs Lent 1751. Nt.
Dale, Joseph. S for highway robbery Summer 1742 R for life Lent 1743. Be.
Dale, Thomas. S s nails at Halesowen Summer 1726. Sh.
Dale, Thomas. S Jan T Mar 1764 *Tryal*. M.
Dale, Thomas. S Feb T Apr 1766 *Ann*. M.
Dale, William. R for America Jly 1709. Db.
Dale, William of St. Martin, Norwich. S Summer 1731. *Nf.

Dale, William. S s gelding Summer 1767 R 14 yrs Lent 1768. Nt.
Dale, William. S Jan-Feb 1774. M.
Dales, John. S s horse Summer 1743 R 14 yrs Lent 1744. Y.
Dales, Robert. S Sep-Oct 1773. M.
Dailey, Ann. S Sep-Oct 1773. M.
Dailey, Charles. S Summer 1760. K.
Daley, Charles. SQS Feb T Mar 1764 *Tryal*. M.
Daily, Daniel. S Feb T Mar 1760 *Friendship*. M.
Dailey als Dally, James. S Mar 1726. Do.
Daily, James (1771). *See* Smith. Ca.
Dayly als Peterson, John, als Gahogan, Walter. S & T for life Sep 1755 *Tryal*. L.
Dailey, John. S Oct T Dec 1767 *Neptune*. L.
Daily, John. SQS Sep 1774. M.
Daley, Mary. R 14 yrs Apr 1747. De.
Daley, Mary. S Dec 1773. M.
Dayly, Nathaniel. T Jly 1723 *Alexander* LC Md Sep 1723. Sy.
Dayley, Richard. S Jun T Dec 1736 *Dorsetshire* to Va. M.
Daley, Rose. S Apr-May 1775. M.
Dayly, Timothy. S Oct T Dec 1724 *Rappahannock* to Va. M.
Dayly, William (1769). *See* Dealy. M.
Dalfee, David. S Jun 1747. L.
Dallaway, Matthew. S May T Aug 1769 *Douglas*. M.
Dalloway, Thomas (1745). *See* Dallow. Wo.
Dallimore, Benjamin. S Mar 1735. Ha.
Dallow, Jane wife of Thomas. S Lent R 14 yrs Summer 1746. Wo.
Dallow, Martha, spinster, als Tomlins, widow. S Oct 1769 *Justitia*. M.
Dallow als Dalloway, Thomas. S Lent R 14 yrs Summer 1745. Wo.
Dally, James (1726). *See* Dailey. Do.
Dally, John. S Norwich for housebreaking Summer 1726 R 14 yrs Lent 1727. Nf.
Daloon als McGuy, Jane. S & T Oct 1730 *Forward* to Va. M.
Dalton, Andrew. S & T Oct 1730 *Forward* LC Potomack Jan 1731. M.
Dolton, Ann. S Mar 1750 TB to Va. De.
Dolton, James. S Apr 1720; escaped from *Honor* in Vigo, Spain. L.
Dalton, James. S Jly T Aug 1721 *Prince Royal* to Va. M.
Dalton, Jane (1744). *See* Aspley. M.
Dalton, John. S Sep-Oct T Dec 1752 *Greyhound*. M.
Dalton, John. T Aug 1769 *Douglas*. Sy.
Dalton, Mary (1719). *See* Reed. L.
Dolton, Michael. S Feb 1765. M.
Dalton, Peter. R for Barbados Feb 1675. L.
Dalton, Sarah wife of James. S Jly T Sep 1767 *Justitia*. M.
Dalton, Thomas. R for highway robbery Lent 1750; ordered to remain in gaol until Summer 1750 Assizes. Ht.
Dalton, Thomas. S Oct-Dec 1754. M.
Dalton, Thomas. S Summer 1756 R 14 yrs Lent T Sep 1757 *Thetis*. Sy.
Dalton, William. S Lent 1735. Ca.
Dalton, William. S Jan-Feb 1773. M.
Damant, John. S Lent 1754. Su.
Damaree, Edmund. S Oct T Dec 1734 *Caesar* but died on passage. M.

Damarin als Dammearon, William of St. Pancras. S s lead Jly-Oct 1740
T Jan 1741 *Harpooner*. M.
Damper, Thomas of Cranbrook. R for Barbados or Jamaica Jly 1712. K.
Danby, Catherine. S Feb T Apr 1743 *Justitia*. M.
Danby, Thomas. S s mare & R 14 yrs Lent 1756. Hu.
Daunce, Edward of Underhill. R for America Jly 1698. Wo.
Dance, Rebecca. S & T Oct 1729 *Forward* LC Va Jun 1730. M.
Dancer, John. S & T Sep 1731 *Smith* LC Va 1732. M.
Dancer, Thomas. R for Barbados Jun 1671. M.
Dancer, Thomas. S Summer 1757 R 14 yrs Lent 1758. Wo.
Dancy, Henry. PT Oct 1697. M.
Danzie, John. S Jly R 14 yrs T Aug 1718 *Eagle* LC Charles Town Mar
1719. M.
Dansie, Joseph. S Lent R 14 yrs Summer 1744. Su.
Danzie, Richard. S Apr T 14 yrs Aug 1718 *Eagle* to Md or Va. L.
Dancey, Thomas (John). S Summer 1740 R Lent 1741 (SP). St.
Dando, Samuel. S Jly 1725. So.
Dandy, James. S s gold ring at Himbleton Lent 1756. Wo.
Dandy, John. S Summer R for Barbados Aug 1663. Ht.
Dane, Daniel of Netteswell. R for Barbados or Jamaica Jly 1702. E.
Dane, Francis. T Sep 1758 *Tryal*. K.
Dane, James. S for perjury Lent 1774 & ordered to remain in gaol one
month before transportation; S Lent 1775 for being at large and
ordered to be transported for remainder of his term. La.
Dane, John of Netteswell. R for Barbados or Jamaica Jly 1702. E.
Danells als Demelan, Joseph. S Lent 1724 R Lent 1725. St.
Danford, John. S & T Aug 1718 *Eagle* LC Charles Town Mar 1719. L.
Danford, Robert. S Summer 1734. Su.
Dangerfield, Richard. S & T 14 yrs Oct 1732 *Caesar* to Va. M.
Dangerfield, Samuel. S Nov T Dec 1770 *Justitia*. L.
Dangerfield, Samuel. S s at Handsworth Summer 1771. St.
Daniell, Abraham. S & TB Apr 1740. G.
Daniel als MacDonagh, Charles. S Sep 1735 T Jan 1736 *Dorsetshire* LC
Va Sep 1736. M.
Daniel, Edward. S Aug 1720. So.
Daniel, Elizabeth of Ash. SQS Oct T Dec 1758 *The Brothers*. Sy.
Daniel, Elizabeth. S s at Bassaleg Lent 1767. Mo.
Daniel, Giles. S Mar 1730. Wi.
Daniel als Acres, Hannah wife of John Acres. S Aug T Sep 1725
Forward LC Annapolis Dec 1725. M.
Daniell, Henry of Milborne St. Andrew, husbandman. R for Barbados
Feb 1672. Do.
Daniell als Disnell, John. LC from *Sukey* Annapolis Sep 1725. X.
Daniel, John of Bristol. Sentence confirmed Oct 1767 (SP). G.
Daniel, John. S Aug 1772. So.
Daniel, Joseph. S May T Jun 1764 *Dolphin*. L.
Daniel, Richard of Taunton, husbandman. R for Barbados Jly 1679. So.
Daniell, Richard. Rebel T 1685.
Daniell, Richard. S s cloth Jan-May T Jun 1738 *Forward* to Md
or Va. M.
Daniell, Thomas. Rebel T 1685.

Daniel, Thomas. T May 1737 *Forward*. K.
Daniel, Thomas. S Feb 1775. L.
Daniel, William. T Oct 1726 *Forward*. E.
Daniel, William. T Dec 1758 *The Brothers*. Sx.
Daniels, Abraham. S Lent 1740. Wo.
Daniels, Benny. S s butter at St. James, Dukes Place, Jan T Apr 1768
　Thornton. L.
Danks, Mary. S Jan 1746. M.
Danks, Mary. S Sep-Oct T Dec 1771 *Justitia*. M.
Danks, Thomas. AT from QS Lent 1766. Wa.
Dann, Elizabeth. AT City Summer 1761. Nl.
Dann, John (1740). *See* Ascot. De.
Dannel, Anne. SQS & TB Jan 1758. So.
Danslow. *See* Denslow.
Danson, John. S May 1719. M.
Danvis, Arthur als John. R for America Aug 1715. L.
Danzie. *See* Dancy.
Darban, Sarah. S Aug T Oct 1726 *Forward* to Va. M.
Darbien, Mary. S May T Jly 1722 *Alexander* to Nevis or Jamaica. M.
Darbin als Broom, Mary. S Apr T Nov 1759 *Phoenix*. M.
Darby, Ann. S Feb-Apr 1746. M.
Darby, Edmund. S s sheep & R 14 yrs Summer 1775. St.
Darby, Elizabeth of Rochford, spinster. SQS Apr T Nov 1759
　Phoenix. E.
Derby, Isaac. S Jly T Oct 1768 *Justitia*. M.
Darby als Darley, James. S May T Jun 1738 *Forward*. L.
Darby, James. S Jly T Nov 1759 *Phoenix*. M.
Darby, John. T Jly 1723 *Alexander* but died on passage. Sx.
Darby, John, als MacDiamod, Owen. S Jan T Feb 1726 *Supply* to
　Md. M.
Darby, Mary (1748). *See* May. M.
Darby, Owen. S Jun 1739. L.
Darby, Rebecca. R for Barbados or Jamaica Dec 1716. M.
Darby, Roger of Reigate. SQS Apr T May 1750 *Lichfield*. Sy.
Darby, Thomas. R (Western Circ) for Barbados Jly 1688. L.
Darby, Thomas. S s mare at Kingswinford Summer 1737 R 14 yrs Lent
　1738. St.
Darby, Thomas. S Sep T Dec 1770 *Justitia*. M.
Darby, William. S Jun 1747. L.
Derbyshire Bess (1769). *See* Roby, Elizabeth. Wa.
Darbyshire, Jonathan of Flixton, weaver. SQS Oct 1761. S for returning
　from transportation Summer 1763 R 14 yrs Lent 1764. La.
Darcy, Luke. S Summer 1742. We.
Dare, Gideon. Rebel T 1685.
Dare, Mary. S Mar 1766. Do.
Dare, Richard. S Jly 1738. De.
Dare, Robert of Stockland. R for Barbados Feb 1690. Do.
Dare, Samuel. Rebel T 1685.
Darey, Mary. S Summer 1760. Bu.
Dark, Grace. TB to Va from QS 1756. De.
Dark, James. S Summer 1757 R 14 yrs Lent 1758. G.

Darke, John. S Feb T Mar 1729 *Patapsco* LC Annapolis Dec 1729. M.
Darke, Joseph. S s at St. Nicholas, Gloucester, Lent 1750. G.
Darken, Isaac. T 14 yrs Dec 1758 *The Brothers*. E.
Darlen, Joseph. S Jly 1775. M.
Darley, James (1738). *See* Darby. L.
Darling, Ann. S Jan T Feb 1742 *Industry*. L.
Darling, Ann (1770). *See* Claxton. M.
Darling, Mones. S for forgery Summer 1762 R for life Lent 1763. Su.
Darling, Richard. S s mare Summer 1752 R 14 yrs Lent 1753. Bd.
Darling, Robert. S Jan-Feb 1773. M.
Darling, Thomas. S May T Jun 1764 *Dolphin*. M.
Darlington, James. S Apr-Jun 1739. M.
Darlow, Thomas. S Apr T May 1750 *Lichfield*. L.
Darlow als Barlow, William. R May-Jly T for life Sep 1755 *Tryal*. M.
Darnell, Francis. S Lent 1744. Db.
Darnell, Mary. TB from QS 1735. De.
Darnell, William. S s shoulder of mutton Apr T Sep 1758 *Tryal* to
    Annapolis. M.
Darnet, William. R City 14 yrs Summer 1765. Y.
Darnton, Eleanor of Newcastle upon Tyne. R for Barbados Feb
    1673. Nl.
Darracott, Richard of Great Torrington. R for Barbados Jly 1677. De.
Darrent, Sarah. S May T Jly 1722 *Alexander* to Nevis or Jamaica. M.
Darrant, William. S s horse Lent R 14 yrs Summer 1742. Li.
Dart, Mary. S Feb-Apr T May 1751 *Tryal*. M.
Dart, William. S Mar 1744. De.
Dartee, Bartholomew. S Apr T Sep 1767 *Justitia*. M.
Darton, Amelia als Milicent. S Feb 1761. L.
Darton, Mary (1671). *See* Lyon. M.
Darvall, Catherine. LC from *Forward* Annapolis Dec 1725. X.
Darvall, John. R for America Aug 1715. L.
Darvall als Neeves, Sarah. S Oct T Nov 1728 *Forward* LC
    Rappahannock Jun 1729. L.
Darvan, Joseph. S & T Dec 1731 *Forward* to Md or Va. M.
Darvey, Andrew. S May-Jly 1749. M.
Daryel als Reily, Jaques. T 14 yrs May 1719 *Margaret* LC Md May 1720;
    sold to Thomas Joneson. Sy.
Dashashire als Duck, Mary. R for Barbados Jly 1680. M.
Dashwood, Richard. T Jly 1723 *Alexander* but died on passage. Sx.
Da Silva, Joseph (1772). *See* Mascada, Francis. M.
D'Aubiney, Alexander. S Jan-Feb 1775. M.
Daunce. *See* Dance.
Dauphney, John. S s sheep at Threxton Summer 1767 R 14 yrs Lent
    1768. Nf.
Davenot, Samuel (1764). *See* Screen. So.
Davenport, Abraham. S May T 14 yrs Jun 1738 *Forward*. L.
Davenporte, John. R for Barbados or Jamaica Dec 1698. L.
Davenport, John (1699). *See* Adsett. M.
Davenport, John of Manchester, tailor. SQS Jan 1746. La.
Davenport, Joseph. S Summer 1763. La.
Davenport, Luke. SQS Oct 1756. M.

Davenport, Mary. S Feb T Apr 1762 *Dolphin*. M.
Davenport, Samuel. S Lent R 14 yrs Summer 1759. Ch.
Davenport, Thomas. S Lent 1723 R 14 yrs Summer 1724 T *Forward* LC
    Annapolis Jun 1725. O.
Davenport, William. S Dec 1764 T Jan 1765 *Tryal*. M.
Daveridge, Sarah. S Apr 1759. So.
Davett, Joseph. S Jan 1749. E.
Davey. *See* Davy.
Davia, John of Newport. R for Barbados or Jamaica Jly 1705. E.
David, Benjamin. S s at Hentland Summer 1773. He.
David, Daniel. S Feb 1774. L.
David als Davis, Evan. S Lent R 14 yrs Summer 1746. Mo.
David, Hugh of Shrewsbury. R for America Jly 1678. Sh.
David, John. S & R 14 yrs Lent 1775. Mo.
David, Lewis. S s clothing at Mynyddisloyn Summer 1746. Mo.
David als Davis, Margaret. S Lent R 14 yrs Summer 1746. Mo.
David, Thomas. SQS & TB Feb 1738. G.
David, Thomas, als Chilcott, Alexander. R 14 yrs Mar 1744. So.
David, Walter. S Lent R 14 yrs Summer 1727. Mo.
David, William. S Lent R for life Summer T Oct 1739
    Duke of Cumberland. E.
David, William. S s iron at Trevethin Summer 1749. Mo.
David, William. R Feb T for life Mar 1764 *Tryal*. M.
Davidge, Nicholas. Rebel T 1685.
Davids, Abraham. S Sep-Dec 1755 T Jan 1756 *Greyhound*. M.
Davids, David. S Sep-Dec 1755 T Jan 1756 *Greyhound*. M.
Davids, Joseph. SQS Jly 1774. M.
Davidson. *See* Davison.
Davis, Ambrose. R 14 yrs Mar 1743. So.
Davis, Amey (1741). *See* Grey. M.
Davis, Andrew of English Bicknor. R for America Mar 1701. G.
Davies, Anne. R for Barbados Dec 1667. M.
Davis, Anne. R for Barbados or Jamaica Feb 1686. M.
Davis, Ann (1695). *See* Bowcher. M.
Davis, Ann. S Aug T Oct 1726 *Forward*. L.
Davis, Ann (1732). *See* Ellis. K.
Davis als Boswell, Ann. S May 1745. L.
Davis, Ann. S Lent 1749. Sy.
Davis, Ann. T Aug 1752 *Tryal*. K.
Davis, Ann. S Sep T Dec 1758 *The Brothers*. M.
Davis, Ann of St. George, Southwark. SQS Jan T Mar 1764 *Tryal*. Sy.
Davis, Ann. S May-Jly 1773. M.
Davis, Arthur. S Lent 1721. Sh.
Davis, Benjamin of Dorrington, blacksmith. R for America Jly 1693. Sh.
Davis, Catherine. S Oct 1741 T Feb 1742 *Industry* to Md. M.
Davis, Catherine. S Jly-Sep T Sep 1742 *Forward*. M.
Davis, Catherine. S Dec 1753-Jan 1754. M.
Davis, Catherine (1758). *See* Wells. M.
Davis, Catherine. S & T Jan 1767 *Tryal*. M.
Davis, Charles. R Jly AT Aug 1685. M.
Davies, Charles. S s at Monmouth Lent 1750. Mo.

Davis, Charles. S May T Sep 1766 *Justitia*. M.

Davis als Davison als Josephson, Charles. S Summer 1768. La.

Davis, Charles. S Sep T for life Oct 1768 *Justitia*. L.

Davis, Charles. R 14 yrs Lent 1774. E.

Davis, Christiana. S Summer 1754 R 14 yrs Lent T May 1755 *Rose*. Sy.

Davis, Christopher. S & T Sep 1731 *Smith* LC Va 1732. M.

Davis, Dan. R Apr 1770. Do.

Davies, David. S s horse Lent R 14 yrs Summer 1727. Sh.

Davies, David. S Lent R 14 yrs Summer 1727. G.

Davis, David. T *Elizabeth* LC Potomack Aug 1729. No.

Davis, David. S s at Pen-y-Clawdd Summer 1736. Mo.

Davis, David. S Summer 1745. Sx.

Davis, David. S Jan 1757 to be T for life. L.

Davis, Diana. S s at Cardington Summer 1751. Sh.

Davies, Edward of Richard Castle. R for Barbados Oct 1663. Sh.

Davies, Edward, aged 15. R for Barbados Feb 1664. M.

Davyes, Edward. R for America Jly 1687. Wa.

Davis, Edward. S Aug T Sep 1725 *Forward* LC Annapolis Dec 1725. L.

Davis, Edward. S Jly 1746. L.

Davis, Edward (1754). *See* Taylor, John. G.

Davies, Edward. S s breeches Summer 1754. He.

Davies, Edward. S Oct T Nov 1762 *Prince William*. M.

Davis, Edward. S & T Nov 1762 *Prince William*. L.

Davis, Edward. T Mar 1764 *Tryal*. M.

Davis, Edward. T Sep 1764 *Justitia*. Sy.

Davies, Edward. S s at Shrewsbury & R 14 yrs Summer 1771. Sh.

Davis, Elinor. R for Barbados or Jamaica Feb 1687. L.

Davies, Elianor. S & T Oct 1730 *Forward* LC Potomack Jan 1731. L.

Davis, Eleanor. S & T Sep 1731 *Smith* LC Va 1732. L.

Davies als Evans, Elianor. S s at Riccards Summer 1745. Sh.

Davis, Elianor. S Lent R 14 yrs Summer 1757. Sh.

Davis, Eleanor. S s at Halford Lent 1767. Sh.

Davis, Eleazar. S & T Sep 1765 *Justitia*. L.

Davis, Elisha. Rebel T 1685.

Davies, Elizabeth. S Jan T Feb 1719 *Worcester* LC Annapolis Jun 1719. L.

Davis, Elizabeth. S Jly 1721 T Mar 1723. Bu.

Davies als Hope, Elizabeth. T Oct 1724 *Forward* LC Md Jun 1725. Sy.

Davis, Elizabeth. T Apr 1732 *Patapsco*. Sy.

Davis, Elizabeth. S & T May 1736 *Patapsco*. L.

Davis, Elizabeth. S Jun-Dec 1738 T Jan 1739 *Dorsetshire* to Va. M.

Davis, Elizabeth (1739). *See* Price. M.

Davis, Elizabeth. S Apr-Jun 1739 to be T 14 yrs. M.

Davis, Elizabeth. S Sep 1740. L.

Davis, Elizabeth. S & T 14 yrs Apr 1741 *Mediterranean*. L.

Davis, Elizabeth. S Feb T Mar 1750 *Tryal*. M.

Davis, Elizabeth. S s shoes at St. Laurence, Reading, Lent 1750. Be.

Davis, Elizabeth. S May-Jly T Sep 1751 *Greyhound*. M.

Davis, Elizabeth. S Feb 1752 to be T for life. L.

Davis, Elizabeth. S Jly 1756. M.

Davis, Elizabeth. T Dec 1758 *The Brothers*. K.

Davis, Elizabeth. T Jly 1770 *Scarsdale*. M.
Davis, Elizabeth. S Jan-Feb 1773. M.
Davis, Elizabeth. S Sep-Oct 1773. M.
Davies, Emanuel. LC from *Forward* Annapolis Jun 1723. X.
Davies, Evan. R for Barbados Oct 1673. L.
Davis, Evan. S Lent R 14 yrs Summer 1743. Sh.
Davis, Evan (1746). *See* David. Mo.
Davis, Evan. S s at Thornbury Lent TB Apr 1751. G.
Davies, Evan. S Summer 1764 R 14 yrs Lent 1765. Sh.
Davis, Evan. S s horse hair at Holt Summer 1768. Wo.
Davis, Francis. S s coat Jun T Dec 1736 *Dorsetshire* to Va. M.
Davis, George. S Lent R 14 yrs Summer 1755. He.
Davies, Gilbert. S Lent 1743. Sh.
Davis als Davison, Grace. S & T Sep 1751 *Greyhound*. L.
Davis, Hannah. S Jly 1746. L.
Davis, Hannah. S s at Tithing of Whistons Lent 1761. Wo.
Davis, Henry. T Oct 1719 *Susannah & Sarah*. L.
Davis, Henry. S Feb T Apr 1739 *Forward* to Va. M.
Davis, Henry. S Oct 1740. L.
Davis, Henry. S & T Oct 1772 *Caesar* to Va. M.
Davis, Hezekiah. PT Summer 1717. G.
Davis, Honor wife of John. S Feb T 14 yrs Mar 1731 *Patapsco* LC Md
    Jun 1731. M.
Davis, Hugh. T Sep 1742 *Forward*. K.
Davis, Hugh. S Aug 1752. So.
Davyes, Humphrey. Rebel T 1685.
Davies, Humphrey of Weobley. R for America Jly 1686. He.
Davis, Isabella. S Nov T Dec 1753 *Whiteing*. L.
Davies, Jacob. S Apr T Jly 1770 *Scarsdale*. L.
Davies, James of Richard Castle. R for Barbados Oct 1663. Sh.
Davies, James. PT Apr R Jly 1675. M.
Davis, James. S Jun-Dec 1745. M.
Davis, James. SQS Feb 1754. M.
Davies, James. S Sep 1754. L.
Davies, James (1758). *See* Roberts. He.
Davis, James. S & T Sep 1766 *Justitia*. L.
Davis, Jane. PT Oct T Dec 1716 *Lewis* to Jamaica. M.
Davis, Jane of Camberwell, spinster. SQS Jan T Mar 1758 *Dragon*. Sy.
Davies, Jane. S s at Cusop Lent 1759. He.
Davis, Jane (1768). *See* Jones, Dorothy. Sh.
Davis, Jane. S Oct T Dec 1769 *Justitia*. M.
Davies, Jane. S & T Dec 1771 *Justitia*. L.
Davis, Jane. S Jan-Feb 1774. M.
Davies, Jenkin. R for Barbados May 1668. M.
Davis als Wheeler, Joan of Colyton, widow. R for Barbados Jly
    1711. De.
Davis, John. R for Barbados Aug 1664. M.
Davis, John of Fisherton Anger. R for Barbados Jly 1667. Wi.
Davies, John. R for Barbados Aug 1670 & Jun 1671. M.
Davyes, John of Long Sutton. R for Barbados Jly 1684. Ha.
Davis, John of Worcester. R for America Feb 1690. Wo.

Davis als Davy, John. R for Barbados or Jamaica Dec 1695 & Jan 1697. M.

Davis, John of Cannock. R for America Jly 1696. St.

Davys, John of Watchett. R for Barbados Feb 1700. So.

Davis als Beard, John of St. Mary le Savoy. R for America Aug 1713. M.

Davis, John. S s horse Lent 1723 R 14 yrs Summer 1724. He.

Davies, John of Bedford. S Summer 1727. *Bd.

Davis, John. S Oct 1727-June 1728 T Jun 1728 *Elizabeth* LC Potomack Aug 1729. M.

Davis, John. T Oct 1729 *Forward*. E.

Davies, John. S & T Oct 1730 *Forward* LC Potomack Jan 1731. L.

Davis, John. T May 1736 *Patapsco*. K.

Davis, John. T Jan 1738 *Dorsetshire*. E.

Davis, John (1739). *See* Roberts. L.

Davis, John. R 14 yrs Mar 1740. So.

Davis, John. S & T Dec 1740 *Vernon*. L.

Davis, John. S Jun T Nov 1743 *George William*. M.

Davis, John. S Oct 1743 T Feb 1744 *Neptune*. L.

Davis, John. S Lent T May 1744 *Justitia*. Bu.

Davis, John. S Dec 1746. L.

Davis, John. S Jly-Dec 1747. M.

Davies, John. S s at Newchurch Lent 1748. Mo.

Davis, John. S s silver at St. Philip & Jacob Lent TB Mar 1748. G.

Davis, John. S Dec 1748 T Jan 1749 *Laura*. M.

Davis, John. S Jly 1750. L.

Davis, John. S Lent R 14 yrs Summer 1751. He.

Davis, John. S Summer T Sep 1751 *Greyhound*. Sy.

Davis, John. S Feb 1752. L.

Davis, John. S for setting fire to a cottage Summer 1752 R 14 yrs Lent 1753. Wa.

Davis, John. S s horse Lent R 14 yrs Summer 1754. Wa.

Davies, John. S Jly-Sep 1754. M.

Davis, John. S s iron wedges Summer 1754. Be.

Davis, John. SQS Coventry Oct 1754. Wa.

Davis, John. S s horse Lent R 14 yrs Summer 1757. No.

Davis, John. S Oct T Dec 1758 *The Brothers*. M.

Davis, John. S Dec 1760. M.

Davis, John. S s silver spoons at Oswestry Lent 1764. Sh.

Davis, John. SQS Jly T Sep 1764 *Justitia*. M.

Davies, John. S s deer Summer 1764 R 14 yrs Lent 1765. G.

Davies, John (1765). *See* Hughes, Robert. Ch.

Davies, John. S Lent 1766. Ch.

Davis, John. S Jly T Sep 1766 *Justitia*. L.

Davis, John. S & T Sep 1766 *Justitia*. L.

Davis, John. S & T Apr 1769 *Tryal*. M.

Davis, John. S & T Apr 1769 *Tryal*. L.

Davis, John of Woking. SQS Jan 1772. Sy.

Davis, John. S Jan-Feb T Apr 1772 *Thornton*. M.

Davis, John. SQS Feb T Apr 1772 *Thornton*. M.

Davies, John. S s at St. Chad, Shrewsbury, Lent 1772. Sh.

Davis, John of St. Paul Covent Garden. SW Oct 1774. M.
Davis, John Evan. SQS Apr 1773. M.
Davies, Jonathan of Layborne. R for Barbados or Jamaica Jly 1688. K.
Davis, Joseph. S Lent 1746. E.
Davies, Joseph of Warrington. SQS May 1750. La.
Davis, Joseph. R 14 yrs Mar 1753. De.
Davis, Joseph. S Apr 1763. L.
Davis, Joseph. SQS Jly T Sep 1764 *Justitia*. M.
Davis, Joseph. S Jan T Feb 1765 *Tryal*. L.
Davis, Luke. S s horse & R 14 yrs Lent 1773. He.
Davis, Margaret. S s iron hoops Apr T Dec 1735 *John* to Md. M.
Davis, Margaret. S Jly-Sep T Sep 1742 *Forward*. M.
Davis, Margaret (1746). *See* David. Mo.
Davis, Margaret. S May-Jly T Sep 1755 *Tryal*. M.
Davies, Margaret. S Summer 1758 R 14 yrs Lent 1759. Sh.
Davis, Martha. S Jan T Feb 1719 *Worcester* LC Annapolis Jun 1719. L.
Davis, Martha (1758). *See* How. Bd.
Davis, Mary. R for Barbados Jly 1674. L.
Davis, Mary. R for Barbados May 1676. L.
Davis, Mary (1685). *See* Cary. M.
Davis, Mary. R for Barbados or Jamaica Dec 1689. L.
Davies als Dawson, Mary. S & T Oct 1722 *Forward* LC Md Jun 1723. L.
Davis, Mary. S Oct T Dec 1724 *Rapppahannock* to Va. M.
Davies, Mary. S Summer 1741. Sh.
Davis, Mary. S Jan T Feb 1744 *Neptune*. L.
Davis, Mary. S Apr 1745. L.
Davis, Mary. S s at St. Owen, Gloucester, Lent 1749. G.
Davis, Mary. S May-Jly T Sep 1751 *Greyhound*. M.
Davis, Mary. S s at Caerwent Summer 1760. Mo.
Davis, Mary. S & R 14 yrs Lent 1770. St.
Davis, Mary. SQS Jan 1774. M.
Davis, Mary. S Jly 1774. L.
Davis, Matthew. S May-Jun T Jly 1753 *Tryal*. M.
Davis, Matthew. SQS Dec 1753. M.
Davis, Michael. S Summer 1756 R 14 yrs Lent T Sep 1757 *Thetis*. Sy.
Davis, Moses. S Jan T Feb 1742 *Industry* to Md. M.
Davis, Nathaniel. R for Barbados Jun 1671. L.
Davis, Peter (1700). *See* Anderson. L.
Davies, Peter. S s at Whittington Summer 1750. Wo.
Davis, Peter. S Jly-Sep 1754. M.
Davis, Philip. S Lent R 14 yrs Summer T Sep 1755 *Tryal*. K.
Davis, Philip. SEK & T Jan 1766 *Tryal*. K.
Davis, Philip of Bristol. R 14 yrs Aug 1773 (SP). G.
Davis, Priscilla. S Nov T Dec 1753 *Whiteing*. L.
Davies, Rachael. S s silver teaspoons at St. Julian, Shrewsbury, Lent 1749. Sh.
Davis, Rachael. S Lent 1754. Ca.
Davis, Rachel. S Feb T Mar 1760 *Friendship*. M.
Davis, Randal. R 14 yrs Aug 1742. So.
Davis, Rebecca. R 10 yrs in plantations Oct 1662. M.
Davis, Rebecca. S Jan-Feb T Apr 1772 *Thornton*. M.

Davys, Richard of Bromyard. R for America Jly 1675. Wo.
Davis, Richard. R for Barbados May 1676. L.
Davis, Richard. R for Barbados or Jamaica Dec 1689. M.
Davis, Richard of St. Chad, Shrewsbury. R for America Feb 1700. Sh.
Davis, Richard of Ilfracombe. R for Barbados Feb 1710. De.
Davis als Hill, Richard. S Mar 1719 to be T to Va. Do.
Davis, Richard. S Jan T Feb 1724 *Anne* to Carolina. M.
Davis, Richard. S Mar 1740. Ha.
Davis, Richard. R 14 yrs Aug 1746. De.
Davis, Richard. S Lent T May 1750 *Lichfield*. Bu.
Davis, Richard. S s at Old Swinford Lent 1753. Wo.
Davis, Richard. S 14 yrs Jan 1755. M.
Davis, Richard. T Sep 1765 *Justitia*. Sy.
Davis, Richard (1766). *See* Harding, John. Wa.
Davis, Richard. S Sep T Dec 1767 *Neptune*. M.
Davis, Richard. S s cloth at Stone Lent 1769. St.
Davies, Richard. S s gelding at Wellington & R 14 yrs Summer
    1771. Sh.
Davis als Devis, Robert of Brampton. R for Barbados Jly 1681. Cu.
Davis, Robert. S Apr 1728. So.
Davis, Robert. S & T Sep 1731 *Smith* LC Va 1732. M.
Davies, Robert. S Summer 1742. Sh.
Davis, Robert. S Apr T Sep 1758 *Tryal* to Annapolis. M.
Davis, Robert of Croydon. SQS May 1764. Sy.
Davies, Samuel. PT Summer 1719. Sh.
Davis, Samuel. T Jly 1723 *Alexander* LC Md Sep 1723. Bu.
Davis, Samuel. S Lent 1724 R 14 yrs Lent 1725. St.
Davis, Samuel. S Dec 1753-Jan 1754. M.
Davis, Samuel. S & T Jan 1766 *Tryal*. L.
Davis, Sarah (1679). *See* Demericke. L.
Davis, Sarah. R for America Aug 1702. M.
Davis, Sara. S Sep 1719 T Oct 1720 *Gilbert* to Md. M.
Davis, Sarah. S s candlesticks Jan-May T Jun 1738 *Forward*. M.
Davis, Sarah wife of Thomas. S Jly-Sep T Oct 1739
    Duke of Cumberland. M.
Davis, Sarah. S Lent T May 1755 *Rose*. E.
Davis, Sarah. S s at Holy Trinity, Gloucester, Lent 1760. G.
Davies, Sarah. S Sep 1760. M.
Davis, Sarah of Bristol. R Nov 1762 (SP). G.
Davis, Sarah. S s at Hereford Lent 1769. He.
Davis, Sarah. S Sep-Oct 1772 to be T 14 yrs. M.
Davies, Susan of Owen by Gloucester. R for Jamaica, Barbados or
    Bermuda Mar 1688. G.
Davis, Susan. R for Barbados Dec 1695 & May 1697 AT Jly 1697. M.
Davies, Thomas of Bath, worsted comber. R for Barbados Jun 1666. So.
Davys, Thomas. R for America Jly 1675. He.
Davies, Thomas of Lydney. R for America Jly 1686. G.
Davice, Thomas. R for Barbados or Jamaica Dec 1698. L.
Davis, Thomas of Upton upon Severn. S s clothing Summer 1719. Wo.
Davies, Thomas. S s at Eye Summer 1722. He.
Davis, Thomas (1725). *See* Guy. Wi.

Davis, Thomas. T Apr 1725 *Sukey* LC Md Sep 1725. Sy.

Davis, Thomas. S Aug 1727 T *Forward* LC Rappahannock May 1728. M.

Davis, Thomas. S Jan-Jun T Jun 1728 *Elizabeth* LC Potomack Aug 1729. M.

Davis, Thomas. S Apr T Sep 1737 *Pretty Patsy* to Md. M.

Davis, Thomas. S Jly T Sep 1737 *Pretty Patsy* to Md. M.

Davis, Thomas. S Jun 1739 to be T 14 yrs. L.

Davis, Thomas of St. Mary, Whitechapel. S s cotton & T Jan 1740 *York*. M.

Davis, Thomas. T Apr 1742 *Bond*. Ht.

Davies, Thomas. S s horse Summer 1743 R 14 yrs Lent 1744. He.

Davis, Thomas. S Feb-Apr 1746 to be T 14 yrs. M.

Davis, Thomas. S s iron chain at Stow Summer TB Aug 1749. G.

Davies, Thomas. S Lent 1754. Sy.

Davies, Thomas. S Dec 1755 T Jan 1756 *Greyhound*. L.

Davies, Thomas. S & R 14 yrs Summer 1759. Sh.

Davis als Baker, Thomas. S Feb T Mar 1764 *Tryal*. M.

Davis, Thomas. S & T Jan 1766 *Tryal*. M.

Davis, Thomas. S s at Tidenham Summer 1767. G.

Davies, Thomas. SQS Sep T Dec 1769 *Justitia*. M.

Davis, Thomas. S s at Chesham Bois Lent T Apr 1770 *New Trial*. Bu.

Davis, Thomas. S May T 14 yrs Jly 1771 *Scarsdale*. L.

Davis, Thomas. S Sep-Oct 1772. M.

Davies als Huskinson, Thomas of Manchester. SQS Oct 1772. La.

Davis, Thomas. S & R 14 yrs Lent 1773. Sh.

Davis, Thomas. S Jly 1773. L.

Davies, Thomas. S s yarn at Baschurch Summer 1774. Sh.

Davies, Thomas. SQS Sep 1774. M.

Davies, Thomas. S for highway robbery & R 14 yrs Summer 1775. St.

Davis, Uriah. S Feb T Apr 1732 *Patapsco* LC Annapolis Oct 1732. M.

Davies, Vincent. S Jly T Aug 1721 *Prince Royal* to Va. M.

Davies, Walter of Shrewsbury. R for Barbados Jly 1664. Sh.

Davies, Walter. S Summer 1742 R 14 yrs Lent 1743. Wa.

Davies, William. R for Barbados Aug 1670. M.

Davies, William of Oswestry. R for America Jly 1675. Sh.

Davis, William of Loughborough. R for America Jly 1678. Le.

Davys, William of Southwark, pinmaker. R (Western Circ) for Barbados Jly 1688. Sy.

Davis, William. S May T Jly 1722 *Alexander*. L.

Davis, William. S Dec 1727. L.

Davis, William. S Feb T Mar 1731 *Patapsco* LC Annapolis Jun 1731. M.

Davis, William. S Summer 1731. Sh.

Davies, William. S Lent R 14 yrs Summer 1732. Sh.

Davies als Pritchard, William. S Feb T Apr 1734 *Patapsco* to Md. M.

Davis, Williim. S Feb T Apr 1734 *Patapsco*. L.

Davis, William. T Apr 1739 *Forward*. K.

Davis, William. S Sep T Oct 1739 *Duke of Cumberland*. L.

Davies, William of Preese. S Lent 1741. Sh.

Davis, William. S Jun T Nov 1743 *George William*. M.

Davies, William. S Oct 1744-Jan 1745. M.

Davis als Hooper als Cooper, William. S Summer 1746 R 14 yrs Lent TB Apr 1747. G.

Davis, William. S Lent R 14 yrs Summer TB Aug 1747. G.

Davis, William. S & T for life Mar 1750 *Tryal*. L.

Davis als Brown, William. S s at Padworth Lent 1751. Be.

Davies, William. S & T Jun 1756 *Lyon*. M.

Davis, William. S Summer 1756. Sy.

Davis, William. S Feb T Mar 1760 *Friendship*. M.

Davis, William. S Jly 1760. M.

Davis, William. S Lent 1761. Sy.

Davis, William. S Mar TB to Va May 1763. Wi.

Davis, William. S & T Sep 1765 *Justitia*. M.

Davis, William. S Jly T 14 yrs Sep 1766 *Justitia*. M.

Davis, William. S Oct 1766 T Jan 1767 *Tryal*. M.

Davis, William. S & R 14 yrs Lent 1768. Bd.

Davies, William (1770). *See* Watson, John. M.

Davis, William. T Jly 1770 *Scarsdale*. M.

Davis, William. S & T Jly 1772 *Tayloe*. M.

Davies, William (1773). *See* Matthews. Co.

Davis, William. S Feb 1773. L.

Davis, William. S Oct 1773. L.

Davis, William. S Apr 1774. L.

Davies, William. S s at Tong Norton Summer 1774. Sh.

Davidson, Catherine. S Jly 1749 to be T for life. L.

Davison, Charles (1768). *See* Davis. La.

Davison, George. S Summer TB Aug 1752. Y.

Davidson, George. T Sep 1764 *Justitia*. Sy.

Davison, Grace (1751). *See* Davis. L.

Davidson, Jan (1762). *See* Davits. Nl.

Davison, Jane. S Jan T Feb 1719 *Worcester* LC Annapolis Jun 1719. L.

Davison, Jane. S & T Sep 1757 *Thetis*. M.

Davison, John. S Sep-Oct 1749. M.

Davison, John. S Sep-Oct T Dec 1771 *Justitia*. M.

Davison, John. SQS Apr 1774. M.

Davison, Margaret (1742). *See* Donahoo. L.

Davison, Margaret. S Summer 1766 R for life Summer 1767. Cu.

Davison, Margaret. R for life Summer 1767. Nl.

Davidson, Mary. R & T 14 yrs Apr 1770 *New Trial*. M.

Davison, Peter. R for Barbados Dec 1683. M.

Davison, Phoebe (1774). *See* Maeks. Nl.

Davison, Ralph. S Lent T Apr 1771. Wa.

Davison, Samuel. Rebel T 1685.

Davison, Samuel. S s cows Lent 1725 AT Summer 1728. Y.

Davison, Thomas. S Jly 1766. De.

Davison, William. S s at Mitcheldean Lent TB Mar 1750. G.

Davison, William. R 14 yrs Mar 1757. De.

Davison als Davy, William. S s sheep at Campsall & R 14 yrs Summer 1768. Y.

Davidson, William. S Sep-Oct 1773. M.

Davits als Davidson als Jacobson, Jan. S City for obtaining money by false pretences Summer 1762. Nl.

Davy, Ann. R for life Mar 1771 TB to Va. De.
Davy, Bartholomew. Rebel T 1685.
Davy, Edward. R 14 yrs Mar 1767 TB to Va. De.
Davy, George. S Mar 1719 to be T to Va. De.
Davy, George. SQS Jly 1751. Nt.
Davy, Honor. S Aug 1734. De.
Davey, James of Stockport, Chesh. SQS Oct 1764. La.
Davy, John (1695). *See* Davis. M.
Davy, John. SQS Jly 1751. Nt.
Davey, John. R 14 yrs Mar 1761. So.
Davy, John. S Summer 1773. Sy.
Davy, Mary, als wife of William Spencer. S Summer 1762. Nf.
Davey, Robert. S Jun 1739. L.
Davy, Robert. S & T for life Sep 1751 *Greyhound*. L.
Davy, Solomon (1734). *See* Stevenson. E.
Davy, Thomas. T Apr 1753 *Thames*. E.
Davy, Thomas. R 14 yrs Jly 1771 TB to Va 1772. De.
Davey, William. R 14 yrs Mar 1765. Co.
Davey, William. TB to Va 1768. De.
Davy, William (1768). *See* Davison. Y.
Davey, William (1773). *See* Matthews. Co.
Dawe, Edward. S Aug 1773. Do.
Dawe, George. S Aug 1773. Do.
Daw, Joan. S s stays at Little Dean Summer 1765. G.
Daw, Joseph. S s sheep Summer 1766 R 14 yrs Lent 1767. He.
Daw, Judith. TB to Va from QS 1738. De.
Daw, Michael. S Feb 1773. L.
Daw, Petronella of Tywordreth, spinster. R for Barbados Jly 1693. Co.
Daw, Robert. Rebel T 1685.
Daw, Samuel. S Mar 1742. Do.
Daw, Thomas. S Mar 1730. De.
Daw, Thomas. T Apr 1762 *Neptune*. K.
Dawe, William. Rebel T 1685.
Dawber, John. S s at Wakefield & R 14 yrs Summer 1768. Y.
Dawes, George. S & T Oct 1729 *Forward* LC Va Jun 1730. M.
Daws, John. S Lent 1752. Bd.
Daws, Robert. T May 1752 *Lichfield*. Sy.
Dawes, Thomas. S Summer 1754. E.
Dawes, Thomas. S Dec 1768 T Jan 1769 *Thornton*. M.
Daws, William. S Lent 1737. Nf.
Dawes, William. R 14 yrs Jly 1767. Ha.
Dawgs, Amy. S & T Dec 1731 *Forward*. L.
Dawkins, John. R for America Jly 1708. Li.
Dawkings, John, als Crispe, George. S Summer 1744 R 14 yrs Lent 1745. E.
Dawkins, John. S Lent 1754 R 14 yrs Summer 1756. Bu.
Dawkins, Mary of Castle Hedingham. R for Barbados or Jamaica Feb 1683. E.
Dawkins, Richard. S Feb T Mar 1729 *Patapsco* LC Annapolis Dec 1729. M.
Dawkins, Richard. T May 1751 *Tryal*. E.

Dawkins, Thomas. S Lent 1774. E.

Dawlen, Ann (1749). *See* Veysey. De.

Dawley, Francis. S Lent 1773. K.

Dawney, Mary wife of Benjamin of Newton on Ouse, clerk. SQS Thirsk as pickpocket Oct 1744 TB May 1745; chose to be transported rather than publicly whipped. Y.

Dawsey. *See* Dorsey.

Dawson, Anne. S Lent R 14 yrs Summer TB to Va Sep 1742. Le.

Dawson, Ann. S Lent 1761. Sy.

Dawson, Anthony. S Lent 1764. Bd.

Dawson, Barbara, spinster, als wife of Mark. R Oct TB Nov 1662. L.

Dawson, Bartholomew of Loughborough. R for America Jly 1678. Le.

Dawson, Bartholomew. R Jly 1679. Db.

Dawson, Christopher of Geyst. R for Barbados Jly 1663 & Jan 1665. Nf.

Dawson, Christopher. S s sheep at Threxton Summer 1767 R 14 yrs Lent 1768. Nf.

Dawson, David. S Summer 1750. Cu.

Dawson, Elizabeth. S Sep T Oct 1719 *Susannah & Sarah* LC Md Apr 1720. L.

Dawson, Elizabeth. S Jan T Feb 1724 *Anne* to Carolina. M.

Dawson, Elizabeth of Warrington, singlewoman. SQS Oct 1768. La.

Dawson, George. S Dec 1733 T Jan 1734 *Caesar* LC Va Jly 1734. L.

Dawson, George. S May T Jly 1771 *Scarsdale*. L.

Dawson, Jacob of Prestwich, weaver. SQS Aug 1757. La.

Dawson, James. S Apr-May T Jly 1771 *Scarsdale*. M.

Dawson, John of Stanton. R for America Mar 1686. Su.

Dawson, John. S Apr T May 1719 *Margaret* but died on passage. L.

Dawson, John of Mattersea. SQS s corn May 1736. Nt.

Dawson, John. S Dec 1742 T Mar 1743 *Justitia*. L.

Dawson als Dodson, John. S Jly 1746. L.

Dawson, John. S s sheep Lent R 14 yrs Summer 1764. Li.

Dawson, John. SQS & T Apr 1766 *Ann*. M.

Dawson, John. TB to Va from QS 1771. De.

Dawson, John. S Apr-Jun T Jly 1772 *Tayloe*. M.

Dawson, John. S Apr 1774. M.

Dawson, Joseph of St. Thomas, Southwark. SQS Jan T Apr 1768 *Thornton*. Sy.

Dawson, Lillingstone. S Jly 1759. Ha.

Dawson, Margaret. S Jly TB Aug 1754. Wi.

Dawson, Mark. R 10 yrs in plantations Oct 1662. M.

Dawson, Mary (1723). *See* Davies. L.

Dawson, Mary. S Jan-Jun T Jun 1728 *Elizabeth* LC Potomack Aug 1729. L.

Dawson, Mary. S Feb-Apr 1746. M.

Dawson, Mary Ann wife of George. ST & T Nov 1762 *Prince William*. L.

Dawson, Nancy als Elizabeth of Bermondsey, spinster. SQS & T Jan 1767 *Tryal*. Sy.

Dawson, Nicholas. T Jun 1728 *Elizabeth* LC Va Aug 1729. E.

Dawson als Luck, Peter of Salford, weaver. SQS Oct 1752. La.

Dawson, Richard. S s at Leek Summer 1774. St.

Dawson, Robert. S Lent 1767. Nf.
Dawson, Samuel. S Lent R 14 yrs Summer 1722. Le.
Dawson, Samuel. S for rape Lent R Summer 1726. Li.
Dawson, Sarah. S Oct T Dec 1724 *Rappahannock* to Va. M.
Dawson, Thomas. S & TB Aug 1740. G.
Dawson, Thomas. S Jly T Sep 1767 *Justitia*. M.
Dawson, Timothy. S Sep-Oct 1773. M.
Dawson, William. S Feb T Mar 1727 *Rappahannock*. L.
Dawson, William. S s sheep Summer 1746 R 14 yrs Lent 1747. Li.
Dawson, William. S s cow & R Lent 1774. Wa.
Dawtrey, William. R for Barbados Mar 1683. M.
Daxon, James. SQS Sep T Dec 1763 *Neptune*. M.
Day, Alice. S Feb T Mar 1731 *Patapsco* LC Annapolis Jun 1731. L.
Day, Andrew. T Nov 1743 *George William*. K.
Day, Ann. S Apr 1734. M.
Day, Ann. S Jan T Feb 1742 *Industry* to Md. M.
Day, Benjamin. T for life Apr 1770 *New Trial*. Sy.
Day, Damaras of Compton Dando, spinster. R for Barbados Jly
  1693. So.
Day, Edward. S Jly T Sep 1766 *Justitia*. M.
Day, Elianor of Burbage. R for America Mar 1682. Le.
Day, Elizabeth (1705). *See* Fuller. Sy.
Day, Elizabeth. S Jan T Feb 1719 *Worcester* LC Annapolis Jun 1719. L.
Day, Elizabeth. S Sep 1756. M.
Dey, Frances. R for America Aug 1715. M.
Day, George. S Jly 1721 T Mar 1723. Bu.
Day, John of Sherborne, husbandman. R for Barbados Feb 1668. Do.
Day, John. S Apr 1723. So.
Day, John. S Oct T Nov 1725 *Rappahannock* LC Rappahannock Apr
  1726. L.
Day, John. S s pork Summer 1741. O.
Day als Bell, John. S s ass at Cockfield Lent 1770. Su.
Day, John. T for life Apr 1770 *New Trial*. Ht.
Day, John. S & T Jly 1772 *Tayloe*. M.
Day, John. S s flour at Wantage Lent 1774. Be.
Day, Joseph. SQS Aug TB Sep 1723. Nt.
Day, Margaret. S s brass at Drayton Lent 1747. O.
Day, Mary of Lambeth. R for Barbados or Jamaica Jun 1699. Sy.
Day, Mary. R Dec 1699 & Aug 1700. M.
Day, Mary (1702). *See* Lloyd. Sy.
Day, Mary. S s coat & T Dec 1734 *Caesar* LC Va Jly 1735. M.
Day, Mary. S Dec 1757 T Mar 1758 *Dragon*. L.
Day, Mary. S Jan 1759. L.
Daye, Penelope. TB to Md 14 yrs Oct 1720. L.
Day, Richard. S Summer 1733. St.
Day, Richard. R 14 yrs Apr 1751. So.
Day, Robert. S Summer 1739. Be.
Day, Robert. S Jan T 14 yrs Apr 1741 *Speedwell*. L.
Day, Robert. S Summer 1763 R 14 yrs Lent TB to Va Apr 1764. Le.
Day, Robert. S s sheep & R 14 yrs Lent 1764. Li.
Day, Robert. S Lent T 14 yrs Apr 1772 *Thornton*. K.

Day, Sarah. PT Oct R Dec 1699. M.
Day, Susanna. S Jly-Sep 1754. M.
Day, Thomas (1693). *See* Wheeler. M.
Day, Thomas. S Apr T 14 yrs Sep 1757 *Thetis*. M.
Day, Thomas. R 14 yrs Aug 1757 TB to Va 1758. De.
Day, William. S Mar 1723. Wi.
Day, William. S & T Sep 1731 *Smith* LC Va 1732. M.
Day, William (1743). *See* Earl. M.
Day, William of Merstham. SQS Oct 1750. Sy.
Day, William. T Aug 1769 *Douglas*. E.
Day, William. S Apr-May T Jly 1771 *Scarsdale*. M.
Day, William. S Mar TB to Va Apr 1775. Wi.
Day, Zacariah. S Lent 1748. E.
Dayly. *See* Daley.
Deacock, Thomas of St. John's. SQS Apr 1752. Sy.
Deacomb, Edward (1699). *See* Wyke. M.
Deacon, Elizabeth wife of Colbert. S Feb T Mar 1731 *Patapsco* LC
   Annapolis Jun 1731. M.
Deacon, Elizabeth. S Mar 1761. L.
Deacon, James of Preston. SQS Jan 1772. La.
Deacon, James of Lambeth. SQS Oct 1774. Sy.
Deacon, John. S Oct-Dec 1739 T Jan 1740 *York* to Md. M.
Deacon, John. S Jly T Oct 1741 *Sea Horse* to Va. M.
Deacon, John. R & T Jly 1770 *Scarsdale*. M.
Deakin als Peacock, Mary. S May T Dec 1735 *John* LC Annapolis Sep
   1736. L.
Deakin, Stephen. S Summer 1759 R 14 yrs Lent 1760. He.
Deacon, Thomas. R for America Mar 1690. Le.
Dekin, Thomas. SL Nov T Dec 1763 *Neptune*. Sy.
Deacome, William (1728). *See* White. Ha.
Deacon, William. S s hogs Lent 1775. Hu.
Deakings als Dickins, Thomas. S s wheat at Hereford Lent 1769. He.
Deal, Ann. S Lent 1745. Sy.
Deale als Reynolds, James. R for Barbados or Jamaica Feb 1687. M.
Deal, James. S Jan 1745. L.
Deal als Dean, John. S Aug T Oct 1726 *Forward* to Va. M.
Deal, Joseph. S s mare at Haresfield Lent R 14 yrs Summer TB Sep
   1736. G.
Deal, Mary (1739). *See* Bolingbroke. M.
Deal als Baker, Mary. S Sep T Oct 1744 *Susannah*. L.
Deale, Richard. R Dec 1765 T Jan 1766 *Tryal*. L.
Deale, Robert of St. James, Bristol. R for Barbados Jly 1684. G.
Deale, William. Rebel T 1685.
Dealey. *See* Deeley.
Dealing, Samuel (1720). *See* Deely. L.
Dealtry, Abraham. R for life for highway robbery Summer 1745. Y.
Dealtry, Margaret. R for Barbados Feb 1675. L.
Deame, William of Church Stretton. R for America Jly 1677. Sh.
Deane, Daniel. S Sep T Dec 1767 *Neptune*. L.
Deane, Daniel. SW & T Jun 1768 *Tryal*. M.

Deane, Elizabeth. S & T Oct 1719 *Susannah & Sarah* LC Annapolis
Apr 1720. L.
Dean, Frances. S Jan T Feb 1744 *Neptune*. L.
Deane, Francis. S & T Oct 1730 *Forward* LC Potomack Jan 1731. M.
Dean, James (1758). *See* Roberts. He.
Dean, Jane. S Jan T Mar 1764 *Tryal*. M.
Deane, Jeremiah, a Quaker. R for plantations Jly 1665. Ht.
Deane, John of Okehampton, husbandman. R for Barbados Apr
1668. De.
Dean, John. R for America Aug 1715. L.
Dean, John (1726). *See* Deal. M.
Dean, John. T Oct 1726 *Forward*. Sy.
Dean, John. S & T May 1736 *Patapsco*. L.
Dean, John. S Mar 1737. Wi.
Dean, John. S Jun-Dec 1745. M.
Dean, John. S Jan T Mar 1750 *Tryal*. L.
Dean, John. S & T for life Mar 1764 *Tryal*. L.
Dean, John. S & T Dec 1769 *Justitia*. M.
Deane, Joseph. S Jan-Jun T Jun 1728 *Elizabeth* LC Potomack Aug
1729. M.
Dean, Josiah. T Jly 1722 *Alexander*. E.
Deane, Joshua. S & T for life Jan 1736 *Dorsetshire* LC Va Sep 1736. L.
Deane, Lidia. S & T Oct 1730 *Forward* LC Potomack Jan 1731. M.
Deane als Baskervile, Mary. S Jan 1656 to House of Correction unless
she consents to be transported. M.
Deane, Mary. S Jan-Jun T Jun 1728 *Elizabeth* LC Potomack Aug
1729. L.
Deane, Mary. S as pickpocket & R Summer 1774. Mo.
Deane, Michael of Hath. R for America Jly 1677. Db.
Deane, Peter. T Nov 1728 *Forward*. Sy.
Deane, Richard. S Feb T Jun 1738 *Forward* to Md or Va. M.
Dean, Richard. S Summer 1754. Sy.
Deane, Samuel, als Edwards, Thomas. S Feb T Apr 1739 *Forward*. M.
Dean, Samuel. S for highway robbery Summer 1749 R 14 yrs Lent
1750. Be.
Dean, Samuel. R Apr 1773. M.
Dean, Sarah. R for Barbados or Jamaica Feb 1687. L.
Dean, Sarah. T Sep 1758 *Tryal*. E.
Dean, Thomas. S Jan T Mar 1764 *Tryal*. L.
Dean als Cook, Thomas. S for false pretences Jly T Sep 1765 *Justitia*. L.
Deane, William. S Mar 1736. Ha.
Deane, William. S Jly-Sep T Oct 1739 *Duke of Cumberland* to Va. M.
Deane, William of Rotherhithe, ship carpenter. SQS Oct T Dec 1771
Justitia. Sy.
Dear. *See* Deer.
Deardsley, Howard (1735). *See* Deasley. L.
Dearing, Hester. S Aug T Oct 1723 *Forward* to Va. M.
Dearing, James. S s at Treethorpe Lent 1773. Nf.
Dearing, Redmond. S Jan T Feb 1726 *Supply* LC Annapolis May
1726. M.
Deering, William. T Oct 1732 *Caesar*. K.

Deasley als Deardsley, Howard. S s coat Feb T Apr 1735 *Patapsco* LC
   Annapolis Oct 1735. L.
Death, Andrew. R for Barbados Jly 1675. M.
Death, John. S Mar 1760. Co.
Death, Thomas. S for burglary Lent 1724 R 14 yrs Lent 1725 (SP). Su.
Death, William. S Aug T Sep 1764 *Justitia*. L.
Debang, Hugh. S Apr T May 1752 *Lichfield*. L.
Debart, Joseph. T 14 yrs Sep 1767 *Justitia*. E.
De Beaufort, Leonard Peter Casalor. S Sep T Oct 1768 *Justitia*. M.
Debee, Joseph. S Dec 1748 T Jan 1749 *Laura*. L.
Debell, Richard. S Apr T Sep 1737 *Pretty Patsy* to Md. M.
Debidge, Ann. S Feb-Apr 1746. M.
Debman, William of Clavering. SQS Jan T Apr 1766 *Ann*. E.
Debnam, Thomas. Rebel T 1685.
Deboe, John. T Jan 1736 *Dorsetshire*. Sy.
De Bruyer, Henry. SQS & T Apr 1769 *Tryal*. M.
Debuck, Mary T Sep 1758 *Tryal*. Sy.
Decelee, Samuel of St. Clement Danes. SW Apr 1774. M.
Deckron, John. LC Va Aug 1729. Sy.
Decruze, John. T Sep 1730 *Smith*. K.
Dee, Richard. T 14 yrs Dec 1753 *Whiteing*. E.
Dee, Sarah. S May T Jly 1722 *Alexander* to Nevis or Jamaica. M.
Dee, Thomas. S Summer 1756 R 14 yrs Lent 1757. Wo.
Deeble, Joseph (1746). *See* Hatch. De.
Deekes, Joseph of Belchamp Otten. SQS Jan T Apr 1759 *Thetis*. E.
Deeks, Richard. S Summer 1743 & committed Lent 1744 for being at
   large after sentence. Su.
Deeks, Thomas. R Summer 1772 for pulling down mills. E.
Deely, Mary. S s at Bromsgrove Summer 1728. Wo.
Dealey, Mary. T Apr 1743 *Justitia*. Sy.
Deely als Dealing, Samuel. S Apr T May 1720 *Honor* LC Port York Jan
   1721. L.
Dealy als Dayly, William. S Sep T Dec 1769 *Justitia*. M.
Deemer, Jeremiah. S Jly-Sep 1754. M.
Deare, Ann. S Jly 1756. M.
Deer, Benjamin. S s at Tuddenham & R Lent 1769. Su.
Deer, Elizabeth. R 14 yrs Jly 1748. Ha.
Dear, Naphthali. S Apr T Jly 1770 *Scarsdale*. L.
Deer, Richard. S Jan T Mar 1750 *Tryal*. L.
Deeves, John (1734). *See* Gormwood, Samuel. E.
Deffett, Joseph. SQS Jly TB Sep 1768. So.
Defoe, Henry. S & T Oct 1732 *Caesar* to Va. M.
De Frayne, James. T Apr 1741 *Speedwell* or *Mediterranean*. Bu.
De Hague, Godfrey. R for Barbados Aug 1668. M.
Delafield, Nicholas. S s at Stoke Church Summer 1752. O.
Delafontain, Mary Ann. S Jly T Aug 1721 *Owners Goodwill* to Md. M.
Delaforce, Joseph. R & T for life Jly 1770 *Scarsdale*. M.
Delahay, John. S s at Llancillo Summer 1774. He.
Delahunt, Rose. SL Jly T Sep 1755 *Tryal*. Sy.
Delamar, Edward. S Nov T Dec 1770 *Justitia*. L.
Delander, Peter. S May 1745. L.

Delane, John. S Oct-Dec 1739 T Jan 1740 *York* to Md. M.
Delaney, Dennis. S Jly 1747. L.
Delany, Margaret (1767). *See* Delany, Martha. M.
Delany, Martha als Margaret. S & T Sep 1767 *Justitia*. M.
Delaney, Mary. S Apr T May 1752 *Lichfield*. L.
Delany, Mary (1760). *See* Brooks. M.
Delaney, Mary. R Dec 1773. M.
Delaney, Richard. R Lent 1775. Sy.
Delany, Robert. S Dec 1742 T Apr 1743 *Justitia*. M.
Delany, Sarah. S Apr 1734. M.
Delaney, Sarah (1736). *See* Richardson. M.
Delapp, Jane (1767). *See* Brown. M.
Delavan, Catherine. S & T Apr 1733 *Patapsco* to Md. M.
Delay, Richard. S s watch case at St. Margaret Patten May T Jun 1768
    Tryal. L.
Delborough, Thomas. R for Barbados Feb 1675. L.
Delfosse, Stephen. S Apr T May 1719. L.
Delight, John. T Oct 1768 *Justitia*. E.
Delirio, Dio (1774). *See* Williams, David. He.
Dell, Edward (1732). *See* Dale. M.
Dell, Joseph. S May 1775. M.
Dellion, James. LC from *Eagle* Charles Town Mar 1719. X.
Dellmore, Elizabeth. S Sep-Dec 1755 T Jan 1756 *Greyhound*. M.
Delloon, James. LC from *Forward* Potomack Jan 1731. X.
Dellow, Abraham of Christchurch. SQS Nov T Dec 1753 *Whiteing*. Sy.
Deloas, Elizabeth. LC from *Forward* Annapolis Jun 1723. X.
Delwyn, William. S Jun T Aug 1769 *Douglas*. L.
Demaine, Rebecca. S Jun-Dec 1745. M.
Demarry, Thomas (1681). *See* Bolton. L.
Demelan, Joseph (1724). *See* Danells. St.
Demericke als Davis, Sarah. R for Barbados Jan 1679. L.
Demerry, Philip. R for Barbados Mar 1681. M.
Demetrius, John. R for Barbados Jun 1663. M.
Demogg, William (1695). *See* Wake. M.
Dempier, Ann (1761). *See* Wade. M.
Dempsey, James. R for life Oct 1772. M.
Dempsey, Pearce. S Aug 1760 L.
Dympsey, Philip of St. Stephen next Launceston, husbandman. R for
    Barbados Feb 1672. Co.
Dempsey, Richard. S & T Sep 1751 *Greyhound*. M.
Dempson, Edward. PT Apr 1692. M.
Dempson, Grace. PT Apr 1692. M.
Demsdale, Sarah. R for Barbados or Jamaica May AT Jly 1697. M.
Demy, John. R for Barbados or Jamaica May 1684. L.
Demy, John. R for Barbados or Jamaica Jan 1693. L.
Denby, George. AT Summer 1748. Y.
Denby, Samuel. T Sep 1766 *Justitia*. M.
Dench, Eleanor. TB to Va from QS 1759. De.
Dendy, Mary of Chertsey. R for Barbados or Jamaica Feb 1684. Sy.
Denell, Pearce. SQS Oct 1765 T Jan 1766 *Tryal*. M.
Denham, Charles (1753). *See* Dunham. Ha.

Denham, John. Rebel T 1685.
Denham, Richard. Rebel T 1685.
Denham, Samuel. Rebel T 1685.
Denish, Priscilla. R for Barbados Jly 1674. L.
Denley, James. T Jan 1738 *Dorsetshire*. K.
Denlon, William. S Feb 1735. M.
Denman, Thomas. R for Barbados Oct 1673. L.
Denmead, John. S Aug 1775. So.
Denmead, Sarah. S Jly 1739 TB to Va Oct 1740. Wi.
Denmead, William. S Aug 1773. So.
Dennett, Nicholas of Sadbury, gunsmith. R for Barbados Feb 1688. De.
Dennett, Susanna. S Summer T from London Sep 1759. Nl.
Dennett, Thomas (1685). *See* Bennett.
Dennett, Thomas. S Sep 1740. L.
Dennick, Nathaniel. Rebel T 1685.
Denning, John. Rebel T 1685.
Denning, John. S s horse & R 14 yrs Lent 1769. G.
Dennis, Catherine (1726). *See* Phillips. M.
Dennis, Francis. SQS Thirsk Apr TB Aug 1738. Y.
Dennis, Henry. S s sheep Summer 1759 R 14 yrs Lent 1760. Bu.
Dennis, Jane. S Feb T Mar 1727 *Rappahannock* to Md. M.
Dennis, John. S Feb-Apr T May 1755 *Rose*. M.
Dennis, John. R 14 yrs Jly 1758 TB to Va 1759. De.
Dinnis, John. S 14 yrs Jly 1766. De.
Dennis, Joseph. T Jly 1723 *Alexander* LC Md Sep 1723. Sy.
Dennis, Joseph. S & T Apr 1733 *Patapsco* LC Annapolis Nov 1733. M.
Dennis, Joshua. S s at Weston on Trent Lent 1739. St.
Dennis, Margaret. S Sep T Oct 1719 *Susannah & Sarah* LC
    Annapolis Apr 1720. L.
Dennis, Mary wife of Thomas of All Saints, Hertford, "an old convict".
    R for Barbados or Jamaica Mar 1698. Ht.
Dennis, Mary (1730). *See* Rusher. M.
Dennis, Richard. T Apr 1731 *Bennett*. E.
Dennys, Robert. R for West Indies Oct 1614. M.
Dennis, Roger. S Oct 1743 T Feb 1744 *Neptune*. L.
Dennis, Thomas. Rebel T 1685.
Dennis, Thomas. S Sep T Oct 1739 *Duke of Cumberland*. L.
Dennis, Thomas. S Lent R 14 yrs Summer 1749. O.
Dennis, Thomas. S Jan-Feb T Apr 1753 *Thames*. M.
Dennis, William (1735). *See* Denney. Nf.
Dennis, William. S Feb 1754. M.
Dennison, Barnaby. S Summer 1735 R 14 yrs Summer 1736. Cu.
Denison, Bartholomew. S Lent R 14 yrs Summer 1756. Ca.
Dennison, Catherine (1735). *See* Hughes. M.
Dennison als Lawler, Catherine. S May-Jly 1748. M.
Dennison, John. S Sep 1760. M.
Dennison, Mathias. S Apr-May T 14 yrs May 1741
    Catherine & Elizabeth to Md. M.
Dennison, Michael. S 14 yrs for receiving Aug 1774. Co.
Dennison, Richard. S Oct T Dec 1771 *Justitia*. L.
Dennison, Thomas. R Jly 1773. M.

Denny, Abraham. T Jan 1741 *Vernon*. E.

Denny, Edward of Hadham. R for Barbados or Jamaica Jly 1677. Ht.

Denny, Mary of St. Clement Danes. S s silver mug & T May 1736 *Patapsco*. M.

Denny, William. R May AT Jly 1697. M.

Denney als Dennis, William. S Summer 1735 for bigamously marrying Sarah Turner while his first wife Mary Green was living. *Nf.

Densham, John Jr. S Mar 1766 TB to Va. De.

Densley, Thomas. R (Home Circ) for Barbados Apr 1663. X.

Danslow, James. S Jan T Feb 1733 *Smith*. L.

Denslow, Mary. S Feb-Apr T May 1751 *Tryal*. M.

Densloe, Richard (1681). *See* Bayly. Do.

Denston, Isabella. S & T Apr 1762 *Neptune*. M.

Denston, Nathaniel of Isle of Ely. R for Barbados or Jamaica Oct 1664. Ca.

Denston, Richard of Burton on Trent. S Lent 1720. St.

Dent, Ann. S & T Oct 1729 *Forward* LC Va Jun 1730. L.

Dent, Benjamin of Westbury on Trim. S s gun Lent TB Mar 1754. G.

Dent, Francis. R 14 yrs Jly 1758. Ha.

Dent, Hainsworth. S Jan T Feb 1726 *Supply* LC Annapolis May 1726. L.

Dent, William (1755). *See* Frazier, Alexander. Y.

Dent, William of Manchester. SQS Oct 1765. La.

Denton, Ann. R for America May 1704. M.

Denton, Grice. S Lent 1737. Y.

Denton, Joseph of Thoresby. SQS East Retford s boots Jan TB Apr 1774. Nt.

Denton, William. LC from *Patapsco* Annapolis Oct 1735. X.

Denyer, Francis. SQS Dec 1774. M.

Depenn, Mary of Whitechapel, spinster. S s watch Jly 1740 T Jan 1741 *Harpooner* to Rappahannock. M.

Deplosh, Peter. S Jly T Aug 1721 *Prince Royal* LC Va Nov 1721. L.

De Poure, Armaine. PT Feb R Mar 1688. M.

De Pree, Bartholomew Marrier. S & T Oct 1732 *Caesar* to Va. M.

Deprose, Mary. S May T Jun 1764 *Dolphin*. M.

Deracke, George. R for Barbados or Jamaica Dec 1695 & Jan 1697. L.

Derbin. *See* Durbin.

Derby. *See* Darby.

Derbyshire. *See* Darbyshire.

Dereham, William. S s horse Lent R 14 yrs Summer 1727 T *Elizabeth* LC Potomack Aug 1729. Be.

Derosse, Elizabeth. S & T Oct 1722 *Forward* to Md. M.

Derricke, John of Clifton. R Jly 1679. G.

Derrin, Mary. S Jan 1735. M.

Derritt, Benjamin. S May-Jun T Jly 1753 *Tryal*. M.

Derrock, Richard. R 14 yrs Aug 1736. So.

Derry, Thomas. S Summer 1763 R 14 yrs Lent TB to Va Apr 1764. Le.

Derry, Thomas. S s sheep & R 14 yrs Lent 1764. Li.

Desborough, John. S s sheep Lent R 14 yrs Summer 1756. Li.

Desborough, William. S s sheep Summer 1760 R 14 yrs Lent 1761 but died in gaol. Hu.

Desbrieres, Rose Langlais. S Feb T Apr 1771 *Thornton*. L.

Desionge, Peter. R May T Jun 1691. M.
Desoe, Mary. R May AT Sep 1684. M.
Dethick, Charles. S for killing sheep R Lent TB Apr 1768. Db.
Deval, George of Croydon. SQS Jan T Apr 1770 *New Trial*. Sy.
Devall, Margaret wife of Joseph. S Feb T 14 yrs Apr 1742 *Bond*. M.
Divall, Robert. S Summer 1774. Sx.
Devan, James of Chatham. S Summer T Oct 1739
  Duke of Cumberland. K.
Devenis, Susannah (1740). *See* Devinois. M.
Devenish, Robert. R for Barbados Oct 1673. L.
Deverall, Jane (1700). *See* Biggs. M.
Devereux, James. S Summer T Sep 1751 *Greyhound*. K.
Devereaux, James. R 14 yrs Dec 1773. M.
Deverson, Peter. R for Barbados Dec 1683. L.
Devett als Dewitt, Edward of Stroud. R for America Feb 1681. G.
Devitt, Hannah (1771). *See* Kay. La.
Devett, James. R Apr 1773. M.
Devey, Joseph. S Summer 1757 R 14 yrs Lent 1758. Wo.
Devie, Lewis. S & T 14 yrs Oct 1732 *Caesar* to Va. M.
Devine, Philip. S Jun-Dec 1745. M.
Devine, Thomas. S & T Sep 1765 *Justitia*. M.
Devinois als Devenis, Susannah of St. Andrew Holborn. S s clothing
  Jly-Oct 1740 T Jan 1741 *Harpooner*. M.
Devis, Robert (1681). *See* Davis. Cu.
Devon, Elizabeth wife of Michael. S Jly-Sep T Oct 1739
  Duke of Cumberland. M.
Devon, Martha. S Aug T Oct 1723 *Forward* to Va. M.
Devon, Philip of St. George, Southwark. R for Barbados or Jamaica Jly
  1702. Sy.
Devotrice, James. S Jly 1774. L.
Devoux, Stephen. S Dec 1764 T Jan 1765 *Tryal*. M.
Dewe, Edward of Warminster, husbandman. R for Barbados Feb
  1665. Wi.
Dew, Elizabeth. S Oct 1733 T Jan 1734 *Caesar* LC Va Jly 1734. M.
Dew, Francis of Plymouth. R for Barbados Dec 1686. De.
Dew, James. Rebel T 1685.
Dew, John. R 14 yrs Jly 1734. Ha.
Dew, Joseph. S Apr T May 1755 *Rose*. L.
Dew als Holloway, Mary. S Feb T Mar 1729 *Patapsco* LC Md Dec
  1729. L.
Dew als Finch, Thomas. S s horse Lent R 14 yrs Summer 1731 (SP). O.
Dew, William. Rebel T 1685.
Dewdney, William. TB to Va from QS 1742. De.
Dewell. *See* Jewel.
Dewes als Jewes, Edward. S for highway robbery R Lent T Apr
  1773. No.
Dewhurst, John. S Summer 1753. La.
Dewhurst, Peter. S 14 yrs Summer 1760. La.
Dewine, William. T 14 yrs Apr 1771 *Thornton*. K.
Dewing als Gill, Ann. R for America Aug 1715. M.
Dewis, William. S for rape Lent R 14 yrs Summer 1739. Wa.

Dewitt, Edward (1681). *See* Devett. G.
Dewitt, Elizabeth. S Apr 1774. M.
Dewitt als Rolls, Francis. PT Jan R May 1677. M.
Dewman, Robert. S Jan-Feb 1773. M.
Dewy, Richard. SQS Feb T Apr 1768 *Thornton*. M.
Dexcon, Sarah. S Dec 1746. L.
Dexter, Edward. SQS Aug TB to Va Oct 1756. Le.
Diamond, Jasper. Rebel T 1685.
Dymond, John. R 14 yrs Aug 1747. De.
Diamond, Mary. S Sep-Oct 1775. M.
Diaper, John. S Jan-Feb T Apr 1771 *Thornton*. M.
Dibble, John. T Oct 1729 *Forward*. Sy.
Dibley, James. S s sheep Lent 1722. Be.
Dibley, Thomas. R 14 yrs Jly TB to Va Sep 1744. Wi.
Dick als Dickenson, George. S Jun T 14 yrs Aug 1769 *Douglas*. L.
Dick, Jane. R Jun T 14 yrs Aug 1769 *Douglas*. M.
Dicke, William of Hankerton. R for Barbados Sep 1665. Wi.
Dickason. *See* Dickerson.
Dickate als Coffee, William. R for Barbados or Jamaica Dec 1699 &
    Aug 1700. L.
Dicken, Sarah. S s at St. Mary, Shrewsbury, Summer 1758. Sh.
Dicken, Silas. S Lent & R for life Apr 1774. Db.
Dickins, Andrew. R (Norfolk Circ) for Barbados Jly 1675. X.
Dickins, Catherine. S Mar 1754.
Dickens, David. S Summer 1749. Sy.
Dickins, Edward. R for Barbados Mar 1683. L.
Dickins, Edward. S & T Dec 1758 *The Brothers*. L.
Dickens, John. R for America Feb 1692. Ru.
Dickings, John. SQS Oct 1752 T Apr 1753 *Thames*. M.
Dickens, John. S Oct 1772. L.
Dickens, Joseph. S s razors at Sheffield Summer 1768. Y.
Dickins, Thomas (1769). *See* Deakings. He.
Dickens, Thomas of St. Martin in Fields. SW Apr 1773. M.
Dickons, William. R for America Jly 1683. Li.
Diccons, William. R for America Jly 1694. No.
Dickens, William. S for highway robbery Lent R 14 yrs Summer
    1750. No.
Dickinson, Abraham. S & R Lent 1723. Y.
Dickinson, Abraham. S City Summer 1732. Y.
Dickinson, Amy. S s cloth at Stroud Summer 1771. G.
Dickenson, Arthur. T May 1719 *Margaret* LC Md May 1720; sold to
    Andrew Bell. Sy.
Dickenson, David. S Aug T Sep 1725 *Forward* LC Md Dec 1725. M.
Dickenson, George of Purton. R for Barbados Feb 1698. Wi.
Dickenson, George (1769). *See* Dick. L.
Dickinson, Guy of St. Martin in Fields. SW Jan 1774. M.
Dickinson, James. T Oct 1726 *Forward*. E.
Dickinson, John of Stroud. S s brass furnace Lent 1719. G.
Dickinson, Joseph. S Sep T Nov 1759 *Phoenix*. M.
Dickinson, Mary. S Jan T Feb 1719 *Worcester* LC Md Jun 1719. L.
Dickenson, Marry (1742). *See* Hale. M.

Dickinson, Rebecca (1700). *See* Maund. M.

Dickinson, Richard. S Summer 1757. Hu.

Dickinson, Robert aged 32, black hair, husbandman. LC from *Gilbert* Annapolis May 1721. X.

Dickenson, Robert. S s harrow teeth at Tettenhall. S & R 14 yrs Summer 1771. St.

Dickenson, Thomas of Willesden. R for America Aug 1713. M.

Dickinson, Thomas. R for America Aug 1715. L.

Dickenson, William of St. Olave, Southwark. R (Newgate) for Barbados Apr TB Oct 1669. Sy.

Dickenson, William. S Sep T Oct 1739 *Duke of Cumberland*. L.

Dickenson, William. T Dec 1753 *Whiteing*. K.

Dickenson, William. S Apr 1764. Fl.

Dickinson, William. S Lent T Apr 1771. Wa.

Dicker, Catherine. S May-Jly 1748. M.

Dickason, John of Croydon. R for Barbados or Jamaica Jly 1710. Sy.

Dickerson, John. S s mare Lent R 14 yrs Summer 1756. Hu.

Dickerson, Nathaniel. T May 1719 *Margaret* LC Md Aug 1719; sold to William Black. Ht.

Dickery, John. S Mar 1719 to be T to Va. So.

Dickie, James. S for assaulting Customs officer on Holy Island Summer 1765; later received free pardon. Du.

Dickins. *See* Dickens.

Dickinson. *See* Dickenson.

Dickman, Benjamin. S s mare Lent R 14 yrs Summer TB Aug 1742. G.

Dickman, William. R 14 yrs Mar 1772. Ha.

Dicks. *See* Dix.

Dicksey. *See* Dixey.

Dickson. *See* Dixon.

Diddimus, Grace wife of Richard. S Mar 1729. De.

Diddimus, Mably. S Mar 1729 TB to Va. De.

Digby, George. T Oct 1723 *Forward*. Ht.

Digby, John. R for Jamaica Aug 1661. L.

Diggenham, John. S Jly T Sep 1755 *Tryal*. L.

Digger, John. S s at Llantrissant Summer 1769. Mo.

Diggin, Peter. S Aug 1751. So.

Diggins, John. S Mar 1760. So.

Diggins, Mary. S s at Raglan Summer 1756. Mo.

Digle, John (1731). *See* Coles. So.

Diggle, Joseph of Birtle, carpenter. S for forgery Lent R 14 yrs Summer 1769. La.

Digle, Richard (1731). *See* Coles. So.

Dighton, Dorothy (1719). *See* Hawkins. L.

Dighton, William. SQS Jan T Mar 1750 *Tryal*. M.

Digweed, John (or William). SQS Apr 1765 R 14 yrs Jly 1766. Ha.

Dikes. *See* Dykes.

Dilkill, Mary. S Feb T May 1767 *Thornton*. M.

Dilks, John. R for America Feb 1700. Le.

Dilkes, John. TB to Md Oct 1721. Le.

Dilkes, Thomas. S Lent 1774. Db.

Dillar, Henry. S Aug 1773. Do.

Dillart als Dilworth, George of Walton upon the Hill. S Lent 1741. La.
Dilling, Penelope, spinster, als wife of Luke. R for Barbados & TB Oct 1667. L.
Dillon, James. S Aug T Sep 1718 *Eagle* to Md or Va. L.
Dillon, James. S Oct 1737 T Jan 1738 *Dorsetshire* to Va. M.
Dillon, John. S Dec 1774. M.
Dilloway, John of Wolverhampton. R for Jamaica, Barbados or Bermuda Feb 1686. St.
Dilly, Alice. S & T Sep 1764 *Justitia*. M.
Dilworth, George (1741). *See* Dillart. La.
Diment, Henry. TB to America from QS 1751. De.
Diment, Samuel. R 14 yrs Mar 1775. De.
Dimmery, Joseph. S s sheep wool at Rodborough Lent 1759. G.
Dimmock, John (1663). *See* Knight. Ht.
Dimock, Peter. S s sow Lent T Apr 1766 *Ann*. Bu.
Dimmock, William. T 14 yrs Apr 1766 *Ann*. Ht.
Dimsdale, Mary. S Feb T Mar 1729 *Patapsco* LC Annapolis Dec 1729. M.
Dimsdale, Rachael. S Apr T Sep 1757 *Thetis*. L.
Dymsdale, Sarah. T Jan 1738 *Dorsetshire*. Sy.
Dimsdell, Zachary Ogden. S as an apprentice prosecuted by his master for breaking & entering Oct T Dec 1736 *Dorsetshire*. M.
Dimsey, James. S Lent 1755. Hu.
Dines, Isaac. T Jun 1727 *Susanna*. E.
Dingle, William. S Aug 1731 TB to Va. De.
Dingley, Mark (1771). *See* Worrall. Ha.
Dinham, George. R 14 yrs Mar TB to Va May 1763. Wi.
Dinham, Joseph (1746). *See* Hatch. De.
Dinner, Samuel. R 14 yrs Jly 1751. Do.
Dinnett, John. Rebel T 1685.
Dinning, John. R 14 yrs Aug 1750. So.
Dinns, Sarah. S Lent 1748. K.
Diplow, Henry. S & T Dec 1731 *Forward* to Md or Va. M.
Dirick, Gertrude. R for Barbados Mar 1683. L.
Discombe, John. S Mar 1726. De.
Disey, Elizabeth (1708). *See* Kinglis. Be.
Disherman, Gabriel. S & T Oct 1730 *Forward* LC Potomack Jan 1731. L.
Disnell, John (1725). *See* Daniell. X.
Disney, Robert. R (Norfolk Circ) for America Jly 1663. X.
Disney, William of St. Mary Whitechapel. S s linen Apr T May 1740 *Essex*. M.
Diston als Cox, Edmund. R for Barbados May 1702. De.
Diston, William. S s mare Lent R 14 yrs Summer 1742. O.
Dyche, James. S s gelding Summer 1772. Db.
Ditch, Lydia. T May 1752 *Lichfield*. K.
Ditch, William of Reading. R for America Feb 1690. Be.
Ditchburn, Elizabeth. LC from *Dorsetshire* Va Sep 1736. X.
Ditchell, Walter of Burnham Overy. R for America Jun 1714. Nf.
Ditcher als Stubbs, Anne. PT Apr 1681 R Sep 1682. M.
Ditcher als Ditchfield, William. S s sheep at Drayton Lent 1724. Sh.
Ditchfield, Robert (1620). *See* Lambert. M.

Ditchfield, Thomas. S Lent 1764. Wa.
Ditchfield, William (1724). *See* Ditcher. Sh.
Divall. *See* Devall.
Dicks, James. SQS & TB Apr 1765. So.
Dixe, John of Ramesbury, husbandman. R for Barbados Jun 1669. Wi.
Dix, Joseph. S Dec 1745. L.
Dicksey, Ann. S Sep 1763. M.
Dixey, Richard. S & T Apr 1725 *Sukey* LC Annapolis Sep 1725. M.
Dixey, William. R for Barbados or Jamaica Jan 1693. L.
Dixon, Anne. S Aug T Sep 1725 *Forward* LC Annapolis Dec 1725. M.
Dixon, Ann (1765). *See* Smith. Sy.
Dixon, Benjamin. S Dec 1749-Jan 1750 T Mar 1750 *Tryal*. M.
Dixon, Benjamin. S s at St. Philip & Jacob Lent TB Apr 1751. G.
Dixon, Catherine. S Jun T Oct 1744 *Susannah*. M.
Dixon, David. S & T Oct 1730 *Forward* LC Potomack Jan 1731. M.
Dickson, Edward (1725). *See* Dyson. M.
Dickson als Johnson, Edward. SQS Jan 1754. M.
Dixon, Eleanor. S Sep-Oct 1774. M.
Dickson, Elizabeth (1668). *See* Wilson. Ht.
Dixon, Elizabeth. SQS & T Sep 1767 *Justitia*. M.
Dixon, Henry. S May-Jly 1749. M.
Dixon, Jane. S Sep 1760. M.
Dixon, Jane wife of Christopher. S Feb s hose at All Hallows, Lombard
    Street T Apr 1768 *Thornton*. L.
Dixon, Jesse. S & T Mar 1760 *Friendship*. L.
Dixon, John of Arksden. R for Barbados or Jamaica Mar 1678. E.
Dickson, John of Wootton. R for America Mar 1680. O.
Dixon, John of Lancaster. R for Barbados Jly 1699. La.
Dixon, John. R for America Aug 1715. M.
Dixon, John. TB 14 yrs Oct 1719. L.
Dixon, John, aged 17, fair. S Jan T Feb 1723 *Jonathan* LC Md Jly
    1724. L.
Dixon, John. S Jan T Feb 1724 *Anne*. L.
Dixon, John. S & T Oct 1729 *Forward* LC Va Jun 1730. M.
Dixon, John. T Sep 1730 *Smith*. Sy.
Dixon, John (1731). *See* Cane. M.
Dixon, John. S Apr T Sep 1737 *Pretty Patsy* to Md. M.
Dixon, John. T Oct 1738 *Genoa*. Sy.
Dickson, John. S s horse Summer 1742 R 14 yrs Lent 1743. Le.
Dixson, John. T Sep 1742 *Forward*. K.
Dixon, John. S for highway robbery at Stapleton Summer TB Aug
    1748. G.
Dixon, John. T Aug 1752 *Tryal*. E.
Dixon, John. SL Oct 1756. Sy.
Dixon, John. S & T Nov 1762 *Prince William*. L.
Dixon, John. S s sheep Lent R 14 yrs Summer 1764. Be.
Dixon, John. S s pimento at St. Mary at Hill Feb T Apr 1768
    Thornton. L.
Dixon, John. T for life Apr 1770 *New Trial*. K.
Dixon, John. S Apr 1773. M.
Dixon, John. S s rags at Brandon Summer 1773. Nf.

Dixon, Jonathan. S Feb T Apr 1769. M.

Dixon, Joseph. S & T Dec 1736 *Dorsetshire*. L.

Dickson, Margaret. S & T Oct 1730 *Forward* to Va. M.

Dixon, Martha. S & T Apr 1733 *Patapsco* LC Annapolis Nov 1733. M.

Dixon, Mary (1726). *See* Blewett. L.

Dixon, Mary (1731). *See* Rowe. M.

Dixon, Mary. LC from *Forward* Potomack Jan 1731. X.

Dixon, Mary. S s at Yarm Lent TB May 1743. Y.

Dixon, Richard. T Apr 1739 *Forward*. Sy.

Dixon, Richard. S Feb-Apr T May 1751 *Tryal*. M.

Dixon, Richard. SQS Oct 1754. M.

Dixon, Robert. S Apr T Jly 1770 *Scarsdale*. L.

Dixon als Pope, Sarah. S Feb 1752. L.

Dixon, Thomas of Dumfries, Scotland. SQS Thirsk s at Great Smeaton etc. Apr 1732. Y.

Dixon, Thomas. S s horse Summer 1752 R 14 yrs Lent 1753. Li.

Dixon, Thomas. S Jun T Sep 1767 *Justitia*. L.

Dixon, Thomas. S s hogs at Waldingfield Lent 1771. Su.

Dickson, William. S Jan T Feb 1719 *Worcester* LC Annapolis Jun 1719. L.

Dixon, William. S Jan T 14 yrs Apr 1743 *Justitia*. M.

Dixon, William. S Dec 1748 T Jan 1749 *Laura*. M.

Dixon, William. AT Lent & Summer 1759. Y.

Dixon, William. T Apr 1771 *Thornton*. Ht.

Dixon, Zachariah. S & T Mar 1760 *Friendship*. L.

Dobbins, Elizabeth. T Jly 1753 *Tryal*. M.

Dobbins, Joseph. R Jun T Aug 1769 *Douglas*. M.

Dobbings, William. S Oct 1744-Jan 1745. M.

Dobbins, William. S s at St. Nicholas, Worcester, Lent 1762. Wo.

Dobbs, Elizabeth. T from Newgate on *Margaret*, sold to Joseph Pettibone Md Sep 1719. X.

Dobbs, James of Hornsey. S s silver spoon & T Dec 1740 *Vernon*. M.

Dobbs, John. S Summer 1745. Su.

Dobbs, John. S Summer 1750 R 14 yrs Lent 1751. No.

Dobbs, Joseph, yeoman. S & R for killing gelding at Stoke Summer T Dec 1770 *Justitia*. Bu.

Dobbs, Thomas. S Apr-May T May 1744 *Justitia*. M.

Dobbs, Thomas. S & T Jly 1770 *Scarsdale*. M.

Dobie, Christian, spinster. SQS s gowns Summer 1767. Du.

Dobey, James. S Feb T Apr 1765 *Ann*. L.

Dobree, Elias. S Feb-Apr T May 1755 *Rose*. M.

Dobson, Francis. S May T Jun 1726 *Loyal Margaret* LC Md Oct 1726. M.

Dobson, Francis. S & T Dec 1734 *Caesar* LC Va Jly 1735. L.

Dobson, Francis. S for assault with intent to rob Summer 1755. Nf.

Dobson, George, barber aged 24, black hair. T Oct 1720 *Gilbert* LC Md May 1721. Sy.

Dobson als Blower, John. T 14 yrs May 1719 *Margaret*; sold to Benjamin Williams Md Sep 1719. E.

Dobson, John, als Herdman, Thomas. S s horse Summer 1733 R 14 yrs Summer 1734. Y. & Nl.

Dobson, Thomas. T Jly 1724 *Robert*. Sy.

Dobson, William. S Jun T Dec 1736 *Dorsetshire* to Va. M.

Docker, John. SQS & T Sep 1766 *Justitia*. M.

Docker, Sarah. SQS Coventry Apr 1765. Wa.

Dockerday, William of St. Saviour, Southwark. SQS Jan 1773. Sy.

Dockerill, James. AT Summer T Oct 1739 *Duke of Cumberland*. Ht.

Dodd, Ann. R 14 yrs Aug 1742. De.

Dodd, Elizabeth of St. Saviour, Southwark, spinster. SQS Apr 1752 *Lichfield*. Sy.

Dodd, Henry. S Dec 1733 T Jan 1734 *Caesar* LC Va Jly 1734. L.

Dodd, John. LC from *Forward* Rappahannock May 1728. X.

Dodd, John. S s iron at Newbury Summer 1728. Be.

Dod, John. T May 1752 *Lichfield*. Bu.

Dodd, Joseph. S Jan T 14 yrs Feb 1719 *Worcester* LC Annapolis Jun 1719. L.

Dodd, Mary. S & T Jan 1756 *Greyhound*. M.

Dodd, Richard of Manaton. R for Barbados Mar 1694. De.

Dodd, Richard. S s sheep Lent R 14 yrs Summer 1753. Bu.

Dodd, Richard. S Feb T Apr 1768 *Thornton*. M.

Dodd, Robert of Adbaston. R for America Feb 1673. St.

Dodd, Robert. T Apr 1765 *Ann*. Ht.

Dodd, Robert. R for life Lent 1775. K.

Dodd, Robert. R 14 yrs s horse Summer 1775. No.

Dodd, Samuel. S & T 14 yrs Sep 1751 *Greyhound*. M.

Dodd, Thomas. R for Barbados or Jamaica Oct 1690. M.

Dodd, Thomas. S Summer T Sep 1751 *Greyhound*. Bu.

Dodd, Thomas. S Sep-Oct T Dec 1771 *Justitia*. M.

Doddimead, William. SQS Jan-Mar TB to Va Apr 1741. Wi.

Dods, John. Rebel T 1685.

Dodds, John. S s at St. Andrew, Auckland, Summer 1772. Du.

Doddy als Dodson, Thomas. R Dec 1698 AT Jan 1699. M.

Dodge, Ann. SQS Jan TB Apr 1766. So.

Dodgson, Matthew. S s horse Summer 1726 R 14 yrs Lent 1729. Y.

Dodsley, Thomas. S for highway robbery Summer 1743 R 14 yrs Lent 1744. No.

Dodson, Katherine (1681). *See* Johnson. M.

Dodson, Francis. S Apr T 14 yrs May 1718 *Tryal* LC Charles Town Aug 1718. L.

Dodson, John (1746). *See* Dawson. L.

Dodson, John. S Feb 1774. L.

Dodson, Lancelot. R for Barbados Dec 1681. L.

Dodson, Mary (1764). *See* Tanner. M.

Dodson, Thomas (1698). *See* Doddy. M.

Dodson, William. R Dec 1698 AT Jan 1699. M.

Doe, Daniel. T Apr 1741 *Speedwell* or *Mediterranean*. E.

Doe, John. T Oct 1721 *William & John*. Sy.

Doe, John. T Oct 1726 *Forward*. E.

Doe, Mary. S Apr TB to Md May 1719. L.

Doe, Mary. S Dec 1745. L.

Doe, Richard of Plymouth. R for Barbados Mar 1686. De.

Doman, Richard. R 14 yrs Jly 1718 to be T to Boston NE. Wi.

Doeman, Thomas. S Aug T Oct 1724 *Forward* to Md. M.
Doggett als Lyons, Elizabeth. S Dec 1741 T 14 yrs Feb 1742 *Industry*. M.
Doggett, Jacob of Camberwell. SQS Apr 1763. Sy.
Doggett, John. S Lent 1740. G.
Doggett, Joseph. R Dec 1774. M.
Dougherty, Constant. R for Barbados or Jamaica Jly 1696. X.
Doherty, John. SQS Dec 1757 T Mar 1758 *Dragon*. M.
Doharty, Matthew. S Feb-Apr T May 1752 *Lichfield*. M.
Doggarty, Patrick. S May-Jly 1774. M.
Doidge, Richard. S Aug 1729. De.
Doolan, John. S Aug 1763. L.
Dolan, John. SQS Apr T Jun 1764 *Dolphin*. M.
Doland, William. S & T Apr 1733 *Patapsco* to Md. M.
Dolbeare, Samuel. Rebel T 1685.
Dole, John of Carle Stoke, husbandman. R for Barbados Jly 1667. Wi.
Doleman, John (1767). *See* Hull, Edward. M.
Dolman, John. S Apr-May T Jly 1771 *Scarsdale*. M.
Doleman, Rebecca, aged 35, dark. S & T Oct 1720 *Gilbert* LC Md May 1721. M.
Doleman, Thomas. Rebel T 1685.
Doleman, Thomas. LC from *Forward* Annapolis Jun 1725. X.
Doleman, Thomas. S Lent R Summer 1731. Db.
Dolman, Thomas. S s at Trentham Summer 1734. St.
Doleman, Thomas. S Jun T Dec 1736 *Dorsetshire* to Va. M.
Dolland, Elizabeth. S Jly T Sep 1767 *Justitia*. M.
Dollard, William. S Aug T Sep 1764 *Justitia*. L.
Dollimore, Thomas. S & T Dec 1767 *Neptune*. M.
Dolline, John. T Sep 1730 *Smith*. E.
Dolling, George. SQS 14 yrs for receiving & TB Apr 1758. So.
Dolling, Mary. S & T Dec 1759 *Phoenix*. L.
Dolling, Thomas. Rebel T 1685.
Dollison, James. R Jun T 14 yrs Aug 1769 *Douglas*. M.
Dollison, Thomas. S Oct 1751-Jan 1752. M.
Dolls, James. S Feb 1752. L.
Dolphin, Elizabeth. S Jan T Apr 1734 *Patapsco* to Md. M.
Dolphin, Joseph. T Jan 1734 *Caesar* LC Va Jly 1734. E.
Dolton. *See* Dalton.
Domat, John. S Aug 1767 TB to Va. De.
Domatt, William Jr. R Apr 1770. De.
Dominicus, John. S Dec 1733 T Jan 1734 *Caesar* LC Va Jly 1734. L.
Domingus, Mary. S Apr T May 1740 *Essex*. L.
Dominy als Smith, Daniel. S s shirt at Kempston Summer 1774. Bd.
Donnald, John. S Lent R 14 yrs & T Summer TB Aug 1736. Y.
Donald, John. R 14 yrs Jly 1749. Co.
Donnald, Thomas. S Aug 1742. Co.
Donald, William. SWK Jan T Apr 1770 *New Trial*. K.
Donaldson, James. S Apr 1763. M.
Donaldson, John. S City Lent 1761. Y.
Donaldson, William. S May 1775. L.
Doncaster, Elizabeth. S Sep-Oct T Dec 1771 *Justitia*. M.
Donegan als Dongan, Patrick. S Apr T Jun 1742 *Bladon* to Md. M.

Doney, Mary (1731). *See* Downing. L.

Dongey, William. S Summer 1749. K.

Donne, Humphrey. S for perjury Jly 1744. So.

Donne, John. AT Summer 1668 & Winter 1669 for attending conventicle. Bd.

Done, John. S Summer 1733 AT Lent 1734. Wo.

Done, John. S s at Bromyard Summer 1737. He.

Donnell, George. R for Barbados Jun 1671. M.

Donnelly, Bryan. S Apr 1763. M.

Donnoly, Hannah. S Sep 1737 T Jan 1738 *Dorsetshire* to Va. M.

Donally, Henry. S Jly T Sep 1767 *Justitia*. M.

Donelly, John. SQS & T Sep 1751 *Greyhound*. M.

Donnolly, John. S Feb T Apr 1766 *Ann*. M.

Donnelly, John. S Oct 1766 T Jan 1767 *Tryal*. M.

Donnala, Michael. T Jly 1770 *Scarsdale*. M.

Donnilly, Patrick. S Jly 1760. M.

Donnelly, Thomas. S Apr T May 1767 *Thornton*. M.

Donning, Thomas. S s at Old Windsor Lent 1757. Be.

Donningson, Thomas of Newcastle upon Tyne. R Mar 1710. Nl.

Donington, Robert. S Jly T Aug 1721 *Prince Royal* but died on passage. M.

Donnington, William. S May-Jly 1746. M.

Donnohow, David. S Lent 1749. K.

Donnahaugh, Dennis. S Summer 1772. E.

Donagha als Donoghue, Florence. R for America Nov 1710. M.

Donahoo als Davison, Margaret. S Jly T Sep 1742 *Forward*. L.

Donnavan, Cornelius. S Feb T 14 yrs Mar 1770 *Tryal*. M.

Donnovan, James of Liverpool, mariner. S for setting fire to Liverpool Gaol Lent R 14 yrs Summer 1770. La.

Donnevan, John (1749). *See* Pyke. De.

Donnevan, John. SQS Oct 1764 T Jan 1765 *Tryal*. M.

Donsley, Anthony. R 14 yrs Mar 1758. De.

Donvilla, Victoire. S May T Sep 1765 *Justitia*. M.

Doody, Joseph. S & T Feb 1744 *Neptune* to Md. M.

Doolan. *See* Dolan.

Dooley, Laurence. SQS Oct 1774. M.

Dooley, Nathaniel. T Sep 1757 *Thetis*. K.

Dooley als Dowley, Valentine. SQS Sep 1772. M.

Doran, Edward. T Jun 1764 *Dolphin*. M.

Doran, John. S May T Jun 1768 *Tryal*. M.

Dore, Edward. S Dec 1733 T Jan 1734 *Caesar* LC Va Jly 1734. L.

Dore, Thomas. R 14 yrs Jly 1728. Ha.

Door, William. S Lent 1764. Li.

Dorey, John of St. George, Southwark. SQS Feb T Jun 1764 *Dolphin*. Sy.

Dorigny, Francis. S Dec 1731. M.

Dorman, Edward. T Sep 1730 *Smith*. K.

Dorman, Elizabeth. S Apr T May 1767 *Thornton*. M.

Dorman als Sims, George. S s mare Summer 1766 R 14 yrs Lent 1767. Su.

Dorman, George of Kingston on Thames. SQS Jan 1775. Sy.

Dorman, Joseph. S Mar 1756. Ha.

Dorman, Timothy of Barking. SQS Oct 1757 T Sep 1758 *Tryal*. E.

Dorman, William. R for America Jly 1693. Ru.

Dormant, Humphrey of Warwick. R for America Jly 1682. Wa.

Dormer, John. S for killing sheep Summer 1742 R 14 yrs Lent T Apr 1743 *Justitia*. Bu.

Dornall, Peter. S Summer 1745 R 14 yrs Summer 1746. Cu.

Dorney, Philip. S Oct T Nov 1728 *Forward* LC Rappahannock Jun 1729. L.

Dorrell, Catherine. S Aug T Sep 1725 *Forward* to Md. M.

Dorell, George of St. Saviour, Southwark. R (Newgate) for Barbados Apr TB Oct 1669. Sy.

Dorrill, George. R for Barbados Jun 1671. M.

Dorrell, Thomas. SQS Oct 1754. M.

Dorrington, Martha. S Lent T May 1755 *Rose*. K.

Dorse, John. S Mar 1740. So.

Dawsey, James. S Apr T May 1750 *Lichfield*. M.

Dorsey, John. S s horse & R 14 yrs Summer TB Sep 1769. Y.

Dawsey, Patrick. S Dec 1749-Jan 1750 T Mar 1750 *Tryal*. M.

Dotterell, William. SQS Jly 1774. M.

Doubt, Roger. S Mar 1765. Co.

Douby als Turby, John. S & T Oct 1730 *Forward* LC Potomack Jan 1731. L.

Dougle, Margaret. S May T Sep 1765 *Justitia*. M.

Dougheda, Rose (1740). *See* Smith. M.

Doughton, Ann. S s cloak Dec 1735 T Jan 1736 *Dorsetshire* LC Va Sep 1736. M.

Doughty, Abigael of Milsom. R for America Mar 1697. Sh.

Doughty, Elizabeth of Thongland, spinster. R for America Jly 1673. Sh.

Doughty, Elizabeth. S Jan 1746. L.

Dowty, Nathaniel. R for Barbados Mar 1683. M.

Doughty, Philip. R Jly 1774. M.

Dowty, Robert of Andover, woolcomber. R for Barbados Jly 1677. Ha.

Doughty, Thomas. S s at Neen Savage Lent 1726. Sh.

Doughty, William. S Lent 1745. *Su.

Douglas, Alexander. R Jly AT Sep 1675. M.

Douglas, Alexander. S Dec 1750. L.

Douglass, Eleanor wife of John. S May T Nov 1743 *George William*. M.

Douglas als Redhead, Elizabeth. S s silver tankard & T May 1736 *Patapsco*. M.

Douglas, Isabel. S Jly 1744. Ha.

Douglas, Isabella (1764). *See* Parkhouse. M.

Douglas, James. S Lent 1754. Su.

Douglas als Sutherland als Watson als Mackenzie, James. S for obtaining money by false pretences Mar 1775. De.

Douglass, John. R Dec 1698 AT Jan 1699. M.

Douglas, John. S Feb T Mar 1727 *Rappahannock* to Md. M.

Douglas, John Hunter (1771). *See* Campbell, Duncan. M.

Douglas, Margaret (1686). *See* Urwin, Isabel. Nl.

Douglas, Margery. S s cloth at Evesham Lent 1745. Wo.

Douglass, Mary, als wife of Roger Allen. S Feb T Jun 1738 *Forward*. M.

Douglas, Rebecca. SL Sep T Dec 1758 *The Brothers*. Sy.

Douglas, Robert. S & T Dec 1752 *Greyhound*. M.

Douglas, Thomas. S Dec 1743 T Feb 1744 *Neptune* to Md. M.

Douglass, William. T Jly 1723 *Alexander* LC Md Sep 1723. Sy.

Douglas, William. T Jun 1764 *Dolphin*. K.

Dousy, Innace. S May T Jly 1771 *Scarsdale*. L.

Douyer, Peter. T 14 yrs Aug 1769 *Douglas*. E.

Dove, Elianor. S Jan-Apr 1749. M.

Dove, John. S for burning barn & poisoning cattle Lent 1725 T Lent 1733. Y.

Dove, John of St. Olave, Southwark. SQS Feb 1757. Sy.

Dove, John. SQS Jly T Sep 1765 *Justitia*. M.

Dove, Mary. S Dec 1727. M.

Dove, Nicholas. T Jun 1740 *Essex*. Sy.

Dove, Richard. S for highway robbery Summer 1753 R 14 yrs Lent 1754; S to hang Summer 1759 for returning from transportation. No.

Dove, Thomas. S Summer 1722 T Oct 1723. Y.

Dove, William. S & T Jly 1770 *Scarsdale*. L.

Dove, William. SQS Dec 1774. M.

Dover, Ann. S & T Sep 1764 *Justitia*. M.

Dovey, Ann. S s at Doddenham Summer 1727. Wo.

Dovey, John. S s at Leigh Lent TB Apr 1753. G.

Dow, Mary (1719). *See* Gray, Martha. L.

Dow, Mary. S for murdering her bastard child Summer 1724 R 14 yrs Lent 1725. Su.

Dow, Thomas. R Summer 1721. Y.

Doway, Peter. S May T Jly 1722 *Alexander*. L.

Dowday, John. S Jly 1775. L.

Dowde, Edward. S Aug 1740. So.

Dowden als Cooke, Giles. S Mar 1721. Do.

Dowden als Hill, John. R Jly 1775. Ha.

Dowding, James. S Apr 1741. So.

Dowding, William. SQS Apr TB Sep 1773. So.

Dowdle, Thomas of St. Olave, Southwark. SQS Feb T May 1750 *Lichfield*. Sy.

Dowdell, William. S Jan T Apr 1762 *Dolphin*. L.

Dowdy, George. S for highway robbery & R 14 yrs Summer 1745. Nl.

Dowers, Oliver. S Lent R 14 yrs Summer TB Aug 1739. G.

Dowgard, Daniel. S Jan T Sep 1737 *Pretty Patsy* to Md.

Dowland, Margaret. S Apr 1761. M.

Dowland, William. LC from *Patapsco* Annapolis Nov 1733. X.

Dowland, William. SQS Oct T Dec 1769 *Justitia*. M.

Dowlas, Mary. TB Oct 1719. L.

Dowle, Jacob. S s handkerchiefs Feb T Apr 1735 *Patapsco* LC Md Oct 1735. L.

Dowle, John. S & T Sep 1731 *Smith* LC Va 1732. L.

Dowell, John. R 14 yrs Summer 1754. Cu.

Dowle, Mary. S Oct 1766 T Jan 1767 *Tryal*. L.

Dowle, Samuel. S Jan T Feb 1765 *Tryal*. L.

Dowell, William. S Summer 1735 R 14 yrs Lent 1736. O.

Dowell, William. S s at St. Mary de Lode, Gloucester, & R 14 yrs Summer 1735 TB May 1736. G.

Dowle, William. S Mar 1752. Do.

Dowler, Anne. S Aug T Oct 1724 *Forward* LC Annapolis Jun 1725. M.

Dowles, Jacob. S & T May 1744 *Justitia*. L.

Dowley, Francis. S s at Wolverhampton Lent 1751. St.

Dowley, Lawrence. S Jan-Feb T Apr 1772 *Thornton*. M.

Dowley, Richard. S Oct T Dec 1771 *Justitia*. L.

Dowley, Valentine (1772). *See* Dooley. M.

Dowley, William of Inkberrow. R for America Jly 1677. Wo.

Dowling, Richard. S Apr 1773. M.

Dowling, Silas. S Sep 1754. L.

Dowman, Jemima. S s handkerchiefs at Etwall Lent 1764. Db.

Downe, Charles. S Apr T May 1767 *Thornton*. M.

Downe, Elizabeth of Chittlehampton, spinster. R for Barbados Jly 1695. De.

Down, James. S Jly 1755 TB to Va. De.

Downe, John. Rebel T 1685.

Downe, Richard of Lindridge, carpenter. R for America Jly 1682. Wo.

Downe, William. T Apr 1771 *Thornton*. K.

Downer, Elizabeth. S Lent R 14 yrs Summer 1754. Sy.

Downes, Abel. LC from *Honor* Port York Jan 1721. X.

Downes, Anne. S Feb T Mar 1730 *Patapsco* LC Annapolis Sep 1730. M.

Downs, Benjamin (1768). *See* Hakins. E.

Downes, Charles. S May 1775. L.

Downes als Vaughan, George. S & T 14 yrs Feb 1740 *York* to Md. M.

Downes, James. S Oct-Dec 1739 T Feb 1740 *York* to Md. M.

Downes, James. S Summer 1771. He.

Downes, John. S Feb T Apr 1765 *Ann*. M.

Downs, John. S May T Sep 1766 *Justitia*. M.

Downes, Joseph. S Oct 1749. L.

Downes, Ralph. S Lent R 14 yrs Summer 1755. St.

Downes, Richard of Hadnall. R for America Jly 1699. Sh.

Downes als Robinson, Susanna. S Jly T Aug 1721 *Prince Royal*. M.

Downes, Thomas. T Apr 1766 *Ann*. E.

Downey, Daniel. S Sep-Oct 1748 T Jan 1749 *Laura*. M.

Downey, James. S for sacrilege Summer 1743 R 14 yrs Summer 1744. Nl.

Downey, Thomas of St. Olave, Southwark. SQS Feb T Mar 1763 *Neptune*. Sy.

Downey, William of Cawston. S Summer 1726. *Nf.

Downham, Thomas of Clyst Honiton, cordwainer. R for Barbados Feb 1698. De.

Downing, Biron. S Lent R 14 yrs Summer 1754. K.

Downing, George. S & T 14 yrs Oct 1730 *Forward* LC Potomack Jan 1731. M.

Downing, George. S Summer 1764. Nt.

Downing, John. S & T Oct 1729 *Forward* LC Va Jun 1730. M.

Downing, John. SQS Feb T May 1751 *Tryal*. M.

Downing als Doney, Mary. S & T Sep 1731 *Smith* LC Va 1732. L.

Downing, Michael (1749). *See* Barnsides. M.

Downing, Nicholas. R 14 yrs Jly 1740. Ha.

Downing, Robert. S Dec 1766 T Jan 1767 *Tryal*. M.

Downton, George. S & T Jly 1772 *Tayloe*. L.

Downton, Mary. S Summer 1760 R 14 yrs Lent 1761. Sh.

Dowse, John. R 14 yrs Jly 1721 T from Southampton 1723. Ha.

Dowse, John (1751). *See* Towers. Be.

Dowset, Joseph. T Apr 1735 *Patapsco*. E.

Dowsett, Paul. R for America Aug 1713. L.

Dowsell, Richard. SQS New Sarum or Warminster & TB to Va Oct 1768. Wi.

Dowsewell, Edward of Purton. R for Barbados Feb 1665. Wi.

Dowson, Martha. S Dec 1762 T Mar 1763 *Neptune*. M.

Dowtch, Robert. T 14 yrs Apr 1769 *Tryal*. K.

Dowty. *See* Doughty.

Doxey, Eleanor. SQS Dec 1768 T Jan 1769 *Thornton*. M.

Doil als Doyle, Bartholomew. S & T Dec 1767 *Neptune* but died on passage. M.

Doyle, Catherine. S Dec 1748 T Jan 1749 *Laura*. M.

Doyle, Elizabeth. S Aug T Oct 1723 *Forward*. L.

Doyle, Elizabeth. S Oct T Nov 1725 *Rappahannock* LC Rappahannock Apr 1726. M.

Doyle, Francis. S Nov T Dec 1770 *Justitia*. L.

Doyle, James. SQS Jun TB Aug 1769. So.

Doyle, Margaret (1735). *See* Conner. M.

Doyle, Margaret. S Lent 1775. K.

Doyle, Mary. T Jun 1768 *Tryal*. M.

Doyle, Michael. SQS Jun T Sep 1767 *Justitia*. M.

Doyle als Heydon, Michael. S Sep T Dec 1767 *Neptune*. M.

Doyle, Patrick. S Apr T Jun 1768 *Tryal*. M.

Doyle, Philip. S Dec 1754. L.

Doyle, Robert. TB to Va from QS 1767. De.

Doyle, Sylvester. SW & T Apr 1769 *Tryal*. M.

Doyle, William. S Jun T Sep 1767 *Justitia*. L.

Dozzington, Elizabeth ((722). *See* Baily. M.

Drake, Ann. SQS Jun T Jly 1753 *Tryal*. M.

Drake, Daniel. S & T Apr 1725 *Sukey* LC Annapolis Sep 1725. M.

Drake, Elizabeth. S Aug T Oct 1724 *Forward* LC Annapolis Jun 1725. M.

Drake, Francis. S Mar 1751. Ha.

Drake, Isaac. R 10 yrs Lent 1656. Sy.

Drake, John of Crewkerne, husbandman. R for Barbados Apr 1668. So.

Drake, John. TB to Va from QS 1742. De.

Drake, John. S Feb 1749. Ha.

Drake, Joshua. TB Oct 1719 T *Susannah & Sarah* but died on passage. L.

Drake, Mary. T Apr 1759 *Thetis*. E.

Drake, Peter of Limerick, Ireland. R for America May 1709 for taking up arms for France. M.

Drake, Richard. Rebel T 1685.

Drake, Robert. SQS Dec 1768 T Jan 1769 *Thornton*. M.

Drake, Thomas. S as pickpocket Summer 1750 R 14 yrs Lent 1751. Wa.

Drake, William. S Apr-Jun T Jly 1772 *Tayloe*. M.

Draper, Elizabeth. SL & T Nov 1762 *Prince William*. Sy.

Draper, James. SQS Mar TB May 1739. Nt.
Draper, James. S s horse Lent R 14 yrs Summer 1756. No.
Draper, John. PT Sep 1672 R Feb 1673. M.
Draper, John. S Feb T Apr 1741 *Speedwell* or *Mediterranean*. M.
Draper, John of Christchurch. SQS s lead coffins & T Jan 1769
  Thornton. Sy.
Draper, Joseph. S Lent 1749. *Su.
Draper, Mary. S Aug 1756. So.
Draper, Robert. S Oct T Dec 1724 *Rappahannock*. L.
Draper, Robert. R 14 yrs Jly 1764. Ha.
Draper, Simon. R Mar TB to Va Apr 1773. Wi.
Draper, Solomon. R 14 yrs Mar 1740. Ha.
Draper, Thomas. R for Barbados Dec 1668. M.
Draper, Thomas. S s handkerchief at St. Bride's Apr T Jun 1768
  Tryal. L.
Draper, Thomas. S s at Worstead Summer 1770. Nf.
Draper, Thomas. S Mar TB to Va Apr 1773. Wi.
Draper, Valentine. R 14 yrs Mar 1740. Ha.
Draper, William of Saffron Walden. R for Barbados or Jamaica Feb
  1684. E.
Draper, William. SQS & TB Jly 1735. So.
Draper, William. S Dec 1748 T Jan 1749 *Laura*. M.
Draper, William. R s sheep Summer 1771. Li.
Drawwater, Michael. S Sep T Dec 1758 *The Brothers*. M.
Drawater, Robert. R 14 yrs Aug 1759 TB to Va. De.
Drain, John. T May 1737 *Forward*. E.
Drayne, Thomas of Ashfield. R for America Jly 1703. Su.
Drayson, Gabriel. S Lent 1773. K.
Drayton, Peter. Rebel T 1685.
Drayton, Samuel. S for highway robbery & R 14 yrs Lent 1773. G.
Draiton, Thomas. S Aug 1750. Do.
Dresser, James. S s at Newcastle under Lyme Lent 1765. St.
Drew, Abraham. R for Barbados Jan 1664. L.
Drew, Acquila. SQS & TB Jan 1758. So.
Drew, Garrat. S Lent R for Barbados Aug 1663. Sy.
Drew, Isaac. S May T Jly 1723 *Alexander* but died on passage. M.
Drew, Jane. TB to Va from QS 1758. De.
Drew, John. R 14 yrs Mar 1721. Wi.
Drew, John. TB to Md 1728. De.
Drew, John. S Jan T Feb 1733 *Smith* to Md or Va. M.
Drew, John. S & T Mar 1764 *Tryal*. L.
Drew als Ridout, John. R 14 yrs Jly 1767. Ha.
Drew, Jonathan. Rebel T 1685.
Drew, Jonathan. S Jan-Jun T Jun 1728 *Elizabeth* LC Potomack Aug
  1729. L.
Drew, Martha. S Feb T Mar 1727 *Rappahannock* to Md. M.
Drew, Martha (1734). *See* Shepherd. M.
Drew, Mary. R for Barbados May 1664. M.
Drew, Richard Jr. SQS Jly TB Aug 1765. So.
Drew, Thomas. R for Barbados Jly 1663. L.
Drew, Thomas, victualler. R for Barbados or Jamaica Feb 1686. L.

Drew, William. S s cloth at Stroud & Tedbury Lent TB Mar 1737. G.
Drew, William. S Mar 1740. De.
Drew, William (1775). *See* Bussett. De.
Druet, Mary wife of Richard. S Lent R 14 yrs Summer 1758. O.
Drewitt, William. S s at Ferry & South Hinksey Lent 1767. Be.
Dribray, Elizabeth (1740). *See* Whitney. M.
Dring, Mark. R for America Feb 1700. Nt.
Dring, Richard. S s cattle Lent R 14 yrs Summer 1759. Li.
Drinkale, Sarah. TB Apr 1719. L.
Drinkrow, John. S May-Jly 1750. M.
Drinkwater, Elizabeth. S Apr 1761. M.
Drinckwater, James of Tamworth. R (Midland Circ) Jly 1679. St.
Drinkwater, Richard. S s sheep at Wick Lent 1729. Wo.
Drinkwater, Richard. R Lent 1729 AT Lent 1731. O.
Drinkwater, Robert of Manchester, calenderer. SQS May 1770. La.
Drinkwater, William. R for Barbados Aug 1664. M.
Drinkwater, William. S & T Oct 1729 *Forward* but died on passage. M.
Driscall, John. S Lent 1744. Db.
Driver, George. S & R Lent 1738. Su.
Driver, Hopkins. S Feb T Mar 1760 *Friendship*. M.
Driver, James. S s bread at Palgrave Lent 1773. Su.
Driver, John. LC from *Forward* Rappahannock May 1728. X.
Driver, John. S Sep 1760. L.
Driver, John. S s bread at Palgrave Lent 1773. Su.
Driver, Thomas. S Lent 1750. Su.
Driver, William. SQS & T Jan 1765 *Tryal*. M.
Drodge, Henry. S & T Apr 1766 *Ann*. M.
Drouse, John (1731). *See* Rouse. L.
Drover, John. S Mar 1731. Ha.
Drower, Robert. Rebel T 1685.
Drown, William. R 14 yrs Aug 1742. De.
Drowning, Thomas. T May 1719 *Margaret*. Sx.
Druet. *See* Drewitt.
Drummer, Alexander. S & T Jan 1722 *Gilbert* LC Annapolis Jly 1722. L.
Drummer, Elizabeth. S Aug T Oct 1723 *Forward* to Va. M.
Drummer, Sarah. S Feb T Apr 1765 *Ann*. M.
Drummond, Daniel. S Lent 1735. Y.
Drummond, Joseph. S Oct 1737 T Jan 1738 *Dorsetshire* to Va. M.
Drumond, Robert. S May T Jly 1722 *Alexander* to Nevis or Jamaica. M.
Drumond, Robert. T Jly 1723 *Alexander*. Sy.
Drumond, Robert. S Dec 1727. M.
Drummond, Sarah. S Aug T Sep 1764 *Justitia*. L.
Drury, Ann. S & T Jan 1736 *Dorsetshire* but died on passage. L.
Drewry, Anthony. S Summer 1742 R 14 yrs Lent 1743. Li.
Drury, Elizabeth. R for Barbados Aug 1679. L.
Drury, Ellis. S s at Stow in the Wold Lent TB Apr 1757. G.
Drewry, Jane. S for infanticide Summer 1749 R 14 yrs Lent T May 1750
    Lichfield. Sy.
Drury, Michael. S Lent R 14 yrs Summer 1758. Li.
Drury, Robert. Died on passage in *Rappahannock* 1726. Li.
Drury, Timothy. S & T Dec 1769 *Justitia*. M.

Dryberry, Thomas. T Dec 1770 *Justitia*. Sy.
Drye, George. R for Barbados Feb 1664. L.
Dryer, Tobias. Rebel T 1685.
Dubden, Valentine. S Oct 1772. L.
Duboyce, John of Beckenham. R for Barbados or Jamaica Mar 1698. K.
Dubrocq, Alexander. T Jan 1741 *Vernon*. K.
Dubrocq, Petre. T Jan 1741 *Vernon*. K.
Ducke, Abigail. R for Barbados Aug 1715. M.
Ducke, John of Thorley. R for Barbados or Jamaica Mar 1694. Ht.
Duck, John Joseph (1774). *See* Bolton. Wo.
Duck, Mary (1680). *See* Dashashire. M.
Duck, Peter of Ashfield. R for America Jly 1703. Su.
Duckett, John. S Sep T 14 yrs Oct 1750 *Rachael*. M.
Duckett, Rachael. S Sep 1740. L.
Duckett, Richard. S s at Ellesborough Lent 1773. Bu.
Duckett, Thomas. S Jan T Apr 1741 *Speedwell* or *Mediterranean*. M.
Duckles, Richard. S Lent 1740. Y.
Duckworth, Mary of Warrington, spinster. SQS Jan 1764. La.
Ducret, John Victior. R Dec 1774 to be T for life. M.
Dudbridge, Richard. T Oct 1724 *Forward*. Sy.
Dudge, William. S Lent R 14 yrs Summer 1730. G.
Dudley, Charles (1672). *See* Wells. M.
Dudley, Edward. S & T Jun 1756 *Lyon*. M.
Dudley, James. S Summer 1775. Wa.
Dudley, John (1774). *See* Poole. Sh.
Dudley, Joseph. S s at Dudley Summer 1771. Wo.
Dudley, Joshua. S for perjury Jun T Jly 1772 *Tayloe*. L.
Dudley, Richard. S Oct-Dec 1754. M.
Dudson, John. S s at Severn Stoke Lent 1728. Wo.
Duedale, Richard (1673). *See* Ewdall. L.
Duel. *See* Jewel.
Duff, Hugh of St. John Evangelist. SW Apr 1773. M.
Duffey, Alice. S Aug T Oct 1724 *Forward* LC Annapolis Jun 1725. M.
Duffey, Andrew. S Jly T Sep 1766 *Justitia*. M.
Duffey, James. S Dec 1772. M.
Duffey, James. SQS Apr 1774. M.
Duffy, Mary. S Oct 1744-Jan 1745. M.
Duffey, Michael of St. Martin in Fields. SW Jan 1774. M.
Duffey als Murray, Patrick. R 14 yrs Jly 1765. Ha.
Duffield, Edward. SQS Jly TB to Md Oct 1739. So.
Duffield, Isabel of Dudley. R for Jamaica, Barbados or Bermuda Feb 1686. St.
Duffield, Jacob. T 14 yrs Aug 1769 *Douglas*. E.
Duffield, James (1754). *See* Jarvis. Nf.
Duffield, John. R for Bermuda Oct 1614. M.
Duffield, William. R Summer 1773. Sy.
Duffin, Ann. S Dec 1774. L.
Duffin, Edward. S Jly T Sep 1757 *Thetis*. M.
Dugannon, Peter. S Summer 1719 T Aug 1720 *Owners Goodwill*. K.
Dugard, Abraham. S Jan-Feb 1775. M.
Duggard, John of Pedmore. R for Barbados Oct 1663. Wo.

Dugard, John. S Jan-Feb 1775. M.
Dugdell, Henry. S Feb T Mar 1764 *Tryal*. M.
Duggen, George. S Lent 1739. Ch.
Duggen, John. S Oct-Dec 1739 T Jan 1740 *York* to Md. M.
Duggan, John (1754). *See* Beefey. L.
Duggan, Joseph. SQS May T Aug 1769 *Douglas*. M.
Duggan, Thomas. S Dec 1773. L.
Duggin, William. S Oct T Dec 1769 *Justitia*. M.
Duggen, William. S s watch at Llantrissant Lent 1770. Mo.
Duggar, George (1742). *See* Pascoe. Co.
Dugmore, Christopher of Sheriff Hales. R for America Jly 1677. St.
Dugmore, Dorcas of West Bromwich. R for America Feb 1681. St.
Dugmore, Edward. T Oct 1741 *Kitty*. K.
Dugmore als Dagmore, Isabel. S s at Gateshead Summer 1773; Martha
  Dugmore acquitted. Du.
Dugmore, Sarah. T May 1744 *Justitia*. K.
Dugmore, Sarah. S Nov T 14 yrs Dec 1763 *Neptune*. L.
Dugmore, Thomas. T Sep 1755 *Tryal*. K.
Dugmore, Thomas. T Jun 1756 *Lyon*. K.
Duke, Catherine. S Jly T Nov 1762 *Prince William*. M.
Duke, Henry. S Mar 1732. So.
Duke, William als Richard. S s poultry at Appleton Lent 1743. Be.
Dukes als Lambe, Ann. R for Barbados Mar 1683. L.
Dukes, Elizabeth. S & T Apr 1765 *Ann*. L.
Dukes, Isaac. S & T Mar 1764 *Tryal*. L.
Dukes, John. S Jly-Sep 1754. M.
Dukes, Richard. S Jly-Sep 1754. M.
Dukesett, Margaret. R Apr TB to Barbados Jun 1668. L.
Dulvey, William. T May 1744 *Justitia*. Sx.
Dumb Jenny (1772). *See* Saytuss, James. M.
Dumble, Thomas. S & T Sep 1757 *Thetis*. L.
Dumbrain, Daniel. T May 1741 *Miller*. K.
Dumbrell, Edward. T May 1719 *Margaret* LC Md May 1720; sold to
  Stephen West. Sy.
Dumerick, George, als Napton, Francis. S Jan-Apr 1749. M.
Dummet, Robert. R 14 yrs Mar 1774. De.
Dumond, Charlotte. SQS Feb T Sep 1765 *Justitia*. M.
Dumontier, Hester of St. Mary Matfellon, journeyman quilter. S Feb to
  be T May 1736 but "brought to bed the night the transports went
  on board & was left behind." M.
Dumount, Anthony. S & T Apr 1725 *Sukey* LC Annapolis Sep 1725. M.
Dumper, Aaron. S Mar TB to Va Apr 1740. Wi.
Dunbarr, Elizabeth. S Oct T Nov 1728 *Forward* LC Rappahannock Jun
  1729. M.
Dunbar, Jonathan. S May-Jly 1773. M.
Dunbar, Thomas. R for highway robbery Dec 1702 (SP). Wi.
Duncalfe, James. S s cloth at Brude Lent 1759. St.
Duncalfe, William. S Feb T Apr 1739 *Forward* to Va. M.
Doncan, Ann. S City Summer 1753. Nl.
Duncombe, Catherine. S Sep 1754. L.
Duncan, Elizabeth wife of John. S Feb T Mar 1758 *Dragon*. M.

Dunkin, Isaac. S Jly 1764. Ha.

Duncombe als Dunken, James. R for Barbados Jan 1693. M.

Dunkin, John. R for Barbados or Jamaica Feb 1687. L.

Duncan, John. S Feb T Apr 1770 *New Trial*. M.

Duncan, John. S Feb 1773. L.

Duncomb, John. S May-Jly 1773. M.

Dunkin, Joseph. T Nov 1725 *Rappahannock* but died on passage. Sy.

Dunkin, Margaret. S Lent 1754. K.

Duncombe, Richard (1723). *See* Newton. Ht.

Duncombe, Samuel. S & T Jan 1739 *Dorsetshire*. L.

Donkan, William. R 14 yrs Summer 1747; S to hang Summer 1751 for
returning from transportation. Y.

Duncastle, Robert. S Dec 1755 T Jan 1756 *Greyhound*. L.

Dunce, John. T Jly 1723 *Alexander* LC Md Sep 1723. Sy.

Dunce, John. T Nov 1725 *Rappahannock* LC Va Aug 1726. Sy.

Dundass, Elizabeth. S Jun-Dec 1745. M.

Dundas, James. S May-Jun T Jly 1753 *Tryal*. M.

Dundass, John, als Gordon, James. S Lent R Summer T 14 yrs Sep 1757
Thetis. Ht.

Dunfield, Edward. S Sep-Oct 1749. M.

Duneford, Catherine. LC from *Patapsco* Annapolis Nov 1733. X.

Dunford, Thomas of Ewell. SQS & T Jan 1767 *Tryal*. Sy.

Dungworth, Abram. S s handkerchiefs at Abingdon Summer 1764. Be.

Dungworth, Ebor als Hebor. S Lent 1755. Y.

Dungworth, John. S Lent 1741. Y.

Dunham als Denham als Durham, Charles. S Mar 1753. Ha.

Dunill, George. S s sheep Lent R 14 yrs Summer 1758. Nt.

Dunk, Edward. S Summer 1748 T Jan 1749 *Laura*. Sx.

Dunk, Thomas. R Summer 1749. Sy.

Dunk, Wilham. T for life Jun 1768 *Tryal*. Ht.

Dunkirk, Matthew. S Lent 1749. Ca.

Dunckley, Joseph. R for Barbados Dec 1683. L.

Dunkley, Sarah of Ingatestone, spinster. S Summer 1745. E.

Dunckley, Thomas. S s sheep Lent R 14 yrs Summer 1759. Bd.

Dunlap, Casper. S Apr 1750. M.

Dunmole, Francis. S Jun 1754. L.

Dunmore, Thomas. SQS Mar TB May 1721. Le.

Dunn, Amy. S Lent T May 1750 *Lichfield*. K.

Dunn, Anne (1719). *See* Jones, Sara. L.

Dunn, Ann. S Jan T Jun 1738 *Forward* to Md or Va. M.

Dunn, Ann. S s at St. Nicholas, Gloucester, Lent 1750. G.

Dunn, Arthur. S May T Jly 1723 *Alexander* to Md. M.

Dunn, Barnaby. SQS Jly 1774. M.

Dunn, Catherine. S Aug 1760. L.

Dunn, Daniel. S s cloth at Old Swinford Lent 1770. Wo.

Dunn, Dennis. T Jan 1738 *Dorsetshire*. Sy.

Dunn, Dennis. T Oct 1738 *Genoa*. K.

Dunn, Edward. T Sep 1765 *Justitia*. M.

Dunn, Elizabeth. S Lent 1748. K.

Dunn, Elizabeth. R & T for life Sep 1766 *Justitia*. L.

Dunn, Francis. S & T Jly 1753 *Tryal*. L.

Dunn, Godfrey. S Aug T Oct 1741 *Sea Horse*. L.

Dun, Henry. LC from *Alexander* Annapolis Sep 1723. X.

Dunne, Henry. SQS Jly 1748 TB Feb 1749. So.

Dunn, Henry. S for obtaining money by false pretences at Aymestrey Summer 1764. He.

Dunn, Horton. S Apr T May 1767 *Thornton*. M.

Dunn, Hugh. S Apr T May 1751 *Tryal*. L.

Dunn, James. T May 1751 *Tryal*. K.

Dunn, James. S Jly 1775. M.

Dun, John. S Aug T Oct 1726 *Forward* to Va. M.

Dunn, John. S s at Kingswinford Summer 1727. St.

Dunn, John. S Feb T Mar 1729 *Patapsco* LC Annapolis Dec 1729. M.

Dunn, John. S Oct 1751-Jan 1752. M.

Dunn, John. SW & T Jan 1769 *Thornton*. M.

Dunn, John. S Dec 1772. M.

Dunn, Joseph. S & T Dec 1734 *Caesar* LC Va Jly 1735. L.

Dunn, Joseph. S Summer 1755 R 14 yrs Lent 1756. St.

Dun, Margaret. S Jan T Feb 1733 *Smith* to Md or Va. M.

Dunn, Mary. S Jly-Sep 1754. M.

Dunn, Mary (1765). *See* Smith. M.

Dun, Mathew. S Feb T Apr 1766 *Ann*. M.

Dunn, Patrick. S Jan-Feb 1773. M.

Dunn, Patrick. S Apr 1773. L.

Dunn, Paul. S Apr-Jun 1739. M.

Dunn als Matthews, Paul. S May T Jly 1770 *Scarsdale*. M.

Dunn, Richard. LC from *Dorsetshire* Va Sep 1736. X.

Dunn, Richard. S Jly T Sep 1764 *Justitia*. M.

Dunn, Richard. SQS & T Apr 1769 *Tryal*. M.

Dunn, Thomas. S Jly T Aug 1721 *Prince Royal* LC Va Nov 1721. L.

Dunn, Thomas. S Feb T Apr 1770 *New Trial*. L.

Dunn, Timothy. R for America Aug 1715. M.

Dunn, William. S Jly 1725. So.

Dunn, William. T Apr 1741 *Speedwell* or *Mediterranean*. Sy.

Dunn, William. S s at St. John Baptist Summer 1765. He.

Dunn, William. R Dec 1765 T for life Jan 1766 *Tryal*. L.

Dunnet, John. S Feb T Apr 1772 *Thornton*. L.

Dunnicombe, Henry. S Aug 1735. De.

Dunning, Alexander. S Oct 1773. L.

Dunning, Ann wife of John of Scarborough, mariner. S s candles Lent TB Aug 1770. Y.

Dunning, Francis. Rebel T 1685.

Dunning, James. S City Lent 1754. Y.

Dunning, Mary. S Apr T Sep 1758 *Tryal* to Annapolis. M.

Dunning, Mary wife of William. SQS Jly T Sep 1767 *Justitia*. M.

Dunning, Samuel. S & R Lent 1762. Ch.

Dunning, William. S Summer 1751 R 14 yrs Lent T May 1752 *Lichfield*. Sy.

Dunstan, Ann of St. Clement Danes, spinster. S s gold coins & T Dec 1740 *Vernon*. M.

Dunstar, Katherine. S Jan T Feb 1726 *Supply* LC Annapolis May 1726. L.

Dunstone, Nicholas of Exeter. R for Barbados Feb 1698. De.
Dunt, Mary. S & T Apr 1725 *Sukey* LC Annapolis Sep 1725. M.
Dunthorne, Samuel. S Jan T Apr 1759 *Thetis*. M.
Dunton, John. R 14 yrs Lent T May 1719 *Margaret* LC Md May 1720;
    sold to John Amslow. Sy.
Dunton, Thomas. T Jan 1734 *Caesar* LC Va Jly 1734. E.
Dunwell, Katherine. S & T Jan 1736 *Dorsetshire* LC Va Sep 1736. L.
Dupe, James of Norwood. R for Barbados Jan 1675. So.
Dupere, Ann. S Sep-Oct T Dec 1771 *Justitia*. M.
Dupree, Ann. S Sep-Oct T Dec 1752 *Greyhound*. M.
Dupree, John. S Sep T Oct 1768 *Justitia*. M.
Durbin, Hannah (1748). *See* Fifoot, Mary. G.
Durbin, Joseph. S & T Mar 1763 *Neptune*. L.
Durdant, Peter (1685). *See* Durden.
Durden, Benjamin. S Dec 1772. M.
Durdin, Jane. S & T Oct 1729 *Forward* but died on passage. M.
Durden, Mary. SQS & T Jan 1766 *Tryal*. M.
Durden als Durdant, Peter. Rebel T 1685.
Durgin, James (1767). *See* Stowers. Be.
Durham, Charles (1753). *See* Dunham. Ha.
Durham als Hunt, Elizabeth. S & T Apr 1733 *Patapsco* LC Md Nov
    1733. M.
Durham, Elizabeth. T Jun 1740 *Essex*. Sy.
Durham, Elizabeth. S Sep T Dec 1758 *The Brothers*. M.
Durham, George. S Jly T Aug 1721 *Prince Royal* to Va. M.
Durham, John. R 14 yrs Summer T Oct 1739 *Duke of
    Cumberland*. Sy.
Durham, John. T Apr 1742 *Justitia* but died on passage. Sx.
Durham, John. S Dec 1750. L.
Durham, John. T 14 yrs Sep 1765 *Justitia*. Sy.
Durham, Mary. S s at Wellford Lent 1759. G.
Durham, Ralph. S s fish at Hedgerley Lent 1773. Bu.
Durham, Robert. S Feb T Mar 1729 *Patapsco* but died on passage. M.
Durham, Stephen. LC from *Forward* Annapolis Jun 1725. X.
Durham, Thomas. S & T Oct 1730 *Forward* but died on passage. M.
Durham, Thomas. S Sep-Oct T Dec 1753 *Whiteing*. M.
Durly, William. S Dec 1727. M.
Durnford, Ambrose. R 14 yrs Mar 1731. Wi.
Durneford, George of Marnehall, blacksmith. R for Barbados Feb
    1683. Do.
Durneford, John of Portsmouth. R for Barbados Mar 1686. Ha.
Durneford, Thomas of Marnehall. R for Barbados Feb 1683. Do.
Durnell, Richard. R for Barbados Apr 1669. M.
Durnill, Isaack. S Jly 1727. Wi.
Durant, Elizabeth wife of Benjamin, als Shewing, Elizabeth, spinster.
    S Feb T Apr 1770 *New Trial*. M.
Durant, James. S s at Whitby Lent TB May 1772. Y.
Durrant, John. S Feb T Apr 1734 *Patapsco*. L.
Durant, John. S s turkeys at North Burlingham Lent 1771. Nf.
Durrant, Richard of Dartford. R for Barbados or Jamaica Jly 1677. K.
Durrell, Thomas Jr. R 14 yrs Jly TB to Va Sep 1750. Wi.

Dust, Francis. S Apr-May 1754. M.
Dust, Samuel. S & T Dec 1752 *Greyhound*. M.
Dust, Samuel. S Jly T Sep 1765 *Justitia*. M.
Dutch, Ann of Battersea, spinster. SQS Oct 1752 T Jly 1753 *Tryal*. Sy.
Dutton, Andrew (1752). *See* Carroll. M.
Dutton, Anne. S Oct 1719. M.
Dutton als Holmes, Elizabeth. T Apr 1742 *Bond*. K.
Dutton, Francis. S s stockings & T Dec 1734 *Caesar* LC Va Jly 1735. M.
Dutton, George. S & T Apr 1765 *Ann*. L.
Dutton, Jane. S & T Apr 1759 *Thetis*. L.
Dutton, John. S s cheese at St. Mary, Shrewsbury, Lent 1764. Sh.
Dutton, Joseph. S Feb T 14 yrs Apr 1734 *Patapsco*. L.
Dutton, Martha. T Apr 1742 *Bond*. K.
Dutton, Richard of Sutton. R for America Jun 1692. St.
Dutton, Thomas. S Oct 1742 T Mar 1743 *Justitia*. L.
Dewty, John. S Lent 1738. Hu.
Duty, Matthew. S Aug T Oct 1724 *Forward* LC Annapolis Jun 1725. M.
Duvall, Peter. PT Jly 1680. M.
Duxon, Hannah. S Dec 1761 T Apr 1762 *Dolphin*. M.
Dwyer, Catherine wife of Mathew. S Sep-Dec 1746. M.
Dwyer, John. S & T Jan 1736 *Dorsetshire* LC Va Sep 1736. L.
Dwyer, Mary, als Ryland, Eleanor. S Apr T Sep 1757 *Thetis*. M.
Dwire, Peter. SQS & T Jly 1773 *Tayloe* to Va. M.
Dyal, Hannah of Bermondsey, spinster. SQS & T Jan 1769 *Thornton*. Sy.
Dyal, Sarah. S Jan-Apr 1748. M.
Dyball, Mary, spinster. S s at Ridlington & R Summer 1770. Nf.
Dyde, Michael (1766). *See* Dye. M.
Dye, Anne. R Jly & Dec 1685. M.
Dye als Thomas als Whitwood, Ann. R for Barbados or Jamaica Dec 1689. M.
Dye, Arthur. R for Barbados or Jamaica Mar 1688. M.
Dye, David of Chigwell. R for Barbados or Jamaica Jly 1696. E.
Dye, John. S Lent 1749. *Su.
Dye, Joseph of Felsham. R for America Feb 1695. Su.
Dye als Dyde, Michael. SQS Dec 1766 T Jan 1767 *Tryal*. M.
Dye, Penelope, aged 23, black hair. S Jan T 14 yrs Oct 1720 *Gilbert* LC Annapolis May 1721. L.
Dye, Richard of Bradfield, cordwainer. R for Barbados Oct 1663. Be.
Dyer, Angelo. S Apr 1773. L.
Dyer, Benjamin. S Jly 1743. De.
Dyer, Elizabeth. S Oct 1757 T Mar 1758 *Dragon*. L.
Dyer, Elizabeth. S Jan 1759. L.
Dyer, Elizabeth. S Dec 1764 T Jan 1765 *Tryal*. M.
Dyer, Francis. SQS May T Jly 1773 *Tayloe* to Va. M.
Dyer, Isaac. Rebel T 1685.
Dyer, James. R 14 yrs Mar 1744. De.
Dyer, James. S Lent 1750. K.
Dyer, John. T Oct 1722 *Forward*. Sx.
Dyer, John, hatmaker aged 21, dark. S Jan T Feb 1723 *Jonathan* LC Annapolis Jly 1724. L.
Dyer, John. S Dec 1766 T Jan 1767 *Tryal*. M.

Dyer, John (1769). *See* Evans. M.

Dyer, Margaret. S May-Jly 1774. M.

Dyer als Latoush, Mary. R Aug AT Oct 1701. M.

Dyer, Moses. S & TB Mar 1732. G.

Dyer, Obadiah. S s geese at Kimbolton Lent 1767. He.

Dyer, Peter of Exeter. R for Barbados Jun 1702. De.

Dyer, Ralph. SQS & TB Apr 1748. So.

Dyer, Richard. Rebel T 1685.

Dyer, Richard. S s peas at Broughton Lent 1758; Martha Dyer
   acquitted. O.

Dyer, Samuel. S Mar 1766. Co.

Dyer, Samuel. S & T Jly 1770 *Scarsdale*. M.

Dyer, Simon. Rebel T 1685.

Dyer, Stephen. S & T Dec 1724 *Rappahannock*. L.

Dyer, Susannah. S & T Oct 1722 *Forward* LC Annapolis Jun 1723. L.

Dyer, Thomas. S Aug 1762. So.

Dyer, Thomas. SQS Oct T Dec 1769 *Justitia*. M.

Dyer, William of Edmonton. R for America Aug 1713. M.

Dyet, Henry. S Mar TB to Va Apr 1741. Wi.

Dyke, Henry. SQS Sep 1773. M.

Dyke, Michael. R 14 yrs Jly 1741. Ha.

Dyke, Moses. S Lent 1757. K.

Dyke, Moses. T Sep 1758 *Tryal*. Sx.

Dyke, Richard. Rebel T 1685.

Dyke, Thomas. S Mar TB to Va Apr 1765. Wi.

Dikes, Henry, als Clarke, James. S Jan 1751. M.

Dikes, John. R for Barbados or Jamaica Feb 1686. L.

Dykes, Martha. S Sep R Dec 1716 T Jan 1717 *Queen Elizabeth* to
   Jamaica. M.

Dykes, Richard (1667). *See* Hallett. Do.

Dykes, Sarah. S s at St. Nicholas, Hereford, Summer 1757. He.

Dyley, Mary (1769). *See* Oyley. L.

Dyon, Mary. S for shoplifting Summer 1721 R 14 yrs Summer 1722 T
   Forward LC Annapolis Jun 1723. Li.

Dyson als Dickson, Edward. S & T Apr 1725 *Sukey* LC Annapolis Sep
   1725. M.

Dyson, Hannah wife of William. AT Lent & Summer 1765. Y.

Dyson, John. S s sheep Summer 1758 R 14 yrs Lent 1759. No.

Dyson, John. S Summer 1766 R 14 yrs Lent 1767. Wo.

Dyson, John. S Summer 1767. No.

Dyson, John of Huyton, linen weaver. SQS Apr 1774. La.

Dyson, Robert of Bradley. R for America Jly 1699. Wo.

Dison, William of Hitchin. R for Barbados or Jamaica Feb 1683. Ht.

Dyson, William. SQS Dec 1755 T Jan 1756 *Greyhound*. M.

Dyster, Edward. S Jan 1755.

E

Eacot als Bryant, Martha. S Mar 1759. Wi.

Eades, Ann. S Sep T Oct 1768 *Justitia*. L.

Eades, George. S Sep T Dec 1767 *Neptune*. M.

Eades, Henry. T Oct 1729 *Forward*. E.

Eades, Isaac. S s clothing Sep T Dec 1736 *Dorsetshire* to Va. M.

Eades, James. T 14 yrs Aug 1769 *Douglas*. E.

Eades, Jane. S May T Jun 1727 *Susanna* to Va. M.

Eades, John. R for Barbados Dec 1668. M.

Eades, John. S Jan-Feb 1773. M.

Eades, Mary. R for Barbados or Jamaica Apr 1690. L.

Eades, Mary. S Jly 1736. M.

Eades, Roger. S Aug T Sep 1727 *Forward* LC Rappahannock May 1728. L.

Eades, Samuel. R Oct 1694 AT Jan 1695. M.

Eades, Thomas. S s iron from warehouse Lent 1741. Wo.

Eadon. *See* Eden.

Eager, Florence. T Dec 1731 *Forward*. Sy.

Eager, Margaret of Christchurch. R for Barbados or Jamaica Jun 1675. Sy.

Eager, Samuel. S Oct 1751-Jan 1752 to be T for life. M.

Egar, Silvester. S Jan-Feb T Apr 1753 *Thames*. M.

Eagle, Edward. S May 1763. M.

Eagle, John of Stepney. S s silver buttons Feb T May 1736 *Patapsco*. M.

Eagles, Edward. S & T Jly 1771 *Scarsdale*. L.

Eales. *See* Eeles.

Ealey. *See* Ely.

Ealing, John. S & T Dec 1724 *Rappahannock*. L.

Ealing, Samuel. T Jun 1738 *Forward*. Sy.

Eaman, Thomas Henry (1771). *See* Enman. Y.

Emes, John. S Apr T Jun 1742 *Bladon*. L.

Eames, John. S s sheep Summer 1743 R 14 yrs Lent T May 1744 *Justitia*. Bu.

Eams, Sarah. SQS Dec 1750. M.

Eames, William. R (Home Circ) for Barbados May 1664. X.

Eamsden, William. SQS & T 1742. Bd.

Eanis, Bryan. T 14 yrs Aug 1752 *Tryal*. E.

Earall, John. Died 1720 on passage in *Margaret*. X.

Eardley, Margery. S & T Mar 1760 *Friendship*. L.

Earland, Mary. S Jly 1724. De.

Earle, Elizabeth. S & T Apr 1733 *Patapsco* to Md. M.

Earle, Elizabeth. S Apr T Jun 1742 *Bladon* to Md. M.

Earle, George. PT Jan 1675. M.

Earl, Isaac. S Aug T Oct 1741 *Sea Horse* to Va. M.

Earle, James. S Feb T Mar 1730 *Patapsco* LC Annapolis Sep 1730. L.

Earle, John. S Aug 1750 TB to Va. De.

Earle, John. S Apr-May T Jly 1771 *Scarsdale*. M.

Earl, Nathaniel. SQS Oct T Dec 1771 *Justitia*. M.

Earle, Richard of St. Neots. R for America Jly 1702. Hu.
Erle, Richard. S & T Oct 1732 *Caesar* to Va. M.
Earle, Richard. S Jly 1771 TB to Va. De.
Earle, Robert. Rebel T 1685.
Earl als Day, William. S Sep T Nov 1743 *George William*. M.
Early, Ann. S Mar 1772 TB to Va. De.
Earley, Mary. S & T Apr 1733 *Patapsco* LC Annapolis Nov 1733. M.
Earos, Jeremiah. LC from *Loyal Margaret* Annapolis Oct 1726. X.
Earp, Thomas (1775). *See* Sharp. Sy.
Earsell, Matthew. R for Barbados or Jamaica Jan 1692. M.
Earsley, Philip (1720). *See* Hazlewood. E.
Easam, James. S 14 yrs for receiving Aug 1772. Co.
Easemond, John. Rebel T 1685.
Eason, John. S May-Jly 1774. M.
Eason, Samuel. T Dec 1769 *Justitia*. M.
Eason, William. S & T Mar 1763 *Neptune*. L.
East, Charles. S May T Jly 1771 *Scarsdale*. L.
East, Daniel. S Sep-Oct 1775. M.
East, Isaac. T Jly 1722 *Alexander*. E.
East, Jane. S Jly 1756. M.
East als Wiggington, John. SQS Dec 1772. M.
East, Samuel. S Jly 1721 T from Southampton 1723. Ha.
East, Samuel. S Oct T 14 yrs Dec 1724 *Rappahannock*. L.
East, William. S s at Cookham Lent 1775. Be.
Eastabrook, Edward. S Mar 1757. De.
Eastbury, James. S 14 yrs for s cloth from bleaching yard at Stow on the
    Wold Lent 1773. G.
Eastell, Thomas. S & R 14 yrs Summer 1772. O.
Easter, Robert (1738). *See* Caston. Le.
Easterby, Elizabeth. SQS Pontefract Apr 1724 T *Supply* LC Md May
    1726. Y.
Eastham, Margaret wife of James of Ormskirk, carpenter. SQS Jly
    1747. La.
Eastoby, William. S Dec 1737 T Jan 1738 *Dorsetshire*. L.
Eastock, Richard (1757). *See* Eatough. La.
Eastlick, Mary. S Jan T Feb 1724 *Anne* to Carolina. M.
Eastlake, Pascoe. S Aug 1772. Co.
Eastlick, Samuel. S May T Jly 1723 *Alexander* LC Annapolis Sep
    1723. M.
Eastman, Edward. S Apr-May T Jly 1771 *Scarsdale*. M.
Eastmead, John Clement. S Lent R 14 yrs Summer T Sep 1751
    Greyhound. E.
Easton, Alice. S for murder of child Lent R 14 yrs Summer 1751. No.
Easton, Frances. SQS Thirsk Apr TB Sep 1742. Y.
Easton, John. S Apr T May 1719 *Margaret*; sold to Richard Snowden
    Md Aug 1719. L.
Easton, Richard. Rebel T 1685.
Easton, Robert. Rebel T 1685.
Easton, Samuel. S Apr T Sep 1757 *Thetis*. L.
Easton, Thomas. S s book May 1735 T Jan 1736 *Dorsetshire* LC Va Sep
    1736. M.

Eastwick, Elizabeth. S Lent 1762. Su.
Eastwood, John of Burnley, weaver. SQS May 1767. La.
Easy, William. S s bread at Long Stanton Lent 1771. Ca.
Eates, Mary. S & T Oct 1720 *Gilbert* to Md. M.
Eaton, Ann. S Sep-Oct 1772. M.
Eaton, Catherine. S Oct-Dec 1754. M.
Eaton, Charles. SQS & T May 1750 *Lichfield*. Ht.
Eaton, Elizabeth. S Aug 1725. M.
Eaton, Elizabeth. S Apr-May T May 1744 *Justitia*. M.
Eaton, Elizabeth. S Dec 1753-Jan 1754. M.
Eaton, Elizabeth. S Jan 1757. M.
Eaton als Royal, Elizabeth. T Dec 1770 *Justitia*. Sy.
Eaton, Francis. T Nov 1741 *Sea Horse*. E.
Eaton, George. SW & T Dec 1767 *Neptune*. M.
Eaton, Grace. S Nov T Dec 1770 *Justitia*. L.
Eaton, James of Waltham Holy Cross. SQS Oct 1754. E.
Eaton, Jane. R for Barbados or Jamaica Nov 1690. L.
Eaton, John. R Summer 1772. Sy.
Eaton, John. S & R Lent 1775. Ch.
Eaton, Josiah. S s at Stone Summer 1736. St.
Eaton, Lawrence. SQS Dec 1757 T Mar 1758 *Dragon*. M.
Eaton, Margaret, als Irish Pegg. S & T Oct 1730 *Forward* LC Potomack
    Jan 1731. L.
Eaton, Martha. S & T Jan 1756 *Greyhound*. L.
Eaton, Mary. S s at Linton Summer 1729. He.
Eaton, Mary wife of George. S Summer T Aug 1771. Wa.
Eaton als Layton, Paul. S Aug T Oct 1724 *Forward* to Md. M.
Eaton, Peter of Camberwell. R for Barbados or Jamaica Mar 1698. Sy.
Eaton, Richard. S Mar 1723. Ha.
Eaton, Robert. S s rags at Chipping Norton Lent 1757. O.
Eaton, Thomas of West Wycombe. R for Barbados or Jamaica Mar
    1697. Bu.
Eatough als Eastock, Richard, linen weaver. SQS Jan 1757. La.
Eatwell, John. R 14 yrs Apr TB to Va Sep 1753. Wi.
Eatwell, William. S Lent 1767. Bu.
Eaves. *See* Eves.
Ebbidge, Robert. S Norwich Summer TB Sep 1760. Nf.
Ebbit, Ann wife of Oliver. S & T Dec 1769 *Justitia*. M.
Ebblewhite, Joseph. AT from QS Summer 1774. Li.
Ebdon, George. Rebel T 1685.
Ecclefield, John. S Lent 1742. Y.
Eccles, Ann. S Feb T Apr 1741 *Speedwell* or *Mediterranean* to Md. M.
Eccles, Philip. S Lent 1740. Y.
Eckleston, John. TB Sep 1742. Y.
Eccleston, Thomas. S Lent R 14 yrs Summer 1730. Wa.
Eccleston, William (1755). *See* Norman. La.
Eccritt, Robert (1774). *See* Ackerett. De.
Eckley, Roger of Chaddesley Corbett. R for America Feb 1713. Wo.
Eddens, John. T Apr 1733 *Patapsco* LC Md Nov 1733. Sy.
Edings, John. S for returning from transportation Lent R Summer
    1757. Hu.

Eddings, Simon. S for deer poaching in Whittlewood Forest & assaulting keepers Summer 1765. No.

Eddowes, Richard. S s at Wem Lent 1768. Sh.

Eddows, Thomas (1734). *See* Esbury. M.

Eddy, Gouge Walter. R 7 yrs Mar 1755. Co.

Eddy, Patrick. S Jly 1761. Co.

Eddy, William. S 14 yrs for receiving Jly 1761. Co.

Edy, William, als Pascoe, Joseph. R 14 yrs Mar 1771 TB to Va. De.

Eden, Isabel. S s at Sunderland Summer 1775. Du.

Eden, Richard. R for America Feb 1683. Wa.

Eden, Sarah (1685). *See* Carter. L.

Eadon, Thomas. S & T Dec 1758 *The Brothers*. M.

Edenbery, James (1729). *See* Kinsman, John. De.

Edes. *See* Eades.

Edgar, Ann. S Sep T Dec 1763 *Neptune*. M.

Edgar, Richard. Rebel T 1685.

Edge, John. S for highway robbery Lent R 14 yrs Summer 1765. St.

Edge, Thomas. S Jan T Feb 1724 *Anne* to Carolina. M.

Edge, Thomas. S s horse Lent R 14 yrs Summer 1737. Y.

Edge, William. S s at Uttoxeter Lent 1759. St.

Edge, William of Lambeth. SQS & T Apr 1766 *Ann*. Sy.

Edge, William. S s 60 half pence & T Apr 1769 *Tryal*. M.

Edgecombe, George. SQS 1774. Ht.

Edgecomb als Elford, John. S Apr 1728. De.

Edgecombe, Mary. R 14 yrs Mar 1756 TB to Va. De.

Edgecombe, Thomas. S s pigs at Newland Summer 1765. Wo.

Edgehill, Richard. Rebel T 1685.

Edgehill, Richard. R Jly 1686. M.

Edghill, Thomas. S Sep T Dec 1769 *Justitia*. M.

Edgele als Ellford, William. S Oct 1753. M.

Edger, William. R 14 yrs Aug 1720. De.

Edgerley, Robert. SQS & T Jly 1753 *Tryal*. M.

Edgers, Mary. S Sep-Oct T Dec 1771 *Justitia*. M.

Edgerton. *See* Egerton.

Edginton als Edgerton, John. S Aug T Oct 1726 *Forward*. L.

Edgley als Hamilton, Ann. S Jly 1760. M.

Egley, John. S Mar 1740. Ha.

Edgley, Mary Magdalen. S Apr 1774. L.

Edgware Bess Hannapenny (1726). *See* Shepherd, Elizabeth. M.

Edinburgh, John. R Feb T 14 yrs Mar 1764 *Tryal*. M.

Ediver als Brooke, John of Barnstaple, husbandman. R for Barbados Jly 1667. De.

Edkins, Thomas. S Lent 1765. Wa.

Edmonds, Ann. S & T Jan 1736 *Dorsetshire* LC Va Sep 1736. L.

Edmonds, Jacob. S & T Feb 1740 *York*. L.

Edmonds, James. Rebel T 1685.

Edmonds, Jeremiah. S Oct T Dec 1724 *Rappahannock*. L.

Edmonds als White, John of New Sarum, husbandman. R for Barbados Apr 1668. Wi.

Edmonds, John of Amersham. R for America Feb 1695. Bu.

Edmonds, John, aged 31, husbandman, dark. T Oct 1720 *Gilbert* LC Md May 1721. Sy.

Edmonds, John. R 14 yrs Jly TB to Va Sep 1759. Wi.

Edmunds, Mary of Newington. R for Barbados or Jamaica Feb 1690. Sy.

Edmunds, Sarah, spinster. S Norwich Summer 1766. Nf.

Edmonds, Thomas. T 5 yrs to Va Nov 1661. L.

Edmonds, Thomas. R for Jamaica Jan 1663. M.

Edmonds, Thomas. R for Barbados Dec 1683. M.

Edmonds, Thomas (1754). *See* Kelly, Edmund. Ha.

Edmonds, William. S s at Shirehampton Lent 1723. G.

Edmonds, William. S Mar 1754. L.

Edmonstone, Robert. S Summer 1742 R 14 yrs Lent 1743. Sh.

Edney, Richard of Bristol. R for Barbados Jun 1666. G.

Edridge, Elizabeth. S Feb T Apr 1742 *Bond* to Potomack. M.

Edsir, Joseph. S for manslaughter Jly 1718 to be T to Va. Ha.

Edward, Robert. T Oct 1726 *Forward*. Sy.

Edwards, Ann. S Sep-Oct T Dec 1752 *Greyhound*. M.

Edwards, Ann. S Jly T Sep 1764 *Justitia*. M.

Edwards als Jones, Ann. S Apr-May 1775. M.

Edwards, Anthony. S Lent 1761. Sy.

Edwards, Bridget wife of Philip. S May T Jly 1770 *Scarsdale*. M.

Edwards, Daniel Jr. of Farnham. SQS Jan 1751. Sy.

Edwards, David. S s clothing at Tenbury Lent 1738. Wo.

Edwards, Edward. S Oct T Dec 1724 *Rappahannock*. L.

Edwards, Edward. S Dec 1745. L.

Edwards, Edward. S Jan-Jun 1747. M.

Edwards, Edward. T Mar 1764 *Tryal*. M.

Edwards, Edward (1764). *See* Peace. M.

Edwards, Edward of St. Martin in Fields. SW & T Jan 1767 *Tryal*. M.

Edwards, Edward. S s sheep & R 14 yrs Lent 1770. G.

Edwards, Elizabeth. PT Aug 1654 R Feb 1656. M.

Edwards, Elizabeth. R for Barbados or Jamaica Oct 1694. L.

Edwards, Elizabeth. R for America Aug 1702 & to be T at her own charge or else executed. L.

Edwards, Elizabeth. S s at Caldicot Lent 1724. Mo.

Edwards als Casey, Elizabeth. S & T Apr 1725 *Sukey* LC Annapolis Sep 1725. M.

Edwards als Lareman, Elizabeth. S Apr-May T May 1744 *Justitia*. M.

Edwards, Elizabeth wife of Joseph. S Feb-Apr 1746. M.

Edwards, Elizabeth. S May-Jly 1750. M.

Edwards, George. S Lent 1742. Mo.

Edwards, George. S Mar 1764. Do.

Edwards, Henry. S Lent 1765. Wa.

Edwards, Henry. S Feb T Apr 1772 *Thornton*. L.

Edwards, James of Hereford. R for America Jly 1682. He.

Edwards, James. S Lent 1750. Su.

Edwards, Joan (1758). *See* Nowel. So.

Edwards, John of Atcham. R for America Jly 1683. Sh.

Edwards, John (2). Rebels T 1685.

Edwards, John. R for Barbados or Jamaica Oct 1694. L.

Edwards, John. S Jly T Aug 1721 *Prince Royal* LC Va Nov 1721. L.
Edwards, John (1730). *See* Lewis. Mo.
Edwards, John. S City Summer 1736. Nl.
Edwards, John. S Jly-Sep T Oct 1739 *Duke of Cumberland* to Va. M.
Edwards, John (1748). *See* Bew. M.
Edwards, John of St. John's. SQS Jan T May 1752 *Lichfield*. Sy.
Edwards, John. S s sheets at Oswestry Lent 1753. Sh.
Edwards, John. S Lent 1755. Ht.
Edwards, John. S s at Penkridge Lent 1757. St.
Edwards, John. S Mar 1765. Ha.
Edwards, John. S Apr T May 1767 *Thornton*. M.
Edwards, John. S Sep T Dec 1767 *Neptune*. L.
Edwards, John, als Howard, Edward. S Apr T Jly 1770 *Scarsdale*. M.
Edwards, John. R Summer 1773. Ht.
Edwards, John. S Sep-Oct 1774. M.
Edwards, Joseph of Evesham. R for America Mar 1683. Wo.
Edwards, Joseph. S May T Jly 1722 *Alexander* to Nevis or Jamaica. M.
Edwards, Joseph of Chelmsford. SQS Apr 1775. E.
Edwards, Margaret. R Oct 1700. M.
Edwards, Margaret. S Feb-Apr T May 1751 *Tryal*. M.
Edwards, Margaret. S Feb T Apr 1765 *Ann*. L.
Edwards, Mark. R 14 yrs Jly TB to Va Aug 1751. Wi.
Edwards als Symmes, Mary. R for Barbados Nov 1668. L.
Edwards, Mary. S & T Oct 1730 *Forward* but died on passage. M.
Edwards als Collett, Mary. S & TB Mar 1732. G.
Edwards, Mary. T Apr 1742 *Bond*. E.
Edwards, Mary. S Sep-Oct T 14 yrs Dec 1752 *Greyhound*. M.
Edwards, Mary (1753). *See* Murphy. M.
Edwards, Mary. S & T Mar 1760 *Friendship*. L.
Edwards, Mary (1761). *See* Welch, Martha. M.
Edwards, Mary. S & T Mar 1763 *Neptune*. L.
Edwards, Mary. SQS Jly T Sep 1764 *Justitia*. M.
Edwards, Mary. R Dec 1765 T 14 yrs Jan 1766 *Tryal*. M.
Edwards, Mary. S May 1768. M.
Edwards, Mary (1772). *See* Tilsey. So.
Edwards, Millicent. S Sep-Oct T 14 yrs Dec 1752 *Greyhound*. M.
Edwards, Philip. R 14 yrs Jly 1745. Ha.
Edwards, Philip. S Summer 1758 R 14 yrs Lent 1759. St.
Edwards, Richard. R 14 yrs Aug 1727 TB to Md. De.
Edwards, Richard. S Lent R Summer 1739 (SP). St.
Edwards, Richard. S Lent R 14 yrs Summer T Sep 1764 *Justitia*. Bu.
Edwards, Richard. S & T Dec 1771 *Justitia*. M.
Edwards, Robert of Cambridge. R for America Jly 1703. Ca.
Edwards, Robert. S Jan 1718 T Feb 1719 *Worcester* LC Annapolis Jun 1719. M.
Edwards, Robert. R 14 yrs Dec 1774. M.
Edwards, Rosanna. S Summer 1774 AT Lent 1775. Wa.
Edwards, Samuel. S Mar 1731 TB to Va. De.
Edwards, Samuel. S s mare Lent R 14 yrs Summer 1765. Sh.
Edwards, Sarah (1733). *See* Pugh. L.
Edwards, Stephen. TB to Va 1728. De.

Edwards, Thomas. R for Jamaica Aug 1661. M.
Edwards, Thomas of Camberwell. R for Barbados Aug 1662. Sy.
Edwards, Thomas. R for Barbados Jun 1670. M.
Edwards, Thomas. S Jan TB to Md or Va Feb 1719. L.
Edwards, Thomas. S Aug 1723. So.
Edwards, Thomas. S Feb T Mar 1727 *Rappahannock* to Md. M.
Edwards, Thomas. T Dec 1736 *Dorsetshire*. Sy.
Edwards, Thomas (1739). *See* Deane, Samuel. M.
Edwards, Thomas. S for assault at Stow Summer 1750. Mo.
Edwards, Thomas. S Summer 1756 R 14 yrs Lent 1757. Sh.
Edwards, Thomas. T 14 yrs Apr 1759 *Thetis*. E.
Edwards, Thomas. S s at Patshull Summer 1763. St.
Edwards, Thomas. S Feb T Apr 1771 *Thornton*. L.
Edwards, Thomas. S Lent 1775. Ht.
Edwards, Walter. S Mar 1740. De.
Edwards, William. Rebel T 1685.
Edwards, William, aged 19, dark. S Jan T 14 yrs Feb 1723 *Jonathan* LC
     Va Jly 1724. M.
Edwards, William. S s at Mangotsfield Summer 1723. G.
Edwards, William. S City Summer 1724 AT Summer 1725. Nl.
Edwards, William. T Oct 1724 *Forward* LC Md Jun 1725. Sy.
Edwards, William. T Nov 1725 *Rappahannock* LC Va Aug 1726. Sy.
Edwards, William. LC from *Patapsco* Annapolis Nov 1733. X.
Edwards, William. S Jan T 14 yrs Apr 1743 *Justitia*. M.
Edwards, William. S s pigs at Dormington Lent 1743. He.
Edwards, William. S Lent R 14 yrs Summer 1746. Mo.
Edwards, William. S Mar 1748. Do.
Edwards, William. S Lent R 14 yrs Summer 1751. He.
Edwards, William. S Lent R 14 yrs Summer 1757. Sh.
Edwardes, William. S Lent 1764. Wa.
Edwards, William. S Mar 1767. Do.
Edwards, William. SW & T Dec 1771 *Justitia*. M.
Edwick, Elizabeth. T Dec 1736 *Dorsetshire*. E.
Edwin, Dorothy. S Jly T Dec 1736 *Dorsetshire* to Va. M.
Edwin, Francis. T Jun 1764 *Dolphin*. Bu.
Edy. *See* Eddy.
Eeg, Hans. S Aug 1763 to be T for life. L.
Eales, Elizabeth. S Jly 1741. M.
Eeles, Mary. S Aug T Oct 1724 *Forward* to Md. M.
Eeles als Pugh, Mary. S Jly T Oct 1741 *Sea Horse* to Va. M.
Eales, Richard. S Aug 1737. Co.
Eles, Samuel. R 12 yrs Jan 1663 (SP). L.
Eeles, Samuel. R for Barbados Jan 1664. M.
Eals, Thomas. S Summer 1759 T Sep 1760 from Whitehaven. We.
Eels, William. S Jly-Sep T Oct 1739 *Duke of Cumberland* to Va. M.
Eales, William. S Jan T Feb 1744 *Neptune*. L.
Effen, Elizabeth. S Apr-Jun T Jly 1772 *Tayloe*. M.
Effoll, Thomas. R for Barbados or Jamaica Oct 1690. M.
Egan, Bernard. S Jan T Feb 1719 *Worcester* LC Annapolis Jun 1719. L.
Eagan, Catherine. S May T Nov 1759 *Phoenix*. M.
Eagan, Nicholas (1741). *See* Hogin. M.

Eagan, William. S May T Jun 1756 *Lyon*. L.

Egan, William. S & T Jan 1767 *Tryal*. M.

Egar. *See* Eager.

Edgerton, Ann wife of Thomas. S Summer 1772. Wa.

Edgerton, Ellenor. R for Barbados or Jamaica May 1691. L.

Egerton, Isaac. S May 1761. M.

Egerton, Peter. S Dec 1766 T Jan 1767 *Tryal*. M.

Egerton als Batt, Philip. S May-Jun T Aug 1752 *Tryal*. M.

Eggabear, William. R 14 yrs Jly 1758. De.

Eggborough, Edward. S s beehive Summer '761. Hu.

Eggett, Judith, spinster. S s at Garveston Lent 1769. Nf.

Eggleston, Richard. T May 1719 *Margaret*; sold to John Gaskin Md Sep 1719. E.

Egleton, William. T Apr 1768 *Thornton*. Bu.

Egley. *See* Edgley.

Eglin, John. S & T Oct 1729 *Forward* LC Va Jun 1730. M.

Eglin, Thomas. Rebel T 1685.

Eglinton, Joseph. S Apr T Oct 1720 *Gilbert*. L.

Eglington, Thomas Durrant. S s silver spoon Lent 1766. Nf.

Eglon, Robert. S Mar 1737. So.

Elber, Henry. S Dec 1774. M.

Elbitt, John. SQS Thirsk Apr 1738. Y.

Elborow, Christopher of Lyddiard Tregoose. R for Barbados Feb 1714. Wi.

Elby, Thomazin. T 14 yrs May 1719 *Margaret* LC Md May 1720; sold to Dr. Charles Carroll. Sy.

Elcombe, Eleazer of Hambledon. R for Barbados Jan 1675. Ha.

Elder, Alexander. S Jan-Feb 1775. M.

Elder, Andrew. S Dec 1774. L.

Elder, Joshua. T Sep 1766 *Justitia*. E.

Elder, William. R for Jamaica Aug 1661. L.

Elder, Worth. S Lent 1744. Su.

Elderkin, William. R for America Aug 1685. Li.

Eldersheire, John. R for America Jly 1683. Wa.

Elderton, Thomas. R Dec 1699 AT Jan 1700. M.

Eldridge, John (1714). *See* Townsend. G.

Eldridge, John. T Apr 1759 *Thetis*. Sx.

Eldridge, John. T 14 yrs Apr 1770 *New Trial*. Sy.

Eldridge, Matthew of Holy Trinity, Guildford. R for Barbados or Jamaica Feb 1690. Sy.

Eldridge, Thomas (1769). *See* Palmer. O.

Eleazer, Jacob. S for perjury Oct T 14 yrs Dec 1771 *Justitia*. L.

Element, Thomas. S Jan T Mar 1764 *Tryal*. M.

Elener Ann (1748). *See* White. M.

Eler. *See* Eller.

Elered, John. R for Barbados or Jamaica Feb 1687. L.

Eley. *See* Ely.

Elgar, Mary. S Aug T Sep 1764 *Justitia*. L.

Elgar, William. S & T Nov 1762 *Prince William*. L.

Elias, Leien. S Feb T Mar 1730 *Patapsco* LC Annapolis Sep 1730. M.

Elias, Thomas. S & T Jly 1770 *Scarsdale*. L.

Elisha, Joseph. T Apr 1725 *Sukey* LC Md Sep 1725. Sy.

Elkin, John. SQS Sep 1768 T Jan 1769 *Thornton*. M.

Elkington, Thomas (1736). *See* Brown. Be.

Elkins, James. S s nails & T Sep 1757 *Thetis*. M.

Elkins, Mary wife of William, als wife of John Wood. S Apr T Sep 1757 *Thetis*. M.

Ellacott, John. S Mar 1743. De.

Ellam, James. R 14 yrs Summer 1754. Y.

Elam, John. S s at Abingdon Lent R 14 yrs Summer 1745. Be.

Ellam, Michael. LC from *Patapsco* Annapolis Nov 1733. X.

Ellard, Samuel. S Apr-May T May 1741 *Catherine & Elizabeth* to Md. M.

Ellard, Saul. S s at Runcton Summer 1771. Nf.

Elcocke, Edward. R for Barbados May 1665. X.

Ellcock, John. S Lent 1755. Wo.

Elcock, Robert. S Lent 1740. Y.

Ellen, Margaret. S & T Jan 1722 *Gilbert* LC Annapolis Jly 1722. M.

Eler, Ann (1754). *See* Brown. M.

Eller, Mary. S Jan T Feb 1724 *Anne*. L.

Ellerbeck, George of Tottington Higher End. SQS for false pretences Jan 1773. La.

Ellershaw, Thomas (1767). *See* Ellishey. Su.

Ellerthorpe, Richard. AT Lent T Oct 1723 *Forward* to Va from London. Y.

Ellerton, John. S s horse Summer 1767 R 14 yrs Summer 1768. Nl.

Ellery, John. R Mar 1773. So.

Elletson als Inman, William. S Lent R 14 yrs Summer 1755. St.

Ellett, Francis. R for Barbados Jly 1674. M.

Ellett, Lewis. S Jly T Aug 1721 *Prince Royal* LC Va Nov 1721. M.

Ellett, Robert. S Mar 1733. De.

Ellford, James (12). Rebels T 1685.

Elford, John (1728). *See* Edgecomb. De.

Elford, Mary. S Feb T Apr 1743 *Justitia*. M.

Ellford, William (1753). *See* Edgele. M.

Ellgood, Christopher of Stebbing. SQS Apr 1754. E.

Elliard, James. S Lent 1741. O.

Ellicks, John. S Oct T Dec 1724 *Rappahannock*. L.

Elligoe, William of Greetham. R for America Feb 1713. Ru.

Ellinger, Israel. S Mar 1757. Ha.

Ellingworth, Thomas (1766). *See* Illingworth. Y.

Ellinor, Thomas of Wilby. R for America Feb 1695. Nf.

Ellyott, Ambrose. S s cow Summer 1749 R 14 yrs Lent 1750. Li.

Elliott, Christopher. S Jan T Feb 1726 *Supply* LC Annapolis May 1726. L.

Elliott, Cornelius. Rebel T 1685.

Elliot, Edmund. T Apr 1768 *Thornton*. Sx.

Elliott, Edward. R for America Aug 1715. L.

Elliot, Edward (Edmond). S Aug T Sep 1725 *Forward* LC Annapolis May 1726. L.

Elliot, Eleanor. S Apr-Jun T Jly 1772 *Tayloe*. M.

Elliott, Enoch. S Lent 1775. Wa.

Elliott, George of Helay in Swaledale. R for Barbados Jly 1685. Y.
Elliott, James of Wisley or Send. S for highway robbery Lent R 14 yrs Summer T Oct 1750 *Rachael*. Sy.
Elliot, John. TB Aug 1738. Y.
Elliott, John. S Jan T Apr 1762 *Dolphin*. L.
Elliott, John. R 14 yrs Aug 1764. De.
Elliott, John of St. Olave, Southwark. SQS & T Jan 1769 *Thornton*. Sy.
Eliot, Joseph. S Aug T Oct 1741 *Sea Horse* to Va. M.
Elliott, Martha. TB to Va from QS 1740. De.
Elliott, Martha. S Dec 1762 T Mar 1763 *Neptune*. M.
Elliott, Mary of St. James, Westminster, spinster. S s shirt & T Feb 1740 *York* to Md. M.
Elliott, Mary. R 14 yrs City Summer 1754. Su.
Elliott, Matthew. Rebel T 1685.
Elliott, Nathaniel. S Lent 1770. G.
Elliott, Richard. SQS Oct 1735 TB to Md Jan 1736. So.
Elliott, Richard. S Apr T May 1750 *Lichfield*. M.
Elliott, Robert. S Jly T 14 yrs Sep 1766 *Justitia*. M.
Elliott, Samuel. S Jun-Dec 1738 T Jan 1739 *Dorsetshire* to Va. M.
Elliott, Samuel. S Sep T Dec 1767 *Neptune*. L.
Elliott, Sarah wife of Thomas. S s apron Dec 1735 T Jan 1736 *Dorsetshire*. M.
Ellyott, Silvester. S to House of Correction unless he consents to be transported Oct 1661. M.
Elliott, Thomas of York City. R for Barbados Jly 1701. Y.
Elliott, Thomas. SQS Jly TB Aug 1754. So.
Elliott, Thomas. S Lent 1775. Sy.
Elliott, William. T May 1737 *Forward*. Sx.
Elliott, William. S Oct 1751-Jan 1752. M.
Elliott, William. S s mare at Caldbeck & R Summer 1771; S for being at large & R Summer 1773. Cu.
Elliott, William. S Summer 1772. Db.
Ellis, Ann wife of Edward. S Summer 1749 R 14 yrs Lent TB Mar 1750. G.
Ellis, Ann. R Sep-Oct T for life Dec 1753 *Whiteing*. M.
Ellis, Ann wife of Robert. S 14 yrs s from bleaching ground at Diss Summer 1773. Nf.
Ellis, Christopher. R 14 yrs Mar 1762 TB to Va. De.
Ellis, Edward. S Oct 1764 T Jan 1765 *Tryal*. M.
Ellis, Elizabeth. S May-Jly 1746. M.
Ellis, Elizabeth. S May T Jun 1756 *Lyon*. L.
Ellis, Elizabeth. S Jan-Feb 1775. M.
Ellis, George. R 14 yrs Jly 1752. De.
Ellis, George of Rotherhithe. SQS Apr 1774. Sy.
Ellis, Isabel. S 14 yrs for receiving Summer 1741. Y.
Ellys, James. S Jan-Feb T Apr 1753 *Thames*. M.
Ellis, Jane. S Oct 1747. L.
Ellis, Jeffery. S Mar 1728. Co.
Ellis, Joane of Newland. R for America Jly 1699. G.
Ellis, John. S Jly T Sep 1718 *Eagle* LC Charles Town Mar 1719. L.
Ellis, John. T Aug 1720 *Owners Goodwill*. K.

Ellis, John. S Feb T Mar 1731 *Patapsco* LC Annapolis Jun 1731. L.
Ellis, John. S Summer 1737. Nf.
Ellis, John. S Summer 1741. Y.
Ellis, John. S Summer 1754 T May 1755 *Rose*. K.
Ellis, John. SQS Dec 1763 T Mar 1764 *Tryal*. M.
Ellis, John (1766). *See* Elley. Nt.
Ellis, John. T 14 yrs Sep 1767 *Justitia*. Sy.
Ellis, John. S 14 yrs for receiving stolen goods from Robert Creswell *(qv)*
    Lent 1775. Su.
Ellis, Joseph. S Aug 1731 TB to Va. De.
Ellis, Joseph. TB Apr 1774. Nt.
Ellis, Margaret of St. Giles in Fields, widow. S 14 yrs for receiving
    stockings & T Jan 1740 *York* to Md. M.
Ellis, Mary, widow. R for America Aug 1685. Le.
Ellis, Mary. LC from *Forward* Annapolis Jun 1725. X.
Ellis, Mary. S s at Goodrich Lent 1762. He.
Ellis, Mary. S Apr T Jun 1768 *Tryal*. M.
Ellis, Matthias. TB to Va from QS 1735. De.
Ellis, Richard. S Lent R 14 yrs Summer 1733. Y.
Ellis, Richard. SWK Oct 1768 T Jan 1769 *Thornton*. K.
Ellis, Robert. S s horse Lent 1719 R 14 yrs Summer 1721 T Oct 1723
    Forward from London. Y.
Ellis als Horston, Robert. S s mare at Woolstone Lent R 14 yrs Summer
    TB Jly 1744. G.
Ellis, Roger. S Mar 1724. So.
Ellis, Sarah. SQS & T Dec 1758 *The Brothers*. Ht.
Ellis, Sarah. S Apr T Jly 1770 *Scarsdale*. M.
Ellis, Thomas, als Holmes, Matthew. S s oxen Lent 1738. Y.
Ellis als Botman, Thomas. R 14 yrs Summer 1748. Y.
Ellis, Thomas. S s breeches at Whittington Lent 1766. Sh.
Ellis, Thomas of Eakering. SQS East Retford s clothing Jan TB Apr
    1774. Nt.
Ellis, Thomas. S Dec 1774. M.
Ellis, Walter. S Mar 1724. Do.
Ellis, William. R for America Jly 1674. Db.
Ellis, William. S s at Hartlebury Summer 1756. Wo.
Ellis, William. S Jly 1760 TB to Va 1761. De.
Ellis, William. T Apr 1768 *Thornton*. Sy.
Ellishey als Ellershaw, Thomas of Garstang, butcher. S s sheep Lent R
    14 yrs Summer 1767. La.
Ellison, Ann. S Oct 1756. L.
Ellison, John. S for forgery Summer 1751 R 14 yrs Lent 1752. La.
Ellmer, John. S s cow & R Summer 1775. Y.
Ellon, William. SQS s shirts Easter 1775. Du.
Ellott, Ann. S s at Langley Summer TB Jly 1763. Db.
Ellott, John of Tronghead. R for Barbados Jun 1675. Cu.
Elms, Edward. T Nov 1725 *Rappahannock*. K.
Elmes, Elizabeth. S Jly-Sep T Sep 1742 *Forward*. M.
Elmes, Mary. R for Barbados May 1664. M.
Elmes, Robert. T Oct 1722 *Forward*. Sx.
Elms, Samuel. S Dec 1733. L.

Elmes, Thomas. S Jly T 14 yrs Aug 1721 *Prince Royal* LC Va Nov 1721. M.

Elmore, Margaret wife of Samuel. S Jan T Feb 1744 *Neptune* to Md. M.

Eylmore, Symon. TB 14 yrs Oct 1719 T *Susannah & Sarah* LC Annapolis Apr 1720. L.

Ellmore, Thomas. T 14 yrs May 1719 *Margaret* LC Md May 1720; sold to Ambrose Nealson. Sy.

Elphy, Joseph. T Dec 1731 *Forward*. K.

Elps, Aaron. S Jly 1720 to be T to Boston NE. Wi.

Elry, John. S s handkerchief at St. Lawrence Jewry Apr T Jun 1768 *Tryal*. L.

Elsden, Benjamin. S s pig at Leiston Lent 1772. Su.

Elsden, John. R 14 yrs Summer 1752. Su.

Elsdon als Elzin, William als Thomas. S Summer 1740; S & R 14 yrs Summer 1748; found at large Summer 1751 & ordered to be transported for remainder of his term. Nf.

Elsigood, William S Norwich Summer 1748. Nf.

Elsegood, William. S Jan-Apr 1749. M.

Elsey, John of St. Sepulchre. S s lead & T May 1740 *Essex* to Md or Va. M.

Elsey, John. S Jly 1741. Ha.

Ellsey, Nicholas. S May-Jun T Jly 1753 *Tryal*. M.

Elsey, Thomas. S s shirt Oct T Dec 1736 *Dorsetshire* to Va. M.

Elsey, Thomas. S Summer 1741 R 14 yrs Lent 1742. Li.

Elsey, William. S 14 yrs Jly 1741. Ha.

Ellsmore, Edward. S Jan-May T Jun 1738 *Forward* to Md or Va. M.

Elsmore, John of Longhope. R for America Jly 1696. G.

Elsmore, Mary. R for Barbados Oct 1673. L.

Ellesmore, William. S s at Walsall Summer 1773. St.

Elsome, Robert. LC from *Supply* Annapolis May 1726. X.

Elsome, William of Welby. R for America Jly 1716. Li.

Elson, Henry. R Lent 1775. Sy.

Elster, William. S Summer 1751. Hu.

Elston, Matthew. SQS Jly TB Aug 1738. Nt.

Elstone, Robert of Crediton. R for Barbados Jly 1683. De.

Elstop, John. S Mar 1721 T from Portsmouth 1723. Ha.

Elsworth, Sarah. S Lent 1721 T Oct 1723 *Forward* to Va from London. Y.

Elt, John of Whiteladies Aston. R for America Jly 1691. Wo.

Eltham, Henry. S 14 yrs Summer 1775. K.

Eltoft, William. S City Summer 1736. Y.

Elton, Joseph of Newent, blacksmith. R for America Jly 1699. G.

Elton als Reynolds, Martha. R for America Aug 1702 & to be transported at her own charge or else executed. L.

Elton als Halton, Thomas. S s horse Lent R 14 yrs Summer 1766. Sh.

Elton, William. S Feb T 14 yrs Apr 1741 *Speedwell* or *Mediterranean*. M.

Elvidge, George of Snenton, boatman. SQS s wine Oct 1762. Nt.

Elwand, Alan of Slowby. R for America Jly 1673. Li.

Elwell, Ann. R 14 yrs Lent 1721. St.

Elwin als Jones, Ann. S Jan T 14 yrs Apr 1741 *Speedwell*. L.

Ellwood als Bable, Ann. S May T 14 yrs Jun 1726 *Loyal Margaret*. M.

Elwood als Cook, Ann. S Sep T Dec 1734 *Caesar* LC Va Jly 1735. M.

Ellwood, Hester. S & T Dec 1731 *Forward* to Md or Va. M.
Elwood, John. S Jan T Feb 1726 *Supply* LC Annapolis May 1726. M.
Ellwood, John. S Sep T Dec 1769 *Justitia*. M.
Elwood, William of Dereham. R for Barbados Aug 1671. Nf.
Elworthy, Elizabeth wife of Simon *(qv)*, als Locke, of Bermondsey. SQS
    Mar 1754. Sy.
Ellworthy, Robert of Chulmleigh, weaver. R for Barbados Jly 1693. De.
Elworthy, Samuel. Rebel T 1685.
Ealey, Easter. SW & T Jan 1769 *Thornton*. M.
Eley, Elizabeth. T May 1719 *Margaret*. Sy.
Ely, John. S Jly TB to Va Sep 1756. Wi.
Elley als Ellis, John. S Summer 1768. Nt.
Ely, William of All Commons. R for Barbados Jly 1681. Wi.
Eley, William. R for America Jly 1686. Li.
Eley, William. R for Barbados or Jamaica Mar 1688. L.
Ealey als Keeley, William. S & T Sep 1765 *Thornton*. M.
Elzin, William (1740 & 1748). *See* Eldson. Nf.
Emanell, John (1737). *See* Place. M.
Emanuel, Aaron. S Apr T Jly 1770 *Scarsdale*. L.
Emanuel, Ralph. S Dec 1774. L.
Emanuel, Samuel. S Jly 1775. M.
Emberson, John. S 14 yrs s from bleaching ground at Yaxley Summer
    1771; wife Sarah acquitted. Hu.
Emblen, James. S Oct 1761. L.
Embling, John. S Dec 1743 T Feb 1744 *Neptune* to Md. M.
Emmerson, Ann. S Sep-Oct 1775. M.
Emmerson, Charles (1735). *See* Amison. St.
Emerson, Francis (1724). *See* Stewart, James. M.
Emerson, Henry of Garbich Thorne *(sic)*. R for America Feb 1695. Nf.
Emmerson, Henry of St. Saviour, Southwark. SQS Nov T Dec 1753
    Whiteing. Sy.
Emerson, Jane. S Summer 1728. Y.
Emerson als Maughan, John of Newcastle upon Tyne. R for Barbados
    Jly 1705. Nl.
Emerson, Mary. S Feb T Mar 1730 *Patapsco* LC Annapolis Sep 1730. L.
Emmerson, Ralph of Barnard Castle. R for Barbados Jly 1698. Su.
Emerson, Thomas. T Dec 1731 *Forward*. Sy.
Emerton, Ann of Bermondsey. R for Barbados or Jamaica Feb 1684. Sy.
Emerton, Frances. S & T Oct 1732 *Caesar*. L.
Emmery, Arthur. S Jly-Sep 1739. M.
Emery, George. S Lent 1747. *Bd.
Emery, Henry. S Sep T 14 yrs Oct 1720 *Gilbert*. L.
Emery, Isaac. S Dec 1733 T Jan 1734 *Caesar* LC Va Jly 1734. M.
Emery, John. T Oct 1722 *Forward* LC Md Jun 1723. Sx.
Emmery, John. SW & T Dec 1769 *Justitia*. M.
Emery, Margery. R Sep 1671 AT Jly 1672 & Oct 1673. M.
Emery, Mary. S Lent TB Sep 1759. Y.
Emes. *See* Eames.
Emley, George. S & T Sep 1731 *Smith* to Va. M.
Emley, John. S & T Sep 1731 *Smith* LC Va 1732. M.
Emley, Mary of Hawkesbury. R for America Mar 1682. G.

Emlyn, Mary. SQS Jan TB Apr 1763. So.
Emmerston, Charles (1735). *See* Amison. St.
Emmett als Russell als Wilkinson, Eleanor. S Jly 1722. So.
Emitt, George. R Oct AT Dec 1688. M.
Emett, John. S Mar 1737. Wi.
Emmett, Nathaniel. SQS Jly 1734. So.
Emmet, Richard. S & T Jly 1771 *Scarsdale*. M.
Emmott, William. S Dec 1753-Jan 1754. M.
Emms, Abraham of Tottington. R for America Jun 1714. Nf.
Emms, Henry. S Lent R 14 yrs Summer 1727. G.
Emms, John. S Lent 1747. Nf.
Emms, Susanna. S Jly-Sep T Sep 1742 *Forward*. M.
Emms, William. S s mare Lent R 14 yrs Summer 1744. Su.
Emon, David. S Apr-May 1775. M.
Empson, Daniel. SQS & T Dec 1767 *Neptune*. M.
Empson, William. S Lent R 14 yrs Summer 1726. St.
Emroe, Christopher. SQS Apr T May 1752 *Lichfield*. M.
Emsden, William. S Lent 1750. Su.
Emtage, John. S Jun-Dec 1745. M.
End, William of Winchcombe, yeoman. R for America Feb 1713. G.
Endacott als Potter, Ann. S Mar 1760 TB to Va. De.
Endacott, Elizabeth. TB to Va from QS 1767. De.
Endersby, Thomas. S Feb-Apr T May 1752 *Lichfield*. M.
Endich, Mary. S for murdering a bastard child Lent 1724 R 14 yrs Lent 1729. Y.
Ends, Elizabeth. S Mar TB Sep 1728. Wi.
Endsor, Edward. S & T Jun 1756 *Lyon*. M.
England, Allen. Rebel T 1685.
England, Charles. R Aug 1775. So.
England, David. S Summer TB Aug 1760. Y.
England, Elizabeth. S Jan T Apr 1759 *Thetis*. M.
England, Elizabeth. T Apr 1762 *Neptune*. Sy.
England, George. R 14 yrs Aug 1762. So.
England, Isaac. TB to Va 1770. De.
England, John. Rebel T 1685.
England, John. R 14 yrs s horse Summer 1721. No.
England, John. S Aug T Sep 1725 *Forward* LC Annapolis Dec 1725. M.
England, John. S Jun 1739. L.
England, Philip. Rebel T 1685.
England, Richard of Littleham, husbandman. R for Barbados Apr 1668. De.
England, Thomas. Rebel T 1685.
England, William. Rebel T 1685.
Engledon, William. S Sep T Oct 1768 *Justitia*. M.
Engleton, Christopher (1730). *See* Ingleton. L.
English, Christian of St. Saviour, Southwark. SQS 14 yrs Oct T Dec 1763 *Neptune*. Sy.
English, Elizabeth (1756). *See* Ward. M.
English, George. S Aug T Sep 1725 *Forward* LC Annapolis Dec 1725. L.
English, James of Diss. S Summer 1731. *Nf.
English, James. T May 1737 *Forward*. K.

English, Jane. AT City Summer 1759. Nl.

English, John. S for ravishing Mary Woolard, spinster, Lent R 14 yrs Summer 1754. Su.

English, Mary. S Dec 1765 T 14 yrs Jan 1766 *Tryal*. M.

English, Rebecca. S Jan-Jun T Jun 1728 *Elizabeth* LC Potomack Aug 1729. M.

Inglish, Sarah. S Apr-May T May 1744 *Justitia*. M.

English, William. S for highway robbery Summer 1729 R 14 yrs Lent 1730. G.

English, William. S Jly 1763. M.

Enman als Eaman, Thomas Henry. S s horse at Coxwold & R for life Lent TB Aug 1771. Y.

Ennis. *See* Innis.

Enoch, William. S s poultry Apr T Jun 1768 *Tryal*. M.

Enos, Richard. PT Sep 1684 R Mar 1685. M.

Enstead, William. S Apr T May 1750 *Lichfield*. M.

Entwistle, Edmund. S Summer 1749 R 14 yrs Lent 1750. La.

Entwisle, Thomas. R 14 yrs Summer 1751. Y.

Enwood, John. S Oct 1773. L.

Enwood, Mary. S Feb-Apr 1746. M.

Eoy, Thomas. T Apr 1741 *Speedwell* or *Mediterranean*. Ht.

Epelby. *See* Appleby.

Eppingstall, John. S Lent 1775. E.

Erby, Elizabeth. R for America Feb 1683. Nt.

Erick, Hans. S Sep T Dec 1763 *Neptune*. M.

Erith, Jeffery of Belchamp St. Paul, victualler. SQS Jan T Apr 1759 *Thetis*. E.

Erkeen, Thomas. S & T Sep 1765 *Justitia*. M.

Erouselle, Philip. S Jun T Aug 1769 *Douglas*. L.

Erskine als Maxwell als Hamilton, Thomas. S Jan-Feb T Apr 1771 *Thornton*. M.

Erskine, Thomas. SQS Sep 1773. M.

Ervin, John. Rebel T 1685.

Erwin. *See* Irwin.

Esbury als Eddows als Eddoways, Thomas. S Sep T Dec 1734 *Caesar* but died on passage. M.

Escott, Mary, widow. SQS Apr TB Aug 1749. So.

Esden, Richard. R for Barbados May 1665. X.

Esling, Samuel. T Jun 1727 *Susanna*. Sy.

Espin, George of Nottingham. R for America Jly 1678. Nt.

Espin, John of Nottingham. R for America Jly 1678. Nt.

Essex, Richard. S for highway robbery at Shalstone & R Summer 1772. Bu.

Essex, William (1753). *See* Williams. M.

Esthers, Sarah of St. Saviour, Southwark, spinster. SQS Apr T May 1750 *Lichfield*. Sy.

Etheridge, Sarah. S May-Jly 1773. M.

Etheridge, Thomas. S & T 14 yrs Oct 1722 *Forward* LC Annapolis Jun 1723. M.

Etteridge, Thomas. S Jly T Sep 1764 *Justitia*. M.

Etherington, John. S s at Cheadle Lent 1764. St.

Etherington, Mary. SQS s handkerchief Oct 1758. Du.
Etherington, Richard. R (Home Circ) for Barbados Apr 1663. X.
Etherington, Terence. S & T Jly 1771 *Scarsdale*. M.
Etherington, William. T Apr 1741 *Speedwell* or *Mediterranean*. Sy.
Eustise, Christopher. S Summer 1724 R Summer TB to Md Jly
    1725. Db.
Eustace, Mary. S Oct 1724. M.
Eustace, Maurice. S for highway robbery Lent R 14 yrs Summer
    1725. Be.
Eustice, Thomas. S Oct 1774. L.
Evan, Jane. S s at Mynyddisluyn Lent 1757. Mo.
Evans, Alice. S Feb T Mar 1731 *Patapsco* LC Annapolis Jun 1731. M.
Evans, Ann. S Apr 1734. M.
Evans, Ann. S for receiving silver mug Feb T May 1736 *Patapsco*. M.
Evans, Anne. S Jly T Oct 1741 *Sea Horse*. L.
Evans, Benjamin. S s handkerchief at St. Mary at Hill Apr T Jun 1768
    Tryal. L.
Evans, Catherine. S Feb-Apr 1746 to be T 14 yrs. M.
Evans, Catherine. S & T Jly 1772 *Tayloe*. M.
Evans, Charles. R Jly 1773. M.
Evans, Charles. R for Barbados Mar 1683. M.
Evans, Charles Abraham of Hammersmith. S Sep 1740. M.
Evans, David. S s hats at Burford Summer 1738. O.
Evans, David. S Summer 1740. Ch.
Evans, Dorothy. T May 1752 *Lichfield*. L.
Evans, Edward. R & TB to Barbados Oct 1667. L.
Evans, Edward. S Feb T Apr 1732 *Patapsco* LC Annapolis Oct 1732. M.
Evans, Edward. S Mar 1733. De.
Evans, Edward. S Dec 1750. L.
Evans, Edward. S Summer T Sep 1751 *Greyhound*. Bu.
Evans, Edward. S s mare at Bridgnorth & R 14 yrs Summer 1770. Sh.
Evans, Edward. S & T Dec 1771 *Justitia*. L.
Evans, Elianor of Bromsgrove. R for America Sep 1671. Wo.
Evans, Elianor (1745). *See* Davies. Sh.
Evans, Eliza wife of Edward. S Lent R 14 yrs Summer 1765 for being at
    large after QS sentence in 1763. Sh.
Evans, Elizabeth. R Mar 1677 & May 1678. M.
Evans, Elizabeth. R Dec 1716 T Jan 1717 *Queen Elizabeth*. M.
Evans, Elizabeth. S Jly 1720. M.
Evans, Elizabeth. S Dec 1727. L.
Evans, Elizabeth. S & T Apr 1733 *Patapsco* LC Annapolis Nov 1733. M.
Evans, Elizabeth wife of Richard. S Dec 1756. M.
Evans, Elizabeth wife of John. S s at Kinnersley Lent 1757. Sh.
Evans, Elizabeth of St. John's, widow. SQS Mar T Apr 1768
    Thornton. Sy.
Evans, Elizabeth. S & T Apr 1769 *Tryal*. L.
Evans, Elizabeth. SQS Dec 1772. M.
Evans, Evan of Broseley. R for America Jly 1686. Sh.
Evans, Evan of Camberwell. SQS for grand larceny Oct T Dec 1769
    Justitia. Sy.

Evans, Evey als Evan. S Jun T Nov 1743 *George William* or Dec 1743 *Neptune*. M.
Evans, Francis. T Sep 1730 *Smith*. Sy.
Evans, George. T for life Dec 1771 *Justitia*. Sy.
Evans, Griffith. S s handkerchiefs at Abergavenny Lent 1726. Mo.
Evans, Griffith. S Lent 1730. Sh.
Evans, Griffith. S s saddle at Bridgenorth Lent 1739. Sh.
Evans, Henry. T Sep 1730 *Smith*. E.
Evans, Henry. SQS Devizes & TB to Va Apr 1754. Wi.
Evans, Henry of St. Margaret, Westminster. SW Apr 1774. M.
Evans, James. S Apr T May 1719 *Margaret*; sold to William Jones Md Aug 1719. L.
Evans, James. T Jly 1722 *Alexander*. Sy.
Evans, James. S Jan 1740. L.
Evans, James. S s at Cholsey Lent 1743. Be.
Evans, James. S Feb 1754. M.
Evans, James. SQS Sep T Dec 1771 *Justitia*. M.
Evans, Jane. R for America Feb 1700. Wa.
Evans, Jane. R for America Aug 1715. L.
Evans, Jane. S May T Jly 1722 *Alexander* to Nevis or Jamaica. M.
Evans, Jane of Newport Pagnell, spinster. S s tablecloth Lent T Apr 1739 *Forward*. Bu.
Evans, Jane. S Jan-Apr 1748. M.
Evans, Jenkin. S s clothing Dec 1735. M.
Evans, Job. T Jly 1724 *Robert* LC Md Jun 1725. Sy.
Evans, John. R for America Aug 1685. No.
Evans, John of Cadbury. R for Barbados Dec 1686. De.
Evans, John. R for America Jly 1688. Wa.
Evans, John. S Aug 1720. So.
Evans, John. S May T Jun 1727 *Susanna*. L.
Evans, John. S Summer 1727 R 14 yrs Summer 1728. G.
Evans, John. S s at Trelleck Grange Summer 1736. Mo.
Evans, John. S Dec 1748 T Jan 1749 *Laura*. M.
Evans, John. S s horse Lent R 14 yrs Summer 1750. Mo.
Evans, John. SQS Jly 1750. M.
Evans, John. S & T Apr 1753 *Thames*. L.
Evans, John. S Lent R 14 yrs Summer 1755. Wo.
Evans, John. S Oct 1756. L.
Evans, John. S & R 14 yrs Apr 1759. Fl.
Evans, John. R 14 yrs Jun 1761. Ha.
Evans, John. S Oct T Dec 1763 *Neptune*. M.
Evans als Fox, John. R 14 yrs s horse Summer 1764. Y.
Evans, John. S & T Apr 1765 *Ann*. L.
Evans als Harris, John. S Dec 1765 T Jan 1766 *Tryal*. M.
Evans, John. S Feb T Apr 1766 *Ann*; apprehended at Dudley, Worcs, & hanged in 1768. M.
Evans, John. SQS Jun T Sep 1766 *Justitia*. M.
Evans, John. R 14 yrs Aug TB to Va Sep 1767. Wi.
Evans, John. S s mare & R 14 yrs Lent 1769. Sh.
Evans als Burges, John. S s pigs at Enville Lent 1773. St.
Evans, John. S Summer 1775. K.

Evans als Jostler, Joseph. S Lent R 14 yrs Summer 1742. St.

Evans, Joseph. S Summer 1749. E.

Evans, Lewis of Higham, husbandman. R for Barbados Sep 1665. So.

Evans, Margaret. R 14 yrs Jly 1733. Ha.

Evans, Margaret (1753). *See* Griffith. Sh.

Evans, Mary. S Feb T Apr 1739 *Forward* to Va. M.

Evans, Mary of St. John Evangelist, spinster. S s Oct 1740 T Jan 1741
Harpooner. M.

Evans, Mary. S Jly T Oct 1741 *Sea Horse* to Va. M.

Evans, Mary (1751). *See* Pitt. M.

Evans, Mary wife of John. S 14 yrs for receiving Lent 1769. Sh.

Evans, Mary Jane. S & T Jan 1766 *Tryal*. M.

Evans, Matthew. R for Barbados May 1665. X.

Evans, Morgan. R for Jamaica Aug 1661. M.

Evans, Morrice. S Summer 1751 R 14 yrs Lent TB Mar 1752. G.

Evans, Morris. T Jan 1765 *Tryal*. M.

Evans, Patrick. S Apr T Oct 1719 *Susannah & Sarah* LC Annapolis
Apr 1720. L.

Evans, Philip. S Jun T Sep 1764 *Justitia*. M.

Evans, Richard of Pontesbury. R for America Sep 1671. Sh.

Evans, Richard of Layton. R for Barbados or Jamaica Jun 1675 & Jly
1677. E.

Evans, Richard. S May T Jly 1723 *Alexander* LC Annapolis Sep 1723. L.

Evans, Richard. S Oct 1727-June 1728 T Jun 1728 *Elizabeth* LC
Potomack Aug 1729. M.

Evans, Richard of Christchurch. S s hat Oct 1740 T Jan 1741
Harpooner. M.

Evans, Richard. S & R 14 yrs Summer 1774. Sh.

Evans, Robert. R for Barbados or Jamaica Dec 1689. M.

Evans, Robert. T Dec 1734 *Caesar*. Bu.

Evans, Robert. S s iron at Kempston Hardwick (Beds) Summer 1758. G.

Evans, Robert. S Jan T Mar 1764 *Tryal*. L.

Evans, Samuel. S Jly-Dec 1747. M.

Evans, Samuel. S s hops at St. Nicholas, Worcester, Lent 1772. Wo.

Evans, Samuel. S s cloth at Rodborough Lent 1773. G.

Evans, Sarah. S May-Jly 1749. M.

Evans, Simon. S s handkerchief Sep T Dec 1736 *Dorsetshire* to Va. M.

Evans, Susanna (1722). *See* Morgan. M.

Evans, Susanna. S Apr 1756. So.

Evans, Susannah. T Oct 1768 *Dorsetshire*. Sx.

Evans, Thomas (1718). *See* Byrch. He.

Evans, Thomas. T Nov 1728 *Forward*. Bu.

Evans, Thomas als Matthew. S s horse Summer 1733 R 14 yrs Summer
1734. Wo.

Evans, Thomas. S & T May 1744 *Justitia*. L.

Evans, Thomas. S s at Bridgnorth Lent 1750. He.

Evans, Thomas. S s horse Lent R 14 yrs Summer 1752. Nt.

Evans, Thomas. R 14 yrs Summer 1754. Y.

Evans, Thomas. S s silver spoon at Oswestry Summer 1755. Sh.

Evans, Thomas. T 14 yrs Apr 1762 *Neptune*. K.

Eavans, Thomas (1764). *See* Bird. Y.

Evans, Thomas. S s silver watch at Old Swinford Lent 1764. Wo.
Evans, Thomas. S Apr-May 1775. M.
Evans, Timothy. S Lent R 14 yrs Summer 1724. G.
Evans, Timothy. S Jan T Mar 1750 *Tryal*. L.
Evans, William (1666). *See* Ewens. De.
Evans, William. R Oct 1694 AT Jan 1695. M.
Evans, William. S Sep T Oct 1719 *Susannah & Sarah* LC Annapolis
  Apr 1720. L.
Evans, William. S Lent 1742. Ch.
Evans, William. LC from *Shaw* Antigua May 1743. Db.
Evans, William. T May 1744 *Justitia*. E.
Evans, William. S Feb T Mar 1750 *Tryal*. M.
Evans, William. S for highway robbery Lent R 14 yrs Summer 1750. Wa.
Evans, William of St. George, Southwark. SQS Jan T Mar 1764
  Tryal. Sy.
Evans, William. S Sep-Oct 1772. M.
Evans, William (1773). *See* Blaney. M.
Evans als Hamilton, William. S & R 14 yrs Summer 1774. St.
Evans, William. S s sheep & R 14 yrs Summer 1775. St.
Evans, William Rixton. S s sheep & R 14 yrs Summer 1774. He.
Evans, Winifred. S Oct T Nov 1725 *Rappahannock* but died on
  passage. M.
Evanson, Thomas. S s at Barrow Summer 1768. Sh.
Evett, Elizabeth. S Apr-Jun 1739. M.
Evatt, Henry. S & T Oct 1729 *Forward* but died on passage. L.
Evatt, Mary (1746). *See* Pidgeon. M.
Eve, Hesther. S for murder of her bastard child Summer 1729 R 14 yrs
  Summer 1730. Li.
Eve, John. S for ripping lead from a house Sep 1756. M.
Evea, Jane. S Jan T Apr 1743 *Justitia*. M.
Evedall, Richard (1673). *See* Udall. L.
Eveleigh, John. TB to Va 1768. De.
Evelin, Thomas. R for Barbados Jun 1671. M.
Everard, Arthur. Rebel T 1685.
Everell, James. S City Summer 1756. Nl.
Everitt als Everill, Andrew. S Lent 1749. Ht.
Everitt, Elizabeth (1749). *See* Oldham. Li.
Everett, James. S Sep T Oct 1744 *Susannah*. L.
Everett, James. S & T Apr 1766 *Ann*. L.
Everett, James. S Lent 1775. E.
Everett, John. T May 1719 *Margaret* but died on passage. Ht.
Everet, John. S s at Oswestry Summer 1727. Sh.
Everett, John. S Feb T Mar 1729 *Patapsco* LC Annapolis Dec 1729. M.
Everett, John. S & T Dec 1731 *Forward*. L.
Everett als Wright, John. SQS Feb T Apr 1766 *Ann*. M.
Everett, Joseph (1744). *See* Rugles. Su.
Everett, Joseph. R 14 yrs Jly 1774. M.
Everett, Robert. S & T Oct 1730 *Forward* LC Potomack Jan 1731. M.
Everitt, William (1749). *See* Oldham. Li.
Everet, William. S Apr 1756. So.
Everett, William. S Dec 1761 T Apr 1762 *Dolphin*. M.

Everill, Andrew (1749). *See* Everitt. Ht.
Everin, Richard. T Nov 1728 *Forward*. Bu.
Evers, Marmaduke. S s at Heworth Lent TB Aug 1755. Y.
Evershett, Thomas. S Jan T Feb 1733 *Smith* to Md or Va. M.
Everton, Job (1757). *See* Overton. Wa.
Every. *See* Avery. M.
Eaves, Ann. S Jly 1736. M.
Eves, Edward. Rebel T 1685.
Eaves, Edward. S s sheep & R 7 yrs Lent 1772. Wa.
Eves, John. T Nov 1759 *Phoenix*. E.
Eves, Joseph. S & T Oct 1732 *Caesar*. L.
Eves, Richard. S Dec 1745. L.
Eves, William. S & T Sep 1751 *Greyhound*. M.
Evins, Henry. T Apr 1770 *New Trial*. E.
Evins, Richard. R for Barbados Oct 1673. L.
Ewdall. *See* Udall.
Ewin, John. S Lent 1746. *Nf.
Ewin, John. S Apr 1761. M.
Ewen, John. SQS Oct T Dec 1767 *Neptune*. M.
Ewin, Richard. SQS Mar TB May 1739. Nt.
Ewen, Robert. R 14 yrs Jly 1744. Ha.
Ewing, Samuel. R 14 yrs Mar 1742. Do.
Ewen, Sarah. PT Jan 1680. M.
Ewen, William. T Jan 1736 *Dorsetshire*. Sx.
Ewens, John. T Apr 1732 *Patapsco*. E.
Ewings, John Jr. S Apr 1767. So.
Ewins, Joseph of Great Hampton. R for America Mar 1710. Wo.
Ewens als Evans, William of Broadhempston, weaver. R for Barbados Jun 1666. De.
Ewens, William. R Lent 1773. K.
Ewer, Thomas. S May T Dec 1734 *Caesar* LC Va Jly 1735. M.
Yure, William. S Oct T Nov 1728 *Forward* LC Rappahannock Jun 1729. L.
Ewers, James of Woodham Walter. R for America Jly 1700. E.
Ewers, Martha. S Jun T Nov 1743 *George William*. L.
Exall, Francis. R for Barbados or Jamaica Jan 1692. L.
Exall, Susannah. S Feb T Apr 1772 *Thornton*. L.
Exelby, John. R 14 yrs Summer T Oct 1739 *Duke of Cumberland*. Sy.
Exell, Ann. S Lent 1754. E.
Exon als Gaines, Francis. R Dec 1698 AT Jan 1699. M.
Extell, Emanuel. S Jan T Apr 1741 *Speedwell* or *Mediterranean*. M.
Eyes, John. S & T Sep 1765 *Justitia*. M.
Eylatt, Francis. S Jly 1735. Co.
Eyles. *See* Iles.
Eyre als Wheeler, James. R 14 yrs Jly TB to Va Sep 1738. Wi.
Eyre, John, als Talbot, Richard. S Jly TB to Va Aug 1762. Wi.
Eyre, John. S Summer 1767. Nt.
Eyre, John. S Oct T Dec 1771 *Justitia*. L.
Eyre, Thomas. T Jun 1727 *Susanna*. Bu.
Eyres. *See* Ayres.
Eyton, Richard. PT Oct 1690.

F

Facer, Joseph. S Summer 1762. No.

Facey, John. Rebel T 1685.

Fackner, Elizabeth. S s at Sunderland Summer 1775. Du.

Fade, William. Rebel T 1685.

Fagan, Catherine. S Dec 1773. M.

Fagan, James. T Sep 1755 *Tryal*. M.

Fagan, John. S Jun 1754. L.

Fagan, John. S Sep-Oct 1775. M.

Fagin, Matthew. SQS Wisbech s sheep & R 14 yrs Sep 1773 (SP). Ca.

Fagan, Michael. SQS Jan 1751. M.

Fagen, Nicholas. S & T Sep 1731 *Smith* LC Va 1732. L.

Fagg, Mary (1697). *See* Booker. L.

Fahee, Thomas. S Apr T May 1752 *Lichfield*. L.

Fairall, John. S Summer 1747. K.

Fairbanke, Elizabeth. R for Barbados or Jamaica May 1691. L.

Fairbank, James. S Jan 1755. L.

Fairburn, Robert. S Aug 1763. L.

Fairchild, Thomas. R for Barbados Aug 1679. L.

Faircliffe, Francis. S Summer 1750. Ca.

Faircloth, Sarah. R for Barbados or Jamaica Dec 1716. L.

Farfax, John. S s at Bromsgrove Lent 1727. Wo.

Fairfax, William of Lincoln. R for America Jly 1678. Li.

Fairfax, William. S & T Jun 1742 *Bladon* to Md. M.

Fairfield, Thomas. S & R Lent 1769. Ch.

Fairing, Daniel. T Apr 1766 *Ann*. E.

Fairley, Ann. S Feb T Mar 1730 *Patapsco* LC Annapolis Sep 1730. L.

Fairley, Susan of Leighton Buzzard. R for America Feb 1688. Bd.

Fairley, Thomas of Morpeth. R for Barbados Jly 1690. Nl.

Fairman, Robert, a Quaker. R for plantations Jly 1665 (SP). Ht.

Fairman, William of Hertford, brewer. SQS 1664 R for Barbados Jly 1665 (PC). Ht.

Fairthorne, Edmund. S Mar 1743. Ha.

Fairweathers, Robert. S Lent 1767. Li.

Fairwell, Anthony. S & T Sep 1764 *Justitia*. M.

Fairy, William. AT Winter 1668. Bd.

Faithfull, Jonathan. T Apr 1731 *Bennett*. Sy.

Faithfull, William. S Summer 1775. Ru.

Falcon, Jacob. S Apr 1745. L.

Faukenbridge, John. S Jly TB Aug 1771. Nt.

Fauconbridge, Richard of Bulwell, framework knitter. SQS s goose at Calverton Apr 1766. Nt.

Fall, John. S Lent R 14 yrs Summer T Sep 1751 *Greyhound*. K.

Fall als Smith, William. S Summer 1765 R 14 yrs Summer 1766 for being at large in Morpeth and Hinckley, Leics, after sentence of transportation. Nl.

Fallowfield, Dorothy. S City for shoplifting at St. Crux Lent 1740. Y.

Falvey, John. S Apr 1727. So.

Fancia, Obadiah. S Feb T Mar 1730 *Patapsco* LC Annapolis Sep 1730. L.
Fancy, Libel. R 14 yrs Aug 1736. Do.
Fanjoy, William. S Sep-Oct 1773. M.
Fann, Elizabeth. S Apr T May 1720 *Honor*. L.
Fan, George. S Aug 1736. Do.
Fann, Owen. S & R 14 yrs Summer 1742. Hu.
Fann, Susanna wife of John. S & T Apr 1725 *Sukey* LC Annapolis Sep 1725. M.
Fann, Thomas. R for Barbados or Jamaica Feb 1687. M.
Fanning, James. S Jun T Aug 1769 *Douglas*. M.
Fanshaw, Sibilla (1725). *See* Hanshaw. M.
Fanside, Ann. S & T Sep 1764 *Justitia*. M.
Fanting, Lewis. S s from Earl of Buckinghamshire Jan T by his own consent Apr 1770 *New Trial*. M.
Fanton, Mary, widow. S Oct T Dec 1767 *Neptune*. L.
Farding als Ferne, James. T Sep 1730 *Smith*. Sy.
Farding, Mary Ann. S Aug 1745. De.
Fardoe, Martha. S Summer 1767 to be hanged and her body dissected and anatomized for drowning a child in a pool of water R 14 yrs Lent 1768. Sh.
Fardo, Richard. S Apr R 14 yrs for Carolina May 1719. L.
Fares als Smith, Catherine. S Jly 1721 T *Owners Goodwill* LC Md Jly 1722. M.
Farfass, William. S Lent R 14 yrs Summer 1722. G.
Farley, Ann. S 14 yrs for receiving goods stolen at Castlemorton Lent 1759. Wo.
Farley, John of Hanley Castle. R for America Jly 1683. Wo.
Farley, John. T 14 yrs Apr 1765 *Ann*. Sx.
Farleys, Henry. S Lent R 14 yrs Summer T Oct 1750 *Rachael*. K.
Farlow als White, William. S Lent R for Barbados May 1664. Sy.
Farmer, Ann (1751). *See* Colley. M.
Farmer, Ann. S Oct T Dec 1767 *Neptune*. M.
Farmer, Bryan. S s at Aston Ingham Lent 1723 AT Summer 1725. He.
Farmer, Christiana. R 10 yrs in plantations Oct 1662. M.
Farmer, Edward. S Lent 1749. K.
Farmer, George. S s horse Summer 1738 R 14 yrs Lent 1739. Li.
Farmer, Helen. R for Barbados Oct 1673. L.
Farmer, John. Rebel T 1685.
Farmer, John. S for forgery Lent R 14 yrs Summer 1746. Sy.
Farmer, John. S s sheep Lent R 14 yrs Summer 1752. Sh.
Farmer, John. S s at Harwell Summer 1763. Be.
Farmer, John Sr. S s at St. Julian, Shrewsbury, Summer 1764; John Farmer Jr. acquitted. Sh.
Farmer, Joseph. S Summer 1733 R 14 yrs Lent 1734. Be.
Farmer, Mary of Manchester. SQS Jan 1757. La.
Farmer, Matthew. S & T Sep 1764 *Justitia*. M.
Farmer, Robert. T May 1751 *Tryal*. Sx.
Farmer, Samuel (2). Rebels T 1685.
Farmer, William. T Apr 1753 *Thames*. K.
Farmworth, John. S s saws Oct T Dec 1736 *Dorsetshire* to Va. M.
Farn, John. S Summer 1725 R Summer 1726. Wa.

Farnaby, Frances. S Lent 1742. Mo.

Farnaby, Ralph. T Apr 1771 *Thornton*. K.

Farnass, Isaac (1754). *See* Furness, William. Y.

Farncombe als Verncombe, Henry. R 14 yrs Mar 1771. So.

Farnam, John. S Lent 1731. Wo.

Farnum, Lawrence. S Dec 1757 T Mar 1758 *Dragon*. M.

Farnham, Robert. S Jan T Apr 1741 *Speedwell* or *Mediterranean*. M.

Farnsworth, Joseph. S s mare Summer 1767 R for life Lent 1768. Nt.

Farnsworth, Samuel. TB Oct 1752. Db.

Farnworth, Thomas. S s at Wolverhampton Lent 1758. St.

Faquar, Alexander. LC from *Forward* Annapolis Jun 1725. X.

Farquhar, John. S Jan T Feb 1724 *Anne* to Carolina. M.

Farr, Alice (1769). *See* Johnson. L.

Farre, Elianor wife of Thomas. AT Jan 1656. M.

Farr, George. S Sep 1754. L.

Farr, Joane. SQS Oct 1732. So.

Farr, Johanna. R for Barbados Jun 1663. M.

Farr, Nathaniel of Horningsham. SQS Warminster Jly TB to Va Oct 1742. Wi.

Farr, Robert. S Mar 1774. Ha.

Farrah. *See* Farrer.

Farrand, William. S s tablecloth at Sherborne Lent 1765. G.

Farraway, Robert. T Aug 1752 *Tryal*. E.

Farrall, Bridget. S May T Jun 1726 *Loyal Margaret* LC Annapolis Oct 1726. M.

Farrell, Edward. S & T Sep 1731 *Smith* LC Va 1732. M.

Farrell, Francis. S s looking glass Oct 1742 T Apr 1743 *Justitia*. M.

Farrell, Francis. S Dec 1749-Jan 1750 T Mar 1750 *Tryal*. M.

Farrell, Francis. S & T Jan 1756 *Tryal*. M.

Farrell, James of Bermondsey. SQS Jan T Mar 1764 *Tryal*. Sy.

Farrell, James. S & T Sep 1765 *Justitia*. L.

Farrell, John. S May T Jun 1726 *Loyal Margaret* but died on passage. M.

Farrell, John. SQS Dec 1764 T Jan 1765 *Tryal*. M.

Farrell, John (1771). *See* Clarke. M.

Farrell, John. S Sep-Oct 1772. M.

Farrell, John of St. Martin in Fields. SW Apr 1773. M.

Farrell, Margaret. SQS Jan T Mar 1764 *Tryal*. M.

Farrell, Margaret (1768). *See* Crow. M.

Farrell, Michael. S Jly T Sep 1767 *Justitia*. M.

Farrell, Peter. T Mar 1758 *Dragon*. L.

Farrell, Peter. S & T Dec 1771 *Justitia*. M.

Farrell, Peter. S Lent 1774. K.

Farrell, Philip. S Dec 1766 T Jan 1767 *Tryal*. M.

Farrell, Philip. S Oct 1775. M.

Farrell, Thomas. SQS Apr T May 1751 *Tryal*. M.

Farrell, William. S Feb T Mar 1731 *Patapsco* LC Annapolis Jun 1731. M.

Farrell, William. S Aug 1764. De.

Farrell, Winifred. S Feb-Apr T May 1755 *Rose*. M.

Farren, William. R 14 yrs for murder & to be T to Va Jly 1718. De.

Farrer, George. S Jan T Feb 1765 *Tryal*. L.

Farrah, James. S Apr T Nov 1759 *Phoenix*. M.

Farrer als Ferrow, James. S Aug 1772. Do.
Farrer als Farrar, Mark. AT Lent 1766. Y.
Farrer, Thomas. S Summer 1755. Y.
Farrer, William. S Lent R 14 yrs Summer 1742 (SP). Ca.
Farrie, John. T Dec 1734 *Caesar*. E.
Farrier, Nicholas. R for America Aug 1715. M.
Farrington, Richard (1753). *See* Reading. He.
Farrington, Samuel. S s horse Lent R 14 yrs Summer 1768. St.
Farrington, Thomas. S Lent 1756. Bu.
Farrington, William. AT from QS Lent 1766. Wa.
Farris als Farrow, James. S Feb-Apr T 14 yrs May 1751 *Tryal*. M.
Farrow als Jackson, Elizabeth. S Oct 1741 T 14 yrs Feb 1742 *Industry*. L.
Farrow, Isabel wife of Richard. S Lent 1745. Y.
Farrow, James (1751). *See* Farris. M.
Farrowe, John of Bulphan. R for Barbados or Jamaica Feb 1696. E.
Farrow, John. S Apr 1745. L.
Farrow, Thomas. S Norwich Summer TB Sep 1754. Nf.
Farthing, Anne. SQS Oct 1732. So.
Farthing, Charles. S Jan 1775. M.
Farthing, John. S Jan-Feb T Apr 1771 *Thornton*. M.
Farthing, Mary. S Jan T Mar 1764 *Tryal*. L.
Farthing, Richard. S & T 14 yrs Jan 1722 *Gilbert* but died on passage. L.
Farthing, Samuel. S Aug 1734. So.
Fathers, John. Rebel T 1685.
Fatty, Mary (1734). *See* Goat. M.
Fauklin, Ann. S Dec 1756. M.
Faulkener, Alice (1739). *See* Jones. M.
Faulkner, Ann. S Aug 1763. L.
Faulkner, James. S Jly T Sep 1764 *Justitia*. M.
Faulkner als Howard, Jane. S Oct-Dec 1750. M.
Faulkner, Jane. S Aug T for life Sep 1764 *Justitia*. L.
Faulkner, John. S Mar TB to Va Apr 1775. Wi.
Folkner, Joseph (Richard). T Jun 1728 *Elizabeth* LC Va Aug 1729. Ht.
Faulkner, Joseph. T May 1767 *Thornton*. Sy.
Falkner, Mary. S Dec 1766 T Jan 1767 *Tryal*. M.
Faulkner, Richard. SQS & T Sep 1751 *Greyhound*. M.
Faulkner, Thomas. R for Barbados Mar 1683. M.
Faulkner, William. S Jan T Feb 1724 *Anne* to Carolina. M.
Fawcett, Edward. R 14 yrs Mar 1742. Co.
Fawcett, James. S Apr 1749. L.
Fawcet, John. ST & T Sep 1764 *Justitia*. L.
Fawcett, Thomas. SQS s wheat Lent 1768. Du.
Fawkes, Edward. S s at Cradly Summer 1724 AT Summer 1726. He.
Fawkes, John. S & T Jan 1739 *Dorsetshire*. L.
Feagins, Nicholas. S & T May 1744 *Justitia*. L.
Feakes, Joyce of Lambeth. R for Barbados or Jamaica Feb 1683. Sy.
Fear, Edmund. R for life Mar 1773. So.
Fear, George. S Dec 1749-Jan 1750 T Mar 1750 *Tryal*. M.
Fear, John. S Lent R 14 yrs Summer 1754. K.
Feare, William. Rebel T 1685.
Fearn, Elizabeth. S Feb T May 1767 *Thornton*. L.

Fearn, Mary (1723). *See* White. K.
Fearnley, Nicholas. S Mar 1755. De.
Fearnley, Sarah. S Lent 1761. Y.
Fearnley, William. S Lent 1732. Y.
Fearson, Ann. T Mar 1758 *Dragon*. Sy.
Feary, Ann. S Feb T Mar 1760 *Friendship*. M.
Feast, Henry, a Quaker. S for attending conventicles Summer 1664 & R
    for plantations Jly 1665 (PC). Ht.
Feathers, Henry. S Jan T 14 yrs Apr 1759 *Thetis*. M.
Feathers, Samuel. T Apr 1766 *Ann*. K.
Featherstone, Ann. S Nov T Dec 1763 *Neptune*. L.
Fetherstone, Elizabeth (1724). *See* Levingstone. Ha.
Fetherstone, Joan. TB to Va from QS 1757. De.
Fetherstone, John of York City. R for Barbados Jun 1675. Y.
Fetherston, John, yeoman. R for America Feb 1692. No.
Featherstone, Millicent (1764). *See* Spratley. M.
Featherstone, Mary, servant to Jonathan Brown of Ware. Taken as
    vagrant in Foxon, Cambs, delivered of bastard child, & T Sep 1730
    Smith. Ht.
Featherstone, Thomas. S May-Jly 1774. M.
Fetherstone, William. S Aug 1767. So.
Felgate, Samuel of Mitton, yeoman. R for Barbados Jly 1685. La.
Fell, Edward. R Lent 1773. E.
Fell, Elizabeth. S Dec 1763 T Mar 1764 *Tryal*. M.
Fell, John. R for Barbados May TB Jun 1668. M.
Fell, Mary (1716). *See* Smith. M.
Fell, Stephen, als Hall, William. S Summer TB Aug 1773. Y.
Fell, William. S Summer 1749. Sy.
Fellaway, Elizabeth. SQS & T Jly 1772 *Tayloe*. M.
Felles, John. S Jan T Feb 1726 *Supply* LC Annapolis May 1726. M.
Fellow, Edward. R 14 yrs Summer 1730 (SP). G.
Fellow, Edward. S s horse Lent R 14 yrs Summer 1768 (SP). St.
Fellows, Henry. S s sheep Lent R 14 yrs Summer 1766. Bu.
Fellows, Jane. R for America Jly 1708. Li.
Fellows, John. S 14 yrs s linen from bleaching yard at Dawley Summer
    1758. Sh.
Fellows, Margaret. S & T Oct 1732 *Caesar*. L.
Fellows, Richard of Whitchurch, tailor. R for America Jun 1714. O.
Fellows, Richard. S as pickpocket Lent R 14 yrs Summer 1730. Wa.
Fellows, Richard. S Lent T Apr 1766 *Ann*. Bu.
Fellows, Thomas. SQS Jly 1769. M.
Felsted, Mark of Tarling. S Lent 1772. E.
Felter, Ann. S & T Apr 1769 *Tryal*. M.
Felter, John (1729). *See* Filter. L.
Feltham, John. R 14 yrs Jly 1773. Ha.
Felton, Dorothy. S Jly T 14 yrs Sep 1737 *Pretty Patsy* to Md. L.
Felton, George. S & T Apr 1733 *Patapsco* LC Annapolis Nov 1733. M.
Felton, John. S Feb 1752. L.
Felton, Mary. S & T Sep 1757 *Thetis*. M.
Felton, Mary. S Jan T Feb 1765 *Tryal*. L.
Felton, Thomas. SQS Feb 1754. M.

Felton, William. S s at Tibberton Lent 1751. Wo.

Fenby, Thomas. S Dec 1774. M.

Fendeloe, Elizabeth (1756). *See* Anderson. Db.

Fendley, Charles. S & T Apr 1766 *Ann.* M.

Fenkell, George. S Summer 1753. Du.

Fenleoo, Rachael of St. Saviour, Southwark, spinster. SQS Mar T 14 yrs
  Apr 1753 *Thames.* Sy.

Fenley, Henry. S Oct 1774. L.

Fenley, John. S & T Sep 1764 *Justitia.* M.

Fenley, Mary. S & T Dec 1758 *The Brothers.* M.

Fenley, Patrick. S Jan-Feb T Apr 1772 *Thornton.* M.

Fenn, Elizabeth. S May T Jly 1722 *Alexander* to Nevis or Jamaica. M.

Fenn, Hugh. S & T Jan 1739 *Dorsetshire.* L.

Fenn, James. T Jan 1736 *Dorsetshire.* K.

Fenn als Welham, James. R for life Lent 1774. K.

Fenn, Martha. S Feb T Mar 1729 *Patapsco* LC Annapolis Dec 1729. L.

Fenne, Thomas. R for Barbados Jly 1668. M.

Fennell, John. R Jun T Aug 1769 *Douglas.* M.

Fennell, Richard. S Lent 1758. No.

Fenner, Hezekiah of Belchamp Walter. SQS Jan 1746. E.

Fennister, Mary (1746). *See* Toasten. L.

Fenny, William. T Apr 1743 *Justitia.* E.

Fenton, Bartholomew. S Sep T Dec 1769 *Justitia.* M.

Fenton, James. S Apr T May 1750 *Lichfield.* M.

Fenton, John of Shelton. R for America Jly 1698. St.

Fenton, John. S Summer 1765. We.

Fenton, Matthew. S Summer 1740. Y.

Fenton, Robert of Birmingham. R for America Jly 1682. Wa.

Fenton, Robert (John). S & T Oct 1730 *Forward* LC Potomack Jan
  1731. L.

Fenton, William. S for highway robbery at Stapleton Summer TB Aug
  1748. G.

Fenton, William. S Jan 1751. M.

Fenton, William. S Apr T Jly 1770 *Scarsdale.* L.

Fenwick, Ann. S Sep T Nov 1762 *Prince William.* M.

Fenwick als Peers, Francis. S Jan T Feb 1719 *Worcester* LC Annapolis
  Jun 1719. L.

Fenwick, John (1742). *See* Parnaby. Y.

Fenwick, Lionel. R Jly AT Oct 1685. M.

Ferbin, Jasper. S Feb T Mar 1730 *Patapsco.* M.

Farguson, Edward. S s horse & R 14 yrs Summer 1768. We.

Ferguson, Isabella. AT City Summer 1758. Nl.

Fergusson, James. S Oct T Nov 1725 *Rappahannock* LC Rappahannock
  Apr 1726. L.

Ferguson, John. S Sep-Dec 1755 T Jan 1756 *Greyhound*: indicted in Apr
  1757 as John Drummond als Forkey for returning from
  transportation. M.

Furguson, John. S Sep 1761. M.

Ferguson, John. SQS Jan T Apr 1770 *New Trial.* M.

Ferguson, Robert. S & T Dec 1771 *Justitia.* L.

Ferguson, Roger. S s horse Summer 1744 R 14 yrs Summer 1746. Du.

Fergison, William. R for Barbados Sep 1669. M.
Ferminer, Hannah. S Sep 1733 T Jan 1734 *Caesar* LC Va Jly 1734. M.
Fernandez, Lewis. S Oct T Nov 1759 *Phoenix*. L.
Ferrand, Sarah. S May T Jly 1771 *Scarsdale*. L.
Ferret, Richard. S Mar 1737. Ha.
Ferriday, Edward. S s gelding Lent 1774. Sh.
Ferrill, Ann. LC from *Sukey* Annapolis Sep 1725. X.
Ferring, Charles. S Apr-May 1754. M.
Ferris, Benjamin. S Mar 1721. Wi.
Ferris, James. S Feb T 14 yrs Mar 1730 *Patapsco* LC Annapolis Sep 1730. M.
Ferris, Thomas. Rebel T 1685.
Ferrow, James (1772). *See* Farrer. Do.
Ferryman, Stephen (1770). *See* Browne, Timothy. La.
Fessand, Zachary. R for America Mar 1697. Ru.
Festrope, Anne. S Jly T 14 yrs Aug 1721 *Prince Royal* LC Va Nov 1721. L.
Fettiplace, George. S Sep T Dec 1770 *Justitia*. M.
Fevil, John. S s at Wokingham Lent 1764. Be.
Fewkes, Mathew. S Mar TB to Va Sep 1744. Wi.
Fewterell, George of Greet. R for America Jly 1675. Sh.
Fewtle, Ward. LC from *Forward* Annapolis Jun 1723. X.
Fiander, Henry husband of Elizabeth. S s sheets May 1736. M.
Fickus, Elizabeth wife of Thomas. S 14 yrs for receiving Apr 1754. So.
Fiddes, Christopher. R City 14 yrs Summer 1758. Y.
Field, Ann. S Apr 1748. L.
Field, Ann. S Dec 1773. L.
Field, Ann. S 14 yrs Jly 1774. L.
Field, Elizabeth of Cobham. R for Barbados Apr 1668. Sy.
Field, Elizabeth of Thatcham, spinster. R for America Jly 1711. Be.
Field, Elizabeth. S Feb T 14 yrs Mar 1727 *Rappahannock*. L.
Field, Elizabeth. S Jan-Jun T Jun 1728 *Elizabeth* LC Potomack Aug 1729. L.
Field, George, R Jly 1775. Ha.
Field, Hannah. SQS & T Sep 1751 *Greyhound*. M.
Field, Hannah. S Feb 1775. L.
Field, Isaac. R 14 yrs Mar 1759. Wi.
Field, James Jr. Rebel T 1685.
Field, James. S Jan-Feb T Apr 1771 *Thornton*. M.
Field, Jane, spinster, als wife of Joseph. R for Barbados or Jamaica Dec 1689. L.
Field, John. Rebel T 1685.
Field, John (1699). *See* Serjeant. L.
Field, John. T Apr 1725 *Sukey* but died on passage. E.
Field, John. S s clothing at Great Farringdon Summer 1749. Be.
Field, John. S Nov T Dec 1763 *Neptune*. L.
Field, John. T 14 yrs Dec 1771 *Justitia*. Ht.
Field, Joseph. R 14 yrs Summer 1757. Y.
Field, Margaret. S Summer 1749. Sy.
Field, Mary of St. Botolph Aldgate. S s silk & T May 1736 *Patapsco*. M.
Field, Mary. S 14 yrs Feb-Apr 1746. M.

Field, Mary. S Dec 1756. M.
Field, Mary. S s at All Saints, Worcester, Summer 1771. Wo.
Field, Mary. S Oct T Dec 1771 *Justitia*. L.
Field, Matthew of St. Margaret, Westminster. SW Apr T May 1767 *Thornton*. M.
Field, Peter. T 14 yrs Apr 1768 *Thornton*. Ht.
Field, Rowland of Hemel Hempstead. S Summer T Oct 1739 *Duke of Cumberland*. Ht.
Field, Samuel. S s goose at Enville Lent 1735. St.
Field, Samuel. S Summer 1767. Wa.
Field, Sarah. T Apr 1765 *Ann*. Sy.
Field, Stephen. S s handkerchief at St. Mary at Hill Apr T Jun 1768 *Tryal*. L.
Field, Thomas of Lambeth. R for Barbados or Jamaica Jly 1688. Sy.
Field, Timothy. R for Barbados Jly 1668. M.
Field, Walter. R for Barbados Jly 1674. M.
Field, William. R for Barbados Nov 1668. L.
Field, William. S & T Oct 1729 *Forward* LC Va Jun 1730. M.
Field, William. S & TB Sep 1753. G.
Field, William. S May 1760. M.
Field, William of Manchester, silk weaver. SQS Aug 1765. La.
Field, William. S Lent 1768. Wa.
Field, William of Rotherhithe. SQS Jan 1773. Sy.
Fielden, Thomas. S Jan T Mar 1764 *Tryal*. M.
Fielder, Ann. S Aug TB to Va Oct 1764. Wi.
Fielder, John. S Jan T Feb 1726 *Supply* LC Annapolis May 1726. L.
Fielder, John. R 14 yrs Jly 1744. So.
Fielder, Price. S Oct 1748 T Jan 1749 *Laura*. L.
Fielder, Priscilla (1681). *See* Wynn. M.
Fielder, Richard. T May 1744 *Justitia*. K.
Fielder, Sarah. S Jan T Feb 1726 *Supply* to Md. M.
Fielder, Sarah (1742). *See* Camell. Sx.
Fielder, Stephen. S Feb 1754. L.
Fielder, William. S Mar 1774. Ha.
Fieldhouse, Joseph. S Feb T Mar 1731 *Patapsco* but died on passage. M.
Fieldhouse, Thomas. S s sheep Lent R 14 yrs Summer 1742. Sh.
Fieldhouse, Thomas. S s at Bromyard Lent 1753. He.
Fielding, Catherine. S Summer T Sep 1755 *Tryal*. Sy.
Fielding, Elizabeth. S Dec 1761. M.
Fielding, John. Died on passage in *Gilbert* 1721. X.
Fielding, John. S Oct 1772. L.
Fielding, Joshua. S & T Dec 1736 *Dorsetshire*. L.
Fielding, Thomas. S & T Sep 1731 *Smith* LC Va 1732. L.
Fielding, William. S Lent 1768. a.
Fielding, Willoughby. S Oct T Dec 1724 *Rappahannock*. L.
Fieldsend, John. S Lent 1756. Y.
Fife, Docia. S & T Jly 1753 *Tryal*. L.
Fife, James. R & T Apr 1770 *New Trial*. M.
Fife, John. S Apr-Jun 1739. M.
Fife, William. S Oct 1756. M.

Fyfield, Eleanor. S for arson at Broughton Lent 1728 & elected T 14 yrs to Barbados. O.

Fifield, Grace. R 14 yrs Jly 1756. Ha.

Fiefield als Pyefield, Susannah. S & T Sep 1757 *Thetis*. M.

Fifoot, Mary als Durbin, Hannah. S & TB Mar 1748. G.

Fiford, William. S Mar 1750. Do.

Figgis, Mary. S Summer 1748 T Jan 1749 *Laura*. Ht.

Figgott, Richard (1752). *See* Simms. G.

Figgote, Thomas. S for highway robbery Lent R 14 yrs Summer TB Jly 1743. G.

Figures, Joseph. S s at Blockley Lent 1729. Wo.

Filbrick, Henry of St. Mary's at Wall, Colchester. SQS Oct T Dec 1753 *Whiteing*. E.

Filby, John. S s mare & R Lent 1766. Nf.

Fileman, Philip. SW & T Dec 1771 *Justitia*. M.

Filewood, John. TB 14 yrs Oct 1719. L.

Filgon als Filgoe, John of Stepney. S s watering can Apr 1740. M.

Filley, John. T Dec 1753 *Whiteing*. K.

Fillimore, Francis. S & T Jly 1753 *Tryal*. L.

Filming, William (1761). *See* Fleming. La.

Filter, John. S Feb T Mar 1729 *Patapsco* LC Annapolis Dec 1729. L.

Finch, Ann. R for America May 1704. M.

Finch, Elizabeth of Fingringhoe, spinster. SQS Jan T Apr 1762 *Neptune*. E.

Finch, Heneage. S Sep-Dec 1746. M.

Finch, John. S Jly 1746. L.

Finch, Samuel. Died on passage in *Rappahannock* 1726. X.

Finch, Sarah. S Sep T Dec 1758 *The Brothers*. M.

Finch, Thomas. PT Apr R for Barbados or Jamaica Aug 1700. M.

Finch, Thomas (1731). *See* Dew. O.

Finch, Thomas. S Apr T Sep 1757 *Thetis*. L.

Finch, William. S Lent T Jun 1756 *Lyon*. E.

Finch, William. S & R 14 yrs Summer 1774. G.

Fincham, Ann. S Lent 1745. Nf.

Fincham, Isaac. S s rabbits at Eriswell Lent 1774. Su.

Fincham, John. T Jun 1740 *Essex*. E.

Fincham, Robert. T Jun 1740 *Essex*. E.

Fincham, William. R for Barbados or Jamaica Mar 1685. L.

Fincher, Charles of Ightham. R for Barbados or Jamaica Jun 1692. K.

Finder, Joseph of St. Saviour, Southwark. SQS Apr T May 1752 *Lichfield*. Sy.

Findme als Foundme, Peter. R 14 yrs Jly 1724. Ha.

Fines, Margaret (1752). *See* Fyance. M.

Fynes, Margery. S Dec 1755 T Jan 1756 *Greyhound*. L.

Finley, Ralph. S Jan T May 1720 *Honor* LC Port York Jan 1721. L.

Finlay, Richard. S Summer 1749. E.

Finley, Robert. S Jun T Sep 1758 *Tryal* to Annapolis. M.

Finlow, Lydia, aged 19, brown hair. S Jan T Feb 1723 *Jonathan* LC Annapolis Jly 1724. L.

Finn, James. S Feb-Apr T May 1755 *Rose*. M.

Finnamore als Boswell, John. S Lent R 14 yrs Summer 1760. O.

Finnee, Ann. S Sep 1736. M.

Finney als Quennell, Elizabeth of Lambeth. R for Barbados or Jamaica Feb 1683. Sy.

Finney, William of Stockport, Chesh. SQS Jan 1761. La.

Finney, William. T for life Dec 1770 *Justitia*. Sy.

Finnick, Francis. S Oct T Dec 1769 *Justitia*. L.

Finnimore, Alexander. S s at South Morton Lent 1759. Be.

Finnimore, Joseph. S Dec 1755 T 14 yrs Jan 1756 *Greyhound*. L.

Finninlay, John. S s cow Summer 1744 R 14 yrs Lent 1745. Li.

Finnis, William. T May 1767 *Thornton*. E.

Firbuck, John. LC from *Forward* Annapolis Jun 1725. X.

Firebeard, Grizle. S Jly TB to Va Aug 1758. Wi.

Firle, Thomas. T May 1737 *Forward*. K.

Firth, Helen (1731). *See* Howsley. Y.

Firth, James. S Summer 1770. Nt.

Firth, Mary of Manchester, widow. SQS Jly 1774. La.

Fish, George. S Norwich Summer 1755. Nf.

Fish, James. S & T Dec 1758 *The Brothers*. M.

Fish, James of Stoke, bargeman. SQS & T Jan 1769 *Thornton*. Sy.

Fish, John. T Jan 1741 *Vernon*. E.

Fish, John. S Feb T Apr 1759 *Thetis*. M.

Fish, Margaret (1764). *See* Hindley. La.

Fish, Mary. S & T Jly 1753 *Tryal*. L.

Fish, Richard. S Mar 1759. Ha.

Fish, Thomas. R 14 yrs Jly 1736. Ha.

Fish, Thomas. S & T Apr 1765 *Ann*. L.

Fish, William. S Dec 1733 T Jan 1734 *Caesar* LC Va Jly 1734. L.

Fisher als Casey, Alexander. S Jan-Apr 1749. M.

Fisher, Andrew. S s iron & Lead at Chapel Hill Lent 1757. Mo.

Fisher, Bethia (Martha), aged 46, dark. S Jan T Feb 1723 *Jonathan* LC Annapolis Jly 1724. L.

Fisher, Catherine wife of Thomas. S for receiving Feb 1758. Ha.

Fisher, Christopher. S May-Jly T Sep 1751 *Greyhound*. M.

Fisher, Edward. S Lent 1763. La.

Fisher, Elizabeth of St. Luke, spinster. S s gowns Jly 1740 T Jan 1741 *Harpooner* to Rappahannock. M.

Fisher, George. S Jan T Feb 1724 *Anne*. L.

Fisher, Giles. S s cloth from tenter & R 14 yrs Lent 1769. G.

Fisher, Hannah of Bristol. R 14 yrs Lent 1774 (SP). G.

Fisher, Henry. S s wheat at Bridstow Lent 1757. He.

Fisher, Isaac. SL & T Sep 1765 *Justitia*. Sy.

Fisher, John. Rebel T 1685.

Fisher, John of North Mimms. R for Barbados or Jamaica Jly 1687. Ht.

Fisher, John. S & T Oct 1722 *Forward* LC Annapolis Jun 1723. M.

Fisher, John. LC from *Rappahannock* at Rappahannock Apr 1726. X.

Fisher, John. S Lent 1735. Y.

Fisher, John. S May-Jly T Sep 1751 *Greyhound*. M.

Fisher, John. S Lent 1757. Le.

Fisher, John. T Apr 1757. Db.

Fisher, John. S Aug 1760. L.

Fisher, John. S s horse & R 14 yrs Summer TB Nov 1762. Y.

Fisher, John. S Jly T Sep 1767 *Justitia*. M.
Fisher, Joseph. R Dec 1699 AT Jan 1700. M.
Fisher, Joseph. S Dec 1737 T Jan 1738 *Dorsetshire*. L.
Fisher, Joseph. S Lent R 14 yrs Summer T Sep 1751 *Greyhound*. Sy.
Fisher, Joseph. S s at Kingswinford Summer 1757. St.
Fisher, Joseph. S 14 yrs s cowtail hair at Whitchurch Lent 1764. Sh.
Fisher, Joseph. R Mar 1773. Ha.
Fisher, Joseph of St. Clement Danes. SW Apr 1773. M.
Fisher, Joseph of St. Martin in Fields. SW Oct 1773. M.
Fisher, Lawrence. S s cloth at Edgmond Summer 1773. St.
Fisher, Margaret. S & T Oct 1722 *Forward* LC Annapolis Jun 1723. M.
Fisher, Mary. R for Barbados Jly 1674. L.
Fisher, Mary. R for Barbados or Jamaica Feb 1686. L.
Fisher, Mary wife of John of Warrington, als Mary Gregory. SQS Jly 1769. La.
Fisher, Matthew. S s sheep & R 14 yrs Summer TB Oct 1763. Y.
Fisher, Richard of Linton. R for America Feb 1673. He.
Fisher, Robert. S Lent 1766. Su.
Fisher, Samuel. SQS & T Apr 1769 *Tryal*. M.
Fisher, Sarah. S Lent T Sep 1757 *Thetis*. K.
Fisher, Thomas. R for Barbados or Jamaica Oct 1690. M.
Fisher, Thomas. S & T Oct 1722 *Forward* LC Annapolis Jun 1723. L.
Fisher als Gallway, Thomas. T Apr 1739 *Forward*. K.
Fisher, Thomas. S Apr-Jun 1739. M.
Fisher, Thomas. S Sep-Oct T Dec 1771 *Justitia*. M.
Fisher, William of Whitsondine. R for America Feb 1713. Ru.
Fisher, William. Died on passage in *Rappahannock* 1726. X.
Fisher, William. S s horse Lent R 14 yrs Summer 1731. No.
Fisher, William. S Summer 1740. Y.
Fisher, William. SQS & T Jly 1741. Bd.
Fisher, William. R 14 yrs Jly 1745. Ha.
Fisher, William. S Mar 1749 R for life & TB to Va Apr 1750. Wi.
Fisher, William. S Apr T Jun 1768 *Tryal*. M.
Fisherman, John (1733). *See* Powell. M.
Fishwick, John of Samlesbury, weaver. SQS Apr 1748. La.
Fiske, Jeremy of Bungay. S Summer 1731. *Su.
Fisk, Mary. S Jan T Feb 1744 *Neptune*. L.
Fison, Henry. S Apr T May 1771 *Tryal*. L.
Fyson, James. S s rabbits at Eriswell Lent 1774. Su.
Fyson, Thomas (1747). *See* Lemon. E.
Fitch, Edward. S Apr-May 1754. M.
Fitch, William. S s shirt at Wokingham Lent 1752. Be.
Fitch, William (1753). *See* Chapman. E.
Fitmouse, Francis. T Jan 1756 *Greyhound*. Ht.
Fitness, Eden. R Summer 1772. Sy.
Fitton, William. R for Barbados Mar 1683. M.
Fitzgerald, Andrew, als Parsons, James, als Mackase, Bartholomew. S Dec 1748 T Jan 1749 *Laura*. M.
Fitzgerald, Andrew. R Feb T for life Apr 1766 *Ann*. L.
Fitzgerald, Catherine. S Dec 1745. L.
Fitzgerald, Eleanor. S Jan-Feb 1773. M.

Fitzgerald, Gerard. R & T 14 yrs Sep 1737 *Pretty Patsy* to Md. M.

Fitzgerald, James of Frensham. SQS & T Apr 1766 *Ann*. Sy.

Fitzgerald, James. S Sep-Oct 1772. M.

Fitzgerald, Jane. S s sheets Feb T May 1736 *Patapsco* to Md. M.

Fitchgarrald, Margaret, aged 22, brown hair. LC from *Jonathan* Annapolis Jly 1724. X.

Fitzgerald, Martin. T Dec 1734 *Caesar*. Sy.

Fitzgerald, Mary. T Sep 1730 *Smith*. Sy.

Fitzgerald, Michael. S & T Apr 1766 *Ann*. L.

Fitzgerald, Thomas. T May 1767 *Thornton*. E.

Fitzgerald, Walter. S Feb-Apr T Jun 1756 *Lyon*. M.

Fitzhitt, Margaret. S & T Apr 1725 *Sukey* LC Annapolis Sep 1725. M.

Fitzhugh, Robert. T Oct 1738 *Genoa*. Sy.

Fitzjohn, Edward. S Summer 1758. No.

Fitzmaurice, Eleanor. S s at Tenbury Summer 1768; husband Edward acquitted. Wo.

Fitzmorris, John. S May-Jly 1773. M.

Fitzpatrick, Catherine. SQS Jan T May 1755 *Rose*. M.

Fitzpatrick, Francis. S Dec 1768 T Jan 1769 *Thornton*. M.

Fitzpatrick, William. S Oct T Dec 1769 *Justitia*. M.

Fitzsimmonds, James. S Jly-Dec 1747. M.

Fitzwater, Joseph. S 14 yrs Jan 1745. L.

Fitzwalter, Mark. S Feb T Apr 1762 *Dolphin*. M.

Flack, Francis of St. Ann, Westminster. S s cloak & T Feb 1740 *York*. M.

Flack, George. S Lent 1748. Ht.

Flack, Jane, widow. S s at St. Nicholas, Ipswich, Lent 1772. Su.

Flack, John. S Jan T Feb 1733 *Smith*. L.

Flack, John. T Jun 1740 *Essex*. Sy.

Flack als Jones, John of Lambeth. S Lent T May 1750 *Lichfield*. Sy.

Flack, John. S s hog at Pampisford Lent 1773. Ca.

Flack, Richard. S Lent R 14 yrs Summer T Oct 1744 *Savannah*. E.

Flack, Richard. S s at Stroud Lent 1772. G.

Flack, William. R Lent 1775. E.

Flackson, Richard. S s horse Lent R 14 yrs Summer TB Jly 1733. G.

Flake, Sarah. SQS May T Jly 1773 *Tayloe* to Va. M.

Flaming, William (1761). *See* Fleming. La.

Flanady, Margaret. S Dec 1768 T Jan 1769 *Thornton*. L.

Flannagan, Andrew. S Apr 1761. M.

Flaningham, Judith. S Feb T Mar 1727 *Rappahannock* to Md. M.

Flannigan, Matthew. S & T Dec 1758 *The Brothers*. M.

Flanigan, Richard. S Apr T Sep 1757 *Thetis*. M.

Flanagan, Thomas. SQS Mar TB May 1724. Nt.

Flannagan, William. S Jan-Feb 1774. M.

Flanck, William. R for Barbados or Jamaica May 1684. L.

Flanders, Mary. S Jly 1760. M.

Flanders, Robert. S s gelding & R 14 yrs Lent 1754; wife Esther acquitted. Bd.

Flant, John. ST & T Dec 1763 *Neptune*. L.

Flathers, Benjamin of St. Paul Covent Garden. SW Jun 1775. M.

Flathers, Edward. S Dec 1774. L.

Flatman, Robert. S Norwich Summer TB Sep 1754. Nf.

Flatt, Henry. S s gelding at Bradwell & R Lent 1773. Su.

Flatt, John of Barsham. S Summer 1731. *Su.

Flatt, John. S & T Sep 1757 *Thetis*. L.

Flavell, Richard. R for America Feb 1683. Wa.

Flax, Samuel. S Dec 1733 T Jan 1734 *Caesar* LC Va Jly 1734. M.

Flaxman, William. S Summer 1744 R 14 yrs Lent 1745 (SP). Nf.

Flaxman, William. SQS Feb 1763. M.

Flaxton, Elizabeth. S Oct T Nov 1728 *Forward* LC Rappahannock Jun 1729. M.

Flaytey, Thomas. S Jly T 14 yrs Sep 1764 *Justitia*. M.

Fleathers, Benjamin of St. George, Southwark. SQS Apr 1751. Sy.

Fleck, John. S Feb-Apr T May 1755 *Rose*. M.

Fleet, Elizabeth wife of Joseph. S Oct 1741 T Feb 1742 *Industry* to Md. M.

Fleet, Elizabeth wife of John Sr. S 14 yrs for receiving goods stolen by Mary Fleet *(qv)* Lent 1765. Nf.

Fleet, Mary. S Lent 1765 R 14 yrs Lent 1766. Nf.

Fleet, William. S for highway robbery at Bradwell Summer 1769. Su.

Fleetwood als Piper, Jane. S & T Apr 1725 *Sukey* LC Annapolis Sep 1725. M.

Fleetwood, Thomas. S May T Jun 1726 *Loyal Margaret* LC Annapolis Oct 1726. M.

Flegg, Bartholomew. S Norwich Summer TB Sep 1758. Nf.

Flegg, Robert. S Summer 1757. Su.

Flemmar als Flemming, William, als Silver Heels. S Jly T Sep 1742 *Forward*. L.

Fleming, Elinor. S Jly T Aug 1721 *Prince Royal* LC Va Nov 1721. M.

Fleming, Elizabeth. S Feb T Mar 1731 *Patapsco* LC Annapolis Jun 1731. L.

Fleming, Henry. S s brass pan at Abbotts Bromley Lent 1769. St.

Fleming, James. S Norwich by special court for rioting Dec 1766 R for life Summer 1767. Nf.

Fleming, James. R Mar 1774. Ha.

Fleming, John. AT City Summer 1755. Nl.

Fleming, John of Bermondsey. SQS Jan T Apr 1765 *Ann*. Sy.

Fleming, Lettice. S Dec 1761 T Apr 1762 *Dolphin*. M.

Flemen, Peter. SQS s horse Mar R 14 yrs & TB Apr 1724. Nt.

Fleming, Susanna. S Sep T Dec 1769 *Justitia*. M.

Fleming, Thomas. R 14 yrs Aug 1739. Co.

Fleming, Thomas. S Summer 1764. Nf.

Fleming, Thomas. R Lent 1775. E.

Flemming, William (1742). *See* Flemmar. L.

Flemming, William. S & T Apr 1753 *Thames*. L.

Fleming als Flaming als Filming, William of Manchester, innholder. S for forgery Lent 1761 R for life Lent 1761. La.

Fleming, William. S s at St. Aldate, Oxford, Lent 1764. O.

Flendell, Joseph. R Jan-Feb T 14 yrs Apr 1772 *Thornton*. M.

Fleppen, John. S for perjury Jly 1774. Do.

Fletcher, Ambrose. S Jan-Jun T 14 yrs Jun 1728 *Elizabeth* LC Potomack Aug 1729. L.

Fletcher, Benjamin. S Lent AT Summer 1720. Y.

Fletcher, Charles. LC from *Forward* Rappahannock May 1728. X.

Fletcher, Eleanor. S Jly 1756. M.

Fletcher, Elizabeth. S May T Jun 1726 *Loyal Margaret* LC Annapolis Oct 1726. M.

Fletcher, Elizabeth. S Jun-Dec 1738 T Jan 1739 *Dorsetshire* to Va. M.

Fletcher als Weeden, Jane. TB 14 yrs Oct 1719. L.

Fletcher, John. S Mar 1719 TB 14 yrs Aug 1720. Le.

Fletcher, John. S & T Oct 1730 *Forward* LC Potomack Jan 1731. L.

Fletcher, John. S & T Jan 1739 *Dorsetshire*. L.

Fletcher, John. S Sep 1754. L.

Fletcher, John. T May 1767 *Thornton*. M.

Fletcher, John. S & T Apr 1769 *Tryal*. M.

Fletcher, Joseph. S s at Market Drayton Lent 1748. Sh.

Fletcher, Joseph. S Jan-Feb T Apr 1772 *Thornton*. M.

Fletcher, Margaret (1746). *See* Smith. M.

Fletcher, Martha wife of Edward. S s wool fleeces Summer 1750. Nf.

Fletcher, Mary. R for Barbados or Jamaica Aug 1700. L.

Fletcher, Mary als Joyce. S Jly T Aug 1721 *Prince Royal* LC Va Nov 1721. M.

Fletcher, Moses. S s at Walsall Summer 1764. St.

Fletcher, Nathaniel, als Black Jack. S & R 14 yrs Summer 1734. Ca.

Fletcher, Ralph. S & TB Mar 1734. G.

Fletcher, Richard. S Lent R 14 yrs Summer 1738. Wa.

Fletcher, Richard. S Lent R 14 yrs Summer 1764. St.

Fletcher, Robert. PT Oct 1686. M.

Fletcher, Rowland. S s at Newport Lent 1750. He.

Fletcher, Samuel. S s at Market Drayton Lent 1748. Sh.

Fletcher, Samuel. S Lent TB Sep 1750. Y.

Fletcher, Thomas. S Mar TB to Va Apr 1754. Wi.

Fletcher, Thomas. R Dec 1765 T 14 yrs Jan 1766 *Tryal*. M.

Fletcher, Thomas. S s mare Lent R 14 yrs Summer 1767 T Apr 1768. Li.

Fletcher, William. R for Barbados or Jamaica May 1684. M.

Fletcher, William. R & T Dec 1734 *Caesar* LC Va Jly 1735. M.

Fletcher, William. TB Apr 1739. Db.

Fletcher, William. S Jan-Jun 1747. M.

Fletcher, William. S Dec 1773. M.

Fletcher, William of Bilborough, coalminer. SQS s fowl Oct 1775. Nt.

Flew, John. R Mar 1774. So.

Flewit, Thomas. AT Summer 1733. Wo.

Flewitt, William. TB Sep 1726. Nt.

Flight, Richard of Kings Sombourne. R for Barbados Jun 1708. Ha.

Flinders, William. S Lent TB Apr 1758. Db.

Fling, John. S Jly-Dec 1747. M.

Fling, John. S Sep-Oct T Dec 1752 *Greyhound*. M.

Flingar, John. S Apr 1727. So.

Flinn, Barnard. S Jan T Apr 1762 *Dolphin*. M.

Flinn, Thomas. S Jan T Apr 1762 *Dolphin*. M.

Flint, David. S Apr-May T May 1744 *Justitia*. M.

Flint, Henry of Midwich. R for America Mar 1688. St.

Flint, John, weaver aged 23, brown hair. S Jan T Feb 1723 *Jonathan* LC Annapolis Jly 1724. M.

Flint, John. SQS Apr T Jly 1772 *Tayloe*. M.

Flint, John. R 14 yrs Lent 1774. Ht.

Flint, Mary Ann wife of Thomas. S Dec 1768 T Jan 1769 *Thornton*. M.

Flint, Richard. S & T Dec 1767 *Neptune*. L.

Flint, Richard. S Jan-Feb 1775. M.

Flint, William. S s heifers at Kirby Cane & R Lent 1772. Nf.

Flintham, Mary. S Apr 1760. M.

Flitcroft, William. S Summer 1757. Y.

Flixon, John of St. George, Southwark. R for Barbados or Jamaica Feb 1686. Sy.

Flixon, William, an old convict. S to be transported 1697. Ht.

Flocker, John. S & T Dec 1770 *Justitia*. L.

Flood, Daniel. S Jan T Mar 1764 *Tryal*. L.

Flood, Frances. SQS Dec 1772. M.

Flood, Francis. S Jan T 14 yrs Feb 1719 *Worcester* LC Annapolis Jun 1719. LM.

Flood, John. T Apr 1741 *Speedwell* or *Mediterranean*. Sy.

Flood, Judith. S Oct 1766 T Jan 1767 *Tryal*. M.

Flood, Matthew of St. James, Westminster. SW Apr 1774. M.

Flood, William. T Jun *Loyal Margaret* LC Md Dec 1726. K.

Florence, Francis. S Sep T Dec 1763 *Neptune*. M.

Florence als Florendine, William. S Lent 1774. Wa.

Florendine, William (1774). *See* Florence. Wa.

Florey, Thomas, aged 19, dark. S & T Oct 1720 *Gilbert* LC Annapolis May 1721. L.

Floud, James (1740). *See* Moor. M.

Flounders, Thomas. SQS Guisborough s iron Jly TB Aug 1751. Y.

Flower, Daniel. R for Barbados or Jamaica Jly 1686. M.

Flower, Eleanor. S Jun T Nov 1743 *George William*. M.

Flower, Frances (1683). *See* Marshall. L.

Flower, James. S Aug TB Sep 1728. So.

Flower, John of Chilcombe, husbandman. R for Barbados Jun 1669. Ha.

Flower, John. R for Barbados Mar 1677. L.

Flower (Fowler), John. Rebel T 1685.

Flower, John. S Lent 1757. K.

Flower, Joseph. T Jun 1728 *Elizabeth* LC Va Aug 1729. E.

Flower, Richard. R for Barbados Jun 1671. L.

Flower, Robert. S Summer 1724 R Summer 1725. Li.

Flower, Samuel of St. Paul Covent Garden. SW Apr 1774. M.

Flower, Stephen. S Mar TB to Va May 1763. Wi.

Flower, William. S Aug T Oct 1726 *Forward* to Va. M.

Flowers, Jane. S Jly-Dec 1747. M.

Flowers, William. S s horse Summer 1746 R 14 yrs Lent 1747. Wa.

Floyd, Anne. S City Summer 1718 R 14 yrs Summer 1720. Nl.

Floyd, Arthur. S May T Jun 1756 *Lyon*. L.

Floyd als Harris, Diana. T Apr 1732 *Patapsco*. K.

Floyde, Henry. R for Barbados Sep TB Oct 1669. L.

Floyd, Henry (1719). *See* Perry. L.

Floyd, John of Christchurch. R for Barbados or Jamaica Jun 1675. Sy.

Floyd, John (1686). *See* Lloyd. E.

Floyd als Lloyd, John of Gloucester. R for America Nov 1694. G.

Floyd, Margaret of Newington. R for Barbados or Jamaica Jun 1684. Sy.

Floyd, Margaret wife of Stainbank. S 14 yrs for receiving tallow Summer 1764; Isabel Floyd acquitted. Du.

Floyd, Mary. S & T Apr 1762 *Dolphin*. L.

Floyd, Richard of Ausley. R for America Jly 1673. Wa.

Floyd, Samuel of Liverpool, tailor. S for forgery & R Lent 1768. La.

Floyd, Susanna. LC from *Honor* Port York Jan 1721. X.

Floyd, Thomas (1691). *See* Williams. M.

Floyd, Thomas. S Jun-Dec 1738 T Jan 1739 *Dorsetshire* to Va. M.

Floyd, Thomas. S Feb-Apr T May 1755 *Rose*. M.

Floyd, William. LC from *Loyal Margaret* Annapolis Oct 1726. X.

Floyd, William. S Feb T Apr 1742 *Bond* to Potomack. M.

Floyd, William. S Summer 1748 R 14 yrs Lent 1749. He.

Flude, Thomas. S Summer 1767. Le.

Fluellin, William. S Jly T Aug 1721 *Prince Royal* to Va. M.

Flurry, Edward. S s shoes Jan-May T Jun 1738 *Forward* to Md or Va. M.

Fluster, Thomas. S Feb 1734. L.

Fluty, John. S Jly T Sep 1765 *Justitia*. M.

Flyfield, George (1763). *See* Morris. Wo.

Foane, Robert. Rebel T 1685.

Foden, Richard. S Jan T Feb 1726 *Supply* LC Annapolis May 1726. M.

Fogarty, Mary. S Feb 1761. M.

Fogarty, Patrick. S Jun 1761. M.

Fogg, Elizabeth. SQS Oct 1762. La.

Fogg als Trigg, John. T Oct 1723 *Forward*. E.

Fogg, Richard. R for America Jly 1687. Db.

Fogg, Richard of Bromley. R for America Jly 1693. St.

Foggett, Mary. S Feb 1729 T *Patapsco* LC Annapolis Dec 1729. M.

Foker, John. T 14 yrs Sep 1764 *Justitia*. E.

Foler, Robert. S Jan 1774. L.

Folgee, Robert. S Jly T Dec 1736 *Dorsetshire* to Va. M.

Folkard, Henry. S Lent 1768. Su.

Follard, James. S Jly T 14 yrs Aug 1718 *Eagle* LC Charles Town Mar 1719. LM.

Follett, John. Rebel T 1685.

Folling, Cecilia. SQS Jun T Jly 1772 *Tayloe*. M.

Folliott, Joseph. S Lent 1775. Wa.

Follitt, William. S & T Mar 1763 *Neptune*. L.

Followfield, John. LC from *Forward* Annapolis Dec 1725. X.

Folon, Robert. S Feb 1774. L.

Folton, Thomas. S Summer 1765. Nl.

Folwell, Mary. S Apr-May T Jly 1771 *Scarsdale*. M.

Food, James. S Lent 1749. Sy.

Food, John. S Lent T Apr 1773. No.

Foot, Anthony. SQS Jan 1754. M.

Foote, Elizabeth. S Feb-Apr 1746. M.

Foot, Esau. T 14 yrs Apr 1769 *Tryal*. Sy.

Foot, George. R 14 yrs Mar 1735. Do.

Foote, John of Maiden Newton, blacksmith. R for Barbados Jly 1667. Do.

Foot, John. Rebel T 1685.

Foot, John. S Mar 1746. De.

Foot, Joseph. SL Jan T Feb 1765 *Tryal*. Sy.

Foot, Magdalen (1731). *See* Bucknell. L.

Foot, Margaret. S Jly T Oct 1723 *Forward*. L.

Foot, Simon. S Mar 1773. Do.

Forbes, Francis. S Sep-Oct 1749. M.

Forbes, Isabella. SQS Jun T Jly 1753 *Tryal*. M.

Forbes, James. S Feb T Mar 1727 *Rappahannock*. L.

Forbes, James. S s horse & R for life Summer 1770. Wo.

Forbess, John. S May-Jly 1773. M.

Force, James. SQS Apr T May 1767 *Thornton*. M.

Forse, Richard. S Mar 1750. Do.

Forcey, Thomas. Rebel T 1685.

Ford, Ambrose. R for Barbados Jly 1675. L.

Ford, Amelia. S & T Aug 1752 *Tryal*. L.

Ford, Ann. SQS & TB Apr 1771. So.

Ford, Ann. S Mar 1773. De.

Ford, Ann. S Lent 1774. K.

Ford, Arthur (2). Rebels T 1685.

Ford, Bowyer. S May T Jun 1727 *Susanna*. L.

Ford, Charles. S & T Jly 1772 *Tayloe*. L.

Ford, Edward. Rebel T 1685.

Foord, Edward. R 14 yrs Lent 1733. St.

Ford, Elizabeth wife of Edward. SQS for Barbados Oct 1664. M.

Ford, Elizabeth. S Aug T Oct 1741 *Sea Horse* to Va. M.

Ford, Francis. S Summer TB Sep 1761. Y.

Ford, George. S Mar 1740. So.

Ford, Isaac. R for Barbados or Jamaica Dec 1689. M.

Ford, James. T Jan 1736 *Dorsetshire* LC Va Sep 1736. Sy.

Ford, James. S Jan T Feb 1744 *Neptune*. L.

Ford, Jeremiah of Reigate. SQS Apr T May 1750 *Lichfield*. Sy.

Ford, John of Takeley. R for Barbados or Jamaica Feb 1696. E.

Ford, John of Bethersden. R for Barbados or Jamaica Jly 1696. K.

Ford, John of Clapham. S Lent T May 1719 *Margaret* LC Md May 1720;
   sold to Timothy Sullivan. Sy.

Ford, John. S Apr 1741. So.

Ford, John. S Jly 1752. De.

Ford, John. S Apr T May 1767 *Thornton*. M.

Ford, John. S for forgery & R 14 yrs Lent 1774. St.

Ford, John. S Sep-Oct 1775. M.

Ford, Joseph. R for America Feb 1692. Db.

Ford, Laurence. R for Barbados or Jamaica Dec 1698. L.

Ford, Margaret. S & T Oct 1722 *Forward* LC Annapolis Jun 1723. M.

Ford, Mary Ann. S Feb-Apr 1746. M.

Ford, Nicholas of Mangotsfield, yeoman. S Mar 1718 as a dangerous, idle
   person, threatening the King's officers and witnesses. Be.

Ford, Nicholas of Siston. S s fish Summer 1718 & noted as above. G.

Ford, Patrick. S Lent 1774. E.

Ford, Richard. R May AT Sep 1684. M.

Foard, Richard. R 14 yrs Summer 1732. St.

Ford, Richard of St. James, Westminster. S s guineas & T Feb 1740 *York* to
   Md. M.

Ford, Richard. S & T Dec 1752 *Greyhound*. M.

Ford, Richard. S Feb 1754. M.
Ford, Richard. S Jan T Apr 1759 *Thetis*. M.
Ford, Roger. S Apr 1753. So.
Ford, Samuel. S Feb T Apr 1769 *Tryal*. M.
Ford, Sarah. S 14 yrs for receiving Lent 1722. G.
Ford, Sarah. S & T Oct 1730 *Forward* LC Potomack Jan 1731. M.
Foard, Thomas of Cromhall. S Summer 1720. G.
Ford, Thomas. S Jan-Jun T Jun 1728 *Elizabeth* LC Potomack Aug 1729. L.
Ford, Thomas. S Lent R 14 yrs Summer 1736. He.
Ford, Thomas. S Dec 1745. L.
Ford, Thomas. S Mar 1749 TB to Va. De.
Ford, Thomas. S Mar 1773. Ha.
Ford, William. S Jan T Feb 1724 *Anne* to Carolina. M.
Ford, William. T Sep 1742 *Forward*. K.
Ford als Fords, William. S s gamecock at Clanfield Lent 1743. O.
Ford, William. S s iron buckles at Wolverhampton Lent 1764. St.
Ford, William. S s at Enville Summer 1772. St.
Forden, William. S May T Jun 1764 *Dolphin*. M.
Forder, Henry. S Mar 1775. Ha.
Forder, William. SQS Apr 1765. Ha.
Fordham, Alice. S Jun T Oct 1744 *Susannah*. M.
Fordham, Edward. S Aug T Sep 1727 *Forward* LC Rappahannock May 1728. L.
Fordham, Hannah. S Apr T Sep 1757 *Thetis*. L.
Fordham, Jacob. S Jan 1751. M.
Fordham, Thomas of Chesterton. R for America Apr 1697. Ca.
Fordham, Thomas. T Jly 1770 *Scarsdale*. M.
Fordham, Thomas. R 7 yrs Lent 1774. E.
Fordington als Forthington, Fortunatus. S Aug 1773. Do.
Fords, James. SQS & TB Mar 1736. G.
Fords, John. S s shirt at Saul Summer TB Sep 1736. G.
Fords, William (1743). *See* Ford. O.
Fore, George of Rotherhithe. SQS Jan 1774. Sy.
Forman, John. T May 1744 *Justitia*. Sx.
Foreman, Mary. S Dec 1753-Jan 1754. M.
Foreman, Peter. S Dec 1753-Jan 1754. M.
Foreman, Richard (1738). *See* Pointer. Wi.
Foreman, Walter. S Sep T Nov 1743 *George William*. M.
Foreman, William. R for Barbados or Jamaica Dec 1693. M.
Forshea als Southward, Eleanor. S Feb T Apr 1762 *Dolphin*. M.
Forsee, Elizabeth. S Jan T Feb 1744 *Neptune* to Md. M.
Foreshoe, Margaret. S Aug T Oct 1741 *Sea Horse* to Va. M.
Forshaw, John of St. Helens within Windle. SQS Apr 1772. La.
Foresight, John. S Jly-Sep 1754. M.
Forey, William. T May 1751 *Tryal*. Sx.
Forge, William. R 14 yrs Summer 1750. Y.
Forgeom, Mary. S & T Oct 1729 *Forward* LC Va Jun 1730. M.
Forly, John. S s hogs Lent 1734. Be.
Forrest als Forrester, Elias. S s from warehouse at Halesowen Lent 1769. Wo.
Forest, Humphrey. S Lent R 14 yrs Summer 1755. Sh.
Forrest, James. S Lent 1742. Sh.

Forrest, Jeremiah. S Summer 1755. Cu.

Forrest, Martin. S Summer 1742 R 14 yrs Lent 1743. Du.

Forrest, Richard of Worcester. S Lent 1720. Wo.

Forrest als Forester, Susan of Portsea, spinster. R for Barbados Jun 1708. Ha.

Forrest, Thomas. S s at Pershore Lent 1726. Wo.

Forester, Ann. S & T Jly 1753. M.

Forrester, Elias (1769). *See* Forrest. Wo.

Forrester, Elizabeth. S s muslin at Stafford Lent 1723 LC from *Robert* Annapolis Jun 1725. St.

Forrester, James. S s shirt at Stone Summer 1752. St.

Forrester, John. S Jly 1763. M.

Forester, Patience. S Dec 1742 T 14 yrs Apr 1743 *Justitia*. M.

Forrester, Susan (1708). *See* Forrest. Ha.

Forrester, William. S s stockings Summer 1750. Cu.

Forrester als Jackson, William als John. R 14 yrs Summer 1758. Cu.

Forsbrook, Richard. S Lent R 14 yrs Summer 1755. Wo.

Forsith, John, als Berkley, William. T for life Apr 1769 *Tryal*. Sy.

Forster. *See* Foster.

Forsyth, Joseph of Ulverstone, joiner. SQS Jly 1750. La.

Fort, Francis. S Feb 1735 T Jan 1736 *Dorsetshire* to Va. M.

Fort, William of Ilminster, sergeweaver. R for Barbados Feb 1699. So.

Fortee, Jacob. S & T Oct 1722 *Forward* LC Annapolis Jun 1723. L.

Forth, John. S s silver tankard Summer 1762. Du.

Forth, John (1769). *See* Heirs. Be.

Forth, Richard. S Oct T Nov 1759 *Phoenix*. M.

Forth als Taylor, Timothy. S Feb 1738. Ha.

Forthington, Fortunatus (1773). *See* Fordington. Do.

Forton, Mary (1727). *See* Clark. M.

Forward, Ambrose. S s goat hair May T Dec 1735 *John* LC Annapolis Sep 1736. M.

Forward, Mary. S Jun 1733 T Jan 1734 *Caesar* LC Va Jly 1734.M.

Foskett, Henry. S Lent 1749. Bu.

Fossett, Dorothy. S & T 14 yrs Oct 1732 *Caesar*. L.

Fossett, Edward. S Sep-Oct 1774. M.

Fosset, Henry. S May T Jun 1764 *Dolphin*. L.

Fossett, John. S s at Thatcham Lent 1729. Be.

Fossett, John. R Apr 1773. M.

Fossett, Joseph of Bermondsey. SQS Jly T Sep 1764 *Justitia*. Sy.

Fossitt, Richard. S Feb T Apr 1739 *Forward* to Va. M.

Fossett, William. S & T Oct 1732 *Caesar* to Va. M.

Foster, Alice. R for Barbados Jun 1671. L.

Foster, Alice. R Sep 1671 AT Oct 1673. M.

Forster, Ann. S Feb T May 1719 *Margaret*; sold to John Gaskin Md Sep 1719. L.

Foster, Anne. S Mar TB to Va May 1763. Wi.

Foster, Charles. S Sep T Oct 1719 *Susannah & Sarah* LC Annapolis Apr 1720. L.

Foster, Daniel. R 14 yrs Summer 1728 (SP). Nf.

Foster, David. S Jly T Aug 1721 *Prince Royal* LC Va Nov 1721. M.

Forster, Edward. S for setting fire to barn Lent R 14 yrs Summer 1736. Li.

Foster, Edward. S Mar 1750 TB to Va. De.

Foster, Edward. S Mar 1761. L.

Foster, Elizabeth. S & T Oct 1729 *Forward* but died on passage. M.

Foster, Elizabeth of Ealing. S s poultry Feb T May 1736 *Patapsco*. M.

Foster, Fortune. S s edging Jan T Apr 1735 *Patapsco* LC Annapolis Oct 1735. L.

Foster, George, waterman. T *Jekyll* LC Barbados Jun 1724. L.

Forster, George. S Apr-May 1754. M.

Foster, George. T Apr 1759 *Thetis*. Sx.

Foster, Henry. S s at Handsworth Summer 1771. St.

Forster, Humphry, aged 17, periwig maker, fair. LC from *Jonathan* Annapolis Jly 1724. X.

Foster, James. Died on passage in *Forward* 1730. X.

Foster, James. S May T 14 yrs Jly 1771 *Scarsdale*. L.

Foster, James. S s at Newcastle under Lyme Lent 1775. St.

Foster als Turner, Jane wife of Thomas Turner of Burton on Trent. R for America Jly 1679. St.

Foster, Jane. S s at Workington Summer 1742. Cu.

Forster, John of St. Maughans. R for America Jly 1678. Mo.

Foster, John. Rebel T 1685.

Foster, John of Chislington. R (Oxford Circ) for America Mar 1701. Ch.

Forster als Hallatt, John. S s horse Summer 1741 R 14 yrs Summer 1742. We.

Forster, John. S Jan-Apr 1749. M.

Foster, John of Warrington, buckle maker. SQS for receiving Jan 1752. La.

Foster, John. T May 1752 *Lichfield*. Sy.

Foster, John. S Jan 1757. L.

Foster, John. S Jan T Feb 1765 *Tryal*. L.

Foster, John. S Summer 1766 R 14 yrs Summer 1767. Cu.

Foster, John. R 14 yrs Summer 1767. Nl.

Foster, John. S s silver mug at St. Sepulchre Sep 1768 T Jan 1769 *Thornton*. L.

Foster, John. SQS & T Apr 1771 *Thornton*. Ht.

Forster, Joseph. SQS Feb T Apr 1772 *Thornton*. M.

Foster, Mary. R for Barbados Sep 1669. M.

Foster, Mary of Benmead, Hambleton, spinster. R for Barbados Jun 1699. Ha.

Foster, Mary. S Jan T Feb 1719 *Worcester* LC Annapolis Jun 1719. L.

Foster, Mary (1730). *See* Williams. M.

Foster als Anderson, Mary, als wife of Richard Wilson. S City as pickpocket Lent 1732 R 14 yrs Summer 1733. Y.

Foster, Mary of Clerkenwell. S s silver spoon & T May 1740 *Essex*. M.

Foster, Mary. S Jan T Feb 1744 *Neptune*. L.

Foster, Mary of Bermondsey, spinster. SQS Jan T Mar 1758 *Dragon*. Sy.

Forster, Mary. S Sep-Oct T Dec 1771 *Justitia*. M.

Forster, Mary. S Jly 1773. L.

Foster, Michael. S Lent R 14 yrs Summer 1759. Li.

Foster, Richard. S & T Dec 1740 *Vernon*. L.

Forster, Robert, als Bell, William. R 14 yrs Summer 1747. Nl.

Forster, Robert. AT City Summer 1758. Nl.

Foster, Robert of Holmepierpoint. SQS s cloak Jan 1769. Nt.

Foster, Rose. T Sep 1766 *Justitia*. M.

Foster, Sampson. S Jly 1719 to be T to Va. Co.

Foster, Samuel. SQS Jan 1765. Ha.

Foster, Sarah (1771). *See* Cooper. M.

Foster, Thomas. S Jun 1739. L.

Foster, Thomas. T Apr 1741 *Speedwell* or *Mediterranean*. Sy.

Foster, Thomas. S Lent R 14 yrs Summer 1751. St.

Foster, Thomas. SL & T Jan 1756 *Greyhound*. Sy.

Forster, Thomas of Barking. SQS Jly T Sep 1766 *Justitia*. E.

Foster, Thomas. S Summer 1767. No.

Foster, William. S Summer T Oct 1723 *Forward* from London. Y.

Forster, William. S s brass stamp May 1735 T Jan 1736 *Dorsetshire* LC Va
Sep 1736. M.

Forster, William. S City Lent 1742. Y.

Forster, William. S s sheep Lent R 14 yrs Summer 1750. Nt.

Forster, William. S Feb-Apr T May 1752 *Lichfield*. M.

Foster, William. S s sheep Lent R 14 yrs Summer 1756. Li.

Foster, William. S Jly 1766. De.

Foster, William of St. Paul Covent Garden. SW Apr 1774. M.

Fostyker, Susan. R for Barbados Oct 1673. M.

Fotherby, Susan (1727). *See* Moses. L.

Fothergill, George. S Summer 1732. Nl.

Fothergill, William. S & T Dec 1731 *Forward* to Md or Va. M.

Fotheringham, James. S s sal ammoniac Summer 1752. Nl.

Foulger, John. S Jan T Feb 1765 *Tryal*. L.

Foulger, Robert. S s at St. James, Bury St. Edmunds, Lent 1775. Su.

Foulham, William. R for America Jly 1694. Li.

Foulk, John. TB Oct 1739. TB Apr 1739. Db.

Fowke, Moses. S Oct 1661 to House of Correction unless he consents to be
transported. M.

Fowke, Sarah. S Summer 1756. Db.

Foulks, Edward. S Sep 1754. L.

Folks, Edward. S s at Maer Summer 1774. St.

Foulkes als Fox, George. S Jun-Dec 1738 T Jan 1739 *Dorsetshire* to Va. M.

Foulkes, James. T Jly 1723 *Alexander* LC Md Sep 1723. Bu.

Folkes, John (1721). *See* Fox. E.

Folks, John. S Feb T Mar 1727 *Rappahannock* to Md. M.

Fokes, John. S Lent T May 1767 *Thornton*. Bu.

Folkes, John. S Feb T Apr 1770 *New Trial*. M.

Foulkes, John. S s sheep at Eversholt & R Lent 1774. Bd.

Fookes, Mary. S s at New Windsor Lent 1751. Be.

Fowkes, Robert. R for Barbados Jun 1671. L.

Fooks, Robert. S Mar 1756. Do.

Fukes, Thomas. SQS Sep 1774. M.

Foulks, William of St. James, Westminster. S s coat & T May 1736
Patapsco. M.

Fowkes, William. S s sheep Lent R 14 yrs Summer 1768. St.

Foulson, Henry. TB Aug 1735 T *Squire* LC Md Apr 1736. Db.

Foulston, Samuel, als Green, John of Bermondsey. R for Barbados or
Jamaica Jly 1715. Sy.

Found als Layfield, William. R 14 yrs Aug 1741. So.

Foundme, Peter (1724). *See* Findme. Ha.

Founds als Laffield, Thomas. S Aug 1741. So.

Fountayne, Aaron of Water Newton. R for Barbados Aug 1671. Hu.

Fountain, Francis. S Feb T Mar 1730 *Patapsco* LC Annapolis Sep 1730. L.

Fountaine, John. S Jly 1733. Do.

Fountain, Mary. S Jan T Apr 1762 *Dolphin*. M.

Fountain, Mary Ann. LC from *Owners Goodwill* Annapolis Jly 1722. X.

Fountaine, Richard. R for Barbados Jly 1675. M.

Fountaine, William. T Apr 1768 *Thornton*. Bu.

Fountenow, Mary. Sep-Dec 1746. M.

Foweracre, James of Taunton St. James. R for Barbados Jly 1678. So.

Fouracres, James (1729). *See* Acres. De.

Fouracres, Richard. Rebel T 1685.

Foweracres, William of Wellington. R for Barbados Jly 1698. So.

Fourcauzey, Peter. S Sep-Oct T Dec 1752 *Greyhound*. M.

Fovargue, John. S Summer 1740 R 14 yrs Lent 1741. Li.

Fowle, Margaret. S Summer R for Barbados Aug 1664. K.

Fowell, Martha. S Jan T Feb 1726 *Supply* LC Annapolis May 1726. M.

Fowell, Susanna (1725). *See* Belchier. M.

Fowke. *See* Foulke.

Fowkes. *See* Foulkes.

Fowler, Ann. S Lent TB Sep 1750. Y.

Fowler, Bartholomew. S Mar 1756. Do.

Fowler, Charles. S Summer 1769. Li.

Fowler als Carter als Clements, Elizabeth. S Sep-Oct 1748 T Jan 1749 *Laura*. M.

Fowler, Elizabeth. S Lent R 14 yrs Summer 1761. Bu.

Fowler, Elizabeth wife of David. S for receiving feather bed T 14 yrs Jun 1764 *Dolphin*. M.

Fowler, George. S s heifers Summer 1769 R 14 yrs Lent 1770. Nt.

Fowler, Hester. S Jan 1746 to be T 14 yrs. M.

Fowler, James. Rebel T 1685.

Fowler, Jane. S s at Bishops Cleeve Summer 1758. G.

Fowler, John Sr. Rebel T 1685.

Fowler, John Jr. Rebel T 1685.

Fowler, John. R for America Feb 1692. Li.

Fowler, John. AT Lent 1747 & tried same session for returning from transportation & found not guilty. Y.

Fowler, John. T Apr 1768 *Thornton*. Sy.

Fowler, John. S May-Jly 1773. M.

Fowler, Joseph. S (Western Circ) Dec 1766 AT Lent 1767. G.

Fowler, Margaret (1768). *See* Sedgware. M.

Fowler, Mary (1677). *See* Toole. L.

Fowler, Mary (1679). *See* Penryn. M.

Fowler, Mary. S Jan-Jun T Jun 1728 *Elizabeth* LC Potomack Aug 1729. L.

Fowler, Mary. S Apr-May T May 1744 *Justitia*. M.

Fowler, Mary (1748). *See* Fowles. M.

Fowler, Richard. T Jun 1764 *Dolphin*. Sx.

Fowler, Thomas. S Dec 1750. L.

Fowler, Thomas. R 14 yrs Mar 1754. Ha.

Fowler, Thomas. S Lent T Sep 1757 *Thetis*. K.

Fowler, Thomas. S & T Sep 1764 *Justitia*. M.

Fowler, Walter (1683). *See* Gilman. Sy.

Fowler, Ward. T Oct 1722 *Forward*. Sx.

Fowler, William. S Lent 1750. Hu.
Fowler, William. T Apr 1766 *Ann*. Ht.
Fowles, Elizabeth (1739). *See* Holmes. M.
Fowles als Fowler, Mary. S May-Jly 1748. M.
Fowles, Samuel Wallis. S Lent 1742. G.
Fowles, Stephen. S Oct T 14 yrs Dec 1724 *Rappahannock*. L.
Fowley, Thomas. S Jly-Sep T Oct 1739 *Duke of Cumberland* to Va. M.
Fownes, John of Cradley. R for America Jly 1681. Wo.
Fox, Alexander. S s wheat at Presteigne Summer 1767. He.
Fox, Andrew. S Summer T Sep 1772. No.
Fox als Turner, Ann. TB Feb 1747. Db.
Fox, Barbara. S & T Oct 1722 *Forward*. L.
Fox, Eleanor. S Dec 1766 T Jan 1767 *Tryal*. M.
Fox, Elizabeth. S & T Oct 1730 *Forward* LC Rappahannock Jan 1731. L.
Fox, Frances. R Dec 1699 & Aug 1700. M.
Fox, George. S & T Apr 1725 *Sukey* LC Annapolis Sep 1725. M.
Fox, George (1738). *See* Foulkes. M.
Fox als Bond, Hannah. S Feb T Mar 1729 *Patapsco* LC Annapolis Dec 1729. M.
Fox, Hannah (1771). *See* Kay. La.
Fox, Humphrey. S s lead Sep T Dec 1736 *Dorsetshire* to Va. M.
Fox, James. S Aug T 14 yrs Sep 1718 *Eagle* LC Charles Town Mar 1719. L.
Fox, James. S Jun-Dec 1738 T Jan 1739 *Dorsetshire* to Va. M.
Fox, James. S for perjury Feb 1773. L.
Fox als Alderidge als Folkes, John. T Aug 1721 *Owners Goodwill*. E.
Fox, John. S & T Oct 1730 *Forward* LC Potomack Jan 1731. M.
Fox, John of St. Giles in Fields. S & T Dec 1740 *Vernon* to Md. M.
Fox, John. T Apr 1742 *Bond*. Sy.
Fox, John. S Summer 1759. Hu.
Fox, John (1764). *See* Evans. Y.
Fox, Laurence. R for America Jun 1686. Li.
Fox, Margaret. S Feb T 14 yrs Sep 1737 *Pretty Patsy* to Md. M.
Fox, Martha. R for Barbados Jun 1671. L.
Fox, Mary. S Sep T Oct 1768 *Justitia*. M.
Fox, Mary. S Feb 1774. L.
Fox, Owen. S 14 yrs for receiving goods stolen in Essex May 1770. M.
Fox, Richard. T Apr 1765 *Ann*. Sy.
Fox, Samuel. S Oct T Dec 1758 *The Brothers*. M.
Fox, Sara. S May T Jun 1726 *Loyal Margaret* LC Annapolis Oct 1726. M.
Fox, Thomas. S Feb T Mar 1730 *Patapsco* LC Annapolis Sep 1730. L.
Fox, Thomas. S & TB Aug 1740. G.
Fox, William. PT Oct 1700. M.
Fox, William. T 14 yrs Dec 1771 *Justitia*. Sy.
Foxall, Elizabeth. R 14 yrs Mar 1771. Do.
Foxley, William of Finchley. S s saddle Feb T May 1736 *Patapsco*. M.
Foxon, William. S Feb T Mar 1758 *Dragon*. L.
Foxworthy, Francis. S for murder Oct 1702 to be T to West Indies (SP). Co.
Foy, James. S Aug 1763. L.
Foy, Margaret (1725). *See* Toy. Sy.
Foy, Margaret. S Feb T Apr 1732 *Patapsco* LC Annapolis Oct 1732. M.
Foy, Patrick. SQS Jly T Sep 1764 *Justitia*. M.

Foy, Rose. S Feb T Apr 1766 *Ann*. M.

Foyle, Thomas. S Jly 1755. Ha.

Foyle, William. S Jly TB to Va Sep 1774. Wi.

Fram, Robert of Newcastle upon Tyne. R for Barbados Jly 1681. Nl.

Frame, Mary. T Apr 1766 *Ann*. K.

Frame, Matthias, a soldier. S s money Feb T Apr 1735 *Patapsco* LC Md
 Oct 1735. M.

Frampton, Joseph. T Jun 1764 *Dolphin*. Sy.

Frampton, Moses. R 14 yrs Mar 1753. Do.

Frampton, Robert. S s horse Summer 1752 R 14 yrs Lent 1753. Be.

France, Daniel. S Lent R 14 yrs Summer TB Aug 1742 T *Shaw* LC
 Antigua May 1743. Db.

France, Henry. R 14 yrs Summer 1747. Y.

France, Mathew of Middleton. SQS Apr 1754. La.

Francis, Andrew. R 14 yrs s mare Summer 1733. Li.

Francis, Basil. R 14 yrs Mar TB to Va Apr 1765. Wi.

Francis, Benjamin of Swardeston. S Summer 1726. *Nf.

Francis, Christopher of Bristol, mariner. R 14 yrs for s from ship in
 distress (SP). Apr 1773. G.

Francis, Dorothy. SQS Sep T Dec 1771 *Justitia*. M.

Francis, Elizabeth. S Aug T Oct 1724 *Forward* LC Annapolis Jun 1725. M.

Francis, Francis. S Summer 1767 R 14 yrs Lent 1768. He.

Francis, George. T Oct 1722 *Forward* LC Md Jun 1723. K.

Francis, Hannah wife of William. S Feb T Apr 1770 *New Trial*. M.

Francis, James (1698). *See* Lane, Richard. De.

Francis, James. S & T Apr 1753 *Thames*. L.

Francis, James. S Oct T Dec 1758 *The Brothers*. L.

Frances, Joan of Quethiock. R for Barbados Jly 1672. Co.

Francis, John. R for Barbados or Jamaica May 1684. L.

Francis, John. S Feb T Mar 1730 *Patapsco* LC Annapolis Sep 1730. L.

Francis, John. S Aug 1735. So.

Franceys, John. S Oct 1735 T Jan 1736 *Dorsetshire* LC Va Sep 1736. M.

Francis, John. SQS New Sarum Jan TB to Va Aug 1752. Wi.

Francis, John. S Lent 1752. Nf.

Francis als French, John. SQS Jun 1761. M.

Francis, John. S & T Jly 1771 *Scarsdale*. M.

Francis, John. T 14 yrs Dec 1771 *Justitia*. E.

Francis, Joseph. SQS New Sarum Jly TB to Va Aug 1769. Wi.

Francis, Margaret of St. Philip, Gloucester, spinster. R for America Jly
 1673. G.

Frances, Margaret wife of Robert of Little Addington. R for America Jly
 1711. No.

Frances, Mary. S Oct 1719 T *Susannah & Sarah* LC Annapolis Apr 1720. L.

Frances, Mary. S s at Alveston Lent TB Apr 1756. G.

Francis, Matthias. S Apr-Jun 1739. M.

Francis, Phebe. S Apr 1773. M.

Francis, Ralph. S s iron spikes in Whitby Docks Lent TB Aug 1757. Y.

Francis, Richard. LC from *Forward* Potomack Jan 1731. X.

Francis, Samuel. S Lent 1754. Su.

Francis, Samuel. S Dec 1760. M.

Francis, Thomas. S Mar 1737. So.

Francis, Thomas. S Dec 1763 T Mar 1764 *Tryal*. M.

Francis, William. S Oct T Dec 1724 *Rappahannock*. L.

Francis als Meggs, William. S Mar TB to Va Apr 1745. Wi.

Francis, William. S Mar 1765. Ha.

Francis, William Caddy. S & T Dec 1736 *Dorsetshire*. L.

Francois, Thomas. R 14 yrs Mar 1764. Ha.

Franck, Anne wife of William of Great Barton, Bury St. Edmunds. R for Barbados Feb 1664. Su.

Frank, Daniel. R for Va May 1622. Sy.

Frankenbridge, John. S Summer 1771. Nt.

Frankish, Matthew. S Summer 1769 R 14 yrs Lent 1770. Nt.

Frankland, Francis. S for highway robbery at Danby & R 14 yrs Summer TB Aug 1774. Y.

Frankland, John. S Lent 1760. Y.

Frankland, John (1763). *See* Walker. La.

Frankland, Samuel of Wimbledon. SQS Jan T Apr 1770 *New Trial*. Sy.

Frankland, Thomas. S for highway robbery at Danby & R 14 yrs Summer TB Aug 1774. Y.

Franklin, Birmingham. S s at Cholsey Lent 1753. Be.

Franklin, Catherine. S May 1775. L.

Franklin, Charles. S Sep 1747. L.

Francklyn, Edward of Bullington Green. R (Western Circ) for America Jly 1700. O.

Franklin, Elizabeth (1731). *See* Woodward. M.

Francklin, John (1721). *See* Windmill. Ht.

Franklain, John. S Mar 1763. Ha.

Franklin, John. S (Western Circ) Dec 1766. G.

Franklin, Mary. S & T Apr 1733 *Patapsco* LC Annapolis Nov 1733. L.

Francklin, Rachael. S Jly T Oct 1741 *Sea Horse* to Va. M.

Franklyn, Richard. S May T 14 yrs Jun 1738 *Forward*. L.

Franklyn, Robert. R & TB to Barbados Oct 1667. L.

Francklyn, Robert. SQS & TB Jan 1725 T *Forward* LC Md Jun 1725. Bd.

Frankling, Robert. S Norwich Summer 1749. Nf.

Franklyn, Samuel. S Dec 1757 T Mar 1758 *Dragon*. M.

Francklyn, Thomas. Rebel T 1685.

Franklin, Thomas. LC from *Rappahannock* at Rappahannock Apr 1726. X.

Franklin, Thomas. S Feb 1773. L.

Franklin, William (1693). *See* Smith. M.

Franks, Elizabeth. T Jly 1724 *Robert* LC Md Jun 1725. Sy.

Franks, Richard. T Sep 1742 *Forward*. E.

Frankus, Charles. Died on passage in *Dorsetshire* 1736. X.

Fratter, Phillis (1737). *See* Phratter. L.

Frazier, Alexander, als Dent, William. S Lent 1755. Y.

Frazer, Charlotte. T Jun 1764 *Dolphin*. Sy.

Frazer, Daniel. SQS Jly T Sep 1764 *Justitia*. M.

Fraizier, Elizabeth. S Feb-Apr 1745. M.

Fraser, George. S Oct T Dec 1769 *Justitia*. L.

Frazer, Henry. S Lent 1773. K.

Frazier, James. S Dec 1763 T Mar 1764 *Tryal*. M.

Frazier als Revett, Jane. S Aug T Oct 1723 *Forward*. L.

Frazier, John. R 14 yrs Summer 1729. Nl.

Frazier, John. S May-Jly 1750. M.

Frazier, John. S s ox Summer 1756 R 14 yrs Lent 1757. La.

Fraser als Friswell als Treswell, Loring John. SQS Apr T Jun 1764
   Dolphin. M.

Frazer, Margaret. S Apr T Jly 1770 *Scarsdale*. L.

Frazier, Mary of St. Margaret, Westminster. SW Jun 1775. M.

Frizer als Smith, Richard. S s horse Summer 1769 R 14 yrs Lent 1770. Wo.

Frazier, Samuel. SQS Jan T Apr 1759 *Thetis*. M.

Frasier, Sarah. S Lent 1763. K.

Frazier, Susan. S Feb T 14 yrs Mar 1730 *Patapsco* LC Annapolis Sep 1730. L.

Frazer, Thomas. S Lent R 14 yrs Summer 1742. Wo.

Frazier, William. S Jan T Feb 1724 *Anne*. L.

Frazier, William (1749). *See* Grace. Bu.

Frazier, William. S Mar 1764. So.

Freame, John. S s at St. Michael, Gloucester, Lent 1772. G.

Frear, Thomas. S & T Sep 1718 *Eagle* LC Charles Town Mar 1719. L.

Frere, Walgrave. S Apr T 14 yrs May 1718 *Tryal* LC Charles Town Aug
   1718. L.

Freckleton, Catherine. S Apr-May T Jly 1771 *Scarsdale*. M.

Frederick als Johannes, Daniel. S Sep-Dec 1755 T Jan 1756 *Greyhound*. M.

Frederick, John. S Apr 1748. L.

Free, Elizabeth. S for Va Aug 1718. M.

Free, John. T Sep 1767 *Justitia*. K.

Freelove, John. S Dec 1733 T Jan 1734 *Caesar* LC Va Jly 1734. M.

Freeman, Alice. T Sep 1730 *Smith*. Sy.

Freeman, Anne (1675). *See* Harris. L.

Freeman, Ann. S Apr T May 1750 *Lichfield*. L.

Freeman, Ann wife of Edward. S s sheep & R 14 yrs Lent 1768; noted as
   having missed transportation ship & ordered to wait until Summer
   1768. Ca.

Freeman, Charles. S Feb T Mar 1730 *Patapsco* LC Annapolis Sep 1730. M.

Freeman, Daniel. S Jan T Feb 1726 *Supply* LC Annapolis May 1726. M.

Freeman, Edward. S Summer 1767. Be.

Freeman, Elizabeth. R for Jamaica Aug 1661. M.

Freeman, Elizabeth. S Oct 1722 T *Forward* LC Annapolis Jun 1723. M.

Freeman, Elizabeth. S Feb-Apr T May 1755 *Rose*. M.

Freeman, Francis. R May TB Jun 1691. M.

Freeman, James of Chailey. R for Barbados or Jamaica Feb 1684. Sx.

Freeman, James. S Jly T Oct 1741 *Sea Horse* to Va. M.

Freeman, James. S Feb 1775. M.

Freman, John. S Aug T Oct 1723 *Forward*. L.

Freeman, John. LC from *Forward* Rappahannock May 1728. X.

Freeman, John. S Dec 1741 T Feb 1742 *Industry* to Md. M.

Freeman, John. S May-Jly 1746. M.

Freeman, John. S May-Jun T Jly 1753 *Tryal*. M.

Freeman, John. T Sep 1757 *Thetis*. K.

Freeman, John. S & T Apr 1766 *Ann*. L.

Freeman, Mary. S May-Jly 1748. M.

Freeman, Mary. S Feb-Apr T May 1751 *Tryal*. M.

Freeman, Mary. S s at Wellington under Wrekin Lent 1758. Sh.

Freeman, Nathaniel. T May 1752 *Lichfield*. E.

Freeman, Samuel. S Apr T May 1751 *Tryal*. L.

Freeman, Thomas (1739). *See* Owen. L.

Freeman, Thomas. S Feb 1752. L.

Freeman, Thomas. S Lent T Sep 1767 *Justitia* from London. Ru.

Freeman, Walter of Raking. R for Barbados or Jamaica Jly 1702. K.

Freeman, William. R Mar 1750. Ha.

Freeman, William (1755). *See* Norman. La.

Freeman, William. S for highway robbery at Luton & R Lent 1774. Bd.

Freemantle, John of Witley. SQS & T Apr 1765 *Ann*. Sy.

Freemantle, William. R 14 yrs Mar 1775. Ha.

Freemore, John. T Sep 1758 *Tryal*. K.

Freestone, Enoch. S Apr 1728. So.

Freestone, Isaac. SQS Jly 1730. So.

Freeston, John. R for America Jly 1708. Le.

Freestone, Walter. S Jly 1718 to be T to Va. So.

French, Alice. S Jun-Dec 1745. M.

French, Baptiste (1766). *See* French, Gasper. M.

French, Benjamin. T May 1744 *Justitia*. Sy.

French, Katherine. S Feb T 14 yrs Apr 1732 *Patapsco* LC Annapolis Oct 1732. L.

French, David. S Sep-Oct 1772. M.

French, Francis. R Dec 1679 AT Feb 1680. M.

French, Gasper als Baptiste. S Jly T Sep 1766 *Justitia*. M.

French, George. SQS Apr 1733. So.

French, George. S & T Apr 1733 *Patapsco* LC Annapolis Nov 1733. L.

French, George. T Jan 1766 *Tryal*. M.

French, James. S Aug 1748. Do.

French, John (1761). *See* Francis. M.

French, Peter. S Feb T Apr 1768 *Thornton*. M.

French, Richard. S Jly 1741. De.

French, Robert. R 14 yrs Aug 1750. So.

French als Thayne, Robert. S s gelding Lent R 14 yrs Summer 1752. Nf.

French, Roger. Rebel T 1685.

French, Samuel. S Aug 1729. De.

French, Thomas of Sarsden. R for America Jly 1675. O.

French, Thomas. S Feb T Mar 1731 *Patapsco* LC Annapolis Jun 1731. M.

French, Thomas. S Nov T Dec 1770 *Justitia*. L.

French, William of Pitchcott. R for Barbados Mar 1679. Bu.

French, William. TB to Va from QS 1737. De.

French, William. S Dec 1774. M.

Freney, Elizabeth. TB to Va from QS 1771. De.

Frenley, John. AT from QS Summer 1765. Nt.

Freshney, John. R for America Jun 1684. Li.

Freshwater, Sarah. R Jan-Feb T Apr 1772 *Thornton*. M.

Freshwater, Thomas. S Jly 1766. Ha.

Freston, Walter. Rebel T 1685.

Fretts, Mary. S May T Jun 1727 *Susanna* to Va. M.

Fretwell, Ann. AT Lent 1760. Y.

Fretwell, William. S Lent 1775. Db.

Frevitt, William. S Lent 1754. Sy.

Frewin, Mary. SQS Apr T May 1752 *Lichfield*. M.

Fricker, John of Frome Selwood, husbandman. R for Barbados Jly 1667. So.

Fricker, John. S Jly 1723. Wi.

Fricker, John. R 14 yrs Jly 1761. So.

Frickland, Robert, aged 39, husbandman, dark. LC from *Gilbert* Annapolis May 1721. X.

Friday, Ann (1759). *See* Giles. M.

Friend, Charles. S Summer 1769 R 14 yrs Lent 1770. Wa.

Frend, John. PT Dec 1691 R Jan 1692. M.

Frind, John (1767). *See* Trend. De.

Friend, John of Bristol. R 14 yrs s from brigantine May 1771 (SP). G.

Friend, Richard of Gasum. R (Midland Circ) for America Feb 1681. Wo.

Frind, Robert. LC Va Aug 1729. Sy.

Friend, Rowland. S Jan T Feb 1733 *Smith*. L.

Friend, Simon. T Apr 1732 *Patapsco*. Sx.

Friend als Rowland, Susannah. S Jan T Feb 1733 *Smith*. L.

Friend, Thomas. S Jan T Feb 1742 *Industry* to Md. M.

Frigatee, Charles. S Apr T May 1755 *Rose*. L.

Frimstone, William. S Summer 1740. Ch.

Frindly, John. S Jan-Apr 1749. M.

Frisby, Ann. S Lent 1765. Li.

Frisby, John. S s sheep Summer 1764 R 14 yrs Lent 1765. Li.

Frisby, William. S Mar TB to Va Apr 1767. Le.

Frisby, William. S & R 7 yrs Summer T Sep 1772 *Trimley* from London. Ru.

Friskney, Edward of Partney. R for America Jly 1673. Li.

Friswell, Loring John (1764). *See* Fraser. M.

Frith, Elizabeth. S & T Oct 1722 *Gilbert* to Md. M.

Frith, Henry. S s sheep Summer 1764 R 14 yrs Lent TB Apr 1765. Db.

Frith, John Jr. of Hornchurch. R for Barbados or Jamaica Jly 1702. E.

Froggatt, Robert. TB Nov 1736. Db.

Frohen, Johanna (1740). *See* Baker. L.

Frosdick, William. TB to Va 1758. De.

Frost, Abraham. S s naval stores Summer 1749. K.

Frost, Elizabeth. TB to Va from QS 1756. De.

Frost, James of Lamarsh. SQS Jan 1770. E.

Frost, John. S Sep T Oct 1719 *Susannah & Sarah* LC Annapolis Apr 1720. L.

Frost, John. S Jun T Sep 1758 *Tryal*. L.

Frost, Joseph. T Nov 1728 *Forward*. Sy.

Frost, Judith. S Oct 1743 T Feb 1744 *Neptune* to Md. M.

Frost, Mary of Woodham. R for Barbados or Jamaica Jly 1679. E.

Frost, Thomas. S Lent R 14 yrs Summer TB to Va Sep 1765. Le.

Frost, William. SQS Jly 1732. So.

Frost, William. S Jly 1738. Ha.

Frost, William of Impington. S Lent 1741. *Ca.

Frost, William. S Jly 1752. De.

Frostick als Harris, Ruth, als Jones, Mary. S & T Jly 1771 *Scarsdale*. M.

Froud, Jane. R & T for life Sep 1766 *Justitia*. M.

Froud, Thomas. T for life Dec 1770 *Justitia*. Sy.

Fry als Hull, Ann. SQS Apr T May 1752 *Lichfield*. M.

Fry, Daniel. R for Barbados Mar 1683. L.

Fry, Edward. S Lent 1750. Ca.

Fry, Elianor, spinster. SQS Warminster Jly TB to Va Oct 1764. Wi.

Fry, Elizabeth (1770). *See* Bailey. M.
Fry, Francis of Empingham. R for America Jly 1678. Ru.
Fry, George. S Aug 1741. So.
Fry, Jane. S & T Oct 1729 *Forward* LC Va Jun 1730. M.
Fry, John. S Mar 1729 TB to Va. De.
Fry, John. T Dec 1753 *Whiteing*. K.
Fry, John. T for life Dec 1771 *Justitia*. Sy.
Fry, Joseph. S Apr 1756. So.
Fry als Monger, Joseph. S Mar 1765. Ha.
Fry, Patience. S Dec 1727. L.
Fry, Patience. S Oct 1741 T Feb 1742 *Industry*. L.
Fry, Richard of Frome, scribbler. SQS Oct 1753 for a second time running
    away and leaving his family chargeable to the parish of Frome TB Apr
    1754. So.
Fry, Richard. S Feb 1775. M.
Fry, Robert. SQS Jly TB Aug 1761. So.
Fry, Thomas. S Mar 1730. So.
Fry, William. S Dec 1727. M.
Fry, William. S Jly-Sep T Oct 1739 *Duke of Cumberland* to Va. M.
Fry, William. R 14 yrs Mar 1740. So.
Fry, William. S Apr T for life May 1750 *Lichfield*. M.
Fry, William. S s horse Lent R 14 yrs Summer 1763. O.
Fryatt, Robert. S Summer 1735. Su.
Fryer, George of Lancaster. R for Barbados Jly 1699. La.
Fryer, Isaac. S Mar 1753. Ha.
Fryer, John. R Dec 1699 & Aug 1700. M.
Fryer, John. T Aug 1721 *Owners Goodwill* LC Md Nov 1721. Ca.
Fryer, John. S Feb T Apr 1742 *Bond* to Potomack. M.
Fryer, John. R 14 yrs Jly 1744 TB to Va 1745. De.
Fryer als Turpin, John. S Feb T 14 yrs Mar 1750 *Tryal*. M.
Fryer, John. S Lent 1764. Li.
Fryer, Joseph. R 14 yrs Apr 1739. So.
Fryer, Joseph. R 14 yrs Summer TB Sep 1750. Y.
Fryer, Leonard of Epping. R for Barbados or Jamaica Mar 1698. E.
Fryer, William. S & T Oct 1732 *Caesar* to Va. M.
Fryer, William. SQS Peterborough s horse Oct 1740. No.
Fryer, William. S & T Jly 1772 *Tayloe*. M.
Fryers, John. R 14 yrs Oct 1772. M.
Fryett, Robert. S & T Jan 1756 *Greyhound*. M.
Fudge, Roger of Stallbridge Weston. R for Barbados Jun 1699. Do.
Fudges, John (1720). *See* Benson. Sy.
Fulbrook, Richard. S s eels at Aldermaston Lent 1757. Be.
Fulford, John. S May-Jly T Sep 1751 *Greyhound*. M.
Fulford, John. S s gun Summer 1753. Wo.
Fulgeram, Thomas. T for life Oct 1768 *Justitia*. Sy.
Fulham, Edward. SQS Feb T Apr 1765 *Ann*. M.
Fulham, Margaret. SWK Jan T Apr 1766 *Ann*. K.
Fulham, Thomas. S Apr-May 1754. M.
Fulker, Mary. S Jan-Jun 1747. M.
Fulker, Zachariah. S s sheep at Shinfield Summer 1744 R 14 yrs Lent
    1745. Be.

Fullagate, Edward. T 14 yrs Nov 1762 *Prince William*. Sy.

Fullager, Elizabeth. T Sep 1767 *Justitia*. K.

Fullagar, John. T May 1751 *Tryal*. K.

Fuller, Bartholomew. S & T Apr 1733 *Patapsco* LC Annapolis Nov 1733. M.

Fuller, Elizabeth. R for Barbados or Jamaica Jly 1687. L.

Fuller als Day, Elizabeth of St. Saviour, Southwark. R for Barbados or Jamaica Jly 1705. Sy.

Fuller als Pulley, Elizabeth. S Apr 1745. L.

Fuller, George of Epping. R for Barbados or Jamaica Jly 1687. E.

Fuller, George. S for burglary Lent R 14 yrs Summer 1738. Be.

Fuller, George. T Jun 1740 *Essex*. Ht.

Fuller, John. R (Home Circ) for Barbados May 1664. X.

Fuller, John. R for Barbados or Jamaica Mar 1685. L.

Fuller, John. S & T Oct 1720 *Gilbert* to Md. M.

Fuller, John. S s gelding Norwich Summer 1726 R 14 yrs Lent 1727. Nf.

Fuller, John. S & T Oct 1732 *Caesar*. L.

Fuller, John. S Lent T May 1750 *Lichfield*. E.

Fuller, John. S May T Jun 1756 *Lyon*. L.

Fuller, John. S s gelding Summer 1765 R 14 yrs Lent T Apr 1766 *Ann*. Bu.

Fuller, Joseph. S s sheet Norwich Summer 1765. Nf.

Fuller, Mary of St. Martin in Fields, spinster. S s household goods Jly 1740 T Jan 1741 *Harpooner*. M.

Fuller, Rebecca. S May-Jly T Sep 1755 *Tryal*. M.

Fuller, Richard of Great Fransham. R for America Mar 1686. Nf.

Fuller, Robert. S Sep T 14 yrs Oct 1744 *Susannah*. M.

Fuller, Robert. T 14 yrs Nov 1759 *Phoenix*. Sx.

Fuller, Samuel. S Jly 1761. So.

Fuller, Sarah. S Jun T Nov 1743 *George William*. M.

Fuller, Sarah. S Sep T Oct 1750 *Rachael*. M.

Fuller, Thomas, als Smith als Shortoe, William. R 14 yrs Mar 1773. So.

Fuller, Thomas. S s beans at Bisham Lent 1774. Be.

Fuller, Turpin. T Apr 1742 *Bond*. E.

Fuller, William. R for Jamaica Aug 1661. M.

Fuller, William. S Jan-Jun T Jun 1728 *Elizabeth* LC Potomack Aug 1729. L.

Fuller, William. T May 1737 *Forward*. E.

Fuller, William. S & R Summer 1745. Su.

Fuller, William. S s mare Lent R 14 yrs Summer 1758. Su.

Fuller, William. S Mar 1759. Ha.

Fullerton, Arthur, aged 19, dark. S Jan T Feb 1723 *Jonathan* LC Annapolis Jly 1724. M.

Fullifull, John. S Aug T Sep 1725 *Forward* to Md. M.

Funge, William of Leatherhead. SQS Jan T Mar 1764 *Tryal*. Sy.

Funnell, John. S s shirts Apr T Dec 1735 *John* LC Annapolis Sep 1736. M.

Furber, John. Rebel T 1685.

Furber, John. SQS & TB Jly 1735. So.

Furber, John. S s at North Nibley Lent 1774. G.

Furber, Joseph (1765). *See* Turner. St.

Furmentine, Elizabeth (1733). *See* Austin. L.

Furnell, John. S Mar 1752. So.

Furness, Ann. S Jan T Feb 1719 *Worcester* LC Annapolis Jun 1719. L.

Furness, Anthony. S for obstructing Customs officers Summer 1737. Nf.

Furnis, James. S Feb T Sep 1737 *Pretty Patsy* to Md. M.
Furness, John. T Apr 1735 *Patapsco*. E.
Furness, William, als Farnass, Isaac. AT Summer 1754. Y.
Furrier, Ann. S Feb 1774. L.
Fursman, Prudence. R 14 yrs Mar 1764. De.
Fury als Garvey, Mary. S Sep-Oct T Dec 1753 *Whiteing*. M.
Furze, Mary wife of George. R 14 yrs Mar 1774. De.
Furse als Vosse, Morris. Rebel T 1685.
Fyance als Fines, Margaret. SQS Jan 1752. M.
Fyfield. *See* Fifield.
Fynes. *See* Fines.
Fyson. *See* Fison.

G

Gabriel, Solomon. S Nov T Dec 1763 *Neptune*. L.
Gadbury, Anne. S Jan T Feb 1724 *Anne* to Carolina. M.
Gadbury, John. S Dec 1766 T Jan 1767 *Tryal*. M.
Gad, John. S for killing gelding Summer 1735. Ca.
Gadd, Robert. SQS & TB Apr 1765. So.
Gadd, Thomas. R for Jamaica Aug 1661. M.
Gaddish, James. T Apr 1759 *Thetis*. Sy.
Gadman, James of Manchester, weaver. SQS Aug 1762. La.
Gadsby, William. R Summer 1774. Sy.
Gaffney, Ann wife of Henry, als Ann Jenkins. S Jun-Dec 1738 T Jan 1739
    Dorsetshire. M.
Gaffney, James. R 14 yrs Aug 1731. So.
Gaffney, Patrick (1744). *See* Casey. M.
Gaffy, Mary. SQS Jly 1774. M.
Gag, Mary. Died on passage in *Dorsetshire* 1736. X.
Gayge, John of Clayhidon. R for Barbados Feb 1684. De.
Gage, John. S Feb T Mar 1731 *Patapsco* LC Annapolis Jun 1731. M.
Gage, Joseph. Rebel T 1685.
Gager, Joseph. S s at Newent Summer TB Aug 1742. G.
Gahagan, Farrant of Rotherhithe. SQS Feb T Apr 1759 *Thetis*. Sy.
Gahagan, John. R for life Jly 1773. M.
Gailks, Mary. T Jan 1736 *Dorsetshire*. Sy.
Gainer, Magdalene. S Aug T Sep 1725 *Forward* LC Annapolis Dec 1725. M.
Gainer als Gehner, Sarah. S & T Jly 1753 *Tryal*. M.
Gainer, Thomas. S Apr-Jun T Jly 1772 *Tayloe*. M.
Gaines, Francis (1699). *See* Exon. M.
Gainsley, Jane. S Jly-Sep T Oct 1739 *Duke of Cumberland* to Va. M.
Gale, Ann. S Mar 1775. Do.
Gale, Charles. R for Barbados or Jamaica Dec 1693. L.
Gale als Silvester, Charles. AT Oct R Dec 1699. M.
Gale, Christopher. S May T Sep 1765 *Justitia*. L.
Gale, Dorothy. S May-Jly 1749. M.
Gale, George. S Mar 1756. Do.
Gale, Jane wife of Thomas. S Jan T Feb 1733 *Smith* to Md or Va. M.
Gale, John (1656). *See* Harvey. L.
Gale, John of South Tawton, husbandman. R for Barbados Feb 1669. De.
Gale, John. Rebel T 1685.
Gale, John. S Mar 1724. Wi.
Gale, John. SQS & TB Oct 1728. So.
Gale, John. R 14 yrs Aug 1742. De.
Gale, John. S May-Jly 1750. M.
Gale, Joseph. Rebel T 1685.
Gale, Leonard of Chippenham, clothworker. SQS New Sarum Jan TB to
    Va Apr 1762. Wi.
Gale, Nicholas. SQS Apr 1754. M.
Gale, Richard. S Jly 1718 to be T to Va. Co.
Gale, Robert. S Mar TB to Va Apr 1765. Wi.

Gale, Robert. S Apr T Jly 1770 *Scarsdale*. L.
Gale, Thomas. S Mar 1759. Wi.
Gale, William. S s horse Lent R 14 yrs Summer 1752. Sh.
Galhampton, Thomas. Rebel T 1685.
Galin, James (1768). *See* Gayler. M.
Galeing, Simon of St. Olave, Southwark. R for Barbados or Jamaica Jly
    1704. Sy.
Gaul, George. R for life for s horse Summer 1768. Nl.
Gall, Samuel. T Apr 1765 *Ann*. E.
Gallagher, Charles (1771). *See* Callagan. M.
Gallant, Ambrose of Orsett. SQS Oct 1742 T Apr 1743 *Justitia*. E.
Gallant, Edward of Heybridge. R for Barbados or Jamaica Feb 1688. E.
Galleof, Ann (1741). *See* Greenhall. M.
Gallery, John of Whitley. R for Barbados or Jamaica Jly 1704. Sy.
Gallon, Robert. R 14 yrs Summer 1747. Nl.
Gallop, James. Rebel T 1685.
Galloway, James. S Jan 1745. L.
Galloway, John (1656). *See* Harvey. L.
Galloway, Richard. S s at Stoke Lent 1751. O.
Galloway, William (1760). *See* Gallyford. De.
Gallway, Thomas (1739). *See* Fisher. K.
Gallyford als Galloway, William. S Jly 1760 TB to Va 1761. De.
Galpin, William. S Mar 1771. Do.
Galsworthy, John (1727). *See* Goldsworthy. De.
Galsworthy, John. TB to Va 1769. De.
Galton, Edward. S Summer 1733 R 14 yrs Summer 1734. Nl.
Galton, Joseph. S Mar 1763. Do.
Gamage, Henry. S Lent 1766. Wa.
Gamage, Stephen. Rebel T 1685.
Gamage, Thomas. Rebel T 1685.
Gambeling, Anne. R for Barbados Mar 1683. M.
Gambell. *See* Campbell.
Gamble, John of Low Worsall. SQS Richmond Jan 1747. Y.
Gamble, John. S Mar TB to Va Apr 1768. Le.
Gamble, Mary. S Summer 1757. Hu.
Gamble, Thomas. S Lent 1749. Sy.
Gamble, Thomas. S Lent 1760. Le.
Gamble, William. S Summer 1757. Le.
Gamble, William. T Oct 1757. Db.
Gambutt, Francis (1685). *See* Gamlyn.
Gamford, William of Dymock. R for Barbados Oct 1663. G.
Gamlin, Edward. S Mar 1737. De.
Gamlyn (Gambutt), Francis. Rebel T 1685.
Gamlin, John (1685). *See* Lease.
Gamling, John (1699). *See* Gayling. M.
Gamlin, Thomas. Rebel T 1685.
Gammins, Elizabeth. S Apr 1747. So.
Gammon, Mary. TB to Va from QS 1748. De.
Gammon, Richard. S May T Sep 1765 *Justitia*. M.
Gamull, Ralph. S & R 14 yrs Lent 1769. Ch.
Ganderd, William. PT Dec 1688. M.

Gandy, Elizabeth. S Aug T Sep 1725 *Forward* LC Annapolis Dec 1725. L.

Gandy, William of Chissington. R for Barbados or Jamaica Dec 1680. Sx.

Gandy, William. S s sheep Summer 1748 R 14 yrs Lent 1749. Wo.

Gane, Aaron. R 14 yrs Aug 1752. So.

Gane (Game), John. S Feb T Mar 1727 *Susanna* to Va. M.

Ganey, James. S Dec 1748 T Jan 1749 *Laura*. M.

Ganfield, John of Chatham. R for Barbados or Jamaica Mar 1698. K.

Gannett, Joseph. S Aug 1750 TB to Va. De.

Garbitt, William. T Dec 1734 *Caesar*. Bu.

Garbutt, Richard. S Apr-Jun T Jly 1772 *Tayloe*. M.

Garcy, John. S & T Oct 1722 *Forward* LC Annapolis Jun 1723. M.

Gard. *See* Guard.

Gardlett als Garnett, John. S s at Shifnal Summer 1736. Sh.

Gardner, Ambrose. S Oct 1744-Jan 1745. M.

Gardener, Ann. TB to Va from QS 1769. De.

Gardner, Anthony. SQS & TB Feb 1738. G.

Gardner, Anthony. S & TB Aug 1739. G.

Gardner, Barbara of Wednesbury. R for Barbados Jly 1664. St.

Gardiner, Charles. S Jly 1718 to be T to Boston NE. Wi.

Gardner, Edward of Bishops Stortford. R for Barbados or Jamaica Mar 1694. Ht.

Gardner, Elizabeth. R Dec 1693 AT Jan 1694. M.

Gardner, Elizabeth wife of Thomas. S s household goods Oct T Dec 1736 *Dorsetshire*. M.

Gardner, Elizabeth. S Jun-Dec 1745. M.

Gardner als Bridgwater, Elizabeth. S Feb-Apr 1746. M.

Gardiner, Elizabeth. SQS Apr T May 1767 *Thornton*. M.

Gardiner, Francis. Rebel T 1685.

Gardner, Francis. S s shoes Jly 1735 T Jan 1736 *Dorsetshire* LC Va Sep 1736. M.

Gardner, George. S s at Finemore Lent 1738. O.

Gardner, George (1768). *See* Walcraft, Thomas. Be.

Gardner, Hannah. R & TB for Barbados Aug 1668. L.

Gardner, Henry. S s at Pershore Summer 1745. Wo.

Gardner, James (1690). *See* Gowen. M.

Gardiner, James. S & T Jan 1722 *Gilbert* LC Annapolis Jly 1722. L.

Gardner, James. S s at Church Down Summer TB Aug 1749. G.

Gardiner, Jane. S & T Sep 1766 *Justitia*. M.

Gardner, John. R for Barbados Jun 1665. M.

Gardner, John. R for Barbados Dec 1667. M.

Gardner, John. R for Barbados May 1672. L.

Gardner, John of Birmingham. R for America Feb 1681. Wa.

Gardner, John. Rebel T 1685.

Gardener, John. S Jly 1754. Ha.

Gardner, John. SQS Jly TB Sep 1759. So.

Gardiner, John. S s cloth from rack at Stroud Summer 1761. G.

Gardiner, John of Christchurch. SQS for s lead coffins & T Jan 1769 *Thornton*. Sy.

Gardner, John. T Aug 1769 *Douglas*. E.

Gardiner, John. T Apr 1771 *Thornton*. Sx.

Gardner, Joseph (Henry). S May T Jun 1727 *Susanna* to Va. M.

Gardner, Margaret (1735). *See* Owen. L.

Gardiner, Mark. SQS Apr T Jly 1772 *Tayloe*. M.

Gardner, Mary. S Lent 1749. E.

Gardner, Matthew Sr. SQS & TB Feb 1738. G.

Gardner, Matthew Jr. SQS & TB Feb 1738. G.

Gardiner, Philis. T Apr 1766 *Ann*. Sx.

Gardner, Rachael. S Apr T May 1719 *Margaret*; sold to Mr. Polla Md Sep 1719. L.

Gardner als Thomas als Williams, Rebecca. S Aug 1727. L.

Gardiner, Richard (1663). *See* Turner. M.

Gardner, Richard. S May-Jly T Sep 1751 *Greyhound*. M.

Gardner, Robert. S Lent R 14 yrs Summer TB Aug 1757. G.

Gardner, Samuel. S May-Jly 1746. M.

Gardiner, Samuel. S s skins at Holt Summer 1764. Wo.

Gardener, Sarah. S Jan-Apr 1749. M.

Gardiner, Sarah. S Oct T Dec 1769 *Justitia*. L.

Gardner, Sarah. S s at Kidderminster Summer 1773. Wo.

Gardner, Solomon. S s at Hartlebury Lent 1724; found at large Summer 1726 & committed for burglary. Wo.

Gardiner, Susannah wife of Luke. S Jly T Oct 1768 *Justitia*. M.

Gardiner, Thomas. R for Barbados or Jamaica Feb 1686. M.

Gardner, Thomas. S for highway robbery Summer 1743 R 14 yrs Lent 1744. Wo.

Gardiner, Thomas. S Oct 1743 T Feb 1744 *Neptune*. L.

Gardiner, Thomas. S s at Blewbury Summer 1752; wife Sarah acquitted. Be.

Gardiner, Thomas. S Apr T May 1755 *Rose*. L.

Gardiner, Thomas. S Mar 1771. Ha.

Gardiner, Thomas. S s cloth at Bisley Lent 1774. G.

Gardiner, William. R Oct TB Nov 1662. L.

Gardiner, William. S Norwich Summer 1746. *Nf.

Gardiner, William. S Summer 1756. Sy.

Gardner, William. S s cloth from rack at Stonehouse Summer 1761. G.

Gardener, William. S s wheat at Bisley Lent 1767. G.

Gardner, William. S s at Nacton Lent 1769. Su.

Gardner, William. S Mar 1774. So.

Gargle, Elizabeth. S Apr-May T Jly 1771 *Scarsdale*. M.

Garish, Thomas. LC from *Alexander* Annapolis Sep 1723. X.

Gariston als Harrison, Mary. LC from *Supply* Annapolis May 1726. X.

Garland, Elizabeth. R for Barbados May 1676. L.

Garland, Elizabeth wife of Edward. S s apron Dec 1735 T Jan 1736 *Dorsetshire* LC Va Sep 1736. M.

Garland, John of Besthorpe. R for Barbados or Jamaica Mar 1697. Nf.

Garland, Sarah. S & T Apr 1759 *Thetis*. L.

Garland, William. SQS Jan TB Sep 1728. So.

Garle, Christopher. S & T Oct 1730 *Forward* LC Potomack Jan 1731. L.

Garlett, Robert of Chatham. R for Barbados or Jamaica Mar 1698. K.

Garlick, William. S Mar TB to Va Apr 1766. Wi.

Garling, John. S s horse Lent R 14 yrs Summer 1740 (SP). Nf.

Garlington, Lidia (1682). *See* Garrington. L.

Garman, Daniel. S Apr 1760. M.

Garment, William. T Apr 1759 *Thetis*. Ht.

Garmson, John of Kemerton. S s geese at Shifnal Summer 1733. Sh.

Garne, John. S s at Winchcombe Summer TB Sep 1755. G.

Garne, Thomas. S s sheep & R 14 yrs Lent 1773. G.

Garner, Elizabeth (1755). *See* Gaudon. M.

Garner, John. S Lent 1774. Wa.

Garner, Joseph. R 14 yrs Summer 1756. Y.

Garner, Leda. S May 1775. L.

Garner, Samuel. S for highway robbery Lent R 14 yrs Summer 1753. No.

Garner als Watson, Sarah, spinster, als wife of Edward Gilden. S Norwich Summer 1752. Nf.

Garner, Thomas (1756). *See* Garnett. Sh.

Garnes, Lewis. S Oct 1773. L.

Garnett, John. SL Jan 1733. Sy.

Garnett, John (1736). *See* Gardlett. Sh.

Garnett, John. S Oct 1744-Jan 1745. M.

Garnett, John. S Jly 1758. Ha.

Garnett, John Jr. of Manchester, hatter. SQS Jan 1764. La.

Garnett, Margaret. S & T Apr 1733 *Patapsco* LC Annapolis Nov 1733. L.

Garnett, Mary wife of John. S & T May 1736 *Patapsco* to Md. M.

Garnett, Richard. S Apr-Jun 1739. M.

Garnett, Thomas of Galeston. R for Barbados Jly 1683. La.

Garnett als Garner, Thomas. S s iron boxes at Bridgnorth Lent 1756. Sh.

Garnon, Judith. S Aug 1763. L.

Garnons, William. R & T for life Jly 1770 *Scarsdale*. M.

Garrard, Robert. S s mare Summer 1750 R 14 yrs Lent T May 1751 *Tryal*. E.

Garraway, Jeremiah. S May T Jly 1723 *Alexander* LC Annapolis Sep 1723. L.

Garrell, William. S Jan-Jun T Jun 1728 *Elizabeth* LC Potomack Aug 1729. M.

Garratt, Bartholomew. S May-Jly 1773. M.

Garrett, Elizabeth (1669). *See* Scruce. L.

Garrett, Elizabeth. T Sep 1757 *Thetis*. K.

Garrett, Gilbert. S & T Sep 1766 *Justitia*. L.

Garrett, Henry. R for America Feb 1683 & Aug 1685. Wa.

Garrett, John. S s sheep Lent R 14 yrs Summer T Aug 1752 *Tryal*. Bu.

Garrett, Joseph. T Oct 1729 *Forward*. E.

Garrett, Joseph. S Jan-Feb 1775. M.

Garrett, Martha. S Sep-Oct T Dec 1752 *Greyhound*. M.

Garrett, Mary. R for Jamaica Jan 1663. M.

Garrett, Mary. S Aug T Oct 1724 *Forward* LC Annapolis Jun 1725. M.

Garratt, Mary. S s silver at Pyrton Lent 1775. O.

Garrett, Philip. S Mar TB to Va Apr 1745. Wi.

Garrett, Philip. S & T Apr 1765 *Ann*. L.

Garrett, Richard. R for life Jly 1774. M.

Garrett, Samuel. S Mar 1763. So.

Garrett als Knowles, Thomas. R for Barbados or Jamaica Mar 1688. M.

Garrett, Thomas. T May 1719 *Margaret*. K.

Garrett, Thomas. S Lent 1763. Wa.

Garret, Valentine. S Mar 1732. Do.

Garrett, William. S & T Dec 1731 *Forward* to Md or Va. M.

Garratt, William. S Lent 1764. Wa.

Garrick, Arthur. SQS Apr T May 1751 *Tryal*. M.

Garrington als Garlington als Arlington, Lidia. R for Barbados Sep 1682. L.

Garris, Anne. R for highway robbery Aug AT Oct 1701. M.

Garrison, Elizabeth. S Lent 1775. E.

Garrison, Thomas. S Lent 1721. St.

Garrold, George (1685). *See* Carrow.

Garroway, Edward. R for Barbados Dec 1667. M.

Garrway, John. T Dec 1752 *Greyhound*. M.

Garside, John. TB to Md Mar 1723. Db.

Garth, George. S s sheep at Marrick Lent R 14 yrs Summer TB Aug 1766. Y

Garth, James. S s sheep at Marrick Lent R 14 yrs Summer TB Aug 1766; Elizabeth Garth respited. Y.

Garth, James. S 14 yrs Jan-Feb 1774. M.

Garthon, Joseph Jr. S s watch at St. Gregory, Norwich & R 14 yrs Summer 1775. Nf.

Garton, John. SQS Aug TB Sep 1723. Nt.

Garton, William. S s gold coins at St. Mildred, Bread Street, Sep T Oct 1768 *Justitia*. L.

Garvey, Mary (1753). *See* Fury. M.

Garvis, Humphrey (1666). *See* Jarvis. Wi.

Garwood, Thomas. S s fish from a trunk Summer 1748. Nf.

Garwood, Thomas. S Lent 1751. Su.

Gascoyne, Elizabeth. SQS Feb T Apr 1770 *New Trial*. M.

Gascoine, John. S s poultry at Witney Lent 1729. O.

Gascoyne, Richard. S Oct T Nov 1728 *Forward* but died on passage. L.

Gascoine, Sarah. S & T Apr 1725 *Sukey* LC Annapolis Sep 1725. M.

Gascoyne als Connor, Sarah. S May T Sep 1757 *Thetis*. L.

Gascoyne, Thomas. R 14 yrs Aug 1749. So.

Gascoyne, William. S Sep-Oct 1749. M.

Gasford, Samuel (1772). *See* Carter. M.

Gash, Cassandra (1704). *See* Hall. Nt.

Gash, Richard. R for Barbados or Jamaica Aug 1700. L.

Gaskin, John. R Jly 1679. Db.

Gaskin, John. TB Aug 1733. Db.

Gasking, Richard als John of Rotherhithe. SQS Jan T Mar 1764 *Tryal*. Sy.

Gaskin, William. S s frock at St. John, Worcester, Summer 1751. Wo.

Gass, Richard of Acton, mariner. R (Western Circ) for Barbados Jly 1698. M.

Gasson, Edmund. T Apr 1731 *Bennett*. K.

Gasson, Henry. T Jan 1736 *Dorsetshire*. Sx.

Gasson, Thomas of Limpsfield. R for Barbados or Jamaica Sep 1669. Sy.

Gassoone, Thomas of Charing. R for Barbados or Jamaica Jly 1678. K.

Gason, William. S Lent 1761. E.

Gastrell, Anthony of Haresfield. R for America Jly 1675. G.

Gastrell, Roger of Uley. R for America Jly 1696. G.

Gatcombe, Thomas. S Mar 1730. So.

Gate, Stephen. S Jan 1751. L.

Gater, Alexander. S Jan T Mar 1760 *Friendship*. M.

Gater, Mary (1671). *See* Cuckeele. M.

Gates als Yeates, George. SQS & T Sep 1765 *Justitia*. M.

Gaytes, Isaac. S Oct-Dec 1729 T Jan 1740 *York* to Md. M.

Gates, Jeremy als Peter, weaver aged 41, dark. S Jan 1723 T *Jonathan* LC Annapolis Jly 1724. M.

Gates, Peter. S & T Oct 1730 *Forward* LC Potomack Jan 1731. L.

Gates, Samuel of Great Canfield, higler. SQS Oct 1773. E.

Gaites, William. R for America Feb 1709. Li.

Gates, William. S s hogs Lent 1756. Nf.

Gates, William. R 14 yrs Jly 1757. Ha.

Gatfield, Margaret. S s handkerchiefs at St. Martin, Worcester, Lent 1772. Wo.

Gatfield, Robert. SWK Oct 1775. K.

Gathwaite, William. S & T Apr 1769 *Tryal*. M.

Gatland, Richard. S May 1734. M.

Gatley, Mary (1728). *See* Boulton. M.

Gaton, Elizabeth. S s at Inkberrow Lent 1724. Wo.

Gaton, Susanna. TB to Va from QS 1740. De.

Gatson, Jane (1766). *See* Loxham, Elizabeth. M.

Gaul. *See* Gall.

Gauntlett, William. S Jly 1734. Ha.

Gauslin, William of Poslingford. R for America Mar 1688. Su.

Gaudon als Garner, Elizabeth. SQS Jan T May 1755 *Rose*. M.

Gawden, Isabel. R for Barbados Mar 1681. M.

Gawdery, Thomas. T Oct 1729 *Forward*. Ht.

Gawdren, John. S Summer 1741 R 14 yrs Lent 1742. Li.

Gawdry, John. SQS Dec 1768 T Jan 1769 *Thornton*. M.

Gawthorn, Samuel. S Feb T Mar 1731 *Patapsco* LC Annapolis Jun 1731. M.

Gawthrope, Richard. S Summer TB Oct 1763. Ca.

Gawton, Philip. S Mar 1735. De.

Gay, Anne. S May T Jly 1723 *Alexander* LC Annapolis Sep 1723. M.

Gay, Charles. R 14 yrs Jly TB to Va Sep 1750. Wi.

Gay, Charles. S s handkerchief at St. Andrew Holborn Sep T Oct 1768 *Justitia*. L.

Gay, Henry. S Summer 1764. G.

Gay, John. Rebel T 1685.

Gay als Johnson, Mary of Bermondsey. R for Barbados or Jamaica Sep 1669. Sy.

Gay, Mary. TB to Va from QS 1757. De.

Gay, Richard. S Aug 1731 TB to Va. De.

Gay, Timothy. SQS Jan-Mar TB to Va Apr 1741. Wi.

Gayer, Andrew. S Jly 1718 to be T to Va. De.

Gayler als Galin, James. S Dec 1768 T Jan 1769 *Thornton*. M.

Gayler, Thomas. S Feb-Apr T May 1755 *Rose*. M.

Gayling als Gamling, John. R Dec 1699 AT Jan 1700. M.

Gaywood, John. S Feb-Apr T May 1751 *Tryal*. M.

Gaywood, William. S Feb 1761. L.

Gazely, John. S Summer 1757. Nf.

Gazey, Samuel. S Summer 1747. Sy.

Geach, Jacob. S Apr 1770. De.

Geach, James. S Aug 1731. Co.

Geake, Robert. S Mar 1754. Co.

Geale, Elizabeth. S Lent T Jun 1756 *Lyon*. K.

Geare, Henry. S & T Nov 1762 *Prince William*. L.

Gear, Solomon. S Mar & Jly 1720 to be T to Boston NE. Wi.

Gear, Solomon. S Mar TB Sep 1728. Wi.

Gearing, John (1752). *See* Gill. So.

Gearing, Thomas. S Oct T Nov 1725 *Rappahannock* LC Rappahannock Apr 1726. L.

Gearish, Thomas. T Jly 1723 *Alexander* LC Md Sep 1723. Ht.

Geary, Eleanor. S & T 14 yrs May 1744 *Justitia*. L.

Geary, Elizabeth. T Jun 1740 *Essex*. K.

Geary, Jane. S Lent 1761. Sy.

Geary, John. S & T Sep 1764 *Justitia*. L.

Gearey, William. S s sheep Summer 1742 R 14 yrs Lent 1743. Wo.

Geaton, William. R 14 yrs Jly 1721. De.

Gee als Geeze, Ann. S s apron Apr T Dec 1735 *John* to Md. M.

Gee, Edward. S Sep T Dec 1758 *The Brothers*. M.

Gee, George. PT Apr R Oct 1673. M.

Gee, Jeremiah. T 14 yrs Apr 1768 *Thornton*. Sy.

Gee, John. S for killing deer in park of Earl of Uxbridge at Rugeley Summer 1744 R 14 yrs Lent 1745. St.

Gee, John. S Jan-Feb 1774. M.

Gee, Richard. S & T Dec 1770 *Justitia*. M.

Geen, Thomas. S Mar 1729. Co.

Geers, Solomon. S Lent R 14 yrs Summer 1731 (SP). G.

Gees, Nicholas. S Mar 1755. Ha.

Geeze, Ann (1735). *See* Gee. M.

Gehner, Sarah (1753). *See* Gainer. M.

Gelson, Jane. S Summer 1755. Du.

Gelvin, William. S Dec 1765 T Jan 1766 *Tryal*. L.

Genders, John, als Banks, Edward. S s sheep & R Lent 1768. Wa.

Gendrier, Francis. S Oct 1761 T Apr 1762 *Dolphin*. M.

Generall, James (1686). *See* Scott. Nl.

Gennett, Margaret wife of William of Gillingham. R for Barbados or Jamaica Feb 1683. K.

Gentt, George. S Jly 1738. De.

Gent, Thomas. R for America Feb 1700. No.

Gent, Thomas. S s sheep Summer 1755 R 14 yrs Lent 1756. Wa.

Gentry, Samuel. S Oct-Dec 1754. M.

Geoffreys. *See* Jeffreys.

George, Ann. S s at Monmouth Lent 1722. Mo.

George, Daniel, als Little John. S Sep 1733 T Jan 1734 *Caesar* LC Va Jly 1734. M.

George, Edmund. S Lent R for life Summer 1763. Nf.

George, Edward Jr. S Aug 1764. So.

George, Elizabeth. S Jan T Feb 1719 *Worcester* LC Annapolis Jun 1719. L.

George als Morgan, Elizabeth wife of George. S Summer 1748 R 14 yrs Lent 1749. Mo.

George, Elizabeth wife of Edward. S Feb 1757. M.

George, George. S s horse Lent R 14 yrs Summer 1759. No.

George, Hannah. S Lent 1763. Nf.

George, Henry. S Mar 1740. Co.

George, John of Abergavenny. R for America Feb 1673. Mo.

George, John. S & T Jan 1736 *Dorsetshire* LC Va Sep 1736. L.

George, John. S Lent R 14 yrs Summer 1768. Be.

George, John. S & R 14 yrs s sheep Lent 1773. Be.

George, Little. S Apr-Jun 1739. M.

George, John. S 14 yrs for receiving Jly TB to Va Sep 1757. Wi.

George, Mary. SQS Jan 1761. M.

George, Philip. S s sheep & R Summer 1774. Mo.

George, Richard. S May-Jly 1773. M.

George, Robert. S & T Sep 1731 *Smith* but died on passage. L.

George, Thomas. S s silver mug Feb T May 1736 *Patapsco* to Md. M.

George, Thomas of St. George the Martyr. S s bedding Jan-May T Jun 1738 *Forward*. M.

George, Thomas. S & TB Aug 1739. G.

George, Thomas. S s at Almondsbury Lent TB Apr 1757. G.

George, Thomas. S s sheep & R Summer 1774. Mo.

George, Walter. S s bullocks Lent 1734. Mo.

George, William. S & T Jly 1772 *Tayloe*. M.

George, William. S Lent 1774. Sy.

George, William. S 14 yrs for receiving sheep stolen at Llanvercha by Thomas & Philip George *(qv)* Summer 1774. Mo.

George, William. S Dec 1774. M.

Georgeson, James of Rotherhithe. SQS Jan T Apr 1760 *Thetis*. Sy.

Jermain, Edward (1731). *See* Jermy. Nf.

Germain, Elizabeth. S & T Jun 1756 *Lyon*. M.

Germain, Henry. S & T Sep 1764 *Justitia*. L.

Germain, Hugh als Hookey. S s horse Summer 1757 R 14 yrs Lent T Apr 1758. Bd.

Jarmain, John. S & T Jan 1739 *Dorsetshire*. L.

German, Edward. S Mar 1753. De.

Jerman, Hugh. S Dec 1727. L.

Jerman, James. Rebel T 1685.

Jerman, Joseph. Rebel T 1685.

German, Mary. S Aug 1734. De.

Germyn, Robert. T Oct 1720 *Gilbert*. E.

Jerman, William. R for Barbados Jly 1668. L.

Germer, Sarah. S Norwich Summer 1737. Nf.

Gerrard, Isaac. T Jly 1723 *Alexander* LC Md Sep 1723. Sy.

Gerrard, Jane. S Jan-Jun T Jun 1728 *Elizabeth* LC Potomack Aug 1729. M.

Gerrard, John. S Apr-May T 14 yrs May 1744 *Justitia*. M.

Gerrard, Rebecca. S Jan T Mar 1750 *Tryal*. L.

Gerrard, Susan of Beaminster. R for Barbados Mar 1686. Do.

Gerrard, Vincent. SQS for attending conventicle Dec 1664. M.

Gerry, Anne. TB to Va from QS 1741. De.

Gery, Isabella wife of Peter. S Oct T Dec 1734 *Caesar* to Va. M.

Gerry, John. TB to Va from QS 1741. De.

Gersey, Philip. S Jly T Aug 1721 *Prince Royal* LC Va Nov 1721. L.

Gervise, Gerrard. S Feb 1754. M.

Gervase, John. S Summer 1752. Y.

Gething, Joseph of Kingswinford. S s at Shifnal Lent 1720; noted as having escaped Lent 1721. Sh.

Gethin, Joseph. S s at Worfield Summer 1769. Sh.

Gethin, William. S s watch at St. Chad, Shrewsbury, Lent 1762. Sh.

Getley, John. R for America Jly 1694. Le.

Gew, George. S Jan T Sep 1737 *Pretty Patsy* to Md. M.

Gew, John. S & T Jly 1771 *Scarsdale*. M.

Gewen, Thomas. T Apr 1732 *Patapsco*. E.

Geyrin, Hannah. S & T Jan 1766 *Tryal*. M.

Ghent, Timothy. SWK Oct T Dec 1771 *Justitia*. K.

Ghost, Joseph. S Jun-Dec 1738 T Jan 1739 *Dorsetshire* to Va. M.

Goast, Mary wife of William. S Dec 1741 T 14 yrs Feb 1742 *Industry*. M.

Giacomo. *See* Jacomo.

Gibb, James. S & T Jan 1722 *Gilbert* to Md. M.

Gibberd, John. S Lent R 14 yrs Summer 1766. O.

Gibbard, Sarah wife of Henry, als Mary Jones, spinster. S Sep T Dec 1769
    Justitia. M.

Gibbard, Thomas. SQS & T Jly 1770 *Scarsdale*. Ht.

Gibbon, John. S Lent R 14 yrs Summer 1760. E.

Gibbon, Thomas. S Jan T Feb 1719 *Worcester* LC Annapolis Jun 1719. L.

Gibbon, William. S Mar 1731 TB to Va. De.

Gibbens, Charles. S Aug 1770. So.

Gibbons, Elizabeth. S Feb T Apr 1742 *Bond* to Potomack. M.

Gibbons, Henry. Rebel T 1685.

Gibbons, Isabella (1747). *See* Notson. M.

Gibbons, John. R Apr TB for Barbados Jun 1669. M.

Gibbons, John. T May 1719 *Margaret* & sold Md Sep 1719 to Patrick
    Sympson & William Black. E.

Gibbons, John. S May T Jly 1722 *Alexander* to Nevis or Jamaica. M.

Gibbons, John. T Dec 1752 *Greyhound*. K.

Gibbons, Mary of St. John Baptist, Hereford. R for Jamaica, Barbados or
    Bermuda Mar 1688. He.

Gibbons, Mary (1697). *See* Wittins. M.

Gibbons, Mary. LC from *Honor* Port York Jan 1721. X.

Gibbons, Mary. S Summer 1758 R 14 yrs Lent 1759. G.

Gibbons, Mary. S Jun T Sep 1767 *Justitia*. M.

Gibbons, Obadiah. S s shirt at Rudford Summer 1767. G.

Gibbons, Samuel. S Oct T 14 yrs Dec 1724 *Rappahannock* to Va. M.

Gibbons, Samuel. T Sep 1758 *Tryal*. Sy.

Gibbins, Samuel. S s at St. Mary de Grace, Gloucester, Lent 1765. G.

Gibbons, Samuel. S Oct T Dec 1769 *Justitia*. L.

Gibbins, Thomas. TB to Md Aug 1724 T *Forward* LC Annapolis Jun
    1725. Db.

Gibbons, Thomas. S s cloth at Stroud Lent 1762. G.

Gibbons, Walter. S Jly 1775. M.

Gibbons, William. S Oct T Nov 1725 *Rappahannock* LC Rappahannock
    Apr 1726. L.

Gibbons, William. S Feb-Apr 1751. M.

Gibbins, William. S Jly 1772. Ha.

Gibbons, William, als Bates, John. R 14 yrs Mar 1775. Ha.

Gibbs, Anne of Chulmleigh, spinster. R for Barbados Jly 1667. De.

Gibbs, Benjamin. S Aug 1731. So.

Gibbs, Charles. S s silver spoon Jan-May T Jun 1738 *Forward*. M.

Gibbs, Elizabeth. S Aug T 14 yrs Oct 1741 *Sea Horse*. L.

Gibbs, James. LC from *Gilbert* Annapolis Jly 1722. X.

Gibbs, James. S for deer poaching in Whittlewood Forest Summer 1765. No.

Gibbs, John (2). Rebels T 1685.

Gibbs, John (1732). *See* King. Ha.

Gibbs, John. S & T Oct 1732 *Caesar* to Va. M.

Gibbs, John. S Oct 1741 T Feb 1742 *Industry*. L.

Gibbs, John. SQS New Sarum Jan TB to Va Apr 1765. Wi.

Gibbs, John. S Dover Apr 1766 T Jan 1769 *Thornton*. K.

Gibbs, Mary. S Feb 1656. M.

Gibbs, Richard. T Oct 1726 *Forward*. Bu.

Gibbs, Sarah. T Jan 1741 *Vernon*. E.

Gibbs, Thomas. R Feb 1687. M.

Gibbs, William. S Sep 1760. L.

Gibney, George of St. Saviour, Southwark. R for Barbados Apr 1668. Sy.

Gibson, Abram. S Sep 1733 T Jan 1734 *Caesar* LC Va Jly 1734. M.

Gibson, Anne. R Sep 1671 AT Jly 1672. M.

Gibson, Ann Sr. S Feb 1729. L.

Gibson, Ann Jr. S Feb T Mar 1729 *Patapsco* LC Annapolis Dec 1729. L.

Gibson, Anthony. S s horse Lent R Summer 1726. Li.

Gibson, Charles. R Dec 1698 AT Jan 1699. M.

Gibson, David of Chipping Wycombe. R for America Jly 1702. Bu.

Gibson, Elizabeth. S Apr T Jun 1768 *Tryal*. M.

Gibson, James. S s at Gloucester Summer 1761. G.

Gibson, James. SQS Sep T Dec 1771 *Justitia*. M.

Gibson, John. R for Barbados Apr 1669. M.

Gibson, John of Cleyhanger. R for Barbados Jun 1716. De.

Gibson, John. S Sep T Dec 1767 *Neptune*. M.

Gibson, John of Carlisle. SQS s harness Lent 1773. Du.

Gibson, Jonathan. S Sep T Nov 1759 *Phoenix*. M.

Gibson, Joseph. S s lead at Tamworth Summer 1750. St.

Gibson, Joseph. S Summer 1764. Nt.

Gibson, Judith. S Apr T May 1752 *Lichfield*. L.

Gibson, Mary. R 14 yrs Jly 1757. Ha.

Gibson, Philip. S 14 yrs Oct 1751-Jan 1752. M.

Gibson, Samuel. S Jly 1774. L.

Gibson, Sarah. S Jly T Aug 1721 *Prince Royal* LC Va Nov 1721. M.

Gibson, Susan (1679). *See* Banser. L.

Gibson, Thomas of Worcester. R for America Jly 1698. Wo.

Gibson, Thomas. S Jan TB to Md or Va Feb 1719. L.

Gibson, Thomas. R 14 yrs Summer 1730 AT Summer 1732. Nl.

Gibson, Thomas. S Summer 1751 R 14 yrs Lent T May 1752 *Lichfield*. Sy.

Gibson, William. S Aug T Oct 1723 *Alexander* to Md. M.

Gibson, William. T Dec 1758 *The Brothers*. E.

Gibson, William. S 14 yrs Lent 1759. Li.

Gibson, William. S Sep T Dec 1770 *Justitia*. M.

Giddins, Edward. R Jly 1773. Ha.

Giddins, George. S Lent R Summer 1739 (SP). Be.

Giddins, John. S Dec 1733 T Jan 1734 *Caesar* LC Va Jly 1734. M.

Giddings, Michael. S Mar TB May 1756. Wi.

Gidley, John. TB to Va from QS 1769. De.

Gidman, Ann. S Summer 1756. Ch.

Gifford, James. S May-Jly 1774. M.

Gifford, William. S Lent T Sep 1758 *Tryal*. Bu.

Giffoy, Charles (John). SQS Oct T Dec 1763 *Neptune*. M.

Gift, Elizabeth. S Jan 1755. L.

Gigg, Thomas. S & T Sep 1731 *Smith* LC Va 1732. L.

Gigle, William. S & T Oct 1732 *Caesar*. L.

Gilbank, Grace. S s tablecloth Lent TB Oct 1748. Y.

Gilbert, Bond. S May T Jly 1722 *Alexander*. L.

Gilbert, Charles. S Feb T Mar 1731 *Patapsco* LC Annapolis Jun 1731. M.

Gilbert, Edward. Rebel T 1685.

Gilbert, Elizabeth, aged 24, dark. S Jly T Oct 1720 *Gilbert* LC Annapolis May 1721. L.

Gilbert, Elizabeth. S 14 yrs Aug 1727 T *Forward* LC Rappahannock May 1728. M.

Gilbert, Frances wife of Thomas. S s watch Oct 1735 T Jan 1736 *Dorsetshire* LC Va Sep 1736. M.

Gilbert, James of All Saints, Worcester. R for America Jly 1678. Wo.

Gilbert, James (1713). *See* Harford. M.

Gilbert, James. S for violent assault Summer 1751. Nf.

Gilbert als Phillips, James John. S Apr-Jun T Jly 1772 *Tayloe*. M.

Gilbert, John (1672). *See* Gilder. M.

Gilbert, John. S for highway robbery Summer 1721 R 14 yrs Summer TB to Md Jly 1722. Db.

Gilbert, John. S Summer 1729 R 14 yrs Summer 1730. Le.

Gilbert, John. S Lent R 14 yrs Summer 1731. Li.

Gilbert als Steel, John of St. Giles in Fields. S s silver buckles Apr T May 1740 *Essex*. M.

Gilbert, John. S s at Barnsley Summer TB Aug 1742. G.

Gilbert, John. S Summer 1756 R 14 yrs Lent 1757. K.

Gilbert, Mary. R for Barbados Mar 1683. L.

Gilbert, Robert. S Jly 1724. Ha.

Gilbert, Samuel. S Jan T Feb 1726 *Supply* LC Annapolis May 1726. M.

Gilbert, Samuel. TB Aug 1740. Db.

Gilbert als Sparkes, Samuel. S Aug 1763. L.

Gilbert, Sarah. T Apr 1741 *Speedwell* or *Mediterranean*. Ht.

Gilbert, Susan wife of John. S Feb T Apr 1734 *Patapsco* to Md. M.

Gilbert, Thomas of Shrewsbury. R for America Jly 1678. Sh.

Gilbert, Thomas. S Jan T Feb 1744 *Neptune*. L.

Gilbert, Thomas. S s sheep Lent R 14 yrs Summer 1749. He.

Gilbert, William. S & T Oct 1722 *Forward* LC Annapolis Jun 1723. L.

Gilbert, William. S Lent R 14 yrs Summer 1763. Li.

Gilbee, Ahaz. S Lent R 14 yrs Summer T Sep 1757 *Thetis*. Bu.

Gilby, Henry. S s hen Lent T Apr 1768 *Thornton*. Bu.

Gilby, John. S for highway robbery Lent R 14 yrs Summer 1746. Ht.

Gilby, Thomas. S s hen Lent T Apr 1768 *Thornton*. Bu.

Gilchrist, Henry. S Jan 1775. M.

Gilden, Sarah (1752). *See* Garner. Nf.

Gilder als Gilbert, John. R for Barbados Feb 1672. M.

Gilding, John. S & R 14 yrs Summer 1767 but died in gaol. Nf.

Gyles, Alexander (1742). *See* Jeals. Ha.

Giles als Friday, Ann. S Jan T Apr 1759 *Thetis*. M.

Giles als Curry, Elizabeth. S Feb T Apr 1732 *Patapsco* LC Annapolis Oct 1732. L.

Giles, Elizabeth. S s butter & cheese at Kingswinford Lent 1768. St.

Giles, Elizabeth. S & R 14 yrs Lent 1769. Be.
Giles, George. S Oct T Nov 1728 *Forward* LC Rappahannock Jun 1729. M.
Giles, George. SQS Apr TB Sep 1768. So.
Giles als Rook, Henrietta Maria. S s gown Jan-May T Jun 1738 *Forward*. M.
Giles, John of Royston. R for Barbados Apr 1668. Ht.
Giles, John of Walkhampton, tinner. R for Barbados Jun 1669. De.
Giles, John. AT Sep 1682. M.
Giles, John Jr. Rebel T 1685.
Giles, John. S May-Jun T Jly 1753 *Tryal*. M.
Giles, John. R 14 yrs Jly TB to Va Aug 1758. Wi.
Gyles, John. S Summer 1759 R 14 yrs Lent 1760. Wo.
Giles, John. S Feb T Apr 1768 *Thornton*. M.
Giles, Leonard. S Mar 1741. Co.
Giles, Mary wife of Thomas. S Apr-Jun 1739. M.
Giles, Mary. S Summer 1745 R 14 yrs Lent 1746. Be.
Giles, Richard. S Aug 1754. Co.
Giles, Richard. T from Bristol by *Maryland Packet* 1761 but intercepted by
    French; T Apr 1763 *Neptune*. Sh.
Giles, Richard. S s wheat at Wellington Lent 1765. Sh.
Giles, Samuel. SQS Jly TB Sep 1768. So.
Giles, Sarah. T Nov 1741 *Sea Horse* but stopped & T Jun 1742 *Bladon*. Sx.
Giles, Thomas. S Lent s sheep & R 14 yrs Summer 1749. Be.
Giles, Thomas. S Lent s at Wytham & R 14 yrs Summer 1762. Be.
Giles, William of Bedwelty. R for America Jly 1675. Mo.
Gyles, William. Rebel T 1685.
Giles, William. R 14 yrs Sep 1718 T Feb 1719 *Worcester* LC Charles Town
    Mar 1719. L.
Giles, William, als Saunders, Charles. S Jly T Aug 1721 *Prince Royal* LC
    Va Nov 1721. M.
Giles, William of Manchester, broadcloth weaver. SQS Jly 1747. La.
Giles, William. S Sep T Nov 1762 *Prince William*. M.
Gilford. *See* Guildford.
Gilgose, Francis. R 14 yrs Mar 1761 TB to Va. De.
Gilham. *See* Gillam.
Gilks, Mary. S Lent 1775. Wa.
Gill, Ann (1715). *See* Dewing. M.
Gill, Catherine. SQS Apr 1773. M.
Gill, Christian of Plympton St. Maurice, spinster. R for Barbados Jly
    1711. De.
Gill, Edward. S Jly 1744. Ha.
Gill, Elizabeth Sr. wife of Ralph Gill Sr. of Stowell Inferior. R for America
    Jly 1683. G.
Gill, Elizabeth Jr. of Stowell Inferior, spinster. R for America Jly 1683. G.
Gill, Elizabeth. S & T Sep 1731 *Smith* but died on passage. M.
Gill, Elizabeth. S Feb-Apr T Jun 1756 *Lyon*. M.
Gill, Elizabeth wife of John. S Aug 1762 TB to Va. De.
Gill, George. S Aug T Sep 1725 *Forward* LC Annapolis Dec 1725. M.
Gill, George. S Aug 1760. L.
Gill, Hezziah. T May 1767 *Thornton*. E.
Gill, Hugh. Rebel T 1685.
Gill, James. S Mar 1730. De.

Gill, John of St. Peter, Worcester. R for America Jly 1679. Wo.
Gill, John. S s horse Summer 1724 R 14 yrs Lent 1729. Y.
Gill als Gearing, John. S for perjury Mar 1752. So.
Gill, Keziah wife of William. S Mar 1755. Ha.
Gill, Margaret. S Feb-Apr T May 1755 *Rose*. M.
Gill, Mary. R & T Dec 1734 *Caesar* LC Va Jly 1735. M.
Gill, Mary. T Oct 1738 *Genoa*. Sy.
Gill, Mary. T Dec 1769 *Justitia*. M.
Gill, Nicholas. Rebel T 1685.
Gill, Ralph Jr. of Stowell Inferior, miller. R for America Jly 1683. G.
Gill, Richard. S & T Sep 1751 *Greyhound*. L.
Gill, Robert. SQS Wisbech s cow & R 14 yrs Sept 1773. Ca.
Gill, Thomas. T Jun 1740 *Essex*. Sy.
Gill, Thomas. S Lent 1749. Nf.
Gill, Thomas. S May T Nov 1759 *Phoenix*. M.
Gill, Thomas. S Oct 1765 T Jan 1766 *Tryal*. M.
Gill, Thomas of Much Hadham. SQS Dec 1767 T Apr 1768 *Thornton*. Ht.
Gill, William. S Summer 1722 T Oct 1723 *Forward* from London. Y.
Gill, William. T May 1744 *Justitia*. K.
Gill als Bass, William, als Taylor, George, als Barber, Samuel. R s horse
    Lent 1761. Le.
Gill, William. T Jan 1765 *Tryal*. M.
Gilham, Emanuel of Hyndon, victualler. R for Barbados Jun 1665.
Gillam, John. S Apr 1743. M.
Gilham, Joseph. S Dec 1737 T Jan 1738 *Dorsetshire*. L.
Gillham, Josiah. Rebel T 1685.
Gillum, Matthew. S Jly 1724. Ha.
Gilham, Peter. S & T Nov 1762 *Prince William*. L.
Gillham, Richard. S Lent 1775. K.
Gilham, Susan. R for Jamaica Aug 1661. L.
Gilham, William. S Oct 1757 T Mar 1758 *Dragon*. M.
Gillard, George. S Mar 1772. So.
Gillard, Humphrey. Rebel T 1685.
Gillard, Salisbury. S Jly T Oct 1741 *Sea Horse*. L.
Gillard, Scipio (1773). *See* Michell. Co.
Gillard, Stephen. S s at Barnwood Lent 1727. G.
Gillars, Anthony (1664). *See* Willis. Bd.
Giller, Ann (1725). *See* Hughes. L.
Gilespy, James. R 14 yrs Summer 1751. Cu.
Gillett, Ann. S Lent 1750. Su.
Gillett, Jane. R for Barbados or Jamaica May 1697. L.
Gillett als Mouth, John. S & T 14 yrs Oct 1732 *Caesar*. L.
Gillett, John. S Mar 1764. So.
Gillett, Mary (1749). *See* Pollard. L.
Gillett, William of Abbots Roothing. R for Barbados or Jamaica Jun 1675
    & Jly 1677. E.
Gillett, William. R for Barbados or Jamaica Oct 1694. L.
Gillett, William. S Lent 1763. Ht.
Gilliard, Elizabeth wife of George of St. George, Southwark. SQS Jan
    1757. Sy.
Gilyard, John. S s at Chapel Alleston, Leeds, Lent 1766. Y.

Gilliard, Stephen. S & TB Aug 1727. G.
Gilliard, William Thompson. S Feb T May 1767 *Thornton*. L.
Gillingham, John. S s at Molscroft Summer 1767. Y.
Gillity, Anne. S s at Kidderminster Summer 1755. Wo.
Gilly, Elizabeth. S s at Sheffield Lent 1769. Y.
Gilley, Joseph. S for forging a will Lent R 14 yrs Summer 1741. Y.
Gillman, John. S Feb-Apr T May 1755 *Rose*. M.
Gilman, Simon. S s cloth at Cold Ashton Lent 1725. G.
Gilman, Susanna. S Jly T Aug 1721 *Prince Royal* LC Va Nov 1721. M.
Gilman, Thomas. S Dec 1774. M.
Gilman als Fowler, Walter of Thursby. R for Barbados or Jamaica Feb
     1683. Sy.
Guilman, William of Reading. R for America Feb 1690. Be.
Gilmer, Jane wife of William. S Summer 1737. We.
Gilmoor, Robert. S Summer 1732. Y.
Gilmore, Samuel. R for Jamaica Feb 1665. M.
Gilpin, Thomas. S for breaking & entering Feb T Apr 1735 *Patapsco* LC
     Annapolis Oct 1735. L.
Gilroy, Andrew. S Summer 1720. Nl.
Gilson, Arthur. S Oct 1751-Jan 1752. M.
Gilson, Jeremiah. S for s from stable Lent R 14 yrs Summer 1725 T *Sukey*
     LC Annapolis Sep 1725. Ca.
Gilson, John (1769). *See* Hale. G.
Jilson, Richard. S Sep-Oct 1774. M.
Gilson, Thomas. S Jan T Apr 1762 *Dolphin*. M.
Gilson, William. S Lent R 14 yrs Summer 764. He.
Gilstone, Mary. LC from *Susannah & Sarah* Annapolis Apr 1720. X.
Gimer, John. S Lent 1755. Ca.
Gingell, Charles (1743). *See* Tanner. G.
Gingel, Dinah. S 14 yrs for receiving Mar TB to Va Oct 1768. Wi.
Gingell, Isaac. R 14 yrs Mar TB to Va Apr 1751. Wi.
Gingell, Thomas of Ledbury. R for America Jly 1677. He.
Gingin als Kingan, John of St. Olave, Southwark. R for Barbados or
     Jamaica Jun 1699. Sy.
Gingen, Mary. R for Barbados or Jamaica Dec 1693. L.
Ginn, Edward. T May 1752 *Lichfield*. E.
Ginn, John. S Lent 1754. Ca.
Ginn, Thomas of St. George, Southwark. SQS May 1754. Sy.
Ginn, Thomas. S Lent 1758. Su.
Ginney, William. S Mar 1738. So.
Girl, Joseph. S Aug T Oct 1741 *Sea Horse* to Va. M.
Gurling, Benjamin. S 14 yrs for receiving Summer 1736. Su.
Girling, Elizabeth. S Oct 1729 T *Forward* LC Va Jun 1730. M.
Gurling, Robert. T Apr 1741 *Speedwell* or *Mediterranean*. E.
Gurton als Kirton, Anthony. SW & T Jan 1766 *Thornton*. M.
Girton, Arthur. R for Jamaica Aug 1661. M.
Gisburne, Christiana. R for Barbados May 1664. M.
Gisop, Samuel. S Lent 1772. Wa.
Gissard, Isaac. S Mar TB to Va Apr 1740. Wi.
Gist, William of Bath, clothworker. R for Barbados Jun 1666. So.
Gittins, John. S s mare Lent R 14 yrs Summer 1752. Fl.

Gittins, Thomas. S Lent R 14 yrs Summer 1751. Sh.

Gittins, William. S s at Chirbury Lent 1765. Sh.

Gittings, William. S s cowhides at Chirbury Lent 1770. Sh.

Glade, Joseph. S Jan T Feb 1724 *Anne*. L.

Gladman, Henry. R for America Aug 1713. L.

Gladman, John. S & T 14 yrs Oct 1732 *Caesar* to Va. M.

Gladstones als Cleghorn, John. S s horse Summer 1738 R 14 yrs Summer 1739. Nl.

Gladwin, Edward. R for Barbados Jly 1668. M.

Gladwin, John. T 14 yrs Dec 1758 *The Brothers*. Ht.

Gladwin, Moses. S Jan T 14 yrs Feb 1726 *Supply* LC Annapolis May 1726. M.

Gladwin, Moses. S Jly T 14 yrs Sep 1737 *Pretty Patsy*. L.

Glanfield, Sarah (1721). *See* Griffith. De.

Glanister, Nathaniel. S May T Jly 1722 *Alexander* to Nevis or Jamaica. M.

Glanister, Thomas. R for Barbados or Jamaica Feb 1686. M.

Glanister, Thomas. S & T Oct 1722 *Forward* LC Annapolis Jun 1723. M.

Glannon, John. S Jan-Feb T Apr 1771 *Thornton*. M.

Glannon, Michael. S Jan-Feb T 14 yrs Apr 1771 *Thornton*. M.

Glanvill, James. Rebel T 1685.

Glascocke, George of Curringham. R for Barbados Apr 1669. E.

Glascock, John of East Donyland. R for Barbados or Jamaica Jly 1712. E.

Glascocke, Richard, aged 26. R for Barbados Feb 1664. L.

Glascock, William. S Dec 1756. M.

Glascow, Elizabeth. S Feb T Mar 1764 *Tryal*. M.

Glascow, Hannah. S Sep T Oct 1750 *Rachael*. M.

Glascoe, William. S Apr 1760. M.

Glasford, Richard, carver aged 18, dark. S & T Oct 1720 *Gilbert* LC Annapolis May 1721. M.

Glaspole, Hugh Edward. S Mar 1754. Ha.

Glaspole als How, Thomas. S Jly 1741. Ha.

Glass, Anthony. S Apr-Jun 1739. M.

Glass, Enoch. S Apr T May 1767 *Thornton*. L.

Glass, Henry. R 14 yrs Mar TB to Va Apr 1772. Wi.

Glass, James. TB to Va from QS 1752. De.

Glass, John. R 14 yrs Aug 1735. De.

Glass, John. S Jun-Dec 1738 T Jan 1739 *Dorsetshire* to Va. M.

Glass, Mary (1697). *See* Williams. M.

Glassbrook, Samuel. S May T Jly 1723 *Alexander* LC Annapolis Sep 1723. L.

Glaswell, John. S Jan 1746. M.

Glazing als Jones, Elizabeth. S Jly 1724. Ha.

Gleaves als Cleaves, Edward of York City. R for Barbados Feb 1697. Y.

Gledhill, Elizabeth. AT Lent 1748. Y.

Gleadhill, Thomas of Deagshelfe, Halifax. R for Barbados Jly 1701. Y.

Gledhill, William. AT Lent & Summer 1765. Y.

Gleed, William of St. Luke. S s thread & T May 1740 *Essex*. M.

Glendinning, Archibald. S Summer 1726. Nl.

Glendining, David of Manchester. SQS May 1755. La.

Glenton, John (1720). *See* Brown, Robert. Y.

Glenton, Robert. S City s gelding at St. Sampson & R 14 yrs Summer 1768. Y.

Glesby, Ann. S May-Jly 1774. M.

Gleve als Glew, Thomas. S Lent TB Apr 1766. Db.

Glew, John. S Dec 1740. L.

Glew, Thomas (1766). *See* Gleve. Db.

Glibbery, John. T May 1751 *Tryal*. Sy.

Gloster, Joseph. S s salt Summer 1753. Wo.

Glover, Benjamin. S s sheep & R 14 yrs Summer 1772. Wo.

Glover, Elizabeth. S Aug T Sep 1725 *Forward* LC Annapolis Dec 1725. M.

Glover, George. T Apr 1741 *Speedwell* or *Mediterranean*. Sy.

Glover, Henry. S Lent 1764. Ch.

Glover, Hugh of Orsett. R for Barbados Apr 1668. E.

Glover, James. S Oct T Nov 1728 *Forward* LC Rappahannock Jun 1729. M.

Glover, John. S & T Oct 1722 *Forward* LC Annapolis Jun 1723. M.

Glover, John. S s cow Lent R 14 yrs Summer 1744. Le.

Glover, John. SQS Warminster Jly TB Aug 1754. Wi.

Glover, John. R Lent 1775. K.

Glover, Joseph. S s at Bromsgrove Lent 1727. Wo.

Glover, Mary. S Oct T Nov 1759 *Phoenix*. M.

Glover als Lightfoot, Richard. S & T Jly 1753 *Tryal*. L.

Glover, Richard of Manchester, weaver. SQS Jly 1772. La.

Glover, Robert. S Lent AT Summer 1734. Wo.

Glover, Samuel. S s horse Lent R 14 yrs Summer 1759. No.

Glover, Sarah. S Dec 1727. M.

Glover, Thomas of Loughborough. R for America Jly 1678. Le.

Glover, Thomas. S for burglary Summer 1739 R 14 yrs Lent 1740. Hu.

Glover, Thomas. S 14 yrs for receiving silver tankard Apr T Jun 1742 *Bladon*. M.

Glover, Thomas of Christchurch. SQS Apr T May 1750 *Lichfield*. Sy.

Glover, Thomas. S Lent R 14 yrs Summer 1756. Wo.

Glover, William. S Jly-Sep T Sep 1742 *Forward*. M.

Gloyne, James. S Mar 1738. Co.

Glynn, Abigail. S Sep T Dec 1758 *The Brothers*. M.

Glynn, Henry. S & T Apr 1725 *Sukey* LC Annapolis Sep 1725. M.

Glyn, James. S Nov T Dec 1770 *Justitia*. L.

Glynn, John. S Apr T Jun 1742 *Bladon* to Md. M.

Glynn, Mary. S & T Dec 1734 *Caesar* LC Va Jly 1735. L.

Glinn, Patrick. S Sep T Nov 1743 *George William*. M.

Glyn, Richard. S Feb 1761. L.

Glyn, Sarah. S Feb 1773. L.

Glynn, Thomas. R 14 yrs Aug 1766. So.

Goacher, James. S Summer T Oct 1744 *Savannah*. Sx.

Goacher, William of Worksop, tailor. SQS East Retford s barley & TB May 1772. Nt.

Goad, Thomas. S Dec 1765 T Jan 1766 *Tryal*. M.

Goast. *See* Ghost. M.

Goat als Fatty, Mary. S Feb T Apr 1734 *Patapsco* to Md. M.

Goater, John. T Apr 1766 *Ann*. Sy.

Goathorne, Richard (1722). *See* Cavery. O.

Goatley, George. S Summer 1732 R Summer 1733 AT Lent 1734. Be.

Godbolt, James. R Jan-Feb T for life Apr 1772 *Thornton*. M.

Godbolt, John. S 14 yrs Norwich for receiving goods stolen by Samuel Mills *(qv)* Summer 1764. Nf.

Godby, Ann wife of Jasper. S Sep-Oct 1773. M.

Godby, Jasper. S Jan 1746 & Sep 1747. L.

Godby, Sarah wife of Francis. S Summer 1758. Hu.

Godard, Adam. S s at Inkberrow Lent 1738. Wo.

Goddard als Wilson, Ann. R Oct 1694 AT Jan 1695. M.

Goddard, Anthony. S Mar 1720 T *Honor* but escaped in Vigo, Spain. L.

Goddard, Edward. R for Barbados Sep 1672 AT Dec 1674. M.

Godard, Edward. S s at St. Peter, Worcester Lent 1738. Wo.

Goddard, Eleanor. S & T Sep 1764 *Justitia*. M.

Goddard, Elizabeth. S Mar 1730. De.

Godard, George. S s at Inkberrow Lent 1738. Wo.

Godard, James. S Apr T Sep 1757 *Thetis*. L.

Goddard, James Jr. S Mar 1773. Do.

Goddard, John. S Sep-Oct 1749 to be T 14 yrs. M.

Goddard, John. S Apr T May 1751 *Tryal*. L.

Goddard, John of Christchurch. SQS Apr T May 1752 *Lichfield*. Sy.

Goddard, Joseph. S Lent 1768. Nf.

Goddard, Mary. S May-Jly T Sep 1755 *Tryal*. M.

Goddard, William. R for Barbados or Jamaica Oct 1688. M.

Goddard, William of Newington. SQS Jan 1751. Sy.

Goddin, Charles. R for Barbados or Jamaica Oct 1694. L.

Goden, Richard. S Lent 1753. *Su.

Godden, Thomas of Luppitt. R for Barbados Jly 1672. De.

Goddin, William. S Jan T Feb 1719 *Worcester* LC Annapolis Jun 1719. LM.

Godden, William. S Mar 1768. Ha.

Godderham, Robert. S s stockings Summer 1765. Nf.

Godfrey, Ann. S & T Jun 1742 *Bladon* to Md. M.

Godfrey, Benjamin. S Jan T Feb 1733 *Smith* to Md or Va. M.

Godfrey, Benjamin. R Jly 1774. M.

Godfrey, Edward. R for Barbados Aug 1664. M.

Godfrey, Elizabeth (1741). *See* Rance. M.

Godfrey, Elizabeth. S Feb T Mar 1758 *Dragon*. M.

Godfrey, Elizabeth wife of William. S 14 yrs for receiving goods from Sarah Swain *(qv)* Summer 1770. Be.

Godfrey, Hugh. R for Barbados Jun 1663. M.

Godfrey, John. S May 1727. M.

Godfry, John. SQS Oct 1754. M.

Godfrey als Henry, John. R Aug 1773. Do.

Godfrey, Joseph. S & T Oct 1729 *Forward* LC Va Jun 1730. M.

Godfrey, Mary. S Dec 1719. M.

Godfrey, Mary (1741). *See* Barrow. M.

Godfrey, Robert. S Apr T Oct 1719 *Susannah & Sarah* LC Annapolis Apr 1720. L.

Godfrey, Robert. SQS Dec 1774. M.

Godfrey, Thomas. T Nov 1762 *Prince William*. E.

Godfrey, William. S Jan-Feb 1774. M.

Godley, Joseph. S Mar 1754. L.

Godman. *See* Goodman.

Godsall, James. S s at Tewkesbury Lent 1775. G.

Godsall, John. Rebel T 1685.

Godsell, Samuel. S s silver buckles at Cheltenham Summer TB Aug 1757. G.

Godsmark, Richard of Steyning. R for Barbados or Jamaica Apr 1668. Sx.
Godson. *See* Goodson.
Godstone, William. R Apr 1773. M.
Godwin. *See* Goodwin.
Goff. *See* Gough.
Goffee, John. S May-Jly 1773. M.
Gohalve, Roger (1685). *See* Hobbs.
Golbay, Art. S s at Islip Summer 1751. O.
Gold. *See* Gould.
Goldby, Noah of Rugby. R for America Jly 1711. Wa.
Goldham, Mary. T Apr 1725 *Sukey* LC Md Sep 1725. Sx.
Golding. *See* Goulding.
Goldring, Jane of Portsmouth, spinster. R for Barbados Jly 1693. Ha.
Goldring, Thomas. T 14 yrs Dec 1758 *The Brothers*. Sx.
Goldsacke, Peter of Cheriton. R for Barbados or Jamaica Jly 1702. K.
Goldsbrough, Sarah wife of John of Northallerton. SQS Easingwold Jan TB Aug 1757. Y.
Goldsborough, Thomas. R for Barbados or Jamaica Feb 1686. M.
Gouldsborough, Thomas. S s mare & R 14 yrs Lent TB to Va Aug 1768. Le.
Goldsby, Edward. S Oct T Nov 1728 *Forward* LC Rappahannock Jun 1729. M.
Goldsmith, Ann. S May T Nov 1759 *Phoenix*. M.
Goldsmith, Elizabeth wife of Thomas. S Jly-Sep T Oct 1739 *Duke of Cumberland*. M.
Goldsmith, Elizabeth. S Aug 1763. L.
Gouldsmith, John. T Jly 1724 *Robert* LC Md Jun 1725. K.
Goldsmith, Samuel. S May 1775. L.
Goldsmith, Thomas. S Jly 1767. Ha.
Goldsmith, William. S Lent 1745. Bd.
Goldsworthy (Galsworthy), John. S Aug 1727 TB to Md. De.
Goldthorpe, Edward. AT Summer 1758. Y.
Goldup, John. T May 1751 *Tryal*. K.
Goldwyer, Robert. R 10 yrs Lent 1655 to be T by Thomas Vincent & Samuel Highland. Sy.
Goll, James. S Norwich Summer 1751. Nf.
Gollidge als Shute, Mary. T Jun 1727 *Susanna*. Sy.
Gollop, Mathew. S Mar 1754. Do.
Golstone, Mary. TB 14 yrs Oct 1719. L.
Golstone, Robert. S & T Oct 1730 *Forward* to Va. M.
Golton, Anne of Dorchester. R for Barbados Mar 1691. Do.
Gom, James. S Apr-Jun T Jly 1772 *Tayloe*. M.
Gommery, Mary. S Aug T Oct 1741 *Sea Horse* to Va. M.
Gomms, Elizabeth. S Aug 1734. De.
Gonderton, Edward. S s greatcoat Lent 1741. O.
Goninon, John. R 14 yrs Jly 1763. Co.
Gooch, John. S s horse Lent 1729 (SP). Su.
Gooch, John of Layton. S Lent T Apr 1772 *Thornton*. E.
Good, Elizabeth of Modbury. R for Barbados Feb 1683. De.
Goode, John. T Oct 1729 *Forward*. K.
Good, Mary. S Jan T Feb 1733 *Smith* to Md or Va. M.
Good, Mary. S Summer 1754. E.

Good, Nathaniel. R for America Jun 1684. No.
Good, Sarah (1681). *See* Chapman. L.
Goode, Thomas. S s at Pauntley Summer 1722. G.
Good, Thomas. S Aug TB to Va Sep 1767. Wi.
Good, Walter of Salcombe. R for Barbados Apr TB Oct 1669. Sx.
Good, William. S Lent T Sep 1757 *Thetis*. Sy.
Goodaire. *See* Goodyear.
Goodall, Elias. R 14 yrs Mar 1775. Ha.
Goodall, Joseph. S Lent 1751. Y.
Goodall, Joseph. R 14 yrs Mar 1775. Ha.
Goodall, Rebecca. S Dec 1733 T Jan 1734 *Caesar* LC Va Jly 1734. L.
Goodall, Thomas. S Lent T Sep 1757 *Thetis*. Bu.
Goodbury, Elizabeth (1735). *See* Tooley. M.
Goodchild, Elizabeth. S Apr T May 1720 *Honor* LC Port York Jan 1721. L.
Goodchild, Peter. R 14 yrs Jly 1759. Ha.
Goodchild, Samuel. S s mare & R 14 yrs Summer 1775. Be.
Goodchild, William. R for America Aug 1715. L.
Goodchild, William. S Lent 1746. E.
Goodday, Peter (1748). *See* Heddye. La.
Gooden, Abraham. Rebel T 1685.
Gooden, Edward of Lancaster. R for Barbados Jly 1699. La.
Gooden, Elizabeth. S Apr 1759. So.
Goodenough, Richard. R Jly 1686. M.
Gooder, Catherine. S Sep T Oct 1739 *Duke of Cumberland*. L.
Gooderham, Henry. S Lent 1758. Su.
Gooderham, Lovet. S Lent 1758. Su.
Gooderham, Mary wife of Henry *(qv)*. S Lent 1758. Su.
Gooderham, William. T Apr 1741 *Speedwell* or *Mediterranean*. E.
Goodfellow, William. S Lent 1765. Hu.
Goodge, Charles. S Sep T Oct 1768 *Justitia*. M.
Goodgroome, Peter. Rebel T 1685.
Goodier. *See* Goodyear.
Goodin, Ann. S Feb-Apr T May 1752 *Lichfield*. M.
Gooding, Margaret. SQS Sep T Dec 1753 *Whiteing*. M.
Gooding, Richard. S s gelding Lent R 14 yrs Summer 1739 (SP). Hu.
Gooding, Samuel of Holsworthy. R for Barbados Jun 1702. De.
Gooding, Simon. SQS Jan TB Apr 1769. So.
Gooding, Thomas. TB May 1721. Le.
Goodin, William. LC from *Forward* Annapolis Dec 1725. X.
Gooding, William. S Jly T Sep 1766 *Justitia*. M.
Goodland, John. R 14 yrs Mar 1768. So.
Goodland, William. Rebel T 1685.
Goodman, Benjamin. R for Barbados Feb 1672. M.
Goodman, Edward. Rebel T 1685.
Godman, Edward. T Oct 1726 *Forward*. Ht.
Godman, Elizabeth. S Sep-Dec 1746. M.
Goodman, Elizabeth. R 14 yrs Jly 1763. M.
Goodman, Grace of Tywordreth, spinster. R for Barbados Jly 1693. Co.
Goodman, Humphrey. R 14 yrs Apr 1759. Co.
Goodman, John. S & T Oct 1732 *Caesar* to Va. M.
Goodman, John. S s sheep Summer 1751 R 14 yrs Lent 1752. Bd.

Goodman, Joseph. S Oct 1751-Jan 1752. M.

Goodman, Lewis. R 14 yrs Mar 1750. Co.

Goodman als Gudburne, Mark. T Oct 1723 *Forward*. K.

Goodman, Martha. R for Barbados Dec 1668. M.

Goodman, Mary. S & T May 1736 *Patapsco*. L.

Goodman, Matthew. Rebel T 1685.

Goodman als Wheeler, Rose. PT Jan 1675 R Mar 1677. M.

Goodman, Samuel. S Lent 1756. Hu.

Goodman, Sarah. S Summer 1766. Wa.

Goodman, Thomas. T Apr 1731 *Bennett*. K.

Goodman, William. R Oct AT Dec 1688. M.

Goodman, William. S s mare Lent R 14 yrs Summer 1746. Bu.

Goodman, William. R s horse Lent 1768. Le.

Goodman, William. R 14 yrs Mar 1768. De.

Goodram, Thomas. S Jan T Feb 1719 *Worcester* LC Annapolis Jun 1719. L.

Goodridge, Gilbert. T Apr 1753 *Thames*. K.

Goodrod, Mary. T Jan 1736 *Dorsetshire*. Sy.

Goods, Benjamin of Hereford. S Lent 1721. He.

Goodson, Catherine. S Jly T Sep 1767 *Justitia*. M.

Godson, Charles. T Sep 1755 *Tryal*. M.

Goodson, John of New Windsor. R for America Feb 1687. Be.

Goodson, Joseph. S & T Sep 1731 *Smith* LC Va 1732. L.

Godson als Clements als King als Collins, Mary. R for America Aug 1715. L.

Godson, Mary. S for returning from transportation & T Jly 1723 *Alexander*. L.

Goodson, Phillip. S for Va Aug 1718. L.

Goodson, Thomas. Rebel T 1685.

Goodspeed, Mary. S & R Summer 1764 T Apr 1765 *Ann*. Bu.

Goodwell, Anne (1682). *See* Parkinson. M.

Goodwin, Ann wife of Francis of Barking. R for America Jly 1700. E.

Goodwin, Ann. S Summer 1738 R 14 yrs Lent 1739. Ru.

Goodwin, Catherine. R & T Jly 1770 *Scarsdale*. M.

Goodwin, Daniel. S Summer 1754. E.

Goodwin, Edward Sr. S Feb T Mar 1731 *Patapsco* to Md. M.

Godwyn, Francis. S & TB to Va Mar 1738. Wi.

Goodwin, Giles. S s at Bishop Frome Summer 1751. He.

Godwin, Hannah. T May 1720 *Honor*. L.

Goodwyn, Henry. S Oct-Dec 1754. M.

Goodwyn, Jane. R for Va s petticoat May 1620. M.

Goodwyn, John. SQS for attending conventicle Dec 1664. M.

Goodwyn, John. R for America Feb 1692. No.

Goodwin als Plumpe, John. R for Barbados or Jamaica Dec 1699. L.

Goodwin als Barlow, John. S s horse Summer 1738 R 14 yrs Summer 1739. Y.

Goodwin, John (1743). *See* Goody. L.

Goodwin, Mary. S Oct 1765 T Jan 1766 *Tryal*. L.

Goodwin, Mary. S Jan-Feb T Apr 1771 *Thornton*. M.

Goodwin, Mary. S Jan-Feb 1773. M.

Goodwin, Matthew. S Feb T Mar 1731 *Patapsco* LC Annapolis Jun 1731. M.

Goodwin, Richard. R 14 yrs for highway robbery Jly 1724. Ha.

Godwin, Richard. T Jan 1766 *Tryal*. M.

Goodwin, Robert of Sternfield. S Summer 1731. *Su.

Goodwin, Sarah. S & T Oct 1732 *Caesar* to Va. M.

Goodwin, Solomon. S Dec 1764 T Jan 1765 *Tryal.* M.

Goodwin, Stephen. S s sheep Lent 1750. Nf.

Goodwin, Thomas. S Mar TB Aug 1720 T *Owners Goodwill* LC Md Jly 1722. Le.

Goodwin, William. S Aug 1725. M.

Goodwin, William. S & T May 1736 *Patapsco.* L.

Godwin, William. S s horse & R 14 yrs Lent 1773. Mo.

Godwin, William. S Mar 1774. So.

Goodey, Henry. S Jun T Sep 1758 *Tryal.* L.

Goody als Goodwin, John. S Feb T Mar 1743 *Justitia.* L.

Goody, John. S Lent 1748. Su.

Goodye, John of Lambeth. SQS Apr T Sep 1751 *Greyhound.* Sy.

Goody, Richard. S Lent T May 1767 *Thornton.* Bu.

Goodier, Benjamin. S s at St. Martin, Worcester, Lent 1735. Wo.

Goodyeare, John of Walton. R for Barbados Jly 1690. Y.

Goodyear, John. S Mar 1732 TB to Va. De.

Goodeare, John. TB to Va from QS 1743. De.

Goodaire, John. S Summer 1759. Y.

Goodyer, Thomas of St. Olave, Southwark. R for Barbados or Jamaica Dec 1680. Sy.

Goose, Ann. S Norwich for shoplifting Summer 1742. Nf.

Goose, John of Rochford. R for Barbados or Jamaica Jly 1710. E.

Goosetree, Joseph of Newcastle under Lyme. S for shoplifting Summer 1740. St.

Goosey, Joseph. S Mar TB to Va Apr 1774. Le.

Gootree, John. S & T Oct 1729 *Forward* but died on passage. M.

Gorbe, William. T Apr 1734 *Patapsco.* Sy.

Gorbett, John. S s silver mug at Sheffield, Yorks, Lent 1764. Db.

Gordon, Alexander. S Sep T Oct 1768 *Justitia.* M.

Gordon, Ann. S Feb T Apr 1739 *Forward* to Va. M.

Gordon, Ann. S & T Apr 1766 *Ann.* M.

Gordon, Charles. S & T Apr 1725 *Sukey* LC Annapolis Sep 1725. M.

Gorden, Elizabeth (1729). *See* Sugg. St.

Gordon, Elizabeth wife of John. S Feb T Apr 1768 *Thornton.* M.

Gordon, Elizabeth. S s from barracks at Scarborough Castle Lent 1775. Y.

Gordon, Frances. S Apr T May 1750 *Lichfield.* M.

Gordon, Isabella. S for shoplifting Summer 1741 R 14 yrs Summer 1742. We.

Gordon, Isabella. R 14 yrs Summer 1742. Cu.

Gordon, James of Epsom. SQS Jan 1754. Sy.

Gordon, James. S Mar 1767. Co.

Gorden, James. S Sep-Oct 1775. M.

Gorden, Jane, aged 50, brown hair. T Oct 1720 *Gilbert* LC Md May 1721. E.

Gordon, Jane. S Summer 1730 AT Summer 1732. Nl.

Gordon, John. S Jly T Aug 1721 *Prince Royal* LC Va Nov 1721. M.

Gordon, John. S Jan T Feb 1726 *Supply* LC Annapolis May 1726. L.

Gordon, John. T Jun 1740 *Essex.* E.

Gordon, John. S Oct 1756. L.

Gordon, John. S May T Sep 1766 *Justitia.* M.

Gordon, John. T Apr 1768 *Thornton.* K.

Gordon, John. R for life Summer 1772. K.

Gordon, Margaret. R 14 yrs Summer TB Aug 1741. Y.
Gordon, Margaret. SQS Oct T Dec 1771 *Justitia*. M.
Gordon, Mary. S Jun 1733 T Jan 1734 *Caesar* LC Va Jly 1734. M.
Gordon, Mary. S Summer 1753. Du.
Gordon, Richard (1760). *See* Handford. M.
Gordon, Thomas. S Jan-Jun 1747. M.
Gordon als Gourden, William. S Summer 1719 AT Summer 1720. Y.
Gordon, William of Newcastle under Lyme. R for America Feb 1713. St.
Gordon, William. S & R City Summer 1726. Nl.
Gordon, William. S Jly-Sep 1754. M.
Gordon, William. S s at St. Mary le Crypt, Gloucester, Lent 1759. G.
Gore, Christopher. T Oct 1721 *William & John*. Sy.
Gore, Daniel. SQS Oct 1750. M.
Gore als Purcell, John. S Sep-Oct T Dec 1752 *Greyhound*. M.
Gorgonna, John Baptista. S & T Sep 1757 *Thetis*. M.
Gorgrave, Richard. S & T Sep 1766 *Justitia*. M.
Gorman, Edward. S Dec 1766 T Jan 1767 *Tryal*. M.
Gorman, Eleanor. S Jun-Dec 1738 T Jan 1739 *Dorsetshire* to Va. M.
Gorman, Lawrence. S Feb 1757. M.
Gorman, Sarah. S Jan 1751. M.
Gorman, Thomas. R 14 yrs Mar 1762. Ha.
Gorman, William. S Jan-Jun 1747. M.
Gormwood, Samuel, als Deeves, John. T Dec 1734 *Caesar*. E.
Gornly, Barnaby. S Jan 1757. M.
Gorridge, Anthony (1772). *See* Gutteridge. No.
Gorsuch, John. LC from *Forward* Annapolis Jun 1725. X.
Gorton, Edward. S s at Whittington Lent 1735. Sh.
Gosdale, James. S Lent 1744. Hu.
Gosdale, Mary. S Lent 1744. Hu.
Gosdin, Mary. S Jan-Jun 1747. M.
Gosgrave, Elizabeth. R for Jamaica Aug 1661. M.
Gosler, John of St. George, Southwark, gent. SQS May 1764. Sy.
Gosling, Ann. S Lent 1759. Su.
Gosling, David. S Lent R 14 yrs Summer 1750. Sh.
Gosling, James (1745). *See* Goswell. E.
Gosling, John. S s horse Summer 1725 R 14 yrs Lent 1726, died on *Loyal Margaret* 1726. St.
Gosling, John. S s horse Summer 1729 R 14 yrs Summer 1730. Li.
Gosling, Josiah. S & T May 1744 *Justitia*. L.
Gosling, Mary. S Feb T Mar 1758 *Dragon*. L.
Gosling als Bailey, Robert. S Lent R 14 yrs Summer 1751; apprehended Lent 1767 for returning from transportation but acquitted. Nf.
Gosling, Samuel. R 14 yrs Mar 1771 TB to Va. De.
Gosling, Thomas (1700). *See* Grove. Be.
Gosling, Thomas. S Feb T Apr 1770 *New Trial* but removed from ship & detained in prison. M.
Gosling, William. S Sep-Oct 1775. M.
Gossage, William. S Apr T Oct 1719 *Susannah & Sarah* LC Md Apr 1720. L.
Gosseloe, Hannah. S Feb T Mar 1731 *Patapsco* LC Annapolis Jun 1731. M.
Gostling, Thomas. S s at Diss & R Lent 1771. Nf.

Goswell als Gosling, James of Duddinghurst. S Summer 1745 R 14 yrs
   Lent 1746; S for returning Lent 1749 R & T for life May 1750 *Lichfield*. E.
Gothard, John Jr. R 14 yrs Mar 1772 TB to Va. De.
Gothard, Sarah. R 14 yrs Mar 1772. De.
Gotobed, John. S s at St. Botolph, Cambridge, Summer 1773. Ca.
Gotray, Hugh. S Jan-Jun 1747. M.
Goud, Robert. S Mar 1771. Ha.
Gouge, Richard. S Aug 1763. L.
Goff, Ann. S s linen Dec 1735 T Jan 1736 *Dorsetshire* LC Va Sep 1736. M.
Gough, Edward. R for Barbados Jun 1671. L.
Goff, Elizabeth. S Jan-Jun 1747. M.
Goffe, George of Aldingbourne. R for Barbados or Jamaica Feb 1683. Sx.
Gough, James. SQS Jly TB to Md Nov 1740. So.
Gough, James. AT Lent 1745. He.
Gough, James. S Jan-Feb 1775. M.
Goffe als Newberry, Joane. S Aug 1720. De.
Gough, John (1770). *See* Newby, Godfrey. Be.
Gough, John. S for forgery & R for life Summer 1773. St.
Goff, Martha wife of John. S Jan T 14 yrs Apr 1759 *Thetis*. M.
Gough als Goff, Mary. S Jun-Dec 1738 T Jan 1739 *Dorsetshire* to Va. M.
Gough, Mary of St. George, Southwark, spinster. SQS Apr T Sep 1751
   Greyhound. Sy.
Gough, Mary. S Apr 1753. So.
Goffe, Nehemiah. Rebel T 1685.
Goff, Richard. R 14 yrs Jly 1771 TB to Va 1772. De.
Gough, Rose wife of Francis. S Feb T Apr 1770 *New Trial*. L.
Goff als Newberry, Thomas. S Mar 1734. De.
Gough, William of Wimborne, butcher. R (Oxford Circ) for America Mar
   1688. Do.
Gough als Goff, William. S Jan T Sep 1737 *Pretty Patsy* to Md. M.
Gould, Edward. S Aug 1736. So.
Gould, Elias. TB to Va from QS 1739. De.
Gould, Elizabeth of Putney, spinster. SQS Apr T May 1752 *Lichfield*. Sy.
Gould, Elizabeth. R Dec 1765 T Jan 1766 *Tryal*. M.
Gould, Elizabeth. S Jan-Feb 1774. M.
Gould, Enoch. Rebel T 1685.
Gould, George. S Summer 1746 R 14 yrs Lent 1747. He.
Gold, George. AT Lent 1748. He.
Gould, James of Methringham. R for America Jly 1673. Li.
Gould, Jane. S Feb T Apr 1770 *New Trial*. L.
Gould, Jane. R 14 yrs Mar 1775. De.
Gould, John. Rebel T 1685.
Gold, John. R for Barbados or Jamaica Jly 1696. X.
Gold als Beadle, John. S & T Apr 1725 *Sukey* LC Annapolis Sep 1725. M.
Gold, John. T Sep 1730 *Smith*. E.
Gold, John. S Dec 1749-Jan 1750 T Mar 1750 *Tryal*. M.
Gould, John. S Apr 1775. So.
Gould, Joseph. T Jly 1770 *Scarsdale*. M.
Gold, Mary. S Feb T Mar 1727 *Rappahannock*. L.
Gould, Mary. S Sep-Oct 1773. M.
Gold, Philip. R for Va Feb 1621. Nf.

Gould, Richard (1731). *See* Pace. E.
Gould, Thomas. Rebel T 1685.
Gold, Thomas. R 14 yrs Mar 1741. Ha.
Gould, William. Rebel T 1685.
Gold, William. PT Jun R Oct 1690. M.
Gould, William. S & T Jan 1756 *Greyhound*. L.
Golden, John of Worsley. SQS Jly 1772. La.
Goulding, Charles. S May 1761. M.
Goulding, Elizabeth. S Jan T 14 yrs Feb 1726 *Supply* LC Annapolis May
  1726. M.
Golding, Frances. S Oct T Nov 1728 *Forward* LC Rappahannock Jun 1729. L.
Golding, Francis (1758). *See* Jaggard. Nf.
Gouldin, George. S Lent 1754. Sy.
Goldin, John. R for Barbados Jly 1675. L.
Golding, Margaret. S Aug 1723. M.
Golding, Margaret (1767). *See* Gowling. Cu.
Goulding, Mary (1741). *See* Nash. M.
Gouldin, Pearcy. S Jly 1763. M.
Goulding, Peter. S Oct 1765 T Jan 1766 *Tryal*. L.
Golding, Richard. S & T Apr 1725 *Sukey* LC Annapolis Sep 1725. M.
Golding, Richard. S Feb T Apr 1772 *Thornton*. L.
Golding, Thomas of Northampton. R for America Jly 1679. No.
Golding, Thomas. S Aug T Oct 1723 *Forward* to Va. M.
Golding, William. S Aug 1752. So.
Gouldson, William. T Sep 1730 *Smith*. E.
Goulstone, Mary. S & T 14 yrs Jan 1722 *Gilbert* LC Annapolis Jly 1722. M.
Goulston, Richard. S May-Jly 1749 to be T for life. M.
Gounley, Jane. T Jan 1766 *Tryal*. L.
Gourden, William (1719). *See* Gordon. Y.
Gourdian, Alexander. R for Barbados Jun 1670. M.
Govey, George. T 14 yrs Nov 1759 *Phoenix*. Ht.
Govier, Anthony. TB to Md from QS 1737. De.
Govier, John of Dorking. SQS Oct T Dec 1767 *Neptune*. Sy.
Govier, Samuel. R 14 yrs Aug 1748. So.
Goward, Mary, spinster. S s at Stagsden & R 14 yrs Lent 1769. Bd.
Gowden, Alexander. T Dec 1753 *Whiteing*. Sx.
Gowen als Gardner, James. PT Jun R Oct 1690. M.
Gowen, James. S Feb T Mar 1729 *Patapsco* LC Annapolis Dec 1729. L.
Gowen, Thomas. S Sep 1715 R & T Dec 1716 *Lewis* to Jamaica. M.
Gower, Elizabeth. AT from QS Summer 1731. St.
Gower, John of Claydon. R for America Mar 1686. Su.
Gower, Philip. S Apr-May 1754. M.
Gower, Thomas. T 14 yrs Sep 1766 *Justitia*. Ht.
Gowers, George of Newington. R for Barbados or Jamaica Jly 1674. Sy.
Gowers, John of Barking. SQS Jan T May 1752 *Lichfield*. E.
Gowery als Gowerly, Thomas. R 14 yrs Summer 1752. Nl.
Gowing, Edward. S Summer 1751. Su.
Gowing, John of Harwell. R for Jamaica, Barbados or Bermuda Feb 1686. Be.
Gowling als Golding, Margaret. S s at Weighton Summer 1767. Cu.
Goyne, Thomas. S Mar 1754 for assaulting a JP on duty to preserve
  stranded ship. Co.

Goyte, Joseph. S s barley at Weford Lent 1723. St.
Grace, Edward. S Jan T Feb 1726 *Supply* LC Annapolis May 1726. M.
Grace, John. R 14 yrs Aug 1724. So.
Grace, John. S Apr 1742. Ha.
Grace, Mary (1741). *See* Grey. M.
Grace, Susan. T Dec 1731 *Forward*. Sy.
Grace, William. S Dec 1745. L.
Grace, William. S Jan-Jun 1747. M.
Grace als Frazier, William. S Lent 1749. Bu.
Gradley, John. S Jan T Jun 1738 *Forward* to Md or Va. M.
Grady, Edward. R for Barbados Aug 1679. M.
Grady, Eleanor. S Feb-Apr T May 1752 *Lichfield*. M.
Grady, John. S Lent 1754. Sy.
Grafton, Henry, als Taylor, Harry. S Jly 1748. L.
Graham, Ann. R for Barbados or Jamaica Aug 1700. L.
Graham, Ann. T Jun 1756 *Lyon*. Ht.
Graham, Charles. S for sacrilege Summer 1743 R 14 yrs Summer 1744. Nl.
Graham, George. S May-Jun T Aug 1752 *Tryal*. M.
Graham als Grimes, Hannah. R & T 14 yrs Jan 1722 *Gilbert* LC Md Jly
    1722. M.
Graham, Henry. S Summer 1754. Y.
Graham, James. S s shoes Jan-May T Jun 1738 *Forward* to Md or Va. M.
Graham, Jane (1735). *See* Henderson. Cu.
Graham, Jane. S Jan T Apr 1743 *Justitia*. M.
Graham, Jeanette of Stanwix. R for Barbados Jly 1683. Nl.
Graham, John (1733). *See* Hall. Cu.
Graham als McBlair als Rutledge als Lawes, John. S s horse Summer
    1738 R 14 yrs Summer 1739. Cu.
Graham als Grimes, John. S Jly T Sep 1757 *Thetis*. M.
Graham, Joseph. SQS & T Apr 1766 *Ann*. M.
Graham als Grimes, Leonard. S s sheep Summer 1757 R 14 yrs Lent
    1758. Nt.
Graham, Martha (1745). *See* Grimes. L.
Graham, Martha of Lambeth, spinster. SQS Jan 1765. Sy.
Graham, Mary. T Apr 1765 *Ann*. Sy.
Graham als Gregg, Mary. SQS Summer 1773. Du.
Graham, Mary. SQS Summer 1774. Du.
Graham, Patrick. S Dec 1760. M.
Graham, Peter. S Apr T 14 yrs Jly 1770 *Scarsdale*. M.
Graham als Grimes, Robert. T Dec 1736 *Dorsetshire*. Sy.
Graham, Robert. S Feb-Apr 1745. M.
Graham, Robert. S Summer 1756. Cu.
Graham, Sarah. S Apr 1761. M.
Graham, Thomas. S Jly T Oct 1723 *Forward*. L.
Graham, Thomas (1753). *See* Grime. Y.
Graham, William. R 14 yrs Summer 1744. Nl.
Graham, William. S & T Apr 1762 *Neptune*. L.
Graham, William. S & T Apr 1766 *Ann*. L.
Graham, William. T Apr 1766 *Ann*. M.
Graham, William. S Summer 1772. Cu.
Granby, Elizabeth. S Lent 1762. Sh.

Granfield, John. S Aug 1764. So.
Granfield, William, als Grinet, Robert. S s asses at Hurley Lent 1770. Be.
Grange, Eunice. T 14 yrs Dec 1758 *The Brothers*. Ht.
Grange, William. T Sep 1764 *Justitia*. E.
Grainger, Elizabeth (1694). *See* Ridgway. M.
Grainger, Elizabeth. S May 1726. M.
Granger, Esther. S Oct 1766 T Jan 1767 *Tryal*. M.
Grainger, Francis. S 14 yrs Dec 1773. L.
Grainger, James. T Dec 1736 *Dorsetshire*. Sy.
Granger, John. TB May 1741. Db.
Grainger, Joseph. S Lent T May 1755 *Rose*. Sy.
Grainger, Joseph of Bedale. SQS Richmond Jan 1775. Y.
Granger, Martin. S s hen at Walsall Lent 1759. St.
Grainger, Mary. S Summer 1759 R 14 yrs Lent 1760. Wo.
Granger, Richard. TB to Va 1768. De.
Granger, Thomas. R for Barbados or Jamaica Dec 1693. L.
Grainger, Thomas of Addington. R for Barbados or Jamaica Jly 1696. Sy.
Grainger, William. T May 1737 *Forward*. E.
Grant, Adam. S Feb-Apr T May 1752 *Lichfield*. M.
Grant, Alexander. SL Jly 1773. Sy.
Grant, Catherine. S Feb T Apr 1732 *Patapsco* LC Annapolis Oct 1732. M.
Grant, Charles. S & T Jan 1736 *Dorsetshire* LC Va Sep 1736. L.
Grant, Christian. S Dec 1749-Jan 1750 T Mar 1750 *Tryal*. M.
Grant, Clementina. S Lent 1740. Y.
Grant, Elizabeth (1699). *See* Barrenclaugh. M.
Grant, James. SQS & TB Oct 1749. So.
Grant, John. S Jly T Aug 1721 *Prince Royal* to Va. M.
Grant, John. S May T Sep 1765 *Justitia*. M.
Grant, John. S s at Cirencester Lent 1774. G.
Grant, Joseph. SQS Feb T Apr 1763 *Thames*. M.
Grant, Margaret wife of John. S May-Jly 1773. M.
Grant, Mary. S Summer T Oct 1750 *Rachael*. Sy.
Grant, Mary. S Aug 1760. L.
Grant, Peter (1764). *See* Holland, Bryan. So.
Grant, Sarah. S May T Jly 1723 *Alexander* LC Annapolis Sep 1723. M.
Grant, Sarah. S Jly T Sep 1755 *Tryal*. L.
Grant, Simon of Bristol. R 14 yrs Sep 1768 (SP). G.
Grant, Susannah. S Feb-Apr 1746. M.
Grant, Thomas. S Sep T Oct 1720 *Gilbert*. L.
Grant, Thomas. TB to Va from QS 1740. De.
Grant, Thomas. S s horse Summer 1762 R 14 yrs Lent 1763. Wa.
Grant, William. S Mar 1720. De.
Grant, William. S for breaking & entering Apr T Jun 1742 *Bladon* to Md. M.
Grant, William. R 14 yrs Aug 1742. So.
Grant, William. T Sep 1764 *Justitia*. Sy.
Grant, William. S s sacks at St. Peter in East, Oxford, Lent 1773. O.
Grantham, Henry of Rotherhithe. SQS Oct 1764 T Jan 1765 *Tryal*. Sy.
Grantham, John. SW & T Oct 1768 *Justitia*. M.
Grantlett, John. S Jly 1718 to be T to Va. Co.
Granwell als Bigge, Thomas. R for Barbados Mar 1681. M.
Grass, Isabel (1739). *See* Gross. Nl.

Grasshoof, Deborah. S s gown Jun T Dec 1736 *Dorsetshire* to Va. M.

Grater, Henry. TB to Va from QS 1741. De.

Gratewood. *See* Greatwood.

Gratton, Joseph. S Summer 1740. Ch.

Gravil, Benjamin. S Mar 1767 TB to Va. De.

Gravel, John. R 14 yrs Mar 1731. Wi.

Graveney, Thomas. S s sheep Lent R 14 yrs Summer 1758 T Apr 1759 *Thetis* as Thomas Grosvenor. Bu.

Gravenor, Philip of Middleton on Hill. R for America Jly 1675. He.

Graves, Elianor. R for Barbados Jun 1671. M.

Graves, Elizabeth. T Sep 1755 *Tryal*. M.

Graves, James. T Jun 1764 *Dolphin*. K.

Graves, Jane (1680). *See* Bassett. Sy.

Graves, Jane (1774). *See* Gray. M.

Graves, John (1722). *See* Scoon. L.

Graves, John. S Oct 1744-Jan 1745. M.

Graves, John. S s gelding & R 14 yrs Lent 1759. Bd.

Graves als Rhodes, John of Crompton. SQS Jun 1767. La.

Graves, Richard. S s mare & R 14 yrs Summer TB to Md Sep 1772. Le.

Graves, Thomas. T 14 yrs Apr 1768 *Thornton*. Sy.

Graves, William of St. James Clerkenwell. S s hats & T Jan 1740 *York*. M.

Gravett, James of Abinger. SQS Jan 1773. Sy.

Grey als Davis als Reason, Amey. S Jly 1741. M.

Gray, Ann of Woolaston. R for America Feb 1713. No.

Grey, Ann. S s sheep Summer 1764 R 14 yrs Lent T Oct 1765. Bd.

Gray, Arthur. S May T Jly 1722 *Alexander* to Nevis or Jamaica. M.

Gray, Catharine. S Dec 1766 T Jan 1767 *Tryal*. M.

Gray, Christopher. Rebel T 1685.

Gray, Christopher. S Lent 1749. Sy.

Gray, Elizabeth. S Feb T Apr 1743 *Justitia*. M.

Gray, Elizabeth. S & T Jan 1756 *Greyhound*. L.

Gray, Elizabeth. T Sep 1758 *Tryal*. K.

Grey, Elizabeth. AT City Summer 1759. Nl.

Gray, Elizabeth, spinster. S s at Burford Summer 1769. O.

Gray, Frances. S & R 14 yrs Summer 1758. Du.

Gray, Francis. S for burglary Lent 1769 R for life Summer 1770. Be.

Gray, George. Rebel T 1685.

Gray, George. S Feb T Mar 1729 *Patapsco*. L.

Grey, Henrietta. SQS Apr 1773. M.

Gray, Henry. S Jly 1721 T Mar 1723. Bu.

Gray, James. S Jly T Sep 1737 *Pretty Patsy* to Md. M.

Gray, James. SQS Jly T Sep 1751 *Greyhound*. M.

Gray, James. SQS New Sarum Jan TB to Va Apr 1754. Wi.

Gray, James. S Mar 1756. Ha.

Gray, James. T 14 yrs Aug 1769 *Douglas*. K.

Gray, James. S Oct T Dec 1771 *Justitia*. L.

Gray als Graves, Jane. SQS Dec 1762 T Mar 1763 *Neptune*. M.

Grey, Jean. S City for perjury Summer 1766; to stand in pillory for an hour before transportation. Nl.

Gray, John, barber aged 29, fair. S Jly T Oct 1720 *Gilbert* LC Md May 1721. M.

Gray, John. S & T Oct 1730 *Forward* LC Potomack Jan 1731. L.

Grey, John. T Apr 1739 *Forward*. E.

Gray, John of Downton, tanner. SQS Marlborough & TB to Va Oct 1742. Wi.

Gray, John. S 14 yrs for receiving Aug 1769. Nl.

Gray, Joseph. S Summer 1742 R 14 yrs Lent 1743. Be.

Gray, Margaret. S & T Oct 1730 *Forward* LC Potomack Jan 1731. M.

Gray, Margaret. SQS Jan 1752. M.

Gray, Martha, als Dow, Mary. S Apr T May 1719 *Susannah & Sarah* LC Md May 1720. L.

Gray, Martha. S Oct 1719. M.

Grey, Martin. S Apr T May 1720 *Honor* but escaped in Vigo, Spain. L.

Gray als Walter, Mary. T Nov 1725 *Rappahannock* LC Va Aug 1726. Sy.

Grey als Grace, Mary. S Jly T Oct 1741 *Sea Horse* to Va. M.

Gray, Matthew (1775). *See* Imber. Wi.

Gray, Rachel. S for shoplifting Summer 1729 R 14 yrs Summer 1730. Li.

Gray, Richard. R for America Jly 1694. Db.

Gray, Richard. S Apr T May 1755 *Rose*. L.

Grey, Richard. S s mare Lent R 14 yrs Summer 1756. No.

Gray, Richard. T Sep 1764 *Justitia*. M.

Gray, Roger of Gosport, mariner. R for Barbados Jun 1708. Ha.

Gray, Samuel. S Feb T Mar 1729 *Patapsco* LC Annapolis Dec 1729. M.

Grey, Samuel. S Jly 1741. Co.

Gray, Samuel. S & R for life Lent T Apr 1773. No.

Gray, Sarah. S Oct T Nov 1725 *Rappahannock* LC Rappahannock Apr 1726. L.

Gray, Sarah wife of Richard. TB Apr 1743. Db.

Gray als Judson, Sarah. S Jan 1757. M.

Gray, Thomas. S Mar TB Apr 1731. Nt.

Grey, Thomas. S City Summer 1740. Nl.

Gray, Thomas. S Apr T May 1750 *Lichfield*. M.

Gray, Thomas. S s malt at Bromley Lent 1757. St.

Gray, Thomas. S May T Aug 1769 *Douglas*. M.

Gray, Thomas. T Aug 1769 *Douglas*. K.

Grey, Thomas. S s at Codrington Lent 1774. G.

Gray, Walter. S Aug T Sep 1764 *Justitia*. L.

Gray, William. SQS for being idle & disorderly Jan 1665. M.

Gray, William. PT Sep 1691 R Jan 1692. M.

Gray, William. S Oct T 14 yrs Nov 1725 *Rappahannock* LC Rappahannock Apr 1726. L.

Gray, William. S Aug 1735. So.

Gray als Jones, William. S Apr-Jun 1739. M.

Grey, William. S Aug T 14 yrs Oct 1741 *Sea Horse* to Va. M.

Grey, William. S Lent R 14 yrs Summer 1742. Ca.

Gray, William. S Feb T Apr 1743 *Justitia*. M.

Gray, William. S Jly 1763. M.

Gray, William. S Jly T Sep 1767 *Justitia*. M.

Graycroft, John. R for America Aug 1715. M.

Graydon, Christopher. T Jun 1738 *Forward*. E.

Grayer, Margaret. R for Barbados Dec 1667. M.

Grayhurst, Mary. S Oct T Dec 1770 *Justitia*. M.

Grayley, Francis. S Sep-Oct 1772. M.

Grayling, John. T Jun 1738 *Forward*. Sx.

Grason, George of Huntingdon. R for America Jly 1683. Hu.

Grayson, John. S Summer 1730. Y.

Grayson, John. S Lent 1761. La.

Grayson, Mary of Kirkdale, spinster. SQS Oct 1744. La.

Grayson, Thomas. S Summer 1730. Y.

Graystock, Charles. S & T Jan 1722 *Gilbert* LC Annapolis Jly 1722. L.

Greaghan, John. S Apr T Sep 1758 *Tryal* to Annapolis. M.

Grear, Ann. S Sep-Oct 1773. M.

Greasley, Peter. S Lent 1761. Nt & Nl.

Greasy, Mery. S Mar 1737. De.

Greatrix, Samuel. S Apr-Jun T Jly 1772 *Tayloe*. M.

Greatwood, James. S Jan-Feb 1773. M.

Gratewood, John. S Aug TB to Va Sep 1767. Wi.

Greatwood, Samuel. SQS Warminster Jly TB to Va Aug 1765. Wi.

Greaves. *See* Greeves.

Greedy, Edmund. S Jly 1722. So.

Greedy, Robert (1688). *See* Sandford. So.

Green als Harvey, Abigall of St. George, Southwark. S Lent T May 1719
  Margaret LC Md May 1720 & sold to Mrs. Bransome. Sy.

Green, Abraham. S & TB to Va Apr 1769. Wi.

Green, Anne. R for Barbados Jly 1680. M.

Greene, Anne (1682). *See* Smyth. L.

Green, Ann. R for Barbados or Jamaica May AT Jly 1697. M.

Green als Rowling, Ann. S Feb T 14 yrs Mar 1727 *Rappahannock*. L.

Green, Ann. S Oct T Nov 1728 *Forward* LC Rappahannock Jun 1729. L.

Green, Ann of St. George, Southwark, spinster. SQS Aug T Dec 1753
  Whiteing. Sy.

Green, Ann or St. Margaret, Westminster. SW Jly T Sep 1767 *Justitia*. M.

Green als Greenough als Greenhalgh als Greena, Ann of Salford. SQS
  Jun 1772. La.

Green, Ann (1774). *See* Clarke. M.

Green als Newman, Ann. S s at Wood Walton Lent 1774. Hu.

Green, Anthony. S & T Dec 1767 *Neptune*. L.

Green, Bartholomew (1688). *See* Kettle. Su.

Green als Tiptee, Bathsheba of St. Mary's, Colchester, spinster. SQS Jan T
  Sep 1758 *Tryal*. E.

Green, Benjamin. S Lent 1768. Wa.

Greene, Bridget (1664). *See* Harding. M.

Green, Charles (1721). *See* Vermin. M.

Green, Charles. T Apr 1741 *Speedwell* or *Mediterranean*. Sy.

Green, Charles. R Jly 1774. M.

Green, Christopher Jr. AT City Lent 1753. Y.

Green, Constance. S s at Burston & R Summer 1769; her husband Cornelius
  Green hanged for same. Nf.

Green, Crispin. S May T Jun 1727 *Susanna* to Va. M.

Green, Daniel. S & TB Apr 1742. G.

Greene, Deborah. R for America Mar 1690. Li.

Green, Edward. R 14 yrs Aug 1724. So.

Green als Smith, Edward of West Ham. SQS Oct T Nov 1762 *Prince
  William*. E.

Green, Edward of St. Saviour, Southwark. SQS Jan T Apr 1765 *Ann*. Sy.

Green, Edward. T 14 yrs Sep 1766 *Justitia*. K.

Green, Edward. T 14 yrs Apr 1768 *Thornton*. E.

Greene, Elizabeth. R for Jamaica Aug 1661. M.

Green, Elizabeth. R for Barbados Feb 1675. L.

Greene, Elizabeth. R for Barbados Jly 1675. L.

Green, Elizabeth (1720). *See* Twelves. Sy.

Green, Elizabeth. T Jly 1724 *Robert* LC Md Jun 1725. Sy.

Green, Elizabeth. R 14 yrs for murder Mar 1725. So.

Green, Elizabeth. S & T Jan 1736 *Dorsetshire* LC Va Sep 1736. L.

Green, Elizabeth. S Oct-Dec 1739 T Jan 1740 *York* to Md. M.

Green, Elizabeth. S Lent 1754. Y.

Green, Elizabeth. S May T Jly 1770 *Scarsdale*. L.

Green, Elizabeth. S Oct T Dec 1770 *Justitia*. M.

Green, Elizabeth wife of Thomas. S 14 yrs for receiving Summer 1775. Wa.

Greene, Emma. R (Norfolk Circ) for America Jly 1663. X.

Green, Francis. S Aug 1763. L.

Greene, George. R for Jamaica Aug 1661. M.

Greene, George. R 10 yrs in plantations Oct 1662. M.

Green, George (1720). *See* Way. E.

Green, George. S Oct T Nov 1725 *Rappahannock* but died on passage. L.

Green, George. T Oct 1738 *Genoa*. Sy.

Green, George. S s at Rotherham Lent 1766. Y.

Greene, Henry of West Haughton, fustian weaver. R for Barbados Jly 1683. La.

Green, Henry. T Jly 1723 *Alexander* LC Md Sep 1723. E.

Green, Henry. S s at Wallingford Lent 1751. Be.

Green, Henry. S Jly T Sep 1757 *Thetis*. L.

Green, Henry (1772). *See* Long. Be.

Green, Henry. S Dec 1772. M.

Greene, James. S s 10 pence Jan 1656; to be whipped & sent to House of Correction unless he agrees to transportation. M.

Green, James. R 14 yrs Jly 1719 to be T to Va. De.

Green, James. T Apr 1739 *Forward*. E.

Green, James. R 14 yrs Aug TB to Va Oct 1739. Wi.

Green, James. S s at St. James Summer TB Aug 1742. G.

Green, James. S Jly 1763. Do.

Green, James. S s gelding at Southwold & R Lent 1770. Su.

Greene, Jane of Cirencester, spinster. R for Barbados Mar 1693. G.

Greene, John. S Jan 1656 to be sent to House of Correction unless he agrees to transportation. M.

Greene, John (1667). *See* Wright. L.

Green, John (1672). *See* Hawkesworth. M.

Green, John. R Dec 1683. M.

Green, John of Bithburn. R for Barbados Jun 1684. Du.

Greene, John of Inworth. R for Barbados or Jamaica Mar 1688. E.

Greene, John. R for Barbados or Jamaica Mar 1688. M.

Greene, John of Harpenden. R for Barbados or Jamaica Jun 1699. Ht.

Green, John (1715). *See* Foulston. Sy.

Green, John. S Sep T Oct 1719 *Susannah & Sarah* LC Annapolis Apr 1720. L.

Green, John. S & T Jan 1722 *Gilbert* LC Annapolis Jly 1722. M.

Green, John. T Oct 1722 *Forward* LC Md Jun 1723. Sy.

Green, John. S Aug T Sep 1725 *Forward*. L.

Green, John. S & T Dec 1734 *Caesar* LC Va Jly 1735. M.

Green, John. S Jly 1736. Ha.

Green, John. S & T 14 yrs Jan 1739 *Dorsetshire*. L.

Green, John. S Oct 1741 T Feb 1742 *Industry* to Md. M.

Green, John. S s sheep at Ducklington Summer 1744 R 14 yrs Lent 1745. O.

Green, John. S Lent 1745. *Su.

Green, John. S Jan-Jun 1747. M.

Green, John. S Lent R 14 yrs Summer 1749. E.

Green, John. S for receiving uncustomed goods with armed band Summer 1749 R 14 yrs Lent T May 1750 *Lichfield*. K.

Green, John. R 14 yrs Mar 1750. Ha.

Green, John. S for highway robbery Lent R 14 yrs Summer TB to Va Sep 1751. Le.

Green, John. S s linen at Bromsgrove Summer 1752. Wo.

Green als Bowdler, John. S s shirt Lent 1754. He.

Green, John. S s wheat at St. Aldates Summer 1757. Be.

Green, John. SQS Oct T Nov 1759 *Phoenix*. M.

Green, John. S Feb 1761. L.

Green, John. S s at St. Mary le Crypt, Gloucester, Lent 1764. G.

Green, John, als Seaman, James. S s mare Lent R 14 yrs Summer 1767. Nf.

Green, John (2). T Oct 1768 *Justitia*. K.

Green, John. S Dec 1768 T Jan 1769 *Thornton*. L.

Green, John. S Lent 1770. No.

Green, John. S Maidstone & T Apr 1771 *Thornton*. K.

Green, John. S Lent 1774. Db.

Green, Joseph. T May 1751 *Tryal*. Sy.

Green, Joseph. S Lent T Sep 1757 *Thetis*. E.

Green, Joseph. T Sep 1758 *Tryal*. Sy.

Green, Joseph. T Nov 1759 *Phoenix*. K.

Green, Joseph. T 14 yrs Sep 1766 *Justitia*. Sy.

Green, Joseph. S Lent R 14 yrs Summer TB to Va Sep 1767. Le.

Green, Joseph. T Jly 1770 *Scarsdale*. L.

Green als Greenaway, Joseph. S & T Jly 1772 *Tayloe*. M.

Green, Joshua. S Lent 1735. Y.

Green, Lawrence. S Aug 1727 T *Forward* LC Rappahannock May 1728. M.

Green, Margaret. S & T Oct 1729 *Forward* but died on passage. L.

Green, Margaret. SQS Apr T May 1751 *Tryal*. M.

Green, Margaret. T Apr 1768 *Thornton*. K.

Green, Mary. S Jly 1720. M.

Green, Mary. S Jan-Apr 1749. M.

Green, Mary. S May-Jly 1750. M.

Green, Mary. SQS Aug 1751. Db.

Green, Mary. S Summer 1761. Nt.

Green, Mary. S Summer 1761. Nl.

Green als Collyer als Waller, Mary. S Jun 1761. M.

Green, Mary. SQS Jly T Sep 1765 *Justitia*. M.

Green, Matthew. S Feb T May 1767 *Thornton*. L.

Greene, Nowell. R Jly 1685. M.

Green, Peter. S s horse Lent R Summer 1726. Nt.

Green, Peter. S 14 yrs for receiving goods stolen at Bromsgrove by John Cox *(qv)* Summer 1752. Wo.

Greene, Richard. R Jly 1674 & Feb 1675. M.

Green, Richard. Rebel T 1685.

Green, Richard. S Feb T Mar 1729 *Patapsco* LC Annapolis Dec 1729. M.

Green, Richard. S s cordial Apr T Dec 1735 *John* LC Annapolis Sep 1736. L.

Green, Richard of Bristol. R 14 yrs Mar 1764 (SP). G.

Green, Richard. S for highway robbery Lent R 14 yrs Summer 1765. Hu.

Green, Richard. SQS Feb T Apr 1768 *Thornton*. M.

Greene, Roger. R 10 yrs Lent 1655 to be T by Thomas Vincent & Samuel Highland. Sy.

Green, Robert. S May T Jun 1727 *Susanna* to Va. M.

Green, Robert. S Norwich Summer 1746. *Nf.

Green, Robert. S Feb 1752. L.

Green, Robert. S Summer 1757. Nf.

Green, Robert. S Lent 1766. Ca.

Green, Robert. S Apr 1773. M.

Green, Samuel. S Lent 1768. Wa.

Green, Sarah. S Jly T 14 yrs Aug 1721 *Prince Royal* LC Va Nov 1721. L.

Green, Sarah. S & T Apr 1759 *Thetis*. L.

Green, Sarah. S s at Clive Summer 1760. Wo.

Green als Man, Sarah. T Jun 1764 *Dolphin*. E.

Greene, Susan (1679). *See* Banser. L.

Greene, Thomas of Stogumber, husbandman. R for Barbados Jly 1667. So.

Greene, Thomas (1682). *See* Wigham. Cu.

Green, Thomas of Broad——-. S Lent 1721. G.

Green, Thomas. S Apr T May 1750 *Lichfield*. M.

Green, Thomas. T 14 yrs Dec 1758 *The Brothers*. E.

Green, Thomas. S Jan T Apr 1762 *Dolphin*. L.

Green, Thomas. S s from Count Haslaugh Jan T Mar 1764 *Tryal*. M.

Green, Thomas. T Jly 1770 *Scarsdale*. M.

Green, Thomas. S Apr 1775. M.

Green, Walker. S Sep T 14 yrs Oct 1722 *Forward* LC Annapolis Jun 1723. L.

Greene, Walter of Quenington. R for Barbados Jly 1664. G.

Green, Walter of Tong. R for America Feb 1716. Sh.

Greene, William of Hardwicke. R for Barbados Jun 1668. G.

Green, William. S s shoes Jun T Dec 1736 *Dorsetshire* to Va. M.

Green, William. S Oct-Dec 1739 T Jan 1740 *York* to Md. M.

Green, William. S Mar TB to Va Apr 1741. Wi.

Green, William. S Norwich for burglary Summer 1749 R 14 yrs Lent 1750. Nf.

Green, William. S Sep-Oct 1749. M.

Green, William of Parr. SQS Jly 1757. La.

Green, William. T 14 yrs Apr 1768 *Thornton*. E.

Green, William of Rotherhithe. SQS & T Apr 1769 *Tryal*. Sy.

Green, William of Colwick. SQS s metal pot Jly 1769. Nt.

Green, William. S 14 yrs for receiving & T Jly 1771 *Scarsdale*. L.

Green, William. S Dec 1772. M.

Green, William. S s at Ellsworth Lent 1773. Ca.

Greena, Ann (1772). *See* Green. La.

Greenaway, Ann wife of John. R Mar TB to Va Apr 1775. Wi.

Greenaway, Hannah of St. Marylebone, widow. S s sheets Oct 1740 T Jan 1741 *Harpooner* to Rappahannock. M.

Greenaway, Henry. S Apr 1749. L.

Greenway, Jane of West Gynge. R for Barbados Jly 1664. Be.

Greenway, John. S s at Wigmore Summer 1764. He.

Greenaway, Joseph (1772). *See* Green. M.

Greenaway, Mary. SQS Jun T Aug 1752 *Tryal.* Sy.

Greenaway, Richard. S s pewter plates at Burford Lent 1750. O.

Greenaway, Thomas (1730). *See* Woodward. G.

Greenway, William. Rebel T 1685.

Greenaway, William. T May 1737 *Forward.* Sx.

Greenaway, William. S Jun 1739. L.

Greenbanke, George. S s watch at Thornton, West Riding, Lent 1768. Y.

Greenfield, John of Patshull. R for America Nov 1694. St.

Greenfield, John. T 14 yrs Sep 1767 *Justitia.* Sx.

Greenfield, John. S s iron at Kingswinford Lent 1768. St.

Greenhalgh, Adam of Breighthurst, weaver. SQS Aug 1757. La.

Greenhalgh, Ann (1772). *See* Green. La.

Greenhalgh, Edward of Manchester, calenderer. SQS Oct 1768. La.

Greenhalgh, Henry. S s fustian Summer 1740. La.

Greenhalgh, John of Wigan, linen weaver. S Summer 1741 R 14 yrs Summer 1742. La.

Greenhalgh, John of Elton. SQS Feb 1755. La.

Greenhall als Galleof, Ann. S & T 14 yrs Apr 1741 *Speedwell* or *Mediterranean.* M.

Greenham, Richard of Bishops Hatfield, sawyer. SQS Sep T Oct 1768 *Justitia.* Ht.

Greenow, Richard. S Lent R 14 yrs Summer 1756. He.

Greenhough, Thomas. S s cheeses at Uttoxeter Lent 1773. St.

Greening, James. S s at Sudely Lent TB Apr 1757. G.

Greenland, Edward. R 14 yrs Apr 1775. So.

Greenland, John. S & T Oct 1722 *Forward* LC Annapolis Jun 1723. M.

Greenland, William. Rebel T 1685.

Greenough, Ann (1772). *See* Green. La.

Greeneslade, Francis of Stogumber, carpenter. R for Barbados Jly 1667. So.

Greenslade, George. TB to Va from QS 1740. De.

Greenslade, Stephen. S Mar 1741. De.

Grinslade, William. R 14 yrs Mar 1754 TB to Va. De.

Greenslade, William. TB to Va 1768. De.

Greenswood, George. S & TB Oct 1745. G.

Greensword als Greenwood, George. S for highway robbery Lent R 14 yrs Summer TB Jly 1743. G.

Greentree, Isabella. T Apr 1762 *Neptune.* Sy.

Greenwater, Margery. AT City Summer 1758. Nl.

Greenwell, Acteon of Bermondsey. SQS Jan T Apr 1770 *New Trial.* Sy.

Greenwell, Acton. S Oct 1775. M.

Greenwood, Ann. SQS Oct 1773. M.

Greenwood, Caroline (1744). *See* Banham. M.

Greenwood, David. S Summer 1744. La.

Greenwood, Elizabeth. S Sep-Oct 1772. M.

Greenwood, George (1743). *See* Greensword. G.

Greenwood, George. SQS Jly T Oct 1768 *Justitia*. M.
Greenwood, James of Conington. S s horse Lent R 14 yrs Dec 1731 (SP). Hu.
Greenwood, Sarah. S Jan T Dec 1736 *Dorsetshire* but died on passage. L.
Greenwood, Thomas of Matson. S s wool combs Lent 1724. Nf.
Greenwood, Thomas. S & R 14 yrs Summer 1772. G.
Greenwood, William. S Jan T Feb 1719 *Worcester* LC Annapolis Jun 1719. L.
Greenwood, William. S for obtaining goods at Wolverhampton by false
   pretences Summer 1768. St.
Greeve, Elizabeth Harriot. SQS Oct 1774. M.
Greeve, Elizabeth wife of John. S for stealing Oct 1768 T Jan 1769
   Thornton; acquitted of setting fire to her husband's house. M.
Greaves, Ann. S Summer 1756. K.
Greaves als Brierly als Rhodes, Ann of Crompton. SQS Jan 1768. La.
Greeves, John. LC from *Gilbert* Annapolis Jly 1722. X.
Greeves als Hollett, Mary of Isleworth, spinster. S s gold coin Sep 1740 T
   Jan 1741 *Harpooner* to Rappahannock. M.
Greaves als Brierly als Rhodes, Mary wife of William of Crompton. SQS
   Jan 1768. La.
Greeves, Robert. S Feb T Apr 1772 *Thornton*. L.
Greaves, William. S Summer 1729. Y.
Greaves, William. S s horse Lent R 14 yrs Summer 1758. Wa.
Gregg, Henry. S s cloth at Brampton Summer 1773. Cu.
Gregg, Mary (1773). *See* Graham. Du.
Greggs. *See* Griggs.
Gregory, Alice. S & T Apr 1733 *Patapsco* LC Annapolis Nov 1733. M.
Gregory, Ann. S Jly-Dec 1747. M.
Gregory, Ann. S Jan T Mar 1758 *Dragon*. M.
Gregory, Anthony. R for Jamaica Mar 1665. L.
Gregory, Anthony. S Jly 1718 to be T to Va. De.
Gregory, Anthony. S & TB to Va Apr 1750. Wi.
Gregory, Benjamin. S Apr 1770. So.
Gregory, Catherine. S Jan-Feb 1773. M.
Gregory, Daniel. R 14 yrs Jly 1775. M.
Gregory, Edward. S May T Jly 1770 *Scarsdale*. M.
Gregory als Walter, Hannah. S & T Jan 1766 *Tryal*. L.
Gregory, Henry. S s yarn at Baschurch Summer 1774. Sh.
Gregory, James. S Apr-May 1744. M.
Gregory, James. S & T Jly 1772 *Tayloe*. L.
Gregory, John of Cheltenham. S Lent 1719. G.
Gregory, John. S Jan-Apr 1749. M.
Gregory, John of Croydon. SQS Oct 1754. Sy.
Gregory, John. S Apr 1757. M.
Gregory, John. S s horse Summer 1757 R 14 yrs Lent TB Oct 1758. Db.
Gregory, Lile. S Lent 1754. Sy.
Gregory als Crane, Lucy. SQS Jly T Sep 1764 *Justitia*. M.
Gregory, Mary. SL & T Sep 1765 *Justitia*. Sy.
Gregory, Richard. S Oct T Nov 1728 *Forward* LC Rappahannock Jun
   1729. M.
Gregory, Richard of St. Olave, Southwark. SQS Feb T Mar 1763 *Neptune*. Sy.
Gregory, Thomas of Mells. R for Barbados Jly 1664. So.
Gregory, Thomas. R Jan AT Feb 1679. M.

Gregory, Thomas. Rebel T 1685.

Gregory, William. S Apr T Oct 1719 *Susannah & Sarah* LC Annapolis Apr 1720. L.

Gresham, Charles of Barking. SQS Jan 1754. E.

Greswold, Joseph. S Apr-May T May 1744 *Justitia*. M.

Gretton, Cadman. S Oct-Dec 1754. M.

Grevill, John. S s sheep Summer TB Aug 1740. G.

Grew, Charles. T Oct 1721 *William & John*. Sy.

Grew als Le Grew, Jane. S & T Oct 1732 *Caesar* to Va. M.

Grew, Joseph. S Sep T Oct 1750 *Rachael*. M.

Grey. *See* Gray.

Greygoose, James. S for shoplifting Lent 1766. Su.

Grice, Denton. S Lent 1736. Y.

Grice, Katherine. S & T Dec 1740 *Vernon*. L.

Grierson, John. S for performing marriages without banns or licence Sep-Dec 1755 T 14 yrs Jan 1756 *Greyhound*. M.

Griffin, Ann. S Lent 1742. St.

Griffin, Edward. TB to Va from QS 1743. De.

Griffin, Edward. S 14 yrs Sep 1756. M.

Griffin, Francis. S Feb T Mar 1730 *Patapsco* LC Annapolis Sep 1730. M.

Griffin, George. S Jly 1724. De.

Griffin, George. S Lent 1754. Nf.

Griffin, Harman of St. Saviour, Southwark. SQS Apr T Sep 1751 *Greyhound*. Sy.

Griffin, Henry. R for Barbados Nov 1668. L.

Griffen, John. LC from *Forward* Annapolis Jun 1725. X.

Griffin, John. S s at Whitbourne Lent 1743. He.

Griffin, John. S 14 yrs for receiving May T Jly 1771 *Scarsdale*. L.

Griffin, John. SQS Apr 1773. M.

Griffen, Joseph. LC from *Forward* Rappahannock May 1728. X.

Griffin, Martha wife of Edward of St. James, Westminster. S s bed linen Jly 1740 T Jan 1741 *Harpooner* to Rappahannock. M.

Griffin, Martha. T Aug 1752 *Tryal*. M.

Griffin, Mary. S Aug 1763. L.

Griffin, Peter. SQS Apr T May 1750 *Lichfield*. M.

Griffin, Philip. S s cereals at Wolverley Lent 1765; his wife Nancy Griffin & Nancy Griffin Jr. acquitted. Wo.

Griffin, Richard. LC from *Forward* Annapolis Dec 1725. X.

Griffin, Robert. S Oct 1740. L.

Griffin, Robert. S Jly 1749. L.

Griffin, Robert. S 14 yrs for receiving & T Sep 1766 *Justitia*. L.

Griffin, Sarah. S Sep T Dec 1734 *Caesar* LC Va Jly 1735. M.

Griffin, Thomas. S & T Sep 1731 *Smith* LC Va 1732. M.

Griffin, Thomas. S s horse Summer 1760 R 14 yrs Lent 1761. Wa.

Griffin, Thomas of Hartwell. S Lent 1763. Bu.

Griffen, Tobias. T Oct 1729 *Forward*. Bu.

Griffin, William. S s at Benson Summer 1737. O.

Griffith, Anne. S Summer 1730. He.

Griffith, Ann. S Feb T Mar 1758 *Dragon*. L.

Griffith als Hatch, Ann. R Apr 1773. M.

Griffith, Christopher. S & R Summer 1737 T Jan 1733 *Dorsetshire*. Bu.

Griffith, Emblin. SQS Feb T May 1752 *Lichfield*. M.
Griffith, Henry. T Apr 1743 *Justitia*. E.
Griffith, James. R for Barbados or Jamaica May 1684. L.
Griffith, James. S Feb 1757. M.
Griffith, John of Norton. R for Barbados Oct 1663. Wo.
Griffith, John. S s at Ellesmere Lent 1762. Sh.
Griffith, Margaret. R Nov 1668 & Apr 1669 TB to Barbados Jun 1669. L.
Griffith als Evans, Margaret wife of Robert. S s at Church Stretton Lent 1753. Sh.
Griffith, Mary (1673). *See* Bromley. M.
Griffith, Mary. T Oct 1726 *Forward*. Sy.
Griffith, Mary. S s cotton Sep 1735 T Jan 1736 *Dorsetshire* LC Va Sep 1736. M.
Griffith, Michael of Nettlested. R for Barbados or Jamaica Jly 1702. K.
Griffith, Michael (1748). *See* Griffith, Thomas. G.
Griffith, Rice of Stratton. R for America Jly 1716. Wa.
Griffith, Robert. S & T Sep 1718 *Eagle* LC Charles Town Mar 1719. L.
Griffith als Glanfield, Sarah. S Mar 1721. De.
Griffith, Sarah. TB Mar 1760. Db.
Griffith, Thomas. PT May R Jly 1687. M.
Griffith, Thomas. S s tobacco at All Saints, Worcester, Lent 1738. Wo.
Griffith, Thomas als Michael. S s horse Summer 1747 R 14 yrs Lent TB Mar 1749. G.
Griffith, Thomas. S Apr 1749. L.
Griffith, William. PT May R Jly 1687. M.
Griffith, William. T Sep 1730 *Smith*. E.
Griffith als Shovel als Shuffle, William. S s clothing & T Dec 1734 *Caesar* LC Va Jly 1735. M.
Griffiths als Parrott, Ann. S Jan-May T Jun 1738 *Forward* to Md or Va. M.
Griffiths, Ann. S Jan-Feb T Apr 1753 *Thames*. M.
Griffiths, Ann. S Summer 1763 R 14 yrs Lent 1764. Mo.
Griffiths, Ann, spinster. S s gloves at All Hallows, Lombard Street, Feb T Apr 1768 *Thornton*. L.
Griffiths, Catherine. S May T Sep 1757 *Thetis*. L.
Griffiths, Eleanor. S s money Oct 1761 T Apr 1762 *Dolphin*; acquitted of burning a house. M.
Griffiths, Elizabeth. S s at St. Woolos Lent 1747. Mo.
Griffiths, Elizabeth. S Lent 1761. Sy.
Griffiths, Frances. S Lent 1731. Sh.
Griffiths, George. S Jan-Feb T Apr 1772 *Thornton*. M.
Griffies, Griffith. S s at Bourton on the Hill Lent R 14 yrs Summer 1765. G.
Griffiths, Henry. S for rape Lent R for life Summer 1767. He.
Griffiths, Henry. S & R 14 yrs Lent 1774. Wo.
Griffiths, James. SL Aug T Sep 1764 *Justitia*. Sy.
Griffis, James. SQS Feb T Apr 1770 *New Trial*. M.
Griffiths, James. S Jan-Feb 1774. M.
Griffiths, John. S Apr T May 1720 *Honor* but escaped at Vigo, Spain. L.
Griffiths, John. S s from Stapleton church Lent 1727. Sh.
Griffiths, John. S Lent 1734. Sh.
Griffiths, John. S s at Hentland Lent R 14 yrs Summer 1737. He.
Griffiths, John. S Sep T Oct 1768 *Justitia*. M.
Griffiths, John. S May T Jly 1771 *Scarsdale*. L.

Griffiths, John. SQS Apr 1773. M.

Griffiths, Mary. S & T Sep 1731 *Smith* LC Va 1732. M.

Griffiths, Mary (1750). *See* Wilkes. L.

Griffiths, Mary. S Jan 1757. L.

Griffiths als Turner, Mary. S s at St. Martin, Worcester, Lent 1772. Wo.

Griffiths, Morgan. S Jan T Apr 1741 *Speedwell* or *Mediterranean*. M.

Griffiths, Morris. SQS Sep 1774. M.

Griffiths, Owen. S Jly T Dec 1736 *Dorsetshire* to Va. M.

Griffiths, Rachael. S s at St. Mary, Shrewsbury, Lent 1767. Sh.

Griffiths, Richard. S May-Jly T 14 yrs Sep 1755 *Tryal*. M.

Griffiths, Robert. S for Va Aug 1718. M.

Griffiths, Samuel. S s at Ledbury Summer 1757. He.

Griffiths, Sarah. S Lent 1760. Db.

Griffis als Butler, Thomas. S & T 14 yrs Oct 1730 *Forward* LC Potomack Jan 1731. M.

Griffiths, Thomas. S Summer 1756 R 14 yrs Lent 1757. He.

Griffiths, Thomas of St. Olave, Southwark. SQS 14 yrs for receiving lead Jan T Aug 1769 *Douglas*. Sy.

Griffiths, Thomas. S Feb T Apr 1770 *New Trial*. M.

Griffiths, Thomas. S s at Bromyard Lent 1771. He.

Griffiths, William. S s hens at Rushall Lent 1765. St.

Griffiths, William. R Jly T for life Sep 1767 *Justitia*. M.

Griffiths, William. S s horse & R 14 yrs Summer 1772. Mo.

Griffiths, William. S s mare & R 14 yrs Summer 1774. Mo.

Grigg, Ann. T Nov 1741 *Sea Horse*. Ht.

Grigg, Elizabeth. T Jun 1764 *Dolphin*. K.

Grigg, James. S Jly 1718 to be T to Va. Do.

Grigg, Margaret (1747). *See* Oldfield. M.

Grigge, Margaret (1754). *See* Clarke. M.

Grigg, Richard. R 14 yrs Apr 1747. De.

Grigg, William. S Feb-Apr T May 1751 *Tryal*. M.

Griggs, George. T Oct 1720 *Gilbert*. E.

Griggs als White, James. S s coat at St. Andrew, Holborn, May T Jun 1768 *Tryal*. L.

Griggs, John. T Nov 1762 *Prince William*. K.

Greggs, Sarah. S Apr T Jun 1768 *Tryal*. M.

Griggs, Thomas. S Jun 1747. L.

Greggs, Walter. S Summer 1743. Cu.

Grigson, James. R Oct 1700 & Aug 1701. M.

Grimbald als Grimbold, Ann. S Summer 1755. Ca.

Grimbald, Elizabeth. S Lent 1749. Nf.

Grime, James of Forest of Rossendale. SQS May 1753. La.

Grime, Jeffery of Newchurch, Rossendale Forest, woollen weaver. SQS Apr 1751. La.

Grime, Oliver of Forest of Rossendale, tailor. SQS May 1753. La.

Grime, Oliver Jr. of Forest of Rossendale. SQS May 1753. La.

Grime, Robert of Rutland. R for America Jly 1683. Ru.

Grime als Graham, Thomas. S Lent TB Aug 1753. Y.

Grimer, George. S Lent 1762 R for life Lent 1763. Wa.

Grimes, Elizabeth wife of Charles. R for America Feb 1700. Le.

Grimes, George. T May 1752 *Lichfield*. K.

Grimes, Hannah (1722). *See* Graham. M.

Grimes, Henry of Norwich. R for America Jun 1714. Nf.

Grimes, James. T Jly 1722 *Alexander*. Sy.

Grimes, John. S May 1726 T *Loyal Margaret* LC Annapolis Oct 1726. M.

Grimes, Leonard (1757). *See* Graham. Nt.

Grimes als Graham, Martha. S Apr 1745. L.

Grimes, Mary (1696). *See* Meachum. Sy.

Grimes, Robert. R for America Mar 1690. Li.

Grimes, Robert (1736). *See* Graham. Sy.

Grimes, Robert. SQS Apr T May 1755 *Rose*. M.

Grimes, Thomas. T Jan 1738 *Dorsetshire*. K.

Grimmer, Charles. S s gelding & R 14 yrs Summer 1737. Nf.

Grimmer, William. S Summer 1757. Nf.

Grimsby, Richard. S Summer 1756. Sy.

Grimshaw, Edmund of Old Accrington, cotton weaver. SQS Apr 1766. La.

Grimshaw, James (1739). *See* Grimson. M.

Grimshaw, Job. S Mar 1761. Ha.

Grimshaw, John. S for highway robbery at Sedgley Summer 1744 R 14 yrs Lent 1745 St.

Grimshaw, Thomas of Manchester. SQS Apr 1759. La.

Grimshire, Josiah. R Lent 1775. K.

Grimshire, Richard. S s sheep Lent R 14 yrs Summer 1768. Be.

Grimson als Grimshaw, James. S Feb T Apr 1739 *Forward* to Va. M.

Grimson, Samuel. T 14 yrs May 1767 *Thornton*. E.

Grimstead, William. S & T Sep 1757 *Thetis*. L.

Grimstead, William. S Oct T Dec 1771 *Justitia*. L.

Grimstone, Samuel. S Feb T Sep 1737 *Pretty Patsy* to Md. M.

Grimwood, Thomas. T 14 yrs Sep 1767 *Justitia*. E.

Grimwood, William. S Lent R 14 yrs Summer 1768. Sh.

Grinald, Thomas. S Jun T Aug 1769 *Douglas*. M.

Grindall, Joseph. S Jly 1775. L.

Grindall, Margaret. T Apr 1734 *Patapsco*. Sy.

Grindley, Elizabeth. S & T Jan 1736 *Dorsetshire* LC Va Sep 1736. L.

Grindy, William. S Lent R for life Summer T Sep 1751 *Greyhound*. Ht.

Grinet, Robert (1770). *See* Granfield. Be.

Grinley, Ann of St. Saviour, Southwark. SQS Jan 1758. Sy.

Grinley, John. S Dec 1737 T Jan 1738 *Dorsetshire*. L.

Grinter, Grace (1760). *See* Hallett. Do.

Grisbrook, Henry. T Jun 1738 *Forward*. Sx.

Grisby, Phebe. S Apr 1720. M.

Greisby, William of Wellor. R for America Jly 1678. Nt.

Grissell, Hannah. S Jan 1757. M.

Grissell, John of Waltham Abbey. R for Barbados or Jamaica Jly 1687. E.

Grist, Charles. S Mar TB to Va Apr 1773. Wi.

Gritton, John. S s wheat at Walford Lent 1773. He.

Gritton, William. S Sep-Oct 1748 T Jan 1749 *Laura*. M.

Grocer, Robert. S Lent 1773. La.

Grocott, John. S s gelding Lent R 14 yrs Summer 1760. Wa.

Grommett, Francis. T Apr 1742 *Bond*. Bu.

Groom, Ann wife of Jacob. S Oct-Dec 1739 T Jan 1740 *York* to Md. M.

Groom, Catherine. SQS Jly TB Aug 1765. So.

Groom, Charles of St. George, Hanover Square. S s hat & T Jan 1740 *York*. M.

Groom, Edward Jr. T Oct 1738 *Genoa*. Bu.

Groom, Elizabeth. S s at St. Mary, Shrewsbury, Summer 1761. Sh.

Groom, Jeremy of St. Leonard, Colchester. R for Barbados or Jamaica Jly 1715. E.

Groom, Jonathan. SQS May T Jly 1771 *Scarsdale*. M.

Groom, Mary. S & T Apr 1741 *Speedwell* or *Mediterranean* to Md. M.

Groome, Thomas. S for mixing vitriol with milk and giving it to Bonard Walker to drink at Thame Lent 1728. O.

Groom, William. S s from warehouse Lent 1745. Nf.

Groom, William. T Sep 1755 *Tryal*. M.

Groom, William. S Sep-Dec 1755 T Jan 1756 *Greyhound*. M.

Groome, Zacharias of Whapload. R for America Jly 1678. Li.

Groshia, Martin. SQS for attending conventicle Dec 1664. M.

Gross als Grass, Isabel. S City Summer 1739. Nl.

Gross, Josiah. S s sheep Lent R 14 yrs Summer 1769. No.

Gross, Sarah. S 14 yrs Apr 1744. M.

Grose, Simon. S Lent 1754. Sy.

Grosvenor, Richard. T Apr 1753 *Thames*. K.

Grosvenor, Thomas (1758). *See* Graveney. Bu.

Grout, Charles. T *Robert* Jly 1724 LC Annapolis Jun 1725. Be.

Grout, Joseph. R 14 yrs Mar 1745. Ha.

Grove, Ann. S Lent R 14 yrs Summer 1755. Wo.

Grove, Daniel. R for Barbados or Jamaica Apr 1690. L.

Grove, James. R for Barbados or Jamaica Aug 1700. L.

Grove, James. S s at Pensack Lent 1765. Wo.

Grove, Jonathan. R for Barbados Aug 1679. M.

Grove, Margaret (1675). *See* Biggs. L.

Grove, Mary. S s at Chetton Summer 1732. Sh.

Grove, Samuel (1740). *See* Hildrup. De.

Grove als Gosling, Thomas of East Hagbourne. R (Western Circ) for America Jly 1700. Be.

Grove, William. S Oct T 14 yrs Dec 1724 *Rappahannock*. L.

Grove, William. S s at Thornbury Lent TB Aug 1727. G.

Grove, William. S May-Jly 1773. M.

Grover, John. T Nov 1741 *Sea Horse*. Ht.

Grover, John. S Summer 1754 R 14 yrs Lent T May 1755 *Rose*. Ht.

Grover, Thomas. R for Barbados or Jamaica Dec 1699 & Aug 1700. L.

Groves, Ann. S Jly-Dec 1747. M.

Groves, Edward of St. Dunstan in West. S s pot & T Feb 1740 *York*. M.

Groves, Henry. T Sep 1730 *Smith*. Ht.

Groves, James. S s at Walsall Lent 1763. St.

Groves, James. S Summer 1775. Wa.

Groves, Jane. T Oct 1723 *Forward*. K.

Groves, John. S Jly 1722. So.

Groves, John (1753). *See* Smith. M.

Groves, Richard. T Oct 1732 *Caesar*. K.

Groves, Sarah (1727). *See* Linny. M.

Groves, Sarah wife of John. S Apr 1773. M.

Groves, William. R for Barbados Jly 1674. L.

Groves, William. S s gelding at Tilehurst Lent R 14 yrs Summer 1736. Be.
Groves, William. S Jun 1747. L.
Groves, William. S Aug T Sep 1764 *Justitia*. L.
Growden, Ann. S Jun-Dec 1738 T Jan 1739 *Dorsetshire* to Va. M.
Grubb, Arabella. S Feb T Apr 1734 *Patapsco*. L.
Grubb, Humphry. S Summer 1746. E.
Grubb, William. S Feb-Apr T Jun 1756 *Lyon*. M.
Grubb, William. S Summer 1767. Bu.
Grundy, James of Lancaster. R for Barbados Jly 1681. La.
Grundy, Robert. S Summer 1754 R 14 yrs Summer 1755. Hu.
Grundy, William of Little Bolton, weaver. SQS May 1753. La.
Gard, Christopher. SQS Jan TB Apr 1772. So.
Guard als Bowhay, Elizabeth. S Aug 1743. Co.
Gubbidge, George. R Feb 1675. M.
Gubbins, Leonard. R 14 yrs Aug 1726. De.
Gudburne, Mark (1723). *See* Goodman. K.
Gudden, Thomas of Northchurch. R for Barbados or Jamaica Jly 1687. Ht.
Gude, Edward. S Mar TB to Md Apr 1771. Le.
Gudgeon, Abraham. S Aug T Oct 1726 *Forward*. L.
Guest, Edmund als Edward. S s mare & gelding & R Lent T May 1770. Wa.
Guest, John. S s lead from St. Dunstan's church, Stepney, May T Nov 1759 *Phoenix*. M.
Guest, Joseph (1724). *See* Jacobs. L.
Guest, Joseph. S Jan 1751. L.
Guffick, Richard. S s at Whitby Lent 1775. Y.
Guildford als Wood, Margaret. S Oct 1768 T Jan 1769 *Thornton*. M.
Gilford, William. S & T Sep 1757 *Thetis*. M.
Guillane, John. T Jun 1742 *Bladon*. Sx.
Gunnis, Edward. S Jan T Feb 1724 *Anne*. L.
Guinnes, William. R for Barbados Jly 1663. L.
Guise, James of Claines. R (Western Circ) for America Jly 1700. Wo.
Guise, Mary. S & T Jan 1739 *Dorsetshire*. L.
Guise, Susanna. S Lent 1761. Wo.
Gullaken, James. S Feb 1774. L.
Gullick, William. S Jly-Sep 1754. M.
Gulliford, John Glew. S Dec 1740. L.
Gulliforth, Ann. S Jan T Sep 1737 *Pretty Patsy* to Md. M.
Gulliver, Thomas Jr. S s shirts at Fringford Lent 1761. O.
Gulliver, Thomas. S s peas at Stoke Lyne Lent 1763. O.
Gullocke, Robert of Ileton, husbandman. R for Barbados Jly 1664. So.
Gullocke, Thomas of Newton St. Loe. R for Barbados Jly 1672. So.
Gullocke, William of Ileton, husbandman. R for Barbados Jly 1664. So.
Gully, John of Withypool. R for Barbados Feb 1699. So.
Gully, John. S & R 14 yrs Lent 1769. G.
Gully, Michael. S Dec 1763 T Mar 1764 *Tryal*. M.
Gulley, Richard. R Jan-Feb T 14 yrs Apr 1772 *Thornton*. M.
Gumbleton, Humphrey. S & T May 1744 *Justitia*. L.
Gumley, Theophilus. R for America Mar 1697. Le.
Gumm, Ann. T Aug 1752 *Tryal*. Sy.
Gummer, Edward of Cadworth. R for Barbados Jly 1715. So.
Gummer, Robert. S Apr 1753. So.

Gummer, Thomas. S for demolishing a mill at Kingsland & R 14 yrs Lent 1775. He.
Gunn, Catherine. S Apr 1773. L.
Gunn, John. S Jly T Sep 1767 *Justitia*. L.
Gunn, John. S Oct 1774. L.
Gunn, Mary. S & T Jly 1772 *Tayloe*. M.
Gunn, Richard. S Summer 1735 R 14 yrs Summer TB Sep 1736. Nt.
Gunn, William. R for Jamaica Aug 1661. M.
Gunnell, Francis, als Gurnell, Thomas. S s horse Lent R 14 yrs Summer 1765. Li.
Gunnell, George. S Jan 1746. M.
Gunnell, John. S Feb 1761. L.
Gunnele, William. S Jun 1754. L.
Gunner, Lewis. R 14 yrs Mar 1730. Ha.
Gunner, Sarah. S Summer T Sep 1751 *Greyhound*. K.
Gunniman, Robert. R 14 yrs for highway robbery Lent 1721. Be.
Gunson, Mary. S Summer 1724 T Summer 1725. Y.
Gunstone, Matthias. S Mar TB to Va Apr 1768. Wi.
Gunter, Thomas. S Lent R 14 yrs Summer 1747. Mo.
Gunton, William. S s at Little Cornard Summer 1774. Su.
Guppy, John. R Aug 1770. Do.
Guppy, Justinian. Rebel T 1685.
Guppy, William (2). Rebels T 1685.
Gurd, John. S Mar TB to Va Apr 1766. Wi.
Gurling. *See* Girling.
Gurnell, Thomas (1765). *See* Gunnell, Francis. Li.
Gurney, Benjamin. T Oct 1732 *Caesar*. Sy.
Gurney, Mary. R for Barbados Mar 1683. M.
Gurr, Thomas. T Apr 1739 *Forward*. Sx.
Gurry, Richard. S Lent R 14 yrs Summer T Sep 1755 *Tryal*. Ht.
Gurry, William. T Sep 1730 *Smith*. Sy.
Gurton. *See* Girton.
Gush, James. S Jun-Dec 1738 T Jan 1739 *Dorsetshire* to Va. M.
Gusseny, Abraham. S Oct 1774. L.
Gutch, Edward. R for Jamaica Aug 1661. L.
Guthrey, Margaret. LC from *Honor* Port York Jan 1721. X.
Gutteridge, Alexander (1742). *See* Guttery. Nl.
Gutteridge als Gorridge, Anthony. S Summer T Sep 1772. No.
Gutteridge, Charles. S Oct 1756. M.
Guttery als Gutteridge, Alexander. S Summer 1742. Nl.
Guttery, James. S Apr T May 1743 *Indian Queen* to Potomack. M.
Guttery, James. S Summer 1751. Cu.
Guy, Anne. R Feb 1673 AT Jun 1674. M.
Guy, George. T Apr 1753 *Thames*. Sy.
Guy, Hannah. S s at Cottingham Summer 1774. Y.
Guy, John. S Oct 1751-Jan 1752. M.
Guy, John. S Aug 1753. De.
Guy, Richard. R for Barbados Feb 1664. M.
Guy, Stephen. S & T Oct 1732 *Caesar* to Va. M.
Guy als Davis, Thomas. S Mar 1725. Wi.
Guy, William of Bere Regis. R for Barbados Jly 1693. Do.

Guy, William. R for Barbados or Jamaica Dec 1699. M.
Guy, William. S & T Oct 1730 *Forward* LC Potomack Jan 1731. M.
Guy, William. S Sep T Oct 1739 *Duke of Cumberland*. L.
Guy, William. S s horse & R 14 yrs Lent 1775. G.
Guyver, Sarah (1735). *See* Smyther. K.
Gwatkins, John of Chatham. S Lent 1745. K.
Gwillim, Ann. S s at Caerleon Summer 1764. Mo.
Gwillim, Lewis. S Apr T Jun 1768 *Tryal*. M.
Gwynn, Bryan. S & T Mar 1750 *Tryal*. L.
Gwinn, James. S & T Oct 1730 *Forward* LC Potomack Jan 1731. M.
Gwyn, James. SL & T May 1767 *Thornton*. Sy.
Gwynn, John. S Apr T May 1751 *Tryal*. L.
Gwynn, John of St. Paul, Covent Garden. SW Oct 1766 T Jan 1767 *Tryal*. M.
Gwynn, Joseph of St. Saviour, Southwark. SQS Mar T Jun 1768 *Tryal*. Sy.
Gwyre, Richard of Aishill, husbandman. R for Barbados Jly 1667. So.
Gynne, William. SQS Dec 1750. M.

H

Habberley, Thomas. S s at More Summer 1749. Sh.

Habberley, William. S for highway robbery Lent R 14 yrs Summer 1744 T Oct 1744 *Savannah*. Bu.

Habin, Joseph. LC from *Patapsco* Annapolis Nov 1733. X.

Hace, Thomas. T May 1767 *Thornton*. K.

Hack, John. R 14 yrs Jly 1752. Ha.

Hacke, Robert. R for Barbados Sep 1669. M.

Hack, Thomas. S s mare at Newbury Lent R 14 yrs Summer 1737. Be.

Hacker als Webb, Elizabeth. R for Barbados or Jamaica Feb 1686. M.

Hacker, Jane. S Sep T Dec 1734 *Caesar* LC Va Jly 1735. M.

Hacker, Jane wife of Thomas. S Sep 1737 T Jan 1738 *Dorsetshire*. M.

Hacker, William. S & T Oct 1730 *Forward* LC Potomack Jan 1731. M.

Hackery, Mary (1740). *See* Toppin. L.

Hackery als Hakary, William. S Aug 1740 TB to Va. De.

Hackett, Charles. T Nov 1725 *Rappahannock* LC Va Aug 1726. E.

Hackett, John of Newport Pagnell, shoemaker. S s fish at Tyringham Lent 1739. Bu.

Hackett, John. S s cloth at Kidderminster Lent 1752. Wo.

Hackett, John. S for forgery Lent R 14 yrs Summer 1753. Le.

Hackett, Peter. S & T Jly 1771 *Scarsdale*. M.

Hackford, John. S s bridle at St. Martin Lent 1759. He.

Hackleton als House, Rebecca, aged 21. R for Barbados Feb 1664. L.

Hackliut, Martha, spinster, als wife of John. R for Barbados Aug 1664. L.

Hackney, Edward. S Lent 1755. K.

Hackney, John. S Dec 1749-Jan 1750 T Mar 1750 *Tryal*. M.

Hackney, William. S Apr-May 1775. M.

Hacksupp, Jane. S Summer 1763. Y.

Haddington, John. SQS Apr T Sep 1758 *Tryal* to Annapolis. M.

Haddock, Francis. S 14 yrs for receiving iron stolen by John Serjeant *(qv)* Lent 1769. St.

Haddock, John. S May T Jly 1770 *Scarsdale*. M.

Haddock, William. S Apr 1748. L.

Haddon, Daniel. S Mar TB to Va Apr 1766. Le.

Haddon, Frances (1749). *See* Phill. Nf.

Haddon, George. R 14 yrs Summer 1751. Cu.

Haddon, Henry. S & TB Aug 1774. Nt.

Hadden, John. S Summer T Sep 1770. Wa.

Hadden, Laurence of St. George, Southwark. SQS & T Jan 1769 *Thornton*. Sy.

Hadon, Noal (1721). *See* Heading. E.

Haddon, Thomas. S Dec 1727. L.

Hadden, William. T Oct 1721 *William & John*. K.

Haddoway (Hathaway), Thomas. R 10 yrs in plantations Oct 1662. M.

Hadfield, Thomas. S for highway robbery Lent R 14 yrs Summer 1739. Y.

Hadley, David. S Sep-Oct 1772. M.

Hadley, Joseph. S s cattle Lent R 14 yrs Summer 1767. St.

Hadley als Wilkins, Martha. S s silver tankard & T May 1736 *Patapsco*. M.

Hadley als Adley, Mary. S Sep-Oct T Dec 1753 *Whiteing*. M.

Hadley, Mary wife of John. S for receiving goods stolen at Halesowen by Shem Hadley *(qv)* Summer 1768. Wo.

Hadley, Shem. S s at Halesowen Summer 1768 R 14 yrs Lent 1769. Wo.

Hadlow, Hercules. S Lent 1754. K.

Hadlow, Mallian. T Jun 1740 *Essex*. K.

Hadwell, John (1764). *See* Hoddy. Wo.

Hafen, Joseph. T Apr 1733 *Patapsco* LC Md Nov 1733. E.

Hagen, Mary. S Jan-Feb 1773. M.

Hagan, Michael of Rotherhithe. SQS & T Jan 1769 *Thornton*. Sy.

Hagon, Samuel. S s from warehouse Summer 1744. Nf.

Hagar, William of Worcester. R for Jamaica, Barbados or Bermuda Mar 1688. Wo.

Hagg, Paul. S Lent TB Apr 1758. Db.

Haggerston, John (1743). *See* Henderson. Nl.

Hagerston, John. R 14 yrs Jly 1766. Ha.

Haggot, John. R Aug 1770 TB to Va. De.

Haggett, William. S Jan-Feb 1773. M.

Haggety, Matthew. S Jan-Feb T Apr 1771 *Thornton*. M.

Hagley, Lewis. Rebel T 1685.

Hags, Robert. T May 1719 *Margaret* LC Md Aug 1719; sold to Patrick Cragin. Sy.

Hague, James. S s handkerchiefs Apr T Dec 1735 *John* LC Annapolis Sep 1736. M.

Haigh als Hays, John. S s horse Summer 1726 R 14 yrs Lent 1729. Y.

Haigh, John. S Lent 1736. Hu.

Haigh, John. AT Summer 1758. Y.

Hague, Susanna. S Oct 1766 T Jan 1767 *Tryal*. L.

Hailstone, Thomas. R 14 yrs Jly TB to Va Aug 1765. Wi.

Haines. *See* Haynes.

Hainsworth, Benjamin. S Jan-Feb 1775. M.

Hainsworth, James. S Apr-May 1775. M.

Hainsworth, Mary. S Norwich Summer 1764. Nf.

Haires, Joseph. R for life for highway robbery Summer 1765. Y.

Hakary, William (1740). *See* Hackery. De.

Hakins als Downs, Benjamin of Inworth. SQS Apr T Oct 1768 *Justitia*. E.

Halcomb, Martha. S Jun T Dec 1736 *Dorsetshire* to Va. M.

Hale, Charles, als Maylin, Daniel. S s at Churchdown Summer 1773. G.

Hale, George. S for highway robbery at Whitchurch Lent R 14 yrs Summer 1767; John Hale hanged. Bu.

Hale als Gilson, John. S s horse Lent R 14 yrs Summer 1769. G.

Hale, John. S s at [Wotton] under Edge Lent 1774. G.

Hale, Joseph. T Dec 1734 *Caesar*. E.

Hale als Dickenson, Mary. S & T Jun 1742 *Bladon* to Md. M.

Hale, Mary wife of Richard *(qv)*. S 14 yrs Summer 1745. Sy.

Hale, Matthew. S & T Mar 1763 *Neptune*. L.

Hale, Matthew. S Summer 1764. Wo.

Hale, Richard. S 14 yrs Summer 1745. Sy.

Hale, Richard of Hanningfield. R 14 yrs Lent T Apr 1772 *Thornton*. E.

Hale, Thomas (1683). *See* Rumsey. L.

Hale, Thomas. S for cutting down a turnpike Lent R 14 yrs Summer 1736. Wo.

Hale, Thomas. S Lent T May 1755 *Rose*. Sy.

Hale, Thomas of Christchurch. SQS Oct 1765 T Jan 1766 *Tryal*. Sy.

Hale, Thomas. S s bread at Shipton Lent 1767. O.

Hale, William. S Apr-May T May 1741 *Catherine & Elizabeth* to Md. M.

Hale, William. T Apr 1743 *Justitia*. Sy.

Hale, William of Kirdford. S Summer T Oct 1750 *Rachael*. Sx.

Hale, William. S Oct 1761. L.

Hale, William. S s cloth Lent 1774. G.

Hales, Abraham. S Apr 1749. L.

Hales, David. T Apr 1769 *Tryal*. E.

Hales, Elizabeth. S Feb T 14 yrs May 1740 *Essex*. L.

Hales, Francis. Rebel T 1685.

Hales, George. S Lent TB Apr 1766. Db.

Hayles, Isabel (1683). *See* Syms. M.

Hales, James. S Lent 1775. E.

Hales, John. S for assisting escape of Samuel Prior *(qv)* Summer 1748 T Jan 1749 *Laura*. K.

Hales, John. S May 1768. M.

Hales, Roger. S Apr 1749. L.

Halewood, James. S s sheep Summer 1756 R 14 yrs Lent 1757. La.

Haley, Alice. S & T Oct 1729 *Forward* LC Va Jun 1730. L.

Hayley, Anne of St. Sepulchre, widow. SQS to Jamaica for attending unlawful religious assembly Jan 1665. M.

Hayley, Carbery. S & T Jly 1753 *Tryal*. M.

Haley, Cornelius. ST & T Jan 1766 *Tryal*. L.

Haley als Poor, Jane. S Feb-Apr T May 1752 *Lichfield*. M.

Haley, Jane, spinster. S s gold coins at St. Lawrence Jewry Jly T Oct 1768 *Justitia*. L.

Haley, Margaret of St. George, Southwark, widow. SQS & T Jan 1766 *Tryal*. Sy.

Haley, Patrick. T Apr 1760 *Thetis*. K.

Haley, Richard. T May 1719 *Margaret* LC Md May 1720; sold to Patrick Sympson. Sy.

Haley, Richard. S Summer 1764; found at large in London Lent 1765 & R 14 yrs Summer 1765. Sh.

Halfeyard, George. Rebel T 1685.

Halfhide, Frances. S Jan-Jun T Jun 1728 *Elizabeth* LC Potomack Aug 1729. M.

Halfknight, William of Blundeston. S Summer 1731. *Su.

Halfnight, William. S Lent 1737. Su.

Halford, Ann wife of George. SQS Aug TB to Va —- 1762. Le.

Halford, John of Halford. R for America Jly 1677. Wa.

Halford, John (1773). *See* Harefoot. Co.

Halford, William. S Jan T Feb 1742 *Industry*. L.

Halfpenny, Michael. S Sep-Oct T Dec 1752 *Greyhound*. M.

Halfpenny, Peter. S Sep-Oct 1749. M.

Halfpenny, Robert. S Aug T Sep 1725 *Forward* LC Annapolis Dec 1725. L.

Hallifax, Lidia. R for Barbados Jly 1675. L.

Hallifax, Simon. R for Barbados Feb 1675. L.

Hall, Abigall wife of John of Manchester, tailor. SQS Jan 1741. La.

Hall, Anne. S Aug T Oct 1723 *Forward* to Va. M.

Hall, Anne. S Jan T 14 yrs Feb 1726 *Supply* LC Annapolis May 1726. M.

Hall, Ann. S Sep T Dec 1734 *Caesar* but died on passage. M.

Hall, Ann. S s money Dec 1735 T Jan 1736 *Dorsetshire* but died on passage. M.

Hall, Ann wife of William. SQS & TB Oct 1737. G.

Hall, Ann. T Jun 1740 *Essex*. E.

Hall, Ann of St. George Bloomsbury, spinster. S s cotton Jly-Oct 1740 T Jan 1741 *Harpooner*. M.

Hall, Ann. S Feb T Apr 1765 *Ann*. M.

Hall, Arnold. S & T Dec 1767 *Neptune*. M.

Hall, Benjamin. R Apr AT Jun 1690. M.

Hall, Benjamin. S Oct 1766. M.

Hall als Gash als King, Cassandra. R for America Jly 1704. Nt.

Hall, Catherine. S Apr 1735. M.

Hall, Charles. S Dec 1719. M.

Hall, Daniel Jr. of Moston. SQS Jan 1775. La.

Hall, Edward. SQS Feb T Apr 1770 *New Trial*. M.

Hall, Edward. S s shirts at Much Marcle Lent 1770. He.

Hall, Eleanor. S Summer 1733 AT Summer 1734. Cu.

Hall, Eleanor. SQS Apr T May 1767 *Thornton*. M.

Hall, Elizabeth. R Jly 1698 AT Jan 1699. M.

Hall, Elizabeth, aged 23, dark. S & T Oct 1720 *Gilbert* LC Annapolis May 1721. M.

Hall, Elizabeth (1722). *See* Abbott. M.

Hall, Elizabeth (1725). *See* Spurrier. M.

Hall, Elizabeth (1754). *See* Smith. M.

Hall, Elizabeth. S Jly-Sep 1754. M.

Hall als Beavis, Elizabeth. S Mar 1756. Do.

Hall, Francis. R for Barbados Feb 1664. L.

Hall, Francis. R for life Jly 1774. M.

Hall, Gabriel. R for America Mar 1697. Le.

Hall, George. S Sep T Oct 1744 *Susannah*. M.

Hall, George. S Oct 1757 T Mar 1758 *Dragon*. M.

Hall, George. S Oct T Nov 1759 *Phoenix*. L.

Hall, George. S s at Upton Bishop Lent 1767. He.

Hall, Gilbert. SQS Mar TB to Md Apr 1742. Le.

Hall, Hannah of St. Luke, spinster. S s gold beads & T Dec 1740 *Vernon*. M.

Hall, Henry. S Feb T Sep 1737 *Pretty Patsy* to Md. M.

Hall, Henry. S Lent 1737. Su.

Hall, Isaac. S Mar 1761. L.

Hall, Isabella. S Jan T Feb 1726 *Supply* LC Annapolis May 1726. M.

Hall als Mascall, Israell. S s at Chieveley Summer 1774. Be.

Hall, James. SQS & TB Dec 1734. Bd.

Hall, James. S & T Aug 1752 *Tryal*. L.

Hall, James. S s sheep Summer 1756 R 14 yrs Lent TB Apr T Aug 1757 *Lux*. Db.

Hall, John of Birmingham. R for America Jly 1674. Wa.

Hall, John of Spelsbury. R for America Feb 1690. O.

Hall, John (1718). *See* Clerke. L.

Hall als Graham als Alexander, John. S s horse Summer 1733 R 14 yrs Lent 1734. Cu.

Hall, John. S s fish Feb T Jun 1738 *Forward*. L.

Hall, John. LC from *Shaw* Antigua Jun 1742. Db.

Hall, John. S Mar 1748. Do.

Hall, John of St. Saviour, Southwark. S Summer 1748 T Jan 1749 *Laura*; found at large & to be transported again Summer 1749. Sy.

Hall, John. SQS Feb T Mar 1750 *Tryal*. M.

Hall, John of Newington. SQS Jan 1751. Sy.

Hall, John. S Apr 1754. So.

Hall, John. S Oct 1757 T Mar 1758 *Dragon*. M.

Hall, John. S Summer 1760. Hu.

Hall, John. R Dec 1765 T Jan 1766 *Tryal*. M.

Hall, John (1772). *See* Sharpless. M.

Hall, John. S Dec 1773. L.

Hall, Jonathan. R & T for life Apr 1770 *New Trial*. M.

Hall, Joseph. S Feb T Mar 1731 *Patapsco* LC Annapolis Jun 1731. L.

Hall, Joseph. S Jun-Dec 1738 T Jan 1739 *Dorsetshire* to Va. M.

Hall, Joseph. S for rape Lent R 14 yrs Summer 1742. Wo.

Hall, Joseph. T Jun 1764 *Dolphin*. E.

Hall, Joseph. S & R 14 yrs Lent 1775. Wo.

Hall, Joshua. S s horse Summer 1732 R 14 yrs Summer 1733. Nl.

Hall, Joshua. S Jun 1733. M.

Hall, Joyce wife of Hector. S Oct T Nov 1728 *Forward* but died on passage. M.

Hall, Margaret. S Jan T Feb 1724 *Ann*. L.

Hall, Margaret (1725). *See* Allis. M.

Hall, Martha. S Jly 1749. L.

Hall, Mary, aged 30. R for Barbados Feb 1664. M.

Hall, Mary. R for America Aug 1715. L.

Hall, Mary. R 14 yrs for Carolina May 1719. L.

Hall, Mary. S Jan T Jun 1726 *Loyal Margaret* but died on passage. M.

Hall, Mary. S Sep 1733. M.

Hall, Mary. S Jun-Dec 1738 T Jan 1739 *Dorsetshire* to Va. M.

Hall, Mary wife of William of Bolton. SQS May 1751. La.

Hall, Mary. SQS Jun T Aug 1752 *Tryal*. M.

Hall, Mary wife of John. AT City Summer 1755. Nl.

Hall, Mary of Braintree, widow. SQS Oct 1760. E.

Hall, Mary wife of John. S Sep-Oct T 14 yrs Dec 1771 *Justitia*. M.

Hall, Mary. S Jly 1773. L.

Hall, Michael. R 14 yrs Summer 1750. Nl.

Hall, Norris. S Aug T Oct 1724 *Forward* LC Annapolis Jun 1725. M.

Hall, Philip, bricklayer to Sir Robert Walpole. S Sep 1735 T Jan 1736 *Dorsetshire* but died on passage. M.

Hall, Ralph of Murton. R for Barbados Jly 1699. Du.
Hall, Rebecca. S Summer 1765 R 14 yrs Lent 1766. Wo.
Hall, Richard. T Jun 1740 *Essex*. Sy.
Hall, Richard. T May 1744 *Justitia*. K.
Hall, Richard. S Oct 1756. L.
Hall, Richard. S Apr-Jun T Jly 1772 *Tayloe*. M.
Halle, Robert of Ottery St. Mary. R for Barbados Sep 1665. De.
Hall, Robert. S & T Oct 1729 *Forward* LC Va Jun 1730. L.
Hall, Samuel of Camberwell. R for Barbados or Jamaica Feb 1684. Sy.
Hall, Samuel. SQS Dec 1755 T Jan 1756 *Greyhound*. M.
Hall, Sarah. S Feb T May 1767 *Thornton*. M.
Hall, Susan. R for America Aug 1715. M.
Hall, Susanna. S Dec 1745. L.
Hall, Thomas of Corsenside. R for Barbados Jly 1682. Nl.
Hall, Thomas of Newbury. R for America Jun 1692. Be.
Hall, Thomas of Barnwell. R for America Feb 1695. Ca.
Hall, Thomas. R for America Feb 1700. Nt.
Hall, Thomas. R for America Mar 1705. L.
Hall, Thomas of North Petherton. R for Barbados Feb 1714. So.
Hall, Thomas. S Aug T Sep 1725 *Forward* LC Annapolis Dec 1725. M.
Hall, Thomas. S Feb T Mar 1731 *Patapsco* LC Annapolis Jun 1731. M.
Hall, Thomas. S Lent 1744. Su.
Hall, Thomas. S Dec 1750. L.
Hall, Thomas. S May-Jun T Jly 1753 *Tryal*. M.
Hall, Thomas. S s silk handkerchief Summer 1756. Du.
Hall, Thomas. S s mare Summer 1757 R 14 yrs Lent 1758. Nf.
Hall, Thomas. S Sep T Dec 1769 *Justitia*. M.
Hall, Thomas. S May T Jly 1771 *Scarsdale*. L.
Hall, Thomas. SQS New Sarum or Marlborough & TB to Va Jan 1774. Wi.
Hall, William of Fulham. R for Barbados May TB Jun 1668. M.
Hall, William. Rebel T 1685.
Hall, William. R for America Jly 1707 & Jly 1709. Li.
Hall, William. S Aug T Oct 1724 *Forward* LC Annapolis Jun 1725. M.
Hall, William. SQS Jan 1738. So.
Hall, William. S May-Jun T Aug 1752 *Tryal*. M.
Hall, William. S s iron at Enstone Lent 1753. O.
Hall, William. S Lent 1754. K.
Hall, William. S Oct T Dec 1763 *Neptune*. M.
Hall, William. R Feb T Mar 1764 *Tryal*. M.
Hall, William. T Jun 1764 *Dolphin*. Sx.
Hall, William. S Feb T Apr 1766 *Ann*. L.
Hall, William. S Lent 1766. Nf.
Hall, William. S s silk at Old Swinford Lent 1770. Wo.
Hall, William. S Oct T Dec 1771 *Justitia*. L.
Hall, William. S Lent T Apr 1772 *Thornton*. E.
Hall, William. S Aug 1772. De.
Hall, William (1773). *See* Fell, Stephen. Y.
Hall, William. S Jan-Feb 1774. M.
Hall, William. S Lent 1775. Ht.
Hall, William. S for highway robbery & R 14 yrs Lent 1775. St.

Hall, William. R 14 yrs Apr 1775 (SP). Be.

Hall, William. S s sheep & R 7 yrs Summer 1775. Li.

Hallam, James. S & T Dec 1740 *Vernon*. L.

Hallam, James of Snenton. SQS s hay Jan 1766. Nt.

Hallcroft, John (1770). *See* Allcroft. Y.

Hallett, Daniel. Rebel T 1685.

Hallett, George. Rebel T 1685.

Hallett als Grinter, Grace. S Mar 1760. Do.

Hallett, Hannah of St. Saviour, Southwark. R for Barbados or Jamaica Jun 1684. Sy.

Hallett, John (1663). *See* West. M.

Hallatt, John (1741). *See* Forster. We.

Hallett, Joseph. Rebel T 1685.

Hallett, Stephen, als Dykes, Richard of Tarrant Hinton, husbandman. R for Barbados Jly 1667. Do.

Hallett, Thomas. Rebel T 1685.

Hallett, William. R for life Aug 1770 TB to Va 1771. De.

Hallifield, Valentine of Fenny Compton. R for America Jly 1673. Wa.

Halliman, Mary. T May 1744 *Justitia*. Sy.

Hallis als Hollis, William. S as pickpocket Lent 1764. Db.

Halliston, William. S Lent 1748. E.

Halliwell, Edmund of Rochdale. SQS Apr 1775. La.

Halliwell, James of Huddersfield. SQS Apr 1775. La.

Halmark, George (1766). *See* Candiland. Sh.

Hallmarke, Thomas of Whitchurch. S Lent R 14 yrs Summer 1734. Sh.

Halls, James. S Lent R 14 yrs Summer 1774. Nf.

Halls, Mordecai. R 14 yrs Mar 1759 TB to Va. De.

Halls, Richard of Wanstead. R for Barbados or Jamaica Feb 1676. E.

Halls, Richard. S Mar 1742. De.

Halsey, Edward. Rebel T 1685.

Halsey, James. S Nov T Dec 1763 *Neptune*. L.

Halstaffe, Thomas. R for Barbados Sep 1677. L.

Halsted, George. S Sep 1731. M.

Halton, Thomas (1766). *See* Elton. Sh.

Halton, William. S Jan-Apr 1749. M.

Halton, William (1764). *See* Hatton. Db.

Ham, George. R 14 yrs Aug 1767. So.

Hamm, Henry. R 14 yrs Jly 1724. De.

Ham, John. Rebel T 1685.

Ham, Richard. S Mar TB Apr 1729. Wi.

Ham, Thomas of Sundridge. R for Barbados Apr 1668. K.

Ham, Thomas. S Mar 1733. Wi.

Hamble, Jane (1755). *See* Hemble. Y.

Hambleton, Arthur. S Feb T Mar 1727 *Rappahannock*. L.

Hambleton, Charles of Burnham. R for America Mar 1686. Bu.

Hambleton, Emanuel. R for Barbados or Jamaica Dec 1698. L.

Hambleton, Francis of South Hanningfield. R for Barbados or Jamaica Jun 1699. E.

Hambleton, Harriott of Warrington, spinster. SQS Apr 1757. La.

Hambleton, John of St. Saviour, Southwark. SQS Jan 1754. Sy.

Hambleton, John (1769). *See* Morris. M.

Hambleton, Mary, als Dutchess of Hambleton or Hamilton of Manchester. SQS Jan 1758. La.

Hambleton, Robert. S Aug T Oct 1724 *Forward* LC Annapolis Jun 1725. L.

Hambleton, Sarah wife of John. S s cambric Lent 1740. He.

Hambleton, William. S Lent T May 1719 *Margaret* LC Md May 1720; sold to Peter Hyat. Sy.

Hambleton, William. S Feb 1754. M.

Hambleton, William. S Feb-Apr T for life May 1755 *Rose*. M.

Hamblett, George. TB Aug 1733. Db.

Hambly, Henry. R 14 yrs Aug 1754. Co.

Hamblyn, Sarah of Shalbourne, widow. R for Barbados Feb 1699. Wi.

Hamblin, William. S s fish Summer 1754. Be.

Hambridge, George. S s blankets at Bisley Lent TB Apr 1751. G.

Hambridge, Richard. S Jun-Dec 1745. M.

Hamilton, Adam. S Summer 1769 R 14 yrs Summer 1770. Be.

Hamilton, Ann of Goosnargh, singlewoman. SQS Jan 1761. La.

Hamilton, Arthur. S Jun T Sep 1758 *Tryal* to Annapolis. M.

Hamilton, Barbara (1766). *See* Clarke. L.

Hamilton, Charlott als Charley of Crompton. SQS Jly 1751. La.

Hamilton, Dutchess of (1758). *See* Hambleton, Mary. La.

Hamilton, George. S & T Jan 1736 *Dorsetshire* LC Va Sep 1736. L.

Hamilton, Henry. S Dec 1763 T Mar 1764 *Tryal*. M.

Hamilton, Jane. S May-Jly 1749. M.

Hamilton, John (1727). *See* Ashton. M.

Hamilton, John. S Jun T Nov 1743 *George William*. M.

Hamilton, John. S Jan-Feb 1773. M.

Hamilton, Margaret wife of Charles. S Apr T May 1767 *Thornton*. M.

Hamilton, Samuel. S Sep 1754. L.

Hamilton, Thomas. SQS Sep 1761. M.

Hamilton, Thomas (1771). *See* Erskine. M.

Hamilton, William. S Dec 1748 T Jan 1749 *Laura*. M.

Hamilton als Scholar als Harris als Smith, William. R Jly T for life Oct 1768 *Justitia*; acquitted for being at large Dec 1769 and sent to Surrey for trial on charge of assault. M.

Hamilton, William (1774). *See* Evans. St.

Hamlen, William. R 14 yrs Mar 1758. De.

Hamlet, Robert (1774). *See* Browne. G.

Hammack, Edward. S Oct T Dec 1771 *Justitia*. L.

Hammersly, Ann wife of Thomas. S & T Oct 1732 *Caesar* to Va. M.

Hammersley, John. T Apr 1766 *Thornton*. Sy.

Hammerton, John. S s horse Summer 1743 R 14 yrs Lent 1744. Be.

Hamerton, Thomas. S s stockings at Hurst Lent 1738. Be.

Hamett, Henry. Rebel T 1685.

Hammett, John of Taunton, yeoman. R for Barbados Jly 1688. So.

Hamet, John. S Apr 1728. De.

Hammett, John. S Lent 1745. La.

Hammett, Joseph (1745). *See* Cleeve. De.

Hamming, John. S Lent R for Barbados May 1664. Sy.

Hammond, Ann. S s at Atcham Lent 1765. Sh.

Hammond, Edward. S Jan-Apr 1749. M.

Hammond, Elizabeth. S Jun-Dec 1738 T Jan 1739 *Dorsetshire* to Va. M.

Hammond, Elizabeth, als wife of Austin Medcalfe. S s at Burton on Trent Lent 1749. St.

Hammond, Elizabeth, spinster. S Dec 1754. L.

Hammond, Elizabeth. T Dec 1758 *The Brothers*. E.

Hammond, Elizabeth wife of John of Newington. SQS Jan T Apr 1760 *Thetis*. Sy.

Hammond, James. S Feb T for life Mar 1750 *Tryal*. M.

Hammond, John. T Jun 1738 *Forward*. Sy.

Hammond, John. S Lent 1750. Bd.

Hammond, John. S Lent 1754. Ca.

Hammond, John. T Jun 1764 *Dolphin*. Sx.

Hammond, Joseph of Farnham. SQS Jly T Aug 1769 *Douglas*. Sy.

Hammond, Lambert. S & T Jan 1739 *Dorsetshire*. L.

Hammond, Mary (1734). *See* Hollis. Bu.

Hammond, Mary. S Feb T Mar 1750 *Tryal*. M.

Hammond, Mary. S Jly 1771. Ha.

Hamond, Priscilla. S s horse Summer 1728 R 14 yrs Lent 1729. Sh.

Hammond, Richard. S Mar 1736. Ha.

Hammond, Richard. T Sep 1766 *Justitia*. M.

Hammond, Richard. S at Hythe & T for life Dec 1769 *Justitia*. K.

Hammond, Thomas. T Sep 1730 *Smith*. K.

Hamond, Thomas. T Jan 1736 *Dorsetshire*. Sy.

Hammond, Thomas. T Sep 1765 *Justitia*. Sx.

Hammond, William. R 14 yrs Jly 1750. Ha.

Hammond, William. SL Nov T Dec 1763 *Neptune*. Sy.

Hammonds, John. S s at Rock Summer 1752. Wo.

Hamonds, Richard of Hopesay. R for America Feb 1681. Sh.

Hamnett, John. S Summer 1762. Ch.

Hamon, Dennis. SQS Apr 1751. M.

Hamper, Robert. S Lent R 14 yrs Summer 1752. Sy.

Hamper, William of Rotherhithe. SQS Jly T Sep 1766 *Justitia*. Sy.

Hampil, John. T 14 yrs Apr 1770 *New Trial*. E.

Hampson als Richmond, Ann. S Lent 1767. La.

Hampson, John, als Haslam, Ellis of Pilkington. SQS Jly 1775. La.

Hampstead, Benjamin. S Summer T Oct 1750 *Rachael*. Sy.

Hampton, Ann. R for Barbados or Jamaica May AT Jly 1697. M.

Hampton, Ester wife of William of Sawbridgworth & Great Hadham, yeoman. Delivered of a child, Sarah, in Hertford Gaol & T Dec 1731. Ht.

Hampton, John. S Lent 1738. Ch.

Hampton, John. S Dec 1746. L.

Hampton, Mary. S & T Oct 1732 *Caesar*. L.

Hampton, Thomas. R Jly 1770. Ha.

Hampton, William. S Feb 1733. Ha.

Hampton, William. S s horse Summer 1740 R 14 yrs Lent 1741. Wa.

Hams als Haynes, William, als Johnson, Thomas. S s wheat at Drayton Bassett Lent 1767. St.

Hams, Bethia. S for highway robbery Lent R 14 yrs Summer T Nov 1741 *Sea Horse*. Bu.

Hams, Edward. S Jan-Apr 1748. M.
Hanby, Richard. S Jly 1774. L.
Hanby, Thomas. S Feb 1774. L.
Hance, William of Edmonton. R for Jamaica Jan 1663. M.
Hancher, William. S s at Dodderhill Summer 1734. Wo.
Hancock, Abraham of Stepney. S for highway robbery Sep R & T Dec 1740 *Vernon*. M.
Hancock, Benjamin. S Summer 1721 T Oct 1723 *Forward* from London. Y.
Hancock, Edward. S Jan T Mar 1750 *Tryal*. L.
Hancock, Elizabeth. R for Barbados or Jamaica Jan 1692. M.
Hancock, Elizabeth. S Dec 1745. L.
Hancock, Giles of Bagpath. S s sheep Summer 1741; found at large & S to hang Lent but R & TB Jly 1742. G.
Handcock, Henry. S & T Apr 1733 *Patapsco* LC Annapolis Nov 1733. M.
Hancock, James (1688). *See* Prist. So.
Hancock, James. S May T Jly 1771 *Scarsdale*. L.
Hancock, James. S & T for life Jly 1772 *Tayloe*. L.
Hancock, John. S Aug T Sep 1725 *Forward* LC Annapolis Dec 1725. M.
Hancock, John. S Mar 1762. So.
Hancock, John. S & R 14 yrs Summer T Sep 1772. No.
Hancock, Joseph. SQS Oct TB Dec 1769. So.
Hancock, Mary. R for Barbados or Jamaica Feb 1686. M.
Hancock als Jones als Archer, Mary. S s at Handsworth Lent 1758. St.
Hancock, Ralph. R for America Jly 1683. Le.
Hancock, Richard. T Oct 1723 *Forward*. Sy.
Hancock, Susannah. S Apr-May T Jly 1771 *Scarsdale*. M.
Hancock, Thomas. S Mar 1765. Ha.
Hancock, William. S Aug 1743 & Mar 1744. So.
Hancock, William. TB to Va from QS 1772. De.
Hancox, Richard. S s sheep Lent R 14 yrs Summer 1742. He.
Hancorne, James. R for Barbados Dec 1683. L.
Hand, Elizabeth. S May-Jly 1749. M.
Hand, Harriot. S Apr 1761. M.
Hand, James. T May 1736 *Patapsco*. Sy.
Hand, Patrick. S Jun-Dec 1745. M.
Hand, Patrick. S Feb 1758. Ha.
ỿHand, Philip. S Oct T Nov 1725 *Rappahannock* to Va. M.
Hand, Thomas. TB to Md Jly 1726. Db.
Hand, William. S Mar TB to Va Apr 1775. Wi.
Handby, John. S & T Sep 1757 *Thetis*. M.
Hanfield, John. S May 1759. M.
Handfield, Thomas. S Feb T Apr 1741 *Speedwell*. L.
Handford, Jane (1754). *See* Rebecco. M.
Handford, Martha. S May-Jly T Sep 1751 *Greyhound*. M.
Handford als Gordon, Richard. S Dec 1760. M.
Handle, William (1763). *See* Hanlow. M.
Handley, Edward. S Lent 1764. Wa.
Handley, George. R for America Aug 1685. Nt.
Handley, Hannah. S Lent TB Mar 1760. Db.
Handley, James. S Summer 1773. Sy.

Handley, John. S Lent 1764. Li.
Handley, John. S Lent 1775. Wa.
Hendley, Michael. S s mare Summer 1763 R 14 yrs Lent 1764. Wa.
Handley, Thomas. S Lent 1757. Ch.
Handley, William. S Aug TB Sep 1728. Nt.
Hands, John. R Dec 1765 T for life Jan 1766 *Tryal*. M.
Handsley, Elizabeth. R for Va for s from Mary Payne Apr 1620. M.
Handy, John (1721). *See* Beaule. M.
Handysides, William of Streatham. SQS May T Jun 1764 *Dolphin*. Sy.
Haney als Heaney, John. S Dec 1742 T Mar 1743 *Justitia*. L.
Hayney, Nicholas. S Jly-Sep T Oct 1739 *Duke of Cumberland* to
    Va. M.
Hanger, John. TB to Va from QS 1767. De.
Hankey, John. S Jan T Feb 1724 *Anne* to Carolina. M.
Hankinson, Edmond of Great Hoole, miller. R for Barbados Jly
    1685. La.
Hanks, Betty, als Plummer, Lydia. S s gown at Berkeley Lent 1769. G.
Hanley, John of South Kirby. R for Barbados Jly 1690. Y.
Hanley, Peter of Ewell. SQS Jan 1751. Sy.
Hanlow als Handle, William. S Dec 1763 T Mar 1764 *Tryal*. M.
Hanmer, Elizabeth (1729). *See* Hanner. M.
Hanna, Daniel. S Jly-Sep T Oct 1739 *Duke of Cumberland* to Va. M.
Hanner als Hanmer, Elizabeth. S Feb T Mar 1729 *Patapsco* to Md. M.
Hannah, Jacob. S s buckles Jun T Dec 1736 *Dorsetshire* to Va. M.
Hannah, James. T Apr 1742 *Bond*. Ht.
Hanna, John. S May-Jun T Aug 1752 *Tryal*. M.
Hanah, Mary. S & T Apr 1733 *Patapsco* LC Annapolis Nov 1733. M.
Hannah, William. S Dec 1749-Jan 1750 T Mar 1750 *Tryal*. M.
Hannaford, John. S Mar 1729 TB to Va. De.
Hannan, Robert. Rebel T 1685.
Hannat, James. T Mar 1742. Ht.
Hanning, John. Rebel T 1685.
Hannis, John (1759). *See* Ennis. G.
Hannis, Thomas. S & TB Mar 1732. G.
Hanns, Thomas. S & T Apr 1725 *Sukey* LC Annapolis Sep 1725. M.
Hans, William. T 5 yrs to Va Nov ?1661. L.
Hanscombe, Thomas. S Lent R for life Summer T Sep 1755 *Tryal*. Ht.
Hansford, John. S Mar 1759. Ha.
Hanshaw, Nicholas, aged 25, fair. T *Gilbert* LC Md May 1721. Sy.
Hanshaw als Fanshaw, Sibilla. S Oct T Nov 1725 *Rappahannock* to
    Va. M.
Hanshaw, William. S & T Sep 1751 *Greyhound*. L.
Hansom, James. S May-Jun T Jly 1753 *Tryal*. M.
Hansom, John. S May-Jun T 14 yrs Jly 1753 *Tryal*. M.
Hanson, Elizabeth. R for Barbados Aug 1679. L.
Hanson, Henry. S Jun T Aug 1769 *Douglas*. M.
Hanson als Higgs, John. S s horse Lent R 14 yrs Summer 1729. Be.
Hanson als Longden als Wagstaffe, Mary. TB Nov 1736. Db.
Hanson, Mary. S May T Jly 1770 *Scarsdale*. L.
Hanson, Richard. S & T 14 yrs Oct 1730 *Forward* LC Potomack Jan
    1731. L.

Hanson, William. R for Barbados Sep 1672. L.

Hansor, Matthew. LC from *Patapsco* Annapolis Dec 1729. X.

Hansua, Peter. S Lent R 14 yrs Summer 1753. Wa.

Hanwell, William. T Apr 1766 *Ann*. Bu.

Hanworthy, John. S Apr 1728. De.

Haper, Peter. T Aug 1721 *Owners Goodwill*. E.

Harbar, William (1765). *See* Herbert. Su.

Harbert als Kirby, Rebecca. R for Barbados Jun 1671. L.

Harbertson, John. S s horse Summer 1738 R 14 yrs Summer 1739. Nl.

Harbin, Joseph. S Mar 1772. Do.

Harbin, Robert. S & T Jan 1739 *Dorsetshire*. L.

Harbine, Susannah. SQS Oct 1773. M.

Harbourne, Benjamin. SQS Jan 1755. M.

Harbridge, John. R for Barbados Jly 1674. M.

Harbridge, John. SW & T Jly 1771 *Scarsdale*. M.

Harbutt, Richard. S Lent T Oct 1765. Bd.

Harcombe, John. Rebel T 1685.

Harcourt, Mary. SQS Feb 1773. M.

Harcot, Peter. S Apr-May 1775. M.

Hard, Dyer. T 14 yrs Apr 1768 *Thornton*. Ht.

Hardacker, William. LC from *Gilbert* Annapolis Jly 1722. X.

Hardbeard, Richard. S s wheat at Bicester Summer 1757. O.

Hardcastle, Mary wife of John. S Oct-Dec 1739 T Jan 1740 *York* to
  Md. M.

Harden, Elizabeth. S Apr-May 1775. M.

Harden, John (1699). *See* Hardy. Ha.

Harden, John. S Dec 1773. L.

Harden, William. T Apr 1759 *Thetis*. K.

Hardyman, Henry. R 14 yrs Mar TB to Va Apr 1769. Wi.

Hardiman, John. Rebel T 1685.

Hardiman als Stringer, Mary. S s at Holt Summer 1768. Wo.

Hardiman, William. S s peas at St. Giles, Reading, Lent 1774. O.

Hardimore, Rebecca. S Sep T Dec 1763 *Neptune*. M.

Harding, Alice. S Jly T Aug 1721 *Prince Royal* LC Va Nov 1721. L.

Harding, Amos. R 14 yrs Aug 1742. De.

Harding, Ann. S Oct T Nov 1759 *Phoenix*. M.

Harding als Greene, Bridget. R for Barbados Aug 1664. M.

Harding, Charles. R for Barbados or Jamaica Dec 1698. L.

Harding, Edward. S & T Jly 1753 *Tryal*. L.

Harding, Edward. S Summer 1761. Bu.

Harding, Elizabeth. R 14 yrs Jly TB to Va Oct 1742. Wi.

Harding, Elizabeth (1744). *See* Pugh. M.

Harding, Francis. S Mar 1744. Do.

Harding, Francis of St. Martin in Fields. SW Apr 1773. M.

Harding, George. Rebel T 1685.

Harding, George. SQS Feb 1774. M.

Harding, Harry Fry. R 14 yrs Jly 1751. Do.

Harding, Henry of Bruton, butcher. R for Barbados Feb 1699. So.

Harding, Isaac of Prescott. SQS Jan 1764. La.

Harding, James. R for Barbados or Jamaica May 1684. L.

Harding, James. S Jly T Sep 1751 *Greyhound*. L.

Harding, James. R for life Mar 1772. Do.

Harding, John. S Mar 1733 T *Patapsco* LC Annapolis Nov 1733. Wi.

Harding, John (1738). *See* Oatway. De.

Harding, John. S Jan T Mar 1764 *Tryal*. M.

Harding, John, als Davis, Richard, als Powell, William als Benjamin. SQS Coventry Apr 1766. Wa.

Harding, John. S Oct T Dec 1771 *Justitia*. L.

Harding, Joseph. S for smuggling tea & obstructing Customs Summer 1737. Nf.

Harding, Martha. S & T May 1740 *Essex*. L.

Harding, Mary. R & T Dec 1716 *Lewis* to Jamaica. M.

Harding, Mary. S Jan T Feb 1719 *Worcester* LC Annapolis Jun 1719. L.

Harding, Mary. S Jun T Aug 1769 *Douglas*. L.

Harding, Michael. T Apr 1768 *Thornton*. M.

Harding, Moses. SQS Calne Oct 1741 TB to Va Apr 1742. Wi.

Harding, Nathaniel. SQS for attending conventicle Dec 1664. M.

Hardin, Robert. S s horse Lent 1725 R 14 yrs Lent 1729. Y.

Harding, Robert. S Mar TB to Va Nov 1748. Wi.

Harding, Robert. R for life Mar 1772. Do.

Harding, Thomas (1699). *See* Newman. So.

Harding, William of Petworth. R for Barbados Aug 1668. Sx.

Harding, William. R Apr 1773. M.

Harding, William. R Lent 1775. Sy.

Hardisty als Hargrave, John of York. R for Barbados Jly 1701. Y.

Hardman, John. T Sep 1730 *Smith*. E.

Hardman, John of Salford, dyer. SQS Jan 1752. La.

Hardware, Ann. S Apr T Sep 1737 *Pretty Patsy* to Md. M.

Hardware, Charles. S & R 14 yrs Lent 1773. St.

Hardwicke, Charles. S & T Dec 1769 *Justitia*. M.

Hardwick, James. S s sheep Lent R 14 yrs Summer 1762. Nt.

Hardwick, John. S s at Newent Lent TB Mar 1735. G.

Hardwick, John. S Oct-Dec 1750. M.

Hardwicke, John. S Jly 1766. Ha.

Hardwick, John. R 14 yrs Mar 1773. So.

Hardwicke, Mary Divet. S Lent 1766. Ca.

Hardy, Andrew. S s coat at St. Andrew Holborn May T Jun 1768 *Tryal*. L.

Hardy, Duncan. S & T Dec 1771 *Justitia*. L.

Hardey, Elizabeth. S Oct T Dec 1724 *Rappahannock*. L.

Hardy, Elizabeth. S Jan T 14 yrs Feb 1742 *Industry* to Md. M.

Hardy, Elizabeth wife of John. S at Hull Summer 1768. Y.

Hardy, Francis. SQS Jly TB Nov 1726. So.

Hardy, Grace. S Mar 1755. Do.

Hardy, James. S s at All Saints, Huntingdon, & R Summer 1773. Hu.

Hardy, Jane, spinster. R for Barbados Jly 1671. Y.

Hardy als Harden, John of Gosport. R for Barbados Jun 1699. Ha.

Hardy, John. S Summer 1728 (SP). Nf.

Hardy, John. S for counterfeiting Summer TB Dec 1739. Y.

Hardy, John. S Aug 1753. Do.

Hardy, John. S Summer 1766. La.

Hardy, John. S s sheep at Stoke Nayland & R 14 yrs Lent 1774. Su.

Hardy, Joseph. S Jly TB to Va Aug 1749. Wi.

Hardy, Mary. T Jun 1740 *Essex*. Sx.

Hardy, Matthew. S Aug 1727 T *Forward* LC Rappahannock May 1728. M.

Hardy, Nathaniel. T Dec 1736 *Dorsetshire*. E.

Hardy, Richard. S s handkerchief at St. Catherine Creechurch Oct 1768 T Jan 1769 *Thornton*. L.

Hardy, Robert. S s sheep Summer 1743 R 14 yrs Summer 1744. Nl.

Hardy, Robert. SQS & TB Jan 1774. So.

Hardy, Samuel. S s at St. Michael, Cambridge, Lent 1769. Ca.

Hardy, Samuel. S Apr-May T Jly 1771 *Scarsdale*. M.

Hardy, Thomas. S s sheep Lent R 14 yrs Summer 1754. Li.

Hardy, Thomas. S s gelding at Downham & R 14 yrs Lent 1774. Nf.

Hare, George of Buckland Brewer. R for Barbados Dec 1673. De.

Hare, Henry. R for Barbados Apr 1668. M.

Hare, Jarvis. R & T 14 yrs Feb 1740 *York*. L.

Hare, John. T Apr 1753 *Thames*. E.

Hare, Mary. R 10 yrs in plantations Oct 1662. M.

Hare, Richard. S May T Sep 1765 *Justitia*. L.

Hair, Robert, aged 21, dark. LC from *Gilbert* Md May 1721. X.

Hare, Sarah wife of James. S Mar 1774. So.

Hare, Thomas. S Aug T Oct 1724 *Forward*. L.

Harebottle, Elizabeth. S Jly 1750. L.

Harefoot als Halford, John. R 14 yrs Mar 1773. Co.

Harfield, William. SQS Oct 1768. Ha.

Harford, Hannah. S s shirts Feb T Apr 1735 *Patapsco* LC Annapolis Oct.

Harford, James. S Sep-Oct 1749. M.

Hartford, John. T Jly 1753 *Tryal*. L.

Harford, John. S for arson Summer 1758 R 14 yrs Lent 1759. No.

Harford, Thomas, als Gilbert, James. R for America Aug 1713. M.

Hargest, William. S & T Oct 1729 *Forward* but died on passage. L.

Hargins, Mathias. S Sep T Oct 1768 *Justitia*. M.

Hardgrave, George. AT Summer 1720. Y.

Hargrave, Isaac. T Nov 1725 *Rappahannock* LC Va Aug 1726. Sy.

Hargrave, John (1701). *See* Hardisty. Y.

Hargrave, Nathaniel. S May T Jly 1770 *Scarsdale*. L.

Hargrave, Solomon, aged 21, fair. S Jan T Feb 1723 *Jonathan* LC Annapolis Jly 1724. M.

Hargrave, Thomas. S s coat at Cirencester Lent 1765. G.

Hargraves, George. S s at Woolley in Royston Lent 1771. Y.

Hargrove, Ann of St. Saviour, Southwark, spinster. R for Barbados or Jamaica Jly 1715. Sy.

Hargrove, Daniel. S s horse Lent R 14 yrs Summer 1768. St.

Hargrove, Elizabeth. S & T Jan 1722 *Gilbert* LC Annapolis Jly 1722. M.

Hargrove, Hester. S s gold ring May T Dec 1735 *John* LC Annapolis Sep 1736. L.

Hargrove, John. S s iron hoops Jun T Dec 1736 *Dorsetshire* to Va. M.

Hargrove, Nathaniel. S & T Apr 1733 *Patapsco* LC Annapolis Nov 1733. M.

Hargrove, Thomas. S Sep 1747. L.

Harker, John. T May 1719 *Margaret* LC Md May 1720; sold to David Bele. Sy.

Harker, John. S s mare Summer 1769 R 14 yrs Lent 1770. Li.

Harker, William. S Dec 1747. L.

Harkney, Edward. T May 1755 *Rose*. K.

Harland, Frances. S Jly-Sep 1754. M.

Harland, Jane. S Feb T Mar 1760 *Friendship*. M.

Harleech, John. S & T Sep 1751 *Greyhound*. L.

Harley, Edmond (1725). *See* Harney, Edward. L.

Harley, John. S Feb-Apr 1746. M.

Harling, John, als Davis als Williams, Richard, als Powell, Benjamin. R for life s horses Lent 1766. Wa.

Harling, Oliver. AT Summer 1755. Y.

Harling, Richard. S Dec 1754. L.

Harlow, Mary. S & T Oct 1722 *Forward* LC Annapolis Jun 1723. M.

Harman, Anne (1682). *See* Carter. M.

Harman, Barbara (1744). *See* Housman. M.

Harman, Edward. S Mar 1758. Wi.

Harman, Hester. SQS Oct 1773 TB Jan 1774. So.

Harman, John of Kensington. S s lambs Jly 1740. M.

Harman, John. S Jan 1745. L.

Harman, John. SW & T Dec 1771 *Justitia*. M.

Harman, Joseph. S Lent 1769. Be.

Harman, Mary. T Oct 1721 *William & John*. K.

Harman, Richard. S & T Sep 1764 *Justitia*. L.

Harman, Robert of Bishops Lydeard. R for Barbados Jun 1687. So.

Harman, Robert. S Apr 1734. So.

Harman, Robert. S Mar TB to Va Apr 1741. Wi.

Harman, Thomas of Calne. R for Barbados Jly 1684. Wi.

Harman, Thomas. T May 1719 *Margaret* LC Md May 1720; sold to John Cornelius. Sy.

Harman, William. S Mar 1737. Wi.

Harman, William. T Jun 1738 *Forward*. Sx.

Harmer, Elizabeth. LC from *Patapsco* Annapolis Dec 1729. X.

Harmer, James. S Norwich Summer 1752. Nf.

Harmer, Kinard. S s at Whittington Lent TB Mar 1750. G.

Harmsworth, Edward. S Mar 1745. Ha.

Harmsworth, Mary, spinster. S Lent 1753; Mary Harmsworth, widow, & Bethania Harmsworth discharged. Be.

Harnaman, Edward of Portsmouth. R for Barbados Jun 1688. Ha.

Harner, William (1741). *See* Turner. Do.

Harnett, Bartholomew. LC from *Caesar* Va Jly 1734. X.

Harney, Edward (Harley, Edmond). S Aug T Sep 1725 *Forward* LC Annapolis Dec 1725. L.

Harnham, John. S Mar 1739. Ha.

Harns, Thomas. LC from *Forward* Annapolis Dec 1725. X.

Harper, Alexander. S Jan-Jun T Jun 1728 *Elizabeth* LC Potomack Aug 1729. M.

Harper, Amos. S for highway robbery & R for life Lent 1774. Y.

Harper, Ann of Worcester, spinster. S Lent 1720. Wo.

Harper, Ann. S Oct 1760. M.

Harper, Anthony. S Jan-Feb T Apr 1753 *Thames*. M.

Harper, Bartholomew. S Oct 1742 T Apr 1743 *Justitia*. M.

Harper, Christopher of St. Saviour, Southwark. SQS Jun T Jly 1753 *Tryal*. Sy.

Harper, Daniel. S s gelding & R 14 yrs Summer 1736. Nf.

Harper, Edward. TB to Md Mar 1723 T *Forward* from London LC Annapolis Jun 1725. Db.

Harper, Edward. S Jan T Feb 1733 *Smith* to Md or Va. M.

Harper, Jane wife of John. SQS Apr 1752. M.

Harper, John. S for highway robbery Summer 1731 R 14 yrs Lent 1732. Be.

Harper, John. S Summer 1774. Sh.

Harper, Joseph. S Lent R 14 yrs Summer 1761. Wa.

Harper, Katherine. T Jun 1727 *Susanna*. K.

Harper, Philip. S & T Apr 1725 *Sukey* LC Annapolis Sep 1725. M.

Harper, Richard. S Lent R 14 yrs Summer 1745. Sh.

Harper, Richard. S 14 yrs s linen from bleaching yard Lent 1762. Nf.

Harper, Richard. S s at Worfield Summer 1763. Sh.

Harper, Sara. S Jan T Feb 1719 *Worcester* LC Annapolis Jun 1719. L.

Harper, Thomas. R for Barbados Mar 1677. L.

Harper, Thomas. T Oct 1723 *Forward*. E.

Harper, William of York. R for Barbados Jly 1699. Y.

Harper, William. S Dec 1733 T Jan 1734 *Caesar* LC Va Jly 1734. L.

Harper, William. S Summer 1746 R 14 yrs Lent 1747. Sh.

Harper, William. S Lent 1766. Bd.

Harper, William. S s heifer Lent R 14 yrs Summer 1770. Sh.

Harpin, Elizabeth. S Sep-Oct T Dec 1771 *Justitia*. M.

Harps, Susanna. S Dec 1742 T Apr 1743 *Justitia*. M.

Harpum, George of Isle of Ely. R for Barbados or Jamaica Oct 1664. Ca.

Harr, Samuel. S Lent 1767. Li.

Harragutt, Ruth. R for Barbados Apr 1669. M.

Harard, John. SQS Mar TB Apr 1773. Nt.

Harrad, Martha. S Oct 1772. L.

Harridge, Abraham (1673). *See* Beaumont. Y.

Harril, Thomas. S Dec 1742 T Apr 1743 *Justitia*. M.

Harriman, Charles (1744). *See* Hart. Su.

Harriman, Mary. S Lent 1731. Sh.

Harringan, Neal. S Jan-Apr 1748. M.

Harrington, Charles. T for life Apr 1768 *Thornton*. E.

Harrington, Edward (1749). *See* Hill. L.

Harrington, George. S Aug 1728. So.

Harrington, James. S Oct-Dec 1750. M.

Harrington, Jeremiah. SQS Apr T Jly 1771 *Scarsdale*. M.

Harrington, John of Hallow. R for Barbados Feb 1665. Wo.

Harrington, John. S Feb T Apr 1739 *Forward* to Va. M.

Harrington als Arrington, Mary. S Feb T Apr 1734 *Patapsco* to Md. M.

Harrington, Thomas. S & T Dec 1767 *Neptune*. M.

Harriott, James. S City Summer 1740. Nl.

Harris, Alexander. R 14 yrs Mar 1764. De.

Harris, Ann (1664). *See* Smith. L.

Harris als Freeman, Anne. R for Barbados Jly 1675. L.

Harris, Anne. R for Barbados or Jamaica Dec 1689. L.

Harris, Ann. R for Barbados or Jamaica May 1691. L.

Harris, Ann. R for Barbados Dec 1693. L.

Harris, Ann. S Jly T Aug 1721 *Owners Goodwill* LC Annapolis Jly 1722. L.

Harris, Ann. S Feb T Mar 1731 *Patapsco* LC Annapolis Jun 1731. M.

Harris, Ann. S Lent 1773. K.

Harris, Ann wife of Edward *(qv)*. R for life for counterfeiting Lent 1775. Sy.

Harris, Catherine (1758). *See* Sullivan. Ha.

Harris, Cesar. S s clothing at Hanwell Lent 1726. O.

Harris, Charles of Rowde. R for Barbados Jly 1698. Wi.

Harris, Christopher of Hemel Hempstead. R for Barbados or Jamaica Jly 1705. Ht.

Harris, Christopher. T Dec 1758 *The Brothers*. Ht.

Harris, Daniel. S Sep 1754. L.

Harris, David of Woolaston. R for America Jly 1677. G.

Harris, Diana (1732). *See* Floyd. K.

Harris, Edward. R for Barbados May 1665. X.

Harris, Edward. PT Jun 1673. M.

Harris, Edward. Rebel T 1685.

Harris, Edward. S Jly 1732. Ha.

Harris, Edward. S Jly T Oct 1741 *Sea Horse* to Va. M.

Harris, Edward. R for life for counterfeiting Lent 1775. Sy.

Harris, Eleanor. S Oct T Nov 1759 *Phoenix*. M.

Harris, Elizabeth. R for Barbados Aug 1664. L.

Harris als Harrison, Elizabeth. R for Barbados Jly 1674. M.

Harris, Elizabeth. R for Barbados or Jamaica Dec 1693. L.

Harris, Elizabeth. R for Barbados or Jamaica Dec 1695 & May 1697. M.

Harris, Elizabeth. R Jly 1702 to be T at her own cost else to be executed. L.

Harris, Elizabeth (1722). *See* Abbott. M.

Harris, Elizabeth. S Sep 1734. M.

Harris, Elizabeth (1739). *See* Rustin. L.

Harris, Elizabeth. S Apr T May 1743 *Indian Queen* to Potomack. M.

Harris, Elizabeth. S Jun T Nov 1743 *George William*. L.

Harris, Elizabeth, spinster. R 14 yrs Lent 1754. Bu.

Harris, Elizabeth Maria. T 14 yrs Oct 1768 *Justitia*. E.

Harris, Erasmus of Great Barrington, cooper. R for Barbados Oct 1663. G.

Harris, Frances. SQS May T Sep 1751 *Greyhound*. M.

Harris, Francis, als Tubb, Jacob. R 14 yrs Aug 1728 TB to Md. De.

Harris, George. S Jly T 14 yrs Aug 1718 *Eagle* LC Charles Town Mar 1719. L.

Harris, George. R 14 yrs Mar 1738. So.

Harris, George. S s at Barnsley Summer TB Aug 1742. G.

Harris, George. S Lent R 14 yrs Summer 1759. Mo.

Harris, George. S s at Trostrey Lent 1772. Mo.

Harris, George. S Mar 1772. Do.

Harris, George. S May-Jly 1774. M.
Harris, Grace. S & T Oct 1732 *Caesar* to Va. M.
Harris, Henry. R for Barbados Mar 1683. L.
Harris, Henry. R 14 yrs Aug 1726. De.
Harris, Henry. S Sep T Nov 1743 *George William*. L.
Harris, Henry. T Apr 1766 *Ann*. K.
Harris als Clerke, Isabel. R for Barbados or Jamaica Oct 1694. L.
Harris, Isabella. S May T Jun 1726 *Loyal Margaret* LC Annapolis Oct
 1726. M.
Harris, James. R for Jamaica Aug 1661. L.
Harris, James. R for America Mar 1705. M.
Harris, James. S s sheets Apr T Jun 1742 *Bladon*. L.
Harris, James. S s wheat Lent 1755. Wo.
Harris, James. SQS & T Jan 1756 *Greyhound*. M.
Harris, James of Christchurch. SQS & T Jan 1769 *Thornton*. Sy.
Harris, James. S Feb T Apr 1770 *New Trial*. L.
Harris, James. R 14 yrs Aug 1772. So.
Harris, James. S Jly 1775. M.
Harris, Jane. R for Barbados Mar 1677 & May 1678. L.
Harris, Jane. S & T Dec 1731 *Forward* to Md or Va. M.
Harris, Jane. SQS Warminster Jly TB to Va Sep 1741. Wi.
Harris als Robinson, John. R for Jamaica Aug 1661. L.
Harris, John. R 10 yrs in plantations Oct 1662. M.
Harris, John (1664). *See* Harvey. M.
Harris, John of Tonge. R for America Sep 1671. Sh.
Harris, John of St. Saviour, Southwark. R for Barbados or Jamaica Feb
 1684. Sy.
Harris, John. Rebel T 1685.
Harris, John. R for America Jly 1686. Li.
Harris, John, baker aged 25, dark. S Jan T Feb 1723 *Jonathan* LC
 Annapolis Jly 1724. M.
Harris, John. T Oct 1726 *Forward*. Sy.
Harris, John. S May T Jun 1727 *Susanna*. L.
Harris, John. S Jan-Jun T Jun 1728 *Elizabeth* LC Potomack Aug 1729. L.
Harris, John. S & T Oct 1730 *Forward* LC Potomack Jan 1731. M.
Harris als Homer, John. T Oct 1732 *Caesar*. K.
Harris, John. R 14 yrs Mar 1744. De.
Harris als Lee, John. S s at St. Woollos Lent 1746. Mo.
Harris, John of St. Nicholas, Chelmsford. SQS Jly T Sep 1751
 Greyhound. E.
Harris, John. S s at Stapleton Lent TB Mar 1752. G.
Harris, John. S Mar 1752. De.
Harris, John. S Mar 1753. Co.
Harris, John. S Summer 1754. K.
Harris, John. S Mar 1755. De.
Harris, John. S Summer T Sep 1755 *Tryal*. E.
Harris, John. S & T Jan 1756 *Greyhound*. M.
Harris, John. S Summer 1758 R 14 yrs Lent 1759. Sh.
Harris, John. S Jun T Sep 1764 *Justitia*. M.
Harris, John (1765). *See* Evans. M.
Harris, John. S Jun T Sep 1767 *Justitia*. L.

Harris, John. R Jly T 14 yrs Sep 1767 *Justitia*. M.
Harris, John. TB to Va 1769. De.
Harris, John. R s sheep Lent 1772. Li.
Harris, John. TB to Va from QS 1772. De.
Harris, John of St. James, Westminster. SW Jun 1774. M.
Harris, John. S Oct 1774. L.
Harris, Joshua of Wolverhampton. R for America Mar 1682. St.
Harris, Judith. S & T Oct 1732 *Caesar* to Va. M.
Harris, Margaret. S Sep T Dec 1763 *Neptune*. M.
Harris, Martha of St. Saviour, Southwark, spinster. SQS Apr 1751. Sy.
Harris als Williams als Sharpe, Mary. R Sep 1682; transportation bond
    with William Carter & Richard Williams. M.
Harris, Mary. R for Barbados Sep 1682. L.
Harris, Mary, aged 21, fair. LC from *Gilbert* Annapolis May 1721. X.
Harris als Wyatt, Mary. S May T Jly 1722 *Alexander* to Nevis or
    Jamaica. M.
Harris, Mary. S Aug T Oct 1724 *Forward* LC Annapolis Jun 1725. M.
Harris, Mary wife of Thomas. S Oct 1741 T Feb 1742 *Industry* to Md. M.
Harris, Mary. S Feb-Apr 1746. M.
Harris, Mary. S Apr 1746. L.
Harris, Mary. S & T Apr 1765 *Ann*. L.
Harris, Mary. SQS Dec 1765. M.
Harris, Mary. T Apr 1770 *New Trial*. L.
Harris, Mary. S & T Jly 1771 *Scarsdale*. M.
Harris, Michael. S Oct-Dec 1754. M.
Harris, Nathaniel. R for plantations Jan 1664 & Jan 1665. L.
Harris, Oughton. LC from *Forward* Annapolis Jun 1725. X.
Harris, Philip. S Mar 1729. Co.
Harris, Reuben. S Jun T Aug 1769 *Douglas*. M.
Harris, Richard. R for Barbados Jan 1693. M.
Harris als Castle, Richard of Botley. R for America Jly 1698. Be.
Harris, Richard. S Mar 1721 T Mar 1723. Bu.
Harris, Richard. SQS Jan TB to Jamaica Sep 1727. So.
Harris, Richard. S s coffee pot at Shrewsbury Lent 1738. Sh.
Harris, Richard. T Apr 1742 *Bond*. K.
Harris, Richard. SQS Marlborough Jan TB to Va Apr 1745. Wi.
Harris, Richard. R 14 yrs Jly TB to Va Nov 1748. Wi.
Harris, Richard. S Lent 1763. E.
Harris, Richard. S s sheep Summer 1764 R 14 yrs Lent 1765. Li.
Harris, Richard (1765). *See* Harris, Thomas. M.
Harris, Robert, als Harrison, John of Haresfield. S s mare Lent 1718; T
    from Berkshire as John Harrison. G.
Harris, Robert. S Mar 1730. Co.
Harris, Robert. S & R 14 yrs Lent 1775. He.
Harris, Ruth. R for Barbados Dec 1693 AT Jan 1694. M.
Harris, Ruth (1771). *See* Frostick. M.
Harris, Sarah. T Oct 1720 *Gilbert*. Sy.
Harris, Sarah. S Jun-Dec 1745. M.
Harris, Sarah. S Jly T Sep 1764 *Justitia*. M.
Harris, Sylvanus. S s at Hinstock Lent 1775. Sh.
Harris, Thomas (2). PT Oct 1672 R Oct 1673. M.

Harris, Thomas of Wimborne, clothier. R (Oxford Circ) for America Mar 1688. Do.

Harris, Thomas. S Apr T Aug 1718 *Eagle* LC Charles Town Mar 1719. L.

Harris, Thomas. S Jly 1718 to be T to Boston NE. Wi.

Harris als Towsey, Thomas. R 14 yrs Jly 1730. Co.

Harris, Thomas. SQS & TB Jan 1734. G.

Harris, Thomas. S & TB Mar 1734. G.

Harris, Thomas. T Jun 1740 *Essex*. Ht.

Harris, Thomas. S Lent 1742. Sh.

Harris, Thomas als Richard. S Jly T Sep 1765 *Justitia*. M.

Harris, Thomas. S Feb T Apr 1770 *New Trial*. L.

Harris, Thomas, als Johnson, Richard. S s carpentry tools at Abingdon Summer 1771. Be.

Harris, Walter. S Summer 1755 R 14 yrs Lent 1756. Sh.

Harris, William. R for plantations Jan 1665. L.

Harris, William. R for Barbados Sep 1672. L.

Harris, William. Rebel T 1685.

Harris, William. R Dec 1698 AT Jan 1699. M.

Harris als Withers, William. T May 1719 *Margaret* LC Md May 1720; sold to Philip Jones. Sy.

Harris, William. T Jly 1722 *Alexander*. Sy.

Harris, William. S Aug TB to Va Sep 1731. Le.

Harris, William. SQS Jly TB to Md Nov 1738. So.

Harris, William. S & TB May 1744. G.

Harris, William. S Apr 1747. De.

Harris, William. S Jan 1751. L.

Harris, William of St. George, Southwark. SQS Apr T Sep 1751 *Greyhound*. Sy.

Harris, William. S Jan 1757. M.

Harris, William. TB to Va from QS 1757. De.

Harris, William. S Jly 1761. So.

Harris, William. T Apr 1765 *Ann*. Sy.

Harris, William. S & T Apr 1766 *Ann*. L.

Harris, William. S s sheep Lent R 14 yrs Summer 1767. Wo.

Harris, William (1768). *See* Hamilton. M.

Harris, William. S Dec 1768 T Jan 1769 *Thornton*. M.

Harris, William of Christchurch. SQS & T Jan 1769 *Thornton*. Sy.

Harris, William. S Jun T Aug 1769 *Douglas*. L.

Harris, William. S s wheat at Sutton under Brailes [Warw] Lent 1774. G.

Harris, William. S Jan-Feb 1775. M.

Harrison, Alice. S City s spoons at St. Martin Lent 1774. Y.

Harrison, Anne. R for Barbados Jan 1665. Y.

Harrison, Ann. S Feb-Apr 1745. M.

Harrison, Ann (1749). *See* Smith. La.

Harrison als Johnson als Williamson, Ann. S Sep 1761. M.

Harrison, Ann. S Sep-Oct 1773. M.

Harrison, Daniel of St. Martin in Fields. SW Oct 1774. M.

Harrison, Elizabeth (1674). *See* Harris. M.

Harrison, Elizabeth. R for America Aug 1702. L.

Harrison, Elizabeth. S May T Jly 1722 *Alexander* to Nevis or Jamaica. M.

Harrison, Elizabeth. S & T Apr 1753 *Thames*. L.

Harrison, Elizabeth. S & T Sep 1757 *Thetis*. M.

Harrison, Elizabeth. S Summer TB Sep 1760. Db.

Harrison, Elizabeth (1764). *See* Owen. La.

Harrison, Francis. S s horse Summer 1766 R 14 yrs Lent 1767. Nt.

Harrison, George. R for Va Aug 1618. Ht.

Harrison, George of Swaildale. R for Barbados or Jamaica Mar 1697. Nf.

Harrison, George of St. John's. SQS Jan T Mar 1758 *Dragon*. Sy.

Harrison, George. S s wood ash at Droitwich Summer 1764. Wo.

Harrison, George. S Jly T Sep 1764 *Justitia*. M.

Harrison, George. S Lent TB Apr 1766. Db.

Harrison als Watson als Jones als Chumley, George. SQS Coventry Apr 1766. Wa.

Harrison, Henry. T Jun 1726 *Loyal Margaret* but died on passage. K.

Harrison, Henry. T Apr 1759 *Thetis*. Sy.

Harrison, Humphrey. S Feb T Apr 1765 *Ann*. L.

Harrison, James. S Jan 1746. L.

Harrison, John. R for Barbados Jun 1666. Y.

Harrison, John. R Feb 1675. M.

Harrison, John of Rainham. R for America Jly 1700. E.

Harrison, John (1718). *See* Harris, Robert. G.

Harrison, John. S Mar 1719 to be T to Va. Wi.

Harrison, John. S Lent 1721. Be.

Harrison, John. S Summer 1723 T Oct 1723 *Forward* from London. Y.

Harrison, John. S Aug T Oct 1726 *Forward*. L.

Harrison, John. T Jan 1736 *Dorsetshire*. Sy.

Harrison, John. TB Feb 1744. Db.

Harrison, John of Great Bolton, weaver. SQS May 1753. La.

Harrison, John. S Summer 1755 R 14 yrs Lent 1756. La.

Harrison, John. S Lent 1765. No.

Harrison, John. S for perjury Summer 1774. Wo.

Harrison, Joseph. S Aug T Sep 1725 *Forward* LC Annapolis Dec 1725. M.

Harrison als Newell, Katherine. R for Jamaica Jan 1663. M.

Harrison, Katherine. S Summer 1748 T Jan 1749 *Laura*. Ht.

Harrison, Margaret (1745). *See* Rawlinson. La.

Harrison, Mary (1724). *See* Hunton. Y.

Harrison, Mary (1726). *See* Gariston. X.

Harrison, Michael. S & T Dec 1740 *Vernon*. L.

Harrison, Nathaniel. T Sep 1758 *Tryal*. K.

Harrison, Ralph. R for Barbados or Jamaica Mar 1685. M.

Harrison, Richard. SQS Oct 1762. La.

Harrison, Robert. S Lent 1741. O.

Harrison, Robert. TB Apr 1749. Db.

Harrison, Robert. R 14 yrs Summer 1758. Y.

Harrison, Robert. SQS Oct T Dec 1770 *Justitia*. M.

Harrison, Rowland. S Dec 1742 T Apr 1743 *Justitia*. M.

Harrison als Sarrison, Sarah. S May-Jun T Jly 1753 *Tryal*. M.

Harrison, Stephen. S Lent 1750. Y.

Harrison, Susan. R Apr TB for Barbados Oct 1669. M.

Harrison, Susanna. S s at Woodchester Summer 1758; Robert Harrison Jr. burnt in the hand & discharged. G.

Harrison, Thomas. PT Aug 1676. M.

Harrison, Thomas (1686). *See* Rowland. St.

Harrison, Thomas Jr. of Sheraton. R for Barbados Jly 1699. Du.

Harrison, Thomas. S Aug T Sep 1725 *Forward* to Md. M.

Harrison, Thomas. S Jan T Feb 1726 *Supply*. L.

Harrison, Thomas. S s horse Lent R 14 yrs Summer TB Sep 1736. Nt.

Harrison, Thomas. S 14 yrs Sep 1750. M.

Harrison, Thomas. S for housebreaking with violence at Fordon & R 14 yrs Lent TB Aug 1770. Y.

Harrison, William. R for Barbados May 1664. M.

Harrison, William. S Summer R for Barbados Aug 1664. K.

Harrison, William of St. Peter, Hertford. R for Barbados or Jamaica Jly 1688. Ht.

Harrison, William. S Summer 1723 T *Forward* LC Annapolis Dec 1725. Cu.

Harrison, William. S s horse Lent R 14 yrs Summer 1747. Li.

Harrison, William. S s horse Summer 1752 R 14 yrs Lent TB to Md Apr 1753. Le.

Harrison, William. S Dec 1760. M.

Harrison, William. S Jly T Nov 1762 *Prince William*. M.

Harrison, William. S Jan T Apr 1770 *New Trial*. M.

Harrison, William of Linton. SQS for fraudulently collecting money Summer 1774. Ca.

Harrison, William. S May 1775. L.

Harristick, Elizabeth of St. George, Southwark, spinster. SQS Apr 1751 *Greyhound*. Sy.

Harriware, Robert. R 14 yrs Lent 1721. G.

Harrold, John. S s at Kingwick Lent 1754. Bu.

Harrold, Martha wife of Edward. S & T Oct 1732 *Caesar* to Va. M.

Harold, Robert. S & R Summer 1734. Su.

Harrold, Susannah. SQS Oct 1751. M.

Harrord als Henrord, Edward. T 14 yrs Sep 1767 *Justitia*. E.

Harrow, Elizabeth. TB May 1745. Y.

Harrow, Joseph. S Summer 1774. Ht.

Harrow, Rebecca (1743). *See* Heroe. K.

Harrup, Anne. S Jly T 14 yrs Aug 1718 *Eagle* LC Charles Town Mar 1719. L.

Harrupp, John. R for Barbados or Jamaica Mar 1685. L.

Harrop, John. T 14 yrs Apr 1768 *Thornton*. Ht.

Harrop, Thomas. S Jan T Feb 1726 *Supply* LC Annapolis May 1726. L.

Harry, Ann. S s at Monmouth Lent 1763. Mo.

Harrey, John of Breinton. S s game cock Summer 1718. He.

Harry, John. S s at Llanhannock Lent 1769. Mo.

Harry, Mordecai of Usk. R for America Mar 1710. Mo.

Harry, William of Abbey Dore. R for America Jly 1677. He.

Harsdell, John. S Dec 1775. M.

Hart, Abigail. S & T May 1736 *Patapsco* to Md. M.

Hart, Abraham. TB to Va from QS 1738. De.
Hart, Arabella. S Oct 1774. L.
Hart als Harriman, Charles. S Lent 1744. Su.
Hart, Edward. S for highway robbery & R 14 yrs Lent 1770. Ca.
Hart, Elizabeth of Bermondsey. R for Barbados or Jamaica Jly 1696. Sy.
Hart, Elizabeth. S & T Dec 1736 *Dorsetshire*. L.
Hart als Carter, Elizabeth. S Jun T Sep 1767 *Justitia*. L.
Hart, Emma of Chulmleigh. R for Barbados Feb 1688. De.
Hart, Fanny. S May 1775. L.
Hart, George. T May 1737 *Forward*. E.
Hart, Henry. R for Barbados May 1668. M.
Harte, Henry. T Nov 1728 *Forward*. K.
Hart, Henry. LC from *Caesar* Va Jly 1734. X.
Hart, Henry. S Mar 1751. De.
Hart, Hyam. S Jly 1744. So.
Hart, Isaac. S Nov T Dec 1770 *Justitia*. L.
Hart, John. Rebel T 1685.
Hart, John. S & T Jan 1722 *Gilbert* LC Annapolis Jly 1722. L.
Hart, John. S Aug 1728 TB to Md. De.
Hart, John. S Aug 1737. So.
Hart, John. S & R Lent T Oct 1738 *Genoa*. Bu.
Hart, John of St. Botolph Aldgate. S s perukes & T May 1740 *Essex*. M.
Hart, John. S Jly 1750. L.
Hart, John. S & T Sep 1764 *Justitia*. L.
Hart, Joseph. R & T Dec 1734 *Caesar* but died on passage. M.
Hart, Joseph. S Mar 1760 TB to Va. De.
Hart, Joseph of St. John Evangelist. SW s leather saddle Jan 1775. M.
Hart, Margaret wife of Daniel. S Sep-Dec 1746. M.
Hart, Mary. S Mar 1758. So.
Hart, Mathew. S Sep-Oct 1773. M.
Hart, Michael (2). S Oct 1756. L.
Hart, Peter. S & T Sep 1731 *Smith* LC Va 1732. M.
Hart, Robert, a Quaker. R for plantations Jly 1665 (SP). Ht.
Hart, Robert. S Feb T Mar 1730 *Patapsco* LC Annapolis Sep 1730. M.
Hart, Thomas of Standlake. R for America Jly 1681. O.
Hart, Thomas. S Lent 1721. St.
Hart, Thomas. S Lent R 14 yrs Summer 1744. Y.
Hart, Thomas. S Summer 1766. Wa.
Hart, Thomas. T 14 yrs May 1767 *Thornton*. E.
Hart, Thomas. S Oct 1774. L.
Hart, Walter. S May T Sep 1765 *Justitia*. L.
Hart, William. S for burglary Lent 1724 R 14 yrs Lent 1725. Su.
Hart, William. R for life Jan 1757. M.
Hart, William. S Summer 1757 R 14 yrs Lent 1758. Wo.
Hart, William. S Jan-Feb T Apr 1772 *Thornton*. M.
Hartcliffe, Thomas of Atherton, nailer. SQS Apr 1752. La.
Hartford. *See* Harford.
Hartley, Christiana. R for Barbados or Jamaica Mar 1688. M.
Hartley, Francis. T Apr 1734 *Patapsco*. K.
Hartley, George. S Summer 1724 R 14 yrs Summer TB Sep 1725. Nt.
Hartley, George of Whitwell. SQS Richmond Jan TB Sep 1759. Y.

Hartley als Hatley, Hannah. S Feb T 14 yrs Mar 1730 *Patapsco* LC Md Sep 1730. L.

Hartley, Harry. S Feb T Apr 1743 *Justitia*. M.

Hartley, Henry of Lostock, miller. R for Barbados Jly 1683. La.

Hartley, James. S & T 14 yrs Sep 1718 *Eagle* LC Charles Town Mar 1719. L.

Hartley, James. S Apr T May 1750 *Lichfield*. M.

Hartley, John. S Feb-Apr T May 1752 *Lichfield*. M.

Hartley, John. S Summer 1752. Su.

Hartley, Sarah. S s linen Dec 1735 T Jan 1736 *Dorsetshire* LC Va Sep 1736. M.

Hartley, Thomas. R Aug AT Oct 1701. M.

Hartley, William. R 14 yrs Summer 1753. Cu.

Hartley, William. T 14 yrs Apr 1768 *Thornton*. K.

Hartley, William. S Lent 1775. Y.

Hartliff, Alice. S Summer 1759. La.

Hartling, John. S s from warehouse Lent R 14 yrs Summer 1769. Wa.

Hartman, William. S Feb 1775. L.

Hartness, George. S s at Swyncombe Summer 1744. O.

Hartnes, William. R Feb 1675. M.

Hartshorne, John. R for America Jly 1688. Le.

Harteshorne, Nathaniel of Denham. R for America Feb 1688. Bu.

Hartshorn, Susannah. S Sep T Nov 1743 *George William*. M.

Hartwell, John. S for highway robbery at Wolverton & R Lent T Apr 1770 *New Trial*. Bu.

Hartwell, Joseph. S Lent 1749. Bd.

Harty, John. Rebel T 1685.

Harvey, Abigall (1719). *See* Green. Sy.

Harvey, Ann. S Oct T Dec 1767 *Neptune*. M.

Harvey, Ann. S Apr T 14 yrs May 1770 *Essex* to Md or Va. M.

Harvy, Benjamin. R May TB Jun 1691. M.

Harvey, Charles. SQS Feb 1774. M.

Harvey, Daniel. S Jun 1747. L.

Harvey, David. S Aug 1773. Co.

Harvey, Edward. S Summer 1749 R 14 yrs Lent T May 1750 *Lichfield*. E.

Harvey, Edward. SQS Apr TB May 1767. So.

Harvey, Edward. R Mar 1773. Co.

Harvey, Elizabeth of Chinnock. R for Barbados Jly 1683. Do.

Harvey, Elizabeth. S Mar 1763 TB to Va. De.

Harvey, Humphrey. R 14 yrs Aug 1767 TB to Va. De.

Harvey, Isabella. S Jan-Feb T Apr 1753 *Thames*. M.

Harvey, James. S for burglary Lent R Summer 1741 (SP). Sh.

Harvey, James. T May 1752 *Lichfield*. Ht.

Harvey als Gale als Galloway, John. R for plantations Feb 1656. L.

Harvey als Harris, John. R 12 yrs for Barbados Jan 1663 & Jan 1664. L.

Harvey, John of Halstead. R for Barbados or Jamaica Feb 1684. E.

Harvey, John. T Oct 1732 *Caesar*. Sy.

Harvey, John. S Mar 1746. So.

Harvey, John. R 14 yrs Jly 1747. Ha.

Harvey, John. S Jly-Dec 1747. M.

Harvey, John. S Jan-Apr 1748. M.

Harvey, John. S s leather at Dursley Lent 1759. G.

Harvey, John. S Jan T Apr 1768 *Thornton*. M.

Harvey, Jonathan. S Mar 1729. Co.

Harvey, Jonathan. T Apr 1770 *New Trial*. E.

Harvey, Martha. R for Barbados Mar 1683. M.

Harvey, Martha. T 14 yrs May 1767 *Thornton*. E.

Harvey als Coates, Mary. S & T Jan 1722 *Gilbert* LC Annapolis Jly 1722. L.

Harvey, Mary wife of Thomas. S & T Apr 1725 *Sukey* LC Annapolis Sep 1725. M.

Harvy, Mary. S Feb T Mar 1729 *Patapsco* LC Annapolis Dec 1729. M.

Harvey, Mary. S Aug 1758. Co.

Harvey, Rebecca. R for America May 1704. L.

Harvey, Richard. S Feb-Apr T Jun 1756 *Lyon*. M.

Harvey, Richard. R 14 yrs Mar 1773. Co.

Harvey, Robert. R for Barbados Sep 1672. L.

Harvey, Robert. S Jly 1731. Wi.

Harvey, Samuel. Rebel T 1685.

Harvey, Sarah. S Jan-Feb T Apr 1771 *Thornton*. M.

Harvey, Sofia. T Apr 1732 *Patapsco*. Sy.

Harvey, Susannah. S Dec 1743 T Feb 1744 *Neptune* to Md. M.

Harvey, Thomas. S Oct T Nov 1725 *Rappahannock* to Va. M.

Harvey, Thomas. TB to Va from QS 1768. De.

Harvey, Thomas. SQS Oct 1771 TB Apr 1772. So.

Harvey, Thomas. S & R for life Summer 1773. St.

Harvey, William. R for Barbados Jly 1680. M.

Harvy, William. Rebel T 1685.

Harvey, William. S Oct T Dec 1724 *Rappahannock* to Va. M.

Harvey, William. S & T Oct 1732 *Caesar* to Va. M.

Harvey, William. S Jly 1740. Ha.

Harvey, William. S Feb-Apr T May 1751 *Tryal*. M.

Harwar, Matthew of Enfield. PT Jan R Mar 1685. M.

Harward als Howard, Anne. S Feb 1656. M.

Harwich, Philip. S Mar 1761. Ha.

Harwood als Churchman, Ann. S Aug T Sep 1725 *Forward* LC Annapolis Dec 1725. L.

Harwood, Elizabeth. S Apr-May 1754. M.

Harwood, George of Livesay. R for Barbados Jly 1679. La.

Harwood, James. S Lent 1753. Nf.

Harwood, John. Rebel T 1685.

Harwood, John. S s at Wentbridge Lent 1723 T Feb 1726 *Supply* LC Md May 1726. Y.

Harwood, John. S Jan 1751. M.

Harwood, John. T Sep 1767 *Justitia*. Sx.

Harwood als Howard, John. SW & T Jan 1769 *Thornton*. M.

Harwood, Leonard. S s at St. Mary, Reading, Lent 1756. Be.

Harwood, Margaret (1727). *See* Taylor. L.

Harwood als Badger als Radford, Mary. S Feb T 14 yrs Mar 1730 *Patapsco* LC Md Sep 1730. M.

Harwood, Mary of St. Martin in Fields, spinster. S s gold coins Oct 1740 T Jan 1741 *Harpooner* to Rappahannock. M.

Harwood, Mary. S Feb T Apr 1770 *New Trial.* L.

Harwood, Robert (1749). *See* Sherrard. L.

Harwood, Sarah. S Apr 1761. M.

Harwood, Thomas. R for Barbados & TB Oct 1667. L.

Harwood, Thomas. S Dec 1719 T May 1720 *Honor* but escaped in Vigo, Spain. L.

Harwood, Thomas. S Summer T Sep 1768. Li.

Harwood, William. T May 1737 *Forward.* E.

Harwood, William. S s horse Lent R 14 yrs Summer 1740 (SP). Hu.

Haseldine, Grace. S Oct T Nov 1759 *Phoenix.* M.

Hasledine, Nathaniel. LC from *Dorsetshire* Va Sep 1736. X.

Haselwood. *See* Hazlewood.

Hasham, John. T for life Apr 1770 *New Trial.* E.

Hasker, John. S Feb T May 1767 *Thornton.* L.

Haskett, Ann. S Aug 1767. Do.

Haskey, John of Stone. R for America Jun 1714. St.

Haskins, Elizabeth (1768). *See* Hoskins. M.

Haskins, Thomas. S Sep-Dee 1755 T Jan 1756 *Greyhound.* M.

Haslam, Ellis (1775). *See* Hampson, John. La.

Haslam, James. S Lent 1769. La.

Haselam als Slice, John of Stafford. S s cow Lent AT Summer 1719. St.

Haslegrave, Martha wife of John. S City 14 yrs for receiving; said John & Robert Haslegrave acquitted. Y.

Haslegrove, John. S Jly T Sep 1764 *Justitia.* M.

Haslehurst, William. S s crockery at Old Swinford Lent 1756. Wo.

Haslip, Thomas. S Sep-Oct 1772. M.

Hassell, Ann. S Sep T Nov 1762 *Prince William.* M.

Hassell, Nicholas. TB to Va from QS 1740. De.

Hassell, Richard. S Dec 1742 T 14 yrs Apr 1743 *Bond.* L.

Hassen, George of North Kelsey. R for America Jly 1673. Li.

Hassey, Ann. S & T Oct 1730 *Forward* LC Potomack Jan 1731. L.

Hastellow, John. S Lent R 14 yrs Summer 1748. Wa.

Hastilow, Susanna. S s table linen at Drayton Bassett Lent 1757. St.

Hastings, Elizabeth. SQS Jan 1751. M.

Hastings, James. S & T Apr 1733 *Patapsco* LC Annapolis Nov 1733. L.

Hastings, John. S Feb T Mar 1727 *Rappahannock.* L.

Hastings, John, als Lord Hastings. S Oct-Dec 1739 T Jan 1740 *York.* M.

Hastings, John. R Summer 1774. Sx.

Hastings, Katherine. S May T Jun 1726 *Loyal Margaret* to Md. M.

Hastings, Martha. S Mar 1754. L.

Hastings, Mary (1740). *See* Steward. M.

Hastings, Mary. SL Oct 1754. Sy.

Hasty, Ann. S Feb-Apr T May 1755 *Rose.* M.

Hasty, Thomas of Millhouse, Haltwistle, shoemaker. R for Barbados Jly 1686. Nl.

Hatch, Ann (1773). *See* Griffith. M.

Hatch, Daniel. S Oct 1765 T Jan 1766 *Tryal.* M.

Hatch als Deeble als Dinham, Joseph. R 14 yrs Aug 1746. De.

Hatch, William. R 14 yrs Mar 1737. De.

Hatch, William. S Dec 1772. M.

Hatcher, George. T Dec 1734 *Caesar.* K.

Hatcher, George. S Jun-Dec 1738 T Jan 1739 *Dorsetshire* to Va. M.
Hatcher, John of Worth. R for Barbados or Jamaica Jly 1696. Sx.
Hatchet, Joseph. S Oct-Dec 1750. M.
Hatchman, George. S Mar 1774. Ha.
Hatchman, John. S & T Sep 1765 *Justitia*. M.
Hatfield, Frances. S Lent 1769. Li.
Hatfield, Joseph of Plaistow. R for Barbados or Jamaica Jly 1702. E.
Hatfield, Mary. TB Apr 1765. Db.
Hatfield, Susanna. S Feb T May 1767 *Thornton*. L.
Hatfield, William. T Sep 1742 *Forward*. K.
Hathaway, Thomas (1662). *See* Haddoway. M.
Hathaway, Thomas (1760). *See* Holloway. G.
Hathaway, William. S s horse Lent R 14 yrs Summer 1743. St.
Hathen, Daniel. S Jan T Mar 1764 *Tryal*. L.
Hather, Christopher of Edwinstow. SQS East Retford s clothing Apr TB
    Dec 1733. Nt.
Hatherick, Robert (1740). *See* Hatherwick. Nl.
Hatherly, Matthew. SQS & TB Jan 1771. Db.
Hatherwick als Hatherick, Robert. S City Summer 1740. Nl.
Hatley, Hannah (1730). *See* Hartley. L.
Hatley, John. S & R 14 yrs Lent 1737. Ca.
Hatsett, Thomas. S for fraud Feb T Apr 1770 *New Trial*. L.
Hatt, Grace. S May-Jly T Sep 1755 *Tryal*. M.
Hatt, John. S Jan-Apr 1749. M.
Hatten, Thomas. S s horse & R 14 yrs Summer 1773. He.
Hatter, John (1733). *See* Walker. M.
Hatter, William (1737). *See* Hatton. M.
Hatterell, Francis. PT Sep 1674. M.
Hatton, Catharine. TB Jun 1738. Db.
Hatton, Edward. S Jun-Dec 1738 T Jan 1739 *Dorsetshire* to Va. M.
Hatton als Hutton, Elizabeth. SQS & T Sep 1766 *Justitia*. M.
Hatten, John, aged 30. R for Barbados Feb 1664. M.
Hatton, John. S May T Jun 1726 *Loyal Margaret* LC Annapolis Oct
    1726. M.
Hatton, Matthew. S Dec 1727. L.
Hatton, Richard. S Oct 1765 T Jan 1766 *Tryal*. L.
Hatton, William of Fisherton Anger. R for Barbados Jly 1667. Wi.
Hatton als Hatter, William. S Jly T Sep 1737 *Pretty Patsy* to Md. M.
Hatton, William. S Jun-Dec 1738 T Jan 1739 *Dorsetshire* to Va. M.
Hatton, William. S s coat at George Inn, Derby, Lent 1764. Db.
Hatton, William. R for life Lent 1773. K.
Haughton. *See* Houghton.
Haulgh, John of Harwood, weaver. SQS Aug 1757. La.
Hault, William. S 14 yrs Jly T Aug 1741 *Betty* from Hull. Nt.
Hauser, Mathew. S Feb T Mar 1729 *Patapsco* to Md. M.
Havard, Ann. S Lent R 14 yrs Summer 1751. He.
Havard, John. S s leather at Abergavenny Lent 1770. Mo.
Havard, William. S s sheep Lent R 14 yrs Summer 1768. Mo.
Haven, Thomas. S Apr T 14 yrs May 1743 *Indian Queen* to
    Potomack. M.
Havener, George of Loughton. SQS Jly 1753. E.

Havergirl, Nathaniel of St. Saviour, Southwark. SQS Apr T Aug 1752 *Tryal*. Sy.

Havers, Elizabeth of Barking. R for Barbados or Jamaica Jly 1710. E.

Havilock, John. S May-Jly 1773. M.

Havitt, Lewis. S Oct 1729. M.

Hawcombe als Holcombe, Thomasine of Tiverton, spinster. R for Barbados Jly 1667. De.

Hawcroft, John (1770). *See* Allcroft. Y.

Haws, Ann. LC from *Elizabeth* Potomack Aug 1729. X.

Hawes, Benjamin. S & T Oct 1729 *Forward* LC Va Jan 1730. L.

Haws, Catherine wife of William. S Jun T Oct 1744 *Susannah*. M.

Hawes, Edward. S Oct 1766 T Jan 1767 *Tryal*. L.

Hawes, George. S Sep-Oct 1774. M.

Hawes, Isaac. S & T Apr 1753 *Thames*. L.

Hawes, James. S Sep T Oct 1750 *Rachael*. M.

Hawes, Jane of Pembury. S Summer T Oct 1739 *Duke of Cumberland*. K.

Hawes, Mary. S Feb T Mar 1731 *Patapsco* LC Annapolis Jun 1731. M.

Hawes, Michael. S & T Apr 1753 *Thames*. L.

Hawes, Richard. S s bread Feb 1738. M.

Hawes, Thomas. S Sep-Oct T Dec 1771 *Justitia*. M.

Hawes, William. S Lent 1749. K.

Hawke, Richard. S 14 yrs Jly 1774. L.

Hawke, William. S Jan-Feb T 14 yrs Apr 1771 *Thornton*. M.

Hawker, Joseph. Rebel T 1685.

Hawker, Joseph. S Mar 1749. So.

Hawker, Timothy. Rebel T 1685.

Hawkeridge, Elizabeth wife of John. S Mar 1738. De.

Hawkes, Elizabeth, spinster. R for America Jly 1706. Wa.

Hawkes, Henry. S Jly T 14 yrs Aug 1721 *Prince Royal* LC Va Nov 1721. M.

Hawks, John. S Lent R 14 yrs Summer 1747. O.

Hawkes, Jonathan. R for Barbados or Jamaica Oct 1690. M.

Hawkes, Joseph. S s sheep Lent R 14 yrs Summer 1745. Bu.

Hawks, Mary. S & T Dec 1724 *Rappahannock*. L.

Hawkes, Robert. S Apr 1754. So.

Hawkes, Thomas. R for America Jly 1694. No.

Hawks, Thomas. S Summer 1761. K.

Hawkes, William. S s clothing Summer 1754. Wo.

Hawkesley, Richard. S Summer R for Barbados Aug 1665. Ht.

Hawkeswood, Richard. S s at Wolverhampton Lent 1727. St.

Hawkesworth als Green, John. PT Sep 1672 R Oct 1673. M.

Hawksworth, William. S Summer 1718 T Lent 1719. Y.

Hawket, James. S Jly T Sep 1765 *Justitia*. M.

Hawkins, Ann. S & T Jan 1736 *Dorsetshire* LC Va Sep 1736. L.

Hawkins, Ann (1744). *See* Wilder. L.

Hawkins, Ann. S Lent 1765. Wa.

Hawkins, Charles Sr. S Lent R 14 yrs Summer 1750. G.

Hawkins, Cornelius. SQS & TB Jan 1758. So.

Hawkins als Dighton, Dorothy. S Jan T Feb 1719 *Worcester* LC Md Jun 1719. L.

Hawkins, Edward of Plaistow. R for Barbados or Jamaica Jly 1702. E.
Hawkins, Elizabeth, aged 21. R for Barbados Feb 1664. M.
Hawkins, Elizabeth. R Dec 1698 AT Jan 1699. M.
Hawkins, Elizabeth. S & T Dec 1731 *Forward*. L.
Hawkins, Elizabeth. T Apr 1732 *Patapsco*. Sy.
Hawkings, Elizabeth. S Mar 1750. Do.
Hawkins, Grace. R for Barbados Dec 1667. M.
Hawkins, Henry (1754). *See* Pugh, Hugh. M.
Hawkins, James. R 14 yrs Aug 1764. Do.
Hawkings, Jane. S Jly 1743. De.
Hawkins, John. S & T Oct 1729 *Forward* LC Va Jun 1730. M.
Hawkins, John. S Jan T Feb 1733 *Smith* to Md or Va. M.
Hawkins, John. S & T May 1744 *Justitia*. L.
Hawkins, John. S May-Jly 1750. M.
Hawkins, John (1767). *See* Allcock. Bu.
Hawkins, John. R Mar 1773. Ha.
Hawkins, John. R for life Lent 1773. Wa.
Hawkins, Joseph. S Jun-Dec 1738 T Jan 1739 *Dorsetshire* to Va. M.
Hawkins, Margaret. S Apr TB May 1718. L.
Hawkins, Margaret. S & T Oct 1732 *Caasar* to Va. M.
Hawkins, Mary. R for Barbados Feb 1664. Su.
Hawkins, Mary. S Aug 1727 T *Forward* LC Rappahannock May 1728. M.
Hawkins, Mary. S & T Jly 1771 *Scarsdale*. M.
Hawkins, Mary. S Oct T Dec 1771 *Justitia*. L.
Hawkins, Peter. S Lent R 14 yrs Summer 1750. G.
Hawkins, Reuben. SQS Feb 1774. M.
Hawkins als Wood, Richard of Stogumber. R for Barbados Feb 1698. So.
Hawkins, Richard (1714). *See* Kerle. De.
Hawkins, Richard. S Sep-Oct 1775. M.
Hawkins, Thomas. S Summer R for Barbados Aug 1663. E.
Hawkins, Thomas. S Aug T Oct 1724 *Forward* LC Annapolis Jun 1725. M.
Hawkins, Thomas. S Mar 1727. Wi.
Hawkins, Thomas Jr. S Lent 1755. Su.
Hawkins, Thomas. TB to Va from QS 1767. De.
Hawkins, Ursula of Walsall. R for America Jly 1662. St.
Hawkins, William. R for Jamaica Aug 1661. M.
Hawkins, William. S Jly 1719 to be T to Va. De.
Hawkins, William. T Nov 1725 *Rapppahannock* LC Va Aug 1726. K.
Hawkins, William. T Jun 1728 *Elizabeth*. Ht.
Hawkins, William. S Jan T Feb 1733 *Smith* to Md or Va. M.
Hawkins, William. S s at Newbury Lent 1752. Be.
Hawkins, William. S s sheep Lent R 14 yrs Summer 1754. Bd.
Hawkins, William. S Feb 1775. L.
Hawkins, William. S s sheep & R 14 yrs Lent 1775. G.
Hawley, Christopher of Exning. R for Barbados Feb 1664. Su.
Hawley, Edward. R for Barbados or Jamaica Feb 1686. L.
Hawley, Joseph of Great Gaddesden, chimney sweep. SQS Oct 1765 T Jan 1766 *Tryal*. Ht.

Hawley, Martha. S Jan T Feb 1719 *Worcester* LC Annapolis Jun 1719. L.
Hawley, Mary. R for Barbados Mar 1677. L.
Hawley, Oliver of Charlton. R for Barbados Jly 1679. K.
Haworth, George. S Summer 1749. La.
Haworth, John of Bury, weaver. SQS Jan 1771. La.
Hawson, Dennis. T May 1751 *Tryal*. M.
Hawther, Mary. S Feb T Apr 1770 *New Trial*. M.
Hawthorn, Richard. S Lent T Apr 1743 *Justitia*. Bu.
Hawton. *See* Houghton.
Hawtrey, William. S s gelding Lent R 14 yrs Summer T Jly 1724
    Robert. Bu.
Hawwood, Anne. S for shoplifting Summer 1736 R 14 yrs Lent
    1737. Wa.
Haye, Charles. S s wheat at St. Lawrence, Ludlow, Summer 1729. Sh.
Hay, Collin. S Jun T Aug 1769 *Douglas*. M.
Hay, Thomas. S s sheep Summer 1758 R 14 yrs Summer 1759 T Sep
    1759 from London. Nl.
Haybarn, Isaac. S Aug 1727 T *Forward* LC Rappahannock May
    1728. M.
Haburn, Lawrence. S Summer 1738. Y.
Heybourne, Richard. R for America Mar 1697. No.
Hayby, William. S s sheep & R 14 yrs Summer 1775. Li.
Haycock, James (1766). *See* White. Wa.
Haycock, Mary wife of John. S s at Tettenhall Summer 1756. St.
Haycock, Sarah. R & T for life Apr 1770 *New Trial*. M.
Haycocks, Edward. S s at All Saints, Worcester, Summer 1750. Wo.
Haycocks, Samuel. S s at Bitterley Summer 1751. Sh.
Haycraft, James. S Apr-May T May 1744 *Justitia*. M.
Haycroft, John. S Lent T Dec 1734 *Caesar*. Bu.
Haydon, Ann (1767). *See* Adams. M.
Hayden, Bartholomew. SQS Apr 1732. So.
Hayden, Daniel of Hemel Hempstead. R for Barbados Aug 1662. Ht.
Haydon, Eleanor. R 14 yrs Aug 1747. So.
Heden, John. S s sheep & R Lent T Oct 1768 *Justitia*. Bu.
Haydon, John. S Sep-Oct T Dec 1771 *Justitia*. M.
Haydon, Mary (1743). *See* Hoden. L.
Heydon, Michael (1767). *See* Doyle. M.
Haydon, Richard. T Sep 1758 *Tryal*. Sy.
Haydon, Samuel. S s handkerchief & T May 1736 *Patapsco* to Md. M.
Hayden, Thomas. S Jan-Apr 1749. M.
Haydon, Thomas. S Apr T May 1750 *Lichfield*. M.
Heydon, William. S Dec 1749-Jan 1750 T Mar 1750 *Tryal*. M.
Hays, Ann wife of Christian. S Apr-Jun 1739. M.
Hayes, Ann. S Lent 1765. Wa.
Hayes als Trail, Christian. S May T Jun 1764 *Dolphin*. L.
Hays, Elizabeth. S Apr 1748. L.
Hayes, Elizabeth of St. Mary le Strand, spinster. SW Apr T Jly 1772
    Tayloe. M.
Hayes, Frances. S Dec 1753-Jan 1754. M.
Hayes, Francis. S Sep 1718. M.
Hayes, George. R s horse Summer 1728 (SP). Nf.

Hayes, Henry. AT Apr 1675. M.

Hayes, Hercules of Portsmouth, mariner. R for Barbados Mar 1686. Ha.

Hayes, James. S Apr T 14 yrs Sep 1718 *Eagle* but died on passage. L.

Heyes, James of Manchester, weaver. SQS Jan 1757. La.

Hayes, John. R for Barbados or Jamaica Mar 1685. M.

Hays, John (1726). *See* Haigh. Y.

Hayse, John. SQS & T May 1750 *Lichfield*. Ht.

Hayes, Margaret (Mary), aged 30, dark. S Jan T Feb 1723 *Jonathan* LC Md Jly 1724. M.

Hays, Mary (1730). *See* Rusher. M.

Hayes, Philip. S Jan T Mar 1743 *Justitia*. L.

Hayes, Philip. S Summer 1764. Bd.

Hays, Philip. S s at Cookham Summer 1768. Be.

Hayes, Robert. T 14 yrs Dec 1753 *Whiteing*. Sy.

Hayes, Samuel. T Oct 1722 *Forward* LC Md Jun 1723. E.

Hayes, Thomas. S s gelding Summer 1727 R 14 yrs Lent 1729. O.

Hayes, Thomas. S Summer 1736 R 14 yrs Lent 1737. Wa.

Hayes, Thomas. SQS Newark on Trent Jly TB Aug 1738. Nt.

Hayes, Thomas. S Apr-May T May 1741 *Catherine & Elizabeth* to Md. M.

Hayes, Thomas. S Jan 1751. L.

Hayes, Thomas. S & T Jan 1756 *Greyhound*. L.

Hayes, William. Rebel T 1685.

Hayes, William. R Dec 1698 AT Jan 1699. M.

Hayes, William of Chatham. R for Barbados or Jamaica Mar 1707. K.

Hayfield, Mary (1769). *See* Heafield. Le.

Hayington, Cuthbert. S s horse Lent R 14 yrs Summer 1753. Nt.

Hayles. *See* Hales.

Hayley. *See* Haley.

Haylin, Mary. S & T Oct 1720 *Gilbert* to Md. M.

Haylock, Abraham. T Dec 1734 *Caesar*. E.

Hayman, Mary. SQS Jly TB Nov 1746. So.

Hayman, Thomas. S & T Jan 1736 *Dorsetshire* LC Va Sep 1736. L.

Hayman, William. S Apr T Sep 1757 *Thetis*. M.

Haymour, Elizabeth. S May-Jly 1748. M.

Haymer, Mary. T May 1744 *Justitia*. Sy.

Haymian, Charles Christian. S at Sandwich Oct 1728 T Jan 1729 *Sally* LC Va Jun 1729. K.

Hayne, Jacob. R 14 yrs Jly 1733. De.

Hayne, John. Rebel T 1685.

Hayne, John Michael, als Thist, Mathias. R 14 yrs Jly 1765. Ha.

Hayne, Philip. R 14 yrs Aug 1772. Co.

Hayne, Thomas. SQS Jly TB Aug 1749. So.

Heyne, William of Thorncombe. R for Barbados Feb 1665. De.

Haines, Ann wife of Samuel. S Sep 1735 T Jan 1736 *Dorsetshire* LC Va Sep 1736. M.

Haynes, Catherine. S Mar 1759. Ha.

Haynes, Catherine. S & T Mar 1763 *Neptune*. L.

Haynes, Charles of Bourton on the Hill. R for America Feb 1687. G.

Haynes, Edward. S s at Tewkesbury Lent 1774. G.

Haynes, Elizabeth. S Aug T Oct 1741 *Sea Horse*. L.

Haynes, Francis. T Apr 1733 *Patapsco* LC Md Nov 1733. Ht.

Haynes, Francis. S Apr T May 1743 *Indian Queen* to Potomack. M.

Haynes, George. R 14 yrs for Carolina May 1719. L.

Haynes, Henry. T 14 yrs Sep 1767 *Justitia*. Sx.

Haines, Isaiah. S s lead from Lady Beauclerk at Somerset House Jan T Mar 1764 *Tryal*. M.

Haynes, James. S & T 14 yrs Mar 1763 *Neptune*. L.

Haynes, John. S & T Sep 1731 *Smith* LC Va 1732. M.

Haines, John. R 14 yrs Mar TB to Va Apr 1741. Wi.

Haynes, John. S May 1745. M.

Haynes, John. S Aug 1754. De.

Haines, John. S & T Apr 1766 *Ann*. L.

Haynes, John. S & T Sep 1766 *Justitia*. L.

Haynes, John. R 14 yrs Aug 1767 TB to Va. De.

Haines, Joseph. T Jun 1764 *Dolphin*. Ht.

Haynes, Joseph. S Apr 1767. So.

Haynes, Richard of Redbourn. R for Barbados or Jamaica Feb 1684 & Feb 1686. Ht.

Haynes, Richard. S s mare Lent R Summer 1725, died on passage in *Rappahannock* 1726.. No.

Haynes, Richard. T Apr 1765 *Ann*. K.

Haynes, Robert. R for Barbados Sep 1669. M.

Hains, Robert (1765). *See* Ainsworth. Bu.

Haynes, Samuel. S Mar 1736. Wi.

Haines, Sarah, aged 25, dark. LC from *Gilbert* Annapolis May 1721. X.

Haines, Sarah. S May T Jly 1722 *Alexander*. L.

Haynes, Thomas. AT for attending conventicle Summer & Winter 1668. Bd.

Haines als Sendry, Thomas Jr. of Pangbourne. R for America Feb 1713. Be.

Haines, Thomas of Prees. S Lent 1741. Sh.

Haynes, Thomas. S Jun-Dec 1745. M.

Haynes, William. Rebel T 1685.

Haines, William. SQS Jan TB Nov 1726. So.

Haynes, William. S Sep-Oct T Dec 1752 *Greyhound*. M.

Haynes, William. S Jan T Apr 1759 *Thetis*. M.

Haynes, William. SQS May 1763. M.

Haynes, William (1767). *See* Hams. St.

Haynes, Winefred. S Apr T May 1719 *Margaret*; sold to John Welch Md Aug 1719. L.

Heynam, Thomas. R 14 yrs Mar 1758. So.

Haynham, Thomas Milton. S Apr 1775. So.

Hayopp, George of Newcastle upon Tyne. R for Barbados Jly 1705. Nl.

Hays. *See* Hayes.

Hayter, John. R 14 yrs Jly 1737. Wi.

Haythorne als Smythhurst, Nathaniel of Leathley. R for Barbados Jun 1675. Y.

Heyton, Ann of St. Saviour, Southwark. R for Barbados or Jamaica Feb 1690. Sy.

Hayton, Anne (1729). *See* Heaton. Cu.

Hayton, Ann. S Feb T Apr 1770 *New Trial*. M.

Hayton, Robert of Great Horkesley. R for Barbados or Jamaica Jly 1705. E.
Hayton, William. S s at Hanley Child Lent 1759. Wo.
Hayward, Anne. T Oct 1722 *Forward*. E.
Hayward, Francis. S Lent R 14 yrs Summer 1757. Sh.
Hayward, Francis. S s at Stirchley Lent 1766. Sh.
Hayward, James. S Mar 1730. Wi.
Hayward, Job. S Aug 1773. So.
Hayward, John of Frogg Mill. R for America Feb 1673. G.
Heyward, John of Tooting. R for Barbados or Jamaica Jun 1675. Sy.
Hayward, John (1768). *See* Haywood. L.
Hayward, John (1771). *See* Howard. M.
Hayward, Joseph (1760). *See* Yearwood. L.
Hayward, Joseph. T Dec 1763 *Neptune*. K.
Hayward, Joseph. S Sep T Dec 1767 *Neptune*. M.
Hayward, Mary. R for Barbados Dec 1667. M.
Hayward, Samuel. S Lent R 14 yrs Summer 1757. Sh.
Hayward, Sarah. S Mar 1755. Ha.
Hayward, Simon. S Mar 1766. De.
Hayward, Thomas of Bourton Shrivenham, blacksmith. R for Barbados Feb 1688. Wi.
Hayward, Thomas. S Mar TB to Va Apr 1765. Wi.
Hayward, Thomas. S Lent 1775. Sy.
Hayward, William of Great Brickhill. S Summer 1720. Bu.
Hayward, William. S s silver at Chipping Norton Summer 1770. O.
Haywarding, John. S Aug 1746 TB to Va Jun 1747. Wi.
Haywood, John. S s beans Lent 1752. St.
Heywood, John. R 14 yrs for killing sheep Summer 1767. Wa.
Heywood, John. S s handkerchief at St. Lawrence Jewry Apr T Jun 1768 *Tryal*. L.
Haywood, Joseph (1760). *See* Yearwood. L.
Heywood, Matthew. S s horse Summer 1749 R 14 yrs Lent 1750. La.
Haywood, Robert. Rebel T 1685.
Haywood, Robert. T Oct 1729 *Forward*. Bu.
Haywood, Thomas (1756). *See* Baker. No.
Haywood, William. S Aug 1720 T Mar 1723. Bu.
Haywood, William. S & T Sep 1755 *Tryal*. L.
Haywood, William. S Feb T Apr 1770 *New Trial*. L.
Hayworth, Thomas. R 14 yrs Summer 1730. Y.
Hazard, John. S Summer 1759 R 14 yrs Lent 1760. Nt.
Hazard, John, aged 26, 5'10" tall, brown complexion, born at Melburn, Derbys. S s cheese from boat at Farnden Lent 1773. Nt.
Hazard, Richard. S & T Oct 1732 *Caesar* to Va. M.
Hazard, Walter. S Jun-Dec 1738 T Jan 1739 *Dorsetshire* to Va. M.
Hazard, William. S Jan-Jun T Jun 1728 *Elizabeth* LC Potomack Aug 1729. M.
Hazard, William. SQS Jly 1774. M.
Hazzard, Zachariah. S s from warehouse Lent R 14 yrs Summer 1739. Li.
Hazell, John. R for life Mar TB to Va Apr 1767. Wi.
Hazell, Robert. SWK Oct 1773. K.

Hazledine, William (1775). *See* Johnson. M.

Haslewood, Elizabeth. PT Jly 1672. M.

Hazlewood, Elizabeth wife of John *(qv)*. R (Western Circ) for Barbados Feb 1699. L.

Hazlewood, Jacob. T Jun 1764 *Dolphin*. E.

Hazlewood, John. R (Western Circ) for Barbados Feb 1699. L.

Hazlewood als Earsly, Philip. T Oct 1720 *Gilbert*. E.

Haselwood, Thomas. S Mar 1752. So.

Haselwood, Thomas. S Mar 1768. So.

Heachstone, William. S Jan T Feb 1726 *Supply* LC Annapolis May 1726. M.

Head, Anne of Newington, spinster. SQS Apr T May 1750 *Lichfield*. Sy.

Head, Edward. T Sep 1742 *Forward*. Ht.

Head, Edward. T Sep 1749. Ht.

Head, James. S May 1761. M.

Head, John. S & T 14 yrs Oct 1730 *Forward* LC Potomack Jan 1731. M.

Head, Robert. S & T Oct 1732 *Caesar* to Va. M.

Head, Samuel. S & T Sep 1742 *Forward*. L.

Head, William. S Sep T Dec 1769 *Justitia*. M.

Headach, Dinah, spinster. S s at Reading Lent 1770. Be.

Headdon, William. S Mar 1733. De.

Headford, John. T Jun 1738 *Forward*. Sy.

Heading, Nower, als Hadon, Noal. T Aug 1721 *Owners Goodwill* LC Md Jly 1722. E.

Headley, James. S Summer TB Sep 1759. Db.

Headley, John. S & T Jan 1722 *Gilbert* LC Annapolis Jly 1722. M.

Headley, John. S 14 yrs for receiving Summer TB Sep 1759. Db.

Headley, Mary. S 14 yrs for receiving Summer 1756. Db.

Headly, Michael. R 14 yrs s horse Lent 1764. Li.

Headley, Rebecca wife of James *(qv)*. S Summer TB Sep 1759. Db.

Headman, William. S Apr 1742. Ha.

Heafield als Hayfield, Mary. S Jly TB to Va Aug 1769. Le.

Heald, John. T Sep 1767 *Justitia*. E.

Hele, Edward. S Mar 1742. De.

Heale, James. Rebel T 1685.

Hele als Coryton, John. S Aug 1767. Co.

Hele, Robert. TB to Va from QS 1743. De.

Heeley, Caleb. S Summer 1769. Wa.

Healey, Edward. S & T Sep 1766 *Justitia*. M.

Healey, Elizabeth. S & T Jan 1766 *Tryal*. M.

Healey, James. S s sheep Lent R Summer 1751. La.

Healey, James (1756). *See* Lees. La.

Healey, John. S Jun T Jly 1772 *Tayloe*. L.

Hely, Joseph. S Jly-Sep 1754. M.

Healy, William. S Summer 1753 R 14 yrs Lent 1754. La.

Healowe, William of Nottingham. R for America Jly 1678. Nt.

Heaney, John (1742). *See* Haney. L.

Heap, Lucian als Resolution. S & R 14 yrs Lent 1775. Ch.

Heape, Samuel of St. Luke. S s candles Apr T May 1740 *Essex* to Md or Va. M.

Heard, Abednego of Cadeleigh. R for Barbados Jly 1679. De.

Heard, Archibald. S & T Jly 1753 *Tryal*. L.

Hurd, Edmund. Rebel T 1685.

Heard, George of Hartland. R for Barbados Jly 1717. De.

Heard, George. R 14 yrs Jly 1735. Co.

Hurd, Hannah of York, spinster. R for Barbados Feb 1697. Y.

Heard, Henry. S Mar 1731 TB to Va. De.

Hurd, James. Rebel T 1685.

Heard, James. T 14 yrs Apr 1768 *Thornton*. E.

Heard, John of Holcombe Burnell. R for Barbados Mar 1691. De.

Herd, Samuel. R for Barbados or Jamaica Dec 1695. L.

Heard, Susan. R for Barbados Dec 1681. L.

Hurd, Thomas. Rebel T 1685.

Hearnden, Thomas. T Apr 1771 *Thornton*. K.

Hern, Aaron. S for highway robbery at Cardington & R 14 yrs Lent 1773. Bd.

Hearn, Bew. S Lent R 14 yrs Summer 1750. O.

Herne, Edward of Ormskirk, tinker. SQS Jly 1765. La.

Hurn, Isaac. S Mar TB to Va Apr 1765. Wi.

Herne, Jeremiah, a Quaker. R for plantations Jly 1665 (SP). Ht.

Hearne, John. S Dec 1753-Jan 1754. M.

Hern, John (1755). *See* Hunn. Nf.

Hearn, John. S Nov T Dec 1763 *Neptune*. L.

Herne, John. SQS & T Jun 1764 *Dolphin*. Ht.

Herne, Mary. SQS Feb 1771. M.

Herne, Peeling. R Jly 1774. M.

Hearne, Thomas. S 7 yrs in Barbados Jun 1671. M.

Herne, Thomas of Ewell. SQS Jan 1751. Sy.

Hearsey, Thomas. R 14 yrs Mar 1767. Ha.

Hearst. *See* Hurst.

Heartgrave, Isaac. LC from *Rappahannock* at Rappahannock Apr 1726. X.

Heartsworth, William. S Summer 1766 R 14 yrs Lent 1767. Bd.

Heasman, George. S Apr 1774. M.

Heater, James. S Aug T Oct 1741 *Sea Horse* to Va. M.

Heath, Bartholomew als James. T Jun 1728 *Elizabeth* LC Va Aug 1729. Sy.

Heath, Charles. S Jly-Dec 1747. M.

Heath, Henry. S & T Oct 1732 *Caesar* to Va. M.

Heath, James. S May T Jly 1723 *Alexander* LC Annapolis Sep 1723. M.

Heath, James (1728). *See* Heath, Bartholomew. Sy.

Heath, James. S for killing sheep Summer 1756 R 14 yrs Lent TB Apr T Aug 1757 *Lux*. Db.

Heath, John. R for America Aug 1713. L.

Heath, John. S s clothing at Clent Summer 1723. St.

Heath, John. T Sep 1730 *Smith*. E.

Heath, John. S Jan T Apr 1759 *Thetis*. M.

Heath, John, als Rutland, James. R 14 yrs Summer 1764. Nt.

Heath, Mary. S Oct 1756. L.

Heath, Richard. R 14 yrs Jly 1748. Ha.

Heath, Robert. S Aug T Sep 1725 *Forward* LC Annapolis Dec 1725. M.

Heath, Robert. T 14 yrs Sep 1766 *Justitia*. K.

Heath, Robert. S s horse Summer 1767 R 14 yrs Lent 1768. St.

Heath, Samuel. S Lent 1764. O.

Heath, Sarah of Beeding or Seale (?Surrey). R for Barbados or Jamaica Mar 1694. Sx.

Heath, Thomas. R for America Feb 1700. Le.

Heath, Thomas. S Oct 1756. L.

Heath, Thomas. S s hat looping at Stone Lent 1769. St.

Heath als Snapp, William. S for highway robbery Lent R 14 yrs Summer 1749. Le.

Heath, William. S Lent R 14 yrs Summer 1752. St.

Heathcote, Isaac. SQS & T Sep 1757 *Thetis*. M.

Heathcote, James. S Apr T May 1720 *Honor* LC Port York Jan 1721. L.

Heathcote, Lydia. T 14 yrs Apr 1759 *Thetis*. Sy.

Heathcote, Lydia. S 14 yrs Summer 1773. Sy.

Heathcote, Robert. S 14 yrs Summer 1773. Sy.

Heathcote, Thomas. T Apr 1759 *Thetis*. Sy.

Heather, Elizabeth. T May 1719 *Margaret* LC Md Sep 1719; sold to Samuel White. Sy.

Heather, Jasper. S Mar 1766. Ha.

Heather, Mary. S Jan T Mar 1764 *Tryal*. L.

Heathfield, John. Rebel T 1685.

Heathfield, Margaret. R for Barbados Sep 1669. M.

Heathfield, Thomas of Croydon. S Lent T May 1750 *Lichfield*. Sy.

Heathier, William. S Mar 1773. Co.

Heathwood, Thomas. S Jly 1764. Ha.

Heaton als Hayton, Anne. S Summer 1729. Cu.

Heaten, Elizabeth. LC from *Forward* Annapolis Dec 1725. X.

Heaton, John. S Jly T Sep 1755 *Tryal*. L.

Heaton, John. S Dec 1764 T Jan 1765 *Tryal*. M.

Heaton, Jonathan. S s from warehouse at Sheffield Lent 1766. Y.

Heaton, Thomas. S for highway robbery at Jarrow & R 14 yrs Summer 1775. Du.

Heaverland, William. S Jun 1754. L.

Heavysides, William. S Summer 1740. Y.

Heayer, Lewis. R for Barbados or Jamaica Mar 1688. L.

Hebb, Matthew. S Feb T Apr 1770 *New Trial*. L.

Hebb, Thomas. S Mar 1773. Ha.

Hebberd, Jehoakim. S Mar TB to Va Apr 1764. Wi.

Heber, John. S Dec 1742 T Apr 1743 *Justitia*. M.

Heckler, Thomas Jr. AT City Summer 1750. Y.

Heckman, Mary of St. John, Wapping, spinster. S s clothing & T Feb 1740 *York* to Md. M.

Heddington, Richard. S for highway robbery Summer 1726 R 14 yrs Lent 1727. O.

Heddye als Goodday, Peter of Manchester. SQS Oct 1748. La.

Heden. *See* Hayden.

Hedge, Charles. S Lent 1763. Wa.

Hedges, William. S Feb T Apr 1769 *Tryal*. M.

Hedgley, Richard. S May T Jly 1722 *Alexander*. L.

Heirs als Ayres als Forth, John. S & R 14 yrs Lent 1769. Be.

Helenford, Phillip. S Jun T Sep 1767 *Justitia*. M.

Hellard, Bryan. R 14 yrs Mar 1764. So.

Helliar, John. R 14 yrs Jly 1728. Ha.

Helliar, Mary, als Awbury, Martha. S Mar 1753. Ha.

Hellier, Richard. R 14 yrs Aug 1742. De.

Hellyer, Robert. Rebel T 1685.

Hellyer, Thomas. Rebel T 1685.

Helliar, William. S Jly 1721. Wi.

Hellier, William. SQS Apr TB Jly 1729. So.

Hellier, William. S Mar 1741. Do.

Helligan, Katherine (1672). *See* Wyat. Co.

Helliwell, John. AT Lent 1766. Y.

Hellum, Dorothy. S & T Oct 1720 *Gilbert* but died on passage. M.

Helman, Stephen. Rebel T 1685.

Helmes, George. R 14 yrs Jly 1724. De.

Helmes, Henry. T Sep 1730 *Smith*. Sy.

Helmsley, William. R 14 yrs Summer 1740. Y.

Helps, John. Rebel T 1685.

Helsteed, George of Bristol. R for Barbados Feb 1697. G.

Helston, Mary. S Mar 1720 T May 1720 *Honor* to York River. L.

Helton, Elizabeth. T May 1723 *Victory*. K.

Hemas, Joseph. S s clothing at Wombourne Lent 1738. St.

Hemble als Hamble, Jane. R 14 yrs Summer 1755. Y.

Hemingway, John. S Summer 1772. Li.

Hemingway, Richard. S s gelding Lent 1746. Y.

Hemmery als Horton, Robert. S Oct T Dec 1769 *Justitia*. L.

Hemmet als Hemmon, John. S Aug 1739. De.

Heming, Francis. S Lent R 14 yrs Summer 1751. Wo.

Heminge, John of Worcester. R for America Jly 1678. Wo.

Hemming, John. SQS Jly T Sep 1764 *Justitia*. M.

Heming, Thomas (1722). *See* Jones. Sh.

Hemming, William. S s mare & R 14 yrs Summer 1772. G.

Hemmings, James. SQS & T Sep 1765 *Justitia*. M.

Hemmings, John. S for receiving stolen goods from his wife Sarah *(qv)* Lent 1767. St.

Hemmings, Sarah wife of John *(qv)*. S for shoplifting Lent R for life Summer 1767. St.

Hemings, Susanna. S & T Oct 1730 *Forward* LC Potomack Jan 1731. M.

Hemmon, John (1739). *See* Hemmet. De.

Hempson, Thomas of Rowley, yeoman. R for America Feb 1713. St.

Hempstead, John. SQS Dec 1766 T Jan 1767 *Tryal*. M.

Hemstock, John (1725). *See* Kempstock. Sy.

Henderson, Archibald. S s sheep Summer 1744. Nl.

Henderson, Elizabeth. S Jan T Feb 1726 *Supply* LC Annapolis May 1726. M.

Henderson als Anderson, James. S s horse Summer 1736 R 14 yrs Summer 1737. Cu.

Henderson, Jane. S Sep-Oct 1775. M.

Henderson als Haggerston, John. S s horse Summer 1743 R 14 yrs Summer 1744. Nl.

Handerson, John. S Apr-May 1754. M.

Henderson, Mary. S City s at Holy Trinity Micklegate Lent 1766. Y.

Henderson, Thomas of Newcastle upon Tyne. R for Barbados Jly 1705. Nl.
Henderson, William. T May 1751 *Tryal*. K.
Hendley. *See* Handley.
Hendon, Susan wife of Lewis. S Feb 1729. M.
Hendrick, John. S Jun T Nov 1743 *George William*. L.
Hendry, Leonard. S May T 14 yrs Jly 1722 *Alexander* to Nevis or Jamaica. M.
Hendry als Remington, Thomas. R for Barbados Sep TB Oct 1669. L.
Hendy, George. S Aug 1740. So.
Hindy, James. S Jly TB to Va Sep 1738. Wi.
Hendy, James. S Feb 1758. Ha.
Hendy, John. SQS Jly 1735. So.
Hendy, Thomas. Rebel T 1685.
Henley, Alice. S May T Jly 1722 *Alexander* to Nevis or Jamaica. M.
Henley, Ann. S Aug T Sep 1725 *Forward* LC Annapolis Dec 1725. L.
Henley, Ardell. S & T Dec 1771 *Justitia*. M.
Henly, Dorothy. S Apr T Oct 1719 *Susannah & Sarah* LC Annapolis Apr 1720. L.
Henley, George. S Lent 1768. Su.
Henly, Hannah. S Aug T Oct 1724 *Forward* LC Annapolis Jun 1725. M.
Henley, James. SQS Apr T May 1767 *Thornton*. M.
Henley, Mary. S Jan-Apr 1749. M.
Henley, Mathew. S & T Dec 1767 *Neptune*. M.
Henly, Ralph (1720). *See* Finley. L.
Henley, Rebecca. S Aug T Sep 1725 *Forward* LC Annapolis Dec 1725. M.
Henley, Sarah. S Jun T Nov 1743 *George William*. L.
Henly, William. S Feb 1758. Ha.
Henley, William. S Oct T Dec 1770 *Justitia*. M.
Henna, William. S Aug 1736. De.
Hennick, Rachael. S Sep 1761. M.
Henning, Jane. S Feb T Apr 1762 *Dolphin*. M.
Henrord, Edward (1767). *See* Harrord. E.
Henry, Elizabeth. TB to Va from QS 1740. De.
Henry, George. S Apr 1742. M.
Henry, John (1773). *See* Godfrey. Do.
Henry, Mary. S Oct T Dec 1767 *Neptune*. M.
Henshaw, Charles. S ec 1741 T Feb 1742 *Industry* to Md. M.
Henshaw, Isabella. Died on passage in *Rappahannock* 1726. X.
Henshaw, John. T Oct 1721 *William & John*. K.
Henshaw, John. S Oct 1765 T Jan 1766 *Tryal*. L.
Henshaw, John. S Sep T Dec 1767 *Neptune*. L.
Henshaw, Joseph. S s at Penkridge Lent 1739. St.
Henshaw, Nicholas. T Oct 1720 *Gilbert*. Sy.
Hensley, John. Rebel T 1685.
Hensley, Joseph. R for Barbados or Jamaica Feb 1687. L.
Hensman, Richard. R for Barbados Feb 1664. L.
Henson, John. Rebel T 1685.
Henson, John. S Aug TB Sep 1770. Le.
Henson, John. S s at Castle Thorpe Lent T Apr 1771 *Thornton*. Bu.

Hensor, John. S Jly 1718 to be T to Boston NE. Wi.

Henzey, Benjamin. S s at Old Swinford Lent 1753. St.

Heppard, William. S Aug 1726. M.

Hepper, John. R for Jamaica Aug 1661 & Oct 1662. M.

Hepworth, John. S Dec 1741 T Feb 1742 *Industry* to Md. M.

Hepworth, Richard. S Summer TB Aug 1749. Y.

Herbert, Anne. S & T Oct 1729 *Forward* LC Va Jun 1730. M.

Herbert, Anne (Hannah). S & T Apr 1733 *Patapsco* LC Annapolis Nov 1733. L.

Herbert, Arthur. S Apr TB May 1719. L.

Herbert, Benjamin. S Feb T Apr 1772 *Thornton*. L.

Herbert, Charles. SQS Apr T May 1767 *Thornton*. M.

Herbert, Elizabeth. R for Barbados Dec 1670. M.

Herbert, Elizabeth. S May T Jun 1727 *Susanna* to Va. M.

Herbert, Elizabeth. S Jan-May T Jun 1738 *Forward* to Md or Va. M.

Herbert, Elizabeth. S Aug T Oct 1741 *Sea__Horse* to Va. M.

Herbert, Henry of Abingdon. R for America Mar 1710. Be.

Herbert, James. S s at Morton Valence Lent TB Mar 1748. G.

Herbert, Mary. S Apr TB May 1719. L.

Herbert, Mary. S Sep-Oct 1748 T Jan 1749 *Laura*. M.

Herbert, Richard. S Aug 1727 T *Forward* LC Rappahannock May 1728. M.

Herbert, Sarah. S & T 14 yrs Jan 1722 *Gilbert* LC Annapolis Jly 1722. M.

Herbert, Thomas. S Oct T Nov 1725 *Rappahannock* LC Rappahannock Apr 1726. M.

Herbert, Thomas. S Sep-Oct T Dec 1771 *Justitia*. M.

Herbert als Harbar, William. S Lent 1765. Su.

Herbert, William. R Apr 1773. M.

Herbert, William. R Jly 1775. M.

Herbert, William. S s silver teaspoon at Ampney Summer 1775. G.

Herd. *See* Heard.

Herdman, Thomas (1733). *See* Dobson. Y.

Herdman, Thomas (1734). *See* Dobson, John. Nl.

Herdon als Heyton, Joan. R for Barbados Lent 1692. Co.

Herreford, Anne. R for Barbados or Jamaica Oct 1690. M.

Heritage, Sarah wife of Richard. S Summer 1772. Wa.

Heritage, Thomas (1687). *See* Hopkins. Wa.

Heritage, Thomas. S s shirt at St. Peter in East, Oxford, Summer 1774. O.

Herman, Richard. S Mar 1725. So.

Hermer, John. S s at St. James, Bury St. Edmunds, Lent 1769. Su.

Hermes, John. T May 1737 *Forward*. K.

Hermitage, George. S Jan-Feb T Apr 1753 *Thames*. M.

Hermitage, Mary. LC from *Forward* Annapolis Jun 1725. X.

Hermitage, Thomas (1725). *See* Armitage. L.

Hermond, William. S Oct 1733 T Jan 1734 *Caesar* LC Va Jly 1734. M.

Herne. *See* Hearne.

Herniman, Humphrey of Burrington, blacksmith. R for Barbados Jun 1702. De.

Herod, George. T Sep 1765 *Justitia*. K.

Heroe als Harrow, Rebecca. T Nov 1743 *George__William*. K.

Heron, Daniel of Newcastle under Lyme. R for America Jly 1699. St.
Heron, Henry. S Sep T Dec 1758 *The Brothers*. M.
Heron, Isaac of Huntingdon. R for America Jly 1700. Hu.
Heron, James. S City Summer 1727. Nl.
Heron, John. S & T Apr 1765 *Ann*. L.
Herring als Brown, Catherine. S May 1745. M.
Herring, Elizabeth. T Apr 1772 *Thornton*. K.
Herring, Henry. S Jan-Feb 1773. M.
Herring, Herbert. R Dec 1699 AT Jan 1700. M.
Herring, James. Rebel T 1685.
Herring, James. S Aug T Sep 1725 *Forward* LC Annapolis Dec 1725. M.
Herring, John. S Apr T Dec 1734 *Caesar* LC Va Jly 1735. M.
Herring, Mary. S & T Jan 1769 *Thornton*. M.
Herring, Michael. S & T Apr 1725 *Sukey* LC Annapolis Sep 1725. M.
Herring, Thomas. Rebel T 1685.
Herringshaw, Ruth. S Feb T Mar 1730 *Patapsco* to Md. M.
Herrington, Roger. T Dec 1771 *Justitia*. Ht.
Herryman, John. S Sep T Oct 1750 *Rachael*. M.
Hersey, Martha. T Nov 1762 *Prince William*. Sy.
Herwick, Joseph. R 14 yrs s horse Summer 1721. No.
Heskett, Joseph. R 14 yrs Jly 1736. Ha.
Heskett als Hesketh, William. T Oct 1750 *Rachael*. M.
Heslam, Edward. S Apr R 14 yrs Aug 1718 T *Eagle* LC Charles Town
    Mar 1719. L.
Heslop, Andrew. S s horse & R 14 yrs Summer 1766. Cu.
Heslop, John, als Anderson, Thomas. S for counterfeiting Summer 1758
    R 14 yrs Summer 1759 T Sep 1759 from London. Nl.
Heslop, Margaret. SQS s gown Lent 1774. Du.
Hesmely, William. S s horse Summer 1739 R 14 yrs Lent 1740. Y.
Hesseter, Hannah. S Feb T Apr 1772 *Thornton*. L.
Hessey, Richard. R 14 yrs Jly 1758. Ha.
Hessill, John. R for America Aug 1715. L.
Hessle, Mary. S City Summer 1749. Y.
Hesslington, William. S Lent 1775. Li.
Hetherington, Andrew, als Black Andrew. S Summer 1729. Y.
Hetherington, John of St. Luke. S s gold & silver & R May 1740
    Essex. M.
Hetherington als Carrodice, Mary. TB Apr 1749. Db.
Hetherington, Robert. SQS s saddle Oct 1755. Du.
Hetherington, Walter. S Aug T Sep 1725 *Forward* LC Annapolis Dec
    1725. M.
Hetherington, William. S s horse Summer 1738 R 14 yrs Summer 1739
    AT Summer 1740. Cu.
Hetherly, William Sr. TB Oct 1738. Db.
Heughan, William. S s silver tankard Summer 1759. Du.
Heverdine, William of Chidham. R for Barbados Apr 1668. Sx.
Hew. *See* Hugh.
Hewby, James. S Jly 1735. M.
Hewes. *See* Hughes.
Heweston, Anne. T Dec 1731 *Forward*. K.

Hewetson, Rowland. S Lent R 14 yrs Summer 1731; found at large & R 14 yrs Summer 1733. Y.

Hewison, Robert. S City for sacrilege Lent & T Summer 1733. Y.

Hewitt, Ann. S Sep T Dec 1736 *Dorsetshire* to Va. M.

Hewet, Ann wife of Thomas. S Feb T Mar 1760 *Friendship*. M.

Huat, Benjamin. S Lent 1767.

Hewitt, Christopher. T Jun 1738 *Forward*. E.

Hewett, Edward. S Oct 1735 T Jan 1736 *Dorsetshire* LC Va Sep 1736. M.

Hewitt, Elizabeth. R for Barbados May 1676. M.

Hewitt, Elizabeth (1719). *See* Tooley. M.

Hewet, Francis. S Mar 1758. So.

Hewitt, Francis. S Lent TB Aug 1760. Y.

Hewett, Henry. S Aug 1742. So.

Hewitt, James. R Dec 1699 AT Jan 1700. M.

Huat, John. R 14 yrs Jly 1740. Wi.

Hewitt, John. S Feb T May 1767 *Thornton*. L.

Hewitt, John of Manchester. S s fish from Lady Egerton Lent R Summer 1767. La.

Hewitt, Joseph. S May T Jun 1738 *Forward*. L.

Hewitt, Lewis. LC from *Forward* Va Jun 1730. X.

Hewit, Mary. S Lent 1759. Ca.

Hewitt, Rachell. S May T Jun 1727 *Susanna* to Va. M.

Hewitt, Robert. T Aug 1720 *Owners Goodwill*. K.

Hewett, Thomas. R Dec 1681 AT Jan 1682. M.

Hewitt, Thomas. S Jan T Feb 1742 *Industry*. L.

Hewitt, Thomas. S Apr T Nov 1759 *Phoenix*. M.

Hewett, William. R for Barbados May TB Jun 1668. M.

Hewett, William. SQS Oct 1773 TB Jan 1774. So.

Hewlet, Samuel. S Apr 1756. So.

Hewlin, William. S s at Meole Brace Summer 1757. Sh.

Hewood, Joseph (1727). *See* Ilewood. L.

Hewson, Edward. T Aug 1721 *Owners Goodwill* LC Annapolis Jly 1722. E.

Hewson, John. T Jly 1723 *Alexander* LC Md Sep 1723. Bu.

Hewson, Mary, als Tompkin, Martha. S Jan T Feb 1719 *Worcester* LC Md Jun 1719. L.

Hewson, Richard. S s brass kettle at Strensham Summer 1773. Wo.

Hewson, Thomas. T Oct 1720 *Gilbert*. E.

Heyward. *See* Hayward.

Heywood. *See* Haywood.

Hiats. *See* Hyatts.

Hibbart, Adam of Jute. R for Barbados Jly 1685. La.

Hibbert, Edward. R 14 yrs Jly TB to Va Aug 1731. Wi.

Hibbert, Henry. S Mar 1733. De.

Hibbert, John. TB Nov 1736. Db.

Hibbard, Samuel. TB Aug 1735 T *Squire* LC Md Apr 1736. Db.

Hibberd, William. S Jan-Feb 1774. M.

Hibbins, Nicholas. S Jly T Dec 1736 *Dorsetshire* to Va. M.

Hibble, John. S Lent 1735. *Su.

Hibbs, Jane. S s at Mangotsfield Summer 1773. G.

Hibbs, Sarah. S s at Mangotsfield Summer 1773. G.

Hichels, Thomas (1743). *See* Hitchels. Ha.

Hick, William. S Summer 1742. Y.

Hicketts, Henry of Westbury. R for Barbados Jly 1704. Wi.

Hickey, Cicily. S Jan T Apr 1762 *Dolphin*. L.

Hickey, Jane. S Oct 1757 T Mar 1758 *Dragon*. M.

Hickey, John. SQS Jly TB Sep 1767. So.

Hickling, William. R for America Feb 1692. Le.

Hickman als Brogden, Ann. S Jly T Oct 1741 *Sea Horse* to Va. M.

Hickman, Elizabeth. S Aug T Oct 1723 *Forward* to Va. M.

Hickman, Elizabeth. S Oct 1730 T *Forward* LC Potomack Jan 1731. M.

Hickman, James. S s sheep & R 14 yrs Lent 1772. Be.

Hickman, John. S Aug 1737. So.

Hickman, John. S Jan-Mar T 14 yrs Jun 1738 *Forward* to Md or Va. M.

Hickman, John. T Nov 1759 *Phoenix*. Sx.

Hickman, John Smith. R for life Lent 1775. Ht.

Hickman, Mary. S & TB to Va Mar 1738. Wi.

Hickman, Noah. S s iron & nails at Sedgley Lent 1774. St.

Hickman, Richard. R for Jamaica Aug 1661. M.

Hickman, Richard. S & T Mar 1760 *Friendship*. L.

Hickman, Sarah wife of Benjamin. S & T Dec 1731 *Forward* to Md or Va. M.

Hickman, Seymour. S Feb 1775. L.

Hickman, Stephen. S Lent R 14 yrs Summer 1754. K.

Hickman, Thomas. S Summer 1732 AT Lent 1733. Wo.

Hickman, William. S Lent R 14 yrs Summer 1751. Sh.

Hicks als Burford, Ann. S Jun-Dec 1738 T Jan 1739 *Dorsetshire* to Va. M.

Hicks, Ann of St. Andrew Holborn, widow. S s clothing & T Dec 1740 *Vernon*. M.

Hicks als White, Ann. S & T Jly 1772 *Tayloe*. M.

Hicks, Cesar of Lorledge. R (Western Circ) for Barbados Jly 1715. G.

Hicks, Daniel. R 14 yrs s horses Jly 1720 T from Portsmouth 1723. Ha.

Hicks, Elias. S s at Mixbury Lent 1763. O.

Hicks, Elizabeth. PT Jly 1680 R Mar 1681. M.

Hicks, Elizabeth. S Sep-Oct 1772. M.

Hixe, Francis of Hornblotton. R for Barbados Feb 1688. So.

Hicks, George. S Jan 1775. M.

Hicks, Henry. T Oct 1726 *Forward*. Ht.

Hicks, James. S May T Jly 1723 *Alexander* LC Annapolis Sep 1723. M.

Hix, John. SQS Jly 1741 TB to Md May 1742. So.

Hix, John. S s at Cirencester Lent TB Apr 1751. G.

Hicks als Hilkes, John. S Oct 1751-Jan 1752. M.

Hicks, John, yeoman. S s at Attleborough Lent 1773. Nf.

Hicks, Joseph. S Mar 1759. Wi.

Hicks, Rebecca. T 14 yrs Apr 1770 *New Trial*. Ht.

Hickes, Richard. T Sep 1731 *Smith*. Bu.

Hicks, Silvia. T 14 yrs Apr 1770 *New Trial*. Ht.

Hicks, Thomas. S Oct T Nov 1725 *Rappahannock* LC Rappahannock Apr 1726. L.

Hicks, Thomas. S May T Jun 1727 *Susannah* to Va. M.

Hicks, Thomas. S Lent R 14 yrs Summer 1758. Wa.

Hicks, Tristram. S Apr 1751. So.

Hicks, William. S Mar 1719 to be T to Va. Wi.
Hicks, William. T Dec 1736 *Dorsetshire*. Ht.
Hicks, William. S Lent 1766. Ca.
Hicks, William. S Mar TB to Va Apr 1773. Wi.
Hickson, Ann (1741). *See* Wayland. M.
Hickson, Benjamin. S Sep 1760. L.
Hickson, John. S Mar 1766. So.
Hickson, Mathew. S Feb T Apr 1770 *New Trial*. M.
Hixson, William of Brickenden. R for Barbados or Jamaica Mar 1698. Ht.
Hide. *See* Hyde.
Hides, Edward. TB Aug 1733. Db.
Hidlam, Thomas. R for life at Peterborough for highway robbery Apr 1773. No.
Higby, Mary. S May-Jly 1748. M.
Higday, Thomas, butcher aged 22, dark. S Sep T Oct 1720 *Gilbert* LC Annapolis May 1721. L.
Higden, John of Wallingford, butcher. S s shirt at Ewelme Lent 1720. O.
Higden, William. Rebel T 1685.
Higgerson, Thomas. R for Barbados Jun 1670. M.
Hickinbotham, John. TB Apr 1739. Db.
Higginbottom, Richard. S Aug T Oct 1726 *Forward*. L.
Higginbotham, Samuel. S Summer 1736 R 14 yrs Summer 1737. Nt.
Higington, Joshua of Manchester. SQS Oct 1750. La.
Higgins, Ann. S Sep-Oct T Dec 1771 *Justitia*. M.
Higgins, Avis (1749). *See* Jones. Ht.
Higgins, David (1678). *See* Powell. Mo.
Higgins, David, als Powell, Thomas of Byford. R for America Jly 1679. He.
Higgins, Edward. S & T Oct 1720 *Gilbert* to Md. M.
Higgins, Hannah. SQS Feb T Apr 1753 *Thames*. M.
Higgins, John of Chapel Chorlton. R for Barbados Oct 1663. St.
Higgins, John (1722). *See* Serjeant. M.
Higgins, John. S Jly 1729. Do.
Higgens, John. S Mar 1741. Wi.
Higgins, John. S s silver cup at St. Swithin, Worcester, Summer 1761. Wo.
Higgins, John. S Oct 1764 T Jan 1765 *Tryal*. M.
Higgins, Joseph. S s handkerchiefs at St. Dunstan in West Oct 1768 T Jan 1769 *Thornton*. L.
Higgins, Mary, aged 40, dark. S Jun T Oct 1720 *Gilbert* LC Annapolis May 1721. L.
Higgins, Mary. S Oct T Nov 1728 *Forward* LC Rappahannock Jun 1729. L.
Higgins, Mary. Died on passage in *Patapsco* 1730. X.
Higgins, Susanna. S Feb T Sep 1737 *Pretty Patsy* to Md. M.
Higgins, Susannah. TB to Va from QS 1760. De.
Higgins, Thomas of Baunton. S Lent TB Mar 1754. G.
Higgins, Thomas. SQS Jan TB Mar 1768. So.
Higgins, Thomas. S s at Holkham & R 14 yrs Lent 1773. Nf.
Higgins, William. S Mar 1719 to be T to Va. Wi.

Higgins, William. S Aug 1720. De.

Higgins, William. T Jly 1722 *Alexander*. K.

Higgins, William. R for life Jan 1757. M.

Higgins, William. S Apr 1765. So.

Higgins, William. S Sep-Oct 1774. M.

Higginson, Charles. S Apr-Jun 1739. M.

Higginson, Eleanor, als wife of C. White. S s hats Sep T Dec 1736 *Dorsetshire*. M.

Higginson, John. S Jly T Sep 1742 *Forward*. L.

Higginson, Joseph of Coventry. R for America Mar 1690. Wa.

Higgison, Joseph. LC from *Susannah & Sarah* Annapolis Apr 1720. X.

Higginson, Joseph. S Apr T Jly 1770 *Scarsdale*. L.

Higginson, Richard. PT May R Jly 1686. M.

Higgonson, William. S Jly T Sep 1757 *Thetis*. M.

Higgs, Elizabeth. S Apr T 14 yrs May 1718 *Tryal* LC Charles Town Aug 1718 L.

Higgs, Elizabeth. S s at Bromsgrove Lent 1765. Wo.

Higgs, George of St. George, Bloomsbury. S s copper plates Sep 1740 T Jan 1741 *Harpooner* to Rappahannock. M.

Higgs, James. T Apr 1732 *Patapsco*. Sy.

Higgs, James. SQS Jan 1752. M.

Higgs, John (1729). *See* Hanson. Be.

Higgs, Mary. T Jun 1742 *Bladon*. Sx.

Higgs, Richard of Bisham. R for America Mar 1688. Be.

Higgs, Susanna. S Sep-Oct T Dec 1752 *Greyhound*. M.

Higgs, Thomas. AT Lent 1735. St.

Higgs, William. SW & T Aug 1769 *Douglas*. M.

High—ey, Mary. PT Jly 1680. M.

Higham/Highams. *See* Hyam/Hyams.

Hyfield, Hannah. S Jan T Feb 1724 *Anne* to Carolina. M.

Highfield, Jane. S May T Dec 1735 *John* LC Annapolis Sep 1736. M.

Highhorne, Samuel of Knighton. R for America Jly 1673. Wa.

Highman, Thomas. S Apr 1770. So.

Highmore, Richard. S Jly 1749. L.

Highton, William. S Feb T Mar 1731 *Patapsco* LC Annapolis Jun 1731. M.

Higlin, Peter. R for Barbados Jun 1671. L.

Hignett, Thomas. S Summer 1765. Wa.

Higton, Paul. S Summer 1768. Nt.

Higwell, Moses. Rebel T 1685.

Hilburn, Robert. S s sheep Summer 1757 R 14 yrs Lent 1758. No.

Hilditch, William. S s sheep & R 14 yrs Lent 1766. Ch.

Hildrup als Grove, Samuel. R 14 yrs Aug 1740 TB to Va. De.

Hilkes, John (1752). *See* Hicks. M.

Hill, Adam of St. Cleer, tailor. R for Barbados Jly 1664. Co.

Hill, Alice of Kattford. R for America Mar 1682. Nt.

Hill, Ann als Nancy of Manchester. SQS Jly 1763. La.

Hill, Ann. S Oct 1765 T Jan 1766 *Tryal*. L.

Hill, Charles of Leybourne. R for Barbados or Jamaica Jly 1688. K.

Hill, Edward. S Mar 1730. Co.

Hill, Edward. S Lent 1749. *Su.

Hill als Harrington, Edward. S Oct 1749. L.

Hill, Elijah. S Sep-Oct T Dec 1771 *Justitia*. M.

Hill, Elizabeth. R for Barbados or Jamaica Jly 1685. M.

Hill, Elizabeth. R 14 yrs Aug 1732 TB to Va. De.

Hill, Elizabeth. T May 1744 *Justitia*. Sy.

Hill, Elizabeth, spinster. S s at Ampthill Summer 1750. Bd.

Hill, Elizabeth. S & T Dec 1771 *Justitia*. M.

Hill, Francis. S for murder at Speen Summer 1737 R for life Lent 1738. Be.

Hill, Francis Carraway of Upton St. Leonard, yeoman. S s wheat Summer TB Aug 1740. G.

Hill, George of Chipping Barnet. R for Barbados Sep 1669. Ht.

Hill, George. SQS Jan TB Apr 1753. So.

Hill, George. S Dec 1765 T Jan 1766 *Tryal*. M.

Hill, Godfrey. S Lent 1773. Db.

Hill, Henry. S Mar 1730. Co.

Hill, Henry. S & T Jan 1739 *Dorsetshire*. L.

Hill, Henry. S Summer 1744. Y.

Hill, Henry. S May-Jly 1749. M.

Hill, Henry of Woodchester. S s cloth Lent TB Mar 1754. G.

Hill, James. TB Aug 1740. Db.

Hill, James. S May-Jly 1749. M.

Hill, James. S s at Madresfield Lent 1751. Wo.

Hill, James. S City Summer 1752. Y.

Hill, James. R 14 yrs Aug TB to Va Oct 1764. Wi.

Hill, Jane (1680). *See* Bassett. Sy.

Hill, Jane. TB to Va from QS 1771. De.

Hill, John. Rebel T 1685.

Hill, John of Stafford. R for America Nov 1694. St.

Hill, John. S Jan T 14 yrs Feb 1719 *Worcester* LC Annapolis Jun 1719. L.

Hill, John. S Jly 1722 for counterfeiting a pass; asked for transporation rather than corporal punishment. De.

Hill, John. S Feb T Mar 1727 *Rappahannock* to Md. M.

Hill, John. SQS Aug TB Sep 1728. Nt.

Hill, John. T Sep 1730 *Smith*. Sy.

Hill, John. R 14 yrs Apr 1742. So.

Hill, John. S Summer 1745. Bu.

Hill, John. S s at Pershore Lent 1749. Wo.

Hill, John of Thaxted, butcher. SQS for fraud Jly 1754. E.

Hill als Conybear als Phillips, John. S Aug 1759 TB to Va. De.

Hill, John. R 14 yrs Aug 1760. So.

Hill, John. S Jun T Sep 1764 *Justitia*. M.

Hill, John. T Apr 1766 *Ann*. Sy.

Hill, John. S Apr 1767. So.

Hill, John. S Apr T May 1767 *Thornton*. M.

Hill, John. S Jly T Sep 1767 *Justitia*. M.

Hill, John. T Apr 1770 *New Trial*. L.

Hill, John (1772). *See* Bowden, William. De.

Hill, John of St. George, Hanover Square. SW Apr 1774. M.

Hill, John of St. Martin in Fields. SW Jun 1774. M.

Hill, John (1775). *See* Dowden. Ha.

Hill, John of Rochdale. SQS Jan 1775. La.

Hill, Joseph. S s shoes at Newcastle under Lyme Lent 1749. St.

Hill, Joseph of Thaxted, butcher. SQS for fraud Jly 1754. E.

Hill, Joseph Jr. SQS Apr TB Sep 1773. So.

Hill, Luke. Died on passage in *Rappahannock* 1726. Li.

Hill als Hilliard, Mary. S Aug T Oct 1724 *Forward* LC Annapolis Jun 1725. M.

Hill, Mary. S Summer 1734 R 14 yrs Lent TB Mar 1735. G.

Hill, Mary. S Sep-Dec 1746. M.

Hill, Mary. S Dec 1749-Jan 1750 T Mar 1750 *Tryal*. M.

Hill, Mary (1771). *See* Twiss. Sh.

Hill, Mary. SQS Apr 1773. M.

Hill, Mary. S Apr-May 1775. M.

Hill, Prudence. R for Barbados Aug 1679. M.

Hill, Richard. R for Barbados Aug 1679. L.

Hill, Richard (1719). *See* Davis. Do.

Hill, Richard. S Dec 1737 T Jan 1738 *Dorsetshire*. L.

Hill, Richard. S Mar 1743. De.

Hill, Richard of Ashtead. SQS Jan T Apr 1765 *Ann*. Sy.

Hill, Richard. AT from QS Lent 1774. Db.

Hill, Robert. S Aug T 14 yrs Oct 1726 *Forward* to Va. M.

Hill, Robert. R 14 yrs Jly TB to Va Oct 1740. Wi.

Hill, Robert of Ashtead. SQS Jan T Apr 1756 *Greyhound*. Sy.

Hill, Robert. S Apr 1774. L.

Hill, Samuel of St. Giles in Fields. S for burglary Feb T 14 yrs May 1740 *Essex*. M.

Hill, Samuel. S s lambs Lent R 14 yrs Summer 1753. Su.

Hill, Samuel. S Mar 1768. Ha.

Hill, Sarah (1697). *See* Borroughs. L.

Hill, Shadrick. S May-Jly 1750. M.

Hill, Shadrack of St. Saviour, Southwark. SQS Jan 1775. Sy.

Hill, Susannah. S Aug 1772 R for life Mar 1773. De.

Hill, Thomas of Westminster. R Aug 1663 (PC). M.

Hill, Thomas. Rebel T 1685.

Hill, Thomas. R 14 yrs Jly 1719 to be T to Va. So.

Hill, Thomas. S & T Oct 1722 *Forward* LC Annapolis Jun 1723. M.

Hill, Thomas. S Feb T Mar 1727 *Rappahannock*. L.

Hill, Thomas. T Oct 1732 *Caesar*. K.

Hill, Thomas. T Aug 1741 *Sally*. Sy.

Hill, Thomas. S for highway robbery Lent R 14 yrs Summer 1743. St.

Hill, Thomas. S Apr 1748. L.

Hill, Thomas. S s sheep Lent R 14 yrs Summer 1753. Su.

Hill, Thomas. S Lent 1755. Ca.

Hill, Thomas Jr. R 14 yrs Summer 1764. Y.

Hill, Thomas. S Feb T Apr 1768 *Thornton*. M.

Hill, Thomas. S for obtaining money by false pretences Jun T Jly 1772 *Tayloe*. L.

Hill, Thomas. R Dec 1773. M.

Hill, Walter. S Apr 1770. De.

Hill, William. R for Va for s bull May 1620. M.

Hill, William of Silverton, husbandman. R for Barbados Jun 1669. De.
Hill, William of Hereford. R for America Jly 1678. He.
Hill, William of Christchurch. R for Barbados or Jamaica Feb 1686. Sy.
Hill, William. S s at Ledbury Lent 1728. He.
Hill, William. S Aug 1741. So.
Hill, William. S s at Much Cowarne Lent 1756. He.
Hill, William of Bingham. SQS s oak Jan AT Lent 1769. Nt.
Hill, William. T Aug 1769 *Douglas*. L.
Hill, William. S Summer 1772. Db.
Hill, William of St. Ann, Westminster. SW Apr 1773. M.
Hillard, John of North Cadbury. R for Barbados Mar 1695. So.
Hillard, Thomas. SQS Jan TB to Jamaica May 1725. So.
Hillary, John. S Feb T Mar 1731 *Patapsco* but died on passage. M.
Hillary, John. R 14 yrs Jly 1773. Ha.
Hillerton, Edward. T May 1751 *Tryal*. K.
Hillaton, Jane. LC from *Sukey* Annapolis Sep 1725. X.
Hilleson, Robert. LC from *Susannah & Sarah* Annapolis Apr
     1720. X.
Hilliard, Ann. S Oct-Dec 1750. M.
Hilliard, Ann. S Jan 1757. M.
Hilliard, Elizabeth. T Jun 1728 *Elizabeth* LC Va Aug 1729. Sy.
Hilliard, Grace (1669). *See* Berry. M.
Hilliard, John. R for Barbados or Jamaica Jly 1686. L.
Hilliard, Mary (1724). *See* Hill. M.
Hilliard, Mary. S & T Apr 1725 *Sukey* LC Annapolis Sep 1725. M.
Hilliard, Philip. S Oct T Nov 1728 *Forward* LC Rappahannock Jun
     1729. M.
Hilliard, Samuel. S Feb T Mar 1731 *Patapsco* to Md. M.
Hilliard, Sarah. LC from *Patapsco* Annapolis Jun 1731. X.
Hilliard, Sarah. S Jly T Oct 1741 *Sea Horse* to Va. M.
Hilliard, Thomas. S Dec 1764 T Jan 1765 *Tryal*. M.
Hillier, John. S Jly T Sep 1764 *Justitia*. M.
Hillier, John. R 14 yrs Mar TB to Va Oct 1768. Wi.
Hillingworth, Richard. S Summer 1772. E.
Hillison, Robert. TB 14 yrs Oct 1719. L.
Hillman, Elizabeth wife of Alexander. S Mar TB to Va Oct 1742. Wi.
Hillman, Elizabeth (1765). *See* Brown. M.
Hillman, Hatwood. S Feb 1749. Ha.
Hillman, James. Rebel T 1685.
Hillman, Margaret. R for Barbados Jun 1671. L.
Hillman, Thomas. R for Barbados or Jamaica Dec 1689. M.
Hills, Elizabeth. T Dec 1736 *Dorsetshire*. Sy.
Hills, Matthew. T Apr 1765 *Ann*. K.
Hills, Matthew. T for life Sep 1766 *Justitia*. K.
Hills, Sarah. T Jun 1738 *Forward*. E.
Hills, Thomas of Laindon. SQS Jly T Oct 1768 *Justitia*. E.
Hills, William of Stockbury. R for Barbados or Jamaica Feb 1676. K.
Hills, William. T Jan 1741 *Vernon*. K.
Hills, William. T Apr 1765 *Ann*. K.
Hilton, Ann. S Feb-Apr T May 1752 *Lichfield*. M.
Hilton, George of Manchester. SQS Jan 1752. La.

Hilton, James. T May 1723 *Victory*. K.
Hilton als Hulton, James of Middle Hulton. SQS Jan 1770. La.
Hilton, John. S Feb T Mar 1731 *Patapsco* LC Annapolis Jun 1731. L.
Hillton, John. S May-Jly 1750. M.
Hilton, Samuel. R for Barbados Jun 1670. M.
Hinch, Joseph. S Jan T Apr 1734 *Patapsco* to Md. M.
Hinchcliffe, John of Leeds. R for Barbados Jly 1699. Y.
Hinchcliffe, Michael. S Lent R 14 yrs Summer 1749. Nt.
Hinchley, Mary. S & T Jan 1769 *Thornton*. M.
Hinchman, John. T Jly 1724 *Robert* LC Md Jun 1725. E.
Hinckman, Charles. S Apr T May 1720 *Honor* but escaped in Vigo,
    Spain. L.
Hind, Charles. SQS Feb T Apr 1766 *Ann*. M.
Hind, Christopher of East Layton, husbandman. SQS Richmond s at
    Stanwick Jan 1736. Y.
Hind, David. S Feb T Apr 1772 *Thornton*. L.
Hinde, Henry of Bolton by the Sands. SQS Jly 1773. La.
Hinde, John of Rainham. R for Barbados or Jamaica Dec 1680. K.
Hind, Mary. S Jan-Feb 1774. M.
Hind, Richard. S Oct T Nov 1762 *Prince William*. M.
Hinde, Thomas. SQS & T Jan 1765 *Tryal*. M.
Hind, William of Sutton. R for Barbados Jly 1699. Y.
Hindley als Fish, Margaret of Manchester, widow. SQS May 1764. La.
Hindley, William. S Jun 1747. L.
Hindmarsh, John. R & T 14 yrs Apr 1770 *New Trial*. M.
Hindmarsh, Mary. S Sep 1737 T Jan 1738 *Dorsetshire* to Va. M.
Hinds, George. S Dec 1766 T Jan 1767 *Justitia*. M.
Hinds, John. S Jan T Feb 1742 *Industry*. L.
Hindes, John. S Mar TB Apr 1754. Le.
Hindes, John. S for highway robbery & R 14 yrs Summer 1774. O.
Hindes, Matthew. S s cow Lent R 14 yrs Summer 1764. Su.
Hynds, Peter. S Feb T May 1736 *Patapsco* to Md. M.
Hindes, Terence. S Oct 1772. L.
Hinds, Thomas. SQS Jly T Sep 1767 *Justitia*. M.
Hindes, William. S Summer 1760. Ca.
Hinds, William. R Dec 1773. M.
Hindson, John als William. S s horse Summer 1739 R 14 yrs Summer
    1740. Cu.
Hindy. *See* Hendy.
Hine, Eleanor. S Apr-May 1754. M.
Hine, John. S Nov T Dec 1753 *Whiteing*. L.
Hinemore, Ann. S May-Jly 1749. M.
Hines, Danby. S Summer 1756. Su.
Hines, Elizabeth. S Feb T Apr 1765 *Ann*. L.
Hines, James. S s silver spoon at St. Botolph Bishopsgate Dec 1768 T
    Jan 1769 *Thornton*. L.
Hines, Jane. S Dec 1768 T Jan 1769 *Thornton*. L.
Hines, John. SQS Feb T Apr 1772 *Thornton*. M.
Hines, John. R 14 yrs Jly 1775. M.
Hynes, John Martin. S Feb T May 1767 *Thornton*. L.
Hines, Thomas. S Lent 1752. Su.

Hingston, William. S Mar 1732 TB to Va. De.

Hinckley, Arthur. R for America Feb 1700. Db.

Hinckley, Francis. T May 1719 *Margaret* LC Md Aug 1719; sold to William Black. Ht.

Hinkley, William. S s at Abbots Bromley Lent 1775. St.

Hincks, Ann (1732). *See* Palmer. M.

Hincks, Sarah. S & T Sep 1767 *Justitia*. L.

Hinks, Thomas. S s horse Summer 1741 R 14 yrs Lent 1742. Wa.

Hinkes, Thomas. S Oct 1766 T Jan 1767 *Tryal*. M.

Hincks, Thomas. S 14 yrs for receiving goods stolen from Lichfield Cathedral Close Lent 1769. St.

Hinks, Thomas. S Summer T Sep 1770. Wa.

Hincks, William. T Jly 1724 *Robert* LC Md Jun 1725. Sy.

Hinkson, Mary. TB to Va from QS 1740. De.

Hinkson, Philip. TB to Va from QS 1740. De.

Hinkson, Richard. LC from *Patapsco* Annapolis Nov 1733. X.

Hinsell, Susanna. R May AT Oct 1678. M.

Hinton, John. S s at Bitterley Lent 1753. Sh.

Hinton, John. S s at Kempsey Summer 1771. Wo.

Hinton, Richard. S s at Hampton Bishop Summer 1750. He.

Hinton, Thomas. SWK Jan 1775. K.

Hinton, Timothy. S Jly-Sep 1754. M.

Hinton, William. S Lent R 14 yrs Summer 1767. G.

Hinton, William. SQS Dec 1773. M.

Hipditch, William. S Dec 1774. M.

Hipkin, Ann wife of Michael of St. George, Southwark. SQS Jan 1751. Sy.

Hipkin, Edward of Spixworth. R for America Jly 1683. Nf.

Hipkins, John. S 14 yrs for receiving Aug TB to Va Sep 1767. Le.

Hipkins, Mary (1679). *See* Stephens. L.

Hipsley, George. R 14 yrs Mar 1731. So.

Hippesley, Henry. S Mar 1749. So.

Hipsey, Elizabeth. S Sep-Oct T Dec 1771 *Justitia*. M.

Hipwell, William. S Jun-Dec 1738 T Jan 1739 *Dorsetshire* to Va. M.

Hipworth, John. S Dec 1755 T Jan 1756 *Greyhound*. L.

Hippworth, Mary (1724). *See* Lees. M.

Hircutt, Mary (1745). *See* Ursin. So.

Hirst. *See* Hurst.

Hiscitt als Hiscott, Benjamin. R 14 yrs Mar 1736. Wi.

Hiscock, John (1744). *See* Wilkins. So.

Hiscock, Roger. S Jly 1732. Wi.

Hiscocks, William. S Lent R 14 yrs Summer 1724. G.

Hiscott, Benjamin (1736). *See* Hiscitt. Wi.

Hiser, John. S Feb T Mar 1730 *Patapsco* to Md. M.

Hitch, John, als Sadler, Mary. T Apr 1742 *Bond*. E.

Hitch, Thomas. S s at Little Newchurch Summer 1770. He.

Hitchcock, Edward. S May 1775. L.

Hitchcock, James. S s at Chieveley Lent 1775. Be.

Hitchcock, John. R & T 14 yrs Jly 1772 *Tayloe*. M.

Hitchcock, Mary. TB to Va 1768. De.

Hitchcock, Roger. LC from *Patapsco* Annapolis Nov 1733. X.

Hitchcock, Thomas. S Dec 1737 T Jan 1738 *Dorsetshire*. L.

Hitchcock, William, als Bristol Jack. R for Barbados or Jamaica Dec 1698. M.

Hitchcox, Robert. S s iron bar at Howley Summer 1772. O.

Hitchcott, John. Rebel T 1685.

Hitchels als Hichels, Thomas. S Mar 1743. Ha.

Hitchin, Robert. R for America Jly 1709. Li.

Hitchin, William. S Lent R 14 yrs Summer 1739. Wa.

Hitchings, Henry. S s at Bitton Lent 1770. G.

Hitchings, Joseph. S & T Apr 1733 *Patapsco* LC Annapolis Nov 1733. L.

Hitchins, Joseph. S Apr-Jun 1739. M.

Hitchings, Richard. S Oct 1761. L.

Hitchins, Richard. S & T Mar 1764 *Tryal*. L.

Hitchins, William. S s lambs at Defford Lent R 14 yrs Summer 1763. Wo.

Hitchman, Mary (1722). *See* Walker. M.

Hitchman, Thomas. S Apr-May 1754. M.

Hitherington, Ann. S Mar 1772. Co.

Hitson, Jane. SQS Oct 1751. M.

Hiver, John. LC from *Patapsco* Annapolis Sep 1730. X.

Hix/Hixe. *See* Hicks.

Hixton als Axall, Thomas. SQS May T Aug 1769 *Douglas*. M.

Hoad, Nicholas. PT Jly 1680. M.

Hoadley, Thomas. T Jan 1738 *Dorsetshire*. K.

Hoadman, Martha. S May-Jun T Jly 1753 *Tryal*. M.

Hore, Ann. R 14 yrs Mar 1752. De.

Hoar, Catherine. S Jan-Jun T Jun 1728 *Elizabeth* to Md or Va. M.

Hoar, Edward. R 14 yrs Aug 1742. Do.

Hoare, Elizabeth. S Jan-Jun T Jun 1728 *Elizabeth* to Md or Va. M.

Hoare, Elizabeth. S Dec 1753-Jan 1754. M.

Hoare, Elizabeth. SW & T Dec 1767 *Neptune*. M.

Hoare als Brown als Kirkman, Elizabeth. S Jan-Feb 1775. M.

Hoar, Hannah. S Oct 1749-Jan 1750. M.

Hoare, Henry. R for life Lent 1775. Sy.

Hoare, John. Rebel T 1685.

Hore, John of Stoke St. Gregory. R for Barbados Feb 1692. So.

Hoar, John. TB to Va from QS 1738. De.

Hoare, Matthew of Pillaton. R for Barbados Jly 1693. Co.

Hoare, Richard. Rebel T 1685.

Hoare, Robert. S Mar 1742. Co.

Hoare, Thomas. Rebel T 1685.

Hoar, Thomas (1720). *See* Mead. Be.

Hoar, Thomas. S Feb 1761. L.

Hoar, Thomas. T Dec 1770 *Justitia*. Sy.

Hoar, Thomas (1772). *See* Oar. So.

Hoare, William. S Jan-Apr 1748. M.

Hoare, William Grenville. S Oct T Dec 1771 *Justitia*. L.

Hoarnden, James. T Appr 1742 *Bond*. K.

Hoasden, John of Curricott. R (Midland Circ) for America Feb 1683. Ht.

Hoasse, Philip als John. S May T Jun 1764 *Dolphin*. L.

Hobbs, Ann. S May T Jly 1723 *Alexander* LC Annapolis Sep 1723. L.

Hobbs, Benjamin. S Mar 1764. Ha.

Hobbs, Daniel. R Jly T for life Sep 1767 *Justitia*. M.

Hobbs, Elizabeth. S & T Oct 1732 *Caesar* to Va. M.

Hobbs, Henry of Cutcombe. R for Barbados Jly 1679. So.

Hobbs, James. S & T Sep 1731 *Smith* LC Va 1732. M.

Hobbs, James. S Sep T Dec 1763 *Neptune*. M.

Hobbs, James. S Jan-Feb 1773. M.

Hobbs, John. R for Jamaica Aug 1661. M.

Hobbs, John. S Aug T Sep 1725 *Forward* LC Annapolis Dec 1725. L.

Hobbs, John. S Mar 1736. So.

Hobbs, John (1740). *See* Hobby. Wo.

Hobbs, John. T 14 yrs Aug 1752 *Tryal*. K.

Hobbs als Barnes, Martha. S & TB Mar 1732. G.

Hobbs, Nicholas. R 14 yrs Mar 1774. So.

Hobbs, Oliver. Rebel T 1685.

Hobbs, Peter of Menheniot. R for Barbados Mar 1694. Co.

Hobs, Richard. R 14 yrs Mar TB to Va Oct 1768. Wi.

Hobbs, Robert. SQS Apr 1774. M.

Hobbs, Roger. Rebel T 1685.

Hobbs, Sara. S Aug T Oct 1726 *Forward*. L.

Hobbs, Sarah. S Feb-Apr 1746. M.

Hobbs, Thomas. S Jly-Sep 1754. M.

Hobbs, William. R 14 yrs & TB to Va Mar 1738. Wi.

Hobbs, William. R 14 yrs Sep 1746. So.

Hobbs, William. S Mar 1764. Ha.

Hobbs, William. T 14 yrs Sep 1767 *Justitia*. E.

Hobby, John. S & T Jan 1736 *Dorsetshire* LC Va Sep 1736. L.

Hobby als Hobbs, John. S Lent TB Apr 1740. G & Wo.

Hobday, Samuel. S Lent 1730. Wo.

Hobday, Samuel. R Summer 1730. O.

Hobler, Mary. S May-Jly 1774. M.

Hoblyn, Christopher. Rebel T 1685.

Hobson, Cuthbert of Crookhouse. R for Barbados Feb 1673. Nl.

Hobson, George. S s horse Summer 1723 R 14 yrs Lent 1729. Y.

Hobson, Hannah. S Oct 1742 T Apr 1743 *Justitia*. M.

Hobson, Margaret. S & T Oct 1730 *Forward* LC Potomack Jan 1731. M.

Hobson, Mary. S Lent 1775. Wa.

Hobson, Richard. S 14 yrs for receiving coal from Henry Carter *(qv)* Lent 1773. O.

Hobson, Robert. S Lent R 14 yrs Summer 17388 Le.

Hobson, Samuel. S Jan-Apr 1749. M.

Hobson, Stephen. R for Barbados Jan 1664. L.

Hobson, Thomas. S Jan-Jun 1747. M.

Hobson, Thomas of Warrington. SQS Apr 1751. La.

Hobson, William. S s pig at Wargrave Lent 1766. Be.

Hoccombe, Andrew. Rebel T 1685.

Hocombe, Thomas. R 14 yrs Jly 1719 to be T to Va. De.

Hockabout, Francis. S May T Jly 1723 *Alexander* LC Annapolis Sep 1723. L.

Hockaday, George. R 14 yrs Jly 1724. De.

Hockaday, John. TB to Va from QS 1765. De.

Hockerdy, Philip. S & T Sep 1764 *Justitia*. L.

Hoccaday, William. S Aug 1731 TB to Va. De.

Huckenhull, Mary Jr. S Feb T Mar 1758 *Dragon*. L.

Hockeridge, William of Chicksands. R for America Jun 1714. Bd.

Hocking, Catherine. R 14 yrs Aug 1724. Co.

Hockingham als Wilmore, Sarah. S Jly 1750. Ha.

Hockley, Thomas. S & T Jan 1765 *Tryal*. M.

Hocklish, John. T 14 yrs Aug 1752 *Tryal*. K.

Hocknell, Daniel. PT Jan 1674 R Feb 1675. M.

Hodd, Thomas. S Apr-Jun T Jly 1772 *Tayloe*. M.

Hodder, Robert. R 14 yrs Jly 1728. Ha.

Hodder, Sarah. S Mar 1774. Wi.

Hodder, William. S Mar 1741. Ha.

Hoddinott, William. R Jly 1686. M.

Hody, Edward. Rebel T 1685.

Hoddy als Hadwell, John. S s at Great Witley Summer 1764. Wo.

Hoddy, Richard. S Apr 1761. M.

Hoden als Haydon, Mary. S Jun T Nov 1743 *George William*. L.

Hodge, Ann. S Aug 1757. So.

Hodge, Eleanor. S Summer 1734. Cu.

Hodge, Francis. S Lent 1746; his wife acquitted & discharged. Ht.

Hodge, Humphrey. Rebel T 1685.

Hodge, John (1695). *See* Jones. M.

Hodge, John. S Mar 1740. De.

Hodge, Samuel. R 14 yrs Aug 1748. Co.

Hodgeon, George. S City Lent 1754. Y.

Hodgeon, Samuel. R 14 yrs Summer 1753. We.

Hodges, Edward. R for Barbados Sep 1669. M.

Hodges, Elizabeth. S Jun-Dec 1738 T Jan 1739 *Dorsetshire* to Va. M.

Hodges, Frances. S & T Dec 1734 *Caesar* LC Va Jly 1735. L.

Hodges, Francis. T 14 yrs Sep 1767 *Justitia*. Ht.

Hodges als Pison, James. S Jly-Dec 1747. M.

Hodges, John. S Jly 1750. L.

Hodges, John. S Sep T Dec 1767 *Neptune*. L.

Hodges, John. S Dec 1774. L.

Hodges, Margaret. R 14 yrs Mar 1737. Wi.

Hodges, Mary. SQS & T Dec 1767 *Neptune*. M.

Hodges, Philip. S Summer 1756 R Summer 1757. Wo.

Hodges, Richard. LC from *Forward* Annapolis Jun 1725. X.

Hodges, Robert of Stanstead Abbots. R for Barbados or Jamaica Jly 1704. Ht.

Hodges, Sara (1697). *See* Wittins. M.

Hodges, Sara. S Feb T Apr 1732 *Patapsco* but died on passage. M.

Hodges, Thomas. R for Barbados Sep 1669. M.

Hodges, Thomas. S s from warehouse at Derby Lent TB Apr 1764. Db.

Hodges, William. S Feb 1733. Ha.

Hodges, William. T Jun 1740 *Essex*. Sx.

Hodgetts, Elizabeth of Sedgley, spinster. S Lent 1719. Wo.

Hodgetts, John of Woverd, Sollers Hope. R for Barbados Oct 1663. He.

Hodgetts, John. S Summer 1759. Wa.

Hodgetts, Margaret of Halesowen, spinster. R for Barbados Oct 1663. Sh.

Hodgkins, Edward. T Oct 1726 *Forward*. Sy.

Hodgkins, John. S Jly TB to Md Oct 1738. Le.

Hodgkins, John. S Jan 1758. M.

Hodgkins, John. S for wounding horse & R Lent T May 1770. Wa.

Hodgkinson, John. S Lent R 14 yrs Summer 1733. Li.

Hodgkinson, John. S Summer 1736 R 14 yrs Lent 1737. O.

Hodgkinson, Mary. S s horse Lent R 14 yrs Summer 1740. Bd.

Hodgman, Edward. S Oct 1756. M.

Hodgson, Brian. S Lent 1746. La.

Hodgson, Elizabeth wife of Isaac, als Elizabeth Swinbank, widow. R 14 yrs Summer 1759. We.

Hodgson, George. S Dec 1735 T Jan 1736 *Dorsetshire* LC Va Sep 1736. M.

Hodgson, Jane. S Apr T Sep 1758 *Tryal* to Annapolis. M.

Hodgson, John. R for America Aug 1685. Le.

Hodgson, John. S s peruke at Much Wenlock Lent 1753. Sh.

Hodgson, John. S Feb R Jun T 14 yrs Sep 1764 *Justitia*. M.

Hodgson, John. S Lent R 14 yrs Summer 1768. St.

Hodgson, John. S s cow at Whickham & R Summer 1772. Du.

Hodgson, Joseph. SQS s pillowslips Easter 1767. Du.

Hodgson, Robert. S s sheep Summer 1737. We.

Hodgson, Samuel. S s steers & R Summer 1773. Li.

Hodgson, Solomon. S Summer 1726 AT Summer 1727. We.

Hodgson, Thomas. S s horse Summer 1720 R 14 yrs Summer 1721. We.

Hodgson als Hudson, William. R for Jamaica Aug 1661. L.

Hodgson, William. S Dec 1750. L.

Hodgson, William. S Feb T 14 yrs Apr 1766 *Ann*. M.

Hodnet, Elizabeth. S Lent R 14 yrs Summer 1766. Sh.

Hodson, James of Pemberton. SQS Oct 1754. La.

Hodson, Mary of Stapleford, spinster. SQS s cloth Jan 1747. Nt.

Hodson, William. LC from *Forward* Annapolis Jun 1725. X.

Hoe, John. R for Barbados or Jamaica Dec 1693 & Jan 1694. M.

Hoffein, Goddard. S 14 yrs Sep-Oct 1773. M.

Hoffman, Mary wife of John. S Apr-May 1775. M.

Hogan, Ann. S Feb 1757. M.

Hogan, John. S Jan T Mar 1764 *Tryal*. M.

Hogin als Eagan, Nicholas. S Feb T Apr 1741 *Speedwell* or *Mediterranean*. M.

Hogan, Sebastian. R Feb T for life Mar 1764 *Tryal*. M.

Hogan, Thomas. LC from *Supply* Annapolis May 1726. X.

Hogborne als Richardson, Grace. S Jly 1730. Wi.

Hogden, Nehemiah. S Summer 1772. K.

Hogden, William (1713). *See* Ogden. M.

Hogg, Andrew of Christchurch. SQS Jan 1773. Sy.

Hog, Catherine. S Oct 1773. L.

Hogg, James. S & T 14 yrs Jan 1722 *Gilbert* LC Annapolis Jly 1722. M.

Hogg, John. S Summer 1772. Wa.

Hogg, Richard. T Apr 1741 *Speedwell* or *Mediterranean*. Sy.

Hogg, Sarah. S & T Dec 1736 *Dorsetshire*. L.

Hoggart, Daniel. S Summer 1765. Li.

Hoggins, Humphrey. R for Barbados Dec 1683. M.

Hoggins, William. R for America Aug 1715. M.

Hoglett, Richard. S & TB Aug 1740. G.

Holbert. *See* Hulbert.

Holbrooke, Francis. T Jun 1727 *Susanna*. K.

Holbrooke, John. S Apr 1742. So.

Holbrook, John. S Jan T Apr 1744 *Neptune* to Md. M.

Holbrook, Robert. TB Apr 1739. Db.

Holcombe, Thomasine (1667). *See* Hawcombe. De.

Holden, Ann of Maids Moreton. S Summer 1723 R 14 yrs Summer 1724
    T *Robert* LC Md Jun 1725. Bu.

Holden, Elizabeth (1725). *See* Scott. M.

Holden, James. S Feb T Mar 1763 *Neptune*. M.

Holden als Alden, John of Foulsham. R for Barbados Jan 1665. Nf.

Holden, John of Scrubby next Alford. R for America Feb 1713. Li.

Holden, John. SQS Coventry Mar AT Sep 1742. Wa.

Holden, John. S Apr T May 1752 *Lichfield*. L.

Holden, John. S Summer 1755. Y.

Holden als Lovegrove, Rebecca. S Sep 1754. L.

Holden, Richard. S Summer 1773. K.

Holden, Robert. T Nov 1725 *Rappahannock* but died on passage. Ht.

Holden, Thomas. S Jly-Dec 1747. M.

Holden, Thomas. SQS & T Jan 1767 *Tryal*. M.

Holder, Charles. S s sheep Summer 1752 R 14 yrs Lent TB Apr 1753. G.

Holder, Edward. S Mar TB May 1770. Le.

Holder, Elizabeth. S Sep T Nov 1743 *George William*. L.

Holder als James, Richard. S s at Great Malvern Lent 1769. Wo.

Holder, Robert. S s brass pot & kettle at Oxendon Summer 1763. G.

Holder, Thomas. SL Oct 1754. Sy.

Holderness, George of Croydon. SQS Jan & Apr 1775. Sy.

Holding, Ann. R for Barbados or Jamaica Dec 1689. M.

Holding, Rebecca wife of George. S Jly-Oct 1740 T 14 yrs Jan 1741
    Harpooner to Rappahannock. M.

Holding, Richard. S s mare at Anderton Lent R 14 yrs Summer
    1766. La.

Holding, William. S s sheep & R 14 yrs Lent 1743. Nf.

Holdsworth, James. S & T Jan 1736 *Dorsetshire* LC Va Sep 1736. L.

Holdsworth, John. S s mare Lent R 14 yrs Summer 1725 T *Sukey* LC
    Md Sep 1725. Ca.

Holdsworth, Joseph. S Dec 1741 T Feb 1742 *Industry* to Md. M.

Holdsworth, Robert. T Jun 1727 *Susanna*. Bu.

Holdesworth, Seth. R for Barbados Feb 1675. L.

Holdsworth, William. S for burglary Lent 1742 R 14 yrs Summer 1743
    AT Lent 1744. Nf.

Holdturn, Thomas. S s at Cannock Summer 1772. St.

Holdy, Ralph of Churchdown. S s sheep Summer 1720. G.

Hole, John. R 14 yrs Mar 1772 TB to Va. De.

Hole, William. R 14 yrs Mar 1759 TB to Va. De.

Holesworth, Richard. SQS Coventry Apr 1745 but escaped. Wa.

Holford, Elizabeth. S Feb T Mar 1729 *Patapsco* LC Annapolis Dec 1729. L.

Holford, Jane. S Nov T Dec 1752 *Greyhound*. L.

Holford, Thomas. S & T Apr 1725 *Sukey* LC Annapolis Sep 1725. M.

Holford, Thomas. S Sep T Nov 1759 *Phoenix*. M.

Holgate, William. S Lent R 14 yrs Summer 1748 T Jan 1749 *Laura*. Ht.

Holl als Bowen, Elizabeth. S Sep 1756. M.

Hollams, John. S Lent R 14 yrs Summer 1755. St.

Holland, Abraham. S Summer 1767. Wa.

Holland als Lee, Ann. S Jly-Sep T 14 yrs Sep 1742 *Forward*. M.

Holland als Shepherd, Ann. S Oct-Dec 1750. M.

Holland, Bryan, als Grant, Peter. R 14 yrs Mar 1764. So.

Holland, Ellen. R for Barbados Jly 1680. M.

Holland, John. R for Jamaica Aug 1661. M.

Holland, John. R for Barbados Aug 1679. L.

Holland, John of Methwold. R for America Mar 1680. Nf.

Holland, John. S May T Jly 1722 *Alexander* to Nevis or Jamaica. M.

Holland, John (1729). *See* Moor. M.

Holland, John. S s cotton twist Lent 1739. La.

Holland, John. S Lent R 14 yrs Summer 1752. Nt.

Holland, John. S Mar TB to Va Apr 1764. Wi.

Holland, John. S & T Jly 1771 *Scarsdale*. L.

Holland, John. S s bread at Bythorn Lent 1773. Hu.

Holland, John. S Jly 1774. Ha.

Holland, Joseph. S Jly T 14 yrs Sep 1765 *Justitia*. M.

Holland als Priest, Mary. S May T Jun 1727 *Susanna* to Va. M.

Holland, Mary. T Dec 1752 *Greyhound*. M.

Holland, Matthew. S s horse Lent R 14 yrs Summer 1726. Li.

Holland, Matthew. R 14 yrs Mar 1749. Do.

Holland, Richard. R for Barbados Aug 1664. L.

Holland, Samuel. S Aug T Oct 1741 *Sea Horse* to Va. M.

Holland, Sarah. S Oct T Dec 1758 *The Brothers*. L.

Holland, Thomas. S s at St. Peter in Barley, Oxford, Summer 1721. O.

Holland, Thomas. S Lent T May 1750 *Lichfield*. K.

Holland, Thomas. S Oct 1751-Jan 1752. M.

Holland, Thomas. S Jan 1757. L.

Holland, Thomas. S Lent R 14 yrs Summer 1765. O.

Holland, William. S Jan-Feb 1775. M.

Hollands, Robert. R 14 yrs Summer T Oct 1739 *Duke of Cumberland*. Sx.

Hollard, Bernard. SQS Apr TB to Md Nov 1738. So.

Hollett, John. R 14 yrs Apr 1742. Ha.

Hollett, Mary (1740). *See* Greeves. M.

Hollett, Thomas of Clapham. R for Barbados or Jamaica Jly 1687. Sy.

Holliday, James. S Apr T May 1720 *Honor* but escaped in Vigo, Spain. L.

Holliday, James. S Lent 1762. Su.

Holliday, John. R Dec 1699 AT Jan 1700. M.

Holliday, John. S s at Tetbury Summer TB Aug 1749. G.

Holliday, Joseph. S Jan T Feb 1719 *Worcester* LC Annapolis Jun 1719. L.

Holliday, Thomas. SQS Oct 1766 T Jan 1767 *Tryal*. M.

Holliday, William of Bisley. R for Barbados Jly 1664. G.

Holliday, William. S Aug T Sep 1764 *Justitia*. L.

Holligg, Ephraim. R Mar TB to Va Apr 1774. Wi.

Hollihead, William. SQS Coventry Aug 1745. Wa.

Hollingberry, Richard. T Nov 1743 *George William*. K.

Hollins, Alice of Manchester, singlewoman. SQS Aug 1762. La.

Hollings, Neomi. S Summer 1739 R 14 yrs Lent 1740. Y.

Hollings, Robert. T Dec 1771 *Justitia*. Sy.

Hollingsworth, William of Harlow. R for Barbados or Jamaica Jly 1674. E.

Hollington, Dixon als Dixley. S s watch at Bridgenorth Summer 1774. Sh.

Hollinworth, Arthur of Warrington, husbandman. SQS Jan 1775. La.

Holehock, William. R for America Aug 1715. M.

Hollis, Alethea. S May-Jun T Aug 1752 *Tryal*. M.

Hollis, John. T Jun 1740 *Essex*. Sy.

Hollis, Mark. S Summer 1750. Bu.

Hollis als Hammond, Mary. T Jan 1734 *Caesar*. Bu.

Hollis, Richard. R for Barbados or Jamaica Jly 1687. M.

Hollis, Richard. R Summer 1773. Sy.

Hollis, Symon. R Dec 1698 AT Jan 1699. M.

Holles als Jenkins, Thomas. S Summer 1740. St.

Hollis, Vincent. S Feb T Apr 1766 *Ann*. M.

Hollis, William (1764). *See* Hallis. Db.

Hollis, William, als Berk, Thomas. SQS Dec 1772. M.

Hollister, John. S Jly T Sep 1755 *Tryal*. L.

Hollow, William. S Summer 1729. Cu.

Holloway, Alice. S Feb 1761. L.

Holloway, Elizabeth. S Jly 1763. Ha.

Holloway, George. S Mar 1721 T Mar 1723. Bu.

Holloway, George. LC from *Dorsetshire* Va Sep 1736. X.

Holloway, George of St. James, Westminster. SW Apr T May 1767 *Thornton*. M.

Holloway als Van Gadwey, Jacob. S Dec 1746. L.

Holloway, Jane (1719). *See* Scott. L.

Holloway, John. Rebel T 1685.

Holloway, John. T Oct 1738 *Genoa*. K.

Holloway, John. S Lent 1750. Bu.

Holloway, John. S May-Jun T Jly 1753 *Tryal*. M.

Holloway, John. S Norwich Lent 1763; found at large & to hang Summer 1764. Nf.

Holloway, Judith. S Feb T 14 yrs Mar 1729 *Patapsco* but died on passage. L.

Holloway, Mary (1729). *See* Dew. L.

Holloway, Mary. S Jan T Feb 1733 *Smith* to Md or Va. M.

Holloway, Mary wife of Anthony. S Dec 1763 T 14 yrs Mar 1764 *Tryal*. M.

Holloway, Robert. S Sep-Oct T Dec 1771 *Justitia*. M.

Holloway, Robin of North Perrot. R for Barbados Jan 1675. So.

Holloway, Susan of Tewkesbury. R for America Jly 1698. G.

Holloway, Thomas of Ivybridge, blacksmith. R for Barbados Apr 1668. De.

Holloway, Thomas. S s cheese Feb T Jun 1738 *Forward* to Md or Va. M.

Holloway, Thomas. S s at Waltham St. Lawrence Lent 1753. Be.

Holloway als Hathaway, Thomas. S s at Uley Lent 1760. G.

Holloway, William. R for Barbados Sep 1672. L.

Holloway, William of Camberwell. R for America Jly 1700. Sy.

Holloway als Jones, William. S Lent R 14 yrs Summer 1757. O.

Hollowell, Mary. R for America Mar 1690. No.

Hollowood, John. T Jun 1738 *Forward*. Sy.

Hollows, Elizabeth. S Summer 1749. Sy.

Holly, James. S Mar 1751. De.

Holly, Sarah. SQS Devizes & TB to Va Apr 1774. Wi.

Holley, William. S Summer 1769. Li.

Hollyer, Richard. R 10 yrs in plantations Oct 1662. M.

Holman, Eli. Rebel T 1685.

Holman, John. S Jan T Feb 1726 *Supply* LC Annapolis May 1726. M.

Hollman, John. T May 1751 *Tryal*. Sy.

Holman, Thomas. T Jun 1738 *Forward*. Sx.

Holman, Thomas. SWK & T Apr 1765 *Ann*. K.

Holman, Thomas. S s sheep at Streatley & R Summer 1774. Bd.

Homby, Joan of Welling. R for Barbados Apr 1668. Ht.

Holmby, Thomas. S Apr T 14 yrs May 1718 *Tryal* LC Charles Town Aug 1718. L.

Holme, Ellen, singlewoman. SQS Apr 1765. La.

Holm, George (1771). *See* Cock, Charles. St.

Home, John. SQS Apr T May 1750 *Lichfield*. M.

Holme, John of Ulverstone. SQS Apr 1768. La.

Holme, Robert. S s horse Lent R 14 yrs Summer 1750. La.

Holmes, Ann. S Summer 1756. Sy.

Holmes, Edward of Huntingdon. R for Barbados Feb 1665. St.

Holmes, Edward. R & T 14 yrs Jly 1770 *Scarsdale*. M.

Holmes, Elizabeth, als wife of John Fowles. S Oct-Dec 1739 T Jan 1740 *York*. M.

Holmes, Elizabeth (1742). *See* Jackson. L.

Holmes, Elizabeth (1742). *See* Dutton. K.

Holmes, Elizabeth. S May T 14 yrs Jun 1765 *Justitia*. M.

Holmes, Frederick. S Feb T Mar 1758 *Dragon*. L.

Holmes, George, shoemaker. R (Western Circ) for Barbados Feb 1699. L.

Holmes, Hannah (1759). *See* Ward, Mary. M.

Holmes, Henry. T 14 yrs Aug 1769 *Douglas*. E.

Holmes, Isaac. R Apr 1773. M.

Holmes, James. S Oct T Nov 1725 *Rappahannock* LC Rappahannock Apr 1726. M.

Holmes, Jane. T Mar 1750 *Tryal*. M.

Holmes, John. R for Barbados May 1676. L.

Holmes, John. R for Barbados or Jamaica Mar 1685. M.

Holmes, John. Rebel T 1685.

Holmes, John. R Dec 1699 AT Jan 1700. M.

Holmes, John of Great Oakley. R for Barbados or Jamaica Jly 1710. E.

Holmes, John. S Feb 1719. M.

Holmes, John. S Aug T Oct 1726 *Forward*. L.

Holmes, John. S Summer 1732. Nl.

Holmes, John. T Jan 1738 *Dorsetshire*. Sy.

Holmes, John. S for highway robbery Summer 1755 R 14 yrs Lent 1756. Wa.

Holmes, John, cordwainer. S s flour at St. Helen's Summer 1757. Be.

Holmes, John, hempdresser. S s flour at St. Helen's Summer 1757. Be.

Holmes als Howmes, John. SQS s spade Summer 1763. Cu.

Holmes, John. S Summer 1766. No.

Holmes, John Jr. R 14 yrs Jly 1771 TB to Va 1772. De.

Homes, Jonas. TB to Md from QS 1737.

Holmes, Joseph. S s at Brewood Lent 1753. St.

Holmes, Joshua. S & T Mar 1760 *Friendship*. L.

Holmes, Lancelot. S s at Astley Lent 1758. Wo.

Holmes, Mary. S for burning a barn & R Summer 1735. Su.

Holmes, Mary. S & T Jan 1736 *Dorsetshire* LC Va Sep 1736. L.

Holmes als Yates als Smith, Mary. S Jun 1743. M.

Holmes, Matthew. S & T Oct 1732 *Caesar* to Va. M.

Holmes, Matthew (1738). *See* Ellis, Thomas. Y.

Holmes, Peter. AT Summer 1748. Y.

Holmes, Rebecca wife of James. S Jan-Feb 1775. M.

Holmes, Richard of Adwalton. R for Barbados Jly 1685. Y.

Holmes, Richard of Great Dunmow. R for America Jly 1700. E.

Holms, Richard. LC from *Patapsco* Annapolis Nov 1733. X.

Holmes, Richard. S Sep-Oct 1772. M.

Holmes, Robert. S & T Jan 1722 *Gilbert* LC Annapolis Jly 1722. M.

Holmes, Robert. T Jly 1724 *Robert* LC Md Jun 1725. Sy.

Holmes, Robinson. S s mare Aug 1764 R 14 yrs Lent TB to Va Apr 1765. Le.

Holmes, Samuel of Langar. SQS s well chain Oct 1759. Nt.

Holmes, Sarah. S s at St. Mary, Reading, Summer 1749. Be.

Holmes, Sarah. S Lent TB Apr 1767. Db.

Holmes, Sarah. S Oct T Dec 1769 *Justitia*. L.

Holmes, Thomas of Leominster. R for America Mar 1710. He.

Holmes, Thomas. S Summer 1732. Y.

Holmes, Thomas. S Lent TB Apr 1741. Y.

Holmes, Thomas. AT Summer 1757. Y.

Holmes, Thomas. S Apr-Jun T Jly 1772 *Tayloe*. M.

Holmes, Thomas. S Summer 1772. Li.

Holmes, William. S Feb T Mar 1729 *Patapsco* LC Annapolis Dec 1729. L.

Holmes, William. S s cloth Summer 1754. Sh.

Holmes, William. S Feb T Mar 1758 *Dragon*. M.

Holmes, William. S Lent T Apr 1768. Li.

Holmstead, James. T May 1719 *Margaret*. Sy.

Holstock, Hannah, aged 21, fair. S & T 14 yrs Oct 1720 *Gilbert* LC Annapolis May 1721. M.

Holstock, John. T Nov 1741 *Sea Horse*. K.

Holstop, Joseph. S & T Jly 1753 *Tryal*. L.

Holt, Edmund. S Summer 1753. La.

Holt, Edmund. S Lent R 14 yrs Summer 1757. St.

Holt, George. S s at Settrington & R for life Lent 1774. Y.

Holt, John. S & R Summer 1727 AT Summer 1728. Y.

Holt als Chiswell, John. S s at Barrowfield Lent 1734. St.

Holt, John. S Lent T May 1750 *Lichfield*. E.

Holt, John. S Summer 1752. Bd.

Holt, John. T Apr 1753 *Thames*. K.

Holt, John als Jockey of Rochdale. SQS Apr 1758. La.

Holt, John. T Sep 1765 *Justitia*. K.

Holt, John. SQS Lent TB Apr 1766. Db.

Holt, John. SQS Jan TB Apr 1766. So.

Holt, Mary. S Feb T Mar 1764 *Tryal*. M.

Holt, Nathaniel. S Mar 1730. Ha.

Holt, Ormond. T Apr 1735 *Patapsco*. E.

Holt, Richard. S s cloth at Kidderminster Lent 1774. Wo.

Holt, Robert. S s from warehouse Summer 1758 R 14 yrs Lent 1759. La.

Holt, Sarah. T Nov 1725 *Rappahannock* LC Va Aug 1726. Sy.

Holt, Simeon (1771). *See* Bird. Nf.

Holt, Susanna wife of Glese als Ralph. S for highway robbery near
  Liverpool Summer 1765 R 14 yrs Lent 1766. La.

Holt, Thomas. R for America Jly 1687. Db.

Holt, Thomas. S Lent 1754. Sy.

Hoult, Thomas. S s mare at Doncaster & R 14 yrs Lent 1768. Y.

Holt, William. S Sep-Oct T Dec 1753 *Whiteing*. M.

Holt, William of Mitcham. SQS 14 yrs & T Jan 1756 *Greyhound*. Sy.

Holt, William. S Lent T May 1770. Wa.

Holtam als Holtham, John. R for Barbados or Jamaica Mar 1685. M.

Holten, Benjamin. R Lent 1773. E.

Holton als Brown, Elizabeth. R for life Lent 1774. Sy.

Holton, John (1751). *See* Orton. M.

Holton, John. S & R 14 yrs Lent 1775. Be.

Holway, William (1730). *See* Alway. So.

Holyhead, William. S Lent 1739. St.

Holyman, Richard. S & T Jly 1772 *Tayloe*. L.

Holyoake, Daniel. S s sheep Lent R 14 yrs Summer 1767. Wa.

Holliocke, John of Adderbury. R for America Mar 1680. O.

Holythorne, Thomas. S for receiving Sep T 14 yrs Dec 1767 *Neptune*. L.

Homan, Anthony. S Summer R for Barbados Aug 1663. K.

Homell, Elizabeth. S Feb T Apr 1765 *Ann*. M.

Homer, John (1732). *See* Harris. K.

Homer, John. S Nov T Dec 1753 *Whiteing*. L.

Homer, Jonathan. S Summer 1759 R 14 yrs Lent 1760. Wo.

Homersham, Charles. R for Barbados or Jamaica Jly 1686. M.

Homes. *See* Holmes.

Homine, John. S Jan T Feb 1742 *Industry*. L.

Homlyn, Thomas. S Mar 1738. So.

Honden, Richard. S & TB Sep 1753. G.

Hone, Ann. SQS Oct 1754. M.

Hone, James. S Jly 1760. Ha.

Honey, John (1726). *See* Oney. M.

Honey, John Jr. T Apr 1770 *New Trial*. K.

Honey, Sarah. SQS Dec 1757 T Mar 1758 *Dragon*. M.
Honeybond, William. R Lent 1773. Ht.
Honour, William. S May-Jun T Aug 1752 *Tryal*. M.
Hood, Esther. T 14 yrs Sep 1767 *Justitia*. Sy.
Hood, Hannah, spinster. S s at St. Nicholas, Norwich, Lent 1769. Nf.
Hood, John Jr. S Lent 1745. Sy.
Hood, John. T Sep 1764 *Justitia*. Sy.
Hood, Michael. TB Sep 1736. Nt.
Hood, Robert of Scarborough. R for Barbadds Jly 1699. Y.
Hood als Pilling, William. T Oct 1720 *Gilbert*. Sx.
Hookam, Martha. S Summer 1733 R 14 yrs Summer 1734. Nt.
Hook als Cofield, Elizabeth. S & T Dec 1734 *Caesar* LC Va Jly 1735. L.
Hooke, John. R for Barbados Jun 1665. M.
Hooke, John. S Norwich Summer 1749. Nf.
Hooke, Nathan. S Norwich Lent 1744. Nf.
Hook, Richard. S Apr-May T Jly 1771 *Scarsdale*. M.
Hook, Stephen. S Summer 1750 R 14 yrs Lent TB Apr 1751. G.
Hook, Thomas. T Sep 1758 *Tryal*. Sy.
Hook, William of St. Margaret, Westminster. SW Oct 1773. M.
Hooker, John. T Oct 1723 *Forward*. Sy.
Hooker, Thomas. S Jly 1736. Ha.
Hooker, William. S Jly 1736. Ha.
Hookins, Simon. S Aug 1764. So.
Hookley, Sarah. S Apr 1748. L.
Hookstood, Joseph. SQS Dec 1774. M.
Hooley, John of Wynrith. R for America Aug 1699. Ch.
Hooley, Matthew. TB to Md Jly 1725. Db.
Hoop, James (1738). *See* Thompson. La.
Hooper, Anthony. S Apr 1767. So.
Hooper, Bernard. R 14 yrs Jly 1730. De.
Hooper, Elizabeth. R 14 yrs Aug 1764. De.
Hooper, Elizabeth. S Oct 1764 T Jan 1765 *Tryal*. M.
Hooper, Elizabeth. S Mar 1773. De.
Hooper, Henry. Rebel T 1685.
Hooper, Henry. R Oct 1694 AT Jan 1695. M.
Hooper, Henry. S Jun-Dec 1738 T Jan 1739 *Dorsetshire* to Va. M.
Hooper, James. S May T 14 yrs Jly 1722 *Alexander* to Nevis or
    Jamaica. M.
Hooper, John (3). Rebels T 1685.
Hooper, John. PT Summer 1719. G.
Hooper, John. S Aug 1726. Do.
Hooper, John. T Apr 1733 *Patapsco*. K.
Hooper, John. TB to Va from QS 1737. De.
Hooper, John. S Feb T Apr 1741 *Speedwell* or *Mediterranean*. M.
Hooper, John. TB to Va from QS 1761. De.
Hooper, John. S Mar TB to Va Apr 1762. Wi.
Hooper, John. S Mar 1764. De.
Hooper, Josiah. S s cloth at Stroud Summer 1774. G.
Hooper, Lawrence. R 14 yrs Aug 1729. De.
Hooper, Mary. S Apr T 14 yrs Aug 1718 *Eagle* LC Charles Town Mar
    1719. L.

Hooper, Mary. S Jan-Feb 1775. M.

Hooper, Richard. Rebel T 1685.

Hooper, Richard. R 14 yrs Aug 1742. De.

Hooper, Richard. S s pigs at Goodrich Lent 1767. He.

Hooper, Robert. TB to Va from QS 1741. De.

Hooper, Robert. T Dec 1763 *Neptune*. M.

Hooper, Roger (1685). *See* Bryant.

Hooper, Samuel. S s at Grimley Summer 1775. Wo.

Hooper, Thomas of Bradley, Kentchurch, yeoman. R for Barbados Jly 1663. He.

Hooper, Thomas of Upper Sapey. R for Barbados Feb 1665. He.

Hooper, Thomas. Rebel T 1685.

Hooper, Thomas of Payhembury. R for Barbados Jun 1687. De.

Hooper, Thomas of Deerhurst, yeoman. S Summer TB Aug 1740. G.

Hooper, William. Rebel T 1685.

Hooper, William (1728). *See* Jones. Be.

Hooper, William (1747). *See* Davis. G.

Hooper, William. S Aug 1748. Co.

Hooper, William. S s sheep Lent R 14 yrs Summer 1749. He.

Hoopham, John. S Jly T Sep 1766 *Justitia*. M.

Hoops, John Jr. AT Lent 1766. Y.

Hooton, John. S Lent 1749. K.

Hopcroft, Robert. S Jan-Feb T Apr 1771 *Thornton*. M.

Hopday, Stephen. T Jun 1740 *Essex*. K.

Hope, Elizabeth (1724). *See* Davies. Sy.

Hope, George. R 14 yrs Summer 1743. Y.

Hope, Matthew. S Feb 1752. L.

Hope, Ralph. S s at North Otterington Lent TB Apr 1774. Y.

Hope, Robert, als Chapman, Richard. R for America Aug 1713. M.

Hope, Stephen. S May T Aug 1769 *Douglas*. M.

Hope, Thomas. SQS Jly T Sep 1751 *Greyhound*. M.

Hope, William. S City Lent 1727 AT Summer 1728. Y.

Hope, William. S s horss Summer 1742 R 14 yrs Lent 1743. Du.

Hope, William. S Lent 1773. K.

Hopegood, Mary. S Oct 1768 T 14 yrs Jan 1769 *Thornton*. M.

Hopgood, Thomas. S Jly 1758 TB to Va 1759. De.

Hopes, John. SQS New Sarum or Warminster & TB to Va Oct 1768. Wi.

Hopkin, George. R for Barbados May 1665. X.

Hopkin, Sarah. S Summer 1768. Y.

Hopkin, Susannah of Broughton, singlewoman. SQS Jan 1743. La.

Hopkins, Ann. S Dec 1733 T Jan 1734 *Caesar* LC Va Jly 1735. L.

Hopkins, Ann of St. Andrew Holborn. S & T May 1736 *Patapsco* to Md. M.

Hopkins, Elizabeth. S Feb T Mar 1727 *Rappahannock* to Md. M.

Hopkins, Elizabeth. S Dec 1733 T Jan 1734 *Caesar* LC Va Jly 1734. M.

Hopkins, Elizabeth. S Oct 1760. M.

Hopkins, James. S May T Jun 1726 *Loyal Margaret* LC Annapolis Oct 1726. M.

Hopkins, James. S Aug T Oct 1726 *Forward* to Va. M.

Hopkins, James. T May 1767 *Thornton*. E.

Hopkins, John. R for Barbados or Jamaica May 1684. L.

Hopkins, John. R for America Feb 1700. No.

Hopkins, John. S for assault on highway Summer 1738 R 14 yrs Lent 1739. Mo.

Hopkins, John. SQS Aug 1747 TB to Va Jly 1748. Le.

Hopkins, John (1753). *See* Williams. De.

Hopkins, John. S Lent 1774. K.

Hopkins, Joseph als John of Forthampton. R for America Feb 1716. G.

Hopkins, Lettice. S Jan T Feb 1724 *Anne*. L.

Hopkins, Margaret. R & T Dec 1716 *Lewis* to Jamaica. M.

Hopkins, Sarah. S Jan T Feb 1724 *Anne* to Carolina. M.

Hopkins als Heritage, Thomas. R for America Jly 1687. Wa.

Hopkins, Thomas (1718). *See* Matthews. M.

Hopkins, Thomas. T Oct 1721 *William & John*. K.

Hopkins als Hughes, Thomas. T Oct 1722 *Forward* LC Md Jun 1723. Sy.

Hopkins, Thomas. S & TB Aug 1727. G.

Hopkins, Thomas. Accused Lent 1737 of returning from transportation but found not guilty & discharged. G.

Hopkins, Thomas. S May-Jly 1774. M.

Hopkins, William. R for Barbados Feb 1675. L.

Hopkins, William of Camberwell. R for Barbados or Jamaica Feb 1684. Sy.

Hopkins, William (1746). *See* Thomas. De.

Hopkins, William. S s at Cheltenham Lent 1758. G.

Hopley, James. S s at St. Martin, Worcester, Lent 1752. Wo.

Hopman, Margaret. LC from *Owners Goodwill* Annapolis Jly 1722. X.

Hoppart, James. S Summer 1765. We.

Hopper, William of Newcastle upon Tyne. R for Barbados Jly 1686. Nl.

Hopping, Ann. S Mar 1752. De.

Hoppit, William. S Apr T May 1755 *Rose*. L.

Hopps, Anthony. S May-Jly 1749. M.

Hopps, Joseph. S May T Jun 1764 *Dolphin*. L.

Hopson, John. LC from *Alexander* Annapolis Sep 1723. X.

Hopson, Richard of Abergavenny. R for America Jly 1678. Mo.

Hopson, Richard. S Feb T Apr 1743 *Justitia*. M.

Hopson, Thomas of St. Mary, Gloucester. R for America Jly 1679. G.

Hopton, Charles. R for Barbados or Jamaica Jly 1687. L.

Hopwood als Orpwood, John. SQS Feb T Apr 1766 *Ann*. M.

Hopwood, William. S Feb-Apr 1746. M.

Horabin, John. S Sep 1740. L.

Horobin, William. S Lent R 14 yrs Summer 1757. St.

Horan, James of Rotherhithe. SQS & T Apr 1765 *Ann*. Sy.

Horden, John. T Dec 1763 *Neptune*. K.

Hordley, Richard (1735). *See* Pugh. He.

Hords, Martha wife of John. S Feb T May 1736 *Patapsco* to Md. M.

Hordust, William. S s at St. Andrew, Worcester, Lent 1729. Wo.

Hore. *See* Hoar.

Horley, Robert. S & T Sep 1757 *Thetis*. L.

Horley, Thomas of Hentland. R for America Nov 1694. He.

Horman, John. Died on passage in *Rappahannock* 1726. X.

Hornbrook, Thomas. R & T 14 yrs Sep 1737 *Pretty Patsy* to Md. M.

Hornby, George. S at Hull s gold coin Summer 1772. Y.

Hornby, Mercy. R & T Dec 1734 *Caesar* LC Va Jly 1735. M.

Hornby, William. S Lent 1757. Sy.

Horn, Benjamin. S s fowls at Witney Summer 1748. O.

Horne, Charles, son of an attorney in King Street. S for assault with sword Dec 1735 T Jan 1736 *Dorsetshire*. M.

Horn, Elizabeth. S Mar 1763. Ha.

Horne, Henry. S Feb-Apr T Jly 1753 *Tryal*. M.

Horne, John (1773). *See* Mayhew. Su.

Horn, Joseph. R 14 yrs Jly 1753. Ha.

Horn, Mary. T Nov 1725 *Rappahannock* LC Va Aug 1726. K.

Horn, Mary. S May-Jun T Jly 1753 *Tryal*. M.

Horne, Mary. S & T Jly 1770 *Scarsdale*. L.

Horne, Mary. T Apr 1771 *Thornton*. M.

Horn, Philip. S Lent 1755. Be.

Horn, Richard. S s sheep Lent R 14 yrs Summer 1763. St.

Horne, Thomas. S Jan T Feb 1726 *Supply* LC Annapolis May 1726. M.

Horne, William. S s rye at Broseley Lent 1726. Sh.

Horn, William (1740). *See* Strugler. Ha.

Horne, William. R 14 yrs Jly 1751. Ha.

Horne, William. S Summer 1757 R 14 yrs Lent 1758. O.

Horn, William. S s sheep at Chelmondiston & R 14 yrs Lent 1774. Su.

Horner, Barthena. T Oct 1720 *Gilbert*. Sy.

Horner, Edward. R for Barbados Mar 1683. M.

Horner, John (1715). *See* Turner. Do.

Horner, Robert. S Sep 1756. M.

Horner, Thomas. S s sheep Mar R 14 yrs Summer TB to Va Apr 1763. Le.

Horney, Thomas. T 21 yrs Apr 1770 *New Trial*. Ht.

Hornsby, Ann. S for shoplifting Summer 1758. Du.

Hornsby, James. S Apr R 14 yrs for Carolina May 1719. L.

Hornsbee als Hornsby, William. S Feb T Apr 1765 *Ann*. M.

Hornstock, John. LC from *Rappahanock* Va Apr 1726. X.

Horrocks, Jane of Little Lever, spinster. SQS Apr 1743. La.

Horrod, Sarah (1756). *See* Whorewood. O.

Horrad, William. S s wheat at Dunstable Summer 1768. Bd.

Horrell, John. S Mar 1758. De.

Horsefall, Luke. T Oct 1729 *Forward*. Ht.

Horseman, Henry. T Oct 1722 *Forward* LC Md Jun 1723. Sy.

Horsepoole, Mary. R for Barbados or Jamaica Jan 1692. L.

Horsey, Andrew. PT Aug 1676. M.

Horsey, John of St. Sepulchre, shoemaker. SQS for attending unlawful religious meeting Jan 1665. M.

Horsey, Mary. S Feb-Apr T May 1751 *Tryal*. M.

Horsey, Richard. S Aug 1764. So.

Horsley, Christian of North Shields, butcher's wife. S for obtaining goods by false pretences Summer 1771 T *Lowther & Senhouse* LC Va May 1772. Nl.

Horsley, James (1733). *See* Wilson. Nl.

Horseley, John. S & T Dec 1759 *Phoenix*. M.

Horson, Thomas. T May 1767 *Thornton*. K.

Horston, Robert (1744). *See* Ellis. G.

Hort, Anthony. R 14 yrs Aug 1750. So.

Horton. *See* Houghton.

Horwood, Edward. T Apr 1741 *Speedwell* or *Mediterranean*. Ht.

Horwood, Thomas. S s sheep Lent R 14 yrs Summer 1754; John Horwood acquitted. Bu.

Horwood. *See* also Whorewood.

Hosegood, George. S Mar 1732. So.

Hosey, Thomas. R for Barbados & TB Oct 1667. L.

Hosier, Ann. S & T Oct 1732 *Caesar* to Va. M.

Hossyer, Robert of Hemel Hempstead. R for Barbados or Jamaica Mar 1707. Ht.

Hosier, Thomas. S Apr T Sep 1718 *Eagle* LC Charles Town Mar 1719. L.

Hoskyn, Francis. S Jly 1729. Co.

Hoskin, Hercules als Argalus. S Apr 1759. Co.

Hoskins, Ann. S Jly T Oct 1741 *Sea Horse*. L.

Hoskins, Ann. S Sep T Nov 1743 *George William*. M.

Hoskins, Catherine. LC from *Loyal Margaret* Annapolis Oct 1726. X.

Hoskins als Haskins, Elizabeth. S May T Jun 1768 *Tryal*. M.

Hoskins, Esther. S May-Jly 1750. M.

Hoskins, Frances. S Oct 1730. M.

Hoskins, Margaret of Exeter, spinster. R for Barbados Feb 1673. De.

Hoskins als Shrub, Samuel. R 14 yrs Mar 1772. So.

Hoskins, Sarah. S & T Oct 1729 *Forward* LC Va Jun 1730. M.

Hoskins, Thomas (1719). *See* Matthews. L.

Hoskins, Thomas. S Aug T Sep 1727 *Forward* LC Rappahannock May 1728. L.

Hoskins, Thomas. S Oct T Nov 1759 *Phoenix*. L.

Hoslamb, Edward. S Sep 1718. M.

Hosler, William. S Lent R 14 yrs Summer 1761. E.

Hotchpitch, William. S May-Jly 1749. M.

Hotton, John. S Apr 1749. L.

Houching, Susan. T Apr 1741 *Speedwell* or *Mediterranean*. E.

Huffe, Eleanor wife of Richard *(qv)* of Stony Stratford. R for Barbados Mar 1679. Bu.

Hough, Hugh. S s at Eccleshall Summer 1774. St.

Hough, James (1750). *See* Cashleake. He.

Huff, Mary wife of William. S Sep T Dec 1763 *Neptune*. M.

Huffe, Richard of Stony Stratford. R for Barbados Mar 1679. Bu.

Hough, William. TB Apr 1765. Db.

Hougham (Huffam), Solomon Jr. S at Sandwich Jun T Aug 1721 *Prince Royal* LC Va Apr 1723. K.

Haughton, Adolphus James. S Sep T Oct 1750 *Rachael*. M.

Horton, Anne. R Apr TB for Barbados Jun 1669. M.

Horton, Charles. R for Barbados May 1676. M.

Hawton, Edward of Worth. R for Barbados or Jamaica Jly 1691. Sx.

Horton, Edward. S s horse Lent R 14 yrs Summer 1734. No.

Houghton, Edward. S Lent 1743. Bd.

Haughton, Elizabeth. S Sep-Oct 1772. M.

Houghton, James. S Feb-Apr T May 1752 *Lichfield*. M.

Houghton, James. S for highway robbery at Hemingford Grey Lent 1771. Hu.
Houghton, John. S Lent 1745. *Su.
Horton, John of Westbury. SQS Marlborough Oct 1755 TB May 1756. Wi.
Horton, John (1760). *See* Bowers. Wo.
Hawton, Joseph. TB to Md 1728. De.
Horton, Joseph. R 14 yrs Jly 1775. M.
Horton, Mark. S May T Jly 1722 *Alexander*. L.
Houghton, Martha. R for Barbados Oct 1673. L.
Houghton, Peter. S Lent 1747. La.
Horton, Richard. S for life Jan 1746. M.
Houghton, Robert of Chesterfield. R for America Jly 1678. Db.
Horton, Robert (1769). *See* Hemmery. L.
Houghton als Horton, Roger. R Aug AT Oct 1700. M.
Houghton, Samuel of Denton. SQS Jan 1741. La.
Haughton, Thomas. R Jan 1656. M.
Horton, Thomas of Bradley. R for America Mar 1683. St.
Houghton als Horton, Thomas. S s at Newent Summer 1733. G.
Horton, Thomas. S Oct-Dec 1754. M.
Horton, Thomas. S Jan-Feb 1774. M.
Haughton, William. S Jly 1747. L.
Houghton, William. S Sep 1760. L.
Haughton, William. S s hens at Wombourne Lent 1767. St.
Haughton, William. S May-Jly 1773. M.
Haughton, William. R 14 yrs Jly 1774. M.
Hoult. *See* Holt.
Hounsby, William. T Sep 1757 *Thetis*. Sy.
Hounsome, William. T 14 yrs Apr 1770 *New Trial*. Sy.
Howse, Edward of Abingdon. R for America Nov 1694. Be.
Howse, James of Farnborough. R for America Jly 1674. Wa.
House, James. S Mar 1773. Do.
Hows, John. S for burglary Lent R 14 yrs Summer T Nov 1741 *Sea Horse*. Bu. & Nf.
House, John. S May T Aug 1769 *Douglas*. M.
Howse, Joseph (1727). *See* Percivall. M.
House, Mary. S & T Sep 1767. M.
House, Rebecca (1664). *See* Hackleton. L.
House, Thomas of St. Paul, Covent Garden. SW Apr T May 1767 *Thornton*. M.
House, Thomas. SQS Apr TB Sep 1768. So.
Howse, William. S Mar R 14 yrs Summer TB to Va Sep 1751. Le.
Housman als Harman, Barbara. S Feb 1744. M.
Houseman, Thomas. S s at Bedwardine Lent 1770. Wo.
Houseman, William of Deptford. S s horse Summer 1746. Sy.
Housion, James of St. Olave, Southwark. SQS Jan 1752. Sy.
Howsley als Firth, Helen. S Lent 1731. Y.
Howsley, John. S Lent 1745. Y.
Howsley, John. S Lent R 14 yrs Summer 1765. Nt.
Houseley, Marella (1772). *See* Berry. Db.
Housley, Richard. S Summer 1769. Db.

Houseley, Samuel (1764). *See* Berry. Db.
Housley, Thomas (1773). *See* Howsell. Nt.
Howsley, William. S Lent 1765. Nt.
Houten, William. S & T Apr 1769 *Tryal*. L.
Hover, Samuel of Colchester. SQS Oct 1743 T May 1744 *Justitia*. E.
Howard, Andrew. Rebel T 1685.
Howard, Anne (1656). *See* Harward. M.
Howard, Anne, aged 20. R for Barbados Feb 1664. M.
Howard, Ann. S Jan T Feb 1719 *Worcester* LC Annapolis Jun 1719. L.
Howard, Ann. S May T Jun 1726 *Loyal Margaret* to Md. M.
Howard, Ann. S Feb-Apr 1746. M.
Howard, Ann. S Sep 1760. L.
Howard, Bridget (1756). *See* Newman. M.
Howard, Christian. LC from *Loyal Margaret* Annapolis Oct 1726. X.
Howard, Daniel of Middleton, weaver. SQS Mar 1767. La.
Howard, Denchier. T Dec 1770 *Justitia*. K.
Howard, Edward of St. Martin, Colchester. SQS Oct 1754. E.
Howard, Edward (1770). *See* Edwards, John. M.
Howard, Eignon. SQS & T Dec 1758 *The Brothers*. Ht.
Howard, Elizabeth. S Jan T Mar 1750 *Tryal*. L.
Howard, Elizabeth. S Apr T Jun 1768 *Tryal*. M.
Howard, George of Cobham. R for Barbados or Jamaica Jun 1699. K.
Howard, Hannah. S & T Apr 1733 *Patapsco* LC Annapolis Nov 1733. M.
Howard, Henry. R for Barbados Jan 1664. L.
Howard, Henry. R for Barbados Sep 1672. L.
Howard, Henry. R 14 yrs Mar 1757. So.
Howard, Henry. ST & T Aug 1769 *Douglas*. L.
Howard, Henry. S Dec 1772. M.
Howard als Crafts, Hester. S Dec 1734. L.
Howard, James. T Oct 1726 *Forward*. E.
Howard, James. SL Jly 1761. Sy.
Howard, Jane (1750). *See* Faulkner. M.
Howard, Jenkin. S Dec 1765 T Jan 1766 *Tryal*. M.
Howard, John. R for Barbados May AT Sep 1684. M.
Howard, John of Hennock (Devon). R for Barbados Jly 1684. Co.
Howard, John of Saham Toney. R for America Mar 1686. Nf.
Howard, John, weaver aged 29, dark. T Oct 1720 *Gilbert* LC Md May
    1721. E.
Howard, John. S Jan T Feb 1726 *Supply* LC Annapolis May 1726. L.
Howard, John. S & T Oct 1729 *Forward* LC Va Jun 1730. L.
Howard, John. S Jun-Dec 1738 T Jan 1739 *Dorsetshire* to Va. M.
Howard, John. S s sheep Summer 1740. Wo.
Howard, John. S Jly T Sep 1751 *Greyhound*. L.
Howard, John (1769). *See* Harwood. M.
Howard als Hayward, John. SQS & T Jly 1771 *Scarsdale*. M.
Howard, John. S s oats at St. Peter, Thetford, Summer 1773. Nf.
Howard, John. S Jan-Feb 1775. M.
Howard, Josias. Rebel T 1685.
Howard, Katherine (1687). See Baulfield, Elizabeth. M.
Howard, Margaret. S Mar 1754. L.

Howard, Martha. S May T Jly 1723 *Alexander* LC Annapolis Sep 1723. M.

Howard, Mary. R Aug 1700. M.

Howard, Mary. S & T Mar 1750 *Tryal*. L.

Howard, Moses. S Summer 1749. Nf.

Howard, Richard of Crediton. R for Barbados Jly 1684. De.

Howard, Richard. T Apr 1739 *Forward*. K.

Howard, Richard. S Jly 1749. L.

Howard, Robert. R for Barbados Dec 1667. M.

Howard, Robert. S & T May 1744 *Justitia*. L.

Howard, Samuel. S for highway robbery Lent R 14 yrs Summer 1766. Bu.

Howard, Sarah. S Apr-May T May 1774 *Justitia*. M.

Howard, Simon. S s fowls at Buckden Lent 1771. Hu.

Howard, Susan of Tring. R for Barbados or Jamaica Feb 1686. Ht.

Howard, Thomas of Wivenhoe. R for America Jly 1700. E.

Howard, Thomas. S Jan-Jun T Jun 1728 *Elizabeth* LC Potomack Aug 1729. L.

Howard, Thomas. S s horse Lent R 14 yrs Summer 1729. G.

Howard, Thomas. S & T Apr 1733 *Patapsco* LC Annapolis Nov 1733. M.

Howard, Thomas. SW & T Apr 1768 *Thornton*. M.

Howard, Thomas. S Summer 1774. E.

Howard, William. R 10 yrs in plantations for counterfeiting Oct 1662. M.

Howard, William. R for America Mar 1705. M.

Howard, William. LC from *Forward* Annapolis Dec 1725. X.

Howard, William. S Dec 1727. M.

Howard, William. S Sep 1737 T Jan 1738 *Dorsetshire* to Va. M.

Howard, William. S Aug 1763. So.

Howard, William of Lambeth. SQS Feb T Apr 1766 *Ann*. Sy.

Howard, William. R Jly 1775. M.

Howarth, William (1758). *See* Cookson. Y.

Howorth, William. S & T Apr 1765 *Ann*. L.

Howburn, Sarah. S for murder of her bastard child Summer 1744 R 14 yrs Summer 1745 AT Summer 1746. Nl.

Howcroft als Howlcroft, Silvanus. S for highway robbery at Sheffield Summer 1767 R 14 yrs Summer 1768. Y.

Howd, John of Newcastle upon Tyne. R for Barbados Jly 1679. Nl.

How, Ann wife of Thomas. R 14 yrs Mar 1746. Ha.

How, Benjamin. SQS Summer 1774. Ht.

Howe, Christopher. S s sheep at Glemsford & R 14 yrs Lent 1774. Su.

How, Edward. T Oct 1768 *Justitia*. K.

Howe, George. PT Feb 1680. M.

How, Isabella. S Dec 1766 T Jan 1767 *Tryal*. M.

How, James. T Oct 1724 *Forward* LC Md Jun 1725. Sy.

How, James. S Feb-Apr 1745. M.

How, James. T 14 yrs Oct 1768 *Justitia*. K.

How, John, a boy. S Summer 1736 R 14 yrs Summer 1737. Wa.

How, John. S Sep-Oct T Dec 1752 *Greyhound*. M.

How als Knapp, John. S s mare Lent R 14 yrs Summer 1757. Le.

How, John. T Oct 1757. Db.

How, John (1774). *See* Channon. De.

How, Joseph. T Nov 1725 *Rappahannock* but died on passage. Ht.

How, Martha, spinster, als wife of John Davis. S s at Dill Summer 1758. Bd.

How, Mary. TB to Va from QS 1740. De.

How, Richard. S Jun 1733. M.

How, Samuel. S Jun-Dec 1738 T Jan 1739 *Dorsetshire* to Va. M.

How, Samuel. T Apr 1742 *Bond*. Ht.

Howe, Thomas of Bagborough, husbandman. R for Barbados Sep 1665. So.

Howe, Thomas. SQS Apr TB to Md Nov 1731. So.

How, Thomas (1741). *See* Glaspole. Ha.

How, Thomas. S Jan-Apr 1749. M.

How, William of Witton le Wear. R for Barbados Jun 1684. Du.

How, William. S & T Apr 1766 *Ann*. L.

Howell, Edward. S s at Wonastow Lent 1746. Mo.

Howell, Elizabeth. R Feb AT Sep 1675. M.

Howell, Elizabeth. S s at Bedwardine Lent 1722. Wo.

Howell, Elizabeth. S s clothing at Bransford Lent 1723. Wo.

Howell, Elizabeth wife of Henry. S Feb T Mar 1731 *Patapsco* LC Annapolis Jun 1731. M.

Howell, Elizabeth (1745). *See* Staveraugh. L.

Howell, Faithfull, widow. S Lent 1752. Nf.

Howell, Francis. S Apr 1748. L.

Howell, Henry. T Apr 1743 *Justitia* but died on passage. Sx.

Howl, James (1773). *See* Town. St.

Howell, John. LC from *Susannah & Sarah* Annapolis Apr 1720. X.

Howell, John. S s at Frocester Lent TB Mar 1735. G.

Howl, John. S s mare Lent R 14 yrs Summer 1767. Wa.

Howell, John. S s at Awre Lent 1772. G.

Howell, Jonathan (1722). *See* Johnson. M.

Howell, Joseph. S Mar 1721. So.

Howell, Joseph. S Jun-Dec 1745. M.

Howell, Margaret. S Jly 1756. M.

Howell, Peter of Kingston on Thames. R for Barbados Jly 1679. Sy.

Howell, Richard. S Mar TB Apr 1729. Wi.

Howell, Richard. S Summer 1767. No.

Howell, Robert. S Mar 1725. So.

Howell, Thomas. Rebel T 1685.

Howell, William of Pedwardine. R for America Jly 1675. He.

Howell, William. R for Barbados or Jamaica Dec 1698. L.

Howell, William of Newington. SQS Jun T Aug 1752 *Tryal*. Sy.

Howell, William. T Jun 1764 *Dolphin*. E.

Howells, Anthony. S Lent R 14 yrs Summer 1741 (SP). He.

Howells, Joseph. S s horse Lent 1731 R 14 yrs Lent 1732 (SP). He.

Howells, Richard. Rebel T 1685.

Howells als Powell, Thomas. S s wheat at Bacton Lent 1757. He.

Hower, Catherine. LC from *Elizabeth* Potomack Aug 1729. X.

Howland, Ann. S Feb T Mar 1764 *Tryal*. M.

Howland, John. S Feb 1757. M.

Howlat, Madis John of Richmond, shoemaker. SQS & T Jan 1767
Tryal. Sy.
Howlett, William. S Aug 1748. So.
Howlett, William. S Oct T Dec 1771 *Justitia*. L.
Howlin als Browne, Richard. R for Barbados or Jamaica Dec 1699 &
Aug 1700. L.
Howsden, Benjamin. S Oct T Dec 1769 *Justitia*. L.
Howsden, Jane. R for America May 1704. M.
Howsden, John of Bermondsey. SQS Apr 1750. Sy.
Howsell als Housley, Thomas, aged 42, 5'5" tall, blackish complexion &
dark brown hair, born at Epworth, Lincs. S s mare at Clayworth & R
14 yrs Lent TB Apr 1773. Nt.
Howson, John. SQS & TB Jly 1723. Bu.
Howson, John. T 14 yrs Apr 1769 *Tryal*. K.
Howson, Mary, als Tomkin, Martha. S Jan T Feb 1719 *Worcester* to
Md. M.
Howton, Alice. S Jly 1720. M.
Hoxen, Henry. S s geese at Much Marcle Lent 1768. He.
Hoxton, Benjamin of Blofield. S s coat Summer 1738. Nf.
Hoyde, Philip. S & T Mar 1750 *Tryal*. L.
Hoye, Joseph. S Aug 1736. De.
Hoye, Mary. S Lent 1748. K.
Hoy, Roger. T Apr 1753 *Thames*. E.
Hoyes, Robert. S s sheep Summer 1757 R 14 yrs Lent 1758. Li.
Hoyle, Henry. SQS Jly TB Sep 1768. So.
Hoyle, Joseph of Uttoxeter. R for Jamaica, Barbados or Bermuda Feb
1686. St.
Hoyle, Samuel. S s cloth from tenter Lent R 14 yrs Summer 1721. Y.
Hoyle, William of Walmersley. SQS Apr 1774. La.
Hoyles, William. S May-Jly 1746. M.
Hoysted, Robert. T Nov 1741 *Sea Horse*. K.
Huat. *See* Hewitt.
Huband, Matthew. S Summer T Sep 1751 *Greyhound*. Sx.
Hubbard, Catherine. S Feb-Apr T May 1755 *Rose*. M.
Hubbard, Elizabeth. S Jly T Aug 1721 *Owners Goodwill* to Md. M.
Hubbard, Elizabeth (1748). *See* Kerr. M.
Hubbard, George. S s silver spoon Lent 1753. Ca.
Hubbard, Henry. S for highway robbery Summer 1753 R 14 yrs Lent
TB Apr 1754. Le.
Hubbard, Henry. S Summer 1762. Su.
Hubbart, James (1692). *See* Smith. K.
Hubbard, James (1736). *See* Hubbard, Samuel. L.
Hubbard, James. S Jan T 14 yrs Apr 1741 *Speedwell*. L.
Hubbard, Jeremiah of Hatfield Peveral. R for Barbados or Jamaica Mar
1707. E.
Hubbard, John. S Jly T Aug 1721 *Prince Royal* to Va. M.
Hubbard, John. T Jun 1764 *Dolphin*. K.
Hubbert, Nathaniel. R for Jamaica Aug 1661. L.
Hubbard, Samuel (James). S & T Jan 1736 *Dorsetshire* LC Va Sep
1736. L.
Huckaby, William. SQS Feb T Mar 1764 *Tryal*. M.

Huckenhull. *See* Hockenhull.

Hucker, John Jr. Rebel T 1685.

Hucker, Tobias. Rebel T 1685.

Hucker, Walter. Rebel T 1685.

Huckle, John (1764). *See* Carpenter. M.

Huckell, Mary of Camberwell, spinster. SQS Jan T Apr 1753 *Thames*. Sy.

Hucklebone als London, Alice. R for Barbados Jun 1665. L.

Hucks, Fouck. T Oct 1723 *Forward*. E.

Hudd, Mary. S Dec 1746. L.

Huddle, Thomas. S Dec 1742 T Mar 1743 *Justitia*. L.

Hudell als Hoodell, Thomas. S Jan-Apr 1749. M.

Huddle, Thomas. S May-Jly 1750. M.

Hudlestone, Charles. S for highway robbery Lent R 14 yrs Summer 1722. Nt.

Hudling, Huuh of Plaistow. SQS Apr T Nov 1762 *Prince William*. E.

Hudman, John. S Oct 1733 T Jan 1734 *Caesar* LC Va Jly 1734. M.

Hudnall, James. T 14 yrs Aug 1752 *Tryal*. K.

Hudson, Alice (1775). *See* Wooton. M.

Hudson, Ann (1736). *See* Hutchinson. M.

Hudson, Ann (1737). *See* Robinson. Nf.

Hudson, Ann of St. Paul, Shadwell, spinster. S s household goods Oct 1740 T Jan 1741 *Harpooner* to Rappahannock. M.

Hudson, Ann. S Apr-Jun T Jly 1772 *Tayloe*. M.

Hudson, Benjamin. R Jly T Sep 1767 *Justitia*. M.

Hudson, Catherine. S Jan T Feb 1719 *Worcester* to Md. L.

Hudson als Archer, Daniel. AT from QS Summer 1767. Nt.

Hudson, Eleanor. S Oct 1730 T Mar 1731 *Patapsco*. L.

Hudson, Elizabeth, als Combot, wife of John. S Jan T Feb 1726 *Supply* LC Annapolis May 1726. M.

Hudson, Elizabeth. S s at Idsall Summer 1757. Sh.

Hudson, Grissell, spinster, als wife of John. R for Barbados Jly 1663, Aug 1664, Jun 1665, Oct 1673 & Jly 1674. L.

Hudson, Isabell wife of John. SQS Thirsk Apr 1742. Y.

Hudson, Jane. S Sep-Dec 1746. M.

Hudson, John of Sodbury. R for America Mar 1680. G.

Hudson, John. R for Barbados or Jamaica Aug 1700. M.

Hudson, John. T Sep 1730 *Smith*. Sy.

Hudson, John. SQS Thirsk Apr 1742. Y.

Hudson, John. S Apr T May 1750 *Lichfield*. M.

Hudson, John. S Oct 1756. L.

Hudson, John. S Jan-Feb 1773. M.

Hudson als Todell, John. S for highway robbery & R 7 yrs Summer T Sep 1773. Wa.

Hudson, John. S s at Stokesley Lent 1774. Y.

Hudson, John. TB Apr 1774. Y.

Hudson, Jonathan. T Jly 1724 *Robert* LC Md Jun 1725. Sy.

Hudson, Jonathan. T May 1737 *Forward*. E.

Hudson, Joseph of Bermondsey. SQS Jan 1752. Sy.

Hudson, Lewis. T Jly 1724 *Robert* LC Md Jun 1725. Sy.

Hudson, Mary. S & T Sep 1731 *Smith* LC Va 1732. M.

Hudson, Peter. S Feb T Mar 1730 *Patapsco* LC Annapolis Sep 1730. M.

Hudson, Philip. SEK & T Sep 1766 *Justitia*. K.

Hudson, Sarah. S Apr 1719. M.

Hudson, Sarah. S Aug T Oct 1726 *Forward* to Va. M.

Hudson, Sarah of St. Mary le Strand, spinster. S s silk & T Dec 1740 *Vernon*. M.

Hudson, Skinner. S Apr T May 1767 *Thornton*. L.

Hudson als Peirce, Thomas. R for Barbados or Jamaica Dec 1693. L.

Hudson, Thomas. S May T Jun 1727 *Susanna* to Va. M.

Hudson, Thomas. S Feb T Mar 1731 *Patapsco* LC Annapolis Jun 1731. L.

Hudson, Thomas. S Jan T 14 yrs Apr 1743 *Justitia*. M.

Hudson, Thomas. S & T Dec 1767 *Neptune*. M.

Hudson, William (1661). *See* Hodgson. L.

Hudson, William of Wymondham. R for Barbados Aug 1671. Nf.

Hudson als Thickhead, William. S Aug T Oct 1724 *Forward* to Md. M.

Hudson, William. T Jun 1740 *Essex*. Sy.

Hudson, William. S Lent 1748. K.

Hudson, William. SQS Jan 1755. M.

Hudson, William. S at Canterbury Apr R Summer 1756. K.

Hudson, William. S for raping Mary, wife of James Speak, Summer 1767 R for life Lent 1768. La.

Hudspeth, William (1769). *See* Todd. Nl.

Huff. *See* Hough.

Huffer, William (1771). *See* Hutchens. Co.

Huffman, Mary. S Dec 1748 T Jan 1749 *Laura*. M.

Huggitt, Charles. T Oct 1729 *Forward*. Sy.

Huggett, Loftius. S Jan T Mar 1750 *Tryal*. L.

Huggate, Richard of Ewhurst. S Lent T May 1750 *Lichfield*. Sy.

Hugitt, William of Leek. R for America Feb 1684. St.

Huggins, Benjamin. S May-Jly 1749. M.

Huggins, David of Almeley, glover. R for America Jly 1673. He.

Huggins als Votier, Elizabeth. S Feb T 14 yrs Mar 1727 *Rappahannock*. L.

Huggins, Francis. S s ram at Newent Lent TB Aug 1727. G.

Huggins, Humphrey. PT Dec 1683. M.

Huggins, John. S Jly 1748. L.

Huggins, Matthew. S Jly 1756. M.

Huggins, William. T May 1737 *Forward*. K.

Hew, John. LC from *Rappahannock* at Rappahannock Apr 1726. X.

Hugh, William. S Mar 1736. De.

Hughes, Abraham. R Lent 1775. Sy.

Hughs, Andrew. T Jly 1724 *Robert* LC Annapolis Jun 1725. Be.

Hughes als Giller, Ann. S Oct T Nov 1725 *Rappahannock* LC Rappahannock Apr 1726. L.

Hughes, Ann. S Jan-Jun T Jun 1728 *Elizabeth* to Md or Va. M.

Hughes, Anne. S Feb T Mar 1730 *Patapsco* LC Annapolis Sep 1730. M.

Hughes, Arthur. T Jun 1764 *Dolphin*. Sx.

Hughes, Batt of Bristol, mariner. S for highway robbery at Great Sankey Lent R 14 yrs Summer 1765. La.

Hughes als Dennison, Catherine. S s pinafores Apr T Dec 1735 *John* LC Annapolis Sep 1736. M.

Hughes, Catherine wife of Jacob. S Oct 1760. M.

Hughes, Charles. R Mar AT May 1688. M.

Hughes, Charles. S Jan T Apr 1743 *Justitia*. M.

Hughes, Christopher of St. Olave, Southwark. R for Barbados Apr 1668. Sy.

Hughes, Christopher. LC from *Loyal Margaret* Annapolis Oct 1726. X.

Hughs, Christopher. S & T Jan 1736 *Dorsetshire* LC Va Sep 1736. L.

Hewes als Huish, David of Braunton. R for Barbados Jun 1708. De.

Hughes als Morris, David. S s sheep & R 14 yrs Lent 1774. He.

Hughes, Deborah. S Jly 1760, taken aboard transport ship but removed to Newgate & shipped later in 1760. M.

Hughes, Edward. R 14 yrs Lent 1721. G.

Hughes, Edward. S Jan 1755. L.

Hughes, Edward. S Sep T Dec 1769 *Justitia*. M.

Hughes als Mason, Edward. R 14 yrs Apr 1770. So.

Hughes, Elizabeth, als Black Bess. S s horse Summer 1726 R 14 yrs Lent 1727. O.

Huse, Elizabeth wife of Richard of St. John's. SQS Jan 1752. Sy.

Hughes, Elizabeth. S & T Dec 1759 *Phoenix*. L.

Hughes, Henry. R 14 yrs Aug 1730. So.

Hughes, Henry. T Dec 1736 *Dorsetshire*. E.

Hughes, Henry. S Jan 1745. L.

Hughes, Henry. S Jan T Apr 1768 *Thornton*. M.

Hughes, Henry. S s at Montford Lent 1770. Sh.

Hughes, Isabella. S Aug T Oct 1726 *Forward*. L.

Hughes, Jacob. S Summer 1728. Sh.

Hughes, Jane. S Apr 1763. L.

Hughes als Piper, John. R for Barbados Jly 1675. M.

Hughes, John. T 14 yrs May 1719 *Margaret* LC Md May 1720; sold to John Summerland. Sy.

Hughes, John. S Oct T Nov 1722 *Rappahannock* to Va. M.

Hughes, John. T Oct 1726 *Forward*. K.

Hughes, John. S Jan-Jun T Jun 1728 *Elizabeth* to Md or Va. M.

Hughes, John. S & T Oct 1729 *Forward* LC Va Jun 1730. L.

Hughes, John. S & T Oct 1732 *Caesar* to Va. M.

Hughes, John. S Feb T Apr 1739 *Forward*. L.

Hughes, John. S s horse Summer 1745 R 14 yrs Lent 1746. Le.

Hughes, John. S Sep-Oct 1748 T Jan 1749 *Laura*. M.

Hughes, John. S Apr T May 1751 *Tryal*. L.

Hughs, John. SWK Jan 1754. K.

Hughes, John. SQS Dec 1754. M.

Hughes, John. S for life Jan 1757. L.

Hughes, John. S Oct T Nov 1759 *Phoenix*. L.

Hughes, John. S Oct 1760. M.

Hughes als Lewis, John. S Apr T Jun 1768 *Tryal*. M.

Hughes, John (1769). *See* Arm, Thomas. Wa.

Hughes, John. S May T Jly 1771 *Scarsdale*. L.

Hughes, John. S Sep-Oct T Dec 1771 *Justitia*. M.

Hughes, John. S s fowls at Stanton Lacy Lent 1774. Sh.

Hughes, John. R Mar 1774. Wi.

Hughes, John. S Jan-Feb 1775. M.

Hughes, Joseph of Stepney. S s lead pipe Oct 1740 T Jan 1741 *Harpooner* to Rappahannock. M.

Hughes, Joseph of Esher. SQS Oct 1772. Sy.

Hughes, Llewellin. S Apr 1763. Fl.

Hewes als Hughes, Lucy. S & T Feb 1740 *York*. L.

Hughes, Martha wife of William. S s cloth at Newbury Summer 1751. Be.

Hughes, Martha. R Summer 1775. Wa.

Hughes, Mary. S & T 14 yrs Oct 1720 *Gilbert* to Md. M.

Hughes, Mary. S May T Jun 1727 *Susanna* to Va. M.

Hughes, Mary. S & T Oct 1729 *Forward* but died on passage. M.

Hughes als Cashell, Mary. S s horse Lent R 14 yrs Summer 1746. G.

Hughes, Mary. S s at Llandenny Lent 1758. Mo.

Hughes, Mary. S Sep 1761 T Apr 1762 *Dolphin*. M.

Hughes, Mary. S Dec 1761. M.

Hughes, Mary. S Jan T Apr 1762 *Dolphin*. L.

Hughes, Michael. SW Jly 1773. M.

Hughes, Michael of St. James, Westminster. SW Oct 1773. M.

Hughes, Nathaniel. S Dec 1765 T Jan 1766 *Tryal*. M.

Hughes, Peter. R & T Apr 1735 *Patapsco* LC Annapolis Oct 1735. M.

Hughes, Peter. S Aug 1754. So.

Hughes, Richard. R Dec 1679 AT Feb 1680. M.

Hughes, Richard. T Oct 1729 *Forward*. Sy.

Hughes, Robert of St. Philip & Jacob. R for America Jly 1696. G.

Hughes, Robert, als Davies, John. S Summer 1765. Ch.

Hughes, Roderick. S s leather at Pontesbury Lent 1751. Sh.

Hughes, Samuel of Horton. R for Jamaica, Barbados or Bermuda Mar 1688. Sh.

Hughes, Samuel. R Oct 1694 AT Jan 1695. M.

Hughes, Samuel. S Oct 1748 T Jan 1749 *Laura*. L.

Hughes, Sarah. S & T Dec 1724 *Rappahannock*. L.

Hughes, Sarah. S s at Ellesmere Lent 1763. Sh.

Hughes, Susanna. S Summer 1766. Wa.

Hughes, Thomas. R 14 yrs Lent 1721. G.

Hughes, Thomas (1722). *See* Hopkins. Sy.

Hughes, Thomas. S s at Stokesay Summer 1737. Sh.

Hughes, Thomas of St. Chad, Shrewsbury. S Lent 1741. Sh.

Hughs, Thomas. S City Summer 1756. Nl.

Hues, Thomas. T May 1767 *Thornton*. K.

Hughes, Thomas. S s at St. Nicholas, Abingdon, Summer 1767. Be.

Hughes, Thomas. S s timber at Wroxton Summer 1773. O.

Hughes, William of Stokesay. R for America Jly 1693. Sh.

Huse, William. S Lent R 14 yrs Summer 1728. Be.

Hughs, William. S Feb T Mar 1730 *Patapsco* to Md. M.

Hughes, William. S Summer 1731. G.

Hughes, William of Oswestry. S Lent 1734. Sh.

Hughes, William. S for shoplifting Lent 1741. Wo.

Hughes, William. R 14 yrs Mar 1748. So.

Hughes, William. S Feb-Apr T for life May 1752 *Lichfield*. M.

Hughes, William. S Oct T Dec 1771 *Justitia*. L.
Hughes, William. S 14 yrs Apr 1773. L.
Hughes, William. S s pigs at Minchinhampton Summer 1773. G.
Hughes, William. S Apr 1774. M.
Hughes, William Sr. S s wheat at Llanvihangel Summer 1774. Mo.
Hughes, William Jr. S s wheat at Llanvihangel Summer 1774. Mo.
Hughill, Thomas. S Mar 1741. Ha.
Hughson. *See* Hewson.
Hugo, Stephen. S Aug 1767. Co.
Huish, David (1708). *See* Hewes. De.
Hugon, Thomas. SQS Wakefield Jan 1725. Y.
Holbert, Margaret. SL Jly 1773. Sy.
Hulins, Thomas (1775). *See* Hulonce. Mo.
Hull, Alice, spinster, als wife of George. R for Jamaica Mar
    1665. L.
Hull, Ann (1752). *See* Fry. M.
Hull, Ann. T Sep 1766 *Justitia*. Sy.
Hull, Bartholomew of Bocking. R for Barbados Aug 1668. E.
Hull, Benjamin. T Jan 1767 *Tryal*. M.
Hull, Edward, als Doleman, John. S Jun T Sep 1767 *Justitia*. M.
Hull, Eleanor. S Sep-Dec 1755 T Jan 1756 *Greyhound*. M.
Hull, Elizabeth. R for Barbados Mar 1681. M.
Hull, Grace of Barking. R for Barbados or Jamaica Jly 1674. E.
Hull, Isaac. S & T Sep 1767 *Justitia*. L.
Hull, John. Rebel T 1685.
Hull, John. S Lent T May 1750 *Lichfield*. E.
Hull, Mary. R for Barbados May 1664. M.
Hull, Richard. T Oct 1719 *Susannah & Sarah*. L.
Hull, Richard. S s at Sandy & R 14 yrs Lent 1771. Bd.
Hull, Samuel. S Aug T Sep 1725 *Forward* LC Annapolis Dec 1725. L.
Hull, Thomas. S Sep 1733. M.
Hull, William of Fishbourne. SQS s sea coal Apr 1774. Sx.
Hulley, Thomas. TB Sep 1754; S to hang Lent 1757 for returning from
    transportation. Db.
Hulman, Frances, spinster. R for Barbados May 1665. X.
Hullman, Isaac. S Sep T 14 yrs Oct 1722 *Forward* LC Annapolis Dec
    1725. L.
Hulls, Mary. S Oct T Nov 1759 *Phoenix*. L.
Hulls, Richard. T Oct 1739 *Duke of Cumberland*. Bu.
Hulme, Augustine of Manchester. SQS Jly 1751. La.
Hulme, Thomas of Manchester, joiner. SQS Jan 1749. La.
Hulse, Samuel. S Mar TB to Va Apr 1766. Le.
Hulonce als Hulins, Thomas. S for highway robbery & R 14 yrs Lent
    1775. Mo.
Hullston, Henry. S Oct 1751-Jan 1752. M.
Hulston, John. S s at Luston Lent 1723. He.
Hulstone, Simon of Chislet. R for Barbados or Jamaica Mar 1698. K.
Hulston, Thomas. R for Barbados Jly 1668. M.
Hulton, James (1770). *See* Hilton. La.
Humber, William of Bullington. R for Barbados Feb 1665. Ha.
Humber, William of Send. SQS & T Apr 1769 *Tryal*. Sy.

Humble, Elizabeth. S Aug 1741. M.

Humble, Issabell. R 14 yrs Summer TB Aug 1751. Y.

Humble, Joseph. S for picking pockets at Annandale, Scotland, Summer 1758. Nl.

Hume, Joseph. S Apr-Jun 1739. M.

Humphrey, Edward. T 14 yrs Apr 1771 *Thornton*. K.

Humphrey, Elizabeth. S Jly 1763. M.

Humphry, George. T Dec 1734 *Caesar*. Sy.

Humphrey, John. T 14 yrs Apr 1768 *Thornton*. K.

Humphry, Thomas. S Dec 1763 T Mar 1764 *Tryal*. M.

Humphrey, Thomas. S Summer 1767. Bu.

Humphrey, William of Probus. R for Barbados Feb 1698. Co.

Humphrey, William. S Lent R 14 yrs Summer 1756. K.

Humphryes, Ann. S Sep-Oct T Dec 1753 *Whiteing*. M.

Humphryes, Charles. S Feb-Apr T May 1755 *Rose*. M.

Humphries, Charles. S 14 yrs for receiving Lent 1768. Wa.

Humfries, David. R 14 yrs Mar 1736. So.

Humphrys, Edward. R May T for life Sep 1758 *Tryal* to Annapolis. M.

Humphreys, Edward. S s at Sheinton Summer 1766. Sh.

Humphreys, Elizabeth. SQS Jly 1740. So.

Humphreys, Elizabeth. S Dec 1753-Jan 1754. M.

Humphreys, Frances. S Feb T 14 yrs May 1740 *Essex*. L.

Humphrays, Gumpay. T Jly 1771 *Scarsdale*. L.

Humphreys, Humphrey. S s cow at Nestrange Lent 1738. Sh.

Humphreys, James. S s gelding Lent R 14 yrs Summer 1764. Ca.

Humphreys, James. S s silver shoe buckles at Caversham Summer 1774. O.

Humphreys, James. R for life Lent 1775. Sy.

Humphreys, John. R for Barbados for s cows Jun 1663. M.

Humphreys, John. S Jly 1721 T Mar 1723. Bu.

Humphreys, John. T May 1723 *Victory*. K.

Humphries, John. S Feb T Apr 1734 *Patapsco* to Va. M.

Humphryes, John. S Lent R 14 yrs Summer T Sep 1755 *Tryal*. Sy.

Humphries, John. S Aug 1767. Do.

Humphries, John. S s at Kinstock Summer 1769. Sh.

Humphrys, John. T Jly 1770 *Scarsdale*. M.

Humphreys, Lewis. S & T Dec 1771 *Justitia*. L.

Humphries, Mary (1762). *See* Price. M.

Humphreys, Mathew. S Lent 1759. Ch.

Humphries, Richard. R Dec 1698 AT Jan 1699. M.

Humphries, Robert. S Dec 1757 T Mar 1758 *Dragon*. M.

Humphreys, Samuel. R Apr 1773. M.

Humfryes, Thomas. R for Barbados Jun 1670. M.

Humphryes, Thomas. Rebel T 1685.

Humphreys, Thomas of Dawley, yeoman. R for America Feb 1714. Sh.

Humphryes, Thomas. S May T Jly 1723 *Alexander* LC Annapolis Sep 1723. M.

Humphreys, Thomas. S Feb 1752. L.

Humphreys, Thomas (1759). *See* Knightley. Wo.

Humphreys, Thomas of Watford. SQS & T Jun 1764 *Dolphin*. Ht.

Humphrys, Thomas. R Mar 1774. So.

Humphreys, William. R for America Jly 1708. Li.

Humphrys, William. S s watch Summer 1759. Su.

Humphrys, William. S Mar TB to Va May 1763. Wi.

Humphreys als Pigeon, William. S s cock at Sedgley Lent 1767. St.

Humphrys, William. S s at Winterbourne Lent 1768. G.

Humphrison, William. S s sheep at Sheriff Hales Summer 1729. St.

Humpston/Humpton, John (1679). *See* Quinton. M.

Hunderboone, Thomas. S s from Ann Hunderboone, widow, Sep T Dec 1767 *Neptune*. M.

Hundy, Thomas. S s at St. Martin, Worcester, Lent 1774. Wo.

Hungate, Charles. T Jun 1727 *Susanna*. Ht.

Hungerford, John. S Feb T Apr 1739 *Forward*. L.

Hunn, Francis. S s gelding Summer 1752 R 14 yrs Lent 1753. Ca.

Hunn als Hern als Williamson, John. S Norwich Summer 1755. Nf.

Hunslay, Robert. R for life s horse Feb 1766. Db.

Hunsley, William. SQS & T Dec 1752 *Greyhound*. M.

Hunsworth, John, aged 22, black hair. LC from *Gilbert* Md May 1721. X.

Hunt, Abraham. Rebel T 1685.

Hunt, Ann of Hamptworth Downton, spinster. R for Barbados Jly 1717. Wi.

Hunt, Ann. S & T May 1740 *Essex*. L.

Hunt, Ann. R 14 yrs Mar 1759. Ha.

Hunt, Barbara. T Dec 1753 *Whiteing*. E.

Hunt, Benjamin. SQS & TB Apr 1729. So.

Hunt, Catherine. S May 1763. M.

Hunt, Charles. S Lent 1766. No.

Hunt, Daniel. S s cloth at Rotherham Lent 1768. Y.

Hunt, Dorothy, aged 21. R for Barbados Feb 1664. M.

Hunt, Edmund. S s cow at Bury St. Edmunds & R Lent 1771. Su.

Hunt, Edward. T May 1736 *Patapsco*. Ht.

Hunt, Edward. S Apr-Jun 1739. M.

Hunt, Edward. S Apr T May 1750 *Lichfield*. L.

Hunt, Elizabeth. AT Lent 1723 T Oct 1723 *Forward* to Va from London. Y.

Hunt, Elizabeth (1733). *See* Durham. M.

Hunt, Francis. R 14 yrs Jly 1775. M.

Hunt als Leech, George of Bury St. Edmunds. R for Barbados or Jamaica Mar 1697. Su.

Hunt, Giles of Worcester. R for America Jly 1708. Wo.

Hunt, Hannah wife of Joseph *(qv)* of St. Albans. S Summer 1749. Ht.

Hunt, Henry. Rebel T 1685.

Hunt, Henry. S Sep-Oct 1749. M.

Hunt, James. T Apr 1735 *Patapsco*. Ht.

Hunt, James. S May-Jun T Jly 1753 *Tryal*. M.

Hunt, James. T 14 yrs Apr 1759 *Thetis*. E.

Hunt, James. S for highway robbery Summer 1769 R 14 yrs Lent 1770. Li.

Hunt, James. S Jan-Feb T Apr 1772 *Thornton*. M.

Hunt, Jane. S s silver mug & T Dec 1734 *Caesar* LC Va Jly 1735. M.

Hunt, Job. Rebel T 1685.

Hunt, John of Camberwell. R for Barbados or Jamaica Mar 1698. Sy.

Hunt, John. R Aug 1700. M.
Hunt, John of Allington. R for Barbados or Jamaica Jly 1715. K.
Hunt, John. S Jun-Dec 1745. M.
Hunt, John. S Jly 1750. Ha.
Hunt, John. S s horse Summer 1750 R 14 yrs Lent 1751. No.
Hunt, John. R Feb T for life Mar 1764 *Tryal*. M.
Hunt, John. S s oats, beans & peas Summer 1765. Nf.
Hunt, John. S s sheep Lent R 14 yrs Summer 1765. He.
Hunt, John of St. Saviour, Southwark. SQS Mar T Jun 1768 *Tryal*. Sy.
Hunt, John of Wootton. R s mare Lent T 14 yrs Apr 1772 *Thornton*. Sy.
Hunt, John. SQS Jun T Jly 1772 *Tayloe*. M.
Hunt, Joseph. T Jan 1734 *Caesar* LC Va Jly 1734. Sy.
Hunt, Joseph of St. Albans. S Summer 1749. Ht.
Hunt, Joyce. R for Barbados Jun 1670. M.
Hunt, Julius. S 14 yrs Apr-May 1744. M.
Hunt, Margaret. SW & T Dec 1767 *Neptune*. M.
Hunt, Marlborough. S Mar TB to Va Oct 1739. Wi.
Hunt als Ipy, Mary. R 14 yrs Aug T Sep 1718 *Eagle* LC Charles Town Mar 1719. L.
Hunt, Mary. S for burning a dwelling Lent R 14 yrs Summer TB Dec 1731. Bd.
Hunt, Mary wife of John. S s shirt & T Dec 1734 *Caesar* LC Va Jly 1735. M.
Hunt, Mary of St. Giles in Fields, spinster. S s cloth Oct 1740 T Jan 1741 *Harpooner* to Rappahannock. M.
Hunt, Matthew. S s iron at Cirencester Lent 1729. G.
Hunt, Maurice. R Dec 1679 AT Feb 1680. M.
Hunt, Rebecca. S & T Jly 1770 *Scarsdale*. M.
Hunt, Richard. S May T Jly 1722 *Alexander* to Nevis or Jamaica.
Hunt, Richard. S Jun T Nov 1743 *George William*. M.
Hunt, Robert. T 14 yrs Sep 1764 *Justitia*. Ht.
Hunt, Robert. T Apr 1765 *Ann*. E.
Hunt, Samuel of St. Martin in Fields. SW Apr 1774. M.
Hunt, Stephen of Tollard Royal. R for Barbados Jun 1666. Wi.
Hunt, Susannah. S Summer 1756. Sy.
Hunt, Thomas. SQS Dec 1754. M.
Hunt, Thomas. S s at Halesowen Summer 1764. Sh.
Hunt, William. R for Barbados Jly 1675. M.
Hunt, William of Chislet. R for Barbados or Jamaica Mar 1698. K.
Hunt, William. S Sep 1733 T Jan 1734 *Caesar* LC Va Jly 1734. M.
Hunt, William. T Oct 1738 *Genoa*. Ht.
Hunt, William. S s gelding Summer 1743 R 14 yrs Lent 1744. Su.
Hunt, William. T 14 yrs Dec 1758 *The Brothers*. K.
Hunt, William. T Sep 1764 *Justitia*. Sy.
Hunt, William. T Sep 1765 *Justitia*. Ht.
Hunt, William Jr. S Mar TB to Va Apr 1766. Wi.
Hunt, William of Bristol. R 14 yrs Apr 1768 (SP). G.
Hunt, William. S for highway robbery Lent R for life Summer 1772. Wa.
Hunt, William. S Jly 1775. M.
Hunter, Adam. S s coat Jan-May T Jun 1738 *Forward* to Md or Va. M.
Hunter, Anthony. S Oct T Dec 1771 *Justitia*. L.

Hunter, Charles. R Summer 1774. Du.

Hunter, Christian. S Feb T Apr 1766 *Ann*. M.

Hunter, David. S & T Jly 1771 *Scarsdale*. L.

Hunter, George. S s at Tanfield Summer 1775. Du.

Huntur, James. T Jun 1740 *Essex*. E.

Hunter, James. SQS Apr T Jly 1771 *Scarsdale*. M.

Hunter, John. S Lent R 14 yrs Summer 1721. St.

Hunter, John. S 14 yrs Oct 1751-Jan 1752. M.

Hunter, John. S Apr 1763. M.

Hunter, Joseph. S Feb 1761. M.

Hunter, Joseph. SQS Oct 1773. M.

Hunter, Martha. AT City Summer 1759. Nl.

Hunter, Robert. S s horse Summer 1736 R 14 yrs Summer 1737. Nl.

Hunter, Thomas. S Jan T Feb 1733 *Smith* to Md or Va. M.

Hunter, Thomas. R 14 yrs Summer 1749. Y.

Hunter, William. SQS Dec 1753. M.

Hunter, William. S Lent 1754. Sy.

Hunter, William. AT City Summer 1755. Nl.

Huntingford, Edward. S Lent AT Summer 1745. Sy.

Huntley, Ann. S Feb T Mar 1727 *Rappahannock* to Md. M.

Huntley, Anne (1729). *See* Moss. Sh.

Huntley, Thomas (1729). *See* Matthews. Sh.

Hunton als Harrison, Mary. S s at Ferrybridge Summer 1724. Y.

Hunton, Mary. S s pewter plates May T Dec 1735 *John* LC Annapolis Sep 1736. M.

Huntresse, John. R for Barbados Jun 1665. L.

Huntridge, Isabel. S Apr T May 1720 *Honor* LC Va Jan 1721. L.

Hurcan als Hurkham, Thomas. R Jly 1774. M.

Hurd. *See* Heard.

Hurdley, John. R Jan-Feb T 14 yrs Apr 1772 *Thornton*. M.

Hurle, John. Rebel T 1685.

Hurley, John. SQS Apr T May 1751 *Tryal*. M.

Hurley, John. S Jan-Feb 1774. M.

Hurley, Mary. S Mar 1766. So.

Hurley, Maurice of Plymouth. R for Barbados Feb 1710. De.

Hurley, Patrick. S May T Jun 1764 *Dolphin*. M.

Hurn. *See* Hearn.

Hurndale, Ann. T Jan 1734 *Caesar*. Bu.

Hurred, John (1767). *See* Wilcocks. De.

Hurren, John. S s mare at Felixstowe & R Summer 1770. Su.

Hurring als Hutsing, John. S Summer 1765. Su.

Hurry, Ann. T Apr 1771 *Thornton*. E.

Hursley, Robert. TB Apr 1766. Db.

Hurst, Andrew. R for Barbados Sep 1672. L.

Hurst, Anne. S & T Oct 1729 *Forward* to Va. M.

Hust, Ann. S May-Jly T Sep 1755 *Tryal*. M.

Hurst, Ann. S May T Sep 1758 *Tryal* to Annapolis. M.

Hurst, Christian. S Jly T Aug 1721 *Prince Royal* LC Va Nov 1721. L.

Hurst, Christopher. SQS Jly T Sep 1767 *Justitia*. M.

Hurst, Elizabeth (1681). *See* Huske. M.

Hurst, Elizabeth wife of Emanuel. S Jan-Feb 1775. M.

Hurst, George. SQS New Sarum Jan TB to Va Apr 1772. Wi.

Hurst, Hannah. S May-Jly 1746. M.

Hurst, Henry. S Dec 1772. M.

Hurst, James. S & T Sep 1755 *Tryal*. L.

Hurst, James. T Sep 1764 *Justitia*. K.

Hearst, John. S Aug 1735. So.

Hurst, John. S Apr 1746. L.

Hurst, John. S Dec 1749-Jan 1750 T Mar 1750 *Tryal*. M.

Hurst, John. S for highway robbery Lent R 14 yrs Summer 1753. No.

Hurst, John. S s tablecloth at Sherborne Lent 1765. G.

Hirst, Jonathan. T Oct 1724 *Forward* LC Md Jun 1725. Sy.

Hurst, Joseph. S Mar TB May 1721. Le.

Hirst, Joshua. AT Summer 1753. Y.

Hurst, Mary. S Summer 1740. Wo.

Hurst, Mary. S Feb T Apr 1772 *Thornton*. L.

Hirst, Michael als Nicholas. S Lent 1775. Y.

Hurst, Nathaniel. SL & T Mar 1763 *Neptune*. Sy.

Hurst, Philips. S May T Jly 1723 *Alexander* LC Annapolis Sep 1723. L.

Hurst, Sarah. S & T Jly 1771 *Scarsdale*. L.

Hurst, William. S for perjury at Feckenham Summer 1758; to be
imprisoned 1 month before transporation. Wo.

Hurt, John. T 14 yrs Aug 1752 *Tryal*. E.

Hurt, Joseph. S & T May 1744 *Justitia*. L.

Hurt, Mary wife of John. S 14 yrs Oct 1751-Jan 1752. M.

Husband, Christopher. S Feb T Mar 1731 *Patapsco* LC Annapolis Jun
1731. M.

Husband, Elizabeth. LC from *Owners Goodwill* Annapolis Jly 1722. X.

Husband, William (1723). *See* Wallis. Y.

Huske, Bartholomew of Earls Colne. R for Barbados Apr 1668. E.

Huske als Hurst, Elizabeth. R Mar AT Apr 1681. M.

Husk, Mary (1718). *See* Scott. L.

Huskinson, Samuel. R 14 yrs Aug 1727 TB to Md. De.

Huskinson, Thomas (1772). *See* Davies. La.

Hussell, William. S s at Churchdown Summer 1768. G.

Husseller, Edward. S & T Oct 1720 *Gilbert* to Md. M.

Hussey, Ann. S Aug T Sep 1725 *Forward* LC Annapolis Dec 1725. L.

Hussey, Benjamin. S Mar 1767. Do.

Hussey, Catherine. T Apr 1769 *Tryal*. M.

Hussey, Hester. S Feb-Apr 1746. M.

Hussey, James. T Apr 1768 *Thornton*. Bu.

Hussey, John of Kingston on Thames. R for Barbados or Jamaica Jly
1677. Sy.

Hussey, John. Rebel T 1685.

Hussey, John. S & T Jan 1765 *Tryal*. M.

Hussey, Mary. S Feb T Mar 1727 *Rappahannock*. L.

Hussey, Mary. S Jan-Jun 1747. M.

Hussey, Mary. S Oct 1773. L.

Hussey, Michael. T Jun 1740 *Essex*. K.

Hussey, Samuel. SQS & T Jan 1765 *Tryal*. M.

Hussey, Thomas of St. Bartholomew, Winchester. R for Barbados Jan
1675. Ha.

Husson, Edward (1750). *See* Dale, John. Nt.

Hust. *See* Hurst.

Hustus, Morris. LC from *Forward* Annapolis Dec 1725. X.

Hutchens. *See* Hutchins.

Hutchford, Elizabeth. T Apr 1771 *Thornton*. K.

Hutchin, Noel of Barley. R for Barbados Apr 1668. Ht.

Hutchin, Thomas. T Nov 1728 *Forward*. Ht.

Hutchins, Anne. R 14 yrs for Carolina May 1719. L.

Hutchins, Anne. S & T Apr 1733 *Patapsco* LC Annapolis Nov 1733. M.

Hutchins, Ann. S s clothing Oct 1735 T Jan 1736 *Dorsetshire* LC Va Sep 1736. M.

Hutchins, Benjamin of Devizes. R for Barbados Jly 1688. Wi.

Hutchins, Charles. S & T Apr 1733 *Patapsco* LC Annapolis Nov 1733. M.

Hutchins, Elizabeth. R for Barbados Aug 1679. M.

Hutchins, Elizabeth. S Apr T May 1720 *Honor* to York River. L.

Hutchins, Jane. S Mar 1757. Ha.

Hutchins, John. Rebel T 1685.

Hutchens, John. Rebel T 1685.

Hutchins, John. S Apr T Oct 1719 *Susannah & Sarah* LC Annapolis Apr 1720. L.

Hutchins, John. S Aug T 14 yrs Oct 1726 *Forward* to Va. M.

Hutchings, John. R 14 yrs Mar 1740. So.

Hutchins, John. S Oct 1749. L.

Hutchins, John. SW & T Jan 1769 *Thornton*. M.

Hutchins als Hutchinson, Joseph of Weston under Lizard. R for America Jly 1698. St.

Hutchins, Margaret. S Jly-Sep T Sep 1742 *Forward*. M.

Hutchins, Mary. R for Barbados Sep 1672. L.

Hutchins, Mary. S Apr T Oct 1719 *Susannah & Sarah* LC Annapolis Apr 1720. L.

Hutchens, Mary. R 14 yrs Mar 1742. De.

Hutchins, Matthew. Rebel T 1685.

Hutchins, Nicholas. R 14 yrs Jly 1721 T from Southampton 1723. Ha.

Hutchins, Richard. S Apr T Aug 1718 *Eagle* LC Charles Town Mar 1719. L.

Hutchings, Robert of Belfast, Ireland. R (Western Circ) for Barbados Jan 1676. X.

Hutchings, Robert. S Jly 1722. So.

Hutchins, Robert. S Aug T Oct 1724 *Forward* LC Annapolis Jun 1725. M.

Hutchens, Samuel. R 14 yrs Mar 1742. De.

Hutchins, Samuel, als Irish Sam. S s fishing net at New Windsor Lent 1775. Be.

Hutchings, Sarah. S May T Jun 1726 *Loyal Margaret* to Md. M.

Hutchins, Stephen (1677). *See* Burbage. So.

Hutchings, Susanna. S Oct T 14 yrs Dec 1724 *Rappahannock* to Va. M.

Hutchens, Thomas. R for Barbados Jly 1674. L.

Hutchins, Thomas. Rebel T 1685.

Hutchins, Thomas of East Grinstead. R for Barbados or Jamaica Jly 1704. Sx.

Hutchings, Thomas. LC from *Forward* Annapolis Jun 1723. X.
Hutchins, Thomas of St. Catherine. S s silver tankard Sep 1740. M.
Hutchins, William of Cherhill. R for Barbados Jan 1675. Wi.
Hutchins, William. Rebel T 1685.
Hutchins, William. S Apr T May 1718 *Tryal* LC Charles Town Aug 1718. L.
Hutchens als Huffer, William. R 14 yrs Aug 1771. Co.
Hutchinson als Hudson, Ann. S s shirts Jun 1736. M.
Hutchinson, Ann. S s sheep Lent R 14 yrs Summer 1750. Nt.
Hutchinson, Benjamin. R for Barbados Aug 1679. M.
Hutchinson, Daniel. S Oct T Dec 1724 *Rappahannock*. L.
Hutchinson, David. S Summer 1719 R 14 yrs Summer 1724. Du.
Hutchinson, David. R 14 yrs Summer 1730. Du.
Hutchinson, Edward. S Summer 1730. We.
Hutchinson, George (1767). *See* Cortis. De.
Hutchinson, Henry, aged 18, fair. S Jly T Oct 1720 *Gilbert* LC Annapolis May 1721. M.
Hutchinson, Isabella of St. James, Westminster, spinster. S s linen Jly 1740. M.
Hutchinson, Jane. S May-Jly 1748. M.
Hutchinson, John. S Jan T Sep 1737 *Pretty Patsy* to Md. M.
Hutchinson, John. S s watch at York Lent TB Aug 1771. Y.
Hutchinson, Joseph (1698). *See* Hutchins. St.
Hutchinson, Mary (1762). *See* Middleton. M.
Hutchinson, Mary. S & T Dec 1770 *Justitia*. M.
Hutchinson, Matthew. R for America Mar 1690. Le.
Hutchinson, Robert of Fine. R for Barbados Jly 1699. Du.
Hutchinson, Robert (1765). *See* Mitchell. M.
Hutchingson, Sarah. LC from *Loyal Margaret* Md Oct 1726. X.
Hutchson, Sarah. S Jan-Jun T Jun 1728 *Elizabeth* LC Potomack Aug 1729. M.
Hutchinson, Simon of Christchurch. S s silk Feb T May 1736 *Patapsco*. M.
Hutchinson, Spendslow of Harwood, shoeman. SQS Apr 1747. La.
Hutchinson, William. S May-Jly 1750. M.
Hutchinson, William. S Feb T Mar 1758 *Dragon*. M.
Hutchinson, William. S s at Homsey Summer TB Aug 1771. Y.
Hutsing, John (1765). *See* Hurring. Su.
Hutson, Daniel. S Dec 1727. L.
Hutson, William of Ruckinge. R for Barbados Apr 1668. K.
Hutton, Anne. S Feb T Apr 1733 *Patapsco* LC Annapolis Oct 1732. M.
Hutton, Ann wife of John. S May T Sep 1757 *Thetis*. M.
Hutton, Anthony of Newmarket. R for Barbados or Jamaica Mar 1697. Su.
Hutton, Benjamin. T Jly 1724 *Robert* LC Md Jun 1725. K.
Hutton, Elizabeth. R for Barbados or Jamaica May 1697. L.
Hutton, Henry. T Jly 1724 *Robert* LC Md Jun 1725. Sy.
Hutton, John. S Jan-Jun T Jun 1728 *Elizabeth* LC Potomack Aug 1729. M.
Hutton, Joseph. R for America Aug 1715. M.
Hutton, Leonard of Cannock. R for America Feb 1684. St.

Hutton, Richard of Newcastle upon Tyne. R for Barbados Jly 1681. Nl.

Hutton, Richard. S Nov T Dec 1752 *Greyhound*. L.

Hutton, Richard. S s mare Lent R 14 yrs Summer T Sep 1757 *Thetis*. Bu.

Hutton, Samuel. S May-Jly 1749. M.

Hutton, Samuel. SQS Jly 1756. M.

Hutton, Susanna. S Oct 1751-Jan 1752. M.

Hutton, Thomas. S & T Jan 1739 *Dorsetshire*. L.

Hutton, William. SQS Coventry Mar 1751. Wa.

Huxley, Mary. S Sep-Oct T Dec 1772 *Greyhound*. M.

Huxtable, William. R 14 yrs Mar 1744. De.

Higham, Elizabeth of Dedham, spinster. SQS Oct 1765 T Apr 1766 *Ann*. E.

Hyam, Emanuel. S May T Jun 1764 *Dolphin*. L.

Higham, Farwell. SQS Jun T Sep 1755 *Tryal*. M.

Hyam, George. T Apr 1741 *Speedwell* or *Mediterranean*. Ht.

Hyan, William. S Dec 1753-Jan 1754. M.

Highams, John. S s sheep Summer 1758 R 14 yrs Lent 1759. Wa.

Hyett, Amy of Eaton, spinster. S Lent 1720. He.

Hyatt, Elizabeth. S Sep-Oct 1773. M.

Hyatt, John of Lambeth. R for Barbados or Jamaica Mar 1694. Sy.

Hiat, John. R 14 yrs Apr 1745. So.

Hyatt, Sarah. S s watch Jly-Sep T Sep 1742 *Forward*. M.

Hyett, Thomas. S to House of Correction unless he agrees to be transported Feb 1663. M.

Hyatt, William. R 14 yrs Apr 1775 (SP). G.

Hiats, John. S Nov T Dec 1752 *Greyhound*. L.

Hyde, Augustine (1687). *See* Austin, William. M.

Hyde, Elizabeth. S Jun-Dec 1745. M.

Hyde, Elizabeth wife of William. S May-Jly 1773. M.

Hide, Henry. T Sep 1730 *Smith*. Ht.

Hide, John. S Feb 1775. M.

Hide, Joseph. S Oct T 14 yrs Dec 1724 *Rappahannock* to Va. M.

Hide, Joseph. S Oct T 14 yrs Nov 1725 *Rappahannock* LC Rappahannock Apr 1726. M.

Hyde, Richard. S & T Dec 1731 *Forward* to Md or Va. M.

Hide, Richard. S & R 14 yrs Summer 1738. La.

Hide, Sarah. S Aug T Sep 1764 *Justitia*. L.

Hide, Simon. S Aug 1750. So.

Hyde, Thomas. S & T Jun 1756 *Lyon*. M.

Hyde, William of Claines. R for America Jly 1682. Wo.

Hyder, Richard of Cobham. R for Barbados or Jamaica Jun 1699. K.

Hyder, Stephen of Rotherfield. SQS for robbery at Ringmer Jan 1768 T Apr 1769 *Tryal*; Keeper of Horsham Gaol fined Apr 1769 for permitting his escape. Sx.

Hyfield. *See* Highfield.

Hyland, Elizabeth. LC Va Aug 1729. Sy.

Hyland, Michael. S Apr T Jly 1770 *Scarsdale*. L.

Hymem, Edward. S Apr 1754. So.

Hymes, Michael. S Sep T Dec 1769 *Justitia*. M.

Hynds. *See* Hinds.

Hynes. *See* Hines.

Hyth, John. S Feb T Apr 1743 *Justitia*. M.

I

Ian, Nathaniel. R for America Aug 1685. Li.

Ibbert, Charles. S Apr-May T Jly 1771 *Scarsdale*. M.

Iden, John. S Summer R for Barbados Aug 1664. K.

Idens, Elizabeth of Lambourn Woodlands, spinster. R for Barbados Feb 1665. Be.

Ignell als Wallis, Richard. S for assaulting Customs officers Lent 1738. Nf.

Igoe, Dennis. R 14 yrs Jly 1766. De.

Iles, John. S s at Tetbury Lent 1728. G.

Eyles, Martha. S Dec 1765 T Jan 1766 *Tryal*. M.

Eyles, Mary. S Feb T Mar 1750 *Tryal*. M.

Isbitt, John of Glasgow, Scotland. SQS Jan 1766. La.

Isles als Eyles, Thomas. S s at Dursley Lent 1768. G.

Isles, William (1714). *See* Wale. G.

Ilewood, Joseph. S Feb T Mar 1727 *Rappahannock*. L.

Ilidge, Benjamin. S s at Wolverhampton Summer 1757. St.

Iliffe, Margaret. S Jly T Sep 1764 *Justitia*. M.

Illford als Shepherd, John. S Dec 1756. M.

Illingworth, Israel. S Lent T Oct 1723 *Forward* from London. Y.

Illingworth, Jonathan. SQS Wakefield Jan 1725 T *Supply* LC Md May 1726. Y.

Illingworth als Chadwick, Richard. S s silver cup at Halifax Lent 1773. Y.

Illingworth als Ellingworth, Thomas. AT Lent 1766. Y.

Ilsen, William (1762). *See* Insell. L.

Imber als Gray, Matthew. S Mar TB to Va Apr 1775. Wi.

Imbey, Mary. S Jun T Oct 1744 *Susannah*. M.

Imer, Richard. S Jan T Feb 1765 *Tryal*. L.

Imeson, John. T Apr 1769 *Tryal*. K.

Immens, James. S Lent 1768. Su.

Impey, Alice. SQS Jun T Aug 1752 *Tryal*. M.

Impey, Thomas. S Apr T May 1740 *Essex*. L.

Inch als Lee, Ann. T Apr 1770 *New Trial*. E.

Inch, John. TB to Va from QS 1749. De.

Inch, John. T for life Apr 1770 *New Trial*. E.

Inckoe, Andrew of Chaddesley. R for America Jly 1686. Wo.

Indoe, James. Rebel T 1685.

Ineon, Richard. S s clothing Feb T May 1736 *Patapsco* to Md. M.

Infield, John of Chelson. R for America Mar 1686. Bd.

Ingersole als Waskett, Ann. S Oct 1740. L.

Ingham, Anne. S Lent R 14 yrs Summer 1720 T Oct 1723 *Forward*. Y.

Ingham, Ann wife of John of Manchester. SQS Jan 1747. La.

Ingle, George. S Summer 1748. *Hu.

Inglebird, William. S May T Sep 1737 *Pretty Patsy* to Md. M.

Ingleby, John of Cannock. R for America Jly 1677. St.

Inglesby, Mary. S Aug T Oct 1741 *Sea Horse* to Va. M.

Ingleson, William. R 14 yrs Summer 1741. Y.

Inglethorpe, Thomas. S s cow at Burton on Trent Lent 1738. St.
Ingleton, Christopher. S Feb T Mar 1730 *Patapsco* LC Annapolis Sep 1730. L.
Ingleton, John. PT Oct 1697. M.
Inglish. *See* English.
Ingmire, Robert, S Oct-Dec 1754. M.
Ingold, Mary. R for Barbados Feb 1672. M.
Ingoll, John. S Dec 1755 T Jan 1756 *Greyhound.* L.
Ingram, Augustus. T Dec 1731 *Forward.* K.
Ingram, Barbara. S Aug T Oct 1723 *Forward.* L.
Ingram, Edward of York Castle. R for Barbados Feb 1673. Y.
Ingram, Elizabeth wife of John. S Jun 1761. M.
Ingram, Elizabeth. S Apr 1773. L.
Ingram, Grace. LC from *Forward* Rappahannock May 1728. X.
Ingram, Jacob of Berkhampstead. SQS & T Apr 1766 *Ann.* Ht.
Ingram, James. S Apr T Sep 1737 *Pretty Patsy* to Md. M.
Ingram, John. R Dec 1699 AT Jan 1700. M.
Ingram, John. S s horse Lent R 14 yrs Summer 1730. No.
Ingram, John. S Jly 1730. Wi.
Ingram, John. SQS Devizes Apr TB to Va May 1763. Wi.
Ingram als Bennett, John. S s at Tidenham Lent 1764. G.
Ingram, John. S Jly T Oct 1768 *Justitia.* M.
Ingram, John. R Summer 1774. E.
Ingram, Joseph. R Lent T for life Apr 1772 *Thornton.* K.
Ingram, Mary, aged 53, brown hair. LC from *Gilbert* Annapolis May 1721. X.
Ingram, Mary. SQS Jly TB to Md Oct 1739. So.
Ingram, Mary. T Sep 1758 *Tryal.* Sy.
Ingram, Mary. S & T Jly 1771 *Scarsdale.* M.
Ingram, Richard. T May 1719 *Margaret* but died on passage. Ht.
Ingram, Richard. S Mar 1737. So.
Ingram, Robert. R for Barbados or Jamaica Dec 1698. L.
Ingram, Robert. T Apr 1732 *Patapsco.* K.
Ingram, William. R for Barbados or Jamaica Dec 1695, Jan 1697 & Dec 1698. L.
Ingram, William of Newport Pagnell. S s mare Summer 1723 R 14 yrs Summer T Jly 1724 *Robert* LC Md Jun 1725. Bu.
Ingram, William. T Jly 1724 *Robert* LC Md Jun 1725. Sy.
Ingram, William. T Dec 1731 *Forward.* K.
Ingram, William. S s sheep Lent R 14 yrs Summer 1759. No.
Inkenbottome, Joseph. R May AT Jly 1697. M.
Inks, John. SQS & T Sep 1766 *Justitia.* M.
Inks, William. SQS & T Sep 1766 *Justitia.* M.
Inmall, John. S s mare Lent R 14 yrs Summer 1768. St.
Inman, Henry. R for Barbados Nov 1668. L.
Inman, Margaret (1675). *See* Ransome. M.
Inman, Millicent of St. George, Southwark. SQS Apr T May 1750 *Lichfield.* Sy.
Inman, Thomas. S s cloth at Knaresborough Lent 1774. Y.
Inman, William (1755). *See* Elleton. St.
Innes, Benjamin, als Jones, John. S Lent R 14 yrs Summer 1758. G.

Innis, David. S & T Dec 1758 *The Brothers*. M.

Ennis, George. S & T Sep 1766 *Justitia*. L.

Innis, James. S & T Jan 1766 *Tryal*. M.

Ennis, Richard, wheelwright aged 20, dark. S Jan T Feb 1723 *Jonathan* LC Annapolis Jly 1724. M.

Innes, Solomon. S Sep 1740. L.

Innis, Walter. S Feb-Apr T May 1751 *Tryal*. M.

Innocent, William (1713). *See* Metkins. M.

Inns, John. T Apr 1769 *Tryal*. Bu.

Inon, Henry. S May T Jly 1723 *Alexander* to Md. M.

Inon, John of Almondsbury & Westbury on Trym. R for America Feb 1681. G.

Inon, John (1698). *See* Thomas. De.

Insell, Elizabeth. S Apr T May 1755 *Rose*. L.

Insell, Silvester. S Feb 1758. Ha.

Incell als Ilsen, William. S & T Apr 1762 *Dolphin*. L.

Instance, Samuel. S Summer 1764. Sh.

Ipy, Mary (1718). *See* Hunt. L.

Ireland als Nichols, Anne. S Apr T May 1720 *Honor* LC Md Jan 1721. L.

Ireland, Edward. S Sep-Oct T Dec 1771 *Justitia*. M.

Ireland, Elizabeth. S Oct T Dec 1769 *Justitia*. L.

Ireland, George Frederick. R 14 yrs Jly 1764. Ha.

Ireland, James. S Mar & Jly 1729. Ha.

Ireland, John. R for Va May 1622. Sy.

Ireland als Chambers, John of Walsall. R for America Feb 1681. St.

Ireland, John. S s sheep Summer 1749. Bd.

Ireland, Joseph. S Jly 1767. Ha.

Ireland, Mary. R for Barbados Jly 1674. L.

Ireland, Mary. S & T Oct 1732 *Caesar* to Va. M.

Ireland, Richard. S Feb T Mar 1764 *Tryal*. L.

Ireland, Thomas. S Nov T Dec 1753 *Whiteing*. L.

Ireland, William. PT Jun R Oct 1673. M.

Ireland, William. S Sep T Dec 1769 *Justitia*. M.

Ireland, Zipora. R for Barbados or Jamaica May 1697. L.

Ireman als Bennett, James. S & T Oct 1732 *Caesar* to Va. M.

Irish Nell (1743). *See* Muckleston, Elizabeth. L.

Irish Pegg (1730). *See* Eaton, Margaret. L.

Irish Sam (1775). *See* Hutchins, Samuel. Be.

Irish, Katherine (1685). *See* Cotterell. M.

Irish, Richard. SQS Jan 1735. So.

Irish, William. R 14 yrs s sheep Summer 1763. Le.

Irlam, Mary wife of Jonathan of Manchester. SQS Apr 1746. La.

Iron, Aaron. S Jun T Sep 1758 *Tryal* to Annapolis. M.

Ironmonger, John. S for highway robbery at Horton & R 14 yrs Summer 1774. Bu.

Ironmonger, Robert. SQS Oct 1774. M.

Irons, William. S for life Feb 1754. M.

Irving, John. S & T Feb 1740 *York*. L.

Irving, Robert. SQS Richmond s silver mug at Scorton Jan TB Sep 1742. Y.

Irvin, William. S Mar 1759. Ha.

Erwin, Esther. S May 1760. M.

Irwing, John. S s at Reading Summer 1722 T *Forward* LC Annapolis Jun 1723. Be.

Isacke, George. R Mar 1618 to be T to Va. M.

Isaac, John. S s handkerchief at St. Peter, Hereford, Lent 1773. He.

Isaac, Lazarus. S & T Jan 1769 *Thornton*. L.

Izack, Samuel. S Feb T Apr 1762 *Dolphin*. M.

Isaac, William. S Apr T May 1720 *Honor* to Md. M.

Isaacs, Isaac of St. Olave, Southwark. SQS Jan 1752. Sy.

Isaacs, James. R Lent 1773. Sy.

Isaacs, John. SQS Jly TB to Md Oct 1739. So.

Isaacs, Lyon (1771). *See* Backarac. M.

Isaacs, Mary. S May T 14 yrs Jun 1733 *Forward*. L.

Isaacs als Jacobs, Rachael. S & T 14 yrs Dec 1740 *Vernon*. L.

Isaacs, Solomon of St. Saviour, Southwark. SQS Jan T Mar 1758 *Dragon*. Sy.

Isaacs als Solomons, Solomon. S Jan T Feb 1765 *Tryal*. L.

Isaacs, Tobias. S Jan T Mar 1743 *Justitia*. L.

Isaacs, William. S Mar 1720 T *Honor* but escaped in Vigo, Spain. L.

Isaacson, Susan. S Oct T Nov 1725 *Rappahannock* LC Rappahannock Apr 1726. L.

Isaackson, William. S Feb T Mar 1731 *Patapsco* LC Annapolis Jun 1731. M.

Isdell, William. S Jly 1774. L.

Isedale, Isabella (1760). *See* Paterson. M.

Isgrigg, William. S Apr T May 1740 *Essex*. L.

Isles. *See* Iles.

Islopp, Mary. R for Barbados Oct 1673. L.

Israel, Isaac. S Mar 1768 TB to Va. De.

Israel, Moses. S as pickpocket Lent R 14 yrs Summer 1766. Sh.

Israel, Sabate. S Nov T Dec 1753 *Whiteing*. L.

Israell, William. R for Barbados Sep TB Oct 1669. L.

Israel, William. TB to Md from QS 1737. De.

Isted, Edward. S Lent 1747. Bu.

Isted, John. S Lent R for Barbados Apr 1663. Sx.

Ive, Charles. S 14 yrs Summer 1752 for receiving goods stolen by John Hartley *(qv)* & William Crissell *(qv)*. Su.

Ives, Abraham. S for robbing Samuel Ives at Castle Camps Lent 1772. Ca.

Ives, Edward. T Jun 1740 *Essex*. Sy.

Ives, Joanna. S Aug T Oct 1726 *Forward* to Va. M.

Ives, John of Castle Camps. SQS Apr 1759. E.

Ives, Lucas. S Lent R 14 yrs Summer 1768. Sh.

Ives als James, William. S Feb T Mar *Patapsco* LC Annapolis Dec 1729. M.

Ives, William. S Summer 1756. Su.

Iverson, Peter. S Aug 1771. So.

Iveson, William. S & T Jly 1770 *Scarsdale*. M.

Ivey, Sampson. R 14 yrs Mar 1756 TB to Va. De.

Ivory, Bryan. S Jan-Apr 1748. M.

Ivory, John. S May & Jly 1720 to be T to Boston NE. Wi.
Ivory, William. S Mar 1752. So.
Izard, Abraham. S May T Jun 1756 *Lyon*. L.
Izard, Ann. S May-Jly T Sep 1751 *Greyhound*. M.

J

Jack above Ground (1763). *See* Adwell, John. M.

Jack, James. T 14 yrs Apr 1769 *Tryal*. Sy.

Jack, Jane. S & T Sep 1731 *Smith* LC Va 1732. M.

Jacklin, Andrew. S s mare & R 7 yrs Summer 1773. Li.

Jackman, Elinor. R for America Feb 1700. Li.

Jackman, John. R for Barbados Oct 1673. L.

Jackson, Anthony. T Apr 1770 *New Trial*. Sy.

Jackson, Bryan. S May-Jly 1749. M.

Jackson, Cecily (1700 & 1704). *See* Labree.

Jackson, David. R 14 yrs Summer 1758. Y.

Jackson, Dorothy. S Apr T May 1755 *Rose*. L.

Jackson, Edward. LC from *Dorsetshire* Va Sep 1736. X.

Jackson, Eleanor. S Oct T Dec 1724 *Rappahannock*. L.

Jackson, Elizabeth (1673). *See* Soe. L.

Jackson, Elizabeth. S & T Oct 1730 *Forward* LC Potomack Jan 1731. L.

Jackson als Martin, Elizabeth. S & T Dec 1740 *Vernon*. L.

Jackson, Elizabeth (1741). *See* Farrow. L.

Jackson als Holmes, Elizabeth. S Jan T Feb 1742 *Industry*. L.

Jackson, Elizabeth wife of John. S s at St. James Summer 1756. St.

Jackson, Elizabeth. SL Jan T Apr 1762 *Dolphin*. Sy.

Jackson als Atkinson, Frances. S s mare Feb 1656. M.

Jackson als Cook als Coates, George of Eynsham. R for Barbados Oct 1663. O.

Jackson, George. T Nov 1759 *Phoenix*. E.

Jackson, George of Great Birch. SQS Jan 1763. E.

Jackson, George of Manchester. SQS Jly 1763. La.

Jackson, George (1765). *See* Johnson. De.

Jackson, Gilbert. R for Barbados Mar 1677. M.

Jackson, Henry. R for Jamaica Aug 1661. M.

Jackson, Henry of Cartmel. SQS Jan 1760. La.

Jackson, Isaac of Clerkenwell. R (Western Circ) for Barbados Mar 1691. M.

Jackson, Isaac of Rotherhithe. SQS & T Jan 1766 *Tryal*. Sy.

Jackson, James. R for America Aug 1715. M.

Jackson, James. S Aug T Oct 1724 *Forward* LC Annapolis Jun 1725. M.

Jackson, James. S Dec 1733 T Jan 1734 *Caesar* LC Va Jly 1734. L.

Jackson, James. S for life Feb 1754. M.

Jackson, James. S Sep 1760. M.

Jackson, James, als Turner, William. S s oxen Summer 1764 R 14 yrs Lent 1765. Hu.

Jackson, James. S & T Apr 1769 *Tryal*. L.

Jackson, James. T Apr 1771 *Thornton*. M.

Jackson, James. S Apr-May T Jly 1771 *Scarsdale*. M.

Jackson, Jane. R for America Mar 1690. Li.

Jackson, Jane, LC from *Patapsco* Annapolis Nov 1733. X.

Jackson als Coxe, John. R for Barbados Oct 1673. L.

Jackson, John (1682). *See* Smathwit. Y.

Jackson, John. PT Jly R Oct 1688. M.

Jackson, John of Offham. R for Barbados or Jamaica Jly 1696. K.

Jackson, John of Shipston on Stour. R for America Feb 1716. Wo.

Jackson, John. S May T Jly 1722 *Alexander*. M.

Jackson als Johnson, John. T Jly 1723 *Alexander* but died on passage. E.

Jackson, John. LC from *Forward* Annapolis Dec 1725. X.

Jackson, John. S Aug T Oct 1726 *Forward*. L.

Jackson, John. S s horse Summer 1731 R 14 yrs Lent 1732. Nf.

Jackson, John. S Lent R 14 yrs Summer 1735. Su.

Jackson, John. S & T Jan 1739 *Dorsetshire*. L.

Jackson, John. S Lent T Nov 1743 *George William*. Bu.

Jackson, John. S Jan-Apr 1749. M.

Jackson, John. SQS Mar TB Apr 1754. Le.

Jackson, John. S s breeches at St. Mary, Shrewsbury, Lent 1757. Sh.

Jackson, John. T 14 yrs Dec 1763 *Neptune*. Sy.

Jackson, John. S Lent R 14 yrs Summer 1764. St.

Jackson, John of Bristol. R 14 yrs s horse Sep 1768. G.

Jackson, John of Kingston on Thames. R Lent R 14 yrs Apr 1772 *Thornton*. Sy.

Jackson, Jonathan. R for America Aug 1715. L.

Jackson, Joseph. SQS & TB Mar 1736. G.

Jackson, Joseph. R 14 yrs Summer 1741. Y.

Jackson, Joseph. S Summer T Oct 1750 *Rachael*. K.

Jackson, Joseph. S s hens at Grimley Lent 1759. Wo.

Jackson, Margaret (1715). *See* Wade. M.

Jackson, Margaret. S Aug T Oct 1724 *Forward* LC Annapolis Jun 1725. L.

Jackson, Mark. S s at Atwick & R Summer 1772. Y.

Jackson, Martha. S Summer 1756. Ch.

Jackson, Martha. S s cloth at Alderbury Lent 1757. Sh.

Jackson als Waller, Mary. S May T Jly 1723 *Alexander*. M.

Jackson, Mary wife of William. S Feb T Apr 1741 *Speedwell* or *Mediterranean*. M.

Jackson, Mary wife of John. S s linen at Bridgenorth Lent 1756. Sh.

Jackson, Mary. T Sep 1758 *Tryal*. Sy.

Jackson, Mary. S Oct 1766 T Jan 1767 *Tryal*. L.

Jackson, Mary. S Lent 1770. Nl.

Jackson, Mary. S Summer T Aug 1771. Wa.

Jackson, Mary. SQS Oct 1773. M.

Jackson, Peter. S s snuff box & R 14 yrs Summer 1754. Du.

Jackson, Richard of LLttle Wakering. R for Barbados or Jamaica Feb 1686. E.

Jackson, Richard. R for Barbados or Jamaica Jan 1692. M.

Jackson, Richard of Croydon. SQS for obtaining money by false pretences Oct 1768 T Jan 1769 *Thornton*. Sy.

Jackson, Robert. R for America Jly 1686. Nt.

Jackson, Robert. T Nov 1741 *Sea Horse*. E.

Jackson, Robert. S & T Feb 1744 *Neptune* to Md. M.

Jackson, Robert. S Lent 1759. Ch.

Jackson, Robert of Aspull, weaver. SQS Jly 1764. La.

Jackson, Robert. S Apr T Jly 1770 *Scarsdale*. L.

Jackson, Roland of Bromsgrove. R for America Jly 1673. Wo.

Jackson, Roland of Bircher. R for America Jly 1687. He.

Jackson, Samuel. S Jan-Jun T Jun 1728 *Elizabeth* LC Potomack Jan 1731. L.

Jackson, Samuel. S Summer 1763. Y.

Jackson, Sarah. S & T Oct 1730 *Forward* LC Potomack Jan 1731. L.

Jackson, Sarah. SQS May T Sep 1766 *Justitia*. M.

Jackson, Susan (1725). *See* Isaacson. L.

Jackson, Thomas of Glentham. R for America Feb 1681. Li.

Jackson, Thomas of Newnham. R for America Mar 1701. G.

Jackson, Thomas. S Aug 1725. M.

Jackson, Thomas. S for highway robbery Summer 1729 R Lent 1730 (SP). Sh.

Jackson, Thomas. S 14 yrs Lent 1730. Y.

Jackson, Thomas. S Jan-Jun 1747. M.

Jackson, Thomas. S May T Jun 1764 *Dolphin*. L.

Jackson, Thomas, als Leeke als Peele, William. S Summer 1764. Nt.

Jackson, Thomas. SQS Thirsk & TB Oct 1764. Y.

Jackson, Thomas. S Jly T Sep 1765 *Justitia*. M.

Jackson, William. Rebel T 1685.

Jackson, William. R Dec 1698 AT Jan 1699. M.

Jackson, William. S Summer 1730 R 14 yrs Lent 1731. Li.

Jackson als Jaquet, William. S & T Dec 1731 *Forward* to Md or Va. M.

Jackson, William. S Oct 1733 T Jan 1734 *Caesar* LC Va Jly 1734. M.

Jackson, William. S Feb 1735 T Dec 1736 *Dorsetshire*. M.

Jackson, William. S & T Dec 1736 *Dorsetshire*. L.

Jackson, William. S & R Lent 1738. Li.

Jackson als South, William. S s silk Jly T Sep 1742 *Forward*. L.

Jackson, William. T May 1751 *Tryal*. K.

Jackson als Chicken, William. S Summer 1752. Nf.

Jackson, William. S May-Jly T Sep 1755 *Tryal*. M.

Jackson, William. S s sheep at Yardley Summer 1761 R 14 yrs Lent 1762. Wo.

Jackson, William. S May T Jly 1770 *Scarsdale*. M.

Jackson, William. S Lent 1775. E.

Jacob, Ann. T Jun 1764 *Dolphin*. K.

Jacob, Elizabeth. S & T Apr 1766 *Ann*. L.

Jacob, George. R for Jamaica Aug 1661. M.

Jacob, Moses. S Lent 1751. Bd.

Jacob, Richard. Rebel T 1685.

Jacob, Solomon. S Jly TB Aug 1754. Wi.

Jacob, Thomas. S to be T to Va Jly 1718. Co.

Jacob, Thomas. R 14 yrs Jly 1721. Wi.

Jacob, Thomas, als Thomas, Jacob. S & T Sep 1766 *Justitia*. M.

Jacob, William. S Mar 1759. Ha.

Jacobs, Cornelius. S Jly-Dec 1747. M.

Jacobs, Frances. S May T Aug 1718 *Eagle* LC Charles Town Mar 1719. L.

Jacobs, Jacob. S Jan-Feb T 14 yrs Apr 1771 *Thornton*. M.

Jacobs, John. SQS Mar TB to Md Apr 1741. Le.

Jacobs, John. S Aug T Oct 1741 *Sea Horse* to Va. M.

Jacobs, Michael. S & T Sep 1757 *Thetis*. M.

Jacobs, Michael. T 14 yrs Dec 1758 *The Brothers*. E.

Jacobs, Moses. S Oct 1744-Jan 1745. M.

Jacobs, Rachael (1740). *See* Isaacs. L.

Jacobs, Sarah. S Jly T Oct 1741 *Sea Horse*. L.

Jacobs, Sarah. S Jly T Sep 1755 *Tryal*. L.

Jacobs, Simon, als Guest, Joseph. S Oct 1724 T *Forward* LC Annapolis Dec 1725. L.

Jacobson, Jan (1762). *See* Davits. Nl.

Jacomo, James. S Jan-Apr 1748. M.

Jacques. *See* Jaques.

Jaffray, Lewis. S Dec 1773. M.

Jaggard, Elizabeth. S Summer 1758. Su.

Jaggard als Golding, Francis. S s mare Lent R 14 yrs Summer 1758. Nf.

Jagger, Benjamin. SQS Bradford Jly 1724 T *Supply* LC Md May 1726. Y.

Jagger, John. S May T 14 yrs Jly 1770 *Scarsdale*. M.

Jagger, Joseph. S Lent 1747. Y.

Jago, Ittai. S Aug 1739. Co.

Jeggo, John. S Summer T Oct 1750 *Rachael*. E.

Jagoe, Valentine. S Summer R for Barbados Aug 1665. K.

Jakeman, William. S s sheep Lent R 14 yrs Summer 1759. Wa.

Jakes. *See* Jaques.

James, Ann of Bermondsey. R for Barbados or Jamaica Mar 1682 & Feb 1683. Sy.

James, Ann. S Jan T 14 yrs Apr 1741 *Speedwell*. L.

James, Ann. S Summer 1748 R 14 yrs Lent TB Mar 1749. G.

James, Benjamin. S for killing sheep Lent R 14 yrs Summer 1763. Wo.

James, Diana wife of William. S Jan-Feb 1775. M.

James, Edward of Camberwell. R for America Jly 1700. Sy.

James, Edward. S Sep-Oct T Dec 1752 *Greyhound*. M.

James, Edward. S s at Mitcheldean Lent 1768. G.

James, Elizabeth wife of William. S & T Oct 1732 *Caesar* to Va. M.

James als Bainton, Esther. S Oct T Nov 1725 *Rappahannock* but died on passage. M.

James, George of Whittleborough Forest. R for America Jly 1716. No.

James, George. S Jly T Aug 1721 *Prince Royal* LC Va Nov 1721. L.

James, George. S Oct 1761 T Apr 1762 *Dolphin*. M.

James, Harris. S Aug T Sep 1725 *Forward* LC Annapolis Dec 1725. L.

James, Henry of Bampton. R for America Nov 1694. O.

James als Newton, Hugh. S Aug 1729. De.

James, James. S & TB Mar 1732. G.

James, James (1758). *See* Roberts. He.

James, James. S Jly 1775. M.

James, John of Garway. R for America Jly 1682. He.

James, John of Margaret Marsh. R for Barbados Jly 1683. Do.

James als Jeanes, John. Rebel T 1685.

James als Beacham, John. AT Dec 1697. M.

James, John. S Mar 1721. De.

James als Willing, John. S Mar 1730. De.

James, John. S & T Dec 1731 *Forward* to Md or Va. M.

James, John (1732). *See* Pearse. Co.

James, John. S Apr-Jun 1739. M.

James, John. SQS Feb T Mar 1750 *Tryal*. M.

James als Rowland, John, als Whitney, James. R 14 yrs Summer 1752. Y.

James, John. SQS Jan TB Feb 1757. So.

James, John. SQS May T Nov 1762 *Prince William*. M.

James, John. S s sheep Lent R 14 yrs Summer 1765. Mo.

James, John (1766). *See* Bartlett, William. Wi.

James, John. S s horse Lent R 14 yrs Summer 1768. G.

James, John. R Mar 1774. So.

James, Joseph. S Dec 1745. L.

James, Joseph. R 14 yrs Jly 1767. Ha.

James, Mary. S Jan T Feb 1733 *Smith* to Md or Va. M.

James als Seeker, Mary. T Jan 1738 *Dorsetshire*. Sy.

James, Mary. S Dec 1750. L.

James, Mary. S Feb-Apr T May 1755 *Rose*. M.

James, Mary. S s iron chains at Kidderminster Summer 1761. Wo.

James, Nathaniel. S Mar 1767. Ha.

James, Peter. S Jly 1763 TB to Va. De.

James, Richard. R Jly AT Aug 1685. M.

James, Richard. R 14 yrs Aug 1728. So.

James, Richard (1769). *See* Holder. Wo.

James, Robert. S May T Sep 1737 *Pretty Patsy* to Md. M.

James, Robert. S Mar 1758. So.

James, Samuel. S s pigs at Monmouth Summer 1750. Mo.

James, Sarah. S s calico Jan T Apr *Patapsco* LC Annapolis Oct 1735. M.

James, Sarah. S Lent 1752. Be.

James, Susan. R for Jamaica Aug 1661. L.

James als Charles, Thomas. PT Summer 1719 in Berkshire, S s horse Lent 1720 & to transport himself within 3 months. Mo.

James, Thomas. S & T Jan 1722 *Gilbert* to Md. M.

James, Thomas. S s oxen at Littleton on Severn Lent TB Mar 1735. G.

James, Thomas. S May T Jun 1738 *Forward*. L.

James, Thomas. SQS & T Dec 1752 *Greyhound*. M.

James als Watkins, Thomas. S s at Birley Lent 1753. He.

James, Thomas. S for life Jan 1755. L.

James, Thomas. S Lent R 14 yrs Summer 1765. G.

James, Thomas. S (Western Circ) Dec 1766. Be.

James, Thomas. R Jly T for life Oct 1768 *Justitia*. M.

James, Thomas. SQS Sep 1773. M.

James, William. S May T Jly 1722 *Alexander* to Nevis or Jamaica. M.

James, William (1729). *See* Ives. M.

James, William. S & TB Aug 1740. G.

James, William. S for highway robbery Lent R for life Summer 1750. O.

James, William. S Aug 1754. So.

James, William. S & T Jan 1766 *Tryal*. L.

James, William. S Sep-Oct 1772. M.

James, William. S Sep-Oct 1773. M.

James, William. S s at Magor Summer 1774. Mo.

Jameson, John. S Sep 1756. M.

Jameson, William. R 14 yrs Summer 1720. Nl.

Janes als Jones, Joseph. S Oct 1764 T Jan 1765 *Tryal*. M.

Jeynes, William. S s lead from Gloucester Cathedral Summer TB Aug 1740. G.

Janney, Samuel (1756). *See* Wood. Nt.

Janson, John. S s mare Summer 1756 R 14 yrs Lent 1757. Nt.

Jakes, Elizabeth. S Sep T Oct 1719 *Susannah & Sarah* LC Annapolis Apr 1720. L.

Jacques, Frances. S Oct T Dec 1724 *Rappahannock* to Va. M.

Jaques, George. S & T Apr 1762 *Dolphin*. L.

Jaques, Thomas. S s sheep & R Summer 1775. Y.

Jaques als Jakes, William. T Sep 1764 *Justitia*. Sy.

Jaquet, William (1731). *See* Jackson. M.

Jarcel, John of Morpeth, yeoman. SQS s clothing Mich 1771. Nl.

Jarlett, John. S Sep T Oct 1768 *Justitia*. M.

Jarman, Daniel. S Jan T Mar 1764 *Tryal*. M.

Jarman, Mary. R 14 yrs Jly 1749 TB to Va. De.

Jarman, Thomas. R 14 yrs Aug 1757 TB to Va 1758. De.

Jarreel, John. S s clothing Summer 1771 LC from *Lowther & Senhouse* Va May 1772. Nl.

Jarrett (Jarrow), Abraham. T Aug 1721 *Owners Goodwill* LC Md Jly 1722. E.

Jerret, Elizabeth. S Mar 1757. Ha.

Jarrett, James. T Nov 1743 *George William*. Sx.

Jarrett, James. S s timber at Stroud Lent 1774. G.

Jarrat, John (1745). *See* Whetten. Wa.

Jarrett, Robert. T Nov 1725 *Rappahannock* but died on passage. K.

Jarret, Thomas. S s at Lydham Lent 1768. Sh.

Jarret, William. T Nov 1741 *Sea Horse*. Sx.

Jarrett, William. T May 1752 *Lichfield*. Sx.

Jarrow, Abraham. *See* Jarrett. E.

Jarrow, Bridget. S Feb R for Barbados Jun 1663. M.

Jarro, Jacob Henriques (1753). *See* Mesquita. L.

Jarvice. *See* Jarvis.

Jarvis, Anne. S Feb T Mar 1729 *Patapsco* LC Annapolis Dec 1729. M.

Jervice, Aron. S & T Dec 1734 *Caesar* LC Va Jly 1735. L.

Jarvis, Benjamin of Stevenage. S Lent 1745. Ht.

Jarvis, Elizabeth. S Feb T 14 yrs May 1740 *Essex*. L.

Jarvys, Henry. R (Home Circ) for Barbados May 1664. X.

Jarvis als Garvis, Humphrey of Hacklestone, victualler. R for Barbados Feb 1665 & Jun 1666. Wi.

Jarvis, Humphrey of Thornbury. R for America Jly 1677. G.

Jarvis, Jacob. S for highway robbery & R Lent T Apr 1768 *Thornton*. Bu.

Jarvis, James. S Apr 1728. So.

Jarvis, James. S s brass & T Dec 1734 *Caesar* to Va. M.

Jarvis als Duffield als Waters, James. S Norwich Summer 1754 R 14 yrs Summer 1755. Nf.

Jarvis, Jane, spinster, als wife of Edward. R for Va Oct TB Nov 1667. L.

Jarvis, John (1679). *See* Cotton. Hu.

Jarvis, John of Alphington. R for Barbados Feb 1690. De.

Jarvis, John, als Black Jack. S & T Jly 1753 *Tryal*. L.

Jarvis, John. S s at Woodstock Lent 1770. O.

Jarvis, Mary. S Jan T Feb 1724 *Anne*. L.

Jervise, Mary. SQS Coventry Apr 1765. Wa.

Jarvis, Michael. R 14 yrs Jly 1743. De.

Jarvis, Paul of Bushbury, carpenter. R for America Mar 1683. St.

Jervis, Richard. S Sep T Oct 1719 *Susannah & Sarah* LC Annapolis Apr 1720. L.

Jervis, Robert of Severnake Park. R for Barbados Feb 1701. Wi.

Jarvas, Simon. S Jan T Feb 1719 *Worcester* LC Annapolis Jun 1719. L.

Jarvis, Thomas. R for Barbados or Jamaica Jly 1687. M.

Jarves, William of Cheshunt. R for Barbados or Jamaica Jly 1696. Ht.

Jarvis, William. S Jan 1755. L.

Jervis, William. S s gelding at Wedgebury & R 14 yrs Summer 1770. St.

Jary, William of Taverham. R for Barbados Aug 1671. Nf.

Jasey, Eliiabeth. PT Feb 1680. M.

Jasper, Joan of Calstock, spinster. R for Barbados Feb 1672. Co.

Jasper, John. S s hair collar at Llanwenarth Summer 1768. Mo.

Jaume, Francois. S Jan T Mar 1764 *Tryal*. L.

Javelow, Charles. R for America Summer 1728 (SP). Ca.

Jay, Elizabeth. S s at St. Chad, Shrewsbury, Lent 1762. Sh.

Jay, Elizabeth. T Sep 1766 *Justitia*. E.

Jay als Vaill, George. S Lent 1749. *Su.

Jay, John. S s at Yarpole Lent 1770. He.

Jey, Richard. R Mar 1606. K.

Jay, Richard. S Jly 1749. L.

Jay, Thomas of ?Modits. R for America Feb 1716. He.

Jay, William. S Lent R 14 yrs Summer 1737. O.

Jaycocks, Thomas. R Jly T 14 yrs Sep 1767 *Justitia*. M.

Jays als Jennings, Richard of Stagsden. R for Barbados Aug 1671. Bd.

Jeagles, William. S Summer T 14 yrs Oct 1750 *Rachael*. Sy.

Jeakens, John. T Dec 1753 *Whiteing*. K.

Jeals als Gyles, Alexander. R 14 yrs Apr 1742. Ha.

Jeanes, John (1685). *See* James.

Jeaves, Thomas. S s wheat at Leighton Buzzard Summer 1770. Bd.

Jebb, John. S 14 yrs Oct 1751-Jan 1752. M.

Jebens, Moses. S Jly 1763. M.

Jeff, William. S s at Topcliffe Summer TB Aug 1767. Y.

Jefferson, Henry. S Oct T Nov 1725 *Rappahannock* LC Rappahannock Apr 1726. M.

Jefferson, James. S Oct 1737 T Jan 1738 *Dorsetshire* to Va. M.

Jefferson, John of Mitcham. SQS Oct 1750. Sy.

Jefferson, John. AT Summer 1765. Nl.

Jefferson, John. S May-Jly 1774. M.

Jefferson, William of Chalke. R for Barbados or Jamaica Feb 1696. K.

Jeffery, Alexander. R 14 yrs Mar 1771. Co.

Jeffry, Ann. TB to Va from QS 1745. De.

Jeffrey, Edward. S Apr 1759. Fl.

Jeffery, Francis. R 14 yrs Aug 1771. So.

Jeffery, John. T Sep 1730 *Smith*. Sx.

Jeffery, Katherine. S s at St. Philip & Jacob Lent 1751. G.

Jeffery, Mary of Horsham. S Summer 1772. Sx.

Jeffery, Richard. SQS Jan 1732. So.

Jeffery, Thomas. T 14 yrs Aug 1769 *Douglas*. K.

Jefford, Benjamin. S Lent 1775. Wa.

Jefford, David of Mansfield. R for America Jly 1673. Nt.

Geoffrys, Ann. S s at Rushberry Lent 1749. Sh.

Jefferys, Benjamin. T May 1744 *Justitia*. K.

Jeffreys, Benjamin. S Feb-Apr T May 1752 *Lichfield*. M.

Jeffryes, Christian. S Aug T Oct 1724 *Forward* LC Annapolis Jun 1725. M.

Jefferies, Elinor. R for Barbados or Jamaica May AT Jly 1697

Jefferys, Elizabeth. AT Oct R Dec 1716 T Jan 1717 *Queen Elizabeth* to Jamaica. M.

Jefferys, Elizabeth. S Sep 1756. M.

Jefferies, Jane. S Apr 1763. M.

Jeffreys, John of Nettlebed. R for America Nov 1694. O.

Jefferies, John. S Jly 1720. Ha.

Jefferys, John. S Mar 1741. De.

Jefferys, John. S Jun T Nov 1743 *George William*. L.

Jafferys, John. S Apr T May 1750 *Lichfield*. M.

Jefferies, John. S Lent R 14 yrs Summer 1756. Nf.

Jefferies, John. R 14 yrs Mar TB to Va Oct 1768. Wi.

Jefferis, Katherine. S & TB Apr 1751. G.

Jefferies, Luke. S Feb 1754. M.

Jefferyes, Mary. S Jly T Sep 1757 *Thetis*. M.

Jeffryes, Richard. S s sheep at Llanrothal Summer 1734. He.

Jefferys, Richard. S s deer Mar 1755. Ha.

Jeffreys, Sarah. S s yarn at Ellesmere Lent 1766. Sh.

Jeffryes, Stephen. Rebel T 1685.

Jeffryes, Susannah (1744). *See* Read. M.

Jefferys, Susan. S s at Mathern Lent 1770. Mo.

Jefferies, Thomas. T from Portsmouth 1723. Ha.

Jefferies, Thomas. S Mar 1766. So.

Jeffries, William of West Ham. SQS Oct 1752 T Dec 1753 *Whiteing*. E.

Jefferys, William. R 14 yrs Mar TB Apr 1755. Wi.

Jeffreys, William. S Lent R 14 yrs Summer 1756. Le.

Jefferys, William. SQS Jly T Sep 1767 *Justitia*. M.

Jeffs, Mary. S Aug T Oct 1726 *Forward*. L.

Jeffs, Thomas. S & R 14 yrs Lent 1766. Bd.

Jeggo. *See* Jago.

Jekyll, Cornelius. S s at Reedham Lent 1773. Nf.

Jelfcock, Joseph. S Lent 1765. Wa.

Jellard, William. R & T Dec 1734 *Caesar* LC Va Jly 1735. M.

Jelley, Mary of Claines, spinster. S Summer 1719. Wo.

Jellicoe, Samuel of Kingsley. R for America Aug 1699. Ch.

Jemison, Eleanor. SQS May T Jun 1768 *Tryal*. M.

Jemitt, Green. S Apr T Jun 1768 *Tryal*. M.

Jenkin, Mathias. S Apr 1723. De.

Jenkin, Morgan of Cullompton. R for Barbados Feb 1690. De.

Jenkin, Thomas. S s iron at Trevethin (Mon) Summer 1749. He.

Jenkins, Anne (1670). *See* Niccols. M.

Jenkins, Anne. LC from *Forward* Rappahannock May 1728. X.

Jenkins, Ann (1738). *See* Gaffney. M.

Jenkins, Ann. S Oct 1765 T Jan 1766 *Tryal*. L.

Jenkins, Charles. S s at St. Michael, Gloucester, Lent 1752. G.

Jenkins, David of Bristol. R for Barbados Feb 1714. G.

Jenkins, Edward. R 14 yrs Aug 1736. De.

Jenkins, Edward. S Lent T May 1751 *Tryal*. Bu.

Jenkins, Edward. S s beans at Cholsey Lent 1766. Be.

Jenkins, Edward. S Oct 1766 T Jan 1767 *Tryal*. M.

Jenkins als Bateman, Elizabeth. S & T Apr 1759 *Thetis*. L.

Jenkins, Ellen. S & R Lent 1737. La.

Jenkins, Frances. S Lent R 14 yrs & T Apr 1760 *Thetis*. Sx.

Jenkins, Hannah. T 14 yrs Sep 1765 *Justitia*. Sy.

Jenkins, Henry of Morchard Bishops, husbandman. R for Barbados
Feb 1665. De.

Jenkins, Henry. S Feb T Apr 1734 *Patapsco*. L.

Jenkins, Henry. S s at Halsfield Summer TB Aug 1748. G.

Jenkins als Browne, Jane. R for Barbados or Jamaica Dec 1695 & May
1697. L.

Jenkins, Jane (1730). *See* Jones. M.

Jenkins, Jane. S & T Oct 1730 *Forward* LC Potomack Jan 1731. M.

Jenkins, Jane. SQS Jly TB Aug 1766. So.

Jenkins, John of Aspley Guise. R for America Jly 1683. Bd.

Jenkings, John. S Jan T 14 yrs Feb 1733 *Smith* to Md or Va. M.

Jenkins, John. S s playhouse tickets Dec 1735 T Jan 1736 *Smith*. M.

Jenkins, John. S Jun-Dec 1738 T Jan 1739 *Dorsetshire* to Va. M.

Jenkins, John. S Jan T Feb 1742 *Industry* to Md. M.

Jenkins, John. R 14 yrs Mar 1764. De.

Jenkins, John. S Lent 1775. Sy.

Jenkins, John. S Sep-Oct 1775. M.

Jenkins, Joseph. S Aug 1727. M.

Jenkins, Joseph. S Dec 1727. M.

Jenkins, Joseph. S & R Lent T Apr 1769 *Tryal*. Bu.

Jenkins, Margaret of Fryerning. SQS Jan 1749. E.

Jenkins, Mary. R for Barbados May 1676. L.

Jenkins, Mary. S Jan-Jun T Jun 1728 *Elizabeth* LC Potomack Aug
1729. L.

Jenkins, Mathew. S Jly T Sep 1766 *Justitia*. M.

Jenkins, Priscilla. R for life Mar TB to Va Apr 1767. Wi.

Jenkins, Richard of Worcester. R for America Jly 1696. Wo.

Jenkins, Richard (1697). *See* Page. M.

Jenkins, Thomas (1697). *See* Road. M.

Jenkins, Thomas. S May T Jun 1727 *Susanna* to Va. M.

Jenkins, Thomas. S s watch Feb T Apr 1735 *Patapsco* to Md. M.

Jenkins, Thomas. S Jan-May T 14 yrs Jun 1738 *Forward* to Md or Va. M.

Jenkins, Thomas (1740). *See* Holles. St.

Jenkins, Thomas. S May-Jly 1750. M.

Jenkins, Thomas. S Apr-May 1754. M.

Jenkins, Thomas. S & T Jly 1770 *Scarsdale*. L.

Jenkins, Thomas. S s mare & R 14 yrs Summer 1771. He.

Jenkins, Thomas. R Jan-Feb T 14 yrs Apr 1772 *Thornton*. M.

Jenkyns, William. T May 1719 *Margaret*; sold to John Nelson, Md. Bu.

Jenkins, William. T *Margaret* from London & sold to John Nelson Md Aug 1719. Li.

Jenkins, William. SQS Bradford Jly 1724 T *Supply* LC Md May 1726. Y.

Jenkins als Jenkinson, William. S Lent 1736. Y.

Jenkins, William. S Summer 1742 R 14 yrs Lent 1743. Mo.

Jenkins, William. S Jly 1744. Ha.

Jenkins, William. S Jun T Sep 1764 *Justitia*. M.

Jenkins, William of Lambeth. SQS Oct T 14 yrs Dec 1771 *Justitia*. Sy.

Jenkins, William. S Apr 1774. L.

Jenkins, William Glover of St. John's. SQS Oct T Dec 1771 *The Brothers*. Sy.

Jenkinson, Edward. S Apr-Jun 1739. M.

Jenkinson, John of Hale, Chesh, husbandman. SQS Apr 1763. La.

Jenkinson, Paul. S Jan-Feb T Apr 1771 *Thornton*. M.

Jenkinson, Richard. S Summer 1755 R 14 yrs Lent 1756. St.

Jenkinson, Thomas. AT Lent 1747. Y.

Jenkinson, William. LC from *Patapsco* Annapolis Oct 1735. X.

Jenkinson, William (1736). *See* Jenkins. Y.

Jenks, Christopher. S Jly T Sep 1757 *Thetis*. M.

Jenks, Mary. S & T Apr 1725 *Sukey* but died on passage. M.

Jenner, Charles. S & T Sep 1764 *Justitia*. L.

Jenner, Samuel of Chevening. S Lent T May 1750 *Lichfield*. K.

Jenner, Samuel. S Lent R Summer T 14 yrs Sep 1755 *Tryal*. Sx.

Jennings als Smith als Pennings als Waters, Abel. T 14 yrs Sep 1766 *Justitia*. K.

Jennings, Ann. S Lent R 14 yrs Summer 1742. Wo.

Jennings, Christopher. S Apr 1763. M.

Jennings, Edward. S Lent R 14 yrs Summer 1745. Ht.

Jennings, Elizabeth. S Aug 1741. M.

Jennings, Elizabeth. AT from QS Lent 1746. G.

Jennings, George. S May-Jly 1773. M.

Jennings, Henry. S s porringer Jan T Apr 1735 *Patapsco* LC Annapolis Oct 1735. L.

Jennings, Henry. S Summer 1761. K.

Jennings, James. S Jan-Feb T Apr 1772 *Thornton*. M.

Jennings, Jane. S Feb T Apr 1741 *Speedwell* or *Mediterranean*. M.

Jenings, John of Hertingfordbury. R for Barbados Apr 1668. Ht.

Jennings, John. R for Barbados or Jamaica Feb 1687. M.

Jennings, John. PT Jan 1694 R for Barbados Dec 1698. M.

Jennings, John. S Apr T May 1752 *Lichfield*. L.

Jennings, John. S Apr-May 1754. M.

Jennings, John. S Summer 1755. Cu.

Jennings, John. S Summer 1768. Wa.

Jennings, John. T Oct 1768 *Justitia*. Sy.

Jennings, Joseph. S s sheep at Eastnor Lent 1727. He.

Jennings, Mary. S Sep-Dec 1746. M.

Jennings, Mary. S Feb-Apr T May 1751 *Tryal*. M.

Jennings, Mary (1754). *See* Anthony. L.

Jennings, Richard (1671). *See* Jays. Bd.

Jennings, Richard. S s horse Lent R 14 yrs Summer 1729. Sh.

Jennings, Richard. S Summer 1740. Be.

Jennings, Richard. R 14 yrs Aug 1774. Co.

Jennings, Robert. Rebel T 1685.

Jennings, Robert of Gravesend. R for Barbados or Jamaica Jun 1699. K.

Jennings, Samuel of Egham. S Lent T May 1750 *Lichfield*. Sy.

Jennings, Thomas. S s mare Lent R 14 yrs Summer 1760. Wa.

Jennings, Thomas. SWK Jly T Oct 1768 *Justitia*. K.

Jennings, William. S May-Jun T Aug 1752 *Tryal*. M.

Jennings, William. S s at Wolverhampton Lent 1764. St.

Jennings, William (1772). *See* White. Ht.

Jennings, William. R Lent 1775. E.

Jennison, John. SW & T Oct 1768 *Justitia*. M.

Jenvey, Peter. S Oct-Dec 1754. M.

Jephson, John. S Jly T Sep 1751 *Greyhound*. L.

Jepp, William. S Lent 1774. E.

Jepson, Henry. S 14 yrs s linen from yard at Bromsgrove Summer 1758. Wo.

Jepson, John. S Summer 1749 R for life Lent T May 1750 *Lichfield*. E.

Jepson, Thomas. R Dec 1681 AT Jan 1682. M.

Jepson, William. S Lent 1761. La.

Jerbin, Jasper. Died on passage in *Patapsco* 1730. X.

Jermain. *See* Germain.

Jerman. *See* German.

Jermy als Jermain, Edward of St. Paul, Norwich. S Summer 1731 R 14 yrs Lent 1732. Nf.

Jermy, Michael. S s gelding Lent R 14 yrs Summer 1758. Nf.

Jarmy, William of Henham. S s wheat Lent 1725. *Su.

Jernell, William. R Oct TB Nov 1662. L.

Jerrachino, Abraham. T Apr 1769 *Tryal*. Sy.

Jerret. *See* Jarrett.

Jervice. *See* Jarvis.

Jessey, Griffith. S Jly 1750. L.

Jessin, Henericke. R for Barbados Sep 1669. M.

Jessop, Abraham. S Lent R 14 yrs & T Summer 1736. Y.

Jessop, Henry. R (Norfolk Circ) for Barbados Jly 1675. X.

Jessope, Isaac of Malmesbury. R for Barbados Jly 1684. Wi.

Jessop, John of Holy Trinity, Guildford. R for Barbados or Jamaica Feb 1686. Sy.

Jessop, Robert. S Sep 1737 T Jan 1738 *Dorsetshire* to Va. M.

Jessop, Samuel. S s mare Lent R 14 yrs Summer 1755. Wa.

Jessup, Thomas. T 14 yrs Apr 1771 *Thornton*. K.

Jessup, William. S s gelding & R Lent 1738. Su.

Jetter, John. S Sep-Dec 1746. M.

Jetter, John Jr. S & T Apr 1753 *Thames*. L.

Jevon, Daniel. S s fowls at Sedgley Summer 1771. St.

Jewell, Christopher. Rebel T 1685.

Jewell, James. S Sep-Oct 1749. M.

Juel, Laurence. R 7 yrs Aug 1774. Co.

Duel, Martha. T Apr 1759 *Thetis*. Sy.

Jewell, Mary. R 14 yrs Aug 1759 TB to Va. De.

Jewell, Melony. S Mar 1729. So.

Jewell, Phillip. S Jan 1746. M.

Jewell, Richard. S Mar 1772. Co.

Dewell, Thomas. SL & T Sep 1766 *Justitia*. Sy.

Jewell, William. R for Barbados Jun 1663. M.

Duell, William. S Feb T for life Apr 1741 *Speedwell* or *Mediterranean*. M.

Jewill, William. TB to Va from QS 1743. De.

Jewell, William. SQS Jun T Jly 1772 *Tayloe*. M.

Jewell, William. S Mar 1773. Co.

Jewers, Ann. S & T Apr 1741 *Speedwell* or *Mediterranean* to Md. M.

Jewers, Johanna. S Apr-May T May 1744 *Justitia*. M.

Jewes, Edward (1773). *See* Dewes. No.

Jewes, Richard. S Aug T Sep 1764 *Justitia*. L.

Jewitson, William. AT Summer 1755. Y.

Jewkes. *See* Jukes.

Juson, Joseph. S Lent 1757. K.

Jex, Edward. S s hogs Lent 1761. Nf.

Jex, Humphrey of Barton Bendish. R for America Feb 1695. Nf.

Jex, Jonathan. S s at Stalham & R for life Lent 1774: Henry & James Jex hanged for same. Nf.

Jiggam, Samuel (1720). *See* Crosse. G.

Jilks, William. S May T Jly 1770 *Scarsdale*. M.

Jilson. *See* Gilson.

Joachim, Robert. S & TB Aug 1754. G.

Jobb, John. S Mar 1730. Ha.

Job, Samuel. S s horse Lent R 14 yrs Summer 1729. G.

Jobb, Thomas. S Mar 1726. De.

Jobson als Barnes als Candler als Lusted, Frances. R for Barbados Jun 1671. M.

Jobson, Margaret wife of Christopher, als Clennell, Mary. S to hang, found pregnant & R Summer 1759. Nl.

Jockam, John. S s at Rendcombe Summer 1771. G.

Joddrell, Elizabeth. R for Barbados Feb 1672. M.

Johannes, Daniel (1755). *See* Frederick. M.

John, Alice Haper. S Apr T Sep 1737 *Pretty Patsy* to Md. M.

John, Evan of Alderton, yeoman. R for America Feb 1713. G.

John, Francis Evan. S s at Llantarnam Summer 1727. Mo.

John, Henry. S s at Llanvaches Lent 1753. Mo.

John, Mary of Newport, spinster. R for America Mar 1683. Mo.

John, Roger. S s iron at Trevethan Lent 1735. Mo.

John, Thomas. S Apr 1775. Co.

John, William. S s heifer at Redwick & R 14 yrs Summer 1771. Mo.

Johns, Ann. S Feb-Apr T May 1751 *Tryal*. M.

Johns, Elias. S Mar 1742. Co.

Johns, John. S Mar 1742. Co.

Johns, Robert. S Jly 1733. De.

Johns, Stephen. S Mar 1742. Co.

Johns, Thomas of Walton on Thames. R for Barbados or Jamaica Jun 1699. Sy.

Johns, Thomas of Godalming. SQS Jly T Aug 1769 *Douglas*. Sy.

Johnson, Alexander. PT Jan R for Barbados or Jamaica Aug 1700. M.

Johnson als Farr, Alice. S Jun T Aug 1769 *Douglas*. L.

Johnson, Andrew. S May-Jun T Jly 1753 *Tryal*. M.

Johnson als Jackson als Harrison, Ann. S & T Feb 1744 *Neptune* to Md. M.

Johnson, Ann wife of John. S Jun T Sep 1758 *Tryal* to Annapolis. M.

Johnson, Ann (1761). *See* Harrison. M.

Johnson, Ann. S & T Nov 1762 *Prince William*. L.

Johnson, Ann. S Nov T Dec 1763 *Neptune*. L.

Johnson, Ann. S Dec 1764 T Jan 1765 *Tryal*. M.

Johnson, Ann. S Sep-Oct 1773. M.

Johnson, Ann. S Feb 1775. L.

Johnson, Anthony. S s at Baswich Lent 1739. St.

Johnson, Anthony. S Sep T Oct 1739 *Duke of Cumberland*. L.

Johnson als Johnston, Archibald of Mussleborough, Scotland. R (Northern Circ) for Barbados Jly 1682. X.

Johnson, Barbara. S Feb T Apr 1734 *Patapsco* to Md. M.

Johnson, Benjamin of Newington. R for Barbados Apr 1668. Sy.

Johnson, Benjamin. S Oct 1727-Jun 1728 T Jun 1728 *Elizabeth* to Md or Va. M.

Johnson, Benjamin. R 14 yrs Oct 1772. M.

Johnson, Bridget. S Jan-Feb T Apr 1753 *Thames*. M.

Johnson, Caleb. R for America Jly 1683. Le.

Johnson als Dodson, Katherine. R for Barbados Mar 1681. M.

Johnson, Charles (1688). *See* Cornish. De.

Johnston, Charles, aged 20, fair. LC from *Jonathan* Annapolis Jly 1724. X.

Johnson, Charles. S Summer 1740. Y.

Johnson, Charles. S Dec 1765 T Jan 1766 *Tryal*. M.

Johnson, Christopher. R for America Aug 1685. Wa.

Johnson, Christopher. S s sheep Lent R 14 yrs Summer 1759. Li.

Johnson, Christopher. S Oct 1773. L.

Johnson als Bogg, Daniel. R Dec 1699 AT Jan 1700. M.

Johnson, Daniel. S Lent R 14 yrs Summer 1748. St.

Johnson, David. S Feb T Apr 1768 *Thornton*. M.

Johnson, David. S Feb 1773. L.

Johnson, Davison. SQS Jly T Sep 1765 *Justitia*. M.

Johnson, Edward. S Feb T Mar 1729 *Patapsco* LC Annapolis Dec 1729. M.

Johnson, Edward. R 14 yrs Summer 1736. O.

Johnson, Edward (1754). *See* Dickson. M.

Johnson, Edward. S Jan T Mar 1760 *Friendship*. M.

Johnson, Edward. S s at Scalby Lent TB Aug 1767. Y.

Johnson, Eleanor. S Feb T Apr 1765 *Ann*. M.

Johnson, Elizabeth (1614). *See* Jones. M.

Johnson, Elizabeth, widow. R for Barbados Aug 1679 & Jly 1680. M.

Johnson, Elizabeth. S Feb T Mar 1727 *Rappahannock* to Md. M.

Johnson, Elizabeth. S & T Oct 1729 *Forward* LC Va Jun 1730. L.

Johnston, Elizabeth. R 14 yrs Summer 1730. Du.

Johnson, Elizabeth. S as pickpocket Lent R 14 yrs Summer TB Aug 1734. G.

Johnson, Elizabeth (1741). *See* Clay. L.

Johnson, Elizabeth als Betty. S Lent R 14 yrs Summer 1754. Sx.

Johnson, Elizabeth. S Jly T Sep 1757 *Thetis*. M.

Johnson, Elizabeth. S Sep T Dec 1758 *The Brothers*. M.

Johnson, Elizabeth. T Apr 1759 *Thetis*. Sy.

Johnson, Elizabeth (1772). *See* Wood. M.

Johnson, Esther (1731). *See* Watson. M.

Johnson, Francis. R for Barbados Dec 1683. M.

Johnson, George. S s horse Lent 1728 R 14 yrs Lent 1729. Y.

Johnson, George. S & T Sep 1731 *Smith* LC Va 1732. L.

Johnson, George. S Oct 1741 T Feb 1742 *Industry*. L.

Johnson, George. S Jly 1749. L.

Johnson als Jackson als Nutcombe, George. R 14 yrs Mar 1765 TB to Va. De.

Johnson, Hannah (1741). *See* Wilson. M.

Johnson, Hannah (1771) *See* Kay. La.

Johnson, Henry of Theydon Garnon. R for Barbados Aug 1662. E.

Johnson, Henry. S & T 14 yrs Sep 1718 *Eagle* LC Charles Town Mar 1719. L.

Johnson, Henry. S Apr T Sep 1737 *Pretty Patsy* to Md. M.

Johnson, Henry. T May 1737 *Forward*. Ht.

Johnson, Henry. R Jly T for life Sep 1767 *Justitia*. M.

Johnson, Hester. SL Jly T Sep 1755 *Tryal*. Sy.

Johnson, Hugh. S Lent 1767. La.

Johnson, Isaac. R for Barbados Dec 1668. M.

Johnson, Isaac. S at Bristol Lent 1772. G.

Johnson, Isabel. S Jun 1733 T Jan 1734 *Caesar* LC Va Jly 1734. M.

Johnson, James. R for Barbados May 1664. M.

Johnson als Thompson, James. S Aug T Sep 1725 *Forward* to Md. M.

Johnson, James. S Oct 1741 T Feb 1742 *Industry* to Md. M.

Johnson, James. S Apr 1763. L.

Johnston, James. S Jan T Mar 1764 *Tryal*. L.

Johnson, James. S May T Jun 1764 *Dolphin*. M.

Johnson, James. S & T Jan 1765 *Tryal*. M.

Johnson als Ingram, James. S & T Jan 1767 *Tryal*. M.

Johnson, Jane of Hurst. R for Barbados or Jamaica Feb 1684. K.

Johnson, Jane (1747). *See* Wilkins. M.

Johnson, Jervase. S s mare Summer 1748 R 14 yrs Lent TB Apr 1749. Db.

Johnson, Johanna (1668). *See* Blewitt. Sy.

Johnson, John. R for Jamaica Aug 1661. M.

Johnson, John. R 10 yrs in plantations Oct 1662. M.

Johnson, John. R for Barbados Jan 1664. L.

Johnson, John. R for Barbados Jun 1666. Y.

Johnson, John (1682). *See* Smathwit. Y.

Johnson, John (2). Rebels T 1685.

Johnson, John of Alstonfield. R (Western Circ) for America Jly 1700. St.

Johnson, John (1723). *See* Jackson. E.

Johnson, John. LC from *Forward* Annapolis Jun 1725. X.

Johnson, John. S Lent 1736. Wo.

Johnson, John. R 14 yrs Aug 1736. De.

Johnson, John. T Dec 1736 *Dorsetshire*. K.

Johnson, John. S Summer 1740. Y.

Johnson, John. R Jan T Apr 1741 *Speedwell* or *Mediterranean* to Md. M.

Johnson, John. S Sep T 14 yrs Oct 1744 *Susannah*. M.

Johnson, John. S Summer 1745. Sx.

Johnson, John. S s horse Summer 1746 R 14 yrs Lent 1747. Wa.

Johnson, John. S s horse Lent R 14 yrs Summer 1750. Su.

Johnson, John. T May 1751 *Tryal*. Sx.

Johnson, John. S May-Jly T Sep 1751 *Greyhound*. M.

Johnson, John. S Lent R 14 yrs Summer 1754. Ht.

Johnson, John. S Summer 1754. Nl.

Johnson, John. SQS & T Sep 1755 *Tryal*. M.

Johnson, John. S Apr T Sep 1757 *Thetis*. M.

Johnson, John. S Oct T Nov 1759 *Phoenix*. L.

Johnson, John (1764). *See* McQuin. K.

Johnson als Johnston, John. S s at Lancaster Summer 1764. La.

Johnson, John (1766). *See* Layt. Su.

Johnson, John of Whatton in Vale. SQS s shirt Jly 1767. Nt.

Johnson, John. S Oct T Dec 1767 *Neptune*. L.

Johnson, John. S Jan-Feb T Apr 1771 *Thornton*. M.

Johnson, John. S & T Jly 1771 *Scarsdale*. M.

Johnson als Howell, Jonathan. S & T Jan 1722 *Gilbert* LC Annapolis Jly 1722. M.

Johnson, Joseph. S as incorrigible rogue Jly 1617. M.

Johnson, Joseph. S Oct 1718. M.

Johnson, Joseph, aged 24, dark. S & T Oct 1720 *Gilbert* LC Annapolis May 1721. L.

Johnson, Joseph. S & T Apr 1725 *Sukey* LC Annapolis Sep 1725. M.

Johnson, Joseph. S Jan-Jun T 14 yrs Jun 1728 *Elizabeth* LC Potomack Aug 1729. L.

Johnson, Joseph. R Feb T 14 yrs Mar 1764 *Tryal*. M.

Johnson, Joseph. S Oct T Dec 1769 *Justitia*. M.

Johnson, Lawrence. S Oct T Nov 1725 *Rappahannock* but died on passage. M.

Johnson als Simpson, Margaret of York. R for Barbados Jly 1681. Y.

Johnson als Mason als Edwards, Margaret of Greenwich. R for Barbados or Jamaica Feb 1696. K.

Johnson, Margaret. S May 1719. M.

Johnson, Martha. S Jly-Sep T Sep 1742 *Forward*. M.

Johnson, Mary (1696). *See* Gay. Sy.

Johnson, Mary. S Jly T Aug 1721 *Prince Royal* LC Va Nov 1721. M.

Johnson, Mary. S & T Oct 1729 *Forward* LC Va Jun 1730. L.

Johnson, Mary. S Feb T Mar 1731 *Patapsco* LC Annapolis Jun 1731. M.

Johnson, Mary. S & T Sep 1731 *Smith* but died on passage. M.

Johnson, Mary (1732). *See* Sullivan. M.

Johnson als Rose als Brasie, Mary. S s money Apr T Dec 1735 *John* LC Annapolis Sep 1736. M.

Johnson als Maritime als Smith, Mary. S & T Jan 1736 *Dorsetshire* LC Va Sep 1736. L.

Johnson, Mary. T Sep 1742 *Forward*. Sy.

Johnson, Mary. S May T Nov 1743 *George William*. M.

Johnson, Mary (1748). *See* Walker. M.

Johnson, Mary. S for shoplifting at Leeds Summer 1749. Y.

Johnson, Mary of St. Saviour, Southwark. SQS Apr T May 1750 *Lichfield*. Sy.

Johnson, Mary (1751). *See* Cole. M.

Johnson, Mary. S Feb 1752. L.

Johnson, Mary. S & T Apr 1753 *Thames*. L.

Johnson, Matthew. S Jun 1761. M.

Johnson als Roch, Matthias. S s silver tankard & T May 1736 *Patapsco*. M.

Johnson, Michael. S Sep-Oct 1748 T Jan 1749 *Laura*. M.

Johnson, Michael. SW & T Jun 1768 *Tryal*. M.

Johnson, Nathan. S May 1662 to House of Correction unless he agrees to be transported. M.

Johnson, Nathaniel. R for Barbados or Jamaica Jly 1686. L.

Johnson, Nathaniel of Cumnor. R for America Mar 1697. Be.

Johnson, Nicholas of Broad Campden. R for America Jly 1675. G.

Johnson, Penelope. R for Barbados Apr TB Jun 1669. L.

Johnson, Peter. S Feb T May 1719 *Margaret*; sold to Matthew Ashley Md Sep 1719. L.

Johnson, Peter, aged 21, dark. LC from *Gilbert* Annapolis May 1721. X.

Johnson, Peter. S Mar 1741. Ha.

Johnson, Phillip. PT Aug 1683. M.

Johnson, Philip. S Jly 1766. Ha.

Johnson, Phillip. S Feb T Apr 1768 *Thornton*. M.

Johnson, Ralph of Hunley, butcher. R for Barbados Jly 1683. Ch.

Johnson, Richard Jr. of Bagworth. R for America Jly 1673. Le.

Johnson, Richard. PT Dec 1691. M.

Johnson, Richard. R for America Aug 1715. L.

Johnson, Richard. T May 1751 *Tryal*. K.

Johnson, Richard. S Summer 1755 R 14 yrs Lent 1756. Li.

Johnson, Richard (1771). *See* Harris, Thomas. Be.

Johnson, Robert. R for Barbados Jly 1674. M.

Johnson, Robert of Stoke, yeoman. R (Chester Circ) for Barbados or Jamaica Mar 1694. St.

Johnson, Robert. PT Oct 1700. M.

Johnson, Robert. S Jly T 14 yrs Aug 1721 *Prince Royal* LC Va Nov 1721. M.

Johnson, Robert. S & T Oct 1722 *Forward* LC Annapolis Jun 1723. L.

Johnson, Robert. S & T Oct 1730 *Forward* LC Potomack Jan 1731. L.

Johnson, Robert. S s at Lidlington Summer 1750 R for life Lent 1751. Bd.

Johnson, Robert of St. Olave, Southwark. SQS May 1754. Sy.

Johnson, Robert. S Summer 1756 R 14 yrs Lent 1757. Sh.

Johnston, Robert. S Summer 1757. Cu.

Johnson, Robert, als Brackien, Lancelot. S s gelding at Leeds Summer 1765 R 14 yrs Summer 1766. Y.

Johnson, Robert. S Jun T Sep 1767 *Justitia*. L.

Johnson, Robert, als Smith, William. S s gelding at Arncliffe & R 14 yrs Summer 1768 TB Apr 1769. Y.

Johnson, Robert. S Feb T Apr 1771 *Thornton*. L.

Johnson, Robert. S s silver tankard at Newport Pagnell Lent 1775. Bu.

Johnson, Samuel of St. George, Southwark. R for Barbados or Jamaica Feb 1683. Sy.

Johnson, Samuel. S Aug T Oct 1724 *Forward* LC Annapolis Jun 1725. M.

Johnson als Cabbige, Samuel. S Aug T Oct 1726 *Forward* to Va. M.

Johnson, Samuel (1730). *See* Burrard. M.

Johnson, Samuel. S s shirt Sep T Dec 1736 *Dorsetshire* to Va. M.

Johnson, Samuel. S s calf skin at Thame Lent 1759. O.

Johnson, Samuel of Twinstead. SQS Oct 1765 T Apr 1766 *Ann.* E.

Johnson, Samuel. T Sep 1766 *Justitia.* Sy.

Johnson, Samuel. S Apr-Jun T Jly 1772 *Tayloe.* M.

Johnson, Sarah. S Jly T 14 yrs Aug 1721 *Prince Royal* LC Va Nov 1721. M.

Johnson, Sarah (1733). *See* Walmsley. M.

Johnson, Sarah. SW & T Jun 1768 *Tryal.* M.

Johnson, Silvan of Woolwich. R for Barbados or Jamaica Feb 1676. K.

Johnson, Thomas of Stondon. R for Barbados or Jamaica Jly 1687 & Jly 1688. Ht.

Johnson, Thomas. R for Barbados or Jamaica Dec 1695 & Jan 1697. M.

Johnston, Thomas of Branston. R for America Jly 1716. No.

Johnson, Thomas (1719). *See* Lattimer. Cu.

Johnson, Thomas. S & T Apr 1725 *Sukey* LC Annapolis Sep 1725. M.

Johnson als Ackfrill, Thomas. S Lent 1727 *Ca.

Johnson, Thomas. S Feb T Mar 1729 *Patapsco* LC Annapolis Dec 1729. M.

Johnson, Thomas. T Apr 1732 *Patapsco.* Sy.

Johnson, Thomas. S & R 14 yrs Mar T May 1736. Bd.

Johnson, Thomas. S Mar TB Apr 1737. Le.

Johnson, Thomas. S Aug T Oct 1741 *Sea Horse* to Va. M.

Johnson, Thomas. S Lent 1748. Sh.

Johnson, Thomas of Shelford. SQS s cheeses Jly 1749. Nt.

Johnson, Thomas. S s horse Summer 1749 R 14 yrs Lent 1750. Su.

Johnson, Thomas. S & T Jly 1753 *Tryal.* M.

Johnson, Thomas. SQS Dec 1763 T Mar 1764 *Tryal.* M.

Johnson, Thomas. S Summer 1764 R 14 yrs Lent 1765. La.

Johnson, Thomas. S Dec 1765 T Jan 1766 *Tryal.* M.

Johnson, Thomas (1767). *See* Hams, William. St.

Johnson, Thomas. S Lent 1768. Ca.

Johnson, Thomas (1771). *See* Smith. Ca.

Johnson, Thomas. S s at Ellesmere Lent 1772. Sh.

Johnson, Thomas. S Lent 1775. K.

Johnson, Thomas. S for highway robbery & R Lent 1775. Y.

Johnson, Timothy. SQS Jan 1773. M.

Johnson, Turner. S Apr T Sep 1757 *Thetis.* L.

Johnson, William. Rebel T 1685.

Johnson, William. R for America Jly 1693. Wa.

Johnson, William. S Jly 1718 T Mar 1723. Bu.

Johnson, William. S & T Oct 1729 *Forward* but died on passage. M.

Johnson, William. S for killing deer in enclosed park Lent TB Mar 1733. G.

Johnson, William. S & T Jan 1736 *Dorsetshire* LC Va Sep 1736. L.

Johnson, William. S Dec 1741 T Feb 1742 *Industry* to Md. M.

Johnson, William. T Apr 1742 *Bond*. Sy.

Johnson, William. S & T Feb 1744 *Neptune*. L.

Johnson, William (1746). *See* Milner, Jacob. Y.

Johnson, William. S Lent 1746. Y.

Johnson, William. S Lent 1749. Bu.

Johnson, William. SQS Dec 1750. M.

Johnson, William of Rotherhithe. SQS & T Jan 1767 *Tryal*. Sy.

Johnston, William of Whickham, yeoman. S s clothing Summer 1767. Du.

Johnson, William. S s handkerchief at St. Mary Woolnoth Feb T Apr 1768 *Thornton*. L.

Johnson, William. S May T Jun 1768 *Tryal*. M.

Johnson, William. R Jly T for life Oct 1768 *Justitia*. M.

Johnson, William (1771). *See* Smith, Henry. Sx.

Johnson, William. S Sep-Oct 1772. M.

Johnson, William (1773). *See* Burke. Ha.

Johnson, William. SQS Oct 1774 TB Apr 1775. So.

Johnson als Hazledine, William. S Jly 1775. M.

Johnston. *See* Johnson.

Joiner. *See* Joyner.

Jolland, Elizabeth wife of Robert. S 14 yrs Sep-Oct 1772. M.

Jolland, John. S Sep-Oct 1772. M.

Jollett, John. S Mar 1729. So.

Joliffe, John. Rebel T 1685.

Jolliffe, Mary of Romsey, spinster. R for Barbados Jly 1693. Ha.

Jollop, Samuel. T Dec 1736 *Dorsetshire*. Sy.

Jolly, Benjamin. S Aug 1753. De.

Jolly, Edward. S s money from Earl Gow Jan T Mar 1758 *Dragon*. M.

Jolly, Henry. S Lent 1749. E.

Jolle, John. R 14 yrs Aug 1734. De.

Jolly, Luke. T Jun 1764 *Dolphin*. M.

Jolly, Mary. S Feb T Mar 1727 *Rappahannock* to Md. M.

Jolly, Samuel. S Sep-Oct T Dec 1752 *Greyhound*. M.

Jonas, Mary (1761). *See* Thompson. L.

Jonas, Thomas. S Sep 1733 T Jan 1734 *Caesar* LC Va Jly 1734. M.

Jones, Alexander. S Aug 1727 T *Forward* LC Rappahannock May 1728. M.

Jones als Faulkner, Alice. S Oct-Dec 1739 T Jan 1740 *York* to Md. M.

Jones, Alice. S Feb T Mar 1760 *Friendship*. M.

Jones, Ann of Abbots Langley. R for Barbados Apr 1668. Ht.

Jones, Anne. R for Barbados & TB Jun 1668. L.

Jones, Ann. R for Barbados or Jamaica May 1697. L.

Jones, Anne. S & T Apr 1725 *Sukey* LC Annapolis Sep 1725. M.

Jones, Ann. T Oct 1732 *Caesar*. Sy.

Jones, Ann wife of Thomas *(qv)*. S for perjury Mar 1733. De.

Jones, Ann (1741). *See* Elwin. L.

Jones, Ann. S Feb T Apr 1741 *Speedwell* or *Mediterranean* to Md. M.

Jones, Ann. S Feb-Apr 1745. M.

Jones, Ann. S Jan-Jun 1747. M.

Jones, Ann. S Nov T Dec 1753 *Whiteing*. L.

Jones, Ann. S Dec 1753-Jan 1754. M.

Jones, Ann (1758). *See* Merritt. L.

Jones, Ann wife of Joseph. S s at Peterchurch Lent 1768. He.

Jones, Ann. S Summer 1769 R 14 yrs Lent 1770. He.

Jones, Ann. S Jan-Feb 1774. M.

Jones, Ann (1775). *See* Edwards. M.

Jones als Higgins, Avis. S Summer 1749 for smuggling tools into Hertford Gaol to assist escape of Owen Jones *(qv)*. Ht.

Jones, Benjamin. S s mare Summer 1758 R 14 yrs Lent 1759. Wa.

Jones, Benjamin. R & T for life Apr 1770 *New Trial*. M.

Jones, Katherine (1685). *See* Cotterell. M.

Jones, Katherine. R Jly AT Dec 1687. M.

Jones, Katherine. R for Barbados or Jamaica May 1691. L.

Jones, Catherine. S Sep 1756. M.

Jones, Catherine. S s watch at Whittington Lent 1769. Sh.

Jones, Charles. Rebel T 1685.

Jones, Charles. T Apr 1735 *Patapsco*. Ht.

Jones, Charles. S Dec 1735 T Jan 1736 *Dorsetshire* to Va. M.

Jones, Charles. S Lent R 14 yrs Summer TB Aug 1740. G.

Jones, Charles. S Lent R 14 yrs Summer 1743. Sh.

Jones, Christopher. R for Barbados or Jamaica Oct 1690. L.

Jones, Christopher (1745). *See* Miller. M.

Jones, Cornelius. S Apr 1748. L.

Jones, Daniel. S Jly T Aug 1721 *Prince Royal* LC Va Nov 1721. M.

Jones, Daniel. S Jan 1757. L.

Jones, David. S s pistols at Kentchurch Summer 1723 AT Summer 1726. He.

Jones, David. S Mar 1729. So.

Jones, David. S & T Jun 1756 *Lyon*. L.

Jones, David. S Lent 1757. K.

Jones, David. T Jun 1764 *Dolphin*. K.

Jones, David. S Summer 1764. He.

Jones, David. SQS Jly TB Aug 1766. So.

Jones, David. S May T Jly 1771 *Scarsdale*. L.

Jones, David. S Oct 1772. L.

Jones, Davy. S & R 14 yrs Summer 1770. Wo.

Jones, Deborah. S Dec 1772. M.

Jones, Dorothy, als Davies, Jane. S s at Great Ness Lent 1768. Sh.

Jones, Edward of Whitchurch. R for America Jly 1698. Sh.

Jones, Edward. T Oct 1724 *Forward* LC Md Jun 1725. Ht.

Jones, Edward. SQS May T Sep 1725 *Forward* LC Annapolis Dec 1725. M.

Jones, Edward. S s at St. Clement, Worcester, Lent 1726. Wo.

Jones, Edward. T May 1744 *Justitia*. E.

Jones, Edward. S Lent 1746 R 14 yrs Lent 1747. He.

Jones, Edward. S Nov T Dec 1753 *Whiteing*. L.

Jones, Edward. S Lent T Jun 1756 *Lyon*. Sy.

Jones, Edward. SQS May T Sep 1764 *Justitia*. M.

Jones als Williams, Edward. S & T Sep 1765 *Justitia*. M.

Jones, Edward. S s at Colwall & R 14 yrs Summer 1770; wife Elizabeth acquitted. He.

Jones, Edward. S s at All Saints, Worcester, Summer 1771. Wo.
Jones, Edward. R & T 14 yrs Jly 1772 *Tayloe*. M.
Jones, Edward. SQS Oct 1773. M.
Jones, Edward of St. Paul, Covent Garden. SW Jun 1774. M.
Jones als Ravell, Edward. R 14 yrs Jly 1775. M.
Jones, Edward. S Sep-Oct 1775. M.
Jones, Elinor. PT to Barbados Jan 1694. M.
Jones als Johnson, Elizabeth. R for West Indies Oct 1614. M.
Jones, Elizabeth. R for Barbados Jun 1670. M.
Jones, Elizabeth. R for Barbados or Jamaica Jan 1692. M.
Jones, Elizabeth (1694). *See* Morgan. M.
Jones, Elizabeth. S May T 14 yrs Aug 1718 *Eagle* LC Charles Town Mar 1719. L.
Jones als King, Elizabeth of Llangibby, widow. S Lent 1720. Mo.
Jones, Elizabeth. S Apr T May 1720 *Honor* to York River, Va. L.
Jones, Elizabeth. S Jly T Aug 1721 *Prince Royal* LC Va Nov 1721. L.
Jones, Elizabeth (1724). *See* Glazing. Ha.
Jones, Elizabeth. S Apr T Dec 1735 *John* LC Annapolis Sep 1736. M.
Jones als Walker, Elizabeth. T Apr 1735 *Patapsco*. K.
Jones, Elizabeth. S s silver spoon Dec 1735 T Jan 1736 *Dorsetshire* but died on passage. M.
Jones als Carnaby, Elizabeth. S Jly T Oct 1741 *Sea Horse* to Va. M.
Jones, Elizabeth. S Lent 1745. *Bd.
Jones, Elizabeth. S Jan-Feb T Apr 1753 *Thames*. M.
Jones, Elizabeth. S for life Jly-Sep 1754. M.
Jones, Elizabeth. S s at Droitwich Lent 1756. Wo.
Jones, Elizabeth. S Summer 1756 R 14 yrs Summer 1757. Wo.
Jones, Elizabeth. S May T Sep 1757 *Thetis*. M.
Jones, Elizabeth. S Sep T Nov 1757 *Phoenix*. M.
Jones, Elizabeth. S & T Mar 1764 *Tryal*. L.
Jones, Elizabeth. S & T Sep 1767 *Justitia*. L.
Jones, Elizabeth. S Oct T Dec 1767 *Neptune*. L.
Jones, Elizabeth. S Jan-Feb T Apr 1771 *Thornton*. M.
Jones, Elizabeth. S Apr-Jun T Jly 1772 *Tayloe*. M.
Jones, Elizabeth. SWK Jly 1772. K.
Jones, Elizabeth. S Oct 1773. L.
Jones, Emanuel. R for Barbados Dec 1668. M.
Jones, Evan. S Feb T Mar 1729 *Patapsco* LC Annapolis Dec 1729. L.
Jones, Evan. S s mare Lent R 14 yrs Summer 1766. Mo.
Jones, Evans of Ryton. R for America Jly 1682. Sh.
Jones, Evans of Worcester. R for America Jly 1693. Wo.
Jones, Francis of East Peckham. R for Barbados or Jamaica Jun 1675. K.
Jones, Francis. S Lent R 14 yrs Summer 1728. Sh.
Jones, George. S Summer R for Barbados Aug 1663. K.
Jones, George of Bricklehampton. S Lent 1721. Wo.
Jones, George. S s woodworking tools Jun T Dec 1736 *Dorsetshire* to Va. M.
Jones, George. R 14 yrs Aug 1742. So.
Jones, George (1766). *See* Harrison. Wa.
Jones, George. S s cloth Lent 1773. He.

Jones, Grace of Reading. S Lent 1722. Be.

Jones, Griffith. S & T Oct 1722 *Forward* LC Annapolis Jun 1723. L.

Jones, Hannah of Coventry, spinster. R for America Feb 1713. Wa.

Jones, Hannah. S Aug T Oct 1724 *Forward* to Md. M.

Jones, Henry. S s bladder at Cheadle Summer 1723 LC from *Robert* Annapolis Jun 1725. St.

Jones, Henry. S Jan T Feb 1726 *Supply* LC Annapolis May 1726. M.

Jones, Henry. S Sep T Oct 1750 *Rachael*. L.

Jones, Henry. S for ripping lead from house Sep 1756. M.

Jones, Henry. S Nov T Dec 1770 *Justitia*. L.

Jones, Henry. S Apr-May T Jly 1771 *Scarsdale*. M.

Jones, Henry. S s sheep at Wolves Newton & R 14 yrs Summer 1771. Mo.

Jones als Maunder, Henry. S Dec 1774. M.

Jones, Hester. S s at Leominster Lent 1722. He.

Jones, Hugh. R for Barbados or Jamaica Jly 1685. L.

Jones, Hugh of Thornham. R for Barbados or Jamaica Jly 1715. K.

Jones, Hugh. R 14 yrs for burglary Summer 1724. Wo.

Jones, Hugh. S & T Jan 1736 *Dorsetshire* LC Va Sep 1736. L.

Jones, Hugh. S s mare Lent R 14 yrs Summer 1764. He.

Jones, Humphrey. R for Barbados Jly 1668. L.

Jones, Humphrey. S Jly T Aug 1721 *Prince Royal* but died on passage. L.

Jones, Humphrey. S May T Jly 1723 *Alexander* LC Annapolis Sep 1723. L.

Jones, Humphry. S Summer 1728 R 14 yrs Summer 1730. Le.

Jones, Isaac of Alvechurch. R for America Jly 1687. Wo.

Jones als Bevan, Isaac of Leominster. R for America Feb 1700. He.

Jones, Isaac. S Feb T Mar 1764 *Tryal*. M.

Jones, Isaac. S s at East Challow Summer 1774. Be.

Jones, Isabella (1733). *See* Bannister. M.

Jones, James of Bradley, Kentchurch, miller. R for Barbados Jly 1663. He.

Jones, James of Burrington, husbandman. R for Barbados Jun 1665. De.

Jones, James. R for America Aug 1715. L.

Jones, James. S Feb T May 1719 *Margaret*; sold to Edward Hearpe Md Sep 1719. L.

Jones, James. S Feb T Jun 1738 *Forward*. L.

Jones, James. S Lent R 14 yrs Summer 1743. St.

Jones, James. SQS Feb T Mar 1750 *Tryal*. M.

Jones, James. S Apr T May 1750 *Lichfield*. M.

Jones als Liscot, James. S s at Stoke Edith & Tarrington Summer 1751. He.

Jones, James. S s at Monmouth Summer 1755. Mo.

Jones, James. S Summer 1757. Sh.

Jones, James. T Apr 1759 *Thetis*. E.

Jones, James. S Lent T May 1770. Wa.

Jones, James. S Sep-Oct T Dec 1771 *Justitia*. M.

Jones, James of St. Paul, Covent Garden. SW Jan 1775. M.

Jones, Jane, spinster, als wife of Richard, aged 40. R for Barbados Feb & Aug 1664. L.

Jones, Jane (1665). *See* Wharton. L.

Jones, Jane of Ludlow. R for Jamaica, Barbados or Bermuda Feb 1686. Sh.

Jones, Jane. S to be T to Va Mar 1719. De.

Jones als Jenkins, Jane. S & T Oct 1730 *Forward* LC Potomack Jan 1731. M.

Jones, Jane. S as pickpocket Lent R 14 yrs Summer 1751. He.

Jones, Jane. S s at Grosmont Lent 1759. Mo.

Jones, Jane. S s at St. Chad, Shrewsbury, Lent 1772. Sh.

Jones, Jane. S Feb 1774. L.

Jones, Jane of Richmond, spinster. SQS Jan 1775. Sy.

Jones, Jeremiah. S Jly T Nov 1762 *Prince William*. M.

Jones, Jervas of Astley. R for Jamaica, Barbados or Bermuda Mar 1688. Wo.

Jones, John. R s horse & to be sent to Va 1649. M.

Jones, John. R for Jamaica Jan 1663. M.

Jones, John of Cheltenham. R for Barbados Feb 1665. G.

Jones, John. R for Barbados Dec 1671. M.

Jones, John. R for Barbados Jly 1674. M.

Jones, John of Powick. R for America Mar 1682. Wo.

Jones, John of Huntingdon. R for Barbados Jly 1683. Ch.

Jones, John (2). Rebels T 1685.

Jones, John of Crewkerne. R for Barbados Jly 1693. So.

Jones als Hodge, John. R for Barbados or Jamaica Dec 1695 & Jan 1697. M.

Jones, John (1697). *See* Rice, Richard. De.

Jones, John. R May AT Jly 1697. M.

Jones, John. R for Barbados or Jamaica Aug 1700. L.

Jones, John. PT Oct 1700. M.

Jones, John of Horsham. R for Barbados or Jamaica Jly 1702. Sx.

Jones, John of Pencoyd. R for America Mar 1710. He.

Jones als Williams, John. R 14 yrs for Carolina May 1719. L.

Jones, John, als Burch, Thomas. S Mar 1720. Do.

Jones, John. S Jly T Aug 1721 *Prince Royal* LC Va Nov 1721. M.

Jones, John. S for returning from T & T Jan 1722 *Gilbert* LC Annapolis Jly 1722. L.

Jones, John. S s sheep at Llandenny & Llanover Lent 1722. Mo.

Jones, John. S May T Jly 1723 *Alexander* LC Annapolis Sep 1723. M.

Jones, John. T Apr 1725 *Sukey* LC Md Sep 1725. Sx.

Jones, John. T Oct 1726 *Forward*. Sx.

Jones, John. T Jun 1728 *Elizabeth* LC Va Aug 1729. Sy.

Jones, John. S & T Oct 1730 *Forward* LC Potomack Jan 1731. M.

Jones, John. S Lent 1731 R 14 yrs Lent 1732 (SP). He.

Jones, John. T Apr 1731 *Bennett*. K.

Jones, John. S Summer 1731. G.

Jones, John. S s horse Summer 1731 R 14 yrs Summer 1732. No.

Jones, John. S & T Sep 1731 *Smith* LC Va 1732. M.

Jones, John. S s horse Lent R 14 yrs Summer 1733. St.

Jones, John. S Dec 1733 T Jan 1734 *Caesar* LC Va Jly 1734. L.

Jones, John. S & T Dec 1734 *Caesar* LC Va Jly 1735. L.

Jones, John. S s wheat at Abergavenny Summer 1735. Mo.

Jones, John. T Dec 1736 *Dorsetshire*. E.
Jones, John (1737). *See* Place. M.
Jones, John. S Oct 1737 T Jan 1738 *Dorsetshire* to Va. M.
Jones, John. S s gun at Castle Frome Lent 1739. He.
Jones, John. S Apr-Jun 1739. M.
Jones, John. T Jun 1740 *Essex*. K.
Jones, John. S Jan T Apr 1741 *Speedwell* or *Mediterranean* to Md. M.
Jones, John. S Aug T Oct 1741 *Sea Horse* to Va. M.
Jones, John. S s at Holy Trinity, Gloucester, Lent 1744. G.
Jones, John. S Summer 1745. Sy.
Jones, John. S Summer 1746. Ht.
Jones, John (1747). *See* Pritchard. Sh.
Jones, John. S Jan-Apr 1748. M.
Jones, John. S Jly 1748. L.
Jones, John (1749). *See* Low. L.
Jones, John. S s cloth at Urdesland Lent 1749. He.
Jones, John. S Lent 1749. Ht.
Jones, John. S Mar 1749 TB to Va. De.
Jones, John (1750). *See* Flack. Sy.
Jones, John. S s at Severn Stoke Summer 1750. Wo.
Jones, John. S s at Whittington Summer 1750. Sh.
Jones, John. S May-Jly T Sep 1751 *Greyhound*. M.
Jones, John. S Feb 1752. L.
Jones, John. S Summer 1754. Wo.
Jones, John. S s at St. Martin Summer 1755. Sh.
Jones, John. S s horse Lent R 14 yrs Summer TB to Va Oct 1756. Le.
Jones, John. S Summer 1756. K.
Jones, John. S Jly T Sep 1757 *Thetis*. M.
Jones, John (1758). *See* Innes, Benjamin. G.
Jones, John. SQS Jan T Apr 1759 *Thetis*. M.
Jones, John. S Lent TB Mar 1760. Db.
Jones, John. S Jan 1761. M.
Jones, John. S s at Chipping Sodbury Summer 1761 R 14 yrs Lent
    1762. G.
Jones, John. S s at Wigmore Summer 1764. He.
Jones, John. S Oct 1765 T Jan 1766 *Tryal*. L.
Jones, John (1766). *See* Pritchard. Sh.
Jones, John of Rotherhithe. SQS & T Jan 1766 *Tryal*. Sy.
Jones, John. R & T Sep 1766 *Justitia*. L.
Jones, John. S Lent R 14 yrs Summer 1767. He.
Jones als Vaughan, John. S Summer 1767. Sh.
Jones, John. S s at Cuddesdon Lent 1769. O.
Jones, John of Manchester, paper mould maker. SQS Apr 1769. La.
Jones, John. T Aug 1769 *Douglas*. Sy.
Jones, John. S Sep-Oct T Dec 1771 *Justitia*. M.
Jones, John of Lambeth. SQS Oct T Dec 1771 *Justitia*. Sy.
Jones, John als Thomas. S s at Speen Lent 1772. Be.
Jones, John. S Sep-Oct 1772. M.
Jones, John of St. George, Southwark. SQS Jan 1773. Sy.
Jones, John. SQS Jan 1773. M.
Jones, John. S Jan-Feb 1773. M.

Jones, John. S s at Cannock Summer 1774. St.

Jones, John (1775). *See* Maybrick, Charles. M.

Jones, Joseph, als Moore, Morice. R for Barbados Jan 1693. M.

Jones, Joseph. S Apr 1747. So.

Jones, Joseph. S Summer 1748 R 14 yrs Lent 1749. Sh.

Jones, Joseph. S s at Clifton Summer 1750. Wo.

Jones, Joseph. S Mar 1751. De.

Jones, Joseph. S Summer 1757 R 14 yrs Lent 1758. Wo.

Jones, Joseph. S s at Dymock Summer 1766. G.

Jones, Joseph. S Sep-Oct 1775. M.

Jones, Lamb. S Jan 1751. L.

Jones, Lewis. R for Barbados Jun 1663. M.

Jones, Margaret. R Apr AT Jun 1690. M.

Jones, Margaret. R for Barbados or Jamaica for burning Newgate Gaol May 1691. L.

Jones, Margaret of Hereford. S Lent 1721. He.

Jones, Margaret (1726). *See* Butler, Ann. M.

Jones, Margaret (1729). *See* Browne. M.

Jones, Margaret. S Mar 1754. L.

Jones, Margaret. S Summer 1758 R 14 yrs Lent 1759. Wa.

Jones, Margaret. S May T Jly 1771 *Scarsdale*. L.

Jones, Martha. S & T May 1736 *Patapsco*. L.

Jones, Martha. S Jly T Sep 1767 *Justitia*. M.

Jones, Martin. S & T Oct 1732 *Caesar* to Va. M.

Jones, Mary. R for Barbados Dec 1668. M.

Jones, Mary of ?Glascall. R for America Mar 1680. He.

Jones, Mary. PT Oct 1700 R Aug 1701. M.

Jones, Mary of St. Thomas Apostle, spinster. R for Barbados Jun 1708. De.

Jones, Mary. S Jly T Sep 1718 *Eagle* LC Charles Town Mar 1719. L.

Jones, Mary, aged 32, black hair. S Jan T Oct 1720 *Gilbert* LC Annapolis May 1721. L.

Jones, Mary. S Apr T May 1720 *Honor* LC Port York Jan 1721. L.

Jones als Simpson, Mary. S 14 yrs Oct 1720. M.

Jones, Mary. S Oct T Dec 1724 *Rappahannock* to Va. M.

Jones, Mary. S Aug T *Forward* LC Rappahannock May 1728. M.

Jones, Mary. S Feb T Mar 1730 *Patapsco* LC Annapolis Sep 1730. L.

Jones, Mary. S Jan T Feb 1733 *Smith*. L.

Jones, Mary. S Aug 1734. De.

Jones, Mary. S & T Jan 1736 *Dorsetshire* LC Va Sep 1736. L.

Jones, Mary. T Dec 1736 *Dorsetshire*. Sy.

Jones, Mary wife of Thomas. S s cloth from Earl of Dunmore Jan-May T Jun 1738 *Forward*. M.

Jones, Mary. S Jly-Sep T Oct 1739 *Duke of Cumberland* to Va. M.

Jones, Mary wife of John. S s at St. Chad, Shrewsbury, Lent 1744. Sh.

Jones, Mary. S Feb-Apr 1745. M.

Jones, Mary. S Apr 1745. L.

Jones, Mary. S s at Lantilio Crossenny Lent 1749. Mo.

Jones, Mary of St. George, Southwark, spinster. SQS Apr T Sep 1751 *Greyhound*. Sy.

Jones, Mary. S Feb 1752. L.

Jones, Mary. S Feb 1754. M.
Jones, Mary. S Feb 1757. M.
Jones, Mary (1758). *See* Baxter. M.
Jones, Mary (1758). *See* Hancock. St.
Jones, Mary. SL Sep T Dec 1758 *The Brothers*. Sy.
Jones, Mary. S Sep 1760. L.
Jones, Mary (1761). *See* Thompson. L.
Jones, Mary. S & T Apr 1762 *Neptune*. L.
Jones, Mary. S May 1763. M.
Jones, Mary. S s at Cleobury Lent 1764. Sh.
Jones, Mary (2). S May T Jun 1764 *Dolphin*. M.
Jones als Walls, Mary. S 14 yrs for receiving Lent 1765. Wa.
Jones, Mary wife of John. SQS Jly T Sep 1765 *Justitia*. M.
Jones, Mary. S Oct 1766 T Jan 1767 *Tryal*. M.
Jones, Mary. S Lent R 14 yrs Summer 1767. Sh.
Jones, Mary. S s at Worfield Summer 1768. Sh.
Jones, Mary (1769). *See* Gibbard, Sarah. M.
Jones, Mary (1770). *See* Rawlinson. M.
Jones, Mary (1771). *See* Frostick, Ruth. M.
Jones, Mary. S s at Raglan Lent 1771. Mo.
Jones, Mary. S May T Jly 1771 *Scarsdale*. L.
Jones, Mary. SQS Feb T Apr 1772 *Thornton*. M.
Jones, Mary. S May-Jly 1773. M.
Jones, Mary. S s sheep & R 14 yrs Lent 1774. He.
Jones, Mary. S Apr 1774. M.
Jones, Mary Ann. TB to Va from QS 1756. De.
Jones, Matthew. R for Barbados or Jamaica Dec 1693. L.
Jones, Matthew. S s horse Lent 1723 R 14 yrs Summer 1724 AT Summer 1726. He.
Jones, Matthew. S Jly T Sep 1764 *Justitia*. M.
Jones, Matthias. S Apr 1773. M.
Jones, Morris. R 12 yrs Jan 1663 (SP). L.
Jones, Maurice. R for Barbados Jan 1664. M.
Jones, Maurice als Morris. S s sheep Lent R 14 yrs Summer 1743. O.
Jones, Morris. S s sheep Lent R 14 yrs Summer 1768. Sh.
Jones, Michael. R Jly AT Sep 1675. M.
Jones, Morgan of Carmarthen. S s greatcoat Lent 1719. Mo.
Jones, Nathaniel. SQS Summer 1773. Du.
Jones, Nehemiah. S Oct 1733 T Jan 1734 *Caesar* LC Va Jly 1734. M.
Jones, Nehemiah. S Apr T May 1750 *Lichfield*. M.
Jones, Nicholas of Wolverhampton. R for America Jly 1678. St.
Jones, Owen of Llanymynech. R for America Jly 1698. Sh.
Jones, Owen (1746). *See* Owen, John. Sh.
Jones, Owen. S Lent 1749. Ht.
Jones, Penelope. S Dec 1743 T Feb 1744 *Neptune* to Md. M.
Jones, Peter. R for Barbados Apr TB Oct 1669. M.
Jones, Philip. S s tallow Lent 1742. Mo.
Jones, Phillip. S Jly 1749. L.
Jones, Philip, als Phillips, John. S s horse & R Lent 1775. Sh.
Jones, Phillis. S Sep-Oct 1749. M.

Jones, Ralph. S Feb T 14 yrs Apr 1735 *Patapsco* LC Annapolis Oct 1735. L.

Jones, Rebecca. S Apr TB May 1718. M.

Jones, Rebecca. S Apr T May 1719 *Margaret*; sold to Edward Mallux Md Sep 1719. L.

Jones, Rebecca. S s at Broseley Summer 1768. Sh.

Jones, Rhees. S s at Oswestry Lent R 14 yrs Summer 1762. Sh.

Jones, Rice. S s horse Lent R 14 yrs Summer 1742. Nt.

Jones, Richard. R 10 yrs in plantations Oct 1662. M.

Jones, Richard. R for Barbados Jun 1665. L.

Jones, Richard. R Feb AT May 1686. M.

Jones, Richard of Rotherhithe. S Lent T May 1719 *Margaret*. Sy.

Jones, Richard. S Jly T Aug 1721 *Prince Royal* to Va. M.

Jones, Richard. S & T Oct 1730 *Forward* LC Potomack Jan 1731. M.

Jones, Richard. S Summer 1731. He.

Jones, Richard of Shoreditch. S s tobacco & T Dec 1740 *Vernon* to Md. M.

Jones, Richard. S s sheep Lent 1741. O.

Jones, Richard. S for burglary Lent R 14 yrs Summer 1741. Wo.

Jones, Richard. S s mare Lent R 14 yrs Summer 1742. Sh.

Jones, Richard. S s at Pitchcombe Summer 1742 R 14 yrs Lent TB Mar 1743. G.

Jones, Richard. S Summer 1748 R 14 yrs Lent 1749. Sh.

Jones, Richard. S Jan-Apr 1749. M.

Jones, Richard. S s sheep Lent R 14 yrs Summer 1752. Sh.

Jones, Richard. S Mar 1756. Ha.

Jones, Richard. SQS Marlborough & TB to Va Oct 1756. Wi.

Jones, Richard. S & T Jan 1767 *Tryal*. M.

Jones, Richard. S & T Jly 1771 *Scarsdale*. M.

Jones, Richard. S s at Deerhurst Summer 1772. G.

Jones, Richard. S Oct 1774. L.

Jones, Robert. S s pillion at Oswestry Summer 1729. Sh.

Jones, Robert. S Aug 1738. So.

Jones, Robert. S for highway robbery Lent R 14 yrs Summer 1750. Wa.

Jones als Mortebois, Robert. S Summer 1751 R 14 yrs Lent T May 1752 *Lichfield*. E.

Jones, Robert. T Sep 1757 *Thetis*. Sx.

Jones, Robert. S Lent 1759. Ch.

Jones, Robert. S Summer 1764. Mo.

Jones, Robert. T Apr 1765 *Ann*. Sx.

Jones, Robert. S s horse Lent R 14 yrs Summer 1767. Sh.

Jones, Robert. S Jly 1774. L.

Jones, Roger. S for highway robbery Lent R 14 yrs Summer 1766. Bu.

Jones, Roland. S & T Sep 1731 *Smith* LC Va 1732. M.

Jones, Rowland. S s tobacco at St. Catherine Cree Sep T Oct 1768 *Justitia*. L.

Jones, Ruth. S Jly T Aug 1721 *Prince Royal*. L.

Jones, Samuel. S & T Oct 1729 *Forward* LC Va Jun 1730. M.

Jones, Samuel. T Dec 1736 *Dorsetshire*. Sy.

Jones, Samuel. S Jun-Dec 1745. M.

Jones, Samuel. R 14 yrs Jly 1747. Ha.

Jones, Samuel (2). S Jly T Sep 1751 *Greyhound*. L.

Jones, Samuel. S Summer 1752 R 14 yrs Lent 1753. Sh.

Jones, Samuel. S s silk twist at West Bromwich Lent 1759. St.

Jones, Samuel. S s at Croft & R for life Summer 1773. He.

Jones, Sarah of Worcester. R for America Mar 1682. Wo.

Jones, Sara, als Dunn, Anne. R 14 yrs for Carolina May 1719. L.

Jones, Sarah. S Feb T Mar 1727 *Rappahannock* to Md. M.

Jones, Sarah. S Jan-Jun T Jun 1728 *Elizabeth* LC Potomack Aug 1729. M.

Jones, Sarah. S Oct-Dec 1739 T Jan 1740 *York* to Md. M.

Jones, Sarah. S Feb-Apr T Jun 1756 *Lyon*. M.

Jones, Sarah. S Apr T Sep 1757 *Thetis*. M.

Jones, Sarah. S Jun T Sep 1758 *Tryal* to Annapolis. M.

Jones, Sarah wife of Jacob. S s at Ellesmere Summer 1761. Sh.

Jones, Sarah. S s at Wombridge Lent 1764. Sh.

Jones, Sarah. S Feb T Apr 1770 *New Trial*. M.

Jones, Sarah. S Jan-Feb 1773. M.

Jones, Sarah. S May-Jly 1773. M.

Jones, Silvester. SQS & T Sep 1751 *Greyhound*. M.

Jones, Simon. SQS & T Jan 1765 *Tryal*. M.

Jones, Simon. S Sep T Dec 1770 *Justitia*. M.

Jones, Simon John. S May T Jly 1722 *Alexander* to Nevis or Jamaica. M.

Jones, Susanna. S Dec 1746. L.

Jones, Thomas Jr. of Warminster. R for Barbados Jly 1664. Wi.

Jones, Thomas of Hereford. R for Barbados Jun 1666. He.

Jones, Thomas of Munsley. R for America Sep 1671. He.

Jones, Thomas. R for Barbados Feb 1675. L.

Jones, Thomas of Hampton Bishop. R for America Jly 1675. He.

Jones, Thomas. R for Barbados Aug 1679. M.

Jones, Thomas. PT Feb R Mar 1688. M.

Jones, Thomas of St. Saviour, Southwark. R for America Jly 1700. Sy.

Jones, Thomas of Evesham. R (Western Circ) for America Jly 1700. Wo.

Jones als Wright, Thomas. R Aug AT Oct 1700. M.

Jones, Thomas. TB 14 yrs Oct 1719. L.

Jones, Thomas (1720). *See* Pritchard. E.

Jones, Thomas. LC from *Susannah & Sarah* Annapolis Apr 1720. X.

Jones als Taylor als Prosser als Heming als Lynes, Thomas. S s at Burford Summer 1722. Sh.

Jones, Thomas. S s cows at Hartlebury Summer 1724. Wo.

Jones, Thomas. LC from *Robert* Annapolis Jun 1725. X.

Jones, Thomas, als Wynn, Henry. S s mare Lent R 14 yrs Summer 1725. Sh.

Jones, Thomas. S Feb T Mar 1729 *Patapsco* LC Annapolis Dec 1729. M.

Jones, Thomas. S Summer 1730. We.

Jones, Thomas. S & T Sep 1731 *Smith* LC Va 1732. M.

Jones, Thomas. S & T Sep 1731 *Smith* LC Va 1732. L.

Jones, Thomas. S for perjury Mar 1733. De.

Jones, Thomas. S & T Apr 1733 *Patapsco* LC Annapolis Nov 1733. L.

Jones, Thomas. T May 1736 *Patapsco*. Sy.

Jones, Thomas. S s at Alveley Summer 1736. Sh.

Jones, Thomas. S s boards Jun T Dec 1736 *Dorsetshire* to Va. M.

Jones, Thomas. S Dec 1737 T Jan 1738 *Dorsetshire*. L.
Jones als Browne, Thomas. S Jun-Dec 1738 T 14 yrs Jan 1739
  Dorsetshire. M.
Jones, Thomas. S s cloth at Sheriff Hales Lent 1743. St.
Jones, Thomas. S Dec 1743 T Feb 1744 *Neptune* to Md. M.
Jones, Thomas. S for highway robbery Summer 1745 R 14 yrs Lent
  1746. Le.
Jones, Thomas. R 14 yrs Jly 1747. Ha.
Jones, Thomas. T Apr 1753 *Thames*. Sx.
Jones, Thomas. S Lent R 14 yrs Summer TB Sep 1755. G.
Jones, Thomas. SQS Dec 1755 T Jan 1756 *Greyhound*. M.
Jones, Thomas. S s iron hinges at Wellington Lent 1756. Sh.
Jones, Thomas. S Jly 1756. Ha.
Jones als Crank, Thomas. S s oatmeal at Whitchurch Summer 1757. Sh.
Jones, Thomas. S Jun T Sep 1758 *Tryal*. L.
Jones, Thomas. S Feb T Mar 1760 *Friendship*. M.
Jones als Taylor, Thomas. S Lent TB Mar 1760. Db.
Jones, Thomas. S Jan T Mar 1764 *Tryal*. L.
Jones, Thomas. S Lent 1764. He.
Jones, Thomas. T Jun 1764 *Dolphin*. Sy.
Jones, Thomas (1765). *See* Parry, Edward. Sh.
Jones, Thomas. S Jan T Feb 1765 *Tryal*. L.
Jones, Thomas. T Apr 1765 *Ann*. Sy.
Jones, Thomas of Manchester. SQS Jly 1766. La.
Jones, Thomas. T Jan 1767 *Tryal*. M.
Jones, Thomas of St. George, Hanover Square. SW Jan T May 1767
  Thornton. M.
Jones, Thomas. R 14 yrs Jly 1767. Ha.
Jones, Thomas. SQS Jly TB Sep 1767. So.
Jones, Thomas. S May T Aug 1769 *Douglas*. M.
Jones, Thomas. T Jly 1770 *Scarsdale*. M.
Jones, Thomas (1772). *See* Collins, John. M.
Jones, Thomas. SQS Apr 1773. M.
Jones, Thomas of Crompton, carpenter. SQS Oct 1773. La.
Jones, Thomas. S Dec 1773. M.
Jones, Thomas. S Lent 1775. Sy.
Jones, Thomas. S Apr 1775. M.
Jones, Timothy. S & T Dec 1731 *Forward* to Md or Va. M.
Jones, Walter. S s at Deveren Summer 1750. He.
Jones, William of Bishops Castle. R for America Jly 1679. Sh.
Jones, William of Broad Clyst. R for Barbados Dec 1686. De.
Jones, William of Camberwell. R for Barbados or Jamaica Jly 1688. Sy.
Jones, William. PT Sep 1691. M.
Jones, William of Welford. R for America Nov 1694. G.
Jones, William of Beaconsfield. R for America Feb 1695. Bu.
Jones, William of Ewloe, potter. R for America Aug 1700. Fl.
Jones, William of Bristol. R for Barbados Feb 1710 & Jly 1711. G.
Jones, William. T Aug 1721 *Owners Goodwill* LC Md Nov 1721. Sy.
Jones, William. S Oct T Dec 1724 *Rappahannock*. L.
Jones, William. S Jan T Feb 1726 *Supply* LC Annapolis May 1726. M.
Jones als Hooper, William. S Lent R 14 yrs Summer 1728. Be.

Jones, William. S Feb T Mar 1729 *Patapsco* LC Annapolis Dec 1729. M.
Jones, William. S Feb T Mar 1730 *Patapsco* LC Annapolis Sep 1730. L.
Jones, William. S s horse Summer 1730 R 14 yrs Lent 1732 (SP). He.
Jones, William. T Sep 1730 *Smith*. Sy.
Jones, William. S & T Apr 1733 *Patapsco* LC Annapolis Nov 1733. M.
Jones, William. S s hams Apr T Dec 1735 *John* LC Annapolis Sep
    1736. M.
Jones, William. S s plates at Madley Summer 1736. He.
Jones, William. S s horse Summer 1736 R 14 yrs Summer 1737. No.
Jones, William. S May T 14 yrs Jun 1738 *Forward*. L.
Jones, William (1739). *See* Gray. M.
Jones, William, als Wright, John. S Sep T Oct 1739
    Duke of Cumberland. L.
Jones, William. TB Aug 1740. Db.
Jones, William. SQS Jly 1741 TB to Md May 1742. So.
Jones, William. S s tallow Lent 1742. Mo.
Jones, William. S Sep T Oct 1744 *Susannah*. M.
Jones, William (1745). *See* Morgan. G.
Jones, William. S Sep 1747. L.
Jones, William. S Jly 1750. L.
Jones, William. S for being at large after sentence of transportation & T
    14 yrs Sep 1751 *Greyhound*. Ht.
Jones, William, als Bullock, John. S Lent R 14 yrs Summer 1752. G.
Jones, William (1753). *See* Reading, Richard. He.
Jones, William. T Sep 1755 *Tryal*. K.
Jones, William. S Feb-Apr T Jun 1756 *Lyon*. M.
Jones, William. T Jun 1756 *Lyon*. K.
Jones, William. S Summer 1756 R 14 yrs Lent T Sep 1757 *Thetis*. Sy.
Jones, William (1757). *See* Holloway. O.
Jones, William. S Feb T Mar 1758 *Dragon*. L.
Jones, William. S Feb 1759. L.
Jones, William. S Apr 1763. Fl.
Jones, William. S Feb T Mar 1764 *Tryal*. M.
Jones, William. S Oct 1764 T Jan 1765 *Tryal*. M.
Jones, William. S Lent R 14 yrs Summer 1767. St.
Jones, William. S Jly T Sep 1767 *Justitia*. M.
Jones, William. S Feb T Apr 1768 *Thornton*. M.
Jones, William. S Sep-Oct T Dec 1771 *Justitia*. M.
Jones, William. S Jly 1773. L.
Jones, William. S s horse & R 14 yrs Summer 1773. Wo.
Jones, William. S s at Sellack Lent 1774. He.
Jones, William. S s silver caster at St. Nicholas, Gloucester, Lent
    1774. G.
Jones, William (2). S May-Jly 1774. M.
Jones, William. S s at Magor Summer 1774. Mo.
Jones, William. S Oct 1774. L.
Jones, William. S Dec 1774. M.
Jones, William. S Apr 1775. M.
Jones, Winifred. S May T Jly 1723 *Alexander* LC Annapolis Sep
    1723. M.
Jordain. *See* Jordan.

Jordan, Ann. S May T Jun 1727 *Susanna* to Va. M.

Jordan, Bridget. S May-Jly T Sep 1755 *Tryal*. M.

Jorden, Christian (1685). *See* Bromfield. L.

Jordan, David (1763). *See* Wilson. We.

Jordan, George. T Jly 1723 *Alexander* LC Md Sep 1723. Sy.

Jordan, Hugh. S Dec 1750. L.

Jordan, James. S Lent 1768. Wa.

Jordan, James. R Mar TB to Va Apr 1773. Wi.

Jordan, Jesse. S for highway robbery Lent R 14 yrs Summer 1765. Be.

Jordaine, John. R for Barbados Jly 1674. M.

Jorden, John of Stibton. R for America Jly 1702. Su.

Jordain als Jurdon, John. S s iron harrow teeth Dec 1771 LC from *Lowther & Senhouse* Va May 1772. Nl.

Jordan, Joseph. S Jan-Feb T Apr 1772 *Thornton*. M.

Jordan, Mary. S & T Jan 1722 *Gilbert* LC Annapolis Jly 1722. M.

Jordan, Mary. Died on passage in *Dorsetshire* 1736. X.

Jordan, Mary (1756). *See* Williams. Sh.

Jordan, Michael. R 14 yrs Mar 1755. So.

Jordan, Rachael. S s mare Summer 1749 R 14 yrs Lent 1750. Mo.

Jordan, Robert. S Feb 1663 to House of Correction unless he agrees to be transported. M.

Jordan, Sarah (1762). *See* Mackrell. Sy.

Jordan, Sarah, als wife of Samuel Blythe. S Dec 1772. M.

Jordan, William. T May 1737 *Forward*. Sy.

Jordan, William. T Jun 1764 *Dolphin*. K.

Jordan, William. TB to Va 1768. De.

Jordan, William. S s mare at South Repps & R Lent 1769. Nf.

Joseph, Henry. S for receiving Feb 1775. L.

Joseph, Isaac. S Feb T Mar 1727 *Rappahannock*. L.

Joseph, Jacob. S Aug T Sep 1727 *Forward* LC Rappahannock May 1728. L.

Joseph, Moses. S Summer 1756 R 14 yrs Lent T Sep 1757 *Thetis*. Sy.

Joseph, William. TB to Va from QS 1767. De.

Josephs, Nathan. SQS Apr T Jly 1772 *Tayloe*. M.

Josephson, Charles (1768). *See* Davis. La.

Joshua, Levi. S Feb T Mar 1727 *Rappahannock* to Md. M.

Joslyn, Jane. S Jly T Sep 1765 *Justitia*. M.

Jostler, Joseph (1742). *See* Evans. St.

Joward, Thomas. TB Aug 1738. Y.

Joy, Daniel. T May 1723 *Victory*. K.

Joy, Mary. S Jan T Feb 1719 *Worcester* LC Annapolis Jun 1719. L.

Joy, Richard of St. Ann, Westminster. SW Jun 1774. M.

Joy, Robert of St. Saviour, Southwark. R for Barbados Aug 1662. Sy.

Joice, Benjamin. S s sheep Lent R 14 yrs Summer 1767. Bu.

Joyce, Christopher. S & T Oct 1730 *Forward* LC Potomack Jan 1731. L.

Joyce, James. S Lent T May 1750 *Lichfield*. K.

Joyce, John of Prescott. SQS Jan 1764. La.

Joice, Mary. S for stealing Oct 1655, pleaded pregnancy, found not pregnant & R Feb 1656. M.

Joyce, William. S 14 yrs Jan 1746. L.

Joydrell, John of Stafford. R for America Jly 1673. St.

Joyner, Edward. R for America Feb 1700. Wa.

Joyner, Edward. T May 1744 *Justitia*. K.

Joyner, John. S s logwood & Tar May 1735 T Jan 1736 *Dorsetshire* LC Va Sep 1736. M.

Joyner als Briant, John. R 14 yrs Aug 1742. Do.

Joyner, John. S 14 yrs Lent 1754. Sy.

Joiner, Joseph. S Oct 1743 T Feb 1744 *Neptune* to Md. M.

Joiner, Thomas. S Lent T May 1750 *Lichfield*. K.

Joiner, William. S Dec 1749-Jan 1750 T Mar 1750 *Tryal*. M.

Joyner, William. T Apr 1766 *Ann*. Sy.

Jubb, Joseph. R 14 yrs Summer 1775. Nt.

Jubb, Mary. S Summer 1764. Nt.

Jubb, Thomas. S Lent 1741. Y.

Jubbs, John of Norwich. R for America Jly 1713. Nf.

Judah, Isaac. S Dec 1749-Jan 1750 T 14 yrs Mar 1750 *Tryal*. M.

Judd, William. T Oct 1729 *Forward*. E.

Jude, Michael. S Apr-May T for life May 1744 *Justitia*. M.

Judge, Jane wife of William. S Summer 1754. Bu.

Judge, Judith. S Jly-Dec 1747. M.

Judge, Thomas. S Jly 1766. Ha.

Judson, Ann. S Jan T Feb 1744 *Neptune*. L.

Judson, Jane wife of William. S & T Apr 1733 *Patapsco* to Md. M.

Jukes, Benjamin. S Dec 1747. L.

Jewkes als Wintour, William of Kingswinford. S for several burglaries Summer 1720. St.

Jewques, William. S & T Oct 1730 *Forward* LC Potomack Jan 1731. L.

Jukes, William. S s silver tea tongs at Kingswinford Lent 1770. St.

Jump, Mary. T Apr 1735 *Patapsco*. E.

Jump, Thomas of Wolvercote. R for America Feb 1716. O.

Jump, William. S Jan 1755. M.

Juncker, John Lewis. S Jly 1749. L.

Jurd, Mary of Farnham, spinster. S Summer 1748 T Jan 1749 *Laura*. Sy.

Jurdon, John. S s at Ampney Crucis Lent 1722. G.

Jurdon, John (1772). *See* Jordain. Nl.

Jury, Anthony. TB to Va from QS 1767. De.

Jury, Ralph. S Lent T May 1750 *Lichfield*. E.

Juson, John. S Feb-Apr 1746. M.

Justice, Henry. S & T May 1736 *Patapsco*. L.

Justice, Hugh. S Aug T Oct 1723 *Forward* to Va. M.

Justice, William. T Apr 1735 *Patapsco*. E.

Justin, Humphrey. Rebel T 1685.

Jutton, James (1765). *See* Sutton. K.

Juxon, Jane. R for Barbados or Jamaica May AT Jly 1697. M.

K

Kaghill. *See* Caghill.

Kaines. *See* Caines.

Kane. *See* Cane.

Karrell. *See* Carrol.

Karwood, Mary. S s at Cassington Summer 1772. O.

Kates als States, Francis. S Aug T Oct 1726 *Forward*. L.

Kates als Symonds, Jane. R Jly AT Sep 1675. M.

Kates, John. S Oct 1748 T Jan 1749 *Laura*. L.

Katherines, Edward. S & T Jan 1722 *Gilbert* LC Annapolis Jly 1722. M.

Katterton, Robert. S Summer 1735. Y.

Kay, Abraham. R 14 yrs for highway robbery Summer 1730. Du.

Kaye, Abraham. S & T Jan 1769 *Thornton*. M.

Kay, Arthur. R 14 yrs Summer 1743. Y.

Kay, Elizabeth of Manchester, singlewoman. SQS Jan 1757. La.

Kay, Francis. S for life Oct-Dec 1750. M.

Kay, Hannah, als wife of James Johnson, als wife of George Fox, als wife of Neal Devitt of Manchester, dyer. SQS Jly 1771. La.

Kay, James (1765). *See* Knott. La.

Kay, James. S & T Dec 1767 *Neptune*. M.

Kay, John (1759). *See* Keen. St.

Kay, Michael. S Lent 1753. Y.

Kay, Thomas of Pendleton. SQS Jan 1743. La.

Kayberry, Thomas. S Lent 1735. Y.

Kayne. *See* Cane.

Keach. *See* Keech.

Keakquet, Robert of Eccleston near Knowsley, husbandman. SQS Apr 1754. La.

Kealty, William. S Feb T Apr 1765 *Ann*. M.

Keate, Thomas. S & T Feb 1744 *Neptune*. L.

Keating, John. T 14 yrs Aug 1752 *Tryal*. K.

Keatler, Stephen. S City Lent 1753. Y.

Keatly. *See* Keightley.

Keaton, Michael. T May 1751 *Tryal*. K.

Keay, Joseph. PT Jan 1685. M.

Kebble, Richard. S s sheep Summer 1757 R 14 yrs Lent T Sep 1758 *Tryal*. Bu.

Kecke, Laurence (1686). *See* King. E.

Keeble, Eleanor. S & T Dec 1734 *Caesar* LC Va Jly 1735. L.

Keable, Henry of Halling. R for Barbados or Jamaica Feb 1676. K.

Keeble, John. S May T Jly 1722 *Alexander* to Nevis or Jamaica. M.

Kibble, John. S Sep 1735 T Jan 1736 *Dorsetshire* LC Va Sep 1736. M.

Keeble, Richard. T May 1737 *Forward*. Sy.

Keeble, Richard. S Feb T Apr 1739 *Forward* to Va. M.

Keeble als Tibley, Robert. S s shirts & T May 1736 *Patapsco* to Md. M.

Keeble, William. S May T Jun 1726 *Loyal Margaret* LC Annapolis Oct 1726. M.

Keech, Richard. Rebel T 1685.

Keach, Thomas. S Summer R for Barbados Aug 1665. Sy.
Keach, Timothy. S s gelding Lent R 14 yrs Summer 1755. Hu.
Keed als Keedy als Kid, William. S City Summer 1740. Nl.
Keefe, David. T May 1737 *Forward*. Sx.
Keefe, Henry. S Jan T Feb 1719 *Worcester* LC Annapolis Jun 1719. L.
Kiffe, Robert. S Oct T Nov 1725 *Rappahannock* LC Rappahannock Apr 1726. M.
Keefs, Rose. S Jan-Feb T 14 yrs Apr 1772 *Thornton*. M.
Keel, George. Rebel T 1685.
Keal, Michael. S Aug 1753. De.
Keele, Robert. R for America Jly 1687. Li.
Keley, Jane. S Feb T Apr 1768 *Thornton*. M.
Keeley, William (1765). *See* Ealey. M.
Keeling, Andrew. S May T Jly 1770 *Scarsdale*. M.
Keiling als Sam, James. S May-Jun T Aug 1752 *Tryal*. M.
Keeling, Katherine, widow. R for Barbados Jly 1674. L.
Keen, Daniel. S & TB Aug 1740. G.
Keen als Cain, John. R 14 yrs Mar 1745. Ha.
Keene, John. S Summer T Sep 1751 *Greyhound*. Bu.
Keen, John. S Mar 1755. So.
Keen als Kay, John. S Lent R 14 yrs Summer 1759. St.
Keene, John. S s cow Summer 1766 R 14 yrs Lent 1767. O.
Keen, John. R Aug 1775. So.
Keene, Ralph of Creacombe. R for Barbados Feb 1688. De.
Keene, Richard. S Jly 1721. Co.
Keene, Richard. S for forging receipt Summer 1762 R for life Lent 1763. Nf.
Keen, Richard. S Lent 1772. G.
Keenleside, Richard of Gainsborough. R for America Jly 1716. Li.
Keep, Andrew. T Apr 1731 *Bennett*. Sx.
Keeping, Philip. Rebel T 1685.
Kegan, Robert. S Dec 1760. M.
Keightley, Christopher. LC from *Caesar* Va Jly 1734. X.
Keithly, Elizabeth (1766). *See* Currell. M.
Keighley, Thomas of Salford. SQS Jly 1747. La.
Keatly, Thomas. R Dec 1773. M.
Keightley, William. R for Jamaica Aug 1661. M.
Keith, Alexander. SQS Jly T Sep 1764 *Justitia*. M.
Keith, Alexander. S Sep-Oct 1773. M.
Keith, Eleanor. S Feb-Apr 1746. M.
Keith, John. T May 1751 *Tryal*. M.
Keith, John. SQS Oct 1764 AT Summer 1765. Du.
Keith, Joseph. S Oct 1756. M.
Keith, Thomas. SQS Jly T Sep 1764 *Justitia*. M.
Kelford, Nicholas. Rebel T 1685.
Kellas, John of Newport Pagnell. R for America Jly 1713. Bu.
Kellby, Joseph. TB May 1721. Le.
Kellett, Charles. T 14 yrs Aug 1752 *Tryal*. Sx.
Kellet, George. S s horse Lent R 14 yrs Summer 1733. St.
Kellett, Jane of Halton, singlewoman. SQS Oct 1754. La.
Kellick, John. T Apr 1765 *Ann*. M.

Kellick, Mary. S s at New Windsor Summer 1758. Be.

Kellihorn, John. R & T Jly 1770 *Scarsdale*. M.

Kelloway, Edward. R for Barbados or Jamaica Jan 1693. L.

Kellaway, Josiah. S Mar 1764. Do.

Kellsall, Samuel. S Lent R 14 yrs Summer 1750. St.

Kelly, Andrew. S Aug 1763. L.

Kelley, Ann. S Sep-Dec 1746. M.

Kelly, Ann. S Feb 1761. M.

Kelly, Ann. S May-Jly 1774. M.

Kelly, Catherine. S Apr T for life May 1743 *Indian Queen* to
     Potomack. M.

Kelly, Catherine. T Apr 1770 *New Trial*. Sy.

Kelly, Cecilly. T Sep 1758 *Tryal*. K.

Kelly, Charles of Charlton. R for Barbados Jly 1679. K.

Kelly, Daniel. S & T Jan 1739 *Dorsetshire*. L.

Kelly, Edmund, als Edmonds, Thomas. R 14 yrs Jly 1754. Ha.

Kelley, Eleanor. S May T Dec 1734 *Caesar* LC Va Jly 1735. M.

Kelly, Francis. S Lent 1775. E.

Kelly, George. R 14 yrs Jly TB to Va Sep 1744. Wi.

Kelly, George. R Feb T for life Mar 1764 *Tryal*. M.

Kelly, George. T Jly 1770 *Scarsdale*. M.

Kelly als Urwin als McLaughton, Grifsey of Manchester. SQS Jly
     1749. La.

Kelley, Hugh, aged 22, fair. S & T Oct 1720 *Gilbert* LC Annapolis May
     1721. M.

Kelly, Hugh. SQS & T Dec 1767 *Neptune*. M.

Kelly, James of Whalley. S Lent R 14 yrs Summer 1742. La.

Kelly, James. S Sep T Dec 1763 *Neptune*. M.

Kelly, James. S Oct 1773. L.

Kelly, Jane. T Dec 1736 *Dorsetshire*. E.

Kelly, John. S Mar 1719 to be T to Va. So.

Kelly, John. S s iron grate Jan T Apr 1735 *Patapsco* LC Annapolis Oct
     1735. M.

Kelley, John. S Summer 1742. We.

Kelly, John. S Sep T Nov 1743 *George William*. M.

Kelly, John. S Mar 1768 TB to Va. De.

Kelly, Lothary. S Sep-Oct T Dec 1753 *Whiteing*. M.

Kelly, Margaret. S & T Dec 1731 *Forward*. L.

Kelly, Mary. S May-Jly 1748. M.

Kelly, Mary. S Oct 1749. L.

Kelly, Mary. S May-Jly 1750. M.

Kelly, Mary. S Feb 1754. M.

Kelly, Matthew. S Apr-May 1754. M.

Kelly, Matthew. S Feb 1761. M.

Kelly, Matthias. S Oct T Dec 1763 *Neptune*. M.

Kelly, Michael. SQS Oct T Dec 1753 *Whiteing*. M.

Kelly, Miles. S Jly T Sep 1757 *Thetis*. L.

Kelly, Patrick. SQS Apr T May 1750 *Lichfield*. M.

Kelly, Patrick. SQS Dec 1766 T Jan 1767 *Tryal*. M.

Kelly, Patrick. S Sep-Oct 1774. M.

Kelly, Peter. S Summer 1754 T May 1755 *Rose*. K.

Kelley, Richard. S Aug T Sep 1725 *Forward* LC Annapolis Dec 1725. M.
Kelley, Richard. T Oct 1768 *Justitia*. K.
Kelly, Samuel. TB to Va 1728. De.
Kelley, Terence. SQS Apr T May 1750 *Lichfield*. M.
Kelly, Thomas. S Jly 1733. Wi.
Kelly, Thomas. S & T Dec 1767 *Neptune*. M.
Kelly, Thomas. S s handkerchief at St. Mary Woolnoth Apr T Jun 1768 *Tryal*. L.
Kelly, Thomas. SQS Sep T Oct 1768 *Justitia*. M.
Kelly, Valentine. S Jan T Jun 1738 *Forward* to Md or Va. M.
Kelly, William. T Oct 1738 *Genoa*. Sy.
Kelly, William. S & T Jly 1771 *Scarsdale*. L.
Kelsey, John. S Sep 1756. M.
Kelsey, John. S for highway robbery Lent R for life Summer 1766. Bu.
Kelsey, Richard Sr. of Romsey, husbandman. R for Barbados Feb 1668. Ha.
Kelsey, Thomas. R for Barbados or Jamaica Dec 1689. M.
Kelsy, William. S Sep-Oct T Dec 1752 *Greyhound*. M.
Kelson, Ann. S Bristol 14 yrs for receiving Lent 1772. G.
Kelson, George Jr. SQS & TB Apr 1774. So.
Keelson, Mary. LC from *Honor* Port York Jan 1721. X.
Kelsworth, John. T Jly 1770 *Scarsdale*. M.
Kem als Butcher, George. R 14 yrs Oct 1772. M.
Keminett, Hannah. S & T Feb 1744 *Neptune* to Md. M.
Kempe, Amey. S & T Oct 1729 *Forward* LC Va Jun 1730. M.
Kemp, Benjamin. S Lent 1729 AT Lent 1731. O.
Kemp, Benjamin. T Jan 1738 *Drsetshire*. E.
Kemp, Cornelius. T 14 yrs Sep 1766 *Justitia*. Sx.
Kemp, Edward. Rebel T 1685.
Kemp, Edward of Crimplesham. R for America Feb 1687. Nf.
Kemp, Edward. S Mar 1756 TB to Va. De.
Kemp, Edward. S Lent T from London Sep 1767 *Justitia*. Ru.
Kemp, Edward. SQS for false pretences Jan TB May 1770. So.
Kemp, Elizabeth. S Summer 1729. Cu.
Kemp, George. S Sep-Oct T Dec 1752 *Greyhound*. M.
Kemp, George. S s horse Lent R 14 yrs Summer 1753. Su.
Kemp, George. R Lent 1773. E.
Kemp, Hannah. SQS Apr 1774. M.
Kemp, Henry. S Lent T Oct 1738 *Genoa*. Bu.
Kemp, James Jr. S & R 14 yrs Lent 1775. Ch.
Kemp, John. S s horse Summer 1736 R 14 yrs Lent 1737. Wo.
Kemp, John. S Lent R 14 yrs Summer 1753. Nt.
Kemp, John. S Feb-Apr T Jun 1756 *Lyon*. M.
Kemp, John. R 14 yrs Mar 1763. De.
Kemp, John. S s at Hereford Lent 1767. He.
Kemp, Joseph. S Lent R for Barbados May 1664. E.
Kemp, Mary. S Feb T Mar 1729 *Patapsco* LC Annapolis Dec 1729. L.
Kemp, Thomas (1728). *See* Keys. M.
Kemp, Thomas. S Feb T Apr 1766 *Ann*. L.
Kempe, William. S Apr 1775. M.
Kemplin, John. Rebel T 1685.

Kempson, John. S Dec 1733 T Jan 1734 *Caesar* LC Va Jly 1734. L.

Kempster, Elizabeth. S Dec 1753-Jan 1754. M.

Kempster, John. S Summer 1750 R 14 yrs Summer T Sep 1751
  Greyhound. Bu.

Kempster, John. R 14 yrs Lent 1774. Ht.

Kempster, Susanna (1725). *See* Belchier. M.

Kempstock, John. T Nov 1725 *Rappahannock* LC Va Aug 1726. Sy.

Kempton, Christopher. S & TB to Va Mar 1761. Wi.

Kempton, Mary. R & T 14 yrs Sep 1737 *Pretty Patsy* to Md. M.

Kempton, Samuel. R Dec 1716 T Jan 1717 *Queen Elizabeth*. L.

Kempton, Thomas. S Sep-Oct 1749. M.

Kempton, Thomas. S for attempted robbery at Wendover & R Lent
  1775. Bu.

Kemis, John of Bishops Cleeve. S s shirts Lent TB Mar 1754. G.

Kemeys, John. S s at Monmouth Lent 1767. Mo.

Kendall, Ann. S & T Apr 1759 *Thetis*. L.

Kendall, George of St. Martin in Fields. S s coal Jly 1740 T Jan 1741
  Harpooner to Rappahannock. M.

Kendall, Isaac. S Lent 1738. Su.

Kendall, James. PT Apr 1700. M.

Kendall, Jane. SQS Mar TB Apr 1755. Le.

Kendall, John of Beaumont. R for Barbados or Jamaica Jun 1692. E.

Kendall, Mary. S Jly-Dec 1747. M.

Kendal, Samuel. S Nov T Dec 1753 *Whiteing*. L.

Kendall, Thomas. T Apr 1759 *Thetis*. Sy.

Kendell, Thomas. S Apr 1760. M.

Kendall, Thomas. S s at Osbaldwick Lent TB Oct 1764. Y.

Kendall, Thomas. R Lent 1774. E.

Kendall, William. S Norwich Summer 1745. Nf.

Kendall, William. S Lent 1750. La.

Kendrick, Ann. S Feb-Apr T May 1752 *Lichfield*. M.

Kendrick, James. SQS & T Jly 1772 *Tayloe*. M.

Kendrick, William. S Apr 1749. L.

Kenear. *See* Kinnear.

Kenly, Arthur. S & T Apr 1725 *Sukey* LC Annapolis Sep 1725. M.

Kenmore, Mary. S s cambric Lent 1740. He.

Kennard, Evelyn wife of John. S Mar 1729. De.

Kennard, George (1710). *See* Booker. Sx.

Kennard, Samuel. S Feb T Mar 1758 *Dragon*. L.

Kennaty. *See* Kennedy.

Kenne, Catherine. S Oct T Nov 1759 *Phoenix*. L.

Kenne, Thomas. S Apr 1749. L.

Kenneday, Bartholomew. S Lent R 14 yrs Summer 1749. Sy.

Kennedy, Edward. SW & T Dec 1769. M.

Kinardy, Frances. T Apr 1743 *Justitia*. K.

Kennedy, Isabel. AT City Summer 1760. Nl.

Kennedy, James. R Apr 1773. M.

Kennedy, John. S May T Jun 1726 *Loyal Margaret* LC Annapolis Oct
  1726. M.

Kennedy als Cosgrove, Lawrence. S s horse & R 14 yrs Lent 1774. La.

Kennedy, Lawrence. R for life s horse Lent 1775. Ch.

Kennedy, Martin. S Feb-Apr T May 1755 *Rose*. M.

Kennedy, Mathew. R & T for life Apr 1770 *New Trial*. M.

Kennedy, Matthew. S Apr-May T for life Jly 1771 *Scarsdale*. M.

Kennedy, Michael. R Feb T for life Mar 1764 *Tryal*. M.

Kennedy, Michael. S & T Dec 1771 *Justitia*. M.

Kennedy, Patrick. S Apr-May T 14 yrs Jly 1771 *Scarsdale*. M.

Kennedy, Peter. S Oct 1774. L.

Kennedy, Philip. S Jan T Mar 1764 *Tryal*. L.

Kennedy, Robert. S Sep T Dec 1770 *Justitia*. M.

Kennedy, Timothy. S Oct 1766 T Jan 1767 *Tryal*. M.

Kennaty, William. S Oct 1774. L.

Kinnett, Benjamin. S Feb T Mar 1729 *Patapsco* LC Annapolis Dec 1729. L.

Kennett, George. S Feb T Jun 1727 *Susanna* to Va. M.

Kennett, Richard of Boldre. R for Barbados Jly 1715. Ha.

Kennewall, Charles. S Jan 1745. L.

Kennick, John. S Dec 1762 T Mar 1763 *Neptune*. M.

Kennick, William, als Lamprey, Thomas of Crediton. R for Barbados Mar 1695. De.

Kennolds, Thomas. T May 1719 *Margaret*; sold to Richard Nelson Md Aug 1719. Sx.

Kenny, James W. S Summer 1756. Hu.

Kenny, Luke. S Feb T Mar 1758 *Dragon*. M.

Kenny, Mary. S & T Dec 1770 *Justitia*. L.

Kenny, Patrick. S Apr-May T Jly 1771 *Scarsdale*. M.

Kenny, William. S & T Jly 1771 *Scarsdale*. M.

Kensington, Martha of Mistley. R for Barbados or Jamaica Jly 1710. E.

Kenstephens, Morgan. S Feb 1738. Ha.

Kent, Ann. T May 1744 *Justitia*. Sy.

Kent, Edward. Rebel T 1685.

Kent, Edward. S Oct T Nov 1728 *Forward* LC Rappahannock Jun 1729. L.

Kent, George of Lanteglos. R for Barbados Feb 1673. Co.

Kent, Grace. S Jan-Feb T Apr 1771 *Thornton*. M.

Kent, Humphrey. TB to Va 1726. De.

Kent, John. S Feb T Mar 1731 *Patapsco* but died on passage. L.

Kent, John. S Mar 1736. Ha.

Kent, John. S s horse Summer 1741 R 14 yrs Lent TB to Md 1742. Le.

Kent, John. S Feb 1744. Ha.

Kent, John. S Jly-Dec 1747. M.

Kentt, John. S Jly 1750. L.

Kent, John. S Summer 1753 R 14 yrs Lent 1754. Su.

Kent, Peter. Rebel T 1685.

Kent, Richard. T May 1752 *Lichfield*. Sx.

Kent, Richard. S Lent 1766. Wa.

Kent, Richard. S s sheep at Quarrendon & R Lent T Apr 1772 *Thornton*. Bu.

Kent, Sarah. R 14 yrs Jly 1740. Ha.

Kent, Stephen. S Aug 1772. De.

Kent, Thomas. S Jan T Feb 1724 *Anne* to Carolina. M.

Kentsbeare, Sarah. S Jly 1766. De.

Kenvin, Evan. S s fowls at Machen Lent 1773. Mo.

Kenzer, John. S Jly 1763. M.

Kenzie, Mary of Newington, spinster. SQS Jan 1775. Sy.

Kerby. *See* Kirby.

Kerle, John. Rebel T 1685.

Kerril late Bennett, Mary. S Apr 1734. So.

Kerle als Hawkins, Richard of Bampton. R for Barbados Feb 1714. De.

Kerley, George. S s horse Lent R 14 yrs Summer 1737. Wa.

Kern, George. S for perjury Summer 1769; to be set on pillory at Maidenhead for an hour before transportation. Be.

Kerr, Alexander. S for aiding escape of prisoners from gaol Summer 1744. Nl.

Kerr, Andrew. S s at Berkeley Lent 1734. G.

Kerr als Hubbard, Elizabeth. S May-Jly 1748. M.

Kerr, James. T Jun 1740 *Essex*. Sy.

Kerrivan, Edward (1766). *See* Carrivan. M.

Kershaw, Thomas. S s horse Summer 1729 R 14 yrs Summer 1730. Le.

Kerslake, Robert. R 14 yrs Aug 1773. De.

Kerslake, William. R 14 yrs Aug 1742. De.

Kersly, John. SQS Apr 1770. Ha.

Kersley, William. S Lent R 14 yrs Summer 1774. Ch.

Kerton. *See* Kirton.

Ketch, Margaret, spinster, als wife of John. R for plantations Jan 1665. L.

Ketch, Susan. R for plantations Jan 1665. L.

Ketcher, Mary. S & T Oct 1732 *Caesar* to Va. M.

Ketcher, Samuel. S Aug T Oct 1724 *Forward* LC Annapolis Jun 1725. L.

Ketling, John. R for Barbados or Jamaica Dec 1698. M.

Kett, Richard. S s worsted at St. Giles, Norwich, Summer 1771; Elizabeth Kett, widow, acquitted. Nf.

Kettle als Green, Bartholomew of Clinsett (sic). R for Barbados Feb 1688. Su.

Kettle, James. TB Oct 1719 T *Susannah & Sarah* but died on passage. L.

Kettle, John. S s sheep Summer 1750 R 14 yrs Lent 1751. Ch.

Kettle, William. S & R 14 yrs Lent 1775. Wo.

Kettleburne, Thomas. R for America Jly 1707. Li.

Kettles, Richard. R for America Aug 1715. M.

Kettlestrings, James. S s at St. Maurice, York, Lent 1751. Y.

Kettlewell, Mary wife of Richard. S Lent 1735. Y.

Kew, Sarah. S Lent TB May 1755. G.

Key, Abraham. S & R Summer 1724. Y.

Key, Anthony. S & T Sep 1731 *Smith* LC Va 1732. L.

Key, John of Nantwich. R for Barbados Sep 1671. Ch.

Key, John. Rebel T 1685.

Key, John. S s horse Lent R 14 s Summer 1746. Nt.

Key, Joseph. R for Barbados or Jamaica Mar 1685. M.

Key, Richard. R 14 yrs Mar 1742. Co.

Key, Silvester of Paston. R for Barbados Aug 1671. Nf.

Key, Thomas. S s mare Summer 1752 R 14 yrs Lent T Apr 1753 *Thames*. Bu.

Key, Thomas. S s at Cannock Lent 1764. St.

Key, William. Rebel T 1685.

Key, William. S May T Jly 1723 *Alexander* to Md. M.

Keys, Elizabeth (1755). *See* Southeran. M.

Keys, George of Newington. R for Barbados Apr 1668. Sy.

Keys als Thornton, John. S Apr 1748. L.

Keys, Miriam. S May T Jun 1726 *Loyal Margaret* LC Annapolis Oct 1726. M.

Keys als Kemp, Thomas. S Oct 1727-Jun 1728 T Jun 1728 *Elizabeth* LC Potomack Aug 1729. M.

Keys, Thomas of St. George Martyr. S s coach fittings Jly-Oct 1740 T Jan 1741 *Harpooner* to Rappahannock. M.

Keys, Thomas. SQS Sep T Dec 1771 *Justitia*. M.

Keys, William. LC from *Alexander* Annapolis Sep 1723. X.

Keysell, George. S Sep T Dec 1769 *Justitia*. M.

Keyte, James. AT Summer 1719. Wo.

Keyte, John of Berkeley. R for America Jly 1687. G.

Keywood, Edward. S s horse & R Summer 1773. Be.

Keywood, Robert. R for America Jly 1688. Li.

Kibble. *See* Keeble.

Kidd, Ann. S & T Oct 1730 *Forward* LC Potomack Jan 1731. L.

Kidd, John of Whittlesford. S s pig Lent 1741. *Ca.

Kidd, John. S Jly 1772. Ha.

Kidd, Richard. S s horse Summer 1743 R 14 yrs Lent 1744. Y.

Kid, William (1740). *See* Keed. Nl.

Kidder, Ann. S Oct T Dec 1769 *Justitia*. M.

Kidder, Edward, als Alchin, John. SWK Apr T Sep 1757 *Thetis*. K.

Kiddy, Anthony. TB Jly 1766. Db.

Kiddy George (1731). *See* Mathews, George. L.

Kidgell, Jane. S Mar 1720. L.

Kidman, John. T Sep 1730 *Smith*. Sy.

Kidman, William of North Somercoates. R for America Jly 1716. Li.

Kidner, Robert of Bromfield. R for Barbados Mar 1686. So.

Kidwell, Dorothy of Great Chart. R for Barbados or Jamaica Mar 1698. K.

Kiffe. *See* Keefe.

Kightley, Mary. PT Feb 1679. M.

Kilbert, John. R Jan-Feb T 14 yrs Apr 1772 *Thornton*. M.

Kilburn, Jeremiah. S & T Sep 1764 *Justitia*. L.

Kilburn, Matthew. SQS Richmond s at Scorton Jan TB Apr 1769. Y.

Kilburn, Reuben. S Apr T Jun 1742 *Bladon* to Md. M.

Kilburne, Richard. S & T Oct 1729 *Forward* LC Va Jun 1730. M.

Kilbourne, Thomas. S s sheep Aug TB 14 yrs to Va Sep 1773. Le.

Kilby, Elizabeth. T Jly 1722 *Alexander*. Sy.

Kilcup, Thomas. S Apr T Sep 1737 *Pretty Patsy* to Md. M.

Kilford, Thomas of Westbury. R for America Jly 1693. G.

Kilgour, Alexander of Harwich. S Lent T Apr 1760 *Thetis*. E.

Kilke, Esther. S Dec 1772. M.

Killam, William. R for Barbados Dec 1667. M.

Killicrees, William (1750). *See* Thompson, John. La.

Killigrew, Cornelius. S Summer 1774. E.

Killigrew, Elizabeth. S Sep-Oct 1749. M.
Killegrew, Hannah. S Jly-Dec 1747. M.
Killmister, Mary. S Oct T Dec 1724 *Rappahannock*. L.
Kilman, Joseph. S s silver cup at Uttoxeter Lent 1773. St.
Kilpatrick als Perry, James. S Jly TB to Va Aug 1752. Wi.
Killpatrick, John. R for Barbados or Jamaica Jan 1692. L.
Kilpatrick, John. S Mar 1726. So.
Kilroy, Bernard. S Feb 1773. L.
Kimber, Edward. S for killing deer in chase & TB to Va Apr 1750. Wi.
Kimber, John. SQS New Sarum Jan TB to Va Apr 1766. Wi.
Kimber, Joseph. S s mare Lent R 14 yrs Summer 1766. O.
Kimber, Mary. S Dec 1761 T Apr 1762 *Dolphin*. M.
Kimber, Mary. SQS Apr TB May 1767. So.
Kimber, Richard. S s ribbon at Abingdon Lent 1752. Be.
Kimber, William. S Summer 1739. Be.
Kimberly, John. S s at Bray Lent R 14 yrs Summer 1737. Be.
Kimble, Richard. S Summer 1766. Wa.
Kimball, Robert of Houghton Conquest. S Lent 1729. *Bd.
Kinchley, Peter. S Sep T Dec 1770 *Justitia*. M.
Kind, Thomas. S Aug T Oct 1726 *Forward* to Va. M.
Kinder, John. S s at Loughton Lent 1774. Bu.
Kinder, Ralph. S s sheep Summer 1746 R 14 yrs Lent TB Feb 1747. Db.
Kindar, Samuel. S s gelding Summer 1767 R 14 yrs Lent TB Apr 1768. Db.
Kinett. *See* Kennet.
King Kago (1764). *See* William, John. M.
King, Andrew. S Apr 1763. M.
King, Ann. S Feb T Apr 1741 *Speedwell*. L.
King, Ann wife of John of Egham. SQS Apr T Sep 1757 *Thetis*. Sy.
King, Ann. S Jan T Mar 1764 *Tryal*. M.
King, Bernard Lipscomb. S Apr 1734. M.
King, Bridget. S & T Dec 1767 *Neptune*. M.
King, Cassandra (1704). *See* Hall. Nt.
King, Katherine. R Dec 1716 T Jan 1717 *Queen Elizabeth* to Jamaica. M.
King als Kingston, Charles. T Jly 1724 *Robert* LC Md Jun 1725. E.
King, Charles. LC from *Patapsco* Annapolis Nov 1733. X.
King, Charles. S & R 14 yrs Lent 1738. Hu.
King, Charles. S Mar 1775. Do.
King, Daniel. S Feb 1761. M.
King, David. PT Apr 1692. M.
King, David of Tonbridge. R for Barbados or Jamaica Mar 1694. K.
King, David. S Jan 1745. L.
King, Deborah. S Oct 1751-Jan 1752. M.
King, Edward. R for Barbados Jly 1663. L.
Kinge, Edward of Loughborough. R for Barbados Feb 1671. G.
King, Edward. R for Barbados Jun 1671. L.
King, Edward. R Summer 1773. Sy.
King, Eleanor. S Sep T Oct 1744 *Susannah*. M.
King, Eleanor wife of James. S 14 yrs Feb 1761. M.
King, Elizabeth (1720). *See* Jones. Mo.

King, Elizabeth. S Jun-Dec 1738 T Jan 1739 *Dorsetshire* to Va. M.
King, Elizabeth. S Feb 1757. M.
King, Elizabeth. S s apron at Hereford Lent 1769. He.
King, Elizabeth. S Apr-Jun T Jly 1772 *Tayloe*. M.
King, Francis of Sible Hedingham. R for America Jly 1700. E.
King, George. S Summer 1741 R 14 yrs Lent 1743. Du.
King, George. SW & T Dec 1767 *Neptune*. M.
King, George. SW & T Aug 1769 *Douglas*. M.
King, George (1771). *See* Watts. Ca.
King, Henry. R Dec 1681 AT Jan 1682. M.
King, Hester. R for Barbados or Jamaica Dec 1693. L.
King als Brown, Hugh. S Summer 1741. Cu.
King, Isaac of Bermondsey. SQS Mar T Apr 1768 *Thornton*. Sy.
King, Jacob. Rebel T 1685.
King, James. S May T Jun 1727 *Susanna* to Va. M.
King, James. T May 1737 *Forward*. Sy.
King, James. S Sep T Nov 1743 *George William*. L.
King, James. T May 1752 *Lichfield*. E.
King, James. S & T Sep 1765 *Justitia*. L.
King, James. SQS Dec 1768 T Jan 1769 *Thornton*. M.
King, Jane. S May-Jly 1746. M.
King, Job. S as pickpocket & R 14 yrs Summer 1769. Be.
King, John. R Dec 1681 AT Jan 1682. M.
King, John. T Oct 1721 *William & John*. K.
King, John. S & T Oct 1729 *Forward* but died on passage. M.
King als Gibbs, John. R 14 yrs Jly 1732. Ha.
King, John. S s bay & R 14 yrs Summer 1737. Nf.
King, John (1738). *See* Wells. M.
King, John of Great Warley. S Lent 1745. E.
King, John. S s mare & R Summer 1745. Su.
King als Kiss, John. S Mar 1747. Ha.
King, John. S Lent 1749. K.
King, John. R 14 yrs Lent 1751. Bd.
King, John. S s cheeses Lent 1753. Su.
King, John of St. George, Southwark. SQS Jan 1754. Sy.
King, John. S Summer 1754. K.
King, John. S Lent T Jun 1756 *Lyon*. K.
King, John. TB to Va from QS 1760. De.
King, John. S s at Linslade & R Summer T Dec 1770 *Justitia*. Bu.
King, John. S Oct 1773. L.
King, John. S s at Bosbury Lent 1774. He.
King, Joseph. T Sep 1730 *Smith*. Sy.
King, Joseph. S Jan-Apr 1749. M.
King als Kecke als White, Laurence of East Ham. R for Barbados or
  Jamaica Feb 1683 & Feb 1686. E.
King, Margaret. S May T Jun 1727 *Susanna* to Va. M.
King, Margaret. S Sep-Oct T Dec 1752 *Greyhound*. M.
King, Margaret. S Apr 1760. M.
King, Mary (1715). *See* Godson. L.
King, Mary. LC from *Alexander* Annapolis Sep 1723. X.
King, Mary (1731). *See* Askew. M.

King, Mary wife of Thomas. S Jun 1733 T Jan 1734 *Caesar* LC Va Jly 1734. M.
King, Mary. S Sep-Dec 1746. M.
King, Mary. S Jan-Apr 1748. M.
King, Mary. SQS Apr T May 1755 *Rose*. M.
King, Mary. S Jly T Nov 1762 *Prince William*. M.
King, Michael. SQS Apr T May 1767 *Thornton*. M.
King, Paul of Grantchester. S s hen Lent 1741. *Ca.
King, Richard. Rebel T 1685.
King, Richard. S s horse Lent R 14 yrs Summer 1746. K.
King, Richard. S s at Bisley Lent 1759. G.
King, Richard. S Jan-Feb 1773. M.
King, Robert of Fornham. R for America Apr 1697. Su.
King, Robert. S s handkerchiefs & T May 1736 *Patapsco* to Md. M.
King, Robert. R 14 yrs Aug 1739. So.
King als Williams, Sarah. S Sep-Oct 1774. M.
King, Susan. S Sep 1735 T Jan 1736 *Dorsetshire* LC Va Sep 1736. M.
King, Thomas. S Mar 1733 T *Patapsco* LC Annapolis Nov 1733. Wi.
King, Thomas of Impington. S s sheep Lent 1741. *Ca.
King, Thomas. S Mar 1752. So.
King, Thomas. S Feb-Apr T May 1755 *Rose*. M.
King, Thomas. S Summer 1757 R 14 yrs Lent 1758. Wa.
King, Thomas. R 14 yrs & TB to Va Mar 1761. Wi.
King, Thomas. S Jan T Apr 1768 *Thornton*. M.
King, Thomas. S Oct 1775. M.
King, William. S Aug 1727. So.
King, William. SQS Jly 1736. So.
King, William. T Sep 1742 *Forward*. E.
King, William. S May-Jly 1750. M.
King, William. S Jan 1757. L.
King, William. S Lent T Apr 1758. Bd.
King, William. S Lent R 14 yrs Summer 1761. E.
King, William of Tooting. SQS Jan T Apr 1765 *Ann*. Sy.
Kingan, John (1699). *See* Gingin. Sy.
Kingden, James. SQS Apr TB to Md May 1742. So.
Kingdom, Arthur. T May 1744 *Justitia*. Sy.
Kingham, John. S Lent T May 1767 *Thornton*. Bu.
Kingham, Thomas. S Apr T May 1720 *Honor* & escaped in Vigo, Spain. L.
Kingham, Thomas. S & T Jan 1722 *Gilbert* LC Annapolis Jly 1722. M.
Kingham, William. R for Barbados Jly 1674. M.
Kinghorn, James. S Apr-May T Jly 1771 *Scarsdale*. M.
Kingked, Alexander. S Summer 1718 R 14 yrs Summer 1720. Nl.
Kinglis als Disey, Elizabeth of Wokingham. R for America Jly 1708. Be.
Kingman, Sarah. R & T 14 yrs Feb 1740 *York*. L.
Kingsberry, Thomas. S & T Oct 1729 *Forward* but died on passage. M.
Kingsbury, Sara. TB 14 yrs Oct 1719 T *Susannah & Sarah* LC Annapolis Apr 1720. L.
Kingsland, David. T Apr 1742 *Bond*. K.
Kingsland, John. T May 1741 *Miller*. K.
Kingsland, Thomas. S Jan T Apr 1741 *Speedwell* or *Mediterranean*. M.

Kingsland, William. S Jan 1767. L.

Kingston, Charles (1724). *See* King. E.

Kingston, George. S May T Jun 1764 *Dolphin*. M.

Kingston, George. SW & T Apr 1768 *Thornton*. M.

Kingston, Isaac. Rebel T 1685.

Kingston als Brown, John. S Dec 1750. L.

Kingston, Mary. S Feb-Apr T Jun 1756 *Lyon*. M.

Kingstone, Thomas. S & T Apr 1733 *Patapsco* LC Annapolis Nov 1733. L.

Kingswood, Samuel of Bexhill. R for Barbados or Jamaica Jly 1710. Sx.

Kinman, John. S Summer 1741. Cu.

Kenear, David. S Oct T Dec 1724 *Rappahannock* to Va. M.

Kinner, Thomas. SQS Oct T Dec 1771 *Justitia*. M.

Kinsett, Roger. T Aug 1752 *Tryal*. Sx.

Kinsey, John (1751). *See* Russell. M.

Kinsman, John, als Edenbery, James. S Aug 1729. De.

Kip, Alice. R Dec 1679 AT Feb 1680. M.

Kipling, Charles. S Summer 1749. Y.

Kipling, Robert. S Apr 1773. L.

Kipling, William. R for life Summer 1774. Du.

Kipping, Mary (1746). *See* Morrit. M.

Kipps, William of Hendon. S s fowls & T Feb 1740 *York* to Md. M.

Kirbee, Anthony (1755). *See* Cubberd. E.

Kirby, Benjamin. S Apr-May T May 1741 *Catherine & Elizabeth* to Md. M.

Kirby, Elizabeth als Betty of Ulverstone, spinster. SQS Jly 1773. La.

Kirby, John of Blacktoft. R for Barbados Jly 1683. Y.

Kirby, John, als Trapp, William. R for Barbados or Jamaica May 1691. M.

Kirby, John. S s sheep Lent R 14 yrs Summer T Sep 1751 *Greyhound*. Bu.

Kirby, John. S Norwich Summer 1764. Nf.

Kirby, Margaret (1745). *See* Meers. L.

Kirby, Margaret wife of Edward. S s sheep & R 14 yrs Lent 1768; missed transport ship & ordered to await next Summer 1768. Ca.

Kerby, Martha. S Oct 1744-Jan 1745. M.

Kirby, Mary (1719). *See* Thirby. L.

Kirby, Mary. S & T Apr 1766 *Ann*. L.

Curby, Paul. SL & T Jan 1767 *Tryal*. Sy.

Kirby, Rebecca (1671). *See* Harbert. L.

Kirby, Richard. S & TB Mar 1750. G.

Kerby, Robert. R for Barbados Feb 1675. L.

Kirby, Robert. S Summer 1755. Nf.

Kirby, Samuel. S Summer 1761. Nf.

Kirby, Thomas. S Dec 1773. M.

Kirbee, William (1755). *See* Cubberd. E.

Kirby, William. S s sheep Lent R 14 yrs Summer 1764; noted as disordered in mind & to remain in custody Lent 1765. Bd.

Kirk, Katherine. R for America Aug 1715. L.

Kirk, Grafton. S Jan-May T 14 yrs Jun 1738 *Forward* to Md or Va. M.

Kirk, John. S Summer 1762. No.

Kirk, John. S Jan-Feb T Apr 1772 *Thornton*. M.
Kirk, John. S Sep-Oct 1773. M.
Kirk, Richard. S Summer 1724 R Summer 1725. Li.
Kirk, Samuel. S s breeches at Walsall Lent 1768. St.
Kirk als Oakley, Sarah. T Jun 1727 *Susanna*. Sy.
Kirk, Sarah. S Sep T Oct 1768 *Justitia*. M.
Kirk, Thomas. S Feb-Apr 1745. M.
Kirk, Thomas. S & T Apr 1765 *Ann*. L.
Kirk, Thomas. S for killing sheep Lent R 14 yrs Summer 1766. Be.
Kirke, Thomas. S Apr-Jun T Jly 1772 *Tayloe*. M.
Kirke, Ursula. R for Barbados Jly 1668. L.
Kirkham, Mary. S s at Wen Lent 1757. Sh.
Kirklin, Mary. S Sep T 14 yrs Dec 1763 *Neptune*. M.
Kirkman, Elizabeth (1775). *See* Hoare. M.
Kirkman, Sarah. S Sep-Oct 1772. M.
Kirkup, Mary. S City Summer 1763. Nl.
Kirkwood, John. S Sep-Oct T Dec 1753 *Whiteing*. M.
Kirton, Anthony (1769). *See* Gurton. M.
Kirton, James. R 14 yrs Apr 1770. So.
Kirton, Mary. R for Barbados Dec 1670. M.
Kirton, Sara. R for Barbados Dec 1667. M.
Kerton, Thomas Jr. of Cheddar. R for Barbados Jly 1688. So.
Kerton, Thomas. R for Barbados or Jamaica Oct 1694. L.
Kirton, William. R for Barbados Oct 1673. M.
Kirwood, Edward. S City Summer 1722. Nl.
Kiss, John (1747). *See* King. Ha.
Kitchin, Elizabeth. S s sheet at North Lydbury Lent 1751. Sh.
Kitchen, Jane. LC from *Honor* Port York Jan 1721. X.
Kitching, John. T Nov 1741 *Sea Horse*. K.
Kitchen, John. S Sep-Dec 1746. M.
Kitchin, John Jr. S s fish from a trunk Summer 1748. Nf.
Kitchen, John. S Mar 1753. De.
Kitchen als Kitchener, John. T Apr 1769 *Tryal*. Bu.
Kitchin, John of Satterthwaite, butcher. S s sheep & R 14 yrs Lent 1770. La.
Kitching, Mary. S Jan T Apr 1762 *Dolphin*. L.
Kitchen, Thomas. S Summer 1769 R 14 yrs Lent 1770. Li.
Kitchener, James. S s sheep at Sundon & R 14 yrs Lent 1774. Bd.
Kitchener, John (1769). *See* Kitchen. Bu.
Kitchener, Mary. ST & T May 1767 *Thornton*. L.
Kitchenside, Abraham. S Jan-Feb 1773. M.
Kitchinman, William. S Sep 1737 T Jan 1738 *Dorsetshire* to Va. M.
Kyte, Dorothy of Penton Grafton. R for Barbados Jly 1678. Ha.
Kite, John. SWK Oct 1757. K.
Kite, Patience. S Apr T 14 yrs May 1718 *Tryal* LC Charles Town Aug 1718. L.
Kite, Richard. S s at St. Helen, Abingdon, Summer 1760. Be.
Kite, Robert. S Sep T Oct 1768 *Justitia*. M.
Kiteley, Benjamin. S Summer T Sep 1751 *Greyhound*. Sy.
Kitling, John. PT Jan 1699. M.
Kitratt, William. S Jly 1740. Ha.

Kitson, James of Rotherhithe. SQS Jan T Apr 1759 *Thetis*. Sy.
Kitson, Mary. SW & T Dec 1767 *Neptune*. M.
Kittoe, Grace. R 14 yrs Mar 1757. Co.
Kitto, John. R 14 yrs Aug 1748. Co.
Klinsmith, Lawrence. S Oct 1727-Jun 1728 T Jun 1728 *Elizabeth*. M.
Knafton, Francis. S Apr-Jun 1739. M.
Knapp, James. S Jly-Sep 1754. M.
Knapp, John. SQS Mar TB Apr 1755. Le.
Knapp, John (1757). *See* How. Le.
Knap, Thomas. LC from *Honor* Port York Jan 1721. X.
Knap, Thomas Jr. S Apr 1739. So.
Knapp, Thomas. S & TB to Va Apr 1750. Wi.
Knapton, Robert. S Sep 1754. L.
Knash. *See* Nash.
Kneebone, Joseph. R for Barbados Jly 1684. Co.
Kneebone, Robert. S Aug 1753. Co.
Kneller, William. R 14 yrs Mar TB to Va Apr 1764. Wi.
Knight, Alexander. S s sheep Summer 1742 R 14 yrs Lent 1743. Wa.
Knight, Ann, aged 23, brown hair. LC from *Gilbert* Annapolis May
    1721. X.
Knight, Ann. R & T Dec 1734 *Caesar* LC Va Jly 1735. M.
Knight, Benjamin. S Aug 1726. Do.
Knight, Charles. S Feb T Apr 1768 *Thornton*. M.
Knight, Christopher. Rebel T 1685.
Knight, Deborah. S Feb T Apr 1732 *Patapsco* LC Annapolis Oct
    1732. M.
Knight, Edward. S s horse Summer 1724 R 14 yrs Lent 1725. St.
Knight, Edward. S Summer 1730. G.
Knight, Elizabeth. S Jan T Feb 1723 *Jonathan* but died on passage. M.
Knight, Elizabeth wife of Henry. S Mar 1740. Ha.
Knight, George. S Apr 1748. L.
Knight, George. SQS Jly TB Aug 1754. So.
Knight, George. S Lent R 14 yrs Summer 1761. Bd.
Knight, Humphrey. R for Barbados Jun 1665. M.
Knight, Isaac. R 14 yrs Mar 1737. So.
Knight, James. T Apr 1735 *Patapsco*. K.
Knight, James. S Jun T Nov 1743 *George William*. L.
Knight, James. R Aug 1770. Wi.
Knight, James. S Oct T Dec 1771 *Justitia*. L.
Knight, James. S s rum Summer 1775. Ch.
Knight als Dimmock, John. S Summer R for Barbados Aug 1663. Ht.
Knight, John of Dudley. R for America Feb 1673. Wo.
Knight, John of Wavendon. R for Barbados Mar 1679. Bu.
Knight, John. R for Barbados Dec 1683. M.
Knight, John. Rebel T 1685.
Knight, John (1721). *See* Smith. K.
Knight, John. TB to Md 1728. De.
Knight, John. LC from *Patapsco* Annapolis Jun 1731. X.
Knight, John. S Lent 1732. Y.
Knight, John. S & T Jan 1736 *Dorsetshire* LC Va Sep 1736. L.
Knight, John. S s at Tilehurst Summer 1744. Be.

Knight, John. S & T for life Aug 1752 *Tryal.* L.
Knight, John. S Nov T Dec 1752 *Greyhound.* L.
Knight, John. S s horse Lent R 14 yrs Summer 1763. Be.
Knight, John. AT Summer 1765. Y.
Knight, John. S Mar TB to Va Apr 1766. Wi.
Knight, John. S Dec 1768 T Jan 1769 *Thornton.* M.
Knight, John. S May T Jly 1770 *Scarsdale.* M.
Knight, John. R for life Mar 1771 TB to Va. De.
Knight, John. R for life Lent 1771 TB to Va. Db.
Knight, John. S s money at Horsley Lent 1772. G.
Knight, John. SQS Apr 1773. M.
Knight, Jonathan. S Apr 1734. So.
Knight, Jonathan. SQS Mar 1748. Le.
Knight, Joseph. S at Dover & T Dec 1769 *Justitia.* K.
Knight, Joseph. S Summer 1775. Ch.
Knight, Mary. S Dec 1733 T Jan 1734 *Caesar* LC Va Jly 1734. L.
Knight, Mary. S & T Sep 1766 *Justitia.* M.
Knight, Mary, spinster. S s watch at St. Stephen, Coleman Street, Sep T
    Oct 1768 *Justitia.* L.
Knight, Mary (1772). *See* Murphy. M.
Knight, Nicholas of Penton. R for Barbados Jan 1676. Ha.
Knight, Peter. SWK Jan T Apr 1772 *Thornton.* K.
Knight, Peter. S Aug 1775. Co.
Knight, Richard of Cardington. R for Barbados Mar 1679. Bd.
Knight, Robert. R for Barbados Aug 1670. M.
Knight, Rose. S Sep T Oct 1719 *Susannah & Sarah* LC Annapolis
    Apr 1720. L.
Knight, Ruth. R Apr AT Jun 1690. M.
Knight, Samuel. Rebel T 1685.
Knight, Sarah. S Aug T Sep 1725 *Forward* LC Annapolis Dec 1725. L.
Knight, Thomas of St. Saviour, Southwark. R for Barbados or Jamaica
    Jly 1687. Sy.
Knight, Thomas (1736). *See* Parker. E.
Knight, Thomas of St. George, Southwark. SQS Apr T May 1752
    Lichfield. Sy.
Knight, Thomas. T Apr 1753 *Thames.* K.
Knight als Rabbetts, Thomas. R 14 yrs Jly 1753. Ha.
Knight, Thomas. S s at Whitchurch Lent 1761 T *Atlas* from Bristol
    1761. Sh.
Knight, Thomas. S Feb 1775. L.
Knight, Walter. S Apr-May 1754. M.
Knight, Walter. S s wheat at Beckley Summer 1768. O.
Knight, William of St. Teath, husbandman. R for Barbados Jun
    1669. Co.
Knight, William of Ardington. S Lent 1721 T *Owners Goodwill* LC
    Annapolis Jly 1722. Be.
Knight, William. T Oct 1726 *Forward.* E.
Knight, William. TB to Va from QS 1738. De.
Knight, William. S for shoplifting Summer 1749 R 14 yrs Lent 1750. Li.
Knight, William. S Lent 1763. E.

Knight, William of Hemel Hempstead, paper maker. SQS Jan T Apr 1768 *Thornton*. Ht.

Knightley als Humphreys, Thomas. S s sheets at Kidderminster Summer 1759. Wo.

Knightley, Walter of St. Saviour, Southwark. R for Barbados or Jamaica Feb 1683. Sy.

Knighton, William. S for setting fire to coal stack & R Lent 1775. Db.

Knights, Emanuel. S Summer 1764. Su.

Knights, James. S & R Lent 1764. Nf.

Knights, Sarah. S Lent 1761. E.

Knights, Thomas. S Summer 1757. Ca.

Kniveton als Kniviston, John. S s sugar Feb T Jun 1738 *Forward*. M.

Nock, George. S & T Jan 1739 *Dorsetshire*. M.

Knock, Thomas. S Jun-Dec 1745. M.

Nock, William of Dudley, nailer. R for America Jly 1663. Wo.

Nocks, Catherine. S Oct T 14 yrs Dec 1724 *Rappahannock*. L.

Knocky als Calvert, Sarah. S Summer 1750. Cu.

Knope, George. SW & T Apr 1769 *Tryal*. M.

Knope, Hannah wife of George. S Oct T Dec 1769 *Justitia*. M.

Knotsmell als Shelton, Elizabeth. S Jan 1757. L.

Knott, Andrew. S for killing the King's carp at Cranbourne Park, Windsor, Summer 1773. Be.

Nott, Bridget. R 14 yrs for murder Lent 1721. He.

Knott, George Wilmott. S s horse & R 14 yrs Lent 1774. Sh.

Knott als Cooper als Kay, James. S s mares Lent R 14 yrs Summer 1765. La.

Nott, Joan. S Mar 1746. De.

Knott, John. PT Aug R Dec 1683. M.

Nott, John of Hereford. R for America Jly 1696. He.

Knott, John. SQS Jly TB to Md Nov 1740. So.

Knott, John. S Sep-Oct T Dec 1771 *Justitia*. M.

Knott, Mary. S Sep 1756. M.

Nott, Randall. SW & T Apr 1770 *New Trial*. M.

Knott, Thomas. SQS Oct 1756. M.

Nott, William Sr. T 14 yrs Apr 1759 *Thetis*. E.

Nott, William Jr. T 14 yrs Apr 1759 *Thetis*. E.

Know, John Jr. T Apr 1765 *Ann*. K.

Knowland. *See* Noland.

Knowler, Shelwin. T Jun 1727 *Susanna*. Sy.

Knowles, Alice. S Mar 1763. Ha.

Knowles, Clement. S s iron at Kingswinford Summer 1772. St.

Knowles, Elizabeth. R Dec 1716 T Jan 1717 *Queen Elizabeth* to Jamaica. M.

Knowles, Elizabeth of Debden, spinster. S Summer 1745. E.

Knowles, John. SQS Jan 1733. So.

Nowles, John. S Oct T Dec 1767 *Neptune*. M.

Knowles, Joseph. S s cloth at Leeds Summer 1773. Y.

Knowls, Samuel. TB Apr 1765. Db.

Knowles, Thomas (1688). *See* Garret. M.

Knowles, Thomas. S Apr-May T Jly 1771 *Scarsdale*. M.

Nowels, Thomas. SQS Dec 1773. M.

Knowles, William. R for Barbados Dec 1683. L.

Knowles, William. S City Summer 1725 but indicted for murder Lent AT Summer 1728. Y.

Knowling, John. S Mar 1750 TB to Va. De.

Knowling, Mary of St. John's, spinster. SQS Feb T Jun 1764 *Dolphin*. Sy.

Knox, Sarah. S Summer 1750. Cu.

Knutson, Hans. S Jun T Sep 1767 *Justitia*. M.

Knipe, Samuel. R for America for coining May 1699. Ch.

Knype, Samuel of Broughton. R (Chester Circ) for America Aug 1699. La.

Kockey, John. R 14 yrs Mar 1771. Co.

Kuming/Kummings. *See* Cummings.

Kynaston, Elizabeth. S s at Whitchurch Lent 1766. Sh.

Kynaston, Mary. S Jun T Aug 1769 *Douglas*. L.

L

Laban, Catherine. S Jan T Feb 1719 *Worcester* LC Annapolis Jun 1719. L.

Laban, George. S Jan T Feb 1742 *Industry* to Md. M.

La Bar, Pierre. S Jly 1752. De.

Labeur, Francis. SWK Oct T Dec 1771 *Justitia*. K.

Labree als Bailey als Jackson, Cecily. R for Barbados or Jamaica Aug 1700 & for America May 1704. L.

Lacey, Benjamin of Worcester. S s bacon Lent 1719. Wo.

Lacy, Edward. S Feb T Mar 1730 *Patapsco* LC Annapolis Sep 1730. L.

Lacy, Elizabeth (1755). See Bear. M.

Lacey, James. S Jly T Aug 1721 *Prince Royal* LC Va Nov 1721. M.

Lacey, James. S Summer 1758. Su.

Lacy, John. S Mar 1720. De.

Lacey, John. S & T Jan 1739 *Dorsetshire*. L.

Lacey, John. S Apr 1760. M.

Lacey, Joseph. Rebel T 1685.

Lacey, Joseph. S Nov T Dec 1752 *Greyhound*. L.

Lacey, Martin. S May-Jly 1749. M.

Lacey, Michael. S Apr 1774. L.

Lacey, Philip. Rebel T 1685.

Lacey, Richard. S Aug 1767. Wi.

Lacy, Robert. R for America Jly 1694. i.

Lacy, Robert Sr. S Mar 1742. De.

Lacey, Robert. R 14 yrs Jly 1758 TB to Va 1759. De.

Lacy, Thomas. S Lent R 14 yrs Summer 1734. Be.

Lacey, Thomas. T Apr 1769 *Tryal*. E.

Lacey, William. Rebel T 1685.

Lacey, William. S Mar 1730. Ha.

Lacey, William. R 14 yrs Jly 1754. Ha.

Lacey, William. R 14 yrs Mar 1771. Wi.

Lachenay, Jean Julian. S Jly 1765 TB to Va 1766. De.

Lack, Francis. S s horse Summer 1730 R Lent 1731. Be.

Lack, John. S for killing sheep & R 14 yrs Lent T Apr 1774. No.

Lackey, Catherine. S May T Aug 1718 *Eagle* LC Charles Town Mar 1719. L.

Lackey, John. T Apr 1735 *Patapsco*. Sy.

Lackington, James. R 14 yrs Mar 1737. So.

Lackrow, John of Harwich. R for Barbados or Jamaica Feb 1690. E.

Lacks als Locks, Mary. S Aug T Oct 1724 *Forward* LC Annapolis Jun 1725. M.

Lacon, Edward of St. Helen, Worcester. S s chimney hook Lent 1719. Wo.

Lacon, Sarah (1755). *See* Redshaw. L.

Lacore, Mary. S Apr T Jun 1768 *Tryal*. M.

Lacruce, John. S Jan T Mar 1763 *Neptune*. M.

Ladd, Elizabeth. S & T Sep 1767 *Justitia*. M.

Ladd, James. S Jly TB to Va Aug 1751. Wi.

Ladd, John of Bishopstraw. R (Oxford Circ) for America Jly 1698. Wi.
Ladd, John. R Lent 1773. E.
Lade, Edward. R Jly 1773. M.
Ladle, Michael. S Sep-Oct 1772. M.
Ladlow. *See* Ludlow.
Ladly, William (1774). *See* Ludly. Du.
Ladmore, Thomas. S Feb T Mar 1731 *Patapsco*. L.
Lads, Joseph. R 14 yrs Jly 1752. Wi.
Ladwicke als Lodwick, William. S s gelding at St. Giles, Cambridge, Summer 1768. Ca.
Laffield, Thomas (1741). *See* Founds. So.
Lagdell, George, als Britten, John of Great Cornard. R for Barbados or Jamaica Mar 1697. Su.
Lagden, George of Stanningfield. R for America Feb 1695. Su.
Lagden, Robert. S Sep T Dec 1769 *Justitia*. M.
Laidlaw, David. R 14 yrs Summer 1750. Nl.
Laidler, Adam als Edward. S s horse Summer 1733 R 14 yrs Summer 1734. Nl.
Laidler, Thomas. S s horse & R for life Aug 1767. Nl.
Laird, Christopher. S Feb T May 1767 *Thornton*. L.
Laitor, Benjamin. LC from *Forward* Annapolis Jun 1725. X.
Lake, John. S Jly 1752. De.
Lake, John. S Lent T Sep 1755 *Tryal*. Bu.
Lake, Lucy. S Sep-Oct 1749. M.
Lake, Matthew. SWK Oct 1774. K.
Lake als Lakey, William. S Norwich s from warehouse Summer 1743. Nf.
Lake, William. S Mar 1768 TB to Va. De.
Lakeland, John. SQS May T Jly 1773 *Tayloe* to Va. M.
Lakey, Hannah. R Lent 1775. K.
Lakey, Robert of Bexwell. R for Barbados Aug 1671. Nf.
Lakey, William (1743). *See* Lake. Nf.
Lakin, Francis. S Summer 1774. St.
Lakin, Isabella. S Jan-Feb T Apr 1771 *Thornton*. M.
Lakin, Robert. S Summer 1774. St.
Lakin, Samuel of Stone. R for America Nov 1694. St.
Lally, John. S Dec 1763 T Mar 1764 *Tryal*. M.
Laman. *See* Lemon.
Lambe, Ann (1683). *See* Dukes. L.
Lamb, Ann. S Lent 1766. O.
Lamb, Anthony. S Aug T Oct 1724 *Forward* LC Annapolis Jun 1725. M.
Lamb, Charles. S for counterfeiting at St. Mary, Reading, Summer 1759 R Lent 1760. Be.
Lamb, Hewitt. LC from *Susannah & Sarah* Annapolis Apr 1720. L. or M.
Lamb, Hugh. S s silver tea canisters Lent R 14 yrs Summer 1755. La.
Lamb, James. T May 1736 *Patapsco*. K.
Lamb, James. T Apr 1739 *Forward*. K.
Lamb, James of Bolton. SQS Jly 1770. La.
Lamb, John of St. George, Bloomsbury. S s feather bed Jan-May T Jun 1738 *Forward*. M.

Lamb, John. S for burglary Summer 1740 R 14 yrs Lent 1741 (SP). St.
Lamb, John. S Oct 1747. L.
Lamb, John. S Lent 1748. Ch.
Lamb, John. S Sep-Oct 1772. M.
Lamb, Joseph. R 14 yrs Mar TB to Va May 1770. Wi.
Lamb, Kennet. TB Oct 1719. L.
Lamb, Luke. S 14 yrs for receiving Aug 1759 TB to Va. De.
Lamb, Sarah. S & T Apr 1762 *Neptune*. M.
Lamb, Thomas. S 14 yrs Apr 1728 TB to Va Oct 1729. Le.
Lambe, Walter of Fisherton Anger. R for Barbados Jly 1667. Wi.
Lambe, William. R for Va Mar 1618. M.
Lamball, John. S & T Apr 1766 *Ann*. L.
Lambden, John. T for life Apr 1769 *Tryal*. E.
Lambert, Anne. R Dec 1699 & Aug 1700. M.
Lambert, Anne. S Summer 1730. We.
Lambert, Daniel. S s at Lyng Lent 1772. Nf.
Lambert, Elizabeth of Leckhampton. R for Jamaica, Barbados or
   Bermuda Feb 1686. G.
Lambert, Elizabeth. S Mar 1755. Ha.
Lambert, James. SQS & TB Jan 1774. So.
Lambert, Jane. S Jan-Jun T Jun 1728 *Elizabeth* LC Potomack Aug
   1729. M.
Lambert, Jeremiah als Jemiah of Laindon Hills. SQS Jly 1754. E.
Lambert, John. S Jly-Sep T Sep 1742 *Forward*. M.
Lambert, John. S Mar 1754. Do.
Lambert, Philip of Laindon Hills. SQS Jly 1754. E.
Lambert als Dichfield, Robert. R for Va Jan 1620. M.
Lambert, Robert. S Lent 1735. *Su.
Lambert, Samuel. S City s silver cup Summer 1770. Y.
Lambert, Thomas. R Apr TB for Barbados Jun 1669. L.
Lambert, Thomas. R for Barbados Aug 1679. L.
Lambert, Thomas. S Mar 1730. Ha.
Lambert, Thomas of Great Baddow, blacksmith. SQS Jan T Sep 1758
   Tryal. E.
Lambert, Thomas. S Jan-Feb 1775. M.
Lambert, William. S Lent R 14 yrs Summer 1748 T Jan 1749 *Laura*. Ht.
Lambert, William of Laindon Hills. SQS Jly 1754. E.
Lambeth, Ann. S Sep T Oct 1750 *Rachael*. M.
Lambeth, Elizabeth (1695). *See* Bates, Joanna. M.
Lambeth, Elizabeth. S Feb T Mar 1731 *Patapsco* LC Annapolis Jun
   1731. M.
Lambeth, Ephraim. S s food at Market Drayton Lent 1772. Sh.
Lambeth, John. Died on passage in *Sukey* 1725. X.
Lambeth, Joseph. S & T Jan 1756 *Greyhound*. M.
Lambeth, Joseph. S Feb T Apr 1766 *Ann*. M.
Lambeth, Thomas. SQS Jly 1774. M.
Lamporne, Edward. S Apr T Dec 1734 *Caesar* LC Va Jly 1735. M.
Lambourn, John als Edward of Nettlebed. S s rings Lent 1720. O.
Lambourne, Matthew. S 14 yrs Feb 1730. M.
Lambourne, Robert. PT Dec 1688. M.
Lamdale, Walter. T Jun 1764 *Dolphin*. M.

Lamley, Francis. S & T Oct 1732 *Caesar* to Va. M.

Lammacraft, Richard. TB to Va from QS 1766. De.

Lamon. *See* Lemon.

Lamotte, Isaac. S Feb T Apr 1770 *New Trial*. L.

Lampard, Thomas. S Dec 1755 T Jan 1756 *Greyhound*. L.

Lamprey, John. S s salt at Banbury Lent 1760. O.

Lamprey, Sarah. S & T Jan 1756 *Greyhound*. M.

Lamprey, Thomas (1695). *See* Kennick, William. De.

Lamprey, Thomas. R for life Aug 1766. So.

Lampring, Bartholomew. T Jly 1722 *Alexander*. Sy.

Lamsdall, Adam. T Sep 1751 *Greyhound*. K.

Lancastell, William (1668). *See* Smith. M.

Lancashire, William. S s at Chipping Lambourn Lent 1751. Be.

Lancaster, James. S Mar TB to Va Apr 1758. Wi.

Lancaster, John. SQS Jly TB to Md Oct 1739. So.

Lancaster, Mary. S & T Dec 1771 *Justitia*. M.

Lancaster, Nathaniel. T Apr 1742 *Bond*. Sy.

Lancaster, Richard of Selby. R for Barbados Feb 1673. Y.

Lancaster, William. S Feb T Mar 1731 *Patapsco* LC Annapolis Jun 1731. L.

Landekin, Thomas. S Nov T Dec 1770 *Justitia*. L.

Lander, Eleanor of Hatfield Peveral, spinster. SQS Oct 1760. E.

Lander, George. S Jan T Feb 1742 *Industry* to Md. M.

Lander, John. SWK Jan T Apr 1765 *Ann*. K.

Lander, Mary. S Lent TB Apr 1759. Db.

Lander, Thomas. S Apr 1719. M.

Landman, James. R May T Jly 1722 *Alexander* to Nevis or Jamaica. M.

Landon, Isaac. S Jan-Feb T Apr 1772 *Thornton*. M.

Landwick als Lodowick, William. S May-Jun T Aug 1752 *Tryal*. M.

Lane, Ann. S Feb T Mar 1727 *Rappahannock* to Md. M.

Lane, Benjamin. S Aug T Sep 1725 *Forward* LC Annapolis Dec 1725. L.

Lane, Charles of Curry Rivel. R for Barbados Jly 1679. So.

Lane, Edward. S Aug 1731 TB to Va. De.

Lane, Edward. S Feb T Apr 1741 *Speedwell* or *Mediterranean* to Md. M.

Lane, Edward. S Lent R 14 yrs Summer 1746. St.

Lane, Elisha. S s at Wolverhampton Summer 1764. St.

Lane, Hannah wife of Edward. S Aug T Oct 1726 *Forward* to Va. M.

Lane, Hannah (1742). *See* Adley. M.

Lane, Humfry. S Aug 1732 TB to Va. De.

Lane, James. S Dec 1749-Jan 1750 T Mar 1750 *Tryal*. M.

Lane, Jane. S & T Oct 1729 *Forward* LC Va Jun 1730. M.

Lane, Jane. S & T Oct 1730 *Forward* LC Potomack Jan 1731. M.

Lane, John of Cleese. R for Barbados Jly 1679. So.

Lane, John. S for burglary Lent R Summer 1741 (SP). Be.

Lane, John. R 14 yrs Mar 1742. Co.

Lane, John (2). S Mar 1757. De.

Lane, John. S s at Wellington Lent 1757. Sh.

Lane, Joseph. S Mar 1738. So.

Lane, Joseph. R 14 yrs Jly 1743. Ha.

Lane, Joseph. S s cloth at Penkridge Summer 1765. St.

Lane, Margery. R Sep TB for Barbados Oct 1669. L.

Lane, Mary. R for Barbados Dec 1681. L.

Lane, Richard, als Francis, James of Ilsington, tinner. R for Barbados Jly 1698. De.

Lane, Robert. S Jly 1719 to be T to Va. So.

Lane, Robert. S for firing haystack Lent R 14 yrs Summer 1730. No.

Lane, Robert. R 14 yrs Jly 1734. Do.

Lane, Robert. T Apr 1753 *Thames*. Sy.

Lane, Sarah. T Nov 1759 *Phoenix*. K.

Lane, Sarah wife of Benjamin. S Feb 1761. M.

Lane als Roberts, Sarah, widow. S s paper at St. Dunstan in West Oct 1768 T Jan 1769 *Thornton*. L.

Lane, Thomas. S s horse Summer 1721 R 14 yrs Summer 1722. Li.

Lane, Thomas (1736). *See* Barber. L.

Lane, Thomas. S Lent 1741. Wo.

Lane, Thomas. S 14 yrs Jly 1749. L.

Lane, Thomas. S Sep 1754. L.

Lane, Thomas. S May T Jly 1771 *Scarsdale*. L.

Lane, William. Rebel T 1685.

Lane, William. S Apr T 14 yrs May 1718 *Tryal* LC Charles Town Aug 1718. L.

Lane, William. S Aug T Oct 1723 *Forward* to Va. M.

Lane, William. S s horse brasses at Suckley Lent 1759. Wo.

Lane, William. S Lent 1763. Wa.

Lane, William. S Feb T Apr 1766 *Ann*. M.

Lane, William. S Jan-Feb 1774. M.

Lane, William. S Summer 1774. Sy.

Lanes, Elizabeth. S Feb-Apr 1746. M.

Lang, Christopher. SQS Oct 1750 TB Apr 1751. So.

Lang, George. S Apr 1739. So.

Lang, James. R 14 yrs Aug 1734. De.

Lang, John. S Mar 1735. De.

Lang, John. R 14 yrs Mar 1744. De.

Lang, William. TB to Va from QS 1736. De.

Langcake, Anthony. R 14 yrs Summer 1735. Cu.

Langcake, Mary. S Summer 1761. Cu.

Langdale, Robert (1669). *See* Langdon. M.

Langdell, Robert of Stagsden. R for Barbados Aug 1671. Bd.

Langdon als Langdale, Robert. R for Barbados Sep 1669. M.

Langenfilden, John. S Sep-Oct T Dec 1752 *Greyhound*. M.

Langfitt, Anthony of Greenwich. R for Barbados Aug 1662. K.

Langford, Edward. S & T Dec 1734 *Caesar* LC Va Jly 1735. L.

Langford, Eleanor. S Sep T Dec 1770 *Justitia*. M.

Langford, George. R for Barbados Jan 1664. L.

Langford, Jacob. TB to Newfoundland from QS 1749; with query if this be a proper destination. De.

Langford, Jane of Roxwell. R for Barbados Aug 1662. E.

Langford, Jane. S s at All Saints, Worcester, Lent 1766. Wo.

Langford, John. Rebel T 1685.

Langford als Sivers, John. S Summer 1731. O.

Langford, Thomas of Ellesmere. S Lent 1741. Sh.

Langham, John of St. Botolph, Bishopsgate. S s thread Apr T May 1740
Essex. M.

Langham, Joseph. S & T Sep 1765 *Justitia*. L.

Langham, Randolph of Monks Kirby. R for America Jly 1678. Wa.

Langham, William. S s at Aldridge Lent 1763. St.

Langley, Edward (1743). *See* Roberts, John. M.

Langley, Elizabeth. S Summer 1733 R Summer 1734. Wo.

Langley, Elizabeth. S Lent 1749. K.

Langley als Plaister, George. R for life Jan 1757. M.

Langley, Gilbert. T Jan 1741 *Vernon*. K.

Langley, John. S Lent 1738. Hu.

Langley, John. S s sheep Summer 1742 R 14 yrs Lent 1743. Hu.

Langley, John. S s at Wednesbury Lent 1748. St.

Langley, John. S Lent 1752. Bd.

Langley, John. R Lent 1775. K.

Langley, Lydia. T May 1744 *Justitia*. E.

Langley, Mary. S May T Jun 1764 *Dolphin*. M.

Langley, Titus. S s horse Lent R 14 yrs Summer 1762. St.

Langley, William of Hellingly. R for Barbados or Jamaica Jly 1710. Sx.

Langley, William. S & T Jan 1722 *Gilbert* LC Annapolis Jly 1722. L.

Langley, William of St. George, Southwark. S Lent R 14 yrs Summer T
Oct 1750 *Rachael*. Sy.

Langley, William. S Sep T Dec 1763 *Neptune*. M.

Langley, William. S s mare Lent R 14 yrs Summer 1765. Hu.

Langsden, Mary. S Lent R 14 yrs Summer T Aug 1752 *Tryal*. Sy.

Langshall, Thomas. R for Barbados Jan 1664. L.

Langstaff, Thomas. S Lent R 14 yrs Summer T Oct 1739
Duke of Cumberland. E.

Langston, Henry. S Lent R 14 yrs Summer 1727 T *Elizabeth* LC
Potomack Aug 1729. Be.

Langston, Jacob of St. Saviour, Southwark. SQS Mar 1754. Sy.

Langston, Robert. S Jan T Apr 1762 *Dolphin*. M.

Lankston, William. S Summer 1758 T Apr 1759 *Thetis*. Bu.

Langton, Elizabeth. S Jly T Aug 1721 *Prince Royal* LC Va Nov 1721. L.

Langton, George Jr. of Bourton Shrivenham. R for Barbados Feb
1688. Wi.

Langton, William. R for America Jly 1688. Nt.

Lanham, Henry (1758). *See* Brown, Thomas. M.

Lanham, John. LC from *Patapsco* Annapolis Jun 1731. X.

Lanham, Sarah. S Lent 1753. Su.

Lank, John. R Summer 1771. Li.

Lanman, Philippa. TB to Va from QS 1738. De.

Lansden, William. S s silver caster at St. Nicholas, Gloucester, Lent
1774. G.

Lansdown, Abraham. S s sheep & R Lent 1769. G.

Lanson, Catherine. S Sep 1756. M.

Lanton, John. R Mar 1766. Ha.

Lantwell, Bernard. SQS Sep T Dec 1767 *Neptune*. M.

Lanyon, Mary. R 14 yrs Jly 1749. De.

Lanyon, William. R 14 yrs Jly 1749. De.

Laphan, James. S Jun 1754. L.

Lappington, Elizabeth. S s money Apr T Jly 1770 *Scarsdale*. M.

Larcher, Joseph. S & T Jly 1771 *Scarsdale*. M.

Lardner, John. S s at Churchill Summer 1774. O.

Lardner, Roger. S Apr T May 1718 LC *Tryal* LC Charles Town Aug 1718. L.

Lardner, Thomas. LC from *Forward* Annapolis Jun 1725. X.

Lareman, Elizabeth (1744). *See* Edwards. M.

Laremon als Lorriman, Michael. S Lent R 14 yrs Summer 1746. G.

Laremore, Daniel. S Jan-Feb 1774. M.

Larey. *See* Leary.

Large, Philip. S Aug T Sep 1725 *Forward* LC Annapolis Dec 1725. L.

Large, Thomas. S Summer 1756. K.

Larke, James (1679). *See* Pritchett. M.

Lark, James. T Apr 1742 *Bond*. E.

Larkham, John. Rebel T 1685.

Larkham, Robert, als Reynolds, Josias. R 14 yrs Mar 1755. So.

Larkin, Ann wife of John. S s iron chain at Long Lent 1757. St.

Larkin, Benjamin. S Apr T Oct 1719 *Susannah & Sarah* LC Annapolis Apr 1720. L.

Larkin, Benjamin. T Sep 1742 *Forward*. E.

Larkin, Eleanor wife of John of Whitby, mariner. SQS Thirsk for receiving Oct 1753 TB Sep 1754. Y.

Larkin, John (1723). *See* Clarkin. E.

Larkin, John. S Aug T Sep 1725 *Forward* LC Annapolis Dec 1725. L.

Larkin, Richard. R for Barbados or Jamaica Dec 1699. L.

Larkin, Richard (1700). *See* Lewis. M.

Larkin als Lewis, Richard. R for America May 1704. M.

Larkin, William, a Quaker. R for plantations Jly 1665 (PC). Ht.

Larkman, Edward. S Summer 1748 T Jan 1749 *Laura*. K.

Larkman, Edward. S Lent 1753. Nf.

Larkworthy, James. S & T Jly 1770 *Scarsdale*. M.

Larmer, George. S Feb 1754. M.

Larner, Ann. S Apr 1774. L.

Larner, Elizabeth. S Jly T Nov 1759 *Phoenix*. M.

Laroach, Ann (1700). *See* Peirce. M.

Laroche, Constantine. T Jan 1769 *Thornton*. M.

La Ross, John. S Feb T Apr 1772 *Thornton*. L.

Larramore, John (1723). *See* Latimer. G.

Larrett, Edmund. S Oct 1742 T 14 yrs Apr 1743 *Justitia*. M.

Larrett, Robert. R for Barbados Jly 1674. L.

Larwill, Robert. R 14 yrs Aug 1726. De.

Lary. *See* Leary.

Lash, Joseph. T Sep 1764 *Justitia*. K.

Lashbrook, Abel. S Mar 1720. De.

Lashbrook, William. S Jan T Jun 1738 *Forward* to Md or Va. M.

Lashford, Thomas. S Mar 1764. Ha.

Lashley, Joseph. S Jan-Feb T Apr 1771 *Thornton*. M.

Lasker, Susan. T Apr 1741 *Speedwell* or *Mediterranean*. E.

Lassam, Ann wife of Richard of Farnham. SQS Apr T Jly 1771 *Scarsdale*. Sy.

Laster, Benjamin of Burwell. S Lent 1724. *Ca.

Late, Honor, aged 28, dark. LC from *Gilbert* Annapolis May 1721. X.
Latham, Elizabeth (1689). *See* Browne. L.
Lathom, Margaret (1745). *See* Warburton. La.
Latham, Priscilla. LC from *Forward* Annapolis Jun 1725. X.
Latham, Richard of Stratton Wedmore. R for Barbados Feb 1690. So.
Latham, Thomas. S s at Walsall Summer 1750. St.
Lathbury, Daniel. R for Barbados Jly 1680. M.
Latimer, Andrew. SQS Apr 1774. M.
Lattimer, David, als Johnson, Thomas. R 14 yrs Summer 1719. Cu.
Latimer als Larramore, John. S s at St. James Lent 1723. G.
Lattimore, Martha. R for life for counterfeiting Lent 1775. Sy.
Lattimore, Stephen. S & T Nov 1762 *Prince William*. L.
Latoush, Mary (1701). *See* Dyer. M.
Latter, John. S May T Sep 1758 *Tryal* to Annapolis. M.
Lattin, John. S Lent R 14 yrs Summer 1739. Wa.
Laud, John. S Lent 1765. Hu.
Laud, William (1770). *See* Lord. No.
Laugham, Francis of Great Saxham. R for Barbados Feb 1664. Su.
Laughlan, Nicholas. S & T Jan 1765 *Tryal*. M.
Laughland, Joseph. S May 1727. M.
Laughty, John. R (Norfolk Circ) for America Jly 1663. X.
Launder, John. SQS Dec 1773. M.
Launder, Philip. S Feb-Apr 1745. M.
Launder, Robert of Dudley. R for America Jly 1691. Wo.
Laundress, Sarah. S Sep 1737. M.
Lawndey, Lewis, a Quaker. R for plantations Jly 1665 (PC). Ht.
Lavan, Hannah. S Lent T Jun 1756 *Lyon*. K.
Lavant, Mary. LC from *Elizabeth* Potomack Aug 1729. X.
Laver, John. Rebel T 1685.
Laver, Richard. S Lent 1754. E.
Laver, Thomas. Rebel T 1685.
Laverick, Ralph. S s sheep Summer 1743 R 14 yrs Lent 1744. Du.
Laverack, Robert. S s horse Lent 1732 R 14 yrs Summer 1733. Y.
Laverick, Walter. AT City Summer 1758. Nl.
Lavers, William. S Mar 1775. De.
Laverstick, Alice als Sarah. S Jan T Feb 1733 *Smith* to Md or Va. M.
Lavess, Samuel. S & T Sep 1764 *Justitia*. M.
Lavinder, Elizabeth. T Dec 1758 *The Brothers*. K.
Lavine, John. S s horse & R 14 yrs Lent 1774. Sh.
Law, John (1719). *See* Lowe. L.
Law, John. S Jun T Aug 1769 *Douglas*. M.
Law, Margaret. S Oct 1766 T Jan 1767 *Tryal*. L.
Law, Samuel. S & R 14 yrs Summer 1760. Bd.
Law, Thomas. S Oct T Dec 1769 *Justitia*. L.
Law, William. S Nov T Dec 1770 *Justitia*. L.
Lawe, William. R 14 yrs Lent T Apr 1772 *Thornton*. E.
Law, William. S for cutting cloth from tenters Lent 1775. Y.
Lawder, John of ?Yatem, Scotland. R (Northern Circ) for Barbados Jly 1679. X.
Laws, Ann of Lambeth, spinster. SQS Jan T Apr 1760 *Thetis*. Sy.

Laws, Elizabeth. S Oct T Nov 1728 *Forward* LC Rappahannock Jun 1729. M.

Lawes, Elizabeth wife of William. S Sep 1733 T Jan 1734 *Caesar* LC Va Jly 1734. M.

Laws, George. S Mar 1773. Ha.

Lawes, John (1738). *See* Graham. Cu.

Laws, John. S Apr 1745. L.

Laws, John. T May 1752 *Lichfield*. K.

Laws, Mary. S Jan T Apr 1759 *Thetis*. M.

Laws, Samuel. S & T Jan 1722 *Gilbert* LC Annapolis Jly 1722. L.

Laws, Samuel. R 14 yrs Mar 1767. Ha.

Laws, Sarah. T May 1737 *Forward*. Sy.

Laws, William. S & R Lent 1775. Y.

Lawford, Adam. R 14 yrs Jly TB to Va Sep 1773. Wi.

Lawford, Sarah, widow, als wife of Adam. R Mar TB to Va Apr 1775. Wi.

Lawin als Lawlin, John. S Jan-Jun 1747. M.

Lawler, Catherine (1748). *See* Dennison. M.

Lawler, Elizabeth. S Jly 1718 but died on passage in *Eagle*. L.

Lawlore, John. T Jun 1740 *Essex*. Sy.

Lawler, John. T Apr 1753 *Thames*. Sy.

Lawler als Butler, Margaret. S Feb T Apr 1741 *Speedwell* or *Mediterranean*. M.

Lawless, James. S Jun-Dec 1738 T Jan 1739 *Dorsetshire* to Va. M.

Lawless, Mary wife of John. SQS & T Jan 1767 *Tryal*. Sy.

Lawless, Mary Ann. S May-Jly 1748. M.

Lawley, Francis. S s at Leigh Lent TB Apr 1753. G.

Lawley, Mary. SQS Feb T Apr 1769 *Tryal*. M.

Lawley, William. S s at Monkhopton Lent 1770. Sh.

Lawlin, John (1747). *See* Lawin. M.

Lawlore. *See* Lawler.

Lawman, Peter. R for Barbados or Jamaica Dec 1695 & Jan 1697. M.

Lawn, Dorothy wife of Charles. S Dec 1742 T Apr 1743 *Justitia*. M.

Lawrane, Domingo. SQS Apr T Jun 1764 *Dolphin*. M.

Lawrence, Anthony. R 14 yrs Mar 1721. Ha.

Lawrence, Benjamin (1723). *See* Lyon. M.

Lawrence, Charles. R & TB for Barbados Oct 1667. L.

Lawrence, Diana. R for Barbados or Jamaica Oct 1694. L.

Lawrence, Edward of Graton, Great Bedwin. R for Barbados Feb 1699. Wi.

Lawrence, Elizabeth. S Jly 1730. Co.

Lawrence, Elizabeth (1745). *See* Cane. M.

Lawrence, Elizabeth. S Oct T Dec 1758 *The Brothers*. L.

Lawrence, Elizabeth. SQS Dec 1774. M.

Lawrence, George. PT Summer 1719. St.

Lawrence, George. SQS Jly 1745 TB Apr 1746. So.

Lawrence, Giles. S Lent R 14 yrs Summer 1732. Be.

Lawrence, Hannah of Ealing. S s poultry Feb T May 1736 *Patapsco* to Md. M.

Lawrence, Henry. S Apr 1753. So.

Lawrence, Henry. S Lent 1756. Bu.

Lawrence, Henry. S Jly T Sep 1765 *Justitia*. M.

Lawrence, Jacob. T Apr 1766 *Ann*. E.

Lawrence, James. S & T Apr 1769 *Tryal*. L.

Lawrence, Jane wife of Robert. S & T Dec 1767 *Neptune*. L.

Lawrence, John of Portsmouth. R for Barbados Jly 1678. Ha.

Lawrence, John (2). Rebels T 1685.

Lawrence, John (1698). *See* Mead. G.

Lawrence, John of Graton, Great Bedwin. R for Barbados Feb 1699. Wi.

Lawrence, John. S Apr T 14 yrs May 1718 *Tryal* LC Charles Town Aug 1718. L.

Lawrence, John (1724). *See* Barnett, Robert. L.

Lawrence, John. S Jun 1733 T Jan 1734 *Caesar* LC Va Jly 1734. M.

Lawrence, John. T Apr 1743 *Justitia*. Sy.

Lawrence, John. S Apr 1748. L.

Lawrence, John of Bermondsey. SQS Apr T May 1750 *Lichfield*. Sy.

Lawrence, John. TB to Va from QS 1766. De.

Lawrence, John. R Jun T 14 yrs Aug 1769 *Douglas*. M.

Lawrence, John. SQS Apr 1773. M.

Lawrence, John. SL Jly 1773. Sy.

Lawrence, Margaret. S Feb T 14 yrs Mar 1730 *Patapsco* LC Annapolis Sep 1730. M.

Lawrence, Martha. S Lent R 14 yrs Summer T Sep 1751 *Greyhound*. Ht.

Lawrence, Mary. S Jan 1757. M.

Lawrence, Mary. S s at Luton Lent 1770. Bd.

Lawrence, Nathaniel. S Sep 1747. L.

Lawrence, Philip. S Jan-Jun T Jun 1728 *Elizabeth* LC Potomack Aug 1729. L.

Lawrence, Rebecca (1746). *See* Woolley. M.

Lawrence, Richard. R 14 yrs Jly 1747. Ha.

Lawrence, Robert of Bromham, butcher. R for Barbados Jly 1667. Wi.

Lawrence, Samuel. R for America Jly 1683. Ru.

Lawrence, Samuel. Rebel T 1685.

Lawrence, Sarah wife of Thomas. S & T Oct 1730 *Forward* LC Potomack Jan 1731. M.

Lawrence, Thomas of Luppitt. R for Barbados Jly 1672. De.

Lawrence, Thomas. Rebel T 1685.

Lawrence, Thomas. S Jly T Sep 1767 *Justitia*. M.

Lawrence als Moulton, William of Huntingdon. R for Jamaica, Barbados or Bermuda Feb 1686. St.

Lawrence, William. S May T Jun 1726 *Loyal Margaret* LC Annapolis Oct 1726. M.

Lawrence, William. S Mar 1730. So.

Lawrence, William. T May 1737 *Forward*. E.

Lawrence, William. S 14 yrs Oct 1744-Jan 1745. M.

Lawrence, William. S Dec 1749-Jan 1750 T Mar 1750 *Tryal*. M.

Lawrence, William. S s from warehouse at Kidderminster Lent 1765. Wo.

Lawrence, William. T 14 yrs Apr 1768 *Thornton*. K.

Lawrence, William. S s handkerchief at St. Peter, Cornhill, Oct 1768 T Jan 1769 *Thornton*. L.

Lawrence, William. S Mar TB to Va Apr 1771. Wi.

Lawrence, William. S s sheep & R 14 yrs Summer 1774. Sh.
Lawrenceson, John. S Mar 1738. So.
Lawrett, Mary. S Jun-Dec 1745. M.
Lawson, Ann of St. Giles in Fields. S s sheet May 1736. M.
Lawson, Ann. S Aug 1757 TB to Va 1758. De.
Lawson, Katherine. R & T Dec 1716 *Lewis* to Jamaica. M.
Lawson, Elizabeth. T May 1751 *Tryal*. Sy.
Lawson, Elizabeth wife of Robert. S at Hull Summer 1768. Y.
Lawson, George. S for highway robbery Lent R 14 yrs Summer 1755 T
    1756. Bd.
Lawson, Isabella. S Jan-Feb 1773. M.
Lawson, James. S s at St. Nicholas, Worcester, Lent 1753. Wo.
Lawsen, John. R for Barbados Jun 1675. Y.
Lawson, John of Huntingdon. R for America Jly 1683. Hu.
Lawson, John. S Oct-Dec 1750. M.
Lawson, John. S 14 yrs for breaking & entering TB Nov 1762. Y.
Lawson, Mary. R (Western Circ) for America Jly 1700. L.
Lawson, Mary. S for housebreaking Lent R 14 yrs & TB Dec 1731. Bd.
Lawson, Matthew. SQS Oct T Dec 1753 *Whiteing*. M.
Lawson, Ralph. SQS Dec 1773. M.
Lawson, Samuel. S Apr T Jly 1770 *Scarsdale*. M.
Lawson als Turner, Sara. S Aug T 14 yrs Oct 1726 *Forward*. L.
Lawson, William. S Sep T Dec 1767 *Neptune*. L.
Lawton, George of Saddleworth, Yorks, clothworker. SQS Apr 1743. La.
Lawton, Moses. S & T Jan 1765 *Tryal*. M.
Lawton, Thomas. S Jan T Feb 1724 *Anne* to Carolina. M.
Lax, Ann (1731). *See* Todd. L.
Lax, George. S & T May 1744 *Justitia*. L.
Laxon, Edmond, aged 22, dark. LC from *Gilbert* Annapolis May
    1721. X.
Laxton, Sarah. S & T 14 yrs Dec 1740 *Vernon*. L.
Laycock, Martha wife of Richard. S Apr-Jun 1739. M.
Laycock, Matthew of Burrill. SQS Thirsk s at Bedale etc. Apr T Oct
    1723 *Forward* to Va. Y.
Laycock, Richard. S Jan T 14 yrs Apr 1741 *Speedwell*. L.
Laydall, James (1677). *See* Tivey. M.
Laye, George (1697). *See* Lee. Bu.
Layfield, John. S Apr T May 1720 *Honor* LC Port York Jan 1721. L.
Layfield, William (1741). *See* Found. So.
Layforton, Anthony. T Mar 1764 *Tryal*. M.
Layston, Elizabeth. S & T Oct 1732 *Caesar* to Va. M.
Layt als Johnson, John. S s mare Summer 1766 R 14 yrs Lent 1767. Su.
Layton, Abraham. T May 1744 *Justitia*. K.
Leighton, Agnes. S Jan T Feb 1726 *Supply* LC Annapolis May 1726. M.
Leighton, James. S s iron at Houghton cum Wyton Lent 1775. Hu.
Leighton, John of Newcastle upon Tyne. R for Barbados Jly 1688. Nl.
Layton, Paul (1724). *See* Eaton. M.
Layton, Paul. S May T Jun 1727 *Susanna* to Va. M.
Leighton, Richard. S Jan T Feb 1726 *Supply* LC Annapolis May
    1726. M.
Layton, Sarah. R for Barbados Aug 1679. L.

Layton, Thomas of Hornchurch. R for Barbados or Jamaica Mar 1694. E.

Lazarus, Isaac. S Feb 1773. L.

Lazarus, Isaac. S s silver spoons at Botesdale Summer 1773. Su.

Lazell, John. S Summer 1773. E.

Lazenby, Thomas. S Oct T Dec 1724 *Rappahannock* to Va. M.

Lazenby, William. S s silver tankard at Sproatley Lent 1772. Y.

Leach. *See* Leech.

Leachford, John. SQS s sheep & T Oct 1765. Bd.

Leacock, David (1770). *See* Allanson. Y.

Leadbeater, Ann. S Aug T Oct 1724 *Forward* LC Annapolis Jun 1725. L.

Leadbeater, Edward. S s gelding Summer 1739 R 14 yrs Lent 1740. Bu.

Leadbeter, John of Manchester. SQS Oct 1769. La.

Leadbeter, Ralph. R for America Mar 1690. Nt.

Leadbeater, William. S for highway robbery Lent R 14 yrs Summer 1739. O.

Leader, Alice. S & T Oct 1730 *Forward* LC Potomack Jan 1731. M.

Leeder, Charles. S Lent R 14 yrs Summer 1752. Nf.

Leader, William. SQS Sep 1677 & T by *Duke of York* with his consent. M.

Leake, James. LC from *Supply* Annapolis May 1726. X.

Leake, John. SQS Dec 1773. M.

Leeke, Thomas, silversmith. R (Western Circ) for plantations Jan 1676. L.

Leeke, William (1764). *See* Jackson, Thomas. Nt.

Leaker, John. Rebel T 1685.

Leakey, John of Wedmore. R for Barbados Feb 1701. So.

Leaky, John. S s from stable Lent R 14 yrs Summer 1739. Wa.

Leeman als Smith, John. S Dec 1750. L.

Leaman, Robert als Robin. S Jly 1760 TB to Va 1761. De.

Leaman, William. TB to Va from QS 1768. De.

Lean, Richard. R 14 yrs Jly 1733. De.

Leane, Robert. S Jly 1718 to be T to Va. Co.

Leper, Matthew. S s mare & R 14 yrs Lent 1736. Nf.

Leer, Abraham. S May-Jly 1774. M.

Leer, Ann. S Mar 1763. Ha.

Lear, Joseph. S Mar 1737. Wi.

Lear, William. S s at Colwich Lent 1729. St.

Leary, Cornelius of Bristol. R 14 yrs for highway robbery Apr 1774. G.

Larey, Jeremiah. S Apr-Jun T Jly 1772 *Tayloe*. M.

Leary, John. S 14 yrs Oct 1772. L.

Leary, Margaret. S Sep T Nov 1762 *Prince William*. M.

Lary, Mary. S Jun T Aug 1769 *Douglas*. L.

Leath, John. T Jly 1724 *Robert*. K.

Leith, John. S Oct T Dec 1767 *Neptune*. M.

Leather, John. S & T Oct 1730 *Forward* LC Potomack Jan 1731. L.

Letherby, Ann. S Apr 1767. So.

Leatherby, Richard. S Jly 1764. Ha.

Leatherstone, Hannah. S Oct 1756. L.

Leathorn, James. S Mar 1733. De.

Leavers, Patience. S Sep T Oct 1750 *Rachael*. M.

Leck, Thomas. R 14 yrs Summer TB Aug 1752. Y.

Le Count, David. S Aug T Sep 1725 *Forward* LC Annapolis Dec 1725. M.

Ledger, John. R 14 yrs Summer 1757. Y.

Ledger, John. S Summer 1757 R 14 yrs Lent 1758. Be.

Ledger, John. S s at Albury Lent 1758. O.

Ledger, Newberry. R 14 yrs Summer T Oct 1739 *Duke of Cumberland*. Sy.

Ledger, Thomas. S Lent 1745. Sy.

Ledgett, Joseph. S Jan T Feb 1724 *Anne* to Carolina. M.

Ledley, John. S Summer 1754 R 14 yrs Lent 1755. Li.

Ledman als Powett, Mary, als wife of Joseph Hudson. S Jun-Dec 1738 T Jan 1739 *Dorsetshire*. M.

Lee, Ann (1742). *See* Holland. M.

Lee, Anne. T Apr 1743 *Justitia*. K.

Lee, Ann (1770). *See* Inch. E.

Lee als Levy, Ann. S Apr-May 1775. M.

Lee, Benjamin of Saulby. R for Barbados Jun 1692. Y.

Lee, Benjamin of St. John's. SQS Jan T Apr 1753 *Thames*. Sy.

Lee, Charles. S 14 yrs for receiving goods stolen by his wife Mary Lent 1765. Nf.

Lee, Daniel. S & T Sep 1757 *Thetis*. M.

Lee als Twyford, Downs. T Sep 1730 *Smith*. Sy.

Lee, Edmond of St. Andrew Holborn. S s coat Jan-May T Jun 1738 *Forward*. M.

Leigh, Edward. S Jan T Feb 1726 *Supply* LC Annapolis May 1726. M.

Lea, Edward. S Summer 1746 R 14 yrs Lent 1747. Sh.

Lee, Edward. S Lent R 14 yrs Summer 1750. Bu.

Lee, Edward. S Jan T Mar 1764 *Tryal*. L.

Lee, Elizabeth. R for Barbados Jan 1693. M.

Lee, Elizabeth, aged 23, dark. LC from *Gilbert* Annapolis May 1721. X.

Lee, Elizabeth. S May 1733. M.

Lee, Ferdinando. S s shoulder of mutton Apr T Jun 1742 *Bladon*. L.

Lee, Francis. PT Jan 1700. M.

Lee, George. Rebel T 1685.

Lee als Laye, George of Amersham. R for Barbados or Jamaica Mar 1697. Bu.

Lee, Gertrude. TB to Va from QS 1740. De.

Lee, Hannah. S Lent 1758. Le.

Lee, James of Milton by Gravesend. R for Barbados Aug 1668 (Newgate). K.

Lee, James. S Jun 1754. L.

Lee, James. SQS Devizes Jly TB to Va Aug 1766. Wi.

Lee, James of Salford. SQS Oct 1766. La.

Lee, James. S May T Jly 1770 *Scarsdale*. M.

Leigh, John. R (Home Circ) Aug 1664. X.

Lee, John of Aylesbury. R for Barbados Aug 1671. Bu.

Lee, John of Stratford Langthorne. R for Barbados or Jamaica Mar 1682 & Feb 1683. E.

Lee, John of Saulby. R for Barbados Jun 1692. Y.

Lee, John. R Dec 1699 & Aug 1700. M.

Lee, John of Farnham. R for America Jly 1700. Sy.
Lee, John. S Mar 1719 TB 14 yrs May 1721. Le.
Lee als Lees, John. S & T Jan 1722 *Gilbert* but died on passage. M.
Leigh, John of Manchester, linen weaver. SQS Oct 1743. La.
Lee, John (1746). *See* Harris. Mo.
Lee, John. S Jly 1749. L.
Lee, John. S Jly T Sep 1751 *Greyhound*. L.
Lee, John. S Summer 1754. Y.
Lee, John. S Mar 1759. Wi.
Lee, John. S Oct T Nov 1759 *Phoenix*. L.
Lee, John. S Feb T Mar 1764 *Tryal*. M.
Lee, John. R 14 yrs Mar 1764. Ha.
Lee als White als Young, John of Croydon. SQS May T Jun 1764
    Dolphin. Sy.
Lea, John. S Lent T Apr 1766 *Ann*. Bu.
Lee, John. T 14 yrs May 1767 *Thornton*. K.
Leay als Lee, Joseph. S s buckles at St. Sepulchre Oct 1768 T Jan 1769
    Thornton. L.
Lee, John of Gravely. SQS s whip Apr T Dec 1770 *Justitia*. Ht.
Lee, John. S Jan-Feb 1774. M.
Lee, Joseph. S Aug T Sep 1725 *Forward* LC Annapolis Dec 1725. M.
Lee, Joseph of Rochdale. SQS Jan 1744. La.
Lee, Joseph. S & T Jly 1770 *Scarsdale*. L.
Lee, Langley. PT Jan R Aug 1700
Lee, Lewis. S Feb T Mar 1731 *Patapsco* LC Annapolis Jun 1731. L.
Lee, Margaret wife of Samuel. S 14 yrs for receiving goods stolen at
    Bridgenorth Summer 1755. Sh.
Lee, Martha. S May T Jun 1756 *Lyon*. L.
Lee, Mary. R for Barbados May 1676. M.
Leighe, Mary of Glovers Stone. R for Barbados Mar 1678. Ch.
Lee, Mary. S Feb T Mar 1729 *Patapsco* LC Annapolis Dec 1729. M.
Lee, Mary. SQS & TB Jly 1735. So.
Lee als Branch, Mary. S Aug 1746. De.
Lee, Mary wife of Charles *(qv)*. S Lent 1765. Nf.
Leigh, Mathew. R 10 yrs Apr 1741. So.
Lee, Matthew. S s cow at Rotherham Lent R 14 yrs Summer 1765. Y.
Lee, Paul of Luton. S s petticoat Lent 1727. *Bd.
Lee, Paul. T Jan 1736 *Dorsetshire*. Ht.
Lee, Peter of Thetford. R for America Feb 1684. Nf.
Lee, Peter. S Oct 1744-Jan 1745. M.
Lee, Philip. T Jan 1734 *Caesar* LC Va Jly 1734. E.
Lee, Rebecca. S & T Dec 1758 *The Brothers*. M.
Lee, Rebecca. S Summer 1769. Li.
Leigh, Richard of Black Notley. R for Barbados or Jamaica Jly 1712. E.
Leigh als Lee, Richard. R 14 yrs Aug 1728. So.
Lee, Richard. S Mar 1738. De.
Lee, Richard. TB to Va 1751. De.
Ley, Robert. SQS Jly TB Sep 1772. So.
Lee, Samuel. R (Western Circ) for Barbados Feb 1692. L.
Lee, Sarah. S Feb-Apr T Jun 1756 *Lyon*. M.
Lee, Sarah. T 14 yrs May 1767 *Thornton*. K.

Lee, Simon. R for Barbados Mar 1681. L.
Lee, Susanna. S Aug T Oct 1724 *Forward* LC Annapolis Jun 1725. M.
Lee, Susannah wife of Thomas. S 14 yrs for receiving Lent 1775. Li.
Lee, Thomas. R for Barbados or Jamaica Dec 1689. M.
Lee als Perry, Thomas. R 14 yrs Jly 1728. Ha.
Lee, Thomas. T Oct 1732 *Caesar*. Sy.
Lee, Thomas. S s at Standish Lent 1736 R 14 yrs Summer TB Oct 1737. G.
Lea, Thomas. S Lent 1742. Sh.
Lee, Thomas. S Summer 1756 R 14 yrs Lent 1757. St.
Lee, Thomas. S Jly 1757. Ha.
Lee, Thomas. T 14 yrs Nov 1762 *Prince William*. K.
Lee, Thomas. Ss handkerchief at Whitchurch Summer 1765. Sh.
Lee, Thomas. S Summer T Sep 1770. Wa.
Lee, Thomas of St. Martin in Fields. SW Oct 1774. M.
Leigh, William. Rebel T 1685.
Lee, William of Stanton. R (Western Circ) for America Jly 1700. G.
Lee, William. LC from *Forward* Rappahannock May 1728. X.
Lee, William. T Apr 1739 *Forward*. Sy.
Lee, William. S Jly T Oct 1741 *Sea Horse* to Va. M.
Lee, William. AT Lent 1748. Y.
Leigh, William. S Summer 1748 T Jan 1749 *Laura*. E.
Lee, William. S s leather pumps at Kinver Lent 1749. St.
Lee, William. S Apr T May 1751 *Tryal*. L.
Lee als Leeworthy, William. S May T Jly 1753 *Tryal*; committed Jun 1758 for returning before expiry of term but acquitted because he was brought to England for court martial & ordered to complete his term. M.
Lee, William. S Oct T Dec 1758 *The Brothers*. L.
Lee, William. S Oct 1774. L.
Lee, William. S Oct 1775. M.
Leech, Andrew. SQS & T Jly 1772 *Tayloe*. M.
Leech, Anne. S Aug T Oct 1723 *Forward* to Va. M.
Leach, Edmund of Manchester, woollen weaver. SQS Nov 1755. La.
Leach, George (1697). *See* Hunt. Su.
Leach, James. SQS Jan 1755. Ha.
Leech, John. R for Jamaica Aug 1661. M.
Leach, John Jr. R for Barbados or Jamaica May 1691. L.
Leach, John of Witham. R for Barbados or Jamaica Mar 1698. E.
Leach, John. SQS Jly 1732. So.
Leech, John. S s sheep Summer 1739. He.
Leech, John. S Summer 1751 R 14 yrs Lent 1752. La.
Leech, John. SQS May T Aug 1769 *Douglas*. M.
Leach, John of Bury, weaver. S s horse & R Summer 1774. La.
Leach, Joseph. S Jan T 14 yrs Feb 1744 *Neptune* to Md. M.
Leach, Lawrence. S s geldings & R 14 yrs Lent 1743. Bd.
Leach, Richard. R Jly T for life Sep 1767 *Justitia*. M.
Leach, Robert of Crediton, weaver. R for Barbados Jly 1667. De.
Leach, Roger. S Summer 1754 R 14 yrs Lent T May 1755 *Rose*. E.
Leach, Simon. S Mar 1725. De.
Leach, Solomon. S Lent T Apr 1771. Wa.

Leech, Thomas. R for Barbados Oct 1673. M.

Leedam, Jonathan (1735). *See* Leetham. Y.

Leeds, Ann. T Apr 1725 *Sukey* LC Md Sep 1725. K.

Leely, Robert. R 14 yrs Aug 1731. So.

Leek. *See* Leak.

Leeman. *See* Leaman.

Leer. *See* Lear.

Lees, George. S s hen at Walsall Lent 1759. St.

Lees, George. S & T Dec 1767 *Neptune*. L.

Lees, George of Manchester. SQS Oct 1773. La.

Lees als Healey als Massey, James of Stretford. S for assault with intent to rob Lent 1756. La.

Lees, Jane wife of William. S Lent R 14 yrs Summer 1747. G.

Lease als Gamlin, John. Rebel T 1685.

Lees, John. S Lent R 14 yrs Summer 1721. St.

Lees, John (1722). *See* Lee. M.

Lees, John. T Jly 1723 *Alexander* LC Md Sep 1723. E.

Lees, John als William. S Lent R 14 yrs Summer 1756. St.

Lees als Hippworth, Mary. S Aug T Oct 1724 *Forward* to Md. M.

Lees, Mary of Manchester, spinster. SQS Apr 1766. La.

Lees, Thomas of Caverswall, tailor. R for America Mar 1701. St.

Lees, Thomas. S Mar 1741. Ha.

Lees, William. S Lent R Summer TB Sep 1735. Nt.

Leeson, Elizabeth. S Apr 1749. L.

Leeson, Esther. S Oct 1773. L.

Leeson, John. T Apr 1769 *Tryal*. K.

Leet, William. S Mar 1756. Ha.

Leetham als Leedam, Jonathan. R 14 yrs Summer 1735. Y.

Leeves, Samuel. R 14 yrs Mar 1775. Do.

Leeworthy, William (1758). *See* Lee. M.

Lefebure, Joshua of Maidstone. S Summer T Oct 1739 *Duke of Cumberland*. K.

Lefevre, Louis. S & T May 1736 *Patapsco* to Md. M.

Lefever, Mary. S & T Apr 1733 *Patapsco* LC Annapolis Nov 1733. M.

Lefoe, Daniel. S & T Oct 1732 *Caesar* to Va. M.

Legate, Henry. S s mare at Bunwell & R Lent 1773. Nf.

Legate als Legget, John. S Feb T Apr 1739 *Forward*. L.

Legay, Louis. S Dec 1774. M.

Leg, Catherine. SQS Jly TB Sep 1772. So.

Legg, Grace. R 14 yrs Aug 1732 TB to Va. De.

Legg, James. S Aug T Oct 1726 *Forward*. L.

Legg, James. R 14 yrs Summer 1730 AT Summer 1732. Nl.

Legg, Jane. S Sep 1735 T Jan 1736 *Dorsetshire* LC Va Sep 1736. M.

Legg, John. S & T Dec 1740 *Vernon*. L.

Legg, Margaret. S for cutting cloth from tenters Lent 1721. Mo.

Legg, Richard. S s at Abergavenny Lent 1728. Mo.

Legg, Solomon. AT from QS Lent 1769. G.

Legg, Thomas. R 14 yrs Jly 1724. Ha.

Legg, William. R 14 yrs Jly 1718 to be T to Va. Do.

Leggatt, Benjamin. S s at St. Giles, Reading, Lent 1757. Be.

Leggett, John. T Apr 1725 *Sukey* but died on passage. Sx.

Legget, John (1739). *See* Legate. L.

Leggatt, Richard of Gleham. R for Barbados or Jamaica Mar 1682. K.

Leggatt, Thomas. S Lent 1745. Sx.

Leggatt, William. S s calf Summer 1742 R 14 yrs Lent 1743. Be.

Legier, Gabriel John. S & TB to Va Mar 1760. Wi.

Lego, Charles. S Apr T May 1752 *Lichfield*. L.

Legrand, John Rodolph. S Jan T Apr 1770 *New Trial*. M.

Le Grand, Louis. S Feb T Mar 1763 *Neptune*. M.

Le Grew, Jane (1732). *See* Grew. M.

Legross, John. S Sep-Oct 1748 T Jan 1749 *Laura*. M.

Le Groves, William. S & T Jly 1771 *Scarsdale*. L.

Lehook, Mary. S & T Dec 1758 *The Brothers*. M.

Lester, Elizabeth of St. Saviour, Southwark. S Summer T Oct 1750
   Rachael. Sy.

Leicester, John. S & T Oct 1732 *Caesar* to Va. M.

Leister, John. S s from bleaching croft Lent 1751. La.

Lester, John. S Mar 1756 TB to Va 1757. De.

Lester, Thomas. SQS Apr TB Sep 1773. So.

Leicester, William of Cobham. R for Barbados or Jamaica Jun 1699. K.

Leidenburgh, Aaron. S Apr 1742. So.

Leigh. *See* Lee.

Leighton. *See* Layton.

Leipman, Levi. S Nov T Dec 1763 *Neptune*. L.

Leith. *See* Leath.

Lelleongreen, Frederick. S Jan-Feb 1774. M.

Lem, John. S s at Wolverhampton Lent 1764. St.

Lemange, Peter of St. Martin in Fields. SW Oct 1766 T Jan 1767
   Tryal. M.

Lemocks, Elizabeth. S Jun-Dec 1738 T Jan 1739 *Dorsetshire* to Va. M.

Lemon, David. S Apr T Jly 1770 *Scarsdale*. L.

Lemon, Elizabeth. R for Jamaica Aug 1661. M.

Lemon, Elizabeth. S & T May 1736 *Patapsco*. L.

Lamon, George. S Aug 1739. So.

Leman, Henry. S Jly 1735 T Jan 1736 *Dorsetshire* LC Va Sep 1736. M.

Lemon, John. S Aug T Sep 1725 *Forward* LC Annapolis Dec 1725. L.

Lemmon, Nicholas of Long Leadenham. R for America Jly 1678. Li.

Lemon als Fyson, Thomas. S Lent R 14 yrs Summer 1747. E.

Laman, William. T Oct 1732 *Caesar*. Ht.

Lemon, William. T Aug 1741 *Sally*. Sy.

Lendon, John. TB to Va from QS 1768. De.

Lennigan, John. R 14 yrs Jly 1763 TB to Va. De.

Lennon, John (1772). *See* Page. Ha.

Lenox als Smith, Mary. S Jly 1724. Ha.

Lennox, William. R Sep 1671 AT Jly 1672. M.

Lenorchan, Ann (1762). *See* Clark. M.

Lent, Thomas. S Lent T Apr 1760 *Thetis*. E.

Lenthal, Samuel. S Apr 1749. L.

Lenthall, Thomas. SQS & TB May 1766. Db.

Lenton, Martha. S Lent 1763. No.

Leo, John William. S Sep-Oct 1772. M.

Leonard, Elizabeth. S May-Jly 1749. M.

Lennard, James. SQS Apr T Sep 1757 *Thetis*. M.
Lenard, John of Lambeth. SQS Jan 1773. Sy.
Lennard, Margaret. R Lent T 14 yrs May 1752 *Lichfield*. Sy.
Leonard, William. S s brass boiler Summer TB Sep 1753. G.
Leonard, William. S Jan-Feb 1774. M.
Leper. *See* Leaper.
Leppard, James. S Dec 1745. L.
Leppingwell, James. S Sep-Oct T Dec 1771 *Justitia*. M.
Lequint, Lewis. R for life Dec 1774. M.
Lermont, John. R 14 yrs Summer 1754. Cu.
Lermount, John. S & T Sep 1766 *Justitia*. M.
Lerosse, Ludovic. R for Barbados or Jamaica Oct 1694. L.
Lervin, William. S May T Jun 1764 *Dolphin*. M.
Lesborough, Richard. S Apr-May T May 1741 *Catherine & Elizabeth*. M.
Lescall, William. SQS Jan 1771. M.
Lescallie, William. S Jan 1775. M.
Lescallott, William. T Apr 1771 *Thornton*. M.
Lesley, Charles. S Summer 1728. Y.
Lestadau, John. S Jan T Mar 1764 *Tryal*. L.
Lester. *See* Leicester.
Lestrange, Thomas. S Jan T Feb 1726 *Supply* LC Annapolis May 1726. M.
Lethbridge, William. S Aug 1739. De.
Letherby. *See* Leatherby.
Letherington, Elizabeth. S & T Dec 1734 *Caesar* LC Va Jly 1735. L.
Letherland, George. S Jan T Apr 1741 *Speedwell* or *Mediterranean*. M.
Letherland, Thomas of Northampton. R for America Jly 1682. No.
Letter, Elizabeth. S Oct 1757 T Mar 1758 *Dragon*. M.
Letteridge, Samuel. S Jun T Sep 1767 *Justitia*. M.
Letts, Elizabeth. S Jun-Dec 1738 T Jan 1739 *Dorsetshire* to Va. M.
Leuty. *See* Lewty.
Le Valley, John. S Jly 1748. L.
Leve, Daniel. S Sep-Dec 1755 T Jan 1756 *Greyhound*. M.
Leven, Edward. T Nov 1743 *George William*. K.
Leaver, Benjamin. S Lent T May 1755 *Rose*. K.
Lever, James. S Sep-Oct 1772. M.
Lever, James. S Jan-Feb 1773. M.
Lever, John of Darwen. SQS Jly 1756. La.
Lever, John of Halliwell, weaver. SQS Oct 1758. La.
Lever, John. S Lent 1767. La.
Lever, Samuel. S for breaking & entering at Richmond Lent TB Aug 1758. Y.
Lever, Thomas of Aughton. S s horse & R Summer 1771. La.
Leverit, James. S Summer T Sep 1757 *Thetis*. Bu.
Leverett, James. S 14 yrs Sep-Oct 1773. M.
Leverett, John. R for America Jly 1686. No.
Leveritt, John. S Apr-May T May 1741 *Catherine & Elizabeth* to Md. M.
Leveridge, John. S Apr-May T 14 yrs Jly 1771 *Scarsdale*. M.
Leveridge, Mary. S Mar 1759. Do.

Leversedge, Allegan. Rebel T 1685.

Leviston, Ann (1762). *See* Wade. M.

Leveston, John. S Summer 1732. Y.

Leveston als Liveston, William of Alnwick. R Mar 1710. Nl.

Levett, John of Newington. R for Barbados Aug 1662. Sy.

Levett, William. S Summer 1735. Nf.

Levit, William. T 14 yrs Oct 1768 *Justitia*. Ht.

Levings, Edward. T Nov 1759 *Phoenix*. Ht.

Levingston. *See* Livingston.

Levins, Isaac. T Jun 1764 *Dolphin*. M.

Levoyer als Lovyer, Daniel. S Sep-Oct T Dec 1752 *Greyhound*. M.

Levy, Abraham. S & T Oct 1730 *Forward* LC Potomack Jan 1731. L.

Levy, Abraham. S Lent T Apr 1772 *Thornton*. Sy.

Levy, Ann (1775). *See* Lee. M.

Levy, Brina. S May T Nov 1762 *Prince William*. M.

Levi, David. S & T Jun 1756 *Lyon*. L.

Levy, Elias. S & T Dec 1771 *Justitia*. L.

Levi, Emanuel. SQS & T Dec 1769 *Justitia*. M.

Levy, Garret. S & T Apr 1753 *Thames*. L.

Levy, Henry. SQS & T Jan 1766 *Tryal*. M.

Levy, Henry. S s hat at St. Botolph, Bishopsgate, Jan T Apr 1768 *Thornton*. L.

Levy, Henry. S & T Dec 1771 *Justitia*. L.

Levi, Hyam. S May T Jun 1756 *Lyon*. L.

Levi, Israel. S Oct 1756. L.

Levi, Jacob. S Jan T Mar 1764 *Tryal*. L.

Levy, Jacob. S May-Jly 1773. M.

Levi, Jeremiah. S Apr 1748. L.

Levi, John. SQS Feb T Apr 1759 *Thetis*. M.

Levy, Judah. S & T Dec 1771 *Justitia*. L.

Levy, Lazarus. S Apr T Jly 1770 *Scarsdale*. L.

Levy, Michael. S May T Jun 1764 *Dolphin*. L.

Levy, Mordecai. SQS Sep 1774. M.

Levy, Moses Simon. S Apr-May T Jly 1771 *Scarsdale*. M.

Levy, Samuel. S May T Aug 1769 *Douglas*. M.

Levy, Solomon. S & T Apr 1766 *Ann*. L.

Levi, Solomon. S May T Jly 1771 *Scarsdale*. L.

Levy, Solomon. S 14 yrs Sep-Oct 1772. M.

Lewen. *See* Lewin.

Lewent als Archer, Mary. S Jan-Jun T Jun 1728 *Elizabeth* to Md or Va. M.

Lewer als Owen, Catherine. S & T Oct 1733 *Forward* LC Potomack Jan 1731. L.

Lewes. *See* Lewis.

Lewen, Abraham. S Aug T Oct 1726 *Forward* to Va. M.

Lewen, John. S & T Oct 1730 *Forward* LC Potomack Jan 1731. L.

Lewen, Joseph. T Jun 1740 *Essex*. E.

Lewin, Mary. T Apr 1733 *Patapsco* LC Md Nov 1733. Sy.

Lewin, Peter. S Sep 1775. M.

Lewin, Ralph. S s sheep & R Lent 1772. Li.

Luing, Susannah. Died on passage in *Susannah & Sarah* 1720.
  L. or M.
Lewin, Susanna. S Summer 1745. Sy.
Lewen, William. S Dec 1746. L.
Lewin, William. S Apr 1761. L.
Lewes, Abraham. S Jly 1773. L.
Lewis, Anne. S Jan T Feb 1726 *Supply* LC Annapolis May 1726. M.
Lewis, Anne. S Aug T Sep 1727 *Forward* LC Rappahannock May
  1728. L.
Lewis, Ann wife of James. S & T Feb 1744 *Neptune* to Md. M.
Lewis, Ann. S Summer 1752 R 14 yrs Lent 1753. Mo.
Lewis, Ann. S Oct T Nov 1759 *Phoenix*. M.
Lewis, Ann. S May 1761. M.
Lewis, Bartholomew. S Aug 1763. L.
Lewis, Katherine. T *Margaret*; sold to William Rowles, Md, Aug
  1719. L or M.
Lewis, Catherine. S s at Henbury Lent 1750. G.
Lewis, Charles. R for Barbados Jly 1675. L.
Lewis, Charles. S May 1722. M.
Lewis, Christopher. S Mar 1725. Do.
Lewis, Christopher. S for housebreaking Summer 1740 R Lent 1741. O.
Lewis, Christopher. T Apr 1759 *Thetis*. M.
Lewis als Ratcliffe, Christopher, als Sneyd, John. TB Mar 1763. Db.
Lewis, Christopher. S Oct T Dec 1769 *Justitia*. M.
Lewis, Daniel. S & T Sep 1751 *Greyhound*. L.
Lewis, Daniel of St. Paul, Covent Garden. SW Apr T Jly 1772 *Tayloe*. M.
Lewis, David. S Lent 1742. St.
Lewis, David. S Summer 1742 R 14 yrs Lent 1743. He.
Lewis, Edward. S May T Jly 1723 *Alexander* LC Annapolis Sep 1723. L.
Lewis, Elizabeth wife of Thomas. S Oct 1727-Jun 1728 T Jun 1728
  Elizabeth LC Potomack Aug 1729. M.
Lewis, Elizabeth of Lambeth, spinster. SQS Apr T Sep 1751
  Greyhound. Sy.
Lewis, Elizabeth. R 14 yrs Jly 1756. Ha.
Lewis, Elizabeth (1757). *See* Chester. Bu.
Lewis, Elizabeth. SL Jly 1773. Sy.
Lewis, Elizabeth. S Apr 1774. M.
Lewis, Fabius. R for life Dec 1774. M.
Lewis, Francis. S Feb T Mar 1731 *Patapsco* but died on passage. M.
Louis, Francis. T Sep 1764 *Justitia*. K.
Lewis, Francis. S Dec 1772. M.
Lewis, Frank als Francis. S Sep-Oct 1773. M.
Lewis als Stephens, Grace of Painswick. R for America Mar 1710. G.
Lewis, Henry of St. Ann, Westminster. SW Apr 1774. M.
Lewis, Hugh. S s sheep Lent R 14 yrs Summer 1767. Sh.
Lewis, Isaac. S Lent R 14 yrs Summer 1748. St.
Lewis, James. S Lent R 14 yrs Summer 1736. He.
Lewis, James. S s at Tidenham Summer 1749. G.
Lewis, James. S Lent R 14 yrs Summer 1751. He.
Lewis, James. SQS Dec 1773. M.

Lewis, Jane wife of Jonathan of Whichenford, yeoman. S s shirt Lent 1719. Wo.

Lewis, Jane. S Sep-Dec 1746. M.

Lewis, Jane. SQS & T Jan 1765 *Tryal*. M.

Lewis, Joan. S 14 yrs for killing sheep at Clifford Summer 1758; Nimrod & Margaret Lewis acquitted. He.

Lewis, John. PT Summer 1655 R 10 yrs Lent 1658. Sy.

Lewes, John. R for Barbados Dec 1670. M.

Lewis, John. Rebel T 1685.

Lewis, John. R for Barbados or Jamaica Jly 1686. M.

Lewis, John. S & T Jan 1722 *Gilbert* LC Annapolis Jly 1722. M.

Lewis, John. S & T Apr 1725 *Sukey* LC Annapolis Sep 1725. M.

Lewis als Edwards, John. S s horse Lent R 14 yrs Summer 1730. Mo.

Lewis, John. T Aug 1741 *Sally*. Sy.

Lewis, John. S s at Pontesbury Lent 1747. Sh.

Lewis, John. S Feb-Apr T May 1752 *Lichfield*. M.

Lewis, John (1758). *See* Baker. Wi.

Lewis, John. S s honey & beeswax at Kinnersley Lent 1762. He.

Lewis, John. S Aug 1763. L.

Lewis, John. S Mar 1764. So.

Lewis, John (1768). *See* Hughes. M.

Lewis, John. S Sep T Oct 1768 *Justitia*. M.

Lewis, John. S Dec 1768 T Jan 1769 *Thornton*. M.

Lewis, John. S Feb T Apr 1769 *Tryal*. M.

Lewis, John. R Jan-Feb T 14 yrs Apr 1772 *Thornton*. M.

Lewis, John. SQS Apr 1773. M.

Lewis, John. S & R 14 yrs Lent 1774. G.

Lewis, John. S s at Shire Newton Lent 1775. Mo.

Lewis, John James. T Dec 1763 *Neptune*. Sx.

Lewis, Joseph. S Lent 1748. St.

Lewis, Joseph. SL Mar T Apr 1772 *Thornton*. Sy.

Lewis, Josiah. S for highway robbery Lent R 14 yrs Summer T Oct 1744 *Savannah*. Bu.

Lewis, Lewis. S Sep-Oct T Dec 1752 *Greyhound*. M.

Lewis, Margaret wife of John. S Feb T Mar 1731 *Patapsco* LC Annapolis Jun 1731. M.

Lewis, Margaret. S s at Worfield Summer 1767. Sh.

Lewis, Martha (1719). *See* McCoy. M.

Lewis, Mary. S Apr T May 1718 *Tryal* LC Charles Town Aug 1718. L.

Lewis, Mary. S Jan-Jun T Jun 1728 *Elizabeth* LC Potomack Aug 1729. L.

Lewis, Mary (1731). *See* Shaw, Alice. M.

Lewis, Mary. T Sep 1755 *Tryal*. M.

Lewis, Mary. S Jan-Feb 1774. M.

Lewis, Nathaniel of Newington. SQS Apr T Sep 1751 *Greyhound*. Sy.

Lewis, Peter. S Lent R 14 yrs Summer 1722. G.

Lewis, Peter. T Apr 1742 *Bond*. Sy.

Lewis, Philip (1766). *See* Bagnon. M.

Lewis als Larkin, Richard. S Feb 1700 but apprehended in Apr 1704 for returning. M.

Lewis, Richard (1704). *See* Larkin. M.

Lewis, Richard. S & T Oct 1730 *Forward* LC Potomack Jan 1731. M.

Lewis, Richard. S s at Tetbury Summer 1750. G.
Lewis, Richard. T Sep 1764 *Justitia*. K.
Lewis, Richard. S Aug 1773. So.
Lewis, Robert. PT Jly 1680. M.
Lewis, Robert. S Summer 1745. Sx.
Lewis, Robert. S Jan-Feb 1775. M.
Lewis als Traherne, Samuel of Tewin, yeoman, a Quaker. S for
    attending conventicles Summer 1664 R for plantations Jly 1665. Ht.
Lewis, Samuel. S Feb T 14 yrs Mar 1729 *Patapsco* LC Annapolis Dec
    1729. M.
Lewis, Sarah of St. George, Southwark, spinster. SQS Feb T Mar 1758
    Dragon. Sy.
Lewis, Sibill wife of John. S s at Abbinghall Summer 1722. G.
Lewis, Susan. R for America May 1704. M.
Lewis, Susanna. TB Oct 1719. L.
Lewis, Thomas. S Oct 1743 T Feb 1744 *Neptune* to Md. M.
Lewis, Thomas. S s horse Summer 1752 R 14 yrs Lent 1753. Mo.
Lewis, Thomas. S s handkerchief Lent 1755. He.
Lewis, Thomas. S s watch at Clifford Summer 1758. He.
Lewis, Thomas. S Jan T Apr 1759 *Thetis*. M.
Lewis, Thomas. S Sep T Dec 1767 *Neptune*. M.
Lewis, Thomas. S Oct 1769. M.
Lewis, Walter. S s at Abergavenny Lent 1758. Mo.
Lewis, William of Dorston. R for America Jly 1687. He.
Lewis, William. S & T Apr 1725 *Sukey* LC Annapolis Sep 1725. M.
Lewis, William. S s at Hill als Hull Summer 1729. G.
Lewis, William. R 14 yrs for highway robbery Jly 1730. Do.
Lewis, William. R 14 yrs Mar 1740. So.
Lewis, William. S Lent R 14 yrs Summer 1751. Mo.
Lewis, William (1759). *See* Ray. M.
Lewis, William. S s at Maisemore Lent 1765. G.
Lewis, William. S May T 14 yrs Sep 1765 *Justitia*. M.
Lewis, William. S s wheat at Ross Lent 1768. He.
Lewis, William. R Lent 1773. K.
Lewitt, Thomas. SQS Aug TB to Va Sep 1751. Le.
Lews, Joseph of Kemerton, yeoman. R for America Feb 1713. Wo.
Lewton, Thomas. S at Bristol Lent 1772. G.
Leuty als Lewty, Thomas. S s at Knaresborough Lent 1773. Y.
Leuty, William. S s leather breeches at Wetherby Lent 1774. Y.
Leyland, Samuel of Ashton in Makerfield. S & R 10 yrs Lent 1775. La.
Leyland, William of Manchester. SQS Apr 1768. La.
Leysons, Richard. S Summer 1752. Hu.
Liberty, Samuel. S Feb T Jun 1738 *Forward* to Md or Va. M.
Liciter, William. S Summer 1756 R 14 yrs Lent 1757. Sh.
Liddell, Elizabeth. S & T Dec 1758 *The Brothers*. M.
Liddle, Isabella. S Sep-Oct 1773. M.
Liddle, John. SQS Jan T Mar 1764 *Tryal*. M.
Liddall, Mary. S Feb T Mar 1730 *Patapsco* LC Annapolis Sep 1730. L.
Lediard, Ann. S Jly-Sep 1754. M.
Liddiard, Sarah. S Oct-Dec 1739 T Jan 1740 *York* to Md. M.

Liggett, William. S s human hair at Holy Cross, Pershore, Summer 1736. Wo.

Lidgley, John. S Lent T Sep 1758 *Tryal*. Bu.

Lidley, Richard (1700). *See* Smith. M.

Lyfe, Joseph. S Lent R 14 yrs Summer 1748. Sy.

Life als Roberts, Robert. T Dec 1763 *Neptune*. Sy.

Lift, Henry. R for Barbados or Jamaica Mar 1685. M.

Light, Esther. S & T Dec 1769 *Justitia*. M.

Light, Hester. S Jly 1771. Ha.

Light, Thomas. R 14 yrs Apr 1765. So.

Light, William. S Aug 1728. So.

Light, William. S MAr 1737. Ha.

Lightbourn, Joseph. T Apr 1739 *Forward*. E.

Lightbourne, Richard. S Summer 1750 R 14 yrs Lent 1751. Wo.

Lightfoot, Daniel. S & T Oct 1732 *Caesar* to Va. M.

Lightfoot, George. S s heifers Lent R 14 yrs Summer 1743. St.

Lightfoot, John. S s horse Summer 1739 R 14 yrs Lent 1740 (SP). Sh.

Lightfoot, Richard. S & T Jly 1753 *Tryal*. L.

Lightfoot, Thomas (1749). *See* Linkherd. Co.

Lightfoot, William (1754). *See* Smith. Li.

Lightwood, Elizabeth. SQS Dec 1756. M.

Lightwood, Mary. SQS Dec 1756. M.

Lile. *See* Lisle.

Lill, Silvester. R for America Jly 1707. Li.

Lillington, Elizabeth (1669). *See* Scruce. L.

Lillington als Linnington, Robert. S Aug 1767. Do.

Lilliston, John. S & R 14 yrs Lent 1735. Nf.

Lilleston, John, als Jones, Robert. S Jan T Feb 1742 *Industry*. L.

Lilly, Ann. S Lent 1765. Nf.

Lilley, George (1773). *See* Thompson. Du.

Lilley, Jeremiah. LC from *Forward* Va Jun 1730. X.

Lilley, John. S Summer R for Barbados Aug 1665. Ht.

Lilley, John of Bury St. Edmunds. R for America Apr 1697. Su.

Lilly, John. S Lent R 14 yrs Summer 1750. Wo.

Lilly, John of Rotherhithe. SQS Jan T Apr 1762 *Neptune*. Sy.

Lilly, John. R 14 yrs s sheep Summer 1766. Li.

Lilly, John Patterson. S Oct 1751-Jan 1752. M.

Lilly, Margaret wife of William of Chelmsford, cordwainer. SQS Jly 1754. E.

Lilley, Richard (1656). *See* Salter. M.

Lilly, Robert. S Lent 1761. Su.

Lilley, Samuel. Died on passage in *Rapppahannock* 1726. Li.

Lilly, Sarah. T Jly 1722 *Alexander*. E.

Lilly, Thomas. S Jly 1754. Ha.

Lilly, Timothy. S Lent R 14 yrs Summer 1750. St & Wo.

Lilly, William. S & T Oct 1732 *Caesar* to Va. M.

Lilley, William. T Sep 1766 *Justitia*. E.

Lyllyman, Robert. T Dec 1731 *Forward*. E.

Limarez, John. S Feb T Mar 1764 *Tryal*. M.

Limbrish, Thomas. T Jun 1728 *Elizabeth*. Sx.

Lymes, Herman. S Jan-Feb 1773. M.

Limes, Margaret. S Jan-Apr 1748. M.
Linakin, John. T Apr 1768 *Thornton*. Sy.
Linakin, Mary. S & T Sep 1764 *Justitia*. M.
Linch. *See* Lynch.
Lincolne, Edward of Kings Hatfield. R for America Jun 1699 & Jly 1700. E.
Lincoln, James. SQS Apr 1752. M.
Lincoln, John. S Norwich s sheep Summer 1764 R 14 yrs Summer 1765. Nf.
Lincoln, Rose. S Jun-Dec 1745. M.
Lincoln, Thomas. S s sheep at Silsoe & R Summer T Jly 1775. Bd.
Lind, Thomas. S Summer 1728. Su.
Lindley, John. S Lent 1753. Y.
Lindley, John. R 14 yrs Summer 1753. We.
Lindley, William. T Sep 1758 *Tryal*. K.
Lindley, William. S s sheep Lent R 14 yrs Summer 1760. Nt.
Lindley, William. S Lent 1761. Nl.
Lindon, Catherine. S Jan 1757. M.
Lindsey, Anthony. R & T Apr 1735 *Patapsco* LC Annapolis Oct 1735. M.
Lindsey, Catherine. S Jly 1760. M.
Lindsay, David, gent. R for America Nov 1706 for entering France without licence. L.
Lindsey, Hugh. S Summer 1732. Nl.
Lyndsey, Jane. S Aug T Oct 1726 *Forward* to Va. M.
Linsey, Jane. S Feb-Apr 1745. M.
Lindsey, John. S s cow Summer 1739. Nl.
Linsay als Millar, Lucretia. S Jan T 14 yrs Apr 1741 *Speedwell*. L.
Linsey, Mary. S Oct 1741 T Feb 1742 *Industry*. L.
Lindsey, Mary. S Oct T Dec 1758 *The Brothers*. M.
Lindsey, Richard. S Jly T Aug 1721 *Prince Royal* LC Va Nov 1721. M.
Lynsey, Thomas. R for Barbados Feb 1672. M.
Lindsey, Thomas. S s clothing & T Dec 1734 *Caesar* LC Va Jly 1735. M.
Linsey, Thomas. S Feb T Apr 1770 *New Trial*. M.
Linsey, William. S & T Jan 1766 *Tryal*. M.
Linsey, William. S & R Summer T Sep 1773. No.
Lyne, Benedictus. S Aug 1772. Co.
Lyne, Richard. Rebel T 1685.
Line, Thomas. S for highway robbery Lent R 14 yrs Summer T Sep 1755
Lines, Mary. S Lent 1767. No.
Lynes, Richard. T Jly 1722 *Alexander*. Bu.
Lynes, Thomas (1722). *See* Jones. Sh.
Lynes, Thomas. S Summer 1757. Nf.
Linford, Samuel. S Dec 1774. L.
Lyng, John. S Apr 1775. M.
Ling, Maurice. T Oct 1729 *Forward*. Sy.
Linguard, Isaac. T Apr 1741 *Speedwell* or *Mediterranean*. Sy.
Lingard, Robert. T Apr 1753 *Thames*. Sy.
Lingham, John. S Lent 1749. Sy.
Lingley, Elizabeth. T Dec 1771 *Justitia*. E.
Lingley als Smith, James. S for highway robbery & R Lent 1738. Su.

Lyneing, William. Rebel T 1685.

Linkherd als Lightfoot, Thomas. S Jly 1749. Co.

Lynley, Henry. S Sep 1740. L.

Linlowe, Elizabeth. R for Barbados Sep 1672. L.

Linnard, Richard. S Oct 1768 T Jan 1769 *Thornton*. M.

Linneke, Anne Mary. S & T Apr 1725 *Sukey* LC Annapolis Sep 1725. M.

Linnerpon, George. S Jly 1772. Ha.

Linnett, Benjamin. TB Sep 1730. Db.

Linnett, Francis, aged 30, dark, weaver. LC from *Jonathan* Md Jly 1724. X.

Linnett, Francis. S for shoplifting Lent R 14 yrs Summer 1772. Wa.

Linney, Charles. SQS & T Jan 1765 *Tryal*. M.

Linney, James. S Summer 1744 R 14 yrs Summer 1745 for murder of Thomas Armsden by hanging him with a cord. Bd.

Linney, John. S Apr T Jly 1770 *Scarsdale*. M.

Linny als Groves, Sarah. S Feb T Mar 1727 *Rappahannock* to Md. M.

Linney, William. S & T 14 yrs Dec 1767 *Neptune*. M.

Linnick als Baker, Robert. S Jan-Feb T Apr 1772 *Thornton*. M.

Linnigin, John. T Sep 1766 *Justitia*. M.

Linnington, Robert (1767). *See* Lillington. Do.

Linsley, John. S for highway robbery Summer 1720 R 14 yrs Summer 1721 AT Lent 1722. Y.

Linsted, Thomas. S Lent 1748. E.

Lintern, Edward. SQS Jan 1744 TB to Md Mar 1745. So.

Linton, Henry. S Jan 1775. M.

Linton, Samuel. SQS Apr T May 1767 *Thornton*. M.

Linvill, John. R Dec 1699 & Aug 1700. M.

Lion. *See* Lyon.

Lipcraft, John (1750). *See* Townley. Nf.

Lypiatt, George. S s sheep Lent R 14 yrs Summer 1766. G.

Lippey, William. R Jly AT Aug 1685. M.

Lippitt, William. R 14 yrs for murder Lent 1721. He.

Lipscombe, Stephen. S s at St. Mary Magdalene, Oxford, Lent 1724 T *Forward* LC Annapolis Jun 1725. O.

Lipscomb, William. R 14 yrs Mar 1747. Ha.

Liptrap, Isaac. R & T 14 yrs Jly 1772 *Tayloe*. M.

Liscot, James (1751). *See* Jones. He.

Lisence, Ruth. LC from *Susannah & Sarah* Annapolis Apr 1720. X.

Lish, Thomas. S Jan-Feb T Apr 1772 *Thornton*. M.

Lishman, Jane. S Sep-Oct 1774. M.

Lisle als Lile, Edward of Buckland Brewer. R for Barbados Jly 1667. De.

Lile, Jane (1742). *See* Green. M.

Lissant, Richard (1685). *See* Nash.

Lissiman, Henry. S Summer 1755. Nf.

Lister, John (1728). *See* Coulson. Y.

Lister, John. S Summer 1753. Ch.

Lister, John. R & T for life Apr 1770 *New Trial*. M.

Lister, John. S for highway robbery & R 14 yrs Lent 1772. Li.

Lister, Mary. T Jun 1738 *Forward*. Sy.

Lyston, Robert. S Mar 1743. Co.

Litchfield, John. R Lent 1774. E.
Litford, Mathew. S Jly 1752. Ha.
Lithgoe, Henry of Etchells. R for Barbados Jly 1683. Ch.
Litners, Thomas. S Oct 1772. L.
Little Bess (1731). *See* Armstrong, Elizabeth. L.
Little John (1733). *See* George, Daniel. M.
Little Ned (1756). *See* Cleeve, Edward. Ha.
Little, Andrew. R 14 yrs Summer 1753. Cu.
Little, Archibald. S Jly 1722. Wi.
Little, Daniel. R for life Sep 1756. M.
Little, Edward. R for Barbados or Jamaica Jly 1685. M.
Little, Elizabeth. T Apr 1732 *Patapsco*. E.
Little, Elizabeth. S Sep-Oct T Dec 1752 *Greyhound*. M.
Little, John. S & T Sep 1731 *Smith* LC Va 1732. M.
Little, John. R 14 yrs Summer 1754. Nl.
Little, Keziah. S Lent T Sep 1757 *Thetis*. Ht.
Little, Matthias. S & TB to Va Mar 1760. Wi.
Little, Ralph. R for Barbados Jun 1665. L.
Little, Thomas. S Dec 1750. L.
Little, Thomas. R Dec 1765 T 14 yrs Jan 1766 *Tryal*. M.
Little, William. S & T Oct 1729 *Forward* but died on passage. M.
Little, William. S Mar 1750. Co.
Little, William. SQS Devizes & TB to Va Apr 1774. Wi.
Littleboy, John. S Jly 1774. L.
Littleford, John. SQS Oct 1751. M.
Littlejohn, Elizabeth. S & T Dec 1771 *Justitia*. M.
Littlejohn, Michael. R 14 yrs Aug 1750. Co.
Littlejohn als Saunders, Wilmot. TB to Va from QS 1745. De.
Littlejohns, William. S Mar 1745. Co.
Littler, Abigail. S Apr 1760. M.
Littleton, Joseph. S & T Sep 1765 *Justitia*. L.
Littlewood, Edward. R 10 yrs Lent 1655; to be T by Thomas Vincent &
    Samuel Highland. Sy.
Litton, Thomas. S Mar 1731 TB to Va. De.
Lively, John. R for Barbados Nov 1668. L.
Lively, Matthew. S Oct T Dec 1734 *Caesar* LC Va Jly 1735. M.
Livermore, Mary. S Lent T May 1750 *Lichfield*. E.
Livermoore, Thomas. TB to Va from QS 1744. De.
Liversidge, Elizabeth (1755). *See* Mills. M.
Livesey, Thomas. S Mar TB to Va Apr 1731. Le.
Livesly, Nathaniel of Charleton. R for America Jly 1677. Li.
Livesson, John. S Jan-Feb T Apr 1771 *Thornton*. M.
Liveston, William (1710). *See* Leveston. Nl.
Livings, Thomas. R 14 yrs Jly 1740. Ha.
Levingston, Anna Maria. S Dec 1746. L.
Levingstone als Featherstone, Elizabeth. R 14 yrs Jll 1724. Ha.
Lluellin, David. S Jun T 14 yrs Nov 1743 *George William*. M.
Lewellin, Elizabeth. S May-Jly 1773. M.
Lluellin, John. S Oct T Dec 1771 *Justitia* L.
Luelling, Samuel. R & T Apr 1735 *Patapsco* LC Annapolis Oct 1735. M.
Llewellin, Samuel. S s calf skins at Trebegg Summer 1756. Mo.

Llewellin, Thomas. S s at Redwick Summer 1742. Mo.
Llewellin, William. S s ox Lent R 14 yrs Summer 1760. Mo.
Lloyd, Ann. S Jan T Feb 1719 *Worcester* LC Annapolis Jun 1719. L.
Lloyd, Anne. S Summer 1719 R Summer 1720. Nl.
Lloyd, David of Bridgenorth. R for America Jly 1696. Sh.
Loyd, David. S Oct 1741 T Feb 1742 *Industry* to Md. M.
Lloyd, Deborah. S for life Feb-Apr 1746. M.
Lloyd, Dorothy wife of Thomas. S Oct T Nov 1759 *Phoenix*. M.
Lloyd, Edward. Rebel T 1685.
Lloyd, Edward of Wolverhampton. S s horse Lent 1717 R 14 yrs Lent
    1720. St.
Lloyd, Edward of Worcester. S Lent 1720. Wo.
Lloyd, Edward. S s fowls at St. George Colgate, Norwich, Summer
    1769. Nf.
Lloyd, Eleanor. S Jly 1761. L.
Lloyd, Elizabeth. R Feb 1675. M.
Lloyd, Elizabeth. S Aug 1727 T *Forward* LC Rappahannock May
    1728. M.
Loyd, Elizabeth. R 14 yrs Mar TB to Va Apr 1767. Wi.
Lloyd, Ellis (1721). *See* Lloyd, Lewis. M.
Lloyd, George. S s shirt Summer 1753. Sh.
Lloyd, Griffith. SW & T Jun 1768 *Tryal*. M.
Lloyd, Hannah. S Lent 1745. *Bd.
Lloyd, James. R for Barbados Mar 1677. L.
Loyd, Jane. T Jun 1727 *Susanna*. K.
Lloyd als Floyd, John of Waltham Cross. R for Barbados or Jamaica
    Feb 1686. E.
Lloyd, John (1694). *See* Floyd. G.
Lloyd, John. S Oct T 14 yrs Nov 1725 *Rappahannock* LC Rappahannock
    Apr 1726. M.
Loyd, John. S Feb T Mar 1727 *Rappahannock*. L.
Lloyd, John. S Dec 1737 T Jan 1738 *Dorsetshire*. L.
Lloyd, John. S Apr-May T May 1744 *Justitia*. M.
Lloyd, John. S May-Jly 1748. M.
Lloyd, John of St. John's. SQS Oct 1750. Sy.
Loyd, John. S Jly 1767. Ha.
Lloyd, Joseph. SQS May 1750. M.
Loyd, Joseph. S Mar TB to Va Apr 1766. Wi.
Lloyd, Joseph of St. Margaret, Westminster. SW Jan T Apr 1772
    Thornton. M.
Lloyd, Joseph. R 14 yrs Jly 1775. M.
Lloyd, Lewis als Ellis. S Jly T Aug 1721 *Prince Royal* LC Va Sep
    1736. M.
Lloyd, Margaret (1721). *See* Price. He.
Lloyd, Mary. R for Barbados Feb 1675. L.
Lloyd als Day, Mary of St. Saviour, Southwark. R for Barbados or
    Jamaica Jly 1702. Sy.
Lloyd, Mary. S Oct 1735 T Jan 1736 *Dorsetshire* LC Va Sep 1736. M.
Lloyd, Mary. S for shoplifting Lent R 14 yrs Summer 1766. Sh.
Lloyd, Matthew. S s oxen & R 14 yrs Summer 1772. Sh.

Lloyd als Maund, Nicholas. S s at Ribbesford & Kidderminster Summer 1761. Wo.

Lloyd, Peter (1751). *See* Love. L.

Lloyd, Richard. S s cloth & T Dec 1734 *Caesar* LC Va Jly 1735. M.

Lloyd, Richard. S s in Montgomeryshire Summer 1767. Sh.

Lloyd, Richard. SQS Sep T Dec 1770 *Justitia*. M.

Lloyd, Richard, als Peak, Daniel. S & R 14 yrs Lent 1773. Ch.

Lloyd, Robert. S & T Apr 1733 *Patapsco* LC Annapolis Nov 1733. M.

Lloyd, Samuel (1768). *See* Floyd. La.

Lloyd, Sarah. S Apr 1773. M.

Lloyd, Stephen. S s at St. Giles, Oxford, Lent 1772. O.

Lloyd, Susanna. S Apr T May 1720 *Honor* to York River. L.

Loyd, Theophilus. S s combed wool Lent 1742. G.

Lloyd, Thomas of Ross. R for America Mar 1683. He.

Lloyd, Thomas. S Oct T Dec 1767 *Neptune*. M.

Lloyd, William. S Jly-Sep T Oct 1739 *Duke of Cumberland* to Va. M.

Lloyd, William. S Oct T 14 yrs Nov 1759 *Phoenix*. L.

Loach, Henry. S Mar 1735. De.

Load, John. S for housebreaking Summer 1725 R 14 yrs Lent 1726 T *Loyal Margaret* but died on passage. St.

Loader, William of Holwell, husbandman. R for Barbados Feb 1672. So.

Loadley, Robert. S Jan-Apr 1748. M.

Lobb, Robert. TB to Va from QS 1737. De.

Lobly, Joshua of Purleigh. SQS Jan 1763. E.

Lock, Benjamin of Upwell. S Summer 1728. *Nf.

Lock, Charles. S & R 14 yrs Summer 1773. O.

Locke, Elizabeth (1754). *See* Elworthy. Sy.

Lock, Elizabeth. S Sep T Dec 1763 *Neptune*. M.

Lock, George. S Mar 1758. So.

Lock, Henry. S Norwich Summer 1759. Nf.

Locke, Isaac. S & T Apr 1769 *Tryal*. L.

Lock, John (2). Rebels T 1685.

Lock, John (1724). *See* Lock, William. M.

Lock, John. S Summer 1757 R 14 yrs Lent 1758. Be.

Lock, John. S May-Jly 1773. M.

Lock, Richard Jr. R Summer 1774. E.

Lock, Robert. S Mar 1756. Do.

Lock, Thomas. R s horse Jun 1730 (SP). Wo.

Locke, William. Rebel T 1685.

Lock, William als John. S Aug T Oct 1724 *Forward* LC Annapolis Jun 1725. M.

Lockbeare, Elias. Rebel T 1685.

Locker, Elizabeth. R for Barbados or Jamaica Dec 1689. M.

Locker, Elizabeth. S Summer 1754. Be.

Lockerby, Thomas. SQS s breeches Michaelmas 1763. Cu.

Lockeskegg, Thomas. T for life Sep 1766 *Justitia*. K.

Lockett, Benjamin. T Apr 1769 *Tryal*. Sy.

Lockett als Lockington als Wilson, Charles. R for life Dec 1774. M.

Lockett, John. S s mare Lent 1725 R 14 yrs Lent 1726. Mo.

Lockett, Jonathan. SQS Coventry Aug AT Oct 1752. Wa.

Lockitt als Brock, Mary. S & T Jly 1771 *Scarsdale*. L.

Lockey, Henry. S Summer 1744. We.
Lockhart, Benjamin. SW & T Dec 1767 *Neptune*. M.
Lockhart, Jane. S Mar 1758. De.
Lockhart, John of Rotherhithe. SQS Jan T 14 yrs Apr 1768 *Thornton*. Sy.
Lockhart, Thomas. AT Summer 1765. Y.
Lockhart, Thomas. SQS Dec 1766 T Jan 1767 *Tryal*. M.
Lockin, Richard. S Feb T Mar 1758 *Dragon*. M.
Lockington, Charles (1774). *See* Lockett. M.
Lockley, John. S Lent 1772. Wa.
Locks, Mary (1724). *See* Lacks. M.
Lockwood, John. S Lent TB Aug 1737. Y.
Lockwood, John. S Summer 1746. Su.
Lockwood, Martha. S Summer 1746. K.
Lockwood, Martha. SQS Aug 1747 TB to Va Jly 1748. Le.
Lockwood, Mary. S Jan-Feb T Apr 1771 *Thornton*. M.
Lockwood, William of Mewell. R for America Jly 1703. Nf.
Lockyer, John. S Mar 1719 to be T to Va. So.
Lockyer, Joseph. R 14 yrs Mar 1738. Do.
Lockyer, Roger. R 14 yrs Aug 1756. So.
Lockyer, Thomas. Rebel T 1685.
Locock, Thomas of Newbury. S for shoplifting Summer 1741. Be.
Locup, Mary. SQS Dec 1772. M.
Lodge, Job. S Mar 1775. Ha.
Lodge, Thomas. SQS & T Sep 1766 *Justitia*. M.
Lodowick, William (1752). *See* Landwick. M.
Lodwick, William (1768). *See* Ladwicke. Ca.
Loes als Willinger, Richard of Ashow. R for America Jly 1716. Wa.
Loffen, Thomas of Bexwell. R for Barbados Feb 1664. Nf.
Logan, Robert. S Oct 1742 T Apr 1743 *Justitia*. M.
Login, William. S Feb-Apr T Jun 1756 *Lyon*. M.
Loggins, Joseph. S s wheat Lent 1742. Mo.
Loggs, Henry. S Lent R 14 yrs Summer T Oct 1750 *Rachael*. Ht.
Loman. *See* Lowman.
Lomas, George. S for forgery Lent R for life Summer 1756. Db.
Lomas, Samuel of Camberwell. SQS Apr T Jly 1772 *Orange Bay*. Sy.
Lomas, Thomas. R for America Jly 1688. Db.
Lomax, George. S for rape Summer 1753 R 14 yrs Lent 1754. La.
Lomax, John of Manchester. SQS Apr 1775. La.
Lombard, Elisha. S s sheep Lent R 14 yrs Summer 1742. O.
Lombart, John. T Apr 1725 *Sukey* but died on passage. K.
Lombar, Richard. S Apr 1741. So.
Lumbard, Robert. Rebel T 1685.
Lumbard, Sarah. S Mar TB to Va Apr 1742. Wi.
Lon, Elizabeth. PT Jan 1699. M.
London, Alice (1665). *See* Hucklebone. L.
London, Charlotte. SQS Jan T Apr 1772 *Thornton*. M.
London, Elener. T Sep 1730 *Smith*. Sy.
London, Eleanor. SQS Apr 1752. M.
London, John. S Sep-Oct 1775. M.
London, Martha. S 14 yrs Jun 1739. L.
London, Mary (1748). *See* Sanders. La.

Lone, Elizabeth. S Dec 1745. L.
Lone, John. S May-Jly 1773. M.
Long, Ann. S Jan-Apr 1748. M.
Long, Anthony. S Lent R 14 yrs Summer 1724. G.
Long, Catherine. S May T 14 yrs Jun 1738 *Forward*. L.
Long, Elizabeth, spinster, als wife of William. R for Jamaica Mar 1665. L.
Long, Elizabeth. R 14 yrs Jly 1741. Co.
Long, Grace. R for Barbados Sep 1672. L.
Long, Grace. S Jan T Apr 1734 *Patapsco* to Md. M.
Long, Hannah, aged 40, black hair. S Jly T Oct 1720 *Gilbert* LC Annapolis May 1721. M.
Long als Green, Henry. S s cloth at Faringdon (Oxon) Lent 1772. Be.
Long, Isaac of St. Saviour, Southwark. SQS Oct T Dec 1767 *Neptune*. Sy.
Long, James of Wootton Underedge. S Lent 1721. G.
Long, John. Rebel T 1685.
Long, John. S & T Sep 1718 *Eagle* LC Charles Town Mar 1719. L.
Long, John. S Apr-May T May 1744 *Justitia*. M.
Long, John. SQS Apr T May 1751 *Tryal*. M.
Long, John. SQS Feb T Apr 1753 *Thames*. M.
Long, John. S s at Llavaches Lent 1753. Mo.
Long, John. S s mare Lent R 14 yrs Summer 1761. Nf.
Long, John. S s at Windermere Summer 1764. We.
Long, Joseph. S Mar 1735. So.
Long, Lewis. S Lent 1740. Wo.
Long, Mary. T Apr 1743 *Justitia*. Ht.
Long, Mary. S Feb 1761. M.
Long, Mary Jane. S & T Oct 1730 *Forward* LC Potomack Jan 1731. M.
Long, Patrick of St. Mary le Strand. S s books & T Dec 1740 *Vernon*. M.
Long, Richard. Rebel T 1685.
Long als Bartelott, Robert. R for life Mar TB to Va Apr 1773. Wi.
Long, Sarah. S Sep 1760. M.
Long, Thomas. S Feb T Apr 1765 *Ann*. L.
Long, William. T Jan 1736 *Dorsetshire*. Ht.
Long, William. S Apr 1745. L.
Longbotham, Eli. R 14 yrs Summer 1763. Y.
Longbottom, Elizabeth. S Sep 1754. L.
Longbridge, Francis. Rebel T 1685.
Longden als Strange als Lownde als Blyth, John; als Brown als Wright, Thomas. S s gelding Summer 1755 R 14 yrs Lent 1756. Nf.
Longden, Joseph. S Jly-Dec 1747. M.
Longden, Mary (1736). *See* Hanson. Db.
Longerwood, John. S Lent 1755. Y.
Longford, Elizabeth. SQS Bristol Apr 1771. G.
Longford, John. S s horse & R 14 yrs Lent 1772. O.
Longford, Michael of Kempton Langley, sergeweaver. R for Barbados Feb 1692. Wi.
Longford, Robert. T Jly 1724 *Robert* LC Md Jun 1725. Sy.
Longham, Christian. S Oct 1751-Jan 1752. M.
Longley, Elizabeth. S Summer 1733 R 14 yrs Summer 1734. Wo.
Longman, Elizabeth. R for Barbados Sep 1672. L.

Longman, Elizabeth (1673). *See* Cutler. L.

Longman, William. S Oct 1661 to House of Correction unless he agrees to be transported. M.

Longman, William. R for Barbados Jly 1675. M.

Longmire, William. S Oct T 14 yrs Nov 1725 *Rappahannock* LC Rappahannock Apr 1726. L.

Longmore, Ann. S Jun-Dec 1738 T Jan 1739 *Dorsetshire* to Va. M.

Longstaff, Henry. S & R Summer 1749 for breaking & entering with intent to kill. Bd.

Longstaff, William. T Sep 1765 *Justitia*. Sy.

Longsworth, Peter. S Feb T Apr 1734 *Patapsco* to Md. M.

Longweaver, William (1768). *See* Webb. So.

Lonsdale, William of Colne, woolcomber. SQS Apr 1770. La.

Loohor, John of St. Giles, Colchester. R for America Jly 1700. E.

Looker, John. S Summer 1750. Ch.

Looker, Richard. S Summer 1750. Ch.

Loome, John. S Jun T Aug 1769 *Douglas*. M.

Looms, Michael of Bermondsey. S Summer T Oct 1750 *Rachael*. Sy.

Loosemore, Henry. S Mar 1721. De.

Lord, Anne. S Aug 1728 TB to Md. De.

Lord, Benjamin. S s from tenters at Alverthorp Summer 1765. Y.

Lord, John of Ombersley. R for America Mar 1682. Wo.

Lord, John of North Pickanham. S s waistcoat Lent 1724. Nf.

Lord, John of Spotland. SQS Apr 1741. La.

Lord, John. T 14 yrs Sep 1767 *Justitia*. E.

Lord, Mary. T Jun 1764 *Dolphin*. Sy.

Lord, Richard of Edgeside in Forest of Rossendale. SQS Apr 1759. La.

Lord als Laud, William. S s gelding & R 14 yrs Summer 1770. No.

Lorrell, Mathew. S Mar TB to Va Apr 1742. Wi.

Lorriman, Richard. R for Barbados or Jamaica Oct 1694. L.

Lorrimer, Richard Francis. T for life Dec 1770 *Justitia*. K.

Loseby, Peter. T May 1752 *Lichfield*. Sy.

Loseby, Richard of Barkby Thorpe. R for America Jly 1673. Le.

Loseby, Thomas. S Aug T Sep 1764 *Justitia*. L.

Loton, Ann. S May-Jly 1774. M.

Lotan, Francis. S Apr T Jun 1768 *Tryal*. M.

Loton, Richard. S for housebreaking Lent R 14 yrs Summer 1762. He.

Loton, Sophia. S Aug T Oct 1741 *Sea Horse* to Va. M.

Lott, Elizabeth. R for Barbados or Jamaica Dec 1695 & May 1697. L.

Lotta, Stephen. T 14 yrs May 1767 *Thornton*. K.

Lottiman, Michael (1746). *See* Laremon. G.

Louis. *See* Lewis.

Louiza, Elizabeth. SWK Oct T Dec 1769 *Justitia*. K.

Louman. *See* Lowman.

Love, Edward of Cranbrook. R for Barbados Apr 1668. K.

Love, James. S Oct T Dec 1767 *Neptune*. M.

Love, John of Cranbrook. R for Barbados Apr 1668. K.

Love, John. T Apr 1742 *Bond*. K.

Love als Lloyd, Peter. S Jan 1751. L.

Love, Thomas. S Apr T 14 yrs May 1718 *Tryal*. L.

Love, Thomas. S Jan T Feb 1726 *Supply* LC Annapolis May 1726. L.

Love, Thomas. S s at Briston Lent 1770. Nf.
Love, William. S Aug 1756. So.
Loveday, Joseph. S & T Dec 1771 *Justitia*. L.
Loveday, Mary. S May T Jun 1726 *Loyal Margaret* LC Annapolis Oct 1726. M.
Loveday, Thomas. SQS & T Aug 1769 *Douglas*. Ht.
Lovegrove, James of Bristol. R 14 yrs Apr 1768 (SP). G.
Lovegrove, John. T Apr 1725 *Sukey* LC Md Sep 1725. K.
Lovegrove, Mary. S s sheep Lent R 14 yrs Summer 1749. Be.
Lovegrove, Rebecca (1754). *See* Holden. L.
Lovegrove, William. S s at St. Lawrence, Reading, Lent 1774. Be.
Lovejoy, Roger. R for Va for s horse Jly 1749. M.
Lovejoy, William. S Oct T Nov 1728 *Forward* LC Rappahannock Jun 1729. M.
Lovelace, Edward. SQS Dec 1763 T Mar 1764 *Tryal*. M.
Loveland, Daniel. SQS May T Aug 1769 *Douglas*. M.
Lovell, Catherine. S & T Sep 1765 *Justitia*. L.
Lovell, Frederick. R 14 yrs Apr 1770. So.
Lovell, James. SQS Oct T Dec 1769 *Justitia*. M.
Lovell, John. R for America Jly 1693. No.
Lovell, John. S Lent 1763. No.
Lovell, John. S & T Sep 1764 *Justitia*. M.
Lovell, Joseph. S Feb-Apr T for life May 1755 *Rose*. M.
Lovell, Richard. S Feb T 14 yrs Apr 1765 *Ann*. M.
Lovell, Robert. S Mar 1737. De.
Lovell, Thomas. S s horse Lent R 14 yrs Summer 1740. Bd.
Lovell, William. SQS Feb T Mar 1750 *Tryal*. M.
Lovell, William. R 14 yrs Aug 1750 TB to Va. De.
Lovelock, Abraham. R 14 yrs Mar TB to Va Nov 1748. Wi.
Lovelock, John. S s at Sandleford Summer 1756; found at large Summer 1758 & ordered to Hampshire for trial on capital charge. Be.
Lovelock, Nathaniel. S Apr 1742. Ha.
Lovely, Martha. T Apr 1769 *Tryal*. Sy.
Loveridge, Bernard. Rebel T 1685.
Loveridge, John. Rebel T 1685.
Loveridge als Spencer, John. R for Barbados or Jamaica Nov 1690. L.
Loveridge, William. Rebel T 1685.
Lovering, John. S Oct 1751-Jan 1752. M.
Lovering, Mary. TB to Va from QS 1740. De.
Loveringham, Richard. S Jan T Feb 1726 *Supply* LC Annapolis May 1726. L.
Loveritt, William. S Lent 1731. Sh.
Lovett, Henry. S Jan-Jun 1747. M.
Lovett, John. S Jan-May T Jun 1738 *Forward* to Md or Va. M.
Lovett, Mary. S Feb T Apr 1759 *Thetis*. M.
Lovett, William. S & T Apr 1733 *Patapsco* LC Annapolis Nov 1733. L.
Lovatt, William. S s at Grindon Summer 1751. St.
Lovett, William. S Aug 1760. So.
Lovey, John. S & T Oct 1729 *Forward* LC Va Jun 1730. M.
Loving, Richard. S Jly 1755 TB to Va 1756. De.
Lovyer, Daniel (1752). *See* Levoyer. M.

Lowe, Anne. R for Barbados Oct 1673. L.

Low, Anne. S & T Oct 1722 *Forward* LC Annapolis Jun 1723. M.

Low, Benjamin. S Jan T Feb 1742 *Industry* to Md. M.

Low, Edmund. S Jly 1747. L.

Low, Elizabeth. PT Oct 1697 R Jly & Dec 1698. M.

Lowe, Elizabeth, aged 19, fair. S & T 14 yrs Oct 1720 *Gilbert* LC Annapolis May 1721. L.

Low, Francis. PT May R Jly 1687. M.

Lowe, Francis of Bermondsey. R for Barbados or Jamaica Jly 1688. Sy.

Lowe, George. TB Apr 1751 T *Happy Jennett* LC Md Oct 1751. Db.

Lowe, James. S Jly 1741. M.

Low, Jane (1738). *See* Billingsly. M.

Lowe, John. R for Barbados or Jamaica Oct 1690. M.

Lowe, John. S Apr T Oct 1719 *Susannah & Sarah* LC Annapolis Apr 1720. L.

Lowe, John. S Lent 1721. St.

Low, John. S Jan T Feb 1742 *Industry* to Md. M.

Low, John. S Dec 1742 T Apr 1743 *Justitia*. M.

Low als Jones als Young als Blinkhorne, John. S Jly 1749. L.

Low, John. S s leaden pump Feb T Mar 1758 *Dragon*. M.

Lowe, John. S & T Mar 1764 *Tryal*. L.

Lowe, John. S Feb T May 1767 *Thornton*. L.

Lowe, Joseph. S s nails at West Bromwich Summer 1773. St.

Low, Mary. S Feb 1729. M.

Low, Mary. S Jan T Apr 1743 *Justitia*. M.

Low, Mary. SQS & TB Oct 1749. So.

Low, Mary. S Apr-May 1754. M.

Low, Mary wife of John. S s at St. Nicholas, Durham, Summer 1765; S & R for life Summer 1766 for being at large at St. Oswald, Durham. Du.

Lowe, Robert. T Oct 1732 *Caesar*. K.

Lowe, Rosanna. SQS Apr T May 1767 *Thornton*. M.

Low, Samuel. S Feb 1752. L.

Lowe, Samuel. S Jan-Feb 1773. M.

Lowe, Sarah. R 14 yrs for highway robbery Summer 1775. Nt.

Lowe, Thomas. S s at Burford Lent 1722. O.

Low, Thomas. S Lent 1748. Ht.

Low, Thomas. S May 1763. M.

Lowe, William. S May T Jly 1771 *Scarsdale*. L.

Lowe, William. R for life at Peterborough for highway robbery Apr 1773. No.

Lowbridge, John. S s at Upton Warren Lent 1758. Wo.

Lowcross, Martha (1733). *See* Poulton. L.

Lowden, Michael. T Apr 1771 *Thornton*. M.

Lowder, Elizabeth. S Feb T Apr 1739 *Forward* to Va. M.

Louder, Jonathan. S s fowls Feb T Mar 1758 *Dragon*. M.

Lowder, Richard. S May-Jly 1748. M.

Lowell, John of Rotherhithe. SQS & T Jan 1766 *Tryal*. Sy.

Lowes, John. S Summer 1732. Nl.

Lowin, Thomas. S Apr-May T May 1741 *Catherine & Elizabeth* to Md. M.

Lowman, Bernard. Rebel T 1685.

Louman, Joseph. TB to Va from QS 1741. De.

Lowman, Michael. S Apr T May 1755 *Rose*. L.

Loman, Robert. S Oct 1757 T Mar 1758 *Dragon*. M.

Lownde, John (1755). *See* Longden. Nf.

Lound, Mary of Aylsham. S Summer 1731. *Nf.

Lowndes, Elizabeth of Stapeley. R for America Jly 1687. Ch.

Lowry, Ann. SQS Sep T Dec 1769 *Justitia*. M.

Lowry, Catherine. S 14 yrs May-Jly 1746. M.

Lowry, Edward. S Dec 1746. L.

Lowry, Edward. S Dec 1749-Jan 1750 T Mar 1750 *Tryal*. M.

Lowry, George. S Summer 1748 T Jan 1749 *Laura*. Ht.

Lowry, Roger. S Mar 1736. De.

Lowson, John. R 14 yrs Summer 1762. Y.

Lowth, James. SQS Mar 1748. Le.

Lowther, John of Rose Causeway, Dalston, gent. R for Barbados Jly 1699. Cu.

Lowther, Robert. S for burglary & attempted rape Summer 1723 R 14 yrs Summer 1724. Du.

Lowther als Reachead, Sarah. S for life Dec 1747. L.

Lowther, William. S Lent 1765. Li.

Loxham, Elizabeth, als Gatson, Jane. S Oct 1766 T Jan 1767 *Tryal*. M.

Lucas, Ann. S & T Sep 1757 *Thetis*. M.

Lucas, Catherine. SQS Oct T Dec 1734 *Caesar* LC Va Jly 1735. M.

Lucas, Charles. Rebel T 1685.

Lucas, Elizabeth wife of Abraham. S Aug 1727 T *Forward* LC Rappahannock May 1728. M.

Lucas, George. S & T Jan 1769 *Thornton*. L.

Lucas, James. S Jun T Jly 1772 *Tayloe*. L.

Lucas, Jasper of Wooton. R for Barbados or Jamaica Jly 1702. Sy.

Luckis, John of Frampton. R for Barbados Jly 1681. Do.

Lucas, John. S s horse Lent R 14 yrs Summer 1755. No.

Lucas, Joseph. T Apr 1735 *Patapsco*. K.

Lucas, Joseph. S s sheep Summer 1749. Cu.

Lukis, Mary. TB to Va from QS 1756. De.

Lucas, Mary. S Apr 1759. So.

Lucas, Nicholas, a Quaker. S Summer 1664 for attending conventicles R for plantations Jly 1665. Ht.

Lucas, Peter. S Jan-Jun T Jun 1728 *Elizabeth* LC Potomack Aug 1729. L.

Lucas, Rachael. S 14 yrs Apr-May 1754. M.

Luckis, Richard of Salcombe. R for Barbados Jly 1679. De.

Lucas, Richard (1775). *See* Tanfield, James. G.

Lucas, Robert. S Summer 1740. Ch.

Lucas, Sarah (1733). *See* Walmsley. M.

Lucas, Stephen. S Lent 1775. K.

Lucas, Susan. R for Barbados Dec 1693 AT Jan 1694. M.

Lucas, Thomas. S & T 14 yrs Sep 1718 *Eagle* LC Charles Town Mar 1719. L.

Lucas, Thomas. T May 1719 *Margaret* LC Md Sep 1719; sold to Peter Galloway. Sy.

Lucas, Thomas. S Aug 1740 TB to Va. De.

Lucas, Thomas (1760 & 1761). *See* Luckes. Cu. & Y.
Lucas, Thomas. S s at Devereaux Summer 1761. He.
Lukies, Thomas. S Aug 1767. Co.
Lucas, Thomas. S & T Jly 1771 *Scarsdale*. L.
Lucas, William. S Jan-Jun T Jun 1728 *Elizabeth* LC Potomack Aug 1729. L.
Lucas, William. S Dec 1733 T Jan 1734 *Caesar* but died on passage. M.
Lucas, William. S Aug TB to Va Oct 1764. Wi.
Lucas, William. S Summer 1769. Db.
Luck, Catherine. S May T Jun 1727 *Susannu* to Va. M.
Luck, George. T Oct 1738 *Genoa*. K.
Lucke, Giles of Ellismore. R for Barbados Jly 1702. He.
Luck, Mary. S May T Jun 1727 *Susanna* to Va. M.
Luck, Peter (1752). *See* Dawson. La.
Luckes als Lucas, Thomas. S s sheep Summer 1760 R 14 yrs Summer 1761. Cu. & Y.
Luckey, Isabella. S Aug T Oct 1726 *Forward* to Va. M.
Luckhurst, William. S Summer T Oct 1750 *Rachael*. K.
Lucocke, Adam of Blickling. R for America Feb 1681. Nf.
Lucey, James. T 14 yrs Aug 1752 *Tryal*. E.
Lucy, William. SQS & T Sep 1766 *Justitia*. M.
Ludbrooke, Sarah. S s at Benacre Lent 1772. Su.
Luddington, Thomas. S Summer 1754. Hu.
Ludford, Francis. S Jan T Apr 1743 *Justitia*. M.
Ludgater, Mary of All Saints, Chichester. R for America for murder of her illegitimate child Jly 1700. Sx.
Ludkins als Atkins, John. S Summer 1759. Nf.
Ludlam, Thomas. S May T Nov 1759 *Phoenix*. M.
Ludlow, Henry. SQS Feb T Apr 1768 *Thornton*. M.
Ludlowe, John. R Apr TB for Barbados Jun 1669. L.
Ladlow, John. SQS s stockings Summer 1768. Du.
Ludlow, Richard. S s at St. Neots Summer 1771. Hu.
Ludly als Ladly, William. R 14 yrs Summer 1774. Du.
Luff, John. LC from *Forward* Rappahannock May 1728. X.
Luffe, John. S s at Martham Lent 1772. Nf.
Luffe, Richard of Basing. R for Barbados Jly 1672. Ha.
Luff, Robert. S Oct 1751-Jan 1752. M.
Lugg, Edward. Rebel T 1685.
Luggervan, Thomas (1729). *See* Richards. Co.
Luing. *See* Lewin.
Luke, Hugh. R Jly 1771. Ha.
Luke, John. S Jly 1752. Ha.
Luke, Joseph. S Mar 1747. Ha.
Luke, William. S Mar 1734. Ha.
Lukies. *See* Lucas.
Lullams, John (1770). *See* Price. Ha.
Lumbard. *See* Lombard.
Lumber, James. SQS Jly 1742 TB to Md Feb 1743. So.
Lumbar, Moses. SQS Jan 1735. So.
Lumley, Abraham. S Jan-Feb T Apr 1753 *Thames*. M.
Lumley, Margaret. S Jly-Sep T Sep 1742 *Forward*. M.

Lumley, Thomas. S Feb 1775. M.

Lumb, Joseph. S s cloth at Halifax Lent 1768; John Lumb acquitted. Y.

Lumm, Joseph. R & T 14 yrs Jly 1772 *Tayloe*. M.

Lumsdale, Edmund. S Summer 1744 R 14 yrs Lent 1745. Li.

Lund, John. R 14 yrs s sheep Lent 1772. Li.

Lundberg, Sven. T 14 yrs Dec 1753 *Whiteing*. Sy.

Lungreen, Anders Hendrick. R & T for life Apr 1770 *New Trial*. M.

Lungreen, Jurgen Lawrence of Liverpool, mariner. S & R for life for murder at Liverpool Lent 1766. La.

Lunn, Ann of St. Paul, Covent Garden, spinster. S s jewelry Jly 1740 T Jan 1741 *Harpooner* to Rappahannock. M.

Lunn, Margaret of Stockton. R for America Mar 1710. Du.

Lunn, Nehemiah. S Lent 1769. Li.

Lunn, Thomas. S s at Rugeley Lent 1763. St.

Lunns, Anthony of Baswich. R for America Jly 1683. St.

Lunt, Bridget of Ormskirk, spinster. SQS Oct 1756. La.

Lupton, George. R s horse Lent 1773. Nt.

Lusby, James. S s sheep Summer 1769 R 14 yrs Lent 1770. Li.

Luscombe, John. TB to Va from QS 1771. De.

Lush, Arthur. Rebel T 1685.

Lush, Henry of Stafford. R for America Jly 1673. St.

Lush, John. Rebel T 1685.

Lush, Mary. R Jly AT Sep 1686. M.

Lush, William. Rebel T 1685.

Lush, William. R Mar 1772. Do.

Lush, William. S Mar 1773. So.

Lushby, William. R Jly 1773. M.

Lusted, Frances (1671). *See* Jobson. M.

Luther, Edward. Rebel T 1685.

Lutterel, Elizabeth. S Apr 1759. So.

Lutterell, James (1759). *See* Baker. M.

Lutton, Paul. LC from *Forward* Annapolis Jun 1725. X.

Lutwich, William. S Dec 1762 T Jan 1763 *Neptune*. M.

Lux, John. R 14 yrs Jly 1721. De.

Luxon, Henry. S Mar 1729. So.

Luxton, Richard of Cheriton Fitzpaine. R for Barbados Mar 1691. De.

Lyall, James (1697). *See* Pritchett. M.

Lycence, Richard. TB 14 yrs Oct 1719. L.

Lyde, Edward. Rebel T 1685.

Lyde, Elizabeth. R 14 yrs Jly 1721 T from Southampton 1723. Ha.

Lyde, Hannah Rutter. SQS & T Sep 1751 *Greyhound*. M.

Lyde, John. Rebel T 1685.

Lyde, Sylvester. Rebel T 1685.

Lydeat, James. S Mar 1733 T *Patapsco* LC Annapolis Nov 1733. Wi.

Lydiatt, Jane. T Sep 1758 *Tryal*. E.

Lye, Elianor of West Molesey, spinster, als wife of Richard. R for Barbados or Jamaica Jly 1674. Sy.

Lyes, Samuel. S s at Fladbury Lent 1767. Wo.

Lyfolly, Richard of Lambeth. SQS Jan T Apr 1760 *Thetis*. Sy.

Lyford, John. S s at St. Mary, Reading, Lent 1759. Be.

Lyford, Thomas of St. Thomas Apostle. R for Barbados or Jamaica Mar 1707. Sy.

Lyford, William. S Jun-Dec 1738 T Jan 1739 *Dorsetshire* to Va. M.

Lyger, James. S & T Sep 1755 *Tryal*. L.

Lynch, Charles. S Jan T Feb 1723 *Jonathan* but died on passage. L.

Lynch, Charles. S & T Apr 1733 *Patapsco* LC Annapolis Nov 1733. M.

Linch, Daniel. TB to Va 1770. De.

Lynch, Disney. SQS Jly T Sep 1751 *Greyhound*. M.

Lynch, Eleanor. T Jun 1764 *Dolphin*. M.

Lynch, Elizabeth wife of David. R 14 yrs Jly 1745. Ha.

Linch, John of Ripley. SQS Jan T Apr 1765 *Ann*. Sy.

Lynch, John. S Jly 1775. L.

Lynch, Mary. S May-Jly 1749. M.

Linch, Michael. S Sep T Dec 1758 *The Brothers*. M.

Lyndsey. *See* Lindsey.

Lyne. *See* Line.

Lyneing. *See* Lining.

Lyner, James of Braintree. R for Barbados or Jamaica Jly 1715. E.

Lynes. *See* Lines.

Lyng. *See* Ling.

Lynley. *See* Linley.

Lynn, Elizabeth, aged 27, brown hair. LC from *Jonathan* Md Jly 1724. X.

Lynn als Bond, Hester. S Sep-Oct 1748 T Jan 1749 *Laura*. M.

Lynn, John. S Apr T 14 yrs May 1718 *Tryal*. L.

Lynn, Nathaniel. S Feb 1719. M.

Lynn, Samuel. R for America Aug 1715. L.

Lynn, Thomas. R Aug AT Oct 1700. M.

Lyon, Ann. R 14 yrs Jly 1763. M.

Lyon als Lawrence, Benjamin. S May T Jly 1723 *Alexander* LC Annapolis Sep 1723. M.

Lyon, Charles. R Jan-Feb T 14 yrs Apr 1772 *Thornton*. M.

Lyon, Elizabeth als Esther. S 14 yrs Aug 1763. L.

Lyon, Jacob. T Apr 1771 *Thornton*. Sy.

Lyon, John. R for Barbados Sep 1672. M.

Lyon als Darton als Carleton, Mary. R for Barbados Dec 1671. M.

Lyon, Mary. S Summer 1755 R 14 yrs Lent 1756. St.

Lyon, Moses. S May T Jly 1770 *Scarsdale*. M.

Lyon, Moses. S Apr 1774. L.

Lion, Thomas. S Dec 1757 T Mar 1758 *Dragon*. L.

Lion, Thomas. S Jan 1759. L.

Lyon, William of Uttoxeter. R for America Jly 1687. St.

Lyon, William. S Sep T Dec 1758 *The Brothers*. M.

Lyons, Abraham. S Jun T Jly 1772 *Tayloe*. L.

Lions, Barnaby. S Jun T Aug 1769 *Douglas*. M.

Lyons, Catherine. S Jan-Feb T Apr 1772 *Thornton*. M.

Lyons, Elizabeth (1741). *See* Doggett. M.

Lyons, Elizabeth. S Apr T Jun 1742 *Bladon* to Md. M.

Lyons, Hugh. LC from *Owners Goodwill* Annapolis Jly 1722. X.

Lyons, Isaac. Sep-Oct T Dec 1753 *Whiteing*. M.

Lyons, John. S 14 yrs for receiving & T Jly 1772 *Tayloe*. L.

Lyons, Joseph. S 14 yrs for receiving & T Jly 1771 *Tayloe*. L.
Lypiatt. *See* Lipiatt.
Lyston. *See* Liston.
Lyth, Robert. S Feb T Apr 1732 *Patapsco* LC Annapolis Oct 1732. L.

Mc

To facilitate easier reference the various spellings given in
original documents as Mc, Mac, Mack, Mag, etc. have been unified as Mc.

McUllister, Edward. S Dec 1749-Jan 1750 T Mar 1750 *Tryal*. M.
McOllester, John. S Lent 1756. E.
McArdell, Henry. S Sep T Oct 1750 *Rachael*. M.
McArter, Alexander John. S Summer 1756. Sy.
McCarter, Mary. S Jan 1751. M.
McCarter, Mary. S s gold coin at Manfield Summer 1772. Y.
McColley, Andrew. S & T Oct 1730 *Forward* LC Potomack Jan 1731. L.
McCollie, John. S Summer 1753. Du.
McAway, Stephen. S Sep T Dec 1769 *Justitia*. M.
McAway, William. S Sep T Dec 1767 *Neptune*. M.
McBee, William. AT 14 yrs Summer 1732. Nl.
McBlair, John (1738). *See* Graham. Cu.
McCape, John of Tottington Upper End, joiner. SQS Oct 1763. La.
McCaib, John of St. Saviour, Southwark. SQS Mar T Jun 1768 *Tryal*. Sy.
McCabe, Sarah. T Jun 1764 *Dolphin*. M.
McCabe, William. R 14 yrs Mar 1764. Ha.
McCahil, Owen. S Summer 1745 R 14 yrs Lent 1746. Sy.
McKool, Elizabeth. S Jan-Jun T Jun 1728 *Elizabeth* to Md or Va. M.
McCall, Elizabeth. S Apr 1760. M.
McCall, James. S Jan T Feb 1765 *Tryal*. L.
McKan, John. S May-Jly 1774. M.
McCan, Sarah. S Lent 1763. No.
McCannon, Frederick. SW & T Apr 1770 *New Trial*. M.
McCarley, Charles. S Jun 1733. M.
McCarter. *See* McArthur.
McCartney, Arthur. S & T Jan 1736 *Dorsetshire* LC Va Sep 1736. L.
McCartney, George. S Summer 1771. Ch.
McCartney, James of St. Paul, Covent Garden. S s clothing & T Dec
  1740 *Vernon*. M.
McCartney, Patrick of Stoke next Guildford. SQS Oct 1760. Sy.
McCartney, Patrick. S Jan T Feb 1765 *Tryal*. L.
McHarty, Daniel. PT Jan 1680. M.
McCarty, Darby. T Jun 1764 *Dolphin*. K.
McCarty, David. SL Jly T Sep 1755 *Tryal*. Sy.
McCarty, James. S May-Jly 1773. M.
McKarty, Lawrence. S Jly 1749. L.
McCarty, Mary. S Feb T Mar 1731 *Patapsco* LC Annapolis Jun 1731. L.
McCarty, Mary of St. James, Westminster, spinster. S s clothing Jly 1740
  T Jan 1741 *Harpooner* to Rappahannock. M.
McCarty, Michael (1771). *See* Creamer. M.
McCasey, William. SQS Apr T May 1767 *Thornton*. M.
McCherry, Edward. S s naval stores Jly 1763. Ha.

McClean. *See* McLean.

McClelland, John. S & T Sep 1764 *Justitia*. M.

McClow, Daniel. S & T Jan 1739 *Dorsetshire*. L.

McCloud, Elizabeth. SL Aug T Sep 1764 *Justitia*. Sy.

McCloud, James. S Feb 1770. M.

McCloud, John. S s at Sherbourne Lent 1727. Be.

McCloud, William. SQS Feb T Apr 1772 *Thornton*. M.

McClough, Daniel. S Feb 1775. L.

McColley/McCollie. *See* McAuly.

McComb, Mary. SQS Oct 1760. M.

McConnell, Mary. S & T Oct 1730 *Forward* LC Potomack Jan 1731. M.

McKonnelly, Michael. S Jan T Mar 1764 *Tryal*. L.

McCoppy, Jane (1722). *See* Bean. M.

McCorie, Elizabeth. LC from *Elizabeth* Potomack Aug 1729. X.

McCormick, Adam. S Feb-Apr 1746. M.

McCormick, Ann. S Feb 1754. L.

McCormick, Francis. S Nov T Dec 1753 *Whiteing*. L.

McCoy, Benjamin. S Jan T Feb 1744 *Neptune* to Md. M.

McCoy, James of St. Giles in Fields. S Jly-Sep T Sep 1742 *Forward*. M.

McCoy, John. S Feb T Apr 1732 *Patapsco* LC Annapolis Oct 1732. L.

McCoy, John. T May 1752 *Lichfield*. Sx.

McCoy als Lewis, Martha. S Sep 1719. M.

McCoy, Mary. S Jan-Jun 1728 T *Elizabeth* LC Potomack Aug 1729. M.

McCoy als Smith, Sarah. SQS Feb 1774. M.

McCoy, William (1746). *See* Camell. So.

McCrew, John. S Sep T Dec 1767 *Neptune*. L.

McCue. *See* McHugh.

McCullock, John. S Dec 1742 T Apr 1743 *Justitia*. M.

McCullogh, Margaret. S Dec 1774. M.

McCullogh, William. S Apr-Jun 1739. M.

McCullock, William. S & T Jan 1766 *Tryal*. L.

McDaniel, Ann. S Oct T Dec 1770 *Justitia*. M.

McDaniel, Daniel. S Jun T Sep 1767 *Justitia*. M.

McDaniel, Elizabeth. S Sep-Oct 1773. M.

McDaniel, Hugh. S Jly T Sep 1764 *Justitia*. M.

McDannel, James. S Apr T Sep 1757 *Thetis*. L.

McDaniel, James. R 14 yrs Jly 1774. M.

McDaniel, John. S Feb T Mar 1730 *Patapsco* LC Annapolis Sep 1730. M.

McDaniel, Mary. S Aug T Oct 1723 *Forward* to Va. M.

McDaniel, Mary. S Dec 1749-Jan 1750 T Mar 1750 *Tryal*. M.

McDannell, Mary. S May-Jun T Jly 1753 *Tryal*. M.

McDaniel, Neal. R 14 yrs Aug 1750 TB to Va. De.

McDaniel, Robert. S Mar 1761. Ha.

McDaniel als McDonald, William. SQS Apr T Sep 1751 *Greyhound*. Sy.

McDermot, Timothy. S Feb T Apr 1765 *Ann*. M.

McDiamod, Owen (1726). *See* Darby, John. M.

McDonagh, Charles (1735). *See* Daniel. M.

McDonald, Alexander. S May-Jun T Jly 1753 *Tryal*. M.

McDonald als McDorell, Andrew. S Jun T Aug 1769 *Douglas*. M.

McDonald, Angus. R 14 yrs Summer 1753. Nl.

McDonald, Ann. S s stays Apr T Jun 1742 *Bladon* to Md. M.
McDonald, Ann. S Jan-Apr 1748. M.
McDonald, Ann. S & T Apr 1762 *Dolphin*. L.
McDonald, Archibald. S Jly T Sep 1751 *Greyhound*. L.
McDonald, Charles. S & T Jan 1769 *Thornton*. M.
McDonald, Christopher. S & T Jan 1765 *Tryal*. M.
McDonald, Elizabeth. S Jan T Feb 1719 *Worcester* LC Annapolis Jun 1719. M.
McDonald, Elizabeth. S & R Summer 1745. Su.
McDonald, James. S Sep 1737 T Jan 1738 *Dorsetshire* to Va. M.
McDonald, James. SQS Apr T Jun 1768 *Tryal*. M.
McDonald, James. S & T Jly 1770 *Scarsdale*. M.
McDonald, James (1772). *See* Brown. L.
McDonald, John. S Jan T Feb 1719 *Worcester* LC Annapolis Jun 1719. L.
Mackdonall, John. TB Apr 1749. Db.
McDonald, John. S Summer 1760 R 14 yrs Lent 1761. Wo.
McDonald, John. S & T for life Jly 1771 *Scarsdale*. M.
McDonald, Margaret. S for perjury Dec 1755 T Jan 1756 *Greyhound*. L.
McDonald, Mary. T Jun 1740 *Essex*. E.
McDonald, Matthew. S Feb T May 1719 *Margaret*; sold to Samuel Chaney Md Sep 1719. L.
McDonald, Neal. S s at North Runcton Summer 1753. Nf.
McDonald, Patrick (1747). *See* Avery. M.
McDonald, Peter. SQS Jan 1754. M.
McDonald, Rachael. S Sep-Oct T Dec 1771 *Justitia*. M.
McDonald, Robert. S & T Sep 1731 *Smith* LC Va 1732. M.
McDonald, Roger. S s meat at St. Dionis Backchurch Oct 1768 T Jan 1769 *Thornton*. L.
McDonald, Sarah. S Oct T Dec 1724 *Rappahannock*. L.
McDonall, Sarah (1733). *See* Randall. L.
McDone, Ephraim. S s from lighter on Thames Oct T Dec 1767 *Neptune*. M.
McDonnack, Edward. S Oct T Dec 1758 *The Brothers*. L.
McDonnell, Edward of Biggleswade. R for America Apr 1697. Bd.
McDonnell, Elizabeth. R for Barbados or Jamaica for coin clipping May 1691. L.
McDonnell, James. S Jly T Oct 1741 *Sea Horse* to Va. M.
McDonnell, James. S Apr-May T May 1744 *Justitia*. M.
McDonnell, John. S & T Sep 1731 *Smith* LC Va 1732. M.
McDonnell, Philip. R for Barbados Dec 1693 AT Jan 1694. M.
McDonough als McDonnell, Henry of Westbury. S Summer 1718. G.
McDorell, Andrew (1769). *See* McDonald. M.
McDormale, Patrick. S Aug 1726. M.
McDougal, James. S Feb T Mar 1764 *Tryal*. M.
McDowgall, John. T Nov 1725 *Rappahannock* but died on passage. Sy.
McDowell, James. S Sep T Dec 1767 *Neptune*. M.
McDuff, John. SQS Jun T Jly 1772 *Tayloe*. M.
McDugdale, Daniel of Little Hormead. R for Barbados or Jamaica Jun 1699. Ht.
McEnnis, Frederick. S Apr T Jun 1742 *Bladon*. L.

McEnny, Andrew. S May T Jun 1738 *Forward*. L.

McEreth als Holme, Elizabeth. S Summer 1731 R 14 yrs Summer 1732. We.

McEther, Timothy. T Oct 1729 *Forward*. Sy.

McFarling, Catherine. S & T Jan 1765 *Tryal*. M.

McFarling, Mary. S for Va Aug 1718. L.

McFarndall, Mark. S Apr 1718. M.

McFaston als McFerston, John. S May T Jly 1722 *Alexander*. M.

McFeast, Mary. S May T Jly 1771 *Scarsdale*. L.

McFeet, John of St. John's, yeoman. SQS & T Jan 1766 *Tryal*. Sy.

McGanley, James. SQS Feb 1774. M.

McGea, Andrew. T Oct 1738 *Genoa*. K.

McGee, Catherine. S Feb T Apr 1765 *Ann*. M.

McGee, Christopher. SQS Sep 1773. M.

McGee, John. S May T Jun 1726 *Loyal Margaret* LC Annapolis Oct 1726. M.

McGee, John. S Oct 1764 T Jan 1765 *Tryal*. M.

McGee, Mary (1765). *See* Carrol. M.

McGee, Mary. S Apr-May T Jly 1771 *Scarsdale*. M.

McGey, Thomas. S & T Apr 1725 *Sukey* LC Annapolis Sep 1725. M.

McGee, Thomas. S s horse Summer 1733 R 14 yrs Summer 1734. Nl.

McGirk, James. S May T Jun 1768 *Tryal*. M.

McGlew, Patrick. S Jly T Sep 1755 *Tryal*. L.

McGowing, John. S & T Jan 1769 *Thornton*. M.

McGrath, Elizabeth (1767). *See* Curray. M.

McGrath, Margaret. S Sep T Nov 1759 *Phoenix*. M.

McGregor, Robert. T Oct 1726 *Forward*. K.

McGrew, James. S Apr T May 1743 *Indian Queen*. L.

McGuffin, Alexander of Bermondsey. SQS Oct T Dec 1763 *Neptune*. Sy.

McGuines, Bernard. R 14 yrs Jly 1765 TB to Va 1766. De.

McGinnis, Charles. S Sep-Oct 1775. M.

McGinnis, John. SQS Jan T Mar 1764 *Tryal*. M.

McGuiness, John. S Summer TB Aug 1771. Nt.

McGinnis, Judith. SQS Oct 1768 T Jan 1769 *Thornton*. M.

McGennis, Thomas. T 14 yrs Apr 1770 *New Trial*. Sy.

McGuinis, William. S Aug T Oct 1723 *Forward* to Va. M.

McGennes, William. T Jun 1764 *Dolphin*. K.

McQuire, Barbara. T Dec 1736 *Dorsetshire*. E.

McGuire, Catherine. S Oct 1748 T Jan 1749 *Laura*. L.

McGuire, Catherine. S Apr 1774. M.

McGuire, Daniel. S Jan-Jun T Jun 1728 *Elizabeth* LC Potomack Aug 1729. M.

McGuire, Dennis. SQS Oct T Dec 1771 *Justitia*. M.

McQuire, Henry. T Apr 1765. K.

McGuire, Lockland. S Jly-Dec 1747. M.

McGueire, Margaret. S Feb T Mar 1760 *Friendship*. M.

McGuire, Martin. S Jan-Feb T Apr 1771 *Thornton*. M.

McGuire, Matthew. S Jan T Feb 1765 *Tryal*. L.

McGuy, Jane. *See* Daloon. M.

McGwin, Daniel (1736). *See* Stockman. L.

McHalfpen, James. S Oct 1756. L.

McHam, Margaret. LC from *Forward* Annapolis Jun 1725. X.

McHarty. *See* McCarthy.

McHobin, Ufane. S Sep 1719. M.

McKew, Henry. S & T Jly 1770 *Scarsdale*. M.

McCue, John. S s iron gates Jan T Jun 1738 *Forward* to Md or Va. M.

McInnes, John. S & T Apr 1766 *Ann*. L.

McIntosh, Anne. PT Oct R & T Dec 1716 *Lewis* to Jamaica. M.

McIntosh, Daniel. S Jan T 14 yrs Apr 1741 *Speedwell*. L.

McIntosh, Daniel. SQS Sep 1754. M.

McIntosh, John. T Nov 1741 *Sea Horse*. K.

McIntosh, Peter. S s at North Runcton Summer 1753. Nf.

McIntosh, William. S & T Sep 1766 *Justitia*. L.

McKan. *See* McCan.

McKase, Bartholomew (1748). *See* Fitzgerald. M.

McKaw, Alexander. S Summer T Oct 1750 *Rachael*. K.

McKay, John. S Apr T May 1743 *Indian Queen* to Potomack. M.

McKay, John. S s sheep Lent R 14 yrs Summer 1758. Li.

McKecky, Joseph (1725). *See* Cuzee. M.

McKee, Patrick. R for Barbados Aug 1670. M.

McKeithley, Christopher. S Sep 1733. M.

McKeny, Daniel. S Apr-May T May 1741 *Catherine & Elizabeth* to Md. M.

McKenny, William. R & T May 1736 *Patapsco* to Md. M.

McKenzie, Alexander. ST & T Apr 1765 *Ann*. L.

McKensie, Andrew. T Apr 1766 *Ann*, K.

McKenzie, Christian. S Sep T Nov 1743 *George William*. M.

McKenzie, Eleanor. S Sep-Oct 1772. M.

McKenzie, James (1773). *See* Watson, Thomas. M.

McKenzie, James (1775). *See* Douglas. De.

McKenzie, John. AT Summer 1765. Nl.

McKenzie, John. T Dec 1771 *Justitia*. Sy.

McKenzie, Mary. S Jan-May T Jun 1738 *Forward* to Md or Va. M.

McKenzie, Penelope. S Apr 1748. L.

McKenzie, Sarah als Mary. S Mar 1754. L.

McKensie, Susanna. S Feb T Apr 1766 *Ann*. M.

McKenzie, William (1773). *See* Williams. M.

McKew. *See* McHugh.

McKinney, Thomas of St. Margaret, Westminster. SW Apr 1773. M.

McKley als McKny, William. T Nov 1725 *Rappahannock* but died on passage. K.

McKoan, James of St. Andrew, Hertford. SQS Aug T Sep 1767 *Justitia*. Ht.

McKonnell. *See* McConnell.

McKonnelly. *See* McConnelly.

McKool. *See* McCall

McKoone, Edward. S Lent R 14 yrs Summer TB Aug 1739. G.

McKullester. *See* McAllister.

McLane. *See* McLean.

McLaughlin als McLinglin, Michael of Harwich. SQS Oct 1765 T Apr 1766 *Ann*. E.

McLaughlin, Barnay. S Mar 1765. Ha.

McLochlen, Cornelius. S Jan-Feb 1774. M.
McLocklin, Edward. S Lent 1730. Sh.
McLocklin, Edward. S s at Chetwynd Lent 1739. Sh.
McLaughland, Hannah (1762). *See* Perry. M.
McLaghlin, Henry. T May 1744 *Justitia*. Sy.
McLaughlin, Jeremiah. S Jan-Apr 1749. M.
McLaughlin als Mason als Thomas, Mary. S 14 yrs Jun-Dec 1745. M.
McGlochlin als Rowler, Mary. SQS & TB Apr 1770. G.
McLaughton, Grifsey (1749). *See* Kelly. La.
McLane, Ann. S May T Jun 1726 *Loyal Margaret* to Md. M.
McLin, Ann. S & T Dec 1731 *Forward* to Md or Va. M.
McLane, David. S May T Jly 1771 *Scarsdale*. L.
McLean, Eleanor. S Oct 1751-Jan 1752. M.
McLeane, Frances. S & T Oct 17331 *Caesar* to Va. M.
McClain, Jane. LC from *Loyal Margaret* Annapolis Oct 1726. X.
McLane, Jane. S Oct 1749. L.
McLyn, John. R for Barbados Mar 1683. M.
McLean als McLearon, John. S Jun 1743. L.
Macklin, John. S s handkerchiefs Summer 1754. Sh.
McLane, Paul. S Dec 1746. L.
McLin, Thomas. S Jan-Apr 1748. M.
McLean, Thomas of Merton. SQS Jan 1772. Sy.
McLean, William. S Jan-May T 14 yrs Jun 1738 *Forward*. M.
McLearon, John (1743). *See* McLean. L.
McMahon als Clarke, Benjamin. S Dec 1749-Jan 1750 T Mar 1750
    Tryal. M.
McMahon, Mary. SQS Feb 1757. M.
Mackmelin, John (1765). *See* Mallon. La.
McMillen, William. S May T Jun 1727 *Susanna* to Va. M.
McMillion, Philip. S Oct T Nov 1728 *Forward* LC Rappahannock Jun
    1729. L.
McMulling, Mary wife of James. S s gowns Sep 1735 T Jan 1736
    Dorsetshire LC Va Sep 1736. M.
McNamara, Jeremiah. S Mar 1762 TB to Va. De.
McNamara, Mary wife of James. S Feb 1757. M.
McNamara, Timothy. S Dec 1766 T Jan 1767 *Tryal*. L.
McNamer, Joseph. SQS Dec 1753. M.
McNara, Simon of Hoo. S Summer T Oct 1750 *Rachael*. Sx.
McNeil, Henry. S Dec 1765 T Jan 1766 *Tryal*. M.
McPherson, Alexander. S Apr T May 1718 *Tryal* LC Charles Town Aug
    1718. L.
McPhearson, Ann. S May-Jly 1749. M.
McQueen, Sarah. T Oct 1726 *Forward*. Sy.
McQuin, Daniel. S Apr 1749. L.
McQuin, John. T Jan 1736 *Dorsetshire*. Sy.
McQuin als McQueen als Johnson, John. T Sep 1764 *Justitia*. K.
McQuire. *See* McGuire.
McRow, Daniel. R Jly AT Oct 1685. M.
McSkinning, Ewen. SQS Apr TB May 1756. So.

M

Mabbett, Anthony. S s at Thornbury Lent 1775. G.

Mabell, John of Scarborough. R for Barbados Jly 1699. Y.

Mabeley, Everard. TB Jun 1738. Db.

Mayby, Ambrose. R 14 yrs Aug 1745. So.

Maby als Manning, Samuel. S Apr 1741. So.

Mabe, William of Much Dewchurch. S Lent 1720. He.

Macclesfield, Thomas. S Aug T Sep 1725 *Forward* LC Annapolis Dec 1725. L.

Mace als Mitchell, Edward. R Sep TB for Barbados Oct 1669. L.

Mace, John. S s at Hingham Summer 1753. Nf.

Mace, John. S s game at Cheltenham Summer 1763. G.

Mace, Thomas. R for Barbados Mar 1681. M.

Mace, William. S Feb-Apr T May 1752 *Lichfield*. M.

Macey, George. Rebel T 1685.

Macey, Jane. S Mar 1755. Do.

Masey, Thomas. R 14 yrs Oct 1772. M.

Maychin, Ann. AT from QS Lent 1739. St.

Mack als Bonten, James als Rip. S s mare at Earith & R 14 yrs Lent 1770. Hu.

Mackey, George. S Sep-Oct 1749. M.

Mackey, George. S Jly T Sep 1767 *Justitia*. L.

Mackey, Patrick. S May-Jly T Sep 1755 *Tryal*. M.

Mackrell, Edward. T Jan 1766 *Tryal*. M.

Mackrell, John. R for Barbados Jly 1674. L.

Mackrell, John. S for burglary Lent R Summer 1730 (SP). Be.

Mackrell als Jordan, Sarah of St. Thomas. SQS Jan T Apr 1762 *Neptune*. Sy.

Macrin, Mary. S Sep 1764. M.

Madberry, Thomas (1664). *See* Medberry. Bd.

Maddell, William. S Lent R 14 yrs Summer T Oct 1744 *Savannah*. E.

Madden, Edward. S Jly T Dec 1773 *Neptune*. M.

Maden, Richard of Butterworth, woollen weaver. SQS Apr 1744. La.

Maddens, Samuel. S Sep-Oct T Dec 1771 *Justitia*. M.

Madder, Edward. S Feb T 14 yrs Apr 1741 *Speedwell* or *Mediterranean*. M.

Maddern, John. S Mar 1755. So.

Madders, John. Rebel T 1685.

Madders, William. TB to Va from QS 1741. De.

Madding, Hannah. ST & T Jan 1767 *Tryal*. L.

Meddison, Job. R for Barbados or Jamaica Dec 1689. L.

Maderson, Rachel. T Sep 1730 *Smith*. Sy.

Maddison, Sarah. S Jly T Sep 1757 *Thetis*. M.

Maddox, Ann. S s at Worthen Lent 1747 AT Lent 1749. Sh.

Maddox, Elizabeth. S Lent 1773. K.

Maddox, Elizabeth. S Apr 1773. M.

Maddox, John of St. Margaret, Westminster. SW Apr T May 1767 *Thornton*. M.

Maddocks, Martha. S Feb T Mar 1758 *Dragon*. M.

Maddocks, Martha wife of William. S Sep T Dec 1769 *Justitia*. M.

Maddox, Mary. S s at Rattlinghope Summer 1775. Sh.

Maddocks, Nathaniel. R 14 yrs Aug 1773. De.

Maddox, Richard. S s at Rowley Regis Summer 1766. St.

Maddox, Samuel. S Lent 1765. No.

Meddocks, William. R 14 yrs Aug 1739. De.

Maddringham, Jane (1745). *See* Watkins. M.

Maddy, William. S s cloth Jan T Jun 1738 *Forward*. L.

Madera, Joshua (1746). *See* Watson. M.

Madge, William. S Mar 1730. De.

Madle, Joseph. S Lent 1775. E.

Madren, Mary. S Aug T Sep 1725 *Forward* LC Annapolis Dec 1725. L.

Madwell, James of Braintree, basket maker. SQS Jan T Apr 1741
    Speedwell or *Mediterranean*. E.

Maeks als Davison, Phoebe of Morpeth, yeoman's wife. SQS s
    handkerchiefs Mich 1774. Nl.

Maer. *See* Myer.

Mager. *See* Major.

Magin, Charles. S Feb T Apr 1765 *Ann*. M.

Magner, Philip. R for Barbados or Jamaica Oct 1690. M.

Magoy, Hugh. TB Aug 1738. Y.

Magrave, Ralph. S Oct 1774. L.

Mahon, John of Rotherhithe. SQS Oct 1762. Sy.

Mahan, Joseph. S Oct T 14 yrs Dec 1769 *Justitia*. M.

Mahone als Bignell, Rose of St. Clement Danes, widow. S s watch Oct
    1740 T Jan 1741 *Harpooner* to Rappahannock. M.

Mahoone als Moore als Murry, Sarah. R for Barbados or Jamaica May
    1697. L.

Mahoney, Florence. S & T Jly 1770 *Scarsdale*. L.

Mahony, Michael. S at Faversham Oct 1765 TB Jan 1766 T Jan 1767
    Tryal. K.

Mahoney, Thomas. SQS May T Jly 1771 *Scarsdale*. M.

Mayd, Ann. R for Barbados Jun 1665.

Maid, James of West Derby. SQS Jan 1775. La.

Maid, Jane. S May-Jly 1774. M.

Maiden, Ann. S & T Dec 1731 *Forward* to Md or Va. M.

Maiden, Richard. R for Barbados or Jamaica Jly 1685. M.

Maidenought, Michael. S Apr T May 1750 *Lichfield*. M.

Maidman, James. T Apr 1732 *Patapsco*. K.

Mail. *See* Male.

Maine, Charles. S Sep T Nov 1743 *George William*. M.

Mayne, Henry. R 14 yrs Jun 1761. Ha.

Main, Henry, apprentice at Hutton near Rudby. S for firing cowshed
    TB Aug 1774. Y.

Mayne, James. S Apr 1770. Co.

Maine, John. T Jun 1728 *Elizabeth*. E.

Mayne als May, John. S & T Dec 1740 *Vernon*. L.

Mayne, John. S Sep-Oct T Dec 1753 *Whiteing*. M.

Maine, Mary. R May T for life Sep 1758 *Tryal* to Annapolis. M.

Mayne, Stephen. S Apr 1753. So.

Mayne, Thomas (1738). *See* Mean. De.

Main, Thomas. S Apr 1759. So.

Mayne, William. SQS Jly TB to Md Nov 1740. So.

Mainwairing, Charles. S Apr T May 1767 *Thornton*. M.

Mainwaring, James. SQS & T Apr 1765 *Ann*. M.

Mainy, Lawrence. T Dec 1736 *Dorsetshire*. K.

Mair. *See* Mare.

Major, George. TB to Va from QS 1729. De.

Major, Hannah. S for perjury Aug 1770 TB to Va. De.

Major, James. SQS Sep T Oct 1768 *Justitia*. M.

Major, James. SQS Jun T Jly 1772 *Tayloe*. M.

Major als Markerson, John. R 14 yrs Mar TB to Va Apr 1766. Wi.

Major, John (1767). *See* Brown. Bd.

Mager, John. S Mar 1772. De.

Major, Sarah. TB to Md from QS 1727. De.

Major, Thomas of Elmswell. R for Barbados Feb 1664. Su.

Major als Markerson, Walter. S Mar 1774. Wi.

Makepeace, Anne. S & T Apr 1733 *Patapsco* LC Annapolis Nov 1733. M.

Makepeace, Elizabeth wife of Stephen. S Feb T Apr 1770 *New Trial*. M.

Makin als Meakin, Ellis als Elias of Manchester. SQS Apr 1747. La.

Makin, John of Moston, weaver. SQS Oct 1752. La.

Makyn, Richard of Carlton in Lindrick. SQS s sheets Jly 1749. Nt.

Malburne, Elizabeth. S Sep 1734. M.

Malcah, Abraham. S Nov T Dec 1770 *Justitia*. L.

Malcolm als Price, Lidia wife of James. S s silver cup Jly T Dec 1735 *John* LC Annapolis Sep 1736. M.

Malcomb, Robert. S Jly T Sep 1765 *Justitia*. M.

Malcona, Robert of Parracombe, husbandman. R for Barbados Apr 1668. De.

Mail, Edmund of St. Saviour, Southwark. SQS & T Jan 1756 *Greyhound*. Sy.

Maile, John. S s sheep Summer 1754 R 14 yrs Lent 1755. No.

Male, Robert. S May T Sep 1766 *Justitia*. M.

Male, Samuel. S Apr 1775. So.

Mayle, William of Northampton. R for America Jly 1716. No.

Maile, William. S s sheep Summer 1754 R 14 yrs Lent 1755. No.

Males, Cornelius. S Sep 1731. M.

Maley, Patrick of St. Clement Danes. SW for false pretences & T Jan 1767 *Tryal*. M.

Malings, Thomas. S s at Tottenhoe Lent 1770. Bd.

Mallabar, John. S s silver spoon Jun T Dec 1736 *Dorsetshire* to Va. M.

Mallard, Benjamin. S Lent R 14 yrs Summer 1731. Wa.

Mallard, Elizabeth. R May 1685 AT May 1688. M.

Mallard, George. T Jan 1741 *Vernon*. E.

Mallard, Joseph. SQS & TB Aug 1738. G.

Mallard, Peter. T Oct 1721 *Wiliam & John*. K.

Mallard, Richard. SQS & TB Aug 1738. G.

Mallard, Stephen. S & T Oct 1730 *Forward* LC Potomack Jan 1731. M.

Malletrat, Edward. SQS for attending conventicle Dec 1664. M.

Mallott, Elizabeth. SQS Coventry Apr 1765.

Mallett, John. S Jan T Feb 1765 *Tryal*. L.
Mallett, Joseph. R 14 yrs Aug 1734. De.
Mallett, William. S Jly T Sep 1767 *Justitia*. M.
Mallick, John. S Mar 1773. Co.
Mallison, Thomas. S Lent R 14 yrs Summer 1758. Bd.
Mallory, Diana. S Lent 1766. Wa.
Mallery, Mathew. T Nov 1743 *George William*. E.
Melleory, Thomas. S s handkerchief at St. Sepulchre Sep T Oct 1768 *Justitia*. L.
Malloes, Robert. S May T Aug 1769 *Douglas*. M.
Mallon als Makmelin, John of Manchester, barber. SQS Apr 1765. La.
Mallows, Sarah. S Oct T Nov 1762 *Prince William*. M.
Mallyon, William of Maidstone. R for Barbados or Jamaica Jly 1674. K.
Malone, Abraham. S May-Jly 1773. M.
Malone, John. S Feb-Apr T May 1752 *Lichfield*. M.
Malone, William of Bermondsey, yeoman. SQS Jly 1765. Sy.
Malony, Daniel. S Oct-Dec 1754. M.
Maloney, Thomas. T Sep 1766 *Justitia*. M.
Maloye. *See* Molloy.
Malsheir als Pepperell, Elizabeth. R Aug AT Oct 1700. M.
Maltby, John. S Summer 1765. Nt.
Malvin, Alexander. AT Summer 1758. Y.
Man. *See* Mann.
Manahay, William. SW & T Apr 1768 *Thornton*. M.
Mancill. *See* Mansell.
Mancroft, John. R for Barbados or Jamaica Jly 1686. M.
Mander, William. S s sheep & R Lent 1768. Wa.
Mandevill, Mary. S May T Jun 1738 *Forward*. L.
Mandeville, Penelope. S Jly T Nov 1762 *Prince William*. M.
Manfield, John. S s turkey Lent 1765. Ca.
Manfield, Stephen. S s at Stow cum Quy & Great Wilbraham Summer 1767. Ca.
Manhall, Elizabeth. S May 1775. L.
Manley, Elizabeth. S Lent TB Aug 1751. Y.
Manley, Hugh. R 14 yrs Mar 1758. De.
Manley, James. S Feb T Mar 1730 *Patapsco* LC Annapolis Sep 1730. M.
Manley, Margaret. TB to Va from QS 1751. De.
Manley, Richard. S & T Sep 1765 *Justitia*. M.
Manley, William. TB to Va from QS 1740. De.
Manly als Mansby, William. S & T 14 yrs Jly 1772 *Tayloe*. M.
Mann, David. S s coat Jan-May T Jun 1738 *Forward* to Md or Va. M.
Man, Deborah, spinster. R for Barbados & TB Oct 1667. L.
Mann, Edward als William. S Jly-Sep 1754. M.
Mann, Elizabeth, spinster. S s at Swannington Lent 1771. Nf.
Mann, Francis. S Jan-May T Jun 1738 *Forward* to Md or Va. M.
Mann, George. SQS Jly TB for life to Va Aug 1774. Le.
Man, Henry. S Aug T Oct 1724 *Forward* LC Annapolis Jun 1725. M.
Mann, Henry. R 14 yrs Mar 1754 TB to Va. De.
Mann, James. S Jun T Sep 1767 *Justitia*. L.
Mann, John. S Oct T Nov 1725 *Rappahannock* LC Rappahannock Apr 1726. L.

Man, Mary. T Aug 1752 *Tryal*. M.

Mann, Mary. S Lent 1774. E.

Mann, Richard. T Jan 1738 *Dorsetshire*. Sy.

Man, Samuel of Great Preston. R for Barbados Jly 1684. Y.

Man, Sarah (1764). *See* Green. E.

Man als Mather, Thomas. R for Barbados Oct 1673. L.

Mann, William. T Apr 1725 *Sukey* LC Md Sep 1725. K.

Mann, William. S s sheep Summer 1753 R 14 yrs Lent 1754. Su.

Mann, William (1754). *See* Mann, Edward. M.

Man, Zachary. R 14 yrs Aug 1728 TB to Md. De.

Mannen, James (1764). *See* Manning. M.

Manners, Andrew. R 14 yrs Summer 1750. Nl.

Manners, Joseph (1681). *See* Ward. Li.

Manners, William. SQS Jan TB Apr 1772. So.

Mannett, James. S Mar TB Apr 1729. Wi.

Manning, Charles. S & T Oct 1729 *Forward* LC Va Jun 1730. L.

Manning, Dorothy of St. Martin in Fields. S s pumps & T May 1740 *Essex*. M.

Manning, Edward. S Apr-Jun T Jly 1772 *Tayloe*. M.

Manning, Elizabeth. S Jun T Sep 1767 *Justitia*. L.

Manning, Elizabeth. SQS Oct 1773. M.

Manning, Hannah. S Lent 1765. Nf.

Manning, Henry. TB to Va 1768. De.

Manning, Humphrey of Hagley, carpenter. S s sea coal Lent 1719. Wo.

Manning als Mannen, James. S Sep 1764 *Justitia*. M.

Manning, James. S s clothing at St. Olave, Hart Street, May T Jun 1768 *Tryal*. L.

Manning, Joan. S Apr 1759. So.

Manning, John. Rebel T 1685.

Manning, John of Honington. R for Barbados or Jamaica Mar 1697. Su.

Manning, John. S Feb 1761. M.

Manning, Margaret. S May T Jun 1727 *Susanna* to Va. M.

Manning, Mary. S Aug 1735. De.

Manning, Mary. S Oct T 14 yrs Dec 1767 *Neptune*; Mary Manning, widow, acquitted. M.

Manning, Rebecca. S Feb T Mar 1730 *Patapsco* LC Annapolis Sep 1730. M.

Manning, Richard. S Sep-Oct T Dec 1752 *Greyhound*. M.

Manning, Samuel. S for highway robbery Lent R 14 yrs Summer 1725 T *Forward* LC Annapolis Dec 1725. Be.

Manning, Samuel. T Apr 1734 *Patapsco*. E.

Manning, Samuel (1741). *See* Maby. So.

Manning, Samuel. S for highway robbery Lent R 14 yrs Summer 1766. No.

Manning als Cowell, Thomas of Tolleshunt. R for Barbados or Jamaica Feb 1696. E.

Manning, William. SQS Jly TB to Md Nov 1738. So.

Manning, William. S Jly T Sep 1764 *Justitia*. M.

Mannings, John. R 14 yrs Aug 1765. So.

Mannings, Mathew. S Mar 1732. Wi.

Manniwell, Joseph. SQS Jan 1754. M.

Mannon, Mary. S Apr-May T Jly 1771 *Scarsdale*. M.

Mansby, William (1772). *See* Manly. M.

Mancill, Edward. S s handkerchiefs at Much Wenlock Lent 1757. Sh.

Mansell, John. S Lent R 14 yrs Summer 1752. Sh.

Mansell, Samuel. S s at St. Chad, Shrewsbury, Lent 1772. Sh.

Mansell, Thomas. S Lent R 14 yrs Summer 1768. St.

Mansell, William. S Feb T 14 yrs Mar 1731 *Patapsco* to Md. M.

Mansill, William. S Lent R 14 yrs Summer 1757. Sh.

Mansen, Thomas. T Apr 1772 *Thornton*. K.

Manser, Allen. S s lambs Summer 1744 R 14 yrs Lent 1745. Sx.

Mancer, James. R 14 yrs Jun 1761. Ha.

Mansfield, David. S Jan-Jun T Jun 1728 *Elizabeth* LC Potomack Aug 1729. M.

Mansfield, Elizabeth. S Jan T Feb 1724 *Anne* to Carolina. M.

Mansfield, Elizabeth wife of Robert. S Jan 1761. M.

Mansfield, Joseph. R for Barbados Dec 1693 AT Jan 1694. M.

Mansfield, Peter of Liston. SQS Apr 1773. E.

Mansfield, Sarah. S Jan T Feb 1719 *Worcester* LC Annapolis Jun 1719. L.

Mansfield, Sarah (1757). *See* Shaw. St.

Mansfield, Thomas. S Dec 1741 T Feb 1742 *Industry* to Md. M.

Manson, Edward. R 14 yrs Mar 1772. Co.

Mantle, David. S at Bristol Lent 1772. G.

Mantle, Edward. S s sheep Lent R 14 yrs Summer 1766. Sh.

Mantle, John. S & T Jan 1769 *Thornton*. M.

Manton, Joseph. S Lent 1744. Db.

Manton, Luke. S Lent 1766. Bd.

Manton, Mary. S & T Sep 1757 *Thetis*. M.

Manton, Samuel. S 14 yrs s ducks Jan 1761. M.

Manton, Samuel. S s at Mepppershall Lent 1771. Bd.

Manton als Strutton als Smith, Sarah. S Jun T Aug 1769 *Douglas*. L.

Manton, Thomas. S Jan 1761. M.

Maplesden, Mary. S Lent T May 1750 *Lichfield*. K.

Mapleton, John. S Oct 1749. L.

Mapp, John. S May T Jly 1723 *Alexander* LC Annapolis Sep 1723. M.

Mapp, William. S s pigs at Middleton Lent 1751. Sh.

Mappett, Charles. S s horse Summer 1746. Sy.

Mapps, Abraham. S Jly 1749. L.

Maraim, Mary. R for Barbados Aug 1664. M.

Maraux, Mathering. S Apr 1767. M.

March, George. T 14 yrs Dec 1771 *Justitia*. E.

March, James. S Lent 1748. K.

March, John. S Dec 1733 T Jan 1734 *Caesar* LC Va Jly 1734. L.

Marchant. *See* Merchant.

Marchinton, Matthew. S Sep-Oct T Dec 1771 *Justitia*. M.

Marckle, Christopher. S May T 14 yrs Jly 1770 *Scarsdale*. M.

Mardin, Humphrey. S Mar 1763 TB to Va. De.

Mare, Thomas. R 14 yrs Jly 1758 TB to Va 1759. De.

Mair, William. LC from *Sukey* Annapolis Sep 1725. X.

Margetroide. *See* Murgatroyd.

Margetts, Thomas. S s beans & peas at Wroxton Summer 1757. O.

Margrave, John. S Jun T Sep 1758 *Tryal*. L.

Maria, James. S Apr T May 1750 *Lichfield*. M.

Marison, Charles (1691). *See* Snelling. Nf.

Maritime, Mary (1736). *See* Johnson. L.

Marjoram, William. S Aug T 14 yrs Sep 1727 *Forward* LC Rappahannock May 1728. L.

Mark, John. S Dec 1754. L.

Mark, John. R Summer 1775. Nl.

Markerson, John (1766). *See* Major. Wi.

Markerson, Walter (1774). *See* Major. Wi.

Markey, James. S & R for life Summer 1773. G.

Markey, William. S & R 14 yrs Lent 1774. G.

Markham, James. S Feb 1754. L.

Markham, Joseph. S Apr T May 1743 *Indian Queen*. L.

Markham, Margaret. S Oct T Nov 1728 *Forward* LC Rappahannock Jun 1729. L.

Markins, Samuel. S Lent 1756. Su.

Markland, Joshua of St. Paul Covent Garden. SW & T Jan 1767 *Tryal*. M.

Marklin, Daniel. TB Aug 1733. Db.

Markram, Thomas. S s hens at Tipton Lent 1757. St.

Markes, Anne. S Mar TB Apr 1734. Wi.

Marks, Elizabeth. S Mar TB to Va Apr 1758. Wi.

Marks, Esther. S Jly T Oct 1768 *Justitia*. M.

Markes, Frances. S & T Oct 1732 *Caesar* to Va. M.

Markes, John. Rebel T 1685.

Marks, Nicholas. S Mar 1734. Co.

Markes, Thomas. Rebel T 1685.

Marks, Thomas. R Summer 1731. O.

Markes, William of North Petherton, husbandman. R for Barbados Feb 1669. So.

Marks als Middleton, William. S & T Oct 1729 *Forward* LC Va Jun 1730. L.

Markson, Sharlotte. S & T Jan 1739 *Dorsetshire*. L.

Marland, Henry. S Feb T Mar 1760 *Friendship*. M.

Marlborough, Francis. S Sep 1737 T Jan 1738 *Dorsetshire* to Va. M.

Marling, Mary. S Apr T Dec 1734 *Caesar* LC Va Jly 1735. M.

Marlock, John. S Dec 1764 T Jan 1765 *Tryal*. M.

Marlow als Murphy, Elizabeth. S Aug T Sep 1725 *Forward* to Md. M.

Marlow, James. R 14 yrs Jly 1737. Ha.

Marlow, John. S for firing wood stack Lent R 14 yrs Summer 1748. No.

Marlow, Mary. S & T Sep 1742 *Forward*. L.

Marlow, William. S Sep-Oct 1746. M.

Marlow, William. T Apr 1770 *New Trial*. K.

Marmun, John. R for Barbados Apr 1669. M.

Marman, John. S s at Woodchester Lent TB Mar 1734. G.

Marmon, John. S Lent R 14 yrs Summer TB Aug 1751. G.

Marman, Margaret. S & T Oct 1732 *Caesar* to Va.M.

Marman, Mary. S Lent TB Apr 1742. G.

Marman, Timothy. S s serge at Chipping Sodbury Lent TB Apr 1757. G.

Marman, William. S s at Woodchester Lent TB Mar 1734. G.

Marr, Ann of St. George, Southwark, spinster. SQS Jan 1772. Sy.

Marr, Robert. S Summer 1756. Su.

Marrat, Charles (1676). *See* Mortall. M.

Marrett, James. S Mar 1729. Wi.

Marratt als May, John of Verran. R for Barbados Mar 1679. Co.

Marian, Nicholas. S Jan-Feb 1773. M.

Marrian, Walter. R Summer 1775. Wa.

Marriman. *See* Merriman.

Marriott, Edward. SQS & T Jun 1756 *Lyon*; acquitted in Apr 1758 of being at large, ordered to complete his term & T Sep 1758 *Tryal* to Annapolis. M.

Marriott, Edward of Greasley. SQS s fowl Jan 1775. Nt.

Marriott, James. S s horse & R Summer 1736. Su.

Marriot, Joseph. S s mare Lent R 14 yrs Summer 1754. Li.

Marriott, Richard. S Jan T 14 yrs Apr 1741 *Speedwell*. L.

Marriott, Samuel. S Mar TB to Va Sep 1731. Le.

Marriott, Samuel. R 14 yrs Dec 1773. M.

Marriott, Samuel of Greasley. SQS s fowl Jan 1775. Nt.

Marriott, William. S Lent 1765. No.

Marrowe, William of Stourbridge. R for America Jly 1691. Wo.

Marsden, James. S Lent 1742 R 14 yrs Lent 1743. La.

Marsden, Jonathan. S s at Almondsbury Summer 1773; wife Sarah acquitted. Y.

Marscey, Nathaniel. S Oct T Nov 1728 *Forward* to Va. M.

Marsey, Timothy of Debden. SQS Apr 1755. E.

Marsh, Daniel. S Oct 1748 T Jan 1749 *Laura*. L.

Marsh, Edward. Rebel T 1685.

Marsh, Elizabeth. TB to Va from QS 1745. De.

Marsh, Francis of Marlborough, husbandman. R for Barbados Feb 1668. Wi.

Marsh, George. T from Bristol by *Maryland Packet* 1761 but intercepted by French; T Apr 1763 *Neptune*. De.

Marsh, George. R 14 yrs Mar 1771. Do.

Marsh, Isabel. R for Barbados Mar 1681. M.

Marsh, John. R for Barbados Mar 1683. M.

Marsh, John. S Mar 1726. Ha.

Marsh, John. S s at Monmouth Lent 1753. Mo.

Marsh, John. S Aug 1755. So.

Marsh, John. S May 1763. M.

Marsh, Mary of St. Martin, Colchester. R for Barbados or Jamaica Jly 1705. E.

Marsh, Mary of St. Olave, Southwark, widow. S Summer T Oct 1739 *Duke of Cumberland*. Sy.

Marsh, Nathaniel. T Dec 1758 *The Brothers*. E.

Marsh, Original. S Dec 1746. L.

Marsh, Phillis. LC from *Worcester* Annapolis Jun 1719. X.

Marsh, Richard. SWK Oct 1773. K.

Marsh, Susan. T Sep 1730 *Smith*. Sy.

Marsh, Thomas (1726). *See* Upham. Ha.

Marsh, Thomas. S Feb T Mar 1729 *Patapsco* LC Annapolis Dec 1729. L.

Marsh, Thomas. S Summer 1737. Wo.

Marsh, Thomas. S Feb 1738. Ha.

Marsh, Thomas. R 14 yrs Mar TB to Va Apr 1741. Wi.

Marsh, Thomas. S s wheat at Balsham Summer 1774. Ca.

Marsh, Walter. S Feb T Mar 1760 *Friendship*. M.

Marsh, William. S Jly 1748. Ha.

Marsh, William. R 14 yrs Aug 1772 TB to Va. De.

Marshall, Aaron. S Feb 1663 to House of Correction unless he consents to be transported. M.

Marshall, Abraham. S Lent 1757. Y.

Marshall, Anne. S Lent 1746. La.

Marshall, Diggory. SQS for attending conventicle Dec 1664. M.

Marshall, Edward. S Aug T Sep 1725 *Forward* LC Annapolis Dec 1725. M.

Marshall, Edward. S & T Feb 1744 *Neptune* to Md. M.

Marshall, Edward. S s sheep & R 7 yrs Lent TB to Md May 1772. Le.

Moorshall, Edward. S Jly 1773. L.

Marshall, Elizabeth. S May 1763. M.

Marshall, Elizabeth. S Feb T Apr 1771 *Thornton*. L.

Marshall, Elizabeth, widow. S s butter at Whitby Lent TB Apr 1773. Y.

Marshall als Whipple als Flower, Frances. R for Barbados Dec 1683. L.

Marshall, George of Totteridge. R for Barbados or Jamaica Jly 1688. Ht.

Marshall, George. S Jly 1722. So.

Marshall, George. T Jly 1722 *Alexander*. E.

Marshall, Henry, aged 32. R for Barbados for burglary in Kent Feb 1664. M.

Marshall, Henry. S for attending conventicles Summer 1764 R for plantations Jly 1665 (PC). Ht.

Marshall, Henry. S Lent 1775. K.

Marshall, Isaac (1727). *See* Mercer, Joseph. Y.

Marshall, Isaiah. S Feb T Mar 1731 *Patapsco* LC Annapolis Jun 1731. M.

Marshall, James. S Feb-Apr T May 1751 *Tryal*. M.

Marshall, James. S & T Dec 1752 *Greyhound*. L.

Marshall, John. R for Barbados or Jamaica Dec 1695 & Jan 1697. L.

Marshall, John. R May AT Jly 1697. M.

Marshall, John. S Jly T 14 yrs Aug 1718 *Eagle* LC Charles Town Mar 1719. L.

Marshall, John. S Summer 1726. Sh.

Marshall als Olave, John. S Sep 1733 T Jan 1734 *Caesar* LC Va Jly 1734. M.

Marshal, John. S Mar 1752. Ha.

Marshall, John. S & T Dec 1767 *Neptune*. L.

Marshall, John. S Apr 1774. M.

Marshall, Joseph of Manchester, leather dresser. SQS Apr 1766. La. *Deleted*.

Marshal, Joseph. S Mar TB to Va Apr 1768. Wi.

Marshall, Lydia. S Sep T Dec 1763 *Neptune*. M.

Marshall, Martha. S Apr T May 1752 *Lichfield*. L.

Marshall, Mary. R Dec 1681 AT Jan 1682. M.

Marshall als Bryant, Mary. R for Barbados Dec 1683. M.

Marshall, Nehemiah. S Feb T Mar 1731 *Patapsco* LC Annapolis Jun 1731. M.

Marshall, Nicholas of Dunkeswell. R for Barbados Feb 1698. De.

Marshall, Rachael. S Dec 1755 T Jan 1756 *Greyhound*. L.

Marshall, Richard. T Oct 1726 *Forward*. Sy.

Marshall, Robert. S Jan T Feb 1726 *Supply* LC Annapolis May 1726. L.

Marshall, Sarah. S Jly T Oct 1741 *Sea Horse*. L.

Marshall, Scoter. S & T Jly 1771 *Scarsdale*. M.

Marshal, Simeon of Rochdale, weaver. SQS Jly 1771. La.

Marshall, Thomas. Rebel T 1685.

Marshall, Thomas. S Jan T Feb 1726 *Supply* LC Annapolis May 1726. L.

Marshall, Thomas. T Apr 1732 *Patapsco*. E.

Marshall, Thomas. SQS Jly 1732. So.

Marshall, Thomas. S Feb 1734. L.

Marshall, Thomas. S & T 14 yrs Jan 1736 *Dorsetshire* but died on passage. L.

Moorshall, Thomas. S Jly 1774. L.

Marshall, William. PT Jly 1680. M.

Marshall, William. S s at Pershore Summer 1742. Wo.

Marshall, William. S s at Acle Summer 1767. Nf.

Marshall, William. S Apr-Jun T Jly 1772 *Tayloe*. M.

Marshall, William. S & T Jly 1772 *Tayloe*. M.

Marshall, William. R for life Summer 1773. Sy.

Marshman, James. R 14 yrs Aug 1771. So.

Marshman, William. SQS Devizes Apr TB to Va Aug 1751. Wi.

Marshmant, James (1760). *See* Pinchin. Ha.

Marsinder, Ann. S Aug T Oct 1741 *Sea Horse* to Va. M.

Marson, John. S for highway robbery Lent R for life Summer 1765. St.

Marston, Phillip. S Mar TB to Va Apr 1768. Le.

Marston, William. T for life Oct 1768 *Justitia*. K.

Martain, John (1750). *See* Martin. Sx.

Martin, Andrew. S Sep 1760. M.

Martin, Andrew. S & T Jan 1767 *Tryal*. M.

Martin, Anthony. PT Aug 1676. M.

Martin, Bartholomew. S Jun T Aug 1769 *Douglas*. M.

Martyn, Benjamin. S Mar 1741. Ha.

Martin, Benjamin of North Fambridge, hawker & pedlar. SQS Oct 1757 T Sep 1758 *Tryal*. E.

Martin, Benjamin. R Jly 1774. M.

Martin, Bryan. S Apr 1748. L.

Martin, Charles. S & T Jun 1756 *Lyon*. M.

Martin, David. R for Barbados Jly 1674. M.

Martin, Edward. S & T Sep 1731 *Smith* LC Va 1732. M.

Martin, Edward. T May 1752 *Lichfield*. Ht.

Martin, Elizabeth. R for Barbados Jan & Jun 1665. L.

Martin, Elizabeth. R for Barbados Aug 1679. M.

Martin, Elizabeth. S & T Apr 1725 *Sukey* LC Annapolis Sep 1725. M.

Martin, Elizabeth. T Oct 1738 *Genoa*. K.

Martin, Elizabeth (1740). *See* Jackson. L.

Martin, Elizabeth of St. Paul, Covent Garden, widow. S s cloaks Dec 1740. M.

Martin, Frances. S Feb T Mar 1730 *Patapsco* LC Annapolis Sep 1730. L.

Martin, Henry. S Mar 1729. Co.

Martin, Henry als William. S & T Dec 1769 *Justitia*. L.

Martin, Henry. SQS Marlborough Oct 1772 TB to Va Apr 1773. Wi.

Martin, Hosea. R s cloth from rack Mar 1750. So.

Martin, James. R for Barbados Mar 1683. L.

Martin, James. T May 1719 *Margaret*; sold to John Richardson Md Sep 1719. E.

Martin, James. S Jun T Oct 1744 *Susannah*. M.

Martin, James of Camberwell. SQS 14 yrs & T Jan 1756 *Greyhound*. Sy.

Martin, James. T Dec 1763 *Neptune*. K.

Martin, James. S Apr 1773. M.

Martin, Jane. S Oct T 14 yrs Dec 1724 *Rappahannock*. L.

Martin, Joan of Croydon. R for Barbados or Jamaica Mar 1698. Sy.

Martayne, John of Newington. R for Barbados Apr 1668. Sy.

Martin, John of Romford. R for Barbados Apr 1668. E.

Martin, John. R Dec 1679 AT Feb 1680. M.

Martin, John of Leeds. R for Barbados Jly 1684. Y.

Martin, John of Abergavenny. R for Jamaica, Barbados or Bermuda Feb 1686. Mo.

Martin, John. S Mar 1724. Wi.

Martin, John. S Oct T Dec 1724 *Rappahannock* to Va. M.

Martin, John. LC from *Forward* Annapolis Jun 1725. X.

Martin, John. R 14 yrs Jly TB to Va Aug 1731. Wi.

Martyn, John. R 14 yrs Aug 1737. De.

Martin, John. S Mar 1739. Co.

Martin, John. S 14 yrs Jly T Aug 1741 *Betty* from Hull. Nt.

Martin, John. S Jan T Feb 1744 *Neptune*. L.

Marten als Martin, John. S s gelding at Drayton Summer 1744. Sh.

Martyn, John. S Apr 1745. So.

Martin, John. SQS Coventry Aug 1745. Wa.

Martin, John. S Jun-Dec 1745. M.

Martin, John. S Dec 1749-Jan 1750 T Mar 1750 *Tryal*. M.

Martin als Martain, John of Battle. S for housebreaking Lent R 14 yrs Summer T Oct 1750 *Rachael*. Sx.

Martin, John. S Feb-Apr T May 1751 *Tryal*. M.

Martin, John. S Apr T May 1752. L.

Martin, John. S s sheep Lent R 14 yrs Summer 1757. Li.

Martin, John. SL & T Sep 1766 *Justitia*. Sy.

Martin, John. S s silver watch at St. Bride's Apr T Jun 1768 *Tryal*. L.

Martin, John. T 14 yrs Apr 1768 *Thornton*. Sx.

Martin, John. S May T Jun 1768 *Tryal*. M.

Martin, John. S Feb T Apr 1770 *New Trial*. L.

Martin, John. S Jly 1773. L.

Martin, John. S Aug 1774. So.

Martin, Jonathan. T Jun 1764 *Dolphin*. K.

Martin, Joseph. T Jun 1727 *Susanna*. Bu.

Martin, Margaret. R for Jamaica Aug 1661. L.

Martin, Margaret of Tuffley. R for America Nov 1694. G.

Martin, Martha. S Summer 1758. Ch.

Martin, Martin. SQS Devizes Apr TB to Va May 1770. Wi.

Martin als Meechin, Mary of Lewisham, spinster. R for Barbados or Jamaica Mar 1698. K.

Martin, Mary. S Aug 1727. M.

Martin, Mary. S Feb T Mar 1730 *Patapsco* LC Annapolis Sep 1730. L.

Martin als Andrews, Mary. S Feb T Apr 1734 *Patapsco* to Md. M.

Martin, Mary. SQS Oct 1754. M.

Martin, Mary. S Jan 1757. L.

Martin, Mary. SL Jan T Mar 1764 *Tryal*. Sy.

Martin, Matthew. S Feb T Apr 1770 *New Trial*. L.

Martin, Oliver. R for life Lent 1773. Sy.

Martin, Petchy als Peachy. S s horse at Worlington & R 14 yrs Lent 1774. Su.

Martin, Peter. AT Lent 1749. Be.

Martin, Richard. S Aug T Sep 1727 *Forward* LC Rappahannock May 1728. L.

Martin, Richard. R 14 yrs Jly 1771 TB to Va Apr 1772. Wi.

Martin, Robert. S Aug T Sep 1725 *Forward* LC Annapolis Dec 1725. M.

Martin, Robert. S Feb-Apr T May 1751 *Tryal*. M.

Martin, Robert. S Jly TB to Va Sep 1757. Wi.

Martin, Sampson. SQS Mar TB Aug 1720 to be shipped to Md from Liverpool. Db.

Martin, Sarah. S Feb T May 1719 *Margaret*; sold to John Gaskin Md Sep 1719. L.

Martin, Sarah. S Jly T Oct 1741 *Sea Horse* to Va. M.

Martin, Sarah. S Sep-Oct 1749. M.

Martin, Sarah, spinster. S & T Jly 1770 *Scarsdale*. L.

Martin, Susanna. R for Barbados Dec 1693 AT Jan 1694. M.

Martin, Susan. R Oct 1694 AT Jan 1695. M.

Martin, Susanna, aged 20, fair. S & T Oct 1720 *Gilbert* LC Annapolis May 1721. M.

Martin, Thomas. S s tools Oct T Dec 1736 *Dorsetshire* to Va. M.

Martin, Thomas. S Mar 1739. Co.

Martin, Thomas. S for highway robbery at Stow in the Wold Lent R 14 yrs Summer TB Jly 1744. G.

Martin, Thomas. S Apr T May 1755 *Rose*. L.

Martin, Thomas. S Mar 1767. Ha.

Martin als Stone, Thomas. R 14 yrs Jly TB to Va Sep 1773. Wi.

Martin, Thomas. S Jly 1773. L.

Martin, Thomas. SQS Jly 1774. M.

Martin, William of Leatherhead. R (Newgate) for Barbados Aug 1668. Sy.

Martyn, William of Burrough Green. R for Barbados Aug 1671. Ca.

Martin, William (1675). *See* Mooreton. L.

Martin, William. Rebel T 1685.

Martin, William of Weare. R for Barbados Jun 1699. So.

Martin, William, aged 20, dark. S Jan T Feb 1723 *Jonathan* LC Annapolis Jly 1724. M.

Martin, William. S Oct T 14 yrs Nov 1725 *Rappahannock* but died on passage. M.

Martyn, William. S Mar 1729 TB to Va. De.
Martin, William. S Mar 1730. De.
Martin, William. T Nov 1741 *Sea Horse*. Sx.
Martin, William. S Summer 1742 R 14 yrs Lent 1743. Hu.
Martyn, William. R 14 yrs Mar 1744. De.
Martin, William. R Lent 1749. E.
Martyn, William. S Aug 1755. Co.
Martin, William (1769). *See* Martin, Henry. L.
Martin, William. S Feb T Apr 1772 *Thornton*. L.
Martin, Zephaniah. S Apr T May 1720 *Honor* LC Port York Jan 1721. L.
Martindale, John. S Jun T Sep 1758 *Tryal*. L.
Martinshrider, David. R for Barbados or Jamaica Dec 1698. M.
Martley, Richard. R 14 yrs Mar 1767 TB to Va. De.
Martney, Carrie. SQS Dec 1750. M.
Marton, James of Broughton, Cartmell. SQS Jan 1768. La.
Martow, Jacob. T Jun 1742 *Bladon*. Sx.
Marvel, Mary. S Aug T Oct 1726 *Forward* to Va. M.
Marvill, Richard. S Aug 1727. M.
Marvell, William. T Oct 1719 *Susannah & Sarah*. L.
Marwick, John. T 14 yrs Sep 1766 *Justitia*. Sx.
Marwood, John. Rebel T 1685.
Marwood, Jonas. S Feb T Mar 1727 *Rappahannock* to Md. M.
Mary, Thomas. LC from *Forward* Rappahannock May 1728. X.
Mascada, Francis, als Car, Peras, als Da Silva, Joseph. R & T for life Jly
    1772 *Tayloe*. M.
Mascall, Ann. S Summer 1758 R 14 yrs Lent 1759. Be.
Mascall, Israell (1774). *See* Hall. Be.
Mascall, John. T Oct 1723 *Forward*. Ht.
Mascall, John. S Lent 1750. Bu.
Mascall, Mary. S Sep T Oct 1750 *Rachael*. M.
Mascall, Richard. S s sheep Lent 1741. O.
Mascall, Richard. S s fish Summer 1754. Be.
Mascall, Thomas. S Summer 1738 R 14 yrs Lent 1739. Be.
Masey. *See* Macey.
Mash, John. S Jan-Feb 1773. M.
Mash, Phillis. S Jan T Feb 1719 *Worcester* to Md. L.
Mash, Richard. S 14 yrs s from bleaching yard at Middleton Lent
    1772. Su.
Masham, Ann. S Oct 1742 T Mar 1743 *Justitia*. L.
Mashman, James. S Sep T Dec 1769 *Justitia*. M.
Maskew, Elizabeth. AT Lent & Summer 1750. Y.
Maskew, Esther. AT Summer 1758. Y.
Maskew, Sarah. AT Summer 1759. Y.
Masland, Robert. S Jan T Feb 1724 *Anne* to Carolina. M.
Mason, Alexander. S s at Claines Summer 1766. Wo.
Mason, Allen. S Mar 1746. Ha.
Mason, Amey. SQS Apr 1773. M.
Mason, Ann. R for Jamaica Aug 1661. M.
Mason, Ann, aged 26, brown hair. S Sep T Oct 1720 *Gilbert* LC
    Annapolis May 1721. L.
Mason, Benjamin. T Jan 1765 *Tryal*. M.

Mason, Katherine (1737). *See* Sutton. Y.

Mason, Charles. Rebel T 1685.

Mason, Charles. R 14 yrs Aug 1767 TB to Va. De.

Mason, Charles. S Lent T Apr 1773. Wa.

Mason, Edward. S & T Jan 1722 *Gilbert* LC Annapolis Jly 1722. M.

Mason, Edward of St. Saviour, Southwark, baker. SQS Apr T May 1750
Lichfield. Sy.

Mason, Edward (1770). *See* Hughes. So.

Mason, Edward of Camberwell. SQS Apr T Jly 1772 *Orange Bay*. Sy.

Mason, Elizabeth of St. Martin in Fields, spinster. S s gold pieces Jly
1740 T Jan 1741 *Harpooner* to Rappahannock. M.

Mason, Elizabeth. S & T Apr 1766 *Ann*. L.

Mason als Nicholls, Elizabeth. S Apr T Jun 1768 *Tryal*. M.

Mason, Elizabeth (1775). *See* Boswell. O.

Mason, Francis. S for highway robbery Lent R 14 yrs Summer 1752. O.

Mason, Francis Knill. S Mar 1757. De.

Mason, George. R 14 yrs Jly 1735. Ha.

Mayson, Hannah. SQS s apron Lent 1768. Du.

Mason, Henry. T Apr 1725 *Sukey* LC Md Sep 1725. Sy.

Mason, James. R Jan 1656. M.

Mason, John. R for America Jly 1683. Li.

Mason, John of Rayne. R for Barbados or Jamaica Jun 1699. E.

Mason, John. R for America Feb 1700. Ru.

Mason, John (1718). *See* Mestee. L.

Mason, John. S for returning from transportation & T Jan 1722 *Gilbert*
LC Annapolis Jly 1722. L.

Mason, John. S Feb T Apr 1734 *Patapsco*. L.

Mason, John. S Apr-Jun 1745. M.

Mason, John. S Lent R 14 yrs Summer 1747. E.

Mason, John. S Summer 1748 R 14 yrs Lent 1749. O.

Mason, John. S s waggon wheel at Great Chawley Summer 1749. Be.

Mason, John. T 14 yrs Oct 1768 *Justitia*. E.

Mason, John. S Apr-Jun T Jly 1772 *Tayloe*. M.

Mason, John. SQS Oct 1773. M.

Mason als Bird, Jonathan of Wood Ditton. S Lent 1760. Ca.

Mason, Joseph. S 14 yrs Feb-Apr 1746. M.

Mason, Margaret (1696). *See* Johnson. K.

Mason, Mary. S May T Jly 1722 *Alexander* to Nevis or Jamaica. M.

Mason, Mary. S Aug T Oct 1741 *Sea Horse* to Va. M.

Mason, Mary (1745). *See* McLaughlin. M.

Mason, Patrick. S Feb T Mar 1727 *Rappahannock* to Md. M.

Mason, Peter. S Feb T Apr 1741 *Speedwell* or *Mediterranean* to Md. M.

Mason, Peter. S May T Nov 1759 *Phoenix*. M.

Mason, Richard. S City s watch at St. Michael le Belfry Lent 1768. Y.

Mason, Robert. S Jly 1724. Ha.

Mason, Robert. T Apr 1725 *Sukey* LC Md Sep 1725. K.

Mason, Robert. S Feb T Apr 1742 *Bond* to Potomack. M.

Mason, Robert. S Mar 1755. De.

Mason, Sarah. R for Barbados Jly 1680. M.

Mason, Thomas. S s at Down Hatherley Summer 1723. G.

Mason, Thomas. S Jan-Jun T Jun 1728 *Elizabeth*. L.

Mason, Thomas of Morley. TB Aug 1735. Db.
Mason, Thomas. S s brass pot at Denchworth Lent 1756. Be.
Mason, Thomas. T Sep 1758 *Tryal*. Sx.
Mason, William of Cannock. R for America Jly 1675. St.
Mason, William of Woodstock. R for America Jly 1683. O.
Mason, William. S Sep 1761. M.
Mason, William of Manchester. SQS Jan 1764. La.
Mason, William. S Apr T May 1767 *Thornton*. L.
Massader, Richard. S Jly 1764. Ha.
Massavet, Conrad. S Jun T Sep 1764 *Justitia*. M.
Massey, Ann. S 14 yrs Oct-Dec 1754. M.
Massey, George. R 14 yrs Jly 1747. Ha.
Massey, James (1720). *See* Mercy. L.
Massey, James (1756). *See* Lees. La.
Massey als Carter, Joyce. S s at Worfield Lent 1764. Sh.
Massey, Margaret (1742). *See* Barrett. M.
Massey, Nathaniel. LC from *Forward* Rappahannock Jan 1729. X.
Massey, Sarah. S Feb T Apr 1743 *Justitia*. M.
Massey, Sarah. S 14 yrs Oct-Dec 1754. M.
Massey, Thomas. R for Barbados Jly 1668. L.
Massey, Thomas. S Summer 1738. Ch.
Massey, William. TB Sep 1753. Db.
Massingham, Charles. S Summer T Oct 1744 *Savannah*. Sy.
Masterman, John (1733). *See* Crab. M.
Masterman, John. T Apr 1743 *Justitia*. E.
Masters, Alice (1675). *See* Powell. L.
Masters, Alice. R for America Aug 1715. M.
Masters, Andrew. R 14 yrs Apr 1775. So.
Masters, Christopher. Rebel T 1685.
Masters, James. S Feb T Mar 1729 *Patapsco* LC Annapolis Dec 1729. L.
Masters, John. S Jly T Sep 1718 *Eagle* but died on passage. L.
Masters, Richard. S Mar 1719 to be T to Va. So.
Masters, Thomas. S Jun T Jly 1772 *Tayloe*. L.
Masterson, Thomas. S Sep-Oct 1748 T Jan 1749 *Laura*. M.
Masterton, John. S Jan 1751. M.
Matcham, Henry. S Dec 1763 T Mar 1764 *Tryal*. M.
Matchett, Isabel. S Feb 1734. M.
Matchett, John (1675). *See* Williams. M.
Matchett, Thomas. R for Barbados Sep 1672. L.
Matchett, Thomas. S s mare Lent R 14 yrs Summer 1752. St.
Matchet, William. SQS & TB Mar 1772. Db.
Mate, Jeremiah. S Lent 1755. Y.
Mates, Cornelius. LC from *Smith* Va 1732. X.
Mates, Joseph. T Dec 1763 *Neptune*. M.
Mather, Margaret of Manchester, widow. SQS Jly 1751. La.
Mather, Thomas (1673). *See* Man. L.
Mather, Thomas of Adlington. SQS Jun 1767. La.
Matkins, Elizabeth. S Apr T Dec 1734 *Caesar* LC Va Jly 1735. M.
Maton, Ann. R 14 yrs Mar TB to Va Apr 1772. Wi.
Matson, William. S Summer 1730. Y.
Matter, Mary Jr. S Jly 1752. De.

Mathews, Abraham. R 14 yrs Jly 1751. Do.

Mathews, Ann. S Feb T Mar 1727 *Rappahannock* to Md. M.

Matthews, Anne (1729). *See* Moss. Sh.

Matthews als Cole, Ann, als wife of Thomas Tobeings. S Feb T Mar 1758 *Dragon*. M.

Matthews, Andrew. S Feb T Mar 1764 *Tryal*. M.

Mathews, Catherine. Died on passage in *Gilbert* 1721. X.

Matthews, Catherine Rebecca. S & T Apr 1762 *Neptune*. L.

Mathews, Christopher. S Jly T Sep 1718 *Eagle* LC Charles Town Mar 1719. L.

Mathews, Christopher. S & T Oct 1720 *Gilbert* to Md. M.

Matthews, Clement wife of Michael. S Oct 1756. M.

Matthews, Daniel. T for life Apr 1769 *Tryal*. K.

Matthews, Darby. T Sep 1766 *Justitia*. M.

Mathews, Dorothy. R for Barbados Mar 1681. M.

Mathewes, Edward. S Summer R for Barbados Aug 1664. K.

Mathews, Edward. S s horse Summer 1739 R Lent 1740 (SP). Sh.

Matthews, Eleanor. S & T Dec 1771 *Justitia*. M.

Mathewes, Elizabeth of Heavitree. R for Barbados Jly 1679. De.

Matthews, Elizabeth of St. Giles in Fields. S & T May 1736 *Patapsco*. M.

Matthews, Elizabeth. S & T 14 yrs Dec 1740 *Vernon*. L.

Mathews, Elizabeth. S Jun T Jly 1772 *Tayloe*. L.

Mathews, George. S Jan-Jun T Jun 1728 *Elizabeth* LC Potomack Aug 1729. M.

Mathews, George, als Kiddy George. S & T Dec 1731 *Forward*. L.

Mathews, Harriot. S Sep T Dec 1770 *Justitia*. M.

Matthews, Henry of Netteswell. R for Barbados or Jamaica Jly 1702. E.

Matthews, Hugh. S Apr 1749. L.

Mathews, James. R for Barbados Oct 1673. L.

Mathews, James. R for Barbados Mar 1677. L.

Matthews, James. S s tools from *John & Margaret* Oct T Dec 1736 *Dorsetshire*. M.

Mathews, James. T May 1737 *Forward*. Sy.

Matthews, James. T Jun 1740 *Essex*. Sy.

Matthews, James. S Lent R 14 yrs Summer 1744. Ca.

Matthews, James. S Feb 1761. L.

Matthews, James. R Aug 1770 TB to Va 1771. De.

Matthews, John. S Jan-Jun T 14 yrs Jun 1728 *Elizabeth* LC Potomack Aug 1729. L.

Mathews, John. S s horse Summer 1728 R 14 yrs Lent 1729. Be.

Matthews, John. S Feb T Mar 1731 *Patapsco*. L.

Matthews, John. S Oct 1733. M.

Matthews, John. S s horse Lent R 14 yrs Summer 1738. Wo.

Matthews, John. S Jun-Dec 1738 T Jan 1739 *Dorsetshire* to Va. M.

Matthews, John. S Oct-Dec 1739 T Jan 1740 *York* to Md. M.

Matthews, John. TB to Va from QS 1740. De.

Mathews, John. S for highway robbery Summer 1740 R Lent 1741 (SP). Wo.

Mathews, John. S s at St. Michael, Gloucester, Lent 1752. G.

Mathews, John. S Summer 1762 R 14 yrs Lent 1763. Wo.

Matthews, John of St. Martin in Fields. SW Jun 1763 T Mar 1764 *Tryal*. M.

Matthews, John. SQS s silk at North Collingham May 1764. Nt.

Matthews, John. S Feb T Apr 1765 *Ann*. L.

Mathews, John. S s at Forthampton Summer 1766. G.

Matthews, John. SW & T Jly 1770 *Scarsdale*. M.

Matthews, Joseph. S Mar TB to Va Apr 1767. Wi.

Matthews, Luke of Plaistow. R for Barbados or Jamaica Jly 1702. E.

Matthews, Margaret. S Jly-Dec 1747. M.

Matthews, Margaret. SW & T Oct 1768 *Justitia*. M.

Matthews, Maria. S Jun T Sep 1758 *Tryal*. L.

Mathews, Mary. S Aug T Sep 1725 *Forward* to Md. M.

Matthews, Mary. S Jan T Feb 1726 *Supply* LC Annapolis May 1726. M.

Matthews, Mary. S & T Dec 1734 *Caesar* LC Va Jly 1735. L.

Matthews, Mary wife of John. S 14 yrs for receiving barley Jan T Apr 1735 *Patapsco*. M.

Matthews als Wright, Mary. S s necklace Oct 1735 T Jan 1736 *Dorsetshire* LC Va Sep 1736. M.

Matthews, Moses. S Jly 1772. Ha.

Mathews, Paul. SQS May T Jun 1768 *Tryal*. M.

Mathews, Paul (1770). *See* Dunn. M.

Mathews, Pater of Rotherhithe. SQS Jan T Apr 1770 *New Trial*. Sy.

Mathews, Rebeccah. S Jly T Oct 1741 *Sea Horse* to Va. M.

Matthews, Richard. S & T Dec 1736 *Dorsetshire*. L.

Mathews, Richard. T May 1737 *Forward*. Sy.

Matthews, Richard. S Apr T Sep 1757 *Thetis*. M.

Matthews, Robert. S s at Linton Summer 1737. He.

Mathews, Samuel. R for Barbados Dec 1683. L.

Mathews, Samuel. T May 1741 *Miller*. K.

Matthews, Sarah. S Jan T Feb 1724 *Anne* to Carolina. M.

Matthews als Paine, Sarah. S Oct T Nov 1728 *Forward* LC Rappahannock Jun 1729. L.

Matthews, Sarah. S Feb T May 1767 *Thornton*. L.

Matthews, Sarah wife of Robert. S 14 yrs for receiving Mar 1775. Do.

Matthews, Thomas. Rebel T 1685.

Mathews, Thomas of Kidderminster. R for America Jly 1693. Wo.

Matthews als Hoskins, Thomas. S Apr T 14 yrs May 1718 *Tryal* LC Charles Town Aug 1718. L.

Matthews als Moss als Huntley, Thomas. S s at Shifnal & Wellington Summer 1729. Sh.

Mattews, Thomas. S Jly 1737. Ha.

Mathews, Thomas. S Lent R 14 yrs Summer TB Aug 1751. G.

Matthews, Thomas. T May 1751 *Tryal*. K.

Mathews, Thomas. S Jun 1761. M.

Matthews, Thomas. SQS Jly 1763. M.

Matthews, Thomas. S May T Jun 1764 *Dolphin*. M.

Matthews, William. SQS for attending conventicle Dec 1664. M.

Mathews, William. Rebel T 1685.

Mathews, William. S Feb 1729. M.

Mathews, William. S Aug 1731. So.

Matthews, William. S s cloth at Meole Brace Lent 1744. Sh.

Matthews, William. S Apr 1748. L.

Matthews, William. T Dec 1752 *Greyhound*. M.

Matthews als Davies als Davey, William. S Mar 1773. Co.

Mathews, William. S Jan-Feb 1775. M.

Mattison, Hugh. S & T Oct 1722 *Forward* LC Annapolis Jun 1723. M.

Mattocks, John. S Jan-Feb 1774. M.

Matts, Roger. SQS Apr T Sep 1758 *Tryal* to Annapolis. M.

Matts, Sarah. LC from *Dorsetshire* Va Sep 1736. X.

Matty, Henry. S Summer 1739 R 14 yrs Lent 1740. O.

Maud als Pickington, Grace. S Jan-Jun 1747. M.

Maudin, Thomas. LC from *Gilbert* Annapolis Jly 1722. X.

Maugham, Jane wife of William. S 14 yrs s cloth Summer 1764. Du.

Maughan, John (1705). *See* Emerson. Nl.

Maughan, Joseph. S s horse Summer 1740 R 14 yrs Lent 1743. Du.

Maugham, Mary. TB to Md Mar 1723 T *Forward* from London LC
   Annapolis Jun 1725. Db.

Maulam, Matthew (1768). *See* Robinson. Du.

Mauley. *See* Morley.

Maulkin, John Jr. TB Apr 1749. Db.

Maund als Philpot, John. T Jan 1765 *Tryal*. M.

Maund, Nicholas (1761). *See* Lloyd. Wo.

Maund, Rebecca wife of Abel of Little Dewchurch. R (Western Circ) for
   America Jly 1700. He.

Maund als Dickinson, Rebecca. PT Oct 1700 R Aug 1701. M.

Maunder, Henry (1774). *See* Jones. M.

Maunder, Mary. S May T Jun 1738 *Forward*. L.

Maunder, Samuel. S Aug 1754. De.

Maunders, Thomas of Halberton. R for Barbados Feb 1690. De.

Maundrell, Francis. S Aug 1754. So.

Maundry, Humphrey. Rebel T 1685.

Maundry, William (1715). *See* Thomas. So.

Mawl, Robert. S s horse Lent R 14 yrs Summer 1751. Nt.

Mawson, Thomas of St. Neot's. R for America Jly 1682. Hu.

Maxey, Benjamin. S for burning a workshop at Wallingford Lent R 14
   yrs Summer 1736. Be.

Maxey, John. S Sep 1733 T Jan 1734 *Caesar* LC Va Jly 1734. M.

Maxfield, John. R 14 yrs Summer TB Aug 1749. Y.

Maxfield, Mary. S Apr-May 1754. M.

Maxwell, John. S Mar 1756. Do.

Maxwell, Thomas (1771). *See* Erskine. M.

May, Ann (1765). *See* Swift. M.

May, Catherine. R 14 yrs Jly 1733. De.

May, Celius. SQS & T Sep 1766 *Justitia*. M.

May, Charles. S Aug 1739. Co.

May, Eleanor. S & T Sep 1764 *Justitia*. M.

May, Elizabeth. T Apr 1742 *Bond*. K.

May, George. S Mar 1768 TB to Va. De.

May, Henry. S Jan T 14 yrs Feb 1719 *Worcester* LC Annapolis Jun
   1719. L.

May, Henry. T Apr 1770 *New Trial*. E.

May, James. R 14 yrs Aug 1754. Co.

May, James, als Mills, Emanuel. S Sep-Oct T Dec 1771 *Justitia*. M.

May, Jane. S & T Dec 1734 *Caesar* but died on passage. L.

May, John (1679). *See* Marratt. Co.

May, John. T Aug 1721 *Owners Goodwill* LC Md Jly 1722. E.

May, John (1740). *See* Mayne. L.

May, John. SQS Apr TB Aug 1747. Le.

May, John. T 14 yrs Dec 1753 *Whiteing*. K.

May, John. S s silver at Newbury Lent 1758. Be.

May, John. S Jly 1764. Ha.

May, John, als Wilmot, Cuckold als Jacob. S Mar 1768. Do.

May, John. R 14 yrs Mar 1772. Co.

May als Cross als Darby, Mary. S May-Jly 1748. M.

May, Peter. R Aug AT Oct 1700. M.

May, Peter. S Oct 1772. L.

May, Richard (1725). *See* Borlase. Co.

May, Richard. S Summer 1749. Sy.

May, Richard. S Aug 1750. Co.

May, Richard. S & T Dec 1767 *Neptune*. M.

May, Robert of Sennington. R for Barbados Feb 1692. Wi.

May, Samuel. S Feb T Apr 1727 *Rappahannock*. L.

May, Samuel. S Jun T Sep 1764 *Justitia*. M.

May, Sarah. S Apr T May 1720 *Honor* LC Va Jan 1721. L.

May, Sarah. S Mar TB to Va Apr 1758. Wi.

May, Sarah. S Aug 1767 TB to Va. De.

May, Susannah. S Jan-Feb T Apr 1771 *Thornton*. M.

May, Thomas of South Weald. R (Newgate) for Barbados Sep 1669. E.

May, Thomas. S Aug 1727. M.

May, Thomas. S for highway robbery & R 14 yrs Lent T Apr 1774. No.

May, Thomas. S Jly 1774. Ha.

May, William of Casingwould. R for Barbados Jun 1694. Y.

May, William of Mortimore. R for America Jly 1700. Ha.

May, William. R 14 yrs Jly 1724. De.

May, William. S Mar 1734. Co.

May, William. S Mar 1737. Co.

May, William. S Mar 1763. Ha.

May, William. S Aug TB to Va Sep 1767. Wi.

May, William. TB to Va from QS 1772. De.

Maybank, Elizabeth. S Jan-Apr 1748. M.

Maybrick, Charles, als Jones, John. S Apr-May 1775. M.

Maychin. *See* Machin.

Maycock, William. S Lent 1773. O.

Mayd. *See* Maid.

Mayer. *See* Myer.

Mayes. *See* Mays.

Mayfield, Jane. R for Barbados or Jamaica May 1697. L.

Mayfield, William. S Lent 1774. Li.

Mayhan, James. S Apr-Jun 1739. M.

Mayham, James. S Jly-Dec 1747. M.

Mayam, Robert, aged 21, dark, weaver. LC from *Gilbert* Annapolis May 1721. X.

Mayham, Thomas. S s stockings Jan T Jun 1738 *Forward* to Md or Va. M.

Mayham, William of Wymondham. R for America Jly 1702. Nf.

Mayhew als Warner, Edmund. S for killing King's carp at Cranbourne Park, Windsor, Summer 1773. Be.

Mayhew, John. S Feb T Mar 1727 *Rappahannock*. L.

Mayhew als Horne, John. S s gelding at Easton & R Lent 1773. Su.

Mayhew, Nathaniel. S & T Dec 1731 *Forward* to Md or Va. M.

Mayhew, Philip. T Nov 1741 *Sea Horse*. E.

Mayhew, Susan. S Lent 1749. *Su.

Maylin, Daniel (1773). *See* Hale, Charles. G.

Maynard, Anne. T Jly 1724 *Robert* LC Md Jun 1725. Sy.

Maynard, Charles Gregory, carpenter. S s at Benet College, Cambridge, & R for life Lent 1774. Ca.

Maynard, James. Rebel T 1685.

Maynard, Jane wife of Joseph. S Sep T Nov 1743 *George William*. M.

Maynard, Samuel. S s candlestick at Great Tew Lent 1753. O.

Maynard, Thomas, als Ransford, Jonathan. T Aug 1720 *Owners Goodwill*. K.

Mayne. *See* Maine.

Mayo, Robert. S & T Oct 1720 *Gilbert* to Md. M.

Mayo, Rosamund. S & T Dec 1731 *Forward* to Md or Va. M.

Mayo, Thomas. S for highway robbery & R Lent 1762. Bu.

Mayo, Thomas. S Jan T Mar 1764 *Tryal*. M.

Mayoris, William. R Jly TB Aug 1755. Wi.

Maze, Benjamin. T Sep 1757 *Thetis*. Sy.

Mays, Elizabeth. S Jun-Dec 1745. M.

Mayes, George. T Apr 1742 *Bond*. Bu.

Mayes, James. S & R 14 yrs Lent 1766. Bd.

Mayes, Philip. R 14 yrs Jly 1733. So.

Mayse, Richard. S Summer 1754. Su.

Mayes, Robert. S Summer 1722 T Oct 1723 *Forward* to Va from London. Y.

Mazey, Thomas (1766). *See* Crowdson. La.

Meaburne, Gerard of Hett. R for Barbados Jly 1698. Du.

Meecham, Benjamin of St. Olave, Southwark. R for Barbados or Jamaica Mar 1694. Sy.

Meacham, Edward. S Feb T Mar 1731 *Patapsco* LC Annapolis Jun 1731. M.

Meachum als Grimes, Mary of Bermondsey. R for Barbados or Jamaica Jly 1696. Sy.

Meachum, Mary als Martha. S s kettle & T Dec 1734 *Caesar* but died on passage. M.

Mead, Ambrose of Wandsworth. R for Barbados or Jamaica Mar 1698. Sy.

Mead, Charles of Royston. R for Barbados or Jamaica Jly 1710. Ht.

Mead, Charles. S Apr T Sep 1758 *Tryal* to Annapolis. M.

Mead, Edward. S Jly 1720 T from Portsmouth 1723. Ha.

Mead, Edward. S Summer 1751 R 14 yrs Lent T May 1752 *Lichfield*. Ht.

Mead, George of Ilminster, weaver. R for Barbados Feb 1698. So.

Mead, George. S Apr T Sep 1757 *Thetis*. M.

Mead, John (2). Rebels T 1685.

Mead als Lawrence, John of St. Peter & James, Gloucester. R for America Jly 1698. G.

Mead, John. S Aug T Oct 1724 *Forward* LC Annapolis Jun 1725. L.

Mead, John. S Apr 1756. So.

Mead, John of Orsett. SQS Apr T Sep 1757 *Thetis*. E.

Meed als Watts, John, als Baker, Rowland. R Lent 1775. E.

Mead, Joseph. R for Barbados Jan 1693. M.

Mead, Margaret. S May T Jun 1727 *Susanna* to Va. M.

Mead, Martha. S Aug T Sep 1725 *Forward* LC Annapolis Dec 1725. M.

Mead, Methuselah. S Mar 1733. So.

Mead, Nicholas. S Oct 1744-Jan 1745. M.

Mead, Nightingale. S s lead Jly 1735 T Jan 1736 *Dorsetshire* LC Va Sep 1736. M.

Mead, Nightingale. SQS Apr T May 1750 *Lichfield*; to be publicly whipped from the Red Lion to the Upper Flask in Hampstead before transportation. M.

Mead, Robert. Rebel T 1685.

Mead, Roger. S May T Jly 1722 *Alexander* to Nevis or Jamaica. M.

Meade, Thomas. Rebel T 1685.

Mead als Hoare, Thomas of Maidenhead. S s shirts Lent 1720 R 14 yrs Lent 1721 T *Owners Goodwill* LC Annapolis Jly 1722. Be.

Mead, Thomas (1741). *See* Watts. K.

Mead, Thomas. S Lent R 14 yrs Summer 1760. E.

Mead, Thomas Jr. S Lent T Apr 1760 *Thetis*. E.

Meade, Thomas. T 14 yrs Apr 1766 *Ann*. E.

Mead, William. Rebel T 1685.

Mead, William. S Lent 1756. Bd.

Meadle, James. S Summer 1746. E.

Meadall, William. S Dec 1749-Jan 1750 T Mar 1750 *Tryal*. M.

Meadowcroft, Mathew of Spotland. SQS Jan 1758. La.

Meadows, Eleanor. S Sep T Dec 1770 *Justitia*. M.

Meadows als Willes, Elizabeth. R May T for life Sep 1758 *Tryal* to Annapolis. M.

Meadows, Thomas. S Dec 1750. L.

Mecum, John. S May-Jly 1774. M.

Meakham, Samuel. S May-Jly 1773. M.

Meakin, Ellis (1747). *See* Makin. La.

Meakin, Thomas (1770). *See* Williamson. Db.

Meakins, John. S Jly T Aug 1721 *Prince Royal* LC Va Nov 1721. M.

Meakings, John. T Sep 1730 *Smith*. E.

Meakins, William. S May T Jly 1722 *Alexander* to Nevis or Jamaica. M.

Meal, Abraham (1770). *See* Myer. L.

Meal, Henry. R 14 yrs Jly 1733. So.

Meal, John of Glodwick, linen weaver. SQS Jan 1741. La.

Meal, John. S Dec 1750. L.

Meal, John. S s watch at Bishampton Lent 1770. Wo.

Meal, Mary. S Sep T Oct 1750 *Rachael*. M.

Meals, Casander wife of John. S Feb T Mar 1763 *Neptune*. M.

Mean als Mayne, Thomas. TB to Va from QS 1738. De.

Mears. *See* Meers.

Mease. *See* Meese.

Mecan, William. S Feb T Apr 1743 *Justitia*. M.

Medberry als Madberry, Thomas of Eaton. R for Barbados Feb 1664. Bd.

Medcalf. *See* Metcalf.

Medcroft, George. S for assault on the highway Summer 1738. O.

Meddison. *See* Maddison.

Medhurst, William. T Jly 1724 *Robert* LC Md Jun 1725. K.

Medley, Peter. S May T Aug 1769 *Douglas*. M.

Medley, Roger. R for Barbados Dec 1671. M.

Medlicot, William. S s oats at Clungunford Lent 1764. Sh.

Medlin, Thomas. S Jly 1741. M.

Mee, Joseph. S Lent 1775. Le.

Meech, Ann. S Aug 1739. Co.

Meechin, Mary (1698). *See* Martin. K.

Meedy, Joseph. T Nov 1728 *Forward*. Sy.

Meake, George. R for Jamaica Aug 1661. M.

Meek, John. S Summer 1754. K.

Meeke, Margaret. R Mar AT May 1688. M.

Meek, Robert. S s sheep Lent R 14 yrs Summer 1765. Su.

Meek, Thomas. S s coat at Colton Lent 1774. St.

Meek, William. S s wheat from barge Lent R for life Summer TB Aug 1757. G.

Meek, William. S & R 14 yrs Summer 1774. G.

Meer, Guy. LC from *Patapsco* Annapolis Nov 1733. X.

Meere, Joseph. S s sheep Lent R 14 yrs Summer 1749. Db.

Meeres, John. S s gelding Jly 1653 R Aug 1655. Sy.

Meers, John. S & T Sep 1731 *Smith* but died on passage. L.

Meers als Kirby, Margaret. S Apr 1745. L.

Mears, Richard. S Jly T Sep 1765 *Justitia*. M.

Mease, Edward of Lincoln. R for America Jly 1678. Li.

Meese, Thomas, a Quaker. R for plantations Jly 1665 . Ht.

Meting, Matthew. T Aug 1720 *Owners Goodwill*. K.

Meetkerke, William of St. Mary le Strand. SW Apr 1773. M.

Meggs, William (1745). *See* Francis. Wi.

Meggs, William. SQS Devizes Apr TB to Va Aug 1762. Wi.

Meier. *See* Myer.

Meirick. *See* Merrick.

Melborne, Thomas. R for America Aug 1685. Db.

Melchman, George. SQS Jan 1665 for the workhouse & to be transported unless his mother provides him with a Master. M.

Melhuish, Agnes. S Mar 1719 to be T to Va. De.

Melhuish, William. S Mar 1740. De.

Mellard, Elizabeth. R for Barbados or Jamaica Mar 1688. M.

Melleory. *See* Mallory.

Meller. *See* Miller.

Mellon, Edward. S Sep T Dec 1769 *Justitia*. M.

Melone, John. S Jan-Apr 1749. M.

Mellor, Richard of Manchester, weaver. SQS Jan 1775. La.

Mellor, William. S s sheep Lent R 14 yrs Summer 1760. Db.

Mellors, Frances wife of Francis of Carlton in Lindrick. SQS s cloth Oct 1759. Nt.

Mells. *See* Mills.

Melshaw, Mary. S Feb T Mar 1731 *Patapsco* LC Annapolis Jun 1731. M.

Melton. *See* Milton.

Meltshaw, Sarah wife of Thomas. S Apr-Jun 1739. M.

Melvin, Elliot of St. Paul, Covent Garden. SW Jan 1773. M.

Melvin, Richard. S Aug 1760. L.

Memory, George. S & T Jly 1770 *Scarsdale*. M.

Menick, Suzanna of Westminster. R Aug 1663 (PC). M.

Mepham, Joseph. T Sep 1742 *Forward*. Sx.

Mercer, Elizabeth. S Jan-Jun 1747. M.

Mercer, James. S & T Mar 1750 *Tryal*. L.

Mercer, Jonas. R 14 yrs Mar 1750. So.

Mercer, Joseph. T Jly 1724 *Robert* LC Annapolis Jun 1725. X.

Mercer, Joseph, als Marshall, Isaac. S Lent 1727 AT to Summer 1727. Y.

Mercer, Peter. S Mar TB to Va May 1770. Wi.

Mercer, Richard. T Apr 1733 *Patapsco* LC Md Nov 1733. K.

Merser, Robert. LC from *Forward* Rappahannock May 1728. X.

Mercer, Samuel. SQS Apr TB Sep 1773. So.

Mercer, Sarah (1766). *See* Bawden. La.

Mercer, William. S for assault & R 14 yrs Summer 1763. Ch.

Marchant, Charles. R 14 yrs Jly TB to Va Aug 1766. Wi.

Merchant, Elizabeth. S & T Jan 1767 *Tryal*. M.

Merchant, Emanuel. Rebel T 1685.

Merchant, George. R for Barbados Jly 1674. M.

Merchant, John of Tunbridge. R for Barbados or Jamaica Jly 1687. K.

Merchant, John. S & T Apr 1766 *Ann*. M.

Marchant, Joseph. S Jan-Feb T Apr 1771 *Thornton*. M.

Merchant, Joseph, aged about 30, fair complexion & light brown hair, 5'2" tall, from Balderton. S for killing sheep at Balderton & R Lent TB Apr 1773. Nt.

Marchant, Mary. S s at Avening Lent 1774. G.

Merchant, Robert. SQS Apr T Jun 1768 *Tryal*. M.

Merchant, Stephen Sr. S 14 yrs May-Jly 1773. M.

Merchant, Stephen Jr. S May-Jly 1773. M.

Marchant, Thomas. T Apr 1735 *Patapsco*. Sx.

Merchant, Thomas. T Sep 1742 *Forward*. Sx.

Merchant, William. Rebel T 1685.

Merchant, William. SQS Feb T Mar 1750 *Tryal*. M.

Mercier, Francis. R Apr 1773. M.

Mercilary, Thomas. R 14 yrs Jly 1758 TB to Va 1759. De.

Mercy als Massey, James. S Apr T May 1720 *Honor* but escaped in Vigo, Spain. L.

Mercey, Thomas. R for Barbados or Jamaica Jan 1692. M.

Mereden. *See* Merriden.

Meredith, Edward. S May-Jly T Sep 1751 *Greyhound*. M.

Meredith, Edward. S s horse Lent R 14 yrs Summer 1763. Sh.

Meredith, Elizabeth. S Lent R 14 yrs Summer 1728. Mo.

Meredith, Elizabeth. R Summer 1731. He.

Meredith, Jane. S s sheep Lent R 14 yrs Summer 1765. Mo.
Meredith, John of Tardebigg. R for America Nov 1694. Wo.
Meredith als Cooke, John. S Summer 1742 R 14 yrs Lent 1743. He.
Meridith, Mary. LC from *Alexander* Annapolis Sep 1723. X.
Meredith, Mary of Whitchurch, spinster. S Lent 1734. Sh.
Meredith, Mary. S s at Meole Brace Lent 1761 T *Atlas* from Bristol. Sh.
Meredith, Richard (1753). *See* Reading. He.
Meredith, Richard. S s at Worthen Lent 1756. Sh.
Meredy, Mary. S May T Jly 1723 *Alexander* to Md. M.
Merla, James (1719). *See* Pascoe. Co.
Merrell, John of Truro. R for Barbados Jly 1678. Co.
Merrick, Griffith. S Jun T Nov 1743 *George William*. M.
Meirick, Mary. S 14 yrs for receiving wool stolen by Eleanor Morgan
  (qv) Summer 1764. He.
Merick, Thomas of Woolhope. R for America Feb 1681. He.
Meyrick, Thomas. S s at Bockleton (Salop) Summer 1768 R 14 yrs Lent
  1769. He.
Merrick, William. Rebel T 1685.
Merriday, Mary. S Oct 1756. L.
Merriden, John. R for Barbados Sep 1682. L.
Mereden, Joseph. S Apr 1773. M.
Merring, Richard. S Jan 1740. L.
Merrison, William. S s mare at Wacton & R Lent 1771. Nf.
Merritt als Walden, Anne. R & T 14 yrs Jan 1722 *Gilbert* LC Annapolis
  Jly 1722. M.
Merritt als Jones als Wright, Ann. S Jun T 14 yrs Sep 1758 *Tryal*. L.
Merritt, Charles. S Apr T May 1767 *Thornton*. M.
Merrett als Willis, Israel. R 14 yrs Aug 1726. So.
Merrit, James Jr. R 14 yrs Mar 1768. Ha.
Merrit als Ostler, John. S s grain at Newbury Summer 1758. Be.
Merrit, Richard. T Dec 1731 *Forward*. Sy.
Merritt, William. S s at Tewkesbury Lent 1760. G.
Merry, Henry. T Jly 1741. Bd.
Merry, James of St. Saviour, Southwark, clogmaker. SQS Jun T Jly 1753
  Tryal. Sy.
Merry, Richard. S Oct 1751-Jan 1752. M.
Merryfield, Samuel. T Jan 1738 *Dorsetshire*. K.
Merryman, John of Heavitree. R for Barbados Jly 1695. De.
Merryman, John. TB Apr 1743. Db.
Merryman, Nicholas of Thame. R for America Jly 1679. O.
Merriman, Thomas. S Dec 1749-Jan 1750 T Mar 1750 *Tryal*. M.
Marriman, Thomas Jr. S Feb T Mar 1750 *Tryal*. M.
Mersey, William. S Jun T Aug 1769 *Douglas*. M.
Merson, George. TB to Va from QS 1740. De.
Mirton, William (1739). *See* Nurton. So.
Murton, William. T Jun 1764 *Dolphin*. Ht.
Merveillean, Peter. R for Barbados Sep 1682. L.
Mesquitta als Jarro, Jacob Henriques. S Nov T Dec 1753 *Whiteing*. L.
Messenger, Elizabeth. S Feb T Mar 1763 *Neptune*. M.
Messenger, James. S Oct 1775. M.

Messenger, John. S Feb T Mar 1729 *Patapsco* LC Annapolis Dec 1729. M.

Messenger, William (1731). *See* Smith. Y.

Missiter, Richard. S & T Dec 1771 *Justitia*. M.

Mestee als Mason, John. R 14 yrs Aug T Sep 1718 *Eagle* LC Charles Town Mar 1719. L.

Medcalfe, Adam. S Feb 1758. Ha.

Metcalf, Elizabeth. S & T Jly 1753 *Tryal*. L.

Metcalfe, George. SQS Northallerton Jly TB Aug 1737. Y.

Medcalf, George. T Apr 1741 *Speedwell* or *Mediterranean*. Sy.

Metcalf, James. SW & T Dec 1771 *Justitia*. M.

Metcalfe, John. S Lent 1735. Y.

Medcalf, Joseph. R 14 yrs Jly 1774. M.

Metcalfe, Michael. S Jun 1733. M.

Metcalfe, Simon of Preston. SQS Thirsk s sheep Apr 1735. Y.

Metcalfe als Smith, Thomas. S Feb-Apr T May 1755 *Rose*. M.

Metcalfe, Thomas. S & T Jan 1769 *Thornton*. M.

Medcalfe, William. R for America Jly 1702. Db.

Metcalfe, William. S Summer 1727. We.

Metcalf, William. SQS Sep T Dec 1771 *Justitia*. M.

Medcalfe, William. R for life Lent 1775. Ht.

Metham, Margaret. S s stockings at Burford Lent 1723. O.

Meting. *See* Meeting.

Metkins als Innocent, William of St. Giles in Fields. R for America Aug 1713. M.

Metkirk, William. SQS Dec 1767; transportation contract made with 3rd Regiment of Foot Guards. M.

Metter, Thomasin. R 14 yrs Jly 1744 TB to Va 1745. De.

Metters, Richard. S Mar 1731 TB to Va. De.

Metton, George of St. George, Southwark. SQS Apr T May 1750 *Lichfield*. Sy.

Metyard, John. Rebel T 1685.

Mewres, Samuel. R 14 yrs Summer 1747. Nl.

Meyer. *See* Myer.

Meynell, Christopher of Long Leadman. R for America Jly 1678. Li.

Michaell, John. S May T Jly 1723 *Alexander* LC Annapolis Sep 1723. L.

Michael, Sarah. S & T Apr 1769 *Tryal*. L.

Michener, John (1722). *See* Mitchel. M.

Mitchiner, Thomas. R Sep T for life Oct 1768 *Justitia*. L.

Mickey, Elizabeth. S & T 14 yrs Dec 1740 *Vernon*. L.

Mickleburgh, Daniel. T Oct 1721 *William & John*. K.

Mickleburgh, John Jr. S Norwich Summer TB Sep 1754. Nf.

Middleditch, Eleanor. S May 1761. M.

Middlemass, William. S Summer T Oct 1723 *Forward* to Va from London. Y.

Middleton, Alexander. S Apr-Jun T Jly 1772 *Tayloe*. M.

Middleton, Ann. T Jun 1764 *Dolphin*. K.

Middleton, Charles. R Jly AT Aug 1685. M.

Middleton, Charles. S Oct 1741 T Feb 1742 *Industry*. L.

Middleton, David. R for America Jly 1693. Db.

Middleton, Elizabeth. T Apr 1770 *New Trial*. E.

Middleton, Frances. S & T May 1736 *Patapsco*. L.
Middleton, Gerrard. R for Barbados or Jamaica May 1684. L.
Middleton, John. S Mar 1724. De.
Middleton als High, John. S s at St. Gregory, Norwich, Summer 1772. Nf.
Middleton, Mary. R for Barbados or Jamaica Dec 1695 & May 1697 AT Jly 1697. M.
Middleton, Mary. T May 1737 *Forward*. E.
Middleton, Mary. S Jly T Sep 1737 *Pretty Patsy* to Md. M.
Middleton als Hutchinson, Mary. S Jan T Apr 1762 *Dolphin*. M.
Middleton, Michael. S May-Jly 1750. M.
Middleton, Ralph. Rebel T 1685.
Middleton, Richard. S Mar 1724. De.
Middleton, Robert of Newington. R for Barbados Aug 1662. Sy.
Middleton, Robert. R for America Jly 1702. Ru.
Middleton, Robert. S s horse Lent 1731 R 14 yrs Lent 1732. Nf.
Middleton, Robert. TB to Va from QS 1741. De.
Middleton, Thomas. R for Va Jly 1618. O.
Middleton, Thomas. Rebel T 1685.
Middleton, Thomas. S Feb T Apr 1732 *Patapsco* LC Annapolis Oct 1732. L.
Middleton, Thomas. S Apr 1748. L.
Midleton, Thomas. S s sheep Lent R 14 yrs Summer 1756. Wa.
Middleton, William of Necton. R for America Mar 1680. Nf.
Middleton, William. R for America Jly 1687. Le.
Middleton, William (1729). *See* Marks. L.
Middleton, William. S May-Jun T Jly 1753 *Tryal*. M.
Middleton, William. S Oct 1773. L.
Middlewood, Mary. S for breaking & entering at Kirby Lent TB Aug 1758. Y.
Midgley, Matthew. S Lent 1727 AT to Summer 1728. Y.
Midwinter, John Jr. S Lent R 14 yrs Summer 1750. G.
Milbourne, Catherine. S Jan T Feb 1719 *Worcester* LC Annapolis Jun 1719. L.
Milburn, Elizabeth. AT Lent 1747. Y.
Milbourne, John. S Summer 1749. Ca.
Milburne, Robert. S City Summer 1727. Nl.
Milbourne, Thomas (1750). *See* Abell. Wo.
Milburne, Thomas (1764). *See* Thompson. Y.
Milcham, William. T May 1719 *Margaret* LC Md May 1720; sold to Widow Newman. Sy.
Mildred, Hannah. S Apr 1749. L.
Mileist, Thomas. T May 1744 *Justitia*. Sy.
Miles, Briant. R 14 yrs Jly 1774. Do.
Miles, Charles. S & Dec 1731 *Forward* to Md or Va. M.
Miles, Charles. S Sep 1740. L.
Miles, Christian. T Dec 1763 *Neptune*. K.
Miles, Elizabeth. S Mar 1761. Ha.
Miles, Elizabeth. S & T Apr 1769 *Tryal*. L.
Miles, George. S & R 14 yrs Summer 1775. Be.
Miles, James. S Mar 1756. Do.

Miles, James. S Jly 1763. Ha.

Miles, John of Horsted Keynes. R for Barbados or Jamaica Jly 1688. Sx.

Miles, John. S Aug T Sep 1725 *Forward* LC Annapolis Dec 1725. M.

Miles, John. LC from *Loyal Margaret* Annapolis Oct 1726. X.

Miles, John. S Jan T Feb 1726 *Supply* LC Annapolis May 1726. L.

Miles, John. S & T Jan 1739 *Dorsetshire*. L.

Miles, John. S Jan-Feb T Apr 1753 *Thames*. M.

Miles, John. SQS Jly 1758. Ha.

Miles, John. S s at Blunham Lent 1772. Bd.

Miles, Mary. T Nov 1743 *George William*. Sx.

Miles, Mary. S Apr T May 1751 *Tryal*. L.

Miles, Mary. T 14 yrs May 1767 *Thornton*. M.

Miles, Peter. S s from bleaching ground at Osmotherley Lent TB Aug 1767. Y.

Miles, Robert. S & TB to Va Mar 1760. Wi.

Miles, Thomas of Marden, Heref. S s sheep Lent 1719. Wo.

Miles, Thomas. LC from *Susannah & Sarah* Annapolis Apr 1720. L. or M.

Miles, Thomas. T May 1736 *Patapsco*. E.

Miles, Thomas. T Jun 1738 *Forward*. Sy.

Miles, Thomas. S for assault with reaping hook Lent 1762. He.

Miles, William. S 14 yrs Mar TB to Va Oct 1729. Le.

Myalls, William. T Apr 1733 *Patapsco*. E.

Miles, William. S Summer 1749 R 14 yrs Lent T May 1750 *Lichfield*. E.

Milford, David. S Feb T Mar 1729 *Patapsco* LC Annapolis Dec 1729. L.

Milford, John. S Mar 1750 TB to Va. De.

Miliom, Stephen. S Jly 1740. Wi.

Milkins, William. S & T Oct 1730 *Forward* LC Potomack Jan 1731. M.

Milksop, Thomas. S Jly T 14 yrs Aug 1718 *Eagle* LC Charles Town Mar 1719. L.

Mill als Bramble, Thomas. TB to Va from QS 1740. De.

Millams, George. SQS Jly T Sep 1766 *Justitia*. Sy.

Millard, Henry. R 14 yrs Apr 1747. So.

Millard, John of Bradford. R for Barbados Jly 1683. Wi.

Millard, John. S Mar 1760. So.

Millard, John. S Jan-Feb T Apr 1772 *Thornton*. M.

Millard, Joseph. S Mar 1764. Ha.

Millard, Peter of Gillingham. R for America Apr 1697. Nf.

Millard, Robert. Rebel T 1685.

Millard, Thomas. S Mar 1764. Ha.

Millard, Thomas. S s cloth at Stroud Summer 1771. G.

Millard, William. S s gelding Lent R 14 yrs Summer 1752. Bd.

Millard, William. SQS Marlborough & TB to Va Oct 1756. Wi.

Millard, William (1769). *See* Miller. G.

Millban, Thomas, als Moore, George. S Mar 1774. So.

Milbank, John. R & T for life Jly 1770 *Scarsdale*. M.

Miller, Andrew. S 14 yrs May 1761. M.

Miller, Ann of Sandon. R for Barbados or Jamaica Jly 1674. E.

Miller, Ann, aged 27, brown hair. T Oct 1720 *Gilbert* LC Md May 1721. Sy.

Miller als Rhodes, Ann of Manchester. SQS Jan 1757. La.

Miller, Anna Maria of St. Ann, Westminster, spinster. S s gown Jly 1740 T Jan 1741 *Harpooner* to Rappahannock. M.

Miller als Milward, Benjamin Jr. S s at Ridgmont Lent R 14 yrs Summer 1767. Bd.

Miller, Charles. S Apr T May 1767 *Thornton*. M.

Miller als Jones, Christopher. S Oct 1744-Jan 1745. M.

Miller, Daniel. S Feb-Apr 1746. M.

Miller, Daniel. R Jly 1763. M.

Miller, Daniel. S & T Dec 1771 *Justitia*. L.

Miller, David. S Summer 1758. Cu.

Miller, David. S Summer T Sep 1759 from London. Nl.

Miller, David als John. S Feb T Apr 1768 *Thornton*. M.

Miller, Dorothy. S Apr T May 1720 *Honor* LC Port York Jan 1721. L.

Miller, Edward. SW & T Jly 1772 *Tayloe*. M.

Miller, Edward of Warrington, linen weaver. SQS Jan 1774. La.

Miller, Elizabeth of Bristol. R for Barbados Feb 1700. G.

Miller als Barefoot, Elizabeth. S Dec 1743 T Feb 1744 *Neptune* to Md. M.

Miller, Ganzelius. T Sep 1766 *Justitia*. Ht.

Miller, George. Rebel T 1685.

Meller, Henry. S s silver spoon at Oxford Lent 1734. Be.

Miller, Hester. S & T Apr 1741 *Mediterranean*. L.

Miller, James. T May 1719 *Margaret* LC Md Aug 1719; sold to William Martin. Ht.

Miller, James. S Summer 1731 R 14 yrs Lent 1732 (SP). Su.

Miller, James (1733). *See* Milner. St.

Miller, Jane. S Jly-Sep T Sep 1742 *Forward*. M.

Miller, John. Rebel T 1685.

Miller, John of Bromsgrove. R for America Jly 1691. Wo.

Miller, John of Chelsea. R (Western Cic) for Barbados Jly 1695. M.

Miller, John. TB Oct 1719 T *Susannah & Sarah* LC Annapolis Apr 1720. L.

Miller, John. Died on passage in *Gilbert* 1721. X.

Miller, John. LC from *Mary* Port York Jun 1721. X.

Miller, John. TB May 1744. Db.

Miller als Sargent, John. S Oct 1749. L.

Miller, John. S Mar TB to Va Apr 1751. Wi.

Miller, John. S Lent T May 1752 *Lichfield*. Sy.

Miller, John. S May T Jun 1756 *Lyon*. L.

Miller, John (2). S Jun T Sep 1764 *Justitia*. M.

Meller, John. S s at Bailby Lent 1766. Y.

Miller, John. S & T Sep 1766 *Justitia*. M.

Miller, John. S Dec 1766 T Jan 1767 *Tryal*. L.

Miller als Crockstone, John. S Sep 1767, escaped while boarding transport ship, recaptured & T Dec 1767 *Neptune*. M.

Miller, John (1768). *See* Miller, David. M.

Miller, Joseph. S Jly T Oct 1741 *Sea Horse*. L.

Miller, Joseph. R 14 yrs Aug 1760. So.

Miller, Joseph. T from Bristol by *Maryland Packet* 1761 but intercepted by French; T Apr 1763 *Neptune*. So.

Miller, Lawrence. S 14 yrs for receiving goods stolen by William Groom *(qv)* Lent 1745. Nf.

Miller, Lawrence. S Aug 1763. L.

Miller, Lucretia (1741). *See* Linsay. L.

Miller, Margaret. S Oct T Nov 1728 *Forward* LC Rappahannock Jun 1729. M.

Miller, Margaret. S May 1775. L.

Miller, Mary. S Aug T Sep 1725 *Forward* LC Annapolis Dec 1725. L.

Miller, Mary. S s sheets Summer 1737. Cu.

Miller, Mary. S s stays Apr T Jun 1742 *Bladon* to Md. M.

Miller, Mary wife of Thomas. S Lent 1748. Ht.

Miller, Mary of Chelmsford, chapwoman. SQS Jly 1749. E.

Miller, Mary (1764). *See* Norton. M.

Miller, Mary of West Derby, spinster. SQS Jly 1769. La.

Miller, Maximilian. R Jan-Feb T Apr 1772 *Thornton*; he and his wife frequently indicted previously. M.

Miller, Nicholas. SW & T Apr 1770 *New Trial.* M.

Miller, Ottwell. R for Barbados Dec 1667. M.

Miller, Richard. R for Barbados Jly 1663. L.

Miller, Richard of Waltham St. Lawrence. R for America Nov 1694. Be.

Miller, Richard of Halberton. R for Barbados Feb 1699. De.

Miller, Richard. T Apr 1739 *Forward.* Sy.

Miller als Browne, Robert of Broadhembury, butcher. R for Barbados Jun 1669. De.

Miller, Robert. S Jly 1748. L.

Millea, Samuel. S Apr T Sep 1757 *Thetis.* M.

Miller als Meller, Sarah, aged 15, brown hair. S & T Oct 1720 *Gilbert* LC Annapolis May 1721. M.

Miller, Solomon. S s horse Summer 1752 R 14 yrs Lent 1753. No.

Miller, Susannah. S & T Oct 1730 *Forward* LC Potomack Jan 1731. L.

Miller, Thomas. TB Aug 1749. Y.

Miller, Thomas. S & T Jly 1753 *Tryal.* M.

Miller, Thomas. T Apr 1766 *Ann.* M.

Miller, Thomas. S Sep T Oct 1768 *Justitia.* M.

Miller, Thomas. S May-Jly 1773. M.

Miller, Thomas Zachariah. S Feb T May 1767 *Thornton.* L.

Miller, William. R 14 yrs Summer 1736. O.

Miller, William. S May T Jun 1738 *Forward.* L.

Miller, William. S Jan T Apr 1743 *Justitia.* M.

Miller, William. R 14 yrs Jly 1749. Do.

Miller als Milner, William. S City Summer 1750. Y.

Miller, William. S Apr 1757. M.

Miller, William. T Dec 1763 *Neptune.* Sy.

Miller, William. S & T Sep 1764 *Justitia.* L.

Miller als Millard, William. S s horse Summer 1769 R 14 yrs Lent 1770. G.

Miller, William. S s at St. Sepulchre, Cambridge, Summer 1772. Ca.

Millers, James. T Apr 1753 *Thames.* E.

Millett, Ann. S Apr T May 1751 *Tryal.* L.

Millett, Caleb. R for Barbados or Jamaica Dec 1698. L.

Millett, Mary. S Sep-Oct T Dec 1771 *Justitia.* M.

Milley, John (1769). *See* Moratt. M.

Millichap, Richard als Edward. S s sheep & R 14 yrs Summer 1773. He.

Millidge, Mary. S s at Frampton Cotterell Lent 1771. G.

Milliford, James. S Mar 1758. De.

Millikin, Mark. S for obtaining goods by false pretences Feb 1775. L.

Millickin, Robert. S Aug T Sep 1725 *Forward* LC Annapolis Dec 1725. M.

Millind, John. LC from *Elizabeth* Potomack Aug 1729. Be.

Milliner, Anne. T Nov 1728 *Forward*. Sy.

Millinor, Thomas. LC from *Mary* Port York Jun 1721. X.

Milliner, William. S & T Jly 1753 *Tryal*. M.

Millington, Giles of Dorking. R for Barbados or Jamaica Jly 1702. Sy.

Millington, James. S Lent R 14 yrs Summer 1745. St.

Millington, John. S Jan-Apr 1749. M.

Millington, Joseph. S s barley at St. Paul, Bedford, Lent 1774. Bd.

Millison, Matthew. S Jly 1775. M.

Millo, Herman. S Oct-Dec 1750. M.

Mills, Abel. R 14 yrs Mar 1742. De.

Mills, Alexander, als Wiltshire, David. S & T Jan 1769 *Thornton*. L.

Mills, Anne (1688). *See* Yates. L.

Mills, Bonaventure of Lancaster. R for Barbados Jly 1699. La.

Mills, Eleanor. T Oct 1723 *Forward*. Sy.

Mills, Eleanor wife of William. S May-Jly 1773. M.

Mills, Elford. S Sep-Oct 1749. M.

Mills, Elizabeth. S Feb T 14 yrs Mar 1730 *Patapsco* LC Annapolis Sep 1730. L.

Mills, Elizabeth wife of William. SQS Jly TB Nov 1746. So.

Mills als Cassody, Elizabeth. S Feb 1754. M.

Mills als Liversidge, Elizabeth. S Feb-Apr T May 1755 *Rose*. M.

Mills, Elizabeth. S Jly 1763. Do.

Mills, Emanuel. S Jan-Apr 1749. M.

Mills, Emmanuel (1771). *See* May, James. M.

Mills, Frances. S Jan T Feb 1719 *Worcester* LC Annapolis Jun 1719. L.

Mills, George of Skelton. R for Barbados Jun 1694. Y.

Mills, George. S s silver spoons at St. Giles, Reading, Lent 1758. Be.

Mills, Gideon. R for Barbados Jun 1665. L.

Mills, Henry. Rebel T 1685.

Mills als Pizey, Henry. S for highway robbery Lent R Summer T for life Oct 1750 *Rachael*. E.

Mills, Isabella wife of Robert. S & T Feb 1744 *Neptune* to Md. M.

Mills, Isabella. S Sep T 14 yrs Oct 1744 *Susannah*. M.

Mills, James. S for highway robbery Lent R 14 yrs Summer 1750. Wa.

Mills, John. R for Barbados or Jamaica Feb 1687. L.

Mills, John of Cobham. R for America Jly 1700. Sy.

Mills, John. S Apr T Aug 1718 *Eagle* LC Charles Town Mar 1719. L.

Mills, John. S s at Stone Summer 1722. St.

Mills, John. S Jan T Jun 1726 *Loyal Margaret* to Md. M.

Mills, John, als Mollying Jack. S Sep 1733 T Jan 1734 *Caesar* LC Va Jly 1734. M.

Mills, John. T Jan 1736 *Dorsetshire*. Sy.

Mills, John of Greenwich. S Lent T May 1750 *Lichfield*. K.

Mills, John. S s horse at Normanton & R 14 yrs Lent 1768. Y.

Mills, John. S s money at Stroud Lent 1770. G.

Mills, John. S Mar 1773. De.

Mills, Joseph. S & T Dec 1771 *Justitia*. L.

Mills, Margaret. S s kettle Feb T Apr 1735 *Patapsco* LC Annapolis Oct 1735. M.

Mills, Martha. S & T Sep 1751 *Greyhound*. L.

Mills als Stephens, Mary. R for Barbados May 1676. L.

Mills, Mary wife of Thomas of St. George, Bloomsbury. S s cotton Oct 1740 T Jan 1741 *Harpooner* to Rappahannock. M.

Mills, Mary. S Oct 1749. L.

Mills, Mary. S Feb T Sep 1767 *Justitia*. M.

Mills, Michael. S Jun T Aug 1769 *Douglas*. L.

Mills, Nathaniel. S & T Jan 1722 *Gilbert* but died on passage. M.

Mills, Nicholas. R 14 yrs Jly 1744 TB to Va 1745. De.

Mills, Richard. S & T Dec 1716 *Lewis* to Jamaica. L.

Mells, Robert. S s from warehouse Summer 1758 R 14 yrs Lent 1759. La.

Mills, Robert. SQS Jan 1761. M.

Mills, Robert. S Mar 1771. So.

Mills, Samuel. S Norwich Summer 1764. Nf.

Mills, Samuel. S Oct 1766 T Jan 1767 *Tryal*. L.

Mills, Sarah. S Lent R 14 yrs Summer 1737. O.

Mills, Sarah. S Sep T Nov 1743 *George William*. M.

Mills, Sebastian. R 10 yrs Lent 1655; to be T by Thomas Vincent & Samuel Highalnd. Sy.

Mills, Thomas of Wateringbury. R for Barbados or Jamaica Mar 1682. K.

Mills, Thomas. Rebel T 1685.

Mills, Thomas. TB Oct 1719. L.

Mills, Thomas of Whittington. S Lent 1721. G.

Mills, Thomas. S s horse Summer 1744 R 14 yrs Summer 1746. Du.

Mills, Thomas. S Mar 1752. Ha.

Mills, Thomas. S Jan 1755. M.

Mills, Thomas. T Sep 1767 *Justitia*. L.

Mills, Vincent. T Oct 1739 *Duke of Cumberland*. Bu.

Mills, William of Whittington. S Lent 1721. G.

Mills, William. LC from *Rappahannock* Rappahannock Apr 1726. X.

Mills, William. S s wheat Lent 1741. O.

Mills, William. S s clothing at Cookham Summer 1743. Be.

Mills, William. S Mar TB to Va Apr 1745. Wi.

Mills, William. S Mar 1755. Do.

Mills, William. AT Summer 1760. Y.

Millson, Thomas. S Sep-Oct 1773. M.

Milner, Edward. T Summer 1739. Y.

Milner, Elizabeth. R for Barbados Dec 1667. M.

Milner, George. S Lent R 14 yrs Summer 1743. St.

Milner, George. AT Summer 1754. Y.

Milner, Jacob als Nathan, als Johnson, William. S s mare Lent 1746. Y.

Milner als Miller, James. S Summer 1733 R 14 yrs Lent 1734. St.

Milner, Jane. AT Summer 1754. Y.

Milner, John. S s cloth Summer 1737. We.

Milner, John. AT Summer 1758. Y.

Milner, Nathan (1746). *See* Milner, Jacob. Y.

Milner, Robert. SQS s peas & beans at Eakring Oct 1766. Nt.

Milner, Thomas. R 14 yrs Summer 1749. Y.

Milner, Thomas. T Dec 1763 *Neptune*. K.

Milner, William (1750). *See* Miller. Y.

Milner, William. AT Summer 1754. Y.

Milsham, John. S Lent R Summer 1739 (SP). Be.

Milsum, Abraham. S s at Siston Lent 1763. G.

Milsome, John. R 14 yrs Mar 1758. So.

Milstead, Edward of Bethersden. R for Barbados or Jamaica Jly 1674. K.

Milston, Thomas. S Apr T Jly 1770 *Scarsdale*. L.

Milton, Anne. S Feb T Mar 1730 *Patapsco* LC Annapolis Sep 1730. M.

Milton, Edward. S Apr 1728. De.

Milton, Henry. SQS Jly T Sep 1767 *Justitia*. M.

Milton, James of Chittlehampton. R for Barbados Feb 1714. De.

Milton, John. T 14 yrs May 1719 *Margaret*; sold to Nathaniel Stinchman Md May 1720. Sx.

Milton, John. S Apr 1765. So.

Melton, Joseph. R for Barbados Sep 1677. L.

Melton, Philip of Faldingworth. R for America Jly 1678. Li.

Melton, Thomas. S Lent 1761. Su.

Milton, William. S Apr 1742. So.

Milward, Benjamin (1767). *See* Miller. Bd.

Milward, Jane. R for America Jly 1693. Wa.

Milward, John. R 14 yrs Summer 1756. Y.

Milward, Richard. Rebel T 1685.

Milwood, Richard. R Jly 1679. Le.

Mims, Mary. S Apr T Oct 1719 *Susannah & Sarah* LC Annapolis Apr 1720. L.

Mince, John als Peter. S May-Jly 1774. M.

Minchell. *See* Minshall.

Mincher, Hannah of St. George, Southwark, widow. R for Barbados or Jamaica Jly 1712. Sy.

Mincher, John. LC Md Sep 1719; sold to Patrick Sympson & William Black. Sy.

Mincher, John. S s malt at Dudley Summer 1764. Wo.

Minchin, Joseph of Highnam, yeoman. R for America Feb 1713. G.

Minett, Matthew. S Feb 1754. L.

Mingham, Benjamin. S Jly 1724. Ha.

Mingis, Martha. S Dec 1753-Jan 1754. M.

Minifie, John. Rebel T 1685.

Minns, Elizabeth wife of John. R for Barbados May 1676. L.

Minns, James. S s sheets at St. Michael Colney, Norwich, Summer 1774. Nf.

Minns, John. R for Barbados Jun 1671. L.

Minsall, Anne (1728). *See* Birch. X.

Minchell, John of Chatham. S Lent T May 1719 *Margaret*; sold to Patrick Sympson Md May 1720. K.

Minshall, Thomas. S s sheep at Stoke upon Tern Lent 1738. Sh.

Minsheare, Roger. AT Aug 1678. M.

Minskipp, Thomas. S May T Jly 1723 *Alexander* LC Annapolis Sep 1723. M.

Minson, Richard. S 14 yrs for receiving Mar 1733. Wi.

Minty, Mary. S & T Jan 1766 *Tryal*. M.

Mirehouse, Joseph (1744). *See* Taylor, John. Y.

Mires. *See* Myers.

Mirton. *See* Merton.

Missiter. *See* Messiter.

Misson, Gretian. S Jan T Feb 1724 *Anne* to Carolina. M.

Mist, John. S Dec 1764 T Jan 1765 *Tryal*. M.

Mitcham, William. T Dec 1770 *Justitia*. K.

Mitchell, Adam. SW & T Jly 1772 *Tayloe*. M.

Mitchell, Benjamin. S Lent R 14 yrs Summer T Aug 1752 *Tryal*. Sy.

Mitchell, Katherine of Abbotskerswell. R for Barbados Feb 1690. De.

Mitchell als Procter, Christian. S Sep T Nov 1743 *George William*. M.

Mitchell, Dorothy. T 14 yrs May 1767 *Thornton*. Sy.

Mitchell, Edward (1669). *See* Mace. L.

Mitchell, Edward. Rebel T 1685.

Mitchell, Elinor. R for Barbados or Jamaica Jly 1685. L.

Mitchell, Elizabeth. R for Barbados or Jamaica Dec 1695. M.

Mitchell, Elizabeth. S Jly-Dec 1747. M.

Michill, George. Rebel T 1685.

Mitchell, George. S Jly-Dec 1747. M.

Mitchell, George. T Oct 1768 *Justitia*. E.

Mitchell, James. S Dec 1727. M.

Mitchell, James. T Sep 1730 *Smith*. Sy.

Mitchell, James. S s watch Feb T Apr 1735 *Patapsco* LC Annapolis Oct 1735. M.

Mitchell, James (1736). *See* Campbell. Cu.

Mitchell, James. S City Summer 1746. Nl.

Mitchell, James. S Lent R 14 yrs Summer 1747. Sy.

Mitchell, James. S Lent 1754. K.

Mitchell, James. S Mar 1754. L.

Mitchell, James. S Mar 1763 TB to Va. De.

Mitchell, James. T Aug 1769 *Douglas*. Sy.

Mitchell, James. S Oct T Dec 1771 *Justitia*. L.

Mitchell, James of St. Martin in Fields. SW Apr T Jly 1772 *Tayloe*. M.

Mitchell, Jane wife of Robert of Epping. R for Barbados or Jamaica Jly 1710. E.

Mitchell, John (2). Rebels T 1685.

Mitchell als Michener, John. S & T Jan 1722 *Gilbert* to Md. M.

Mitchell, John (1727). *See* Avis. M.

Mitchell, John. T Sep 1730 *Smith*. K.

Mitchell, John. S Apr-Jun 1739. M.

Mitchell, John of St. Paul, Covent Garden. S s coal scuttle & T Jan 1740 *York*. M.

Mitchell, John. S Jly 1750. L.

Mitchell, John. S Apr T May 1767 *Thornton*. L.

Mitchell, John. S May T Jly 1771 *Scarsdale*. L.

Mitchell, John. SQS Jly TB Aug 1771. So.
Mitchell, John. S Sep-Oct T Dec 1771 *Justitia*. M.
Mitchell, Joseph. S Summer 1740. Y.
Mitchell, Mary. R for Barbados or Jamaica May 1697. L.
Mitchell, Peter. S s sheet at Potton Lent 1771. Bd.
Mitchell, Ralph. S & T Jly 1771 *Scarsdale*. M.
Mitchell, Richard. R 14 yrs Mar 1743. So.
Mitchell, Richard. R 14 yrs Jly 1743. De.
Mitchell, Richard. S Mar 1758. So.
Mitchell, Richard. R for life Jly 1763. M.
Mitchell, Robert. Rebel T 1685.
Mitchell als Hutchinson, Robert. T Sep 1765 *Justitia*. M.
Mitchell, Samuel. R 14 yrs Aug 1742. Do.
Mitchel, Samuel. S Oct T Dec 1769 *Justitia*. L.
Mitchell, Sarah. S Summer 1741. Y.
Mitchell, Sarah of Lambeth, spinster. SQS Feb 1757. Sy.
Mitchell, Sarah. S Feb T Apr 1765 *Ann*. L.
Mitchell, Sarah. S Mar 1774. So.
Michell als Gillard, Scipio. S Mar 1773. Co.
Mitchell, Thomas. Rebel T 1685.
Mitchell, Thomas. R for Barbados or Jamaica Oct 1694, Dec 1695 & Jan 1697. M.
Mitchell, Thomas. AT Lent 1749. Be.
Mitchell, Thomas. S s poultry at All Hallows Lombard Street Feb T Apr 1768 *Thornton*. L.
Michell, William of Kingston on Thames. R (Newgate) for Barbados Aug 1668. Sy.
Mitchell, William. R for Barbados Jly 1674. M.
Mitchell, William. S Mar 1739. Co.
Mitchell, William. S Apr-May T May 1744 *Justitia*. M.
Mitchell, William. T Jly 1770 *Scarsdale*. M.
Mitchell, William. S Sep-Oct T Dec 1771 *Justitia*. M.
Mitchells, Jacob. S Feb T Apr 1770 *New Trial*. M.
Mitchelson, James. S s at Bishopwearmouth Summer 1765; wife Mary acquitted. Du.
Mitchiner. *See* Michener.
Mitton, John of Pemberton, butcher. SQS Jan 1774. La.
Mitton, Samuel of Ashworth, weaver. SQS Jan 1774. La.
Mitton, William. AT Summer 1757. Y.
Mixon, William. S Mar 1732 TB to Va. De.
Mote, Elizabeth. S Feb T Mar 1729 *Patapsco* LC Annapolis Dec 1729. M.
Moate, John. S Lent R 14 yrs Summer T Sep 1751 *Greyhound*. K.
Mobbs, Elizabeth. S & T Jan 1722 *Gilbert* LC Annapolis Jly 1722. L.
Mobbs, Elizabeth. S Jly T Sep 1737 *Pretty Patsy* to Md. M.
Mobbs, Martha. S & T Jan 1739 *Dorsetshire*. L.
Mobbs, Philip. T Apr 1732 *Patapsco*. Sy.
Mobbs, Thomas. S Aug T Oct 1724 *Forward* LC Annapolis Jun 1725. M.
Mobson, William of Didcot. R for America Jly 1699. Be.
Mock, John. S Mar 1775 De.
Moco Jack (1734). *See* Traviss, John. M.

Modesty, Thomas. S May T Jun 1727 *Susanna* to Va. M.

Moffatt, Alexander. S Lent 1747. Y.

Moffett, Samuel. S Oct T Dec 1771 *Justitia*. L.

Moge, Joseph. S Jan T Feb 1733 *Smith* to Md or Va. M.

Mogridge, John (2). Rebels T 1685.

Mogridge, John. S Mar 1766 TB to Va. De.

Muggeride, Joseph. S Aug 1732 TB to Va. De.

Mockridge, Mary wife of William. S May T Nov 1743 *George William*. M.

Moggridge, Richard (1728). *See* Burman. So.

Moggridge, Samuel (1729). *See* Burman. So.

Moggridge, Timothy. R 14 yrs Mar 1730. So.

Mohnn, Catherine (1755). *See* Moon. L.

Moisey, William. S Mar 1734. Co.

Mole, Thomas. S Lent 1775. E.

Mowls, Ann. S Feb 1761. L.

Moles, George. R for Barbados Dec 1671. M.

Molesworth, Joseph. S s at Wolverhampton Lent 1768. St.

Moley, Ann (1743). *See* Stone. M.

Molieure, John. T Dec 1734 *Caesar* LC Va Jly 1735. Ht.

Molineux, Edward. S Feb T May 1719 *Margaret* but died on passage. L.

Mollynex, John of Liverpool, butcher. S s silver spoons Summer 1736. La.

Molineaux, Jonathan. S May T Jun 1726 *Loyal Margaret* LC Annapolis Oct 1726. M.

Molineux, Richard. S s silver cup at Killington Summer 1768. Y.

Molineux, Robert of Castle. R for Barbados Jly 1685. La.

Molineux, Sapcott. R for Va Jly 1618. O.

Moll, Francisco. S Jan T Apr 1762 *Dolphin*. L.

Mol, John. SQS Aug 1752 TB to Md Apr 1753. Le.

Molland, William. R 14 yrs Aug 1727 TB to Md. De.

Mollett, Edward. S Oct 1737 T Jan 1738 *Dorsetshire* to Va. M.

Maloye, Lawrence. T Jan 1766 *Tryal*. M.

Molloy, Mary. S Jly T 14 yrs Aug 1721 *Prince Royal* LC Va Nov 1721. M.

Mulloy, Mary. S Oct 1756. M.

Molloy, Roger. S Jan 1775. M.

Mollying Jack (1733). *See* Mills, John. M.

Molney, Peter. S & T Jan 1767 *Tryal*. L.

Molson. *See* Moulson.

Molton. *See* Moulton.

Momford. *See* Mumford.

Monday. *See* Munday.

Money, Edward of Reading. R for America Feb 1690. Be.

Money, Robert of Fornham. R for America Apr 1697. Su.

Money, Roger. R for Barbados Aug 1664. M.

Moneypenny, Hugh. S Jan T Apr 1762 *Dolphin*. L.

Monford, Richard. S Aug 1758. So.

Monford, Thomas. T Jun 1727 *Susanna*. Bu.

Monger, Joseph (1765). *See* Fry. Ha.

Monger, Sarah. S Nov T 14 yrs Dec 1753 *Whiteing*. L.

Monk, Ann. S Feb 1754. L.

Monk, Ann. S Feb-Apr T May 1755 *Rose*. M.

Monk, Ann. S May-Jly 1774. M.

Monke, Elizabeth. S Apr T Dec 1735 *John* LC Annapolis Sep 1736. M.

Monk, Elizabeth. T Apr 1759 *Thetis*. Sy.

Monk, George. S Sep 1737 T Jan 1738 *Dorsetshire* to Va. M.

Monk, George. T Jun 1740 *Essex*. E.

Monk, George. S Summer 1755 R 14 yrs Summer 1756. E.

Munk, Jane. S Sep T Dec 1770 *Justitia*. M.

Monk, John. S Apr-May 1754. M.

Monk als Williams, John. S Feb T Apr 1768 *Thornton*. M.

Monk, Joseph (1773). *See* Richards. L.

Monk, Joseph. S May-Jly 1773. M.

Monk, Martha. S Sep T Oct 1744 *Susannah*. M.

Monk, Mary. S for arson Lent R 14 yrs Summer 1749. He.

Moncke, Richard. R for America Feb 1683. Li.

Monk, Rinaldo. S 14 yrs Mar TB to Va Apr 1742. Wi.

Monke, Thomas of Kingswinford. R for America Mar 1701. St.

Monkhouse, Jane wife of William, als Jane Murray. S May T Sep 1765 *Justitia*. M.

Munkhouse, John of Brackenthwaite. R for Barbados Feb 1673. Cu.

Munckton, Joseph. S Apr 1741. So.

Monmouth, Charles William of Panteg. R for America Jly 1698. Mo.

Monro, Jane. S s pewter pot Feb T Jun 1738 *Forward* to Md or Va. M.

Monroe, John. AT Summer 1765. Nl.

Monro, John. R & T for life Jly 1770 *Scarsdale*. M.

Monroe, Joseph. SWK & T May 1750 *Lichfield*. K.

Monroe, Margaret. S Jun T Oct 1744 *Susannah*. M.

Monro, Margaret. S May-Jly 1774. M.

Monro, Mary. SQS Feb T Mar 1750 *Tryal*. M.

Munroe, Robert. S Jan 1751. L.

Montague, Elizabeth. S Apr T Sep 1737 *Pretty Patsy* to Md. M.

Mountague, Francis. R (Home Circ) for Barbados Aug 1665. X.

Mountague, Margaret. S Jan-Jun T Jun 1728 *Elizabeth* LC Potomack Aug 1729. L.

Montague, Thomas. AT Sep 1682. M.

Montague, Thomas. R Apr 1690. M.

Mountague, William (1774). *See* Mounty. Wi.

Montear, Martha. S Aug T Oct 1724 *Forward* LC Annapolis Jun 1725. L.

Monteeth, Robert. S for highway robbery at Whitburn & R 14 yrs Summer 1773. Du.

Monter, Sarah. T Apr 1766 *Ann*. M.

Montford, Robert. S Lent 1773. E.

Montgomery, Alexander. R 14 yrs Dec 1773. M.

Montgomery, Andrew. S Jly 1740. Ha.

Montgomery, Eleanor. S May T Jun 1756 *Lyon*. L.

Montgomery, Elizabeth wife of William. S for shoplifting Summer 1742 R 14 yrs Lent 1743. Wa.

Montgomery, Ester. S Oct T Dec 1724 *Rappahannock* to Va. M.

Montgomery, Frances. R 14 yrs Jly 1747. Ha.

Montgomery, George Frederick. SQS Feb T May 1767 *Thornton*. M.

Montgomery, Hannah wife of Andrew. S & T Oct 1730 *Forward* LC Potomack Jan 1731. M.

Montgomery, John of Aston. SQS Aug T Sep 1766 *Justitia*. Ht.

Montgomery, Margaret. S Feb T Apr 1770 *New Trial*. M.

Montross, Francis. S Aug T Oct 1724 *Forward* LC Annapolis Jun 1725. M.

Mooden als Moody, Elizabeth wife of Thomas. S Jun-Dec 1738 T Jan 1739 *Dorsetshire*. M.

Moody, Andrew. S s iron hoops Jun T Dec 1736 *Dorsetshire* to Va. M.

Moody, Charles. T Oct 1726 *Forward*. Sy.

Moody, Eleanor. S Apr 1718. M.

Moody, Elizabeth. S Apr T Aug 1718 *Eagle* LC Charles Town Mar 1719. L.

Moody, Elizabeth (1738). *See* Mooden. M.

Moody, Elizabeth als Betty. S Aug TB to Va Sep 1767. Wi.

Moody, James. Rebel T 1685.

Moody, James of Newington. SQS Feb T 14 yrs May 1767 *Thornton*. Sy.

Moody, John. S Nov T Dec 1752 *Greyhound*. L.

Moody, John. R May T for life Sep 1758 *Dragon*. M.

Moody, John. S Lent 1763. Ht.

Moody, John. S & T Dec 1771 *Justitia*. L.

Moody, John. S s wine at Pursley Lent 1774. G.

Moody, Richard. S for firing haystack Summer 1729 R 14 yrs Summer 1730. No.

Moody, Samuel. S Lent 1754. K.

Moody, Samuel. S Jly T Sep 1766 *Justitia*. L.

Moody, Thomas. R 14 yrs Jly 1733. So.

Moody, William. S Summer 1719 R 14 yrs Summer 1720. Y.

Moody, William. R 14 yrs Jly 1735. Ha.

Moody, William. S Jly T Sep 1764 *Justitia*. M.

Moon als Moor, Ann. S Summer 1738 R 14 yrs Summer TB Dec 1739. Y.

Moon als Mohnn, Catherine. S Jan 1755. L.

Moon, George. S Apr T Jun 1742 *Bladon*. L.

Moon, Thomas. S Oct T Dec 1758 *The Brothers*. L.

Mooney, John. S Feb T 14 yrs Mar 1750 *Tryal*. M.

Mooney, Nicholas. T Oct 1768 *Justitia*. Sy.

Mooney, Richard. S Jly-Sep 1754. M.

Moore, Aaron. TB to Va from QS 1744. De.

Moor, Ann (1738). *See* Moon. Y.

Moore, Ann. S Feb-Apr T May 1755 *Rose*. M.

Moore, Ann. S Dec 1757 T Mar 1758 *Dragon*. M.

Moore, Anthony. S Dec 1733 T Jan 1734 *Caesar* but died on passage. L.

Moore, Arthur. S Feb T Mar 1731 *Patapsco* LC Annapolis Jun 1731. M.

Moore, Charles. S & T Oct 1720 *Gilbert* to Md. M.

Moore, Charles. S Oct 1749. L.

Moore, Christopher of Dodcott. R for Barbados Mar 1682. Ch.

Moore, Christopher. R for Barbados Dec 1683. M.

Moore, Daniel. S Dec 1762 T Mar 1763 *Neptune*. M.

Moore, Diana (1774). *See* Cripps. O.

Moore, Dorothy. R for Barbados Oct 1673. L.

Moore, Dorothy. R for Barbados Mar 1677. L.

Moore, Edward Jr. R 14 yrs Jly 1735. Wi.

Moore, Edward. S Mar TB to Va Apr 1742. Wi.

Moore, Eleanor als Nell. S as pickpocket Summer 1755 R 14 yrs Lent 1756. He.

More als Baldwin, Elizabeth. R for Barbados Apr 1669. M.

Moor, Elizabeth, als Paul, Margaret. R for America Aug 1715. L.

Moor, Elizabeth. S Aug T Sep 1725 *Forward*. L.

Moore, Elizabeth. S Feb 1752. L.

Moore, Elizabeth (1754). *See* Baker. M.

Moor, Elizabeth wife of Isaac. S & R Lent 1765. Nf.

Moore, George of Cheam. R for Barbados or Jamaica Mar 1680. Sy.

Moore, George. S s at Wokingham Lent 1764. Be.

Moore, George (1774). *See* Millban, Thomas. So.

More, Guy. S Apr 1733. M.

Moore, Henry. S s horse Summer 1753 R 14 yrs Lent 1754. No.

Moore, Isaac of Modbury. R for Barbados Jly 1695. De.

Moore, James. Rebel T 1685.

Moor, James of St. John's. S Summer T Oct 1750 *Rachael*. Sy.

Moore, James. S & T Jly 1753 *Tryal*. L.

Moore als Floud, Jane of St. Giles in Fields, widow. S s beer Jly 1740 T Jan 1741 *Harpooner* to Rappahannock. M.

Moore, Jane. S Jan-Feb 1774. M.

Moore, John. S Jun 1621. M.

Moore, John. R for Barbados or Jamaica Dec 1689. L.

Moore, John (1698). *See* Richardson. K.

Moor, John. S Summer 1718 R 14 yrs Summer 1721 T Oct 1723 *Forward* from London. Y.

Moor, John. S & T Jan 1722 *Gilbert* LC Annapolis Jly 1722. M.

Moor, John. TB to Md from QS 1727. De.

Moore, John. S Mar TB Sep 1728. Wi.

Moor als Holland, John. S Feb T Mar 1729 *Patapsco* LC Annapolis Dec 1729. M.

Moore, John. S Sep 1733 T Jan 1734 *Caesar* LC Va Jly 1734. M.

Moore, John. TB to Va from QS 1734. De.

Moore, John. S Lent 1741. Y.

Moore, John. S Lent 1748. *Nf.

Moore, John. S Lent R 14 yrs Summer 1748. No.

Moore, John. S Dec 1749-Jan 1750 T Mar 1750 *Tryal*. M.

Moor, John. S Summer 1750 R 14 yrs Lent TB Apr 1751. G.

Moore, John. S Mar 1753. Co.

Moore, John. S Oct 1766 T Jan 1767 *Tryal*. L.

More, John. S Summer 1767. Nf.

Moore, John. T 14 yrs Oct 1768 *Justitia*. E.

Moore, John. S Jun T 14 yrs Aug 1769 *Douglas*. M.

Moore, John, als Stone, Samuel. R Aug 1770. So.

Moore, John. S Feb T Apr 1771 *Thornton*. L.

More, Joseph (1738). *See* Morey. Sy.

Moore, Joseph. TB Sep 1749. Db.

Moore, Joseph. R 14 yrs Mar 1757. De.

Moore, Mary. T Jan 1736 *Dorsetshire*. Sx.

Moore, Mary. S s at Newcastle under Lyme Summer 1767. St.

Moore, Morice (1693). *See* Jones, Joseph. M.

Moore, Moses. Rebel T 1685.

Moor, Nicholas. S & T Dec 1771 *Justitia*. M.

Moore, Peter. R Lent 1775. K.

Moor, Rebecca. S & T Jan 1722 *Gilbert* but died on passage. L.

Moore, Richard. S & T Apr 1733 *Patapsco* LC Annapolis Nov 1733. M.

More, Richard. T Apr 1742 *Bond*. Sy.

Moore, Richard. R Mar 1774. So.

Moore, Robert. S Feb 1754. L.

Moore, Robert. SQS & T Sep 1766 *Justitia*. M.

Moor, Robert als William. S s horse at Aldborough & R 14 yrs Lent 1770. Y.

Moore, Samuel als James. S Lent 1748. *Nf.

Moore, Sarah (1697). *See* Mahoone. L.

Moore, Sarah. TB to Va from QS 1740. De.

Moore, Sarah. S Feb T Apr 1759 *Thetis*. M.

Moor, Susanna. S Apr 1719. M.

Moore, Thomas. Rebel T 1685.

Moore, Thomas of Hornchurch. R for Barbados or Jamaica Jun 1699. E.

Moore, Thomas. T Oct 1720 *Forward*. Sy.

Moore, Thomas. R 14 yrs Mar 1738. So.

Moore, Thomas, als Stew, John. S for highway robbery Lent R 14 yrs Summer 1743. O.

Moore, Thomas Jr. S s mare Lent R 14 yrs Summer 1752. Fl.

Moore, Thomas (1753). *See* Rogers. Wo.

Moore, Thomas of St. George, Southwark. SQS Jly 1765 T Jan 1766 *Tryal*. Sy.

More, Thomas. SQS Summer 1775. Ht.

Moor, Timothy. S Jan-Jun T Jun 1728 *Elizabeth* LC Potomack Aug 1729. M.

Moore, Timothy of Rotherhithe. SQS Feb T Apr 1759 *Thetis*. Sy.

Moore, William of Durham City. R for Barbados Jly 1690. Du.

Moore, William of Overton. R for Barbados Feb 1702. Ha.

Moore, William. R 14 yrs Aug 1720. De.

Moor, William. S Oct T Nov 1725 *Rappahannock* but died on passage. M.

Moore, William. S Jan T 14 yrs Feb 1726 *Supply* LC Annapolis May 1726. L.

Moore, William. S Dec 1733 T Jan 1734 *Caesar* LC Va Jly 1734. L.

Moore, William. SQS Jan 1734. So.

Moore, William. S & T Jan 1739 *Dorsetshire*. L.

Moore, William of Manchester. SQS Jan 1748. La.

Moore, William. S Apr 1748. L.

Moore, William. S Summer 1753. Su.

Moore, William. S Sep T Dec 1758 *The Brothers*. M.

Moore, William. SQS Apr T May 1767 *Thornton*. M.

Moore, William Sr. T May 1767 *Thornton*. Sy.

Moore, William Jr. T May 1767 *Thornton*. Sy.

Moor, William (1770). *See* Moor, Robert. Y.

Moore, William. S Nov T Dec 1770 *Justitia*. L.
Moor, William. S s rabbits in warren at South Cave Summer 1771. Y.
Moore, William. S Aug 1773. So.
Moore, William. S Jan-Feb 1774. M.
Moore, William. S Apr 1774. L.
Moores, John. R for life Sep 1756. M.
Moores, Mathew. S Lent 1760. Ch.
Moores, Richard. S s mare at Hogshaw & R Summer T Oct 1768
  Justitia. Bu.
Moores, Thomas. R for life Sep 1756. M.
Morfield, William. T Apr 1742 *Bond*. K.
Mooring als Grey, William. S & T Sep 1757 *Thetis*. M.
Moorshall. *See* Marshall.
Moot, John. S s at Walsham-le-Willows Lent 1773. Su.
Mopsey, Ann. R for life Mar 1771. So.
Moraa, William. S City Summer 1719 AT Summer 1720. Y.
Moratt als Milley, John. SW & T Jan 1769 *Thornton*. M.
Morcombe, Josias. S Aug 1726. De.
Morcomb, Nathaniel (1725). *See* Power. De.
Mordecai, Moses. T Sep 1758 *Tryal*. Sy.
Mordicai, Samuel. S & T Apr 1769 *Tryal*. L.
Morden als Shields, Elizabeth. S Jan T Feb 1724 *Anne* to Carolina. M.
Mordoe, William. S for returning from transportation Lent R 14 yrs
  Summer 1750. La.
Mordrum, Henry. SQS Summer T Jly 1770 *Scarsdale*. Ht.
More. *See* Moore.
Moreby, Richard. S Oct T Dec 1724 *Rappahannock* to Va. M.
Morehane, Joseph. R Jly T for life Sep 1767 *Justitia*. M.
Morehouse, William Jr. of Middleton. S s gun Summer 1738. Nf.
Morein, John. S Apr T Sep 1758 *Tryal* to Annapolis. M.
Moreland. *See* Morland.
Moreman, Mary, spinster, als wife of William of St. Saviour, Southwark.
  R for Barbados Jly 1679. Sy.
Morestly als Mosely, Joseph. S Feb-Apr T May 1752 *Lichfield*. M.
Moretman, Edward (1726). *See* Mortimore. X.
Morton, Abraham of Lambeth. R for Barbados or Jamaica Feb
  1684. Sy.
Moreton, Benjamin. S s at Ellenhall Summer 1769 R 14 yrs Lent
  1770. St.
Moreton, Caleb. S Lent R 14 yrs Summer 1756. Wo.
Moreton, Charles. S Feb T Sep 1737 *Pretty Patsy* to Md. M.
Moreton, Christopher. S Feb T Apr 1771 *Thornton*. L.
Morton, Daniel. S Aug TB Oct 1732. Le.
Morton, Edward. Rebel T 1685.
Morton, Elizabeth. S Lent 1769. Y.
Morton, George. S s mare at Almondsbury Lent R 14 yrs Summer
  1766. Y.
Morton, George. T May 1767 *Thornton*. E.
Moreton, Henry. S for housebreaking Summer 1734 R 14 yrs Lent 1735
  AT Summer 1736. He.
Moreton, James. S Jun T Aug 1769 *Douglas*. M.

Moreton, John. S s deer from enclosed park Lent R 14 yrs Summer 1738. Db.

Moreton, Mark. S s sheep Lent R 14 yrs Summer TB Sep 1754. Db.

Morton, Mary wife of Robert. S Sep-Oct 1772. M.

Morton, Richard of Foulby. R for Barbados Jly 1688. Y.

Moreton, Rose. LC from *Caesar* Va Jly 1734. X.

Morton, Samuel, aged 21, fair, painter. LC from *Jonathan* Annapolis Jly 1724. X.

Moreton, Samuel. S Jly T 14 yrs Sep 1737 *Pretty Patsy*. L.

Moreton, Sarah. S Summer 1775. Wa.

Mooreton als Martin, William. R for Barbados Jly 1675 & May 1676. L.

Moreton, William. S May T Jun 1726 *Loyal Margaret* LC Annapolis Oct 1726. M.

Moreton als Seabright, William. S s at Enville Lent 1764. St.

Morey, James. S Dec 1768 T Jan 1769 *Thornton*. L.

Moorey, John. T Sep 1767 *Justitia*. Sy.

Morey als More, Joseph. T Jun 1738 *Forward*. Sy.

Morey, Stephen. S Jly 1741. De.

Morey, William. S Mar 1750 TB to Va. De.

Morfitt, George. S s at Middleton Lent TB Aug 1768. Y.

Morfoot, John. S for assault with intent to rob Lent 1754. Hu.

Morgan, Alice. R Jan AT Feb 1679. M.

Morgan, Chandos. S s silver at Ross Lent 1751. He.

Morgan, Charles. S Nov T Dec 1763 *Neptune*. L.

Morgan, Charles. S s tea chest at St. Bride's Sep T Oct 1768 *Justitia*. L.

Morgan, Christopher (1716). *See* Teddall. M.

Morgan, David. S & T Mar 1760 *Friendship*. L.

Morgan, David. R Jun 1761 to be transported during the King's pleasure. M.

Morgan, Dorcas. R for Barbados or Jamaica Mar 1685. L.

Morgan, Edward of Newport Pagnell. S & R 14 yrs Summer 1723. Bu.

Morgan, Edward. T Jan 1736 *Dorsetshire*. Sy.

Morgan, Eliner. T Jly 1723 *Alexander* LC Md Sep 1723. Bu.

Morgan, Eleanor. S Jan T Feb 1742 *Industry* to Md. M.

Morgan, Eleanor. S s cloth Lent 1754. He.

Morgan, Elianor. S s at Kington Summer 1764. He.

Morgan, Eleanor wife of John, als Eleanor Walker, spinster. S May T Aug 1769 *Douglas*. M.

Morgan als Jones, Elizabeth. PT to Barbados Jan 1694. M.

Morgan, Elizabeth. S Aug T Sep 1725 *Forward* LC Annapolis Dec 1725. M.

Morgan, Elizabeth (1748). *See* George. Mo.

Morgan, Elizabeth. S & T Sep 1767 *Justitia*. L.

Morgan, Elizabeth. SQS Dec 1768. M.

Morgan als Williams, George. R for America Aug 1715. M.

Morgan, George. S for burglary Lent R 14 yrs Summer 1763. Mo.

Morgan, Henry. S s horse & R 14 yrs Summer 1775. Mo.

Morgan, James of Brislington, husbandman. R for Barbados Feb 1673. So.

Morgan, James. S s at Tetbury Lent 1725. G.

Morgan, James. S Lent 1740. Mo.

Morgan, James. S & TB Aug 1740. G.

Morgan, James. R Aug 1770. So.

Morgan, James. S Feb T Apr 1772 *Thornton*. L.

Morgan, Jane. S Oct 1744-Jan 1745. M.

Morgan, Jane. S Jan-Jun 1747. M.

Morgan, Job. S Mar 1734. De.

Morgan, John. S Jan 1656 to House of Correction unless he agrees to be transported. M.

Morgan, John. R for Barbados or Jamaica Mar 1685. L.

Morgan, John of Bridfort, wigmaker. R for America Mar 1698. He.

Morgan, John. S Aug T 14 yrs Sep 1727 *Forward* LC Rappahannock May 1728. L.

Morgan, John. S Summer 1730. G.

Morgan, John. S Summer 1732. Nl.

Morgan, John. S s at St. Mary Magdalene, Bridgenorth, Summer 1736. Sh.

Morgan, John. S s horse Summer 1737 R 14 yrs Lent 1738. He.

Morgan, John. S for burglary Lent 1739 R 14 yrs Lent 1740 (SP). Wo.

Morgan, John. S s horse Summer 1739 R 14 yrs Lent 1740 (SP). Sh.

Morgan, John. S Oct-Dec 1739 T Jan 1740 *York* to Md. M.

Morgan, John. S Aug 1750. So.

Morgan, John. SQS Jan 1754. M.

Morgan, John. SL Oct 1754. Sy.

Morgan, John. S Sep T Nov 1759 *Phoenix*. M.

Morgan, John. S Aug 1763. L.

Morgan, John. S s cowtail hair at Whitchurch Lent 1764. Sh.

Morgan, John (1767). *See* Willington. Sh.

Morgan, John, als Crate, Jack. S s watch at Wormbridge Lent 1770. He.

Morgan, John, als Morris, Thomas. S Jan-Feb 1774. M.

Morgan, Joseph. S Jan-Jun T Jun 1728 *Elizabeth* LC Potomack Aug 1729. M.

Morgan, Martha. S s at Weobley Lent 1770. He.

Morgan, Mary. S s shirt Jan T Apr 1735 *Patapsco* LC Annapolis Oct 1735. M.

Morgan, Mary wife of George. S Jan T Apr 1743 *Justitia*. M.

Morgan, Mary. S Lent R 14 yrs Summer T Aug 1752 *Tryal*. Sy.

Morgan, Mary. S s at Christchurch Lent 1775. Mo.

Morgan, Mary wife of William. S s horse & R 14 yrs Summer 1775. G.

Morgan, Matthew. R Feb AT May 1686. M.

Morgan als Slade, Moses. S Mar TB to Va Apr 1773. Wi.

Morgan, Richard. R for Barbados Dec 1668. M.

Morgan, Richard. R for Barbados Dec 1670. M.

Morgan, Richard. TB 14 yrs Oct 1719. L.

Morgan, Richard. R 14 yrs Lent 1721. G.

Morgan, Richard. S for highway robbery Lent R 14 yrs Summer 1741 (SP). He.

Morgan, Richard. S Summer 1746 R 14 yrs Lent 1747. He.

Morgan, Richard. S Jan-Feb 1775. M.

Morgan, Robert. S Apr T Oct 1719 *Susannah & Sarah* LC Annapolis Apr 1720. L.

Morgan, Robert. S Aug T Oct 1726 *Forward* to Va. M.

Morgan, Sara. S & T Sep 1718 *Eagle* LC Charles Town Mar 1719. L.
Morgan, Sarah. S Sep T Dec 1734 *Caesar* but died on passage. M.
Morgan, Sarah. S Sep 1756. M.
Morgan, Sarah. SQS Feb T Apr 1772 *Thornton*. M.
Morgan, Sarah of Bristol. R 14 yrs Apr 1774 (SP). G.
Morgan als Evans, Susanna. S May T Jly 1722 *Alexander* to Nevis or Jamaica. M.
Morgan, Thomas of Longtown. R for America Sep 1671. Sh.
Morgan, Thomas of Hockluffe. R for America Mar 1680. Bd.
Morgan, Thomas. S s sheep Lent R 14 yrs Summer 1742. He.
Morgan, Thomas. S Summer 1745 R 11 yrs Lent 1746. Mo.
Morgan, Thomas. SQS & TB Jan 1747. So.
Morgan, Thomas. SQS Oct T Dec 1753 *Whiteing*. M.
Morgan, Thomas. S s at Newchurch Lent 1764. Mo.
Morgan, Thomas. S May T Jun 1768 *Tryal*. M.
Morgan, Thomas. R 14 yrs Jly 1774. M.
Morgan, Walter of Panteg. S s shears Summer 1719. Mo.
Morgan, William. R for Barbados or Jamaica Dec 1695 & Jan 1697. M.
Morgan, William. S Aug T Oct 1724 *Forward* LC Annapolis Jun 1725. M.
Morgan, William. S Jly 1728. Ha.
Morgan, William (1739). *See* Williams. G.
Morgan, William. S s at Hanley Castle Summer 1743. Wo.
Morgan als Jones, William. S s at Longhope Summer TB Oct 1745. G.
Morgan, William. S Summer T Sep 1751 *Greyhound*. Sy.
Morgan als Stevens, William. R 14 yrs Aug 1757. So.
Morgan, William. S Apr R May T Nov 1762 *Prince William*. M.
Morgan, William. S Jly 1763. M.
Morgan, William. S Jan T Feb 1765 *Tryal*. L.
Morgan, William. S (Western Circ) Dec 1766 AT Lent 1767. G.
Morgan, William (1769). *See* Pritchard. He.
Morgan, William. S s at Woolaston Lent 1770. G.
Morgan, William. S Lent 1775. Wa.
Moring, Elias. S & T Sep 1765 *Justitia*. L.
Morin, Rogers. S Dec 1762 T Mar 1763 *Neptune*. M.
Moring, Thomas. S Feb T Apr 1741 *Speedwell* or *Mediterranean*. M.
Morland, Edward (1730). *See* Morley. Du.
Morland, Eleanor. S Jly 1774. L.
Moreland, John. SW & T Oct 1768 *Justitia*. M.
Moreland, William. S s brass knocker Feb T Jun 1738 *Forward* to Md or Va. M.
Morley, Ann wife of Joseph, als Ann Wylett, spinster. S Jan T Apr 1766 *Ann*. M.
Morley, Edward (1679). *See* Smith. Nf.
Morley als Morland, Edward. R 14 yrs s mare Summer 1730. Du.
Morley, Frances of St. Sepulchre, spinster. S for attending attending unlawful religious assembly Jan 1665. M.
Morley, John of Barton Regis. R for America Feb 1684. G.
Morley, John. Rebel T 1685.
Morley, John. S Summer 1751 R 14 yrs Lent 1752. Nt.
Morley, John. S Oct 1751-Jan 1752. M.

Morley, Joseph. S & T Jan 1767 *Tryal*. L.

Morley, Mary (1749). *See* Brown. M.

Morley, Robert (1682). *See* Wilson. Nl.

Morley, Shadreck. Rebel T 1685.

Morley, Thomas. S Lent 1754. Su.

Morley, Thomas. S for highway robbery at South Kilvington & R 14 yrs Lent TB Aug 1771. Y.

Mauley, William of Colne. SQS Jan 1775.

Moronie, John (1775). *See* Roley. M.

Murphet, Edward. R 14 yrs Lent 1721. Wo.

Morphew, John. T May 1744 *Justitia*. E.

Morray. *See* Murray.

Morrell, Benjamin of Hallingbury. R for Barbados or Jamaica Jun 1692. E.

Morrell, Elizabeth. S Oct 1727-Jun 1728 T Jun 1728 *Elizabeth* LC Potomack Aug 1729. M.

Morrell, John. S Mar 1719 to be T to Va. De.

Murrall, John. S Lent R 14 yrs Summer 1751. St.

Morrell, Mary, als Cambridge Moll. R for Barbados or Jamaica Oct 1694. L.

Murrell, Muriel. T Dec 1731 *Forward*. Sy.

Murrell, Robert. S s meal at Kenninghall Lent 1772. Nf.

Murrell, Sarah. S & T 14 yrs Apr 1741 *Speedwell* or *Mediterranean*. M.

Murrell als Brooks als Sneechall, Sarah. S & T Apr 1765 *Ann*. L.

Murrell, Sarah, spinster. S & R s at St. Andrew, Norwich, Summer 1773. Nf.

Murrell, Susanna (1722). *See* Stewart. M.

Morrice. *See* Morris.

Morris, Abraham of Warrington. SQS May 1753. La.

Morris, Ang. PT Oct 1700. M.

Morrice, Ann (1741). *See* Williams. L.

Morris, Ann wife of William. S 14 yrs for receiving Mar 1772. Do.

Morris, Augustin. R for Barbados or Jamaica Aug 1700. M.

Morris, Bartholomew. S & T Apr 1725 *Sukey* LC Annapolis Sep 1725. M.

Morris, Benjamin. S & T Apr 1765 *Ann*. L.

Morris, Catherine wife of Richard. S Oct T Dec 1767 *Neptune*. L.

Morris, David. S s at Berkeley Lent 1723. G.

Morris, David. R for life Lent 1774. Sy.

Morris, David (1774). *See* Hughes. He.

Morris, Edward. S Nov T Dec 1763 *Neptune*. L.

Morris, Eleanor. S Sep-Oct 1749. M.

Morris, Elizabeth. R for Barbados or Jamaica Mar 1688. M.

Morris, Elizabeth. S Aug T Oct 1724 *Forward*. L.

Morris, Elizabeth wife of John of Eagle Court, Strand. S Sep 1735 T Jan 1736 *Dorsetshire* LC Va Sep 1736. M.

Morris, Elizabeth. S s at St. Andrew, Worcester, Lent 1738. Wo.

Morris, Elizabeth. AT Summer 1742. Wo.

Morris, Elizabeth. S & T Dec 1759 *Phoenix*. L.

Morris, Elizabeth. S s at St. Chad, Shrewsbury, Lent 1768. Sh.

Morris, Evan. S s heifer Lent R 14 yrs Summer 1765. Sh.

Morris, Frances, widow, als wife of John of St. Saviour, Southwark. R for Barbados or Jamaica Jly 1702. Sy.

Morris als Flyfield als Whittimore als Wittingham, George. S s mare at Dudley Summer 1763 R 14 yrs Lent 1764. Wo.

Morris, George. S s at St. Mary Magdalene, Bridgenorth, Lent 1769. Sh.

Morris, Hanna. S Summer 1724 R 14 yrs Lent 1725. St.

Morris, Hannah of St. Saviour, Southwark, spinster. SQS Apr 1751. Sy.

Morris, Hannah. S Jly T Sep 1755 *Tryal*. L.

Morris, Henry. PT Summer 1717. G.

Morris, James. S s at Neen Savage Lent 1758. Sh.

Morris, James. T Jun 1764 *Dolphin*. K.

Morris, James of Camberwell. SQS Feb 1773. Sy.

Morris, Jane. S Dec 1745. L.

Morris, John of Southchurch. R for Barbados Aug 1668 (Newgate). E.

Morris, John. S Apr T May 1718 *Tryal* LC Charles Town Aug 1718. L.

Morris, John. S s at Shirenewton Lent 1725. Mo.

Morrice, John. S Mar TB Apr 1729. Wi.

Morris, John. S s at St. Helen, Worcester, Lent 1736. Wo.

Morris, John. S s at Drayton Lent 1736. Sh.

Morris, John. S Feb T Sep 1737 *Pretty Patsy* to Md. M.

Morris, John. S Jan T Jun 1738 *Forward* to Md or Va. M.

Morris, John. R for life Jly TB to Va Oct 1742. Wi.

Morris, John. S Jun-Dec 1745. M.

Morris, John. S Sep-Oct 1748 T Jan 1749 *Laura*. M.

Morris, John. S Jun 1754. L.

Morris, John. R 14 yrs s sheep Lent 1761. Li.

Morris, John. S s at Over Swell Lent 1764. G.

Morris, John. S 14 yrs s cloth from rack at Oswestry Summer 1764. Sh.

Morris, John. S Jly T Sep 1764 *Justitia*. M.

Morris, John. S & T Jan 1765 *Tryal*. M.

Morris, John of Clifton cum Glapton, butcher. SQS s fowls Jly 1766. Nt.

Morris als Hambleton, John. S May T Aug 1769 *Douglas*. M.

Morris, John. S s silk handkerchiefs at Rotherham Lent 1770. Y.

Morris, John. S & T Jly 1770 *Scarsdale*. M.

Morris, John. S s fowls at Stanton Lacy Lent 1774. Sh.

Morris, John. S for killing sheep at Penn & R 14 yrs Lent 1775. Bu.

Morris, Joseph. S Mar 1768. Ha.

Morris, Margaret. S Jan-Apr 1749. M.

Morris, Margaret, als wife of Henry Powell. S 14 yrs for receiving snuff stolen by Thomas Morris *(qv)* Lent 1751. He.

Morris, Mary. R for Barbados Jly 1675. L.

Morris, Mary (1719). *See* Reed. L.

Morris, Mary. S Apr-Jun 1739. M.

Morris, Mary. S Apr 1759. Fl.

Morris, Mary. R Feb T for life Apr 1762 *Dolphin*. M.

Morris, Morgan. S Sep 1770. M.

Morris, Philip of Wolverhampton. R for America Mar 1682. St.

Morrice, Richard. S Lent R 14 yrs Summer 1754. Ht.

Morris, Richard. S Oct T Nov 1759 *Phoenix*. L.

Morris, Richard. S s ewe & R Lent 1775. Le.

Morris, Robert of Chelmsford. SQS Jan T Jun 1756 *Lyon*. E.

Morris, Ruth. S Sep-Oct T Dec 1752 *Greyhound*. M.
Morris, Sarah. S Apr T Sep 1757 *Thetis*. M.
Morris, Silvan. PT Jan R Mar 1685. M.
Morris, Thomas. R for Barbados Dec 1670. M.
Morris, Thomas of Ausley. R for America Jly 1673. Wa.
Morris, Thomas of Spalding. R for America Jly 1679. Li.
Morris, Thomas of Cowlesfield, Whiteparish. R for Barbados Feb
    1710. Wi.
Morris, Thomas. S Aug 1723. So.
Morris, Thomas. S 14 yrs Aug 1727 T *Forward* LC Rappahannock May
    1728. M.
Morris, Thomas. S & T Dec 1736 *Dorsetshire*. L.
Morris, Thomas. R & T 14 yrs Sep 1737 *Pretty Patsy* to Md. M.
Morris, Thomas. S Apr 1747. So.
Morris, Thomas. S s snuff at All Saints, Hereford, Lent 1751. He.
Morris, Thomas. T May 1752 *Lichfield*. E.
Morris, Thomas. T Sep 1765 *Justitia*. M.
Morris, Thomas. S & T Jly 1771 *Scarsdale*. M.
Morris, Thomas (1774). *See* Morgan, John. M.
Morris, Thomas. S Lent 1774. Sy.
Morris, William of Creek, Caerwent. R for Barbados Jun 1668. Mo.
Morris, William. R (Norfolk Circ) for Barbados Jly 1675. X.
Morris, William. S & T Oct 1730 *Forward* LC Potomack Jan 1731. L.
Morris, William. T Oct 1738 *Genoa*. Sy.
Morris, William. S s sheep Lent R 14 yrs Summer 1743. Mo.
Morris, William. S s pig at Withington Lent 1769. G.
Morris, William. S s at Holmer Lent 1771. He.
Morrish, Sarah. S Mar 1763 TB to Va. De.
Morrish, Thomas of Tavistock. R for Barbados Jly 1672. De.
Morrish, William. S Mar 1772. De.
Morrison, Effa. S Jly T Sep 1765 *Justitia*. M.
Morrison, John. S Lent 1748. Y.
Morrison, Lucy. SQS Jan T May 1755 *Rose*. M.
Morrison, Samuel. S Jun T Nov 1743 *George William*. M.
Morrit, Mary wife of Edward, als Mary Kipping. S 14 yrs May-Jly
    1746. M.
Morrow, John. S Lent R 14 yrs Summer 1743. St.
Morry. *See* Morey.
Morse, Charles. S Summer T Sep 1751 *Greyhound*. Sy.
Morse, Dinah. S Lent 1761. Sy.
Morse, John. Rebel T 1685.
Morse, John. T Oct 1720 *Gilbert*. E.
Morse, Paul. Rebel T 1685.
Morse, Richard. T Dec 1736 *Dorsetshire*. K.
Morse, William of Upton St. Leonard. R for America Feb 1716. G.
Morse, William. S Mar 1729. So.
Morse, William. S Jan-Apr 1748. M.
Mortall als Bowyer als Marrat, Charles. R May AT Aug 1676. M.
Mortar, Richard of Inworth. R for Barbados or Jamaica Jun 1699. E.
Mortebois, Robert (1752). *See* Jones. E.

Mortimer, Edward. SQS Bradford Jan 1725 T *Supply* LC Md May 1726. Y.

Mortimor als Chandler, Luke. S s money with menaces Summer 1740 R 14 yrs Lent T Jly 1741. Bd.

Mortimer, Roger. Rebel T 1685.

Morton. *See* Moreton.

Moseley, Charles. S Sep-Oct 1749. M.

Moseley, Hannah. S & T Apr 1762 *Neptune*. L.

Moseley, John of Coventry. R for America Jly 1716. Wa.

Moseley, Joseph. S Lent 1749. Sx.

Mosely, Joseph (1752). *See* Morestly. M.

Moseley, Paul. SWK Jan T Apr 1768 *Thornton*. K.

Moseley, Richard. T Apr 1742 *Bond*. Sy.

Moseley, Thomas. LC from *Patapsco* Annapolis Sep 1730. X.

Moses, Benjamin. S Jan T Feb 1726 *Supply* LC Annapolis May 1726. M.

Moses, Jacob. S Jan T Apr 1762 *Dolphin*. L.

Moses, Jacob. S Aug 1763. L.

Moses, Jacob. S & T Apr 1769 *Tryal*. L.

Moses, Joseph. S Jly 1761. L.

Moses, Samuel. S & T Jan 1767 *Tryal*. L.

Moses, Solomon. S Dec 1773. L.

Moses als Fotherby, Susan. S Feb T Mar 1727 *Rappahannock*. L.

Moses, Susan. S Oct 1733 T Jan 1734 *Caesar* LC Va Jly 1734. M.

Moses, Thomas. T Apr 1725 *Sukey* but died on passage. E.

Moses, William. S May T Jun 1738 *Forward*. L.

Moses, William. S Mar 1775. Ha.

Mosesly, George. R 14 yrs Mar 1751. Ha.

Moss, Ann of Royton, spinster. SQS Apr 1752. La.

Moss, Charles. S s breeches at Cirencester Summer 1771. G.

Moss, Christopher. S Dec 1727. L.

Moss, Francis. SQS Apr T May 1767 *Thornton*. M.

Moss, Jarvis of Milton in Prittlewell. SQS Jan 1767 T Apr 1768 *Thornton*. E.

Moss, John. S s gelding Lent R 14 yrs Summer 1742. O.

Moss, John. S Apr 1759. So.

Moss, Peter. S Jan-Apr 1748. M.

Moss, Philip. S s at Weston Market Lent 1773. Su.

Mosse, Richard. S Mar 1746. So.

Moss, Robert. T Sep 1742 *Forward*. E.

Moss, Sarah wife of William. S May T Jly 1770 *Scarsdale*. L.

Moss, Thomas (1729). *See* Matthews. Sh.

Moss, Thomas. T Dec 1734 *Caesar*. K.

Moss, Thomas. T Dec 1771 *Justitia*. Sy.

Moss, William. S 14 yrs Lent 1730. Y.

Moss, William. S Feb T Apr 1732 *Patapsco* LC Annapolis Oct 1732. L.

Mosten, John. S Apr T May 1750 *Lichfield*. M.

Motherby, Charles. S May T Jly 1723 *Alexander* LC Annapolis Sep 1723. M.

Motley, Mary. PT Jan 1675. M.

Motley, Robert. R for Jamaica Mar 1665. L.

Motley, Robert. R for Barbados Jly 1674. M.

Motley, William. R for Barbados Jly 1675. L.
Motley, William. R Mar AT Apr 1677. M.
Motley, William. PT Feb 1682. M.
Motloe, William. S Summer TB Sep 1732. G.
Mott, John. S Jly 1773. Ha.
Mott, Joseph. S Lent 1775. E.
Mott, Richard. SQS Jly 1763. Ha.
Mott, Richard. R 14 yrs Mar 1773. Ha.
Mott, William of Lambourne. R for Barbados or Jamaica Feb 1676. E.
Moucheau, Michael. S for wounding Customs officers Summer
    1742. Nl.
Mould, Daniel. R 14 yrs Aug 1748. De.
Mould, Jeremiah. T Sep 1766 *Justitia*. Ht.
Mould, Martin. SQS Sep 1754. M.
Mould, William. S Aug T Oct 1724 *Forward* LC Annapolis Jun 1725. M.
Moulden, Daniel. S & T Lent 1729. Y.
Moulden, Thomas. S & T Jan 1722 *Giibert* to Md. M.
Moulder, John. S Jan T Feb 1733 *Smith* to Md or Va. M.
Molder, Mary. S Lent 1741. O.
Moulding, James. S Jan T Sep 1737 *Pretty Patsy* to Md. M.
Molding, William. S Lent 1749. Bd.
Moulding, William of St. George, Southwark. SQS Jan 1752. Sy.
Moule, Edward. S Lent R 14 yrs Summer 1747. E.
Moule, John. S s sheep Summer 1740. Wo.
Moule, Thomas of Coton. R for America Mar 1686. Ca.
Molson, Joseph. S Jun T Jly 1772 *Tayloe*. L.
Moulson, Robert. S Aug T Sep 1725 *Forward* LC Annapolis Dec 1725. L.
Moulson, William. T Sep 1730 *Smith*. E.
Molton, Humphrey. Rebel T 1685.
Moulton, Samuel. S Jan T 14 yrs Feb 1723 *Jonathan* to Md. M.
Moulton, William (1686). *See* Lawrence. St.
Molton, William. R May AT Jly 1697. M.
Moulton, William. S Lent 1765. Su.
Mounslow als Barnett, John of Fulham. S Oct 1740 T Jan 1741
    Harpooner to Rappahannock. M.
Mount, John. S s gelding Summer 1757 R 14 yrs Lent 1758. Nf.
Mount, John. R Lent 1775. K.
Mount, Jonas. R Lent 1774. K.
Mount, Thomas. S & T Jan 1736 *Dorsetshire* but died on passage. L.
Mountague. *See* Montague.
Mountaine, Mary. S & T Jan 1722 *Gilbert* LC Annapolis Jly 1722. M.
Mountfield, Robert (1738). *See* Mimford. M.
Mountsley, Mary (1686). *See* Pinck. Sy.
Mountstephen, Lawrence of Payhembury. R for Barbados Jun 1669. De.
Mountstephen, Samuel. Rebel T 1685.
Mountstephen, William of Payhembury, husbandman. R for Barbados
    Sep 1665. De.
Mounty als Mountague, William. S Mar 1774. Wi.
Mouse, Humphrey (1758). *See* Moushell. Co.
Moushell als Mouse, Humphrey. S Mar 1758. Co.
Mouth, John (1732). *See* Gillett. L.

Mow, Rachel. S Dec 1727. L.

Mowburn, George of Skelton. S s at Hilton Lent TB Aug 1770. Y.

Moy, Richard. S Nov T Dec 1770 *Justitia*. L.

Moyes als Pearson, John. S Lent R 14 yrs Summer 1755. Su.

Moyle, Richard Sr. S Apr 1775. Co.

Moyser, William. S Lent TB Apr 1741. Y.

Muckaway, Thomas. S Feb T Apr 1771 *Thornton*. L.

Mucklehone, James. T Dee 1753 *Whiteing*. E.

Muckleroy, Bartholomew. S Feb T Apr 1765 *Ann*. M.

Muckleston, Elizabeth, als Irish Nell. S Sep 1743. L.

Muckley, Humphrey. R for America Jly 1687. Wa.

Mudd, Bartholomew of Laindon. R for Barbados or Jamaica Mar 1707. E.

Mudeford, Daniel. S s at Old Windsor Lent 1723. Be.

Mudford als Munford, Robert. Rebel T 1685.

Mudgett, Elizabeth wife of Thomas of Ealing. S s rags Apr 1740. M.

Mugford, Francis. S Mar 1755. De.

Muggeride. *See* Moggridge.

Mulbens, Joseph. T from Bristol by *Maryland Packet* 1761 but intercepted by French; T Apr 1763 *Neptune*. Wi.

Mulbury, James. S Sep T Nov 1743 *George William*. L.

Mulford, David. R Lent 1775. Sy.

Mull, James. SL & T Jan 1767 *Tryal*. Sy.

Mullens. *See* Mullins.

Mullett, William. R 14 yrs Mar 1736. Do.

Mullett, William. S Mar 1720. Do.

Mullener, John. S Jan T Apr 1743 *Justitia*. M.

Mulliner, Thomas. S s gelding at Stratton & R 14 yrs Summer 1773. Nf.

Mulling, Patrick. S Oct-Dec 1750. M.

Mullings, Ann. S Jly 1748. L.

Mullens, Daniel. SL & T Jly 1771 *Scarsdale*. Sy.

Mullins, George. Rebel T 1685.

Mullens, Henry. S & TB to Va Mar 1761 but then picked for Army service. Wi.

Mullins, James. S Dec 1749-Jan 1750 T Mar 1750 *Tryal*. M.

Mullins, James. S Jly T Sep 1755 *Tryal*. L.

Mullens, John. T May 1736 *Patapsco*. E.

Mullens, John. S & TB to Va Mar 1761. Wi.

Mullins, John. SQS Apr T Jun 1764 *Dolphin*. M.

Mullins, Joseph. Rebel T 1685.

Mullins, Margaret. S & T Apr 1741 *Speedwell* or *Mediterranean*. M.

Mullens, Mary of Croydon, spinster. SQS Apr 1763. Sy.

Mullins, Matthew. S Lent T Jun 1756 *Lyon*. K.

Mullins, Richard. T for life Oct 1768 *Justitia*. Sy.

Mullens, Robert. Rebel T 1685.

Mullens, Thomas. S Sep-Dec 1755 T Jan 1756 *Greyhound*. M.

Mullis, John. S Jly 1766. De.

Mully, John. T Oct 1722 *Forward*. E.

Mulzar, John of Feering. R for Barbados or Jamaica Jly 1691 & Jun 1692. Sx.

Mumford, Charles. S Lent 1759. Wa.

Mumford als Waters, Margaret. S Feb T Mar 1729 *Patapsco* LC Annapolis Dec 1729. M.

Mumford als Mountfield, Robert. S Jun-Dec 1738 T Jan 1739 *Dorsetshire*. M.

Momford, Thomas. TB Sep 1745. Db.

Mumford, William of Manchester. SQS Jly 1752. La.

Mumpman, Ann. S Sep-Oct 1748. M.

Munckton. *See* Monkton.

Munday, David. S Mar 1727. Wi.

Munday, Edward of Westbury. SQS Marlborough Oct 1755 TB May 1756. Wi.

Munday, Frances. S May-Jly 1748. M.

Munday, James. S Dec 1749-Jan 1750 T Mar 1750 *Tryal*. M.

Munday, Richard of West Wycombe. R for Barbados or Jamaica Mar 1697. Bu.

Munday, Richard. S Feb-Apr T Jun 1756 *Lyon*. M.

Munday, Richard. S Feb T Mar 1764 *Tryal*. M.

Monday, Richard als Edward. S Mar 1772. Ha.

Munday, Thomas (1734). *See* Williams. Do.

Mundy, Thomas. S Lent 1751. Su.

Monday, William. S s sheep & R 14 yrs Lent 1745. Hu.

Munden, James. S & T Sep 1765 *Justitia*. M.

Mundle, John. T Apr 1766 *Ann*. M.

Munfie, John of Marshwood. R for Barbados Feb 1683. Do.

Munford, Robert (1685). *See* Mudford.

Mungay, Thomas. S Summer T Sep 1772. No.

Munger, Thomas. S s sheep Summer 1766 R 14 yrs Lent 1767. Wa.

Munk. *See* Monk.

Munn, Joseph of Hatfield. R for Barbados or Jamaica Jly 1696. Ht.

Munn, William. S May T Jun 1726 *Loyal Margaret* but died on passage. M.

Mun, William. S s at Aston Lent 1764. Sh.

Munnery, John of Washington. R for Barbados or Jamaica Jly 1715. Sx.

Munns, James. S s at Westwick Lent 1773. Nf.

Munns, Joshua. S Jly T Sep 1766 *Justitia*. L.

Munns, Thomas of Bluntisham. S Lent 1731. *Hu.

Munro. *See* Monro.

Munson, Richard. LC from *Patapsco* Annapolis Nov 1733. X.

Munt, Elizabeth. S Summer 1748 T Jan 1749 *Laura*. E.

Munt, Jane. R for life Feb 1775. M.

Muntford, Ann. S Oct 1733 T Jan 1734 *Caesar* LC Va Jly 1734. M.

Murdock, Alexander. S Sep-Dec 1755 T Jan 1756 *Greyhound*. M.

Murdock, John. S & T Apr 1765 *Ann*. L.

Murgatroyd, Elizabeth. T Oct 1724 *Forward* LC Md Jun 1725. Sy.

Murgatroyd, Joseph. S Apr T Sep 1757 *Thetis*. L.

Margetroide, Michael. R 14 yrs Aug 1729. De.

Murgett, Edward of Baconsthorpe. R for America Feb 1681. Nf.

Murland, John. S Summer 1754. Nf.

Murphet. *See* Morphet.

Murphil, John Lawrence. S Dec 1757 T Mar 1758 *Dragon*. M.

Murphy, Ann. S Apr 1746. L.

Murphey, Bridget. S Aug 1730. So.
Murphy, Edward. S May T Jun 1764 *Dolphin*. M.
Murphy, Edward. SQS Apr T Jly 1772 *Tayloe*. M.
Murphy, Eleanor. S Jly 1773. L.
Murphy, Elizabeth (1725). *See* Marlow. M.
Murphy, Garrett of Rotherhithe. SQS Feb T Apr 1759 *Thetis*. Sy.
Murphy, James. S Sep-Oct T Dec 1753 *Whiteing*. M.
Murphy, James. S Jan T Mar 1764 *Tryal*. M.
Murphy, James. ST & T Apr 1766 *Ann*. L.
Murphy, Jeremiah. S Feb-Apr T May 1751 *Tryal*. M.
Murphy, John. S & T 14 yrs Oct 1722 *Forward* LC Annapolis Jun
    1723. M.
Murphy, John of St. George, Bloomsbury. S s silver spoon Sep 1740 T
    Jan 1741 *Harpooner* to Rappahannock. M.
Murphy, John. R 14 yrs Jly 1750. Ha.
Murphy, John. S Feb T Apr 1770 *New Trial*. M.
Murphy, John. S Apr-May T Jly 1771 *Scarsdale*. M.
Murphy, John. S & T Dec 1771 *Justitia*. M.
Murphy, Lawrence. S Feb T 14 yrs Apr 1765 *Ann*. M.
Murphy, Margaret. S Feb T Mar 1760 *Friendship*. M.
Murphy, Mary. S Dec 1749-Jan 1750 T Mar 1750 *Tryal*. M.
Murphy als Edwards, Mary. S Sep-Oct T 14 yrs Dec 1753 *Whiteing*. M.
Murphy, Patrick. S May T Sep 1766 *Justitia*. M.
Murphy, Patrick. SW & T Jly 1771 *Scarsdale*. M.
Murphy, Sarah. S & T May 1736 *Patapsco*. L.
Murphy, Thomas. S Sep 1754. L.
Murphy, Thomas. T Dec 1770 *Justitia*. Sy.
Murfey, Timothy. T May 1755 *Rose*. E.
Murphy, William. S Lent R 14 yrs Summer 1754. K.
Murfey, William. T Sep 1764 *Justitia*. Ht.
Morray, Adam. R 14 yrs Summer 1774. Nl.
Murray, Brien. SQS Oct T Dec 1770 *Justitia*. M.
Murray, Elizabeth. S Dec 1747. L.
Murrey, Francis of Marsh Gibbon. R for America Jly 1693. Bu.
Murry, Henry. S & T Jan 1722 *Gilbert*. L.
Murray, Jane (1765). *See* Monkhouse. M.
Murray, John. R Dec 1698 AT Jan 1699. M.
Murray, John. S Sep T Dec 1770 *Justitia*. M.
Murray, Judith. S Jun-Dec 1738 T 14 yrs Jan 1739 *Dorsetshire* to Va. M.
Murry, Mary (1733). *See* Thomas. M.
Murray, Matthew. S Jan-Feb T Apr 1771 *Thornton*. M.
Murray, Richard. S Nov T Dec 1752 *Greyhound*. L.
Murray, Robert. S 14 yrs Apr 1763. M.
Morray, Roger. S & T Oct 1729 *Forward* LC Va Jun 1730. M.
Murry, Sarah (1697). *See* Mahoone. L.
Murrell. *See* Morrell.
Murrick, Elizabeth. SQS Oct 1751. M.
Murrow, Mary. S Summer 1745 AT Summer 1746. Nl.
Murthwaite, Ann. S s at Westward Summer 1769. Cu.
Murtogh, Bryan. S Apr-Jun 1739. M.
Murton. *See* Merton.

Musgrave, Andrew. S Apr-May T Jly 1771 *Scarsdale*. M.
Musgrave, John. S s mare Lent R 14 yrs Summer 1742. G.
Musgrave, Maria. S Lent 1769. Be.
Musgrave, Nathaniel. Rebel T 1685.
Musgrove, Edward of Winterbourne. S s gold coin Lent TB Mar 1754. G.
Musgrove, John of Newington. R (Newgate) for Barbados Apr TB Oct 1669. Sy.
Musgrove, John. S & TB Aug 1742. G.
Musgrove, Thomas. S s horse & R 14 yrs Summer 1769. Be.
Musket, James. S Apr T May 1743 *Indian Queen*. L.
Muskett, William. S for attempted smuggling Lent 1738. Nf.
Muskman, John. S Lent AT Summer 1139. Y.
Mussedy, Thomas of Wambury. R (Western Circ) for America Jly 1710. G.
Mussen, James. S May T Sep 1766 *Justitia*. M.
Musters als Pawles, Munday. S Jan T Mar 1764 *Tryal*. M.
Musto, Thomas. S Lent TB Apr 1742. G.
Muston, Richard Joseph. S Jan-Feb T Apr 1771 *Thornton*. M.
Mutchmore, Walter of Linkenhorne, tinner. R for Barbados Jly 1664. Co.
Mutes, Mary. S Feb T Mar 1727 *Rappahannock* to Md. M.
Mutlow, Sarah. T Jun 1764 *Dolphin*. M.
Muttit, Elizabeth (1668). *See* Shales. Su.
Muttlebury, John. Rebel T 1685.
Mutton, Mary. S Dec 1766 T Jan 1767 *Tryal*. M.
Muzzle, Joseph. S Summer 1747 R 14 yrs Lent 1748. Sy.
Myalls. *See* Miles.
Myer als Meale, Abraham. S Apr T Jly 1770 *Scarsdale*. L.
Maer, Alexander. S May T Jun 1764 *Dolphin*. L.
Meyer, Christopher. S & T Dec 1759 *Phoenix*. M.
Meyer, Henry. Rebel T 1685.
Meier, John. R 14 yrs Mar 1764. De.
Mayer, John (1767). *See* Brown. Bd.
Myer, Samuel. S Sep T 14 yrs Oct 1722 *Forward*. L.
Mayer, William. TB to Va from QS 1772. De.
Myers, Ann. S & T Dec 1767 *Neptune*. L.
Mires, Catherine. S Summer 1754. Cu.
Myers, Daniel. AT Summer 1720. Y.
Myers, Edward. T Aug 1720 *Owners Goodwill*. K.
Miers, Emanuel. S & R 14 yrs Summer 1774. Wo.
Myres, Hannah. S Summer 1775. Y.
Myers, John. S Dec 1755 T Jan 1756 *Greyhound*. L.
Myers, Joseph. S Lent 1771. La.
Myers, Mary. S May 1719. M.
Myers, Mary. S May-Jly 1748. M.
Mires, Mary. S Summer 1754. Cu.
Miers, Sarah. S & T Apr 1725 *Sukey* LC Annapolis Sep 1725. M.
Mires, Thomas. S s sheep at Quarrendon & R Lent T Apr 1772 *Thornton*. Bu.
Myers, William. S Feb-Apr T May 1755 *Rose*. M.
Myers, William. S & T Jan 1756 *Greyhound*. L.
Myford, Elizabeth. S Jly 1763. M.

N

Nabb als Nabbs, Elizabeth. S Lent 1770. La.

Nabbs, Thomas. S s at Wolverhampton Lent 1772. St.

Nabrick, Andrew. Rebel T 1685.

Naden, Richard of Donhead. R (Midland Circ) for America Jly 1678. St.

Naden, Robert of Alstonfield, yeoman. R for America Feb 1713. St.

Naden, Thomas of Wallspring. R (Midland Circ) for America Jly 1678. St.

Naden, Thomas of Aldridge. R for America Feb 1684. St.

Naden, Thomas of Blakeley, weaver. S Lent R 14 yrs Summer 1764. La.

Naggington, Robert. S s corn at Childs Ercall Lent 1775. Sh.

Naggs, Sarah. T May 1719 *Margaret* LC Md May 1720; sold to Peter Galloway. Sy.

Naisby, Frances of Whitby, spinster. SQS Guisborough s at Coatham & Marske Jly 1734. Y.

Naish, John. S Mar TB to Va Apr 1741. Wi.

Naish, Susan of Maidstone. S Lent 1745. K.

Naish, William. R 14 yrs Mar 1731. Wi.

Naley, Patrick. S Lent 1760. K.

Nalfing, Philip. S Aug 1727 T *Forward* LC Rappahannock May 1728. M.

Nancy, Elizabeth. S Mar 1756. Co.

Nanny, Martin. S & T Sep 1731 *Smith* LC Va 1732. M.

Nantford, Francis. R for Barbados Feb 1672. M.

Napett, Samuel. S Lent 1768. Su.

Napkin, Hannah. T Mar 1752 *Lichfield*. Ht.

Napper, John. S Jly 1764. Ha.

Napton, Francis (1749). *See* Dumerick, George. M.

Narder, James. S & T Jly 1753 *Tryal*. M.

Narroway, William. S Apr T Sep 1757 *Thetis*. L.

Nary, Andrew. S Feb 1774. L.

Nasey, Richard. S Lent R for Barbados May 1664. E.

Nash als Nass, Abraham. S 14 yrs Apr-Jun 1739. M.

Nash, Ann wife of John. S Feb T Mar 1763 *Neptune*. M.

Nash, Diana. SQS Oct 1768 T Jan 1769 *Thornton*. M.

Nash, Elizabeth. S Feb T Apr 1734 *Patapsco*. L.

Nash, John. S & T Jan 1722 *Gilbert* LC Annapolis Jly 1722. M.

Nash, John. S s sheep Summer 1752 R 14 yrs Lent TB Apr 1753. Db.

Nash, John (1773). *See* Burvill, Richard. K.

Nash als Goulding, Mary. S 14 yrs & T Apr 1741 *Speedwell* or *Mediterranean* to Md. M.

Nash, Mary wife of John. S Aug TB to Va Sep 1767. Wi.

Nash, Mary. S Summer T Aug 1771. Wa.

Nash, Matthew. S Sep-Dec 1755 T Jan 1756 *Greyhound*. M.

Nash als Lissant, Richard. Rebel T 1685.

Knash, Richard. S Jly T Oct 1741 *Sea Horse*. L.

Nash, Sarah. SQS & T Sep 1764 *Justitia*. M.

Nash, Susannah. S Dec 1768 T Jan 1769 *Thornton*. M.

Nash, Thomas. R for Jamaica Aug 1661. M.

Nash, Thomas. S s at Colne St. Dennis Lent TB Aug 1727. G.
Nash, Thomas. S Summer 1758 R 14 yrs Lent 1759. Bd.
Nash, William. S Jun-Dec 1738 T Jan 1739 *Dorsetshire* to Va. M.
Nash, William. S Lent 1773. K.
Nashion, Thomas. Rebel T 1685.
Nason, John of St. George, Southwark. S Summer 1746. Sy.
Nass, Abraham (1739). *See* Nash. M.
Naston, John, als Taylor, Colonel. SQS Jan 1754. M.
Nathan, Bernard. S Jan T Apr 1762 *Dolphin*. L.
Natt, John (1718). *See* Platt. M.
Natt, John. S Apr-May T Jly 1771 *Scarsdale*. M.
Navell, James. Rebel T 1685.
Nawnton, James (1715). *See* Compton. M.
Naylor, Ann, als Mary wife of John Vesper. S & T Oct 1730 *Forward* LC
  Potomack Jan 1731. M.
Nealer, Elizabeth. R for America Jly 1707. Wa.
Nailor, Elizabeth. S Sep T Oct 1744 *Susannah*. L.
Naylor, Esther (1738). *See* Stephens. M.
Naylor, George of Barking. R for Barbados or Jamaica Jun 1699. E.
Naylor, James. S s cloth at Wigan & R 14 yrs Lent 1770. La.
Naylor, John. S Lent 1748. E.
Nailor, Mary (1752). *See* Strange. Sy.
Naylor, Nathaniel. S s at Halifax Summer 1767. Y.
Naylor, Robert. R for America Feb 1700. Db.
Naylor, Susannah. S Dec 1772. M.
Nailer, William. S for highway robbery Summer 1768. Wa.
Neale, Ann of St. Giles in Fields, spinster. S s sheets Sep 1740 T Jan
  1741 *Harpooner* to Rappahannock. M.
Neale, Anna Maria of Whitechapel. S Jly-Sep T Sep 1742 *Forward*. M.
Neal, Christopher. S s gelding & R Lent 1766. Nf.
Neale, Connell. S Jan T Apr 1759 *Thetis*. M.
Neil als O'Neil, Cornelius. S Sep-Oct T Dec 1771 *Justitia*. M.
Neal, Daniel. S May-Jly 1774. M.
Neal, Edward. S Summer 1753 R 14 yrs Lent 1754. Nf.
Neale, Elizabeth. R for Barbados Mar 1683. M.
Neale, Hannah. R for Barbados Sep 1669. M.
Neale, John. R for Barbados Apr 1669. M.
Neale, John. S Summer 1743. Nf.
Neale, John. S Lent 1757. K.
Neale, John. S s sheep Lent R 14 yrs Summer 1766. No.
Neal, John. S Feb T Apr 1768 *Thornton*. M.
Neale, John. SQS Oct T Dec 1770 *Justitia*. M.
Neale, Joseph. S Lent R 14 yrs Summer 1766. Hu.
Neal, Laurence. S & T Oct 1729 *Forward* LC Va Jun 1730. L.
Neal, Mary. S s shirts Apr T Dec 1735 *John* LC Annapolis Sep 1736. M.
Neal, Paul. S 14 yrs for receiving horseshoes T Dec 1758 *The
  Brothers*. M.
Neale, Rebecca (1721). *See* Butlas. L.
Neale, Richard. S Jly-Sep T Oct 1739 *Duke of Cumberland* to Va. M.
Neale, Richard. S Oct T Dec 1769 *Justitia*. M.
Neale, Samuel. S & R 14 yrs s sheep Lent 1769. G.

Neale, Sarah. S Lent T Jly 1748. Bd.

Neale, Sarah. S Lent 1757. Hu.

Neale, Susannah. S & T Jly 1753 *Tryal*. L.

Neal, Thomas. S Jun 1733. M.

Neal, Thomas. T Jan 1741 *Vernon*. E.

Neal, Thomas. S Aug T Oct 1741 *Sea Horse* to Va. M.

Neal, Thomas. R Lent 1749. Ht.

Neale, Thomas. S & TB Aug 1754. G.

Neale, William. PT Aug 1676 R Mar 1677. M.

Neale, William. S Sep T Oct 1739 *Duke of Cumberland*. L.

Neale, William. S Feb-Apr T May 1752 *Lichfield*. M.

Neale, William. S Oct T Nov 1759 *Phoenix*. L.

Neale, William. SQS New Sarum Jan TB to Va Mar 1760. Wi.

Nealer. *See* Naylor.

Neaton, Edward. S Lent 1775. K.

Neave. *See* Neve.

Nebard, Samuel. S Lent 1765. Su.

Neckless, George. S s at Shaw Summer 1750. Be.

Need, William. S Jun 1754. L.

Needham, James. S Oct 1749. L.

Needham, John. S Jly 1750. L.

Needum, Mary. R for Barbados Aug 1679. L.

Needham, Thomas. S Jly T 14 yrs Aug 1718 *Eagle* LC Charles Town
    Mar 1719. L.

Needham, Thomas. S Dec 1748 T Jan 1749 *Laura*. M.

Needham, William. S Lent TB Mar 1760. Db.

Needham, William. S Feb 1775. L.

Needs, John. Rebel T 1685.

Needum. *See* Needham. L.

Negle, Thomas. S Lent R 14 yrs Summer TB Aug 1747. G.

Neighbours, Joseph of Bristol. R 14 yrs Nov 1765 (SP). G.

Neilson, Neils. S Sep 1760. M.

Nell, Ann. S Lent 1739 R 14 yrs Lent 1740. Y.

Nelms, Mary. S s at Dursley Lent AT Summer 1772. G.

Nelson, Ann. S Feb T Apr 1742 *Bond* to Potomack. M.

Nelson, Ann. S & T Apr 1753 *Thames*. L.

Nelson, Ann (1762). *See* Wade. M.

Nelson, Eleanor. S Jly T Sep 1755 *Tryal*. L.

Nelson, Henry, poulterer. S & T Oct 1720 *Gilbert* LC Annapolis May
    1721. M.

Nelson, Hugh. S Summer 1738 R 14 yrs Lent 1739. St.

Nelson, James. S Summer 1754. Nf.

Nelson, John. PT Jly 1689. M.

Nelson als Raynard, John. S Summer 1736 R 14 yrs Summer 1737. Y.

Nelson, John. S Lent 1761. No.

Nelson, Joseph. R for Barbados May 1665. X.

Nelson, Peter. SQS for fraud Oct T Dec 1771 *Justitia*. M.

Nelson, Richard. S s silver tankard Summer 1719. G.

Nelson, Robert. S Apr T Oct 1719 *Susannah & Sarah* LC Annapolis
    Apr 1720. L.

Nelson, Thomas. S Sep T Oct 1719 *Susannah & Sarah* from London LC Annapolis Apr 1720. Nl.

Nelson, Thomas (1772). *See* Nicholson. Y.

Nelson, Thomas. S Sep-Oct 1775. M.

Nelson, William. R for Barbados Jan 1665. Y.

Nelson, William of Hompton. R for Barbados Jly 1671. Y.

Nelson, William. S Summer 1744 R 14 yrs Lent 1745. E.

Neptune, Ann. S & T Jan 1767 *Tryal*. M.

Nesbitt, Elizabeth. S Feb-Apr T May 1751 *Tryal*. M.

Nesbitt, James. T 14 yrs Aug 1752 *Tryal*. K.

Nesbitt, James. T Sep 1764 *Justitia*. K.

Nesbitt, William. S & T Dec 1767 *Neptune*. L.

Nesson, John (1719). *See* Easton. M.

Nest, John. LC from *Margaret* Md Sep 1719 & sold to John Baldwin. Sy.

Nethercliffe, John. S Jan T Feb 1733 *Smith*. L.

Nethercliffe, William. S Lent T May 1752 *Lichfield*. Bu.

Nethercote, John. S Lent R 14 yrs Summer 1737. No.

Netherwood, William. S Jly T Dec 1736 *Patapsco* to Md. M.

Netheway, Elizabeth. S for shoplifting Summer 1721 R 14 yrs Summer 1723 AT Lent 1724. He.

Nettleton, John. R for America Jun 1684. Li.

Neve, John. S Lent 1753. Nf.

Neave, John. S s at St. Benedict, Cambridge, & R 14 yrs Summer 1774. Ca.

Neve, Samuel. R for Barbados Sep 1682. L.

Nevell. *See* Nevill.

Nevers, Thomas (1772). *See* Bevers. Y.

Neves, Daniel. S Apr-Jun 1739. M.

Neves, Thomas. S Aug T Oct 1726 *Forward* to Va. M.

Nevill, Katherine. R for Barbados Mar 1681. L.

Nevill, Eleanor. S Dec 1765 T Jan 1766 *Tryal*. M.

Nevell, John. LC from *Rappahannock* Rappahannock Apr 1726. X.

Nevell, John. S Feb-Apr T Jun 1756 *Lyon*. M.

Nevill, Mary. R for Barbados Jly 1674. M.

Nevill, Mayes. S s geldings at Foulsham & R Lent 1770. Nf.

Nevill, Thomas. S Feb T Mar 1731 *Patapsco* LC Annapolis Jun 1731. M.

Nevinson, John of Wortley. R for Barbados Jly 1679. Y.

Nevison, Margaret. R for Barbados Apr 1669. M.

New, Richard. S Lent 1728 AT Lent 1731. O.

Newall, Thomas of Manchester. SQS May 1764. La.

Newbee. *See* Newby.

Newbell, Joseph. S s horse Lent R 14 yrs Summer 1753. Li.

Newberry, Edward of Brixham. R for Barbados Jan 1682. De.

Newberry, Elizabeth wife of Thomas Jr. S Jun-Dec 1745. M.

Newberry, Elizabeth. TB to Va from QS 1756. De.

Newberry, Jacob. PT Oct 1700. M.

Newberry, James. S & T Dec 1740 *Vernon*. L.

Newberry, Joane (1720). *See* Goffe. De.

Newberry, John. R Mar 1772 TB to Va. De.

Newberry, Joseph. Rebel T 1685.

Newberry, Robert. S Mar 1738. De.

Newberry, Robert. S Mar 1741. Do.

Newberry, Robert. T 14 yrs Nov 1759 *Phoenix*. Sy.

Newberry, Thomas (1734). *See* Goff. De.

Newbert, Ann. S s at Wellington Lent 1759 & ordered to be transported one month after delivery of her child. Sh.

Newbowl, George. T May 1751 *Tryal*. K.

Newbole, Henry. S & T Oct 1732 *Caesar* to Va. M.

Newbald, John of Tettenhall. R for America Jun 1714. St.

Newbolt, William. R for Barbados or Jamaica Aug 1700. M.

Newborne, James. S Aug T Oct 1724 *Forward* LC Annapolis Jun 1725. M.

Newborn, Thomas. S Summer 1746. E.

Newbound, Thomas. R for life Apr 1774 (SP). Ca.

Newbound, William. R for life Apr 1774 (SP). Ca.

Newby, Bever. S Feb T Sep 1737 *Pretty Patsy* to Md. M.

Newbee, Edward. S 14 yrs Sep 1750. M.

Newby, Elizabeth (1750). *See* Wanless. M.

Newby, Godfrey, als Gough, John, als Barrett, Thomas. S s asses at Hurley Lent 1770. Be.

Newby, James. LC from *Dorsetshire* Va Sep 1736. X.

Newby, John. S & R 14 yrs Lent 1738. Nf.

Newby, Sarah. SQS & T Sep 1755 *Tryal*. M.

Newby, Thomas. S s sheep Lent R 14 yrs Summer 1749. Le.

Newcomb, Elisha. S for highway robbery Lent R 14 yrs Summer 1749. Le.

Newcombe, Frances. S & T 14 yrs Jan 1769 *Thornton*. M.

Newcombe, John. S & T Oct 1729 *Forward* LC Va Jun 1730. M.

Newcombe, Joseph. R 14 yrs Jly 1721 T from Southampton 1723. Ha.

Newcomb, Mary of St. Andrew, Holborn, widow. S s saucepan Jly-Oct 1740 T Jan 1741 *Harpooner* to Rappahannock. M.

Newcombe, Robert. S & T Oct 1729 *Forward* but died on passage. M.

Newcombe, Robert (1766). *See* Smith, John. M.

Newcombe, Samuel. S s beef at Stroud Lent 1765. G.

Newcomb, Timothy. S Mar TB to Va Apr 1740. Wi.

Newcombe, William. S Lent R 14 yrs Summer 1765. G.

Newdale, Robert. S s at Halesworth Summer 1726. St.

Newell, Katherine (1663). *See* Harrison. M.

Newell, Elizabeth (1745). *See* Wyatt. M.

Newell, Francis. S s horse Lent R Summer 1721. Be.

Newell, Isabella. S Jly 1734. M.

Newell, James. S s at Newington Summer 1773. O.

Newell, John. S Feb 1739. M.

Newell, John. S Lent 1775. K.

Newell, Luke. T Apr 1739 *Forward*. K.

Newill, Margaret. S & T 14 yrs Apr 1741 *Speedwell* or *Mediterranean*. M.

Newell, Richard. S s at St. Philip & Jacob Summer 1750. G.

Newell, Sarah. R for Barbados or Jamaica Oct 1694. M.

Newell, Sarah (1727). *See* Williams. M.

Newell, William. S Feb T 14 yrs Apr 1732 *Patapsco* LC Annapolis Oct 1732. M.

Newell als Blackhead, William. S Sep T Dec 1734 *Caesar* LC Va Jly 1735. M.

Newell, William. S Sep-Dec 1746. M.

Newey, John of Killingworth. R for America Jly 1678. Wa.

Newey, John. R for America Jly 1683. Wa.

Newey, John. SW & T Jan 1769 *Thornton*. M.

Newey, John. S Lent T Apr 1771. Wa.

Newey, Margaret, spinster, als wife of John of Lambeth. R for Barbados or Jamaica Jly 1677. Sy.

Newey, William of Tamworth. R (Midland Circ) Jly 1679. St.

Newham, John of Dekesdon. R for America Apr 1697. Hu.

Newhouse, Cornelius. S 14 yrs Oct 1751-Jan 1752. M.

Newhouse, Joseph of York. R for Barbados Jly 1690. Y.

Newington, Robert. R 14 yrs Jly 1763. M.

Newington als Bowen als Reeve, Sarah. S s at St. Lawrence, Reading, Lent 1727 T *Elizabeth* LC Potomack Aug 1729. Be.

Newins, Letitia wife of John of St. Paul, Covent Garden. SW Apr 1773. M.

Newland, Henry. S May-Jly 1774. M.

Newland, James. S s watch Jly-Sep T Sep 1742 *Forward*. M.

Newland, James. R & T for life Jly 1770 *Scarsdale*. M.

Newland, James. S Feb T Apr 1772 *Thornton*. L.

Newland, John (1719). *See* Rowland. L.

Newland, John. T Dec 1731 *Forward*. Sy.

Newland, William. S May T Jly 1771 *Scarsdale*. L.

Newlove, Sarah of St. Giles in Fields, spinster. S s plates & T Dec 1740 *Vernon*. M.

Newman, Ann. S Jly T 14 yrs Sep 1737 *Pretty Patsy*. L.

Newman, Ann (1774). *See* Green. Hu.

Newman als Howard, Bridget. S Oct 1756. M.

Newman, Daniel. T Jun 1740 *Essex*. E.

Newman, Edward. SQS May 1753. Ha.

Newman, Edward. S Oct 1773. L.

Newman, Elizabeth. LC from *Alexander* Annapolis Sep 1723. X.

Newman, Henry of Marshfield. R for America Jly 1675. G.

Newman, James. S & T Sep 1766 *Justitia*. L.

Newman als Biggs, Jane. T Sep 1764 *Justitia*. E.

Newman, John of Great Gidding. R for America Feb 1664. Hu.

Newman, John. Died on passage in *Loyal Margaret* 1726. X.

Newman, John. S s skins at Rotherfield Peppard Lent 1753. O.

Newman, John. R for life Jly 1773 TB to Va Jan 1774. Wi.

Newman, John Thomas. T Jan 1767 *Tryal*. M.

Newman, Joseph. R 14 yrs Mar 1731. Wi.

Newman, Maria. S May-Jun T Aug 1752 *Tryal*. M.

Newman als Colthropp, Mary. R for Barbados or Jamaica Dec 1695 & May 1697. L.

Newman als Worth, Michael. LC from *Dorsetshire* Va Sep 1736. X.

Newman, Michael. S Jan T Mar 1764 *Tryal*. L.

Newman, Nash. SQS & T Dec 1771 *Justitia*. M.

Newman, Richard (1719). *See* Yeoman. L.

Newman, Richard of St. Martin in Fields. S s shirts & T Dec 1740 *Vernon*. M.

Newman, Robert. R for Jamaica Aug 1661. L.

Newman, Robert. S Feb T Mar 1729 *Patapsco* LC Annapolis Dec 1729. M.

Newman, Robert. S s at St. Philip & Jacob Summer TB Sep 1736. G.

Newman, Thomas. R for Barbados Mar 1683. M.

Newman als Harding, Thomas of Cucklington, linenweaver. R for Barbados Feb 1699. So.

Newman, Thomas. S & T Oct 1719 *Susannah & Sarah* LC Annapolis Apr 1720. L.

Newman als Smith, Thomas. S Jun-Dec 1745. M.

Newman, Thomas. S Lent R 14 yrs Summer T Sep 1757 *Thetis*. Ht.

Newman, Thomas. S & T Dec 1767 *Neptune*. L.

Newman, Thomas. S s shoes at Melbourn & R 14 yrs Summer 1775. Ca.

Newman, William. TB to Md from QS 1728. De.

Newman, William. S Jly-Dec 1747. M.

Newman, William. S & T Jly 1753 *Tryal*. L.

Newman, Willmot wife of William. TB to Va from QS 1732. De.

Newman, Zachary of Melksham, fuller. R for Barbados Jun 1666. Wi.

Newmarsh, Jonathan. S Aug T Oct 1726 *Forward*. L.

Newnham, Francis. S s gelding at Beetly & R 14 yrs Summer 1775. Nf.

Newport, John. S Oct T Dec 1724 *Rappahannock*. L.

Newport, John. S Mar 1761. L.

Newport, Richard (1732). *See* Pearce. Do.

Newport, Susanna. S Aug T Oct 1723 *Forward*. L.

Newson, John. S Feb T Apr 1770 *New Trial* but removed from ship & ordered to be detained. M.

Newstead, Abigail. R 14 yrs Aug T Sep 1718 *Eagle* LC Charles Town Mar 1719. L.

Newsted, Abigail. T Apr 1759 *Thetis*. Sy.

Newstead, Thomas. S s gelding & R 14 yrs Summer 1742. Nf.

Newth, Sarah wife of John. S s at Bitton Lent TB Mar 1747. G.

Newton, Ann wife of Joseph. S 14 yrs Summer 1757 for receiving stolen goods from Mary Airson *(qv)*. Du.

Newton, Augustine of Hoxton. S Oct 1661 to House of Correction unless he agrees to be transported. M.

Newton, Charles. S Dec 1742 T 14 yrs Mar 1743 *Justitia*. L.

Newton, Daniel. S Jly 1718 to be T to Va. De.

Newton, Edward of Hale. R for America Jly 1678 & Jly 1679. Li.

Newton, George. SQS Sep 1774. M.

Newton, Hugh (1728). *See* James. De.

Newton, James. R for Barbados Jun 1665. M.

Newton, James. PT Oct 1676 R Mar 1677. M.

Newton, James. S Apr-May 1775. M.

Newton, John of Hillington. R for Barbados Feb 1664. Nf.

Newton, John. Died on passage in *Susannah & Sarah* 1720. X.

Newton, John. R 14 yrs Jly 1733. So.

Newton, John. S Oct 1757 T Mar 1758 *Dragon*. M.

Newton als Wood als Chantler, Joseph. S & R 21 yrs Lent 1765. Ch.

Newton, Joseph. S s watch at Thornhill Lent 1773. Y.

Newton, Mary of Hitchin. R for Barbados or Jamaica Jly 1710. Ht.
Newton, Mary of Manchester, spinster. SQS Oct 1771. La.
Newton, Rachael. S Aug 1754. So.
Newton als Duncombe, Richard. T Jly 1723 *Alexander* LC Md Sep 1723. Ht.
Newton, Richard. S Summer 1730. Y.
Newton, Richard of Rotherhithe. SQS Jan 1755. Sy.
Newton, Stephen. S Jly T Aug 1721 *Prince Royal* LC Va Nov 1721. L.
Newton, Susan of Fordham, widow. R for Barbados or Jamaica Jly 1715. E.
Newton, Thomas of New Sleeford. R for America Feb 1713. Li.
Newton, Thomas. TB May 1734 T *Squire* LC Md Aug 1735. Db.
Newton, Thomas. S Jan T 14 yrs Mar 1758 *Dragon*. M.
Newton, Thomas. S Summer 1769 R 14 yrs Lent 1770. Nt.
Newton, William. R 14 yrs Summer 1730. Y.
Newton, William. S Aug 1763. So.
Newton, William. S s mare Lent R 14 yrs TB to Va Sep Summer 1765. Le.
Newton, William. SW & T Jan 1769 *Thornton*. M.
Newton, William. SQS Jly 1774. M.
Niblett, James. R Dec 1698 AT Jan 1699. M.
Niblett, Joel. S Jan T Feb 1744 *Neptune* to Md. M.
Niccoli als Niccolin, William. S & T Dec 1771 *Justitia*. M.
Nice, Charles. S s coat Apr T Dec 1735 *John* LC Annapolis Sep 1736. L.
Nichol, Edward. S Nov T Dec 1753 *Whiteing*. L.
Nichollus, Elizabeth. S Jly T Sep 1765 *Justitia*. M.
Nicholas, George of St. Sepulchre. S for forgery Jan 1722 & R for T on *Happy Return* to Va. M.
Nicholas, James. PT Aug 1688. M.
Nicholas, John. S s skins at North Lydbury Summer 1755. Sh.
Nicholas, John. S Mar 1766. So.
Nicholas, Mathew (1698). *See* Nicholls. Co.
Nicholas, Robin of Staplehurst. S Lent 1745. K.
Nicholas, Thomas. S s lamb Summer 1749 R 14 yrs Lent 1750. He.
Nicholas, William. R 14 yrs for murder Mar 1753. Co.
Nicholls, Allan. PT Feb R for Barbados Sep 1672. M.
Niccolls als Jenkins, Anne. R for Barbados Jun 1670. M.
Nichols, Anne (1720). *See* Ireland. L.
Nichols, Ann. S Feb T Mar 1729 *Patapsco* LC Annapolis Dec 1729. M.
Nicholls, Ann. S Mar 1742. Co.
Nicholls, Ann. S Lent 1745. Nf.
Nicholls, Daniel (1775). *See* Nicholson. M.
Nicholls, Edward. S 14 yrs Sep-Oct 1774. M.
Niccolls, Elizabeth. R & T Dec 1716 *Lewis* to Jamaica. M.
Nicolls, Elizabeth of St. Mary le Strand, spinster. SW Jly T Sep 1767 *Justitia*. M.
Nicholls, Elizabeth (1768). *See* Mason. M.
Nicholls, Emanuel. S Sep-Oct 1749. M.
Nicholls, Emanuel. R 14 yrs Mar 1762. Co.
Nicholls, George. S Sep T Oct 1750 *Rachael*. L.
Nicholls, George. S Apr T May 1752 *Lichfield*. L.

Nicholls, Henry. T Oct 1726 *Forward*. K.
Nicholls, Humphrey. S s at Claverly Lent 1735. Sh.
Nicholls, James. R for Barbados or Jamaica Oct 1688. M.
Nicholls, James. S Feb T Apr 1734 *Patapsco*. L.
Nicholls als Cryer, Jane. S Dec 1755 T Jan 1756 *Greyhound*. L.
Nicholls, Joan. R for Barbados or Jamaica May 1684. L.
Nicholls, Joanna. S Apr T Sep 1737 *Pretty Patsy* to Md. M.
Niccolls, John. R for Barbados Jly 1668. L.
Nicholls, John of Egloshayle. R for Barbados Feb 1684. Co.
Nicholls, John. S & T Oct 1722 *Forward* LC Annapolis Jun 1723. L.
Nicholls, John. S s sheep at Hagley Summer 1724. Wo.
Nicholls, John. S Lent T May 1750 *Lichfield*. K.
Nichols, John. R 14 yrs Jly 1751. Ha.
Nicholes, John. S & R 14 yrs Summer 1773. Sh.
Nicholls, Jonathan. S May T Sep 1765 *Justitia*. L.
Nicholls, Joseph. S May T Sep 1766 *Justitia*. M.
Nicholls, Joseph. R & T for life Apr 1770 *New Trial*. M.
Nicholls, Mark. R 14 yrs Mar 1742. Co.
Nicholls, Martha. S Apr T 14 yrs May 1718 *Tryal* LC Charles Town Aug
    1718. L.
Nicholls, Mary. S Lent R 14 yrs Summer 1746. St.
Nicholls, Mary wife of John of Lambeth. S Summer T Oct 1750
    Rachael. Sy.
Nichols, Mary. SQS & T Dec 1752 *Greyhound*. M.
Nicholls als Nicholas, Mathew of Gwermop, tinner. R for Barbados Jly
    1698. Co.
Nicholls, Matthias. S for life Oct-Dec 1750. M.
Nicholls, Nathaniel. S Feb T Apr 1742 *Bond*. L.
Niccols, Paul of Bickleton. R for Barbados Feb 1665. G.
Nicholls, Philip. TB to Va from QS 1749. De.
Nickolls, Richard. R Summer 1728 (SP). Nf.
Nicholls, Richard. S Sep 1740. L.
Nicholls, Richard. T May 1741 *Miller*. K.
Nicholls, Richard. S Apr T May 1751 *Tryal*. L.
Nicholls, Richard. SQS Dec 1762 T Mar 1763 *Neptune*. M.
Nicholls, Robert. S Feb T Apr 1742 *Bond*. L.
Nichols, Robert. S Dec 1775. M.
Niccolls, Thomas. R for Barbados or Jamaica Dec 1698. L.
Niccolls, Thomas, aged 22, fair, weaver. S Jan T Feb 1723 *Jonathan* LC
    Annapolis Jly 1724. M.
Nicholls, Thomas. SQS Jan 1738. So.
Nicholls, Thomas. TB Sep 1743. Db.
Nicholls, Thomas. S for being at large after sentence of transportation
    Summer 1746 R Lent 1747. Wa.
Nichols, Walter. S Mar 1751. Ha.
Nicholls, Walter. S Mar 1754. L.
Nicholls, Walter of St. George, Southwark. SQS & T Jan 1769
    Thornton. Sy.
Nicholls, William. S & T Apr 1725 *Sukey* to Md. M.
Nicholls, William. S Mar 1732. Co.
Nicholls, William. S Jly 1748. L.

Nicholls, William. S Jly 1763. M.

Nicholls, William. S Jun T Aug 1769 *Douglas*. L.

Nicholls, William. S s linen at Kidderminster Lent 1771. Wo.

Nichollus. *See* Nicholas.

Nicholson, Ann. S Sep-Oct 1748 T Jan 1749 *Laura*. M.

Nicholson, Anthony. TB to Va 1770. De.

Nicholson, Bartholomew. S & T Oct 1730 *Forward* LC Potomack Jan 1731. L.

Nicholson als Nichols, Daniel. S Jan-Feb 1775. M.

Nicholson, Edmund. S Sep T Dec 1763 *Neptune*. M.

Nichollson, Edward. S Jly T Oct 1741 *Sea Horse*. M.

Nicholson, Eleanor. AT Summer 1759. Y.

Nicholson, Elizabeth. S City s at St. Crux Lent 1740. Y.

Nicholson, George. S s horse Summer 1750 R 14 yrs Summer 1752. Du.

Nicholson, George. S Apr 1774. M.

Nicholson, Hannah wife of William. S City Lent 1740. Y.

Nicholson, James of Uttoxeter. S Lent 1720. St.

Nicholson, Jane. S & T Jan 1739 *Dorsetshire*. L.

Nicholson, John. Died on passage in *Sukey* 1725. X.

Nicholson, John. LC from *Forward* Rappahannock Jun 1729. X.

Nicholson, John. TB to Va from QS 1756. De.

Nicholson, John. SQS s shirts Summer 1766. Du.

Nicholson, John. S Lent 1772. Li.

Nickolson, Patrick. S Dec 1764 T Jan 1765 *Tryal*. M.

Nicholson als Nelson, Thomas. S s at Whitby Lent TB May 1772. Y.

Nicholson, William. T Apr 1741 *Speedwell* or *Mediterranean*. Sy.

Nicholson, William. S Jly T Sep 1767 *Justitia*. M.

Nicholson, William. SL Mar T Apr 1772 *Thornton*. Sy.

Nicklow, Elizabeth. ST & T Dec 1763 *Neptune*. L.

Nicks, John. T Nov 1759 *Phoenix*. K.

Nickson. *See* Nixon. M.

Night. *See* Knight.

Nightingale als Taylor als Taverly, Ann. R 14 yrs Summer TB Sep 1754. Y.

Nightingale, Matthew. SQS Jly T Sep 1764 *Justitia*. M.

Nightingale, Peter. S Lent R 14 yrs Summer 1758. Le & No.

Nightingale, William of Hatfield Peveral. SQS Oct T Dec 1753 *Whiteing*. E.

Nimmo, John. SQS Feb 1773. M.

Nisbee als Surrey, Susanna. S Dec 1753-Jan 1774. M.

Nisbett, Richard. S Feb 1775. L.

Nisbett, William. S Lent R 14 yrs Summer T Sep 1751 *Greyhound*. Sy.

Nickson, Alice wife of Henry of Greenhalgh with Thistleton, hatter. SQS Jan 1752. La.

Nixon, Francis. S Sep-Oct 1772. M.

Nixon, Jane. AT City Summer 1759. Nl.

Nickson, John. S Oct T 14 yrs Nov 1728 *Forward* to Va. M.

Nixon, Laurence. R for America Feb 1692. Db.

Nixon, Margaret. S s at St. Nicholas, Durham, Summer 1772. Du.

Nixon, Richard of Whitechapel. S for breaking & entering & T May 1736 *Patapsco*. M.

Nixon, Richard. S s horse Summer 1737 R 14 yrs Summer 1738. Cu.

Nixon, Robert. R 14 yrs Summer 1731 AT Summer 1732. Cu.

Nixon, Robert. T Sep 1758 *Tryal*. Sy.

Nixon, Susanna. SQS May T Sep 1776 *Justitia*. M.

Nickson als Nixon, Thomas. R for Barbados Jun 1663. M.

Nixon, William. R 14 yrs Summer 1758. Cu.

Nixon, William. S s sheep Summer 1744 R 14 yrs Summer 1745. Cu.

Nokes, James. S Jan T Mar 1764 *Tryal*. M.

Noakes, Jeremiah. SL & T Jan 1766 *Tryal*. Sy.

Nokes John. R 14 yrs Jly TB to Va Oct 1742. Wi.

Noakes, Stephen Jr. SQS New Sarum Jan TB to Va Apr 1766. Wi.

Noar, William. T Apr 1739 *Forward*. Ht.

Nobbs, John. S Lent 1743. *Su.

Nobbs, Samuel. S Norwich Summer 1759. Nf.

Noble, Elizabeth (1691). *See* Busby. L.

Noble, George. SWK Jly T Sep 1765 *Justitia*. K.

Noble, John. SQS for attending conventicle Dec 1664. M.

Noble, John. S s gelding Summer 1736 R 14 yrs Lent 1737. Nf.

Noble, Mark. T Jun 1727 *Susanna*. E.

Noble, Mark. S Summer 1754. Bu.

Noble, Phyllis. S Jan T Feb 1726 *Supply* LC Annapolis May 1726. M.

Noble, Simon. R for Barbados Jly 1677. Y.

Noble, Susannah. T May 1719 *Margaret* LC Md May 1720; sold to Jonathan Prasher. Sy.

Nobody als Parsley, Mary of St. George, Southwark, spinster. SQS Jan 1751. Sy.

Nock. *See* Knock.

Nockliss, Mary. S & T Sep 1757 *Thetis*. M.

Nockolds, Elizabeth. S Norwich as pickpocket Summer 1749. Nf.

Nocks. *See* Knocks.

Nodder, John. S Feb T Mar 1731 *Patapsco* LC Annapolis Jun 1731. M.

Noddy, Francis (1740). *See* Cocking. Co.

Noden, John. S for highway robbery & R 14 yrs Summer 1775. Sh.

Noel. *See* Nowell.

Nokes. *See* Noakes.

Noland, Andrew. S Feb T Mar 1731 *Patapsco* LC Annapolis Jun 1731. L.

Nowland, Ann. S Feb 1731. L.

Noland, Bridget. S & T Aug 1718 *Eagle* LC Charles Town Mar 1719. L.

Knowland, Catherine (1757). *See* Bourne. L.

Knowland, Katherine. S Oct T Dec 1770 *Justitia*. M.

Knowland, Eleanor. S Jan-Feb 1774. M.

Knowland, James. S Mar 1750 TB to Va. De.

Knowland, James. S Lent 1764. Db.

Knowland, William. T Apr 1762 *Neptune*. K.

Nolder, Mary of Rotherhithe. R for Barbados or Jamaica Feb 1684. Sy.

Noller, Elizabeth. S May T Jly 1723 *Alexander* LC Annapolis Sep 1723. L.

Nolloth, William. S s at Badingham Lent 1769. Su.

Nolton, James. S & T Oct 1730 *Forward* LC Potomack Jan 1731. L.

Noone, Fortunatus (1675). *See* Pearce. Be.

Noon, Henry. Rebel T 1685.

Noon, John. S Oct-Dec 1754. M.

Noon, Mary. S & T Dec 1724 *Rappahannock*. L.

Noon, Thomas of Farnfield. R for America Feb 1713. Nt.

Noon, William. S Oct 1741 T Feb 1742 *Industry*. L.

Nooney, James. S Jan T Mar 1764 *Tryal*. L.

Noraway, Thomas. S Lent 1738. Bu.

Norbury, Elizabeth. S 14 yrs Jan-Feb 1774. M.

Norbury, Hester. S Jan T Mar 1750 *Tryal*. L.

Norcott, John. PT Jan R Dec 1698. M.

Norcott, John. S Jan T Feb 1733 *Smith*. L.

Nordis, Catherine (1767). *See* Smith. M.

Nordon, Joseph of South Milford. R for Barbados Jly 1699. Y.

Norfolk Bob (1753). *See* Boar, Robert. E.

Norford, James. S s handkerchiefs Summer 1746. O.

Norgate, Nathaniel. S Jan T 14 yrs Apr 1741 *Speedwell*. L.

Norgate, Sarah of St. Saviour, Southwark, spinster. R for Barbados or
  Jamaica Jly 1674. Sy.

Norgrave, Joseph. S s mare Summer 1755 R 14 yrs Lent 1756. No.

Nork, William. S s at Wolverhampton Lent 1728. St.

Norman, Anna Maria. S Lent 1745. K.

Norman als Penington, Charles. R Oct 1694 AT Jan 1695. M.

Norman, Elizabeth. R (Home Circ) for America Aug 1664. X.

Norman, Elizabeth. S Jly T Oct 1741 *Sea Horse* to Va. M.

Norman, Elizabeth. S Feb T Apr 1765 *Ann*. M.

Norman, George. R 14 yrs Mar 1766 TB to Va. De.

Norman, Hanna (1722). *See* Starky. M.

Norman, Henry. R 14 yrs Mar 1746. Ha.

Norman, Henry. AT from QS Summer 1768. Nt.

Norman, Henry (1769). *See* Tindell. M.

Norman, James. S Mar 1766. Ha.

Norman, John (1722). *See* Perry. M.

Norman, John of Whepstead. S Lent 1725. Su.

Norman, John. S Aug 1765. So.

Norman, Mary. T May 1736 *Patapsco*. Ht.

Norman, Mary. S May-Jly T Sep 1751 *Greyhound*. M.

Norman, Peter. S Jun 1739. L.

Norman, Philip. S Mar 1771. So.

Norman, Robert. R for Barbados Mar 1683. L.

Norman, William. Rebel T 1685.

Norman, William. S Mar R 14 yrs & TB Sep 1727 T *Forward* LC
  Rappahannock May 1728. Nt.

Norman, William. S Dec 1743 T Feb 1744 *Neptune* to Md. M.

Norman als Freeman als Eccleston, William of Liverpool, butcher. SQS
  Oct 1755. La.

Nornevill, John. SQS & T Dec 1767 *Neptune*. M.

Norridge. *See* Norwich.

Norrington, Thomas (1769). *See* Bessom. G.

Norris, Batchellor. S Lent 1775. Sx.

Norris, Frances. S May-Jly T Sep 1755 *Tryal*. M.

Norris, Francis. S Oct 1773. L.

Norris, George. R 14 yrs Apr 1742. Ha.

Norris, James. S s handkerchief at St. Sepulchre Sep T Oct 1768 *Justitia*. L.

Norris, John. R Oct 1694 AT Jan 1695. M.

Norris, John. S Mar 1755. De.

Norris, John. S Oct 1756. M.

Norris, Letitia. SQS & privately whipped Apr T Nov 1759 *Phoenix*. M.

Norris, Mary. S Jly T 14 yrs Oct 1741 *Sea Horse* to Va. M.

Norris, Michael of London. R (Western Circ) for Barbados Feb 1699. L.

Norris, Philip. S Mar 1755. So.

Norris, Richard. S Mar 1761. L.

Norris, Richard. T 14 yrs Apr 1765 *Ann*. Sy.

Norris, Robert. T Jan 1741 *Vernon*. K.

Norris, Thomas. S Aug 1734. So.

Norris, Thomas. SQS Feb T Mar 1750 *Tryal*. M.

Norris, William. S Mar 1725. Wi.

Norris, William. T Apr 1742 *Bond*. Sy.

Norris, William. S s at Diss Summer 1770. Nf.

Norson, Jervis. LC from *Susannah & Sarah* Annapolis Apr 1720. X.

North, Catherine. S s shoes & T May 1736 *Patapsco* to Md. M.

North, Edward. SQS Oct T Dec 1769 *Justitia*. M.

North, Elizabeth. T Oct 1721 *William & John*. K.

North, Elizabeth. S s money from Lord Glenorchy & T May 1736 *Patapsco*. M.

North, James. SQS Mar 1750 T *Happy Jennett* LC Md Oct 1751. Db.

North, James. S Mar 1775. Ha.

North, John. R Feb 1675. M.

North, John. S s sheep Summer 1750 R 14 yrs Lent 1751. Db.

North, John. S Apr 1773. M.

North, Jonathan. S s sheep & R Summer 1775. Y.

North, Joseph. S s horse Summer 1736 R 14 yrs Lent 1737. Li.

North, Mary. R for Barbados Jly 1680. M.

North, Mary. S Apr T May 1720 *Honor* LC Port York Jan 1721. L.

North, Mary wife of John of Shoreditch. S s gown Apr T May 1740 *Essex*. M.

North, Richard of Speen. R for America Jly 1698. Be.

North, Thomas of Kidbrook. S Lent 1745. K.

North, Thomas. S Sep-Oct 1748 T Jan 1749 *Laura*. M.

North, Thomas. S for highway robbery Summer 1765 R for life Lent 1766. Li.

North, Thomas. SQS & T Apr 1769 *Tryal*. M.

North, William of Hursley. R for Barbados Feb 1665. Ha.

North, William. S & T 14 yrs Sep 1718 *Eagle* LC Charles Town Mar 1719. L.

North, William. SQS Sep 1774. M.

Northam, Gervas. TB 14 yrs Oct 1719. L.

Northcote, Hazell. TB to Va from QS 1726. De.

Northcote, James. R for life for buggery Aug 1771. Co.

Northcott, William. R for Barbados Sep 1669. M.

Northmore, William. S Mar 1763 TB to Va. De.

Northover, Nicholas of St. Ann. R (Western Circ) for Barbados Feb 1698. L.

Norton, Elizabeth of Deddington. R for America Nov 1694. O.

Norton, Hannah. S Aug T Sep 1725 *Sukey* LC Annapolis Dec 1725. M.

Norton, Hester. S Lent R 14 yrs & T Summer 1736. Y.

Norton, James. S Apr T May 1750 *Lichfield*. L.

Norton, John. SQS Dec 1768 T Jan 1769 *Thornton*. M.

Norton, John. S Feb 1774. L.

Norton als Notman als Miller, Mary. S Jan T Mar 1764 *Tryal*. M.

Norton, Mary. S Feb T Apr 1765 *Ann*. M.

Norton, Mary wife of George. S Sep-Oct 1773. M.

Norton, Richard. S Aug 1727 T *Forward* LC Rappahannock May 1728. M.

Norton, Robert. Rebel T 1685.

Norton, Thomas. Rebel T 1685.

Norton, Thomas. S May 1775. L.

Norton, William. S Aug 1720. So.

Norvil, Robert. S s horse Summer 1742 R 14 yrs Summer 1743 AT Summer 1744. Nl.

Norwidge, Robert. S & T Apr 1733 *Patapsco* LC Annapolis Nov 1733. L.

Norwood, Francis. T May 1723 *Victory*. K.

Norwood, Richard. S May T Jun 1727 *Susanna* to Va. M.

Norwood, Robert of Milton next Gravesend. R for life Lent 1775. K.

Noseley, Thomas. S Feb T Mar 1730 *Patapsco* to Md. M.

Noss als Nurse, William. R 14 yrs Mar 1750. Do.

Notere, Michael. S & T Aug 1752 *Tryal*. L.

Notman, Mary (1764). *See* Norton. M.

Notson als Gibbons, Isabella. S Jan-Jun 1747. M.

Nott. *See* Knott.

Nottage, John. S Lent 1775. E.

Nottingham, James. T Sep 1755 *Tryal*. Bu.

Nottingham, Robert. S Summer 1742. Y.

Nottingham, William. S & T Dec 1767 *Neptune*. M.

Nowden, Ann. S & T Oct 1732 *Caesar* to Va. M.

Noel, Dignory. S Mar 1767. Ha.

Nowell, Esther. SQS & T Dec 1769 *Justitia*. M.

Nowell, George. Rebel T 1685.

Nowell, James. R 14 yrs Jly 1744. So.

Nowel als Edwards, Joan. S Mar 1758. So.

Noel, John. S Aug 1720. So.

Nowell, Lamprey. S Sep 1760. M.

Noell, Michael. R for America Jun 1684. Li.

Nowels. *See* Knowles.

Nowis, Percival. Rebel T 1685.

Nowles. *See* Knowles.

Noyes, Richard, als Black Dick of Liddington. R for Barbados Feb 1701. Wi.

Noyes, William of Swallowcliffe. R for Barbados Jun 1669. Wi.

Noyes, William. S Lent 1774. Li.

Nucke, Richard of Wellington. R for Jamaica, Barbados or Bermuda Mar 1668. Sh.

Nugent, Andrew. R Lent 1750 but ordered to remain in gaol Summer 1750. Ht.

Newgent, Edward. R for Barbados or Jamaica Feb 1687. M.

Nugent, Edward. S Aug 1727 T *Forward* LC Rappahannock May 1728. M.

Nugent, John. SW & T Apr 1768 *Thornton*. M.

Nugent, Patrick. S May-Jun T 14 yrs Jly 1753 *Tryal*. M.

Nugent, Philip. S Jun T Sep 1764 *Justitia*. M.

Nugent, William. SQS Sep T Dec 1763 *Neptune*. M.

Nunn, Elizabeth. S Oct 1766 T Jan 1767 *Tryal*. M.

Nun als Powell, James. S Jly T Aug 1721 *Prince Royal* LC Va Nov 1721. L.

Nunn, John. R Oct 1694 AT Jan 1695. M.

Nunn, William. S Jan T Feb 1765 *Tryal*. L.

Nunny, Thomas. S s at Llavaches Lent 1753. Mo.

Nurcombe, William of Luxborough, butcher. R for Barbados Jly 1667. So.

Nurse, Catherine. S Oct 1772. L.

Nurse, John. R for Barbados Aug 1664. M.

Nourse, Philip. S s wheat at Upton Bishop Lent 1768. He.

Nurse, William (1750). *See* Noss. Do.

Nurton, William. S Apr 1739. So.

Nussey, William. S Summer 1740. Y.

Nutbrown, John. S Jan 1751. M.

Nutbrown, Miles. S Jan 1751. M.

Nutcombe, George (1765). *See* Johnson. De.

Nutkins, Thomas. S Jan-Apr 1749. M.

Nutley, Henry. S Mar TB to Va May 1763. Wi.

Nutley, Hugh. TB Aug 1718. L.

Nutt, John (1718). *See* Platt. L.

Nutt, Sarah, aged 22, brown hair. S Jan T 14 yrs Feb 1723 *Jonathan* LC Annapolis Jly 1724. M.

Nutt, Thomas. S s at Clifton Lent 1723. G.

Nuttall, George. S Lent 1769. La.

Nuttall, John of Elton, crofter. SQS Jan 1765. La.

Nutall, Richard (1662). *See* Smith. M.

Nutall, Robert. S Feb T Mar 1729 *Patapsco* but died on passage. L.

Nuttall, Thomas. R 10 yrs in plantations Oct 1662. M.

Nuttal, Thomas of Middle Hulton. SQS Jan 1754. La.

Nuthall, Thomas. S for killing sheep at Penn & R 14 yrs Summer 1770. St.

Nutter, Elizabeth. S Apr-May 1775. M.

Nutter, Helen of Charterhouse Lane, London, spinster. R for West Indies May 1614. M.

Nutter, Richard. S Lent R Summer 1752. La.

Nutter, Sarah. S Summer 1768. Y.

Nuttier, James. R for Barbados Jun 1666. Y.

Nutting, Thomas of Bishops Hatfield or St. Albans. R for Barbados Aug 1662. Ht.

Nuttin, Thomas of Hitchin. R for Barbados or Jamaica Jun 1692. Ht.

O

Oadley, Sarah (1765). *See* Pritchard. M.

Oadway als Valentine, Mary. S Oct-Dec 1750. M.

Oakam, James of Rotherhithe. SQS Oct 1765 T Jan 1766 *Tryal*. Sy.

Oakden, George. R s horse Lent 1772. Wa.

Oaker, Francis. R (Norfolk Circ) for America Jly 1663. X.

Oaker, Henry (1715). *See* Turner. Do.

Okes, Hannah. S Aug 1740. So.

Oakes, Jeremiah. S Summer 1762. Ch.

Oakes, John. S City Summer 1746. Y.

Oakes, Samuel. SQS Coventry Apr 1766. Wa.

Oakes, Thomas. S Sep-Dec 1746. M.

Oakes, William of Bromsgrove. R for Barbados Jly 1664. Wo.

Okie, John. S Jly 1758 TB to Va 1759. De.

Okey als Sessions, William of Kingham. R for America Jly 1675. O.

Oakford, Josiah. S Mar TB to Va Apr 1764. Wi.

Oakley, Alice. S Oct T Nov 1728 *Forward* LC Rappahannock Jun 1729. M.

Oakley, Benjamin. S Feb T Apr 1770 *New Trial*. L.

Oakley, Benjamin. S Feb T Apr 1770 *New Trial*. Sy.

Oakley, Christopher. S Sep T Oct 1739 *Duke of Cumberland*. L.

Oakley, Francis. R for Barbados Dec 1668. M.

Oakley, George. SW & T Jan 1769 *Thornton*. M.

Oakley, Hugh. S Jly T 14 yrs Aug 1718 *Eagle* LC Charles Town Mar 1719. M.

Oakley, Samuel. T May 1751 *Tryal*. Sy.

Oakley, Sarah (1727). *See* Kirk. Sy.

Oakeley, Thomas. S & T Oct 1729 *Forward* LC Va Jun 1730. M.

Oakley, Thomas. S Feb T Mar 1730 *Patapsco* LC Annapolis Sep 1730. L.

Oakley, Thomas. S Apr T May 1751 *Tryal*. L.

Oakley, Thomas. S Lent R 14 yrs Summer 1756. Ca.

Oakly, Thomas. S s gelding at Wolverton & R Lent T Apr 1770 *New Trial*. Bu.

Oakley, William. S s sheep Summer 1752 R 14 yrs Lent 1753. Ru.

Oar als Hoar, Thomas. R for life Mar 1772. So.

Oasie, William. S Mar 1773. Co.

Oates, Elizabeth. S & T Mar 1763 *Neptune*. L.

Oates, Mary. S Jly T Aug 1721 *Prince Royal* LC Va Nov 1721. M.

Oatley, Margaret. S Oct 1760. M.

Otridge, James. SQS Apr TB May 1756. So.

Oatridge, James. R Mar TB to Va Apr 1767. Wi.

Oatway, Elizabeth. SQS Jly TB Aug 1765. So.

Oatway als Harding, John. S Mar 1738. De.

Obbins, Robert. S & R 14 yrs Lent 1743. Nf.

Obney, Robert. S Jly 1749. L.

O'Brien, Dennis. SQS Jly T Oct 1768 *Justitia*. M.

O'Brien, Edward. SW & T Jun 1768 *Tryal*. M.

O'Bryan, Eleanor. S Sep-Dec 1755 T Jan 1756 *Greyhound*. M.
O'Bryan, James. S 14 yrs for receiving Lent 1765. Wa.
O'Bryan, James. R 14 yrs Mar 1765 TB to Va. De.
O'Brien, Jane als Katherine. S Dec 1763 T Mar 1764 *Tryal*. M.
O'Bryan, Judith. S Jly 1750. Ha.
O'Brien, Loramy. S Jan 1761. M.
O'Brien, Mary (1766). *See* Ovins. M.
O'Brien, Thomas. S May-Jly 1749. M.
O'Bryan, Walter. T Oct 1738 *Genoa*. Sy.
Obryan, William. S Jly 1718 to be T to Va. Co.
O'Brian, William. S May-Jly 1750. M.
O'Brien, William. S Jly T Sep 1766 *Justitia*. M.
O'Brien, William. S Sep-Oct 1773. M.
Ockford, Nathaniel. SQS & TB Jan & Mar 1734. G.
Ockleford, Mary. S Sep T Nov 1759 *Phoenix*. M.
Ockram, Vincent. S Mar 1736. Ha.
O'Conner, Philip Charles. S May T Jun 1726 *Loyal Margaret* but died
   on passage. M.
O'Conner, Timothy. S Dec 1772. M.
Odderway, James. S Jan-Apr 1749. M.
Oddy, Francis. S Jan T Feb 1726 *Supply* LC Annapolis May 1726. L.
Oddy, Miles. TB to Md Aug 1729. Db.
Odele, Edward. T 14 yrs Sep 1764 *Justitia*. Sy.
Odell, Edward. SQS Sep T Dec 1770 *Justitia*. M.
Odell, Elizabeth. S May T Aug 1769 *Douglas*. M.
Odell, John. LC from *Elizabeth* Potomack Aug 1729. No.
Odell, Simon. S for highway robbery Lent R 14 yrs Summer 1731. Bd.
Odell, William. LC from *Elizabeth* Potomack Aug 1729. No.
Odew, Hester. S Nov T Dec 1753 *Whiteing*. L.
Odford, Thomas. S Jly 1724. Do.
Odger, William. S Mar 1773. Co.
Oggers, James. S Dec 1731. M.
Odgers, John Jr. S Aug 1738. Co.
Odum, James. S Lent 1747. O.
Odwyn, Samuel. R for Barbados Sep 1669. M.
Oferman, Anthony. LC from *Forward* Annapolis Jun 1723. X.
Offer, John. S s handkerchief at St. Bride's Sep T Oct 1768 *Justitia*. L.
Offerton, William of Bungay. R for Barbados Feb 1664. Su.
Offery, Mathias. T Aug 1721 *Owners Goodwill*. E.
Ogborn, Robert of St. James, Westminster. SW Jan 1775. M.
Ogden, Elizabeth (1765). *See* Stanfield. M.
Ogden, James of Bolton. SQS Jun 1767. La.
Ogden, Joanna. S Aug T Sep 1725 *Forward* to Md. M.
Ogden, John. S Jun 1761. M.
Ogden, John. S Feb T Apr 1765 *Ann*. M.
Ogden, John of Bolton. SQS Jun 1767. La.
Ogden, John of Manchester. SQS Apr 1769. La.
Ogden, Judith (1750). *See* Butler. M.
Ogden, Thomas of Salford. SQS Jun 1772. La.
Ogden als Hogden, William of Stepney. R for America Aug 1713. M.
Ogden, William. SQS Oct 1750. M.

Ogden, William of Manchester, hatter. SQS Jan 1763. La.

Ogden, William of Manchester, hatter. SQS Oct 1774. La.

Oghen, Hugh. R for Barbados & TB Oct 1667. L.

Ogilby, Catherine. S & T Apr 1733 *Patapsco* LC Annapolis Nov 1733. M.

Ogleby, George. R for Barbados or Jamaica Mar 1688. M.

Ogleby, George. S May-Jly 1746. M.

Ogilby, George. S Sep-Oct T Dec 1752 *Greyhound*. M.

Ogilby, Thomas. S & T Dec 1771 *Justitia*. M.

Ogle, Alexander. S City Summer 1736. Nl.

Ogle, Katherine. R Feb 1675. M.

Ogle, Eleanor. S 14 yrs Sep-Oct 1775. M.

O'Hara, Ann (1740). *See* Connelly. M.

Okentree, John. R for Barbados or Jamaica Aug 1700. L.

Oland, William. S s at Wyck and Abson Lent TB Mar 1750. G.

Olave, John (1733)) *See* Marshall. M.

Old, John. R 14 yrs Mar 1742. Do.

Old, John. S Mar 1749. Do.

Oldasey, Stephen. LC from *Forward* Annapolis Jun 1725. X.

Oldbury, Mark. S Oct 1774. L.

Oldbury, Samuel. S Jan T Feb 1742 *Industry* to Md. M.

Olden, William. R Feb 1675. M.

Oldfield, Eleanor. S Feb T 14 yrs Mar 1730 *Patapsco* LC Annapolis Sep 1730. M.

Oldfield, John. S & T Feb 1719 *Worcester* LC Annapolis Jun 1719. L.

Oldfield, John. S Lent 1768. Nf.

Oldfield, Margaret wife of Michael, als Margaret Grigg. S Jan-Jun 1747. M.

Oldham als Walker als Everitt, Elizabeth wife of William *(qv)*. SQS Lincoln Mar 1749. Li.

Oldham, Elizabeth. S Apr-May 1754. M.

Oldham, Ellen of Manchester, spinster. SQS Jan 1764. La.

Oldham, John of Chester. R for Barbados or Jamaica Mar 1694. Ch.

Oldham als Walker als Everitt, William. SQS Lincoln Mar 1749. Li.

Olding, John. S Feb 1758. Ha.

Olding, Joseph. R 14 yrs Mar 1772. Ha.

Oldin, William of Croydon. SQS Oct 1754. Sy.

Oldis, Sarah. R 14 yrs Mar 1771. Do.

Oldman, Robert. S Apr 1749. L.

Oldridge. *See* Aldridge.

Olford, Hugh. S & T Aug 1718 *Eagle* LC Charles Town Mar 1719. L.

Oliphant, James. S Sep 1733 T Jan 1734 *Caesar* LC Va Jly 1734. M.

Olive, Frances. S s waistcoat Oct T Dec 1736 *Dorsetshire* to Va. M.

Olive, John. S Dec 1766 T Jan 1767 *Tryal*. L.

Olive, William of Devizes. R for Barbados Jun 1699. Wi.

Oliver, Archibald. S Jan T Feb 1724 *Anne* to Carolina. M.

Oliver, Daniel als Jacob. S Apr 1769. De.

Oliver, Evan. SQS & T Sep 1766 *Justitia*. M.

Oliver, Hannah (1741). *See* Courtney. M.

Oliver, Isaac. R for Barbados Aug 1664. L.

Oliver, Isaac. R for Barbados Dec 1667. M.

Oliver, Jacob (1769). *See* Oliver, Daniel. De.

Oliver, John. S Feb T Mar 1730 *Patapsco* LC Annapolis Sep 1730. L.
Oliver, John. S Feb T Apr 1735 *Patapsco* LC Annapolis Oct 1735. M.
Oliver, John. R Lent 1772. Wa.
Oliver, Joseph of Wotton under Edge. R for America Jly 1708. G.
Oliver, Mary. S Feb T Mar 1727 *Rappahannock* to Md. M.
Oliver, Mary. S Apr 1773. L.
Olliver, Nicholas of Burnham. R for Barbados or Jamaica Mar 1698. E.
Oliver, Nicholas of Camberwell. R for Barbados or Jamaica Jun
   1699. Sy.
Oliver, Nicholas. T Sep 1742 *Forward*. K.
Oliver als Osborn, Simon als Samuel. R 14 yrs Mar 1744. So.
Oliver, Thomas. S s at Wolverley Lent 1728. Wo.
Oliver, Thomas. S s horse Summer 1733 R 14 yrs Summer 1734. Nl.
Oliver, Thomas. S Dec 1753-Jan 1754. M.
Oliver, William. SQS Mar 1720, stayed because of infirmity & TB to Md
   Aug 1720. Db.
Olliver, William. S s money Summer 1729. Nl.
Oliver, William. T 14 yrs Dec 1753 *Whiteing*. E.
Oliver, William. S Jun 1754. L.
Oliver, William. S Jun T Sep 1764 *Justitia*. M.
Olley, John. S Norwich Summer 1768. Nf.
Olloway, Isiah. T Apr 1741 *Speedwell* or *Mediterranean*. Ht.
O'Marsh, Catherine, spinster, als wife of James. S 14 yrs Feb-Apr
   1746. M.
O'Marsh, James. S 14 yrs Feb-Apr 1746. M.
O'Marsh, Robert. S Feb-Apr 1746. M.
O'Marsh, Thomas. S Feb-Apr 1746. M.
Ombler, Dorothy of Dunham. SQS s gold & silver Jan 1736. Nt.
Omerton, John. S Apr 1773. L.
O'Neal, Charles. S Apr 1763. L.
O'Neil, Charles of St. Martin in Fields. SW Jan 1773. M.
O'Neil, Cornelius (1771). *See* Neil. M.
O'Neal, Ferdinando. S for perjury Feb T Apr 1739 *Forward* to Va. M.
O'Neal, Henry. S s horse Summer 1751 R 14 yrs Summer 1752. Du.
O'Neale als Bowen, Honor. R for Barbados Jun 1671. L.
O'Niel, James. S Feb T Apr *Ann*. M.
O'Neale, Margaret. S Feb T Mar 1731 *Patapsco* LC Annapolis Jun
   1731. M.
O'Neal, Owen. SQS May T Sep 1751 *Greyhound*. M.
Onesby, Sara. R for Barbados Oct 1673. M.
Oney als Honey, John. S Jan T Feb 1726 *Supply* LC Annapolis May
   1726. M.
Oney, Samuel. T Sep 1730 *Smith*. Ht.
Ong, James. SQS May T Sep 1764 *Justitia*. M.
Onyon, Catherine (1726). *See* Arnold. M.
Onion, Edward. S Aug T Sep 1764 *Justitia*. L.
Onyon, Elizabeth. R Aug 1715 & Dec 1716 T Jan 1717 *Queen
   Elizabeth*. M.
Onion, Henry. LC from *Alexander* Annapolis Sep 1723. X.
Onion, Hester. S & T 14 yrs Jly 1753 *Tryal*. L.
Onion, Thomas. S & T Jly 1753 *Tryal*. L.

Onion, Thomas. S Lent 1763. E.

Onion, William of Huddersfield. SQS Jly 1752. La.

Onions, Joseph. S s dishes at Wednesbury Lent 1757. St.

Onyons, William. R for Barbados Sep 1669. M.

Ooler, James. S Jly T Sep 1764 *Justitia*. M.

Openshaw, John of Blackrod. SQS Jly 1753. La.

Oppenhein, Jacob. S & T Sep 1757 *Thetis*. L.

Orage, Thomas. S s wheat at All Saints, Newmarket, Summer 1773. Ca.

Orum, Benjamin of South Kilworth. R for America Feb 1713. Le.

Oram, John. Rebel T 1685.

Oram, John. S Summer 1768. Wa.

Oram, Samuel. S Feb T Sep 1737 *Pretty Patsy* to Md. M.

Orchard, Abigail wife of Charles. S s gowns Sep T Dec 1736 *Dorsetshire*. M.

Orchard, Christopher. R Jly AT Aug 1685. M.

Orchard, George. R (Norfolk Circ) for Barbados Jly 1675. X.

Orchard, James. S & T Dec 1731 *Forward* to Md or Va. M.

Orchard, James. S Aug 1741. So.

Orchard, John. S May T Jun 1726 *Loyal Margaret* LC Annapolis Oct 1726. M.

Orchard, John. R 14 yrs Mar 1766. So.

Orchard, Sarah. S Jly 1755. Ha.

Orchard, Thomas (1685). *See* Archett.

Orchard, Thomas. S Mar 1725. Wi.

Orchard, Thomas. S Apr 1756. So.

Orchard, Thomas. SQS Apr 1774. M.

Orchard, William. S Mar 1765. Ha.

Ord, Dorothy. S Jan-Jun T 14 yrs Jun 1728 *Elizabeth* LC Potomack Aug 1729. L.

Orde, Elizabeth of Morpeth. SQS s clothing Summer 1771 LC Va from *Lowther & Senhouse* May 1772. Nl.

Ord, Richard (1735). *See* Taylor, Ralph. Nl.

Ord, Robert. R 14 yrs for highway robbery Summer 1730. Du.

Ord, Robert. SQS & T Jly 1773 *Tayloe* to Va. M.

Ordery, Mary (1748). *See* Smith. M.

Orford, Mary. S Jun T Oct 1744 *Susannah*. M.

Organall, William. S & R Lent 1736. Su.

Orgar, Edward. S Lent 1775. E.

Orme, Andrew. S & T Sep 1765 *Justitia*. M.

Orme als Riley, James. TB Aug 1741 T *Shaw* LC Antigua Jun 1742. Db.

Orme, Robert of Burton on Trent. R for America Feb 1673. St.

Ormand, David. S s horse Summer 1766 R 14 yrs Lent 1767. Li.

Ormond, Jane. S s at Newport Summer 1762. Mo.

Ormand, Mary. S City & R Lent 1735. Y.

Ormsbey, Edward. LC from *Dorsetshire* Va Sep 1736. X.

Orocke, William of Ouseburn. R for Barbados Jly 1684. Nl.

Oronsko, Henry. R 14 yrs Mar 1766 TB to Va. De.

Orpwood, John (1766). *See* Hopwood. M.

Orpwood, William of Reading, bargeman. S 14 yrs Summer 1741. Be.

Orr als Cunningham, William. S for highway robbery & R 14 yrs Summer 1773. Nl.

Orrell, John of Wigan, linen weaver. S Summer 1741 R 14 yrs Summer 1742. La.

Orrell, Thomas. R for Barbados Sep 1669. M.

Orrett, George (1766). *See* Aldred. La.

Orrick, Mary wife of John. S Jun 1733 T Jan 1734 *Caesar* LC Va Jly 1734. M.

Orrox, Elizabeth. S & T Sep 1764 *Justitia*. L.

Orton, Johanna. LC from *Forward* Annapolis Dec 1725. X.

Orton, John. T Nov 1725 *Rappahannock* but died on passage. Ht.

Orton als Holton, John. S Jan 1751. M.

Oreton, Thomas of Worcester. R for America Jun 1692. Wo.

Orton, Thomas of Salwarpe. R for America Nov 1694. Wo.

Orton, Thomas the younger. S Mar TB 14 yrs to Va Apr 1773. Le.

Orton, William. R 14 yrs Mar 1744. So.

Osbaldston, Robert. S Feb T Apr 1741 *Speedwell* or *Mediterranean*. M.

Osband, James. SQS Jan TB Apr 1775. So.

Osborne, Ann (1663). *See* Platt. L.

Osborne, Ann of St. James, Colchester. R for Barbados or Jamaica Feb 1684. E.

Osborne, Ann. S & T Apr 1753 *Thames*. L.

Osborn, Anna Maria. S Jan-May T Jun 1738 *Forward* to Md or Va. M.

Osborn, Charles. S Mar 1730. Co.

Osborne als Potter, Elizabeth. R for Barbados Jly 1681. So.

Osborne, Elizabeth (1697). *See* Starre. L.

Osborne, Elizabeth. T Sep 1764 *Justitia*. M.

Osbourne, George. S Jun 1721. M.

Osborn, George. S for perjury at Ipswich Assizes Summer 1744; to stand in pillory at Bury St. Edmunds one hour on Market Day before transportation. Su.

Osborne, George. SQS Bristol Apr 1771. G.

Osborn, George. S s at Holy Trinity, Cambridge, Summer 1775. Ca.

Osborn, Hannah. S Lent 1772. Wa.

Osborne, John of Leicester. R Jly 1679. Le.

Osburn, John. T Oct 1726 *Forward*. Sx.

Osborn, John of Bunwell. S s coat Summer 1728. *Nf.

Osborne, John. T Sep 1730 *Smith*. E.

Osborn, John (1744). *See* Oswald. Nl.

Osborne, John. S Summer 1750. Ca.

Osborne, John Jr. S Lent R 14 yrs Summer 1752. Su.

Osborn, John. T Sep 1758 *Tryal*. E.

Osborne, John of Bristol. R for life Jun 1772 (SP). G.

Osborn, Joseph. S Jan-Feb 1773. M.

Osborne als Chisnell, Martha of Colchester, widow. SQS Apr T Sep 1758 *Tryal*. E.

Osborne, Mary of Ardley, spinster. SQS Jan 1761. E.

Osborn, Moses. Rebel T 1685.

Osborn, Philip. S s lead at Melchborne Summer 1774. Bd.

Osborne, Richard. R for Barbados or Jamaica Feb 1686. L.

Osborn, Sarah. S Sep-Oct T Dec 1752 *Greyhound*. M.

Osborn, Simon als Samuel (1744). *See* Oliver. So.

Osborne, Thomas. R for America Feb 1692. Nt.

Osburn, Thomas. S s at Newport Lent 1764. Sh.

Osborne, Thomas (1774). *See* Perkins. Wa.

Osborn, Walter. Rebel T 1685.

Osborne, William. S Feb-Apr T May 1751 *Tryal*. M.

Osborn, William. S Feb T Apr 1770 *New Trial*. L.

Osborne, William. SQS Bristol Apr 1771. G.

Osborne, William Jr. S & R Summer T Sep 1773. Wa.

Osgood, James. R 14 yrs Mar 1752. So.

Osman, Alice. R 14 yrs Mar TB to Va Apr 1746. Wi.

Osman, Elizabeth. S s at Burford Lent 1758. O.

Osman, John of Southwick. R for Barbados Feb 1701. Ha.

Osmond, Anne. TB to Va from QS 1743. De.

Osmond, Edward of Crediton, blacksmith. R for Barbados Jly 1672. De.

Osmond, Edward. R 14 yrs Apr 1747. De.

Osmonds, John. T May 1755 *Rose*. Sy.

Osmore, Sarah wife of Richard of St. Olave, Southwark. R for Barbados Jly 1679. Sy.

Ostler, John (1758). *See* Merrit. Be.

Osler, Mary. S Mar 1766. Do.

Osler, William. S Mar 1762. So.

Ostrow, William. S Apr-May T May 1741 *Catherine & Elizabeth* to Md. M.

Oswald als Osborn, John. S City for bigamy Summer 1744. Nl.

Othello (1772). *See* Burrell, George. Wi.

Othen, Samuel. S Jan-Feb 1775. M.

Othy, Jane. AT Summer 1764. Du.

Otridge. *See* Oatridge.

Otter, Francis. S Sep-Oct 1748 T Jan 1749 *Laura*. M.

Otter, John. SQS Jan 1665 for attending unlawful religious meeting and refusing to give his abode saying his habitation was with God. M.

Otter, William. S Summer 1765. Nf.

Ottey, Abell. S Oct 1741 T Feb 1742 *Industry*. L.

Ottley, Susannah. R for pulling down mills Summer 1772. E.

Oulsden, John. R for Barbados Jly 1675. M.

Outwood, Richard. S s hats Sep T Nov 1759 *Phoenix*. M.

Over, Henry. S Jly 1729. Ha.

Over, Humphry. R 14 yrs Jly 1739. Ha.

Over, John of Fordingbridge. R for Barbados Jly 1672. Ha.

Overbury, Robert. S Apr 1746. L.

Overan, John. R Summer 1773. Sy.

Overen als Overend, Stephen. S Lent 1721 T Oct 1723 *Forward* from London. Y.

Overhill, John (1699). *See* Owell. E.

Overington, Thomas. T Apr 1733 *Patapsco*. Sx.

Overs, Sarah. S Sep 1737 T Jan 1738 *Dorsetshire* to Va. M.

Overton als Everton, Job. S s mare Lent R 14 yrs Summer 1757. Wa.

Overton als Tucker, John. R for Barbados Jan 1693. M.

Overton, John. SQS Sep T Dec 1771 *Justitia*. M.

Overton, John als William. S s at Christchurch Summer 1774. Mo.

Overton, Mathew. S s at Holwell Summer 1766. O.

Overton, Thomas. S Jan T Feb 1742 *Industry* to Md. M.

Overton, Thomas. S s sheep Lent R 14 yrs Summer 1766. Wa.

Overton, William. S for killing calf Summer 1750. Nf.

Ovins, Gilbert. T for life Apr 1766 *Ann.* Sy.

Ovins als O'Brien, Mary. T Jan 1766 *Tryal.* M.

Ovis, William. S Jly T Oct 1741 *Sea Horse* to Va. M.

Owell als Overhill, John of Rayleigh. R for Barbados or Jamaica Jun 1699. E.

Owen, Benjamin. S Sep T Dec 1767 *Neptune.* M.

Owen, Catherine (1730). *See* Lewer. L.

Owen, David. R for Barbados or Jamaica Dec 1698. L.

Owen, Edward. S Lent 1774. K.

Owen, Elizabeth of St. Olave, Southwark. R for Barbados or Jamaica Jly 1674. Sy.

Owen, Elizabeth. R for Barbados Dec 1681. L.

Owen, Elizabeth. S Apr T May 1719 *Margaret*; sold to Edward Smith Md Aug 1719. L.

Owen, Elizabeth. S Jan-Apr 1748. M.

Owen als Belford, Elizabeth of St. Saviour, Southwark, spinster. SQS Jan T Apr 1753 *Thames.* Sy.

Owen als Harrison, Elizabeth of Culcheth, spinster. SQS May 1764. La.

Owen, George. S s silver Jan-May T Jun 1738 *Forward* to Md or Va. M.

Owen, Henry. R for Barbados Aug 1664. M.

Owen, Henry. S May T Jly 1723 *Alexander* LC Annapolis Sep 1723. L.

Owen, Hugh. S Jly 1763. M.

Owen, James. S Feb T 14 yrs Apr 1732 *Patapsco* LC Annapolis Oct 1732. L.

Owen, Jane. T Jun 1740 *Essex.* Sy.

Owen, Jane wife of John. S Oct 1766 T Jan 1767 *Tryal.* M.

Owen, Jane, spinster. R s horsehair at Whittington Lent 1769. Wo.

Owen, John. S & T Oct 1729 *Forward* but died on passage. M.

Owen, John. S & T Oct 1732 *Caesar* to Va. M.

Owen, John. S & T Dec 1734 *Caesar* but died on passage. L.

Owen, John, als Jones, Owen. S Summer 1746 R 14 yrs Lent 1747. Sh.

Owen, John of Worsley, weaver. SQS May 1755. La.

Owen, John. S Feb T May 1767 *Thornton.* L.

Owen als Gardner, Margaret. S Feb T 14 yrs Apr 1735 *Patapsco* LC Annapolis Oct 1735. L.

Owen, Mary. S & T Oct 1722 *Forward* LC Annapolis Jun 1723. M.

Owen, Mary. S Jun-Dec 1745. M.

Owen, Mary. S Summer 1764. Sh.

Owen, Peter. S Lent R for life Summer 1747. Wo.

Owen, Richard. S for highway robbery Lent R 14 yrs Summer 1743. Wo.

Owen, Robert of St. Ann, Westminster. SW Oct 1774. M.

Owen, Samuel. S Jan 1745. L.

Owen, Stephen of Hellingly. R for Barbados or Jamaica Mar 1698. Sx.

Owen, Susan. S s at Talkmon Lent 1729. Sh.

Owen, Thomas. R for Barbados Jun 1665. M.

Owen, Thomas. S Feb T Mar 1729 *Patapsco* LC Annapolis Dec 1729. L.

Owen als Freeman, Thomas. S Jun 1739. L.

Owen, Thomas. S Lent TB May 1755. G.

Owen, Thomas. S s at Brampton Bryan Summer 1762. He.

Owen, Thomas. S Mar TB to Va Apr 1766. Le.

Owen, William. R 14 yrs s naval stores Lent T May 1750 *Lichfield*. K.

Owen, William. T Dec 1752 *Greyhound*. M.

Owen, William. S s cow at Tickhill & R 14 yrs Lent 1770. Y.

Owens, Hannah. S Oct 1744-Jan 1745. M.

Owens, James of Wigmore. R for America Jly 1678. He.

Owens, James of Titley. R for America Feb 1684. He.

Owens, Michael. S Dec 1737. L.

Owens, Susanna. S s at Kinnersley Lent 1760. He.

Owens, William. S & T Jly 1753 *Tryal*. M.

Owens, William. S Feb 1774. L.

Owle, William. S s at Stourbridge Lent 1726. Wo.

Owles, Joseph. S s sheep Lent R 14 yrs Summer 1768. Wo.

Owram, James als John. S City Lent 1765. Y.

Owsman, Moses. S Oct T 14 yrs Dec 1724 *Rappahannock*. L.

Oxborough, Elizabeth. R for Barbados or Jamaica Dec 1716. L.

Oxden, Richard. R Jly 1686. M.

Oxen, William. SQS Feb T Apr 1766 *Ann*. M.

Oxford, John. S Jan-Jun T Jun 1728 *Elizabeth* LC Potomack Aug 1729. M.

Oxley, Anthony. S Summer 1765 R 14 yrs Lent TB Apr 1766. Db.

Oxley, James. T Oct 1720 *Gilbert*. Sx.

Oxley als Williams, Margaret. S Feb T Mar 1731 *Patapsco* LC Annapolis Jun 1731. M.

Oxley, Thomas. S Apr-May T May 1741 *Catherine & Elizabeth* to Md. M.

Oxtoby, William. R 14 yrs Jly 1775. M.

Oyer, James. T May 1750 *Lichfield*. K.

Oyley als Dyley, Marik. S & T Jan 1769 *Thornton*. L.

Oyston, Joseph. S s horse Summer 1745 R 14 yrs Summer 1746. Du.

P

Paice, Ashwood. SQS Apr T May 1755 *Rose*. M.

Payce, James. S Nov T Dec 1752 *Greyhound*. L.

Paice, John. T Apr 1741 *Speedwell* or *Mediterranean*. E.

Pace als Gould, Richard. T Apr 1731 *Bennett*. E.

Pace, Robert (1748). *See* Price. L.

Pacey, Edward of Helpingham. R for America Jly 1678. Li.

Pacey, Joseph. S s sheep Summer 1752 R 14 yrs Lent 1753. Nt.

Pack, John. R for America Feb 1692. Wa.

Pack, John. R 14 yrs Mar 1767. Do.

Packenden, Robert. S Lent R for Barbados Apr 1663. Sx.

Packer, Elizabeth. S Jan-Feb 1775. M.

Packer, James. S Jun-Dec 1738 T Jan 1739 *Dorsetshire* to Va. M.

Packer, John. TB Oct 1764. Db.

Packer, William. S Aug TB to Va Oct 1764. Wi.

Packet, Elizabeth. S Lent 1760. Bd.

Padderson, John. S Lent 1737. Ca.

Paddison als Patrickson, Thomas. R 14 yrs Summer 1732 AT Summer 1740. Cu.

Paddison, William. S s sheep Lent R 14 yrs Summer 1747. Li.

Paddock, Elizabeth. R 14 yrs Aug 1754. So.

Paddock, Richard. S Lent 1735 T Feb 1739 *(sic)*. Bd.

Paddon, Anthony of East Ogwell, mason. R for Barbados Jly 1667. De.

Pady, Thomas. S Summer 1749. E.

Pafford als Reynold, Thomas. R for Barbados or Jamaica Mar 1688. L.

Pagans, Thomas. S Summer 1749. Sy.

Page, Abraham of Grantchester. S s ducks Lent 1741. *Ca.

Page, Adam. S Aug 1720. So.

Page, Ann wife of William of Bridgenorth, "corvisor". S Summer 1733. Sh.

Page, Ann, als Willis, Mary. S Jly-Dec 1747. M.

Page, Ann. S & T Sep 1767 *Justitia*. L.

Page, Edward. R for Barbados Feb 1672. M.

Page, Edward. T Apr 1735 *Patapsco*. Sy.

Page, Elias. S for assault with intent to rob Summer 1741. Sh.

Page, Elizabeth. R for Barbados Sep 1670. L.

Page, Elizabeth (1727). *See* Stafford. Sy.

Page, Elizabeth. S & T Oct 1732 *Caesar* to Va. M.

Page, Grace. S Jly T Aug 1721 *Prince Royal* LC Va Nov 1723. M.

Page, Henry. R Oct TB Nov 1662. L.

Page, Henry. S Summer 1746. K.

Page, Henry of St. Paul, Covent Garden. SW Jly 1773. M.

Page, James (1739). *See* Pain. L.

Page, Jane. S Oct 1756. L.

Page, John. R Jly 1686. M.

Page, John. S & T Jan 1722 *Gilbert* LC Annapolis Jly 1722. M.

Page, John. S s jewellery Jan T Jun 1738 *Forward* to Md or Va. M.

Page, John. S Lent 1743. Nf.

Page, John. S Apr-May 1754. M.
Page, John. S Feb-Apr T Jun 1756 *Lyon*. M.
Page, John. S s sow Lent 1763. Nf.
Page, John. S Sep T for life Oct 1768 *Justitia*. L.
Page als Lennon, John. S Mar 1772. Ha.
Page, John. S Lent T Apr 1774. No.
Page, Jonathan. T Jly 1724 *Robert* LC Annapolis Jun 1725. K.
Page, Joseph. S Feb T May 1719 *Margaret*; sold to John Buckingham
    Md Aug 1719. L.
Page, Joseph. SQS & T Sep 1767 *Justitia*. Ht.
Page, Joshua. T Sep 1742 *Forward*. E.
Page, Judith. S Oct-Dec 1750. M.
Page, Lucas of Romford. R for Barbados or Jamaica Feb 1696. E.
Page, Margaret. S Oct T Nov 1728 *Forward* LC Rappahannock Jun
    1729. M.
Page, Mark. S Feb T Jun 1738 *Forward* to Md or Va. M.
Page, Mary. S & T 14 yrs Sep 1742 *Forward*. L.
Page, Mary. S Jly T Nov 1762 *Prince William*. M.
Page, Matthew. S Mar 1767. Do.
Page, Richard. R for Barbados Jun 1663. M.
Page, Richard. R for Barbados Jan 1693. M.
Page als Jenkins, Richard. PT Dec 1697. M.
Page, Richard. T Apr 1768 *Thornton*. K.
Page, Robert. S Oct T Nov 1725 *Rappahannock* LC Rappahannock Apr
    1726. L.
Page, Samuel. PT Apr R Jly 1675. M.
Page, Sarah. T Jly 1723 *Alexander* but died on passage. E.
Page, Sarah. S Feb T Mar 1731 *Patapsco* LC Annapolis Jun 1731. M.
Page, Sarah wife of James. S Summer 1766. No.
Page, Sarah. R & T Jly 1770 *Scarsdale*. M.
Page, Thomas. T Jan 1738 *Dorsetshire*. K.
Page, Thomas. S Apr-May T May 1744 *Justitia*. M.
Page, Thomas. T 14 yrs Apr 1768 *Thornton*. Sx.
Page, Thomas. R & T 14 yrs Jly 1772 *Tayloe*. M.
Page, William. Rebel T 1685.
Page, William. S & T Dec 1724 *Rappahannock*. L.
Page, William. S & T Oct 1729 *Forward* but died on passage. M.
Page, William. R 14 yrs Mar TB to Va Apr 1766. Wi.
Page, William. S s watch at Aspley Guise Summer 1773. Bd.
Pagelas, Elizabeth. S Sep T Dec 1770 *Justitia*. M.
Pagett, Edward. S Jly 1775. L.
Pagitt, Elizabeth. T Oct 1722 *Forward*. Ht.
Paget, Henry. R 14 yrs Aug TB to Va Oct 1764. Wi.
Pagett, John. S for highway robbery Lent 1757 R 14 yrs Lent 1760. St.
Pagett, John. S s sheep & R 14 yrs Summer 1768 T Jan 1769. No.
Pagett als Curtis, Martha. S Oct T Nov 1728 *Forward* LC Rappahannock
    Jun 1729. L.
Pagram, Mary. S Feb-Apr 1746. M.
Paice. *See* Pace.
Pail als Parsons, William. S s pig Lent 1730. Wo.
Pain. *See* Payne.

Painter, Edward. S Nov T Dec 1753 *Whiteing*. L.

Painter, George. S Jan T Apr 1741 *Speedwell* or *Mediterranean* to Md. M.

Painter, James. S for highway robbery at Kinver Lent R 14 yrs Summer 1744. St.

Painter, John (1764). *See* Pinchin. M.

Painter, John. S s at Cheltenham Lent 1764. G.

Painter, Sarah. S & T Apr 1759 *Thetis*. L.

Painter, Stephen of Mewan. R for Barbados Jly 1684. Co.

Painter, Thomas. S & T Apr 1759 *Thetis*. L.

Painter, Thomas. S s sheep & R Lent 1774. O.

Painter, William. R for Barbados or Jamaica May 1697. L.

Peisley, Thomas (1725). *See* Wilks. M.

Pakes, William. S Summer T Dec 1737 *Dorsetshire*. Bu.

Pales, Edward. T Jly 1723 *Alexander* LC Annapolis Sep 1723. Bu.

Palfreman, Thomas. R for America Mar 1697. Db.

Palfrey als Parfrey, Jonathan of Huntspill. R for Barbados Jly 1698. So.

Palfry, Robert Simons. S Lent 1749. Nf.

Pallatt, Elizabeth. LC from *Forward* Rappahannock Jun 1729. X.

Pallett, William (1774). *See* Aylett. Ht.

Palley, John. S Aug T Oct 1726 *Forward*. L.

Pallister, Richard. R Summer 1732. Y.

Pallister, William. R for life Jan 1757. M.

Palmer, Alice. S May T Jun 1764 *Dolphin*. L.

Palmer, Andrew. Rebel T 1685.

Palmer, Ann (1727). *See* Rook. M.

Palmer als Hincks, Ann. S Feb T 14 yrs Apr 1732 *Patapsco* LC Annapolis Oct 1732. M.

Palmer, Ann. S Apr 1748. L.

Palmer, Benjamin of Seavington St. Michael, husbandman. R for Barbados Jun 1666. So.

Palmer, Bridget. S Summer 1761. K.

Palmer, Catherine. S Feb T Mar 1758 *Dragon*. M.

Palmer, Catherine. S s sheep & R 14 yrs Lent T Sep 1768. Li.

Palmer, Elizabeth. S Dec 1743 T Feb 1744 *Neptune* to Md. M.

Palmer, Elizabeth. S May-Jly 1748. M.

Palmer, Frances, spinster. S s at Burford Summer 1769. O.

Palmer, George. S Mar 1756. Ha.

Palmer, Hannah (1732). *See* Wallis. M.

Palmer, Henry. S Jan-Feb 1773. M.

Palmer, Hester wife of John. S Jly T Sep 1757 *Thetis*. M.

Palmer, James. S Feb T Apr 1742 *Bond* to Potomack. M.

Palmer, James. S Nov T Dec 1763 *Neptune*. L.

Palmer, Jane. AT Summer 1742. Wo.

Palmer, Joan. R for Barbados Sep 1672. L.

Palmer, John of Olcester. R for America Jly 1677. Wa.

Palmer, John (2). Rebels T 1685.

Palmer, John of West Tilbury. R for Barbados or Jamaica Mar 1688. E.

Palmer, John. S & T Oct 1732 *Caesar*. L.

Palmer, John. S Apr 1734. So.

Palmer, John. SQS Jly TB to Md Nov 1738. So.

Palmer, John. S Summer 1741 R 14 yrs Lent 1742. Le.

Palmer, John. S Lent 1764. Nt.

Palmer, John. S Oct 1765 T Jan 1766 *Tryal*. L.

Palmer, Lewis of Hemel Hempstead. R for Barbados or Jamaica Jly 1705. Ht.

Palmer, Mary. S & T Oct 1729 *Forward* LC Va Jun 1730. L.

Palmer, Mary. S Dec 1755 T Jan 1756 *Greyhound*. L.

Palmer, Mary. SQS Dec 1756. M.

Palmer, Nicholas. Rebel T 1685.

Palmer, Philip. S Apr 1742. So.

Palmer, Rachael. S Jan T Feb 1744 *Neptune*. L.

Palmer, Rebecca. S Lent TB Apr T Aug 1757 *Lux*. Db.

Parmer, Robert. R 14 yrs Jly 1734. Ha.

Palmer, Sarah. S Apr T 14 yrs May 1718. L.

Palmer, Sarah. S May T Jun 1756 *Lyon*. L.

Palmer, Thomas of Wickford. R for Barbados or Jamaica Jly 1702. E.

Palmer, Thomas. LC from *Sukey* Annapolis Sep 1725. X.

Palmer, Thomas. S Mar TB to Va Sep 1727. Le.

Palmer, Thomas. S Aug 1739. Do.

Palmer, Thomas, an old convict. S s sheep Summer 1748 R 14 yrs Lent 1749. Nf.

Palmer, Thomas. S Apr T May 1750 *Lichfield*. M.

Palmer, Thomas. S Aug 1750. So.

Palmer als Eldridge, Thomas. S Summer 1769 R 14 yrs Lent 1770. O.

Palmer, Thomas. R Mar 1775 (SP). Su.

Palmer, Thomas. S s sheep at Watlington & R Lent 1775. Nf.

Palmer, William of Kilsby. R for America Jly 1674. No.

Palmer, William of Lichfield. S Lent 1720. St.

Palmer, William. SQS Jan 1732. So.

Palmer, William. T Jan 1734 *Caesar* LC Va Jly 1734. E.

Palmer, William. S Sep-Oct T Dec 1753 *Whiteing*. M.

Palmer, William. S Summer 1757. Nf.

Palmer, William. SQS May 1774. M.

Palmerstone, Henry. S & T Sep 1765 *Justitia*. M.

Palser als Whitmore, John. S s at Wotton under Edge Lent 1770. G.

Palser, Thomas. S s at Wotton under Edge Lent TB Apr 1756. G.

Palson. *See* Paulson.

Panckhurst, Thomas. T Apr 1753 *Thames*. K.

Pangriffiths, Thomas James. R s sheep Jly T Oct 1768 *Justitia*. M.

Panker, Joseph of Bermondsey. SQS Jan 1755. Sy.

Panks, Sarah. R 14 yrs for Carolina Apr TB May 1718. L.

Pannery, Honor. S May T Jun 1738 *Forward*. L.

Pannifer, William. S Summer 1756. Su.

Pant, Christopher. S Summer 1760 TB Mar 1761. Ca.

Pantall, Thomas. S Summer 1748 R 14 yrs Lent 1749. He.

Panting, Richard. S s billet wood at Shipton Summer 1772. O.

Pantree, John. S Feb T 14 yrs Mar 1730 *Patapsco* LC Annapolis Sep 1730. M.

Pantry, Robert. S Lent 1761. Sy.

Pape, Robert. S Oct T Dec 1767 *Neptune*. M.

Papper, James. S for rape Summer 1752 R 14 yrs Lent 1753. Bd.

Papper, Sampson. R 14 yrs Mar 1738. De.

Papps, Gideon. S Jly TB Aug 1754. Wi.

Papworth, William of Reach. R for America Feb 1695. Ca.

Paradice, Francis Jr. S Jly 1766 TB to Va Apr 1767. Wi.

Paramour, Phoebe. T May 1751 *Tryal*. K.

Parrimore, William of Lambeth. S Lent T May 1719 *Margaret* LC Md May 1720; sold to John Gaskin. Sy.

Pardoe, Elizabeth. S & T 14 yrs Oct 1732 *Caesar*. L.

Pardo, Mary. S Jan 1746. L.

Pardon, Catherine. SQS Feb T Apr 1771 *Thornton*. M.

Parden, John. LC from *Elizabeth* Potomack Aug 1729. X.

Pardon, Sarah. S Feb T Mar 1760 *Friendship*. M.

Pardon, Thomas of Bermondsey. SQS Jan T Apr 1753 *Thames*. Sy.

Parfect, Robert. S May T Sep 1766 *Justitia*. M.

Parfett, Christopher. T Apr 1739 *Forward*. Sy.

Parfit, Joanna. SQS Jan TB Apr 1775. So.

Parfitt, Richard. SQS Apr 1732. So.

Parford, William. S Apr 1746. L.

Parfrey, Jonathan (1698). *See* Palfrey. So.

Pargiter, William. S s hog Summer T Aug 1752 *Tryal*. Bu.

Parris, Charles. PT Jly 1680. M.

Paris, Daniel. S & T Sep 1755 *Tryal*. L.

Paris, Jane. S Aug T Sep 1725 *Forward* to Md. M.

Parris, John. S Jan T Apr 1762 *Dolphin*. L.

Parris, John. S & T Dec 1771 *Justitia*. L.

Paris, Mary of Rotherhithe, spinster. SQS & T Jan 1766 *Tryal*. Sy.

Paris, Richard. T Apr 1734 *Patapsco*. K.

Paris, Robert. SW & T Apr 1769 *Tryal*. M.

Parish, Alexander, aged 57, black hair, tallow chandler. S & T Oct 1720 *Gilbert* LC Annapolis May 1721. M.

Parish, Benjamin. S Summer 1756. Bu.

Parish, George. S May-Jly 1749. M.

Parish, James of St. Martin in Fields. SW Apr 1774. M.

Parish, Jane. LC from *Forward* Annapolis Dec 1725. X.

Parish, John. S Lent 1766 R for life Lent 1767. Nf.

Parish, Thomas (1738). *See* Sickle. Ca.

Parish, Thomas of St. Ann, Westminster. SW Apr 1773. M.

Parish, William of St. Osyth. R for Barbados or Jamaica Jun 1675 & Jly 1677. E.

Parke, John. R for Barbados Dec 1681. L.

Parke, Peter (1663). *See* Preston. M.

Parke, Richard. S s mare at Shendall Summer 1767 R 14 yrs Summer 1768. Y.

Parke, Simpson. S Lent 1755. K.

Parke, Thomas (1713). *See* Poits. Be.

Park, William. S Mar 1764. So.

Parker, Abraham of York Castle. R for Barbados Feb 1673. Y.

Parker als Parkin, Amos of Westleigh, mariner. R for Barbados Jly 1667. De.

Parker, Andrew. T Nov 1741 *Sea Horse*. E.

Parker, Andrew. S City Lent 1755. Y.

Parker, Ann (1753). *See* Stewart. La.

Parker, Ann. S Apr 1760. M.
Parker, Ann wife of Henry. S 14 yrs for receiving Summer 1775. Wa.
Parker, Augustine of Cuxton. R for Barbados or Jamaica Jun 1699. K.
Parker, Austin. S s cheeses at Sutton Lent 1750. Be.
Parker, Baldwin. Rebel T 1685.
Parker, Benjamin. S Lent 1736. Su.
Parker, Benjamin. S s ducks at Penkridge Lent 1753. St.
Parker, Catherine. S May T Sep 1766 *Justitia*. M.
Parker, Charles. R for Barbados May 1665. X.
Parker, Charles. PT Jan 1677. M.
Parker, Charles. S Mar 1726. De.
Parker, Charles of Stockport, Cheshire. S s handkerchiefs & R 14 yrs
    Lent 1769. La.
Parker, Edward. T Oct 1738 *Genoa*. Sx.
Parker, Elizabeth. S & T Jan 1722 *Gilbert* LC Annapolis Jly 1722. L.
Parker, Elizabeth. S Mar 1730. Ha.
Parker, Elizabeth. S Apr 1760. M.
Parker, Francis. T 14 yrs Oct 1768 *Justitia*. K.
Parker, George. S Summer 1740. Y.
Parker, Grace. S Jly T Sep 1718 *Eagle* LC Charles Town Mar 1719. L.
Parker, Hannah. S & T Sep 1766 *Justitia*. M.
Parker, Henry. S s fowls at Witney Summer 1748. O.
Parker, James. R for Barbados Mar 1677. L.
Parker, James. Rebel T 1685.
Parker, James. S for perjury Aug 1759. Co.
Parker, John. R for Barbados May 1665. X.
Parker, John of Harewood. R for America Jly 1699. He.
Parker, John. S Lent T Oct 1723 *Forward* from London. Y.
Parker, John. Died on passage in *Alexander* 1723. X.
Parker, John. Died on passage in *Rappahannock* 1726. X.
Parker, John. S Jan-Jun T Jun 1728 *Elizabeth* to Md or Va. M.
Parker, John. T Jan 1734 *Caesar* LC Va Jly 1734. Sy.
Parker, John. AT Lent 1735. St.
Parker, John. S s shirts Apr T Dec 1735 *John* LC Annapolis Sep
    1736. M.
Parker, John of Hill Deverill. S Mar TB to Va Apr 1740. Wi.
Parker, John. S Mar TB to Va Apr 1741. Wi.
Parker, John. S Lent R 14 yrs Summer 1749. No.
Parker, John. S s wine at Woolhampton Lent 1759. Be.
Parker, John. S Feb T Mar 1764 *Tryal*. M.
Parker, John. R 14 yrs Summer 1766. Li.
Parker, John. S Lent R 14 yrs Summer 1766. Wa.
Parker, John. SQS May T Aug 1769 *Douglas*. M.
Parker, John. S Summer 1773. Db.
Parker, Jonathan. S Sep 1765 T Jan 1766 *Tryal*. M.
Parker, Jonathan of Ratcliffe upon Soar. SQS s cloth Jly 1766. Nt.
Parker, Joseph. S Dec 1737 T Jan 1738 *Dorsetshire*. L.
Parker, Joseph. S Jan T Mar 1750 *Tryal*. L.
Parker, Joseph. S Oct T Dec 1767 *Neptune*. L.
Parker, Joseph. S s wooden hoops at Dudley Summer 1774. Wo.
Parker, Josiah. SQS & TB Mar 1736. G.

Parker, Margaret. S s at Burford Lent 1751. O.
Parker, Martha. R for Barbados Oct 1673. L.
Parker, Martha. PT for shoplifting Summer 1717. Wo.
Parker, Martha. S s at Stone Lent 1723. St.
Parker, Mary, widow. R for Barbados Jly 1674. L.
Parker, Mary. R for America Aug 1702. L.
Parker, Mary. S Jan T Feb 1724 *Anne*. L.
Parker, Mary. S Lent 1729. Be.
Parker, Mary. T Oct 1729 *Forward*. Sy.
Parker, Mary. S Oct-Dec 1750. M.
Parker, Mary of Great Dunmow, spinster. SQS Jly T Sep 1766
    Justitia. E.
Parker, Mary. S s at St. Mary, Stafford, Lent 1772. St.
Parker, Michael. S s at Wakefield & R Lent 1774. Y.
Parker, Ralph of Battersea. R for Barbados Jly 1679. Sy.
Parker, Richard. Rebel T 1685.
Parker, Richard. S Sep T Oct 1750 *Rachael*. L.
Parker, Richard (1753). *See* Bugg. Li.
Parker, Robert. S Oct T Dec 1770 *Justitia*. M.
Parker, Robert. S Apr-May T Jly 1771 *Scarsdale*. M.
Parker, Ruth. S s candlesticks & T May 1736 *Patapsco* to Md. M.
Parker, Samuel. S s horse Lent R 14 yrs Summer TB Dec 1733. Nt.
Parker, Samuel. S Apr 1748. L.
Parker, Sarah. S & R Lent 1774. O.
Parker, Stephen of Yeave. R for America Nov 1694. G.
Parker, Stephen. T Oct 1722 *Forward* LC Md Jun 1723. Ht.
Parker, Susanna. S Jan T Mar 1750 *Tryal*. L.
Parker, Thomas. R for Jamaica Jan 1663. M.
Parker, Thomas. T Apr 1725 *Sukey* but died on passage. Sx.
Parker als Knight, Thomas. T Dec 1736 *Dorsetshire*. E.
Parker, Thomas. R 14 yrs Summer 1747. Y.
Parker, Thomas. S Summer 1748 R 14 yrs Lent 1749. Be.
Parker, Thomas. S s at Stone Summer 1759. St.
Parker, Thomas. TB Sep 1759. Y.
Parker, Thomas. S s mare at Stokesley & R for life Lent 1769. Y.
Parker, Thomas (1772). *See* Ward. M.
Parker, William. R for Va Oct 1670. O.
Parker, William. Rebel T 1685.
Parker, William of Corscombe. R for Barbados Jly 1693. Do.
Parker, William of Yeave. R for America Nov 1694. G.
Parker, William of Albrighton. S Summer 1720 escaped Lent 1721. Sh.
Parker, William. S Jun-Dec 1738 T Jan 1739 *Dorsetshire* to Va. M.
Parker, William. S Dec 1756. M.
Parker, William. R 14 yrs Mar 1758. De.
Parker, William. S for perjury Lent R 14 yrs Summer 1758. Li.
Parker, William. R 14 yrs s sheep Summer 1766. Wa.
Parker, William. S s handkerchief at St. Dunstan in East Dec 1768 T
    Jan 1769 *Thornton*. L.
Parker, William. S Sep-Oct 1772. M.
Parker, William. S Jly 1773. L.
Parker, William (1774). *See* Blaker. Sx.

Parkes, Ann. S Apr 1756. So.

Parks, Edward. S Feb T Mar 1729 *Patapsco* LC Annapolis Dec 1729. L.

Parkes, George. S Lent 1764. Wa.

Parkes, Giles. S Jly 1774. L.

Parkes, Isaac. S s iron bars at Old Swinford Lent 1753. St.

Parkes, James. S s iron at Kingswinford Lent 1729. St.

Parks, James. S Jan-May T Jun 1738 *Forward* to Md or Va. M.

Parks, Joane of Rowley Regis. R for America Jly 1679. St.

Parks, John. S Summer 1737 R 14 yrs Summer 1738. Wa.

Parkes, John. S s at Mavesyn Ridware Lent 1744. St.

Parkes, John. S s at Derby Summer 1764. Db.

Parkes, Joseph. S Summer 1772. Wa.

Parks, Sampson. T May 1755 *Rose*. K.

Parkes, Samuel. S Summer 1745 R 14 yrs Lent 1746. St.

Parkes, Thomas. R for America Jly 1708. Li.

Parks, William. S Summer 1749 R 14 yrs Lent 1750. St.

Parkhouse als Douglas, Isabella. S & T Sep 1764 *Justitia*. M.

Parkhouse, Thomas. R 14 yrs Jly 1752. De.

Parkhurst, James. T 14 yrs Apr 1771 *Thornton*. Sx.

Parkin, Amos (1667). *See* Parker. De.

Parkin, Edward of Hertford, tailor, a Quaker. SQS for Barbados 1664 R for plantations Jly 1665. Ht.

Parkins. *See* Perkins.

Parkinson als Goodwell, Anne. R Sep 1682. M.

Parkinson, Benjamin. S for highway robbery & R 14 yrs Summer 1768; found at large at St. Lawrence, York, & R for life Lent 1770. Y.

Parkinson, David Jr. AT Summer 1758. Y.

Parkinson, James. S Nov T Dec 1753 *Whiteing*. L.

Parkinson, John of Warrington. SQS Oct 1749. La.

Parkinson, Mary wife of Thomas. S 14 yrs for receiving Summer 1758 but later pardoned. Du.

Parkway als Wooten, Robert. PT to Barbados Jan 1694. M.

Parlby, Thomas. S Norwich Summer TB Sep 1758. Nf.

Parley, Daniel. SQS Jly 1755. Db.

Parlour, John. S Summer 1749 R 14 yrs Lent 1750. He.

Parlow, Edward. R Jly AT Aug 1685. M.

Parlo, James. S s sheep & R 14 yrs Summer 1772. He.

Parlow, Thomas. R Jly AT Aug 1685. M.

Parnaby als Fenwick, John of Bedale. SQS Northallerton Jly 1742. Y.

Purnell, Ann. R 14 yrs Apr 1770. So.

Parnell, Elizabeth. S Lent T May 1752 *Lichfield*. Sy.

Parnell, Nurse. S May-Jly 1773. M.

Parnell, Richard. S s at Bromsgrove Lent 1729. Wo.

Parnel, Robert. S s sheep Lent R 14 yrs Summer 1742. No.

Parnell, Robert. S Norwich for being at large after sentence of transportation Summer 1762 TB Oct 1763. Nf.

Purnell, Samuel. S Dec 1766 TB to Va Apr 1767. Wi.

Parnell, Stephen. S Mar 1741. Ha.

Parquot, Frances. S Feb 1719. M.

Parr, Daniel. R for America Jly 1687. Wa.

Parr, John of Reading. R for America Nov 1694. Be.

Parr, John. SQS Apr T Jly 1771 *Scarsdale*. M.

Parr, Peter of Warrington, weaver. SQS Oct 1764. S Lent R for life Summer 1767 for returning from transportation. La.

Parr, Thomas. R for Jamaica Aug 1661. M.

Parr, Thomas. S Lent 1763. K.

Parr, William (2). R for America Jly 1687. No.

Parr, William of Salford, printer, SQS Aug 1760. La.

Parris. *See* Paris.

Parratt, Adam. R for Barbados Dec 1667. M.

Parrett, Alice (1664). *See* Turralll L.

Parrott, Ann (1738). *See* Griffiths. M.

Parrott, Charles. S Sep 1737 T Jan 1738 *Dorsetshire* to Va. M.

Parrott, Edward. S May T Jly 1722 *Alexander* to Nevis or Jamaica. M.

Parrott, Elizabeth. S Apr T May 1752 *Lichfield*. L.

Parrott, Gawin of Brampton, yeoman. R for Barbados Jly 1683. Cu.

Perrott, Jacob. S Mar 1749. Co.

Parrott, John. S s shirts Apr T Dec 1735 *John* LC Annapolis Sep 1736. M.

Perrot, John. R for life Jly 1771 TB to Va Apr 1772. Wi.

Perrot, John. S Oct T Dec 1771 *Justitia*. L.

Parrott, John Jr. T 14 yrs Dec 1771 *Justitia*. Sy.

Parrott, Joshua of Kensworth. R for Barbados or Jamaica Jly 1715. Ht.

Parrott, Leonard. S Lent TB May 1745. Y.

Perrott, Roger. T May 1767 *Thornton*. K.

Parrott, Thomas. S Oct T Nov 1728 *Forward* but died on passage. M.

Parrot, Thomas. T Jan 1734 *Caesar*. Bu.

Parrott, Thomas. S Summer 1759 R 14 yrs Lent 1760. Li.

Perrott, William. S Dec 1768 T Jan 1769 *Thornton*. M.

Parry, Ann. S May T Jun 1727 *Susanna* to Va. M.

Parry, Edward, als Jones, Thomas. S s mare Lent R 14 yrs Summer 1765. Sh.

Parry, Elizabeth. S s at Broseley Lent 1763. Sh.

Parry, Henry. S s shirts at Abergavenny Summer 1724. Mo.

Parry, James. S for demolishing John Parry's water mill at Kingsland & R 14 yrs Lent 1775. He.

Parry, John. S s at St. Peter, Hereford, Lent 1727. He.

Parry, John. S s sheep at Caldicote Lent 1729. Mo.

Parry, John (1767). *See* Sparey. St.

Parry, John. R for life Lent 1774. K.

Parry, John S s oxen & R Summer 1774. Mo.

Parry, Margaret. R 12 yrs Jan 1663 (SP). L.

Parry, Margaret. R for Barbados Jan 1664. M.

Parry, Mathew (1696). *See* Preece. He.

Parry, Rowland. S s at Grosmont Summer 1751. Mo.

Parry, Thomas. S s at Bobbington Lent 1727. St.

Parry, Thomas. SQS May T Sep 1766 *Justitia*. M.

Parry, Thomas. S Apr T May 1767 *Thornton*. L.

Parry, Thomas. T Apr 1770 *New Trial*. Bu.

Parry, Thomas. S for demolishing water mill of John Parry & R 14 yrs Lent 1775. He.

Parry, William. S Lent 1724 R 14 yrs Lent 1725. Sh.

Parry, William. S Lent R 14 yrs Summer 1727. Mo.

Parsingham als Parsons, John. R Jun T Aug 1769 *Douglas*. M.

Parsley, Francis. S Summer 1719 AT Lent 1720. Wo.

Parsley, Henry. S Feb 1752. L.

Parsley als Cockney, John. S s soap from warehouse at St. Philip & Jacob Summer TB Aug 1738. G.

Parsley, Mary (1751). *See* Nobody. Sy.

Parslow, Edward. S & R Lent 1774. O.

Parsons, Angel. S Mar TB to Va Apr 1767. Wi.

Parsons als Reed, Christian of Bromley, spinster. R for Barbados or Jamaica Jly 1702. K.

Parsons, Edward. S Lent R 14 yrs Summer 1758. He.

Parsons, Elizabeth. R Oct AT Dec 1688. M.

Parsons, Elizabeth. S & T Apr 1725 *Sukey* LC Annapolis Sep 1725. M.

Parsons, Elizabeth. T Jan 1734 *Caesar* LC Va Jly 1734. E.

Parsons, Elizabeth of St. John, Wapping. S s money Jly-Sep T Sep 1742 *Forward*. M.

Parsons, Elizabeth. S Jan T Feb 1744 *Neptune* to Md. M.

Parsons, Elizabeth. SQS Jly TB Aug 1766. So.

Parsons, George of Huntley. S s money Summer 1718. G.

Parsons als Ruffler, George. R 14 yrs Apr 1747. So.

Parsons, George. S Jun 1747. L.

Parsons als Couch, George. R Aug 1770. Co.

Parsons, James. T Apr 1739 *Forward*. Sy.

Parsons, James (1748). *See* Fitzgerald. M.

Parsons, James. S s mare at Gayton & R 14 yrs Summer 1774. Nf.

Parsons, Joan, spinster. S 1654 R Feb 1656. M.

Parsons, John. R for Barbados May 1676. L.

Parsons, John (3). Rebels T 1685.

Parsons, John of St. Agnes, tinner. R for Barbados Mar 1695. Co.

Parsons, John. S Mar 1729. So.

Parsons, John. SQS Jan 1730. So.

Parsons, John. S Jly 1730. Wi.

Parsons, John. S Feb T Mar 1731 *Patapsco* LC Annapolis Jun 1731. M.

Parsons, John. S Mar 1740. So.

Parsons, John. TB to Va from QS 1743. De.

Parsons, John. S Mar 1745. De.

Parsons, John (1769). *See* Parsingham. M.

Parsons, Jonathan. R for Barbados Dec 1683. L.

Parsons, Margaret. S May-Jly 1773. M.

Parsons, Mary. S Feb T Mar 1731 *Patapsco* LC Annapolis Jun 1731. M.

Parsons, Mary. S Jun-Dec 1738 T Jan 1739 *Dorsetshire* to Va. M.

Parsons, Mary. S Dec 1761 T Apr 1762 *Dolphin*. M.

Parsons, Richard. R 14 yrs Aug 1727. So.

Parsons, Richard. S Lent R 14 yrs Summer 1749. K.

Parsons, Robert. S s wheat at St. Philip & Jacob Lent 1726. G.

Parsons, Robert. T Apr 1766 *Ann*. K.

Parsons, Samuel of St. Luke. S s household goods & T May 1740 *Essex*. M.

Parsons als Williams als Willis, Sarah. S s at St. George Lent 1761. G.

Parsons, Thomas. Rebel T 1685.

Parsons, Thomas. R & T Dec 1716 *Lewis*. L.

Parsons, Thomas. S Jly TB to Va Aug 1765. Wi.

Parsons, Thomas. S Jly 1765. Do.

Parsons, Thomas. T Apr 1769 *Tryal*. Sx.

Parsons, William. S May T 14 yrs Jly 1723 *Alexander* LC Annapolis Sep 1723. M.

Parsons, William. S s wheat at St. Philip & Jacob Lent 1726. G.

Parsons, William. S Jan-Jun T Jun 1728 *Elizabeth* LC Potomack Aug 1729. M.

Parsons, William (1730). *See* Pail. Wo.

Parsons, William. S for highway robbery Summer 1761 R 14 yrs Lent 1762. No.

Parsons, William. SQS Coventry Apr 1765. Wa.

Parsworth, Thomas. S s at Alveston Summer 1729. G.

Partin, Thomas. S Lent 1749. Sy.

Partington, Ann of Liverpool, singlewoman. SQS Jan 1763. La.

Partington, George. S Lent 1759. Wa.

Partington, John. S Summer R for Barbados Aug 1665. K.

Partington, John of Castleton, Rochdale, blacksmith. S Lent 1756. La.

Parton, William. S for burglary Summer 1723 R 14 yrs Lent 1725. Sh.

Partridge als Paternoster, Catherine wife of Stephen. S s gowns & T May 1736 *Patapsco*. M.

Partridge, Isabel, spinster. R for Barbados Jly 1684. Y.

Partridge, John. Rebel T 1685.

Partridge, Joseph. S Apr-Jun 1739. M.

Partridge, Joseph. S Mar TB to Va Apr 1754. Wi.

Partridge, Love. SQS Apr 1733. So.

Partridge, Mary. T Sep 1730 *Smith*. Sy.

Partridge, Matthew of Romford. SQS Jan T May 1750 *Lichfield*. E.

Partridge, Richard. SQS & T Sep 1766 *Justitia*. M.

Partridge, Sarah. S Aug T Sep 1725 *Forward* to Md. M.

Partridge, Susan. R for Barbados Dec 1668. M.

Partridge, Thomas. S & TB Apr 1742. G.

Parvey, Charles of Orsett. R for Barbados Sep 1669 (Newgate). E.

Pascoe als Duggar, George. S Aug 1742. Co.

Pascoe als Merla, James. R 14 yrs for Va Jly 1719. Co.

Pascoe, John. S Aug 1731. Co.

Pascoe, Joseph (1771). *See* Edy, William. De.

Pascoe, Nathaniel. R Aug 1771. Co.

Paschoe, Sarah of Roach. R for Barbados Feb 1688. Co.

Pass, Joshua. S Jan T Mar 1763 *Neptune*. M.

Pass, Samuel. S s at Newcastle under Lyme Lent 1734. St.

Passenger, Jonathan. R 14 yrs Mar 1744. De.

Passmore, Mary. S & T Apr 1733 *Patapsco* LC Annapolis Nov 1733. M.

Pasmore, Rosamund. R for Barbados or Jamaica May AT Jly 1697. M.

Pasmore, Thomas. R for Barbados or Jamaica May AT Jly 1697. M.

Paston, James. S Apr 1763. L.

Patch, John. S Sep-Oct 1773. M.

Pate, Charity. R 14 yrs Aug 1742. Co.

Pate, John. T Sep 1730 *Smith*. K.

Pateman, Ann wife of John. S Apr 1761. M.

Paternoster, Catherine (1736). *See* Partridge. M.

Paternoster, Joseph (1731). *See* Peterson. M.

Patience, John. S Apr T May 1719 *Margaret*; sold to Patrick Sympson & William Black Md Sep 1719. L.

Patience, John of St. Martin in Fields. SW Jly T Sep 1767 *Justitia*. M.

Patience, William. S Apr T May 1719 *Margaret*; sold to Richard Snowden Md Aug 1719. L.

Patience, William (1758). *See* Clarke, Thomas. Wi.

Patman, Edward. T Apr 1753 *Thames*. Sx.

Patman, Robert. S Lent 1754. Ca.

Patmore, Benjamin. T Aug 1769 *Douglas*. E.

Patmore, Benjamin. S Lent 1775. K.

Patrick, George. S s cider at Burton on Trent Summer 1727. St.

Pattrick, Richard. R for America Jly 1707. Li.

Patrick, Thomas of Esher. S Summer 1748 T Jan 1749 *Laura*. Sy.

Patrickson, Thomas (1732). *See* Paddison. Cu.

Patten als Pottinger, Jane. S & T Oct 1729 *Forward* but died on passage. L.

Patten, James. Rebel T 1685.

Pattenden, John. S for sending threatening letters Summer 1760 R 14 yrs Lent 1761. K.

Pattenger, Letitia. SQS Jan TB Apr 1766. So.

Paterson als Anderson als Isedale, Isabella. S Oct 1760. M.

Patterson, James. S Dec 1762 T Mar 1763 *Neptune*. M.

Pattison, Jane. S Oct T Nov 1725 *Rappahannock* but died on passage. M.

Paterson, Jane. S s handkerchief Summer 1755. Du.

Patterson, John of St. Margaret, Ipswich, cordwainer. S Summer 1732. Su.

Patterson, John of St. Martin in Fields. S s stockings & T Jan 1740 *York*. M.

Pattison, John. R 14 yrs Mar 1751. Ha.

Pattison, Mary, spinster. S Lent 1760. Bu.

Paterson, Peter. T Apr 1771 *Thornton*. Sy.

Paterson, Robert. T Nov 1741 *Sea Horse*. K.

Patterson, Robert. S s mare & R Summer 1772. Nl.

Paterson, Robert. TB to Va from QS 1772. De.

Paterson, Susanna. T Apr 1734 *Patapsco*. Sy.

Paterson, Thomas. S City Summer 1726. Nl.

Pattison, William. S Jun 1739. L.

Pattison, William. R Jly T Sep 1767 *Justitia*. M.

Patterson, William of Albourne. S Summer 1772. Sx.

Pattin, Anne, spinster, als wife of John. R for Barbados Jly 1663. L.

Pattin, John. S Jan 1751. L.

Pattinson, William. R 14 yrs Mar 1743. De.

Pattson, John. R Lent 1773. K.

Patty, Charles. S for Va Jly 1718. Co.

Patty, David. S Mar 1737. De.

Paty, John. S Aug 1753. De.

Patty, John. TB to Va from QS 1771. De.

Paul, Benjamin. S & T Jly 1753 *Tryal*. L.

Paul, Benjamin. S May T Jun 1764 *Dolphin*. L.

Paul, Dorothy. S for highway robbery Summer 1749. Nl.

Paul, Ely. S Jan-Apr 1748. M.

Paul, Gabriel. S Jan-Apr 1748. M.

Paul, John (1749). *See* Woolcock. Co.

Paul, Jonathan. S s horse Summer 1749 R 14 yrs Lent 1750. Su.

Paul, Joseph. Rebel T 1685.

Paul, Margaret. R for Barbados or Jamaica May 1684. L.

Paul, Margaret (1715). *See* Moor, Elizabeth. L.

Paull, Mary. PT Aug 1678. M.

Paul, Mary. S May T Jly 1723 *Alexander* LC Annapolis Sep 1723. M.

Paul, Mary. S Oct T Nov 1759 *Phoenix*. L.

Paull, Peter. R for Barbados or Jamaica May AT Jly 1697. M.

Paul, Rawson. S Aug T Sep 1725 *Forward* LC Annapolis Dec 1725. L.

Paul, Richard. Rebel T 1685.

Paul, Robert. Rebel T 1685.

Paul, Samuel. Rebel T 1685.

Paul, Samuel. R Summer 1774. Du.

Paul, William. SQS Apr T Sep 1758 *Tryal* to Annapolis. M.

Paul, William. S s at East Dereham Summer 1767. Nf.

Paul, William. S City Lent 1771. Y.

Pauldock als Balldock, William. S Jan T Mar 1764 *Tryal*. M.

Paulson, Francis. S Lent 1743. *Su.

Palson, Sarah wife of William. S Feb T Apr 1741 *Speedwell* or *Mediterranean*. M.

Pauntin, John. LC from *Forward* Annapolis Jun 1725. X.

Pavett, Joseph. S s mare Lent R 14 yrs Summer 1748. E.

Paviour, Benjamin. SQS Jan 1734. So.

Paviour, John. S & T Oct 1732 *Caesar* to Va. M.

Pavier, John Jr. R 14 yrs Aug 1765. So.

Pawlet, Jane (1680). *See* Steward. M.

Pawlet, Munday (1764). *See* Musters. M.

Pawley, George. S Nov T Dec 1763 *Neptune*. L.

Pauson, Mary. R for America Jly 1686. Li.

Porson, Sarah. S & T Dec 1771 *Justitia*. M.

Paxford, Richard. S Jan 1719. M.

Paxman, John. S s at Bungay Lent 1774. Su.

Paxton, Charles. S May-Jly 1749. M.

Paxton, Daniel. LC from *Sukey* Annapolis Sep 1725. X.

Paxton, Elizabeth. S Feb-Apr T May 1751 *Tryal*. M.

Paxton, Thomas. R for America Jly 1709. Li.

Paxton, William. S Jly T 14 yrs Aug 1718 *Eagle* LC Charles Town Mar 1719. L.

Paxton, William. SQS 1766. Du.

Payce. *See* Pace.

Paies, Robert. T 14 yrs Oct 1768 *Justitia*. Sx.

Paine, Abraham. R 14 yrs Aug 1747. So.

Payne, Ambrose. S s watch at Ixworth Summer 1774. Su.

Pain, Anne. S Oct T Nov 1725 *Rappahannock* LC Rappahannock Apr 1726. M.

Payne, Benjamin. S May T Jly 1771 *Scarsdale*. L.

Payne, Burry. S & T Jly 1770 *Scarsdale*. L.

Payne, Constabella. S s silver caster Jly T Dec 1735 *John* LC Annapolis Sep 1736. M.

Pain, Charles. TB to Va 1758. De.

Paine, Edward. S Sep 1740. L.

Paine, Edward. S Jan-Jun 1747. M.

Payne, Edward. S Lent R 14 yrs Summer 1760. Sy.

Payne, Elizabeth. S Lent R for Barbados May 1664. E.

Payne, Elizabeth. S Jly T Aug 1721 *Owners Goodwill* LC Annapolis Jly 1722. M.

Payne, Elizabeth. SQS Apr T Jly 1771 *Scarsdale*. M.

Paine, George. S for burglary at St. Laurence, Reading, Summer 1736. Be.

Payne, George. T Aug 1769 *Douglas*. L.

Pain, Hannah. S Aug T Oct 1724 *Forward* to Md. M.

Payne, Henry of Cheshunt. R for Barbados Aug 1662. Ht.

Paine, Henry. SW & T Jly 1772 *Tayloe*. M.

Payne, James. Rebel T 1685.

Pain als Page, James. S & T Jan 1739 *Dorsetshire*. L.

Payne, Jane. S s gowns at Newent Summer TB Aug 1749. G.

Paine, Joan of Bristol. R for Barbados Jun 1666. G.

Pain als Waldron, Joan. R 14 yrs Mar 1748. De.

Pane, John, aged 12. R for Barbados Feb 1664. M.

Paine, John als Thomas. T Jly 1724 *Robert* LC Md Jun 1725. E.

Payne, John. S & T Sep 1731 *Smith* LC Va 1732. M.

Paine, John (1736). *See* Venner. K.

Payn, John. S s gold rings at Cuddesdon Summer 1737. O.

Payne, John. S Oct T Dec 1758 *The Brothers*. L.

Paine, John. S May T Jun 1764 *Dolphin*. L.

Paine, Joshua. S Oct T Nov 1728 *Forward* LC Rappahannock Jun 1729. M.

Payne, Martha. S 14 yrs Jly-Dec 1747. M.

Payne, Mary. S s at Dymoke Sumer TB Jly 1743. G.

Pain, Mary. R 14 yrs Mar 1744. De.

Paine, Matthew. T Jan 1738 *Dorsetshire*. K.

Paine, Peter. T Apr 1770 *New Trial*. E.

Paine, Richard of Pershore, yeoman. R for America Jun 1714. Wo.

Payne, Richard. SL & T Sep 1767 *Justitia*. Sy.

Payne, Robert. S Mar TB Oct 1732. Le.

Payne, Robert. S s at Cirencester Lent 1774. G.

Payne, Samuel. S for highway robbery Lent R 14 yrs Summer 1750. O.

Paine, Sarah (1728). *See* Matthews. L.

Pain, Stephen. T Apr 1765 *Ann*. K.

Payne, Thomas. R Dec 1698 AT Jan 1699. M.

Payne, Thomas, aged 33, dark. S & T Oct 1720 *Gilbert* LC Annapolis May 1721. M.

Paine, Thomas. S Summer T Oct 1726 *Forward*. Bu.

Payne, Thomas. R 14 yrs Jly 1737. Wi.

Paine, Thomas. S Lent R 14 yrs Summer 1757. Le.

Paine, Thomas. T Oct 1757. Db.

Paine, Thomas. S s mare Lent R 14 yrs Summer 1758. Nf.

Pain, Thomas. S s handkerchief at St. Dunstan in East Dec 1768 T Jan 1769 *Thornton*. L.

Paine, William. R for Barbados & TB Oct 1667. L.

Payne, William. S Jly T Aug 1721 *Prince Royal* to Va. M.

Payne, William. S & T Mar 1750 *Tryal*. L.

Payne, William. T 14 yrs Apr 1765 *Ann*. K.

Payne, William. S Sep-Oct T 14 yrs Dec 1771 *Justitia*. M.

Payne, William. R Lent 1773. K.

Payson, John. R May T Jun 1691. M.

Payton, Edward. SQS Jan TB Feb 1749. So.

Peybody, John. R for Barbados Dec 1683. M.

Pebody, John. S Aug TB for life to Va Sep 1773. Le.

Peace, Charles. R 14 yrs Summer 1753. Y.

Peace als Edwards, Edward. SQS Jly T Sep 1764 *Justitia*. M.

Peace, John. S Lent R Summer 1742. Db.

Peach, Ann wife of John. S Oct 1744-Jan 1745. M.

Peach, Joseph. TB Aug 1741 T *Shaw* LC Antigua Jun 1742. Db.

Peach, Samuel. TB Sep 1750. Db.

Peach, William. Died on passage in *Sukey* 1725. X.

Peacham als Perry, Mary of St. Ann, Westminster, spinster. S s bed linen & T Dec 1740 *Vernon*. M.

Peachy, Daniel. S & T Jly 1753 *Tryal*. L.

Peacocke, Edward of Elkington. R for America Jly 1673. Li.

Peacock, Edward of Camberwell. SQS Jan 1752. Sy.

Peacock, Elizabeth. S s sheep Lent R 14 yrs Summer 1742. Li.

Peacock, Elizabeth. T Sep 1757 *Thetis*. Sy.

Peacock, Jeffery. R Summer 1728 (SP). Nf.

Peacock, Jeremiah. S Feb 1761. L.

Peacock, John. S Lent 1765. Li.

Peacock, John. S s mare & R 14 yrs Lent 1773. Li.

Peacock, Mary (1735). *See* Deakin. L.

Peacock, Richard. S Feb T Mar 1730 *Patapsco* but died on passage. L.

Peacock, Richard. S Feb-Apr T May 1751 *Tryal*. M.

Peacock, Stephen. S for burglary Lent R 14 yrs Summer 1740. Bd.

Peacock, Thomas. S s sheep & R 14 yrs Lent 1754. Bd.

Peacock, Thomas. T Jan 1756 *Greyhound*. Ht.

Peacocke, William. R Aug 1661 & Oct 1662 TB for Jamaica Nov 1662. L.

Peacock, William. T Oct 1720 *Gilbert*. Sx.

Peacock, William. S Lent R 14 yrs Summer T Aug 1752 *Tryal*. Sy.

Peacock, William. S Dec 1754. L.

Peacod, Richard. S & T Jan 1736 *Dorsetshire* LC Va Sep 1736. L.

Peadle als Read, Richard. T Apr 1770 *New Trial*. Sx.

Peak, Daniel (1773). *See* Lloyd. Ch.

Peake, Dorothy. S Apr 1761. L.

Peak, Elizabeth. S & T Oct 1732 *Caesar* to Va. M.

Peak, Frances. S & T Jly 1753 *Tryal*. L.

Peake, George. S Summer 1758 T Apr 1759 *Thetis*. Bu.

Peak, James. T Apr 1733 *Patapsco* LC Annapolis Nov 1733. Bu.

Peak, Jane. S & T Oct 1722 *Forward*. L.

Peake, John. S Summer T Sep 1751 *Greyhound*. Sy.

Peake, Rebecca of St. Paul, Covent Garden, widow. S s gown & T Jan 1740 *York*. M.

Peake, Richard. TB to Va from QS 1736. De.

Peake, Samuel. SQS Oct 1766 T Jan 1767 *Tryal*. M.

Peak, Sarah. S Oct 1749. L.

Peake, Thomas. R for Barbados Jun 1663. M.

Peake, Thomas. S & R Summer 1745. Su.

Peake, Thomas. R Jly T 14 yrs Sep 1767 *Justitia*. L.

Peake, William of St. James, Clerkenwell. S s sheep & T Feb 1740 *York*. M.

Peale. *See* Peele.

Pearce, Abram. S Sep 1733 T Jan 1734 *Caesar* to Va. M.

Pierce, Abraham. S Jun-Dec 1738. M.

Pearse, Andrew. T May 1751 *Tryal*. M.

Peirce als Laroach, Ann. R Aug AT Oct 1700. M.

Peirce, Ann. S Feb T May 1719 *Margaret*; sold to Patrick Sympson & William Black Md Sep 1719. L.

Pearse, Ann. T Apr 1739 *Forward*. K.

Pearce, Benjamin of Bristol. R 14 yrs s from ship in distress Apr 1773. G.

Pearce, Charles. T May 1755 *Rose*. Sy.

Pearce, Charles. S Jan T Mar 1764 *Tryal*. L.

Pierce, David. T Aug 1721 *Owners Goodwill*. E.

Perce, Edmund. T Apr 1742 *Bond*. K.

Pearse, Edward. S Mar 1748. De.

Pierce, Edward. S Lent R 14 yrs Summer 1758. Sh.

Pearce, Edward. T Dec 1771 *Justitia*. Sx.

Peirce, Elizabeth. R for Barbados Jly 1663. L.

Pears, Elizabeth of St. Andrew, Worcester. R for Barbados Jly 1702. Wo.

Pearce, Elizabeth. S Jly 1730. Co.

Pearce, Elizabeth. S Jly 1733. De.

Pierce, Elizabeth. S & T 14 yrs Apr 1753 *Thames*. L.

Pearce als Noone, Fortunatus of Newbury. R for America Jly 1675. Be.

Peers, Francis (1719). *See* Fenwick. L.

Pierce, George. S Aug 1726. De.

Pearse, George. R 14 yrs Aug 1752. So.

Pierce, George. S s sheep & R 14 yrs Lent 1769. G.

Pearce, Gilbert. S Dec 1763 T Mar 1764 *Tryal*. M.

Pearce, Henry. R May 1699 (SP). Do.

Peirce, Henry. R (Western Circ) for Barbados Jun 1699. L.

Peirce, Isaac of Lambeth. S Summer T Oct 1739 *Duke of Cumberland*. Sy.

Peirce, James. Rebel T 1685.

Pearce, James. SQS Feb T Mar 1760 *Friendship*. M.

Pearce, James. S & T Jly 1770 *Scarsdale*. L.

Pearce, Jane. S & T Jan 1722 *Gilbert* LC Annapolis Jly 1722. L.

Pearce, Jane. S & T Apr 1725 *Sukey* LC Annapolis Sep 1725. M.

Pierce als Price, John. R for Barbados & TB Oct 1667. L.

Pearse, John of Sowton, feltmaker. R for Barbados Feb 1669. De.

Pearce, John. S Summer 1722 R 14 yrs Summer 1724. Du.

Pearse, John. S Aug 1731 TB to Va. De.

Pearse als James, John. R 14 yrs Aug 1732. Co.
Pearce, John. SQS Jly 1740. So.
Pearse, John. R 14 yrs Mar 1742. Co.
Pearse, John. LC from *Shaw* Antigua May 1743. Db.
Pearse, John. R 14 yrs Jly 1743. De.
Pearce, John. S Summer 1752. Su.
Pearce, John. S & TB May 1755. G.
Pearce, John. S Oct 1772. L.
Pearce als Pinfold, Joseph. R 14 yrs Mar 1775. Ha.
Pearse, Mary. S Aug T Sep 1725 *Forward* LC Annapolis Dec 1725. M.
Pearse, Mary. R 14 yrs Aug 1726. De.
Pearce, Mary. S Lent R Summer 1739 (SP). Be.
Pierce, Mary. T Sep 1758 *Tryal.* Sy.
Pearce, Morrice. S & T Jan 1765 *Tryal.* M.
Peirce, Millicent. S Jly 1741. M.
Pearse, Peter. S for burglary Summer 1744 R 14 yrs Lent 1745. Su.
Pearse, Philip. S Apr 1765. So.
Pearse, Richard. S Feb 1663 to House of Correction unless he agrees to
  be transported. M.
Pearce, Richard. R for Barbados Jun 1671. M.
Pearce als Newport, Richard. R 14 yrs Jly 1732. Do.
Peirce, Richard. S Mar 1739. Wi.
Pearce, Richard. S Jly TB to Va Sep 1741. Wi.
Pearse, Richard. SQS Jan TB Feb 1749. So.
Pearce, Richard. R Jan-Feb T 14 yrs Apr 1772 *Thornton.* M.
Pearce, Robert (2). Rebels T 1685.
Pearce, Robert. S & T Apr 1725 *Sukey* LC Annapolis Sep 1725. M.
Pearce, Robert. R 14 yrs Jly 1725. Wi.
Pearse, Robert. S Mar 1754. Do.
Pearce, Sarah. S Aug 1735. So.
Pearce, Sarah. S May-Jun T Aug 1752 *Tryal.* M.
Peirse, Thomas. R for West Indies Oct 1614. M.
Peirce, Thomas (1693). *See* Hudson. L.
Peirce, Thomas. R Oct 1696. M.
Pearce, Thomas. R for Barbados or Jamaica Aug 1700. M.
Pierce, Thomas. S Jly T Aug 1721 *Prince Royal* LC Va Nov 1721. L.
Pierce, Thomas. S Oct T Nov 1728 *Forward* LC Rappahannock Jun
  1729. L.
Pearce, Thomas. R 14 yrs Jly 1733. Co.
Pearce, Thomas. S Jan T Apr 1735 *Patapsco* LC Annapolis Oct 1735. M.
Pierce, Thomas. T Nov 1743 *George William.* E.
Pearce, Thomas. S Jan 1761. M.
Pearce, Thomas. S Mar 1761. L.
Pearce, Thomas. S s sheep Lent R 14 yrs Summer 1766. Sh.
Pearce, Thomas. S s wool at North Nibley Lent 1774. G.
Pearce, Thomas. S Apr 1774. L.
Pearce, William of Hornsey. R for Barbados or Jamaica Mar 1685. M.
Pearse, William. S Jly T Sep 1718 *Eagle* LC Charles Town Mar 1719. L.
Pearse, William. S Aug T Oct 1723 *Forward* to Va. M.
Peirce, William. T Apr 1725 *Sukey* LC Md Sep 1725. Bu.
Pearce, William. S Jly 1725. Ha.

Pearse, William. R 14 yrs Aug 1732. Co.

Pearse, William. S Aug 1737. De.

Pearce, William the elder. SQS Jan 1767. Ha.

Pearce, William the younger. SQS Jan 1767. Ha.

Pearce, William. S Feb T Apr 1771 *Thornton*. L.

Peirse, William. S Dec 1774. L.

Pearcehouse, Thomas. SQS May T Jly 1773 *Tayloe* to Va. M.

Peircemore, Rebecca. S May T Sep 1737 *Pretty Patsy* to Md. M.

Pearcey, Ann. T Apr 1735 *Patapsco*. E.

Pearcey, Charles of St. George, Southwark. R Lent T 14 yrs Apr 1772 *Thornton*. Sy.

Piercy, Charles. S s sheep & R Lent 1772. Wa.

Piercy, Elizabeth. S Summer 1737 R 14 yrs Summer 1738. Wa.

Pearsey, Henry. S Aug 1727 T *Forward* LC Rappahannock May 1728. M.

Peircy, John. Rebel T 1685.

Piersey, John of Lawton. SQS Jan 1741. La.

Piercy, John. S Summer 1750 R 14 yrs Lent 1751. Be.

Piercy als Cooper, John. S Apr T May 1755 *Rose*. L.

Peircy, Richard. Rebel T 1685.

Peircy, William. S Lent R 14 yrs Summer 1732. Be.

Pearciball, Mary. S & R 14 yrs Summer 1746. Nf.

Peirey, John. T Sep 1730 *Smith*. Sy.

Pearkey, Mary. T Apr 1739 *Forward*. K.

Pearles, Uriah. S s gelding Summer 1754. Bd.

Peirman, Thomas. S Apr 1742. Ha.

Pears. *See* Pearce.

Pearslow, John. ST & T Jan 1769 *Thornton*. L.

Pearson, Ambrose. S Nov T Dec 1753 *Whiteing*. L.

Pearson, Ann of St. Olave, Southwark, spinster. SQS Jan 1758. Sy.

Pearson, Charles. S 14 yrs Lent 1755. Sy.

Pierson, Diana. S Jly 1757. M.

Pearson, Edward. SW & T Jun 1768 *Tryal*. M.

Pearson, Francis. S Summer 1738 R 14 yrs Lent 1739. Le.

Pearson, George. S Summer 1729 R 14 yrs Summer 1730. Wa.

Pearson, Hugh. R 14 yrs Summer 1730 AT Summer 1732. Nl.

Pearson, James of Malmesbury. R for Barbados Jly 1688. Wi.

Pearson, James. T Sep 1758 *Tryal*. Sx.

Pearson, James. R Mar 1775 (SP). Su.

Pearson, James. S s sheep at North Banham & R Lent 1775. Nf.

Pearson, John. S Jly 1722. Wi.

Pearson, John. S s horse Summer 1738 R 14 yrs Lent 1739. Wa.

Peirson, John. S 14 yrs Jan 1745. L.

Pearson, John. R 14 yrs Summer 1747. We.

Pearson, John. T May 1751 *Tryal*. K.

Pearson, John. S for forgery Lent R 14 yrs Summer 1752. Ca.

Pearson, John (1755). *See* Moyes. Su.

Peirson, John. S Dec 1755 T Jan 1756 *Greyhound*. L.

Pearson, John. R 14 yrs s horse Summer 1766. We.

Pearson, Joseph. T 14 yrs Apr 1766 *Ann*. E.

Pierson, Joseph. T 14 yrs Apr 1769 *Tryal*. Sx.

Pearson, Matthew. S Lent 1751. Y.

Pearson, Nathaniel. S Apr T May 1752 *Lichfield*. L.

Peirson, Rachel. S Jan T Feb 1726 *Supply* LC Annapolis May 1726. M.

Peirson, Richard. T May 1719 *Margaret* LC Md May 1720; sold to George Harman. Sy.

Pearson, Robert. R for Barbados Jun 1666. Y.

Pearson, Robert of Great Markham. R for America Jly 1678. Nt.

Pearson, Sarah. R for Barbados Dec 1683. L.

Pearson, Temple. R 14 yrs Summer 1760. We.

Pearson, Thomas. R 14 yrs City Summer 1740. Nl.

Pearson, Thomas of Manchester. SQS Jan 1775. La.

Pierson, William. S & T Sep 1751 *Greyhound*. M.

Pearson, William. S s sheep at Sheffield & R 14 yrs Summer 1768. Y.

Peart, John. S Lent 1758. Nf.

Peart, Thomas. S Oct 1751-Jan 1752. M.

Peasant, Dedereux. R for Barbados or Jamaica Dec 1699. L.

Pease, John. S Feb-Apr T Jun 1756 *Lyon*. M.

Peate, John. SQS Feb T May 1752 *Lichfield*. M.

Peat, Richard Denton. S Dec 1753-Jan 1754. M.

Peate, William. R for Barbados May 1664. M.

Peate, William of Halling. R for Barbados or Jamaica Feb 1690. K.

Peate, William. S Aug TB to Va Sep 1727. Le.

Peaten, John. LC from *Gilbert* Annapolis Jly 1722. X.

Peates, William. T Oct 1726 *Forward*. E.

Peaty, Thomas. S Lent 1742 AT Summer 1742. O.

Pebworth als Smith, Mary. S Jly-Dec 1747. M.

Pebworth, Matthew of Witney. S Lent 1720. O.

Pebworth, Robert. S s at Burford Lent R 14 yrs Summer 1736. O.

Peck, Ann. T Oct 1750 *Rachael*. M.

Pecke, David of Towcester. R for America Jly 1679. No.

Peck, Edward. SQS Apr T May 1755 *Rose*. M.

Peck, James. S Feb T Mar 1731 *Patapsco* LC Annapolis Jun 1731. M.

Pecke, Jane. R for Barbados Dec 1670. M.

Peckard. *See* Pickard.

Peckett, John. R for Barbados Apr 1668. L.

Peckham, Sarah wife of Moses. S Jly 1748. Ha.

Pecod, Thomas. R 14 yrs Mar 1760. Wi.

Pect, Elizabeth (1734). *See* Richardson. M.

Pedder, Charles. SQS Feb T Apr 1765 *Ann*. M.

Pedder, John. S Feb T Mar 1729 *Patapsco* LC Annapolis Dec 1729. M.

Peddington, John. S Apr-May T Jly 1771 *Scarsdale*. M.

Pediello, Pedro of Bishops Hatfield. R for Barbados or Jamaica Jly 1715. Ht.

Pedrick, Charles (1688). *See* Cornish. De.

Pead, Joseph. S Oct 1766. L.

Peed, Nehemiah of Wotton under Edge. R (Western Circ) for Barbados Feb 1699. G.

Peeke, John (1760). *See* Cripps. So.

Peale, Charles. S & T for life Jan 1736 *Dorsetshire* LC Va Sep 1736. L.

Peale, Edward. SQS s potatoes Easter 1775. Du.

Peal, George. S s gelding Summer 1722 R 14 yrs Summer 1724. Du.

Peale, James. T May 1752 *Lichfield*. Sy.

Peele, James. S Oct T Dec 1771 *Justitia*. L.

Peel, Jeremiah. S s cloth from tenters & R Lent 1762. Y.

Peel, John. S & R Lent 1768. Ch.

Peel als Bolley, Polyna. S Dec 1736. L.

Peele, Thomas. S & T Jly 1770 *Scarsdale*. M.

Peele, William (1764). *See* Jackson, Thomas. Nt.

Peelina, Ralph. S Feb 1672 & to be considered for transportation. M.

Pearless, Samuel. T May 1741 *Miller*. K.

Peerlesse, William of Brasted. R for Barbados Apr 1668. K.

Peers. *See* Pearce.

Pegden, John. T Apr 1732 *Patapsco*. K.

Pegden, William. T Oct 1729 *Forward*. Sy.

Pegg, William. S Summer T Oct 1757. Db & Le.

Pegg, William. S & T Apr 1769 *Tryal*. L.

Peirce. *See* Pearce.

Peirey. *See* Pearey.

Peirman. *See* Pearman.

Peirson. *See* Pearson.

Peisley. *See* Paisley.

Pelham, William, aged 30, black hair. LC from *Gilbert* Md May 1721. X.

Pell, Gerrard. S Jly T Sep 1718 *Eagle* LC Charles Town Mar 1719. L.

Pell, Juliana. R Jly AT Oct 1685. M.

Pell, Richard. T May 1737 *Forward*. Sy.

Pell, William. S s sheep Lent R 14 yrs Summer 1759. Li.

Pellett, John of Shipley. SQS s tame fowls Apr 1774. Sx.

Pelling, John. T 14 yrs Aug 1752 *Tryal*. K.

Pellingham, Jane. R for Barbados Dec 1671. M.

Pells, John. S s at Thorington Summer 1773. Su.

Pelsome, Ellinore. R for Barbados or Jamaica Oct 1694. L.

Pelson, Edward. S Summer 1720. G.

Pelter, James. S Jly T Sep 1766 *Justitia*. M.

Pember, Catherine. S Dec 1733 T Jan 1734 *Caesar* LC Va Jly 1734. L.

Pemberton, Isaac. R & T for life Apr 1770 *New Trial*. M.

Pemberton, James. S Summer 1740. La.

Pemberton als Pendry als Pendrick als Pendroon, Jane. S & T Oct 1729
    Forward LC Va Jun 1730. M.

Pemberton, John. S s horse Summer 1750 R 14 yrs Lent 1751. Db.

Pemberton, William. LC from *Happy Jennett* Md Oct 1751. Db.

Pembrooke, Arthur. R for Barbados Mar 1683. M.

Penbrook, Grace. S s mare at Bray Lent R 14 yrs Summer 1736. Be.

Pendell, John. LC from *Honor* Port York Jan 1721. X.

Pendal, John. T *Rappahannock* 1726 but died on passage. Li.

Pendlebury, Margaret of Manchester. SQS Apr 1743. La.

Pendrill, Elianor. S & T Oct 1729 *Forward* but died on passage. L.

Penfold, Thomas of West Hoathly. S Summer 1772. Sx.

Penfold, William. T Apr 1741 *Speedwell* or *Mediterranean*. Sx.

Penford, Daniel. S Jly 1736. Ha.

Pengelly, Alexander. S Mar 1732. So.

Pengelly, Hannah. S Summer 1745. K.

Pengilly, John. TB to Va from QS 1738. De.

Pengelly, Thomas. R for life Mar 1771 TB to Va. De.

Penn, Amy. T 14 yrs Apr 1768 *Thornton.* K.

Penn, Daniel (1687). *See* Brookes. L.

Pen, Hannah. LC from *Forward* Annapolis Jun 1725. X.

Penn, John. S Lent 1749. Ht.

Penn, Mary. LC from *Patapsco* Annapolis Oct 1735. X.

Penn, Matthew. S Summer T Sep 1751 *Greyhound.* Sy.

Penn, Samuel. S Lent T May 1770. Wa.

Penn, Susanna. S Aug T Sep 1764 *Justitia.* L.

Penn, Thomas of Felpham. R for Barbados Aug 1662. Sx.

Pennard, Sarah. S Feb T Mar 1727 *Rappahannock* to Md. M.

Pennell, Thomas. S Lent R 14 yrs Summer 1745. Wo.

Pennell, Thomas. S Dec 1746. L.

Pennill, Elizabeth. S Oct 1744-Jan 1745. M.

Pennings, Abel (1766). *See* Jennings. K.

Pennington, Charles (1695). *See* Norman. M.

Pennington, Henry of Lancaster, brazier. SQS Apr 1767. La.

Pennington, John. S Jan T Apr 1741 *Speedwell* or *Mediterranean.* M.

Pennington, John of Gravely. SQS s sheets Jan 1775. Ht.

Penniston, Henry, aged 30, dark, weaver. LC from *Gilbert* Md May 1721. X.

Pennithorne, Peter. SQS for false pretences Dec 1760. M.

Pennithorne, Peter. S Nov T Dec 1763 *Neptune.* L.

Pennock, William. T 14 yrs Apr 1768 *Thornton.* E.

Penny, Benjamin. T Apr 1771 *Thornton.* Sy.

Penny, Edward. S Norwich Summer 1734. Nf.

Penny, Elizabeth. S Jly 1752. De.

Penny, Elizabeth (1764). *See* Perry. M.

Penny, George. R 14 yrs Mar 1731. Wi.

Penny, Hannah. Died on passage in *Loyal Margaret* 1726. X.

Penny, Henry. S Mar TB to Va Apr 1762. Wi.

Penny, John of East Chinnock, husbandman. R for Barbados Feb 1668. So.

Penny, John of Farningham. R for Barbados or Jamaica Mar 1682. K.

Penny, John. PT Oct R Dec 1698. M.

Penny, Joseph. S Apr 1751. So.

Penney, Joseph. S Mar 1768. So.

Penny, Martha. S Apr T Jun 1742 *Bladon* to Md. M.

Penny, Thomas. S Dec 1743 T Feb 1744 *Neptune* to Md. M.

Penny, William. T May 1737 *Forward.* Sy.

Penny, William. SQS Jan 1738. So.

Penny, William. T Apr 1766 *Ann.* K.

Pennyfather, Michael. S Sep T Nov 1743 *George William.* L.

Pennylow, John of St. Ann, Westminster. S Feb T May 1736 *Patapsco.* M.

Penpraise, James. S Sep-Oct T Dec 1752 *Greyhound.* M.

Penprose, Daniel (1725). *See* Williams. Co.

Penrice, Lawrence. S & T Sep 1751 *Greyhound.* L.

Penrice, Robert. S s at Hanbury Summer 1759. Wo.

Penryn als White als Fowler als Taffe, Mary. R Jan AT Feb 1679. M.

Penson, William. S Feb T Apr 1766 *Ann.* M.

Penstone, Thomas. S Mar 1761. Ha.

Pentycost, Eleanor wife of John. S Feb T Mar 1758 *Dragon*. M.

Pentecost als Pentecross, James. S for false pretences Oct T Dec 1767 *Neptune*. L.

Penticost, Richard. T Jan 1741 *Vernon*. Sx.

Pention, Ann. S as pickpocket Lent R 14 yrs Summer TB Aug 1734. G.

Pentlow, Mary wife of William. SQS Apr 1763. M.

Peppen, Walter of Stogumber, blacksmith. R for Barbados Feb 1690. So.

Pepper, Anthony. S Summer 1745. Cu.

Pepper, Francis. S s gelding Summer 1766 R 14 yrs Lent 1767. No.

Pepper, Jasper. S Aug TB to Va Sep 1731. Le.

Pepper, Mary (1748). *See* Smith. M.

Pepper, Phillis of Middleham, widow. SQS Northallerton Jly TB Sep 1754. Y.

Pepper, Richard (1754). *See* Pippin. M.

Pepper, Thomas. T Apr 1725 *Sukey* LC Md Sep 1725. K.

Pepperell, Alexander. PT Oct R Dec 1698. M.

Pepperell, Elizabeth (1700). *See* Malsheir. M.

Pepperell, Mary. S Mar 1758. De.

Peravall, Thomas. R for Barbados or Jamaica Oct 1688. M.

Perce. *See* Pearce.

Perceval, James. S Lent 1745. Db.

Percivall als Howse, Joseph. S Dec 1727. M.

Percival, Thomas. PT Dec 1688. M.

Percival, Thomas. R for Barbados for coin clipping Dec 1693 AT Jan 1694. M.

Percival, Thomas. T Sep 1757 *Thetis*. Sy.

Perdue. *See* Purdue.

Periam, Bernard. Rebel T 1685.

Perira, Joseph (1772). *See* Mascada, Francis. M.

Perkin, Lionel. SQS Jly TB to Md Nov 1740. So.

Parkins, Anne. S Mar 1720. De.

Perkins, Ann. S Sep T Dec 1734 *Caesar* LC Va Jly 1735. M.

Perkins, Ann. S Jun-Dec 1745. M.

Perkins, Ann. T Jan 1756 *Greyhound*. L.

Perkins, Ann. R Jun T for life Aug 1769 *Douglas*; one of this name sentenced to hang in 1769 for returning from transportation. M.

Perkins, Benjamin. SQS Oct T Dec 1763 *Neptune*. M.

Perkins, Charles. S & T Dec 1731 *Forward*. L.

Perkins, Edward of Whilton. R for America Jly 1678. No.

Perkins, Edward. R for Barbados or Jamaica Mar 1685. M.

Perkins, Elizabeth. PT Dec 1699 R Aug 1700. M.

Perkins, George (1727). *See* Pinfold. M.

Perkins, Hannah. S & T Jan 1722 *Gilbert* LC Annapolis Jly 1722. M.

Perkins, Henry. LC from *Mary* Port York Jun 1721. X.

Perkins, James of Whilton. R for America Jly 1678. No.

Perkins, Jane of Kingston on Thames. R for America Jly 1700. Sy.

Perkins, John. S Aug 1727. M.

Perkyns, John. S & T Oct 1730 *Forward* LC Potomack Jan 1731. L.

Perkins, John. S & T May 1736 *Patapsco*. L.

Perkins, John. S s banknotes at Canwell Lent 1766. St.

Perkins, Joseph. S Jan-Jun T 14 yrs Jun 1728 *Elizabeth* LC Potomack Aug 1729. M.

Perkins, Mary. T *Margaret* & sold to Patrick Sympson & William Black Md Sep 1719. L or M.

Perkins, Mary (1730). *See* Siggins. M.

Perkins, Mary. S Apr T May 1740 *Essex.* L.

Perkins, Mary. S May-Jun T Jly 1753 *Tryal.* M.

Perkins, Richard. Rebel T 1685.

Perkins, Richard. R 14 yrs Jly 1738. De.

Perkins, Richard. T Apr 1753 *Thames.* Sy.

Perkins, Robert. R & T Dec 1716 *Lewis.* L.

Perkins als Osborne, Thomas. S for assault Lent 1774. Wa.

Perkins, William. S Apr 1747. De.

Perkins, William. S Summer T Sep 1751 *Greyhound.* K.

Perkins, William. S Lent 1754. K.

Perkins, William. R Mar 1770. Ha.

Perkes, John of Stourbridge. R for America Feb 1681. Wo.

Perks, William. S for highway robbery & R 14 yrs Lent 1769. He.

Perleigh, Abraham. S Aug 1723. So.

Perrier, Peter. S Apr 1774. L.

Perrin, John. S s from church at Walton on Hill Lent 1746 R 14 yrs Lent 1747. La.

Perryn, John. T Sep 1764 *Justitia.* E.

Perryn, Philip. S s at St. Nicholas Lent 1772. Be.

Peryn, Samuel of Axbridge, husbandman. R for Barbados Feb 1673. So.

Perrin, Sarah. S Oct 1761. L.

Perrin, Thomas. S May T Jun 1727 *Susanna.* L.

Perring, John of East Grinstead. R for Barbados or Jamaica Jun 1675. Sx.

Perring, Peter. TB to Va from QS 1768. De.

Perrott. *See* Parrott.

Perry, Ann. S Jan 1746. M.

Perry, Ann. S s at Seighford Summer 1755. St.

Perry, Barnaby. S Feb T Mar 1731 *Patapsco* LC Annapolis Jun 1731. L.

Perry, Benjamin. S 14 yrs Aug 1727. M.

Perry, Catherine. S Aug T Oct 1723 *Forward* to Va. M.

Perry, Cavalier. T Apr 1731 *Bennett.* Ht.

Perry, Christopher. S Mar 1728. Co.

Perry, Edward. T Oct 1722 *Forward* LC Md Jun 1723. Sx.

Perry, Edward. S s horse Summer 1740 R Lent 1741; S to hang Lent 1743 for being at large. St.

Perry, Edward. S 14 yrs for receiving goods stolen by Samuel Brown *(qv)* Lent 1746. Hu.

Perry, Edward. S Sep-Oct T Dec 1752 *Greyhound.* M.

Perry, Elizabeth. R for Barbados or Jamaica May 1697. L.

Perry, Elizabeth. T Apr 1733 *Patapsco* LC Md Nov 1733. Sy.

Perry, Elizabeth wife of William. S Aug 1745. So.

Perry als Penny, Elizabeth wife of William. S May T Jun 1764 *Dolphin.* M.

Perry, George. S Feb 1738. Ha.

Perry, George. S Sep T Oct 1750 *Rachael.* M.

Perry, George. R 14 yrs Mar TB to Va Apr 1768. Wi.

Perry als McLaughland, Hannah. S May T Nov 1762 *Prince William*. M.

Perry als Floyd, Henry. S Jan T Feb 1719 *Worcester* LC Annapolis Jun 1719. L.

Perry, Isabella wife of Peter. LC from *Caesar* Jly 1735. X.

Perry, James (1752). *See* Kilpatrick. Wi.

Perrey, John of Wellington, husbandman. R for Barbados Jun 1666. So.

Perry, John of Upton St. Leonard. R for America Feb 1716. G.

Perry als Norman, John. S & T Oct 1722 *Forward* to Md. M.

Perry, John. S for destroying looms Summer 1730 R 14 yrs Lent 1731 (SP). G.

Perry, Joseph. S Apr T May 1770 *Lichfield*. M.

Perry, Martha of Wethersfield, spinster. SQS Jly T Aug 1752 *Tryal*. E.

Perry, Martha. S Jan 1757. M.

Perry, Mary (1740). *See* Peachum. M.

Perry, Mary. S Dec 1741 T Feb 1742 *Industry* to Md. M.

Perrey, Mary Frances. S May T Jun 1764 *Dolphin*. M.

Perry, Nicholas. S Mar 1728. Co.

Perry, Peter. S Summer 1749. Sy.

Perry, Priscilla. S Apr T Sep 1757 *Thetis*. M.

Perry, Ralph. S Aug 1737. So.

Perry, Richard. T Apr 1765 *Ann*. E.

Perry, Robert of Great Bedwin, Wilts. S s razor Summer 1719 R 14 yrs Lent 1721 T *Owners Goodwill* LC Annapolis Jly 1722. Be.

Perry, Samuel. S s at Mendham Summer 1753. Nf.

Perry, Simon. T 14 yrs Apr 1769 *Tryal*. K.

Perry, Strongfaith. S & T Oct 1730 *Forward* LC Potomack Jan 1731. M.

Perry, Thomas of Wincanton. R for Barbados Jly 1715. So.

Perry, Thomas of St. Leonard. S s guinea Summer 1718. G.

Perry, Thomas (1728). *See* Lee. Ha.

Perry, Thomas. S for breaking highway toll barrier at Norton Lent 1735. He.

Perry, Thomas. S Lent 1737. Y.

Perry, Thomas. S Jan-Apr 1749. M.

Perry, Thomas. SQS Feb T Jun 1756 *Lyon*. M.

Perry, Thomas. S & R 14 yrs Lent 1773. Wo.

Perry, William. S Apr T Oct 1719 *Susannah & Sarah* LC Annapolis Apr 1720. L.

Perry, William. T May 1737 *Forward*. K.

Perry, William. S Jan T Apr 1741 *Speedwell* or *Mediterranean*. M.

Perry, William. S & T Jan 1769 *Thornton*. M.

Perry, William. S May T Aug 1769 *Douglas*. M.

Perriman, Betty. S Aug 1771. So.

Perryman, Robert. LC from *Eagle* Charles Town Mar 1719. X.

Perryment, William. S Jan T Feb 1744 *Neptune*. L.

Pessey, David (1769). *See* Price. M.

Pester, Thomas. Rebel T 1685.

Petals als Petts, William. R for Barbados Sep 1669. M.

Petch, Robert (1772). *See* Anderson. Y.

Petchy, Elizabeth (1723). *See* Beechy. E.

Peter Boy (1765). *See* Bowyer, Peter. Do.

Peter, Abraham. T Apr 1770 *New Trial*. L.

Peters, Anne, aged 28. R for Barbados Feb 1664. L.

Peters, Daniel. S Mar TB to Va Apr 1766. Wi.

Peters, John. T May 1737 *Forward*. K.

Peters, John. S s plough chain Lent 1765. Hu.

Peters, Joseph of St. Runwald, Colchester. SQS Oct 1754. E.

Peters, Otto. S Dec 1733 T Jan 1734 *Caesar* LC Va Jly 1734. M.

Peters, Richard. S s at Bewdley Lent 1756. Wo.

Peters, Robert. R Jan AT Feb 1679. M.

Peters, Solomon. S May T Nov 1759 *Phoenix*. M.

Peters als Weller, Thomas. S Lent R for Barbados Apr 1663. Sx.

Peters, William. S & T Oct 1722 *Forward* LC Annapolis Jun 1723. M.

Peterson, Andrew of White Waltham. R for America Nov 1694. Be.

Peterson, Christopher. S Jan T 14 yrs Mar 1743 *Justitia*. L.

Peterson, John (1755). *See* Dayly. L.

Peterson als Paternoster, Joseph. S & T Dec 1731 *Forward* to Md or Va. M.

Peterson, Richard of Whitechapel. S s handkerchief Sep 1740 T Jan 1741 *Harpooner* to Rappahannock. M.

Peterson, William. S Jan T Apr 1768 *Thornton*. M.

Pether, John. T 14 yrs Apr 1771 *Thornton*. Sy.

Pether, Thomas. R 14 yrs Apr 1775. So.

Petheway, Elizabeth. PT for shoplifting Summer 1725. He.

Petman, John. S Feb T Apr 1770 *New Trial*. M.

Peto, Thomas. S Oct 1774. L.

Pett, Anne. S Lent R 14 yrs Summer 1735. Su.

Pett, John. R for Barbados or Jamaica Mar 1685. L.

Pettifer, John. S s sheep Lent R 14 yrs Summer 1749. Wa.

Pettifer, John, aged 31, born at Oakham, 5'5" tall. S s lambs & R Summer T Sep 1775 *Rebecca* from London to Baltimore. Ru.

Pettyford, Charles. S & R 14 yrs Lent 1774. G.

Pettiford, Elizabeth. S & T Oct 1720 *Gilbert* to Md. M.

Pettin, Ann wife of Robert. S Jan-Feb 1775. M.

Pettingale, Richard. S Summer R for Barbados Aug 1664. Sy.

Pettis als Petworth als Read als Cade, Ann, aged 26. R for Barbados Feb 1664. L.

Pettit, Ann (1758). *See* Petty. L.

Pettit, John of Stevenage. R for Barbados or Jamaica Jly 1704. Ht.

Pettet, John. AT City Summer 1758. Nl.

Pettit, Michael. S Lent 1763. Nf.

Pettit, Sarah. S Jan 1761. M.

Pettitt, Sarah of Earls Colne, spinster. SQS Apr 1774. E.

Pettit, Thomas. S & T Sep 1731 *Smith* LC Va 1732. M.

Petit, Thomas. T May 1752 *Lichfield*. K.

Petts, Elizabeth. S Jly 1748. Ha.

Petts, Mary. S Jly 1748. Ha.

Petts, William (1669). *See* Petals. M.

Pettey, Ann of St. Martin in Fields, spinster. S Apr T May 1740 *Essex*. M.

Petty als Pettit, Ann. S Oct T 14 yrs Dec 1758 *The Brothers*. L.

Petty, Francis. S Lent 1726 R Lent 1727. Su.

Petty, Henry. S Jly 1762. Ha.

Petty, Isabella. S Feb-Apr T May 1755 *Rose*. M.

Petty, Thomas. S Mar 1724. Wi.

Petworth, Ann (1664). *See* Pettis. L.

Peverley, Alexander. LC from *Patapsco* Annapolis Oct 1732. X.

Peaverley, John. S Feb T 14 yrs Apr 1732 *Patapsco* to Md. M.

Peverley, Rebecca. SQS Jun T Jly 1772 *Tayloe*. M.

Pevett als Goddard, Elizabeth. S Feb 1757. M.

Pew. *See* Pugh.

Pewter, John. T 14 yrs Sep 1767 *Justitia*. E.

Pewter, Samuel. T Jly 1723 *Alexander* LC Md Sep 1723. Sy.

Pewter, Thomas. S Mar 1729. So.

Pewteres, Jane of Tarrington. R for America Jly 1675. He.

Pewtriss, William. S s wheat at Pendock Lent 1768. Wo.

Peybody. *See* Peabody.

Peyton, Ann. T Apr 1734 *Patapsco*. Sy.

Peyton, Ann wife of Richard. S Dec 1760. M.

Peyton, Edward. SQS Jly T Sep 1765 *Justitia*. M.

Peyton, George. S Dec 1748 T Jan 1749 *Laura*. L.

Pharaoh, Thomas. S s punch bowl at St. Catherine Coleman Feb T Apr 1768 *Thornton*. L.

Phelps, Edward. S s leather breeches Summer TB Sep 1753. G.

Philps, Hugh of Lyme Regis. R for Barbados Feb 1714. Do.

Phelps, John. S Mar 1745. De.

Phelps, John. S Dec 1756. M.

Phelps, Mary. S Lent 1748. Sy.

Phelps, Thomas. S s at Selwick Lent 1752. He.

Phelps, Thomas. S s lambs & R 14 yrs Lent 1775. Be.

Phelpes, William. Rebel T 1685.

Phelps, William. S Lent TB Mar 1731. G.

Phelps, William. S s at Bisley Lent TB Apr 1747. G.

Phenix. *See* Phoenix.

Phenlo, Lydia (1723). *See* Finlow. L.

Phesant, James. S & T Oct 1722 *Forward* to Md. M.

Phill als Haddon, Frances. S Norwich Summer 1749. Nf.

Phillips, Anne. R for Barbados Sep 1669. M.

Phillips, Ann. S Apr-May T May 1744 *Justitia*. M.

Phillips, Ann. S Mar 1755. Ha.

Phillips, Ann. S Dec 1755. L.

Phillips, Benjamin. S s at Pedmore Lent 1773. Wo.

Phillips, Benjamin. S Dec 1774. L.

Phillips, Charles. S & T Oct 1729 *Forward* LC Va Jun 1730. M.

Phillips, Cicely. S Aug 1740 TB to Va. De.

Phillips, Daniel. R for Barbados or Jamaica May 1697. L.

Phillips, David (1769). *See* Thomas. G.

Phillips, Edward of Camberwell. R for America Jly 1700. Sy.

Phillips, Edward. S Apr T May 1750 *Lichfield*. M.

Phillips, Edward. S Apr T May 1751 *Tryal*. L.

Phillips, Edward. T Sep 1767 *Justitia*. E.

Phillips, Edward. R 14 yrs Dec 1774. M.

Phillips, Elizabeth. S Jan T Feb 1724 *Anne*. L.
Phillips, Elizabeth. S Mar 1743. Ha.
Phillips, Elizabeth. S Jly 1749. L.
Phillips, Elizabeth. S Jly 1774. L.
Phillips, Emma of Lambourn Woodland. R for Barbados Jun 1666. Be.
Phillips, Emma of Epping. R for Barbados or Jamaica Jly 1677. E.
Phillips, Evan. S Lent R 14 yrs Summer 1760 T 1761 *Atlas* from
    Bristol. He.
Phillips, Evan. S s gelding at Cleobury & R 14 yrs Summer 1771. Sh.
Phillips, Fidelia. R for Barbados Aug 1664. M.
Phillips, George. AT from QS Lent 1766. Wa.
Phillips, Hannah. S Jun-Dec 1745. M.
Phillips, Isaac. S Dec 1768 T Jan 1769 *Thornton*. M.
Phillips, James of St. John, Worcester. S Summer 1719. Wo.
Phillips, James. S & T Apr 1725 *Sukey* but died on passage. M.
Phillips, James. S & T Oct 1732 *Caesar* to Va. M.
Phillips, James. SW & T Jan 1769 *Thornton*. M.
Phillips, James. R Jly 1774. Ha.
Phillips, James John (1772). *See* Gilbert. M.
Phillips, Jane. S Dec 1756. M.
Phillips, Jane. S Summer 1764. G.
Phillips, John of Milverton, husbandman. R for Barbados Jly 1664. So.
Phillips, John of Bury St. Edmunds. R for America Apr 1697. Su.
Phillips, John (1729). *See* Thinwood. Sy.
Phillips, John. S Apr T Sep 1737 *Pretty_Patsy* to Md. M.
Phillips, John. T Jan 1738 *Dorsetshire*. E.
Phillips, John of Hadley. S s saws Jly 1740. M.
Phillips, John. S s cloth from tenters at Leominster Summer 1745. He.
Phillips, John. S Jan-Apr 1749. M.
Phillips, John. S s sheep Lent R 14 yrs Summer 1751. Bd.
Phillips, John. S Apr-May 1754. M.
Phillips, John (1759). *See* Hill. De.
Phillips, John. S Lent 1760. Bu.
Phillips, John. SQS & T Sep 1766 *Justitia*. M.
Phillips, John. S & T Dec 1767 *Neptune*. L.
Phillips, John. S Jan T Apr 1768 *Thornton*. M.
Phillips, John. T 14 yrs Apr 1768 *Thornton*. E.
Phillips, John. S for highway robbery & R for life Summer 1770 T Aug
    1771. Wa.
Phillips, John. S Mar 1771. Ha.
Phillips, John. S May-Jly 1773. M.
Phillips, John. S s at Keysoe & R Summer 1774. Bd.
Phillips, John (1775). *See* Jones, Philip. Sh.
Phillips, Joseph of St. Saviour, Southwark. SQS 14 yrs Jan T Apr 1760
    Thetis. Sy.
Phillips, Joseph. S Oct T Dec 1771 *Justitia*. L.
Phillips, Margaret of Congleton, spinster. R for America Mar 1690. Ch.
Phillips, Mary. PT Aug 1676 R Mar 1677. M.
Phillips als Brown, Mary, als Dennis, Catherine. S May T Jun 1726
    Patapsco LC Annapolis from *Loyal Margaret* Oct 1726. M.
Phillips, Mary. T Dec 1753 *Whiteing*. Sx.

Phillips, Mary. S Jan 1757. M.
Phillips, Mary. S & T Mar 1764 *Tryal*. L.
Phillips, Mary. S Feb T Apr 1772 *Thornton*. L.
Phillips, Moses. S Mar 1772. Ha.
Phillips, Moses. S Jly 1774. L.
Phillips, Paul. T Oct 1722 *Forward* LC Md Jun 1723. Sx.
Phillips, Philip. S Lent R 14 yrs Summer 1768. He.
Phillips, Ralph. S for demolishing dwelling house Lent R 14 yrs Summer 1728. G.
Phillips, Richard (1724). *See* Solly. Sh.
Phillips, Richard. S Mar TB to Va Apr 1754. Wi.
Phillips, Richard. S Feb T Apr 1766 *Ann*. L.
Phillips, Samuel. S Jan T Feb 1742 *Industry*. L.
Phillips, Samuel. SW & T Jan 1769 *Thornton*. M.
Phillips als Woolen, Sarah. S s at Wormsley Lent 1748. He.
Phillips, Silas. Rebel T 1685.
Phillips, Stephen. T Oct 1721 *William & John*. Sy.
Phillips, Thomas of Charleton. R for Barbados Feb 1665. Bu.
Phillips, Thomas. PT Jun R Oct 1673. M.
Phillips, Thomas of Iver. R for America Jly 1702. Bu.
Phillips, Thomas of St. John's. SQS Apr T May 1750 *Lichfield*. Sy.
Phillips, Thomas of Bristol. R 14 yrs s ox Mar 1767 (SP). G.
Phillips, Thomas. S Sep T Dec 1767 *Neptune*. M.
Phillips, Thomas. S & T Dec 1771 *Justitia*. M.
Phillips, Thomas. S Mar 1774. So.
Phillips, Thomas. S s timber at Cwmcarvan Summer 1774. Mo.
Phillips, Thomas. AT from QS Lent 1775. Li.
Phillips, Timothy. S & R 14 yrs Lent 1770. G.
Phillips, Walter. Rebel T 1685.
Phillips als Williams, William of Redwick. R for Barbados Jun 1668. Mo.
Phillips, William. R for Barbados Jun 1670. M.
Phillips, William. S Jan T Feb 1719 *Worcester* LC Annapolis Jun 1719. L.
Phillips, William. S & T Apr 1725 *Sukey* LC Annapolis Sep 1725. M.
Phillips, William of Abbots Bromley. S s horse Summer 1729 R Lent 1730 (SP). St.
Phillips, William. S Oct T Dec 1734 *Caesar* LC Va Jly 1735. M.
Phillips, William. S Norwich Summer 1737. Nf.
Phillips, William. S Aug 1740 TB to Va. De.
Phillips, William. S & T Dec 1740 *Vernon*. L.
Phillips, William. S & TB Aug 1754. G.
Phillips, William. S s sheep Lent R 14 yrs Summer 1766. St.
Phillips, Wilmot wife of William. S Aug 1758. Co.
Phillipson, John. S Jun-Dec 1738 T Jan 1739 *Dorsetshire* to Va. M.
Phillis, Alexander of Stogumber, husbandman. R for Barbados Sep 1665. So.
Phillis, Joseph. S s cloth Jan T Jun 1738 *Forward* to Md or Va. M.
Philoe, Thomas. S s at East Dereham & R Summer 1773. Nf.
Philpot, George. S Norwich Summer 1768. Nf.
Philpott, Henry. T May 1752 *Lichfield*. K.

Philpott, Jane (1747). *See* Wilkins. M.

Philpot, Mary. S Lent 1763. Sy.

Philpott, Thomas. S s at Worthen Summer 1734. Sh.

Philpotts, Edward. S s tablecloth Summer 1753. He.

Philwood, John. LC from *Susannah & Sarah* Annapolis Apr 1720. X.

Phineas, Joseph. S Jun T Sep 1767 *Justitia*. L.

Phinnimore, John. Rebel T 1685.

Phippe als Phipps, John. S Oct 1655. M.

Phippen, William. Rebel T 1685.

Phipps, Dinah. S & R 14 yrs Lent 1774. Be.

Phipps, George. S s breeches at Stow on the Wold Lent TB Apr 1751. G.

Phipps, James. S Lent 1763. Bu.

Phipps, John of Braughin. R for Barbados or Jamaica Jun 1699. Ht.

Phipps, John. S Feb T 14 yrs Mar 1727 *Rappahannock* to Md. M.

Phipps, Mary wife of Edward. S s sheep Lent R 14 yrs Summer 1768. Mo.

Phipps, Stephen. R 14 yrs Jly 1731. Ha.

Phipps, Stephen. S s at Broad Rissington Lent TB Apr 1751. G.

Phipps, William. R for America Mar 1680. Wo.

Phipps, William of Farnham. S for highway robbery Lent R 14 yrs Summer 1746. Sy.

Phippy, John. R for Jamaica Aug 1661. M.

Phenix, Alice. S May T Jly 1722 *Gilbert* to Md. M.

Phenix, Caroll. S Nov T Dec 1752 *Greyhound*. L.

Phoenix, Walter. S Aug T Oct 1726 *Forward*. L.

Phratter, Phillis. S Jly T 14 yrs Sep 1737 *Pretty Patsy*. L.

Piceford, Robert. R 14 yrs Mar 1742. Do.

Pickard, Jane. R 14 yrs Mar 1745 TB to Va. De.

Pickard, John, aged 13. S for firing dwelling Summer 1756 R 14 yrs Lent 1757. Hu.

Pickard, Thomas. R for life s horse Lent 1774. Wa.

Peckard, William. S Mar 1720. De.

Peckard, William. TB to Va from QS 1737. De.

Pickard, William. SQS Coventry Mar 1751. Wa.

Pickell, Henry. R for life Lent 1773. Ht.

Pickerell, William of Sandhurst. R for Barbados or Jamaica Feb 1696. Sx.

Pickering, Benjamin (1766). *See* Clark, John. Wa.

Pickering, John. T Jun 1728 *Elizabeth* LC Va Aug 1729. Sy.

Pickering, John. T May 1751 *Tryal*. E.

Pickering, John. S Lent 1762. Ch.

Pickering, John. SQS Feb 1774. M.

Pickering, John Christopher. T May 1736 *Patapsco*. K.

Pickersgill, Thomas. S for perjury Lent 1760; to stand in pillory one hour and to be imprisoned 2 months before transportation TB Aug 1760. Y.

Pickett, James. S Jan-Jun T Jun 1728 *Elizabeth* LC Potomack Aug 1729. M.

Picket, John, a Quaker. R for plantations Jly 1665 (SP). Ht.

Pickett, William. S Lent R 14 yrs Summer 1724 T *Forward* LC
   Annapolis Jun 1725. O.
Pickford, Joseph. S for smuggling brandy under arms Jly 1725. Do.
Pickford, Mark. R 14 yrs Mar 1737. So.
Pickington, Grace (1747). *See* Maud. M.
Pickles, John. AT Lent T Oct 1723 *Forward* from London. Y.
Pickles, John. S s from warehouse Summer 1758 R 14 yrs Lent 1759. La.
Pickills, Thomas. S City Lent AT Summer 1775. Y.
Pickmore, Thomas. S s from Brasenose College, Oxford, Lent 1722. O.
Pickstock, John. S Summer 1757. Ch.
Pickton, John. S & T Apr 1725 *Sukey* LC Annapolis Sep 1725. M.
Picton, Margaret. T Apr 1735 *Patapsco*. Sy.
Piddesley, Matthew of Shobrooke. R for Barbados Feb 1673. De.
Piddington, Edward. S for highway robbery Summer 1758 R 14 yrs Lent
   1759. No.
Piddington, John. S s at St. Aldate, Oxford, Lent 1764. O.
Piddle, James. S Mar 1720. Do.
Pigeon, James. S s sheep Summer 1764 R 14 yrs Lent 1765. Wo.
Pidgeon, John. S Jan-Jun T Jun 1728 *Elizabeth*. L.
Pigen, John. S Lent 1773. Nt.
Pidgeon, Mary wife of John, als Mary Evatt. S Sep-Dec 1746. M.
Pigeon, Mary. S s wine at St. Mary, Shrewsbury, Lent 1762. Sh.
Pidgeon, William. S Summer 1755. Y.
Pigeon, William (1767). *See* Humphreys. St.
Pidgley, James. R Oct AT Dec 1688. M.
Pierce. *See* Pearce.
Piercy. *See* Pearcey.
Pierpoint, John. S Jly T Sep 1718 *Eagle* LC Charles Town Mar 1719. L.
Pierson. *See* Pearson.
Pigg, Joseph. S Jly-Sep T 14 yrs Sep 1742 *Forward*. M.
Piggott, Daniel. SQS & TB Dec 1734. Bd.
Pigot, George of Chertsey. SQS Jan 1767. Sy.
Piggot, John (1769). *See* Scott. M.
Piggott, John. S Summer 1737. Su.
Piggott, John. T 14 yrs Apr 1765 *Ann*. Ht.
Piggott, Mary. S Sep T Oct 1744 *Susannah*. L.
Piggott, Mary. SQS Jun T Jly 1772 *Tayloe*. M.
Piggott, Ralph. T Apr 1743 *Justitia*. Ht.
Piggott, Richard. R for Barbados Sep 1672. L.
Pigott, Thomas. T May 1737 *Forward*. Sx.
Piggott, William. R for Barbados Dec 1670. M.
Pigget als Clarke, William. S for smuggling tea Summer 1737. Nf.
Piggot, William. T Sep 1742 *Forward*. Sx.
Pyke, Eilzsha als Letitia als Alicia. S Jun 1739. L.
Pyke, John. S May T Sep 1737 *Pretty Patsy* to Md. M.
Pyke als Donnevan als Bonnevan, John. S Mar 1749 TB to Va. De.
Pike als Butcher, John. S s horse & R Lent 1774. G.
Pike, Joseph. S Apr 1739. So.
Pike, Mary. S Mar 1761. So.
Pike, Oliver. R (Home Circ) for Barbados Apr 1663. X.
Pike, Robert. S Aug 1773. De.

Pyke, Ruben. S s horse Lent R 14 yrs Summer 1726. G.

Pike, Sarah. S Mar 1761. So.

Pyke, Thomas. R 14 yrs Aug 1736. Do.

Pyke, William. SL Oct 1754. Sy.

Pikeman, Benjamin. S Mar 1739. Wi.

Pilbean, John. S Sep-Oct 1775. M.

Pilborow, John. R for Barbados or Jamaica Jly 1685. L.

Pilcher, ——- of Lyming. R for plantations Feb 1656. K.

Pilcher, William. SQS at Rye s horse & R Jan T Sep 1757 *Thetis*. Sx.

Pyle, William. S Mar 1720. Do.

Pilgrim, Richard. S Jan T Feb 1742 *Industry*. L.

Pilker, Francis. T Apr 1734 *Patapsco*. Sy.

Pilkington, Anne. S Apr 1719. M.

Pilkington, John of Mitton, yeoman. R for Barbados Jly 1685. La.

Pilkington, Richard of Ainsdale within Walton, husbandman. SQS Jan 1765. La.

Pilkington, Thomas. T 14 yrs Apr 1769 *Tryal*. K.

Pilkington, William. R for America Jun 1684. Db.

Pilkington, William. S s at Goldcliff Summer 1734. Mo.

Pilkington, William. S s gelding at St. Clement, Oxford, & R for life Summer 1770. O.

Pilley, John of Anston, cooper. SQS s staves Jan 1733 TB Mar 1734. Nt.

Pilling, Jonathan of Manchester. S s horse & R 14 yrs Summer 1772. La.

Pilling, William (1720). *See* Hood. Sx.

Pillsworth, John of Theydon Garnon. SQS Jly T Sep 1751 *Greyhound*. E.

Pilmer, William. S Aug T Sep 1764 *Justitia*. L.

Pilsbury als Spilsbury, George, formerly of Stafford, now of Manchester, gardener. SQS Jly 1751. La.

Pilsbury, John. S s horse Lent R 14 yrs Summer 1753. Wa.

Piman, William. S Jly T Oct 1723 *Forward*. L.

Pimble, Sarah. S Aug T Sep 1725 *Forward* to Md. M.

Pimm, Emanuel. S & T Dec 1734 *Caesar* LC Va Jly 1735. L.

Pim, Thomas. T May 1752 *Lichfield*. K.

Pinchest, John. S s handkerchief at All Hallows Barking Jly T Oct 1768 *Justitia*. L.

Pinchin, Anne of Potterne, spinster. SQS New Sarum Jan TB May 1756. Wi.

Pinchen, Francis. S Mar 1724. Wi.

Pinchin als Marshmant, James. S Mar 1760. Ha.

Pinchin, John. S Oct 1756. L.

Pinchin als White als Painter, John. S Oct 1764 T Jan 1765 *Tryal*. M.

Pinchin, Mary of Potterne, spinster. SQS New Sarum Jan TB May 1756. Wi.

Pinchin, William of Chalfield Magna, mason. R for Barbados Jun 1666. Wi.

Pinckard, Richard of Bierton. R for America Feb 1688. Bu.

Pinkeny, Isaac. S s wheat at Halesworth Lent 1771. Su.

Pinckney, Jemima. S City Lent 1750. Y.

Pindar, Elizabeth. S Jan T Apr 1759 *Thetis*. M.

Pindar, John. S Apr T May 1720 *Honor* to York River. L.

Pindar, Rachael. S Oct T Dec 1769 *Justitia*. L.
Pinder, William of New Malton. SQS Easingwold for setting fire to shed Jan 1735. Y.
Pyne, Charles. S Jan T Apr 1770 *New Trial*. M.
Pyne, Richard. Rebel T 1685.
Piner, Ann. S & T Oct 1730 *Forward* LC Potomack Jan 1731. L.
Pyner, John. SQS Jly 1774. M.
Piner, Thomas. S Aug T Oct 1726 *Forward* to Va. M.
Pyner, Thomas. S Feb-Apr T May 1751 *Tryal*. M.
Pyner, William of St. Saviour, Southwark. SQS Jan 1773. Sy.
Pynes, Mary (1697). *See* Waters. M.
Pinfield, John. S Lent T Apr 1771. Wa.
Pinfield, William. S s at Rushock Lent 1764. Wo.
Pinfold, George of Farnham. R for Barbados or Jamaica Mar 1682. Sy.
Pinfold als Perkins, George. S Feb T Mar 1727 *Rappahannock* to Md. M.
Pinfold, Joseph (1775). *See* Pearce. Ha.
Pingrey, Francis of Tenbury. R for America Mar 1688. Wo.
Pink Percy (1772). *See* Pinke, Thomas. G.
Pinck als Mountsley, Mary of St. Saviour, Southwark. R for Barbados or Jamaica Feb 1686. Sy.
Pink, Richard. T May 1751 *Tryal*. Sx.
Pincke, Robert of Portsmouth. R for Barbados Jun 1708. Ha.
Pinke, Thomas, als Pink Percy of Bristol. R 14 yrs Jun 1772 (SP). G.
Pingstone, John. S Aug 1735. De.
Pinkstone, Thomas. R for life Feb 1775. M.
Pynn, William of ?Treverough. R for Barbados Jun 1708. De.
Pinn, William. S Jan T Feb 1726 *Supply* LC Annapolis May 1726. L.
Pinn, William of Wimbledon. S Summer 1748 R 14 yrs Lent 1749. Sy.
Pinncaw, Mary. S Oct 1744-Jan 1745. M.
Pinner, Edward. S Lent 1753. Bu.
Pinner, Elizabeth. S Apr T Jun 1742 *Bladon* to Md. M.
Pinner, John. R for Barbados Apr TB Jun 1669. M.
Pynner, John of Lambourne. R (Newgate) for Barbados Sep 1669. E.
Pinney, Azarias. Rebel T 1685.
Pinney, Francis. S Mar 1758. So.
Pinney, John. Rebel T 1685.
Pinney, John. S Mar 1746. So.
Pinnick, Ann. S 14 yrs for receiving & T Jly 1771 *Scarsdale*. L.
Pinegar, Humphrey of Driffield. S Summer 1720. G.
Pinnigar, Joseph. S Mar TB to Va Apr 1771. Wi.
Pinnock, Henry. S Oct T Dec 1758 *The Brothers*. L.
Pinnock, William Sr. SQS Devizes Apr TB to Va Aug 1749. Wi.
Pinson, Roger. R for Jamaica Mar 1665. L.
Pinson, Samuel. Rebel T 1685.
Pinson, Thomas. R 14 yrs Jly 1741. Ha.
Pinton, William als Frampton. R Jly 1773. Ha.
Pinyard, William. AT Summer 1756. Y.
Piper, Elizabeth. T Apr 1765 *Ann*. K.
Piper, Francis. R Oct 1694 AT Jan 1695. M.
Piper, James (1741). *See* Pyechly. M.

Piper, Jane (1725). *See* Fleetwood. M.
Piper, John (1675). *See* Hughes. M.
Pyper, John. R 14 yrs Aug 1764. Co.
Piper, Joseph of Andover, weaver. R for Barbados Jun 1666. Ha.
Piper, Nicholas (1722). *See* Robson. St.
Piper, Richard. S Feb 1752. L.
Piper, Richard. S Jly 1753. Ha.
Pyper, Thomas. R 14 yrs Aug 1764. Co.
Pipkin als Pitkin, William. S s mare Lent R 14 yrs Summer 1742. O.
Pipp, Joseph. S Mar 1774. Wi.
Pippen, John. S for Va Jly 1718. So.
Pipping, Nathaniel. S Feb T Mar 1731 *Patapsco* LC Annapolis Jun 1731. M.
Pippin, Richard. R 14 yrs Lent 1721. G.
Pippin als Pepper, Richard. S Apr-May 1754. M.
Pipson, John. S s sugar at St. Dunstan in East Jly T Oct 1768 *Justitia*. L.
Pisano, Joseph. S & T Dec 1769 *Justitia*. M.
Pissey, John. T Apr 1770 *New Trial*. Sy.
Pisson, Edward (1757). *See* Smith. Ha.
Pison, James (1747). *See* Hodges. M.
Pitcher, Edward. S Jan-Jun T Jun 1728 *Elizabeth* LC Potomack Aug 1729. L.
Pitcher, James. S Mar 1774. So.
Pitcher, Martha. T Jun 1764 *Dolphin*. E.
Pitchey, George. T Sep 1758 *Tryal*. E.
Pitchfield, Thomas. T Apr 1739 *Forward*. E.
Pitchford, William. S s at Claverley Summer 1767. Sh.
Pitchland, Richard. S Mar 1767. Ha.
Pitfield, Sarah. S Oct T Nov 1759 *Phoenix*. M.
Pitford, John. R for Barbados Dec 1693 AT Jan 1694. M.
Pitkin, William (1742). *See* Pipkin. O.
Pitman, Henry. Rebel T 1685.
Pitman, James of Bishops Stortford. S Summer 1745. Ht.
Pitman, Jesse. R 14 yrs Aug 1751. So.
Pitman, John. S Jly T Sep 1767 *Justitia*. M.
Pitman, Mary. S Jly T Sep 1766 *Justitia*. M.
Pittman, Richard. R 14 yrs Mar 1752. So.
Pitman, Samuel. R 14 yrs Aug 1751. So.
Pitman, Thomas. S May T Jly 1722 *Alexander*. L.
Pitman, Thomas. S Dec 1768 T Jan 1769 *Thornton*. M.
Pitney, John. S Mar 1725. So.
Pitt, George. S Jly T Sep 1766 *Justitia*. L.
Pitt, John of Rockland Tofts. R for Barbados Jan 1665. Nf.
Pitt, John. S s sheep Lent R 14 yrs Summer 1742. O.
Pitt, John of St. Saviour, Southwark. SQS Jly T Sep 1766 *Justitia*. Sy.
Pitt, Joseph. S Lent 1749. Sy.
Pitt als Evans, Mary. SQS Feb 1751. M.
Pitt, Richard. S Lent R 14 yrs Summer 1760 T 1761 *Atlas* from Bristol. He.
Pitt, Richard. R Jly 1774. M.
Pitt, Thomas. Rebel T 1685.

Pitt, Thomas of Horsley. S s cloth Lent TB Mar 1754. G.
Pitt, William of Albrighton. R for America Jly 1679. Sh.
Pitt, William Moss. R 14 yrs Mar TB to Va Apr 1773. Wi.
Pittam, John. S Jly 1763. M.
Pittard, Mary. S Mar 1740. So.
Pittard, Thomas. Rebel T 1685.
Pitter, Thomas. SQS May TB to Md Oct 1739. So.
Pitts, Charles. S Feb 1754. M.
Pitts, Francis. S Summer 1737 T Jan 1738 *Dorsetshire*. Bu.
Pitts, Jane. TB to Va from QS 1740. De.
Pitts, Jeremiah. S s mare Lent R 14 yrs Summer 1745. Nf.
Pitts, John of Northampton. R for America Jly 1682. No.
Pitts, John. Rebel T 1685.
Pitts, John. S Jly T Aug 1721 *Prince Royal* LC Va Nov 1721. L.
Pitts, John, a boy. S Summer 1736 R 14 yrs Summer 1737. Wa.
Pitts, Matthew. S Lent R 14 yrs Summer 1742. Ru.
Pitts, William. Rebel T 1685.
Pittwood, Richard of Exeter. R for Barbados Mar 1694. De.
Pixley, John of St. Margaret, Ipswich. S Summer 1732. Su.
Pixley, Robert. LC from *Caesar* Va Jly 1734. X.
Pixley, Thomas. S Jly 1775. L.
Pizey, Henry (1750). *See* Mills. E.
Place, Anne, spinster. S s at Assington & R Summer 1771; Samuel Place
    hanged. Su.
Place als Jones als Emanell, John. S Feb T Sep 1737 *Pretty Patsy* to
    Md. M.
Place, John. S s mare at Preston on Weald Moors Lent R 14 yrs
    Summer 1762. Sh.
Place, William. T Sep 1765 *Justitia*. K.
Plackett, John. S Apr T May 1751 *Tryal*. L.
Plaister als Plaisted, Mary. S s at Sonning Lent 1766. Be.
Plaistow, Samuel. R Jly 1773. M.
Playne, James. S s tallow Lent TB May 1755. G.
Plane, Moses of Rotherhithe. SQS Jan T Mar 1764 *Tryal*. Sy.
Playne als Playden, Thomas of Thurrock. R for Barbados or Jamaica
    Jly 1688 & Feb 1690. E.
Plane, Thomas of Rotherhithe. SQS Jan T Mar 1764 *Tryal*. Sy.
Plank, Sarah. S & T Sep 1757 *Thetis*. L.
Plank, William. S Summer 1757 R 14 yrs Lent 1758. Be.
Plant, Elizabeth. S May T Jly 1723 *Alexander* to Md. M.
Plant, James. S s at Whitchurch Summer 1726. Sh.
Plant, James. S Summer 1775. Y.
Plant, John. S Oct T 14 yrs Nov 1725 *Rappahannock* LC Rappahannock
    Apr 1726. L.
Plaser, Christopher (1738). *See* Ploser. E.
Plaster, Thomas. S Lent R 14 yrs Summer 1765. O.
Plater, Maria of St. James, Westminster, spinster. S s clothing Oct 1740
    T Jan 1741 *Harpooner* to Rappahannock. M.
Platt, Ann, spinster, als wife of John Osborne. R for Barbados Jly
    1663. L.
Platt, Elizabeth. S May T Jun 1727 *Susanna* to Va. M.

Platt, James of Ditton, weaver. SQS Oct 1753. La.

Platt, John. R for Barbados or Jamaica Dec 1693. M.

Platt als Nutt, John. S Apr T 14 yrs May 1718 *Tryal* LC Charles Town Aug 1718. L.

Platt, John. S Feb T Apr 1732 *Patapsco* LC Annapolis Oct 1732. M.

Platt, John. S Summer 1751 R 14 yrs Lent 1752. St.

Platt, John (1751). *See* Burgess. La.

Platt, John. S Apr 1774. M.

Platt, Joseph. T Jan 1765 *Tryal*. M.

Platt, William. S Lent 1748. E.

Platt, William. S s at Eccleshall Lent 1771. St.

Platton, Samuel. S & T Sep 1765 *Justitia*. M.

Platts, John. R for Barbados Sep 1682. L.

Playden, Thomas (1690). *See* Playne. E.

Player, Henry. S Apr 1765. So.

Playne. *See* Plane.

Pleadwell, Margaret. R for Barbados or Jamaica Jan 1693. L.

Pleasants, Charles. T Sep 1766 *Justitia*. M.

Please, Elizabeth. S for Va Mar 1719. De.

Please, John. TB to Va from QS 1768. De.

Pledge, William. T May 1719 *Margaret* LC Md Sep 1719; sold to Patrick Sympson & William Black. K.

Pledger, John of All Saints, Colchester. R for Barbados Jly 1678 & 1679. E.

Plenty, Richard of Battersea. R for Barbados Aug 1662. Sy.

Plessis, Nicholas. S Jan T Apr 1762 *Dolphin*. M.

Plevey, Thomas. S Lent R 14 yrs Summer 1764. He.

Plew, John. S & T Oct 1732 *Caesar*. L.

Plews, Robert of Angram Cote, East Witton. SQS Richmond s at Bedale Jan 1727. Y.

Plisson, Peter of Milton next Gravesend. R for Barbados or Jamaica Jly 1674. K.

Plodd, John Henry. S Jly 1773. L.

Ploser als Plaser, Christopher. T Jan 1738 *Dorsetshire*. E.

Plott, James of Tetsworth. R for America Nov 1694. O.

Plow, Susanna. S Lent 1756. Su.

Plowman, Mary. S Jan T Feb 1726 *Supply* LC Annapolis May 1726. M.

Plowman, Mary. S Mar 1735. So.

Plowman, Moses. S Mar 1740. Do.

Plowman, Richard (1750). *See* Street. Wi.

Plowman, Robert. S Sep-Oct T Dec 1752 *Greyhound*. M.

Plowman, Thomas. S May T Jly 1722 *Alexander* to Nevis or Jamaica. M.

Plowman, William. S Aug T Oct 1726 *Forward*. L.

Plowman, William. S Mar 1740. Do.

Plowright, Mary. S May T Jun 1726 *Loyal Margaret* LC Annapolis Oct 1726. M.

Ploughwright, Thomas. R for Barbados Aug 1664. M.

Pluckrose, John. T Nov 1741 *Sea Horse*. E.

Plum, Frederick. S Lent R 14 yrs Summer T Dec 1763 *Neptune*. K.

Plumb, John. S Feb 1773. L.

Plumb, Thomas. S Lent 1735. *Su.

Plumley, George. Rebel T 1685.

Plumbly, Matthew. S Feb T Mar 1727 *Rappahannock*. L.

Plumer, Ann. S Dec 1775. M.

Plummer, Charles. S Apr T May 1718 *Tryal*. L.

Plummer, Daniel. T Jan 1738 *Dorsetshire*. K.

Plummer, Elizabeth. R for Barbados Aug 1679. L.

Plummer, Francis. Rebel T 1685.

Plummer, Isaac. T May 1719 *Margaret* LC Md May 1720; sold to William Davies. Sy.

Plummer, Joseph. S s beans Lent 1738. Y.

Plummer, Lydia (1769). *See* Hanks, Betty. G.

Plummer, Mary. S May-Jly T Sep 1755 *Tryal*. M.

Plummer, Mary. S Dec 1756. M.

Plomer, Richard. R for America Aug 1685. Nt.

Plummer, Richard. SQS Jan 1738. So.

Plomber, Samuel. T Jly 1722 *Alexander*. E.

Plumber, Samuel. S May T Sep 1766 *Justitia*. M.

Plummer, Thomas of Elsenham. R for Barbados or Jamaica Jly 1715. E.

Plummer, William. S Summer R for Barbados Aug 1664. K.

Plumer, William. SQS Sep 1772. M.

Plumpe, John (1699). *See* Goodwin. L.

Plummeridge, Edward. T Apr 1766 *Ann*. Bu.

Plumridge, John. S Summer 1741. Be.

Plumridge, Richard of White Waltham. R for America Jly 1678. Be.

Plumsey, William, als Warwick, Joseph. R 14 yrs Jly 1737. Ha.

Plunkett, Ann. S s human hair Sep 1735 T Jan 1736 *Dorsetshire* LC Va Sep 1736. M.

Plunket, James. S May T Jun 1756 *Lyon*. L.

Plunket, Mary. S Nov T Dec 1770 *Justitia*. L.

Plunkett, Robert of Christchurch. SQS Jan 1751. Sy.

Plymouth, Susanna. S Jly 1749. L.

Pobgee, William. S Summer 1772. Sy.

Pocock, Charles. S Jan T Feb 1744 *Neptune*. L.

Pocock, John. S s cheeses at Sutton Lent 1750. Be.

Pocock, Robert. S Summer T Sep 1751 *Greyhound*. Sy.

Podmore, George. T for life Oct 1768 *Justitia*. K.

Poe, George. S Jly 1741. De.

Poe, John. S & T for life Mar 1750 *Tryal*. L.

Poe, Samuel. S Lent R 14 yrs Summer 1752. Nt.

Poinctain, John. S Aug T Oct 1724 *Forward* to Md. M.

Pointer, John. S Apr T May 1755 *Rose*. L.

Pointer, John. SQS Jan-Mar TB to Va Apr 1741. Wi.

Pointer als Foreman, Richard. SQS Warminster Jly TB to Va Sep 1738. Wi.

Pointer, Thomas. S Jan T Feb 1733 *Smith* to Md or Va. M.

Poynter, William of St. Clements. R for Barbados Jly 1678. Co.

Poynting, John. R 14 yrs Aug 1751. So.

Poynting, Richard. SQS Jan 1744 TB to Md Mar 1745. So.

Poynting, Stephen. SQS Apr TB May 1756. So.

Poits als Pows als Parke, Thomas of Bray. R for America Feb 1713. Be.

Poke, Mary, als Banks als Hill, Hannah. S May T Jly 1722 *Alexander*. M.

Poker als Rand als Cole, John. S Jan-Apr 1749. M.

Poland, Abraham. S Sep-Oct 1748 T Jan 1749 *Laura*. M.

Poland, Christian. S Jan T Apr 1743 *Justitia*. M.

Polin, William. S s handkerchief at St. Catherine Creechurch Oct 1768 T Jan 1769 *Thornton*. L.

Polkinghorne, James. R 14 yrs Mar 1772. Co.

Polkinhorne, William. S 14 yrs Mar 1744. De.

Pollard, Abraham. Rebel T 1685.

Pollard, Andrew. S Lent 1761. E.

Pollard, Ann. S Lent 1757. Y.

Pollard, Catherine. S & T 14 yrs Sep 1737 *Pretty Patsy* to Md. M.

Pollard, Elizabeth. SQS Dec 1768 T Jan 1769 *Thornton*. M.

Pollard, John. S Lent 1761. K.

Pollard, John. S s sheep & R 14 yrs Lent T Sep 1768. Li.

Pollard, John. SQS Apr T Jly 1771 *Scarsdale*. M.

Pollard, Jonathan. S for highway robbery Summer 1764 R 14 yrs Lent 1765. La.

Pollard als Gillett, Mary. S Apr 1749. L.

Pollard, Mary. S Feb T Apr 1772 *Thornton*. L.

Pollard, Mary. S Apr-May 1775. M.

Pollard, Nicholas. S Apr 1723. De.

Pollard, Thomas. R 14 yrs Apr 1770. So.

Pollard, William. S Jan T Mar 1750 *Tryal*. L.

Pollett, Edward, aged 20, fair. S Jan T Feb 1723 *Jonathan* LC Annapolis Jly 1724. L.

Pollet, Elizabeth. S Aug 1757. So.

Pollett, Richard. PT Summer 1719. Be.

Pollet, Thomas. S Aug 1741. So.

Pollett, Thomas of Winwick with Holme. SQS Jly 1757. La.

Pollet, William. S Oct 1774. L.

Polley, John of Burling. R for Barbados Apr 1668. K.

Polock, James. S Apr-May T Jly 1771 *Scarsdale*. M.

Polson. *See* Poulson.

Polton. *See* Poulton.

Pomeroy, George. S Apr 1728. De.

Pomeroy, James. Rebel T 1685.

Pomroy, John. S & T Oct 1722 *Forward* LC Annapolis Jun 1723. L.

Pomeroy, John. S Dec 1737 T Jan 1738 *Dorsetshire*. L.

Pomeroy, Samuel. Rebel T 1685.

Pomroy, Samuel. S Jun-Dec 1738 T Jan 1739 *Dorsetshire* to Va. M.

Pomfrett, Edward. S Sep-Oct 1749. M.

Pomfret, Elizabeth wife of William. S Jun T Sep 1764 *Justitia*. M.

Pomfret, Henry. T 14 yrs Apr 1768 *Thornton*. E.

Pomfrett, Thomas. Rebel T 1685.

Pomfrett, Thomas of St. Clement Danes. S s violin Oct 1740 T Jan 1741 *Harpooner* to Rappahannock. M.

Pomfrey, Elizabeth. S Oct T Nov 1759 *Phoenix*. L.

Pomfrey, James. S Feb T Mar 1730 *Patapsco* but died on passage. M.

Pomfrey, Susanna. S s at Wantage Summer 1724. Be.

Pond, Bryan. R 14 yrs Aug 1726. So.

Pond, Elizabeth. T Sep 1730 *Smith*. Sy.

Pong, Lettice. S Jan 1746. M.

Pont, Anne. S Summer R for Barbados Aug 1663. K.

Pont, John. T Nov 1743 *George William*. E.

Pont, Margaret. S Summer R for Barbados May 1664. Sx.

Ponting, Edward. S Summer 1768. G.

Poole, Abraham. S s sheep at Hodnet Lent R 14 yrs Summer 1762. Sh.

Poole, Anne. R for Barbados May 1665. X.

Poole, Benjamin. R for Barbados May 1676. L.

Poole, Daniel, aged 19. R for Barbados Feb 1664. L.

Pool, Edward. S s at Shenstone Summer 1761. St.

Poole als Robinson, George. S Jan T Feb 1719 *Worcester* LC Annapolis Jun 1719. L.

Poole, George. S Jun T Aug 1769 *Douglas*. L.

Poole, Grace. S Jly 1724. De.

Poole, James. S May 1744. L.

Pool, James (1771). *See* Cook, Charles. St.

Poole, Jeremy. Rebel T 1685.

Poole, John. R for Barbados Jan 1664. L.

Poole, John. Rebel T 1685.

Poole als Powell, John. S Jan T Feb 1733 *Smith* to Md or Va. M.

Poole als Dudley, John. S s sheep & R Lent 1774. Sh.

Poole, Joseph. S s heifer Summer 1769. Ch.

Poole, Josiah. S Jly T Oct 1741 *Sea Horse* to Va. M.

Poole, Lewis. S & T Jan 1736 *Dorsetshire* LC Va Sep 1736. L.

Poole, Mary. R Dec 1716 T Jan 1717 *Queen Elizabeth* to Jamaica. M.

Pool, Mary wife of John. S Feb T May 1736 *Patapsco* to Md. M.

Poole, Rachel of St. Giles in Fields, spinster. S silverware Apr T May 1740 *Essex*. M.

Poole, Richard. S & R 14 yrs Lent 1769. He.

Pool, Robert. S Mar 1724. So.

Poole, Robert. S & T Sep 1764 *Justitia*. M.

Poole, Sarah. S Jan-Jun T Jun 1728 *Elizabeth* LC Potomack Aug 1729. M.

Poole, Silvester. Rebel T 1685.

Poole, Simon. Rebel T 1685.

Poole, Susannah. S & T Oct 1722 *Forward* LC Annapolis Jun 1723. L.

Poole, Thomas. T May 1719 *Margaret* LC Md Sep 1719; sold to Patrick Sympson & William Black. E.

Poole, Thomas. R 14 yrs Aug TB to Va Sep 1753. Wi.

Poole, Thomas. S for obtaining goods in Shrewsbury by false pretences Summer 1769. Sh.

Pooley, John. S Lent R 14 yrs Summer 1742. Nf.

Pooley, Richard. PT Jun 1674. M.

Pooley, Thomas. S Lent R 14 yrs Summer 1757. Nf.

Pooley, William of St. Margaret, Rochester. R for Barbados Aug 1662. K.

Pooley, William. S s silver spoon at Bray Summer 1755. Be.

Poon, Peter. S for highway robbery Lent R 14 yrs Summer T Sep 1757 *Thetis*. Bu.

Poor, Abraham. S & T Oct 1720 *Gilbert*. L.

Poor, Arthur. SQS Apr T Sep 1758 *Tryal* to Annapolis. M.

Poore, George. R Jly AT Sep 1675. M.

Poor, Henry. S Mar TB to Va Apr 1768. Wi.

Poor, Jane (1752). *See* Haley. M.

Pope, Dorothy of Landrake. R for Barbados Jly 1684. Co.

Pope als Bull, Edward. R Apr 1770. Do.

Pope, Elizabeth als Mary. S Jly 1724. De.

Pope, Francis. S Feb T May 1736 *Patapsco* to Md. M.

Pope, Garrett. S s at Abergavenny Summer 1729. Mo.

Pope, George. S Apr T Jun 1742 *Bladon* to Md. M.

Pope, Humphrey. Rebel T 1685.

Pope, Isaac. T Jun 1738 *Forward*. Sx.

Pope, James of Dulver. R for Barbados Jly 1684. Co.

Pope, John of Angmering. R for Barbados Aug 1662. Sx.

Pope, John (2). Rebels T 1685.

Pope, John. R Dec 1716 T Jan 1717 *Queen Elizabeth* to Jamaica. M.

Pope, John. S & T Apr 1725 *Sukey* LC Annapolis Sep 1725. M.

Pope, John. S Lent 1774. K.

Pope, Joseph. S s at Aston Tirrold Lent 1750. Be.

Pope, Mary (1724). *See* Pope, Elizabeth. De.

Pope, Maurice. S Mar 1772. Ha.

Pope, Robert. R for Barbados Feb 1672. M.

Pope, Sarah (1752). *See* Dixon. L.

Pope, Thomas of Candlemarsh, husbandman. R for Barbados Jly 1667. Do.

Pope, Thomas. R for life Aug 1740. So.

Pope, William. S s mare & R 14 yrs Lent 1737. Ca.

Pope, William. S Lent R Summer 1748 T Jan 1749 *Laura*. Sy.

Pope, William. S Jly 1749. L.

Pope, William. S Sep-Oct T Dec 1752 *Greyhound*. M.

Pope, William. S Oct T Nov 1759 *Phoenix*. L.

Popham als Rowsall, Henry of Morchard Bishop, husbandman. R for Barbados Sep 1665. De.

Popham, Samuel. S Aug 1750. So.

Popley, William. S Oct 1737 T Jan 1738 *Dorsetshire* to Va. M.

Popple als War, Betty. S Aug 1753. Do.

Pople, Charles. Rebel T 1685.

Popplewell, John. S Sep-Oct 1774. M.

Popplewell, Mary wife of Thomas. ST & T Nov 1762 *Prince William*. L.

Popplewell, Timothy. S s sheep Lent 1738. Y.

Porch, George Jr. of Sutton at Hone. R for Barbados or Jamaica Mar 1688. K.

Porson. *See* Pawson.

Port, Ann. S Jan T Feb 1726 *Supply* LC Annapolis May 1726. L.

Porte, Henry. S Dec 1773. L.

Port, John of Sutton, watchmaker. R for America Mar 1698. Ch.

Porter, Daniel. T Oct 1722 *Forward* LC Md Jun 1723. Sy.

Porter, Daniel. S Oct T Dec 1771 *Justitia*. L.

Porter, Edward. S Feb T Apr 1742 *Bond* to Potomack. M.

Porter, Elizabeth. S Jan T Feb 1719 *Worcester* LC Annapolis Jun 1719. L.

Porter, Elizabeth (1735). *See* Cahill. Y.
Porter, Elizabeth (1747). *See* Bargess. La.
Porter, Francis. T Apr 1768 *Thornton*. Sy.
Porter, Jasper. R 14 yrs Jly 1725. Wi.
Porter, John. S s at Cannock Lent 1735. St.
Porter, John. S Feb-Apr T May 1752 *Lichfield*. M.
Porter, John. SW & T Jun 1768 *Tryal*. M.
Porter, Luke. Rebel T 1685.
Porter, Margaret. SQS & T Sep 1766 *Justitia*. M.
Porter, Margaret. S Lent 1771. La.
Porter, Martha. LC from *Alexander* Annapolis Sep 1723. X.
Porter, Martha. T Dec 1736 *Dorsetshire*. Sy.
Porter, Mary. T Apr 1734 *Patapsco*. Sy.
Porter, Mary. S Summer 1740. Sh.
Porter, Mary. S & T Jan 1756 *Greyhound*. M.
Porter, Mary. S Jly 1773. L.
Porter als Pourcher, Matthew of Stamford Rivers or High Ongar. R for
    Barbados or Jamaica Jly 1678. E.
Porter, Mathew. Rebel T 1685.
Porter, Rebecca. S Jly 1748. L.
Porter, Richard. S Feb T Mar 1731 *Patapsco* LC Annapolis Jun 1731. L.
Porter, Robert. R for Barbados Aug 1676. Fl.
Porter, Solomon. SQS Apr 1754. M.
Porter, Solomon. SQS May T Jly 1771 *Scarsdale*. M.
Porter, Tabitha. R Oct AT Dec 1688. M.
Porter, Thomas of St. Saviour, Southwark. SQS Mar T Apr 1768
    Thornton. Sy.
Porter, William. T Apr 1741 *Speedwell* or *Mediterranean*. Sy.
Porter, William of Great Crosby, bricklayer. SQS Apr 1755. La.
Porter, William. R 14 yrs Mar 1766. So.
Porter, William. T 14 yrs Apr 1768 *Thornton*. K.
Porter, William. S Oct 1772. L.
Portes, Margaret wife of John. S s at Newport Summer 1733. Sh.
Portess, William. S Lent T May 1750 *Lichfield*. K.
Portland, James. T Apr 1766 *Ann*. K.
Portman, Richard. S s at Nightwick & Broadway Lent 1737. Wo.
Portnell, John. Rebel T 1685.
Portobello, Elizabeth (1741). *See* Thornton. M.
Portus, John. S for highway robbery Lent R 14 yrs Summer TB Aug
    1736. Y.
Post, John of Shoreham. R for Barbados or Jamaica Jly 1710. K.
Postlewaite, Hugh. S Feb T Apr 1739 *Forward* to Va. M.
Postlethwaite, Thomas. S s mare Lent R 14 yrs Summer 1768. Nt.
Poston, John. S s at Grimley Lent 1729. Wo.
Postons, William. S s at Middleton on Hill Lent 1736. He.
Potley, Christopher. R for Va Jly 1618. O.
Pott, Humphrey of Lichfield. R for America Jun 1692. St.
Pott, John. S Lent R 14 yrs Summer 1749. Le.
Pott, William of Fewston. R for Barbados Jly 1690. Y.
Potten, John (1732). *See* Potter. Sh.
Potter, Ann (1760). *See* Endacott. De.

Potter, Charles. S Apr 1760. M.
Potter, Edward. R for Barbados Jun 1665. M.
Potter, Elisha. R 14 yrs Summer 1741. Y.
Potter, Elizabeth (1681). *See* Osborne. So.
Potter, George. S Sep-Oct 1749. M.
Potter, George. S Summer 1757. Cu.
Potter, Henry (1750). *See* Clarke. Be.
Potter, James. S for highway robbery Summer 1743 R 14 yrs Lent 1744. Nf.
Potter, Jeremiah. S s at Chesham Lent 1754. Bu.
Potter, John. S Oct 1727-Jun 1728 T Jun 1728 *Elizabeth* LC Potomack Aug 1729. M.
Potter als Potten, John. S s at Nash Summer 1732. Sh.
Potter, John. S Aug 1739. So.
Potter, John of Stepney. S s books & T Feb 1740 *York* to Md. M.
Potter, John of St. Ann, Westminster. SW Oct 1766 T Jan 1767 *Tryal*. M.
Potter als Clayton, John. S Mar TB to Va Apr 1767. Wi.
Potter, John. S s at St. Matthew, Ipswich, & R Summer 1775. Su.
Potter, Lawrence. LC from *Mary* Port York Jun 1721. X.
Potter, Martin. S Lent 1767. Li.
Potter, Richard of Hunnington. R for America Jly 1683. Su.
Potter, Richard. S Nov T 14 yrs Dec 1763 *Neptune*. L.
Potter, Sarah of Middleton. SQS 14 yrs for receiving Apr T Sep 1758 *Tryal*. E.
Potter, Thomas. S s silver mug at Cold Kirby Summer TB Aug 1765. Y.
Potter, William. T Oct 1723 *Forward*. Sy.
Potter, William. T May 1737 *Forward*. K.
Potter, William. T Apr 1739 *Forward*. E.
Potter, William. S Feb 1752. L.
Potter, William. S s at St. Peter Mancroft, Norwich, Summer 1770. Nf.
Potter, William. S Aug 1773. De.
Potter, Zachariah. S Jun T Dec 1736 *Dorsetshire* to Va. M.
Pottinger, Henry of Kingston on Thames. R for Barbados or Jamaica Jly 1688 & Feb 1690. Sy.
Pottinger, Jane (1729). *See* Patten. L.
Pottinger, William. S Jly 1738. Ha.
Pottle, James. SQS Dec 1755 T Jan 1756 *Greyhound*. M.
Pottle, Matthew. Rebel T 1685.
Pottle, William. S s mare at Bracknell Lent R 14 yrs Summer 1737. Be.
Potts, Abraham of Blithfield. R for America Feb 1716. St.
Potts, Edmund. S Jan-Apr 1749. M.
Potts, Francis. S Jly 1765. Ha.
Potts, George. S Dec 1750. L.
Potts, Henry. R for America Jly 1686. Db.
Potts, Thomas, merchant. R for Barbados Mar & Dec 1683. L.
Pulson, Cicely (1744). *See* Slaney, Mary. Sh.
Polson, Elizabeth. S Apr T May 1718 *Tryal*. L.
Poulson, Elizabeth. S Oct-Dec 1754. M.
Poulsum, Mary. S Mar TB to Va Apr 1772. Wi.
Poulter, John. S 14 yrs Sep-Oct 1746. M.
Poulter, Owen. T Apr 1741 *Speedwell* or *Mediterranean*. E.

Poultney, Thomas. T Jun 1740 *Essex*. Sy.

Poulton, George of Great Baddow. SQS Jan T Sep 1758 *Tryal*. E.

Poulton, Isaac. R 14 yrs Oct 1772. M.

Pulton, John. T Nov 1741 *Sea Horse*. Sx.

Poulton als Lowcross, Martha. S & T Apr 1733 *Patapsco* LC Annapolis Nov 1733. L.

Poulton, Samuel. S Feb-Apr 1745. M.

Polton, William. T May 1741 *Miller*. K.

Pound, Daniel. S Lent 1756. Bu.

Pound, John. R for Jamaica Feb 1665. M.

Pound, John. S Mar 1725. Wi.

Pound, John. R 14 yrs Mar 1773. Do.

Pourcher, Matthew (1678). *See* Porter. E.

Poushett, William (1748). *See* Bushell. L.

Povey, Ann. R for Barbados or Jamaica May 1697. L.

Pow, Frederick. S Dec 1764 T Jan 1765 *Tryal*. M.

Powd, Thomas. R 14 yrs & TB to Va Mar 1760. Wi.

Powditch, George of St. George, Southwark. SQS Jan T Apr 1770 *New Trial*. Sy.

Powell, Aaron of Axford. R for Barbados Jly 1717. Wi.

Powell, Aaron. S May & Jly 1720 to be T to Boston NE. Wi.

Powell als Masters, Alice. R for Barbados Jly 1675. L.

Powell, Anne, aged 27, dark. S & T Oct 1720 *Gilbert* LC Annapolis May 1721. M.

Powell, Anthony. T Apr 1762 *Neptune*. Ht.

Powell, Arthur. S Summer 1754. Sh.

Powell, Benjamin (1766). *See* Harding, John. Wa.

Powell, Betty wife of David. S Lent TB Apr 1740. G.

Powell, Catherine of Nash, spinster. S Summer 1720. Mo.

Powell, Charles. SQS Feb T Mar 1760 *Friendship*. M.

Powell, Daniel. S s at Pangbourne Lent 1748 AT Lent 1749. Be.

Powell, Edward. T 14 yrs Apr 1759 *Thetis*. Sy.

Powell, Eleanor. S Jan T Feb 1733 *Smith*. L.

Powell, Eleanor. S 14 yrs Apr 1760. M.

Powell, Eleanor. T Jan 1767 *Tryal*. M.

Powell, Eleanor. S Dec 1772. M.

Powell, Elizabeth (1724). *See* Candy. M.

Powell, Elizabeth. S & T Apr 1725 *Sukey* LC Annapolis Sep 1725. M.

Powell, Elizabeth. S Aug T Sep 1725 *Forward* to Md. M.

Powell, Elizabeth. S s gowns Sep T Dec 1736 *Dorsetshire* to Va. M.

Powell, Elizabeth. S Oct 1742 T 14 yrs Apr 1743 *Justitia*. M.

Powell, Elizabeth. S s at Bromyard Lent 1774. He.

Powell, Evan. S s horses & R for life Summer 1774. St.

Powell, George. S & T Oct 1729 *Forward* LC Va Jun 1730. M.

Powell, George. S Lent R 14 yrs Summer TB Aug 1749. G.

Powell, Hannah. S Lent R Summer T Oct 1739 *Duke of Cumberland*. K.

Powell, Hester. S Feb T Mar 1730 *Patapsco* but died on passage. M.

Powell, Humphrey. R 14 yrs Summer 1750. Y.

Powell, Jacob. Rebel T 1685.

Powle, James of Dilwyn. R for America Feb 1673. He.

Powell, James (1721). *See* Nun. L.

Powell, James. S s lead Feb T Jun 1738 *Forward* to Md or Va. M.
Powell, James. T Aug 1752 *Tryal*. Sy.
Powell, James. S Lent 1755. Y.
Powell, James. S s cloth Lent R 14 yrs Summer 1768. St.
Powell, James. S Apr T Jly 1770 *Scarsdale*. L.
Powell, Jane. S Apr 1760. M.
Powell, Jeremiah. S Feb 1774. L.
Powell, John of St. Saviour, Southwark. R for Barbados or Jamaica Jly
    1688. Sy.
Powell, John. S s horse Lent R 14 yrs Summer 1723. G.
Powell, John. S s horse at Llanvihangel Crucorney Lent R Summer
    1729. Mo.
Powell, John (1733). *See* Poole. M.
Powell als Fisherman, John. S & T Apr 1733 *Patapsco* LC Annapolis
    Nov 1733. M.
Powell, John. S & T Apr 1733 *Patapsco* LC Annapolis Nov 1733. M.
Powell, John. S s beer Jly 1740 T Jan 1741 *Harpooner* to
    Rappahannock. M.
Powell, John. S Summer 1757 R 14 yrs Lent 1758. Sh.
Powell, John. S Lent R 14 yrs Summer 1758. He.
Powell, John. T Apr 1762 *Neptune*. Sy.
Powell, John. SQS Oct 1763. M.
Powell, John. S s silver spoons at Claines Lent 1764. Wo.
Powell, John. S s silk at Leeds Summer 1765 R 14 yrs Summer 1766. Y.
Powell, John. S Lent R 14 yrs Summer 1768. Mo.
Powell, John of St. Margaret, Westminster. SW Jan 1773. M.
Powell, John. R Mar 1773. So.
Powell, Joseph. S Feb-Apr T May 1755 *Rose*. M.
Powell, Joseph. S s cows Summer 1763 R 14 yrs Lent 1764. Wa.
Powell, Luke. S & T Sep 1731 *Smith* LC Va 1732. M.
Powell, Margaret (1751). *See* Morris. He.
Powell, Margaret. S & R Lent 1772. Ch.
Powell, Mary of Derrender, spinster. R for Barbados Oct 1663. He.
Powell, Mary. R Dec 1716 T Jan 1717 *Queen Elizabeth* to Jamaica. M.
Powell, Michael. Rebel T 1685.
Powell, Richard. T 5 yrs to Va Nov 1661. L.
Powell, Richard. R for Jamaica Jan 1663. M.
Powell, Richard of Ness. R for America Sep 1671. Sh.
Powell, Richard. S s at Penkridge Lent 1739. St.
Powell, Richard Jr. S Lent R 14 yrs Summer 1756. Sh.
Powell, Richard. S Oct T Nov 1762 *Prince William*. M.
Powell, Richard (1774). *See* Richard. St.
Powell, Robert. S Jly T Nov 1762 *Prince William*. M.
Powell, Robert. S Oct 1764 T Jan 1765 *Tryal*. M.
Powell, Roger. R for Va Jly 1618. O.
Powell, Samuel. S Oct-Dec 1739 T Jan 1740 *York* to Md. M.
Powell, Sarah. S & T Oct 1732 *Caesar* to Va. M.
Powell, Sarah. S s handkerchief Jan T Apr 1735 *Patapsco* LC Annapolis
    Oct 1735. M.
Powell, Sarah. S s at St. Clement, Worcester, Summer 1765. Wo.
Powell, Sarah. S Apr-May T Jly 1771 *Scarsdale*. M.

Powell, Susan. R for Barbados or Jamaica May AT Jly 1697. M.

Powell, Susannah. S s at Horton Lent 1774. Bu.

Powell, Thomas. R for Barbados Jun 1671. M.

Powell, Thomas. R for Barbados Mar 1677. L.

Powell, Thomas, als Higgins, David of Llanellen. R for America Jly 1678. Mo.

Powell, Thomas (1679). *See* Higgins. He.

Powell, Thomas of North Marston. R for America Feb 1716. Wi.

Powell als Tutcher, Thomas. S Jan 1726 T *Loyal Margaret* LC Annapolis Oct 1726. M.

Powell, Thomas. T Jun 1726 *Loyal Margaret* LC Md Dec 1726. K.

Powell, Thomas. S Oct T Nov 1728 *Forward* but died on passage. L.

Powell, Thomas. S Lent 1732. Mo.

Powell, Thomas. S s at Astley Abbotts Summer 1734. Sh.

Powell, Thomas. T May 1744 *Justitia*. K.

Powell, Thomas. R 14 yrs Aug 1748. De.

Powell, Thomas (1757). *See* Howells. He.

Powell, Thomas. S Summer 1766 R 14 yrs Lent 1767. Wa.

Powell, William of Bobbing. R for Barbados or Jamaica Feb 1676. K.

Powell, William. Rebel T 1685.

Powell, William. S Summer 1730. He.

Powell, William. T Sep 1730 *Smith*. Sy.

Powell, William. S s oxen at Bridstow Lent 1739. He.

Powell, William. S Sep T Oct 1744 *Susannah*. M.

Powell, William. S Lent TB May 1755. G.

Powell, William. S s bacon at Llanwenarth Summer 1762. Mo.

Powell, William. S Oct 1764 T Jan 1765 *Tryal*. M.

Powell, William (1766). *See* Harding, John. Wa.

Powell, William. T Sep 1767 *Justitia*. E.

Power, Edward, aged 16, fair, shoemaker. LC from *Gilbert* Md Jly 1722. X.

Power, Edward (1767). *See* Bowers, John. Ha.

Power, Joseph. S Summer 1768. Wa.

Power als Morcomb, Nathaniel. S Mar 1725. De.

Powett, Mary (1738). *See* Ledman. M.

Powis, Elizabeth. S Oct T Nov 1759 *Phoenix*. L.

Powis, Samuel. S s plowshare at Chaddesley Corbett Lent 1773. Wo.

Pows, Thomas (1713). *See* Poits. Be.

Powis, Thomas. S & T Dec 1736 *Dorsetshire*. L.

Powles, Thomas. S s at Ross Summer 1770. Sh.

Powley, Samuel. S s at St. Peter Mancroft, Norwich, Summer 1772. Nf.

Pownell, Christopher of Blandford, tailor. R (Oxford Circ) for America Mar 1698. Do.

Pownall, John. T Sep 1730 *Smith*. E.

Powney, Thomas. S s at Wokingham Lent 1750. Be.

Powney, William. S Jan T Apr 1770 *New Trial*. M.

Powning, John. S Lent 1749. K.

Poyer, James. R 14 yrs Aug 1773. So.

Poyner, Ann. R for Barbados Jun 1671. L.

Poynton, William of North Lopham. R for America Feb 1687. Nf.

Pracer, Henry, als Symes, William of Andover or Broughton, carpenter. R for Barbados Jun 1666. Ha.

Pracey, Thomas. S Jly 1763. M.

Pragge, Thomas. PT Mar 1699. M.

Prangnell, Robert Jr. S Jly 1743. Ha.

Prankitt, Robert. S Jan-Jun 1747. M.

Pratt, Alexander of Detchon, yeoman. SQS s cloth Easter 1775. Nl.

Pratt, Francis. T Apr 1735 *Patapsco*. Ht.

Pratt, Francis. R 14 yrs Summer 1758. Y.

Pratt, Francis. R for life Mar 1773. Ha.

Pratt, Henry. SQS Richmond s cowhide Jan TB Aug 1765. Y.

Pratt, James. S Feb T Apr 1741 *Speedwell* or *Mediterranean*. M.

Pratt, James. S Apr T Jun 1742 *Bladon* to Md. M.

Pratt, John. S 14 yrs Aug 1727 T *Forward* LC Rappahannock May 1728. M.

Pratt, John. S City Lent 1752. Y.

Pratt, John. T Apr 1766 *Ann*. K.

Pratt, Randolph. S Summer 1735 T *Dorsetshire* LC Va Jan 1736. Bu.

Pratt, Roger. S for fraud Feb T Apr 1770 *New Trial*. L.

Pratt, Sarah. T Jan 1767 *Tryal*. M.

Pratt, Thomas. S Oct 1772. L.

Pratt, William. T Jly 1724 *Robert* LC Md Jun 1725. E.

Pratt, William. T Jly 1770 *Scarsdale*. M.

Prawl, Thomas of St. Saviour, Southwark. SQS Jan T Apr 1765 *Ann*. Sy.

Prawley, John (1741). *See* Sprangley. So.

Precious, Elizabeth. LC from *Dorsetshire* Va Sep 1736. X.

Pretious als Browne, Jane. R for Barbados or Jamaica Dec 1695 & May 1697. L.

Preece, Edward, als Parry, Mathew of Almeley. R for America Jly 1696. He.

Preece, Edward (1774). *See* Bowen. Sh.

Preece, Henry. S Summer 1755 R 14 yrs Lent 1756. Sh.

Preece, Sarah. S 14 yrs Summer 1755 for receiving goods stolen by Henry Preece at Bridgenorth. Sh.

Preece, Thomas. S Lent 1740. He.

Prees, William. S s mare Summer 1767 R 14 yrs Lent 1768. Wo.

Pregnall, Joshua. S Jly T Oct 1741 *Sea Horse* to Va. M.

Prentice, William. S Summer 1758 T Apr 1759 *Thetis*. Bu.

Prescott, George. SQS & T Dec 1771 *Justitia*. M.

Prescott, Henry of Thornton. SQS Jan 1758. La.

Prescott, Mary. T Jun 1764 *Dolphin*. E.

Prescott, Mary wife of James of Widford, shovelmaker. SQS Apr 1774. E.

Prescott, Nathan. S Lent 1757. La.

Prescott, William. SQS Coventry Mar AT May 1745. Wa.

Presgrave, Jeremiah. S s horse Summer 1721 R 14 yrs Summer 1722 T *Forward* LC Annapolis Jun 1723. Ru.

Presgrove, Thomas. S Oct 1748 T Jan 1749 *Laura*. L.

Pressly, John. R 14 yrs Aug 1746. Wi.

Presstand, George. SQS Oct 1774. M.

Prestage, Andrew. S s at Wootton Lent 1773. O.

Prestidge, John. T Jun 1740 *Essex*. Ht.

Prestman. *See* Priestman.

Preston, Ann. S Aug 1760. L.

Preston, Charles. S for threatening to accuse the Marquis of Caernarvon of sodomy Jun T Sep 1767 *Justitia*. M.

Preston, Dorothy. S Feb T Apr 1742 *Bond*. L.

Preston, Edward. R Jan AT Feb 1679. M.

Preston, Edward, aged 20, dark, periwig maker. S & T Oct 1720 *Gilbert* LC Annapolis May 1721. M.

Preston, James, waterman. T *Jekyll* LC Barbados Jun 1724. L.

Preston, Johanna. S Dec 1768 T Jan 1769 *Thornton*. M.

Preston, John. T Apr 1735 *Patapsco*. E.

Preston als Budbrook, John. R 14 yrs Mar 1744. De.

Preston, John. S s sheep Lent R 14 yrs Summer 1768. G.

Preston, Mary (1774). *See* Suggs. M.

Preston, Paul. S May-Jly 1773. M.

Preston als Steward als Parke, Peter. R for Jamaica Jan 1663. M.

Preston, Robert of Walton, weaver. S Lent 1741. La.

Preston, Thomas. S Apr 1761. L.

Preston, Thomas. S Jly T Sep 1764 *Justitia*. M.

Preston, Thomas. S s sheep Summer 1766 R 14 yrs Lent 1767. St.

Preston, William James. S Feb T Mar 1764 *Tryal*. M.

Prestwich, Sarah of Manchester, singlewoman. SQS Apr 1752. La.

Prestwood, Richard. S s at Claverley Lent 1748. Sh.

Pretty, Eleanor. S & T Dec 1770 *Justitia*. M.

Pretty, George. S s mare Lent R 14 yrs Summer 1764. No.

Pretty, Henry. R for Jamaica Aug 1661. M.

Pretty, Sarah. S Oct T Dec 1770 *Justitia*. M.

Prew, John. Rebel T 1685.

Prew, William. T Apr 1742 *Bond*. Sy.

Prewett, John. S s sheep & R Lent 1174. G.

Pruett, William. S Oct T Nov 1728 *Forward* LC Rappahannock Jun 1729. L.

Price, Anne. R Dec 1681 AT Jan 1682. M.

Price, Anne. S Lent 1739 R 14 yrs Lent 1740 for suffering an infant child to perish from want. Wa.

Price, Ann als Hannah als Johanna. S Jan 1740. L.

Price, Ann. S Lent 1761. Wa.

Price, Ann. S Apr T May 1767 *Thornton*. L.

Price, Benjamin. S Apr T May 1720 *Honor* LC Port York Jan 1721. L.

Price, Benjamin. S Lent R 14 yrs Summer 1738.

Price, Caleb. R for America Jly 1708. Wa.

Price, Catherine, aged 30, dark. LC from *Gilbert* Annapolis May 1721. X.

Price, Daniel. S s banknotes at Over Norton Lent 1770. O.

Price, Daniel als Dan. S Lent 1774. Sh.

Price, David. S Lent R 14 yrs Summer 1738. St.

Price als Pessey, David. S Sep T Dec 1769 *Justitia*. M.

Price, David. S s horse & R 14 yrs Lent 1774. Sh.

Price, David. S s horse & R 14 yrs Summer 1775. Mo.

Price, Edward. LC from *Owners Goodwill* Annapolis Jly 1722. X.

Price, Edward (1723). *See* Bray. Mo.

Price, Edward. S Aug T Oct 1726 *Forward*. L.
Price, Edward. S s at Clifton Summer 1747. O.
Price als Brice, Edward. R 14 yrs Aug 1753. So.
Price, Edward. S Jly 1763. M.
Price, Edward. S Sep-Oct T Dec 1771 *Justitia*. M.
Price, Edward. S Mar TB to Va Apr 1773. Le.
Price, Elizabeth. R for America May 1704. L.
Price als Davis, Elizabeth. S Oct-Dec 1739 T Jan 1740 *York* to Md. M.
Price, Elizabeth. S Jan T Feb 1742 *Industry* to Md. M.
Price, Elizabeth. S s at Ross Lent 1753. He.
Price, Elizabeth. S Feb T Apr 1765 *Ann*. M.
Price, Elizabeth wife of Samuel. S Sep-Oct 1774. M.
Price, Hannah (1740). *See* Price, Ann. L.
Price, Henry. S Lent TB Mar 1731. G.
Price, Henry of St. Olave, Southwark. SQS Jan T Apr 1759 *Thetis*. Sy.
Price, Hugh. SQS Jun T Jly 1772 *Tayloe*. M.
Price, James. Rebel T 1685.
Price, James of Little Hereford. R for America Mar 1710. He.
Price, James of Almeley. R (Chester Circ) for America Jly 1711. He.
Price, James. S Sep T Nov 1743 *George William*. M.
Price, James. S Apr 1748. L.
Price, Jane wife of John. S 14 yrs for receiving goods stolen at
    Leominster Lent 1765. He.
Price, James. T Jan 1766 *Tryal*. M.
Price, Jane. R Mar AT Apr 1677. M.
Price, Johanna (1740). *See* Price, Ann. L.
Price, John. S Feb 1663 to House of Correction unless he consents to be
    transported. M.
Price, John (1667). *See* Pierce. L.
Price, John. R for Barbados Apr TB Jun 1668. L.
Price, John. R for Barbados Jly 1668. M.
Price, John of Worcester. S Lent 1720. Wo.
Price, John. S s at St. Mary le Crypt, Gloucester, Summer 1726. G.
Price, John. S s horse Lent R 14 yrs Summer 1728. Sh.
Price, John. S Jan-Jun T Jun 1728 *Elizabeth* LC Potomack Aug 1729. L.
Price, John. S s at St. John the Baptist, Gloucester, Lent 1735. G.
Price, John. S Summer 1743 R 14 yrs Lent 1744. Mo.
Price, John. S Apr 1745. L.
Price, John. AT Summer 1748. Mo.
Price, John. S s at Penrhos Summer 1752. Mo.
Price, John. T Apr 1753 *Thames*. M.
Price, John. S & T Jly 1753 *Tryal*. L.
Price, John. S Sep-Oct T Dec 1753 *Whiteing*. M.
Price, John. S May-Jly T Sep 1755 *Tryal*. M.
Price, John. SQS Apr T Sep 1758 *Tryal* to Annapolis. M.
Price, John. SL & T Apr 1760 *Thetis*. Sy.
Price, John. S & R for life Mar 1766. Fl.
Price, John. S Oct 1768 T Jan 1769 *Thornton*. M.
Price als Lullams, John. SQS Jan 1770. Ha.
Price, John. S Feb T Apr 1770 *New Trial*. L.
Price, John. S s lamb & R Lent 1774. Sh.

Price, Joseph. S & T Oct 1729 *Forward* LC Va Jun 1730. L.
Price, Joseph. S Nov T Dec 1770 *Justitia*. L.
Price, Lidia (1735). *See* Malcolm. M.
Price als Russell, Margaret. S & T 14 yrs Sep 1718 *Eagle* LC Charles
  Town Mar 1719. L.
Price, Margaret. T Oct 1720 *Gilbert*. Sy.
Price als Lloyd, Margaret of Ross. S Lent 1721. He.
Price, Marina. S Sep T Oct 1739 *Duke of Cumberland*. L.
Price, Mary. R Aug AT Oct 1700. M.
Price, Mary. S Jly T Aug 1721 *Prince Royal* LC Va Nov 1721. M.
Price, Mary. S Oct T Nov 1728 *Forward* but died on passage. L.
Price, Mary. S Oct 1740. L.
Price, Mary. T May 1744 *Justitia*. Sy.
Price als Humphries, Mary. S Feb T Apr 1762 *Dolphin*. M.
Price, Mary. S s at Cogges Summer 1767. O.
Price, Mary. SQS Apr T Jly 1772 *Tayloe*. M.
Price, Mary. S s at Whittington Summer 1772. G.
Price, Maurice of West Horndon. R for Barbados Jly 1679. E.
Price, Nathaniel. T May 1737 *Forward*. Sy.
Price, Peter. S Oct 1748 T Jan 1749 *Laura*. L.
Price als Thrift als Church, Peter. S Apr T May 1767 *Thornton*. M.
Price, Peter. SQS Sep T Dec 1771 *Justitia*. M.
Price, Philip. S Feb T Mar 1731 *Patapsco* LC Annapolis Jun 1731. M.
Price, Rees. S for counterfeiting coins Lent R Summer 1733 (SP). Sh.
Price, Rees. S Mar 1762. So.
Price, Rees. S s horse & R 14 yrs Summer 1775. Mo.
Price, Richard of Thurrock. R for Barbados or Jamaica Jly 1688 & Feb
  1690. E.
Price, Richard. S s at Taynton Summer 1729. G.
Price, Richard. S Feb T Apr 1734 *Patapsco* to Md. M.
Price, Richard. S Summer 1750 R 14 yrs Lent TB Apr 1751. G.
Price als Sterry, Richard of St. Saviour, Southwark. SQS & T Jan 1767
  Tryal. Sy.
Price, Richard. SW & T Apr 1768 *Thornton*. M.
Price, Robert. S Oct 1748 T Jan 1749 *Laura*. L.
Price, Robert. SW & T Apr 1769 *Tryal*. M.
Price, Samuel. S & T May 1736 *Patapsco*. L.
Price, Samuel. SQS May T Nov 1759 *Phoenix*. M.
Price als Cock-Her-Plump, Sarah. T Oct 1726 *Forward*. Sy.
Price, Sarah (1766). *See* Print. M.
Price, Sarah of St. James, Westminster, spinster. SW Jan 1773. M.
Price, Simon. S & T Jly 1772 *Tayloe*. M.
Price, Stephen. S & T Jun 1742 *Bladon* to Md. M.
Price, Thomas. R for America Aug 1715. M.
Price, Thomas. S Apr T May 1720 *Honor* LC Port York Jan 1721. L.
Price, Thomas. LC from *Gilbert* Annapolis Jly 1722. X.
Price, Thomas. SQS Jan TB to Md Feb 1743. So.
Price, Thomas. S Summer 1763 R 14 yrs Lent 1764. St.
Price, Thomas. S & T for life Jly 1771 *Scarsdale*. M.
Price, Thomas. S Jun T Jly 1772 *Tayloe*. L.
Price, Thomas. S Sep-Oct 1773. M.

Price, Thomas. S for perjury Feb 1774. L.
Price, William of Newport. R for America Feb 1673. Mo.
Price, William. R 14 yrs Aug T Sep 1718 *Eagle*. L.
Price, William (1724). *See* Barnes. Mo.
Price, William. LC from *Sukey* Annapolis Sep 1725. X.
Price, William. S 14 yrs Oct-Dec 1750. M.
Price, William. S s at Kyre Summer 1755. Wo.
Price, William. S Apr 1760. M.
Price, William. S Apr 1761. M.
Price, William. S 14 yrs s fish at Speen Lent 1769. Be.
Price, William. S s ram Summer 1769 R 14 yrs Lent 1770. He.
Price, William. S s at Berkeley Lent 1770. G.
Price, William. S Jly 1775. L.
Prick, Rachael. S May T Nov 1743 *George William*. M.
Pricket als Tate, Michael. S & R 14 yrs Lent 1769. O.
Prickle, Richard. S May T Jun 1727 *Susanna* to Va. M.
Pricklow, John of Godalming. SQS Oct 1761. Sy.
Priddon, Thomas. T Jan 1741 *Vernon*. K.
Pride, Shadrake. T Apr 1770 *New Trial*. E.
Pridmore, Thomas. S s lead & T Dec 1734 *Caesar* LC Va Jly 1735. M.
Priest, Abraham. T 1724 *Robert* LC Md Jun 1725. Bu.
Priest, Ann. S Sep T Oct 1750 *Rachael*. M.
Priest, Catherine. R for America Aug 1715. L.
Priest, Catherine. LC from *Forward* Annapolis Jun 1723. X.
Priest, Daniel. T 1724 *Robert* LC Md Jun 1725. Bu.
Priest, Henry. Rebel T 1685.
Priest als Hancock, James of Wiveliscombe. R for Barbados Feb 1688. So.
Preest, James. S Lent T May 1736 *Patapsco*. Bu.
Priest, James (1743). *See* Tatton. Joseph. Ht.
Priest, John. S s at Sutwell Summer 1734. Be.
Priest, John. R & T for life Apr 1770 *New Trial*. M.
Priest, Laurence. Rebel T 1685.
Priest, Mary (1727). *See* Holland. M.
Priest, Naomi. S Mar 1729 TB to Va. De.
Priest, Nathaniel of Hereford. R for Jamaica, Barbados or Bermuda Feb 1686. He.
Priest, Thomas. Rebel T 1685.
Priest, Thomas. R for life Summer 1772. Sy.
Priest, William. Rebel T 1685.
Priest, William. S Lent 1731. O.
Priest, William. S s sheep Summer 1746 R 14 yrs Lent TB Aug 1747. Le.
Priestland, Elizabeth. S Summer 1760. Ca.
Priestland, William. S s cattle Lent R 14 yrs Summer 1764. Wa.
Priestly, Robert. S Summer 1734 R 14 yrs Lent TB Mar 1734. G.
Priestly, Sarah. S s sheep & R 14 yrs Lent T Sep 1768. Li.
Prestman, Elizabeth. S Jan 1757. M.
Prestman als Priteman, James. S May T Jly 1722 *Alexander* to Nevis or Jamaica. M.
Priestman, James. S & T Dec 1731 *Forward* to Md or Va. M.
Priestman, William. S Lent 1722. Y.

Prigg, Elizabeth. S Sep-Oct T Dec 1752 *Greyhound*. M.

Prigg, James. S Lent 1759; accused with Samuel Prigg now at large. G.

Prim, Thomas. R for America Jun 1684. Li.

Prime, William. S *See* 1775. M.

Primrose, Robert. R for America Jly 1708. Li.

Primus, Thomas. T Oct 1721 *William & John*. K.

Prince, Andrew. S Jly 1764. Ha.

Prince, Anne. R Oct AT Oct 1701. M.

Prince, Elizabeth. PT Apr R Oct 1673. M.

Prince, George. R 14 yrs Mar 1743. Ha.

Prince, Hannah wife of Robert of St. Botolph Aldgate. S s watches & T Dec 1740 *Vernon*. M.

Prince als Bates, John. R for Barbados May 1676. M.

Prince, John. R for Barbados Mar 1683. M.

Prince, John. S s at Newbury Lent 1751. Be.

Prince, Joseph. S Oct 1727-Jun 1728 T Jun 1728 *Elizabeth* LC Potomack Aug 1729. M.

Prince, Martin. T Jly 1722 *Alexander*. Sy.

Prince, Mary of Newport, Isle of Wight. R for Barbados Jly 1693. Ha.

Prince, Richard. S for burning dwelling Lent R 14 yrs Summer 1735. Su.

Prince, William. S Jly T Sep 1765 *Justitia*. M.

Prince, William. S s from tenters at Leeds Summer 1766 R 14 yrs Summer 1767. Y.

Priney, Peter. LC from *Elizabeth* Potomack Aug 1729. X.

Pring, Cyprian. R 14 yrs Mar 1767 TB to Va. De.

Pringell, John of Bitton. R for America Jly 1693. G.

Print als Price, Sarah. S & T Jan 1766 *Tryal*. M.

Prior, Ann. S Feb 1752.

Prior, Elizabeth. S May-Jly 1774. M.

Pryor, Francis, a Quaker. S for attending conventicles Summer 1664 R for plantations Jly 1665. Ht.

Prior, George. S Summer 1757. Nf.

Prior, Hannah. SQS Dec 1772. M.

Pryor, Isaac. Rebel T 1685.

Prior, John of St. George, Southwark. R for Barbados Apr 1668. Sy.

Prior, John. Rebel T 1685.

Pryor, John. S Feb 1719. M.

Prior, John. S for assisting escape of Samuel Prior *(qv)* Summer 1748 T Jan 1749 *Laura*. K.

Prior, John. S 14 yrs for receiving Lent T May 1750 *Lichfield*. Sy.

Pryer, Mary. PT Jan 1700. M.

Pryor, Matthew. Rebel T 1685.

Pryor, Samuel. S for smuggling Summer 1747 but taken from Maidstone Gaol by Samuel Pritchett als Sam the Tinker. K.

Prior, William of Towlesham. R for America Jly 1683. Nf.

Prior, William. S s sheep Summer 1741. Be.

Pryor, William. S Mar 1772. Ha.

Pritchard, Ann. S for burglary Lent R 14 yrs Summer 1741. He.

Pritchard, Arnold. S Dec 1768 T Jan 1769 *Thornton*. M.

Pritchard, Charles. S Mar 1755. So.

Pritchard, Edward. S Aug T Oct 1723 *Forward* to Va. M.

Pritchard, Elizabeth. S Jly-Sep 1754. M.

Pritchard, Ezechiel. S s horse Lent R 14 yrs Summer 1741 (SP). He.

Pritchard, Henry. R for Barbados Sep 1669. M.

Pritchard, Israel. R for Barbados or Jamaica Aug 1700. L.

Pritchard, Jacob. SQS Devizes & TB to Va Apr 1765. Wi.

Pritchard, James (1697). *See* Pritchett. M.

Pritchard, James. S s hog at Michaelchurch Summer 1758. He.

Pritchard, James. S s sheep Summer 1767 R 14 yrs Lent 1768. He.

Pritchard, James. S & R 14 yrs Lent 1770. G.

Pritchard, James. SW & T Jly 1770. M.

Pritchard, Jane. R Dec 1695. M.

Pritchard, Jane. S s at Kinnersley Lent 1764. Sh.

Pritchard, John of Kill. R for Barbados Jly 1672. So.

Pritchard, John. S Summer 1739. He.

Pritchard als Jones, John. S Lent R 14 yrs Summer 1747. Sh.

Pritchard, John. S s at St. Owen, Hereford, Lent 1756. He.

Pritchard, John. S s shoes at Walford Lent 1760. He.

Pritchard, John. S Dec 1765 T Jan 1766 *Tryal*. M.

Pritchard als Jones, John. S s at St. Martin Summer 1766. Sh.

Pritchard, John. S May-Jly 1773. M.

Pritchard, John. S Apr 1775. M.

Pritchard, Jonas of Worth. R for Barbados or Jamaica Jly 1696. Sx.

Pritchard, Margaret. R for America Aug 1715. M.

Pritchard, Martha. S Feb 1757. M.

Pritchard, Mary. S Summer 1723 R 14 yrs Lent 1725. Sh.

Pritchard, Philip of Worth. R for Barbados or Jamaica Jly 1696. Sx.

Pritchard, Richard of Layborne. R for Barbados or Jamaica Jly 1688 & Feb 1690. K.

Pritchard, Richard. S s sheep at Goytre Lent 1726. Mo.

Pritchard, Richard. S Jly T Oct 1741 *Sea Horse* to Va. M.

Pritchard, Robert. S Lent R 14 yrs Summer 1748. Wo.

Pritchard, Samuel. S & T Oct 1730 *Forward* LC Potomack Jan 1731. L.

Pritchard als Oadley, Sarah. S May T Sep 1765 *Justitia*. M.

Pritchard, Sarah. S Sep-Oct T Dec 1771 *Justitia*. M.

Prichard als Jones, Thomas. T Oct 1720 *Gilbert* but died on passage. E.

Pritchard, Thomas of Lambeth. SQS Jan 1775. Sy.

Pritchard als Cadogan, William of Caldicote. R for America Jly 1675. Mo.

Pritchard, William. T Dec 1731 *Forward*. Sy.

Pritchard, William (1734). *See* Davies. M.

Pritchard, William. S s at Condover Summer 1748 AT Lent 1749. Sh.

Pritchard, William. S Feb-Apr T May 1751 *Tryal*. M.

Pritchard, William. S s at St. Owen, Hereford, Lent 1756. He.

Pritchard als Morgan, William. S for obtaining leather at Ledbury by false pretences Lent 1769. He.

Pritchard als Williams, William. S s at Upper Bullingham Lent 1772. He.

Pritchet, David, aged 24, dark, shoemaker. S Jan T Feb 1723 *Jonathan* LC Annapolis Jly 1724. L.

Pritchett als Pritchard als Lyall als Larke, James. R May AT Jly 1697. M.

Pritchett, John. S & T 14 yrs Sep 1737 *Pretty Patsy* to Md. M.

Priteman, James (1722). *See* Prestman. M.

Pritchet, John. TB Apr 1771. Db.

Probert, Alice. S Aug T Oct 1724 *Forward* LC Annapolis Jun 1725. M.

Probert, Howell of Bromfield. R for America Jly 1678. Sh.

Probert, Thomas. S s handkerchief at Ewyas Harold Summer 1723 AT Summer 1725. He.

Probert, Thomas. AT from QS Summer 1744. Mo.

Probert, Thomas. SW & T Apr 1768 *Thornton*. M.

Probeart, Thomas. S Apr 1774. L.

Probart, William. S Feb 1757. M.

Probert, William. S Lent T Apr 1768 *Thornton*. Bu.

Probuts, William of Orsett. SQS Apr T Sep 1757 *Thetis*. E.

Proby, Thomas. S Jly-Sep T Oct 1739 *Duke of Cumberland* to Va. M.

Proctor, Abigail. SQS s coal from Sir James Lowther Easter 1774. Du.

Procter, Christian (1743). *See* Mitchell. M.

Procter, Christopher. S & T Dec 1740 *Vernon*. L.

Procter, Elizabeth. S Sep T Dec 1763 *Neptune*. M.

Procter, John. S s at Banham Lent 1772. Nf.

Procter, John. R Apr 1773. M.

Procter, Margaret. S & T Oct 1730 *Forward* LC Potomack Jan 1731. L.

Procter, Mary. S Sep T Nov 1743 *George William*. M.

Proctor, Richard of Preston. SQS May 1756. La.

Proctor, Sarah. S Jun T Aug 1769 *Douglas*. L.

Prockter, Thomas, aged 23. R for Barbados Feb 1664. M.

Procter, Thomas. S for highway robbery & R 14 yrs Lent 1773. Li.

Procter, William. S Apr-Jun T Jly 1772 *Tayloe*. M.

Proles, Nathaniel. SQS Jly 1741 TB to Md May 1742. So.

Prophett, John. S s at Whiteladies Aston Summer 1734. Wo.

Prosey, William. S Apr 1748. L.

Prosser, Ann. S Lent R 14 yrs Summer 1759. He.

Prosser, Charles. S Feb T 14 yrs Mar 1730 *Patapsco* LC Annapolis Sep 1730. L.

Prosser, Elizabeth (1719). *See* Stephens. Mo.

Prosser, James. R for life Jan 1757. M.

Prosser, James. S s at Madresfield Lent 1766. Wo.

Prosser, John. S Summer 1743 R 14 yrs Lent 1744. Mo.

Prosser, Jonathan. S for highway robbery Lent R for life Summer 1764. O.

Prosser, Roger. R 14 yrs Lent 1721. Mo.

Prosser, Sarah. S Feb 1754. M.

Prosser, Thomas (1722). *See* Jones. Sh.

Prosser, Thomas. S Feb-Apr T May 1752 *Lichfield*. M.

Prosser, Thomas. S s saddle at Peterchurch Lent 1753. He.

Prosser, William. S Lent R 14 yrs Summer TB Aug 1749. G.

Prosser, William. S Summer 1760. Mo.

Prothero, Evan (1737). *See* Thomas, John. G.

Protherow, John. R 14 yrs Mar 1774. So.

Prytherow als Prytherch, Silvanus. S s gelding at Llanwenarth Summer 1761 R 14 yrs Lent 1762. Mo.

Proudfoot, Matthew. T Mar 1750 *Tryal*. M.

Proudman, Daniel. S Mar TB to Va Sep 1727. Le.
Provost, Mary. S & T Apr 1741 *Mediterranean*. L.
Prowse, John. TB to Va from QS 1740. De.
Prowse, Roger of Exeter. R for Barbados Mar 1694. De.
Prowse, William of Nether Stowey. R for Barbados Feb 1683. So.
Prowse, William (2). Rebels T 1685.
Pruett. *See* Prewett.
Pryor. *See* Prior.
Prytherch, Silvanus (1761). *See* Pritherow. Mo.
Puckering, Edward. S Jly T Sep 1755 *Tryal*. L.
Puckett, Francis. Rebel T 1685.
Puddle, Hannah. R & T 14 yrs Jly 1770 *Scarsdale*. M.
Puddy, William. SQS & TB Apr 1763. So.
Pudiphas, Samuel. S Lent 1775. Ht.
Puggesley, John. SQS & TB Jly 1735. So.
Puggesley, William. SQS Oct 1735 TB to Md Jan 1736. So.
Pew, Anne. S Aug T Oct 1724 *Forward* LC Annapolis Jun 1725. M.
Pugh, Ann. S Jly 1748. L.
Pugh, Arabella of Bristol. R Oct 1761 (SP). G.
Pugh, Daniel. S Dec 1753-Jan 1754. M.
Pugh, David. S Lent R 14 yrs Summer 1748. Wo.
Pew, David. S s pigs at Tidenham Summer TB Aug 1749. G.
Pugh als Harding, Elizabeth. S Sep T Oct 1744 *Susannah*. M.
Pugh, Hugh, als Hawkins, Henry. S Apr-May 1754. M.
Pugh, Hugh. T Sep 1758 *Tryal*. Sy.
Pugh, John. S s at Bishops Castle Lent 1750. He.
Pugh, John William. S Jan-Feb 1774. M.
Pew, Margaret. S Jan T Feb 1726 *Supply* LC Annapolis May 1726. L.
Pugh, Mary (1741). *See* Eales. M.
Pugh, Mary. S Feb 1754. L.
Pugh, Philip. S Feb T Mar 1730 *Patapsco* LC Annapolis Sep 1730. M.
Pugh als Hordley, Richard. S s wheat at Pencombe Summer 1735 R 14
    yrs Lent 1736. He.
Pugh, Richard. S May 1775. M.
Pew als Edwards, Sarah. S & T Dec 1736 *Dorsetshire*. L.
Pugh, Simon of Wandsworth. SQS Jan 1763. Sy.
Pugh, William. S s at Alveston Summer 1729. G.
Pugsley, George. S Mar 1752. De.
Puin, Richard. S Lent 1748. Sy.
Pulford, Brian. R May AT Jly 1697. M.
Pulford, Thomas. S Lent R 14 yrs Summer 1751. St.
Pulford, William of Thornham. R for Barbados Feb 1664. Su.
Pulham, Ann. R for America May 1704. L.
Pulham, Robert of Kedington. R for America Feb 1687. Su.
Pullham, Sarah. S & R 14 yrs for arson Lent 1770. G.
Pulham, Thomas. S s at Chedworth Summer TB Aug 1738. G.
Pulisson, Roger. R for Barbados Jly 1674. M.
Pulla, Dominique. S & T Sep 1731 *Smith* LC Va 1732.
Pullen, Charles. S Oct 1774. L.
Pullen, John. R 14 yrs Aug 1736. So.
Pullin, John (1757). *See* Ayling. Sx.

Pullein, John. S Jly T 14 yrs Sep 1764 *Justitia*. M.

Pullen, Joseph. T 14 yrs Sep 1766 *Justitia*. K.

Pullen, Richard. S & TB Aug 1754. G.

Pullen, Richard. SW & T Apr 1771 *Thornton*. M.

Pulleyn, Robert. S s cloth from tenters & R Lent TB Aug 1755. Y.

Pullen, Samuel. R Summer 1773. Sy.

Pullen, William. S Summer 1745. K.

Pullen, William. S Mar 1752. So.

Pullenger, William. S Jan-Apr 1748. M.

Pullor, Joseph. S May-Jly 1750. M.

Puller, Walter. S s sheepskins at Basildon Lent 1753. Be.

Pulley, Elizabeth (1745). *See* Fuller. L.

Pulley, Susanna. SQS Oct 1755 TB May 1756. So.

Pulman, Mary. S Mar 1730. De.

Pulman, William of Martock. R for Barbados Feb 1683. So.

Pulpitt, William. T May 1751 *Tryal*. Sx.

Pulsevir, Catherine. TB to Va from QS 1738. De.

Pump, Jeremiah. S Apr T Jun 1768 *Tryal*. M.

Puncheon, Lawrence. S Mar 1773. Co.

Punt, Augustine. R for Barbados Jly 1675. M.

Punter, John. R 14 yrs Mar 1749. So.

Punter, Thomas. S Lent TB May 1755. G.

Purcell, Henry. T Jan 1734 *Caesar* LC Va Jly 1734. Sy.

Purcell, John of Bitton. R for America Jly 1693. G.

Purcell, John (1752). *See* Gore. M.

Purcell, William. R for Barbados Aug 1664. M.

Purchase, George. S & T Apr 1725 *Sukey* LC Annapolis Sep 1725. M.

Purchase, Richard. S s at Wolverhampton Summer 1763. St.

Purchase, William. T 14 yrs Oct 1768 *Justitia*. Sy.

Purdem, Thomas. T Jly 1770 *Scarsdale*. M.

Purdon, Meriel. S s carpet Dec 1735 T Jan 1736 *Dorsetshire* but died on passage. M.

Purdue, Charles. S & T 14 yrs Sep 1718 *Eagle* LC Charles Town Mar 1719. L.

Perdue, Charles. S Oct 1751-Jan 1752. M.

Purdue, Thomas. S 14 yrs for receiving hens stolen by John Snow *(qv)* Lent 1766. Be.

Purie, William. LC from *Sukey* Annapolis Sep 1725. X.

Purland, Margaret wife of Mathew. S 14 yrs Norwich for receiving Summer 1749. Nf.

Purland, Mathew. S 14 yrs Norwich for receiving goods from Celia Taylor *(qv)* Summer 1749. Nf.

Purlement, Elizabeth wife of William. S & T Jan 1769 *Thornton*. M.

Purnell. *See* Parnell.

Purney, John. S & T Jan 1769 *Thornton*. L.

Purney, Mary Sr. S Sep 1737 T Jan 1738 *Dorsetshire* to Va. M.

Purney, Mary Jr. S Sep 1737. M.

Purney, Richard. S Feb 1754. M.

Purney, Thomas. S s handkerchief at St. Michael, Wood Street, May T Jun 1768 *Tryal*. L.

Purse, Ann, spinster, als wife of John Biggerton. R for Barbados Feb & Aug 1664. L.

Purse, Bernard. SQS Jan TB to Md Oct 1737. So.

Pursely, John of St. George, Southwark. R for Barbados or Jamaica Jly 1702. Sy.

Pursly, John. S 14 yrs Jan 1751. M.

Purser, Catherine. S Nov T Dec 1752 *Greyhound*. L.

Purser, Joseph. S Jun T Nov 1743 *George William*. L.

Purser, Richard. S May T Sep 1765 *Justitia*. M.

Purslake, John. S to Va Jly 1718. De.

Purtle, Thomas. S Feb T Mar 1731 *Patapsco* LC Annapolis Jun 1731. M.

Purton, Henry of Shalbourne. R for Barbados Feb 1699. Wi.

Perton, Winifred wife of Henry. S 14 yrs Summer 1764 for receiving wool stolen by Eleanor Morgan *(qv)*. He.

Purvis, Ann. S Dec 1753-Jan 1754. M.

Purvis, James of St. George, Bloomsbury. S s stays Jly 1740 T Jan 1741 *Harpooner* to Rappahannock. M.

Purvas, Ralphe. S s horse Mar R 14 yrs & TB Apr 1724. Nt.

Putland, Elizabeth. T Nov 1741 *Sea Horse*. Bu.

Putnam, James. S Summer T Sep 1764 *Justitia*. Bu.

Putnam, Mary wife of John. S & T Jly 1771 *Scarsdale*. M.

Putnam, William (1772). *See* Puttenham. Ht.

Putt, Grace of D——-, widow. R for Barbados Jly 1688. So.

Putt, Richard. S Lent 1759. No.

Putten, Daniel. S & T Jly 1753 *Tryal*. L.

Puttenden, John. T Dec 1753 *Whiteing*. K.

Puttenham als Putnam, William of Aldenham. R Summer 1772. Ht.

Puttman, James. Rebel T 1685.

Puttman, William. Rebel T 1685.

Puttyford, John. S Dec 1761 T Apr 1762 *Dolphin*. M.

Puy, William. PT Jan 1700. M.

Pyall, David. SWK Apr T Jly 1772 *Orange Bay*. K.

Pyall, John. SWK Apr T Jly 1772 *Orange Bay*. K.

Pybee, Alexander. S Jun T Nov 1743 *George William*. L.

Pybus, Richard. R for Barbados Jan 1665. Y.

Pycroft, John of Basford, framework knitter. SQS s sheets Jan TB Apr 1773. Nt.

Pye, John. T Sep 1730 *Smith*. Sy.

Pye, John. S for violent assault Summer 1751. Nf.

Pye, John. S s at Maulden Lent 1772. Bd.

Pye, Mary. S Apr T Sep 1737 *Pretty Patsy* to Md. M.

Pye, Richard. S s at Claines Summer 1752. Wo.

Pye, William. S 14 yrs Summer 1760. E.

Pyechly als Piper, James. S Jly T Oct 1741 *Sea Horse* to Va. M.

Pyke. *See* Pike.

Pyne. *See* Pine.

Pyner. *See* Piner.

Q

Quale, Edward. T Aug 1721 *Owners Goodwill* LC Annapolis Jly 1722. Sy.

Queal, John. S Aug 1767. So.

Quail, Richard. S & T Sep 1731 *Smith* LC Va 1732. M.

Queel, Robert. SQS Jan TB Apr 1765. So.

Quant, Henry. Rebel T 1685.

Quant, William of Pitminster. R for Barbados Feb 1690. So.

Quantrill, Prettyman. T 14 yrs Apr 1770 *New Trial*. E.

Quarindon, William. S for life Oct 1744-Jan 1745. M.

Quarles, John. R for Barbados Aug 1679. L.

Quarrington, Henry of Ivinghoe. R for America Mar 1698. Bu.

Quarterman, John. S Oct 1741 T Feb 1742 *Industry* to Md. M.

Queen, Richard. S Jly T Aug 1721 *Prince Royal* to Va. M.

Quelsh, John of Bray. R for America Mar 1680. Be.

Quelch, Moses. S Lent T May 1751 *Tryal*. Bu.

Quelsh, William. SQS & T Apr 1766 *Ann*. M.

Querk, John of Little Crosby, tailor. SQS Oct 1758. La.

Querk, Margaret of Ormskirk, spinster. SQS Jan 1764. La.

Querri, Richard. S Oct T Dec 1770 *Justitia*. M.

Quick, Elizabeth. S Mar 1721. De.

Quick, Henry. Rebel T 1685.

Quick, Hugh. S Lent 1738. Bd.

Quick, John. Rebel T 1685.

Quick, John. SQS Jly TB to Md Nov 1738. So.

Quick, Robert. S Apr 1728. De.

Quick, Robert. S Mar 1764. Do.

Quick, Roger. S Mar 1775. De.

Quick, Thomas. Rebel T 1685.

Quick, Thomas. S Jly 1718 to be T to Va. De.

Quickley, Bartholomew. S Sep-Dec 1746. M.

Quimby, Peter. S Apr T May 1755 *Rose*. L.

Quinn, Edward. S & T Apr 1725 *Sukey* LC Annapolis Sep 1725. M.

Quynn, John. T Apr 1742 *Bond*. K.

Quin, John. SQS Feb T Apr 1753 *Thames*. M.

Quin, Margaret. S Feb T Mar 1750 *Tryal*. M.

Quin, Margaret (1762). *See* Sollowin. M.

Quin als Bulger, Mary. S Sep-Oct 1749. M.

Quin, Mary (1758). *See* Bricklebank. L.

Quin, Patrick. S & T Sep 1765 *Justitia*. M.

Quin, Richard. T Oct 1722 *Forward*. E.

Quin, Thomas. S Oct 1761 T Apr 1762 *Dolphin*. M.

Quinn, Thomas. S & T Dec 1771 *Justitia*. M.

Quin, William. SQS Jly T Sep 1765 *Justitia*. M.

Quin, Winifred. S Feb-Apr T Jun 1756 *Lyon*. M.

Quincey, John. S Jly 1761. L.

Quinnell, Ann of Steyning, spinster. S Summer 1739 T Jan 1741 *Vernon*. Sx.

Quennell, Elizabeth (1683). *See* Finney. Sy.

Quesnell, Magdalen. S Aug T Oct 1726 *Forward* to Va. M.

Quint, Andrew. R Apr 1747. De.

Quint, Crisset. S s sheet Apr T Dec 1735 *John* LC Annapolis Sep 1736. L.

Quinton als Humpston als Humpton, John. R Jan AT Feb 1679. M.

Quinton, John. S Mar 1765 TB to Va. De.

Quinton, Thomas. S s at Micklefield Lent 1771. Su.

Quittenden, Sarah. S Summer T Sep 1751 *Greyhound*. K.

Quitty, Daniel. S Jan T Feb 1719 *Worcester* LC Annapolis Jun 1719. M.

R

Rabbetts, Thomas (1753). *See* Knight. Ha.

Rabnett, James. S Feb-Apr T May 1751 *Tryal*. M.

Raby, Richard. S s bread at Kenninghall & R 14 yrs Lent 1774. Nf.

Race, Charles. SWK Jan 1775. K.

Race, Thomas. S s cloth at Thornton Summer TB Aug 1771. Y.

Rack, John. T Apr 1735 *Patapsco*. Sy.

Rackett, Alice. S Feb T Apr 1742 *Bond* to Potomack. M.

Rackley, Elizabeth. S (Western Circ) Dec 1766 AT Lent 1767. G.

Rackley, James. S Jly T Oct 1768 *Justitia*. M.

Radborn, John. S Dec 1753-Jan 1754. M.

Radborne als Ambrose, Thomas. S Dec 1753-Jan 1754. M.

Radcliff, James. R 14 yrs Summer 1757. Y.

Radcliffe, John. S s cloth from tenters Lent 1775 but T deferred. Y.

Radcliff, Joseph. T 14 yrs Aug 1752 *Tryal*. E.

Radcliffe, Mary. S Mar 1752. De.

Radcliffe, Thomas. S Lent R Summer TB Sep 1757. Db.

Raddall, Charles. S Mar 1730. De.

Rade, Thomas. S May-Jly T Sep 1755 *Tryal*. M.

Radford, Anne. TB to Va from QS 1731. De.

Radford, Cornelius. Rebel T 1685.

Radford, George. TB to Va from QS 1738. De.

Radford, John. S Jan-Feb 1773. M.

Radford, Mary (1730). *See* Harwood. M.

Radford, Mordecai of Ashby de la Zouch. R for America Jly 1678. Le.

Radford, Richard. R 14 yrs Aug 1757. De.

Radford, Sarah wife of Samuel. S & T Jly 1771 *Scarsdale*. M.

Radford, Thomas. S Lent 1736. Wo.

Radford, Walter. S Mar 1738. De.

Radish, Alse. Died on passage in *Sukey* 1725. X.

Radely, Charles. S s brass kettle at Fairford Lent TB Mar 1737. G.

Radley, George. T Oct 1726 *Forward*. E.

Radley, Joseph. T Aug 1752 *Tryal*. Ht.

Radley, Thomas. S & T Sep 1765 *Justitia*. L.

Radmore, Edward. R 14 yrs Jly 1749 TB to Va. De.

Radwell, Bernard. T Apr 1766 *Ann*. Bu.

Radwell, Johanna. S Apr 1720. M.

Radwell, Robert. S 14 yrs Jly-Dec 1747. M.

Radwell, Thomas. SQS Mar TB Dec 1731. Bd.

Rafford, William. S Aug 1727. M.

Ragan. *See* Regan.

Ragg, Isaac. TB Oct 1719 T *Susannah & Sarah* LC Annapolis Apr 1720. L.

Ragg, Susanna. T Aug 1721 *Owners Goodwill*. Ca.

Ragman, Wilmot of Kings Nympton, spinster. R for Barbados Jun 1665. De.

Rainbird, Joseph. T May 1751 *Tryal*. K.

Rainbow, Charles. S Summer 1766 R 14 yrs Lent 1767. Bd.

Rainbow, Robert. Died on passage in *Rappahannock* 1726. X.

Rainbow, Robert. T Jan 1734 *Caesar*. Bu.

Rayne, George. R 14 yrs Jly 1724. Ha.

Raine, James. SQS Thirsk s barley Apr TB Aug 1765. Y.

Rane, Ralph of St. Mary le Savoy. S s gun Apr T May 1740 *Essex*. M.

Raine, Sarah. LC from *Honor* Port York Jan 1721. X.

Raine, Simon. S Jan-Jun T Jun 1728 *Elizabeth* LC Potomack Aug 1729. M.

Raynes, John. S s sheep Lent R 14 yrs Summer 1755. Le.

Raines, William. S Jly TB to Va Sep 1759. Wi.

Rainforth, George Jr. S Summer 1748 R 14 yrs Lent 1749. He.

Rainor, John. TB Apr 1753. Db.

Rainsbury, Mary. S Aug T Oct 1724 *Forward* LC Annapolis Jun 1725. M.

Raynsdon, John. S Apr 1748. L.

Raynsford, Richard. R for America Jly 1686. Li.

Rainsfrow, Thomas. S Apr T Jun 1768 *Tryal*. M.

Rairdon. *See* Reardon.

Raise, William. T Feb 1765 *Tryal*. Sx.

Rakes, Weston. S for life Oct 1751-Jan 1752. M.

Rakestraw, John. LC from *Robert* Annapolis Jun 1725. X.

Rall, John. S for Va Jly 1718. De.

Rallins. *See* Rawlins.

Ralph als Symons, Catherine als Christian als Kitty. S Mar 1752. Co.

Ralph, James. S & T Oct 1729 *Forward* LC Va Jun 1730. L.

Ralph, John. S for housebreaking Summer 1723 R Lent 1725 (SP). Su.

Ralph, John. T Apr 1725 *Sukey* but died on passage. E.

Ralph, John. S Apr-May 1754. M.

Ralph, John. T Dec 1763 *Neptune*. K.

Ralph, Thomas. S Lent 1761. K.

Ralph, William. S Apr 1756. So.

Ralphs, Richard. S Jly T Aug 1721 *Prince Royal* LC Va Nov 1721. M.

Ramage, James. R 14 yrs Summer 1755. Cu.

Rambell, Lewis of Bermondsey. SQS Mar T Apr 1768 *Thornton*. Sy.

Rambridge, Susanna. S Sep 1733. M.

Ramley, John. S Summer 1747 AT to Summer 1748. Y.

Rampley, James. S Lent 1764. Su.

Ramsbottam, James. S Lent 1768. La.

Ramsbotham, John of Manchester. SQS Jan 1758. La.

Ramsbottom, Nicholas. S 14 yrs for receiving Lent 1765. La.

Ramsbottom, Ralph. S for poisoning cow at Wrightington & R 14 yrs Lent 1769. La.

Ramsden, Francis. SQS & T Jly 1741. Bd.

Ramsden, Margaret. R for Barbados Jun 1665. L.

Ramsden, Robert of Marton on Moor. R for Barbados Jly 1671. Y.

Ramsden, Squire. AT Summer 1757. Y.

Ramsden, Thomas. SQS & T Jly 1741. Bd.

Ramsden, William. S & R 14 yrs Summer 1742. Bd.

Ramsey, Ann. S Feb-Apr T May 1751 *Tryal*. M.

Ramsey, George als John. S May T Jun 1764 *Dolphin*. M.

Ramsey, Hannah. S Oct T 14 yrs Dec 1724 *Rapppahannock*. L.

Ramsey, Henry. S Mar 1774. Ha.

Ramsay, Robert. S Jan-Jun T Jun 1728 *Elizabeth* LC Potomack Aug 1729. L.

Ramshaw, George. S Lent 1731. Y.

Ramshaw, Mary. S Jun 1733 T Jan 1734 *Caesar* LC Va Jly 1734. M.

Rance als Godfrey, Elizabeth. S & T Apr 1741 *Speedwell* or *Mediterranean*. M.

Rance, Mary. S Apr-Jun T Jly 1772 *Tayloe*. M.

Rance, Noble. S & T Oct 1719 *Susannah & Sarah* but died on passage. L.

Rance, Richard. S & T Sep 1765 *Justitia*. M.

Rand, Benjamin. S & T Oct 1729 *Forward* LC Va Jun 1730. M.

Rand, John. R May T Jun 1691. M.

Rand, John (1749). *See* Poker. M.

Rand, William. T 14 yrs Aug 1752 *Tryal*. E.

Randle, Aaron. S Aug 1727 TB to Md. De.

Randall, Abraham. R for Barbados May 1665. X.

Randoll, Amos of Martock, carpenter. R for Barbados Jan 1675. So.

Randall, Ann. S Jan-Feb T Apr 1771 *Thornton*. M.

Randall, Bartholomew. Rebel T 1685.

Randoll, Katherine, spinster, als wife of Edward of West Molesey. R for Barbados or Jamaica Jly 1674. Sy.

Randall, Charles. S for highway robbery Summer 1754 R 14 yrs Lent 1755. Wa.

Randall, Christopher. R for Barbados Sep 1672. L.

Randall, Elizabeth. S Sep-Dec 1755 T Jan 1756 *Greyhound*. M.

Randall, George. S Jly T Oct 1741 *Sea Horse*. L.

Randall, Henry. Rebel T 1685.

Randole, John of Camberwell. R for America Jly 1700. Sy.

Randall, John. S Sep T Oct 1719 *Susannah & Sarah* but died on passage. L.

Randall, John. S & T Apr 1725 *Sukey* LC Annapolis Sep 1725. M.

Randall, John. T Nov 1725 *Rappahannock* LC Va Aug 1726. Sy.

Randall, John. S Oct 1740. L.

Randall, John. R 14 yrs Mar 1752. De.

Randall, John. S for highway robbery Summer 1754 R 14 yrs Lent 1755. Wa.

Randall, John. S & T Apr 1765 *Ann*. L.

Randall, John. R & T 14 yrs Apr 1770 *New Trial*. M.

Randall, Mary (1727). *See* Smith. M.

Randall, Mary. S Jun-Dec 1745. M.

Randal, Mary. S s at Ombersley Lent 1764. Wo.

Randall, Nicholas. T Jly 1724 *Robert* LC Md Jun 1725. Bu.

Randall, Richard of Oakham. R for America Jly 1678. Ru.

Randall, Richard. S & T Jan 1739 *Dorsetshire*. L.

Randall, Richard. R Lent 1774. Ht.

Randall, Robert. S s at Clewer Summer 1752. Be.

Randall als Mackdonall, Sarah. S & T Apr 1733 *Patapsco* LC Annapolis Nov 1733. L.

Randoll, Sarah. T Sep 1742 *Forward*. K.

Randall, Thomas. T May 1719 *Margaret* LC Md May 1720; sold to Philemon Lloyd Esq. Sy.

Randall, Thomas. S s at Caerwent Lent 1720. Mo.

Randall, Thomas. S Jan T Feb 1726 *Supply* LC Annapolis May 1726. M.

Randall, Thomas. T Jun 1727 *Susanna*. Sy.

Randall, Thomas. T Jun 1727 *Susanna*. Ht.

Randall, Thomas. S Jly 1730. Co.

Randle als Randall, Thomas. S s horse Summer 1760 R 14 yrs Lent 1761. Wo.

Randall, Thomas of Leatherhead. R 14 yrs s gelding Lent T Apr 1772 *Thornton*. Sy.

Randall, Thomas. S Mar 1773. Ha.

Randall, William. R for Barbados or Jamaica Oct 1694. L.

Randall, William. S Jan T Feb 1744 *Neptune*. L.

Randall, William. S s sheep Lent R 14 yrs Summer 1749. Wa.

Randall, William. S Lent R 14 yrs Summer T Oct 1750 *Rachael*. K.

Randall, William. S s at Martin Hussingtree Lent 1752. Wo.

Randall, William. S s sheep Summer 1754 R 14 yrs Lent 1755. Wa.

Randles, Robert. S s at Atcham Lent 1767. Sh.

Rands, Symon of West Harling. R for America Mar 1680. Nf.

Ranford, Edward. S s mare Lent R 14 yrs Summer 1721. Sh.

Ranger, Job. R 14 yrs Jly TB to Va Sep 1744. Wi.

Ranger, John. S Jly 1758. Ha.

Ranger, Luke. S Dec 1767 T Apr 1768 *Thornton*. L.

Ranger, Philip of Warminster. R for Barbados Jly 1664. Wi.

Ranger, Thomas. S for Va Jly 1718. Ha.

Rank, Martin. T Sep 1767 *Justitia*. E.

Rankey, Margaret. S & T Oct 1732 *Caesar*. L.

Rankin, Paul. S Jan-Jun 1747. M.

Rann, Elizabeth. S Dec 1733 T 14 yrs Jan 1734 *Caesar* but died on passage. L.

Ran, Henry. S Mar 1748. Ha.

Ransey, George. LC from *Forward* Annapolis Jun 1725. X.

Ransford, John. S May T Jun 1727 *Susanna*. L.

Ransford, John. S for obstructing Customs officers Summer 1737. Nf.

Ransford, Jonathan (1720). *See* Maynard, Thomas. K.

Ransom, Elizabeth. S Jly T Oct 1768 *Justitia*. M.

Ransome als Inman, Margaret. R Feb 1675. M.

Ransome, William of Farnhamm. SQS Jly T Aug 1769 *Douglas*. Sy.

Ransome, William. S s at Aldborough Lent 1773. Nf.

Ranson als Bickley als Chickley, Sarah; als Sarah the Cork Cutter of St. Sepulchre, spinster. S for assault & robbery & T May 1740 *Essex*. M.

Ranson, William. T Apr 1759 *Thetis*. Bu.

Rant, James. S s sheep at Needham & R 14 yrs Summer 1771. Nf.

Ranton, Richard. S Dec 1745. L.

Raper, Ralph. S Lent 1731. Y.

Raper, Richard. S at Canterbury Apr R Summer 1756. K.

Rapier, Mary. R for Barbados or Jamaica Jly 1685. M.

Rapson, Andrew. Rebel T 1685.

Rapson, Thomas. T Jun 1764 *Dolphin*. K.

Rash, Joseph. S s malt Sep T Dec 1736 *Dorsetshire* to Va. M.

Rash, Mary. S & T Dec 1734 *Caesar* to Va. M.

Rashfield, Jacob. S May T Jun 1727 *Susanna* to Va. M.

Rashfield, Joseph. S Feb T Mar 1727 *Rappahannock*. L.

Rasker, Christopher of Fordington. R for Barbados Mar 1679. Do.

Rassall, Thomas. S Apr-Jun 1739. M.

Ratcliffe, Anne. R 14 yrs Aug 1739. De.

Ratcliffe, Charles. S 14 yrs for receiving goods stolen at St. Chad by John Cope *(qv)* Lent 1766. St.

Ratcliffe, Charles. S s at Burton on Trent Lent 1770. St.

Ratcliffe, Christopher (1763). *See* Lewis. Db.

Ratcliffe als Butterworth, Edward of Park Yate, Ipstones. R for America Jly 1698. St.

Ratcliffe, Elizabeth. R for Barbados or Jamaica Mar & Jly 1685. L.

Ratcliff, Henry. PT Oct 1698. M.

Ratcliffe, Mary. TB Aug 1741. Db.

Ratcliffe, Robert of West Retford. R for America Jly 1678. Nt.

Ratcliffe, Thomas. S Jan 1656 to House of Correction unless he agrees to be transported. M.

Ratifie, William. LC from *Forward* Rappahannock May 1728. X.

Ratley, John. S s sheep Summer 1748 T Apr 1749. Bd.

Rattenbury, Alice (1661). *See* Stewkley. M.

Rattenbury, William. S Jly 1765 TB to Va 1766. De.

Raughton, Joseph of Worcester. R for Jamaica, Barbados or Bermuda Feb 1686. Wo.

Raughton, Thomas of Worcester. R for Jamaica, Barbados or Bermuda Feb 1686. Wo.

Ravell, Edward (1775). *See* Jones. M.

Raven, Anne, aged 34, dark. S & T Oct 1720 *Gilbert* LC Annapolis May 1721. M.

Raven, George. S Aug T Oct 1726 *Forward*. L.

Raven, Hannah. S Dec 1742 T Mar 1743 *Justitia*. L.

Raven, Henry, aged 37, black hair, locksmith. S Dec 1719 T Oct 1720 *Gilbert* LC Annapolis May 1721. M.

Raven, Margaret. S Oct 1729 T *Forward* LC Va Jun 1730. M.

Raven, Mary (1664). *See* White. L.

Raven, Thomas of St. Saviour, Southwark. SQS & T Jan 1766 *Tryal*. Sy.

Raven, William. S Aug 1728 TB to Va Oct 1729. Le.

Raven, William. S & T Apr 1733 *Patapsco* to Md. M.

Ravenhill, John of St. Paul, Covent Garden. S s ham Apr T May 1740 *Essex*. M.

Ravenscroft, Frances. S Jan T Feb 1733 *Smith* to Md or Va. M.

Ravins, Stephen. S & R 14 yrs Lent 1773. Be.

Raw, Thomas. T May 1744 *Justitia*. E.

Rawbone, Edward. Rebel T 1685.

Rawbone, Thomas. S s at Tadmarton Summer 1766. O.

Rawden, Agar. S City s at St. Mary Bishophill Lent 1774. Y.

Rawkins, John. S Jly TB to Va Aug 1769. Wi.

Rawle, David. S Mar 1746. So.

Rawles, Joseph. S Lent 1775. E.

Rawlett, William. S Apr T May 1750 *Lichfield*. L.

Rawlington, Elizabeth. T Jan 1766 *Tryal*. M.

Rawlins, Charles. S May T Jun 1727 *Susanna* to Va. M.

Rawlins, David. S Lent 1730. Wo.

Rawlins, Elizabeth. S & T Oct 1729 *Forward* LC Va Jun 1730. M.

Rawlings, James. R for Barbados Jly 1680. M.

Rawlins, James. S s woodworking tools Feb T Apr 1735 *Patapsco* LC Annapolis Oct 1735. M.

Rawlins, John of St. George, Southwark. R for Barbados Apr 1668. Sy.

Rawlins, John. S Summer 1744 R 14 yrs Lent 1745 (SP). Nf.

Rawlings, John. S Oct 1756. L.

Rawlins, Margery of St. Olave, Southwark. R for Barbados Aug 1668. Sy.

Rawlins, Nathaniel. S & T Nov 1762 *Prince William*. L.

Rawlins, Thomas. S Aug T Sep 1725 *Forward* LC Annapolis Dec 1725. M.

Rawlings, Thomas. S Lent 1746. Sx.

Rallins, Thomas. S s at Cold Aston Summer 1756 R 14 yrs Lent TB Aug 1757. G.

Rawlings, William, aged 25, dark, tailor. LC from *Gilbert* Annapolis May 1721. X.

Rawlinson, John. S s horse Lent R 14 yrs Dec 1731 (SP). Hu.

Rawlinson als Harrison, Margaret wife of William of Stockport, Cheshire. SQS Apr 1745. La.

Rawlingson, Mary wife of John. SQS Richmond s cloth at Bedale Jan TB Aug 1766. Y.

Rawlinson als Jones, Mary. S Feb T Apr 1770 *New Trial*. M.

Rawlinson, William. S Feb T Apr 1734 *Patapsco* to Md. M.

Rawse, John. S s horse & R Lent 1737. Li.

Rawson, Daniel. S Mar 1763 TB to Va. De.

Rawson, Elizabeth. S Jly T Aug 1721 *Prince Royal* LC Va Nov 1721. M.

Rawson, William. R for Barbados or Jamaica Jly 1685. L.

Rawthorne, John. S & T Jan 1756 *Greyhound*. L.

Ray, Charles. S 14 yrs Feb 1731. M.

Ray, Daniel. S & T Sep 1731 *Smith* LC Va 1732. M.

Ray, John. T Sep 1730 *Smith*. Sy.

Ray, William. S for highway robbery Lent R 14 yrs Summer 1725 T *Forward* LC Annapolis Dec 1725. Be.

Ray als Lewis, William, als Cockran, James. S Feb T Apr 1759 *Thetis*. M.

Raybourn, Ann. T May 1751 *Tryal*. K.

Rayer, Thomas. S & R 14 yrs Lent 1774. G.

Raymond, Ann. R for Barbados or Jamaica May 1697. L.

Raymond, John. S & T Jly 1772 *Tayloe*. L.

Raymond, Rebecca. S Jly T Oct 1741 *Sea Horse* to Va. M.

Raynard. *See* Reynard.

Rayner, Barnaby. S s naval stores Jly 1763. Ha.

Rayner, Edward. R for America Jly 1687. Le.

Rayner, Elizabeth. S & T Oct 1732 *Caesar* to Va. M.

Rayner, John. R Summer 1749. Sy.

Reyner, John. S for highway robbery Lent R 14 yrs Summer 1752. Nf.

Rayner als Reyner, Joseph. AT Summer 1749. Y.

Rayner, Rowland of St. George, Southwark. R for Barbados Aug 1662. Sy.

Rayner, Sarah. S Aug T Sep 1725 *Forward* LC Annapolis Dec 1725. L.

Rayner, William of Halstead. SQS Oct 1761 T Apr 1762 *Neptune*. E.

Rayton, Joseph. SQS Jun T Jly 1772 *Tayloe*. M.

Rea, Matthew. S s at St. Martin, Worcester, Lent 1750. Wo.

Rea, William of Worcester. R for America Jly 1673. Wo.

Reay, James. SQS s clock Easter 1775. Du.

Reech, James. R for Barbados Aug 1664. L.

Reachead, Sarah (1747). *See* Lowther. L.

Reachford, John. S s sheep Lent R 14 yrs Summer 1765. Bd.

Read, Ann (1664). *See* Pettis. L.

Reed, Ann. S & T Oct 1730 *Forward* LC Potomack Jan 1731. L.

Read, Ann. S Sep 1737 T Jan 1738 *Dorsetshire* to Va. M.

Read, Ann. S Jan T Mar 1763 *Neptune*. M.

Reed, Anthony. T Apr 1766 *Ann*. K.

Read, Benjamin. S Aug 1727 T *Forward* LC Rappahannock May 1728. M.

Read, Calvin. R for Barbados Dec 1671. M.

Reed, Christian (1702). *See* Parsons. K.

Read, Christian, als wife of William Barrow. S Sep T Dec 1763 *Neptune*. M.

Read, Christian. S Apr 1773. L.

Reid, David. S Jly T Sep 1767 *Justitia*. M.

Reed, Edward. S Aug 1727. So.

Read, Edward. S Lent 1768. Nf.

Reed, Elizabeth. S Jan 1746. M.

Read, Elizabeth. S Lent 1763. Sy.

Read, Elizabeth. R Summer 1773. Sy.

Read, Ely. S Oct T Dec 1724 *Rappahannock* to Va.

Read, Esau or Isaiah. S Summer 1744. He.

Reade, Francis. S Apr T May 1719 *Margaret*; sold to Henry Wright Md Aug 1719. L.

Reed, Francis. SQS Apr 1774. M.

Reade, George. R May T Jun 1691. M.

Read, Hannah. S & T Dec 1752 *Greyhound*. M.

Reed, Hannah of Springfield. S Lent R 14 yrs Summer 1760. E.

Read, Henry of Hornchurch. S Lent T Apr 1760 *Thetis*. E.

Reed als Reeves, James. R Dec 1716 T Jan 1717 *Queen Elizabeth*. M.

Reed, James Jr. S Aug 1727. So.

Read, Jane. R for Barbados or Jamaica Dec 1689. M.

Reed, John of Charlton. R for Barbados Jly 1686. Nl.

Reed, John. S Apr 1723. De.

Read, John. S Jly R 14 yrs TB Dec 1734. Bd.

Read, John. T Apr 1742 *Bond*. K.

Read, John. S Apr T Jun 1742 *Bladon* to Md. M.

Read, John. S Apr T May 1743 *Indian Queen*. L.

Read, John. S Jan T Feb 1744 *Neptune* to Md. M.

Read als Sweep, John. S Jly-Dec 1747. M.

Read, John. S Lent R 14 yrs Summer TB Aug 1748. G.

Read, John. S Lent T May 1750 *Lichfield*. Sx.

Read, John. S Summer 1752 for perjury by swearing that James Blewitt murdered a bastard child borne by Mary Read; to stand in pillory at Gloucester on Market Day before transportation. G.

Reed, John of St. Philip & Jacob. S s linen caps Lent TB Mar 1754. G.

Read, John. S Summer 1757. Su.

Read, John. S Lent 1764. Li.

Read, John (1765). *See* Reeder. La.

Read, John. S s beaver hats at St. Sepulchre Oct 1768 T Jan 1769 *Thornton*. L.

Reed, John. TB Nov 1769. Db.

Read, John. S & T Dec 1771 *Justitia*. M.

Reed, John. S Mar 1773. Ha.

Read, John. R Lent 1774. Sx.

Read, Jonathan. S Summer R for Barbados Aug 1664. Sy.

Reed, Joseph. S for Va Mar 1719. Co.

Reed, Joseph. S & T Jan 1756 *Greyhound*. L.

Reed, Joseph. S Oct 1766 T Jan 1767 *Tryal*. L.

Reed als Sumner, Margaret. S Feb 1773. L.

Reed, Margaret. SQS Dec 1773. M.

Reed, Martin. T 14 yrs Nov 1759 *Phoenix*. Sy.

Reed als Morris als Dalton, Mary. S & T Feb 1719 *Worcester* LC Annapolis Jun 1719. L.

Reed, Mary. T Apr 1743 *Justitia*. Sy.

Read, Mary. S Sep 1747 but died before being transported. L.

Reed, Mary. S & T Jly 1771 *Scarsdale*. L.

Reed, Mary. TB to Va from QS 1773. De.

Reed, Moses of Edenbridge. R for America Jly 1700. K.

Reed, Michael. S Aug TB Sep 1736. Nt.

Read, Michael. S Sep-Oct T Dec 1753 *Whiteing*. M.

Read, Nicholas. R Mar 1774. Wi.

Read, Osmond. Rebel T 1685.

Read, Rachel of High Lea, Chesh, singlewoman. SQS May 1757. La.

Read, Rebecca. S May T Jun 1726 *Loyal Margaret* LC Annapolis Oct 1726. M.

Reed, Richard. S & T Oct 1722 *Forward* LC Annapolis Jun 1723. M.

Read, Richard (1770). *See* Peadle. Sx.

Read, Robert of Thurnby. R for America Jly 1678. Le.

Reed, Robert. S City Summer 1723. Nl.

Read, Robert. S Jly 1724. De.

Read, Robert. S Dec 1733 T Jan 1734 *Caesar* LC Va Jly 1734. L.

Read, Robert. SQS May T Sep 1766 *Justitia*. M.

Read, Robert. S Lent 1769. Nf.

Read, Robert. S Summer 1773. Ht.

Read, Samuel. T Dec 1734 *Caesar*. E.

Read, Sarah wife of Joseph. S s linen at Old Swinford Lent 1756. Wo.

Read, Stephen of Mitton, yeoman. R for Barbados Jly 1685. La.

Read, Stephen. S Lent R 14 yrs Summer 1748 T Jan 1749 *Laura*. Sx.

Read, Susan. T from Newgate *Margaret*; sold to Patrick Sympson & William Black Md Sep 1719. X.

Read als Jeffryes, Susannah. S Apr-May T May 1744 *Justitia*. M.

Read, Susanna. S Sep-Dec 1746. M.

Read, Thomas. R for Barbados or Jamaica Oct 1690. M.
Read, Thomas. R Dec 1698 AT Jan 1699. M.
Read, Thomas. S May-Jly T Sep 1755 *Tryal*. M.
Read, Thomas. S Summer 1758 R 14 yrs Lent 1759. He.
Read, William. R Feb 1675. M.
Read, William. Rebel T 1685.
Read, William. S for Boston NE Jly 1718. Ha.
Read, William. S May T 14 yrs Jun 1727 *Susanna*. L.
Read, William. S Jun T Dec 1736 *Dorsetshire* to Va. M.
Read, William. T Apr 1741 *Speedwell* or *Mediterranean*. Sx.
Read, William. S Mar 1752. So.
Read, William. S s sheep Lent R 14 yrs Summer 1769. No.
Read als Skeet, William. R Jly 1771. Ha.
Reader, Andrew of Bradfield St. George. R for America Feb 1688. Su.
Reader, Benjamin. T Jan 1738 *Dorsetshire*. K.
Reeder, John. T May 1737 *Forward*. Sx.
Reeder als Read, John. S Lent 1765. La.
Reader, Thomas. S Lent 1775. Y.
Reading, Elizabeth of St. George, Southwark. R for Barbados Apr TB
    Oct 1669. Sy.
Reading, George. S s handkerchief at St. Margaret, New Fish Street,
    May T Jun 1768 *Tryal*. L.
Reddin, James. S May T Sep 1766 *Justitia*. M.
Reading, Lambeth. SW & T Dec 1769 *Justitia*. M.
Reading, Richard, als Jones, William, als Farrington als Meredith,
    Richard. S s at Huntingdon Lent 1753. He.
Ready, Peter. S Sep-Dec 1755 T Jan 1756 *Greyhound*. M.
Ready, Thomas. SW & T Apr 1771 *Thornton*. M.
Rairdon, Bartholomew. SQS & T Jan 1765 *Tryal*. M.
Reardon, John. T Apr 1766 *Ann*. M.
Reason, Amey (1741). *See* Grey. M.
Reason, Bartholomew. S Nov T Dec 1770 *Justitia*. L.
Reason, John. Rebel T 1685.
Reason, Thomas. S Mar TB to Va Apr 1740. Wi.
Reason, William. S Sep-Oct T Dec 1771 *Justitia*. M.
Reavell. *See* Revell.
Reay, John. S Lent 1733 AT Lent 1734. St.
Rebecco als Handford, Jane. S Dec 1753-Jan 1754. M.
Reculus, Lionel. S Feb-Apr T May 1755 *Rose*. M.
Redbeard, Thomas. Rebel T 1685.
Redbeard, William. Rebel T 1685.
Redbrooke, William. S Jan T Mar 1763 *Neptune*. M.
Reddall, John. S Lent 1754. Bu.
Reddall, Mary wife of Samuel. S Summer 1772. Wa.
Reddall, William. S Lent 1766. Wa.
Reddalls, John. S Summer T Oct 1757. Db & Le.
Reddiford, James. S & R 14 yrs Lent 1769. G.
Riddiford, Thomas. S (Western Circ) Dec 1766 AT Lent 1767. G.
Reddin. *See* Reading.
Redford, Richard. T Jan 1741 *Vernon*. Sx.
Redford, William. S Jly 1766. Ha.

Redge, Emblyn of Bexley. R for Barbados Jly
1679. K.
Redhead, Elizabeth (1736). *See* Douglas. M.
Redhead, Elizabeth wife of William. S 14 yrs for receiving Lent
1765. G.
Redhead, James of Cartmell. SQS Jan 1741. La.
Redhead, Love. S City Summer 1753. Nl.
Redhead, Thomas. S Jly 1750. L.
Redman, James. R for life Mar TB to Va Apr 1767. Wi.
Redman, John. R 14 yrs Mar 1774. Do.
Redman, Letitia. S Dec 1727. M.
Redman, Martha. S & T Sep 1731 *Smith* but died on
passage. L.
Redman, Mary. S & T Dec 1767 *Neptune*. M.
Redman, Thomas. LC from *Forward* Annapolis Jun 1723. X.
Redmond, Francis. R & T Sep 1766 *Justitia*. M.
Redriff, John. T May 1767 *Thornton*. M.
Redrup, Daniel. S Jan T Feb 1742 *Industry* to Md. M.
Redshaw als Lacon, Sarah. S Jly T Sep 1755 *Tryal*. L.
Redwood, Henry. S Aug 1720. So.
Redwood, Thomas. Rebel T 1685.
Redwood, William. S Dec 1772. M.
Redwood, William. S Dec 1773. M.
Reed. *See* Read.
Reeder. *See* Reader.
Rees, Evan. S s coat at Oswestry Lent 1724. Sh.
Reese, John. S s at Llangattock Lent 1729. Mo.
Reece, John. S s at Grosmont Lent 1751. Mo.
Rees, John. T Jan 1756 *Greyhound*. M.
Rees, John. S Jly T Sep 1765 *Justitia*. M.
Rees, Mary. S s at Llanvaches Lent 1756. Mo.
Rees, Roger of Worcester. R for Jamaica, Barbados or Bermuda Mar
1688. Wo.
Reece, Thomas. S Summer 1738 R 14 yrs Lent 1739. He.
Rees, William. S s at Usk Summer 1759. Mo.
Rees, William. S s oxen & R 14 yrs Lent 1775. He.
Reeve, Ann. S Summer 1758. Nf.
Reeve, Dina als Diana of Downham Market. R for America Mar
1686. Nf.
Reeve, John. S Summer 1755. Su.
Reeve, John. S Lent R 14 yrs Summer 1767. Nf.
Reeve, Joseph. T Nov 1743 *George William*. K.
Reve, Robert. T Apr 1741 *Speedwell* or *Mediterranean*. E.
Reeve, Sarah (1727). *See* Newington. Be.
Reeve, Thomas. S & TB to Va Apr 1764. Le.
Reeve, William. S s iron vice at Witchingham Lent 1770. Nf.
Reeves, Abraham. S s bacon Jan-May T Jun 1738 *Forward* to Md
or Va. M.
Reeves, Arabella. R Jly 1686. M.
Reeves, Edmund. S & T Apr 1753 *Thames*. L.
Reeves, Elizabeth (1699). *See* Barrenclaugh. M.

Reeves, Elizabeth wife of George. S Jan T Feb 1733 *Smith* to Md or Va. M.

Reeves, George. S & T Oct 1730 *Forward* LC Potomack Jan 1731. M.

Reeves, George. S Apr-May T May 1741 *Catherine & Elizabeth* to Md. M.

Reeves, James (1716). *See* Reed. M.

Reeves, James. S s shoes Summer 1760. Be.

Reeves, John. Rebel T 1685.

Reeves, John. S May T Sep 1765 *Justitia*. L.

Reeves, Joseph. S May T Jly 1722 *Alexander*. L.

Reeves, Joseph. S Summer 1772. K.

Reeves, Mary. S Apr 1765. So.

Reeves, Richard. S Jan-Feb 1773. M.

Reeves, Robert. Rebel T 1685.

Reeves, Robert. S Jan T Feb 1724 *Anne* to Carolina. M.

Reeves, Robert. S & T Jly 1770 *Scarsdale*. M.

Reeves, Thomas. S s at Merton College, Oxford, Lent 1724 T *Forward* LC Annapolis Jun 1725. O.

Reaves, Thomas. S Summer 1741. St.

Reeves, William. R for Jamaica Aug 1661. M.

Reeves, William. S Summer 1741. Sh.

Regan, Andrew. S & T Jly 1770 *Scarsdale*. L.

Regan, Bartholomew. SW & T Apr 1769 *Tryal*. M.

Ragan, James. SQS Feb T Mar 1750 *Tryal*. M.

Rigan, John. LC from *Elizabeth* Potomack Aug 1729. X.

Regan, Mary. S Dec 1764 T Jan 1765 *Tryal*. M.

Ragan, William. S Oct 1773. L.

Reid. *See* Read.

Reidman, Thomas. S & T Oct 1722 *Forward* to Md. M.

Reily, Jaques (1719). *See* Daryel. Sy.

Relief, John. S Sep 1718. M.

Rellett, John. T Apr 1772 *Thornton*. Sx.

Remfry, Richard. R Aug 1775. Co.

Remmington, Robert of Uppingham. R for America Jly 1678. Ru.

Remington, Thomas (1669). *See* Hendry. L.

Remmett, Sarah. TB to Va from QS 1743. De.

Rendall, David. S Apr 1728. So.

Rendall, Judith. R 14 yrs Mar 1775. Do.

Rendell, Samuel. R 14 yrs Mar 1773. De.

Rendall, William. S Mar 1755. De.

Rennet, Joseph (1739). *See* Barrow. De.

Renshaw, Henry. S Dec 1762 T Mar 1763 *Neptune*. M.

Renshaw, Isabella. S May T Sep 1766 *Justitia*. L.

Renton, William. S May T Jly 1722 *Alexander* to Nevis or Jamaica. M.

Resden, John. S Mar 1765. Ha.

Restall, George. S Nov T Dec 1770 *Justitia*. L.

Retallack, Richard. S Mar 1753. Co.

Reth, William. S Mar 1729. Co.

Revell, Hannah. S Dec 1737 T Jan 1738 *Dorsetshire*. L.

Revel, James. T Apr 1771 *Thornton*. Sy.

Revell, John. S Oct T Nov 1725 *Rappahannock* LC Rappahannock Apr 1726. L.

Revell, John. T Apr 1731 *Bennett*. E.

Revell, Samuel. R for America Jly 1707. Db.

Reavell, Sophia. S Sep T 14 yrs Oct 1768 *Justitia*. L.

Revill, William. TB Aug 1741 T *Shaw* LC Antigua Jun 1742. Db.

Revell, William. S Summer 1763. Nl.

Revers. *See* Rivers.

Revett, Jane (1723). *See* Frazier. L.

Revord, John. SQS Jan 1751. M.

Rew, Isaac. SQS & TB Oct 1733. G.

Rewell, Jane. R 14 yrs for Carolina May 1719. L.

Rex als Rix, Charles. S May-Jun T Jly 1753 *Tryal*. M.

Raynard, John (1736). *See* Nelson. Y.

Reyner, Joseph (1749). *See* Rayner. Y.

Reynold, Samuel. R for Barbados Sep 1672. L.

Reynold, Thomas (1688). *See* Pafford. L.

Reynolds, Ann. T Sep 1742 *Forward*. K.

Reynolds, Ann. T Apr 1771 *Thornton*. K.

Reynolds, Arnold. S Apr T May 1719 *Margaret*; sold to Ambrose Nelson Sr. Md Sep 1719. L.

Reynolds, Arnold (1730). *See* White, John. L.

Reynolds, Arnold of Stepney. S s sails & T Jan 1740 *York* to Md. M.

Reynolds, Constantine. S Jan T Mar 1750 *Tryal*. L.

Reynolds, Edward. R & TB for Barbados Aug 1668. L.

Reynolds, Edward. S Jan T Feb 1719 *Worcester* LC Annapolis Jun 1719. L.

Reynolds, Edward. S Feb T Apr 1770 *New Trial*. L.

Reynolds, Elizabeth. S 14 yrs Jun 1739. L.

Reynolds, Emanuel. S Summer 1737. Nf.

Reynolds, Gabriel. R for Jamaica Aug 1661. L.

Reynolds, George. S & T Oct 1732 *Caesar* to Va. M.

Reynolds, George. S & T Apr 1769 *Tryal*. L.

Reynolds, Hannah. S & T Sep 1731 *Smith* but died on passage. L.

Reynolds, Hannah wife of John. S s cloth at Leominster Lent 1738. He.

Reynolds, Henry. S s mare & R 14 yrs Lent 1737. Nf.

Reynolds, Henry. TB to Va from QS 1742. De.

Reynolds, Isaac. S Oct T Dec 1758 *The Brothers*. L.

Reynolds, James (1687). *See* Deale. M.

Reynolds als Bush, James. S & T Oct 1730 *Forward* LC Potomack Jan 1731. M.

Reynolds, James. S Lent R 14 yrs Summer TB Oct 1745. G.

Reynolds, John. S Lent R for Barbados May 1664. E.

Reynells, John. Rebel T 1685.

Reynolds, John. S Dec 1727. M.

Reynolds, John. S Aug 1746. Ha.

Reynolds, John. S 14 yrs for receiving Lent 1758. Bd.

Reynolds, John. SQS May T Sep 1764 *Justitia*. M.

Reynolds, John. T Sep 1766 *Justitia*. Sx.

Reynolds, Jonathan. S Norwich s cloth from tenters Summer 1726 R 14 yrs Lent 1727. Nf.

Reynolds, Joseph. S s horse Lent R 14 yrs Summer 1726. Mo.

Reynolds, Josias (1755). *See* Larkham, Robert. So.

Reynolds, Martha (1702). *See* Elton. L.

Reynolds, Mary. S Aug 1727 T *Forward* LC Rappahannock May 1728. M.

Reynolds, Miles. S Feb T May 1767 *Thornton*. M.

Reynolds, Moses. S s at Stapleton Lent 1739. G.

Reynolds, Nicholas. SQS Jan 1754. M.

Reynolds, Richard. T Sep 1758 *Tryal*. Sx.

Reynolds, Richard (1767). *See* Chevening, James. Sy.

Reynolds, Robert. S Summer 1749. Su.

Reynolds, Samuel. S for destroying looms Summer 1730 R 14 yrs Lent 1731. G.

Reynolds, Stephen. S Jly 1723. Wi.

Reynolds, Thomas. R & TB for Barbados Aug 1668. L.

Reynolds, Thomas of Stepney. R for America Aug 1713. M.

Reynolds, Thomas. T May 1719 *Margaret*; sold to Richard Nelson Md May 1720. Sx.

Reynolds, Thomas. S Oct 1733 T Jan 1734 *Caesar* LC Va Jly 1734. M.

Renalls, Thomas. T Apr 1741 *Speedwell* or *Mediterranean*. E.

Reynolds, Thomas. T Apr 1753 *Thames*. Sx.

Reynolds, Thomas. R Jly 1774. Ha.

Reynolds, Thomas. S Summer 1775. Db.

Reynolds, William. R for Barbados May TB Jun 1668. M.

Reynolds, William. R (Western Circ) for Barbados Jun 1699. L.

Reynolds, William. S s leather from warehouse Summer 1740. St.

Reynolds, William. S Summer T Sep 1751 *Greyhound*. Sy.

Reynolds, William. S Feb 1752. L.

Reynolds, William. S & R Summer 1761. Bu.

Road, Ann. R 14 yrs Mar 1771. Do.

Rhode, John. S City Summer 1731. Y.

Rode, Richard. S Summer 1759 R Lent 1760. Ca.

Rhode, Richard. S s gelding Summer 1769 R 14 yrs Lent 1760. Ca.

Road als Jenkins, Thomas. PT Dec 1697. M.

Rhodenhurst, Mary. S Lent 1774. Sh.

Rhodes, Ann (1757). *See* Miller. La.

Rhodes, Ann (1768). *See* Greaves. La.

Roades, Benjamin. LC Md Sep 1719; sold to Mrs. Polea. Sy.

Rhodes, Francis of Worcester. R for Jamaica, Barbados or Bermuda Mar 1688. Wo.

Rhoades, James. S 14 yrs Bristol for receiving Lent 1772. G.

Rhodes, Jervis. S Feb T 14 yrs Mar 1730 *Patapsco* LC Annapolis Sep 1730. M.

Rhodes, John. S Feb T Mar 1758 *Dragon*. M.

Rhodes, John (1767). *See* Graves. La.

Rhodes, John (1775). *See* Clayton, James. Y.

Rodes, Mary wife of John. S s money bag at St. Michael, Gloucester, Lent 1753. G.

Rhodes, Mary (1768). *See* Greaves. La.

Rhodes, Robert. R for America Jly 1687. Li.

Rhodes, Robert. S Jly T Aug 1721 *Prince Royal* LC Va Nov 1721. M.

Rodes, Robert. AT from QS Summer TB Oct 1764. Db.

Rhodes, Samuel. S Sep-Oct 1772. M.

Rhodes, Thomas. R for life for highway robbery Summer 1772. Sy.

Rhodes, Thomas. S Feb 1773. L.

Roades, William. T Aug 1752 *Tryal*. Sx.

Rice, Alexander. S Feb T Apr 1765 *Ann*. M.

Rice, Ann wife of John. S Sep 1737 T Jan 1738 *Dorsetshire* to Va. M.

Rice, David. S Sep 1754. L.

Rice, Dick (1762). *See* Snell, Benjamin. M.

Rice, Elizabeth. S Jly 1750. L.

Rice, Elizabeth wife of John. S Jun T Sep 1758 *Tryal* to Annapolis. M.

Rice, Elizabeth wife of James. S May T Nov 1762 *Prince William*. M.

Rice, Elizabeth. SQS May T Jun 1768 *Tryal*. M.

Rice als Bully, George of St. Margaret, Westminster. S s timber & T Dec 1740 *Vernon*. M.

Rice, James. S s at Abingdon Lent 1772. Be.

Rice, James. S s at Coney Weston Lent 1775. Su.

Rice, Mary. R Apr TB for Barbados Jun 1669. M.

Rice, Mary. S Jan T Feb 1742 *Industry* to Md. M.

Rice, Mary. TB to Va 1751. De.

Rice, Mary. T Sep 1757 *Thetis*. Sy.

Rice, Mary. S Jan-Feb 1774. M.

Rice, Nathaniel. S s lead at Tamworth Summer 1750. St.

Rice, Richard, als Jones, John of Tiverton, brickmaker. R for Barbados Feb 1697. De.

Rice, Simon. S Mar 1766 TB to Va. De.

Rice, Stephen. SW & T Dec 1771 *Justitia*. M.

Rice, Thomas of Gislingham. R for America Mar 1680. Su.

Rice, Thomas of Ewell. R for Barbados or Jamaica Jly 1704. Sy.

Rice, Thomas. S & T Oct 1722 *Forward* LC Annapolis Jun 1723. L.

Rice, Thomas of Formby. S & R Lent 1775. La.

Rice, Valentine. R 14 yrs Mar 1735. De.

Rice, Walter. R 14 yrs Mar 1758. So.

Rice, William. S Apr T Dec 1735 *John* LC Annapolis Sep 1736. M.

Rice, William. S Mar 1736. De.

Rice, William. S Jly T Sep 1755 *Tryal*. L.

Rice, William. SQS Oct 1766 T Jan 1767 *Tryal*. M.

Rice, William. S Jly 1770. Ha.

Rice, William. R 14 yrs Summer 1774. Ch.

Rich, Daniel. S Apr T May 1750 *Lichfield*. L.

Rich, Elizabeth. T Oct 1729 *Forward*. Sy.

Rich, Elizabeth. S Apr 1745. L.

Rich, Henry. LC from *Sukey* Annapolis Sep 1725. X.

Rich, John. S Feb T Mar 1730 *Patapsco* LC Annapolis Sep 1730. M.

Rich, John. R 14 yrs Mar 1731. Wi.

Rich, John. T May 1752 *Lichfield*. Sy.

Rich, Jonathan. T Aug 1721 *Owners Goodwill*. E.

Rich, Joseph of Melksham, mason. R for Barbados Feb 1714. Wi.

Rich, Samuel. S & T Dec 1771 *Justitia*. M.

Rich, Samuel. R Mar 1773. So.

Rich, Thomas of Selling. R for Barbados or Jamaica Jun 1699. K.

Rich, Thomas of Heathfield. R for America Jly 1700. Sx.

Ritch, William (1730). *See* Richards. Mo.

Richacraft, Thomas, aged 25, dark. LC from *Gilbert* Annapolis May 1721. X.

Ritchard, Ann. S Oct 1761. L.

Richard, John John. S s at Llanarth Lent 1767. Mo.

Richard, Mary (1774). *See* Bandy. Le.

Richard als Powell, Richard. S s horses & R for life Summer 1774. St.

Richard, Robert of Chudleigh. R for Barbados Jly 1688. De.

Richard, William John. S s at Llanarth Lent 1767. Mo.

Richards, Alice. S Aug 1752. Co.

Richards, Ann wife of Jenkins. S Jly T Sep 1765 *Justitia*. M.

Richards, Anthony. T Sep 1767 *Justitia*. E.

Richards, Charles. SQS Jly 1774. M.

Richards, Christopher. Rebel T 1685.

Richards als Tanner, Edward. S Jly 1730. Co.

Richards, Edward. S Jun T Sep 1758 *Tryal*. L.

Richards, Edward. S Feb T Apr 1766 *Ann*. M.

Richards, Elizabeth. S Dec 1727. M.

Richards, Elizabeth. T Jun 1728 *Elizabeth* LC Va Aug 1729. Sy.

Richards, Elizabeth. S for breaking & entering Oct T Dec 1736 *Dorsetshire*. M.

Richards, Elizabeth. S Summer 1756 R Summer 1757. Wo.

Richards, Elizabeth wife of Henry. S Apr 1763. M.

Richards, Elizabeth. S Apr T Jly 1770 *Scarsdale*. M.

Richards, Elizabeth. S s handkerchiefs at Kidderminster Lent 1772. Wo.

Richards, Elizabeth. S Bristol Lent 1772. G.

Richards, Francis of St. John's. SQS Jan T Mar 1758 *Dragon*. Sy.

Richards, Frederick. S & T Apr 1766 *Ann*. M.

Richards, Henry. S Mar 1738. De.

Richards, Humphrey of Armitage. R for America Mar 1682. St.

Richards, James. S Oct 1748 T Jan 1749 *Laura*. L.

Richards, Job. S s at Dudley Lent 1774. Wo.

Richards, John of Giggende. R (Western Circ) for America Jly 1700. Sh.

Richards, John. S Aug 1737. De.

Richards, John. S Mar 1755. Do.

Richards, John. T 14 yrs May 1767 *Thornton*. Sy.

Richards, Joseph. S s at Brewood Lent 1757. St.

Richards als Monk, Joseph. S Jly 1773. L.

Richards, Lucy. S & T Dec 1758 *The Brothers*. L.

Richards, Margaret. S Jan-Feb T Apr 1753 *Thames*. M.

Richards, Margaret. S Aug 1760. L.

Richards, Mary. S Jan T Feb 1726 *Supply* LC Annapolis May 1726. M.

Richards, Mary. S Sep-Oct 1748 T Jan 1749 *Laura*. M.

Richards, Paul (1749). *See* Stephens. St.

Richards, Richard, aged 26, dark. S & T Oct 1720 *Gilbert* LC Annapolis May 1721. M.

Richards, Richard (1766). *See* Richardson. Sh.

Richards, Richard. SQS Apr T Jly 1772 *Tayloe*. M.

Richards, Robert. Rebel T 1685.

Richards als Bartley, Robert of Truro. R for Barbados Feb 1698. Co.

Richards, Samuel. S s at Lainbridge Lent 1728. Wo.

Richards, Samuel. S s silver caster at St. Nicholas, Gloucester, Lent 1774. G.

Richards, Sarah. S Jan T Mar 1758 *Dragon*. L.

Richards, Sarah. S Jan 1759. L.

Richards, Stephen. SQS Apr T May 1751 *Tryal*. M.

Richards, Thomas. R for America Jly 1707. Wa.

Richards, Thomas. SQS Jan TB to Jamaica Sep 1727. So.

Richards als Luggervan, Thomas. S Jly 1729. Co.

Richards, Thomas. S s at Daywell (Salop) Lent 1750. He.

Richards, William (1678). *See* Stone. De.

Richards als Ridge als Ritch, William. S Lent 1730. Mo.

Richards, William. S Mar 1738. So.

Richards, William. S Summer 1740. Wo.

Richards, William. AT Lent 1748. St.

Richards, William. S Sep-Oct T Dec 1753 *Whiteing*. M.

Richards, William. S s at Llanwenarth Summer 1768. Mo.

Richardson, Alexander. S Apr T Jly 1770 *Scarsdale*. L.

Richardson, Anne. R Jly & Dec 1698 AT Jan 1699. M.

Richardson, Anne. S Jly T Aug 1721 *Owners Goodwill* to Md. M.

Richardson, Charles. S for killing sheep Summer 1756 R 14 yrs Lent 1757. Bu.

Richardson, Charles. S & R Lent 1764. Nf.

Richardson, Charles. SQS Sep T Dec 1767 *Neptune*. M.

Richardson als Capstick, Daniel. S Feb T May 1719 *Margaret*; sold to Henry Wright Md Aug 1719. L.

Richardson, Daniel (1750). *See* Curtis. M.

Richardson, Dawney. AT Lent 1759. Y.

Richardson, Edward. R for Barbados Jly 1680. M.

Richardson, Edward. S Summer 1742 R 14 yrs Summer 1743. We.

Richardson, Elizabeth. R for Barbados Jly 1680. M.

Richardson, Elizabeth (1721). *See* Smith. M.

Richardson als Bundy, Elizabeth. S & T Oct 1730 *Forward* LC Potomack Jan 1731. M.

Richardson als Pect als Taylor, Elizabeth. S Jly T Dec 1734 *Caesar* LC Va Jly 1735. M.

Richardson, Elizabeth. S Jly T Sep 1751 *Greyhound*. L.

Richardson, Francis. S Lent 1741. Ch.

Richardson, George. TB Apr 1765. Db.

Richardson, Grace (1730). *See* Hogborne. Wi.

Richardson, Henry. T May 1737 *Forward*. E.

Richardson, James. SQS s shirts Easter 1765. Du.

Richardson, Jane wife of Joseph. S Feb T Apr 1770 *New Trial*. L.

Richardson, John of Christchurch. R for Barbados or Jamaica Jly 1677. Sy.

Richardson, John. R for America Jly 1683. Nt.

Richardson, John of Curedale. R for Barbados Jly 1685. La.

Richardson, John (1697). *See* Taylor. Db.

Richardson als Moore, John of Eltham. R for Barbados or Jamaica Mar 1698. K.

Richardson, John. S Jan-Jun T Jun 1728 *Elizabeth* to Md or Va. M.

Richardson, John, servant of Lady Rachel Morgan. S s coffee pot May 1735 T Jan 1736 *Dorsetshire* LC Va Sep 1736. M.

Richardson, John. S Jun T Nov 1743 *George William*. L.

Richardson, John. SQS Apr TB Aug 1749. So.

Richardson, John. S for highway robbery Summer 1754 R 14 yrs Lent 1755. Li.

Richardson, John of Fishlake, wheelwright. SQS s shirt at East Drayton Jan 1755. Nt.

Richardson, John. R 14 yrs Summer 1758. Y.

Richardson, John of Aylesbury. S Lent 1763. Bu.

Richardson, John. T Apr 1766 *Ann*. M.

Richardson, John. S s at Shenstone Lent 1772. St.

Richardson, John. S Apr 1774. M.

Richardson, Joseph. S Sep T Oct 1739 *Duke of Cumberland*. L.

Richardson, Joseph. S s horse Lent R 14 yrs Summer 1756. Sy.

Richardson, Margaret. R for Bermuda s gold ring May 1620. M.

Richardson, Martha. S Feb T Apr 1765 *Ann*. M.

Richardson, Mary. S Aug T Sep 1725 *Forward* LC Annapolis Dec 1725. M.

Richardson, Mary wife of William. S Aug 1727. M.

Richardson, Mary. S Aug 1727 T *Forward* LC Rappahannock May 1728. M.

Richardson, Mary. T Jan 1741 *Vernon*. E.

Richardson, Mathew. S s shoes Summer 1741 R 14 yrs Summer 1743. Du.

Richardson, Nathaniel. S Summer 1740 R 14 yrs Lent 1741 (SP). Be.

Richardson, Nicholas. S Lent 1775. Sx.

Richardson, Nightingale. S Summer 1754. Be.

Richardson als Richards als Andrews als Clewit, Richard. S s at St. Chad, Shrewsbury, Lent 1766. Sh.

Richardson, Richard. S Feb T Apr 1768 *Thornton*. M.

Richardson, Richard. S May 1775. L.

Richardson, Robert of Eaton. R for Barbados Feb 1664. Bd.

Richardson, Robert. S Oct 1743 T Feb 1744 *Neptune* to Md. M.

Richardson, Samuel. S Lent 1738. Ca.

Richardson, Samuel. S Lent 1755. Ca.

Richardson, Sarah. S s silver buttons Apr 1735 T *John* LC Annapolis Sep 1736. M.

Richardson als Delaney, Sarah. S Feb 1736. M.

Richardson, Sarah. SQS Marlborough Oct 1767 TB to Va Apr 1768. Wi.

Richardson, Thomas. T Apr 1725 *Sukey* but died on passage. Sx.

Richardson, Thomas. S Mar TB to Va Sep 1727. Le.

Richardson, Thomas. S & T Jly 1753 *Tryal*. L.

Richardson, Thomas. S s at Albrighton Summer 1757. Sh.

Richardson, Thomas. S s flour Lent 1758. Be.

Richardson, Thomas. T Jun 1764 *Dolphin*. Sy.

Richardson, Thomas. S Jly T Sep 1767 *Justitia*. M.

Richardson, Thomas. S s sheep at St. Oswald, Durham, & R for life Summer 1768. Du.

Richardson, Thomas. S Lent 1775. Y.

Richardson, William. R Dec 1698 AT Jan 1699. M.

Richardson, William. R for America Aug 1715. M.
Richardson, William. S & T Jun 1756 *Lyon*. L.
Richardson, William. ST & T Apr 1765 *Ann*. L.
Richardson, William. S Apr T May 1767 *Thornton*. L.
Richardson, William. S & T Dec 1767 *Neptune*. L.
Richardson, William. S City s spoon at St. Crux & R 14 yrs Lent 1770. Y.
Richardson, William. T 14 yrs Dec 1771 *Justitia*. Sy.
Richens, Jane. S Sep-Oct T Dec 1752 *Greyhound*. M.
Richens, John. S Apr T May 1750 *Lichfield*. M.
Riches, Simeon. S s turkeys from North Burlingham Lent 1771. Nf.
Richeson, Thomas. T Jan 1736 *Dorsetshire*. Sy.
Richman, John. R Summer 1728 (SP). Bu.
Richman, John. S Jly 1734. Wi.
Richmond, Ann. S for life for firing corn at Ryton TB Sep 1761. Y.
Richmond, Ann. S & T Mar 1763 *Neptune*. L.
Richmond, Ann (1767). *See* Hampson. La.
Richmond, Edward. S Feb 1775. M.
Richmond, Francis. S & T Dec 1731 *Forward* to Md or Va. M.
Richmond, Jane, aged 17, fair. S Jan T Feb 1723 *Jonathan* LC Annapolis Jly 1724. M.
Richmond, John. SQS Apr 1774. M.
Richmond, Mary. S Feb 1754. L.
Richmond, William (1718). *See* Swan. Y.
Richmond, William. S Jan-Feb 1774. M.
Rick, William. T May 1767 *Thornton*. M.
Rickard, Lawrence. T Oct 1729 *Forward*. Ht.
Rickerby, Thomas. S Summer 1742. Nf.
Rickitt, Thomas of Southwell, miller. SQS Southwell Jly TB Sep 1773. Nt.
Rickett, William (1740). *See* Rocart. M.
Rickett, William. S Sep T Oct 1750 *Rachael*. L.
Ricketts, Edward. R for America Feb 1692. Nt.
Rickets, Edward of Tewkesbury. S Lent 1720. G.
Ricketts, Elizabeth. S Apr T Nov 1759 *Phoenix*. M.
Ricketts, John. T Jly 1723 *Alexander* LC Md Sep 1723. Sy.
Ricketts, John. S Dec 1749-Jan 1750 T Mar 1750 *Tryal*. M.
Ricketts, John. S Feb-Apr T May 1755 *Rose*. M.
Ricketts, Thomas. R 14 yrs Lent TB Mar 1737. G.
Ricketts, Thomas. S Jly T 14 yrs Sep 1737 *Pretty Patsy*. L.
Rickets, Thomas. T 14 yrs Dec 1758 *The Brothers*. E.
Ricketts, William of Dagenham. R for Barbados or Jamaica Feb 1686. E.
Ricketts, William. R 14 yrs Mar 1740. So.
Ricketts, William. S Lent T Nov 1743 *George William*. Bu.
Ricketts, William. S Jan T Feb 1744 *Neptune* to Md. M.
Ricketts, William. S Lent R 14 yrs Summer 1750. No.
Rickets, William. T 14 yrs Dec 1758 *The Brothers*. E.
Ricks, James. T Oct 1722 *Forward*. Sy.
Ricks, Sarah wife of William. S Lent 1723 R 14 yrs Lent 1724 T *Robert* LC Annapolis Jun 1725. Be.

Ricks, William. S for highway robbery Lent 1723 R 14 yrs Lent 1724 T *Forward* LC Annapolis Jun 1725. Be.

Rixon, Jacob. T Nov 1743 *George William*. Ht.

Rickson, John. LC from *Elizabeth* Potomack Aug 1729. X.

Riddall, Thomas. S & TB Mar 1732. G.

Riddle, Richard. S for highway robbery Lent R 14 yrs Summer 1725 T *Rappahannock* LC Rappahannock Apr 1726. X.

Riddlesdon, William. R for America Aug 1715. M.

Riddlesden, William. R for being at large before expiry of sentence of transportation & T Oct 1720 *Gilbert* to Md. M.

Rider. *See* Ryder.

Ridewood, Richard. R for Barbados Jan 1664. L.

Ridge, Andrew. S Summer 1756 R 14 yrs Lent T Sep 1757 *Thetis*. Sy.

Ridge, Mary. S & T 14 yrs Apr 1753 *Thames*. L.

Ridge, Sarah (1747). *See* Crispe. M.

Ridge, William (1730). *See* Richards. Mo.

Riges, Victory. S & T Jly 1770 *Scarsdale*. M.

Ridgley als Bartelott, George. R for life Mar TB to Va Apr 1773. Wi.

Ridgeley, Richard. S & T Oct 1730 *Forward* LC Potomack Jan 1731. M.

Ridgely, William (1668). *See* Smith. M.

Ridgway, Edward, aged 13. R for Barbados Feb 1664. M.

Ridgway als Grainger, Elizabeth. R for pregnancy Dec 1693 AT Jan 1694. M.

Ridgway, James. S Oct 1661 to House of Correction unless he agrees to be transported. M.

Ridgway, James. S Summer 1769. Ch.

Ridgeway, John. S Oct T Nov 1759 *Phoenix*. L.

Ridgway, John. S Mar 1775. De.

Ridgeway, Nicholas. R for Barbados Feb 1664. L.

Ridgway, Sarah (1719). *See* Scott. L.

Ridgway, Thomas. S & TB Mar 1731. G.

Ridgway, William. PT Oct 1672 R Oct 1673. M.

Ridgway, William. S Lent TB Mar 1731. G.

Ridgway, William. S for killing sheep Lent R 14 yrs Summer 1768. Be.

Ridgway, William. S Mar 1775. De.

Riding, Henry. S Summer 1766. La.

Rideing, Roger of Liverpool. SQS May 1753. La.

Riding, Thomas. S s at Wem Lent 1751. Sh.

Rydings, John. S s horse Lent R 14 yrs Summer 1726. St.

Ridley, John. R Jly 1774. M.

Ridley, Thomas. R for Barbados Jun 1671. M.

Ridley, Thomas. S Lent 1719. Y.

Ridley, William. R Mar 1755. Co.

Ridout, Elizabeth. S Mar 1768. Do.

Ridout, John (1767). *See* Drew. Ha.

Ridout, Thomas. R for life Jan 1757. M.

Riell, Robert. S Summer 1748 R 14 yrs Lent 1749. Sy.

Rigby, Elinor. PT Apr R Oct 1673. M.

Rigby, Elizabeth. S Apr T May 1720 *Honor* to York River. L.

Rigby, Elizabeth. S & R Lent T May 1737 *Forward*. Bu.

Rigby, George. S 14 yrs s from bleaching ground Summer 1773. La.

Rigby, James. SQS Feb 1773. M.

Rigby, John. S Jun-Dec 1738 T 14 yrs Jan 1739 *Dorsetshire* to Va. M.

Rigby, Nicholas. S Jan-Feb 1774. M.

Riggens, William. S May T Jly 1722 *Alexander* to Nevis or Jamaica. M.

Rigglesworth, William (1774). *See* White. M.

Riggs, John. R for Jamaica Aug 1661. L.

Riggs, William. R for Barbados Dec 1683. L.

Riggs, William. R for Barbados or Jamaica Dec 1698. L.

Righteous, Ellen, spinster. S s at Necton & R Lent 1771. Nf.

Rigley. *See* Wrigley.

Rigmaiden, William. R 14 yrs Jun 1761. Ha.

Rygman, John. S May T Sep 1766 *Justitia*. L.

Rigsby, Jane. S Jan T Feb 1733 *Smith* to Md or Va. M.

Riley, Ann of Warrington, spinster. SQS Oct 1763. La.

Riley, Ann. SQS Dec 1764 T Jan 1765 *Tryal*. M.

Ryley, Ann. T Apr 1771 *Thornton*. Sy.

Ryley, Francis. S Lent R 14 yrs Summer 1750. Le.

Ryley, George. S May T Jun 1727 *Susanna* to Va. M.

Riley, George of St. Martin in Fields. SW Jun 1775. M.

Riley, Grace. S Dec 1753-Jan 1754. M.

Riley, James (1741). *See* Orme. Db.

Riley, James. SL Dec 1755 T Jan 1756 *Greyhound*. Sy.

Ryley, James. SWK Apr T Jly 1772 *Orange Bay*. K.

Ryley, John of Birmingham. R for America Feb 1681. Wa.

Ryly, John. S Apr T 14 yrs Aug 1718 *Eagle* to Md or Va. L.

Riley, John. SQS Oct 1722. M.

Ryley, John. S & T Jan 1739 *Dorsetshire*. L.

Riley, John. S Jly-Sep 1754. M.

Riley, John. SQS Coventry Oct 1754. Wa.

Riley, John. T Sep 1758 *Tryal*. K.

Riley, John. SQS & T Sep 1764 *Justitia*. M.

Riley als Barrett, Joseph. S Apr-May 1754. M.

Ryley, Margaret. S Jan-Apr 1748. M.

Riley, Mary. S Feb T Apr 1743 *Justitia*. M.

Riley, Mary. S May-Jly 1749. M.

Riley als Bulger, Mary. S Oct 1751-Jan 1752. M.

Riley als Barrett, Mary. S 14 yrs Apr-May 1754. M.

Riley, Michael. S Feb 1754. L.

Riley, Philip. S & T Jly 1753 *Tryal*. L.

Riley, Philip. R May T for life Sep 1758 *Tryal* to Annapolis. M.

Riley, Richard. S May T Sep 1765 *Justitia*. M.

Riley, Sarah. S Lent R 14 yrs Summer 1736. Le.

Ryley, Sarah. S May-Jly 1749. M.

Ryley, Sarah. SQS Jan T May 1755 *Rose*. M.

Riley, Thomas. S Apr T Sep 1757 *Thetis*. M.

Ryley, William. S s horse Lent R 14 yrs Summer 1753. Nt.

Ryley, William (1772). *See* Rous. Ca.

Riley, William. S Sep 1775. M.

Rhimes, Mary. S Nov T Dec 1753 *Whiteing*. L.

Rymes, William. S Aug 1726. M.

Rimes, William. T Sep 1742 *Forward*. Ht.

Rimes, William. T Sep 1749. Ht.
Rimmer, Jane of Lytham, spinster. SQS Apr 1742. La.
Rimmer, John. S s at Ewelme Summer 1742. O.
Rimmington, John. S & T Mar 1764 *Tryal*. L.
Rinch, Thomas of Lancaster. SQS Jan 1765. La.
Ring, Daniel. SQS Jan TB Feb 1757. So.
Ring, Richard. S May-Jly 1773. M.
Ring, William. S Lent 1754. K.
Ringing, John. S Feb T Apr 1772 *Thornton*. L.
Ringrose, Moses. LC from *Forward* Annapolis Jun 1725. X.
Ripley, William. S & T Dec 1736 *Dorsetshire*. L.
Ripping, Robert. T Oct 1722 *Forward* LC Annapolis Jun 1723. Sx.
Rippon, Henry. S Jly T Sep 1767 *Justitia*. L.
Rippon, Richard. S & T Oct 1732 *Caesar* to Va. M.
Rippon, William. S Jly T Aug 1721 *Prince Royal* LC Va Nov 1721. L.
Ripton, Robert Jr. S Summer 1740 R 14 yrs Summer 1743. Du.
Riscombe, Benjamin. R 14 yrs Aug 1751. So.
Risdale, William. S Oct 1772. L.
Risdon, Lawrence. S Mar 1758. De.
Risley, William. S Sep 1760. L.
Rison, Martha. S Jly 1748. L.
Ritchie, Peter. S Jan T Feb 1765 *Tryal*. L.
Rithock, Sarah. S Apr-Jun 1739. M.
Riton. *See* Wrighton.
Ritson, John. S & R Summer 1772. Cu.
Rivers als Scott, Benjamin. SL Sep T Dec 1758 *The Brothers*. Sy.
Rivers, Elizabeth. S Aug T Oct 1726 *Forward* to Va. M.
Rivers, Elizabeth. S Oct 1756. M.
Rivers, Robert. R Dec 1773. M.
Revers, Roberts. S s at Badminton Lent 1772. G.
Rivers, William. S s sheep at West Ilsley Summer 1738. Be.
Rives, Edward. PT Dec 1674 R Feb 1675. M.
Rives, James. T Apr 1742 *Bond*. K.
Ryves, Mary. R for Barbados or Jamaica Mar 1685. M.
Rivett, Robert of Wootton. R for America Jly 1702. Nf.
Riviere, Louis. S 14 yrs for receiving goods from Lord Baltimore's house
    Feb T Apr 1766 *Ann*. M.
Rivington, Francis. R for America Jly 1686. Le.
Rix, Charles (1753). *See* Rex. M.
Rix, Henry of St. John Maddermarket, Norwich. S Summer 1731. *Nf.
Rix, James, aged 28, brown hair. LC from *Jonathan* Annapolis Jly
    1724. X.
Rixon. *See* Rickson.
Roache, Eleanor. S 14 yrs Sep-Oct 1774. M.
Roche, Elizabeth of Stogumber, spinster. R for Barbados Jly 1695. So.
Roach, Elizabeth. S & T Oct 1730 *Forward* LC Potomack Jan 1731. L.
Roach, Elizabeth wife of John. S Jan T Apr 1762 *Dolphin*. M.
Roach, James. S Oct 1751-Jan 1752. M.
Roach, John. S Sep-Oct 1748 T Jan 1749 *Laura*. M.
Roach, John. S s at St. Philip & Jacob Summer TB Aug 1749. G.
Roach, John. S for highway robbery Lent R 14 yrs Summer 1750. Ch.

Roach, John. S Dec 1761 T Apr 1762 *Dolphin*. M.

Roch, Matthias (1736). *See* Johnson. M.

Roche, Mary. S Apr T Dec 1735 *John* LC Annapolis Sep 1736. M.

Roach, Richard. SQS Apr 1773. M.

Roach, Robert. S s wigs Feb T Apr 1735 *Patapsco* LC Annapolis Oct 1735. L.

Roach, Samuel. S Sep T Oct 1744 *Susannah*. M.

Roach, Sarah. S Dec 1775. M.

Roach, William. R for Barbados or Jamaica Jly 1686. M.

Road. *See* Rhode.

Roadley, Samuel of Sutton Bonington. SQS s barley Jan 1765. Nt.

Roanes, Samuel. S Lent T Apr 1768 *Thornton*. Bu.

Robb, Peter. R Summer 1772. Sy.

Robert *[no other name given]*, vagrant. S s at Woolhampton Lent 1752. Be.

Robert, John. R for Jamaica Jan 1663. M.

Roberts, Ann. LC from *Forward* Annapolis Jun 1725. X.

Roberts, Anne. S & T Apr 1733 *Patapsco* LC Annapolis Nov 1733. M.

Roberds, Ann (1735). *See* Taylor. X.

Roberts, Arnold. S Lent 1730. He.

Roberts, Charles. R for Barbados Dec 1683. L.

Roberts, Charles. S Jly-Dec 1747. M.

Roberts, Charles. T Jun 1764 *Dolphin*. K.

Roberts, Charles. S Oct T Dec 1771 *Justitia*. L.

Roberts, David. R Jly T 14 yrs Sep 1767 *Justitia*. M.

Roberts, Dorothy. S Feb T Mar 1743 *Justitia*. L.

Roberts, Edward. R for America Jun 1684. X.

Roberts, Edward (1686). *See* Thomas. G.

Roberts, Edward. S Feb T 14 yrs Mar 1729 *Patapsco* LC Annapolis Dec 1729. M.

Roberts, Edward. S s horse & R 14 yrs Summer 1774. Sh.

Robarts, Elinor. R for Barbados May 1666. L.

Roberts, Eleanor. S Nov T Dec 1753 *Whiteing*. L.

Roberts als Harrison, Elizabeth. S Jan T Feb 1724 *Anne* to Carolina. M.

Roberts, Elizabeth. S & T Sep 1731 *Smith* LC Va 1732. L.

Roberts, Elizabeth. S for murder of her bastard child Summer 1748 R 14 yrs Lent 1749. No.

Roberts, Elizabeth. S Sep-Oct T Dec 1752 *Greyhound*. M.

Roberts, Elizabeth wife of Hopkin. S Dec 1764 T Jan 1765 *Tryal*. M.

Roberts, Evan. S s colt Lent R 14 yrs Summer 1764. Sh.

Roberts, Francis. T Jly 1724 *Robert* LC Md Jun 1725. Sy.

Roberts, Francis. TB May 1772. Db.

Roberts, George. S Summer 1755 R 14 yrs Summer 1756. Sx.

Robarts, Griffith. R for Barbados May 1676. M.

Roberts, Henry. S s clothing at Welford Lent 1768. G.

Roberts, Henry. S s pig at Lydney Lent 1772. G.

Roberts, Hugh of Hodnet. R for America Jly 1691. Sh.

Roberts, Hugh. S Sep 1747. L.

Roberts, Hugh. S s skins at St. Julian, Shrewsbury, Summer 1771. Sh.

Roberts, Isaac. S s shilling at Newbury Lent 1771. Be.

Roberts, James. R for America Feb 1692. Db.

Roberts, James. S May T Jun 1726 *Loyal Margaret* LC Annapolis Oct 1726. M.

Roberts, James. R 14 yrs Aug 1726. De.

Roberts, James. S Aug 1735. So.

Roberts als Davies als James als Dean, James. S Summer 1758 R for life Lent 1759. He.

Roberts, James. S s horse & R 14 yrs Summer 1774. Sh.

Roberts, Jane (1734). *See* Taylor. M.

Roberts, Joan. TB to Va from QS 1740. De.

Roberts, John. R for America Jly 1693. Nt.

Roberts, John of Winchcombe, cordwainer. R for America Feb 1700. G.

Roberts, John. S Summer 1720 but escaped by Lent 1721. Wo.

Roberts, John. S Lent R 14 yrs Summer 1722. G.

Roberts, John. S May T Jly 1722 *Alexander* to Nevis or Jamaica. M.

Roberts, John. T Apr 1725 *Sukey* LC Md Sep 1725. Sy.

Roberts, John. S & T Sep 1731 *Smith* but died on passage. M.

Roberts, John. S s clothing at Petton Lent 1737. Sh.

Roberts als Davis, John. S & T Jan 1739 *Dorsetshire*. L.

Roberts, John. R 14 yrs Summer 1739. Sy.

Roberts, John, als Langley, Edward. S Dec 1743 T Feb 1744 *Neptune*. M.

Roberts, John. S Aug 1751. So.

Roberts, John. S s bacon Summer 1753. Sh.

Roberts, John. S Lent R 14 yrs Summer 1755. O.

Roberts, John of Kirkby Lonsdale (Westmorland), currier. S Lent 1756. La.

Roberts, John. S Mar TB May 1756. Wi.

Roberts, John. S Feb T Apr 1765 *Ann*. L.

Roberts, John of St. James, Westminster. SW & T Jan 1767 *Tryal*. M.

Roberts, John. S s clothing at St. Giles Cripplegate Feb T Apr 1768 *Thornton*. L.

Roberts, John of St. Saviour, Southwark. SQS Mar T Apr 1768 *Thornton*. Sy.

Roberts, John. SQS Dec 1768 T Jan 1769 *Thornton*. M.

Roberts, John. S Sep T Dec 1769 *Justitia*. M.

Roberts, John of St. Martin in Fields. SW Jly 1773. M.

Roberts, Jonathan, aged 28, fair. S Jan T Feb 1723 *Jonathan* LC Annapolis Jly 1724. M.

Roberts, Lawrence. S City Lent R 14 yrs Summer 1739. Y.

Roberts, Margaret. R May TB Jun 1691. M.

Roberts, Margaret. S & T Apr 1725 *Sukey* to Md. M.

Roberts, Margaret. S Aug T Sep 1725 *Forward* LC Annapolis Dec 1725. M.

Roberts, Marjory of Hitchin. R for Barbados or Jamaica Jly 1688. Ht.

Roberts, Mary. S as pickpocket Summer 1729 R 14 yrs Summer 1730. Wa.

Roberts, Mary. T Sep 1730 *Smith*. Sy.

Roberts, Mary. S Lent TB Apr 1742. G.

Roberts, Mary. S s sheep at Bedwellty Summer 1761 R 14 yrs Lent 1762. Mo.

Roberts, Mary. S s shoes at St. Mary, Shrewsbury, Lent 1766. Sh.

Roberts, Mary. S s at St. Julian, Shrewsbury, Lent 1770. Sh.

Roberts, Mary. S Jan-Feb T Apr 1771 *Thornton*. M.
Roberts, Morris (1741). *See* Roberts, Robert. Sh.
Roberts als Robertson, Peter. S s breeches at Usk Lent 1753. Mo.
Robarts, Peter. S Mar 1757. Co.
Roberts, Peter. S Summer 1769. Ch.
Roberts, Philip. T Sep 1730 *Smith*. K.
Roberts, Phoebe. S s at Monmouth Lent 1769. Mo.
Roberts, Richard of Dowdeswell. R for America Jly 1677. G.
Roberts, Richard of Kentisbeare. R for Barbados Jly 1688. De.
Roberts, Richard. S s at Shifnal Lent 1736. Sh.
Roberts, Richard. S May T Jun 1764 *Dolphin*. M.
Roberts, Richard. T Apr 1765 *Ann*. Ht.
Roberts, Richard. S Sep-Oct 1772. M.
Roberts, Richard. R Lent 1774. K.
Roberts, Robert. S Jly T 14 yrs Aug 1718 *Eagle* LC Charles Town Mar 1719. L.
Roberts, Robert (1724). *See* Life. Sy.
Roberts, Robert als Morris of St. Chad, Shrewsbury. S Lent 1741. Sh.
Roberts, Samuel. S Mar 1749 R for life & TB to Va Apr 1750. Wi.
Roberts, Sarah. S Feb T Mar 1727 *Rappahannock*. L.
Roberts, Sarah wife of John of St. Saviour, Southwark. SQS Apr T Sep 1751 *Greyhound*. Sy.
Roberts, Sarah (1769). *See* Lane. L.
Roberts, Thomas. R for Jamaica Feb 1665. M.
Roberts, Thomas of Chipping Camden. R for Jamaica, Barbados or Jamaica Mar 1688. G.
Roberts, Thomas. S & T Oct 1719 *Susannah & Sarah* LC Annapolis Apr 1720. L.
Roberts, Thomas. S s horse Lent R 14 yrs Summer 1733 (SP). Wo.
Roberts, Thomas. S s at St. Mary Virgin, Oxford, Lent 1747. O.
Roberts, Thomas. S s at Boddington Lent R 14 yrs Summer 1762. G.
Roberts, Thomas. S Jly 1774. L.
Roberts, William of Bloverdstone. R for Barbados Aug 1676. Ch.
Roberts, William. S Feb T Mar 1727 *Rappahannock* to Md. M.
Roberts, William. S Aug 1727. M.
Roberts, William. S & T Sep 1731 *Smith* LC Va 1732. L.
Roberts, William. S Jan T 14 yrs Feb 1733 *Smith*. L.
Roberts, William. S & T Dec 1734 *Caesar* LC Va Jly 1735. L.
Roberts, William (1736). *See* Robertson. X.
Roberts, William. S Apr 1760. M.
Roberts, William. S s horse & R Apr 1762. Fl.
Roberts, William. S Lent 1763. Li.
Roberts, William. S Aug 1763. Fl.
Roberts, William. S Feb T Apr 1768 *Thornton*. M.
Roberts, William. S s horse & R 14 yrs Summer 1768. Wo.
Roberts, William. S Sep-Oct T Dec 1771 *Justitia*. M.
Roberts, William (1772). *See* Robinson. M.
Robertson, Andrew. S s horse Lent R 14 yrs Summer 1752. Nf.
Robertson als Robinson, Ann. R for Barbados or Jamaica Dec 1689. M.
Robertson, Ann. S Feb-Apr T May 1755 *Rose*. M.
Robertson, George. Rebel T 1685.

Robertson, Hanna. S Summer 1761. Nf.

Robertson, Isabella. S & T Jan 1739 *Dorsetshire*. L.

Robertson, Isabella. R 14 yrs Summer 1766. Li.

Robertson, James. T Jun 1738 *Forward*. Sx.

Robertson, John. S Mar 1754. L.

Robertson, John. S s at St. Chad, Shrewsbury, Lent 1772. Sh.

Robertson, John. S 14 yrs Dec 1774. L.

Robertson, Peter (1753). *See* Roberts. Mo.

Robertson, William. LC Md Sep 1719; sold to Mordecai Price. Sy.

Robertson als Roberts, William. LC from *Dorsetshire* Va Sep 1736. X.

Robertson, William. S Summer 1759 T from London Sep 1759. Nl.

Robbins, Aaron. R 14 yrs Jly TB to Va Aug 1752. Wi.

Robins, Allen. R for Barbados Aug 1679. L.

Robbins, Anne. S Oct 1719. M.

Robins, George. SQS & TB Oct 1737. G.

Robins, James. R for Barbados Dec 1693 AT Jan 1694. M.

Robbins, James. R 14 yrs Aug 1727. So.

Robbins, Jephtha. R 14 yrs Mar 1759 TB to Va. De.

Robins, John. Rebel T 1685.

Robins, John. S & T 14 yrs Oct 1732 *Caesar* to Va. M.

Robbins, John. R 14 yrs Jly 1744 TB to Va 1745. De.

Robbins, John. R Jly 1770. Ha.

Robins, Joseph. Rebel T 1685.

Robins, Mary (1755). *See* Woodbegood. M.

Robbins, Mathew. S Mar 1746 TB to Va Jan 1747. Wi.

Robins, Philip. S Lent R 14 yrs Summer 1767. G.

Robins, Richard. T Jan 1741 *Vernon*. E.

Robins, Thomas. S s mare Lent R 14 yrs Summer 1725. G.

Robbins, Thomas. S Mar 1730. Do.

Robins, Valentine. S & T 14 yrs Oct 1732 *Caesar* to Va. M.

Robinson, Alexander. Rebel T 1685.

Robinson, Andrew. S Feb-Apr 1745. M.

Robinson, Ann (1689). *See* Robertson. M.

Robinson, Ann. S & T Oct 1730 *Forward* LC Potomack Jan 1731. M.

Robinson, Ann. S s edging Apr T Dec 1735 *John* LC Annapolis Sep 1736. M.

Robinson als Hudson, Ann. S Summer 1737. Nf.

Robinson, Ann. S Jan 1741. M.

Robinson, Ann. T Dec 1753 *Whiteing*. Sy.

Robinson, Ann. S Feb-Apr T May 1755 *Rose*. M.

Robinson, Ann. S Sep T 14 yrs Oct 1768 *Justitia*. L.

Robinson, Barbara. S Jan-Feb T Apr 1753 *Thames*. M.

Robinson, Benjamin. S Dec 1773. M.

Robinson, Blaze. S May T Jun 1764 *Dolphin*. M.

Robinson, Bridget. SWK Oct 1757 T Sep 1758 *Tryal*. K.

Robinson, Brittain. S Oct 1768 T Jan 1769 *Thornton*. M.

Robinson, Catherine (1730). *See* Waters. M.

Robinson, Catherine. S & T 14 yrs Aug 1752 *Tryal*. L.

Robinson, Charles. S s gold coin at Manfield Summer 1772. Y.

Robinson, Christopher of York. R for Barbados Jly 1699. Y.

Robinson, Christopher. S & T Apr 1762 *Neptune*. L.

Robinson, Edward of Pilton. R for America Jly 1678. No.

Robinson, Edward. S Jan T 14 yrs Feb 1719 *Worcester* LC Md Jun 1719. L.

Robinson, Edward. S & T Sep 1764 *Justitia*. M.

Robinson, Elinor. S Dec 1733 T Jan 1734 *Caesar* LC Va Jly 1734. L.

Robinson, Elizabeth (1700). *See* Welch. M.

Robinson, Elizabeth. S May T Jly 1723 *Alexander* LC Annapolis Sep 1723. L.

Robinson, Elizabeth. S Apr-May T May 1744 *Justitia*. M.

Robinson, Elizabeth als Betty. S s at Leigh Lent 1760. Wo.

Robinson, George. R for America Jly 1709. No.

Robinson, George (1719). *See* Pool. L.

Robinson, George. S Lent T Oct 1723 *Forward* from London. Y.

Robinson, George. S Lent R Summer 1731. Db.

Robinson, George. S Feb T Apr 1766 *Ann*. L.

Robinson, George of Elston. SQS s wool & TB Apr 1773. Nt.

Robinson, Hannah. S & T 14 yrs Apr 1741 *Speedwell* or *Mediterranean*. M.

Robinson, Hannah. S Dec 1746. L.

Robinson, Henry. R for Barbados Feb 1675. L.

Robinson, Henry. S Apr 1746. L.

Robinson, Henry. S Jan T Apr 1762 *Dolphin*. M.

Robinson, Henry. S for receiving & T 14 yrs Jly 1771 *Scarsdale*. L.

Robinson, Hester. S & T Jan 1736 *Dorsetshire* but died on passage. L.

Robinson, James. S May-Jun T 14 yrs Jly 1753 *Tryal*. M.

Robinson, James. ST & T Apr 1770 *New Trial*. L.

Robinson, James of St. Saviour, Southwark. SQS Oct 1774. Sy.

Robinson, Jane of Hucknell Torkend. R for America Mar 1682. Nt.

Robinson, Jane. S & T Dec 1734 *Caesar* LC Va Jly 1735. L.

Robinson, Jane. S Jan-Feb 1774. M.

Robinson, Jeremiah. S & T Jly 1753 *Tryal*. L.

Robinson, John (1661). *See* Harris. L.

Robinson, John of Twywell. R for America Jly 1674. No.

Robinson, John. T Jly 1722 *Alexander*. Sy.

Robinson, John. S May T Jly 1723 *Alexander* LC Annapolis Sep 1723. L.

Robinson, John. S May T Jun 1726 *Loyal Margaret* LC Annapolis Oct 1726. M.

Robinson, John S Oct T Nov 1728 *Forward* to Va. M.

Robinson, John. S s horse Lent R 14 yrs Summer 1732. Li.

Robinson, John. S s horse Summer 1737 R 14 yrs Lent 1738. Li.

Robinson, John. S Lent AT Summer 1739. Y.

Robinson, John of St. George, Hanover Square. S s spoons Sep 1740 T Jan 1741 *Harpooner* to Rappahannock. M.

Robinson, John. S Apr T 14 yrs May 1743 *Indian Queen* to Potomack. M.

Robinson, John. S for highway robbery Summer 1743 R 14 yrs Lent 1744. Nt.

Robinson, John. S Jan 1746. M.

Robinson, John. S Lent 1748. E.

Robinson, John. S Dec 1748 T Jan 1749 *Laura*. M.

Robinson, John. S City s silver mug Lent 1749. Y.

Robinson, John. S Oct 1751-Jan 1752. M.
Robinson, John. S for highway robbery Lent R 14 yrs Summer 1752. Ch.
Robinson, John. S s at Shenstone Lent 1752. St.
Robinson, John. S Feb 1754. L.
Robinson, John. S s bread & mutton at Badgworth Lent TB Apr 1756. G.
Robinson, John. S & T Sep 1765 *Justitia*. M.
Robinson, John. R Dec 1765 T for life Jan 1766 *Tryal*. L.
Robinson, John. S s sheep at Romanby & R 14 yrs Lent TB Aug 1768. Y.
Robinson, John. T Apr 1769 *Tryal*. Ht.
Robinson, John. S & T Dec 1769 *Justitia*. L.
Robinson, John. T 14 yrs Dec 1770 *Justitia*. Sy.
Robinson, John. SQS Feb 1773. M.
Robinson, John. S Sep-Oct 1773. M.
Robinson, John. S Jan-Feb 1774. M.
Robinson, Joseph of Dartford. R for Barbados or Jamaica Jun 1684. K.
Robinson, Joseph. S s horse Mar R 14 yrs & TB Apr 1724. Nt.
Robinson, Joseph. S Summer 1724 R 14 yrs Lent 1725 T *Sukey* LC Annapolis Sep 1725. Be.
Robinson, Joseph. S & T 14 yrs Oct 1730 *Forward* LC Potomack Jan 1731. M.
Robinson, Joseph. S & T Oct 1732 *Caesar* to Va. M.
Robinson, Joseph. S Jan-Feb T Apr 1753 *Thames*. M.
Robinson, Joseph. S & T Apr 1765 *Ann*. L.
Robinson, Joseph. S s at Chester & R 14 yrs Summer 1775. Du.
Robinson, Josias. R Summer 1721. Y.
Robinson, Leonard. S Feb T Mar 1730 *Patapsco* LC Annapolis Sep 1730. L.
Robinson, Margaret. S Aug T Oct 1726 *Forward* to Va. M.
Robinson, Margaret. S Oct 1742 T Mar 1743 *Justitia*. L.
Robinson, Margaret. AT Summer 1764. Du.
Robinson, Margery. S Dec 1727. M.
Robinson, Martha. S Jan T Sep 1737 *Pretty Patsy* to Md. M.
Robinson, Mary (1679). *See* Stephens. L.
Robinson, Mary of St. Saviour, Southwark, spinster. R for Barbados or Jamaica Jun 1692. Sy.
Robinson, Mary. PT Oct R Dec 1699. M.
Robinson, Mary. AT from QS 1726 & died on *Loyal Margaret* 1726. St.
Robinson als Bisse, Mary. S s clothing Jly-Sep T Sep 1742 *Forward*. M.
Robinson, Mary. S Jly T Sep 1755 *Tryal*. L.
Robinson, Mary. S May T Nov 1762 *Prince William*. M.
Robinson, Mary. S Sep T Nov 1762 *Prince William*. M.
Robinson, Mary. S May T Jun 1764 *Dolphin*. M.
Robinson, Mary, spinster. S s at St. Mary, Huntingdon, Lent 1772. Hu.
Robinson, Matthew. S s horse Lent R 14 yrs Summer 1749. Li.
Robinson als Robson als Maulam, Matthew. S s breeches at Hurworth Summer 1768. Du.
Robinson, Michael. S & T Nov 1762 *Prince William*. L.
Robinson, Michael. S Aug 1763. L.

Robinson, Nathaniel. R 14 yrs Mar 1760 TB to Va. De.

Robinson, Peter. S 14 yrs for highway robbery in St. George, Hanover Square, Apr 1732; to be T to Md or Pa by James Thompson of Tower Hill. M.

Robinson, Reuben. S s mare Lent R 14 yrs Summer 1758. Le.

Robinson, Richard. T May 1719 *Margaret* LC Md May 1720; sold to William Anderson. Sy.

Robinson, Richard. S Sep T Dec 1734 *Caesar* LC Va Jly 1735. M.

Robinson, Robert. R for Barbados or Jamaica Jly 1686. M.

Robinson, Robert. T Jly 1724 *Robert* LC Md Jun 1725. Sy.

Robinson, Robert of St. Saviour, Southwark. SQS Oct T Dec 1752 *Greyhound*. Sy.

Robinson, Robert. T Jly 1753 *Tryal*. Sy.

Robinson, Robert. S & T Dec 1759 *Phoenix*. M.

Robinson, Rose. S May 1745. M.

Robinson, Samuel. S Summer TB Sep 1740. Y.

Robinson, Sarah wife of John of St. Olave, Southwark. R for Barbados or Jamaica Jly 1715. Sy.

Robinson, Sarah. S & T Sep 1765 *Justitia*. M.

Robinson, Sarah. S Lent 1768. Wo.

Robinson, Susanna (1721). *See* Downes. M.

Robinson, Thomas of Peterborough. R for America Jly 1687. No.

Robinson, Thomas. S s at Penkridge Summer 1724. St.

Robinson, Thomas. S s at Shawbury Lent 1738. Sh.

Robinson, Thomas of St. John's. SQS Apr T May 1750 *Lichfield*. Sy.

Robinson, Thomas. S Oct 1751-Jan 1752. M.

Robinson, Thomas. S Feb T Apr 1765 *Ann*. M.

Robinson, Thomas. S Feb T Apr 1768 *Thornton*. M.

Robinson, Thomas of Wandsworth. SQS for grand larceny Oct T Dec 1769 *Justitia*. Sy.

Robinson, Thomas. S Lent 1774. Db.

Robinson, Timothy. Died on passage in *Forward* 1730. X.

Robinson, William. R Jly AT Sep 1675. M.

Robinson, William. T May 1719 *Margaret*. Ht.

Robinson, William, aged 21, ruddy, fisherman. S & T Oct 1720 LC from *Gilbert* Md May 1721. L.

Robinson, William. S & T Oct 1722 *Forward* LC Annapolis Jun 1723. M.

Robinson, William. T Apr 1732 *Patapsco*. Sx.

Robinson als Thompson als Toes, William. S s horse Lent R 14 yrs Summer 1733. Y.

Robinson, William. S for forging deeds Lent R Summer 1733 (SP). He.

Robinson, William. S Norwich Summer 1734. Nf.

Robinson, William. S Jun-Dec 1738 T Jan 1739 *Dorsetshire* to Va. M.

Robinson, William. S Apr-May T May 1744 *Justitia*. M.

Robinson, William. S City s handkerchief at Holgate Lent 1745. Y.

Robinson, William. S & T Aug 1752 *Tryal*. L.

Robinson, William. S Feb-Apr T May 1755 *Rose*. M.

Robinson, William. S Apr 1763. M.

Robinson, William. S Jan T Feb 1765 *Tryal*. L.

Robinson, William. TB to Va from QS 1767. De.

Robinson, William. S Feb T Apr 1768 *Thornton*. M.

Robinson, William. S s mare & R Lent 1768. Wa.
Robinson, William. SQS & T Jly 1772 *Tayloe*. M.
Robinson als Roberts, William. SQS & T Jly 1772 *Tayloe*. M.
Robinson, William. S Summer 1773. Sy.
Robkins, James. S for highway robbery Lent R 14 yrs Summer 1760. Nf.
Robnut, Edward. S Lent T Apr 1772 *Thornton*. Ht.
Robotham, George. S for killing deer at Uttoxeter Lent 1762. St.
Rowbotham, George of Manchester. SQS Apr 1763. La.
Robson, Alice. S Lent 1765. Li.
Robson, George. S s gelding & R Summer 1772. Nl.
Robson, Jacob. S s silver spoon at Sunderland Summer 1775. Du.
Robson, John. R 14 yrs Summer 1747. Nl.
Robson, John. AT City Summer 1758. Nl.
Robson, John (1770). *See* Soulsby, Thomas. Nl.
Robson, Mary. AT City Summer 1760. Nl.
Robson, Mary. S Lent 1775. Li.
Robson, Matthew (1768). *See* Robinson. Du.
Robson, Peter. SQS Jly 1754. Du.
Robson, Thomas, als Piper, Nicholas. S s horse Lent R 14 yrs Summer
    1722. St.
Robson, William. R for Barbados Jan 1665. Y.
Robson, William. R 14 yrs Summer TB Aug 1741. Y.
Robuctine, Hannah. S Apr 1749. L.
Roby, Elizabeth. S Lent T May 1755 *Rose*. Sy.
Roby, Elizabeth, als Derbyshire Bess. S for highway robbery Lent R 14
    yrs Summer 1769. Wa.
Roby, William. S Jly TB to Va Aug 1751. Wi.
Rocart als Rickett, William of Hillingdon. S s fowls Feb 1740. M.
Roche. *See* Roach.
Rochester, Elizabeth. S Summer 1754. Du.
Rochester, Robert. S Lent 1735. *Su.
Rochester, Stephen (1736). *See* Russell. K.
Rochford, John. S Jly T 14 yrs Aug 1718 *Eagle* LC Charles Town Mar
    1719. L.
Rotchford, Thomas. S Dec 1764 T Jan 1765 *Tryal*. M.
Rock, Edward. SQS Mar TB Aug 1720 to be shipped to Md from
    Liverpool. Db.
Rock, Edward. SW & T Aug 1769 *Douglas*. M.
Rock, John. S Apr-May 1754. M.
Rock, Joseph. S s mare & R 14 yrs Summer 1772. St.
Rock, Mary, widow. S s ham at St. Botolph Bishopsgate Apr T Jun 1768
    Tryal. L.
Rock, Samuel. SQS Mar TB Aug 1720 to be shipped to Md from
    Liverpool. Db.
Rock, Sarah. S May-Jun T Aug 1752 *Tryal*. M.
Rockett, Robert. S Sep T 14 yrs Oct 1744 *Susannah*. M.
Rodan, Martha. LC Va Aug 1729. K.
Rodd, Dorothy wife of George. SQS Jan 1754. Ha.
Rodd, John. S Mar 1757. Co.
Rodd, Robert Sr. S Mar 1732 TB to Va. De.
Rodda als Rodder, John. S Aug 1773. Co.

Roddam, Barbara. S Summer 1762. Du.

Roddery, Jane. S Lent 1769. La.

Rodger, Ann. S s at Sheffield & R 14 yrs Lent 1771. Y.

Roding, William. SQS Mar R 14 yrs & TB Aug 1738. Nt.

Rodway, Stephen. Rebel T 1685.

Roe. *See* Rowe.

Roebuck, Thomas. AT Lent & Summer 1765. Y.

Roffe, Edward. S Mar 1722. Ha.

Roff, Robert. S s sheep Summer TB Jly 1742. G.

Rogers, Abraham. SQS Jan TB Apr 1755. So.

Rogers, Alexander of Spalding. R for America Jly 1679. Li.

Rogers, Ann. R May TB Jun 1691. M.

Rogers, Arnold of St. Saviour, Southwark. S Summer 1746. Sy.

Rogers, Benjamin. S Oct 1733 T Jan 1734 *Caesar* LC Va Jly 1734. M.

Rogers, Charles. R 14 yrs Jly 1775. M.

Rogers, Edward. T Apr 1753 *Thames*. Sx.

Rogers, Elinor. R for Barbados or Jamaica Jly 1686. M.

Rogers, Elianor. S s linen at St. Chad, Shrewsbury, Summer 1756;
accused with Sarah, wife of Joshua Rogers, who was hanged. Sh.

Rogers, Francis. S s handkerchief at All Hallows Barking Jan T Apr
1768 *Thornton*. L.

Rogers, Grace. S Apr T May 1719 *Margaret*; sold to James Smith Md
Aug 1719. L.

Rogers, Hannah. R & T Dec 1716 *Lewis* to Jamaica. M.

Rogers, Henry. T Dec 1753 *Whiteing*. Sx.

Rogers, James. S Feb T 14 yrs Mar 1731 *Patapsco* LC Annapolis Jun
1731. L.

Rogers, James. T Oct 1739 *Duke of Cumberland*. Bu.

Rogers, James. S Aug 1767. So.

Rogers, James. R 14 yrs Aug 1775. So.

Rogers, Jane, widow. R for Barbados Nov 1668. L.

Rogers, Joan wife of William. S s at Monmouth Lent R 14 yrs Summer
1761. Mo.

Rogers, John of Hennock, husbandman. R for Barbados Feb 1668. De.

Rogers, John (2). Rebels T 1685.

Rogers, John. S Jan T Feb 1719 *Worcester* LC Annapolis Jun 1719. L.

Rogers, John. T Jly 1724 *Robert* LC Md Jun 1725. K.

Rogers, John. S for burglary Summer 1725 R 14 yrs Lent 1726. Sh.

Rogers, John. R 14 yrs Jly 1730. De.

Rogers, John. S & T Sep 1731 *Smith* LC Va 1732. L.

Rogers, John. S s butter May T Dec 1735 *John* LC Annapolis Sep
1736. L.

Rogers als Barber, John. S Mar 1757. So.

Rogers, John. T Dec 1763 *Neptune*. Sy.

Rogers, John (1772). *See* Walding. Wa.

Rogers, John. R 14 yrs Oct 1772. M.

Rogers, John. S Mar 1774. De.

Rogers, John. S Feb 1775. L.

Rogers, Jonathan. S Feb T Apr 1739 *Forward*. L.

Rodgers, Joseph. S for coining in gaol Summer 1721 R 14 yrs Summer
TB Jly 1722. Db.

Rogers, Joseph. S s brass Jan T Apr 1735 *Patapsco* LC Annapolis Oct 1735. L.

Rogers, Mary. S s cloth at Oswestry Lent 1770. Sh.

Rogers, Michael. S Jan-Feb T Apr 1772 *Thornton*. M.

Rogers, Philip. S Apr T May 1750 *Lichfield*. M.

Rogers, Richard. R for Barbados Dec 1670 & Jun 1671. M.

Rogers, Richard. S Feb T 14 yrs Mar 1730 *Patapsco* LC Annapolis Sep 1730. M.

Rogers, Robert. R Sep 1682. M.

Rogers, Robert (1684). *See* Scull. E.

Rogers, Robert. S Sep-Oct T Dec 1752 *Greyhound*. M.

Rogers, Sarah. T Apr 1760 *Thetis*. Sy.

Rogers, Stephen. R for Va for murder Apr 1617 because he is a carpenter. M.

Rogers, Stephen. S Aug 1767. So.

Rogers, Thomas of Fisherton Anger, cutler. R for Barbados Jan 1682. Wi.

Rogers, Thomas of Wimborne, clothworker. R (Oxford Circ) for America Jly 1688. Do.

Rogers, Thomas. R May TB Jun 1691. M.

Rogers, Thomas of Chadwell. R for Barbados or Jamaica Mar 1698. E.

Rogers, Thomas. S Mar 1725. De.

Rogers, Thomas. S s horse Lent R 14 yrs Summer 1729. Sh.

Rogers, Thomas. S Feb T 14 yrs Mar 1730 *Patapsco* LC Annapolis Sep 1730. M.

Rogers, Thomas. S Summer 1749 R 14 yrs Lent T May 1750 *Lichfield*. K.

Rogers, Thomas of Mitcham. SQS Oct 1750. Sy.

Rogers als Moore, Thomas. S s at Upton Warren Lent 1753. Wo.

Rodgers, Thomas. S s mare Lent R 14 yrs Summer 1769. Li.

Rogers, Thomas. S s cloth at Rodborough Lent 1774. G.

Rogers, William. S Jan T Feb 1726 *Supply* LC Annapolis May 1726. M.

Rogers, William. S Dec 1733 T Jan 1734 *Caesar* LC Va Jly 1734. L.

Rogers, William, servant in King's Confectionary. S s spoons Jan T Apr 1735 *Patapsco* LC Annapolis Oct 1735. M.

Rogers, William. T Aug 1741 *Sally*. Sy.

Rogers, William. S Apr T May 1752 *Lichfield*. L.

Rohick, Barnaby. S & T Jan 1736 *Dorsetshire* LC Va Sep 1736. L.

Rolfe, Edward. S at Ipswich s silver watch Sep 1772. Su.

Rolph, Elizabeth. S s wheat at Bicester Summer 1757. O.

Rolf, John. T Jun 1742 *Bladon*. Sx.

Rolfe, John of Berhampstead St. Peter. SQS Apr T May 1767 *Thornton*. Ht.

Rolfe, Mary. T Apr 1741 *Speedwell* or *Mediterranean*. Sx.

Rolphe, Peregrine of Hatfield. R for Barbados or Jamaica Jly 1687. Ht.

Rolfe, Thomas. T Oct 1721 *William & John*. K.

Rolfe, Thomas. T Apr 1734 *Patapsco*. Ht.

Rolph, Thomas. S s ewe Summer 1772. K.

Rolph, William. R for Barbados or Jamaica Oct 1690. M.

Rolls. *See* Rowles.

Rolph. *See* Rolfe.

Rolt, John. S for killing sheep Summer 1766 R 14 yrs Lent T May 1767 *Thornton*. Bu.

Romane, Elizabeth. S Oct T Nov 1728 *Forward* LC Rappahannock Jun 1729. M.

Romanstoe, John. R for America Jly 1686. Wa.

Rond, Susan of Lambeth. R for Barbados or Jamaica Jly 1677. Sy.

Roney, Alice wife of John. S & T 14 yrs Jan 1765 *Tryal*. M.

Roning, John of Reigate. SQS Apr T May 1750 *Lichfield*. Sy.

Ronsewell, Thomas. Rebel T 1685.

Rood, Edward. R 14 yrs Jly 1752. Ha.

Roof, Sarah. S Sep T Dec 1734 *Caesar* but died on passage. M.

Rook als Palmer, Ann. S May T Jun 1727 *Susanna* to Va. M.

Rooke, Henry. Rebel T 1685.

Rooke, Henry. S May-Jly 1748. M.

Rook, John. S Mar 1774. Ha.

Rooke, Joseph. S Lent R 14 yrs Summer 1755. St.

Rooke, Ralph. S for Va as incorrigible rogue & vagabond Aug 1618. M.

Rooke, Richard Jr. R for life Summer 1772 for murdering a 3-day old child by exposing it in a yard at Winstone. G.

Rooke, Susannah (1770). *See* Cary. M.

Rook, Thomas. S Lent 1763. Wa.

Rook, Thomas. S Apr-Jun T Jly 1772 *Tayloe*. M.

Rook, William. T Oct 1726 *Forward*. Ht.

Rook, William. S & T Sep 1765 *Justitia*. M.

Rooker, William. S Jan-Feb 1775. M.

Rookes, Elizabeth. S Jly-Sep T Oct 1739 *Duke of Cumberland*. M.

Room, John. S Jan-Feb T Apr 1753 *Thames*. M.

Roose. *See* Rouse.

Rooston, George. S s mare Lent R 14 yrs Summer 1765. Li.

Root, George. S Feb T Apr 1765 *Ann*. M.

Rootham, John. T Jan 1736 *Dorsetshire*. E.

Roper, Henry. Rebel T 1685.

Roper, James. S Summer T Aug 1771. Wa.

Roper, Richard. S Feb T Mar 1730 *Patapsco* LC Annapolis Sep 1730. M.

Roper, Richard. S Apr T Jun 1742 *Bladon*. L.

Rorke, John. S & T Apr 1753 *Thames*. L.

Rosamond, John. S for highway robbery Lent R 14 yrs Summer 1725 T *Forward* LC Annapolis Dec 1725. Be.

Roscow, William. S Mar TB Apr 1737. Le.

Roscowdrick, Thomas. S Jly 1727 & Mar 1728. Co.

Rose, Edward. R 14 yrs Jly 1747. Ha.

Rose, Francis. S s sheep Lent R 14 yrs Summer 1746. E.

Rose, George. S Feb T Mar 1727 *Rappahannock* to Md. M.

Rose, George. T Aug 1752 *Tryal*. M.

Rose, Henry. S Sep T Dec 1767 *Neptune*. L.

Rose, Jacob. S Oct 1760. M.

Rose, James. SQS Jan-Mar TB to Va Apr 1741. Wi.

Rose, James. S s mare & R 14 yrs Lent 1743. Ca.

Rose, James of Bermondsey. SQS Jly T Sep 1766 *Justitia*. Sy.

Rose, Jeremiah of Croydon. SQS Jan 1775. Sy.

Rose, John. S Jly T Aug 1721 *Prince Royal* LC Va Nov 1721. L.

Rose, John of Newington. SQS Jan 1751. Sy.

Rose, Joseph. S Mar 1720. L.

Rose, Mary (1735). *See* Johnson. M.

Rose, Mary. S Lent T Apr 1759 *Thetis*. Bu.

Rose, Rebecca wife of Pasq. R for Barbados or Jamaica Jly 1686. M.

Rose, Richard. T May 1719 *Margaret*; sold to Patrick Sympson Md May 1720. Sx.

Rose, Richard. S May T Jun 1727 *Susanna* to Va. M.

Rose, Sarah. T Oct 1721 *William & John*. K.

Rose, Thomas. S Apr T May 1750 *Lichfield*. L.

Rose, Thomas. S Apr TB to Va Apr 1750. Wi.

Rose, Thomas. S Apr-May 1754. M.

Rose, Thomas. S Dec 1757 T Mar 1758 *Dragon*. M.

Rose, Thomas. S Feb 1758. Ha.

Rose, Thomas. R 14 yrs for highway robbery Summer 1758. Ru.

Rose, William, yeoman. R (Western Circ) for Barbados Jly 1695. L.

Rose, William, aged 31, dark, husbandman. S Jan T Feb 1723 *Jonathan* LC Annapolis Jly 1724. M.

Rose, William. S Jly 1740. Wi.

Rose, William. S Dec 1748 T Jan 1749 *Laura*. L.

Rose, William. SQS Jly 1756. M.

Rose, William. S s at Conisborough Lent 1764. Y.

Rose, William of Dorking. SQS & T Apr 1765 *Ann*. Sy.

Rose, William. S Summer 1767 R for life Lent 1768. O.

Rosebrooke, Richard of Great Yeldham. R for Barbados or Jamaica Jly 1702 & Jly 1704. E.

Roseden, Susan of Gateshead, spinster. R for Barbados Feb 1673. Du.

Rosewell, Sarah wife of John. S Aug 1759. So.

Rosier, John. S s fish Summer 1754. Be.

Rosier, John. S Lent R 14 yrs Summer 1766. Be.

Roskronge, Ann. S Jly 1741. Co.

Ross, Alexander. S Nov T Dec 1763 *Neptune*. L.

Ross, Alexander. S & T Jan 1769 *Thornton*. L.

Ross, Andrew. S Jan T 14 yrs Feb 1765 *Tryal*. L.

Ross, Ann. S Oct 1765 T Jan 1766 *Tryal*. M.

Rosse, Catherine. S & T Aug 1718 *Eagle* LC Charles Town Mar 1719. L.

Ross, Charles. SQS Sep T Dec 1767 *Neptune*. M.

Ross, Elizabeth. S May T Sep 1766 *Justitia*. M.

Ross, Esther wife of Edward. S Jun T Sep 1764 *Justitia*. M.

Ross, Henry. T Jun 1738 *Forward*. Sx.

Ross als Bass, Jane. S Apr 1746. L.

Rosse, John. S Lent R for Barbados May 1664. E.

Ross, John (1702). *See* Bradney. Bu.

Rosse, John. S & T Oct 1730 *Forward* LC Potomack Jan 1731. M.

Ross, John. S City s flannel Summer 1750. Nl.

Ross, John. T Sep 1757 *Thetis*. E.

Ross, John. R 14 yrs Mar TB to Va Apr 1769. Wi.

Ross, Margaret. S Summer 1755. Du.

Ross, Margaret of Wandsworth, spinster. SQS Jan T Apr 1770 *New Trial*. Sy.

Ross, Penelope wife of Peter. S & T Sep 1731 *Smith* LC Va 1732. M.

Ross, Peter. S Lent R 14 yrs Summer 1750. G.
Ross, Peter. SL Aug 1763. Sy.
Ross, Thomas. S Dec 1742 T Mar 1743 *Justitia*. L.
Ross, William. S s at St. Philip & Jacob Lent TB Apr 1751. G.
Ross, William. S Jan T 14 yrs Feb 1765 *Tryal*. L.
Rossak, Thomas. SW & T Jan 1769 *Thornton*. M.
Rossen, James. S Lent R 14 yrs Summer 1728. Sh.
Rosser, Aaron of Penalt. R for America Jun 1714. Mo.
Rosser, William. S Summer 1730. Mo.
Rossiter als Vaters, Catherine. S Mar 1740. So.
Rosseter, Elizabeth. S Jly 1773. L.
Rossiter, Hannah. S Dec 1741 T Feb 1742 *Industry* to Md. M.
Rosseter, John. Rebel T 1685.
Rossiter, John. S for Va Jly 1718. So.
Rositor, John. S May T Jun 1726 *Loyal Margaret* LC Annapolis Oct 1726. M.
Rossiter als Vaters, John. S Mar 1740. So.
Rossiter, Nicholas. SQS & TB Jly 1735. So.
Rosseter, Samuel. S Oct T Dec 1763 *Neptune*. M.
Rossum, Mary. S Jun T Nov 1743 *George William*. M.
Roste, Hannah. S Feb-Apr 1745. M.
Rotheram, Joseph. S & R Summer T Sep 1770. Wa.
Rotherton, John. Rebel T 1685.
Rothwell, Richard of Wigan, weaver. SQS Jan 1767. La.
Rotters, John. R for America Aug 1715. L.
Roughsedge, William. S Lent 1763. La.
Rouncevall, John. S Mar 1734. De.
Round, John. R for America Feb 1702. No.
Round, Thomas. S s at Bray & Winkfield Lent 1761. Be.
Round, Thomas. S 14 yrs for receiving Jly 1766. Ha.
Roundy, David. T May 1744 *Justitia*. Sy.
Rouse, Francis. S Apr TB May 1719. L.
Rouse, John. PT Apr R Jly 1675. M.
Rouse als Drouse, John. S & T Dec 1731 *Forward*. L.
Rouse, John. S Jly 1737. Wi.
Rowsse, John. T May 1751 *Tryal*. Sy.
Rouse, Mary (1741). *See* Smith. M.
Rous, Robert. S for assault at St. Giles, Shrewsbury, Lent 1758. Sh.
Rouse, Sarah. S & T Sep 1764 *Justitia*. M.
Roose, William. R 14 yrs for Va for counterfeiting Jly 1719. Co.
Rouse, William. S Jly T Aug 1721 *Prince Royal* but died on passage. M.
Rous als Ryley, William. S s mare at St. Andrew the Great, Cambridge, & R 14 yrs Summer 1772. Ca.
Rousser, Lewis. S Feb-Apr T Jun 1756 *Lyon*. M.
Routh, Christopher. SQS Thirsk Apr TB Oct 1748. Y.
Routledge, Richard. TB Aug 1765. Y.
Rowdon, Sarah. S May T Aug 1769 *Douglas*. M.
Rowden, Thomas. T Jun 1738 *Forward*. E.
Rowden, William. S Summer 1741. Wo.
Rowding, John. S & TB to Va Apr 1769. Wi.
Rowe, Anne. S Feb 1731. L.

Rowe, Ann. S Jan T Feb 1744 *Neptune* to Md. M.

Rowe, Christopher. Rebel T 1685.

Row, Edward. SQS Apr T Jly 1772 *Tayloe*. M.

Rowe, George. T from Bristol by *Maryland Packet* 1761 but intercepted by French; T Apr 1763 *Neptune*. So.

Roe, Hannah. R Lent 1773. Sy.

Roe, Hugh. S Aug 1720. So.

Roe, James of Bewdley. R for America Mar 1710. Wo.

Row, James. S & R 14 yrs Mar 1765 TB to Va. De.

Roe, John. R for America Jly 1688. Nt.

Roe, John, aged 22, dark. LC from *Gilbert* Md May 1721. X.

Rowe, John. S s at Sheinton Summer 1734. Sh.

Rowe, John. T Apr 1743 *Justitia*. Sy.

Roe, John. S Sep T Oct 1750 *Rachael*. M.

Roe, John. S s looking glass at St. Mildred Poultry Oct 1768 T Jan 1769 *Thornton*. L.

Roe, John. S Jly T Oct 1771 *Sea Horse*. L.

Rowe, Mary, als wife of John Cane als Dixon. S & T Sep 1731 *Smith* LC Va 1732. M.

Roe, Mary. S Feb 1744. Ha.

Roe, Nicholas. R 14 yrs Apr 1747. So.

Rowe, Peter. Rebel T 1685.

Roe, Robert. S Summer TB Aug 1740. G.

Rowe, Samuel. S Lent R 14 yrs Summer 1737. Le.

Row, Thomas. R 14 yrs Aug 1736. De.

Row, William. Rebel T 1685.

Row, William of Husborne Crawley. S s gun barrel Summer 1724. *Bd.

Row, William. S s sheep Lent R 14 yrs Summer 1742. Sh.

Rowe, William. S s horse Lent R 14 yrs Summer 1762. Wa.

Row als Roe, William. S Feb T Apr 1765 *Ann*. M.

Row, William. S Oct 1772. L.

Rowell, Edward. S Feb 1663 to House of Correction unless he agrees to be transported. M.

Rowell, Edward. S Jan-Jun T Jun 1728 *Elizabeth* LC Potomack Aug 1729. M.

Rowell, Francis. S Apr T May 1752 *Lichfield*. L.

Rowell, Nicholas. R for America Jly 1694. No.

Rowell, Randolph. S s sheep Lent R 14 yrs Summer 1742. No.

Rowland, Catherine. S Feb T Mar 1743 *Justitia*. L.

Rowland, David. S s wheat at Presteigne Summer 1767. He.

Rowland, Edward. S 14 yrs Aug 1727 T *Forward* LC Rappahannock May 1728. M.

Rowland, Elizabeth. LC from *Forward* Annapolis Jun 1723. X.

Rowland, Elizabeth. S Summer T Sep 1751 *Greyhound*. K.

Rowland, Elizabeth. S Nov T Dec 1752 *Greyhound*. L.

Rowland als Rowling, Elizabeth. S Lent 1767. Su.

Rowland als Rowlin, Hannah. S Jan-Apr 1748. M.

Rowland, John. R Dec 1716 T Jan 1717 *Queen Elizabeth* to Jamaica. M.

Rowland als Newland, John. TB Oct 1719 T *Susannah & Sarah*. L.

Rowland, John. S for shoplifting Summer 1731 R 14 yrs Summer 1732. Wa.

Rowland, John (1752). *See* James. Y.

Rowland, John of Newington. SQS Mar T Apr 1753 *Thames*. Sy.

Rowland, John. S May T Jun 1764 *Dolphin*. L.

Rowland, John. SQS Feb 1774. M.

Rowland, Philip. S Sep-Oct 1775. M.

Rowland, Richard (1730). *See* Smith, John. Wo.

Rowland, Robert. R for Barbados Apr TB Jun 1669. L.

Rowland, Samuel. SQS East Retford s gold coins Jan TB Apr 1727. Nt.

Rowland, Samuel of Warsop. SQS s money Jan TB Apr 1774. Nt.

Rowland, Sarah wife of James. S s at Holy Trinity, Cambridge, Summer 1775. Ca.

Rowland, Susannah (1733). *See* Friend. L.

Rowland als Harrison, Thomas of Kingswinford, blacksmith. R for America Jly 1686. St.

Rowland als Rowlat, Thomas. S Jan 1734. M.

Rowland, Thomas of Croydon. SQS Jan 1752. Sy.

Rowland, Thomas. SQS Sep T Dec 1763 *Neptune*. M.

Rowland, Thomas. S Mar 1771 TB to Va. De.

Rowland, Thomas. S Lent 1773. Db.

Rowland, William of Piddington. R for Barbados Oct 1663. O.

Rowland, William. S s sheep Summer 1744 R 14 yrs Summer 1745. Cu.

Rowlandson, William. R for Barbados Jan 1679. L.

Rowlat, Thomas (1734). *See* Rowland. M.

Rowler, Mary (1770). *See* McGlochlin. G.

Rowles, Daniel. T 14 yrs Dec 1771 *Justitia*. Ht.

Rolls, Francis (1677). *See* Dewitt. M.

Rolls, Francis. S Aug 1753. Do.

Rolls, James. S Jly 1752. Ha.

Rolls, John. S Dec 1737 T Jan 1738 *Dorsetshire*. L.

Rolls, John. S Summer 1772. Sy.

Rolles, William. S Jly 1750. Ha.

Rowles, William. SQS Devizes Apr TB to Va Sep 1767. Wi.

Rowlet, John. S Lent T Sep 1755 *Tryal*. Bu.

Rowley, Ann. S Summer 1772. Wa.

Rowley, Edward. S Lent 1736. Wo.

Rowley, Henry. S Lent R 14 yrs Summer 1737. Wo.

Rowley, James of Warwick. R for America Jly 1678. Wa.

Rowley, John. R for America Feb 1700. Wa.

Roley als Moronie, John. S Sep-Oct 1775. M.

Rowley, Joseph. R for Barbados May 1676. M.

Rowley, Stephen. S Mar TB Oct 1732. Le.

Rowley, Thomas. S & T Sep 1751 *Greyhound*. M.

Rowley, Thomas. S Dec 1773. M.

Rowley, William. S Jun T Sep 1764 *Justitia*. M.

Rowling, Ann (1727). *See* Green. L.

Rowling, Elizabeth (1767). *See* Rowland. Su.

Rowlin, Hannah (1748). *See* Rowland. M.

Rowling, Thomas. SQS & T Jly 1772 *Tayloe*. M.

Rowlins, James. S Oct T Dec 1769 *Justitia*. L.

Rowlinson, James of Shevington. SQS Apr 1774. La.

Rowsall, George. Rebel T 1685.

Rowsall, Henry (1665). *See* Popham. De.

Rowsell, John. S & T Dec 1758 *The Brothers*. L.

Roy, Jane. SQS s linen Easter 1774. Du.

Royal, Elizabeth (1770). *See* Eaton. Sy.

Royce, Robert. S by special court Norwich for riot Dec 1766 R for life Summer 1767. Nf.

Roycroft, Elizabeth (1686). *See* Wilson. L.

Royle, James of Manchester, fustian cutter. SQS Apr 1774. La.

Royley, Mary. S Dec 1733 T Jan 1734 *Caesar* LC Va Jly 1734. M.

Royston, Abraham. S s gelding at Frankley Lent R 14 yrs Summer 1737. Wo.

Royston, Elizabeth. S Feb-Apr T Jun 1756 *Lyon*. M.

Royston, Robert. R for Barbados or Jamaica May 1697. L.

Royton, John. S & T Jan 1722 *Gilbert* LC Annapolis Jly 1722. M.

Rubbery, John. R (Home Circ) for Barbados Aug 1663. X.

Ruby, Thomas. S Oct 1741 T 14 yrs Feb 1742 *Industry* to Md. M.

Rudd, Burlingham of Poringland. S s horse Summer 1728. *Nf.

Rudd, John. S Dec 1727. M.

Rudd, John. S s linen at Winfarthing Summer 1769. Nf.

Rudd, Timothy. S s watches at St. Nicholas, Worcester, Lent 1767. Wo.

Rudd, William. S Mar 1773. De.

Rudder, Thomas. S s cloth Lent 1774. G.

Rudderford, Margaret. TB Aug 1740. Db.

Ruddiford, Mary. R for America Jly 1694. Le.

Ruddle, Samuel. Rebel T 1685.

Rudge, Eleanor. T Oct 1768 *Justitia*. Sy.

Rudge, Thomas. S s at Hope Mansell Lent 1758. He.

Rudge, William. AT from QS Summer T Aug 1771. Wa.

Rudkin, Edward. S Lent 1763. Sy.

Rudman, Thomas of Mells. R for Barbados Jan 1675. So.

Reaudolph, Mary. S Jun T Sep 1767 *Justitia*. M.

Rudram, Thomas. S Summer 1757. Nf.

Rue, William. S & R Lent 1772. Ch.

Ruffhead als Seabright, Thomas. S s cows Summer 1765 R 14 yrs Lent 1766. Bd.

Ruffhead, William. S Oct 1774. L.

Ruffler, George (1747). *See* Parsons. So.

Ruflett, James. R Jly 1736. M.

Rugby, Andrew. S Feb T Apr 1741 *Speedwell*. L.

Ruggles, James. S for life Oct 1744-Jan 1745. M.

Rugles als Everett, Joseph. S Lent R 14 yrs Summer 1744. Su.

Ruggles, William. S Apr T May 1755 *Rose*. L.

Rugmar, Mary. R for Barbados Jly 1674. M.

Ruitty, Daniel. TB Feb 1719. L.

Ruly, John. LC from *Eagle* Charles Town Mar 1719. X.

Rumball, Charles of Stapleford Tawney. R for Barbados or Jamaica Jun 1684. E.

Rumbold, Thomas. SQS Jly 1768. Ha.

Rumbow, Edward. S Jan-Apr 1748. M.

Rummel, Leonard. S s at Speen Summer 1742. Be.

Rumney, Andrew. S Summer 1746. Cu.

Rumpson, John. R 14 yrs Mar 1768. So.

Rumsey, Ann of St. George, Southwark, spinster. R for Barbados or Jamaica Jly 1705. Sy.

Rumsey, John. S Aug T Oct 1722 *Forward* to Md. M.

Rumsey, John. S Feb T Mar 1730 *Patapsco* but died on passage. M.

Rumsey als Hale, Thomas, gent. R for Barbados Mar 1683. L.

Rundle, Richard. S Mar 1737. Co.

Runniard, Ann wife of Henry. S Aug 1764. Do.

Runsberg, John. S 14 yrs Apr-May 1741. M.

Rush, Mary. LC from *Caesar* Va Jly 1735. X.

Rushbrooke, Benjamin. T Dec 1734 *Caesar*. E.

Rusher als Hays als Dennis, Mary. S & T Oct 1730 *Forward* LC Potomack Jan 1731. M.

Rushfield, Fairfax. R 14 yrs & TB Dec 1734. Bd.

Rushing, Jane. S May-Jly 1749. M.

Ruskin, Thomas of Enfield. S s gate Jly 1740 T Jan 1741 *Harpooner* to Va. M.

Ruskton, Thomas. S Summer 1771. St.

Russ, Mary. S s from parish church at Tetbury Summer 1768. G.

Russell, Alexander. S Feb T Apr 1732 *Rappahannock* LC Annapolis Oct 1732. M.

Russell, Ann. R for Va Oct 1618. X.

Russell, Ann. S Feb 1752. L.

Russell, Ann. S Jun T Sep 1767 *Justitia*. L.

Russell, Cornelius. SQS & TB Apr 1774. So.

Russell, David of St. Martin in Fields. SW Jan T Apr 1772 *Thornton*. M.

Russell, Eleanor (1722). *See* Emmett. So.

Russell, Elizabeth. LC from *Forward* Annapolis Jun 1723. X.

Russell als Brown, Elizabeth. S Oct T 14 yrs Nov 1725 *Rappahannock* LC Rappahannock Apr 1726. L.

Russell, Elizabeth. T Apr 1753 *Thames*. Sy.

Russell als Wright, Frances. R for Barbados May 1676. L.

Russell, Francis. R for Barbados Dec 1681 & Sep 1682. L.

Russell, George. Rebel T 1685.

Russell, George of St. Martin in Fields. SW Jun 1775. M.

Russell, Hannah. S May T Sep 1765 *Justitia*. M.

Russell, James. AT Oct R & T Dec 1716 *Lewis* to Jamaica. M.

Russell, James. S Mar TB to Va Apr 1741. Wi.

Russell, Jane of St. Giles in Fields. S s clothing Oct 1742 T Apr 1743 *Justitia*. M.

Russell, John of Westerham. R for Barbados or Jamaica Jly 1710. K.

Russell als Kinsey, John. S Feb-Apr T May 1751 *Tryal*. M.

Russell, John. T Apr 1762 *Neptune*. Sy.

Russell, John Jr. SQS New Sarum or Marlborough & TB to Va Jan 1774. Wi.

Russell, Jonathan, aged 21, dark, glassgrinder. S Jan T Feb 1723 *Jonathan* LC Annapolis Jly 1724. M.

Russell, Joseph. S Oct T Dec 1771 *Justitia*. L.

Russell, Margaret (1718). *See* Price. L.

Russell, Mary (1718). *See* Price. M.

Russell, Nicholas. SEK & T Jly 1771 *Scarsdale*. K.

Russell, Robert of Redston Ferry. R for America Feb 1700. Wo.

Russell als Russen, Robert. R Mar 1774. Ha.

Russell, Sarah. S & T Jly 1753 *Tryal*. L.

Russell als Rochester, Stephen. T Jan 1736 *Dorsetshire*. K.

Russell, Susanna. S Aug T Oct 1724 *Forward* LC Annapolis Jun 1725. M.

Russell, Thomas. R (Home Circ) for Barbados or Jamaica May 1664. X.

Russell, Walter of Uttoxeter. R for Jamaica, Barbados or Bermuda Feb 1686. St.

Russell, William. PT Jly 1680. M.

Russell, William. Rebel T 1685.

Russell, William of Tardebigge. R for America Nov 1694. Wo.

Russell, William. R 14 yrs Aug 1748. De.

Russell, William. SQS Feb 1757. Sy.

Russell, William. S (Western Circ) Dec 1766. Be.

Russell, William. S s cows & R Lent TB Apr 1768. Db.

Russell, William. S for rape Lent 1771. Ht.

Russell, William. S Feb 1774. L.

Russen, Robert (1774). *See* Russell. Ha.

Russen, Thomas of Dudley. R for America Jly 1691. Wo.

Russet, James. S Feb T Apr 1742 *Bond*. L.

Rust, Argentine. Rebel T 1685.

Rust, William. S Summer 1753 R 14 yrs Lent 1754. E.

Rustead, Richard. S & T Nov 1762 *Prince William*. L.

Rusted, Robert. T Oct 1726 *Forward*. E.

Rustin als Harris, Elizabeth. S & T Jan 1739 *Dorsetshire*. L.

Rustin, Mary. S Jun T Sep 1758 *Tryal*. L.

Ruston, Alice. S Summer T Aug 1771. Wa.

Ruston, Robert. S Lent 1773. Db.

Rutherford, John. S Summer 1761. Cu.

Rutherford, John. S & T Apr 1766 *Ann*. M.

Rutherford, Mary. S Jly T Oct 1741 *Sea Horse* to Va. M.

Rutherford, Richard. S Jly T Oct 1741 *Sea Horse* to Va. M.

Rotherford, Robert. S for highway robbery at Stow in the Wold Lent R 14 yrs Summer TB Jly 1744. G.

Ruth, Jacob. SQS Dec 1751. M.

Rutland, James (1764). *See* Heath, John. Nt.

Rutland, Jonathan of Bridgewater. R for America Jly 1700. So.

Rutland, Joseph. S Lent R 14 yrs Summer T Sep 1757 *Thetis*. Bu.

Rutland, Richard of Bridgewater. R for America Jly 1700. So.

Rutland, William. S Lent 1751; wife Alice Rutland acquitted. Su.

Rutlege, John (1738). *See* Graham. Cu.

Routledge, Richard. S s mare at Stokesley Lent R 14 yrs Summer 1765. Y.

Rutlidge, Thomas. S & T Dec 1770 *Justitia*. M.

Rutlege, Thomas. S Apr 1773. M.

Rutledge, William. S s sheep Lent 1753 R 14 yrs Lent 1754. Nf.

Rutley, Robert. S Summer 1757 R 14 yrs Lent T Apr 1760 *Thetis*. Sx.

Rutliss, Wharton. S & T May 1736 *Patapsco*. L.

Rutson, Richard. R 14 yrs Summer 1756. Cu.

Rutt, Christopher. T from Bristol by *Maryland Packet* 1761 but intercepted by French; T Apr 1763 *Neptune*. Wi.

Rutt, James. S Jun T Nov 1743 *George William*. L.

Rutt, John. R 14 yrs Jly 1734. Ha.

Rutter, Amy wife of Philip *(qv)*. SQS Oct 1735 TB to Md Jan 1736. So.

Rutter, Ann wife of Samuel. S Jan-May T 14 yrs Jun 1738 *Forward*. M.

Rutter, George. S Summer 1767. Bu.

Rutter, John. S Apr 1728. So.

Rutter, John. T Nov 1728 *Forward*. K.

Rutter als Asplin, Minah. S & R 1775 for being at large at St. Julian, Shrewsbury, while under sentence of transportation. Sh.

Rutter, Philip. SQS Oct 1735 TB to Md Jan 1736. So.

Rutter, Samuel. Rebel T 1685.

Rutter, Thomas. S & T Jan 1767 *Tryal*. M.

Ruttree, Ann of Oxford, spinster. R for America Mar 1707. O.

Ryan, Daniel. S Dec 1763 T Mar 1764 *Tryal*. M.

Ryan, Jeremiah. S Feb T Mar 1730 *Patapsco* LC Annapolis Sep 1730. M.

Ryan, John. R for Barbados or Jamaica Jly 1696. X.

Ryon, John. S & T Sep 1731 *Smith* LC Va 1732. L.

Ryan, John. S Feb T Apr 1765 *Ann*. M.

Ryan, John of Bristol. R 14 yrs Apr 1774 (SP). G.

Ryan, Mary. S 14 yrs May-Jly 1750. M.

Ryan, Mary wife of John. S Feb T Apr 1765 *Ann*. M.

Ryan, Richard. S Jan-Apr 1749. M.

Ryan, Thomas. S & T May 1736 *Patapsco* to Md. M.

Ryan, Thomas. SQS Feb 1751. M.

Ryan, Thomas. S Aug 1763. L.

Rycroft, Elizabeth. R for Barbados Dec 1681. L.

Rycroft, Elizabeth (1686). *See* Wilson. L.

Rycroft, John. AT from QS Lent 1773. Nt.

Rycroft, Thomas. S s at Whitchurch Summer 1755. Sh.

Ryde, Job. R for Barbados Jun 1663. M.

Rider, Ann. S Sep T Nov 1743 *George William*. M.

Rider, Anthony of Stafford. R for America Jun 1692. St.

Rider, Frances. S s ring Apr T Dec 1735 *John* LC Annapolis Sep 1736. L.

Ryder, James. S Apr T Jly 1770 *Scarsdale*. M.

Ryder, Jane. S Jan T Mar 1750 *Tryal*. L.

Ryder, John. S & T Dec 1724 *Rappahannock*. L.

Rider, John. S Apr-Jun 1739. M.

Ryder, John. S Jan-Apr 1748. M.

Ryder, John. S Jun 1767. M.

Ryder, Mary. S May-Jly 1748. M.

Ryder, Robert. S May T Jun 1727 *Susanna* to Va. M.

Rider, William. S Aug 1760. L.

Rider, William. T 14 yrs Sep 1764 *Justitia*. E.

Ryder, William. T Sep 1766 *Justitia*. M.

Rydings. *See* Ridings.

Rye, George. S Sep-Oct 1772. M.

Ryecroft, Henry. S Oct T Nov 1759 *Phoenix*. L.

Ryer, James. S & T Jly 1772 *Tayloe*. M.

Ryland, William. S Feb T Mar 1731 *Patapsco* but died on passage. M.
Rylett, Edward. S for killing sheep Lent R 14 yrs Summer 1768. Be.
Ryley. *See* Riley.
Rymas, Matthias. S Jan-Apr 1749. M.
Rymer, George. S Sep-Oct 1772. M.
Rymer, Martha. S Oct T Nov 1728 *Forward* LC Rappahannock Jun 1729. L.
Rymer, Roger. S City s silver shoe buckle Lent 1764. Y.
Rymes. *See* Rimes.

S

Sabin, Robert of Barking. SQS Oct 1757 T Sep 1758 *Tryal*. E.

Sable, John. S Lent R 14 yrs Summer 1760. Ht.

Sach, John. R Lent 1773. E.

Sacheverill, Thomas of Marlborough. R (Oxford Circ) for America Mar 1697. Wi.

Sacheverel, Thomas. S for highway robbery Summer 1743 R for life Lent 1744. O.

Sacke, Sidrach of St. Stephen Branwell, husbandman. R for Barbados Feb 1665. Co.

Sacker, George (1773). *See* Thacker. Nf.

Sacker, John, als Smith, William. S Oct-Dec 1754. M.

Sadd, Joseph. R 14 yrs Jly TB to Va Aug 1752. Wi.

Sadd, Thomas. S s sheep Lent 1746. K.

Sadd, William. S Apr 1725. M.

Sadler, Anne, aged 19, brown hair. S & T Oct 1720 *Gilbert* LC Annapolis May 1721. M.

Sadler, Daniel. T Apr 1739 *Forward*. E.

Sadler, Humphry. S s at St. Paul, Bedford, Lent 1772. Bd.

Sadler, Isabella. S Jan T Feb 1742 *Industry*. L.

Sadler, Jane. R for Barbados Sep 1677 & Jan 1679. L.

Sadler, Jane (1680). *See* Steward. M.

Sadler, Joseph. S Jly 1760 T from Bristol by *Maryland Packet* 1761 but intercepted by French; T Apr 1763 *Neptune*. De.

Sadler, Mary (1742). *See* Hitch, John. E.

Sadler, Philip. T May 1736 *Patapsco*. Sy.

Sadler, Ralph. R 14 yrs s mare Summer 1730. Du.

Sadler als Cartwright, Ralph. S & T Dec 1758 *The Brothers*. M.

Sadler, Richard. S s horse Lent R 14 yrs Summer 1752. Nt.

Sadler, Samuel of Stoke Newington. R for Barbados Mar 1683. M.

Sadler, Thomas. R Oct 1673 & Feb 1675. M.

Sadler, William. R for Barbados Feb 1675. L.

Saffell, Samuel. T Apr 1732 *Patapsco*. E.

Sage, Henry of Theydon Bois. R for Barbados Apr 1668. E.

Sage, James. S May-Jly 1773. M.

Sage, Robert. SQS Apr 1774. M.

Sage, Thomas. ST & T Aug 1769 *Douglas*. L.

Sagemuller, John Diederick. S Feb T Mar 1750 *Tryal*. M.

Sago, John. S May-Jun T Aug 1752 *Tryal*. M.

Saint, John Egerton. S for assault on Earl of Radnor Jly 1756. M.

Saintree, John. S & T Jan 1765 *Tryal*. M.

Saires. *See* Sayers.

Sale, Mary. S May-Jly 1748. M.

Sale, Thomas. SQS Jan T Apr 1768 *Thornton*. M.

Sales, Thomas. S s horse Summer 1738 R 14 yrs Lent TB May 1739. Nt.

Salisbury, Ann. S Jly T Sep 1766 *Justitia*. L.

Salsbury, Mary. S Dec 1731. M.

Salisbury, Morris. S Mar 1750. Do.

Salisbury, Robert of Bolton by Sands. S Summer 1758 R 14 yrs Lent 1759. La.
Salisbury, Thomas. Rebel T 1685.
Salsbury, William. S Mar 1733 T *Patapsco* LC Annapolis Nov 1733. Wi.
Salisbury, William. S Jly T Sep 1765 *Justitia*. L.
Salkeld, Thomas. S Dec 1727. L.
Sallis, Andrew. S Summer TB Aug 1740. G.
Salloway, John. S Summer R for Barbados Aug 1663. Sy.
Salloway, Robert of Oakerton, butcher. R for America Mar 1680. O.
Sallows, Robert. T Sep 1742 *Forward*. E.
Sallway, John. TB to Va 1770. De.
Sallway, Mary. LC from *Honor* Port York Jan 1721. X.
Sally, John. PT Oct 1676 R Mar 1677. M.
Salman. *See* Salmon.
Salmon, Elianor of Stratfield Mortimer. R for America Mar 1697. Be.
Salman, James of Stratton. R for Barbados Jly 1677. So.
Salmon, John. T Jun 1740 *Essex*. E.
Salmon, John. T Apr 1742 *Bond*. Sy.
Salmon, John. S Apr T Jun 1742 *Bladon*. L.
Salmon, John. S s gelding & R Summer 1774. Wa.
Salmon, Mary. S Feb T Apr 1732 *Patapsco* LC Annapolis Oct 1732. M.
Salmon, Mary. T Jan 1736 *Dorsetshire*. Sy.
Salmon, Mary. T Apr 1741 *Speedwell* or *Mediterranean*. Sy.
Salmon, Michael. S Jun-Dec 1738 T Jan 1739 *Dorsetshire* to Va. M.
Salmon, Richard. S Jan 1746. M.
Salmon, Richard. S Jun 1747. L.
Salmon, Rowland. S Feb T Mar 1727 *Rappahannock*. L.
Salmon, Samuel. S May T Jly 1723 *Alexander* LC Annapolis Sep 1723. M.
Salmon, Samuel. S & T Oct 1729 *Forward* LC Va Jun 1730. M.
Salmon, Thomas of Burgleid, weaver. R for America Feb 1713. Nt.
Salmon, Walter. TB to Va from QS 1751. De.
Salt, Hannah. AT from QS Summer 1772. Db.
Salt, Henry. S Summer TB to Va Oct 1764. Le.
Salt, Richard of Walsall. R (Western Circ) for America Jly 1700. St.
Salt, William. SQS & T Jly 1771 *Scarsdale*. M.
Salter, Benjamin. S Mar 1760. Do.
Salter, Charles. SQS & T Sep 1766 *Justitia*. M.
Salter, Elizabeth wife of Mathew. S Dec 1742 T Jan 1743 *Justitia*. M.
Salter, Hannah. T Oct 1732 *Caesar*. Sy.
Salter, Henry. T Jly 1724 *Robert* LC Md Jun 1725. Sy.
Salter, James. Rebel T 1685.
Salter, Jemima. S & T Apr 1735 *John* LC Annapolis Sep 1736. M.
Soulter, John. R for America Feb 1700. Db.
Salter, John. LC from *Forward* Annapolis Jun 1725. X.
Salter, John. S Jan-Jun T Jun 1728 *Elizabeth* LC Potomack Aug 1729. L.
Salter, John. TB to Va from QS 1741. De.
Salter, Mary. T Nov 1725 *Rappahannock* LC Va Aug 1726. Sy.
Salter, Nicholas. Rebel T 1685.
Salter als Lilley, Richard. R Jly 1656. M.
Salter, Richard, aged 28. R for Barbados Feb 1664. M.

Salter, Samuel of Bromley. S Lent 1745. K.
Salter, Thomas of Clayhiddon. R for Barbados Jly 1679. De.
Salter als Brown, Thomas. T Aug 1720 *Owners Goodwill*. K.
Salter, Thomas. S & T Oct 1729 *Forward* LC Va Jun 1730. L.
Salter, Thomas. S & R Lent 1775. Wo.
Salterwaite, Charles. S for highway robbery Lent R for life Summer 1764. Wa.
Saltmarsh, John of Moulsham, cordwainer. SQS Jan T May 1750 *Lichfield*. E.
Saltmarsh, Thomas. R for Barbados or Jamaica Jly 1685. L.
Salton, John. S City Summer 1724 AT Summer 1725. Nl.
Sam, John. Rebel T 1685.
Same, George. T Jly 1724 *Robert*. E.
Same, John. S Sep 1733" M.
Sammarell, Henry. SL Aug 1763. Sy.
Samples, James of Liverpool, flax dresser. S Lent 1755. La.
Sampson, Bartholomew. S Aug 1754. Co.
Sampson, James. S Dec 1760. M.
Sampson, John. S Summer 1759 R 14 yrs Lent 1760. Li.
Sampson, John. T Aug 1769 *Douglas*. E.
Sampson, Jonathan. T Apr 1771 *Thornton*. K.
Sampson, Mary. S Lent 1760. Wa.
Sampson, Michael. S Aug T for life Sep 1764 *Justitia*. L.
Sampson, Peter. R for Barbados Jun 1670. M.
Sampson, Richard. S Feb-Apr T Jun 1756 *Lyon*. M.
Sampson, Richard. S Feb R Jun T Sep 1764 *Justitia*. M.
Sampson, Sarah. S & T Oct 1732 *Caesar* to Va. M.
Sampson, Thomas. S & T Oct 1729 *Forward* LC Va Jun 1730. L.
Sampson, Thomas. S 14 yrs Feb 1774. L.
Sampson, William. S Apr 1774. M.
Sampson, William. S s at South Elmham & R Lent 1775. Su.
Sams, Alice wife of Benjamin of St. George, Southwark. SQS Apr T Sep 1751 *Greyhound*. Sy.
Samuel, Myers. S Jan 1740. L.
Samuel, Nathan. S Lent T May 1755 *Rose*. Sy.
Samuell, Roger. R for Barbados Dec 1683. M.
Samuel, Samuel. S Jun T Jly 1772 *Tayloe*. L.
Samuel, Thomas. T 14 yrs Sep 1767 *Justitia*. Ht.
Sandells, John. S Lent R 14 yrs Summer 1764. Sh.
Sandalls als Sandland, Joyce. S Lent 1763. Wa.
Sanders. *See* Saunders.
Sanderson. *See* Saunderson.
Sandford, Abraham of Uley. R for America Jly 1696. G.
Sandford, Benjamin. S & T Oct 1730 *Forward* LC Potomack Jan 1731. L.
Sandford, John of Okehampton (Devon), als Greedy, Robert of Wiveliscombe, blacksmith. R for Barbados Jly 1688. So.
Sanford, Priscilla. S Mar 1720. Do.
Sandford, William. S s mare Lent R 14 yrs Summer 1766. O.
Sandland, Joyce (1763). *See* Sandalls. Wa.
Sands, Ann. T Sep 1755 *Tryal*. M.
Sands, Elizabeth, aged 40, black hair. LC from *Gilbert* Md May 1721. X.

Sands, Frances. S Oct T 14 yrs Dec 1724 *Rappahannock* to Va. M.

Sands, John of Lambeth. SQS Oct 1750. Sy.

Sandys, Robert. Rebel T 1685.

Sandys, Samuel. S Apr 1774. M.

Sandy, John. S Lent 1754. Bd.

Sandy, Thomas. SQS & TB Apr 1754. So.

Sanger, Sarah. S Apr 1773. L.

Sanger, Stephen. S & T May 1736 *Patapsco*. L.

Sanguin, Thomas. S Mar 1752. De.

Sansome, George (1665). *See* Chippett. X.

Sansom, Joan of Whitechapel, spinster. R for Bermuda Jly 1614. M.

Sansom, William. R Feb 1758. Ha.

Sansom als Sanson, William. R 14 yrs Jly 1765. Ha.

Santon, Richard. S for highway robbery Summer 1736 R 14 yrs Summer 1737. Y.

Sany, Thomas. S s at Bray Summer 1772. Be.

Sarah the Cork Cutter (1740). *See* Ranson, Sarah. M.

Sarcott, Francis. T Oct 1722 *Forward* LC Md Jun 1723. Sy.

Sares, Ann. S s at St. John Baptist, Gloucester, Summer 1742. G.

Sargent/Sargeant. *See* Serjeant.

Sargery, John of St. Paul, Covent Garden. S s forks Jly 1740 T Jan 1741 *Harpooner* to Rappahannock. M.

Sarrison, Sarah (1753). *See* Harrison. M.

Sartain. *See* Sertain.

Sasser, John. T Apr 1743 *Justitia* but died on passage. E.

Sassier, Ann. LC from *Mary* Port York Jun 1721. X.

Satchell, George. T Jly 1722 *Alexander*. Sy.

Satcher, Thomas. S & T Oct 1729 *Forward* LC Va Jun 1730. M.

Satcher, Thomas. S & T Jan 1739 *Dorsetshire*. L.

Satchwell, James. R for America Jly 1694. No.

Satchwell, Matthew. S s cow Lent R 14 yrs Summer 1769. Wa.

Satchwell, Sarah (1735). *See* Bailey. M.

Satterfield, Sarah. S Aug T 14 yrs Sep 1727 *Forward* LC Rappahannock May 1728. L.

Satturlee, James. S Apr 1754. So.

Satterly, Solomon. R 14 yrs Aug 1736. De.

Satton, Joseph, als Priest, James. T Apr 1744. Ht.

Sauce, John. LC from *Caesar* Va Jly 1734. X.

Saul, Henry. S & T Jly 1772 *Tayloe*. M.

Saul, John. R 14 yrs Summer 1729. Cu.

Saul, Sarah. S Mar 1732 TB to Va. De.

Saul, Thomas. S Jan T Feb 1719 *Worcester* LC Annapolis Jun 1719. M.

Saunders, Abraham. S Summer 1745 R 14 yrs Lent 1746. Bd.

Sanders, Abraham (1771). *See* Sanders, Benjamin. L.

Saunders, Alice, spinster, als wife of John. R for Barbados Aug & Sep 1664. L.

Saunders, Ann. S Dec 1756. M.

Saunders, Ann. S Oct T Nov 1759 *Phoenix*. L.

Saunders, Ann, spinster. S s money at St. Sepulchre Sep T Oct 1768 *Justitia*. L.

Saunders, Ann, widow. S s at Husborne Crawley Lent 1773. Bd.

Sanders, Barley. S s at Dudley Lent 1775. Wo.

Sanders, Benjamin als Abraham. S Feb T Apr 1771 *Thornton*. L.

Sanders, Catherine. S Jan T 14 yrs Feb 1733 *Smith*. L.

Saunders, Catherine. S Feb 1757. M.

Saunders, Catherine. S Jun T Sep 1767 *Justitia*. M.

Saunders, Charles (1721). *See* Giles, William. M.

Saunders, Charles. S Jly T Oct 1741 *Sea Horse* to Va. M.

Saunders, Daniel. SQS Chippenham & TB to Va Apr 1769. Wi.

Saunders, Edward of Romsey. R for Barbados Jly 1677. Ha.

Saunders, Elizabeth. S Apr T Aug 1718 *Eagle* LC Charles Town Mar 1719. L.

Saunders, Elizabeth. S Jan-Apr 1748. M.

Saunders, Elizabeth. S & T Apr 1765 *Ann*. L.

Saunders als Thompson, Elizabeth. S & T Apr 1766 *Ann*. L.

Saunders, George. S Jan-Jun T Jun 1728 *Elizabeth* LC Potomack Aug 1729. L.

Saunders, Hannah. S Oct 1760. M.

Saunders, Hannah. S s at Cannock Summer 1768. St.

Sanders, Henry. S Lent R 14 yrs Summer 1748. St.

Sanders, Henry. T Nov 1762 *Prince William*. E.

Saunders, Henry. T Sep 1767 *Justitia*. E.

Saunders, Humphrey. Rebel T 1685.

Saunders, James. S for Boston NE Jly 1718. Ha.

Saunders, James. TB to Va from QS 1740. De.

Saunders, James. S Feb-Apr T May 1751 *Tryal*. M.

Saunders, John of Plumpstead or Brasted. R for Barbados or Jamaica Jly 1674. K.

Saunders, John. Rebel T 1685.

Saunders, John of Kingston on Thames. R for Barbados or Jamaica Jly 1702. Sy.

Saunders, John. S & T Apr 1725 *Sukey* to Md. M.

Saunders, John. T Apr 1735 *Patapsco*. Sx.

Sanders, John. S Summer 1743. Nf.

Saunders, John. S Summer 1753 R 14 yrs Lent 1754. K.

Saunders, John of Bermondsey. SQS Jan T Apr 1765 *Ann*. Sy.

Sanders, John. S Summer 1768. Wa.

Saunders, John. TB to Va 1768. De.

Saunders, John. S s at Earl Soham Lent 1773. Su.

Saunders, Joseph. PT Jan 1675. M.

Saunders, Joseph. LC from *Forward* Va Jun 1730. X.

Saunders, Joseph. S Jly 1744. L.

Saunders, Lion. SW & T Dec 1771 *Justitia*. M.

Saunders, Lucey. S Oct 1761. L.

Saunders, Lucretia. S & T Mar 1760 *Friendship*. L.

Sanders als Burton als London, Mary of Radcliffe, widow. SQS Jan 1748. La.

Sanders, Mary. S Mar 1750. Co.

Sanders, Mary. TB to Va from QS 1751. De.

Saunders, Mary. S Jly-Sep 1754. M.

Sanders, Mary. S Mar 1758. De.

Saunders, Matthew. S Oct T Dec 1734 *Caesar* LC Va Jly 1735. M.

Sanders, Peter. S Lent 1754. Sx.

Saunders, Richard. S Jan-May T Jun 1738 *Forward* to Md or Va. M.

Sanders, Richard. S s shirts Summer 1753. Wo.

Saunders, Richard. S May T Sep 1757 *Thetis*. M.

Saunders, Robert. S Jan T Sep 1737 *Pretty Patsy* to Va. M.

Saunders, Robert. S Summer 1753; wife Catherine acquitted. Bu.

Sanders, Sarah. S Dec 1733 T Jan 1734 *Caesar* LC Va Jly 1734. L.

Saunders, Stephen of St. Mary le Bow. S s pistols Jly 1740 T Jan 1741
   Harpooner to Rappahannock. M.

Saunders als Cooke, Susanna. S Jly T Oct 1741 *Sea Horse* to Va. M.

Saunders, Thomas. Rebel T 1685.

Saunders, Thomas of Bromsgrove. R for America Jly 1691. Wo.

Saunders, Thomas. R 14 yrs for Carolina May 1719. L.

Saunders als Basely, Thomas. R 14 yrs Aug 1724. Co.

Saunders, Thomas. S Aug 1727. So.

Saunders, Thomas. S & T Oct 1729 *Forward* LC Va Jun 1730. M.

Saunders, Thomas. S Feb 1733. Ha.

Saunders, Thomas (1739). *See* Saunderson. M.

Sanders, Thomas. TB to Va from QS 1741. De.

Saunders, Thomas. S Lent 1743. Ca.

Saunders, Thomas. S s sheep & R Lent 1774. He.

Saunders, Thomas. S Mar 1774. Co.

Saunders, William of Plumpstead or Brasted. R for Barbados or
   Jamaica Jly 1674. K.

Saunders, William (2). Rebels T 1685.

Sanders, William. T Oct 1729 *Forward*. E.

Saunders, William. S Aug 1731. Co.

Saunders, William. S & T Dec 1736 *Dorsetshire*. L.

Sanders, William. S & TB to Va Apr 1750. Wi.

Saunders als Saunderson, William. S City Summer 1750. Y.

Saunders, William. S Apr-May 1754. M.

Saunders, William. S Jan T Mar 1760 *Friendship*. M.

Saunders, William. S Jun T Sep 1767 *Justitia*. L.

Saunders, Wilmot (1745). *See* Littlejohn. De.

Saunderson, Charles. S s sheep Lent R 14 yrs Summer 1764. Li.

Sanderson, Elias of Rucking. R for plantations Feb 1656. K.

Sanderson, John of Lewisham. R for Barbados or Jamaica Jun 1699. K.

Sanderson, John. S s horse Summer 1742 R 14 yrs Summer 1743. Nl.

Sanderson, John (1747). *See* Clark, Thomas. Y.

Saunderson, Joseph. S & T Oct 1729 *Forward* to Va. M.

Sanderson, Margaret wife of John of Woodstock. R for America Mar
   1688. O.

Saunderson, Thomas. S s horse Lent 1726 R 14 yrs Lent 1729. Y.

Saunderson als Saunders als Alexander, Thomas. S Apr-Jun 1739. M.

Saundry, Alexander (1745). *See* Bonython. Co.

Savage, Ann. S & T Sep 1731 *Smith* LC Va 1732. M.

Savage, Ann. S City Lent 1752. Y.

Savage, Bartholomew. S Sep 1760. M.

Savage, Cane of St. James, Clerkenwell, yeoman. S for breaking &
   entering Jly 1740 T Jan 1741 *Harpooner* to Rappahannock. M.

Savage, Constant wife of Robert. S Aug 1764. Do.

Savage, Edward. R for Barbados Jan 1665. Y.

Savage, Edward. R 14 yrs Aug 1726. So.

Savage, Francis. Rebel T 1685.

Savage, Henry. S Dec 1773. M.

Savage, James. T Jun 1740 *Essex*. Sx.

Savage, James. S Jan 1757. L.

Savage, John of Alton. R for Barbados Feb 1701. Ha.

Savage, John. S Jly 1720. Ha.

Savage, John. T Oct 1721 *William & John*. K.

Savage, John. S Lent R Summer T 14 yrs Sep 1755 *Tryal*. Sx.

Savage, John. S Oct 1757 T Mar 1758 *Dragon*. M.

Savage, Joseph. S Apr 1747. De.

Savage als Bailey, Mary. S Aug T Sep 1725 *Forward* LC Annapolis Dec 1725. L.

Savadge, Mathias of Manchester. SQS Jly 1749. La.

Savage, Maurice. S (Western Circ) Dec 1766 AT Lent 1767. G.

Savadge, Patrick of Manchester. SQS Jly 1749. La.

Savage, Richard. S Lent 1749. Sx.

Savage, Sarah. S Feb-Apr T May 1752 *Lichfield*. M.

Savage, Thomas. S Apr-Jun 1739. M.

Salvidge, Thomas. SQS & TB Jan 1758. So.

Savidge, Thomas. R 14 yrs Apr 1767. So.

Savage, William. S Lent T May 1755 *Rose* for breaking into Maidstone Gaol to release a prisoner. K.

Savage, William. S Aug 1767. So.

Savaree, Elizabeth of Barking, spinster. R Summer T Oct 1739 *Duke of Cumberland*. E.

Savell. *See* Saville.

Saverin, John. S & T Jan 1765 *Tryal*. M.

Saville, Ann. S s stookings at Stow Summer TB Aug 1749. G.

Savell, Ann, widow, als Brown, Thomas *(sic)*. S Jly T Sep 1765 *Justitia*. M.

Saville, Edward. T Aug 1721 *Owners Goodwill*. E.

Savill, Israel. S Summer 1718 TB with Peter How of Whitehaven, merchant. Cu.

Savell, James. S May T Sep 1737 *Pretty Patsy* to Md. M.

Saville, John. S Sep-Oct T Dec 1771 *Justitia*. M.

Savile, Richard. T Nov 1728 *Forward*. K.

Savill, Thomas. S s chinaware Jan-May T Jun 1738 *Forward* to Md or Va. M.

Saville, Thomas. S Feb T May 1767 *Thornton*. M.

Savil, William. T Nov 1743 *George William*. E.

Savory, Ann wife of Edward. S Aug 1759. So.

Savoy, Gabriel. S Jun T 14 yrs Sep 1758 *Tryal*. L.

Sawcer, William (1771). *See* Baker. De.

Sawford, Francis of Cradley. R for Jamaica, Barbados or Bermuda Mar 1688. He.

Sawyer, Charles. S Jan 1757. L.

Sawyer, Charles. SQS Jan T Apr 1771 *Thornton*. M.

Sawyer, Edmund. S s at Biggleswade Lent 1773. Bd.

Sawyer, Frances. S s pillowcases at St. Martin, Oxford, Summer 1774. O.

Sawyer, Henry. T Oct 1723 *Forward*. Ht.
Sawyer, James. R 14 yrs Jly 1746 TB to Va Jan 1747. Wi.
Sawyer, John. T 14 yrs Apr 1769 *Tryal*. Sy.
Sawyer, Samuel. S Summer R 14 yrs Nov 1736 (SP). Su.
Sawyer, Thomas. S (Western Circ) Dec 1766 AT Lent 1767. G.
Sawyer, William. T Oct 1738 *Genoa*. K.
Sawyer, William. R 14 yrs Jly 1746 TB to Va Jan 1747. Wi.
Saxbee, Samuel. Rebel T 1685.
Saxelby, Mary of Arnold, spinster. SQS s geneva Jly 1765. Nt.
Saxon, George of Barking. SQS Jan T Sep 1758 *Tryal*. E.
Say, Ephraim of Bradford. SQS Warminster Jly TB to Va Oct 1742. Wi.
Say, James. R 14 yrs Jly TB to Va Nov 1748. Wi.
Say, John. Rebel T 1685.
Say, Jonas. Rebel T 1685.
Say, Richard. SQS Warminster Jly TB to Va Sep 1741. Wi.
Sayce, John of Ludlow. R for America Jly 1675. Sh.
Sayer, George. S at Kings Lynn s linen Summer 1754 TB at
    GLCRO. Nf.
Saires, Edward. T Apr 1735 *Patapsco*. Sx.
Seyers, John. S Jan 1746. M.
Saires, Thomas. T May 1751 *Tryal*. Sx.
Sayers, William. T May 1767 *Thornton*. Sy.
Sayers, William of Woodham Mortimer. R for Barbados or Jamaica Feb
    1686. E.
Sayes, John. S Summer 1725 R 14 yrs Lent 1726. Sh.
Sayse, John. S s horse Lent R 14 yrs Summer 1727. Sh.
Saythuss, James, als Dumb Jemmy. R Jan-Feb T Apr 1772 *Thornton*. M.
Sayward, Mary. S Apr-Jun 1739. M.
Saywood, Penitent, spinster. R for America Feb 1700. Nt.
Scadding, Elizabeth. TB to Va from QS 1758. De.
Scadding, John. SQS Jan TB May 1770. So.
Scadgell, Richard. R 14 yrs Jly 1721 T from Southampton 1723. Ha.
Scayle, John of Aston Rowant. R for America Jly 1698. O.
Scales, Frances. R for Barbados or Jamaica Aug 1700. M.
Scales, Richard. T Jan 1736 *Dorsetshire*. K.
Scales, Richard. S May T Jun 1738 *Forward*. L.
Scalthropp, John. R for Barbados May 1676. M.
Scam, John. S Aug 1754. De.
Scam, William. R 14 yrs Aug 1754. De.
Scammell, Edward. R 14 yrs Mar TB to Va Apr 1742. Wi.
Scammell, John. S Mar TB to Va Apr 1762. Wi.
Scamell, Sarah (1742). *See* Camell. Sx.
Scamp, Elizabeth. S Mar 1745. Ha.
Scamp, James. S Mar 1745. Ha.
Scamp, John. S Mar 1745. Ha.
Scamp, Mary. S Mar 1745. Ha.
Scamp, Mary (1765). *See* White. Wo.
Scamp, Susannah. S Mar 1745. Ha.
Scampey, Philip (1764). *See* Abraham. M.
Scampey, William (1755). *See* Bowyer. L.
Scandon, John. S Feb T Apr 1766 *Ann*. L.

Scandrell als Scandrett, Thomas. S s corn at Wigmore Summer 1723. He.

Scandrett, Henry. SQS Oct 1766 T Jan 1767 *Tryal*. M.

Scarborough, James. S Jan 1755. M.

Scarborough, James. S Sep-Oct 1773. M.

Scarborough, Joseph. S for Va Jly 1718. De.

Scarborough, Lawrence. S May T Sep 1765 *Justitia*. M.

Scarborough, Thomas. T May 1751 *Tryal*. Sx.

Scarcity, William. S Sep 1735 T Jan 1736 *Dorsetshire* LC Va Sep 1736. M.

Scarenbone, John Peter of St. Martin in Fields. S s silver Feb T May 1736 *Patapsco*. M.

Scarfe, Jeremiah. T Oct 1768 *Justitia*. E.

Scarisbrick, John of Lancaster. SQS Jly 1755. La.

Scarl, Sarah, spinster. S s at Thorpe Summer 1770. Nf.

Scarlett, Catherine. S Feb-Apr T May 1755 *Rose*. M.

Scarlet, Peter. S s at Pershore Summer 1768. Wo.

Scarlett, Richard. R for Barbados or Jamaica Mar 1685. M.

Scarlett, Stephen. R Lent 1774. Sy.

Scarlett, William. T Dec 1753 *Whiteing*. K.

Scarr, William. S Apr 1775. M.

Scarrell, Nicholas (1727). *See* Scarrett. De.

Scarritt, Anne. S Jan T Feb 1724 *Anne* to Carolina. M.

Scarrett, George. S Jan-Apr 1748. M.

Scarratt, Mary. S Summer 1741. St.

Scarrett als Scarrell, Nicholas. R 14 yrs Aug 1727 TB to Md. De.

Scattergood, William. S Lent R 14 yrs Summer 1750. Be.

Schau, Claus Johnson. S & T Mar 1760 *Friendship*. L.

Schlutingt, Claus. S Feb 1761. M.

Schultin, John. S Lent 1758. Hu.

Scholar, William (1768). *See* Hamilton. M.

Scholcroft, James. S Lent 1751. La.

Scholes, Daniel. S Summer 1748 R 14 yrs Lent 1749. G.

Scholes, John. S Sep-Dec 1746. M.

Scoles, John. S Summer 1752 R 14 yrs Lent 1753. Li.

Scholfield, Thomas of Bury, woollen weaver. SQS Jan 1750. La.

Schovell. *See* Shovel.

Schults, Gotolph of St. Clement Danes. SW Jan 1773. M.

Scievyer, Samuel. SQS Warminster Jly TB to Va Sep 1774. Wi.

Skofield, Elizabeth. S for murder of her bastard child Lent 1724 R Lent 1725. Su.

Scowfield, Jervase. S s mare & R for life Lent 1773. Li.

Scofield, John of Derby. R Jly 1679. Db.

Scolfield, John. S & T Aug 1752 *Tryal*. L.

Scofield, Robert. R for Barbados Jan 1693. M.

Scofield, William. SQS Coventry Apr 1765. Wa.

Scole, Jane. S Sep T Dec 1734 *Caesar* LC Va Jly 1735. M.

Scoon als Spooner als Crow als Graves, John. S Jan T Jly 1722 *Alexander*. L.

Score, Joseph. S Mar 1766. Do.

Scoresby, John. S s horse Lent 1726 R 14 yrs Lent 1729. Y.

Scother, Ann. T May 1744 *Justitia*. Ht.

Scott, Andrew. S Feb T Mar 1730 *Patapsco* LC Annapolis Sep 1730. L.

Scott, Ann. S Jly T Sep 1755 *Tryal*. L.

Scot, Barrade. LC from *Robert* Annapolis Jun 1725. X.

Scott, Benjamin (1758). *See* Rivers. Sy.

Scott, Catherine. S Apr-May 1754. M.

Scot, Celia. S Jan T Apr 1759 *Thetis*. M.

Scott, Edward. S & T Apr 1725 *Sukey* LC Annapolis Sep 1725. M.

Scott, Edward. S Jun 1733. M.

Scott, Edward. S s horse Lent R 14 yrs Summer 1758. No.

Scott, Edward. S s mare Lent R 14 yrs Summer 1758. Le.

Scott, Eleanor. AT City Summer 1759. Nl.

Scott, Elizabeth, spinster. R & TB for Barbados Oct 1667. L.

Scott, Elizabeth. R for Barbados Sep 1682. L.

Scott, Elizabeth. S Mar TB May 1721 T *Owners Goodwill* LC Md Jly 1722. Le.

Scott als Holden, Elizabeth. S & T Apr 1725 *Sukey* LC Annapolis Sep 1725. M.

Scott, Elizabeth, als wife of Robert Bridgewater. S & T Oct 1730 *Forward* LC Potomack Jan 1731. M.

Scott, Elizabeth of St. John's. SQS Jan T Apr 1765 *Ann*. Sy.

Scott, George (1718). *See* Scott, John. Nl.

Scott, George. S & T Oct 1732 *Caesar*. L.

Scott, George of Braintree. SQS Oct 1764 T Apr 1765 *Ann*. E.

Scott, Hannah (1774). *See* Brown. L.

Scott, Isabel wife of John. LC from *Dorsetshire* Va Sep 1736. X.

Scott als Generall, James of Gostonfield Head. R for Barbados Jly 1686. Nl.

Scott, James. T Dec 1731 *Forward*. Sy.

Scott, James. T Apr 1742 *Bond*. Ht.

Scott, James. S Sep 1756. M.

Scott als Holloway, Jane. S Feb T May 1719 *Margaret*; sold to Patrick Sympson & William Black Md Sep 1719. L.

Scott, Jane. S Jun-Dec 1745. M.

Scott als Trott, John of Lambeth. R for Barbados or Jamaica Jly 1677. Sy.

Scott, John. R for Barbados or Jamaica Dec 1716. M.

Scott, John als George. S Summer 1718 TB Summer 1719. Nl.

Scott, John. S Mar 1730. De.

Scott, John. T Apr 1732 *Patapsco*. E.

Scott, John. S s silver pot Jan T Apr 1735 *Patapsco* LC Annapolis Oct 1735. M.

Scott, John. S & R for life Summer 1737 T Oct 1738 *Genoa*. Bu.

Scott, John. S Jan T 14 yrs Feb 1742 *Industry* to Md. M.

Scott, John. T Apr 1742 *Bond*. E.

Scott, John. S s mare Summer 1750 R 14 yrs Lent 1751. Su.

Scott, John. R 14 yrs City Summer 1757. Nl.

Scott als Piggot, John. S Sep T Dec 1769 *Justitia*. M.

Scott, Judith (1673). *See* Trott. L.

Scott, Judith. S Aug 1760. L.

Scott, Margaret, spinster, als wife of William of St. Olave, Southwark. R for Barbados or Jamaica Feb 1676 & Jly 1677. Sy.

Scott, Mary. R for Barbados Jly 1663. L.

Scott als Husk, Mary. S & T 14 yrs Sep 1718 *Eagle* LC Charles Town Mar 1719. L.

Scott als Waller, Mary. S Jan T Feb 1742 *Industry*. L.

Scott, Mary wife of Cornelius of Bromley. S Lent R 14 yrs Summer 1745. K.

Scott, Mary. S Dec 1757 T Mar 1758 *Dragon*. M.

Scott, Mary. S Apr T Nov 1759 *Phoenix*. M.

Scott, Mary wife of John. S Feb 1770. M.

Scott, Nathaniel. S Feb 1770. M.

Scott, Nicholas of Aslacton. R for Barbados or Jamaica Mar 1697. Nf.

Scott, Nicholas. S Lent 1763. E.

Scott, Richard of Threlkeld. R for Barbados Jly 1671. Cu.

Scott, Richard. R for Barbados or Jamaica Dec 1695 & Jan 1697. M.

Scott, Richard. S Feb T Mar 1729 *Patapsco* LC Annapolis Dec 1729. M.

Scott als Ridgway als Windham, Sarah. S Feb 1719. M.

Scott, Thomas. R for Barbados Jun 1665. M.

Scott, Thomas. SQS Apr 1719. Du.

Scott, Thomas. S for buggery with mare Lent R 14 yrs Summer TB Aug 1748. G.

Scott, Thomas. S & T for life Sep 1755 *Tryal*. L.

Scott, Thomas. SQS s coat Easter 1770. Du.

Scott, Thomas of Newark on Trent. SQS s stockings Oct 1770 TB Apr 1771. Nt.

Scott, Thomas. S Dec 1774. M.

Scott, William. R 14 yrs Summer 1732. Nl.

Scott, William. T Apr 1741 *Speedwell* or *Mediterranean*. E.

Scot, William. S Aug T Oct 1741 *Sea Horse*. L.

Scott, William. SQS Feb T Mar 1760 *Friendship*. M.

Scott, William. S Jly T Nov 1762 *Prince William*. M.

Scott, William. R 14 yrs Mar 1767 TB to Va. De.

Scott, William of 6th Regiment of Foot. SQS Jly 1773. La.

Scott, William. S Aug 1774. So.

Scourse, Judith. S Aug 1757. So.

Scovell, Thomas. S Lent R 14 yrs Summer TB Aug 1738. G.

Scowfield. *See* Scofield.

Scowlcroft, William. R 14 yrs s horse Summer 1770. Ch.

Scragg, Thomas of Cheddleton. R for America Jly 1699. St.

Scratchard, Gervase. R for America Mar 1690. Nt.

Scratchley, Francis. S Aug TB to Va Oct 1739. Wi.

Screen als Davenot, Samuel. SQS Jly TB Sep 1764. So.

Scringing, James (1719). *See* Cringin. M.

Scriven, George. S Apr T Jun 1742 *Bladon* to Md. M.

Scriven, James. S Apr 1754. So.

Scriven, John. R for Barbados Jun 1665. L.

Scriven, John Sr. S Apr 1754. So.

Scriven, John Jr. S Apr 1754. So.

Skriven, Mark. S s at Bredon Lent 1753. Wo.

Scriven, Robert. S Mar 1760. Ha.

Scriven, Thomas. S for perjury Summer 1760. St.

Scrivenor, George. T Apr 1762 *Dolphin*. M.

Scrivener, John. S Apr T May 1752 *Lichfield*. L.

Scrivener, Peter. R for Barbados May 1665. X.

Scroggs, Robert. S Lent R 14 yrs Summer 1750. Be.

Scruce als Lillington als Garrett, Elizabeth. R Sep TB for Barbados Oct 1669. L.

Scrugion als Austin als Stevens, John of Bristol. R for Barbados Jun 1666. G.

Scruton, Robert. S 14 yrs Apr 1746. L.

Skudamor, Jonathan. R for Barbados Jun 1670. M.

Scudder, John. R Summer 1772. E.

Scuffam, Mary. S Aug T 14 yrs Oct 1726 *Forward*. L.

Scupham, Thomas. S & R Lent 1738. Li.

Scull als Rogers, Robert of Wakes Colne. R for Barbados or Jamaica Feb 1684. E.

Skull als Scull, William. S 14 yrs for receiving Aug 1771. So.

Scullfer, William. S Jan T Feb 1765 *Tryal*. L.

Scully, Ann. S Apr 1774. M.

Sculthorpe, John. S Oct T Nov 1725 *Rappahannock* LC Rappahannock Apr 1726. M.

Scupham. *See* Scuffam.

Scurfield, William. S s horse Summer 1741 R 14 yrs Summer 1742. Nl.

Scurrier, Richard. S & T Apr 1725 *Sukey* to Md. M.

Scurrier, William. Rebel T 1685.

Scutt, John. S Summer 1751 R Lent T May 1752 *Lichfield*. Sx.

Scutt, John. R 14 yrs Mar TB to Va Apr 1764. Wi.

Scutt, Mary (1741). *See* Wilson, Hannah. M.

Seabright, Thomas (1765). *See* Ruffhead. Bd.

Seabright, William (1764). *See* Moreton. St.

Seabrooke, Thomas. S Oct 1748 T Jan 1749 *Laura*. L.

Seabrook, William. S & T Oct 1730 *Forward* LC Potomack Jan 1731. L.

Seaburn, Sarah. T May 1751 *Tryal*. K.

Seaborn, William. S Summer 1749. E.

Seager als Boxer, Benjamin. S s at Kinver Summer 1774. St.

Seagar, Richard of Mitcham. R Feb T May 1719 *Margaret* LC Md Sep 1719; sold to William Black. Sy.

Seager, Thomas. R Jly 1774. Ha.

Seagoe als Wilson, Margaret. S Jun-Dec 1738 T Jan 1739 *Dorsetshire*. M.

Segrave, James. SQS & T Jan 1765 *Tryal*. M.

Seagrave, John. S Feb T Mar 1758 *Dragon*. L.

Seagrove, William. T May 1744 *Justitia*. Sx.

Seagry, Richard of Epsom. SQS Mar 1754. Sy.

Seakin, Edward. T Jly 1722 *Alexander*. K.

Seal, Ann. S s at English Bicknor & R 14 yrs Summer 1771. G.

Seale, Frances. PT Oct 1700. M.

Seale, Matthias. T Nov 1762 *Prince William*. E.

Seal, Thomas of Lindfield. R for America Jly 1700. Sx.

Seale, William. S s iron at Walsall Lent 1735. St.

Seale, William of St. James, Clerkenwell. S s dishes & T Feb 1740 *York*. M.

Seal, William. S Jly-Dec 1747. M.

Seeley, George of Oxford. R for Barbados Mar 1703. O.

Sealy, Hannah. S Jan T Feb 1733 *Smith*. L.
Seeley, John. R Feb 1675. M.
Sealey als Cooksley, Mary of Dunster. R for Barbados Mar 1686. So.
Seely, Robert of Freckenham. R for Barbados Feb 1664. Su.
Sealy, Simon. R 14 yrs Apr 1767. So.
Seaman, James (1767). *See* Green, John. Nf.
Seaman, Jane wife of William. S Sep-Oct 1773. M.
Seaman, Mary. T Jly 1722 *Alexander*. K.
Seaman, Robert. Rebel T 1685.
Seamer. *See* Seymour.
Seamore. *See* Seymour.
Seer, James. SQS Devizes & TB to Va Apr 1765. Wi.
Sear, Richard. T Jan 1738 *Dorsetshire*. Sy.
Seare, Stephen of Flaxley. R for America Mar 1680. G.
Sear, Thomas. T Apr 1770 *New Trial*. Bu.
Searle, Benjamin of Bitton. R for America Jly 1693. G.
Searle, George. Rebel T 1685.
Searle, George. T Apr 1725 *Sukey* LC Md Sep 1725. Ht.
Searle, James. S May-Jly 1746. M.
Searle, John. T Oct 1729 *Forward*. E.
Searle, Simon. R 14 yrs Jly 1749 TB to Va. De.
Searle, Thomas. PT May 1700. M.
Searle, Thomas. S Mar 1751. De.
Searle, Thomas. S s mare & R 14 yrs Summer 1754. Du.
Searle, Thomas Sr. S Mar 1773. De.
Searle, Thomas Jr. S Mar 1773. De.
Searle, William. Rebel T 1685.
Serles, Thomas. TB May 1739. Nt.
Seers, Bernard. S May-Jun T Aug 1752 *Tryal*. M.
Sears, George. S Apr 1746. L.
Seares, George. S Sep-Dec 1755 T Jan 1756 *Greyhound*. M.
Sears, Giles. T Dec 1734 *Caesar*. Sy.
Sears, Mary Ann. S Sep-Oct 1774. M.
Sears, Moses. SQS Apr T May 1755 *Rose*. M.
Sears, Robert. S & T Jan 1736 *Dorsetshire* LC Va Sep 1736. L.
Seares, William. S Feb T Apr 1765 *Ann*. L.
Sease, Robert. Rebel T 1685.
Seaton, John. S & T Jan 1722 *Gilbert* to Md. M.
Ceaton, John. SQS Dec 1766 T Jan 1767 *Tryal*. M.
Seaton, Rachel, als wife of Thomas Sharpe. S City Lent 1733. Y.
Seavell, Ann. S & T May 1736 *Patapsco* to Md. M.
Seaver, Valentine. S & T Sep 1731 *Smith* LC Va 1732. L.
Seaward. *See* Seward.
Seawell. *See* Sewell.
Seckington, James. S s mare & R 14 yrs Lent T Oct 1768 *Justitia*. Bu.
Seddon, Francis. S Summer 1740. La.
Seddon, George. S s horse Summer 1743 R 14 yrs Lent 1747. La.
Seddon, Isaac. T Apr 1732 *Patapsco*. Sy.
Seddon, John. S Apr 1763. L.
Seddon, Nathan. T Apr 1732 *Patapsco*. Sy.
Sedgware als Fowler, Margaret. S Oct 1768 T Jan 1769 *Thornton*. M.

Sedgwick, James. S May T Jly 1722 *Alexander* to Nevis or Jamaica. M.

Sedgewick, John. S City Lent 1744. Y.

Sedgwicke, John. T Sep 1755 *Tryal*. M.

Sedgwick, Martha. T Jun 1740 *Essex*. Sy.

Sedgwick, Richard. S 14 yrs Apr-Jun 1739. M.

Sedgewick, Robert of Croydon. R for Barbados or Jamaica Jly 1688 & Feb 1690. Sy.

Sedgworth, Ann. SQS Thirsk Oct TB Nov 1743. Y.

See, Peter. S Lent 1736. Hu.

Seeker, Mary (1738). *See* James. Sy.

Seers. *See* Sears.

Selby, Edward of St. George, Southwark, carpenter. SQS May 1764. Sy.

Selby, Frances of St. Andrew Holborn, widow. S s lead pipe & T Dec 1740 *Vernon*. M.

Selby, James. S s at Wokingham Summer 1752. Be.

Selby, John of Hayton. SQS s wheat May TB Sep 1728. Nt.

Selby, John. R 14 yrs Jly 1728. Ha.

Selby, John. SQS East Retford May TB Sep 1728. Nt.

Selby, Joseph. R 14 yrs Mar TB to Va Apr 1768. Wi.

Selby, Mary. S Apr T May 1720 *Honor* to York River. L.

Selby, William. T Apr 1739 *Forward*. Sy.

Selerate, John (1750). *See* Sellersat. E.

Self, Betty wife of ——-. S & TB to Va Mar 1738. Wi.

Selfe, Robert of Rodden. R for Barbados Mar 1680. So.

Selfe, William. Rebel T 1685.

Sell, William. S Jan-Feb 1774. M.

Seller, William. S Feb 1775. L.

Sellers, Thomas of Bermondsey. S Summer T Oct 1739 *Duke of Cumberland*. Sy.

Sellers, William als Henry. S s at St. Aldate, Oxford, Lent 1764. O.

Sellersat als Selerate, John. S Summer T Oct 1750 *Rachael*. E.

Sellick, Elizabeth. TB to Va from QS 1746. De.

Sells, James. S Feb T Apr 1772 *Thornton*. L.

Selly, John. S s gelding & R 14 yrs Lent 1738. Ca.

Selley, John. S s at Clun Summer 1761. Sh.

Selley, John. S s sheep Lent R 14 yrs Summer 1765. Sh.

Selly, Samuel. SQS Jly 1741 TB to Md May 1742. So.

Selvie, George. S Apr-May 1754. M.

Selway, George. R 14 yrs Mar 1772. So.

Selwood, Elizabeth. S May-Jun T Jly 1753 *Tryal*. M.

Selwood, Richard. Rebel T 1685.

Selwood, Sara. S for Va Jly 1718. So.

Sellwood, Sarah. S Mar TB to Va Apr 1775. Wi.

Sellwood, William. Rebel T 1685.

Sendry, Thomas (1713). *See* Haines. Be.

Seneca, Mary. S Jan-May T Jun 1738 *Forward* to Md or Va. M.

Senior, Jane. S 14 yrs Aug 1727 T *Forward* LC Rappahannock May 1728. M.

Senior, Richard. R 14 yrs Summer 1751. Y.

Senturelli, Joseph. S Jan T Mar 1750 *Tryal*. L.

Septon, Judith wife of George. S Jun 1744. M.

Sergeason. *See* Surgison.

Serjeant, Elizabeth of St. Mary le Strand, spinster. SW Jly T Sep 1767 *Justitia*. M.

Sargent, Frances. S Jan-Feb T Apr 1771 *Thornton*. M.

Sarjeant, George of Halstead. SQS Apr T Aug 1769 *Douglas*. E.

Serjeant, Hugh. T Jun 1728 *Elizabeth*. K.

Sargeant, Hugh. LC from *Elizabeth* Va Aug 1729. Le.

Sargeant, John. R Feb 1675. M.

Serjeant als Field, John. R for Barbados or Jamaica Dec 1699. L.

Serjeant als Higgins, John. S & T Jan 1722 *Gilbert* LC Annapolis Jly 1722. M.

Sargent, John (1749). *See* Miller. L.

Serjeant, John. S Apr 1760. M.

Serjeant, John. S s iron at Wolverhampton Lent 1769. St.

Serjeant, John. T Apr 1769 *Tryal*. E.

Serjeant, John. SWK Apr 1775. K.

Serjeant, Robert. S Oct T Nov 1725 *Rappahannock* but died on passage. M.

Serjeant, Susanna. S Aug T Oct 1723 *Forward* to Va. M.

Sagent, Thomas. S Feb 1738. Ha.

Serjeant, Thomas. S Jan-Feb T Apr 1771 *Thornton*. M.

Sarjant, Thomas. S Summer 1774. Sx.

Sergeant, William of Peterstow. R for America Feb 1681. He.

Serjeant, William. T Oct 1726 *Forward*. E.

Serjeant, William. S Apr TB Jun 1728. Le.

Serjeant, William. S & T Sep 1731 *Smith* LC Va 1732. M.

Sartain, James of Westbury. SQS Marlborough Oct 1755 TB May 1756. Wi.

Sertain, Thomas. SQS Devizes May TB to Va Oct 1764. Wi.

Servant, Mary. S Sep-Oct 1772. M.

Sessions, William (1675). *See* Okey. O.

Seth, Lewis. R 14 yrs Mar 1774. Co.

Seth, Lewis. R 14 yrs Apr 1774. La.

Severight, George. T Apr 1753 *Thames*. Sy.

Severn, Thomas. S Jan T Feb 1724 *Anne* to Carolina. M.

Sevier, Elizabeth. S Mar 1733. So.

Seville, Mary. S Jly 1724. Ha.

Seaward, Ann wife of Roger. S Jly T Nov 1762 *Prince William*. M.

Seward, James. R 14 yrs Aug 1771. So.

Seward, Martin. R for Barbados or Jamaica Apr 1690. L.

Seaward, Mathew (1755). *See* Steward. De.

Seward, Samuel. T Apr 1725 *Sukey* LC Md Sep 1725. E.

Sewell, Jeremy. PT Jun R Oct 1673. M.

Sewell, John. T Jun 1738 *Forward*. E.

Sewell, Margaret. S Summer 1741. Cu.

Seawell, Mary. T Jun 1740 *Essex*. Sy.

Sewell, Thomas. SQS for false pretences Summer 1765. Du.

Sexey, George. S Jly 1758. Do.

Sexton, John. S Norwich s sheep Summer 1747 R 14 yrs Lent 1748. Nf.

Sexton, John. S s at Beaconsfield Lent T Apr 1771 *Thornton*. Bu.

Sexton, Nathaniel. T Sep 1742 *Forward*. E.

Sexton, Richard of Winchcombe. R for America Jly 1675. G.
Sexton, Thomas. R Jly 1686. M.
Sexton, Thomas. T Jan 1736 *Dorsetshire*. E.
Seyers. *See* Sayers.
Seymour, Anne. R for Barbados Apr 1669. M.
Seamore, Anne. R for Barbados Sep 1672. L.
Seymour, Ann. S Apr 1761. M.
Seymour, Benjamin Ambrose. SQS Feb T Apr 1766 *Ann*. M.
Seymour, Charles Stewart. S Jun 1739. L.
Seymour, Elizabeth. S Oct T Dec 1770 *Justitia*. M.
Seymour, George. R for Barbados Aug 1679. L.
Seymour, George. T Sep 1758 *Tryal*. K.
Seymour, John, aged 30. R Feb 1664. L.
Seymour, John, aged 40. R Feb 1664. L.
Seymore, John. Rebel T 1685.
Seamor, John. S Lent 1745. *Su.
Seymour, John. S Mar 1751. De.
Seymour, John. S peas s at West Shefford Lent 1759. Be.
Seymour, John. S & T Dec 1767 *Neptune*. M.
Seymour, Mary wife of Thomas. S Jun-Dec 1738 T Jan 1739
    Dorsetshire. M.
Seymour, Mary. S Aug 1739. Do.
Seamer, Nicholas. S Mar 1744. De.
Seymour, Richard als Robert of Shenfield. R for Barbados or Jamaica
    Jly 1710. E.
Seymour, Robert. R 14 yrs Jly TB to Va Oct 1742. Wi.
Seamour, Thomas. LC from *Patapsco* Annapolis Nov 1733. X.
Seymore, William of Alvechurch. R for America Mar 1680. Wo.
Seymour, William. S & T Apr 1725 *Sukey* LC Annapolis Sep 1725. M.
Seymour, William. S Jan-Feb T Apr 1772 *Thornton*. M.
Seymour, William. R 14 yrs Aug 1774. Co.
Sha——, Thomas, aged 28, dark, carpenter. LC from *Gilbert* Md May
    1721. X.
Shacklady, George of Formby. SQS Oct 1767. La.
Shackleton, Edward. S Jun T Sep 1758 *Tryal*. L.
Shackleton, Margaret. S Lent 1751. La.
Shakleton, Thomas. T 14 yrs Sep 1765 *Justitia*. Sy.
Shackley, James of Spaldwick. R for America Apr 1697. Hu.
Shacksford, John. R for Barbados or Jamaica Dec 1698. L.
Shadbolt, William. S Lent T May 1755 *Rose*. Ht.
Shaddock, Charles. S Mar 1742. De.
Shaddows, David. S for life Oct 1744-Jan 1745. M.
Shadwell, John. S Jan T Feb 1765 *Tryal*. L.
Shaen, William. S Aug 1760. L.
Shaftoe, Edward. S & T Oct 1730 *Forward* LC Potomack Jan 1731. M.
Shafton, Henry. SQS Jly TB Aug 1738. Nt.
Shailor, James. S s at Wantage Lent 1763. Be.
Shakerly, Sampson. T Oct 1723 *Forward*. Sy.
Shakespeare, John. S Summer 1759 R 14 yrs Lent 1760. Wo.
Shakespear, Samuel. SW & T Aug 1779 *Douglas*. M.
Shakspeare, William of Dudley. R for America Jly 1687. Wo.

Shakespear, William. S & T Sep 1766 *Justitia*. L.

Shale, John. S s window frames at Darlaston Summer 1763. St.

Shale, Robert. Rebel T 1685.

Shale, Sarah. S & T Oct 1729 *Forward* LC Va Jun 1730. M.

Shales, Daniel. R Feb T for life Mar 1764 *Tryal*. M.

Shales als Muttit, Elizabeth of St. Clement, Ipswich. R (Home Circ) Apr 1668. Su.

Shales als Bayley, John. S Jan T Feb 1726 *Supply* LC Annapolis May 1726. L.

Shales, John. R 14 yrs Mar 1764. Ha.

Shallett, Francis. R for America Aug 1685. Nt.

Shamble als Wells, Elizabeth Mary. S Jan T Feb 1742 *Industry* to Md. M.

Shambler, John. S Feb T Apr 1742 *Bond* to Potomack. M.

Shand, Philip. LC from *Rappahannock* Rappahannock Apr 1726. X.

Shanks, Elizabeth. S Jly T 14 yrs Aug 1721 *Prince Royal* LC Va Nov 1721. L.

Shanks, John. S Dec 1733 T Jan 1734 *Caesar* LC Va Jly 1734. M.

Shanks, Robert. R 14 yrs Jly 1737. Wi.

Shanks, Sarah. SQS Oct 1762. La.

Shann, William. S Jan-Jun T 14 yrs Jun 1728 *Elizabeth* LC Potomack Aug 1729. L.

Shanning, Mary wife of Robert. S Lent R 14 yrs Summer 1729. Be.

Shapland, Grace. TB to Va from QS 1740. De.

Shapley, Andrew. S Jly 1722. De.

Shaplin, William. Died on passage in *Rappahannock* 1724. X.

Sharborn. *See* Sherbourne.

Shard, Emanuel. S Dec 1727. M.

Share, John. S s sheets at Old Swinford Summer 1751. Wo.

Shargold, Robert of Shrewton. R for Barbados Jan 1676. Wi.

Sharkey, Lewis. S Dec 1774. L.

Sharlow, Elizabeth. S Aug T Oct 1724 *Forward* LC Annapolis Jun 1725. M.

Sharman, Henry. S for highway robbery Lent R 14 yrs Summer 1730. No.

Sharman, Thomas of Leighton Buzzard. S Lent 1729. *Bd.

Sharpe, Christopher. S Jly 1749. L.

Sharp, Eleanor. S & T Jan 1766 *Tryal*. M.

Sharpe, Elias. S Oct T Nov 1725 *Rappahannock* LC Rappahannock Apr 1726. M.

Sharpe, Elizabeth of North Newnton. R for Barbados Jly 1664. O.

Sharpe, Elizabeth of Cheshunt. R for Barbados or Jamaica Feb 1686. Ht.

Sharp, Elizabeth. S Jan T 14 yrs Apr 1759 *Thetis*. M.

Sharp, Elizabeth. S s at Tetbury Summer 1768. G.

Sharpe, Frances. S Jan T Feb 1733 *Smith* to Md or Va. M.

Sharp, James. R 14 yrs Summer 1751. Cu.

Sharpe, John. S Feb T Apr 1732 *Patapsco* LC Annapolis Oct 1732. L.

Sharp, John, a boy. S Summer 1736 R 14 yrs Summer 1737. Wa.

Sharp, John. S s from tenters at Sowerby Lent 1772. Y.

Sharpe, Mary (1682). *See* Harris. M.

Sharp als Alston, Mary. S & T Oct 1732 *Caesar* to Va. M.

Sharpe, Mary wife of Richard. S Jly TB to Va Aug 1766. Le.

Sharpe, Rachel (1733). *See* Seaton. Y.

Sharp, Rachael. S Lent 1773. Li.

Sharp, Robert. S & T Sep 1731 *Smith* but died on passage. M.

Sharp, Robert. S Lent 1757. Y.

Sharpe, Robert. S at Dover & T Dec 1770 *Justitia*. K.

Sharpe, Samuel of Rainham. R for Barbados or Jamaica Mar 1682 & Feb 1683. E.

Sharpe, Sarah. PT Mar R Aug 1701. M.

Sharp, Thomas. R for America Aug 1715. L.

Sharp, Thomas. S Feb 1730. L.

Sharpe, Thomas. S Lent R 14 yrs Summer 1733. Y.

Sharp, Thomas. T Apr 1741 *Speedwell* or *Mediterranean*. Bu.

Sharp, Thomas. S Lent 1758. No.

Sharpe, Thomas. S s at Tidenham Summer 1759. G.

Sharp, Thomas. SQS Oct 1771 TB Apr 1772. So.

Sharp als Earp, Thomas. R Summer 1775. Sy.

Sharpe, William. R for America Feb 1700. Nt.

Sharpe, William. TB Apr 1719. L.

Sharp als Sharper, William. T Nov 1725 *Rappahannock* LC Va Aug 1726. E.

Sharpe, William. S Summer 1735. Cu.

Sharp, William. S Dec 1737 T Jan 1738 *Dorsetshire*. L.

Sharpcliff, Thomas. S & T Apr 1733 *Patapsco* LC Annapolis Nov 1733. M.

Sharpells, Henry. S s iron hoops Feb T Apr 1735 *Patapsco* LC Annapolis Oct 1735. M.

Sharper, William (1725). *See* Sharp.

Sharples, John of Samlesbury. SQS May 1756. La.

Sharpless, Catherine (1748). *See* Brooks. M.

Sharpless als Sweet, John of Whitechapel. S Apr T May 1740 *Essex*. M.

Sharpless als Hall, John. S Apr-Jun T Jly 1772 *Tayloe*. M.

Sharpley, James. S Apr-May 1775. M.

Sharwell, John. S Oct T Dec 1767 *Neptune*. M.

Shattersley, John of Clifton. R for America Jly 1679. G.

Shaw, Alice, als Lewis, Mary. S & T Sep 1731 *Smith* but died on passage. M.

Shaw, Ann. S Dec 1737 T Jan 1738 *Dorsetshire*. L.

Shaw, Ann wife of John. AT City Summer 1755. Nl.

Shoare, Bartholomew. R for Jamaica Aug 1661. M.

Shaw, Charles. R 14 yrs Dec 1774. M.

Shaw, David. S Lent 1767 R Lent 1768. G.

Shaw, Dorothy. S Feb T Apr 1734 *Patapsco*. L.

Shaw, Edward. S Sep 1719. M.

Shaw, Edward. S s barley & corn at Weeford Lent 1760. St.

Shaw, Elizabeth. S s clothing Jan T Jun 1738 *Forward* to Md or Va. M.

Shaw, Elizabeth (1775). *See* Westfield. G.

Shaw, Emanuel. S Summer 1769. Mo.

Shaw, George. SQS Mar TB Aug 1720 to be shipped to Md from Liverpool. Db.

Shaw, George. S Feb T Mar 1727 *Rappahannock*. L.
Shore, Isaac. S Summer T Sep 1751 *Greyhound*. Sx.
Shore, James. S s horse Lent R 14 yrs Summer 1737. Y.
Shaw, James. S Jan T Feb 1744 *Neptune*. L.
Shawe, James, formerly of Stockport, Chesh, now of Manchester, gardener. SQS Jly 1751. La.
Shaw, Jane. S Sep 1761. M.
Shaw, John. R for Barbados or Jamaica Dec 1695 & Jan 1697. M.
Shaw, John. S Jan T Feb 1719 *Worcester* LC Annapolis Jun 1719. L.
Shaw, John. S Jly 1732. Ha.
Shore, John. T Oct 1750 *Rachael*. M.
Shaw, John. S s at Wolverhampton Lent 1751. St.
Shaw, John. S s sheep Lent R 14 yrs Summer 1759. Li.
Shaw, John. SW & T Dec 1771 *Justitia*. M.
Shaw, Jonathan of Lancaster. R for Barbados Jly 1699. La.
Shaw, Jonathan. SQS 14 yrs Mar 1718, escaped & recaptured, TB to Md from Liverpool Sep 1720. Db.
Shaw, Jonathan. TB Aug 1733. Nt.
Shaw, Joseph. S Summer 1741. Wo.
Shaw, Joseph. S Lent 1764. Wa.
Shaw, Mary. S Jun-Dec 1745. M.
Shaw, Mary (1753). *See* Straw. K.
Shaw, Philip. S s horse Summer 1729 R 14 yrs Summer 1730. Li.
Shaw, Robert. S & T Oct 1730 *Forward* LC Potomack Jan 1731. L.
Shaw, Samuel of Brampton Brearley. R for Barbados Jun 1675. Y.
Shaw, Samuel of Northampton. R for America Jly 1682. No.
Shaw, Samuel. S & T Apr 1725 *Sukey* LC Annapolis Sep 1725. M.
Shaw, Samuel. S Feb T Apr 1772 *Thornton*. L.
Shaw als Mansfield, Sarah. S s at Newcastle under Lyme Lent 1757. St.
Shaw, Thomas of Ottley. R for Barbados Jun 1675. Y.
Shaw, Thomas of Taunton. R for Barbados Mar 1694. So.
Shawe, Thomas. R May AT Jly 1697. M.
Shaw, Thomas. S s at Northleach Lent 1725. G.
Shawe, Thomas. S Lent R 14 yrs Summer 1742 T *Shaw* LC Antigua May 1743. La.
Shaw, Thomas (1750). *See* Crags. L.
Shaw, Thomas of St. Olave, Southwark. SQS Jan 1751. Sy.
Shaw, Thomas. S Lent T Apr 1774. No.
Shaw, Walter. R & T Dec 1716 *Lewis* to Jamaica. M.
Shaw, Walter. S Oct 1765 T Jan 1766 *Tryal*. M.
Shaw, William. S Jly T Aug 1721 *Prince Royal* but died on passage. L.
Shaw, William. Died on passage in *Sukey* 1725. X.
Shaw, William of St. Ann, Westminster. S s books & T May 1736 *Patapsco*. M.
Shaw, William. S Oct-Dec 1739 T Jan 1740 *York* to Md. M.
Shawbridge, Robert. S Mar 1742. Do.
Shay, Jarvis als Gervase. S Apr T May 1752 *Lichfield*. L.
Shays, Mary (1742). *See* White. M.
Sheaf, William. S Jan-Apr 1749. M.
Sheal, John. S Mar 1736. So.
Shean. *See* Sheen.

Sherer, John. T Jun 1764 *Dolphin*. K.
Shearing, Mary. R Summer 1772. Sy.
Shearing, Stephen. S Mar 1741. Ha.
Shearman. *See* Sherman.
Sheers, Elizabeth. S Aug 1757. So.
Shears, Isaac. S Sep-Oct 1775. M.
Sheeres, John of St. Olave, Southwark. R for America Jly 1700. Sy.
Sheers, John. TB to Md from QS 1737. De.
Shears, Leonard. S Aug 1772. So.
Shears, Mary (1730). *See* Cox. L.
Shears, Mary. S Mar 1761. L.
Shiers, Richard of St. Martin in Fields. SW Apr 1773. M.
Shears, Thomas. R Apr 1775. So.
Sheave, Robert. R 14 yrs Aug 1739. Do.
Sheels, John of Torksey. R for America Jly 1716. Li.
Sheene, George of Newington. SQS Oct 1768 T Jan 1769 *Thornton*. Sy.
Shean, James. S Apr 1773. L.
Shean, Joseph. S Mar 1742. Do.
Sheen, Mary. S & T Dec 1731 *Forward*. L.
Sheen, William. S Jan-Feb 1774. M.
Sheepy, John. S & T Jly 1718 *Worcester* LC Charles Town Mar 1719. L.
Sheereman. *See* Sherman.
Sheat, Josias. S Aug 1723. So.
Sheffield, Isaac. S & T Jly 1753 *Tryal*. L.
Sheffield, John of Plympton St. Mary, weaver. R for Barbados Apr
    1668. De.
Sheffield, John. T Apr 1731 *Bennett*. E.
Sheffield, John. S s fish at Godmanchester Lent 1769. Hu.
Sheffield, Joseph. S May 1761. M.
Sheffield, Samuel. SQS Jan 1752. M.
Sheffield, Thomas. S May-Jun T Aug 1752 *Tryal*. M.
Sheffield, Thomas. S s sheep & R Summer 1775. Db.
Sheffield, William. S s at Shinnington Lent 1765. G.
Sheinton, John. S Summer 1757 R 14 yrs Lent 1758. Wo.
Sheldon, Andrew of Charlbury. R for Barbados Jly 1666. O.
Sheldan, Andrew of Darlaston. S Lent 1742. St.
Sheldon, Benedict of Reading. R for Barbados Feb 1665. Be.
Sheldon, John of Dudley, nailer. R for America Mar 1683. Wo.
Shelden, John. S Lent TB Apr 1766. Db.
Sheldon, Mary. S Sep-Oct 1772. M.
Sheldon, Thomas. S Oct T Dec 1767 *Neptune*. M.
Sheldon, William of Handsworth, nailer. R for America Jly 1683. St.
Sheldrick, Elizabeth. S & T Oct 1732 *Caesar*. L.
Shelley, Jacob of St. Mary, Colchester. S Lent R Summer 1745. E.
Shelley, John of Alresford. R for Barbados or Jamaica Jly 1710. E.
Shelley, Philip. S Summer 1760 R 14 yrs Lent 1761. E.
Shelley, Susannah. T Apr 1770 *New Trial*. E.
Shelly, Thomas. R 14 yrs Jly 1728. Ha.
Shelock, James. R for life Sep 1756. M.
Shelton, Edward. T Dec 1753 *Whiteing*. K.
Shelton, Elizabeth (1757). *See* Knotsmell. L.

Shelton, Hannah. S Jan T Apr 1762 *Dolphin*. M.

Shelton, Henry. S & T Dec 1731 *Forward* to Md or Va. M.

Shelton, James. S Feb 1761. L.

Shilton, John. S & R for life Lent 1774. Wa.

Shelton, John. S Jan 1775. M.

Shelton, Jonas. S Lent TB Apr 1758. Db.

Shelton, Mary Sr. S s at Leominster Lent 1748. He.

Shelton, Mary Jr. S s at Leominster Lent 1748. He.

Shelton, Mary (1751). *See* Burge. Sy.

Shelton, Robert of Ardleigh. R for Barbados or Jamaica Jly 1715. E.

Shelton, Walter. S & T Jan 1722 *Gilbert* LC Annapolis Jly 1722. M.

Sheppard, Ambrose. R for Barbados Jun 1666. Y.

Shepherd, Ann (1750). *See* Holland. M.

Shepherd, Ann (1774). *See* Whitaker. La.

Shepard, Charles. S Summer 1746. K.

Sheppard, Charles. T Apr 1753 *Thames*. E.

Shepheard, Charles. S & R for life Lent 1773. Wo.

Shepherd, Conrad. S Oct 1773. L.

Sheppard, David of Bristol. R 14 yrs Aug 1769 (SP). G.

Shepherd, Dorothy. S Nov T Dec 1753 *Whiteing*. L.

Shepherd, Elizabeth, als Edgware Bess Hannapenny. S May T Jun 1726 *Loyal Margaret* LC Md Oct 1726. M.

Shepherd, Elizabeth. S & T Oct 1729 *Forward* LC Va Jun 1730. M.

Shepherd, Elizabeth wife of Philip. S & T Dec 1731 *Forward* to Md or Va. M.

Sheppard, Elizabeth. S Mar 1750 TB to Va. De.

Shepherd, Francis. R for Barbados Oct 1673. L.

Sheppard, George. SQS Apr TB May 1756. So.

Sheppard, Giles. R 14 yrs Aug 1748. So.

Sheppard, Hannah. S & T May 1736 *Patapsco*. L.

Sheppard, James. Rebel T 1685.

Shepherd, James. S s at Claines Summer 1766. Wo.

Shepherd, John. S s wooden drawer Sep 1735 T Jan 1736 *Dorsetshire* LC Va Sep 1736. M.

Shepherd, John (1756). *See* Illford. M.

Shepheard, John. T Dec 1758 *The Brothers*. K.

Shepherd, Margaret. S Jan T Feb 1726 *Supply* LC Annapolis May 1726. L.

Shepherd als Drew, Martha. S s cloth & T Dec 1734 *Caesar* but died on passage. M.

Sheppard, Mary, widow. R for Barbados or Jamaica Oct 1694. L.

Sheppeard, Mary. S Jly T Aug 1721 *Owners Goodwill* LC Annapolis Jly 1722. M.

Sheppard, Mary. T May 1737 *Forward*. Sy.

Sheppard, Mary. S Apr 1747. De.

Shepherd, Mary. T Dec 1753 *Whiteing*. Sy.

Shepherd, Richard. S s cloth & T Dec 1734 *Caesar* LC Va Jly 1735. M.

Shepherd, Robert of Hundersfield. SQS Jan 1770. La.

Sheppard, Robert. S Apr 1774. M.

Shepherd, Samuel. S Feb T Mar 1730 *Patapsco* LC Annapolis Sep 1730. M.

Shepherd, Sara. S Feb T Apr 1732 *Patapsco* LC Annapolis Oct 1732. M.
Shepherd, Thomas. S Aug T Oct 1724 *Forward* LC Annapolis Jun 1725. M.
Shepherd, Thomas. S & T Apr 1725 *Sukey* to Md. M.
Shepherd, Thomas. S Jly TB Sep 1726. Nt.
Shepherd, Thomas. S & T Jan 1766 *Tryal*. L.
Sheppard, Tobias. S Aug 1657 to House of Correction unless he agrees to be transported. M.
Sheppard, William. Rebel T 1685.
Shepard, William. T Jly 1723 *Alexander* LC Md Sep 1723. Ht.
Shepherd, William. S Feb T 14 yrs Mar 1750 *Tryal*. M.
Shepherd, William. S s handkerchief at St. Mary Woolnoth Feb T Apr 1768 *Thornton*. L.
Sheppard, William of St. Olave, Southwark. SQS & T Jan 1769 *Thornton*. Sy.
Shepherd, William of Wimbledon. R s gelding Lent T 14 yrs Apr 1772 *Thornton*. Sy.
Sheppard, William. R Jly 1774. Ha.
Sheppardson, John. S s dishes at Stitnam Lent TB Apr 1773. Y.
Shepton, John. R Mar 1606. K.
Sharborn, John. S May T Sep 1765 *Justitia*. M.
Sherborne, Sarah (1721). *See* Tarborne. M.
Sherbourne, Thomas. R Dec 1698 AT Jan 1699. M.
Sherdon, Paul. T *Rappahannock* from London LC Va Apr 1726. Li.
Sherridan, Catherine. T Sep 1755 *Tryal*. M.
Sheridan, John. S May T Jun 1764 *Dolphin*. M.
Sheriff, Matthew. S Lent T May 1737 *Forward*. Bu.
Sherriff, William. S for Va Mar 1719. Wi.
Sherland, John. R for Barbados or Jamaica Jly 1687. M.
Sherland, William. R 14 yrs Jly 1729. Ha.
Sherles, John. S s horse Summer 1737 R 14 yrs Summer TB Aug 1738. Nt.
Sherley. *See* Shirley.
Sherlock, John. S s at Chetwynd Summer 1727. Sh.
Sherlock, Ralph. S Sep T Oct 1750 *Rachael*. M.
Sherlock, Silvia. S 14 yrs Aug 1727 T *Forward* LC Rappahannock May 1728. M.
Sherlock, Simon. S May T Jun 1727 *Susanna*. L.
Sherlock, William. S Jan 1751. M.
Shurman, Charles. LC from *Patapsco* Annapolis Oct 1735. X.
Shearman, Elizabeth. S Feb T Apr 1765 *Ann*. M.
Shearman, John. S Jly 1750. Ha.
Sherman, Rachael. S Feb T Apr 1762 *Dolphin*. M.
Sherman, Samuel of Arundel. R for Barbados or Jamaica Jly 1705. Sx.
Sherman als Clayton, Susannah. S Apr T May 1767 *Thornton*. M.
Sheereman, William. SQS Jan 1755. M.
Sherrard, Bernard. SQS Dec 1768 T Jan 1769 *Thornton*. M.
Sherrard, Francis. S & T Oct 1732 *Caesar*. L.
Sherrard, George. S s at Wolverhampton Summer 1770. St.
Sherrard, James. T Jly 1722 *Alexander*. Sy.
Sherrard, John. S Dec 1753-Jan 1754. M.

Sherrard, Nathaniel. S Oct 1751-Jan 1752. M.
Sherrard als Harwood, Robert. S Apr 1749. L.
Sherrord als Sherrard als Sherring, William. R 14 yrs Mar 1758. Do.
Sherrar, William. SW & T Jly 1772 *Tayloe*. M.
Sherratt, John. S & R 14 yrs Lent 1769. Ch.
Sherringe, Robert of Forston, R for Barbados Jun 1669. Do.
Sherring, William. S s gelding from Duke of Grafton Lent R 14 yrs
    Summer 1751. Su.
Sherring, William (1758). *See* Sherrord. Do.
Sherrington, William. S & T Oct 1732 *Caesar*. L.
Sherry, Jane. R for Barbados or Jamaica May AT Jly 1697. M.
Sherry, William. Rebel T 1685.
Sherryer, William. T Dec 1753 *Whiteing*. Sx.
Sherston, John. T Apr 1743 *Justitia*. Ht.
Shervill, John, als Tom Thumb. S & T Jan 1756 *Greyhound*. L.
Sherwell, William of Modbury, weaver. R for Barbados Mar 1686. De.
Sherwood, Benjamin. S Jan T Sep 1737 *Pretty Patsy* to Md. M.
Sherwood, John. R for America Jly 1694. Wa.
Sherwood, John. R 14 yrs Jly TB Aug 1755. Wi.
Sherwood, John. S Oct T Nov 1759 *Phoenix*. L.
Sherwood, William. R for Barbados May & Aug 1668. M.
Shettle, Mahaleel. S Aug T Oct 1724 *Forward* to Md. M.
Shettleworth, Thomas. S Summer T Oct 1750 *Rachael*. E.
Shewill, John of Much Birch. S Summer 1719. He.
Shewing, Elizabeth (1770). *See* Durant. M.
Shewswood, John. S Feb T 14 yrs Oct 1730 *Forward* LC Potomack Jan
    1731. M.
Shields, Dennis. S Dec 1765 T Jan 1766 *Tryal*. M.
Shields, Elizabeth (1724). *See* Morden. M.
Shields, Elizabeth. S Jly-Sep T Sep 1742 *Forward*. M.
Shields, Elizabeth, spinster. S 14 yrs at Bristol for receiving Lent
    1772. G.
Shields, Henry. S May T Sep 1766 *Justitia*. L.
Shields, Mary. S Summer 1742. Y.
Shields, Mary. S 14 yrs Apr 1773. M.
Shields, Michael. T Apr 1753 *Thames*. Sx.
Shields, Patrick. S May-Jly 1774. M.
Shields, Paul. S Sep-Oct T Dec 1752 *Greyhound*. M.
Shields, Robert. T May 1737 *Forward*. K.
Shillingford, Jacob. T 14 yrs Sep 1767 *Justitia*. E.
Shillingford, William. S Lent 1756. Y.
Shilton. *See* Shelton.
Shin als Slim, Abraham. SW & T Jly 1771 *Scarsdale*. M.
Shinfield, Martin. R for Barbados Mar 1677. L.
Shingfield, Mary. R for Barbados Oct 1673. L.
Shinler, John. Rebel T 1685.
Shinningfield, Hugh. R for Barbados Feb 1675. L.
Shinwell, Samuel. S s at Penn Summer 1727. St.
Shipley, George. T Dec 1763 *Neptune*. K.
Shipley, John. AT Summer 1754. Y.
Shipley, Richard of Over Haddon. R for America Feb 1713. Db.

Shipley, Robert. R for Barbados Dec 1670. M.

Shipman, William of Northampton. R for America Jly 1678. No.

Shipmarsh, Robert (1691). *See* Welsh. K.

Shipen, Nathaniel. S & TB Aug 1754. G.

Shipper, William. S Jan 1745. L.

Shipton, Robert of St. Michael, Oxford. R for America Feb 1713. O.

Shirley, Elizabeth. R for America Aug 1715. M.

Shirley, John. R 14 yrs Jly 1774. M.

Shirley, Mary, als Davis, Catherine. S & T May 1744 *Justitia*. L.

Sherley als Blyth, Thomas. R Dec 1698 AT Jan 1699. M.

Shirston. *See* Sherston.

Shoebotham, Thomas. S s at Leek Lent 1750. St.

Shoebridge, John. S Jan T Feb 1726 *Supply* LC Annapolis May 1726. M.

Shoebrooks, William. S Aug 1773. So.

Shoesmith, Robert. Rebel T 1685.

Shone, Katherine. S s sheep Lent R 14 yrs Summer 1742. Sh.

Shonk, John. S Summer 1759 R 14 yrs Lent T Apr 1760 *Thetis*. E.

Shooter, Charles. S & T 14 yrs Apr 1741 *Mediterranean*. L.

Shooter, John of Putney. R for Barbados or Jamaica Jly 1715. Sy.

Shore. *See* Shaw.

Shores, Edward. S & T for life Mar 1750 *Tryal*. L.

Shores, William. S Jan-May 1738. M.

Shoreton, Mathew. T Nov 1743 *George William*. Ht.

Shorland, Peter. Rebel T 1685.

Short, Aron. T Sep 1730 *Smith*. Sx.

Short, Edward. R Dec 1698 AT Jan 1699. M.

Shorte, George of Cow Cross, yeoman. R for West Indies Sep 1614. M.

Short, George. S Feb T Apr 1768 *Thornton*. L.

Short, Jane. S Jly T Aug 1721 *Owners Goodwill* LC Annapolis Jly 1722. L.

Short, John of Sturminster Newton. R for Barbados Feb 1701. Do.

Short, John. S Aug T Sep 1725 *Forward* LC Annapolis Dec 1725. L.

Short, John. R 14 yrs Aug 1752. So.

Short, Nicholas. S s lead Jan T Apr 1735 *Patapsco* LC Annapolis Oct 1735. M.

Short, Philip. R 14 yrs Dec 1773. M.

Short, Richard. PT Apr R Jly 1675. M.

Short, Richard. R 14 yrs Mar 1759. Ha.

Short, Richard. SW & T Jan 1769 *Thornton*. M.

Short, Thomas. S & T Oct 1730 *Forward* LC Potomack Jan 1731. L.

Shorter, Anne. S May T Jly 1722 *Alexander* to Nevis or Jamaica. M.

Shorter, Henry of Sevenoaks. R for Barbados or Jamaica Jly 1688 & Feb 1690. K.

Shorter, John. R for Barbados or Jamaica Oct 1694. L.

Shorter, Martha. R for Barbados or Jamaica Oct 1694. L.

Shorter, Rebecca of Hurst. R for America Jly 1691. Be.

Shorthouse, Elizabeth. AT from QS Lent 1775. Db.

Shortoe, George. S Mar 1773. So.

Shortoe, William (1773). *See* Fuller, Thomas. So.

Shotland, Daniel. PT May R for Barbados or Jamaica Aug 1700. M.

Shotton, James. S s pumps at Dudley Lent 1772. Wo.

Shoug, John. S s fowls Summer 1739. Be.
Shove, Henry of Worth. R for Barbados or Jamaica Jly 1696. Sx.
Shovell, John. S Jly T Aug 1721 *Prince Royal* LC Va Nov 1721. M.
Schovell, Philip. S Jan-May T Jun 1738 *Forward* to Md or Va. M.
Shovel, William (1734). *See* Griffith. M.
Show, William. SQS Bradford Jan 1725. Y.
Showle, Thomas. S & TB Aug 1739. G.
Showell, Thomas. S & T Dee 1771 *Justitia.* L.
Showring, James. S Aug 1754. So.
Shrieve, John. S Lent R 14 yrs Summer 1747. E.
Shreve, Robert. R for America Jly 1694. Wa.
Shrive, Thomas. S Lent 1721. G.
Shrimplin, John. S Summer 1749. E.
Shrimpton, William. S & T 14 yrs Oct 1730 *Forward* LC Potomack Jan
    1731. M.
Shrobb, Edward. R Summer 1773. Ht.
Shrons, Godfrey. S Lent 1763. K.
Shropshire, John. R for America Mar 1690. Db.
Shropshire, Mary. S Sep T Dec 1736 *Dorsetshire* to Va. M.
Shrouder, John. R for America Jly 1694. Le.
Shrub, Samuel (1772). *See* Hoskins. So.
Shuckley, Thomas (1688). *See* Shutler. Do.
Shuffle, William (1734). *See* Griffith. M.
Shufflebottom, Elizabeth. S Oct 1737 T Jan 1738 *Dorsetshire* to Va. M.
Shuker, Betton. S s sheep Lent R 14 yrs Summer 1768. Sh.
Shuler, John. S Jun T Aug 1769 *Douglas.* L.
Shurman. *See* Sherman.
Shute, Ann. S & T Apr 1741 *Mediterranean.* L.
Shute, Hannah. S & T Dec 1759 *Phoenix.* L.
Shute, Henry. S for Va Jly 1718. De.
Shute, Jane. TB to Va from QS 1759. De.
Shute, John Gilbert. S Aug 1767. So.
Shute, Mary (1727). *See* Gollidge. Sy.
Shutler als Shuckley, Thomas of Blandford, innholder. R (Oxford Circ)
    for America Mar 1688. Do.
Shuttleworth als Shuttlewood, John. S & R Lent 1775. Le.
Sibballs, Robert. S s pewter pots Dec 1735 T Jan 1736 *Dorsetshire* LC Va
    Sep 1736. M.
Siberry, John. S s sheep Lent R 14 yrs Summer 1750. Li.
Sibley, Henry. S s watch at Maulden & R Lent 1775. Bd.
Sibley, Richard. R 14 yrs Mar 1765. Co.
Siborn, Thomas of Christchurch. SQS s lead coffins Jan 1769. Sy.
Sibre, Samuel. S Apr 1748. L.
Sibson, Peter. SQS s coal from Sir James Lowther Easter 1774. Du.
Sipthorp, Alexander. S s at Walton & R Summer 1772. Bu.
Sibthorpe, Ann. SQS & T Jly 1771 *Scarsdale.* M.
Sibthorpe, John. T Jun 1728 *Elizabeth.* Ht.
Sibthorpe, William. S Jly 1756. M.
Sickle als Parish, Thomas of Bottisham. S s gelding Summer 1738. Ca.
Sickwell als Aldis, William. S Dec 1733 T Jan 1734 *Caesar* LC Va Jly
    1734. M.

Sidaway, Samuel. S Sep-Oct T Dec 1753 *Whiteing*. M.

Siday, Elizabeth wife of William. S 14 yrs for receiving Feb T Apr 1771 *Thornton*. L.

Siday, John. S Lent 1754. E.

Siddall als Siddah, John of Bawtry. SQS East Retford s brandy Jan TB May 1724. Nt.

Siddale, Richard. T Apr 1725 *Sukey* LC Md Sep 1725. Sy.

Siddell, Sarah (1767). *See* Boast. M.

Sidden, Joseph. SQS Mar TB Aug 1720 to be shipped to Md from Liverpool. Db.

Sidnell, Abraham. S s at Marshfield Summer TB Aug 1748. G.

Sidnell, John. S May T Jun 1764 *Dolphin*. M.

Sidow, John. LC from *Robert* Annapolis Jun 1725. X.

Sidwell, Jonathan. R 14 yrs Mar 1773. So.

Sidwell, William. S & T 14 yrs Oct 1720 *Gilbert* to Md. M.

Siggins als Perkins, Mary. S Feb T Mar 1730 *Patapsco* to Md. M.

Sikkard, Mary. S & T Apr 1733 *Patapsco* to Md. M.

Silcock als Chamber, Ann. S Jan-Apr 1748. M.

Silcock, Jacob. TB Sep 1765. Db.

Silcox, Susan. S Mar 1724. Wi.

Silke, John (1685). *See* Thompson. L.

Silk, John. T Apr 1765 *Ann*. Bu.

Silk, Mary. S & T Apr 1733 *Patapsco* LC Annapolis Nov 1733. M.

Silk, Thomas. TB to Va from QS 1738. De.

Silkwood, Margaret. S Aug T 14 yrs Sep 1725 *Forward* LC Md Dec 1725. M.

Silley, Sarah. S Apr T Sep 1737 *Pretty Patsy* to Md. M.

Silly, Thomas. R 14 yrs Aug 1720. De.

Silsby, James. T Jan 1765 *Tryal*. M.

Silver Heels (1742). *See* Flemmar, William. L.

Silver, Ann. R 14 yrs Oct 1772. M.

Silver, Isaac. S May T Nov 1759 *Phoenix*. M.

Silver, John. S Jun T Nov 1743 *George William*. M.

Silver, Thomas, aged 20, dark, husbandman. LC from *Jonathan* Md Jly 1724. X.

Silver, William. T Sep 1758 *Tryal*. Sy.

Silvester, Charles (1699). *See* Gale. M.

Silvester, John. S s lead Jun T Sep 1767 *Justitia*. L.

Silvester, John. T Apr 1769 *Tryal*. E.

Silvester, Richard. T 14 yrs Sep 1764 *Justitia*. Sy.

Silvester, Richard. S & R 14 yrs Summer 1774. St.

Silvester, Thomas. SQS Apr 1773. M.

Silvey, Aaron. S Oct 1772. L.

Silvy, Thomas of Warrington. SQS Jan 1775. La.

Simberell als Simberlen, Francis. R 14 yrs Dec 1773. M.

Simcock, George. S s cloth at Gnosall Summer 1745. St.

Simcock, Theophilus. S s at Penn Lent 1773. Bu.

Symcocks, William of Condover. R for America Jly 1677. Sh.

Simkins. *See* Simpkins.

Simmons. *See* Symonds.

Simms, Elizabeth, als wife of William Terry. S Jly-Sep 1754. M.

Sims, George (1766). *See* Dorman. Su.

Syms, Henry. Rebel T 1685.

Simms, Henry. S May 1745. M.

Syms, Isaac. R for Barbados or Jamaica Oct 1694. L.

Syms als Hayles, Isabel. R for Barbados Dec 1683. M.

Syms, Isabella. T Jun 1738 *Forward*. Sy.

Simms, James. S Apr T Jly 1770 *Scarsdale*. M.

Simms, Jane. S May-Jly 1748. M.

Sims, John (1737). *See* Smith. L.

Simms, John. S Apr T May 1750 *Lichfield*. M.

Syms, John. S Mar 1752. Do.

Simms, Joseph. SQS Dec 1764 T Jan 1765 *Tryal*. M.

Symmes, Mary (1668). *See* Edwards. L.

Sims, Mary. S Mar TB to Va Aug 1749. Wi.

Syms, Richard. R for Jamaica Aug 1661. L.

Simms als Figgott, Richard. S for stabbing mare Summer 1751 R 14 yrs
    Lent TB Mar 1752. G.

Sims, Richard. SQS Jan 1765. Ha.

Syms, Thomas of Oldham. S s lace Summmer 1736. La.

Syms, William. S Mar 1750 TB to Va. De.

Simner, Mary of Whiston, spinster. SQS May 1764. La.

Simon, Isaac. S Lent 1739. Ch.

Simon, John. Rebel T 1685.

Simon, John. S Jan-Feb T Apr 1753 *Thames*. M.

Simon, Joseph. S Apr 1742. Ha.

Simonitz, George. S Lent R 14 yrs Summer 1742. Y.

Simons. *See* Symonds.

Simpcoe, Jane. PT Oct 1685. M.

Simper als Crop, Sarah. S Mar 1733 LC from *Patapsco* Md Nov
    1733. Wi.

Simpkin, Ruth. S Lent 1748. Sx.

Simkin, Thomas. S & T Oct 1729 *Forward* LC Va Jun 1730. M.

Simkins, Edward. S May T Jun 1726 *Loyal Margaret* LC Md Oct
    1726. M.

Simpkins, Edward. SQS Devizes & TB to Va Apr 1750. Wi.

Simpkins, Hannah. S Oct 1748 T Jan 1749 *Laura*. L.

Simpkinson, Robert. S Dec 1749-Jan 1750 T Mar 1750 *Tryal*. M.

Simpron, Robert. T Dec 1736 *Dorsetshire*. E.

Simpson, Alexander. R 14 yrs Mar 1764. De.

Simpson, Andrew. T Oct 1732 *Caesar*. E.

Simpson, Ann (1692). *See* Smith. M.

Simpson, Anne. S Jly T Aug 1721 *Prince Royal* LC Va Nov 1721. M.

Simpson, Ann. S Dec 1746. L.

Simpson, Anne. R 14 yrs City Summer 1747. Nl.

Simpson, Ann. S Lent R 14 yrs Summer 1751. Db.

Simpson, Ann. S Feb 1775. L.

Simpson, Catherine wife of Charles. S Jun-Dec 1738 T Jan 1739
    Dorsetshire. M.

Simpson als Willcockson, Charles als Thomas. S Lent R 14 yrs Summer
    1749. St.

Simpson, Daniel. S Summer 1751 R 14 yrs Lent T May 1752 *Lichfield*. Sy.

Simpson, Daniel. S for highway robbery & R 14 yrs Summer 1772. O.

Simpson, Elizabeth. S Oct T Nov 1759 *Phoenix*. L.

Simpson, George. S s horse Lent R 14 yrs Summer 1754. Nt.

Simpson, Henry. S Lent T Oct 1723 *Forward* from London. Y.

Simpson, Israel. S s peruke at St. Mary Magdalene, Bridgenorth, Summer 1736. Sh.

Simpson, James. S Oct T Nov 1728 *Forward* LC Rappahannock Jun 1729. L.

Simpson, James of St. George, Southwark, mariner. SQS Nov T Dec 1753 *Whiteing*. Sy.

Simpson, James. S for forging will & R 14 yrs Summer 1760; later chosen for Army service. Du.

Simpson, James. S Lent 1763. Ht.

Simpson, James. R Jly T 14 yrs Sep 1767 *Justitia*. M.

Simpson, Jane. T Jun 1727 *Susanna*. K.

Simpson, Jeremiah. S Apr 1775. M.

Simpson, John of Besford. R (Western Circ) for America Jly 1700. Wo.

Simpson, John. AT Oct R & T Dec 1716 *Lewis* to Jamaica. M.

Simpson, John. S Aug T Oct 1723 *Forward*. L.

Simpson, John. LC from *Elizabeth* Potomack Aug 1729. X.

Simpson, John. S Summer 1733 R 14 yrs Summer 1734. Y.

Simpson, John. R 14 yrs City Summer 1734. Nl.

Simpson, John. S Jan-Feb T Apr 1753 *Thames*. M.

Simpson, John. S Dec 1756. M.

Simpson, John. S Summer 1757. Su.

Simpson, John. S Jan T Feb 1765 *Tryal*. L.

Simpson, Jonathan. S Feb 1761. M.

Simpson, Joseph. S s at Knaresborough Lent 1773. Y.

Simpson, Margaret (1681). *See* Johnson. Y.

Simpson, Mary (1720). *See* Jones. M.

Sympson, Mary. S Aug T Oct 1724 *Forward* LC Annapolis Jun 1725. L.

Simpson, Mary als Alice, wife of James of Woodplumpton. SQS Apr 1741. La.

Simpson, Mathew. S Jan T Feb 1742 *Industry* to Md. M.

Simpson, Richard. S s at St. Matthew, Ipswich, & R Summer 1775.

Simpson, Richard. S for burglary Lent R 14 yrs Summer 1728. St.

Simpson, Richard. R 14 yrs Summer 1729. Nl.

Simpson, Samuel. S Lent 1759. Li.

Simpson, Stathey. LC from *Owners Goodwill* Annapolis Jly 1722. X.

Simpson, Thomas of Wadhurst. R for Barbados or Jamaica Feb 1686. Sx.

Simpson, Thomas of Middlewich. R (Oxford Circ) for America Mar 1701. Ch.

Simpson, Thomas. T Oct 1721 *William & John*. K.

Sympson, Thomas. S & T Jan 1722 *Gilbert* LC Annapolis Jly 1722. L.

Simpson, Thomas. S s at Layton Lent 1729. Sh.

Simpson, Thomas. AT Lent 1748; S for being at large after sentence of transportation Lent R 14 yrs Summer 1750. Y.

Simpson, Thomas. S Summer 1762 R 14 yrs Lent 1763. Nt.

Simpson, William. T Aug 1720 *Owners Goodwill*. K.

Sympson, William. R 14 yrs Mar 1731. Wi.

Simpson, William. LC from *Smith* Va 1732. X.

Simpson, William. S Summer 1742 R 14 yrs Lent 1743. La.

Simpson, William. S Apr 1748. L.

Simpson, William. S Summer 1749 R 14 yrs Lent T May 1750
  Lichfield. K.

Simpson, William (1763). *See* Watson, George. M.

Sinclear, Anthony. T Jly 1722 *Alexander*. Sy.

Sinclare, James of Monmouth, gunsmith. R for America Mar 1688. Mo.

Sinclare, John of Monmouth. R for America Mar 1688. Mo.

Sinclear, Margaret. SWK Jly 1774. K.

Sinclair, William. T May 1751 *Tryal*. Sy.

Sinden, Edward. R Summer 1774. Sx.

Siney, John. T for life Jly 1770 *Scarsdale*. Sy.

Sinfield, William. LC from *Mary* Port York Jun 1721. X.

Sinfield, William. S s sheep Lent R 14 yrs Summer 1765. No.

Singer, Elliot. S Jun T Sep 1758 *Tryal*. L.

Singer, Isaac. SQS & T Jly 1773 *Tayloe* to Va. M.

Singer, Michael. S May-Jly 1774. M.

Singer, Robert. R Jun T Aug 1769 *Douglas*. M.

Singer, Thomas. S May-Jly 1774. M.

Singing Jenny (1745). *See* Smith, Jane. L.

Singleton, Ann. S Sep T Dec 1770 *Justitia*. M.

Singleton, Bridget. S Feb 1773. L.

Singleton, Bridget. S Jan-Feb 1775. M.

Singleton, Edward. SQS Mar TB Sep 1726. Nt.

Singleton, Edward. S & T Sep 1757 *Thetis*. M.

Singleton, James of St. Olave, Southwark. R for Barbados Aug 1662. Sy.

Singleton, Sarah. S s aprons Jun T Dec 1736 *Dorsetshire* to Va. M.

Sincklowe, Jane. R for Barbados or Jamaica Jly 1685. M.

Sinnott, Richard. S Feb T Apr 1765 *Ann*. M.

Sinton, Robert. S s horse & R 14 yrs Lent 1775. Y.

Sipthorpe. *See* Sibthorpe.

Sirbin, David. R for Barbados Dec 1668. M.

Sircomb, Thomas. R 14 yrs Aug 1731 TB to Va. De.

Sise, Sarah. SQS Oct 1768 T Jan 1769 *Thornton*. M.

Siseland, William. S Oct 1766 T Jan 1767 *Tryal*. L.

Sisson, Francis. R for America Jly 1688. Li.

Sissons, John. AT Lent T Oct 1723 *Forward* from London. Y.

Sithern, John. SQS Coventry Aug AT Sep 1742. Wa.

Sivers, John (1731). *See* Langford. O.

Skagg, Elizabeth wife of Richard. S & T Oct 1730 *Forward* but died on
  passage. M.

Skane, Christian. S Aug TB to Va Sep 1767. Wi.

Skarnley, John. S Sep 1775. M.

Skate, Lucy. S Jun 1754. L.

Skatt, Timothy Featherstonehaugh. S Jly 1774. L.

Skea, John. S Lent R 14 yrs Summer 1759. St.

Skeet, William (1771). *See* Read. Ha.

Skeats, John. R 14 yrs Jly 1743. Ha.

Skeele, William. S Feb T May 1767 *Thornton*. L.

Skegg, George. T Apr 1741 *Speedwell* or *Mediterranean*. Ht.

Skegg, William. T Apr 1741 *Speedwell* or *Mediterranean*. Ht.

Skeggs, James. S s sheep Lent R 14 yrs Summer T Sep 1755 *Tryal*. E.

Skelhorne, Samuel. S Lent 1774. Wa.

Skelt, John. S Feb 1754. L.

Skelton, Eleanor. S Summer 1749. K.

Skelton, John. S Summer 1718 R 14 yrs Summer 1721 T Oct 1723 *Forward* from London. Y.

Skelton, John. S s at St. George Colgate, Norwich, Summer 1775. Nf.

Skelton, Judith of Wood Walton. R for America Mar 1686. Hu.

Skelton, Mary. SQS Feb T Apr 1772 *Thornton*. M.

Skelton, Richard. SQS Oct TB to Md Nov 1738. So.

Skelton, Susannah, spinster. S & T Dec 1767 *Neptune*. L.

Skelton, William. AT Summer 1755. Y.

Sketchley, Thomas. S Mar TB to Va Apr 1767. Le.

Skidmore, Joseph. R 14 yrs Lent 1721. St.

Skyff, John. Rebel T 1685.

Skill, John. R for Barbados or Jamaica Mar 1698. E.

Skill als Thompson, John. S & T Jan 1722 *Gilbert* LC Annapolis Jly 1722. M.

Skillam, Isaac of Fladbury. S s sheets Summer 1718. Wo.

Skillam, Isaac. S s clothing at Worcester Summer 1724. Wo.

Skillard, William. TB to Va 1768. De.

Skillett, Thomas. S s sheep at Great Gidding & R 14 yrs Lent 1775. Hu.

Skillington, William. R Dec 1698 AT Jan 1699. M.

Skinner, Ann. S Feb T Mar 1758 *Dragon*. M.

Skinner, Ann wife of John of St. Saviour, Southwark. SQS Oct T Nov 1762 *Prince William*. Sy.

Skinner, Anthony. S Aug 1734. De.

Skinner, Edward. S Aug 1736. De.

Skinner, Elizabeth. S Mar 1751. De.

Skinner, Isaac. S Lent 1768; found at large in Bures & S to hang Lent 1769. Su.

Skinner, James. S Mar 1729. So.

Skinner, Moses. R 14 yrs Jly 1767. Ha.

Skinner, Robert. S Mar 1729. So.

Skinner, Thomas. S s mare & R 14 yrs Summer 1771. No.

Skinner, William of Kidderminster, yeoman. R for America Feb 1713. Wo.

Skinner, William. S Aug 1736. De.

Skipton, William (1729). *See* Boddy. Y.

Skuce, Catherine. S 14 yrs for receiving Lent 1768. G.

Skuse, James. R 14 yrs Aug TB to Va Sep 1753. Wi.

Skylight, Margaret. S Dec 1743 T Feb 1744 *Neptune* to Md. M.

Skyrme, John. S Oct 1744-Jan 1745. M.

Skyrrell, Richard. T Jun 1738 *Forward*. Ht.

Slack, David. S for forgery Lent R 14 yrs Summer 1770. St.

Slack, John. S s mare at Halifax Lent 1765. Y.

Slack, Mary (1733). *See* Stanley. St.

Slack, Stephen of Retford. R for America Jly 1678. Nt.

Slack als Slark, Thomas. S s shoes Lent 1755. Be.
Slad, William. LC from *Sukey* Annapolis Sep 1725. X.
Slade, Humphrey. Rebel T 1685.
Slade, John. Rebel T 1685.
Slade, John. SQS New Sarum Jan TB to Va Apr 1740. Wi.
Slade, John. S Lent R 14 yrs Summer 1755. O.
Slade, Mary (1753). *See* Whitaker. M.
Slade, Moses (1773). *See* Morgan. Wi.
Slade, Richard. S Apr 1770. So.
Slade, William. SQS & TB Apr 1755. So.
Slader, Matthew. R for Barbados Jun 1670. M.
Slake, John. S Mar 1772. Do.
Slam, James (1752). *See* Keiling. M.
Slamer, Elizabeth. S Lent 1769. Li.
Slaney, Mary, als Pulson, Cicely, als Taylor, Mary. S s at Newport Lent
    1744. Sh.
Slape, Thomas. SQS Oct TB to Md Nov 1738. So.
Slark, Thomas (1755). *See* Slack. Be.
Slate, Ann. S Apr T May 1743 *Indian Queen* to Potomack. M.
Slate, Frances. S Oct T Dec 1724 *Rappahannock* to Va. M.
Slate, George. T Jan 1736 *Dorsetshire*. K.
Slate, James. S Jan-Apr 1749. M.
Slate, John Jr. of St. Olave, Southwark. R for Barbados Sep 1669. Sy.
Slater, Isaac. S Summer 1756. K.
Slater, John. S s at Burton Lent 1745. St.
Slater, John. S Jan-Apr 1749. M.
Slater, Joshua. R for Barbados Jly 1675. L.
Slater, Margaret. S s at Leek Lent 1755. St.
Slater, Robert. S for evasion of excise duty Summer 1757 R 14 yrs Lent
    1758. La.
Slater, William. TB Apr 1743. Db.
Slater, William. S s handkerchief at Barnard Castle Summer 1768. Du.
Slates, William. T Apr 1725 *Sukey* LC Md Sep 1725. Sy.
Slatford, Joseph. S Apr 1773. L.
Slaughter, Henry of Rotherhithe. R for Barbados or Jamaica Feb
    1683. Sy.
Slaughter, John. PT Jun R Oct 1673 AT Jun 1674. M.
Slaughter, John. S s silver cup at Leominster Summer 1757. He.
Slaughter als Stoughter, John. S s sheep Lent R 14 yrs Summer 1764. Li.
Slaughter, Mary. T Apr 1732 *Patapsco*. E.
Slaughter, Mary. S Jly-Sep 1754. M.
Slaughter, Rebecca. S & T Jan 1722 *Gilbert* LC Annapolis Jly 1722. M.
Slaughter, Robert. R for Barbados Jun 1663. M.
Slavin, Cornelius. S Sep T 14 yrs Oct 1768 *Justitia*. M.
Slaving, Elizabeth. S Apr T Jun 1768 *Tryal*. M.
Slayman, Cornelius. R for Barbados Dec 1693 AT Jan 1694. M.
Slaytor, Mary. S Lent 1740. Y.
Sleath, Joseph. S Jly T Sep 1767 *Justitia*. L.
Slee, Thomas. S Apr 1734. So.
Sleeman, William. TB to Va 1770. De.

Sleightholme, Thomas. S s sheep at Great Broughton Summer 1764 R 14 yrs Lent TB Aug 1765. Y.

Slice, John (1719). *See* Haselam. St.

Slider, Mary. S May T Jun 1726 *Loyal Margaret* LC Annapolis Oct 1726. M.

Slight, John of St. Paul, Covent Garden. SW for false pretences Jan 1775. M.

Slim, Abraham (1771). *See* Shin. M.

Slim, John (1726). *See* Axton, Samuel. M.

Sloan, Ann. S & T Oct 1722 *Forward*. L.

Slocombe, Benjamin. S Mar 1730. So.

Slocombe, George. SQS Oct TB to Md Nov 1738. So.

Slocombe, Henry of Huish Champflower. R for Barbados Jan 1675. So.

Slocombe, Isaac. R 14 yrs Mar 1773. So.

Slocombe, John (1728). *See* Simmons. So.

Slocomb, Sarah. S Mar 1757. So.

Slote, John of Lambeth. SQS Jan T Mar 1764 *Tryal*. Sy.

Slowe als Abraham, Ann wife of Thomas. R for Barbados Mar 1683. L.

Slow, Edward. S Jan T Feb 1733 *Smith*. L.

Slow, John of Stanground. R for America Feb 1688. Hu.

Slowly, John. R 14 yrs Aug 1753. De.

Sly, John. R 14 yrs Mar 1757. So.

Slye, Robert. Rebel T 1685.

Slye, Robert. S s spoons at St. John, Gloucester, Lent 1772. G.

Slye, Thomas. S May T Jly 1723 *Alexander* LC Annapolis Jun 1725. L.

Sly, William. S Lent R Summer 1726. No.

Smaddall als Smeddell, Richard. S City s at North Street Lent 1766. Y.

Smaldy, John. S & T Dec 1731 *Forward* to Md or Va. M.

Smale, Elizabeth. TB to Va from QS 1736. De.

Smale als Stevens, Elizabeth. S Mar 1762 TB to Va. De.

Smale, John. TB to Va 1728. De.

Smale, Joseph. TB to Va from QS 1737. De.

Smale, Mary. TB to Va from QS 1740. De.

Small, Dorrell. S May T 14 yys Jun 1738 *Forward*. L.

Small, Francis. R for Barbados Mar 1681. M.

Small, James. R 14 yrs Mar 1754 TB to Va. De.

Small, Mary. S s cloaks Feb T May 1736 *Patapsco* to Md. M.

Small, Mary. S s hemp yarn at Rodington Summer 1767. Sh.

Small, Robert. S Dec 1763 T Mar 1764 *Tryal*. M.

Small, Thomas. T Dec 1767 *Neptune*. K.

Small, Tobias of Romford, woolcomber. SQS Jan T May 1750 *Lichfield*. E.

Small, William. SQS Mar 1752. Ha.

Smallacombe, Thomasin. R 14 yrs Mar 1742. Co.

Smalley, George. S s sheep Summer 1750 R 14 yrs Lent 1751. Le.

Smallman, Ann. S Summer 1756 R 14 yrs Lent 1757. Wo.

Smallman, John. S Feb T Mar 1764 *Tryal*. M.

Smalman, Martha. S Mar 1720 T *Honor* LC Port York Jan 1721. L.

Smalman, Mary of St. Saviour, Southwark. R for Barbados or Jamaica Jly 1677. Sy.

Smallman, William. S s at Pershore Lent 1774. Wo.

Smallpass, Richard. S 14 yrs Summer T Oct 1750 *Rachael*. Sy.

Smallridge, Samuel. R 14 yrs Aug 1773. De.

Smallwood, Joseph. TB Feb 1770. Db.

Smart, Ann. S s at New Windsor Lent 1744 R 14 yrs Lent 1745. Be.

Smart, Charles of Edial. R for America Jly 1696. St.

Smart, Francis. S s at Kidderminster Summer 1764. Wo.

Smart, Gabriel. Rebel T 1685.

Smart, Hanna (1722). *See* Starky. M.

Smart, James. S for highway robbery Summer 1755 R 14 yrs Lent 1756;
S to hang Lent 1759 for returning from transportation. No.

Smart, John. S Mar 1750. Ha.

Smart, John. R 14 yrs Mar 1758. So.

Smart, John. SQS Jan TB Mar 1768. So.

Smart, Jonas. S Feb T May 1719 *Margaret*; sold to William Martin Md
Sep 1719. L.

Smart, Mary. S Jan 1745. L.

Smart als Aviland, Richard of Brimpsfield. R for Barbados Jly 1664. G.

Smart, Robert of Knadeby. R for Barbados Jly 1683. We.

Smart, Sarah. S Sep T Dec 1763 *Neptune*. M.

Smart, Stephen. S s at Kidderminster Summer 1764. Wo.

Smart, Thomas. R Summer 1728 (SP). Nf.

Smart, William. S Summer 1751. Nl.

Smathwit als Johnson als Jackson, John of Pennistone. R for Barbados
Jly 1682. Y.

Smeddell, Richard (1766). *See* Smaddall. Y.

Smee, Robert. S for burglary Lent R 14 yrs Summer T Oct 1750
Rachael. E.

Smeeton, David. S for highway robbery Summer 1767 R 14 yrs Lent
1768. No.

Smeeton, John of St. George, Southwark. SQS Jan T Mar 1764 *Tryal*. Sy.

Smeeton, Robert. S s horse Lent R 14 yrs Summer 1752. Li.

Smelley, John. S Lent 1756. E.

Smethurst, Elizabeth wife of Ralph of Unsworth, husbandman. SQS
Jan 1750. La.

Smethurst, John. R 14 yrs Summer 1740. La.

Smethurst, Thomas of Pilkington. SQS Oct 1753. La.

Smethurst, William. T Dec 1753 *Whiteing*. K.

Smith, Abel (1766). See Jennings. K.

Smith, Abraham. S Aug T Oct 1724 *Forward* LC Annapolis Jun 1725. L.

Smith, Abraham of Wiswell. SQS Oct 1747. La.

Smith, Adam. Rebel T 1685.

Smith, Alexander. S Lent AT Summer 1730. Y.

Smith, Alexander. S Lent 1737. Bd.

Smith, Alexander. S Feb T Apr 1768 *Thornton*. M.

Smith, Alice. S & T Mar 1763 *Neptune*. L.

Smith, Alice. SQS Jan T Apr 1768 *Thornton*. M.

Smith, Ambrose. R for Va or East Indies Jun 1618. M.

Smith, Amy. S Norwich Summer 1764. Nf.

Smith, Andrew. T Sep 1730 *Smith*. E.

Smith, Ann, spinster, als wife of Michael Harris. R for Barbados Aug
1664. L.

Smith, Anne of Cobham. R for Barbados Apr 1668. Sy.

Smyth, Anne als Swift. R for Barbados Oct 1673. L.

Smyth, Anne. R for Barbados Dec 1681. L.

Smyth als Greene, Anne. R for Barbados Sep 1682. L.

Smith als Simpson, Ann. PT Apr 1692. M.

Smith, Ann. R for Barbados or Jamaica Dec 1693. L.

Smith, Ann (1695). See Bowcher. M.

Smith als Vanderson, Ann. R & T Dec 1716 *Lewis*. M.

Smith, Anne. S Jly T 14 yrs Aug 1718 *Eagle* but died on passage. L.

Smith, Ann, aged 27, dark. S Apr T Oct 1720 *Gilbert* LC Annapolis May 1721. L.

Smith, Anne. S May T Jly 1722 *Alexander*. L.

Smith als Bryan, Anne. S & T Oct 1729 *Forward* LC Va Jun 1730. M.

Smith, Ann als Elizabeth. S & T Oct 1730 *Forward* LC Potomack Jan 1731. L.

Smith, Ann. S City Summer 1733. Nl.

Smith, Ann. S Feb T Apr 1734 *Patapsco* to Md. M.

Smith, Ann. S s cloth & T Dec 1734 *Caesar* LC Va Jly 1735. M.

Smith, Anne. S City Summer 1735. Nl.

Smith, Ann. T May 1736 *Patapsco*. Ht.

Smith, Ann. S Norwich for perjury Summer 1736. Nf.

Smith, Ann. S Dec 1737 T Jan 1738 *Dorsetshire*. L.

Smith, Ann of St. Paul, Covent Garden, spinster. S s linen & T Dec 1740 *Vernon*. M.

Smith, Ann wife of Charles. S Feb T Apr 1741 *Speedwell* or *Mediterranean*. M.

Smith, Ann. S Feb-Apr 1746. M.

Smith, Ann. S Dec 1748 T Jan 1749 *Laura*. L.

Smith, Ann of Tryerning. SQS Jan 1749. E.

Smith als Harrison, Ann, als Walton als Walker, Esther of Latham. SQS Oct 1749. La.

Smith, Ann. S Dec 1753-Jan 1754. M.

Smith, Ann of Great Birch, spinster. SQS Jan T Apr 1760 *Thetis*. E.

Smith als Dixon, Ann. SL & T Sep 1765 *Justitia*. Sy.

Smith, Ann. R Dec 1765 T for life Jan 1766 *Tryal*. M.

Smith, Ann. S Jly T Sep 1767 *Justitia*. M.

Smith, Ann of Bermondsey, spinster. SQS 14 yrs Oct T Dec 1771 *Justitia*. Sy.

Smith, Ann. S Jan-Feb 1774. M.

Smith, Anthony. S s at St. Nicholas, Worcester, Summer 1736. Wo.

Smith, Anthony. S Lent R 14 yrs Summer TB Aug 1751. G.

Smith, Anthony. S May T Jun 1768 *Tryal*. M.

Smith, Barwell, S Oct-Dec 1754. M.

Smith, Benjamin of Burton on Hill. R for America Feb 1687. G.

Smith, Benjamin. S Jly T 14 yrs Aug 1718 *Eagle* LC Charles Town Mar 1719. L.

Smith, Benjamin. S for life Oct 1751-Jan 1752. M.

Smith, Benjamin. S Lent T Jun 1756 *Lyon*. K.

Smith, Benjamin. S Lent 1760. Y.

Smith, Benjamin. S Jan T Feb 1765 *Tryal*. L.

Smith, Benjamin. T 14 yrs Apr 1768 *Thornton*. Sy.

Smith, Benjamin. S s at St. Michael, New Malton, & R 14 yrs Lent TB Aug 1770. Y.

Smith, Bryan. R for America Feb 1700. Li.

Smith, Brian. R for America Jly 1708. Li.

Smith, Katherine of Westbury. R for America Mar 1680. G.

Smith, Katherine (1687). *See* Baulfield, Elizabeth. M.

Smith, Catherine (1721). *See* Fares. M.

Smith, Catherine. T Apr 1741 *Speedwell* or *Mediterranean*. Sy.

Smith, Catherine. TB to America from QS 1751. De.

Smith als Nordis, Catherine. S & T Sep 1767 *Justitia*. M.

Smith, Catherine. S & T Dec 1769 *Justitia*. M.

Smith, Catherine. R Lent 1773. Sy.

Smyth, Charles. R for Barbados Oct 1673. L.

Smith, Charles. T May 1744 *Justitia*. K.

Smith, Charles. S Dec 1749-Jan 1750 T Mar 1750 *Tryal*. M.

Smith, Charles. S Lent R 14 yrs Summer 1750. Li.

Smith, Charles. S Oct 1761. L.

Smith, Charles. S Jly T Sep 1764 *Justitia*. M.

Smith, Charles. S Lent 1767. Nf.

Smith, Charlotte wife of Samuel of Bloomsbury. S s household goods & T Dec 1734 *Caesar* LC Va Jly 1735. M.

Smith, Charlotte. T Jan 1738 *Dorsetshire*. Sy.

Smith, Charlotte. S Apr T Jun 1768 *Tryal*. M.

Smyth, Christopher. R for Barbados Sep 1682. L.

Smith, Christopher. S Jan T 14 yrs Feb 1744 *Neptune* to Md. M.

Smith, Claudius. S Jly 1723. Wi.

Smith, Daniel of St. James, Colchester. S Lent 1745. E.

Smith, Daniel, als Denny, William. S s gelding Summer 1755 R 14 yrs Lent 1756. Hu.

Smith, Daniel (1774). *See* Dominy. Bd.

Smith, David. SQS Dec 1762 T Mar 1763 *Neptune*. M.

Smith, Deborah. R Jly 1702 to be T at her own expense or otherwise executed. M.

Smith, Deborah. Died on passage in *Gilbert* 1721. X.

Smith, Dickey of Pontefract, slater. R for Barbados or Jamaica Mar 1694. Y.

Smith, Dorothy. S City Summer 1733. Nl.

Smith als Morley, Edward of Munford. R for Barbados Mar 1679. Nf.

Smith, Edward of Leigh, yeoman. R for America Feb 1700. St.

Smith, Edward. S for poaching deer in Bere Forest Mar 1741. Ha.

Smith, Edward. S Dec 1749-Jan 1750 T Mar 1750 *Tryal*. M.

Smith, Edward. S Lent R 14 yrs Summer 1752. Sy.

Smith, Edward. S May-Jun T Jly 1753 *Tryal*. M.

Smith, Edward. S & T Jan 1756 *Greyhound*. M.

Smith, Edward als Pisson. S Jly 1757. Ha.

Smith, Edward (1762). *See* Green. E.

Smith, Edward als Edmund. S s horse Lent R 14 yrs Summer 1764. G.

Smith, Edward. S s at Clifton Summer 1766. G.

Smith, Edward. S Jan-Feb T Apr 1771 *Thornton*. M.

Smith, Edward. S for perjury Feb T Apr 1771 *Thornton*. L.

Smith, Edward. S Jan-Feb T Apr 1772 *Thornton*. M.

Smith, Edward. SQS Thirsk s at Alne Apr TB May 1772. Y.

Smith, Eleanor. S Apr T Sep 1737 *Pretty Patsy* to Md. M.

Smith, Eleanor. S Jun T Aug 1769 *Douglas*. L.

Smith, Elias. R for Barbados or Jamaica Feb 1687. L.

Smith, Elizabeth. R Jan 1656. M.

Smith, Elizabeth. R for Jamaica Aug 1661. L.

Smyth, Elizabeth. PT Aug 1676 R Mar 1677. M.

Smith, Elizabeth of Dagenham. R for Barbados or Jamaica Jly 1677. E.

Smith, Elizabeth, spinster, als wife of John of St. Olave, Southwark. R for Barbados or Jamaica Mar 1680. Sy.

Smith, Elizabeth. R for Barbados Dec 1693 AT Jan 1694. M.

Smith, Elizabeth (1700). *See* White. Nf.

Smith, Elizabeth. R for Barbados or Jamaica Aug 1700. L.

Smith, Elizabeth. S Jan T Feb 1719 *Worcester* LC Annapolis Jun 1719. L.

Smith, Elizabeth. S Apr T May 1720 *Honor* LC Va Jan 1721. L.

Smith, Elizabeth. S Jly T Aug 1721 *Prince Royal* LC Va Nov 1721. M.

Smith als Richardson, Elizabeth. S Jly T Aug 1721 *Prince Royal* LC Va Nov 1721. M.

Smith, Elizabeth. S May T Jly 1723 *Alexander* LC Annapolis Sep 1723. M.

Smith, Elizabeth (2). S Oct T Dec 1724 *Rappahannock* to Va. M.

Smith, Elizabeth (1730). *See* Smith, Ann. L.

Smith, Elizabeth. S Feb T Mar 1730 *Patapsco* LC Annapolis Sep 1730. L.

Smith, Elizabeth wife of John. S & T Dec 1731 *Forward* to Md or Va. M.

Smith, Elizabeth. T Oct 1732 *Caesar*. E.

Smith, Elizabeth. S s apron Jan T Apr 1735 *Patapsco* LC Md Oct 1735. M.

Smith, Elizabeth. S Dec 1735 T Jan 1736 *Dorsetshire* LC Va Sep 1736. M.

Smith, Elizabeth wife of Thomas. S & T Jan 1736 *Dorsetshire* but died on passage. L.

Smith, Elizabeth. S s earrings & T May 1736 *Patapsco* to Md. M.

Smith, Elizabeth. S Jly 1736. M.

Smith, Elizabeth. S May T Jun 1738 *Forward*. L.

Smith, Elizabeth of St. Giles in Fields, spinster. S s stockings & T Jan 1740 *York*. M.

Smith, Elizabeth. S Oct-Dec 1750. M.

Smith, Elizabeth. S Mar 1753 with special TB. L.

Smith, Elizabeth. T Apr 1753 *Thames*. M.

Smith als Hall, Elizabeth. S Apr-May 1754. M.

Smith, Elizabeth. S Jly-Sep 1754. M.

Smith, Elizabeth (1757). *See* Collins.

Smith, Elizabeth (1762). *See* Clements. M.

Smith, Elizabeth. S 14 yrs for receiving from George Smith Lent 1762. Wo.

Smith, Elizabeth. T Apr 1762 *Neptune*. E.

Smith, Elizabeth. S Lent 1763. Hu.

Smith, Elizabeth (1772). *See* Wood. M.

Smith, Elizabeth Jr. S Mar 1772. Co.

Smith, Elizabeth. S Lent T Apr 1772 *Thornton*. K.

Smith, Elizabeth. LC from *Lowther & Senhouse* Va May 1772. Nl.

Smith, Elizabeth. R Summer 1773 being found quick with child. Sy.
Smith, Elizabeth wife of John. S s at Old Swinford Summer 1774. Wo.
Smith, Elizabeth. S Jan-Feb 1775. M.
Smith, Emanuel. S Lent 1741. Wo.
Smith, Frances. LC from *Forward* Annapolis Dec 1725. X.
Smith, Frances wife of Richard. S & T Oct 1730 *Forward* LC Potomack
 Jan 1731. M.
Smith, Frances. S Jly 1745. Ha.
Smith, Francis. Rebel T 1685.
Smith, Francis. S Jan T Feb 1719 *Worcester* LC Md Jun 1719. L.
Smith, Francis (1739). *See* Brooks. M.
Smith, Francis. S for killing deer at Uttoxeter Lent 1762. St.
Smith, Francis. S & T Apr 1762 *Neptune*. L.
Smith, Gabriel. S for highway robbery & R 14 yrs Lent 1775. G.
Smith, George of Bircham. R for Barbados Feb 1664. Nf.
Smith, George. Rebel T 1685.
Smith, George of Hornchurch. R for Barbados or Jamaica Feb 1686. E.
Smith, George. R for Barbados or Jamaica Feb 1686. M.
Smith, George of Weobley. R for America Jun 1714. He.
Smith, George. S May T Jun 1727 *Susanna* to Va. M.
Smith, George. S Feb T Mar 1730 *Patapsco* LC Annapolis Sep 1730. L.
Smith, George. S Summer 1731. Y.
Smith, George. T Apr 1732 *Patapsco*. Ht.
Smith, George. S & T Dec 1734 *Caesar* LC Va Jly 1735. L.
Smith, George. S City Lent 1742. Y.
Smith, George of Little Bolton, weaver. SQS May 1753. La.
Smith, George. S Summer 1756. Sy.
Smith, George. S Mar 1763. Ha.
Smith, George. R 14 yrs Aug 1767. Wi.
Smith, George. R Mar 1773. So.
Smith, Gideon. T 14 yrs Aug 1769 *Douglas*. E.
Smith, Giles of Beaminster. R for Barbados Jly 1672. Do.
Smith, Gittos of Berkhampstead. R for Barbados or Jamaica Jly
 1710. Ht.
Smith, Hannah. T Nov 1725 *Rappahannock* LC Va Aug 1726. Sy.
Smith, Hannah wife of Samuel. S Aug 1756. So.
Smith, Hannah. S Sep-Oct 1774. M.
Smith, Hannah. S Dec 1774. M.
Smith, Henry. S Mar 1730. So.
Smith, Henry. S & T Oct 1732 *Caesar*. L.
Smith, Henry. R 14 yrs Summer 1749. Y.
Smith, Henry of Little Hallingbury. SQS Oct 1749 T May 1750
 Lichfield. E.
Smith, Henry. S s sheep at Hanbury Lent 1752. Wo.
Smith, Henry. S s wheat at Caversham Lent 1759. O.
Smith, Henry. S Mar 1762. Ha.
Smith, Henry (1763). *See* Talbott. Db.
Smith, Henry. S & T Sep 1765 *Justitia*. L.
Smith, Henry. S & R 14 yrs Lent 1771. La.
Smith, Henry, als Johnson, William. T Dec 1771 *Justitia*. Sx.
Smith, Henry. S Lent 1773. K.

Smith, Henry. S s turkeys at Rishangles Summer 1773. Su.
Smith, Henry. S Jan-Feb 1774. M.
Smith, Henry. SQS Apr 1774. M.
Smith, Hester (1740). *See* Benham. Ha.
Smith, Honor. S Dec 1762 T Mar 1763 *Neptune*. M.
Smith, Humfrey. R 14 yrs Mar 1731. Wi.
Smith, Humphry. SQS Dec 1755 T Jan 1756 *Greyhound*. M.
Smith, Isaac. R for Barbados or Jamaica Feb 1686. M.
Smith, Isaac. S Mar 1733 T *Patapsco* LC Annapolis Nov 1733. Wi.
Smith, Isaac. S Jly 1734. Wi.
Smith, Isaac. S s at Oldbury Lent TB Mar 1747. G.
Smith, Ivingo. S s wheat at Compton Summer 1742. Be.
Smith, James. R for Jamaica Aug 1661. M.
Smith, James. R for Barbados Oct 1673. M.
Smith, James. Rebel T 1685.
Smith, James of Sonning. R for Jamaica, Barbados or Bermuda Feb
    1686. Be.
Smith, James. R for Barbados or Jamaica Apr 1690. M.
Smith als Hubbart, James of Ightham. R for Barbados or Jamaica Mar
    1698. K.
Smith, James of Iwade. R for Barbados or Jamaica Mar 1698. K.
Smith, James (1702). *See* Bessicke. Sy.
Smith, James. LC from *Robert* Annapolis Jun 1725. X.
Smith, James. S s horse Lent 1727 R 14 yrs Lent 1729. Y.
Smith, James. S Feb T Mar 1729 *Patapsco* LC Annapolis Dec 1729. M.
Smith, James. T Sep 1730 *Smith*. Sx.
Smith, James (1738). *See* Tipping. He.
Smith, James (1738). *See* Lingley. Su.
Smith, James. S Mar 1743. Ha.
Smith, James of Rossendale, wool weaver. SQS Jan 1746. La.
Smith, James. S Jan 1751. M.
Smith, James. S s at All Saints, Worcester, Lent 1751. Wo.
Smith, James. S May T Jun 1756 *Lyon*. L.
Smith, James. T from Bristol by *Maryland Packet* 1761 but intercepted
    by French; T Apr 1763 *Neptune*. Ch.
Smith, James. S Jan T Apr 1762 *Dolphin*. M.
Smith, James. S & T Mar 1764 *Tryal*. L.
Smith, James. S Summer 1764 R 14 yrs Lent 1765. La.
Smith, James. S Aug T Sep 1764 *Justitia*. L.
Smith, James. T 14 yrs Apr 1765 *Ann*. Sy.
Smith, James. S s horse Lent R 14 yrs Summer 1765. St.
Smith, James. S Dec 1765 T Jan 1766 *Tryal*. L.
Smith, James. S s clothing at Wilton Lent TB Aug 1766. Y.
Smith, James. SL & T Sep 1766 *Justitia*. Sy.
Smith, James of Bolton in the Moors. SQS Jun 1767. La.
Smith, James. S Jly T Sep 1767 *Justitia*. M.
Smith, James. SW & T Apr 1768 *Thornton*. M.
Smith, James. S s at Aston Clinton Summer T Oct 1768 *Justitia*. Bu.
Smith, James of Croydon. SQS for false pretences Oct 1768 T Jan 1769
    Thornton. Sy.
Smith, James. S s at Over Worton & Shiplake Lent 1769. O.

Smith, James of St. Saviour, Southwark. SQS Jan T Apr 1770 *New Trial*. Sy.

Smith, James. S Feb T Apr 1770 *New Trial*. L.

Smith als Daily, James. S s at Wood Ditton Lent 1771. Ca.

Smith, James. S s cochineal at Stroud Lent 1773. G.

Smith, James. S May 1775. L.

Smyth, Jane, spinster. R & TB for Barbados Oct 1667. L.

Smith, Jane. S 14 yrs Apr-Jun 1739. M.

Smith, Jane, als Singing Jenny. S Apr 1745. L.

Smith, Jane wife of Gabriel of Wakering, yeoman. SQS Jly 1749. E.

Smith, Jane. S Summer 1749. Sy.

Smith, Jane. S May T Jun 1764 *Dolphin*. M.

Smith, Jane. S Apr-May T Jly 1771 *Scarsdale*. M.

Smith, Jasper. PT Jun R Oct 1673 & Jly 1674. M.

Smith, Jasper. S s horsehair at Godmanchester Lent 1771. Hu.

Smith, Jeremiah. S Aug 1727 T *Forward* LC Rappahannock May 1728. M.

Smith, Jeremiah. S Summer 1760. K.

Smith, Johanna. R May AT Oct 1678. M.

Smyth, John of Ewell. R for Barbados Aug 1662. Sy.

Smith, John. R 12 yrs Jan 1663. L.

Smith, John. R for Barbados Jan 1664. M.

Smith, John. R for Barbados Aug 1664. M.

Smith, John. R for Barbados Apr 1669. M.

Smith, John of Luffeswick. R for America Jly 1674. No.

Smith, John (1678). *See* Court. Wa.

Smith, John. R for Barbados Aug 1679. L.

Smith, John of Stratford Langthorne. R for Barbados or Jamaica Mar 1682 & Feb 1683. E.

Smith, John of Cradley. R for America Mar 1682. Wo.

Smith, John. R for Barbados or Jamaica Mar 1683 & May 1684. M.

Smith, John (3). Rebels T 1685.

Smith, John. R for America Aug 1685. Wa.

Smith, John. R for Barbados or Jamaica Feb 1686. M.

Smith, John of Shrewsbury, butcher. R for America Mar 1698. Sh.

Smith, John. R for Barbados or Jamaica Dec 1699 & Aug 1700. L.

Smith, John of Lulham. R for America Mar 1701. He.

Smith, John of Martin on Trent. R for America Feb 1713. Li.

Smith, John (1719). *See* Brown. K.

Smith, John, aged 53, carpenter. S & T 14 yrs Oct 1720 *Gilbert* LC Annapolis May 1721. M.

Smith, John. S Jly T Aug 1721 *Prince Royal* LC Va Nov 1721. L.

Smith als Knight, John. T Oct 1721 *William & John*. K.

Smith, John. T Oct 1722 *Forward*. E.

Smith, John. SQS Skipton Jly 1723. Y.

Smith, John. S Mar R 14 yrs & TB Sep 1725. Nt.

Smith, John. S Jan 1726 T *Supply* LC Annapolis May 1726. M.

Smith, John. T Oct 1726 *Forward*. E.

Smith, John (1727). *See* Wilson. L.

Smith, John. T Jun 1727 *Susanna*. K.

Smith, John. S & T Oct 1729 *Forward* LC Va Jun 1730. M.

Smith, John. S Feb T Mar 1730 *Patapsco* LC Annapolis Sep 1730. M.
Smith, John. S Lent AT Summer 1730. Y.
Smith, John. S for forgery Summer 1730 R 14 yrs Lent 1731. Wa.
Smith, John, als Rowland, Richard. R s horse Jun 1730 (SP). Wo.
Smith, John. S Aug 1734. So.
Smith, John, a boy. S s linen Apr T Dec 1735 *John* LC Md Sep 1736. M.
Smith, John. S s sheepskins at Bridgnorth Summer 1735. Sh.
Smith als Sims, John. S Jly T 14 yrs Sep 1737 *Pretty Patsy*. L.
Smith, John. R 14 yrs Aug 1737. So.
Smith, John. TB to Va from QS 1738. De.
Smith, John. T Oct 1739 *Duke of Cumberland*. Bu.
Smith, John of St. Martin in Fields. S s waistcoat & T Jan 1740 *York*. M.
Smith, John. SQS Jly 1741 TB to Md May 1742. So.
Smith, John. S Jly T Oct 1741 *Sea Horse* to Va. M.
Smith, John. T Nov 1741 *Sea Horse*. Ht.
Smith, John. T Sep 1742 *Forward*. Ht.
Smith, John. T Nov 1743 *George William*. E.
Smith, John. S & T May 1744 *Justitia*. L.
Smith, John. T May 1744 *Justitia*. E.
Smith, John. S Oct 1744-Jan 1745. M.
Smith, John. S Jan 1745. L.
Smith, John. SQS Marlborough Jan TB to Va Apr 1745. Wi.
Smith, John. S Feb-Apr 1745. M.
Smith, John. S Apr 1745. L.
Smith, John. R 14 yrs Apr 1745. So.
Smith, John. S May-Jly 1746. M.
Smith, John of Low Worsall. SQS Richmond Jan 1747; warrant for his
   apprehension for returning from transportation Oct 1748. Y.
Smith, John. S s at Wolverhampton Summer 1748. St.
Smith, John. S Summer 1749. Sx.
Smith, John. T Sep 1749. Ht.
Smith, John (1750). *See* Leeman. L.
Smith, John. SQS Apr T May 1750 *Lichfield*. M.
Smith, John. S Summer T Oct 1750 *Rachael*. E.
Smith, John. S s at St. Helen, Worcester, Lent 1751. Wo.
Smith, John. AT Summer 1751. Cu.
Smith, John. S for highway robbery Summer 1751 R 14 yrs Lent T May
   1752 *Lichfield*. Bu.
Smith, John. SQS Apr T May 1752 *Lichfield*. M.
Smith, John. S Apr T May 1752 *Lichfield*. L.
Smith, John. T Aug 1752 *Tryal*. K.
Smith, John. S Nov T Dec 1752 *Greyhound*. L.
Smith, John of St. John's. SQS Jan T Apr 1753 *Thames*. Sy.
Smith als Groves, John. S Jan-Feb T Apr 1753 *Thames*. M.
Smith, John. S Summer 1753 R 14 yrs Lent 1754. Ht.
Smith, John. S Lent TB Mar 1754. G.
Smith, John. S Summer 1754 T May 1755 *Rose*. K.
Smith, John. S Summer 1755 R 14 yrs Lent 1756. Li.
Smith, John. SQS & T Sep 1755 *Tryal*. M.
Smith, John. S & T Jan 1756 *Greyhound*. M.

Smith, John of Warrington. S for highway robbery Lent R 14 yrs Summer 1756. La.

Smith, John. S s aprons at St. Martin, Worcester, Lent 1756. Wo.

Smith, John (2). S Lent T Sep 1757 *Thetis*. K.

Smith, John. S Apr T Sep 1757 *Thetis*. L.

Smith, John. S & T Sep 1757 *Thetis*. M.

Smith, John. T Sep 1758 *Tryal*. Sy.

Smith, John. S s bacon Jan T Apr 1759 *Thetis*. M.

Smith, John. S for false pretences Lent 1759. Wo.

Smith, John. S & T Mar 1760 *Friendship*. L.

Smith, John. S & T Apr 1762 *Neptune*. L.

Smith, John. S Oct T Dec 1763 *Neptune*. M.

Smith, John (2). S Jan T Mar 1764 *Tryal*. L.

Smith, John. S Mar 1764. Ha.

Smith, John. S s hogs at Claines Lent 1764. Wo.

Smith, John. S s mare Summer 1764 R 14 yrs Lent 1765. Sh.

Smith, John. S Aug T Sep 1764 *Justitia*. L.

Smith, John. S & T Sep 1764 *Justitia*. L.

Smith, John. S Mar TB to Va Apr 1765. Wi.

Smith, John. T Apr 1765 *Ann*. K.

Smith, John. S s fowls at West Bromwich Lent 1765. St.

Smith, John. S Lent 1765. Su.

Smith, John. S Jly T Sep 1765 *Justitia*. M.

Smith, John of St. John, Hertford. SQS Oct 1765 T Jan 1766 *Tryal*. Ht.

Smith, John, als Newcombe, Robert. S Feb T Apr 1766 *Ann*. M.

Smith, John. S Summer 1766 R 14 yrs Lent 1767. Su.

Smith, John. S s sheep Summer 1766 R 14 yrs Lent T May 1767 *Thornton*. Bu.

Smith, John. AT Lent 1767. G.

Smith, John. S Summer 1767 R 14 yrs Lent 1768. Li.

Smith, John (1768). *See* Woollard, William. Sy.

Smith, John. SQS May T Jun 1768 *Tryal*. M.

Smith, John. R Jly T 14 yrs Oct 1768 *Justitia*. M.

Smith, John. SW & T Jan 1769 *Thornton*. M.

Smith, John. S Jun T Aug 1769 *Douglas*. L.

Smith, John. SW & T Aug 1769 *Douglas*. M.

Smith, John (1772). *See* Young. M.

Smith, John. S Feb T Apr 1772 *Thornton*. L.

Smith, John. S s silver at Shenstone Summer 1772. St.

Smith, John. R Jly 1773. M.

Smith, John. R Summer 1773. K.

Smith, John. S Summer 1774. La.

Smith, John. S s cloth from tenters at Heptonstall & R Summer 1774. Y.

Smith, John. S Jly 1774. Do.

Smith, John. S 14 yrs Sep-Oct 1774. M.

Smith, John. S 14 yrs Jly 1775. L.

Smith, John. S s horse & R 14 yrs Summer 1775. G.

Smith, John. S for highway robbery & R 14 yrs Summer 1775. Be.

Smith, John Adam. S s mare Lent R for life Summer 1768. Be.

Smith, Jonas. S Lent T May 1737 *Forward*. Bu.

Smith, Jonathan. S Jan T Jun 1738 *Forward* to Md or Va. M.

Smith, Jonathan. S Oct 1749. L.

Smith, Jophenix. S Aug T Sep 1725 *Forward* to Md. M.

Smith, Joseph of Newington. R for Barbados Apr 1668. Sy.

Smith, Joseph of Woodford. R for Barbados or Jamaica Jly 1674. E.

Smith, Joseph. S & T Sep 1718 *Eagle* LC Charles Town Mar 1719. L.

Smith, Joseph. S & T Oct 1722 *Forward* LC Annapolis Jun 1723. M.

Smith als Ashburn, Joseph. S Aug T Oct 1724 *Forward* LC Md Jun 1725. L.

Smith, Joseph. S Feb T Mar 1729 *Patapsco* LC Annapolis Dec 1729. M.

Smith, Joseph (1738). *See* Smithson. L.

Smith, Joseph. S Norwich s cloth Summer 1742. Nf.

Smith, Joseph. S s at St. Mary, Stafford, Lent R 14 yrs Summer 1744. St.

Smith, Joseph. S Jan 1746. M.

Smith, Joseph. S Jan 1751. L.

Smith, Joseph. S & T Aug 1752 *Tryal.* L.

Smith, Joseph. S Mar 1757. De.

Smith, Joseph. T Sep 1764 *Justitia.* K.

Smith, Joseph. S May T Sep 1766 *Justitia.* M.

Smith, Joseph. S s sheep Summer 1766 R for life Lent T May 1767 *Thornton.* Bu.

Smith, Joseph als Thomas. S Feb T May 1767 *Thornton.* M.

Smith, Joseph. S Feb T Apr 1768 *Thornton.* M.

Smith, Joseph. S & R 14 yrs Mar TB to Va Apr 1769. Wi.

Smith, Joseph. S Oct T Dec 1769 *Justitia.* L.

Smith, Joseph. S s at St. Chad, Shrewsbury, Lent 1770. Sh.

Smith, Joseph. T Dec 1771 *Justitia.* E.

Smith, Joseph. S Jan-Feb T Apr 1772 *Thornton.* M.

Smith, Joseph. S May-Jly 1773. M.

Smith, Joshua. S Norwich Summer 1766. Nf.

Smith, Judith. S & T Oct 1729 *Forward* LC Va Jun 1730. L.

Smith, Lawrence of Barley Booth in Pendle Forest. SQS Apr 1772. La.

Smith, Levy. SQS Marlborough Oct 1766 TB to Va Apr 1767. Wi.

Smith, Loomus. S Summer 1758. Su.

Smith, Louisa. T Apr 1770 *New Trial.* L.

Smith, Luke. S Oct T Dec 1724 *Rappahannock.* L.

Smith, Luke. T Apr 1765 *Ann.* M.

Smith, Lyon. S Oct 1765 T Jan 1766 *Tryal.* M.

Smith, Maisey. AT City Summer 1758. Nl.

Smith, Margaret. R for America Jly 1683. Nt.

Smith, Margaret. S Jan R & T 14 yrs Feb 1719 *Worcester* LC Annapolis Jun 1719. L.

Smith, Margaret. S Oct 1737. M.

Smith, Margaret. S Oct 1744-Jan 1745. M.

Smith, Margaret. S Jun-Dec 1745. M.

Smith, Margaret als Fletcher. S Sep-Dec 1746. M.

Smith, Margaret. S Dec 1756. M.

Smith, Margaret. AT City Summer 1759. Nl.

Smith, Margaret. S Jly 1760. M.

Smith, Margery of Exeter. R for Barbados Mar 1694. De.

Smith, Mark. R for Barbados Jun 1671. M.

Smith, Martha. S Jly T Aug 1721 *Prince Royal* LC Va Nov 1721. M.

Smith, Martha wife of Thomas. S Jly-Sep T Oct 1739 *Duke of Cumberland*. M.

Smith, Martha. S Summer 1744. Ht.

Smith, Marthe. S Jly 1745. Ha.

Smith, Martha. S Jan-Feb T Apr 1753 *Thames*. M.

Smith, Martha. S Oct 1772. L.

Smith, Mary. R for Jamaica Aug 1661. M.

Smith, Mary. R for Barbados Jun 1671. M.

Smith, Mary. R for Barbados Mar 1681. M.

Smith, Mary. R for Barbados or Jamaica May 1691. L.

Smith, Mary of Exeter. R for Barbados Mar 1694. De.

Smith, Mary. R for Barbados or Jamaica Oct 1694. L.

Smith, Mary of Nottingham, spinster. R (Oxford Circ) for America Jly 1699. Nt.

Smith, Mary. R for America Aug 1715. M.

Smith als Fell, Mary. R & T Dec 1716 *Lewis*. M.

Smith, Mary. S Apr T 14 yrs May 1718 *Tryal* LC Charles Town Aug 1718. L.

Smith, Mary. S Sep 1719. M.

Smith, Mary. S Jly T Oct 1720 *Gilbert* to Md. M.

Smith, Mary (1722). *See* Walker. M.

Smith, Mary. S & T Jan 1722 *Gilbert* LC Annapolis Jly 1722. M.

Smith, Mary. S s at Leominster Lent 1722. He.

Smith, Mary (1724). *See* Lenox. Ha.

Smith, Mary. S Jan T Feb 1724 *Anne*. L.

Smith als Randall, Mary. S 14 yrs Aug 1727 T *Forward* LC Va May 1728. M.

Smith, Mary. S Dec 1727. M.

Smith, Mary. S & T Oct 1730 *Forward* LC Potomack Jan 1731. M.

Smith, Mary. S Feb T 14 yrs Mar 1731 *Patapsco* LC Annapolis Jun 1731. M.

Smith, Mary. S & T Sep 1731 *Smith* LC Va 1732. L.

Smith, Mary. S Feb T Apr 1734 *Patapsco*. L.

Smith, Mary. S May T Dec 1734 *Caesar* LC Va Jly 1735. M.

Smith, Mary. S & T Dec 1734 *Caesar* but died on passage. M.

Smith, Mary. S s breeches Apr T Dec 1735 *John* LC Annapolis Sep 1736. M.

Smith, Mary. S s shirts Sep T Dec 1735 *John* to Md. M.

Smith, Mary (1736). *See* Johnson. L.

Smith als Busco, Mary. S Jun T Dec 1736 *Dorsetshire* to Va. M.

Smith, Mary. S Jly 1737 T Jan 1738 *Dorsetshire* to Va. M.

Smith als Rouse, Mary. S Jly T Oct 1741 *Sea Horse* to Va. M.

Smith, Mary. S Jly T Oct 1741 *Sea Horse* to Va. M.

Smith, Mary (1743). *See* Holmes. M.

Smith, Mary. S s at Wolverhampton Lent 1744. St.

Smith, Mary. S Sep T Oct 1744 *Susannah*. M.

Smith, Mary. S Dec 1746. L.

Smith, Mary (1747). *See* Pebworth. M.

Smith als Ordery als Pepper, Mary. S Jan-Apr 1748. M.

Smith, Mary. S Jly 1750. L.

Smith, Mary. SQS Dec 1750. M.

Smith als Brown, Mary. S Jan 1751. M.
Smith als Cox als Brown, Mary. S May-Jun T Jly 1753 *Tryal*. M.
Smith, Mary. T Sep 1755 *Tryal*. L.
Smith, Mary. S Apr 1756. So.
Smith, Mary. SQS Jan 1757. M.
Smith als Richardson, Mary. S Feb 1757. M.
Smith, Mary. S Sep T Dec 1758 *The Brothers*. M.
Smith, Mary. S Apr 1760. M.
Smith, Mary of Low Leyton. SQS Jly 1761. E.
Smith, Mary. S Lent 1763. Sy.
Smith, Mary. S Jly 1763. M.
Smith, Mary. S Dec 1763 T Mar 1764 *Tryal*. M.
Smith als Dunn, Mary. S Jly T Sep 1765 *Justitia*. M.
Smith, Mary. S & T Apr 1766 *Ann*. L.
Smith, Mary. S & T Dec 1767 *Neptune*. L.
Smith, Mary. S s at St. Mary, Stafford, Summer 1770. St.
Smith, Mary. S Sep-Oct 1772. M.
Smith, Mary. S Jan-Feb 1773. M.
Smith, Mary. S May-Jly 1773. M.
Smith, Mary. S Sep-Oct 1773. M.
Smith, Mary. S Lent 1774. K.
Smith, Mary. S May 1775. L.
Smith, Mary. R for life Summer 1775. Wa.
Smith, Mary. S s at Deerhurst Summer 1775. G.
Smith, Mary. S Sep-Oct 1775. M.
Smith, Matthew of St. Michael, Oxford. S Summer 1720. O.
Smith, Mathew. S Mar 1768. Ha.
Smith, Michael. T May 1719 *Margaret*; sold to Peter Galloway Md May
    1720. K.
Smith, Michael. S & T Feb 1740 *York*. L.
Smith, Middlemore. S Jun-Dec 1738 T Jan 1739 *Dorsetshire* to Va. M.
Smyth, Miles. R for Barbados May 1676. M.
Smith, Nathaniel. R 14 yrs Summer T Oct 1729 *Duke of
    Cumberland*. Sy.
Smith, Nicholas. Rebel T 1685.
Smith, Ophelia (1720). *See* Smith, Winifred. M.
Smith, Parker. S s deer from Earl of Uxbridge at Rugeley Summer 1744
    R 14 yrs Lent 1745. St.
Smith, Patrick. S for rape Lent R 14 yrs Summer 1767. Hu.
Smith, Peter. S s gelding at Tuckford & R 14 yrs Summer 1770. Sh.
Smith, Philip. Rebel T 1685.
Smith, Rachael. R for America Aug 1715. L.
Smith, Ralph. R for Barbados Dec 1693 AT Jan 1694. M.
Smith, Ralph. R 14 yrs Lent 1721. St.
Smith, Ralph. R 14 yrs s horse Lent 1767. Ch.
Smith, Randall. S s horse Summer 1753 R 14 yrs Lent 1754. Wa.
Smith, Rebecca. S Jan-Feb T Apr 1772 *Thornton*. M.
Smith als Nuttall, Richard. R 10 yrs in plantations Oct 1662. M.
Smith, Richard. R for Barbados Dec 1683. M.
Smith, Richard. R for Barbados or Jamaica Jan 1693. L.
Smith als Lidley, Richard. R for Barbados or Jamaica Aug 1700. M.

Smith, Richard of Barston. R for America Feb 1713. Wa.

Smith, Richard (1720). *See* Cook, Pendell. L.

Smith, Richard. S s flour at Lechlade Summer 1729. G.

Smith, Richard. S Feb T Mar 1730 *Patapsco* LC Annapolis Sep 1730. L.

Smyth, Richard. S s mare at Frampton on Severn Lent R 14 yrs Summer TB Sep 1736. G.

Smith, Richard. S Jun-Dec 1738 T Jan 1739 *Dorsetshire*. M.

Smith, Richard. S Lent 1741. O.

Smith, Richard. T Nov 1743 *George William*. K.

Smith, Richard of Bermondsey, mariner. SQS Jan T Apr 1753 *Thames*. Sy.

Smith, Richard. S Lent 1754. Y.

Smith, Richard. S Apr-May 1754. M.

Smith, Richard als Anderson als Williams als Sturgis. S s horse Lent R 14 yrs Summer 1755. Le.

Smith, Richard. S s mares Lent R 14 yrs Summer 1756. No.

Smith, Richard of Liverpool. S s tankard Lent R 14 yrs Summer 1760. La.

Smith, Richard. S Apr 1763. M.

Smith, Richard. S Oct 1764. M.

Smith, Richard. S Jan T Feb 1765 *Tryal*. L.

Smith, Richard. S & T Jan 1767 *Tryal*. M.

Smith, Richard. T Apr 1768 *Thornton*. K.

Smith, Richard (1769). *See* Frizer. Wo.

Smith, Richard. S s at Almondsbury Summer 1769. G.

Smith, Richard. S Sep T 14 yrs Dec 1770 *Justitia*. M.

Smith, Richard. SW & T Jly 1772 *Tayloe*. M.

Smith, Richard. S Apr 1773. L.

Smith, Robert. R (Midland Circ) for America Jly 1674. X.

Smyth, Robert. R for Barbados May 1676. L.

Smith, Robert of Ross. R for America Mar 1680. He.

Smith, Robert. Rebel T 1685.

Smith, Robert. R for Barbados or Jamaica Jan 1693. L.

Smyth, Robert. of Nettlebed. R for America Nov 1694. O.

Smith, Robert. R (Western Circ) for Barbados Feb 1699. L.

Smith, Robert. S Mar 1725. Wi.

Smith, Robert. S Jan-Jun T Jun 1728 *Elizabeth* LC Potomack Aug 1729. M.

Smith, Robert. TB to Md Aug 1729. Db.

Smith, Robert. S & T Dec 1731 *Forward* to Md or Va. M.

Smith, Robert. R 14 yrs Summer 1732. Nl.

Smith, Robert. S Jly T Oct 1741 *Sea Horse* to Va. M.

Smith, Robert. AT Lent 1749. Be.

Smith, Robert. S & T Mar 1760 *Friendship*. L.

Smith, Robert (1766). *See* Bradshaw. M.

Smith, Robert. S Lent 1767. Nf.

Smith, Robert. R 14 yrs Aug 1767. So.

Smith, Robert. S & T Dec 1769 *Justitia*. L.

Smith, Robert of St. James, Westminster. SW Apr 1774. M.

Smith, Roger of Bristol. R for Barbados Feb 1701. G.

Smith, Roger. T Aug 1721 *Owners Goodwill*. E.

Smith als Drogheda, Rose. S & T May 1740 *Essex* to Md or Va. M.
Smith, Samuel. R Oct AT Dec 1688. M.
Smith, Samuel. R Oct 1694 AT Jan 1695. M.
Smith, Samuel. S s cows Summer 1735. Ca.
Smith, Samuel. S s horse Summer 1736 R 14 yrs Lent 1737. Li.
Smith, Samuel of Moreley. S s heifer Summer 1738. Nf.
Smith, Samuel. S Summer T Sep 1751 *Greyhound.* Sy.
Smith, Samuel. T Mar 1758 *Dragon.* L.
Smith, Samuel. S Summer 1764. Nt.
Smith, Samuel. S s sheep Summer 1766 R 14 yrs Lent 1767. O.
Smith, Samuel. SQS s stockings at West Stockwith Oct 1766 AT Lent
    1767. Nt.
Smith, Samuel. S & T Jly 1770 *Scarsdale.* M.
Smith, Samuel. S s mare at Rockland All Saints & R 14 yrs Lent
    1772. Nf.
Smith, Samuel. S s at Kidderminster Summer 1772. Wo.
Smith, Samuel (1774). *See* Stringer. Wo.
Smith, Sara (1677). *See* Bowen. M.
Smith, Sarah. S Jan T Feb 1719 *Worcester* LC Annapolis Jun 1719. L.
Smith, Sarah. S Apr 1734 T Dec 1735 *Caesar* LC Va Jly 1735. M.
Smith, Sarah. S Summer 1734. Hu.
Smith, Sarah. Died on passage in *Dorsetshire* 1736. X.
Smith, Sarah. T Oct 1744 *Savannah.* Ht.
Smith, Sarah. SQS Jly T Sep 1751 *Greyhound.* M.
Smith, Sarah, spinster, als Elizabeth wife of Samuel. S s stockings at
    Fairford Summer TB Sep 1755. G.
Smith, Sarah. S Apr T Sep 1757 *Thetis.* M.
Smith, Sarah. S Summer TB Sep 1757. Db.
Smith, Sarah. S Jan T Apr 1762 *Dolphin.* L.
Smith, Sarah. SQS Feb T Apr 1762 *Dolphin.* M.
Smith, Sarah. S & T Apr 1762 *Neptune.* L.
Smith, Sarah. S Jan T Mar 1764 *Tryal.* M.
Smith, Sarah (1769). *See* Manton. L.
Smith, Sarah. S & T Jly 1771 *Scarsdale.* L.
Smith, Sarah. S for perjury Dec 1773. L.
Smith, Sarah (1774). *See* McCoy. M.
Smith, Sarah. S May-Jly 1774. M.
Smith, Sharpisis. S s wheat at Compton Summer 1742. Be.
Smith, Simon of Wigtoft. R for America Mar 1682. Li.
Smith, Simon. S Sep-Oct T Dec 1753 *Whiteing.* M.
Smith, Smith (1756). *See* Avery, Smith. G.
Smith, Solomon. SQS Feb T May 1751 *Tryal.* M.
Smith, Stephen. S Mar 1739. Ha.
Smith, Stephen. SL Apr 1753. Sy.
Smith, Stephen. S s sheep Summer 1758 R 14 yrs Lent 1759. Nf.
Smith, Stephen. SQS May T Sep 1764 *Justitia.* M.
Smith, Susan, widow. R for Barbados Mar 1681. L.
Smith, Susannah. S Apr T May 1720 *Honor* LC Port York Jan 1721. L.
Smith, Susanna (1722). *See* Stewart. M.
Smith, Susan. S Jly T Dec 1735 *John* LC Annapolis Sep 1736. M.
Smith, Susanna. S May-Jly 1748. M.

Smith, Susanna. S Apr-May 1754. M.

Smith, Susanna. S Jly T Sep 1755 *Tryal*. L.

Smith, Susannah. S Oct T Nov 1759 *Phoenix*. L.

Smith, Susannah. S Lent 1766 found pregnant by jury R Summer 1767. Bu.

Smith, Susannah. SQS New Sarum or Marlborough & TB to Va Jan 1774. Wi.

Smith, Terence. S Apr 1761. M.

Smyth als Swingfield, Thomas. R for Barbados Jan 1664. L.

Smith, Thomas. R for Barbados Jun 1666. Y.

Smith als Alexander, Thomas of Bridge Trafford, husbandman. R for America Aug 1672. Ch.

Smith, Thomas of Sneston. R for America Jly 1678. Le.

Smith, Thomas. R for Barbados Aug 1679. M.

Smith, Thomas. R for Barbados or Jamaica Mar 1685. M.

Smith, Thomas. R for America Aug 1685. Wa.

Smith, Thomas of Bradwell. R for America Feb 1688. Su.

Smith, Thomas of Bishops Norton. R for America Jun 1692. G.

Smith, Thomas of Hentland. R for America Nov 1694. He.

Smith, Thomas of Grantham. R (Western Circ) for Barbados Jly 1698. Li.

Smith, Thomas. R Dec 1698 Dec 1699 & Aug 1700. M.

Smith, Thomas. R for America Aug 1715. M.

Smith, Thomas. S & T 14 yrs Sep 1718 *Eagle* LC Charles Town Mar 1719. L.

Smith, Thomas (1720). *See* Butler. L.

Smith, Thomas. S Jly T Aug 1721 *Prince Royal* LC Va Nov 1721. M.

Smith, Thomas. S & T Oct 1722 *Forward* LC Annapolis Jun 1723. L.

Smith, Thomas. Died on passage in *Alexander* 1723. X.

Smith, Thomas. T Nov 1725 *Rappahannock* but died on passage. Sy.

Smith, Thomas. S May 1727. L.

Smith, Thomas. S Dec 1727. M.

Smith, Thomas. S s at Treddington Summer 1728. Wo.

Smith, Thomas. S s at St. Clement, Oxford, Lent 1735 AT Summer 1736. O.

Smith, Thomas. S Norwich 14 yrs for receiving Summer 1736. Nf.

Smith, Thomas. S 14 yrs Apr-Jun 1739. M.

Smith, Thomas. S Jun 1739. L.

Smith, Thomas. T Apr 1741 *Speedwell* or *Mediterranean*. Bu.

Smith, Thomas. AT Summer 1742. O.

Smith, Thomas. S & T Feb 1744 *Neptune*. L.

Smith, Thomas (1745). *See* Newman. M.

Smith, Thomas. S s silver tankard at Lancaster Lent 1746. La.

Smyth, Thomas. S s coalpit ropes at Stapleton Lent TB Mar 1749. G.

Smith, Thomas. S Apr 1749. L.

Smith, Thomas. S May-Jly 1749. M.

Smith, Thomas. S Apr T May 1750 *Lichfield*. L.

Smith, Thomas. R 14 yrs Jly 1750. Ha.

Smith als Broach, Thomas. SQS May T Sep 1751 *Greyhound*. M.

Smith, Thomas. T May 1751 *Tryal*. K.

Smith, Thomas. S Lent R 14 yrs Summer 1752. He.

Smith, Thomas. S & T Jly 1753 *Tryal*. L.
Smith, Thomas of Deptford. SQS Jan 1754. Sy.
Smith, Thomas. S s sheep Summer 1754 R 14 yrs Lent 1755. Li.
Smith, Thomas (1755). *See* Metcalfe. M.
Smith, Thomas. S Lent R 14 yrs Summer 1755. Wa.
Smith, Thomas. S s mare Summer 1755 R 14 yrs Lent 1756. Hu.
Smith, Thomas. S s sheep Summer 1758 R 14 yrs Lent TB Apr 1759. Db.
Smith, Thomas. T 14 yrs Dec 1758 *The Brothers*. K.
Smith, Thomas. S Feb T Mar 1760 *Friendship*. M.
Smith, Thomas. S Lent 1761. E.
Smith, Thomas. SEK & T Sep 1764 *Justitia*. K.
Smith, Thomas. S s at Low Worsall Lent 1765. Y.
Smith, Thomas. SQS Marlborough Oct 1766 TB to Va Apr 1767. Wi.
Smith, Thomas (1767). *See* Smith, Joseph. M.
Smith, Thomas. S Lent R 14 yrs Summer 1767. He.
Smith, Thomas. T May 1767 *Thornton*. K.
Smith, Thomas. S Jun T Sep 1767 *Justitia*. L.
Smith, Thomas. R Jly T Sep 1767 *Justitia*. L.
Smith, Thomas. R Jly T for life Sep 1767 *Justitia*. M.
Smith, Thomas. SQS Warminster or New Sarum & TB to Va Oct 1768. Wi.
Smith, Thomas. S at Folkestone & T Dec 1769 *Justitia*. K.
Smith als Coffery, Thomas. S Apr-May T Jly 1771 *Scarsdale*. M.
Smith, Thomas. S Jly 1771. Ha.
Smith als Johnson als Crane, Thomas. S s sheep at Brabaham & R 14 yrs Summer 1771. Ca.
Smith, Thomas. S & T Dec 1771 *Justitia*. M.
Smith, Thomas. S s horse & R 14 yrs Summer 1772. Sh.
Smith, Thomas (1775). *See* Wilson, John. Ru.
Smith, Thomas. S Lent 1775. Wa.
Smith, William of Stroud or Marden. R for plantations Feb 1656. K.
Smith, William, minister. SQS Mar 1656 for notorious & lewd acts in remote parts of England. M.
Smith als Ridgely, William. R for Barbados Jly 1668. M.
Smith als Lancastell, William. R for Barbados Aug 1668. M.
Smyth, William. of North Petherton, husbandman. R for Barbados Dec 1673. So.
Smith, William of Dodford. R for America Jly 1678. No.
Smith, William. R Dec 1683. M.
Smith, William. R for America Jun 1684. No.
Smith, William (3). Rebels T 1685.
Smith als Franklin als Babington, William. R for Barbados Dec 1693 & Dec 1694. M.
Smith, William of Fornham. R for America Apr 1697. Su.
Smith, William, als Carrott, John. R for Barbados or Jamaica May 1697. M.
Smith, William of Sandbach, nailer. R for America Mar 1698. Ch.
Smith als Williams, William. R for Barbados or Jamaica Dec 1699 & Aug 1700. L.
Smith, William. R for America Feb 1700. Wa.

Smith, William. PT Mar 1701. M.
Smith, William of Richmond. R for Barbados or Jamaica Jly 1715. Sy.
Smith, William of Ledbury. S Lent 1720. He.
Smith, William. S Apr T May 1720 *Honor* LC Port York Jan 1721. L.
Smith, William. S s at Barnwood Lent 1722. G.
Smith, William. S Aug T Oct 1723 *Forward* to Va. M.
Smith, William. S & T Dec 1724 *Rappahannock*. L.
Smith, William. T Nov 1725 *Rappahannock* LC Va Aug 1726. K.
Smith als Clark, William. S May T Jun 1726 *Loyal Margaret* to Md. M.
Smith, William. LC from *Supply* Annapolis May 1726. X.
Smith, William. T Oct 1726 *Forward*. Bu.
Smith, William. S s cock at Pishill Lent 1727. O.
Smith, William. R 14 yrs Jly 1728. Ha.
Smith, William. S Feb T Mar 1731 *Patapsco* LC Annapolis Jun 1731. M.
Smith, William. T Apr 1731 *Bennett*. Ht.
Smith, William. AT from QS Summer 1731. St.
Smith als Messenger, William. R 14 yrs Summer 1731. Y.
Smith, William. S Lent 1733. Y.
Smith, William. S Feb T Apr 1735 *Patapsco* LC Annapolis Oct 1735. M.
Smith, William. T Apr 1735 *Patapsco*. Ht.
Smith, William. S s cistern Sep T Dec 1736 *Dorsetshire* to Va. M.
Smith, William. S Jly TB to Va Oct 1740. Wi.
Smith, William of Ealing. S s caps Sep 1740 T Jan 1741 *Harpooner* to Va. M.
Smith, William. S s at Woodcote Lent 1743. Sh.
Smith, William. S Apr T May 1743 *Indian Queen*. L.
Smith, William. S Lent R 14 yrs Summer 1744. Wo.
Smith, William. S Summer 1748 T Jan 1749 *Laura*. E.
Smith, William. S Jan-Apr 1749. M.
Smith, William. S Jly 1749. L.
Smith, William. S Jan T Mar 1750 *Tryal*. L.
Smith, William. S May-Jly T Sep 1751 *Greyhound*. M.
Smith, William. T Apr 1753 *Thames*. Sx.
Smith, William (1754). *See* Sacker. M.
Smith, William. S s from Sir Peter Soames Lent 1754. Bd.
Smith als Lightfoot, William. S s horse Summer 1754 R 14 yrs Lent 1755. Li.
Smith, William. S Sep 1754. L.
Smith, William. S s rope Lent 1755. Be.
Smith, William. R 14 yrs Summer T Jun 1756 *Lyon*. Sy.
Smith, William. S Lent 1757. Le.
Smith, William. T Apr 1757. Db.
Smith, William. S s at Walsall Summer 1757. St.
Smith, William. S s gelding Summer 1758 R 14 yrs Lent T Apr 1759 *Thetis*. Bu.
Smith, William. S Oct T Dec 1758 *The Brothers*. L.
Smith, William. S Mar 1760 TB to Va. De.
Smith, William. S s horse Summer 1761 R 14 yrs Lent 1762. Sh.
Smith, William. S Dec 1761 T 14 yrs Apr 1762 *Dolphin*. M.
Smith, William. S May 1763. M.
Smith, William, als Turner, John. R Jly 1763. M.

Smith, William. S s mare Summer 1764 R 14 yrs Lent 1765. St.
Smith, William. S Aug TB to Va Oct 1764. Wi.
Smith, William. S Aug T Sep 1764 *Justitia*. L.
Smith, William (1765). *See* Fall. Nl.
Smith, William. SQS & T Apr 1765 *Ann*. M.
Smith, William. S Jly T Sep 1765 *Justitia*. M.
Smith, William. S s sheep Summer 1766 R 14 yrs Lent T May 1767
  Thornton. Bu.
Smith, William. S Oct 1766 T Jan 1767 *Tryal*. L.
Smith, William. S Aug TB to Va Sep 1767. Le.
Smith, William (1768). *See* Hamilton. M.
Smith, William (1768). *See* Johnson, Robert. Y.
Smith, William. S Lent 1768. Su.
Smith, William. S for forgery at Houghton le Spring & R for life
  Summer 1769. Du.
Smith, William. R Apr 1770. Do.
Smith, William. S Jly 1770. Nl.
Smith, William. AT from QS Lent 1771. Li.
Smith, William. S & T Jly 1771 *Scarsdale*. M.
Smith, William. S s at Bywell & R Summer 1771 T
  Lowther & Senhouse LC Va May 1772. Nl.
Smith, William. SQS Oct T Dec 1771 *Justitia*. M.
Smith, William (1772). *See* Todd. Nl.
Smith, William. S s at Cannock Lent 1772. St.
Smith, William of Newington. R 14 yrs s gelding Lent T Apr 1772
  Thornton. Sy.
Smith, William. S Sep-Oct 1772. M.
Smith, William (1773). *See* Fuller, Thomas. So.
Smith, William (2). S Jan-Feb 1773. M.
Smith, William. S Apr 1773. M.
Smith, William. S for shoplifting at South Shields Summer 1773. Du.
Smith, William. S Feb 1774. L.
Smith, William. S Dec 1774. L.
Smith, William Watkins. S Lent 1763. Ht.
Smith, Winifred als Ophelia. S Jly 1720. M.
Smith, Zachary. S s canvas at Bridgnorth Lent 1724. Sh.
Smitham, Stacey. S Jly T Aug 1721 *Owners Goodwill* to Md. M.
Smither, John. S Summer R for Barbados Aug 1665. Sy.
Smyther als Guyver, Sarah. T Apr 1735 *Patapsco*. K.
Smithergill, John. R for America Jly 1694. No.
Smithers, Ann. S Feb 1773. L.
Smithers, Elizabeth. S Lent T Sep 1757 *Thetis*. K.
Smithiard, Giles, gardener aged 21. R for Barbados Feb 1664. L.
Smytheman, Samuel. S Apr-May T May 1744 *Justitia*. M.
Smithiman als Aston, Thomas. S s flax at Wolverhampton Summer
  1750. St.
Smithson, John. S Mar 1761. L.
Smithson als Smith, Joseph. S Jan T Jun 1738 *Forward*. L.
Smithson, Mary, aged 26, brown hair. LC from *Gilbert* Md May 1721. X.
Smithson, William. S Feb T Apr 1769 *Thornton*. M.
Smythurst, Nathaniel (1675). *See* Haythorne. Y.

Smithurst, William. S Jly T 14 yrs Aug 1721 *Prince Royal* LC Va Nov 1721. L.

Smout, John. S & T Dec 1767 *Neptune*. M.

Smowing, Thomas. S s at Radley Lent 1775. Be.

Smurfitt, Thomas of York. R for Barbados Jly 1671. Y.

Snaesby, James. S & T Jan 1736 *Dorsetshire* LC Va Sep 1736. L.

Snagg, Thomas. S Lent T May 1719 *Margaret* LC Md May 1720; sold to Peter Galoway. Sy.

Snail, William. S Lent 1737. Su.

Snailam, Richard. S Lent TB Apr 1756. Db.

Snailum, Thomas. SQS Jly TB Sep 1772. So.

Snailes als Snailhouse, Hannah. S Feb T Apr 1732 *Patapsco* LC Annapolis Oct 1732. M.

Snalham, Henry (1773). *See* Snellham. La.

Snape, Mary wife of Edward. S Lent 1767. Wa.

Snape, Nathaniel. S & T Dec 1734 *Caesar* LC Va Jly 1735. L.

Snape, William. S s sheep Lent R 14 yrs Summer 1752. St.

Snapp, William (1749). *See* Heath. Le.

Snawden, Robert of York Castle. R for Barbados Feb 1673. Y.

Snaxton, Elizabeth of Croydon. R for Barbados or Jamaica Jun 1699. Sy.

Snead, Elizabeth. R for Barbados Feb 1675. L.

Sneyd, John (1763). *See* Lewis, Christopher. Db.

Sneed, Robert. S Oct 1741 T Feb 1742 *Industry*. L.

Sneechall, Sarah (1765). *See* Murrell. L.

Sneesby, Richard. S Lent 1773. K.

Snell, Bejamin, als Rice, Dick. S & T Apr 1762 *Neptune*. M.

Snell, James. S Lent 1746. Su.

Snell, James. TB to Va 1769. De.

Snell, Mary. R for Barbados Dec 1681 & Sep 1682. L.

Snell, Richard. T Jly 1724 *Robert* LC Md Jun 1725. Sy.

Snell, Richard. S Feb T Mar 1729 *Patapsco* LC Annapolis Dec 1729. M.

Snell, Thomas. R Jan 1656. M.

Snell, Thomas. T 14 yrs Dec 1758 *The Brothers*. K.

Snellham als Snalham, Henry of Longton. SQS Apr 1773. La.

Snelling, James. S s worsted at St. Giles, Norwich, Summer 1771. Nf.

Snelling, John. S Summer 1757. Nf.

Snelling, Rebecca. R for Barbados Dec 1670. M.

Snelling als Marison, Thomas of Barton Turf. R for America Aug 1691. Nf.

Snellock, James. S & T Sep 1751 *Greyhound*. M.

Snipe, Elizabeth of Maidstone. R for Barbados Apr 1668. K.

Snook, George. SQS Apr TB May 1770. So.

Snooke, Henry. Rebel T 1685.

Snook, Richard. Rebel T 1685.

Snooke, Thomas of Stalbridge. R for Barbados Jly 1678. Do.

Snooke, Thomas. Rebel T 1685.

Snoud, William of Heston. R for highway robbery & T 14 yrs Feb 1740 *York*. M.

Snow, Erasmus John. T Nov 1759 *Phoenix*. Sy.

Snow, George. Rebel T 1685.

Snowe, Henry of Sampford Courtenay. R for Barbados Feb 1669. De.

Snow, John. T Jly 1723 *Alexander* LC Md Sep 1723. Bu.

Snow, John. T Apr 1734 *Patapsco*. E.

Snow, John. S s poultry at Sandleford Lent 1766. Be.

Snow, John Brown. S Lent R 14 yrs Summer 1768. G.

Snow, Robert of Hertford. S as accessory to murder Summer 1745 R 14 yrs Lent 1746. Ht.

Snow, William. R 14 yrs Jly 1766. De.

Snowden, Edward. R 14 yrs Summer 1743. Y.

Snowden, Matthew. S Lent TB Sep 1740. Y.

Sockett, Andrew. S Sep 1761. M.

Sockett, Martha. S Summer 1773. Sy.

Soddi, Elizabeth. R & T 14 yrs Jly 1770 *Scarsdale*. M.

Soden, John. S Apr T Oct 1719 *Susannah & Sarah* LC Annapolis Apr 1720. L.

Soe als Jackson, Elizabeth. R for Barbados Oct 1673. L.

Sogg, Elizabeth. SQS Jan TB Apr 1769. So.

Sollis, Elizabeth. S & T Sep 1731 *Smith* LC Va 1732. M.

Solace, John. S s at Quenington Lent 1758. G.

Solace, Joseph. S s at Quenington Lent 1758. G.

Solding, John. SQS Lent TB Apr 1766. Db.

Soleby, Thomas. T Sep 1764 *Justitia*. Ht.

Sollon, James. S Jan 1746. L.

Sollowin als Quin, Margaret. R Feb T for life Apr 1762 *Dolphin*. M.

Solly als Phillips, Richard. S s sheep at Llanvair Waterdine Lent 1724. Sh.

Solme, Jacob. T Apr 1741 *Speedwell* or *Mediterranean*. E.

Solomon, Aaron. S Sep-Oct 1772. M.

Solomon, Abraham. S Oct 1748 T Jan 1749 *Laura*. L.

Solomon, Alley. T 14 yrs Apr 1770 *New Trial*. E.

Solomon, Barnard. S May T Jun 1764 *Dolphin*. L.

Solomon, Barnard. S 14 yrs for receiving Oct 1773. L.

Solomon, Benjamin (1774). *See* Solomon, Wolfe. Co.

Solomon, David. S Nov T Dec 1752 *Greyhound*. L.

Solomon, Emanuel. S Feb-Apr T May 1751 *Tryal*. M.

Solomon, Hyam. S & T Jly 1770 *Scarsdale*. L.

Solomon, Isaac. S May T Nov 1762 *Prince William*. M.

Solomon, Joshua. S Feb 1774. L.

Solomon, Robert, als Blind Isaac. S Dec 1750. L.

Solomon als Abrahams, Samuel. SQS Jan T Apr 1766 *Ann*. M.

Solomon, Saunders. S & T Mar 1760 *Friendship*. L.

Solomon, Wolfe als Benjamin, als Wolfe, Solomon. S Aug 1774. Co.

Solomons, Joseph (1774). *See* Abrahams. L.

Solomons, Lazarus. S Oct T Dec 1771 *Justitia*. L.

Solomons, Rachael. SL & T Sep 1765 *Justitia*. Sy.

Solomons, Solomon (1769). *See* Isaacs. L.

Solomons, Solomon. S Jan-Feb T Apr 1771 *Thornton*. M.

Somarell. *See* Summerell.

Somerhays. *See* Summerhayes.

Somes, John of Selling. R for America Jly 1700. K.

Somes, Sarah. S 14 yrs Apr 1745. L.

Somes, Thomas. S May T Jun 1727 *Susannah*. M.

Sommers. *See* Summers.

Somner, Jonas (1667). *See* Sumner. L.

Sonee, Ann. S Jan T Feb 1744 *Neptune* to Md. M.

Sonne, Susan. PT Aug 1678. M.

Soper, James. Rebel T 1685.

Sopitt, William. S City Summer 1740. Nl.

Sorrell, Daniel. S Mar 1737. So.

Sorrell, John. S Summer 1756 R 14 yrs Lent 1757. o.

Sorrell, Joseph. S & R at Rochester, Kent, Lent 1763. E.

Soukes, Rowland. S May T Sep 1766 *Justitia*. M.

Soul, John. S Lent 1774. Wa.

Soul, Thomas. S & R 14 yrs Lent 1763. G.

Soulsby, John. S s mare at Rookby & R 14 yrs Summer 1768 TB Apr
1769. Y.

Soulsby, Thomas, als Robson, John. S s gelding at Elswick & R
Summer 1771 T *Lowther & Senhouse* LC Va May 1772. Nl.

Soulter. *See* Salter.

Souper, Robert. S Jly T Aug 1721 *Prince Royal* LC Va Nov 1721. L.

South, Francis. S Lent 1766. Nt.

South, John. S Feb 1752. L.

South, Mary. S Jan T Feb 1733 *Smith* to Md or Va. M.

South, Samuel. SQS for gambling at cards Jan 1761. Sy.

South, Samuel. S & T Apr 1762 *Neptune*. M.

South, Thomas. R 14 yrs Jly 1744. Ha.

South, William (1742). *See* Jackson. L.

Southake, Cyprian of Faccombe, scrivener. R for Barbados Jly 1681. Ha.

Southall, Edward of Cleobury Mortimer. S s sheep at Kidderminster
Summer 1719. Wo.

Southall, Elizabeth. S Oct 1766 T Jan 1767 *Tryal*. L.

Southall, Joseph. S s at Dudley Summer 1771. Wo.

Southall, Solomon. S Aug T Sep 1725 *Forward* LC Annapolis Dec
1725. L.

Southam, Thomas of St. Martin in Fields, wigmaker. SW Apr 1773. M.

Southam, Thomas of St. Martin in Fields, labourer. SW Apr 1773. M.

Southerby, Mary. S Oct-Dec 1754. M.

Southerland. *See* Sutherland.

Southeran als Keys, Elizabeth. S Sep-Dec 1755 T Jan 1756
Greyhound. M.

Southen, Thomas. T May 1736 *Patapsco*. E.

Southerne als Southwell, Thomas. S (Western Circ) Dec 1766. Be.

Southan, William. S s at St. Martin, Worcester, Lent 1775. Wo.

Southernwood, Anne. S Aug T Oct 1724 *Forward* LC Annapolis Jun
1725. L.

Southerton, Richard. T May 1737 *Forward*. Sy.

Southier, James, gent. R for America Nov 1706 for entering France
without licence. L.

Southray, Samuel. S Mar 1752. So.

Southurst, Robert (1766). *See* Sudders. La.

Southward, Eleanor (1762). *See* Forshea. M.

Southwell, John. T Apr 1742 *Bond*. E.

Southwell, Thomas (1766). *See* Southerne. Be.

Southwood, John. R 14 yrs Aug 1742. De.

Soutter, William. T Aug 1720 *Owners Goodwill*. K.

Sowdell, William. R for Barbados Mar 1677. L.

Sowden, Benjamin. S Jly 1774. L.

Sowden, Michael. SQS Jan 1771. M.

Sowerbutts, Ellen wife of Richard *(qv)*. SQS Jan 1765. La.

Sowerbutts, Richard of Ormskirk, blacksmith. SQS Jan 1765. La.

Sowgate, James of Great Holland. R for Barbados or Jamaica Jun 1692. E.

Sowray, Malachy. S Feb T Mar 1731 *Patapsco* LC Annapolis Jun 1731. M.

Sowton, Mary. S Feb T Sep 1737 *Pretty Patsy* to Md. M.

Spackman, Charles. S Apr T May 1751 *Tryal*. L.

Spackman, Margaret. S for arson & R 14 yrs Summer 1743; died in prison. Ca.

Spackman, Rebecca. T Apr 1768 *Thornton*. L.

Spacy, John. S s sheep at Dalton & R 14 yrs Lent 1768. Y.

Spain, Augustin. T Jun 1740 *Essex*. K.

Spaish, James. S s sheep Lent R 14 yrs Summer 1767. Be.

Spalding, Elizabeth. S May-Jly 1749. M.

Sparey als Parry, John. S Lent R 14 yrs Summer 1767. St.

Sparribell, Isaac. SQS Warminster or New Sarum TB to Va Oct 1768. Wi.

Spariner, Richard. T Sep 1730 *Smith*. K.

Sparke, Benjamin. Rebel T 1685.

Sparke als Zouch, Elizabeth. R for Barbados Mar 1681. L.

Sparke, John. TB to Va from QS 1732. De.

Sparke, Samuel. S Lent 1751. Su.

Sparke, Thomas. S Summer 1720. Y.

Sparke, William. R 14 yrs Aug 1746. De.

Sparks, Alice. T Jly 1723 *Alexander* LC Md Sep 1723. Sy.

Sparkes, Charles. S Feb T Apr 1770 *New Trial*. L.

Sparks, Edward of St. George, Southwark. SQS Apr T Jly 1770 *Scarsdale*. Sy.

Sparkes, Henry. S Summer 1754. E.

Sparkes, John, aged 26. R for Barbados Feb 1664. L.

Sparkes, John. S Aug T Oct 1724 *Forward* LC Annapolis Jun 1725. M.

Sparkes, Margaret. S Feb T Apr 1734 *Patapsco* to Md. M.

Sparks, Mary. R 14 yrs Aug 1734. De.

Sparkes, Samuel. S Dec 1754. L.

Sparkes, Samuel (1763). *See* Gilbert. L.

Sparks, Sarah. S Jan-Jun 1747. M.

Sparkes, William. S s bacon Jan-May T Jun 1738 *Forward* to Md or Va. M.

Sparkes, William. T Jun 1740 *Essex*. Sy.

Sparkes, William. S Jly T Sep 1755 *Tryal*. L.

Sparkman, Samuel. R 14 yrs Jly 1758. Ha.

Sparrow, Elizabeth. R for Barbados Jun 1671. L.

Sparrow, James. S s pigs at Rougham Lent 1771. Nf.

Sparrow, John. S Mar 1774. Do.

Sparrow, John. PT Oct R Dec 1698. M.

Sparrow, John. S s copper Lent 1765. Ca.

Sparrow, Joseph. S for highway robbery & R Lent 1738. Su.

Sparrow, Joseph. T May 1752 *Lichfield*. Sy.

Sparrow, Joseph. S Feb T Apr 1765 *Ann*. M.

Sparrow, Mary (1754). *See* Walker. L.

Sparrow, Robert. S & T Jan 1756 *Greyhound*. M.

Sparrow, William. S Aug 1752. So.

Sparry. *See* Sperry.

Spavold, John. S for highway robbery Lent R 14 yrs Summer 1767 T Apr 1768. Li.

Spaw, Esther (1732). *See* Thacker. M.

Spawl, John. S & T Dec 1731 *Forward* to Md or Va. M.

Spaul, John. S s horse Lent R 14 yrs Summer 1740 (SP). Nf.

Spaul, Thomas. S & T Oct 1730 *Forward* LC Potomack Jan 1731. M.

Spawfoot, William. S May T Jun 1727 *Susanna*. L.

Spawford, Mary. S Feb T Mar 1727 *Rappahannock* to Md. M.

Speake, Mary. S Summer 1729 R Lent 1730 (SP). Sh.

Spear, Joseph. S Apr T 14 yrs Aug 1718 *Eagle* LC Charles Town Mar 1719. L.

Spearin, James. S Feb T Apr 1765 *Ann*. L.

Spearing, John. Rebel T 1685.

Spearman, Mary, aged 17, fair. S & T 14 yrs Oct 1720 *Gilbert* LC Md May 1721. M.

Speciall, Edward. R Aug 1700. M.

Speck, John. S s watches at Tetbury Summer 1764. G.

Spedding, William. S Apr 1775. M.

Speed, Benjamin. S Apr T May 1718 *Tryal* LC Charles Town Aug 1718. L.

Speed, Benjamin. S & T Oct 1720 *Gilbert* to Md. M.

Speed, Francis. S Feb T Mar 1730 *Patapsco* but died on passage. L.

Speed, John Jr. R 14 yrs Mar 1725. So.

Speed, Mary. S May T Jun 1756 *Lyon*. L.

Speed, Richard. S Mar 1740. So.

Speed, Simon. S & T Jly 1770 *Scarsdale*. M.

Speed, Thomas. Rebel T 1685.

Speight, Christopher. S Oct T Nov 1759 *Phoenix*. M.

Speight, Mary wife of Stephen. S Summer 1756. Y.

Spence, Andrew. S s mare Summer 1722 R 14 yrs Summer 1724. Du.

Spence, James. Rebel T 1685.

Spence, Thomas. R 14 yrs Summer 1730. Y.

Spenceley, George. S s at Whitby Lent R 14 yrs Summer TB Aug 1765. Y.

Spenceley, John. S s hood Jan T Apr 1735 *Patapsco* LC Annapolis Oct 1735. M.

Spencer, Ann, als Browne, Mary of St. Saviour, Southwark. R for Barbados or Jamaica Jly 1688. Sy.

Spencer, Ann. SQS Jan 1767. Ha.

Spencer, Arthur. S 14 yrs Apr 1747. So.

Spencer, Edward of Walmsley, weaver. SQS Aug 1759. La.

Spencer, Edward. S Jan-Feb 1775. M.

Spencer, Elianor of Barking. R for Barbados or Jamaica Jly 1710. E.
Spencer, Elizabeth. S Jly 1773. L.
Spencer, Henry of Watford. R for America Jly 1678. No.
Spencer, James. S Sep T Oct 1750 *Rachael*. L.
Spencer, Jane. R 14 yrs Aug 1747. So.
Spencer, Jane wife of William. S Feb T May 1767 *Thornton*. M.
Spencer, John. R Feb 1675. M.
Spencer, John (1690). *See* Loveridge. L.
Spencer, John. S s gelding Lent R 14 yrs Summer 1754. Bd.
Spencer, John. SW & T Jun 1768 *Tryal*. M.
Spencer, John. S s bullock & R Summer 1768. Nf.
Spencer, John. S s at Bolnhurst & R 14 yrs Lent 1771. Bd.
Spencer, John. S Lent 1773. Db.
Spencer, Laurence. T Apr 1742 *Bond*. E.
Spencer, Martha. S Mar 1720. Do.
Spencer, Martin of Maghull. SQS Apr 1769. La.
Spencer, Mary. S Jan-Apr 1749. M.
Spencer, Mary (1762). *See* Davy. Nf.
Spencer, Mary. S Sep-Oct 1772. M.
Spencer, Moses. S s box at St. Botolph Aldgate Sep T Oct 1768
    Justitia. L.
Spencer, Robert of Ilford. R for Barbados or Jamaica Jly 1702. E.
Spencer als Spicer, Robert. S s iron at Rowley Lent 1769. St.
Spencer, Rowland. S s gold rings at Ombersley Lent 1753. Wo.
Spencer, Thomas of Witham. R for Barbados or Jamaica Feb 1690. E.
Spencer, Thomas. R 14 yrs Jly 1763. Ha.
Spencer, William of Neen Savage. R for America Jly 1673. Sh.
Spencer, William. S & T Jan 1722 *Gilbert* but died on passage. M.
Spencer, William. S Feb T Mar 1730 *Patapsco* LC Annapolis Sep
    1730. M.
Spencer, William of Kinoulton, weaver. SQS s cock Oct 1759. Nt.
Spender, John. S Mar TB Oct 1735. Wi.
Sperring, John of St. Cuthbert, Wells, tailor. R for Barbados Jan
    1676. So.
Sparry, Ann. R for America Jly 1687.
Sperrey, William. R for Barbados Aug 1670. M.
Spettigue, Burchett. S for Va Jly 1718. De.
Spice, Richard. S Mar 1747. Ha.
Spicer, Elizabeth. S Apr-Jun T Jly 1772 *Tayloe*. M.
Spicer, Francis. S Feb T Mar 1730 *Patapsco* LC Annapolis Sep 1730. M.
Spicer, George. S & T Sep 1765 *Justitia*. L.
Spicer, Jane. S Feb T Apr 1769 *Tryal*. M.
Spicer, John. SQS Warminster Jly TB to Va Sep 1741. Wi.
Spicer, Jonathan. S Apr 1773. M.
Spicer, Robert. S Aug T Oct 1724 *Forward* LC Annapolis Jun 1725. M.
Spicer, Robert (1769). *See* Spencer. St.
Spicer, Samuel. S Lent 1768. Su.
Spicer, Thomas. S Jun T Aug 1769 *Douglas*. L.
Spikeman, William of Modbury. R for Barbados Jly 1695. De.
Spiller, Richard. Rebel T 1685.
Spiller, Robert of Ottery St. Mary. R for Barbados Jly 1717. De.

Spilsbury, George (1751). *See* Pilsbury. La.

Spindle, John. S Oct 1732. M.

Spindler, Richard. S Jun T Sep 1767 *Justitia*. L.

Spines, Thomas. R Jly T for life Sep 1767 *Justitia*. M.

Spinke, Jeffry. S Lent 1743. *Su.

Spink, John. SQS East Retford & TB May 1739. Nt.

Spink, John (1756). *See* Wray. Y.

Spink, Robert. T Aug 1769 *Douglas*. M.

Spinks, Daniel of St. Olave, Southwark, carpenter. SQS Jan 1751. Sy.

Spinks, James. S & R Lent 1765. Nf.

Spinks, Thomas. S Oct T Dec 1771 *Justitia*. L.

Spinner, Thomas. S Summer 1733 R 14 yrs Summer 1734. Wo.

Spire, Andrew. R for Barbados Aug 1679. M.

Spires, Deborah. S May T Jun 1727 *Susanna* to Va. M.

Spires, William. S Sep-Oct 1772. M.

Spiring, John. S Mar 1738. So.

Spittle, John. R Jan 1679 & Sep 1682. M.

Spittle, Richard of Wellridge. R for Barbados Jly 1681. Do.

Spittle, Robert. T May 1751 *Tryal*. Sy.

Spivey, James. S Apr T May 1751 *Tryal*. L.

Spoke, Ann. S for arson Summer 1757 R for life Lent 1758. Be.

Spooner, John (1722). *See* Scoon. L.

Spooner, John. S s agricultural tools at Howe Lent 1775. Nf.

Spooner, Peter. T Jan 1734 *Caesar* LC Va Jly 1734. E.

Spours, John. S & T Jly 1772 *Tayloe*. L.

Sprackland, James of Lyme Regis. S for Va Jly 1718. Do.

Spragg, Abraham. S Summer 1749 R 14 yrs Lent 1750. Wo.

Spragg, John. S & T Sep 1765 *Justitia*. L.

Spragg, Samuel Jr. S Jly 1766. Ha.

Spraggs, Thomas. S Summer 1741. Sh.

Sprague, John Jr. S Mar 1764. So.

Sprague, Michael. S Apr T 14 yrs May 1767 *Thornton*. M.

Sprake, John (2). Rebels T 1685.

Sprangley als Prawley, John. SQS Jly 1741 TB to Md May 1742. So.

Spratlye, James, aged 17, dark. T Oct 1720 *Gilbert* LC Md May 1721. Sy.

Spratley, Millicent, als Featherstone, Ann wife of James. S Jan T Mar
  1764 *Tryal*. M.

Spratt, Francis of Wootton. R for America Mar 1680. O.

Spratt, John of Newington near Sittingbourne. R for Barbados or
  Jamaica Mar 1707. K.

Spratt, Joseph. S Mar 1752. So.

Spratt, Philemon. SQS Jly 1742 TB to Md Feb 1743. So.

Spratt, Richard of Kennington. R for Barbados or Jamaica Dec 1680. K.

Spratt, Sarah. S Mar 1737. Ha.

Spratt, Sarah. S Mar TB to Va Apr 1772. Wi.

Spratt, Thomas. S s horse Summer 1750 R 14 yrs Lent 1751. Le.

Spratt, William. S Apr 1754. So.

Spreadbarrow, John. T May 1741 *Miller*. K.

Spreate, William. Rebel T 1685.

Spriggs, Stephen. SL Jan T Mar 1758 *Dragon*. Sy.

Sprightley, Hannah. S Sep-Dec 1746. M.

Sprigmore als Caddell, Elizabeth of St. Martin in Fields, spinster. SW & T Jan 1767 *Tryal*. M.

Spring, Robert. TB to Va from QS 1741. De.

Spring, Solomon. R Mar & Oct 1688. M.

Springett, Hester. S Sep-Oct T Dec 1753 *Whiteing*. M.

Springett, William. S s at Monmouth Lent 1770. Mo.

Springthorp, Ruth. S Aug T Sep 1725 *Forward* LC Annapolis Dec 1725. L.

Sproat, Joseph. S s watch Summer 1773. Nl.

Sprosly, Henry. PT May R Oct 1688. M.

Sproson, John. S Feb T Apr 1771 *Thornton*. L.

Spruce, Apswell. SQS Sep T Dec 1769 *Justitia*. M.

Spruce, John of Waterstock. R for America Feb 1700. O.

Spry, John. S Aug 1739. De.

Spurgeon, Ann. LC from *Margaret* & sold to Rosanna Lees Md Sep 1719. X.

Spurgeon, James. S Feb T May 1719 *Margaret*; sold to Richard Snowden Md Sep 1719. M.

Spurgeon, John. S Oct 1727-Jun 1728 T 14 yrs Jun 1728 *Elizabeth* LC Potomack Aug 1729. M.

Spurgeon, William. S Feb T May 1719 *Margaret*; sold to Richard Snowden Md Aug 1719. L.

Spurham, George. S Jan T Apr 1743 *Justitia*. M.

Spurling, Elizabeth. S Apr 1749. L.

Spurling, Mary. S Aug T Oct 1726 *Forward*. L.

Spurling, Nicholas. S Apr 1749. L.

Spurr, Moses. S for aiding escape from gaol Summer 1764. Nt.

Spurr, Thomas. R for America Jly 1709. Nt.

Spurr, William of East Bridgeford, framework knitter. SQS s cloth Jly 1764. Nt.

Spurrier als Hall, Elizabeth. S Aug T Sep 1725 *Forward* LC Annapolis Dec 1725. M.

Spurry, John. S Aug 1766. So.

Spurway, Daniel. R 14 yrs Aug 1742. De.

Spurway, Robert. Rebel T 1685.

Squelpyn, Abraham. R & TB Lent 1655. Sy.

Squire, Anne. S Apr T May 1719. L.

Squire, John. S Lent TB Apr 1766. Db.

Squire, Peter. S Mar 1760. Ha.

Squire, Robert. T Apr 1733 *Patapsco*. K.

Squire, Robert. S s gelding at Leighton Buzzard & R 14 yrs Lent 1769. Bd.

Squire, Thomas. S s at Christchurch, Oxford, Lent 1722. O.

Squire, William. R 14 yrs Aug 1772 TB to Va. De.

Squires, James of St. Olave, Southwark. SQS Apr 1774. Sy.

Squires, Mary. S Oct 1761. L.

Squires, Robert. S Jan T Apr 1743 *Justitia*. M.

Squires, William. S Oct 1764 T Jan 1765 *Tryal*. M.

Squirrell, Elizabeth of St. Giles, Colchester. S Lent 1745. E.

Stabler, John. S Apr 1760. M.

Stacey, Alice, spinster, als wife of Robert. R for Barbados Aug 1664. L.

Stacey, John of Chedzoy. R for Barbados Feb 1683. So.
Stacey, John of Worth. R for Barbados or Jamaica Jly 1696. Sx.
Stacey, Thomas. S s at Tilehurst Lent R 14 yrs Suumer 1745. Be.
Stacy, William. R 14 yrs Jly 1755 TB to Va 1756. De.
Stack, Richard. TB to Va from QS 1766. De.
Stackpool, George. S Dec 1741 T Feb 1742 *Industry* to Md. M.
Stackwell, John, aged 25. R for Barbados Feb 1664. M.
Staddon als Stanton, John. R 14 yrs Aug 1742. De.
Staddon, William. T Jun 1764 *Dolphin*. K.
Staddow, John. S Jan 1746. L.
Stader, Robert. S & T Oct 1730 *Forward* LC Potomack Jan 1731. M.
Stader, Thomas. S & T 14 yrs Oct 1730 *Forward* LC Potomack Jan 1731. M.
Stades, John. LC from *Mary* Port York Jun 1721. X.
Stafford, Ann. S Sep-Dec 1755 T Jan 1756 *Greyhound*. M.
Stafford, Ann. S Apr T May 1767 *Thornton*. L.
Stafford als Page als Terry, Elizabeth. T Jun 1727 *Susanna*. Sy.
Stafford, Hannah. S Lent TB Mar 1772. Db.
Stafford, John. S Feb T Apr 1766 *Ann*. L.
Stafford, John. T Apr 1770 *New Trial*. L.
Stafford, Matthew, aged 27, brown hair. S & T Oct 1720 *Gilbert* LC Annapolis May 1721. M.
Stafford, Nathaniel of St. Saviour, Southwark. SQS Jan T Jun 1764 *Dolphin*. Sy.
Stafford, Thomas Jr. S Lent 1756. Bu.
Stafford, William als John. R for Barbados or Jamaica Oct 1688. M.
Stafford, William. R Oct 1694 AT Jan 1695. M.
Stagg, Grace (1742). See Thomas. Wi.
Stagg, John. S Norwich Summer 1758 R Lent 1759 but died in prison. Nf.
Stainbank, William. S & T Aug 1725 *Forward* LC Annapolis Dec 1725. L.
Stiner, Jacob. S Jan T Feb 1765 *Tryal*. L.
Stayner, Richard. T Sep 1730 *Smith*. Ht.
Stains, Benjamin of Great Baddow. S Lent 1745. E.
Staynes, Daniel. R Dec 1699 AT Jan 1700. M.
Staines, Elizabeth. R for Barbados Jan 1679. L.
Staines als Allen, Elizabeth. R for Barbados Mar 1681. M.
Stanes, Ezekiel. T Apr 17441 *Speedwell* or *Mediterranean*. Ht.
Staines, Ruth. R for Barbados or Jamaica May 1691. L.
Staines, Thomas. T May 1737 *Forward*. Ht.
Stains, William. S s sheep Lent R 14 yrs Summer 1754. No.
Staines, William. S & T Jly 1770 *Scarsdale*. M.
Stainforth, Isaac. S Lent 1758. Y.
Stainton, John of Wrenthorpe, Wakefield, yeoman. R for Barbados Jly 1699. Y.
Stainton, Mary. S Summer 1744. Cu.
Staley, Andrew. Rebel T 1685.
Stallard, Sarah. S s at Torrington Lent 1769. He.
Stallard, William. S Dec 1764 T Jan 1765 *Tryal*. M.
Stammers, John. R Lent 1775. E.

Stamp, Roger. S Aug 1746. De.
Stamper, Robert. T 14 yrs Aug 1752 *Tryal*. Sy.
Stamps, William. S Jan T Apr 1768 *Thornton*. M.
Stanborough, John. S May T Jly 1722 *Alexander* to Nevis or Jamaica. M.
Stanburn, Robert. R 14 yrs Aug 1730. So.
Stanbury, Ann. S Jan 1746. L.
Stanbury, Gerthrud. S Jan 1724. M.
Stanbury, John. S Mar 1756. Co.
Stanbury, Roger. R for Jamaica Aug 1661. M.
Stanbury, William. S Mar 1733. De.
Standeford, William. S Oct T Nov 1759 *Phoenix*. L.
Standerwick, Nathaniel. Rebel T 1685.
Standfad, Mary. T Apr 1743 *Justitia*. Sy.
Standfast, Richard. T Oct 1729 *Forward*. K.
Standitch, Mary. T Oct 1738 *Genoa*. K.
Standidge, Sarah. S & T Jly 1753 *Tryal*. M.
Standley, Humphry. R 14 yrs Mar TB to Va Apr 1775. Wi.
Standworth, Henry. S Lent R 14 yrs Summer 1745. St.
Stanfart, John. TB to Va from QS 1740. De.
Stanfield, Elizabeth. S Apr T May 1743 *Indian Queen* to Potomack. M.
Stanfield als Ogden, Elizabeth. R Dec 1765 T Jan 1766 *Tryal*. M.
Stanford, Augustine. R for Barbados Sep 1672. L.
Stanford, Elizabeth. S Jan-Feb 1774. M.
Stanford, James. R 10 yrs in plantations Oct 1662. M.
Stanford, Margaret. T Aug 1720 *Owners Goodwill*. K.
Stanford, William. S Jun-Dec 1738 T Jan 1739 *Dorsetshire* to Va. M.
Stanford, William. S Lent 1748. E.
Stangroom, Susannah. S s at Terrington St. Clement Lent 1769. Nf.
Stanhope, John. S s horse Lent R 14 yrs Summer 1756. La.
Staniell, Edward. R for Barbados Feb 1675. L.
Staniford, Walter. T Jly 1770 *Scarsdale*. M.
Stanland, John of Clerkenwell. S s iron & T May 1736 *Patapsco* to Md. M.
Stanley, Anne. S Lent 1739. Ch.
Stanley als Alder, Ann. S Jly T Sep 1765 *Justitia*. M.
Stanley, Edward. S s at Stone Lent 1743. St.
Stanley, Edward (1772). *See* Stanlins. Wo.
Stanley, James. S Feb T Sep 1737 *Pretty Patsy* to Md. M.
Stanley, James. S Dec 1743 T Feb 1744 *Neptune* to Md. M.
Stanley, James. R 14 yrs Aug 1764. Do.
Stanley, Johanna. PT Apr R Oct 1673 AT Jun 1674. M.
Stanley, John of Cambridge. R for America Jly 1702. Ca.
Stanley, John. S s iron mortar Jun T Dec 1736 *Dorsetshire* to Va. M.
Stanley als Brown, John. S Jan-Jun 1747. M.
Stanley, John. S s sheep Lent R 14 yrs Summer 1748. Wa.
Stanley, John of Chetham, gardener. SQS May 1753. La.
Stanley, John. S & T Sep 1755 *Tryal*. L.
Stanley, John. S Oct T Dec 1767 *Neptune*. L.
Stanley, John. S Lent 1772. La.
Stanley, John. R 14 yrs Jly TB to Va Sep 1773. Wi.
Stanley, Mary. R for Barbados Dec 1668. M.

Stanley als Slack, Mary. S as pickpocket Lent 1733. St.

Stanley, Mary. SQS Jly 1750. M.

Stanley, Nathaniel. T Sep 1730 *Smith*. Ht.

Stanley, Peter. S Jun T Sep 1764 *Justitia*. M.

Stanley, Samuel. S s mare Summer 1765 R 14 yrs Lent 1766. Li.

Stanley, Temperance. S May T Jun 1726 *Loyal Margaret* LC Annapolis Oct 1726. M.

Stanley, Thomas. R (Midland Circ) for America Jly 1678. X.

Stanley, Thomas. S s kettle at Sherborn St. John (Hants) Summer 1734. Be.

Stanley, Thomas. S Lent R Summer T for life Sep 1751 *Greyhound*. Sy.

Stanley, Thomas. SQS Coventry Oct 1754. Wa.

Stanley, Thomas (1772). *See* Adams. M.

Stanley, Thomas. S Summer 1775. Wa.

Stanley, William. T May 1719 *Margaret* LC Md Aug 1719; sold to Patrick Sympson. Ht.

Stanely, William. T Sep 1758 *Tryal*. K.

Stanley, William. SQS Dec 1766 T Jan 1767 *Tryal*. M.

Stanlins als Stanley, Edward. S s handkerchiefs at Bromsgrove Summer 1772. Wo.

Stanmore, Elizabeth. S & T Sep 1765 *Justitia*. L.

Stanard, —onking. LC from *Elizabeth* Potomack Aug 1729. X.

Stannard, Elizabeth. S Lent R 14 yrs Summer 1767. Su.

Stennard, Lawrence. S Mar 1736. De.

Stannard, Stephen. SEK & T Dec 1771 *Justitia*. K.

Stanners, George. S s sheep Summer 1773 R 14 yrs Summer 1754. Du.

Stanney, William of New Windsor. R for Jamaica, Barbados or Bermuda Feb 1686. Be.

Stannifer, Mary. S Sep-Dec 1746. M.

Stanning, John. S & T Jan 1736 *Dorsetshire* LC Va Sep 1736. L.

Stanninot, William. S Apr T May 1751 *Tryal*. L.

Stannum, John of Preston. R for Barbados or Jamaica Feb 1683. K.

Stansbury, Jonathan. S s horse Summer 1766 R 14 yrs Summer 1768. He.

Stansbury als Boucher als Burcher, Mary als Margaret. S & T 14 yrs May 1744 *Justitia*. L.

Stansfield, James. S Summer 1760. La.

Stansfield, James. S s horse at Bradford & R Lent 1774. Y.

Stanton, Adam. S Apr-Jun 1739. M.

Stanton, Anne. S Dec 1727. M.

Stanton, Charles. SQS Warminster Jly TB to Va Aug 1752. Wi.

Stanton, Elizabeth. S Jan T Feb 1733 *Smith*. L.

Stanton, James. S Jan-Feb 1775. M.

Stanton, John. T Oct 1726 *Forward*. K.

Stanton, John (1742). *See* Staddon. De.

Stanton, John. S Apr T for life May 1750 *Lichfield*. M.

Stanton, John. S s wheat at All Saints, Newmarket, Summer 1773. Ca.

Stanton, Peter. S & T May 1740 *Essex*. L.

Staunton, William. Rebel T 1685.

Stanton, William of Bermondsey. R for Barbados or Jamaica Jly 1702. Sy.

Stanton, William. T Nov 1728 *Forward*. Ht.

Stanyland, Thomas. S s horse Summer 1725 R 14 yrs Lent 1729. Y.

Stanzell, Nicholas. PT May R Dec 1699 & Aug 1700. M.

Staple, Abraham. R Jan 1656. M.

Staple, Leonard. Rebel T 1685.

Stapler, John. S Mar 1754. L.

Staples, Ann wife of Robert. S Feb T Apr 1770 *New Trial*. M.

Staples, Daniel. S Jan T Mar 1743 *Justitia*. L.

Staples, James. S s at Newbury Lent 1723. Be.

Staples, John. S Lent 1771. Li.

Staples, Mary. S Jly-Sep T Sep 1742 *Forward*. M.

Staples, Mathew. S Feb 1775. L.

Staples, William. S Apr-May T May 1744 *Justitia*. M.

Stapleton, Benjamin. R 14 yrs Apr 1767. So.

Stapleton, Charles. S Jan T Feb 1733 *Smith* to Md or Va. M.

Stapleton, Sarah. S Jan T Feb 1733 *Smith* to Md or Va. M.

Stapleton, Thomas. S May T Jun 1768 *Tryal*. M.

Stapleton, William. S Sep T Dec 1769 *Justitia*. M.

Stapling, Ambrose. R for Barbados or Jamaica Feb 1686. M.

Starbuck, Richard. S s at Rodborough Summer TB Aug 1757. G.

Starkey, George. S May T Jun 1727 *Susanna* to Va. M.

Starky als Norman als Smart, Hanna. S & T Oct 1722 *Forward* LC Annapolis Jun 1723. M.

Starkey, John. S May T Jly 1722 *Alexander* to Nevis or Jamaica. M.

Starkey, Richard. R 14 yrs Aug 1754. So.

Starkey, Sarah (1721). *See* Tarborne. M.

Starkie, William. R for Barbados Jan 1664. L.

Starling, Edward. S May-Jly 1773. M.

Starling, Elizabeth. S & T Oct 1729 *Forward* but died on passage. M.

Starling, George. R for Barbados May 1676. M.

Starling, Sarah. S Oct T Dec 1724 *Rappahannock*. L.

Starlin, Thomas (1750). *See* Startin. Y.

Starnell, William of Hornchurch. R for Barbados or Jamaica Mar 1678. E.

Starre als Osborne, Elizabeth. R for Barbados or Jamaica May 1697. L.

Starr, Joan, spinster. S 1661 R for Barbados Apr 1663. Sx.

Starr, John of Waltham Cross. SQS Jan T Sep 1758 *Tryal*. E.

Starr, Sarah. R 14 yrs Mar 1775. Wi.

Starr, Stephen. R (Home Circ) for Barbados Aug 1663. X.

Starr, William. S Apr T Sep 1737 *Pretty Patsy* to Md. M.

Stars, John. S for false pretences May T Jun 1768 *Tryal*. L.

Start, John. S Oct T Nov 1728 *Forward* LC Rappahannock Jun 1729. M.

Startin als Starlin, Thomas. R 14 yrs Summer 1750. Y.

State, Edward. S Jly-Sep 1754. M.

States, Francis (1726). *See* Kates. L.

Statham, Thomas of Badwell Ash. R for Barbados or Jamaica Mar 1697. Su.

Stather, William. S & T Apr 1762 *Neptune*. M.

Staunton. *See* Stanton.

Stave, Sarah. S Lent 1746. Su.

Staveley, Elizabeth. S Sep 1760. L.

Staveraugh als Howell, Elizabeth. S May 1745. L.
Stavey, William. LC from *Rappahannock* Rappahannock Apr 1726. X.
Staynes. *See* Staines.
Stead, James. S Feb T Apr 1769 *Tryal*. M.
Steadman, Ann. S Jan T Feb 1742 *Industry*. L.
Steadman, Catherine. S Jly T Oct 1741 *Sea Horse* to Va. M.
Stedman, Christopher. T May 1737 *Forward*. Sx.
Steadman, James. S Apr T Jun 1742 *Bladon*. L.
Stedman, John Sr. T May 1737 *Forward*. Sx.
Stedman, John Jr. T May 1737 *Forward*. Sx.
Stedman, Samuel. S & T Dec 1758 *The Brothers*. L.
Stedman, William. R Summer 1773. Sy.
Steads, Richard. S Summer 1769. Li.
Stearn, Joseph. S s at St. George, Botolph Lane, Jly T Oct 1768
  Justitia. L.
Stebbing, Aaron. S s at Diss Lent 1773. Nf.
Stebbing, Thomas. S Summer 1754 R 14 yrs Lent T Jun 1756 *Lyon*. E.
Stebbins, John (1675). *See* Stubbings. M.
Stebbs, John. S s gelding Summer 1756 R 14 yrs Lent 1757. Wa.
Steddall, Elizabeth. T Sep 1742 *Forward*. K.
Steed, Samuel. S Summer 1749. K.
Steele, Alice (1678). *See* Williams. G.
Steale, Anthony. S Summer 1724. Nl.
Steel, Charles. S for false pretences Jun T Jly 1772 *Tayloe*. L.
Steele, Elizabeth. S & R Summer 1765. Ch.
Steele, James. S s sheep Lent R 14 yrs Summer 1768. G.
Steele, John. S Sep T Oct 1719 *Susannah & Sarah* LC Annapolis Apr
  1720. L.
Steel, John. S Oct T 14 yrs Nov 1725 *Rappahannock* LC Rappahannock
  Apr 1726. L.
Steel, John (1740). *See* Gilbert. M.
Steel, John. S s iron spikes from Lord Ravensworth Summer 1757. Nl.
Steel, John. S Summer 1772. K.
Steel, John. R 14 yrs Summer 1774. Du.
Steele, Joseph. S Summer T Sep 1755 *Tryal*. Sy.
Steele, Joseph. S Feb T Apr 1765 *Ann*. M.
Steel, Mary of Cuckfield, spinster. S Lent 1750. Sx.
Steel, Mary. S Jan-Feb T Apr 1753 *Thames*. M.
Steele, Mary. S Apr 1774. L.
Steele, Michael. S s at Whickham Summer 1766. Du.
Steele, Ralph. S Summer 1732 R 14 yrs Summer 1733. Nl.
Steel, Richard. S May-Jly T Sep 1751 *Greyhound*. M.
Steel, Richard. T Jly 1753 *Tryal*. M.
Steele, Samuel of Westbury. R for America Mar 1680. G.
Steele, Sarah. R for Barbados or Jamaica May 1691. M.
Steale, Thomas of Wanstead. R for Barbados or Jamaica Jly 1696. E.
Steele, Thomas. T Apr 1732 *Patapsco*. K.
Steele, Thomas (1771). *See* Webb. Ha.
Steele, William. SW & T 1767 *Neptune*. M.
Steel, William. S Apr T Jun 1768 *Tryal*. M.
Steel, William. SW & T Jly 1771 *Scarsdale*. M.

Steale, William. S Sep-Oct 1772. M.

Steere, Daniel. T Oct 1726 *Forward*. Sy.

Steere, Elizabeth of Plymouth. R for Barbados Jly 1679. De.

Steer, Hugh. S 14 yrs for receiving Mar 1773. De.

Steer, John Sr. S Mar 1744. So.

Steer, Thomas. S Lent 1775. Sx.

Steeres, John. R for Barbados or Jamaica Jly 1686. M.

Steers, John. T Aug 1769 *Douglas*. Sy.

Steeres, Mary of Birmingham. R for America Jly 1682. Wa.

Steers, William. T 14 yrs Dec 1770 *Justitia*. Sy.

Stelfox, Sarah. S 14 yrs for receiving Lent 1771. La.

Stempston, John. T Sep 1755 *Tryal*. M.

Stennard. *See* Stannard.

Stennett, Absolom. S & T Dec 1752 *Greyhound*. L.

Stennings, William. S Summer R for Barbados Aug 1664. K.

Stenson, James als William. S Summer 1749. Sy.

Stent, Deborah. S Apr T 14 yrs Aug 1718 *Eagle* LC Charles Town Mar 1719. L.

Stent, Henry, a Quaker. R for plantations Jly 1665 (PC). Ht.

Stent, Thomas. T Sep 1742 *Forward*. Sy.

Stent, Thomas. S Lent 1775. Sy.

Stenting, Edward. T Jan 1734 *Caesar*. Bu.

Stenton, George. SQS Apr 1775. Du.

Stenton, Richard of Southwell, gardener. SQS 10 yrs s bed linen Jan 1735. Nt.

Stephens. *See* Stevens.

Stephenson. *See* Stevenson.

Steps, Peter. S Feb 1719 T *Worcester* LC Annapolis Jun 1719. L.

Steptoe, William. S s blanket at Witney Summer 1760. O.

Sturney, John. R 14 yrs Mar 1775. Ha.

Sterney, Susanna. S Jan-Feb T Apr 1753 *Thames*. M.

Sterry, Richard (1767). *See* Price. Sy.

Stevens, Abraham. SQS Coventry Sep 1746. Wa.

Stevens, Amelia. T Sep 1755 *Tryal*. M.

Stevens, Ann. S Feb T Apr 1742 *Bond* to Potomack. M.

Stevens, Catherine. S & T Apr 1762 *Neptune*. M.

Stevens, Charity. S for Va Jly 1719. Co.

Stephens, Charles (1708). *See* Weaver. G.

Stephens, Daniel. S Jun T Sep 1758 *Tryal* to Annapolis. M.

Stevens, Edward of Cothelstone, blacksmith. R for Barbados Jan 1675. So.

Stephens, Edward of Henley on Severn. S s pigs Lent 1720. G.

Stevens, Edward. S Lent R 14 yrs Summer 1760. Sy.

Stephens, Elias. Rebel T 1685.

Stevens, Elias. R Oct 1694 AT Jan 1695. M.

Stephens als Prosser, Elizabeth of Llanelly, Brecon. S s clothing Lent 1719. Mo.

Stevens, Elizabeth. S & T Jan 1736 *Dorsetshire* but died on passage. L.

Stephens als Naylor, Esther. S s coffee pot Jan-May T Jun 1738 *Forward*. M.

Stevens, Francis. S Jly 1771. Ha.

Stevens, George. S Feb T Apr 1772 *Thornton*. L.

Stephens, Grace (1710). *See* Lewis. G.

Stephens, Grace. S Mar 1752. So.

Stephens, Hanna wife of Edward of Broxbourne. R for Barbados or Jamaica Feb 1683. Ht.

Stevens, Henry. S Jan-Jun 1747. M.

Stevens, Henry. S Dec 1750. L.

Stephens, Isaac. S s at Stroud Lent TB Apr 1757. G.

Stevens, James. S Jly 1727. Wi.

Steavens, James. T Jan 1734 *Caesar* LC Va Jly 1734. Sy.

Stevens, James. S s clothing at Wokingham Summer 1742. Be.

Stevens, James. SQS & T Jly 1772 *Tayloe*. M.

Stephens, Jane (1679). *See* Vosse. L.

Stevens, Jane (1755). *See* Blynn. L.

Stevens, Joan. S for shoplifting Lent R 14 yrs Summer 1722. Wa.

Stevens, John (1666). *See* Scrugion. G.

Stephens als Billing, John of St. Saviour, Southwark. R for Barbados or Jamaica Mar 1682. Sy.

Stevens, John. R for Barbados or Jamaica Nov 1690. L.

Stephens, John (1710). *See* Williams. Co.

Stevens, John. S Aug T Sep 1725 *Forward* LC Annapolis Dec 1725. L.

Stevens, John. S Feb 1729 T *Patapsco* LC Annapolis Dec 1729. M.

Stevens, John. S s silver seals Feb T Jun 1738 *Forward*. L.

Stevens, John. S s horse Lent R 14 yrs Summer 1738. Wa.

Stevens, John. S 14 yrs Apr-Jun 1739. M.

Stephens, John. S Apr-Jun 1739. M.

Stephens, John. S Summer 1740. Mo.

Stephens, John of St. Paul, Covent Garden. S Oct 1740 T Jan 1741 *Harpooner* to Rappahannock. M.

Stephens, John. T Nov 1741 *Sea Horse*. E.

Stephens, John of Trowbridge. SQS Devizes Apr TB to Va Oct 1742. Wi.

Stephens, John. S Mar 1743. So.

Stevens, John. S Sep T Nov 1743 *George William*. L.

Stevens, John. S Jan T Mar 1750 *Tryal*. L.

Stephens, John. S Sep T Oct 1750 *Rachael*. M.

Stevens, John. S for perjury & T Sep 1755 *Tryal*. L.

Stevens, John. T Sep 1755 *Tryal*. M.

Stevens, John. S s at Shrivenham Summer 1758. Be.

Stephens, John. T Apr 1759 *Thetis*. Ht.

Stevens, John. S Nov T Dec 1763 *Neptune*. L.

Stevens, John. S s sheep Summer 1764 R 14 yrs Lent T Oct 1765. Bd.

Stevens, John. S & T Dec 1771 *Justitia*. M.

Stevens, John. R Lent 1775. K.

Stevens, Jonas. S s coat at Temple Guiting Summer 1765. G.

Stephens, Joseph. R for Barbados or Jamaica Dec 1693. L.

Stevens, Joseph. S s lead Feb T Apr 1735 *Patapsco* LC Annapolis Oct 1735. L.

Stevens, Joseph. S Sep-Dec 1755 T Jan 1756 *Greyhound*. M.

Stephens, Joseph. S & T Apr 1766 *Ann*. M.

Stevens, Joseph, als Stephens, Richard. S s from Earl of Thanet & T Dec 1767 *Neptune*. M.

Stephens, Joseph. S s cloth at Bromsgrove Summer 1768. Wo.

Stephens, Luke. S for highway robbery & R 14 yrs Summer 1773. Be.

Stephens, Mary (1676). *See* Mills. L.

Stephens als Robinson als Hipkins, Mary. R for Barbados Aug 1679. L.

Stephens, Mary. S & T Jan 1722 *Gilbert* LC Annapolis Jly 1722. M.

Stephens, Mary wife of John. S & T Apr 1725 *Sukey* LC Annapolis Sep 1725. M.

Stevens, Mary. S Oct T Nov 1725 *Rappahannock* LC Rappahannock Apr 1726. M.

Stevens, Mary. SQS Jun T Jly 1753 *Tryal*. M.

Stephens, Mary. SQS Apr TB May 1767. So.

Stephens, Mary. S & T Dec 1767 *Neptune*. L.

Stephens als Richards, Paul. S s pumps at Kinver Lent 1749. St.

Stephens als Trink, Peter. S Mar 1752. Co.

Stevens, Philip. S & T Oct 1732 *Caesar* to Va. M.

Stevens, Philip. S s at Ross Summer 1742. He.

Stevens, Richard. PT Apr R Jly 1675. M.

Stephens, Richard. Rebel T 1685.

Stevens als Timms als Times, Richard of Milton Keynes. R for America Jly 1713. Bu.

Stephens, Richard. S Feb T Mar 1730 *Patapsco* LC Annapolis Sep 1730. L.

Stephens, Richard. S Dec 1733 T Jan 1734 *Caesar* LC Va Jly 1734. M.

Stevens, Richard. S s cows Lent R 14 yrs Summer 1748 T Jan 1749 *Laura*. E.

Stevens, Richard of Putney. SQS Jan T Apr 1753 *Thames*. Sy.

Stevens, Richard. S Aug 1762. So.

Stephens, Richard (1767). *See* Stevens, Joseph. M.

Stevens, Robert. T Jun 1727 *Susanna*. Sy.

Stephens, Robert. R 14 yrs Jly 1728. Ha.

Stevens, Robert. T Jun 1738 *Forward*. E.

Stephens, Robert. S & TB Aug 1740. G.

Stevens, Robert. S Aug T Oct 1741 *Sea Horse* to Va. M.

Stephens, Robert. S Mar 1772. So.

Stephens, Roger. S May T Jly 1723 *Alexander* LC Annapolis Sep 1723. M.

Stevens, Sarah. R for America May 1774. M.

Stevens, Stephen. S Aug 1739. So.

Stevens, Susanna wife of Thomas. S Oct 1736. M.

Stephens, Thomas of Cirencester. R for America Jly 1696. G.

Stephens, Thomas of St. Margaret near Rochester. R for America Jly 1700. K.

Stevens, Thomas. S Jan T Feb 1719 *Worcester* LC Annapolis Jun 1719. L.

Stevens, Thomas. T Apr 1732 *Patapsco*. Sx.

Stephens, Thomas. TB to Va from QS 1735. De.

Stevens, Thomas. S Oct T Dec 1736 *Dorsetshire* to Va. M.

Stevens, Thomas. T Apr 1742 *Bond*. Sy.

Stevens, Thomas. S Summer 1757 R 14 yrs Lent 1758. G.

Stephens, Thomas. S Dec 1763 T Mar 1764 *Tryal*. M.

Stevens, Thomas. S s at St. Helen, Abingdon, Lent 1765. Be.

Stephens, Thomas. T Jan 1766 *Tryal*. M.

Stevens, Thomas. T May 1767 *Thornton*. K.
Stevens, Thomas. S & R Summer 1774. Wa.
Stephens, Walter. R for Barbados or Jamaica Dec 1693. L.
Stevens, William. PT Jan 1675. M.
Stephens, William. R for America Jly 1688. No.
Stevens, William of Egham. R for Barbados or Jamaica Feb 1696. Sy.
Stephens, William. R & T Dec 1716 *Lewis*. M.
Stevens, William. S for Va Jly 1718. De.
Stevens, William. S Aug T Sep 1725 *Forward* LC Annapolis Dec 1725. M.
Stephens, William. S Oct T Nov 1728 *Forward* but died on passage. M.
Stephens, William. S s sheep Lent 1734. Wo.
Stevens, William. SQS & T May 1750 *Lichfield*. M.
Stevens, William (1757). *See* Morgan. So.
Stephens, William. S Jan T Apr 1768 *Thornton*. M.
Stevens, William of Bermondsey. SQS Jan 1770. Sy.
Stevens, William. R Lent 1775. Sy.
Stephenson, Ann. S Summer 1763. Nl.
Stephenson, Ann. S May-Jun 1774. M.
Stevenson, Arthur. R for life Dec 1774. M.
Stevenson, Barnabas. R 14 yrs s horse Lent 1762. Li.
Stephenson, Daniel. S s cow at Eccleshall, Yorks, Lent R 14 yrs Summer TB Oct 1764. Db.
Stevenson, Edward (1664). *See* Stimpson. Nf.
Stephenson, Elizabeth. S Jan 1757. M.
Stevenson, George. TB Apr 1765. Db.
Stevenson, James. S Summer 1754 R 14 yrs Lent T May 1755 *Rose*. Sy.
Stephenson, John. S Lent 1749. E.
Stevenson als Davy, Solomon. T Dec 1734 *Caesar*. E.
Stephenson, Susanna. S & T Jun 1756 *Lyon*. L.
Stephenson, Thomas. R for Barbados or Jamaica Mar 1685. M.
Stephenson, Thomas (1713). *See* Stimpson. Li.
Stevenson, Thomas. S Dec 1748 T 14 yrs Jan 1749 *Laura*. M.
Stephenson, Thomas. S Summer 1751. Nl.
Stevenson, William. S s iron bars at Wolverhampton Lent 1728. St.
Stevenson, William. S s cow at Stone Lent 1735. St.
Stephenson, William. S for shoplifting Lent R 14 yrs Summer 1758. Li.
Stevenson, William. T Dec 1758 *The Brothers*. K.
Stevenson, William. S s at St. Michael Lent 1761 T *Atlas* from Bristol. St.
Stephenson, William. S s at Cottingham Summer 1766. Y.
Steventon, George. S s barley at Wellington Summer 1768. Sh.
Steventon, Titus. S 14 yrs for receiving Summer 1741. Sh.
Steventon, William. S 14 yrs for receiving Summer 1741. Sh.
Stew, John (1743). *See* Moore. O.
Steward, Anne. PT Aug 1678. M.
Steward, Charles. T Oct 1726 *Forward*. E.
Steward, Daniel. S May-Jly T Sep 1751 *Greyhound*. M.
Steward, Elizabeth. S May T Jly 1723 *Alexander* LC Annapolis Sep 1723. M.
Steward, Elizabeth. S for shoplifting Summer 1753. Du.

Steward, George. S Summer T Sep 1751 *Greyhound*. E.
Steward, George. SQS Apr 1774. Ha.
Steward, James. S Aug T Sep 1727 *Forward*. L.
Steward, James. S & T Dec 1740 *Vernon*. L.
Steward, James. T Apr 1770 *New Trial*. Sy.
Steward als Pawlett als Sadler, Jane. R Jly 1680. M.
Steward, Jane of Bermondsey. R for Barbados or Jamaica Mar 1682 & Feb 1683. Sy.
Steward, John. R Oct 1694 AT Jan 1695. M.
Steward als Cowper, John. R 14 yrs Summer 1758. Y.
Steward, John. S Jun T Aug 1769 *Douglas*. L.
Steward, John. S Lent 1774. Y.
Steward, Margaret. S as pickpocket Lent 1729 R 14 yrs Lent 1730. Y.
Steward als Hastings, Mary of St. George, Hanover Square. S s stewpan Sep 1740 T Jan 1741 *Harpooner* to Rappahannock. M.
Steward als Seaward, Mathew. S Mar 1755. De.
Steward, Miriam. S Norwich Summer TB Sep 1758. Nf.
Steward, Peter (1663). *See* Preston. M.
Steward, Stephen Jr. S Lent R Summer 1725 T *Rappahannock* but died on passage. Li.
Steward, William. S Sep T Oct 1768 *Justitia*. M.
Stewart, Alexander. S Sep-Dec 1746. M.
Stewart, Alexander. S for highway robbery Lent R 14 yrs Summer 1766. No.
Stewart, Alexander. S s at Belford Summer 1769. Nl.
Stewart als Parker, Ann of Latham, spinster. SQS May 1753. La.
Stewart, Charles. S Feb T Apr 1732 *Patapsco* LC Annapolis Oct 1732. L.
Stewart, Charles. S Lent 1766. Ca.
Stewart, Charles. SQS & T Sep 1766 *Justitia*. M.
Stewart, Dorothy. T Sep 1758 *Tryal*. Sx.
Stewart, Duncan. S Jan-Jun T Jun 1728 *Elizabeth* to Md or Va. M.
Stuart, Elizabeth. S Jun-Dec 1738 T Jan 1739 *Dorsetshire* to Va. M.
Stewart, Francis. S Apr T 14 yrs May 1718 *Tryal* LC Charles Town Aug 1718. L.
Stewart, Hannah, als Yorkshire Hannah of St. Pancras, spinster. S s watch Sep 1740 T Jan 1741 *Harpooner* to Rappahannock. M.
Stuart, Hugh. S s cloth at Brampton Summer 1773. Cu.
Stewart, James. S May T Jly 1723 *Alexander* LC Annapolis Sep 1723. L.
Stewart, James, als Emerson, Francis. S Aug T Oct 1724 *Forward* LC Annapolis Jun 1725. M.
Stewart, James. S May T Jun 1726 *Loyal Margaret* LC Annapolis Oct 1726. M.
Stewart, James. S & T Jan 1767 *Tryal*. M.
Stewart, James. R 14 yrs Jly 1775. M.
Stewart, Jane als Jennett als Jenny of Fishwick, singlewoman. SQS Apr 1750. La.
Stewart, John of Northwich. R for Barbados or Jamaica Mar 1694. Ch.
Stewart, John. S Jan-Jun T Jun 1728 *Elizabeth* LC Potomack Aug 1729. L.
Stewart, John. T Apr 1743 *Justitia* but died on passage. K.
Stewart, John. S Feb 1754. L.

Stewart, John. S Feb T May 1767 *Thornton*. M.

Stewart, John. S Summer 1774. E.

Stewart, Joseph. R 14 yrs Jly 1738. De.

Stewart, Mary. S & T Oct 1729 *Forward* LC Va Jun 1730. L.

Stuart, Mary, widow. S Summer 1746. Nl.

Stewart, Mary. S Apr T Sep 1757 *Thetis*. M.

Stewart, Peter of Manchester. SQS Nov 1747. La.

Stuart, Peter. SQS s gown Summer 1769. Du.

Stewart, Robert. S s at St. Philip & Jacob Summer TB Aug 1738. G.

Stewart, Robert. S s horse Summer 1756 R 14 yrs Summer 1757. Nl.

Stewart, Sarah. S Sep T Oct 1744 *Susannah*. L.

Stewart als Murrell als Smith, Susanna. S May T Jly 1722 *Alexander*. M.

Stewart, Violatte of Garstang, spinster. SQS Jan 1755. La.

Stewart, William. S Oct-Dec 1739 T Jan 1740 *York* to Md. M.

Stewer, Frances. TB to Va from QS 1762. De.

Stewkley als Crowley als Cowley als Rattenbury, Alice. R for Jamaica
   Aug 1661. M.

Stewkly, William. R for America Jly 1686. Li.

Stibbard, Thomas. S s sheep Summer 1758 R 14 yrs Lent 1759. Nf.

Stibbs, Elizabeth. S Jan T Feb 1724 *Anne* to Carolina. M.

Stichbury, Alexander. S Apr T May 1750 *Lichfield*. M.

Stichbury, Isaac. S Apr 1749. L.

Styck, Dorothy (1768). *See* Aston. Sh.

Stickland, Henry. S Mar 1766. Do.

Stickland, Josiah. S Aug 1742. Do.

Stickwood, Jonathan. S s at Great Wilbraham & R 14 yrs Lent TB Apr
   1769. Ca.

Stidfold, John. R 14 yrs Apr 1756. So.

Stiff, Abraham. S Apr 1749. L.

Stiffe, Elizabeth. S Feb T May 1719 *Margaret*. L.

Stiff, John. SQS Oct 1761 T Apr 1762 *Dolphin*. M.

Stife, Richard. SQS Jan T Apr 1768 *Thornton*. M.

Stiff, Thomas. S s sheep Summer 1759 R 14 yrs Lent 1760. G.

Stiffney, John. S s shirt Jan T Apr 1735 *Patapsco* LC Annapolis Oct
   1735. M.

Stiggard, Mary of Debden, spinster. SQS Apr T May 1755 *Rose*. E.

Stigwood, Walter. S Summer 1748. Ca.

Stiles. *See* Styles.

Still, Andrew. S Oct T Dec 1767 *Neptune*. M.

Still, Elizabeth. R for America Aug 1715. L.

Still, James. R 14 yrs Aug 1747. De.

Still, Mary. R for Barbados or Jamaica Aug 1700. L.

Still, Richard. S & T Feb 1744 *Neptune* to Md. M.

Still, Richard. S May-Jun T Jly 1753 *Tryal*. M.

Still, William. S Aug T 14 yrs Oct 1726 *Forward* to Va. M.

Still, William. S s hens Summer 1741. O.

Stilling, Thomas of Heverland. R for America Jly 1682 & Jly 1683. Nf.

Stillita, Jane. S & T Apr 1725 *Sukey* to Md. M.

Stilton, John. PT Feb 1680. M.

Stimpson als Stevenson, Edward of Swaffham. R for Barbados Feb
   1664. Nf.

Stimson, Ralph. S s sheep Summer 1758 R 14 yrs Lent 1759. Li.

Stimson, Richard. S s sheep Lent R 14 yrs Summer 1752. Li.

Stimpson als Stephenson, Thomas of Saleby. R for America Feb 1713. Li.

Stiner. *See* Stainer.

Stinnard, Joseph. S Mar 1723. Wi.

Stint, Richard. S Sep-Oct 1772. M.

Stitchborne, Richard of Frant. R for Barbados or Jamaica Jun 1699. Sx.

Stoakes. *See* Stokes.

Stock, Ana. S Mar 1772. So.

Stock, George. R for America Aug 1715. M.

Stock, John. TB Aug 1738. Nt.

Stock, John. T Nov 1741 *Sea Horse*. E.

Stock, Samuel. T Sep 1758 *Tryal*. E.

Stockbridge, Herbert. S Summer 1761. Cu.

Stockdale, Daniel. S Apr T May 1740 *Essex*. L.

Stockdale, Elianor. S Jly T Aug 1721 *Prince Royal* LC Va Nov 1721. M.

Stockdale, Elizabeth. S Oct T 14 yrs Dec 1763 *Neptune*. M.

Stockdale, Thomas. R for Barbados Sep 1682. L.

Stocker, Francis of Croydon. R for Barbados or Jamaica Dec 1680 & Mar 1682. Sy.

Stocker, Lydia of Knighton. R for Barbados or Jamaica Feb 1690. Sy.

Stocker, William. S 14 yrs for receiving goods from John Worley *(qv)* Lent 1755. Be.

Stockhill, John. S 14 yrs for receiving Lent TB Aug 1758. Y.

Stockin, Elizabeth wife of Edward of Bury St. Edmunds. R (Oxford Circ) for America Jly 1681. Su.

Stockman als MacGwin, Daniel. S & T 14 yrs Jan 1736 *Dorsetshire* LC Va Sep 1736. L.

Stocks, John. S Mar TB Aug 1738. Nt.

Stocks, Thomas. S Summer 1753. Y.

Stockton, William. S for assault at Handsworth Lent 1744. St.

Stockwell, James. S & T Oct 1729 *Forward* LC Va Jun 1730. M.

Stockwell, John, aged 25. R for Barbados Feb 1664. M.

Stockwell, John. S & T Dec 1731 *Forward*. L.

Stockwell, Thomas. S s wheat at Prestbury Lent 1774. G.

Stothart als Armstrong, James. R 14 yrs Summer 1753. Nl.

Stoddart, Joseph of Skirton, mariner. SQS Jan 1749. La.

Stoddard, Martha wife of Peter. S Jly T Sep 1767 *Justitia*. M.

Stutherd, Thomas. S Summer 1733 R 14 yrs Summer 1734. Y.

Stoakley, John. R for America Aug 1715. M.

Stoakes, Anne. S Feb T Mar 1729 *Patapsco* LC Annapolis Dec 1729. M.

Stokes, Edward. T Apr 1732 *Patapsco*. Ht.

Stokes, Elizabeth. S Jly 1750. Ha.

Stokes, Francis. S Lent TB Mar 1772. Db.

Stoakes, John. T Oct 1722 *Forward* LC Md Jun 1723. Ht.

Stokes, John. S Lent R 14 yrs Summer T Oct 1739 *Duke of Cumberland*. E.

Stokes, John of Writtle. S Lent 1745. E.

Stoakes, John. S May-Jun 1753. M.

Stokes, Joseph. R 14 yrs Jly 1734. Wi.

Stokes, Margaret wife of Richard. S Aug 1727 T *Forward* LC Rappahannock May 1728. M.
Stokes, Margaret. S & T Jan 1769 *Thornton*. M.
Stokes, Richard. S Aug 1738. So.
Stokes, Robert. S Mar 1752. Ha.
Stokes, Robert. S Feb T May 1767 *Thornton*. M.
Stoakes, Thomas of Oxford. R for Barbados Feb 1665. O.
Stoakes, William. R for Barbados Jan 1664. L.
Stokes, William of Bradford. SQS Warminster Jly TB to Va Oct 1742. Wi.
Stokes, William. S Jly 1749. L.
Stokes, William. S s at Eaton Socon & R 14 yrs Lent 1772. Bd.
Stokes, William. SW & T Jly 1772 *Tayloe*. M.
Stoakes, Zachary of Upton on Severn. R for Barbados Feb 1665. Wo.
Stolery, Brice. T Sep 1758 *Tryal*. E.
Stone als Booth als Moley, Ann. S Jan T Apr 1743 *Justitia*. M.
Stone, Elizabeth wife of Robert. S Sep 1733 T *Caesar* LC Va Jly 1734. M.
Stone, Elizabeth. S Summer TB Jly 1763. Db.
Stone, Francis. R for Barbados Aug 1670. M.
Stone, George. S Aug 1737. De.
Stone, Henry of Hockworthy. R for Barbados Jly 1683. So.
Stone, Hercules. T Apr 1771 *Thornton*. Sy.
Stone, James. S Lent R 14 yrs Summer T Oct 1744 *Savannah*. Sx.
Stone, James, a marine. SQS at Canterbury & R 14 yrs Sep 1748. K.
Stone, James. S Mar 1750. So.
Stone, James. S Jan-Feb 1773. M.
Stone, John of Oldland. R for America Mar 1680. G.
Stone, John. Rebel T 1685.
Stone, John. SQS Jan TB Feb 1749. So.
Stone, John. S Feb T Apr 1765 *Ann*. M.
Stone, John. T Apr 1768 *Thornton*. Sy.
Stone, Martha wife of Stephen. S Aug 1756. So.
Stone, Mary (1765). *See* Vender. M.
Stone, Mathew. S Mar 1752. Do.
Stone, Nicholas. S Lent 1749. Sy.
Stone als Clefts, Philip. SQS New Sarum Jan TB to Va Apr 1742. Wi.
Stone, Samuel (1770). *See* Moore, John. So.
Stone als Butler, Susan. R for Jamaica Mar 1665. L.
Stone, Thomas. S Summer R for Barbados Aug 1664. Sy.
Stone, Thomas. S for Va Jly 1718. So.
Stone, Thomas. R 14 yrs Aug 1740 TB to Va. De.
Stone, Thomas. TB to Va from QS 1743. De.
Stone, Thomas. SQS Jan TB May 1770. So.
Stone, Thomas (1773). *See* Martin. Wi.
Stone als Richards, William of Sandford. R for Barbados Jly 1678. De.
Stone, William. R Dec 1698 AT Jan 1699. M.
Stone, William. S Mar 1726. De.
Stone, William. S Summer 1735 R 14 yrs Summer 1736. Db.
Stone, William. S Feb T Apr 1741 *Speedwell* or *Mediterranean*. M.
Stone, William. S Mar 1755. So.
Stone, William. S Dec 1765 T Jan 1766 *Tryal*. L.

Stone, William. R 14 yrs Jly 1773. Ha.
Stoneham, James. S Jan T Feb 1719 *Worcester* LC Annapolis Jun 1719. L.
Stonehill, John. S Aug 1748. De.
Stonehouse, William. S Jan 1746. M.
Stoneman, William. S Mar 1739. Co.
Stoner, Francis. S Oct 1751-Jan 1752. M.
Stoner, Sarah. S Jly-Sep 1754. M.
Stoner, Sarah. S Sep 1754. L.
Stones, Rebecca, als Armstrong, Frances, of Edwalton, spinster. SQS as bad, loose and indolent Jan TB Apr 1773. Nt.
Stonilake, Mary. S Jly 1752. De.
Stoning, Edward. S Mar 1752. De.
Stonnell, David. S Jly 1734. M.
Stonell, Richard. S s at West Wycombe & R Summer 1773. Bu.
Stoodley, James of Symondsbury. R for Barbados Jun 1708. Do.
Stoodley, John. Rebel T 1685.
Stooke, Robert. S Aug 1745. De.
Stool, Mary. T May 1750 *Lichfield*. Sx.
Stop, John. S s sheep Summer 1765 R 14 yrs Lent T Apr 1766 *Ann*. Bu.
Stopard, Thomas. S Summer 1726. Sh.
Stopper, Margaret. R for Barbados Aug 1679. M.
Stopps, Thomas of Hornchurch. R Lent T Apr 1772 *Thornton*. E.
Storer, Henry. S s horse Summer 1744 R 14 yrs Lent TB May 1745. Db.
Storer, Henry of Wirksworth. SQS Jan 1764. Db.
Storer, John. S Apr-May T May 1741 *Catherine & Elizabeth* to Md. M.
Storer, Samuel. R 14 yrs Jly 1775. M.
Storer, Thomas. S Jun T Nov 1743 *George William*. M.
Storer, Thomas. S s at South Repps Lent 1773; William Storer acquitted. Nf.
Storer, William. SQS Summer TB Oct 1764. Db.
Storey, Ann. S & T Oct 1730 *Forward* LC Potomack Jan 1731. M.
Story, Catherine, aged 35, dark. S Jly T 14 yrs Oct 1720 *Gilbert* LC Annapolis May 1721. M.
Storey, Elizabeth. R for Barbados or Jamaica Oct 1694. L.
Story als Wright, Elizabeth. S Jly T 14 yrs Aug 1718 *Eagle* LC Charles Town Mar 1719. L.
Storey, Henry. S Jan T Apr 1735 *Patapsco* LC Annapolis Oct 1735. M.
Storey, James. S Jan 1775. M.
Story, John. R for America Jly 1694. Li.
Story, John. Died on passage in *Gilbert* 1721. X.
Story, John. S & T Jan 1722 *Gilbert* LC Annapolis Jly 1722. M.
Storey, John. T Jan 1734 *Caesar* LC Va Jly 1734. Sy.
Storey, John. S at Hull s sheep at West Ella Summer 1764 R 14 yrs Lent 1765. Y.
Storie, Richard. R for Bermuda for s mare Jly 1614. M.
Story, Thomas. R 14 yrs for Boston NE Jly 1718. Wi.
Story, Thomas. S Lent 1750 R 14 yrs Lent 1751. Le.
Story, William. R 14 yrs Apr 1742. Ha.
Storey, William. S Dec 1774. M.
Stork, Thomas. S & T Lent 1729. Y.

Storm, Michael. S Apr T May 1750 *Lichfield*. L.

Storman, Samuel. R 14 yrs Jly 1725. Ha.

Storr, Thomas. T Jan 1738 *Dorsetshire*. Sy.

Storrow, William of House of Correction at Thirsk. SQS Guisborough s
    shirts Jly 1775. Y.

Stothart. *See* Stoddart.

Stothers, John of Rotherhithe. SQS Jan 1775. Sy.

Stott, Elizabeth wife of Henry. S & T Jan 1766 *Tryal*. M.

Stott, George. S Mar 1763. So.

Stott, James of Manchester, weaver. SQS Jan 1761. La.

Stott, John. S for forgery at Leeds & R 14 yrs Lent 1768. Y.

Stot als Atherton, Richard. S s horse & R 14 yrs Lent 1775. Sh.

Stoughter, John (1764). *See* Slaughter. Li.

Stoughton, Thomas. R & T Dec 1716 *Lewis*. L.

Stoughton, Thomas. S Jly T Aug 1718 *Eagle* LC Charles Town Mar
    1719. L.

Stourton, Robert. S Lent 1774. Wa.

Stow, Abraham. S s chickens at Polstead Lent 1775. Su.

Stow, Jane. S Apr T May 1750 *Lichfield*. L.

Stowe, Mary Anne (1762). *See* Bunney. M.

Stowell, George. S Oct T Dec 1771 *Justitia*. L.

Stower, John. Rebel T 1685.

Stower, Robert of Barrington. R for Barbados Jun 1708. So.

Stowers als Durgin, James. S Dec 1766 R 14 yrs Lent 1767. Be.

Stowman, Ann. S Dec 1753-Jan 1754. M.

Stowman, William. T Jun 1742 *Bladon*. Sx.

Stracey, Ann. S Dec 1746. L.

Stradling, Edward. R 14 yrs Aug 1747. So.

Strafford, Susanna. S Dec 1755 T Jan 1756 *Greyhound*. L.

Strahan, Robert. S May-Jly 1773. M.

Strait, George. S Feb T Apr 1739 *Forward*. L.

Strang als Strong, Thomas of Bickington. R for Barbados Feb 1698. De.

Strangbridge, Christopher. S Jan T Sep 1737 *Pretty Patsy* to Md. M.

Strange, Katherine wife of Elias. S Feb T Mar 1731 *Patapsco* LC
    Annapolis Jun 1731. M.

Strange, Edward. S s fish at Syston Lent TB Apr 1757. G.

Strange, John (1755). *See* Longden. Nf.

Strange als Naylor, Mary of St. Michael, Queenhithe, widow. SQS as
    incorrigible rogue & feloniously returning to Southwark after being
    passed to her settlement Apr T Aug 1752 *Tryal*. Sy.

Strange, Thomas. S Lent T Apr 1771. Wa.

Strangeways als Strangwish, John. S Summer 1737 R 14 yrs Summer
    1738. Nl.

Strangis, Arthur. S Mar 1730. So.

Strangwich, Anthony of Ware. R for Barbados or Jamaica Jun 1684. Ht.

Strangwish, John (1737). *See* Stangeways. Nl.

Stratford, John. T Aug 1741 *Sally*. Sy.

Stratford, John of Hemel Hempstead. R for Barbados or Jamaica Jun
    1684. Ht.

Stretton, Elizabeth. S Lent R for Barbados Aug 1663. K.

Stratton, John of Aylesbury. R for America Jly 1683. Bu.

Stretton, John. R for America Feb 1700. Le.

Streton, Thomas of St. Michael, Colchester. S Lent R Summer 1745. E.

Stratton, Thomas. S May-Jun T Aug 1752 *Tryal*. M.

Stratton als Strutton, William. S Oct 1757 T Mar 1758 *Dragon*. M.

Stratton, William. S s at Keysoe Summer 1772. Bd.

Stratton, William. S for rape at Sporle Summer 1773 R 14 yrs Summer 1775. Nf.

Straw als Shaw, Mary. T Apr 1753 *Thames*. K.

Strawbridge, Richard. LC from *Forward* Annapolis Jun 1725. X.

Streak, Francis. R Lent 1774. K.

Stream, John. SQS Oct T Dec 1771 *Justitia*. M.

Streck, John. R for America Aug 1715. L.

Street, Abraham. S Mar 1764. Do.

Street, Ann. S Jan-Feb T Apr 1772 *Thornton*. M.

Street, Diana wife of Henry. S for breaking & entering Sep T Dec 1736 *Dorsetshire*. M.

Street, Edith. SQS Oct TB to Md Nov 1731. So.

Street, Henry. T Jan 1738 *Dorsetshire*. Sy.

Street, John. S Mar 1749 TB to Va. De.

Street, Lawrence. SQS New Sarum or Marlborough & TB to Va Jan 1774. Wi.

Street, Rebecca wife of John. S s gown Jan T Apr 1735 *Patapsco* LC Annapolis Oct 1735. M.

Street als Plowman, Richard. S & TB to Va Apr 1750. Wi.

Street, William. S Mar TB to Va Apr 1741. Wi.

Street, William. S Mar 1750. So.

Street, William. S s boots Lent 1765. Hu.

Stretham, William. S Aug T Oct 1723 *Forward*. L.

Streton/Stretton. *See* Stratton.

Strickett, Arthur. T Apr 1743 *Justitia*. Ht.

Strickland, Anthony of St. George, Southwark. R for Barbados Apr 1668. Sy.

Strickland, George. R for life Mar 1771. So.

Strickland, John. S s at Heversham Summer 1740. We.

Stride, Joseph. R Feb T for life Mar 1764 *Tryal*. M.

Striger, Joseph. S Feb T Apr 1765 *Ann*. M.

Stringer, Ann. S Oct-Dec 1739 T Jan 1740 *York* to Md. M.

Stringer, Elizabeth. S Apr T Dec 1735 *John* LC Annapolis Sep 1736. L.

Stringer, George. T Dec 1731 *Forward*. Sy.

Stringer, Hannah wife of John. S Lent 1749. Bd.

Stringer, James. R for Va Nov 1618. M.

Stringer, John. R 14 yrs s horse Summer 1724. St.

Stringer, John. S Jan T Feb 1726 *Supply* LC Annapolis May 1726. M.

Stringer, Mary. T Nov 1725 *Rappahannock* LC Va Aug 1726. Sy.

Stringer, Mary. T Apr 1753 *Thames*. K.

Stringer, Mary (1768). *See* Hardiman. Wo.

Stringer, Michael. T Dec 1731 *Forward*. Sy.

Stringer, Peter. S Apr 1774. M.

Stringer, Ralph. S s lead pipe & T May 1736 *Patapsco* to Md. M.

Stringer, Robert. S s at Minster Lovell Lent 1747. O.

Stringer, Thomas of Camberwell. R for Barbados or Jamaica Jly 1677. Sy.

Stringer, Thomas. S for highway robbery Summer 1761 R 14 yrs Lent 1762. No.

Stringer, William. S Sep T Dec 1767 *Neptune*. M.

Stringfellow, Thomas of Hoar Cross. R for Barbados Jly 1664. St.

Strinkner, William. S s horse Summer 1735 R 14 yrs Summer 1736. Wa.

Stritch, Walter of Sutton at Hone. R for Barbados Jly 1678 & Jly 1679. K.

Strode, Edward. S & T Jan 1767 *Tryal*. M.

Strong Will (1750). *See* Williams, William. Co.

Strong, Charles. Rebel T 1685.

Strong, Charles. S Aug 1758. So.

Strong, James. S May T Jun 1727 *Susanna* to Va. M.

Strong, Jane. S Jly-Dec 1747. M.

Strong, John. S Jly 1748. L.

Strong, John. S May-Jly T Sep 1751 *Greyhound*. M.

Strong, John. R 14 yrs Aug 1772. Co.

Strong, Mary (1740). *See* Anderson. M.

Strong, Peter. T 14 yrs Sep 1757 *Thetis*. E.

Strong, Thomas (1698). *See* Strang. De.

Strong, Thomas. S Jan-Apr 1749. M.

Strong, Thomas. S Mar 1754. L.

Strong, William. S Mar 1768. Ha.

Strongarm, William. S & T Sep 1731 *Smith* LC Va 1732. M.

Strotton, Thomas. S Mar 1740. Do.

Strotten, Thomas. R 14 yrs Jly 1773. Ha.

Stroud, Ann. S Sep T Dec 1769 *Justitia*. M.

Stroud, Martha of Reading, spinster. R for America Mar 1697. Be.

Strood, Richard. S Summer 1751 R 14 yrs Lent T May 1752 *Lichfield*. K.

Stroud, Richard. SQS & T Jly 1770 *Scarsdale*. Ht.

Stroud, Thomas of Northampton. R for America Jly 1678. No.

Strude, William. T Sep 1764 *Justitia*. K.

Strout, Jasper. R 14 yrs Aug 1759. Co.

Strowte, John. S Mar 1740. Co.

Strowder, John (1686). *See* Crowder. St.

Strudell, Michael. T Apr 1759 *Thetis*. Sy.

Strudwick, George. R Lent 1773. Sy.

Strudwick, Thomas. T 14 yrs Dec 1771 *Justitia*. Sy.

Strudwick, William. T Jan 1738 *Dorsetshire*. Sy.

Strugler als Horn, William. R 14 yrs Jly 1740. Ha.

Strutt, Daniel. R & T 14 yrs Apr 1770 *New Trial*. M.

Strutt, Elizabeth, als wife of John Boseden. S Oct 1766 T Jan 1767 *Tryal*. M.

Strutt, Mary wife of Samuel of Worksop. R for America Mar 1682. Nt.

Strutt, Sarah. S Jun T Aug 1769 *Douglas*. M.

Strutton, John. R for Barbados or Jamaica Jan 1692. M.

Strutton, Sarah (1769). *See* Manton. L.

Strutton, William. S Jly T Sep 1751 *Greyhound*. L.

Strutton, William (1757). *See* Stratton. M.

Stryce, Silver. S Apr T May 1750 *Lichfield*. L.

Stuart. *See* Stewart.

Stubberfield, John of Portsmouth, feltmaker. R for Barbados Mar 1679. Ha.

Stubbing, John. T Sep 1757 *Thetis*. E.

Stubbins, Hannah. T Apr 1753 *Thames*. K.

Stubbings als Stebbins, John. PT Apr R Jly 1675. M.

Stubbings, John. S May T Jun 1727 *Susanna* to Va. M.

Stubbins, John. S s mare Summer 1739 R 14 yrs Lent 1740 (SP). Nf.

Stubbins, William of Lambeth. SQS Jan 1755. Sy.

Stubbs, Anne (1681). *See* Ditcher. M.

Stubbs, Ann. S Sep 1756. M.

Stubbs, Ann. S Feb T Apr 1762 *Dolphin*. M.

Stubbs, Frances wife of John. S 14 yrs Sep 1756. M.

Stubbs, John. S May T Dec 1734 *Caesar* LC Va Jly 1735. M.

Stubbs, John. S May T Sep 1737 *Pretty Patsy* to Md. M.

Stubbs, John. S Oct 1756. M.

Stubbs, Mary. S Summer 1749. Sy.

Stubbs, Samuel. R for Barbados or Jamaica Dec 1699 & Aug 1700. L.

Stuckey, Pasche. Rebel T 1685.

Stuckey, Robert. Rebel T 1685.

Studd, William. S Lent R 14 yrs Summer 1767. Su.

Studder, Elizabeth. S for breaking & entering Sep T Dec 1736 *Dorsetshire*. M.

Studder, Henry. S Jly-Sep T Oct 1739 *Duke of Cumberland* to Va. M.

Studder, John. S Jly-Dec 1747. M.

Studham, Thomas. R for Barbados Sep 1669. M.

Studman, Thomas of Otterden. R for Barbados Aug 1662. K.

Stuford, Mary. SQS Jly 1730. So.

Stupple, John. T Sep 1758 *Tryal*. K.

Sturgeon, John. T Apr 1739 *Forward*. Ht.

Sturgeon, Obediah. S Feb T Sep 1737 *Pretty Patsy* to Md. M.

Sturgeon, William. S Oct 1744-Jan 1745. M.

Sturgis, Abram. R Sep 1671 AT Oct 1673. M.

Sturgis, Jane. R Sep 1671 AT Jly 1672 & Oct 1673. M.

Sturgis, John. S Aug 1747 TB to Va Jly 1748. Le.

Sturgis, Richard (1755). *See* Smith. Le.

Sturges, William. S Jan T Feb 1726 *Supply* to Md. M.

Sturney. *See* Sterney.

Sturrick, John. Rebel T 1685.

Sturt, Elizabeth. S Feb T Apr 1741 *Speedwell* or *Mediterranean*. M.

Sturt, George. S s cloth at St. Margaret Lothbury Feb 1768. L.

Sturt, John. S & T Dec 1734 *Caesar* LC Va Jly 1735. L.

Sturt, John. S Dec 1737 T Jan 1738 *Dorsetshire*. L.

Sturt, Robert. T May 1719 *Margaret*; sold to John Welch Md May 1720. Sx.

Sturte, Thomas. S for highway robbery Mar 1654 R for plantations Aug 1655. Sy.

Sturt, Thomas. T 14 yrs Aug 1752 *Tryal*. K.

Sturt, Thomas. S 14 yrs for receiving Mar 1768. Ha.

Stutherd. *See* Stoddart.

Styers, Thomas. S Jun T Sep 1758 *Tryal*. L.

Stile, Betty. S Mar 1721. So.
Style, Charles. S Aug 1758. So.
Stiles, Elizabeth. S Jly T Aug 1721 *Prince Royal* LC Va Nov 1721. M.
Styles, Eliza. S & TB Aug 1740. G.
Stiles, Felitia of Manchester, spinster. SQS Feb 1756. La.
Stiles, James of St. Martin in Fields. S s stockings & T Jan 1740
  York. M.
Stiles, Jane. S & T Jan 1739 *Dorsetshire*. L.
Styles, Joane. S & TB Aug 1740. G.
Stiles, John. S Jan T Apr 1735 *Patapsco* LC Annapolis Oct 1735. M.
Stiles, John. S Mar 1765. Ha.
Styles, John A. T Oct 1732 *Caesar*. Sx.
Stiles, Mary. S Jan-Jun T Jun 1728 *Elizabeth* LC Potomack Aug 1729. M.
Styles, Mary. S & TB Aug 1740. G.
Stiles, William of Stamford le Hope. SQS Apr T May 1752 *Lichfield*. E.
Styles, William. S Jly 1773. L.
Stiling, John. S Mar 1766. So.
Styling, Mary. S Mar 1761. So.
Sucklin, Balthazar. R for Barbados or Jamaica Aug 1700. M.
Sudders als Southurst als Sutcliffe, Richard. S s mare at Manchester
  Summer 1765 R 14 yrs Lent 1766. La.
Suddery, John. S & TB to Va Mar 1738. Wi.
Sudler, Ralph. S Summer 1740. Sh.
Suffold, William of Danbury. R for Barbados or Jamaica Feb 1690. E.
Suffolk, John. S for forgery Summer 1767 R 14 yrs Lent 1768. He.
Suffolk, Richard. S Summer 1772. Wa.
Sugar, Edward. SQS Jly TB Aug 1771. So.
Sugar, John of Newcastle under Lyme. R for Barbados Feb 1665. St.
Sugg als Gorden, Elizabeth. S to hang Summer 1729 for being at large
  in Bilston after sentence of transportation passed in London in
  August 1723. St.
Suggs als Preston, Mary. S May-Jly 1774. M.
Sulch, John. Died on passage in *Sukey* 1725. X.
Suledge, Samuel. S Jan-Feb T Apr 1771 *Thornton*. M.
Sullinge, Edward. S Feb T May 1767 *Thornton*. M.
Sullinge, Richard. S Feb T May 1767 *Thornton*. M.
Sullivan, Catherine of St. George, Southwark, widow. SQS May
  1754. Sy.
Sullivan als Harris, Catherine. SQS Jly 1758. Ha.
Sullivan, Cornelius. S Sep-Oct 1749. M.
Sullivan, Daniel. S Jan 1740. L.
Sullivan, Dennis. S Jan-Feb 1773. M.
Sullivan, Elizabeth. S Jun T Oct 1744 *Susannah*. M.
Sullivan, Herbert. SQS Sep T Oct 1750 *Rachael*. M.
Sullivan, Isabella. SQS Apr 1773. M.
Sullivan, James. S Sep-Oct T Dec 1771 *Justitia*. M.
Sullivan, John. R Dec 1765 T for life Jan 1766 *Tryal*. M.
Sullivan, John. S Feb T Apr 1771 *Thornton*. L.
Sullivan, Martin. S Sep-Oct 1749. M.
Sullivan als Johnson, Mary. S & T Oct 1732 *Caesar* to Va. M.
Sullivan, Roger. SQS Dec 1773. M.

Sullivan, Timothy. S Apr 1749. L.

Sully, Elizabeth. S Aug 1752. So.

Sully, Joshua. Rebel T 1685.

Sully, Richard of Milverton. R for Barbados Jly 1683. So.

Somer als Somner, Jonas. R for Barbados Oct 1667. L.

Somarell, Benjamin. S s at Mangotsfield Lent TB Mar 1737. G.

Somerel, Jane. S s tablecloth at Newport Lent 1763. Sh.

Somarell, Stephen. S s at Mangotsfield Lent TB Mar 1737. G.

Summerfield, Joseph. S s waistcoat at Old Swinford Lent 1765. Wo.

Summerfield, Joseph. S Lent R 14 yrs Summer 1768. Sh.

Summerfield, Thomas. S s waistcoat at Old Swinford Lent 1765. Wo.

Summerfield, William. S May T 14 yrs Jly 1723 *Alexander* LC Md Sep 1723. M.

Summerhayes, Ann. S 14 yrs for receiving Oct T Dec 1771 *Justitia*. L.

Somerhays, John (1732). *See* Summers. So.

Summers, John. R (Home Circ) Aug 1664. X.

Summers, John of St. Saviour, Southwark. R for Barbados or Jamaica Feb 1686. Sy.

Somers, John of St. Thomas Apostle, Exeter, worsted comber. R for Barbados Feb 1690. De.

Somers als Somerhays, John. S Mar 1732. So.

Summers, John. S Dec 1748 T Jan 1749 *Laura*. L.

Somers, Joseph. S Mar 1721. Do.

Sommers, Joseph. T Apr 1753 *Thames*. M.

Summers, Mary (1774). *See* Wellbrand. M.

Summers, Samuel. S Mar 1736. De.

Sommers, Sarah. TB to Va from QS 1738. De.

Sommers, Sarah. S Jan-Feb T Apr 1753 *Thames*. M.

Summers, Sarah. S Jly 1755 TB to Va 1756. De.

Summers, Thomas. SQS Oct 1767 TB Mar 1768. So.

Sumersbye, Sarah wife of John. S s at Burford Lent 1762. O.

Summerton, Hester. S Feb-Apr 1746. M.

Somerton, John. S Apr 1765. So.

Summerville, James. S Summer 1751. Nl.

Somervell, Thomas. R for Va s horse Jly 1749. M.

Sumner, James of Ulnes Walton. SQS May 1753. La.

Sumner, Margaret. S & T Dec 1769 *Justitia*. M.

Sumner, Margaret (1773). *See* Reed. L.

Sumner, Mary of Penwortham. SQS May 1756. La.

Sumner, Stephen. SQS Apr TB to Md May 1742. So.

Sumner, William of Penwortham. SQS Apr 1741. La.

Sumner, William. S s clocks at New Windsor Lent 1773. Be.

Sumners, Thomas. S Feb 1773. L.

Sunderland, Frances. S May 1719. M.

Sunderland, Nathaniel. R for Barbados May AT Sep 1684. M.

Sunderland, William. S s cloth from tenters at Halifax & R Summer 1774. Y.

Sundrey, Francis. S Lent 1740. He.

Sunley, Richard. S City s silver at St. Helen's Lent 1774. Y.

Sunley, Thomas. S s sheep Summer 1725 AT Summer 1727. Y.

Surcoat, Francis. LC from *Forward* Annapolis Jun 1723. X.

Surfill, John of West Buckland. R for Barbados Jan 1682. So.

Surgeon, John. T 14 yrs May 1767 *Thornton*. Sx.

Sergeason, John. S Summer 1748. Nl.

Surnett, Richard. R for Barbados Apr 1669. M.

Surry, John. S May T Sep 1766 *Justitia*. M.

Surry, Ruth. S Jly T Dec 1736 *Dorsetshire* to Va. M.

Surrey, Susanna (1754). *See* Nisbee. M.

Surridge, Richard. T Oct 1729 *Forward*. E.

Surtis, John. S Summer 1757. Cu.

Sutcliffe, James. S Oct T Nov 1728 *Forward* LC Rappahannock Jun 1729. M.

Sutcliff, Margaret. SQS Feb T Apr 1772 *Thornton*. M.

Sutcliffe, Richard (1766). *See* Sudders. La.

Sutcliffe als Sutlow, Samuel of Manchester, weaver. SQS Apr 1747. La.

Sutcliffe, William. S as pickpocket Lent R 14 yrs Summer 1721 T *Forward* from London Oct 1723. Y.

Suter, Joseph. S s sheep & R Lent T Sep 1772 *Trimley* from London. Ru.

Sutur, Thomas. T Aug 1752 *Tryal*. K.

Sutherland, Ann. SQS Jan 1761. M.

Southerland, Barnard. Died on passage in *Dorsetshire* 1736. X.

Sutherland, James (1775). *See* Douglas. De.

Southerland, Jane. S Oct 1766 T Jan 1767 *Tryal*. L.

Sutherland, John of Camberwell. R Lent T 14 yrs Apr 1772 *Thornton*. Sy.

Sutherland, Margaret. S May-Jly 1748. M.

Sutherland, Margaret. S Sep 1756. M.

Sutlow, Samuel (1747). *See* Sutcliffe. La.

Sutron, William. T Apr 1735 *Patapsco*. K.

Sutton, Abram. S Feb T Sep 1737 *Pretty Patsy* to Md. M.

Sutton, Anne. R for Barbados Oct 1673. L.

Sutton, Anne wife of William. SQS New Sarum Jan TB to Va Aug 1752. Wi.

Sutton als Mason, Katherine. AT Lent 1737. Y.

Sutton, Edward of Basingstoke. R for Barbados Jan 1676. Ha.

Sutton, Edward. S & T Oct 1732 *Caesar* to Va. M.

Sutton, Edward. S Jly 1750. Ha.

Sutton, Edward. T Nov 1759 *Phoenix*. E.

Sutton, Elizabeth. S s tankard Apr T Jun 1742 *Bladon* to Md. M.

Sutton, George. S Oct 1735 T Jan 1736 *Dorsetshire* LC Va Sep 1736; indicted in 1734 for robbery with brother John who was executed; mother Mary Sutton gave evidence. M.

Sutton, George. S Lent 1754. Ch.

Sutton, Hannah. S Jun 1733 but transportation stopped Sep 1733. M.

Sutton als Jutton, James. SWK Jan T Apr 1765 *Ann*. K.

Sutton, John of Wedmore. R for Barbados Jan 1676. So.

Sutton, John. R for Barbados Jly 1680. M.

Sutton, John. R Mar & Oct 1688. M.

Sutton, John. PT Sep 1691. M.

Sutton, John. T Dec 1736 *Dorsetshire*. E.

Sutton, John. S s mare Lent R 14 yrs Summer 1737. St.

Sutton als Andrews, John. SQS Jly TB to Md Nov 1738. So.

Sutton, John. S Mar 1739. Wi.

Sutton, John. S Jan T Mar 1750 *Tryal*. L.

Sutton, John. S Lent 1750. Ca.

Sutton, John. S & T Sep 1757 *Thetis*. M.

Sutton, John. T for life Dec 1770 *Justitia*. Sy.

Sutton, Jonathan. Rebel T 1685.

Sutton, Joseph. T Jly 1723 *Alexander* LC Md Sep 1723. Sy.

Sutton, Joseph of St. James, Westminster. SW Jan 1775. M.

Sutton, Mary. S Apr T May 1719 *Margaret*. L.

Sutton, Robert. S & T Oct 1722 *Forward* LC Annapolis Jun 1723. L.

Sutton, Samuel. S Sep-Oct T Dec 1752 *Greyhound*. M.

Sutton, Sarah. S Feb 1656. M.

Sutton, Sarah of Fordingbridge. R (Oxford Circ) for America Feb 1716. Ha.

Sutton, Thomas. S Dec 1745. L.

Sutton, Thomas. S Feb T Apr 1769 *Tryal*. M.

Sutton, Thomas. S s at Sheffield Lent 1773. Y.

Sutton, Thomas. S s at Snaith & R 14 yrs Summer 1774. Y.

Sutton, William of Lewisham. R for Barbados or Jamaica Feb 1686. K.

Sutton, William. SQS Devizes Apr TB to Va Aug 1766. Wi.

Sutton, William. S Dec 1766 T Jan 1767 *Tryal*. M.

Swaby, Joseph James. S May-Jly 1750. M.

Swadlowe, Margaret. R Feb 1675. M.

Swaff, Margaret. R for America Jly 1686. Nt.

Swaine als Coleman, Edward. R for Barbados Aug 1679. M.

Swayne, Elizabeth, widow. R for plantations Jan 1665. L.

Swaine, George. S s at Repps Lent 1775. Nf.

Swain, Giles. S s iron drag chain Summer TB Sep 1753. G.

Swaine, James. SQS Feb T Mar 1764 *Tryal*. M.

Swaine, Richard. T Jun 1727 *Susanna*. Bu.

Swain, Robert. S s yarn at Condover Summer 1769. Sh.

Swain, Sarah. S s at Speen Summer 1770. Be.

Swaine, William. S s cistern Sep 1736. M.

Swaine, William. T Sep 1765 *Justitia*. Sx.

Swainman, Lawrence (1726). *See* Wainman. Sy.

Swains, John. S Lent R 14 yrs Summer 1737. St.

Swainson, Rowland. S Oct T 14 yrs Nov 1725 *Rappahannock* to Va. M.

Swailes, John. S & T Lent 1729. Y.

Swales, John. S Summer T Sep 1759 from London. Nl.

Swallow, Richard. S Summer 1740. Y.

Swann, Christie. S May-Jly 1773. M.

Swan, Elizabeth. T Jun 1740 *Essex*. K.

Swan, Elizabeth. S Dec 1749-Jan 1750 T Mar 1750 *Tryal*. M.

Swan, Jane. S City Summer 1736. Nl.

Swan, Mary. S Sep T Dec 1734 *Caesar* to Va. M.

Swan, Mary. S s stockings Jun T Dec 1736 *Dorsetshire* but died on passage. M.

Swan, Mary. S Apr 1761. M.

Swan, Peter. S Feb-Apr 1746. M.

Swan, Priscilla. S Jly-Dec 1747. M.

Swan, Ralph. S Summer TB Sep 1757. Db.

Swan, Robert. S Lent 1761. E.

Swan, Thomas. S s cloth from tenters Summer 1718 R 14 yrs Summer 1721 T *Forward* from London Oct 1723. Y.

Swann, Thomas of Cold Cam, Kilburn. SQS Thirsk s from bleaching yard at Scawton Oct 1756 TB Aug 1757. Y.

Swaney, John. S Oct 1748 T Jan 1749 *Laura*. L.

Swannock, John. S Feb T Mar 1750 *Tryal*. M.

Swans, James of Strelley. SQS s horse gear Apr 1737. Nt.

Swansby, Richard. LC from *Alexander* Annapolis Sep 1723. X.

Swanscombe, Richard. S Apr-May T Jly 1771 *Scarsdale*. M.

Swanskin, John. SQS & T Apr 1766 *Ann*. M.

Swanson, Elizabeth. S May-Jun T Jly 1753 *Tryal*. M.

Swanson, Jane. S Sep-Oct 1748 T Jan 1749 *Laura*. M.

Swanson, Thomas. S Jan T Feb 1733 *Smith*. L.

Swanton, Rowland. Died on passage in *Rappahannock* 1726. X.

Swart, Michael. S Dec 1743 T Feb 1744 *Neptune* to Md. M.

Swawbrook als Beakley, Magdalen. S Feb-Apr 1745. M.

Sweep, John (1747). *See* Read. M.

Sweet, John (1740). *See* Sharpless. M.

Sweet, Robert Jr. Rebel T 1685.

Sweet, William. Rebel T 1685.

Sweeting, Henry, a Quaker. R for plantations Jly 1665 (PC). Ht.

Sweething, Nathaniel. S Sep-Oct T Dec 1752 *Greyhound*. M.

Sweeting, Samuel. Rebel T 1685.

Sweetman, Ann. S & T Jan 1722 *Gilbert* LC Annapolis Jly 1722. L.

Sweetman, Edward. S Apr T May 1750 *Lichfield*. M.

Swetman, George of Brockenhurst. R for Barbados Mar 1686. Ha.

Swetman, John. S May T Jun 1726 *Loyal Margaret* but died on passage. M.

Sweetman, John. T 14 yrs Sep 1767 *Justitia*. Sx.

Sweetman, Richard Matthew. ST & T Nov 1762 *Prince William*. L.

Swetman, Robert. R for America Aug 1685. Wa.

Swetman, Thomas. S s sheep Summer 1744 R 11 yrs Lent 1745. Wa.

Sweetman, William. R for Barbados Jun 1671. L.

Sweetman, William. S & T Sep 1731 *Smith* LC Va 1732. M.

Swetland, Peter. S Mar 1739. Do.

Swetland, Peter. S Mar 1751. De.

Swift, Anne (1673). *See* Smyth. L.

Swift, Ann. S Jly T Oct 1741 *Sea Horse* to Va. M.

Swift, Ann wife of James, als Ann May, spinster. S & T Sep 1765 *Justitia*. M.

Swift, Eleanor. SQS Dec 1762 T Mar 1763 *Neptune*. M.

Swift, Elizabeth (1727). *See* Ball. L.

Swift, Elizabeth. S Oct-Dec 1754. M.

Swift, Gabriel. S s fish basket from Thames Dec 1735 T Jan 1736 *Dorsetshire* but died on passage. M.

Swift, Jeremiah. S Jan T Mar 1750 *Tryal*. L.

Swift, John. S 14 yrs Mar TB to Va Oct 1729. Le.

Swift, John. S Lent 1763. Nt.

Swift, John. S May 1763. M.

Swift, John. S & T Apr 1769 *Tryal*. L.

Swift, Richard. S for receiving candles May T 14 yrs Jun 1764 *Dolphin*. M.

Swift, Samuel. T Sep 1755 *Tryal*. M.

Swift, Thomas. S Lent 1735 for bigamously marrying Elizabeth Dugmore at All Saints, Hereford. He.

Swift, William. S Feb T Apr 1766 *Ann*. M.

Swigg, William. R 14 yrs Aug 1760. Co.

Swigg, William. S Aug 1771. Co.

Swinbank, Elizabeth (1759). *See* Hodgson. We.

Swinburn, Richard. S May T Jly 1723 *Alexander* to Md. M.

Swindells, Elizabeth. S & R Lent 1775. Ch.

Swindles, John. S s gold coins at Leominster Summer 1772. He.

Swindels, Lancelot. S Summer 1756. Ch.

Swindon, White. S Jly 1722. Wi.

Swingfield, Thomas (1664). *See* Smyth. L.

Swingley, John of Hemel Hempstead. R for Barbados Jly 1677, 1678, 1679. Ht.

Swingwood, James. S & T Dec 1759 *Phoenix*. M.

Swinne, Rose, aged 44. R Feb 1664. L.

Swinney, Ann. S & T Apr 1759 *Thetis*. L.

Swinney, Bridget. S Feb 1773. L.

Swinney, Edmund. S May T Sep 1765 *Justitia*. L.

Swinney, Edward. S Sep 1719. M.

Swinney, James Rigley. S Feb T Apr 1765 *Ann*. M.

Swynny, Roger. R Dec 1681 AT Jan 1682. M.

Swinshead, Job. S Summer 1767. Wa.

Swinstead, Hambleton of Ware. R for Barbados Jly 1679. Ht.

Swinston, Francis. S Jan-Apr 1748. M.

Swinton, John. S Dec 1745. L.

Swinton, John. S & T Dec 1758 *The Brothers*. L.

Swinyard, Edward. S Summer 1756. K.

Swiselman, Ernest. S Aug 1727 T 14 yrs *Forward* LC Rappahannock May 1728. M.

Sydenham, John Jr. S Aug 1749. So.

Syer, Robert. S s at West Ilsley Lent 1737. Be.

Sikes, Edward of Asher. R for America Jly 1678. Db.

Sykes, Elizabeth. S & T Mar 1763 *Neptune*. L.

Sykes, Francis. S Oct T Dec 1736 *Dorsetshire* to Va. M.

Sikes, John. R for America Jly 1693. Db.

Sykes, John. S Apr 1745. L.

Sykes, Nathaniel. SQS Apr 1773. M.

Sykes, Thomas. R for Barbados Dec 1671. M.

Sykes, William. S Jly T Oct 1741 *Sea Horse* to Va. M.

Sykes, William. R & T 14 yrs Apr 1770 *New Trial*. M.

Symes, Henry. Rebel T 1685.

Symes, James. S Aug 1773. De.

Symes, John of West Kingston, husbandman. R for Barbados Apr 1668. Do.

Symes als White, John. TB to Va 1769. De.

Symes, Joseph. R 14 yrs Aug 1772. So.

Symes, Mary, widow. SQS Jan 1733. So.

Symes, Richard. Rebel T 1685.

Symes, Thomas. R 14 yrs Jly 1744. So.

Symes, William (1666). *See* Pracer, Henry. Ha.

Simons, Abraham. S Sep-Oct 1772. M.

Symonds, Ann of Northleigh. R for Barbados Jly 1681. So.

Simmonds, Ann. S Jly T Dec 1734 *Caesar* LC Va Jly 1735. M.

Symonds, Ann. T Jan 1738 *Dorsetshire*. Sy.

Simmons, Anne. S Apr 1745. L.

Simonds, Ann. S May T Sep 1757 *Thetis*. M.

Simons, Catherine. S & T Feb 1744 *Neptune* to Md. M.

Simmonds, Charles, a little boy. S May 1735 T Jan 1736 *Dorsetshire* LC
 Va Sep 1736. M.

Symons, Christian als Kitty (1752). *See* Ralph. Co.

Simons, David. S May-Jly 1774. M.

Simmonds, Edward. T for life Apr 1769 *Tryal*. K.

Symonds, Elizabeth wife of Richard of Burford. R for Barbados,
 Jamaica or Bermuda Feb 1686. O.

Symonds, Elizabeth of Tipton, widow. R for Barbados, Jamaica or
 Bermuda Feb 1686. St.

Symonds, Elizabeth. T May 1719 *Margaret*; sold to Gustavus Hesseline
 Md May 1720. Sx.

Simonds, Elizabeth. Died on passage in *Margaret* 1720. X.

Simmons, Elizabeth. S Mar 1755. De.

Symons, Elizabeth. S Apr 1767. So.

Simmonds, Elizabeth. S Feb 1774. L.

Symmons, Frances of St. Paul, Shadwell, spinster. S & T Dec 1740
 Vernon. M.

Symonds, Francis. R for Barbados or Jamaica Jly 1686. M.

Symonds, Hannah. S & T Apr 1725 *Sukey* LC Annapolis Sep 1725. M.

Simmons, James. S Summer 1775. K.

Symonds, Jane (1675). *See* Kates. M.

Symons, John. R for Barbados Feb 1665. M.

Symons, John. R Feb 1675. M.

Symonds, John. R for Barbados or Jamaica Dec 1693. L.

Simonds, John of Crawley. R for America Jly 1700. Sx.

Simmons, John of Caister. R for America Jly 1716. Li.

Simons, John. S for Boston NE Jly 1718. Wi.

Symonds, John. T Nov 1725 *Rappahannock* but died on passage. K.

Simmons als Slocomb, John. R 14 yrs Aug 1728. So.

Symonds, John. T Oct 1729 *Forward*. E.

Simmons, John. S Feb T Mar 1730 *Patapsco* LC Annapolis Sep 1730. L.

Symonds, John. R 14 yrs Mar 1735. So.

Symons, John. R 14 yrs Apr 1741. So.

Symonds als Simmons, John of Winterborne. S Summer TB Jly
 1742. G.

Simons, John. S s horses Summer 1749 R 14 yrs Lent 1750. Nf.

Symonds, John. S Lent T Apr 1753 *Thames*. Bu.

Symonds, John. SQS Feb T Mar 1760 *Friendship*. M.

Simmons, John. S s sheep Lent R 14 yrs Summer 1760. No.

Simmonds, John. S & T Sep 1765 *Justitia*. M.

Symonds, John. R & T 14 yrs Apr 1770 *New Trial*. M.

Simmons als Symonds, John. S Apr 1773. M.

Simmons, John. SQS Dec 1774. M.

Simmons, Joseph. S Lent 1764. Li.

Simmons, Love. S Oct 1751-Jan 1752. M.

Simonds, Margaret. S Aug T Oct 1726 *Forward* to VV. M.

Simmonds, Margaret. S Apr 1756. So.

Simonds, Mary. S Jan T Feb 1742 *Industry* to Md. M.

Simmons, Nicholas. S Lent 1773. Sy.

Symonds, Peter. S Dec 1727. M.

Symonds, Peter. S Dec 1737 T Jan 1738 *Dorsetshire*. L.

Symons, Richard. Rebel T 1685.

Symonds, Robert. R for Barbados Aug 1668. M.

Simmons, Robert. S s watch Summer T Dec 1763 *Neptune*. Bu.

Symonds als Simmons, Samuel. S s at Ingham Lent 1769. Nf.

Simmonds, Sarah. S & T May 1744 *Justitia*. L.

Simmons, Sarah. SQS Jly T Nov 1762 *Prince William*. M.

Simons, Simon. S Sep-Oct 1772. M.

Symonds, Thomas. R for Barbados Jly 1675. L.

Simmons, Thomas. S & T 14 yrs Jan 1736 *Dorsetshire* LC Va Sep
  1736. L.

Simmonds, Thomas. T Apr 1743 *Justitia* but died on passage. Sx.

Symons, Thomas. S Summer 1743 R 14 yrs Lent TB May 1744. G.

Symmonds, Thomas. S s mare Lent R 14 yrs Summer 1756. Nf.

Simmons, Thomas. S s at Ambrosden Lent 1759. O.

Symonds, Thomas of St. Paul, Covent Garden. SW Oct T Dec 1763
  Neptune. M.

Symonds, Vincent. S Jan-Jun 1747. M.

Symonds, William. TB Oct 1719 T *Susannah & Sarah* LC Annapolis
  Apr 1720. L.

Symonds, William. T Jly 1723 *Alexander* LC Md Sep 1723. Sy.

Symonds, William. SQS Apr 1730. So.

Simmonds, William (1735). *See* Butler. M.

Simmonds, William. S s money Jan T Jun 1738 *Forward*. L.

Simmonds, William. S s pot Feb T Jun 1738 *Forward* to Md or Va. M.

Simmons, William. S Summer T Sep 1751 *Greyhound*. K.

Symonds, William. S Apr T Sep 1757 *Thetis*. M.

Simmonds, William. SQS May T Sep 1766 *Justitia*. M.

Simmons, William. S Feb T Apr 1768 *Thornton*. M.

Simmonds, William. T 14 yrs Apr 1770 *New Trial*. Sy.

Symonds, William. S Aug 1774. Co.

Synnamon, Thomas. S Feb 1719. M.

Syvett, Joseph. R for Barbados Oct 1673. L.

T

Tabellier, Lewis of Datchet. S Lent T Oct 1726 *Forward*. Bu.

Tabor, Philip of Richmond. SQS 14 yrs Mar T Apr 1753 *Thames*. Sy.

Tabor, William. R for Barbados Mar 1677. L.

Tackett, Edward. T Sep 1731 *Smith*. Bu.

Tackle, Abednego. S Mar 1750. So.

Tackle, John. S Mar 1750. So.

Tadlock, Dorothy. TB Oct 1719 T *Susannah & Sarah* LC Annapolis Apr 1720. L.

Taafe, Elizabeth. S Apr T Jly 1750 *Tryal*. M.

Taffe, Henry. S Apr T Jly 1770 *Scarsdale*. M.

Taffe, Mary (1677). *See* Toole. L.

Taffe, Mary (1679). *See* Penryn. M.

Tagg, Daniel. S Sep-Oct T 14 yrs Dec 1753 *Whiteing*. M.

Tagg, Hester. S Lent 1748. E.

Tailby, John. S Aug TB to Va Sep 1767. Le.

Tainton, William. S s at Standish & R 14 yrs Summer 1768 but died in gaol. G.

Talborn, Elizabeth. S Oct T Dec 1758 *The Brothers*. L.

Talbott, Benjamin. S Feb T Apr 1766 *Ann*. L.

Talbot, Elizabeth. R & T Jly 1770 *Scarsdale*. M.

Talbot, Francis. R for life Dec 1773. M.

Talbot, Henry. S s tankard at Wolverhampton Summer 1762. St.

Talbott als Smith, Henry. TB Mar 1763. Db.

Talbot, James. S Summer 1756. Su.

Talbott, Jane. S Summer R for Barbados Aug 1664. E.

Talbot, John. S Apr-Jun 1739. M.

Talbot, John. S May T Sep 1766 *Justitia*. M.

Talbot, Mary. S May-Jly 1773. M.

Talbott, Richard of Titherley, husbandman. R for Barbados Apr 1668. Ha.

Talbot, Richard (1762). *See* Eyre, John. Wi.

Talbott, Thomas. S Jan T Feb 1744 *Neptune*; executed after 1751. M.

Talbot, Thomas. S s horse Summer 1754 R 14 yrs Lent 1755. Wa.

Tall, Mary. S Apr 1742. Ha.

Tallant, Patrick. S & T Sep 1751 *Greyhound*. M.

Talent, Richard. R for Barbados or Jamaica May 1697. L.

Tallard, John. S Lent 1735. *Su.

Tallmarsh, William. S May T Jly 1722 *Alexander* to Nevis or Jamaica. M.

Talloway, Elizabeth. S Sep 1744. M.

Talloway, Samuel. S s sheep & R Lent 1771. Li.

Tally, Thomazine als Elizabeth. R for Barbados or Jamaica Mar 1688. M.

Talley, William. T Jan 1749 *Laura*. L.

Talmige, John. S Feb-Apr T May 1741 *Tryal*. M.

Talmy als Tolmy, John, als Blind Jack the Kidnapper. S Feb T Apr 1772 *Thornton*. L.

Tame, John. S Summer T Sep 1755 *Tryal*. Sy.

Tame, John. S (Western Circ) Dec 1766. Be.

Tamplin, Anthony. S Oct 1751-Jan 1752. M.

Tandy, John Merry. S & R 14 yrs Lent 1769. Wo.

Tanfield, James, als Lucas, Richard. S s sheep & R 14 yrs Summer 1775. G.

Tanfield, Richard. SQS May 1754. M.

Tankard, Edward. S May T Jly 1722 *Alexander* to Nevis or Jamaica. M.

Tanklin, John. S & T Dec 1758 *The Brothers*. L.

Tanner als Gingell, Charles. S s horse Summer 1742 R 14 yrs Lent TB Mar 1743. G.

Tanner, Charles. S Feb T Apr 1743 *Justitia*. M.

Tanner, Christopher William. S Feb T Apr 1765 *Ann*. M.

Tanner, Edward (1730). *See* Richards. Co.

Tanner, Elizabeth of Newington by Sittingbourne. R for Barbados or Jamaica Jly 1696. K.

Tanner, George. S 14 yrs for receiving from C.W. Tanner *(qv)* Feb T 14 yrs Apr 1765 *Ann*. M.

Tanner, Gilbert. TB to Va from QS 1740. De.

Tanner, Jane of Ducklington. R for America Feb 1684. O.

Tanner, John Sr. S s cloth Lent R 14 yrs Summer 1729. G.

Tanner, John. R 14 yrs Apr 1770. De.

Tanner, Lucy. S Oct 1744-Jan 1745. M.

Tanner, Martin Peter. S Feb T Mar 1730 *Patapsco* LC Annapolis Sep 1730. L.

Tanner, Mary. S & T Oct 1729 *Forward* LC Va Jun 1730. M.

Tanner, Mary. S s lambs Summer 1742 R 14 yrs Lent TB Mar 1743. G.

Tanner als Taylor als Williams als Dodson, Mary. S Feb T Mar 1764 *Tryal*. M.

Tanner, Maurice. S Feb 1663 to House of Correction unless he agees to be transported. M.

Tanner, Samuel. TB to Va from QS 1756. De.

Tanner, Stephen. R 14 yrs Apr TB to Va Sep 1753. Wi.

Tanner, Thomas. S Feb T Apr 1741 *Speedwell* or *Mediterranean*. M.

Tanner, Tobias. S Jan T Feb 1719 *Worcester* LC Md Jun 1719. LM.

Tanner, William of Ducklington. R for America Mar 1680. O.

Tanner, William. S Apr 1728. So.

Tapfield, John. R for Barbados May 1665. X.

Tapling, John. S Oct-Dec 1754. M.

Taplin, John. S Jly 1765. Ha.

Taplin, John. S May T Jun 1768 *Tryal*. M.

Tapling als Tyler, William. R 14 yrs Aug 1727 TB to Md. De.

Tap, Elizabeth. S Sep 1761. M.

Tapp, Henry. SQS Feb 1773. M.

Tapp, Richard. TB to Va 1770. De.

Tapper, James. R Mar 1755. Co.

Tapper, Joseph. S Jly T Sep 1757 *Thetis*. M.

Tapper, Richard. Rebel T 1685.

Tapper, William. S 14 yrs for receiving Mar 1755. Co.

Tappin, James. S s mare & R 14 yrs Lent 1775. O.

Tapping, John. R for Barbados Apr 1668. L.

Tappin, John. S Sep T Oct 1750 *Rachael*. L.

Tapping, Thomas. S Lent 1775. Be.

Tapscott, William. Rebel T 1685.

Tapsell, Mary. T Sep 1758 *Tryal*. K.

Tarbock, George. S Lent 1751. La.

Tarborne als Sherborne als Starkey, Sarah. S Jly T Aug 1721
Prince Royal. M.

Tarleton, Elizabeth. R for Barbados Jan 1679. L.

Tarlton, Mary wife of John of St. Saviour, Southwark. R for Barbados or
Jamaica Jly 1715. Sy.

Tarnell, Mary of Navestock. R for Barbados Jly 1679. E.

Tarner, John. S & TB Mar 1731. G.

Tarr, John. S s at Biggleswade Summer 1771. Bd.

Tarr, Thomas. S Jly 1744. De.

Tarr, William. S Jly 1749 TB to Va. De.

Tarrant, Henry. S & T Sep 1731 *Smith* LC Va 1732. M.

Tarrant, John. S Apr-May 1754. M.

Tarrant, Thomas. SQS Marlborough Oct 1767 TB to Va Apr 1768. Wi.

Tarrant, William. R 14 yrs Aug 1739. So.

Tarrs, William of Shinfield. R for America Mar 1680. Be.

Tart, Mary wife of Thomas. S s cast iron at Leighton Lent 1750. He.

Tarver, John. S Summer 1748 R 14 yrs Lent 1749. O.

Task, Deborah. S & T Apr 1769 *Tryal*. L.

Tasker, David. T Apr 1735 *Patapsco*. K.

Tasker, George of Marylebone. S & T Dec 1740 *Vernon* to Md. M.

Tasker, Grace. S Dec 1762 T Mar 1763 *Neptune*. M.

Tasker, Margaret. S Summer 1763. Ch.

Tasker, William. R for America Jly 1686. No.

Tasker, William. S May-Jly 1750. M.

Taster, Ann of Watford. R for Barbados or Jamaica Mar 1680. Ht.

Tasewell als Tausewell, Nicholas. S for smuggling brandy Jly 1725. Do.

Taswell, William of Sittingbourne. R for Barbados or Jamaica Jun
1684. K.

Tatchwell, John. PT Jly 1679. M.

Tate, George. S Feb T Mar 1727 *Rappahannock* to Md. M.

Tate, James. S & T Oct 1729 *Forward* LC Va Jun 1730. L.

Tate, John. R 14 yrs Summer 1753. Nl.

Tate, Margaret of St. Martin in Fields, spinster. SW Jun 1775. M.

Tate als Taylor, Mary. S Sep 1733 T Jan 1734 *Caesar* LC Va Jly 1734. M.

Tate, Mary. S & T Apr 1741 *Speedwell* or *Mediterranean*. M.

Tate, Michael (1769). *See* Pricket. O.

Tate, Rosamond. T Sep 1765 *Justitia*. M.

Tate, Thomas. S City Summer 1736. Nl.

Tate, William. S May T Sep 1765 *Justitia*. M.

Tatem, William. S s at Chelsworth Summer 1773; James Tatem
acquitted. Su.

Tatham, Thomas. S Nov T 14 yrs Dec 1770 *Justitia*. L.

Tatler, Joseph. SQS Feb T May 1767 *Thornton*. M.

Tattersall, Edmund of Lancaster Castle. S for life Summer 1773. La.

Tattershell, James. S May T Jun 1727 *Susanna* to Va. M.

Tattle, Margery. R for Barbados Dec 1668. M.

Tatton, Ellen wife of John of Gorton, wheelwright. SQS Apr 1769. La.

Tatton, Joseph, als Priest, James. T Nov 1743 *George William*. Ht.
Taubman, Thomas of St. Saviour, Southwark. SQS Jan T Mar 1764
 Tryal. Sy.
Taught, John. T Jun 1738 *Forward*. Sx.
Taulton, John. S Oct T Nov 1728 *Forward* LC Rappahannock Jun
 1729. M.
Taunch, Robert. R 14 yrs for Carolina May 1719. L.
Taunton, Giles of Thornbury, blacksmith. R for Barbados Mar 1663. G.
Taunton, Samuel. R for Barbados Jun 1663. M.
Tausewell, Nicholas (1725). *See* Tasewell. Do.
Taverner, George. S & T Oct 1730 *Forward* LC Potomack Jan 1731. M.
Taverner, George. T Dec 1753 *Whiteing*. E.
Taverner, John. S s horse Summer 1762 R 14 yrs Lent 1763. Li.
Taverner, Joseph. S Feb T Mar 1730 *Patapsco* but died on psaage. M.
Taverner, Sarah. S Feb T Mar 1729 *Patapsco* LC Annapolis Dec 1729. L.
Taverner, Thomas. R for Barbados Dec 1693 AT Jan 1694. M.
Tay, Thomas. S s at Adderbury Summer 1769. O.
Taylor, Abraham. SQS Sep 1772. M.
Taylor, Agnes (1762). *See* Brookes. M.
Taylor, Alexander. SQS Jan 1755. M.
Taylor, Alice. S City s lead Summer 1732. Nl.
Taylor, Alice. S Lent 1766. La.
Taylor, Ann of Brisol. R for Barbados for murder of her bastard Feb
 1700. G.
Tayler, Ann. T Nov 1728 *Forward*. Bu.
Taylor, Anne. S Jan T Feb 1733 *Smith* to Md or Va. M.
Taylor als Roberds, Ann. LC from *Caesar* Va Jly 1735. X.
Taylor, Ann wife of John. Died on passage in *Caesar* 1735. X.
Taylor, Ann. T Nov 1762 *Prince William*. E.
Taylor, Ann. S Lent 1774. Sh.
Taylor, Ann wife of James *(qv)* of Manchester. SQS Apr 1774. La.
Taylor, Celia. S Norwich Summer 1749. Nf.
Taylor, Charles. S s at St. Swithin, Worcester, Summer 1737. Wo.
Taylor, Charles. SW & T Jan 1767 *Tryal*. M.
Taylor, Charles. R 14 yrs Apr 1770. So.
Taylor, Christopher. LC from *Patapsco* Annapolis Oct 1732. X.
Taylor, Colonel (1754). *See* Naston, John. M.
Taylor, Cordelia. S Apr T 14 yrs May 1743 *Indian Queen* to
 Potomack. M.
Taylor, Daniel. S Jly T Aug 1721 *Prince Royal* LC Va Nov 1721. L.
Taylor, Edmund of Upper End, Tottington. SQS Nov 1755. La.
Taylor, Edward. R for Barbados Aug 1664. L.
Taylor, Edward of Quidenham. R for America Mar 1709. Nf.
Taylor, Edward. S Sep 1733 T Jan 1734 *Caesar* LC Va Jly 1734. M.
Taylor, Edward. T Apr 1735 *Patapsco*. Sy.
Taylor, Edward. S s clothing at Burford Summer 1738. O.
Taylor, Edward. S & T Feb 1741 *Speedwell* or *Mediterranean*. M.
Taylor, Edward. T Apr 1765 *Ann*. M.
Taylor, Edward. S s at St. Peter, Worcester, Summer 1770. Wo.
Taylor, Edward. S Oct T Dec 1771 *Justitia*. L.
Tayler, Edward. S s at Walsoken Summer 1772. Nf.

Taylor, Edward. S s at Powick Summer 1773. Wo.

Taylor, Edward. S & R for life Summer 1773. St.

Taylor, Elias. S Lent 1763. Ht.

Taylor, Elizabeth of Pedmore. R for America Jly 1675. Wo.

Taylor als Wild, Elizabeth. S & T Oct 1732 *Caesar* to Va. M.

Taylor, Elizabeth (1734). *See* Richardson. M.

Taylor, Elizabeth. S & T Dec 1734 *Caesar* but died on passage. M.

Taylor, Elizabeth. S s petticoat Apr T Dec 1735 *John* LC Md Sep 1736. M.

Taylor, Elizabeth. S Lent 1741. Wo.

Taylor, Elizabeth. S Sep T Oct 1750 *Rachael*. M.

Taylor, Elizabeth als Wiseman. S Dec 1753-Jan 1754. M.

Taylor, Elizabeth. T Sep 1764 *Justitia*. K.

Taylor, Ely. S 14 yrs Jan-Apr 1748. M.

Taylor, Esther. S Feb-Apr T Jun 1756 *Lyon*. M.

Taylor, Francis. R 14 yrs Mar 1731. So.

Taylor, Francis. S Apr 1748. L.

Taylor, Francis. S Summer 1752 R 14 yrs Lent 1753. Sh.

Taylor, Garrick. SQS & T 1741. Bd.

Taylor, George. R for America Aug 1685. Wa.

Tayler, George of Nottingham. R for America Feb 1713. Nt.

Taylor, George. S Jly 1728. Ha.

Taylor, George. SQS & TB Mar 1736. G.

Taylor, George (1759). *See* Alsop, Joseph. Db.

Taylor, George (1761). *See* Gill, William. Le.

Taylor, George. S Feb T Mar 1764 *Tryal*. M.

Taylor, George of Spotland, woollen weaver. SQS Apr 1766. La.

Taylor, George. S Jly 1771. Ha.

Taylor, Hannah. R for America Jly 1686. Nt.

Taylor, Harry (1748). *See* Grafton, Henry. L.

Taylor, Henry. S Feb T Apr 1732 *Patapsco* LC Annapolis Oct 1732. L.

Taylor, Henry. S Mar TB to Va Apr 1732. Wi.

Taylor, Henry. S Sep 1754. L.

Taylor, Henry. S for perjury at St. Lawrence, Reading, Lent 1768. Be.

Taylor, Ishmael. S s shoes Sep 1735 T Jan 1736 *Dorsetshire* LC Va Sep 1736. M.

Tayler, James of Newark on Trent. R for America Jly 1678. Nt.

Tayler, James. S Lent R 14 yrs Summer 1745. Sx.

Taylor, James. S & TB to Va Apr 1764. Le.

Taylor, James. S s sheep Lent R 14 yrs Summer 1764. No.

Taylor, James of Walls, Rossendale Forest. SQS Jan 1765. La.

Taylor, James. S s at Welland Lent 1766. Wo.

Taylor, James. T 14 yrs May 1767 *Thornton*. Ht.

Taylor, James. SQS Jun T Sep 1767 *Justitia*. M.

Taylor, James. S Summer 1772. Sy.

Taylor, James. SQS Sep 1772. M.

Taylor, James of Manchester. SQS Apr 1774. La.

Taylor, Jane of Westminster. R Aug 1663 (PC). M.

Taylor, Jane. T Nov 1728 *Forward*. Sy.

Taylor, Jane. S Feb T Mar 1731 *Patapsco* LC Annapolis Jun 1731. L.

Taylor, Jane als Roberts. S Sep T Dec 1734 *Caesar* to Va. M.

Taylor, Jane wife of John. S Lent T Apr 1773. Wa.

Taylor, Jeremiah. S Mar 1765. Ha.

Taylor, John of Aylesford. R for Barbados Aug 1662. K.

Taylor, John. R Feb 1675. M.

Tayler als Richardson, John. R for America Mar 1697. Db.

Tayler, John of Ashbourne in Pecco. R for America Feb 1713. Db.

Taylor, John. S for Boston NE Jly 1718. Ha.

Taylor, John. S Apr T Oct 1719 *Susannah & Sarah* LC Md Apr
  1720. L.

Taylor, John. S Jly 1722. Do.

Taylor, John. S Jan T Feb 1724 *Anne*. L.

Taylor, John. S Oct T Dec 1724 *Rappahannock* to Va. M.

Taylor, John. S & T Oct 1730 *Forward* LC Potomack Jan 1731. L.

Taylor, John. S & T Apr 1733 *Patapsco* LC Annapolis Nov 1733. L.

Taylor, John. S s cane Jly 1735 T Jan 1736 *Dorsetshire* LC Va Sep
  1736. M.

Taylor, John. S s horse Summer 1736 R 14 yrs Lent 1737. He.

Taylor, John. S Summer 1740. St.

Taylor, John. T Nov 1741 *Sea Horse*. E.

Tayler, John. S s sheep Lent R 14 yrs Summer TB to Va Sep 1742. Le.

Taylor, John, als Mirehouse, Joseph. S Summer 1744. Y.

Taylor, John. S to hang Lent 1745 for being at large in Lapley before
  expiry of 14 year sentence of transportation. St.

Taylor, John. S & R 14 yrs Lent 1747. Bu.

Taylor, John. S for life 1749. M.

Taylor, John. S & T Apr 1753 *Thames*. L.

Taylor, John, als Davis, Edward. S & TB Mar 1754. G.

Tayler, John. S s deer Mar 1755. Ha.

Taylor, John of Walmsley. SQS Nov 1755. La.

Taylor, John. SQS Apr T Jun 1764 *Dolphin*. M.

Taylor, John. SQS May TB Sep 1764. So.

Taylor, John. S Jly T Sep 1764 *Justitia*. M.

Taylor, John. S Jly T Sep 1766 *Justitia*. M.

Taylor, John. T Sep 1767 *Justitia*. K.

Taylor, John. S 14 yrs for receiving sheep stolen by his wife Mary *(qv)*
  Lent 1768. Ca.

Taylor, John. T Jun 1768 *Tryal*. M.

Taylor, John. S s cloth at Stroud Summer 1770. G.

Taylor, John. S s horse & R 14 yrs Summer 1773. He.

Taylor, John. R Jly 1774. M.

Taylor, John. S s mare & gelding & R 14 yrs Lent 1775. Li.

Taylor, Joseph. R for Barbados or Jamaica Apr 1690. L.

Taylor, Joseph. S Jan T Feb 1726 *Supply* LC Annapolis May 1726. M.

Taylor, Joseph. S s horse Summer 1730 R 14 yrs Lent 1731. Be.

Taylor, Joseph. R 14 yrs Summer 1751. Cu.

Taylor, Joseph. S 14 yrs s from bleaching yard at Bromsgrove Summer
  1756. Wo.

Taylor als Turner, Joseph. S Feb T Mar 1764 *Tryal*. M.

Taylor, Joseph of Mortlake. SQS & T Jan 1766 *Tryal*. Sy.

Taylor, Joseph. T Apr 1771 *Thornton*. Sy.

Taylor, Judith. S Jun 1747. L.

Taylor, Margaret (1715). *See* Wade. M.

Taylor als Harwood, Margaret. S Feb T Mar 1727 *Rappahannock*. L.

Taylor, Margaret. S Oct 1749. L.

Tayler, Martin. T Oct 1720 *Gilbert*. Sy.

Taylor, Mary. R Jly & Dec 1698 AT Jan 1699. M.

Taylor, Mary. S Aug 1720 T Mar 1723. Bu.

Taylor, Mary (1733). *See* Tate. M.

Taylor, Mary. S & T Dec 1734 *Caesar* LC Va Jly 1735. L.

Taylor, Mary wife of William. S s plates Sep T Dec 1736 *Dorsetshire*. M.

Taylor, Mary (1744). *See* Slaney. Sh.

Taylor, Mary. S Sep-Oct 1748 T Jan 1749 *Laura*. M.

Taylor, Mary. S Apr-May 1754. M.

Taylor, Mary (1764). *See* Tanner. M.

Taylor, Mary wife of John. S s sheep & R 14 yrs Lent 1768; missed transportation ship & ordered to take next Summer 1768. Ca.

Taylor, Matthew. AT Lent & Summer 1765. Y.

Taylor, Michael Thomas. R for life Lent 1773. E.

Taylor, Philip of Newent. R for America Mar 1701. G.

Taylor, Ralph, als Ord, Richard. R 14 yrs Summer 1735. Nl.

Taylor, Richard of Tonge. R for America Sep 1671. Sh.

Taylor, Richard. S May 1672 & to be considered for transportation. M.

Tayler, Richard. T Apr 1725 *Sukey*. Sy.

Taylor, Richard. T Dec 1731 *Forward*. K.

Tayler, Richard. S Apr 1742. So.

Taylor, Richard. R (Western Circ) Dec 1766. G.

Taylor, Robert Jr. of Leeds. R for Barbados Jly 1683. Y.

Taylor, Robert. R for America Jun 1684. Li.

Taylor, Robert. R Dec 1699 & Aug 1700. M.

Taylor, Robert. S Lent 1756. Y.

Taylor, Robert. S Mar 1761. Ha.

Taylor, Robert. S Feb T Apr 1768 *Thornton*. M.

Taylor, Robert (1772). *See* Alcock. E.

Taylor, Samuel. S Dec 1749-Jan 1750 T Mar 1750 *Tryal*. M.

Taylor, Samuel of Stapleford, framework knitter. SQS s fowls & TB Apr 1771. Nt.

Taylor, Samuel. SQS Apr 1773. M.

Taylor, Samuel. S s chickens at Dunton Lent 1774. Bd.

Taylor, Sarah. R for Barbados or Jamaica Oct 1690. M.

Taylor, Sarah. S s at Bucklebury Summer 1729. Be.

Taylor als Brown, Sarah. S Apr T May 1743 *Indian Queen* to Potomack. M.

Taylor, Sarah. S Jun T Nov 1743 *George William*. L.

Taylor, Sarah. S Mar 1758. So.

Taylor, Sarah. S Apr-May 1775. M.

Taylor, Solomon. S Apr T Sep 1757 *Thetis*. L.

Taylor, Stephen of Newcastle uon Tyne. R for Barbados Jly 1682. Nl.

Taylor, Stephen. R 14 yrs Aug 1742. De.

Taylor, Susan. PT Jan R Feb 1675. M.

Taylor, Susannah. S Jan 1745. L.

Taylor, Thomas of Wokingham. R for America Jly 1691. Be.

Taylor, Thomas (1722). *See* Jones. Sh.

Taylor, Thomas. Died on passage in *Sukey* 1725. X.
Taylor, Thomas. T Sep 1730 *Smith*. Sy.
Taylor, Thomas. S & T Sep 1731 *Smith* LC Va 1732. M.
Taylor, Thomas. R 14 yrs Jly 1733. De.
Taylor, Thomas. S Feb T Apr 1734 *Patapsco* to Md. M.
Taylor, Thomas. S & R Lent 1738. Su.
Taylor, Thomas. S Feb T Apr 1739 *Forward*. L.
Taylor, Thomas. S Apr-May T May 1741 *Catherine & Elizabeth* to Md. M.
Taylor, Thomas. S Lent 1750. Y.
Taylor, Thomas. S Oct T Nov 1759 *Phoenix*. L.
Taylor, Thomas (1760). *See* Jones. Db.
Taylor, Thomas. S Aug 1760. L.
Taylor, Thomas. S Lent 1761. Sy.
Taylor, Thomas. S & T Jly 1770 *Scarsdale*. L.
Taylor, Thomas. S s gelding & R Lent TB Aug 1771. Db.
Taylor, Thomas. S s silver ring at Tewkesbury Summer 1772. G.
Taylor, Thomas. S s horse & R 14 yrs Summer 1774. Sh.
Taylor, Thomas. S Lent 1775. Sy.
Taylor, Timothy (1738). *See* Forth. Ha.
Taylor, Walter of Cirencester. R for Barbados Mar 1693. G.
Taylor, William. R for plantations Jan 1665. L.
Taylor, William (1679). *See* Tutfold. Sx.
Taylor, William of Wanscombe. R for Barbados or Jamaica Jly 1696. K.
Taylor, William. S for Va Jly 1718. De.
Taylor, William. Died on passage in *Rappahannock* 1726. Li.
Taylor, William. TB to Va from QS 1729. De.
Taylor, William of Biggleswade. S Lent 1729. *Bd.
Taylor als Burleigh, William. S & T Oct 1729 *Forward* LC Va Jun 1730. L.
Taylor als Barrett, William. R 14 yrs Jly TB to Va Aug 1731. Wi.
Taylor, William. S s at St. Nicholas, Hereford, Lent 1735. He.
Taylor, William. TB to Md from QS 1737. De.
Taylor, William. S Lent 1741. Wo.
Taylor, William. T Nov 1743 *George William*. Ht.
Taylor, William. T Apr 1744. Ht.
Taylor, William. S Jan 1745. L.
Taylor, William. S Oct 1748 T Jan 1749 *Laura*. L.
Taylor, William. S Jan-Apr 1749. M.
Taylor, William. S s at Newbury Lent 1752. Be.
Taylour, William. S s pigs at Bransford Summer 1752. Wo.
Taylor, William. SQS Feb 1754. M.
Taylor, William. S 14 yrs for receiving Lent 1760. Wa.
Taylor, William. S s cloth at Moreton Say Summer 1761. Sh.
Taylor, William. S City s horse Lent R 14 yrs Summer 1764. Y.
Taylor, William. T Jun 1764 *Dolphin*. K.
Taylor, William. T 14 yrs Sep 1766 *Justitia*. E.
Taylor, William. S Dec 1766 T Jan 1767 *Tryal*. M.
Taylor, William. S & T Jan 1767 *Tryal*. M.
Taylor, William. S s handkerchief at St. Peter Westcheap Jan T Apr 1768 *Thornton*. L.

Taylor, William. S s poultry at All Hallows Lombard Street Feb T Apr 1768 *Thornton*. L.

Taylor, William. S Apr T Jly 1770 *Scarsdale*. M.

Taylor, William of Warrington. SQS May 1770. La.

Taylor, William. SQS & T Apr 1771 *Thornton*. Ht.

Taylor, William. S s iron axes at Headington Lent 1772. O.

Taylor, William of St. George, Southwark. S Lent T Apr 1772 *Thornton*. Sy.

Taylor, William. S Lent T Apr 1773. Wa.

Taylor, William. SQS May T Jly 1773 *Tayloe* to Va. M.

Tea, Elizabeth. S & T 14 yrs Jan 1736 *Dorsetshire* LC Va Sep 1736. L.

Tee, John. S Mar 1755. Ha.

Tee, Joseph. S Mar 1754. Ha.

Teague, John of Moreton. R for America Jly 1683. Sh.

Teage, Peter. S Mar 1731. Co.

Teape, Robert. Rebel T 1685.

Teape, Walter. Rebel T 1685.

Tear, Edward. R for Barbados or Jamaica Dec 1693. M.

Tearer, Robert. S Mar 1755. Ha.

Tearne, Thomas (1675). *See* Treane. M.

Teasdale, George. S s sheep at Luddam & R Summer 1772; wife Ann acquitted. Nf.

Tebbutt, William. S Lent T May 1755 *Rose*. K.

Tebby, John. S s sheep Summer 1752 R Lent T Apr 1753 *Thames*. Bu.

Tebby, Thomas. S Lent R 14 yrs Summer 1748. O.

Teckoe, Richard. S Lent 1755. Sh.

Tecton, Thomas. R for America Jly 1694. No.

Teddall als Morgan, Christopher. R & T Dec 1716 *Lewis* to Jamaica. M.

Tedder als Tudor, George. S s harness at Llanwern Lent 1729. Mo.

Tedar, Joseph. S & T Mar 1760 *Friendship*. L.

Tedder, Richard of Aylesford. S Lent T May 1719 *Margaret*; sold to Patrick Sympson Md May 1720. K.

Tidder, Richard. S Lent R 14 yrs Summer 1728. Sh.

Teddy, John. R Summer 1773. Sy.

Tedstill, Christopher. S s tablespoon at Bromsgrove Summer 1772. Wo.

Tedstell, John. S s at Stotherton Lent 1761 T *Atlas* from Bristol 1761. Sh.

Telley, William. S Jan T Feb 1742 *Industry*. L.

Tellier, John. R Jly 1686. M.

Telsted, Mark. T Apr 1772 *Thornton*. E.

Tempest, Joshua. S Lent 1774. Y.

Temple, John. S Aug T Oct 1726 *Forward*. L.

Temple, John. S Dec 1765 T Jan 1766 *Tryal*. L.

Temple, Mary wife of John. S Aug T Sep 1725 *Forward* LC Md Dec 1725. M.

Temple, William. PT Oct 1684 R Mar 1685. M.

Temple, William. R for Barbados or Jamaica Dec 1695 & Jan 1697. M.

Templeman, Edward. S & T Dec 1731 *Forward*. L.

Templeman, Henry. T Jly 1723 *Alexander* LC Md Sep 1723. Sy.

Templer, James. S Oct 1774. L.

Tennant, Elizabeth. SQS s coal from Sir James Lowther Easter 1774. Du.

Tennant, Judith. SQS & T Jan 1767 *Tryal*. M.

Tennant, Susanna wife of Moses. S Norwich Summer 1752. Nf.

Teno, Elizabeth wife of Thomas. S Sep T Dec 1734 *Caesar* LC Va Jly 1735. M.

Tenpenny, Nathaniel. S Feb T Mar 1764 *Tryal*. M.

Teppell, Mary. S Apr T Jun 1768 *Tryal*. M.

Terrell, John of Tettenhall. R for America Jly 1683. St.

Terrill, Susan. R Oct 1690. M.

Terrett, Catherine. T Jun 1726 *Loyal Margaret* LC Md Dec 1726. K.

Terratt, William of Drayton. R for Barbados Oct 1663. Sh.

Territt, William. S Sep T Dec 1767 *Neptune*. L.

Terry, Ann. S Sep T for life Oct 1744 *Susannah*. M.

Terry, Elizabeth (1727). *See* Stafford. Sy.

Terry, Elizabeth. S Oct-Dec 1750. M.

Terry, Elizabeth (1754). *See* Simms. M.

Terrey als Toursey, Francis. SQS for attending conventicle Dec 1664. M.

Terry, George of St. Mary, Guildford. R for Barbados or Jamaica Jly 1712. Sy.

Terry, George. SW & T Jan 1769 *Thornton*. M.

Terry, John. SQS for attending conventicle Dec 1664. M.

Terrey, John. R for Barbados or Jamaica Jly 1686. M.

Terry, Martha. S & T Jun 1742 *Bladon* to Md. M.

Terry, Mary wife of James. S Apr-May 1775. M.

Terrey, Richard of Bermondsey. R (Newgate) for Barbados Apr 1669. Sy.

Terrey, Richard. R for Barbados Jly 1674. L.

Terry, Samuel. S & T Dec 1759 *Phoenix*. L.

Terry, Stephen. T 14 yrs Oct 1768 *Justitia*. K.

Terry, Thomas. T Oct 1768 *Justitia*. Sy.

Tessiman, George of Nosterfield. SQS Northallerton s sheep at Snape Jly 1719 but discharged for lameness. Y.

Tessimond, William (1726). *See* Bell. Y.

Tetherly, Richard. R 14 yrs Aug 1740 TB to Va. De.

Tetley, William. S Lent 1775. Db.

Tew, Michael. S s at Cirencester Summer 1729. G.

Tue, Whitehill (1739). *See* Wadmen. So.

Tew, William. S for forgery & R Lent 1775. Wa.

Teward, John of Sittingbourne. R for Barbados or Jamaica Feb 1684. K.

Tewksbury, John of Gosport. R for Barbados Feb 1699. Ha.

Thacker als Spaw, Esther. S Feb T Apr 1732 *Patapsco* LC Md Oct 1732. M.

Thacker, George. S s game birds at Stone & Checkley Lent 1764. St.

Thacker als Sacker, George. S s at Downham Lent 1773. Nf.

Thacker, Jane. R 14 yrs Jly 1747. Ha.

Thacker, William. S & T Jly 1770 *Scarsdale*. M.

Thackeray, William. S May-Jun T Jly 1753 *Tryal*. M.

Thackerill, Edward. S Oct T for life Nov 1759 *Phoenix*. L.

Thackham, William. S Feb T Apr 1743 *Justitia*. M.

Thaire, John of Frimley. R (Newgate) for Barbados Sep 1669. Sy.

Thane, James Wallis. R 14 yrs Jly 1774. M.

Thaine, Robert. R 14 yrs Summer 1729. Nl.

Thayne, Robert (1752). *See* French. Nf.

Tharpe, Joseph. S Lent 1754. K.

Thatcher, Abraham. SQS Jan TB Apr 1750. So.

Thatcher, Anne. S May T 14 yrs Jly 1722 *Alexander*. L.

Thatcher, Elizabeth. S Oct 1757 T Mar 1758 *Dragon*. M.

Thatcher, Henry. R Mar 1774. So.

Thatcher, John. R Mar 1774. So.

Thatcher, Mary. S May T 14 yrs Jly 1722 *Alexander*. L.

Thatcher, Thomas. LC from *Gilbert* Annapolis Jly 1722. X.

Thatchwell als Turner, John. R for Barbados Aug 1679. M.

Thaxton, Susannah. S & T Oct 1732 *Caesar* to Va. M.

Thackston, Thomas of Bromley. R for Barbaaos or Jamaica Jly 1696. K.

Thayer, William. S Summer 1739 R 14 yrs Lent 1740 (SP). O.

Theast, John. S Mar 1763 TB to Va. De.

Theed, Richard of Woodford. S for highway robbery Summer 1745 R 14
    yrs Lent 1746. E.

Theed, Thomas. T Jan 1734 *Caesar* LC Va Jly 1734. E.

Theobald, Hannah of St. Peter Mancroft, Norwich. S Summer
    1731. *Nf.

Theobald, Robert (1765). *See* Clodd. Su.

Theron als Thorn, Isaac. S Dec 1746. L.

Thetford, Edward. S Aug T Sep 1725 *Forward* LC Annapolis Dec
    1725. M.

Thickhead, William (1724). *See* Hudson. M.

Thimbleby, Samuel. T Jun 1728 *Elizabeth*. E.

Thinwood als Phillips, John. T Oct 1729 *Forward*. Sy.

Thirby als Kirby, Mary. S Apr TB to Md May 1719. L.

Thirchild als Child, Edward. S s mare at Richards Castle Summer 1758
    R 14 yrs Lent 1759. Sh.

Thirske, Elizabeth. AT Lent & Summer 1750. Y.

Thirtle, Bartholomew. S Summer 1757. Nf.

Thistle, Richard (1715). *See* Thornbury. L.

Thomas, Abraham. Rebel T 1685.

Thomas als Adams, Alice. S Feb 1719 T *Worcester* LC Annapolis Jun
    1719. L.

Thomas, Anne of Pinchead. R for Barbados Jly 1679. So.

Thomas, Ann (1689). *See* Dye. M.

Thomas, Ann. S & T Aug 1718 *Eagle* LC Charles Town Mar 1719. L.

Thomas, Ann. S Jun-Dec 1738 T Jan 1739 *Dorsetshire* to Va. M.

Thomas, Ann. S Feb-Apr 1746. M.

Thomas, Ann. S Jan-Apr 1748. M.

Thomas, Ann. S Aug 1758. Co.

Thomas, Ann. S Sep-Oct T Dec 1771 *Justitia*. M.

Thomas, Blanch. R for Barbados Mar 1681. M.

Thomas, Catherine. S May 1763. M.

Thomas, Charles. S Jly 1736. M.

Thomas, Charles. S Sep-Oct 1773. M.

Thomas, Charles. S s mare & R 14 yrs Summer 1774. Mo.

Thomas, David of Westleigh. R for Barbados Jly 1667. De.

Thomas, David. Rebel T 1685.

Thomas, David. S s at North Lydbury Lent 1728. Sh.

Thomas als Phillips, David of Bristol. R for life for returning from transportation May 1769 (SP). G.

Thomas, David. S s horse & R 14 yrs Summer 1775. Mo.

Thomas, Diana. S Dec 1727. M.

Thomas, Dorothy. R for Barbados Aug 1679. L.

Thomas, Dorothy. R for Barbados Jly 1680. M.

Thomas, Edmond. S s handkerchief at St. Mary Woolchurch Haw Apr T Jun 1768 *Tryal*. L.

Thomas, Edward. R Apr TB for Barbados Jun 1669. L.

Thomas als Roberts, Edward of Newnham. R for Jamaica, Barbados or Bermuda Feb 1686. G.

Thomas, Edward. S & T Jan 1722 *Gilbert* LC Annapolis Jly 1722. M.

Thomas, Edward. T Oct 1724 *Forward* LC Md Jun 1725. K.

Thomas, Edward. S Lent 1742. Mo.

Thomas, Edward. S & T Apr 1769 *Tryal*. L.

Thomas, Edward. S s sheep & R 14 yrs Lent 1770. Mo.

Thomas als Williams, Edward. S at Bristol Lent 1772. G.

Thomas, Elias. S for obtaining goods by false pretences May 1775. L.

Thomas, Elizabeth. LC from *Forward* Annapolis Jun 1725. X.

Thomas, Elizabeth, widow. S & T Dec 1767 *Neptune*. L.

Thomas, Elizabeth wife of William. S 14 yrs at Bristol for receiving Lent 1772. G.

Thomas, Ellen of Manchester, singlewoman. SQS Oct 1771. La.

Thomas, George. S & T Dec 1731 *Forward* to Md or Va. M.

Thomas, George (1773). *See* Toms. Do.

Thomas als Stagg, Grace of Hale, Hants, spinster. SQS Marlborough & TB to Va Oct 1742. Wi.

Thomas, Griffith of Probus. R for Barbados Feb 1699. Co.

Thomas, Griffith. S Oct 1749. L.

Thomas, Griffith. S Lent 1769. Be.

Thomas, Hannah. SQS & T Sep 1751 *Greyhound*. M.

Thomas, Henry. R for Barbados Aug 1664. M.

Thomas, Henry of Adderbury. R for America Jly 1693. O.

Thomas, Henry. S May-Jly 1746; S Dec 1746 for being at large but acquitted as "casualty of seas" & ordered to be transported again. M.

Thomas, Henry. S s wheat at Church Hanney Lent 1760; James Thomas discharged. Be.

Thomas, Hester. S Jly TB Aug 1755. Wi.

Thomas, Hugh. S Feb T Mar 1730 *Patapsco* LC Annapolis Sep 1730. L.

Thomas, Isaac. S Mar 1736. De.

Thomas, Isaac of St. Ann, Westminster. S s tankard & T May 1736 *Patapsco*. M.

Thomas, Jacob (1766). *See* Jacob, Thomas. M.

Thomas, James. S Lent T May 1719 *Margaret*; sold to Richard Chaney Md May 1720. Sy.

Thomas, James. S Jan-Feb T Apr 1771 *Thornton*. M.

Thomas, James. SQS & TB Jan 1773. So.

Thomas, James. S s turkey at St. Margaret Lent 1773. He.

Thomas, Jane. R 14 yrs Aug 1728. So.

Thomas, Jane. T Apr 1743 *Justitia*. K.

Thomas, Jane wife of John. S s at Monmouth Lent 1763. Mo.

Thomas, Joan, aged 25. LC from *Jonathan* Annapolis Jly 1724. X.

Thomas, John. R for Jamaica Aug 1661. M.

Thomas, John. R 10 yrs in plantations Oct 1662. M.

Thomas, John of Llanthewy Skirrid. R for America Feb 1687. Mo.

Thomas, John, als Blackguard Jack. PT Jun 1698. M.

Thomas als Bonady als Inon, John of Bideford. R for Barbados Jly 1698 & Feb 1699. De.

Thomas, John. R 14 yrs for Carolina May 1719. L.

Thomas, John, als Baker, Lewis. R 14 yrs for Va s horse Jly 1718. De.

Thomas, John. S s iron at Bridstow Lent 1722. He.

Thomas, John. S s at Wargrave Summer 1722 T *Forward* LC Md Jun 1723. Be.

Thomas, John. S Summer 1731. He.

Thomas, John. R 14 yrs Aug 1734. So.

Thomas, John. S Mar 1735. De.

Thomas, John, als Prothero, Evan. S s mare at St. Philip & Jacob Summer 1736 R 14 yrs Lent TB Mar 1737. G.

Thomas, John. S Feb T Jun 1738 *Forward* to Md or Va. M.

Thomas, John. R 14 yrs Summer T Oct 1739 *Duke of Cumberland*. Sy.

Thomas, John of St. Chad, Shrewsbury. S Lent 1741. Sh.

Thomas, John. S Mar 1743. Co.

Thomas, John. S Jun T Nov 1743 *George William*. M.

Thomas, John. S Apr T May 1750 *Lichfield*. M.

Thomas, John. T Apr 1753 *Thames*. Ht.

Thomas, John. S for returning from transportation Summer 1759 T 14 yrs Apr 1760 *Thetis*. E.

Thomas, John. S Apr 1763. L.

Thomas, John. S s watch at Holy Cross Lent 1764. Sh.

Thomas, John. ST & T Jun 1764 *Dolphin*. L.

Thomas, John. SQS & T Jan 1765 *Tryal*. M.

Thomas, John. T Apr 1765 *Ann*. M.

Thomas, John. SL & T Sep 1765 *Justitia*. Sy.

Thomas, John. S Oct 1766. M.

Thomas, John (1768). *See* Umpisson. Wo.

Thomas, John. S s mare & R 14 yrs Lent 1769. He.

Thomas, John. S & T Dec 1769 *Justitia*. L.

Thomas, John. S s at Dowlas Summer 1773. He.

Thomas, John. S Feb 1775. L.

Thomas, Joseph. S s sheep Summer 1764 R 14 yrs Lent 1765. He.

Thomas, Judith. R for Jamaica Aug 1661. L.

Thomas, Margaret. R for Barbados Jun 1671. M.

Thomas, Margaret. S & T Dec 1731 *Forward*. L.

Thomas, Margaret. S s at Pontesbury & R 14 yrs Summer 1770. Sh.

Thomas, Mary wife of David of Horton. R for Jamaica, Barbados or Bermuda Feb 1686. Sh.

Thomas als Murry, Mary. S Jan T Feb 1733 *Smith* to Md or Va. M.

Thomas, Mary (1745). *See* MacLaughlin. M.

Thomas, Mary. S Lent R 14 yrs Summer TB Aug 1751. G.

Thomas, Mary. S Sep-Oct T Dec 1754 *Whiteing*. M.

Thomas, Mary. S s sheep at Bedwellty Summer 1761 R 14 yrs Lent 1762. Mo.

Thomas, Matthew of Bisbury. R for Barbados Feb 1665. Sh.

Thomas, Matthew. R for Barbados or Jamaica Jan 1692. M.

Thomas, Matthew. S for housebreaking Summer 1734 R 14 yrs Lent 1735 AT Summer 1736. He.

Thomas, Michael. S s clothing at Old Sodbury Lent 1767. G.

Thomas, Philip. S Jun 1733 T Jan 1734 *Caesar* LC Va Jly 1734. M.

Thomas, Rebecca (1727). *See* Gardner. L.

Thomas, Richard, a Quaker. R for plantations Jly 1665 (PC). Ht.

Thomas, Richard. S & T Apr 1725 *Sukey* LC Annapolis Sep 1725. M.

Thomas, Richard. S May-Jly 1750. M.

Thomas, Richard. S Summer 1756. K.

Thomas, Richard. R for life Jly TB to Va Aug 1758. Wi.

Thomas, Richard. S Jly 1764. Ha.

Thomas, Richard. S s sheep & R 14 yrs Lent 1770. Mo.

Thomas, Richard. S Feb T Apr 1772 *Thornton*. L.

Thomas, Richard. S & R 14 yrs Summer 1774. Be.

Thomas, Robert of Nannerth. R for America Aug 1700. Fl.

Thomas, Robert. S Feb T Apr 1734 *Patapsco* to Md. M.

Thomas, Samuel. S s at Stanton on Wye Summer 1766. He.

Thomas, Samuel. S s clothing at Old Sodbury Lent 1767. G.

Thomas, Samuel. S s horse & R Lent 1775. Sh.

Thomas, Sarah of St. Saviour, Southwark. R for Barbados or Jamaica Jly 1696. Sy.

Thomas, Smalman. S & T Dec 1731 *Forward*. L.

Thomas, Thomas. S Mar 1743. Co.

Thomas, Thomas. S Apr-May T Jly 1771 *Scarsdale*. M.

Thomas, Walter of Bristol. R for Barbados s horse Feb 1700. G.

Thomas, Walter. S s oxen at Newchurch Summer 1738. Mo.

Thomas, William. R for Barbados or Jamaica Mar 1685. M.

Thomas als Maundry, William of Cudworth. R for Barbados Jly 1715. So.

Thomas, William of Michaelston, Glam, yeoman. S s oxen at Abergavenny Summer 1719. Mo.

Thomas, William. S for shoplifting Lent R 14 yrs Summer 1722. Wa.

Thomas, William, aged 28, brown hair. LC from *Jonathan* Md Jly 1724. X.

Thomas, William. S s cow at Monmouth Lent 1726. Mo.

Thomas, William. LC from *Loyal Margaret* Annapolis Oct 1726. X.

Thomas, William. LC from *Patapsco* Annapolis Nov 1733. X.

Thomas, William (1736). *See* Beer. So.

Thomas, William. S Aug 1736. De.

Thomas als Hopkins, William. R 14 yrs Mar 1746. De.

Thomas, William. S Jan-Apr 1749. M.

Thomas, William of Sittingbourne. S Lent T May 1750 *Lichfield*. K.

Thomas, William. S Mar 1754. Co.

Thomas, William. S Aug 1754. Co.

Thomas, William. S Sep 1756. M.

Thomas, William. T Nov 1759 *Phoenix*. Sx.

Thomas, William. S Mar 1761 TB to Va. De.

Thomas, William. S Lent 1763. Wa.

Thomas, William (1770). *See* Wharton. M.

Thomas, William (1774). *See* Williams, Thomas. G.

Thomas, William. S Jan-Feb 1775. M.

Thomas, William. S Apr 1775. M.

Thomas, Winifred. S s at Bassaleg Lent AT Summer 1736. Mo.

Thomason, William of Warrington, linen weaver. SQS Apr 1772. La.

Thomlinson. *See* Tomlinson.

Thompson, Alexander. S s horse Lent R 14 yrs Summer 1744. Y.

Thomson, Alexander. R 14 yrs Summer 1744. Nf.

Thompson, Alexander. S & T Mar 1760 *Friendship*. L.

Thompson, Alice, aged 21, dark. S Sep T Oct 1720 *Gilbert* LC Md May
    1721. L.

Thompson, Alice. S Feb 1761. L.

Thompson, Andrew. S Summer 1749. K.

Thompson, Andrew. SL Jan 1773. Sy.

Thompson, Ann. R & T Dec 1716 *Lewis*. M.

Thompson, Ann. S Feb T Mar 1731 *Patapsco* LC Annapolis Jul 1731. M.

Thompson, Ann. S & T Jan 1736 *Dorsetshire* LC Va Sep 1736. L.

Thompson, Ann. S Jly-Sep T Oct 1739 *Duke of Cumberland*. M.

Thompson, Ann. S Feb-Apr 1746. M.

Thompson, Ann. S Nov T Dec 1763 *Neptune*. L.

Thompson, Ann wife of Thomas Jr. S 14 yrs for receiving Jly 1773. Ha.

Thompson, Ann. S Apr-May 1775. M.

Thompson, Anthony. S & T Oct 1729 *Forward* but swam away at
    Gravesend. M.

Thompson, Benjamin. AT City Lent 1731 to Lent 1732. Y.

Thompson als Yates, Charles. T Aug 1720 *Owners Goodwill*. K.

Thompson, Charles. S May T Dec 1734 *Caesar* LC Va Jly 1735. M.

Thompson, Cuthbert. R for life for highway robbery Summer 1765. Nl.

Thompson, Daniel. S Jun T Sep 1764 *Justitia*. M.

Thompson, Dorothy. S & T Dec 1724 *Rappahannock*. L.

Thompson als Blake, Edward. PT Aug R Dec 1689. M.

Thompson, Edward. T May 1737 *Forward*. Sy.

Thompson, Edward. S Summer 1745. Nf.

Thompson, Edward. S Lent R 14 yrs Summer 1752. O.

Thompson, Edward. S s horse Lent R 14 yrs Summer 1764. G.

Thomson, Edward. S Mar 1766. Ha.

Thompson, Edward. S Lent 1775. K.

Thompson, Elianor of Newcastle upon Tyne, spinster. R for Barbados Jly
    1705. Nl.

Thompson, Elizabeth. R Dec 1716 T Jan 1717 *Queen Elizabeth*. L.

Thompson, Elizabeth (1734). *See* Austin. X.

Thompson, Elizabeth. S Jly 1750. Ha.

Thompson, Elizabeth. S Jan-Feb T Apr 1753 *Thames*. M.

Thompson, Elizabeth als Betty. S Feb 1758. Ha.

Thompson, Elizabeth. S Sep T Nov 1759 *Phoenix*. M.

Thompson, Elizabeth (1766). *See* Saunders. L.

Thompson, Elizabeth. S Sep-Oct 1774. M.

Thompson, Francis. S s sheep at Richmond & R 14 yrs Lent TB Aug
    1771. Y.

Thompson, George of Botcherby, yeoman. R for Barbados Jly 1683. Cu.

Thompson, George of Binegar, barber surgeon. R for Barbados Feb
    1698. So.

Thompson, George. S s horse Lent 1726 R 14 yrs Lent 1729. Y.

Thompson, George. S s horse Lent R 14 yrs Summer 1739. Nt.

Thompson, George. S Oct 1744-Jan 1745. M.

Thompson, George. S s tankard at Market Weighton Lent 1768. Y.

Thompson als Lilley, George. S s at St. Nicholas, Durham, Summer 1773. Du.

Thompson, Grace. S May-Jly 1773. M.

Thompson, Hannah of St. Catherine, spinster. S s petticoat Jan 1739 T Jan 1740 *York*. M.

Thompson, Henry of Holverston. R for America Feb 1688. Nf.

Thompson, Henry of Leybourne. R for Barbados or Jamaica Jly 1688. K.

Thompson, Henry. S Jan T Feb 1719 *Worcester* LC Md Jun 1719. L.

Thompson, Hester. S May-Jly 1750. M.

Thompson, James. S Apr TB to Md May 1719. L.

Thompson, James. S Lent R 14 yrs Summer 1734. Wa.

Thompson als Hoop, James. S Summer 1738. La.

Thompson, James (1749). *See* Brown. M.

Thompson, James. S Apr 1749. L.

Thompson, James. S & T Apr 1753 *Thames*. L.

Thompson, James. S Summer 1755 T 14 yrs Jun 1756 *Lyon*. Sy.

Thompson, James. S s sheep Summer 1757 R 14 yrs Lent 1758. Li.

Thompson, James. S s at Greatham Summer 1766. Du.

Thompson, James of St. George, Hanover Square. SW Apr T May 1767 *Thornton*. M.

Thompson, James. S s handkerchief at St. Mildred Poultry Oct 1768 T Jan 1769 *Thornton*. L.

Thompson, James. T Apr 1770 *New Trial*. E.

Thompson, James. S Mar 1773. Ha.

Thompson, Jane. S Feb 1719. L.

Thompson, Jane wife of James. S Oct 1744-Jan 1745. M.

Thompson, Jane wife of John of Bermondsey. SQS Oct T Dec 1758 *The Brothers*. Sy.

Thompson, Jenkin of Great Marlow. R for America Feb 1684. Bu.

Thompson, Jeremiah. S Lent T May 1767 *Thornton*. Bu.

Thompson, John. R Sep TB for Barbados Oct 1669. L.

Thompson als Silke, John. R for Barbados or Jamaica Jly 1685. L.

Thompson, John. R for Barbados or Jamaica Feb 1686. L.

Thompson, John of Cirencester. R for Jamaica, Barbados or Bermuda Mar 1688. G.

Thompson, John. R for Barbados or Jamaica May 1691. L.

Thompson, John. R for Barbados or Jamaica Oct 1694, Dec 1695 & Jan 1697. L.

Thompson, John. R Dec 1699 AT Jan 1700. M.

Thompson, John. R for America Aug 1713. L.

Thompson, John (1722). *See* Skill. M.

Thompson, John. S Lent 1725 but died by Summer 1725. Y.

Thompson, John. S & T Oct 1729 *Forward* LC Va Jun 1730. M.

Thompson, John. R 14 yrs s mare Summer 1730. Du.

Thompson, John. S s coat Feb T May 1736 *Patapsco* to Md. M.

Thompson, John. S s leather at Hexham Summer 1738. Nl.

Thompson, John. S as pickpocket Summer 1739 R 14 yrs Lent 1740. Li.

Thompson, John (1740). *See* Wilson. La.

Thompson, John. T Jun 1740 *Essex*. Sy.

Thompson, John. S Mar 1748. Ha.

Thompson, John, als Killicrees, William. S Summer 1750 R 14 yrs Lent 1751. La.

Thompson, John. S Summer 1750. Y.

Thompson, John. S Jly-Sep 1754. M.

Thompson, John. S May T Jun 1756 *Lyon*. L.

Thompson, John of Wood Ditton. S s lead from Earl of Aylesford Lent 1760. Ca.

Thompson, John. S s sheep Summer 1762 R 14 yrs Summer 1763. Cu.

Thompson, John. S Summer TB Oct 1764. Y.

Thompson, John. S s sheep Summer 1765 R 14 yrs Lent 1766. O.

Thompson, John. SQS Thirsk s shirt Apr TB Aug 1766. Y.

Thompson, John. S s coat at St. Botolph Aldgate May T Jun 1768 *Tryal*. L.

Thompson, John. T for life Oct 1768 *Justitia*. Sy.

Thompson, John. SL Jly 1773. Sy.

Thompson, John. S s lead at Albury Summer 1773. O.

Thompson, John. R 14 yrs Jly 1774. M.

Thompson, Joseph. S Jan-Jun 1747. M.

Thompson, Joseph. S s sheep & R 14 yrs Lent 1754. Bd.

Thompson, Joseph. S Apr T May 1755 *Rose*. L.

Thompson, Joseph. T Jly 1770 *Scarsdale*. M.

Thompson, Judith. S May T Jun 1726 *Loyal Margaret* to Md. M.

Thompson, Judith. S s at St. George Lent 1768. G.

Thompson, Luke. S s at Market Weighton Lent 1772. Y.

Thompson, Margaret. SQS Stokesley s apron Jly TB Aug 1766. Y.

Thompson, Margaret. R 14 yrs City Summer 1767. Y.

Thompson, Mary. S Oct T Nov 1728 *Forward* but died on passage. M.

Thompson, Mary. S & T Oct 1730 *Forward* LC Potomack Jan 1731. L.

Thompson, Mary of Langtree, spinster. SQS Apr 1751. La.

Thompson, Mary. S Apr-May 1754. M.

Thompson, Mary. S Aug 1760. L.

Thompson als Jones als Jonas, Mary. S Jly 1761. L.

Thompson als Brown, Mary. S Sep T Nov 1762 *Prince William*. M.

Thompson, Mary. S Summer 1764. Du.

Thompson, Matthew. R for life for highway robbery Suumer TB Aug 1758. Y.

Thompson, Nicholas. S Jly T Oct 1741 *Sea Horse* to Va. M.

Thompson, Patrick. S s horse Summer 1729 R 14 yrs Summer 1730. Li.

Thompson, Richard of Leverton. R for America Jly 1673. Li.

Thompson, Richard. T *Owners Goodwill* LC Md Nov 1721. Ca.

Thompson, Richard, als Cruddess, William. SQS Apr 1754. Du.

Thompson, Richard. S s at Eynsham Summer 1757. O.

Thompson, Richard. S May 1760. M.

Tompson, Richard. S Norwich s silver spoon Summer 1768. Nf.

Thompson, Richard. S Apr 1775. M.

Thompson, Robert. S Jan T 14 yrs Feb 1719 *Worcester* but died on passage. L.

Thompson, Robert (2). T Oct 1729 *Forward*. Sy.

Thompson, Robert. S & T May 1740 *Essex*. L.

Thompson, Robert. S Lent TB Aug 1752. Y.

Thompson, Robert. R 14 yrs Summer 1756. Y.

Thompson, Robert (1761). *See* Crampton. La.

Thompson, Samuel. S Sep-Oct 1748 T Jan 1749 *Laura*. M.

Thompson, Samuel, als Crew, Simon. S Sep-Oct 1749. M.

Tompson, Samuel. S Aug TB Sep 1770. Le.

Thompson, Samuel of Noton, Northumberland, chapman. SQS Oct 1775. La.

Thompson, Sarah. SQS Apr TB Sep 1768. So.

Thompson, Stephen. S Jly T Oct 1741 *Sea Horse*. L.

Thompson, Susanna. S 14 yrs for receiving Lent 1722. G.

Thompson, Susanna. S Dec 1747. L.

Thompson, Thomas. S & T Oct 1730 *Forward* LC Potomack Jan 1731. M.

Thompson, Thomas. S Lent R 14 yrs Summer 1747. Nt.

Thompson als Milburn, Thomas. S s mare at Malton Summer 1764 R 14 yrs Lent 1765. Y.

Thompson, Thomas. S & T Apr 1765 *Ann*. L.

Thompson, Thomas. S Nov T Dec 1770 *Justitia*.L.

Thompson, Thomas Jr. S Jly 1773. Ha.

Thompson, William. R for Barbados Dec 1671. M.

Thompson, William. R for Barbados or Jamaica Dec 1698. L.

Thompson, William. S May 1719. M.

Thompson, William. S Jly T Aug 1721 *Prince Royal* but died on passage. M.

Thompson, William. S May T Jun 1726 *Loyal Margaret* to Md. M.

Thompson, William. S s at Stoke Prior Summer 1728. Wo.

Thompson, William (1733). *See* Robinson. Y.

Thompson, William. S & T Apr 1733 *Patapsco* LC Annapolis Nov 1733. M.

Thompson, William. S s at Twyford Lent R 14 yrs Summer 1736. Be.

Thompson, William. S Jan-May 1738. M.

Thompson, William. S s sheep Summer 1741 R 14 yrs Lent 1742. Li.

Thompson, William. S Jan-Apr 1748. M.

Thompson, William. S Dec 1748 T Jan 1749 *Laura*. L.

Thompson, William of Marefield. S for highway robbery Lent T 14 yrs Oct 1750 *Rachael*. Sx.

Thompson, William. S Lent 1753. Ch.

Thompson, William. S Apr 1765. So.

Thompson, William. S Lent 1766. Ca.

Thompson, William. T 14 yrs Oct 1768 *Justitia*. Sy.

Thompson, William. SQS & T Jly 1773 *Tayloe* to Va. M.

Tompson, William. S & R Lent AT Summer 1774. Wa.

Thompson, Zacharias. R for Barbados or Jamaica Feb 1686. M.

Thompson, Zachariah. S for killing sheep Summer 1742 R 14 yrs Lent 1743. Su.

Thompson, Zachariah. SQS Jun T Sep 1767 *Justitia*. M.

Thomson. *See* Thompson.

Thonge, Richard. T Apr 1733 *Patapsco* LC Annapolis Nov 1733. Bu.

Thorburn, James. S Summer 1754. K.

Thorley, Jane. SQS & T Apr 1766 *Ann*. M.

Thorley, Thomas. R 14 yrs Summer 1750. Y.

Thorman, Thomas. S s clothing at Blackfriars Dec 1768 T Jan 1769 *Thornton*. L.

Thornally, Francis. T Apr 1770 *New Trial*. K.

Thornaway, James. S s harrow teeth at Tettenhall & R 14 yrs Summer 1771. St.

Thornberry, Daniel. R for Barbados or Jamaica Dec 1716. L.

Thornberry, Edward. R for Barbados or Jamaica Dec 1716. L.

Thornbury, Mary. S s at St. Peter, Worcester, Lent 1773. Wo.

Thornbury als Thistle, Richard. R for America Aug 1715. L.

Thorne, Ann. S s plates Sep 1735. M.

Thorne, Daniel. S Apr-Jun T 14 yrs Jly 1772 *Tayloe*. M.

Thorne, Francis of Camberwell. R for Barbados or Jamaica Feb 1696. Sy.

Thorne, George. S & T Oct 1722 *Forward* LC Annapolis Jun 1723. M.

Thorn, Isaac (1746). *See* Theron. L.

Thorne, Jane. S May-Jly 1748. M.

Thorne, John of Rewe. R for Barbados Mar 1686. De.

Thorne, John. R 14 yrs Mar 1730. So.

Thorn, John. S Aug 1737. De.

Thorne, John. R 14 yrs Jly 1759. Wi.

Thorn, Robert. T Apr 1732 *Patapsco*. Sy.

Thorn, Robert. S Feb-Apr T May 1751 *Tryal*. M.

Thorne, John. T Oct 1729 *Forward*. E.

Thorne, John. S Apr T May 1752 *Lichfield*. L.

Thorne, John. T Sep 1758 *Tryal*. K.

Thorne, Richard. S Aug 1731. So.

Thorne, Sarah. S & T Oct 1730 *Forward* LC Potomack Jan 1731. M.

Thorn, Sarah. TB to Va from QS 1768. De.

Thorne, Thomas of Fordingbridge, husbandman. R for Barbados Feb 1668. Ha.

Thorne, Thomas. SQS Jan TB Jly 1735. So.

Thorne, William. SQS Apr TB to Md Nov 1731. So.

Thorn, William. S Mar 1737. De.

Thorn, William. S Lent R 14 yrs Summer 1752. Be.

Thorne, William. S Aug 1756. So.

Thorne, William. S & T Nov 1762 *Prince William*. L.

Thorner, James. S Mar 1752. Do.

Thornham, Thomas. SW & T Dec 1767 *Neptune*. M.

Thornhill, Benjamin (1771). *See* Thornton. M.

Thornhill, Hallsworth. S s mare Summer 1756 R 14 yrs Lent 1757. Li.

Thornivel, Thomas. S for highway robbery at Burton on Trent & R 14 yrs Summer 1768. St.

Thornley, John. S s horse & R 14 yrs Lent 1775. St.

Thornley, John. R 14 yrs Apr 1775 (SP). Be.

Thornley, Peter of Little Hulton, yeoman. SQS May 1770. La.

Thornton, Ann. S s at Brompton Summer TB Aug 1771. Y.

Thornton als Thornhill, Benjamin. S Jan-Feb T Apr 1771 *Thornton*. M.

Thorneton, Blackstone of Camberwell. R for Barbados or Jamaica Jly 1687. Sy.

Thornton, Christopher. SQS Jly T Sep 1764 *Justitia*. M.

Thornton als Portobello, Elizabeth. S Jly T Oct 1741 *Sea Horse* to Va. M.

Thornton, George. S s gelding Lent R 14 yrs Summer 1725. Nf.

Thornton, Jane, als Black Jenny. S May T Jly 1723 *Alexander* LC Annapolis Sep 1723. L.

Thornton, Jane wife of Joseph. S Feb T Mar 1729 *Patapsco* LC Md Dec 1729. M.

Thornton, John (1748). *See* Keys. L.

Thornton, John. S Jan-Apr 1749. M.

Thornton, Joseph. S Summer 1765. Y.

Thornton, Mary of Rotherhithe, widow. SQS & T Apr 1769 *Tryal*. Sy.

Thornton, Richard. PT Feb 1675. M.

Thornton, Samuel. S Summer 1765. Y.

Thornton, Sarah. S Jun T Sep 1758 *Tryal*. L.

Thornton, Susanna. S May-Jly 1746. M.

Thornton, Thomas. S Jly T Sep 1757 *Thetis*. L.

Thornton, Thomas. S s at St. Paul, Bedford, Summer 1771. Bd.

Thorowgood, George. S Lent R 14 yrs Summer T Aug 1752 *Tryal*. Sy.

Thorrowgood, John, a Quaker. R for plantations July 1665 (PC). Ht.

Thurowgood, John. R for Barbados or Jamaica Mar 1685. L.

Thorowgood, Mary. T Sep 1767 *Justitia*. Ht.

Thoroughwood, Richard of Bloxham, yeoman. R for America Feb 1713. O.

Thorovit als Thorowitz, Louisa. S & T Dec 1731 *Forward* to Md or Va. M.

Thorpe, Edward. S Jly 1765. Ha.

Thorpe, Helen. R for Jamaica Aug 1661. L.

Thorpe, Henry. S Aug T Oct 1724 *Forward* LC Annapolis Jun 1725. L.

Thorp, Isachar of Manchester. SQS Jan 1760. La.

Thorpe, James. S Aug 1763. L.

Thorpe, John. R & TB for Barbados Aug 1668. L.

Thorpe, John. S s snuff at St. Helen, Worcester, Lent 1749. Wo.

Thorpe, John. S Apr T for life May 1750 *Lichfield*. M.

Thorpe, John. S Jan-Feb T Apr 1753 *Thames*. M.

Thorp, John. SQS Jan T May 1755 *Rose*. M.

Thorp, John. SQS & T Apr 1766 *Ann*. M.

Thorp, Joseph of Manchester. SQS Jan 1760. La.

Thorpe, Josiah. S s horse Summer 1750 T May 1751 *Tryal*. K.

Thorpe, Richard of Newton, husbandman. SQS Apr 1752. La.

Thorpe, Richard. S s coat at St. Bride's Feb T Apr 1768 *Thornton*. L.

Thorpe, Thomas. S Lent 1737. Y.

Thorp, Thomas. S & R Summer 1768. Su.

Thorpe, William. T 14 yrs Nov 1762 *Prince William*. E.

Thorrington, John. T May 1744 *Justitia*. K.

Threadwell, Joseph. T Jan 1738 *Dorsetshire*. Sy.

Thredgall, John. T Dec 1736 *Dorsetshire*. E.

Threed, William. T Jun 1727 *Susanna*. Sy.

Thresher, James. T Sep 1731 *Smith*. Bu.

Thresher, Richard. T Sep 1730 *Smith*. Sx.

Thrift, Elizabeth. S Dec 1748 T Jan 1749 *Laura*. M.

Thrift, Hester of St. James, Westminster. S s stockings Jly 1740 T Jan 1741 *Harpooner* to Rappahannock. M.

Thrift, James. S & T Dec 1752 *Greyhound*. L.

Thrift, John. S Summer 1772. Sy.

Thrift, Peter (1767). *See* Price. M.

Thrift, William. S s at Bray Lent 1757. Be.

Throup, James. S & T Jly 1771 *Scarsdale*. M.

Thrower, Henry. S Lent 1761. Su.

Thrustlecock, John (1757). *See* Cock. Sh.

Thurby als Kirby, Mary. S Feb T May 1719 *Margaret*; sold to Patrick Sympson & William Black Md Sep 1719. M.

Thurland, Mary. R & T Dec 1716 *Lewis* to Jamaica. M.

Thurland, Thomas. R for America Aug 1715. L.

Thurloe, George. R City for life Summer 1758. Y.

Thurman, Charles. S s shirt Feb T Apr 1735 *Patapsco* to Md. M.

Thursby, Anthony. TB Oct 1764. Db.

Thursby, Sarah, servant of St. Martin in Fields. S s clothing to dress as a man in order to ship to Jamaica & T Dec 1734 LC Va Jly 1735. M.

Thursdale, Anthony. S s linen at Whitwell Summer 1764. Db.

Thurston, Anne of Lewisham, spinster. R for Barbados or Jamaica Jun 1675 & Jly 1677. K.

Thurston, George of Thetford. R for America Feb 1684. Nf.

Thurston, John. S s gelding Summer 1752 R 14 yrs Lent 1753. Ca.

Thurstan, John. S s at Beedon Lent 1759. Be.

Thurston, Mary. S Oct T 14 yrs Nov 1759 *Phoenix*. L.

Thurston, William. S s mare Lent R 14 yrs Summer 1754. Nf.

Thurston, William (1769). *See* Webber. Nf.

Thwaits, John. S s gold coin at South Cave & R Summer 1772. Y.

Thwaites, William. R Jan-Feb T for life Apr 1772 *Thornton*. M.

Tibballs, James. R for Barbados Aug 1668. M.

Tibballs, Samuel. S Jan-Feb 1774. M.

Tibbett, Elizabeth. S Feb-Apr 1745. M.

Tibbet, John. S Maa 1740. So.

Tibble, William. R for Barbados Jun 1670. M.

Tibbs, John. S & T Apr 1725 *Sukey* LC Annapolis Sep 1725. M.

Tibbs, John. T 14 yrs Nov 1759 *Phoenix*. Sy.

Tibbs, William. R for America Aug 1715. L.

Tibbworth, Susannah. T Sep 1767 *Justitia*. Ht.

Tibley, Robert (1736). *See* Kebell. M.

Tice, Robert of Wood Dalling. S Summer 1726. *Nf.

Ticehurst, Thomas. SEK Apr T Sep 1757 *Thetis*. K.

Ticken, Peter. Rebel T 1685.

Tickner, Peter. S Jly-Dec 1747. M.

Tickner, Peter. S Sep-Oct T for life Dec 1753 *Whiteing*. M.

Tickner, William. S & T Sep 1731 *Smith* LC Va 1732. L.

Tidbury, Joseph. R Dec 1774. M.

Tidcombe, William. R 14 yrs Mar 1762. So.

Tidd, Henry. S Aug 1748. Co.

Tidder. *See* Tedder.

Tydey, Thomas. T Sep 1730 *Smith*. Sx.

Tidey, William. T 14 yrs Apr 1768 *Thornton*. Sx.

Tidmarsh, Grace. T May 1737 *Forward*. Sy.

Tiernon, Joseph. SQS Feb T Apr 1769 *Tryal*. M.

Tiffen, Joseph. S May-Jun T Aug 1752 *Tryal*. M.

Tifoot, Mary, als Durbin, Hannah. S Lent 1749. G.

Tiggins, Thomas. S Mar 1759. Ha.

Tigh. *See* Tye.

Tigwell, Thomas. R 14 yrs Apr 1742. Ha.

Tilborow, William Jr. of Ilesfield, husbandman. R for Barbados Feb 1668. Ha.

Tilbury, Anne. S Oct T Nov 1728 *Forward* but died on passage. M.

Tillbry als Tillbree, Sarah. S Feb T Mar 1731 *Patapsco* LC Annapolis Jun 1731. M.

Tildsley, William (1754). *See* Tinsley. Y.

Till, John. R May TB for Barbados Jun 1668. M.

Till, John of Rickmansworth. SQS Summer 1763. Ht.

Till, John. S s at Beoley Lent 1775. Wo.

Till, Martha. T Apr 1759 *Thetis*. Sx.

Till, William. S s skin Lent 1733. St.

Till, William. S & T Sep 1765 *Justitia*. M.

Tillaboo, John. S at Bristol Lent 1771. G.

Tillard, Elizabeth. S Oct T Nov 1728 *Forward* but died on passage. M.

Tillett, William. S Sep T Dec 1767 *Neptune*. L.

Tillewar, James of St. John's. SQS Jan T Mar 1764 *Tryal*. Sy.

Tilley, Abraham. S s wool at Wotton Under Edge. Lent 1768. G.

Tilley, Ann. S Summer 1755. Du.

Tilley, Christopher of North Nibley. R for Jamaica, Barbados or Bermuda Feb 1686. G.

Tilley, Edward. R & TB for Barbados Aug 1668. L.

Tillie, James. S Dec 1754. L.

Tilly, James. S Lent T Apr 1773. No.

Tiley, John. R Jly AT Sep 1675. M.

Tilley, John. Rebel T 1685.

Tilley, John of Glastonbury, woolcomber. R for Barbados Feb 1688. So.

Tilley, Joseph. SQS Jan 1730. So.

Tiley, Marmaduke. S 14 yrs Jly 1736. Ha.

Tilly, Mary (1735). *See* Collins. L.

Tilley, Richard of Exeter. R for Jamaica Apr 1664 (SP). De.

Tilly, Simon. S Mar 1750. Co.

Tilley, William. S Feb T 14 yrs Mar 1729 *Patapsco* but died on passage. M.

Tilley, William. SQS Jan 1730. So.

Tillison, William. SL May T Jun 1764 *Dolphin*. Sy.

Tillotson, Miles of Haslingden. SQS Apr 1774. La.

Tillott, John. S s gelding at Little Cornard & R Summer 1775. Su.

Tilman, Martha. S Dec 1757 T Mar 1758 *Dragon*. M.

Tilsey als Edwards, Mary. SQS Apr TB Sep 1772. So.

Tilsley, John. S Lent R 14 yrs Summer 1758. Sh.

Tilson, Henry. R Apr 1734. M.

Tillson, Roger of Bury St. Edmunds. R for Barbados Aug 1671. Su.

Timberwell, George of Lambeth. SQS Apr T Sep 1751 *Greyhound*. Sy.

Timer als Timewell, Ann. R 14 yrs Apr 1747. De.

Times, Richard (1713). *See* Stevens. Bu.

Timewell, Ann (1747). *See* Timer. De.

Timleh, Mary. S Jly 1775. M.

Timmings, Edward. S Summer 1757 R 14 yrs Lent 1758. St.

Timmins, Lawrence. SQS Sep 1773. M.

Timmons, John. S City Summer 1769. Y.

Tims, Elizabeth wife of Joseph. S Sep T 14 yrs Oct 1744 *Susannah*. L.
Timmes, Henry. S s horse Feb 1656. M.
Tims, Jane wife of Thomas of Denton, tailor. SQS Apr 1742. La.
Timms, John. S s horse Lent R 14 yrs Summer 1750. G.
Timms, John. S Oct T Dec 1758 *The Brothers*. L.
Tims, Philip. R for Barbados or Jamaica Mar 1698. E.
Timms, Richard (1713). *See* Stevens. Bu.
Timothy, John. Rebel T 1685.
Timperley, Robert. S 14 yrs Feb 1757. M.
Tymperley, Thomas. R for life Sep 1768. Y.
Tymson, James of Stoke by Guildford. R for Barbados or Jamaica Jly
    1705. Sy.
Timson, Moan. LC from *Forward* Annapolis Jun 1723. X.
Timpson, Thomas. T Oct 1722 *Forward* LC Md Jun 1723. Sy.
Timpson, William. S Sep 1731. M.
Tindell als Norman, Henry. S Jun T Aug 1769 *Douglas*. M.
Tindall, Thomas. S & TB Aug 1740. G.
Tindy, Richard. S Apr T May 1751 *Tryal*. L.
Tingle, James. T Jly 1722 *Alexander*. Sy.
Tingle, Simon of Gainsborough. R for America Jly 1678. Li.
Tink, Garence Jr. R 14 yrs Aug 1755. Co.
Tink, John Jr. S Aug 1767. Co.
Tinker, Michael. S Summer 1749. Ca.
Tinley, John of Mansfield. SQS s shirt Jly 1765. Nt.
Tinley, John. S May T Jun 1768 *Tryal*. M.
Tinling, Robert. S Summer 1765. Cu.
Tinsey, John. R Jly T for life Oct 1768 *Justitia*. M.
Tinsley, Ann. S Feb 1754. L.
Tinsley, John. R 14 yrs Jly 1765. Ha.
Tinsley, John. S s at Wolverhampton Lent 1767. St.
Tinsley, Thomas. S & T Oct 1722 *Forward* LC Annapolis Jun 1723. L.
Tinsley als Tildsley, William. R 14 yrs Summer 1754. Y.
Tinson, Duke. R 14 yrs Mar 1731. Wi.
Tipper, James. R 14 yrs Apr 1747. De.
Tipper, John. T Sep 1742 *Forward*. K.
Tipper, Mary. S Lent TB Apr T Aug 1757 *Lux*. Db.
Tippett, Abraham. S Jan-Feb T Apr 1753 *Thames*. M.
Tippett, Jane. R Aug 1770. Co.
Tippett, Matthew. S s lead Jly 1735 T Jan 1736 *Dorsetshire* LC Va Sep
    1736. M.
Tippett, Thomas. S for Va Jly 1718. So.
Tipping, Francis. S & T Apr 1766 *Ann*. M.
Tipping als Smith, James. S Lent R 14 yrs Summer 1738. He.
Tipping, John. S Apr-Jun 1739. M.
Tipping, Mary (1725). *See* Bennett. M.
Tipping, Thomas of Ashton, innkeeper. SQS Jly 1748. La.
Tipping, Thomas. S Feb T Apr 1770 *New Trial*. M.
Tipler, Ann wife of John. S Feb T Mar 1729 *Patapsco* LC Annapolis
    Dec 1729. M.
Tiptee, Bathsheba (1758). *See* Green. E.
Tipton, Elizabeth. S Jan T Feb 1742 *Industry*. L.

Tipton, Francis. S & R 14 yrs Lent 1773. Sh.

Tireman, John. S & T Dec 1771 *Justitia*. M.

Tisdall, Charles. S & T Oct 1730 *Forward* LC Potomack Jan 1731. M.

Tisdell, Elizabeth. R for Barbados or Jamaica Jly 1686. M.

Tisdale, Rebecca. S & T Nov 1762 *Prince William*. L.

Tisdell, William Adams. S Mar 1759 TB to Va. De.

Tisden, Mary. S Jan T Apr 1734 *Patapsco* to Md. M.

Tisely, John. T for life Sep 1766 *Justitia*. K.

Tison. *See* Tyson.

Tissant, James. LC from *Forward* Annapolis Jun 1723. X.

Titchborn, Ann. S Sep-Oct T 14 yrs Dec 1752 *Greyhound*. M.

Titchborne, Elizabeth wife of Henry. S Dec 1757 T Mar 1758 *Dragon*. M.

Titherington, Elizabeth. R for Barbados Dec 1695 & May 1697. M.

Titman, William. S Summer 1725 R Summer 1726. No.

Titmus, William of Stevenage, butcher. SQS Apr T Sep 1765 *Justitia*. Ht.

Titten, Richard. S Oct 1751-Jan 1752. M.

Tittle, William. S Apr T 14 yrs May 1718 *Tryal* LC Charles Town Aug 1718. L.

Tiverton, Joseph. T 14 yrs Sep 1766 *Justitia*. E.

Tiverton, William. Rebel T 1685.

Tivey als Laydall, James. R Mar AT Apr 1677. M.

Tizard, Elizabeth. S Aug 1754. Do.

Tizard, Henry. Rebel T 1685.

Tizard, John. S & T 14 yrs Oct 1730 *Forward* LC Potomack Jan 1731. M.

Tizzard, John. S Oct-Dec 1739 T Jan 1740 *York* to Md. M.

Toale. *See* Toll.

Toamy, William. S Mar 1766. Ha.

Toasten als Fennister, Mary. S Dec 1746. L.

Tobeings, Ann (1758). *See* Matthews. M.

Tobin, Edward. R Oct 1694 AT Jan 1695. M.

Tobin, Garrett. S s at Bridgenorth Lent 1749. Sh.

Tobin, James. S Apr-May 1754. M.

Tobin, Walter. R 14 yrs Jly 1763 TB to Va. De.

Todd als Lax, Ann. S & T Sep 1731 *Smith* LC Va 1732. L.

Todd, Charles. S Summer TB Aug 1771. Nt.

Todd, David. S Dec 1743 T Feb 1744 *Neptune* to Md. M.

Todd, Disney. S Aug T 14 yrs Oct 1726 *Forward*. L.

Todd, James of Brozbourne. R 14 yrs Lent T Apr 1772 *Thornton*. Ht.

Todd, John of Etton. R for Barbados Jly 1679. Y.

Todd, John of Horseheath. S Lent 1760. Ca.

Todd, Richard. S Lent R 14 yrs Summer 1738. St.

Todd, Robert. R for Barbados or Jamaica Mar & Jly 1685. L.

Todd, Robert. S Summer 1732. Nl.

Todd, Robert. AT Summer 1740. Y.

Todd, Samuel. S Summer TB Aug 1760. Y.

Todd, Sarah. S Apr T for life May 1755 *Rose*. L.

Todd, Thomas. S Aug T Oct 1724 *Forward* LC Annapolis Jun 1725. M.

Todd, William. S s horse Summer 1720 R 14 yrs Summer 1721. Nt.

Todd, William. T Oct 1726 *Forward*. Sy.

Todd, William. S Lent 1743. Y.

Todd, William. AT Summer 1764. Du.

Todd, William. SQS Feb T Apr 1768 *Thornton*. M.

Todd als Hudspeth, William. S s books Summer 1769. Nl.

Todd als Smith, William. S Summer 1772. Nl.

Todell, John (1773). *See* Hudson. Wa.

Todhunter, Thomas of Orton. R for Barbados Jly 1683. We.

Todman, John. T Jun 1728 *Elizabeth*. Sx.

Toes. *See* Tose.

Toft, James. S & T Jly 1753 *Tryal*. M.

Toft, William of Warrington. SQS Oct 1763. La.

Toleard, Ursula. LC Md Sep 1719 & sold to Jonathan Prather. Sy.

Tolhurst, John. T Sep 1742 *Forward*. K.

Tolhurst, John. T 14 yrs Sep 1766 *Justitia*. K.

Toale, George. S Lent 1747. Bd.

Toll, Thomas of St. George, Southwark. R for Barbados or Jamaica Feb 1684. Sy.

Tollerfield, William. R 14 yrs Jly 1752. Do.

Tolley, John. S s pigs at Claines Lent 1766. Wo.

Tollington, William. SQS May 1774. M.

Tolman, Samuel of St. Michaelchurch. R for Barbados Feb 1688. So.

Toleman, Timothy. Rebel T 1685.

Tolmy, John (1772). *See* Talmy. L.

Tom Thumb (1756). *See* Shervill, John. L.

Tomkins. *See* Tompkins.

Tomkinson, Thomas. R for America Feb 1692. Db.

Tomlin, Elizabeth. S s clothing Jan T Apr 1735 *Patapsco* LC Md Oct 1735. L.

Tomlin, John. S for obtaining money by false pretences Jly 1774. L.

Tomlin, Mary. S & T Oct 1732 *Caesar*. L.

Tomlin, Mary. S Nov T Dec 1752 *Greyhound*. L.

Tomlin, Richard. S Apr T Jly 1770 *Scarsdale*. M.

Tomlin, Thomas. T Jly 1723 *Alexander* LC Md Sep 1723. Bu.

Tomlin, William. TB 14 yrs Jly 1723 T *Alexander* LC Md Sep 1723. Bu.

Tomlin, William. T Apr 1725 *Sukey* LC Md Sep 1725. K.

Tomlin, William. T 14 yrs Apr 1768 *Thornton*. E.

Tomlins, Frances. R for America Aug 1715. L.

Tomlins, George. S Sep-Oct 1774. M.

Tomlins, Martha (1719). *See* Dallow. M.

Tomlinson, Edward. S s saddle at Penkridge Summer 1751. St.

Thomlinson, James. R for Barbados Feb 1664. L.

Tomlinson, James. S Jan 1733. M.

Tomlinson, John. S Aug 1752 TB to Md Apr 1753. Le.

Tomlinson, John. S Oct T Nov 1759 *Phoenix*. L.

Tomlinson, John of East Retford. S s cloth at Normanton Apr 1770. Nt.

Thomlinson, Joseph. R Oct TB Nov 1662. L.

Tomlinson, Joseph. S Dec 1743 T Feb 1744 *Neptune* to Md. M.

Tomlinson, Michael. SQS Oct 1766 T Jan 1767 *Tryal*. M.

Tomlinson, Richard of Newborough in Lathom. S Summer 1754. La.

Tomlinson, Thomas. S Lent T Oct 1738 *Genoa*. Bu.

Tomblinson, William. S for highway robbery & R 14 yrs Lent 1773. Li.

Tommey, Dorothy. R for Jamaica Mar 1665. L.

Tompkin, Martha (1719). *See* Hewson, Mary. L.

Tompkins, Benjamin. R for Barbados Jly 1675. M.

Tompkins, Elizabeth. R for Barbados or Jamaica Aug AT Oct 1700. M.

Tompkins, Henry. T 14 yrs Dec 1753 *Whiteing*. Sy.

Tomkins, John. S Nov T Dec 1763 *Neptune*. L.

Tomkins, Joseph. S 14 yrs Lent 1757 for receiving goods from Benjamin Leggatt *(qv)*. Be.

Tomkyns, Thomas. S s beans & peas at Wroxton Summer 1757. O.

Tomkyns, Thomas. S s at St. John Baptist, Hereford, Lent 1770. He.

Tomkins, William. R for America Jly 1694. No.

Tomkins, William. S s at Pencombe Summer 1749. He.

Toms, Christiana (1726). *See* Cambell. M.

Toms, David. S Apr 1747. De.

Toms, Edward. R for life Lent T Apr 1772 *Thornton*. K.

Toms, Elizabeth. S s at Oxenhall Summer 1770. G.

Toms als Thomas, George. S Aug 1773. Do.

Toms, James. S Jly T Nov 1759 *Phoenix*. M.

Toms, John. R for America Jly 1694. Li.

Toms, John. S Apr-May T May 1741 *Catherine & Elizabeth* to Md. M.

Toms, John. S Mar 1750. So.

Toms, Sarah. S Mar 1767. Do.

Tongison, Mary. S Oct T Nov 1725 *Rappahannock* LC Va Apr 1726. M.

Tongue, Charles. T Apr 1743 *Justitia*. Sy.

Tongue, John. S Aug T Sep 1725 *Forward* LC Annapolis Dec 1725. L.

Tongue, Mary. T Apr 1743 *Justitia*. Sy.

Tonge, Mary wife of William of Manchester. SQS Jan 1745. La.

Tonkyn, John. S Summer 1751 R for life Lent T Jun 1756 *Lyon*. Sy.

Tonkins, James. R 14 yrs Mar 1768. Co.

Tonks, Aaron. S Lent 1766. Wa.

Tonks, William. S & R 14 yrs Summer 1774. St.

Tony, Anthony. S s coat from Duke of Montrose & T May 1736 *Patapsco*. M.

Toogood, James. S Mar 1749. So.

Towgood, James. S Aug 1772. Do.

Toogood, John. R 14 yrs Mar 1749. Do.

Touk, Richard. S Mar 1768 TB to Va. De.

Tool, Christian. S Aug T Oct 1726 *Forward* to Va. M.

Toole, Christopher. TB to Va from QS 1734. De.

Tool, David. T Apr 1768 *Thornton*. K.

Toole, James of St. Paul, Covent Garden. SW Apr T May 1767 *Thornton*. M.

Toole als White als Taffe als Fowler, Mary. R for Barbados Mar 1677. L.

Tole, Richard. TB to Va from QS 1736. De.

Toole, Thomas. S Feb T Apr 1768 *Thornton*. M.

Tooley als Hewitt, Elizabeth. S Feb T May 1719 *Margaret*; sold to Peter Hyat Md Sep 1719. L.

Tooley als Goodbury, Elizabeth, als wife of Cuthbert Walton. S Dec 1735 T Jan 1736 *Dorsetshire* LC Va Sep 1736. M.

Tooley, Fool. S Sep-Dec 1746. M.

Tooley als Tuley, John. S Lent R 14 yrs Summer 1754. Ht.

Tooley, Mary. S Feb T Apr 1765 *Ann*. M.

Toombes, Ann. R Sep 1671 AT Oct 1673. M.

Tombs, Edward. S Lent 1762. Wa.

Tombs, Francis. R 14 yrs Jly 1753. Ha.

Tombs, James. S Mar 1736. De.

Toombes, John. SQS Apr T May 1767 *Thornton*. M.

Toone, James. S Jly 1721 T from Southampton 1723. Ha.

Toone, William. S Summer 1758. Le.

Tupe, Edward of Downton, husbandman. R for Barbados Feb 1668. Wi.

Toop, Joseph. S Mar 1740. Do.

Toope, Nicholas of Rattery, cordwainer. R for Barbados Jun 1665. De.

Toop, William. R 14 yrs Mar 1752. So.

Tooth, Mary. T Apr 1732 *Patapsco*. Sy.

Tooth, William of St. Olave, Southwark. R for Barbados or Jamaica
   Mar 1682 & Feb 1683. Sy.

Tooworth, Ann (1744). *See* Webb. M.

Topham, John of St. Saviour, Southwark. R for Barbados or Jamaica
   Feb 1696. Sy.

Topham, Sarah. S May-Jly 1773. M.

Tophurst, Francis. S Dec 1764 T Jan 1765 *Tryal*. M.

Topp, William. SQS Apr TB to Md May 1742. So.

Topping, Henry of Chester. R for America Aug 1700. Ch.

Topping, Henry. S Summer 1757 R 14 yrs T Sep 1758 *Tryal*. Bu.

Topping, James. S Lent 1757. K.

Topping, John. S 14 yrs Jly 1775. L.

Topping, Joyce wife of Edward. S & T Apr 1762 *Neptune*. M.

Toppin als Hackery, Mary. S Apr T May 1740 *Essex*. L.

Topping, William. S s handkerchief Oct 1735 T Jan 1736 *Dorsetshire* LC
   Va Sep 1736. M.

Topps, Susanna. S Lent T May 1755 *Rose*. Sy.

Torrince, Abraham. S May T Jun 1764 *Dolphin*. M.

Tose, Henry of Holcombe. R for Barbados Jly 1679. De.

Toes, William (1733). *See* Robinson. Y.

Tosswick als Tossick, James. S s gelding Summer 1757 R 14 yrs Summer
   1758. Du.

Tottle, Jasper. S 14 yrs Mar 1746. So.

Tootell, John. S Summer 1768. Wa.

Tootell, Robert. S Summer 1768. Wa.

Totell, Samuel. Rebel T 1685.

Totty, Frances (1723). *See* Allen. M.

Totty, James. S Summer 1740. St.

Tough, John of Newcastle upon Tyne. R for Barbados Jun 1694. Nl.

Toulson, Clement, gent. R Feb AT Jun 1673. M.

Tounch, Robert. S 1718. M.

Toursey, Francis (1664). *See* Tersey. M.

Tovell, Robert. S Lent 1760. Su.

Tovey, Ann. S Dec 1765 T Jan 1766 *Tryal*. M.

Tovey, Hannah. SQS Sep T Dec 1770 *Justitia*. M.

Tovey, Henry of Portsmouth, ropemaker. R for Barbados Jly 1678. Ha.

Toovey, John. T May 1767 *Thornton*. Sy.

Tovey, Richard. R Jan 1693. M.

Toovey, Thomas. S Mar 1752. Ha.

Towell, Anthony. S Lent 1738. Hu.

Towl, James (1773). *See* Town. St.

Towle, Peter. S s horse Lent 1728 R 14 yrs Lent 1729. Y.

Towell, Thomas. R Jun T Aug 1769 *Douglas*. M.

Towers, Charles. S Oct 1724. M.

Towers, Daniel. S Lent 1766. Be.

Towers, James. S & T Dec 1767 *Neptune*. M.

Towers, Jane. T Oct 1723 *Forward*. E.

Towers als Dowse, John. S s cereals at Cookham Summer 1751. Be.

Towers, John. S Feb T Mar 1764 *Tryal*. M.

Towers, John of Ulverstone. SQS Oct 1773. La.

Towers, Mary. S Summer 1758. Nf.

Towers, Richard of Brill. S Lent T Oct 1726 *Forward*. Bu.

Towers, Thomas. PT Oct 1672 R Oct 1673. M.

Towler, Thomas. SQS Richmond Jan 1738. Y.

Towler, Walter of Shipdam. R for America Jly 1682. Nf.

Town als Towl als Howl als Craddock, James. S & R 14 yrs Lent 1773. St.

Towndry, Robert. S Summer 1718 T Lent 1719. Y.

Townes, Martha. S Jan T Feb 1724 *Anne*. L.

Towning, William. TB to Va 1768. De.

Townley als Upcroft, John. S Norwich for highway robbery Summer 1750 R 14 yrs Lent 1751. Nf.

Townley, Mary, aged 21, dark. S Jly T Oct 1720 *Gilbert* LC Annapolis May 1721. L.

Townley, Mary. S Feb-Apr T Jun 1756 *Lyon*. M.

Townsend, Alexander. Rebel T 1685.

Townsend, Christopher. R for Barbados Sep 1672. L.

Townsend, Edward, als Eldridge, John of Stow on Wold. R for America Feb 1714. G.

Townsend, Elizabeth. R for Barbados or Jamaica Mar 1685. M.

Townsend, Elizabeth. S Jly T Sep 1751 *Greyhound*. L.

Townsend, Erasmus. R for Barbados or Jamaica Oct 1694. L.

Townsend, Jacob. S Jly T Nov 1759 *Phoenix*. M.

Townsend, James. S Apr 1775. M.

Townsend, Mary. S May T Jly 1722 *Alexander* to Nevis or Jamaica. M.

Townsend, Mary. R 14 yrs Aug 1737. So.

Townesend, Thomas of Bagshot. R for Barbados or Jamaica Jly 1677. Sy.

Townsend, Thomas. Rebel T 1685.

Townsend, Thomas. S s at Cirencester Lent 1722. G.

Townsend, Thomas. S s sheep Lent R 14 yrs Summer 1742. Wa.

Townsend, Thomas. S Mar 1742. De.

Townsend, Thomas. S Lent R 14 yrs Summer 1765. G.

Townsend, Thomas. S Jly T Sep 1767. L.

Townsend, Thomas. S & R 14 yrs Summer 1772. G.

Townsend, William. S s at South Cerney Lent 1768. G.

Towser, George (1766). *See* White. Ht.

Tozer, John. R 14 yrs Aug 1749. So.

Towzer, Richard. S Mar 1751. Ha.

Towsey, Thomas (1730). *See* Harris. Co.

Toy, Margaret. T Apr 1725 *Sukey* LC Md Sep 1725. Sy.

Toy, Samuel. S May T Jun 1756 *Lyon*. L.

Toynton, Gervase. R for America Jly 1709. Li.

Tracey, Catherine. S & T Apr 1733 *Patapsco* LC Annapolis Nov 1733. M.

Tracey, Catherine. S Feb T Apr 1759 *Thetis*. M.

Tracey, Dorothy. S Jan-Apr 1749. M.

Tracy, Francis. PT Aug 1687 R Mar 1688. M.

Tracey, George. T Oct 1738 *Genoa*. K.

Tracey, John of Liverpool. S for highway robbery Summer 1765 R 14 yrs
Lent 1766. La.

Tracey, Mary. S & T Dec 1734 *Caesar* LC Va Jly 1735. L.

Tracey, Robert. S s at St. Peter in Barley, Oxford, Summer 1721. O.

Tracey, Robert. S & T Jan 1736 *Dorsetshire* LC Va Sep 1736. L.

Traffick, Jeremiah of Tenterden. S Lent 1745. K.

Trafford, Charles. S Sep T Dec 1767 *Neptune*. M.

Trahern, Mary. S Lent R 14 yrs Summer 1736. He.

Traherne, Samuel (1664). *See* Lewis. Ht.

Trahern, Thomas. S s tobacco at Ashperton Lent 1761 T *Atlas* from
Bristol. He.

Traherne, William of Bromyard or Bockleton. S Lent 1721. He.

Trail, Christian (1764). *See* Hayes. L.

Trainer, John. S s handkerchief at St. Martin Ludgate May T Jun 1768
Tryal. L.

Trainer, Patrick. S 14 yrs Apr 1773. M.

Trayner, Tristram. S Summer R for Barbados Aug 1663. K.

Trallacke, Frances. R for plantations Jan 1665. L.

Tranceys, Richard. S & T Oct 1730 *Forward* to Va. M.

Trangmore, Sara. R for Barbados Mar 1677. L.

Tranter, Mary. S Dec 1774. M.

Trantom, John. S s at Whitchurch Summer 1745. Sh.

Trantum, Samuel. S Oct 1774. L.

Trapnell, John. TB to Va from QS 1750. De.

Trapp, William (1691). *See* Kirby, John. M.

Trappall, Simon. T Oct 1723 *Forward*. K.

Trask, Benjamin. Rebel T 1685.

Trask, Susannah. TB to Va 1769. De.

Travel, Thomas. S s money Lent 1754. G.

Travers, Elizabeth. S Feb T Mar 1727 *Rappahannock* to Md. M.

Traverse, John of Plymouth. R for Barbados Jly 1695. De.

Traverse, John. T Apr 1766 *Ann*. Sy.

Travers, Phillis. T Dec 1736 *Dorsetshire*. Sy.

Travillion, Simon. S & T May 1736 *Patapsco*. L.

Traviss, John, als Moco Jack. R & T Apr 1734 *Patapsco* to Md. M.

Treviss, John. S Dec 1765 T Jan 1766 *Tryal*. M.

Trevis, John. SW & T Apr 1771 *Thornton*. M.

Travis, Joseph. S s linen Jan-May T Jun 1738 *Forward* to Md or Va. M.

Trevis, Philip. S Feb-Apr T Jun 1756 *Lyon*. M.

Trevis, Richard. R for Barbados Jan 1664. L.

Trevis, William. S Lent 1774. Li.

Trayford, Thomas. SQS Feb T Apr 1766 *Ann*. M.

Treacle, George. S Jun 1743. L.

Treadwell, John. S Lent R 14 yrs Summer 1758. O.

Tredwell, Richard. S & T Apr 1733 *Patapsco* LC Annapolis Nov 1733. L.

Treane als Tearne, Thomas. R for Barbados Jly 1675. M.

Treble, William. S s at Trimborough Summer 1772. Su.

Tredeage, Thomas. S s yarn at Stroud Lent 1758. G.

Tredgit, William of Peterborough. S Lent 1734. Hu.

Tredway, Thomas. R for Barbados Jun 1663. M.

Tree, Robert. S Lent R 14 yrs Summer 1756. Ht.

Tree, Thomas. R 14 yrs Mar 1744. So.

Treen, Joseph. S Aug T 14 yrs Oct 1726 *Forward*. L.

Treene, Nowell. PT Aug 1685. M.

Tregilgas, Edward. S Aug 1756. Co.

Tregonning, Richard. S Aug 1743. Co.

Tregowith, John. S Jly 1760 but then R for fleet service. De.

Treharn, James. S s at Frampton Cotterell Lent 1771. G.

Treise, John. R 14 yrs Aug 1731. Co.

Tremain, Martha wife of Peter. S Sep 1733 T Jan 1734 *Caesar* LC Va Jly 1734. M.

Tremayne, Mary. R for Barbados Jun 1665. L.

Tremble, George. T 14 yrs Apr 1768 *Thornton*. Sy.

Trimble, John. S & T 14 yrs Dec 1769 *Justitia*. M.

Trimble, William. S & T Dec 1769 *Justitia*. M.

Trembley, Corney. T Jun 1764 *Dolphin*. M.

Trenarry, Richard. S Mar 1742. Co.

Trenchard, Aaron. SQS Jun TB Aug 1769. So.

Trend als Frind, John. R 14 yrs Aug 1767 TB to Va. De.

Trentham, John. S s sheep Lent 1722. O.

Trenton, Edward. S Sep-Oct T Dec 1752 *Greyhound*. M.

Trepine, Judith. SQS Sep 1756. M.

Tresize, Charles. S Jly 1766. De.

Tresler, John. T Apr 1770 *New Trial*. Sy.

Trestrayle, William of Kenwyn, fuller. R for Barbados Feb 1672. Co.

Treswell, Loring John (1764). *See* Fraser. M.

Trethewey, John (1753). *See* Warne. Co.

Trethewey, Joseph. R 14 yrs Aug 1758. Co.

Trethewey, Thomas. S Aug 1773. Co.

Treton, Henry. S Mar TB to Va Apr 1740. Wi.

Trevascus, Arthur. R 14 yrs Mar 1731. Co.

Trevett, Charles. PT Dec 1691 R Jan 1692. M.

Trevett, Noah. S Lent 1756. Sy.

Trevillian, Mary wife of Simon. S Jan T Feb 1733 *Smith* to Md or Va. M.

Trevis. *See* Travis.

Trevit, John. R 14 yrs Mar 1753. Do.

Trevith, Mary. T Jun 1756 *Lyon*. Sy.

Trevitt, Robert. T Jun 1728 *Elizabeth* LC Va Aug 1729. Sy.

Trevor, Thomas. R for America Aug 1713. M.

Treweek, Nicholas. S Aug 1743. Co.

Trewhitt, William. S Jly R 14 yrs Summer TB Sep 1726. Nt.

Tribe, Anthony. R 14 yrs for Boston NE Jly 1718. Ha.

Trickens, Mary. S Apr 1773. L.

Tricket, Edward. S Feb T 14 yrs Apr 1766 *Ann*. M.

Tricks, Lewis. Rebel T 1685.

Trix, Robert. S & T May 1719 *Margaret* from London. Li.

Tricky, Joseph. PT Oct 1701. M.

Triest, Peter. S s from Lord Baltimore Feb T Apr 1766 *Ann*. M.

Trigg, Daniel. S Feb T Apr 1770 *New Trial*. L.

Trigg, John (1723). *See* Fogg. E.

Trigger, Mary. S May T 14 yrs Jun 1726 *Loyal Margaret* but died on passage. M.

Triggs, Elizabeth. T Jan 1767 *Tryal*. M.

Trimble. *See* Tremble.

Trimby, Stephen. R 14 yrs Mar 1773. Do.

Trimlett, Ann. S Dec 1733 T Jan 1734 *Caesar* LC Va Jly 1734. M.

Trimlin, Thomas. SQS Jan-Mar TB to Va Apr 1741. Wi.

Trimnell, John. S Mar 1725. Wi.

Trimnell, Richard. S Jan T Mar 1750 *Tryal*. L.

Trindall, Nathaniel of Bloxham. R for America Feb 1716. Sh.

Trink, Peter (1752). *See* Stephens. Co.

Triphook, Joseph. S Jly 1720 T from Portsmouth 1723. Ha.

Triponet, John Francis of St. Sepulchre, goldsmith. SQS Jan 1665 to be T to Jamaica for attending unlawful religious assembly. M.

Trip, John. T Jun 1740 *Essex*. Ht.

Tripp, Thomas. S Lent 1743. *Su.

Tripp, William. T Oct 1778 *Genoa*. K.

Trippett, Joseph. T Aug 1769 *Douglas*. M.

Trippett, William. PT Jun R Oct 1690. M.

Trippitt, William. S Apr T Jun 1768 *Tryal*. M.

Trippup, John of Kingston on Thames. R Feb 1719. Sy.

Triquett, Peter. S Apr T Jun 1742 *Bladon*. L.

Tristram, James. S Summer 1732. Wo.

Tristram als Tristrum, Joseph. S Summer 1754. Ht.

Tristram, Thomas of Yarmouth, mariner. R (Western Circ) for Barbados Feb 1714. Nf.

Tritton, Daniel. LC from *Robert* Annapolis Jun 1725. X.

Trives, Robert. S Jan-Feb T Apr 1772 *Thornton*. M.

Trivet, Mary. S Summer T Sep 1755 *Tryal*. Sy.

Troale, Anne. S & T Apr 1725 *Sukey* to Md. M.

Trolley, John. R for America Jly 1688. Nt.

Troope, Edward. R for Barbados or Jamaica May 1697. L.

Troop, Isabella. AT City Summer 1758. Nl.

Troop, William. S for killing sheep Mar R 14 yrs & TB to Va Apr 1774. Le.

Trotman, George. SQS Feb T Apr 1768 *Thornton*. M.

Trotman, John. S s cloth at Bisley Summer 1774. G.

Trott, John (1677). *See* Scott. Sy.

Trott, John. T Jly 1722 *Alexander*. Bu.

Trott, John. S Mar 1724. So.

Trott, Judith. R for Barbados Oct 1673. L.

Trott, Richard. T for life Apr 1770 *New Trial*. K.

Trot, Samuel. S Mar 1755. So.

Trott, Thomas. Rebel T 1685.

Trotter, Abraham. S Jun T Oct 1744 *Susannah*. M.

Trotter, Elizabeth. S Feb 1729. M.
Trotter, Jacob. S City Summer 1740. Nl.
Trotter, James. S Mar 1759 TB to Va. De.
Trotter, James. S s gelding at Kingston Summer 1770. He.
Trotter, James. S Jan-Feb T Apr 1772 *Thornton*. M.
Trotter, John. T Jun 1740 *Essex*. E.
Trotter, Richard. R 14 yrs City Summer 1750. Nl.
Trottle, Robert. S for Va Jly 1718. Do.
Trow, John. S s sheep at St. Lawrence Lent 1729. Sh.
Trow, John. S & T Jly 1753 *Tryal*. L.
Troward, Edward. S Feb 1757. M.
Trowell, Eleanor. SQS Mar TB Apr 1763. Le.
Trowell, John. R for Barbados Apr 1669. M.
Troy, William. R & T for life Apr 1770 *New Trial*. M.
Trubbs, George. Rebel T 1685.
Trubody, Theophilus. S Mar 1729 TB to Va. De.
Trubshaw, Ann. T Sep 1758 *Tryal*. K.
Truckey, Joseph. R for Barbados or Jamaica Aug 1701. M.
True, John. S & T Jan 1769 *Thornton*. M.
True, Thomas. S Apr 1765. So.
Trueboy, Richard. S May T Jun 1726 *Loyal Margaret* to Md. M.
Truebridge, Mary. R Oct 1772. M.
Truelock, Giles of Bermondsey. SQS Oct 1761. Sy.
Trulock, James. SQS Devizes May TB to Va Oct 1764. Wi.
Truelove, John of Worcester. R for America Jly 1698. Wo.
Truelove, Robert. S s at Wokingham Lent 1764. Be.
Trueman, Alice. S Jan 1751. L.
Trueman, Jane. S Dec 1765 T Jan 1766 *Tryal*. M.
Trueman, Robert. S s at Melish Summer 1767. Nl.
Trueman, Sarah. S Aug T Oct 1723 *Forward*. L.
Trueman, Thomas. T Apr 1743 *Justitia*. K.
Trueman, William. S Jly T Sep 1765 *Justitia*. M.
Truhitt, Roger. R for life City Summer 1755. Nl.
Trull, John (1755). *See* Vizard. G.
Trull, Mary. S s at Credenhill Summer 1762. He.
Trump, Humphrey. Rebel T 1685.
Trump, James. T Dec 1763 *Neptune*. Sy.
Trump, Richard. T Apr 1741 *Speedwell* or *Mediterranean*. Sx.
Truren, John. Rebel T 1685.
Truslove, Samuel. S & TB to Va Aug 1768. Le.
Truss, John. T Apr 1753 *Thames*. E.
Trussell, Ann. S Jun 1761. M.
Trussin, Elizabeth wife of George. S Sep T Oct 1750 *Rachael*. M.
Trusty, John. S Jan-Feb 1774. M.
Trygoal, John. S Mar TB to Va Apr 1765. Wi.
Tubb, Jacob (1728). *See* Harris, Francis. De.
Tubb, Thomas. S s at Bletchley Summer 1751. O.
Tuck, Henry. S Mar 1771 TB to Va. De.
Tuck, James. S Mar 1720 & Mar 1721. Do.
Tuck, John. S Mar 1737. So.
Tuck, Joseph. R Summer 1728 (SP). Hu.

Tuck, Philip. R Mar 1772 but dead by April 1772. Wi.

Tucker, Edward. S Jan-Apr 1749. M.

Tucker, Elizabeth of St. Olave, Southwark. R for Barbados or Jamaica Feb 1676 & Jly 1677. Sy.

Tucker, Elizabeth. S Jan T Feb 1724 *Ann*. L.

Tucker, Emanuel. SWK Oct 1772. K.

Tucker, Freelove. R 14 yrs Mar 1763. So.

Tucker, Gabriell. R May AT Jly 1697. M.

Tucker, George. S Nov T Dec 1763 *Neptune*. L.

Tucker, Grace. PT Apr R Oct 1673 AT Jun 1674. M.

Tucker, Grace. R 14 yrs Mar 1742. Co.

Tucker, Gregory. SQS Feb T Apr 1766 *Ann*. M.

Tucker, Henry. Rebel T 1685.

Tucker, James. S Jly TB Aug 1755. Wi.

Tucker, James of St. James, Westminster. SW Jan 1775. M.

Tucker, John. TB to Va from QS 1740. De.

Tucker, John. S Mar 1744. De.

Tucker, John. R 14 yrs Jly 1749. Ha.

Tucker, John. S s at Newnham Lent 1774. O.

Tucker, Joseph. S Oct 1772. L.

Tucker, Lewis. S Mar 1729. Do.

Tucker, Mary. S Mar 1760. So.

Tucker, Peter. S Mar 1732 TB to Va. De.

Tucker, Richard. R for Barbados Feb 1672. M.

Tucker, Richard. SQS Oct 1735 TB to Md Jan 1736. So.

Tucker, Robert. S Apr 1723. So.

Tucker, Robert. R 14 yrs Jly 1740. Do.

Tucker, Robert. R 14 yrs Aug 1754. De.

Tucker, Roger of Alfington. R for Barbados Feb 1690. De.

Tucker, Thomas. S Aug 1734. De.

Tucker, Thomas. S Jan 1751. M.

Tucker, William of Oldland. R for America Mar 1680. G.

Tucker, William. Rebel T 1685.

Tucker, William. S Apr 1727. So.

Tucker, William. S 14 yrs Lent 1755. Sy.

Tucker, William of St. Saviour, Southwark. SQS Feb 1775. Sy.

Tuckey, John. S Lent T Apr 1773. Wa.

Tuckey, Thomas. Rebel T 1685.

Tuckfield, Elizabeth. S Sep 1736. M.

Tuckfield, James of Exeter. R for Barbados Apr 1668. De.

Tudor, Frances. S Feb T Apr 1771 *Thornton*. L.

Tudor, George (1729). *See* Tedder. Mo.

Tudor, Hervey als Slingsby. S & T Jly 1772 *Tayloe*. M.

Tuder, Richard. T May 1719 *Margaret*; sold to Patrick Sympson & William Black Md Sep 1719. K.

Tudor, Samuel. R Jly T for life Oct 1768 *Justitia*. M.

Tudor, Woodward. S Oct T Nov 1728 *Forward* LC Va Jun 1729. M.

Tue. *See* Tew.

Tuffield, William. T Oct 1729 *Forward*. K.

Tuffnell, James. S Jan 1775. M.

Tuffnal, James. S Jly 1775. L.

Tuft, John. R 14 yrs Summer 1748. Y.
Tuft, Thomas. S s geldings at Park Gate Lent R 14 yrs Summer 1761. St.
Tugby, John. TB Feb 1770. Db.
Tugman, James. S Summer T Sep 1755 *Tryal*. Sy.
Tugwell, Elizabeth. S Dec 1773. M.
Tulley, Ralph of Portslade. R for Barbados or Jamaica Jly 1677. Sx.
Tully, Susanna wife of William. S Oct T Dec 1763 *Neptune*. M.
Tummer, John. S s sow Lent 1763. Nf.
Tummon, Thomas. S s sheep Summer 1742 R 14 yrs Lent 1743. Y.
Tunbridge, Samuel. S Dec 1749-Jan 1750 T Mar 1750 *Tryal*. M.
Tunicliff, Ann. S Jun 1761. M.
Tuniola, Margaret. S Feb 1761. M.
Tunningley, John. S s cow at Brierly & R 14 yrs Lent 1770. Y.
Tunstall, John of Eccleston or Knowsley, yeoman. SQS Apr 1742. La.
Tunstall, William. R 14 yrs s sheep Lent 1762. Li.
Tupe. *See* Toope.
Turbett, Hannah. S s household goods Sep T Dec 1736 *Dorsetshire*. M.
Turbutt, Isaac. S & T May 1736 *Patapsco*. L.
Turbett, Mary. S Summer T Sep 1751 *Greyhound*. Sy.
Turbutt, William. S 14 yrs Oct 1744-Jan 1745. M.
Turby, John (1730). *See* Douby. L.
Turk, Esau. S s cloth at Rodborough Lent 1772. G.
Turker, William. T May 1755 *Rose*. Sy.
Turle, James. Rebel T 1685.
Turle, John. Rebel T 1685.
Turmidge, John of Steeple cum Stangate. R for Barbados or Jamaica Feb 1696. E.
Turnbull, Hannah. AT City Summer 1755. Nl.
Turnbull, John. S Lent 1763. E.
Turnbull, William. S Jan-Apr 1748. M.
Turner, Abraham. R for Barbados or Jamaica Oct 1694. L.
Turner, Abraham of Middleton, woollen weaver. SQS Jan 1754. La.
Turner, Alice, spinster. R & TB for Barbados Oct 1667. L.
Turner, Anne. S Dec 1727. M.
Turner, Ann. S Aug 1736. So.
Turner, Ann (1747). *See* Fox. Db.
Turner, Ann. S Sep-Oct 1748 T Jan 1749 *Laura*. M.
Turner, Ann. S Aug 1750. So.
Turner, Ann. S Apr 1754. So.
Turner, Ann. S Mar 1758. So.
Turner, Ann Harvey. R Jly T for life Oct 1768 *Justitia*. M.
Turner, Arthur of St. Botolph Aldgate. S s leed & T Dec 1740 *Vernon*. M.
Turner, Augustine. S s mare & R 14 yrs Lent 1738. Nf.
Turner, Charles. S s at Stroud Lent 1770. G.
Turner, Daniel. S Jun T Sep 1767 *Justitia*. L.
Turner, Edward. S Lent 1724 R 14 yrs Lent 1725 died on passage in *Sukey*. Be.
Turner, Elizabeth. S Aug T Oct 1726 *Forward* to Va. M.
Turner, Elizabeth. S Feb T Apr 1732 *Patapsco* LC Annapolis Oct 1732. M.
Turner, Elizabeth. S Sep T Oct 1739 *Duke of Cumberland*. L.

Turner, Elizabeth. S Summer 1754 R 14 yrs Lent T May 1755 *Rose*. Sy.

Turner, Elizabeth. SQS Feb T Apr 1766 *Ann*. M.

Turner, Elizabeth wife of John of St. Olave, Southwark. SQS Jly T Aug 1769 *Douglas*. Sy.

Turner, Elizabeth. S Sep-Oct 1775. M.

Turner, Elizabeth (1775). *See* White. La.

Turner, Frances. S Feb T May 1767 *Thornton*. M.

Turner, Francis. S & T Jan 1739 *Dorsetshire*. L.

Turner, George. S City Summer 1723. Nl.

Turner, George. S Aug T 14 yrs Oct 1726 *Forward*. L.

Turner, George. S Summer 1759 R 14 yrs Lent T Apr 1760 *Thetis*. Sy.

Turner, George. R 14 yrs Mar 1764. De.

Turner, George. S Lent R 14 yrs Summer 1768. Wo.

Turner, Isaac. S s at Sheffield Lent R 14 yrs Summer 1766. Y.

Turner, Isaac. S s shovel at Timworth Lent 1775. Su.

Turner, James of Shrewsbury. R for America Jly 1686. Sh.

Turner, James. S Apr-Jun 1739. M.

Turner, James. S Dec 1764 T Jan 1765 *Tryal*. M.

Turner, James. S s horse Summer 1764 R 14 yrs Lent 1765. Li.

Turner, Jane (1679). *See* Foster. St.

Turner, Jane. T Dec 1770 *Justitia*. Sy.

Turner, John. R for Barbados Dec 1667. M.

Turner, John of Halesowen. R for Barbados Feb 1671. Sh.

Turner, John. R Jly 1673. M.

Turner, John (1679). *See* Thatchwell. M.

Turner als Colly, John of Manchester, husbandman. R for Barbados Jly 1679. La.

Turner, John of Cudworth, butcher. R for Barbados Feb 1699. So.

Turner, John of Woodford. R for Barbados or Jamaica Jly 1702. E.

Turner, John. R for America Jly 1708. Le.

Turner, John als Horner, als Oaker, Henry of Stockland. R for Barbados Jly 1715. Do.

Turner, John. S Jan T Feb 1719 *Worcester* LC Annapolis Jun 1719. L.

Turner, John of Churchdown. S s sheep Summer 1720. G.

Turner, John. S Mar TB Apr 1729. Wi.

Turner, John. S for highway robbery Summer 1731 R Lent 1732. Su.

Turner, John. S Feb T Apr 1732 *Patapsco* LC Annapolis Oct 1732. L.

Turner, John (1736). *See* Turner, Stephen. L.

Turner, John. S s horse Lent R 14 yrs Summer 1737. Nt.

Turner, John. S Lent R 14 yrs Summer 1738. Wa.

Turner, John of Lawton with Kenyon. SQS Apr 1749. La.

Turner, John of St. Michael, Colchester, husbandman. SQS Jly 1749. E.

Turner, John. R 14 yrs Mar 1750. Ha.

Turner, John. S Lent 1750. Ca.

Turner, John. T 14 yrs Aug 1752 *Tryal*. E.

Turner, John (1763). *See* Smith, William. M.

Turner, John. SQS Apr T Jun 1768 *Tryal*. M.

Turner, John. T Apr 1769 *Tryal*. Sy.

Turner, John. SQS Oct T Dec 1770 *Justitia*. M.

Turner, Joseph. S Oct T Nov 1725 *Rappahannock* to Va. M.

Turner, Joseph. SQS Jan 1730. So.

Turner, Joseph (1764). *See* Taylor. M.
Turner als Furber, Joseph. S s at Bradley Summer 1765. St.
Turner, Joseph. S Jly T Sep 1766 *Justitia*. M.
Turner, Joseph of Farnham. SQS Jly T Aug 1769 *Douglas*. Sy.
Turner, Mary. S Jly T Nov 1759 *Phoenix*. M.
Turner, Mary. S Feb T Apr 1766 *Ann*. M.
Turner, Mary (1772). *See* Griffiths. Wo.
Turner, Matthew. PT Apr R Jly 1675. M.
Turner, Matthew. T Apr 1733 *Patapsco* LC Md Nov 1733. Sx.
Turner, Philip. R 14 yrs Aug 1739. So.
Turner, Philip. T 14 yrs Dec 1753 *Whiteing*. Sy.
Turner als Gardiner, Richard. R for Barbados Jun 1663. M.
Turner, Richard. Rebel T 1685.
Turner, Richard. T Oct 1720 *Gilbert*. Sy.
Turner, Richard Jr. S s at Windsor Summer 1724 T *Forward* LC Md Jun 1725. Be.
Turner, Richard. S Jan T Apr 1741 *Speedwell* or *Mediterranean*. M.
Turner, Richard. T Sep 1742 *Forward*. K.
Turner, Samuel. T May 1744 *Justitia*. E.
Turner, Samuel. S Mar 1759 TB to Va. De.
Turner, Samuel. S Summer 1761. K.
Turner, Samuel. S Dec 1762 T Mar 1763 *Neptune*. M.
Turner, Samuel. T Apr 1772 *Thornton*. E.
Turner, Sara (1726). *See* Lawson. L.
Turner, Sarah, als Bryan, Ann. S Dec 1765 T Jan 1766 *Tryal*. M.
Turner, Stephen. S Aug T Oct 1726 *Forward*. L.
Turner, Stephen als John. S & T May 1736 *Patapsco*. L.
Turner, Stephen. SQS Devizes & TB to Va Apr 1765. Wi.
Turner, Susan (1727). *See* Chaplain. St.
Turner, Susan wife of John. S Oct 1737 T Jan 1738 *Dorsetshire* to Va. M.
Turner, Thomas. S (Home Circ) for Barbados Apr 1663. X.
Turner, Thomas of Hempstead. R for America Jly 1687. G.
Turner, Thomas. S & T Apr 1725 *Sukey* LC Annapolis Sep 1725. M.
Turner, Thomas. S Feb T Mar 1729 *Patapsco* LC Annapolis Dec 1729. M.
Turner, Thomas. S Lent R 14 yrs Summer 1750. Sh.
Turner, Thomas. S Summer 1753 R 14 yrs Lent 1754. E.
Turner, Thomas. S Jun T Sep 1758 *Tryal*. L.
Turner, Thomas of St. Paul, Covent Garden. SW & T Jan 1767 *Tryal*. M.
Turner, William. R for Barbados Aug 1664. L.
Turner, William. R for Barbados Aug 1664. M.
Turner, William of Woodstock. R for America Mar 1710. O.
Turner, William. T Aug 1721 *Owners Goodwill*. E.
Turner, William. T Oct 1721 *William & John*. K.
Turner, William. S s mare at Badminton Summer 1736 R 14 yrs Lent TB Mar 1737. G.
Turner, William Sr. S Jly TB to Va Oct 1740. Wi.
Turner, William Jr. S Jly TB to Va Oct 1740. Wi.
Turner, William. S Mar 1741. De.
Turner als Harner, William. R 14 yrs Jly 1741. Do.
Turner, William. S Sep-Oct 1748 T Jan 1749 *Laura*. M.

Turner, William. S Jan T Mar 1750 *Tryal*. L.

Turner, William. S Lent T Apr 1760 *Thetis*. K.

Turner, William (1764). *See* Jackson, James. Hu.

Turner, William. S & T Apr 1765 *Ann*. L.

Turner, William. S Lent R 14 yrs Summer 1768. Wo.

Turner, William. SQS Jan TB Apr 1769. So.

Turner, William. T 14 yrs Apr 1769 *Tryal*. Sy.

Turner, William. S Summer 1770. We.

Turner, William. SQS Sep 1772. M.

Turner als Borroughs, William. S & R 14 yrs Summer 1774. St.

Turnham, Thomas. S Lent T Apr 1739 *Forward*. Bu.

Turnam, Thomas. ST & T Jly 1770 *Scarsdale*. L.

Turnpenny, Samuel of St. Margaret, Westminster. SW Jun 1774. M.

Turpin, Daniel (1749). *See* Whiteing. Be.

Turpin, Elizabeth. S Jan T Feb 1719 *Worcester* LC Md Jun 1719. L.

Turpin, John (1750). *See* Fryer. M.

Turpin, John. S s tea chest at St. Martin Orgar Sep T Oct 1768
    Justitia. L.

Turpin, Oliver of Barnet. R for Barbados Jly 1678 & 1679. Ht.

Turpin, Thomas. T Jun 1727 *Susanna*. Bu.

Turpin, Tirwhite. R for America Jly 1694. Li.

Turpitt, Mary. TB to Va from QS 1750. De.

Turquaire, Alexander. S s human hair at Burford Lent 1723. O.

Turrall als Parrett, Alice. R for Barbados Feb 1664. L.

Turrell, John of Great Leighs. SQS Jan 1763. E.

Turrell, Mary of Kingston on Thames. S Lent 1773. Sy.

Turtle, William Sr. R Summer 1772. Sy.

Turton, Mary. S Jly T Sep 1755 *Tryal*. L.

Turvel, Ann. S Apr-May T Jly 1771 *Scarsdale*. M.

Turvey, Edward of Plymouth. R for Barbados Dec 1686. De.

Turvie, James. T May 1744 *Justitia*. E.

Turvey, Joseph. S & T Dec 1767 *Neptune*. L.

Turvey, William. S & T Dec 1771 *Justitia*. M.

Tustey, Thomas. R for plantations Jan 1665. L.

Tustin, Thomas. S Jly TB to Va Oct 1740. Wi.

Tutcher, Thomas (1726). *See* Powell. M.

Tutfold als Taylor, William of Petworth. R for Barbados Jly 1679. Sx.

Tutin, Daniel. S Mar TB May 1724. Nt.

Tutt, Jacob. S Jly 1733. Ha.

Tutt, Susan. R for Barbados Jly 1675. M.

Tuxworth, Thomas. S s sheep Summer 1758 R 14 yrs Lent 1759. Li.

Twaite, Sampson. S s at St. Philip & James Lent TB Apr 1753. G.

Twaites, William. S & T Dec 1740 *Vernon*. L.

Twanmey, John. S Sep-Oct 1773. M.

Twells, Alice. T Aug 1741 *Sally*. Sy.

Twelves als Green, Elizabeth, aged 22, black hair. T Oct 1720 *Gilbert* LC
    Md May 1721. Sy.

Twelves, George. S Jan T Feb 1719 *Worcester* LC Annapolis Jun 1719. L.

Twelves, George. TB Sep 1750. Db.

Twiddy, Mary. S & T Jan 1722 *Gilbert* LC Annapolis Jly 1722. M.

Twiggs, Peter. S s horse Lent R 14 yrs Summer 1744. Le.

Twine, Thomas. SQS Marlborough & TB to Va Oct 1756. Wi.
Twinney, William. S s cloth Mar 1725. Wi.
Twisdale, Roger. LC from *Worcester* Annapolis Jun 1719. X.
Twiss als Twist als Hill, Mary wife of William. S s at Hodnet Summer 1771. Sh.
Twist, Benjamin. S Jly T Oct 1741 *Sea Horse*. L.
Twist, Charles of Plymouth. R for Barbados Mar 1686. De.
Twist, Mary (1771). *See* Twiss.
Twist, Thomas. S Feb T Apr 1742 *Bond*. L.
Twitt, Katherine wife of Robert. S Feb T Mar 1729 *Patapsco* LC Annapolis Dec 1729. M.
Twyford, Downs (1730). *See* Lee. Sy.
Twyford, Henry. T Jly 1770 *Scarsdale*. M.
Twyner, John of Wadhurst. R for Barbados Sep 1669 (Newgate). Sx.
Twyner, John. S Dec 1768 T Jan 1769 *Thornton*. M.
Tyas als Tyce, Edward. S Norwich s mare Summer 1743 R 14 yrs Lent 1744. Nf.
Tyce, Edward (1743). *See* Tyas. Nf.
Tycer, Benjamin. R 14 yrs & T Aug 1718 *Eagle* LC Charles Town Mar 1719. L.
Tigh, Henry. T Dec 1770 *Justitia*. Sy.
Tye, Mary of Blackmore. R for Barbados or Jamaica Jly 1688 & Feb 1690. E.
Tye, Robert. S s mare at Witnesham & R Lent 1770. Su.
Tyer, John. T Sep 1764 *Justitia*. K.
Tyers als Beard, Ann. S s plates Sep 1735 T Jan 1736 *Dorsetshire* LC Va Sep 1736. M.
Tyers, Richard. S Jly T Sep 1757 *Thetis*. L.
Tyers, Sarah. S Jan T Mar 1750 *Tryal*. L.
Tyler, Edward. S as accessory before housebreaking & R 14 yrs Summer 1772. G.
Tyler, Hannah. S Apr T Oct 1719 *Susannah & Sarah* LC Md Apr 1720. L.
Tiler, Hannah. R 14 yrs Mar 1737. Ha.
Tyler, James. R for Barbados Jly 1663. L.
Tyler, John. T Sep 1730 *Smith*. E.
Tyler, John. S Jly 1749. L.
Tyler, John. SQS May 1753. Ha.
Tyler, John. S Summer 1754 R 14 yrs Lent T May 1755 *Rose*. Sy.
Tyler, Joseph. S Oct 1751-Jan 1752. M.
Tyler, Margaret of Cirencester. R for America Jly 1683. G.
Tyler, Mary. S May T Jun 1726 *Loyal Margaret* LC Annapolis Oct 1726. M.
Tyler, Mary wife of George. S Lent 1755. Wo.
Tyler, Mary. S Apr 1774. L.
Tyler, Thomas. S Summer R for Barbados Aug 1664. Sy.
Tyler, William (1727). *See* Tapling. De.
Tyler, William. R Lent 1774. Sx.
Tyley, John. SQS & TB Apr 1754. So.
Tyne, Sarah. S Sep T Oct 1768 *Justitia*. M.
Tyner, Joseph. S Lent 1766. Wa.

Tyrrell, Adam. R 14 yrs Jly 1721. Wi.

Tyrell, Elizabeth. S Summer 1759 R 14 yrs Lent T Apr 1760 *Thetis*. K.

Tyrrell, Francis. S s sheep & R 14 yrs Lent T May 1772. No.

Tyrrell, Thomas. S Aug 1754. De.

Tysoe, James. S & R Summer T Sep 1770. Wa.

Tysoe, Richard. SQS Coventry Aug 1765. Wa.

Tison, Henry (1751). *See* Fison. L.

Tyson, Joseph. S s cloth from tenters & R Lent 1771. Y.

Tyson, Lewis. S Apr T May 1719 *Margaret*; sold to William Pridall Md Aug 1719. L.

Tythe, Mary. SQS & T Sep 1751 *Greyhound*. M.

Tyther, John of Sarnesfield. R for America Mar 1680. He.

Tyther, John. S s mare at Little Wenlock Lent R 14 yrs Summer 1736. Sh.

U

Udall, John. S Oct-Dec 1750. M.
Ewdall als Evedall, Richard. R for Barbados Oct 1673. M.
Uden, William. R for life Lent 1773. K.
Udith, James. S Apr T Jun 1768 *Tryal*. M.
Uffell, Roger. S Jly 1738. Ha.
Uffleman, Peter. T Oct 1722 *Forward*. K.
Uggles, Richard. S Lent R 14 yrs Summer 1761. E.
Ulph, Charles. T Dec 1753 *Whiteing*. E.
Ulph, John. S Lent 1749. *Su.
Ulph, Samuel (1723). *See* Usk. M.
Umble, Margaret. PT Oct R & T Dec 1716 *Lewis* to Jamaica. M.
Umpisson als Thomas, John. S s at Ribbesford Lent 1768. Wo.
Uncle, Benjamin Jr. of Albury. SQS & T Apr 1765 *Ann*. Ht.
Uncles, Elizabeth wife of William als Joseph als John of St. Saviour, Southwark. SQS Oct 1774. Sy.
Uncles, Thomas. R for America Jly 1708. Wa.
Underhill, George. S Apr 1745. L.
Underhill, Henry. S Dec 1748 T Jan 1749 *Laura*. M.
Underhill, James. S Lent R 14 yrs Summer 1767. St.
Underhill, Joseph. S s at Tettenhall Summer 1756. St.
Underhill, Mary. TB to Va from QS 1738. De.
Underhill, Robert Jr. S for Va Jly 1718. De.
Underhill, William. S for Va Jly 1718. De.
Underhill, William. S Lent R 14 yrs Summer 1756. St.
Underwood, Ann (1770). *See* Claxton. M.
Underwood, Anthony. S Jan T Sep 1737 *Pretty Patsy* to Md. M.
Underwood, Christopher. SQS New Sarum or Warminster & TB to Va Oct 1768. Wi.
Underwood, Dorothy (1768). *See* Aston. Sh.
Underwood, Elizabeth. S Lent TB Mar 1731. G.
Underwood, Humphrey. R for Barbados Feb 1664 (SP). M.
Underwood, Jacob Fosbrook of Hertingfordbury or North Mimms. S Lent 1745. Ht.
Underwood, John. S Jly TB to Va Sep 1744. Wi.
Underwood, John. S Lent R May 1752 *Lichfield*. Sy.
Underwood, John. S May-Jun T Jly 1753 *Tryal*. M.
Underwood, John. SQS Jun T Jly 1753 *Tryal*. M.
Underwood, John. S & T 14 yrs Dec 1770 *Justitia*. L.
Underwood, Thomas. S s mare Lent R 14 yrs Summer 1769. Ca.
Underwood, William. PT Jly 1680. M.
Underwood, William. S s coat at All Saints, Worcester, Summer 1757. Wo.
Underwood, William. SQS New Sarum or Warminster & TB to Va Oct 1768. Wi.
Unite, John Jr. S s ginlocks at Bromwich Lent 1767. St.
Unsworth, John of Winstanley, collier. SQS Oct 1752. La.
Unsworth, John of Manchester. SQS Jly 1763. La.

Unthank, Daniel of Upsall. S s at Hilton Lent TB Aug 1770. Y.
Unwin, Francis. S Feb T Apr 1770 *New Trial*. M.
Unwin, John. S Jly T Aug 1721 *Prince Royal* LC Va Nov 1721. M.
Unwin, Joseph. S Lent 1774. Ch.
Upchurch, John. S Summer 1745 R 14 yrs Lent 1746. Sy.
Upcroft, John (1751). *See* Townley. Nf.
Updale, Elizabeth. T Oct 1724 *Forward*. K.
Upfield, George. S Mar 1726. Ha.
Upgood, John. S & T Apr 1766 *Ann*. M.
Upham, Comfort of St. Olave, Southwark, spinster. SQS Mar 1754. Sy.
Upham, John. T Apr 1742 *Bond*. Sy.
Upham, Robert. R Lent 1775. Sy.
Upham als Marsh, Thomas. S Mar 1726. Ha.
Upham, Thomas. SQS Apr T Jly 1772 *Tayloe*. M.
Uphill, William. R 14 yrs Apr 1742. So.
Uppington, Elizabeth. SQS Sep 1754. M.
Upington, William. S Aug 1750. So.
Upson, Mary of St. Peter, Colchester. S Jan T Jun 1756 *Lyon*. E.
Upton, Edward. S Aug 1763. L.
Upton, Elizabeth. S Jan T Feb 1724 *Anne* to Carolina. M.
Upton, Elizabeth. S Dec 1754. L.
Upton, George. SQS Feb T May 1752 *Lichfield*. M.
Upton, Hannah. S Lent TB Apr 1768. Db.
Upton, John. SW & T Apr 1768 *Thornton*. M.
Upton, Nicholas. R May TB Jun 1691. M.
Upton, Thomas. S s tankard & T Dec 1734 *Caesar* LC Va Jly 1735. M.
Upton, William. S Lent TB Apr 1742. G.
Upwin, John. T Apr 1742 *Bond*. E.
Uren, Elizabeth. TB to Va from QS 1735. De.
Uren als Calebna, Jane. S Mar 1773. Co.
Uridge, Ruth wife of Luke. R Lent 1772. Wa.
Urlin, Elizabeth of Iver. R for Barbados Feb 1664. Bu.
Urquhart, William. S Jun T Sep 1758 *Tryal* to Annapolis. M.
Urry, James. S Mar 1736. So.
Urry, James. R 14 yrs Mar 1763. So.
Ursin als Hircutt, Mary. S Apr 1745. So.
Urton, John. S Jan T Feb 1773 *Smith* to Md or Va. M.
Urvoy, Toussaint Felix. S Jan T Apr 1762 *Dolphin*. L.
Urwin, Grifsey (1749). *See* Kelly. La.
Urwin, Isabel, als Douglas, Margaret of Newcastle. R for Barbados Jly
    1686. Nl.
Urwin, Susanna. S Apr 1748. L.
Usborne, Thomas of Ightham. R for Barbados or Jamaica Jun 1692. K.
Useley, Barbara (1733). *See* Cornelius. M.
Usher, Isaac. S Feb T Mar 1764 *Tryal*. M.
Usher, John. SQS s linen Lent 1772. Du.
Usher, Sarah. T Oct 1722 *Forward*. E.
Usk als Ulph, Samuel. S May T Jly 1723 *Alexander* LC Annapolis Sep
    1723. M.
Utber, John. T Sep 1730 *Smith*. Sy.
Utley, John. S Lent 1773. La.

V

Vager, George. T Jun 1727 *Susanna*. Sx.

Vagg, Edward. Rebel T 1685.

Vails, Zachary of Witham. R for Barbados or Jamaica Feb 1696. E.

Vainwright. *See* Wainwright.

Veil, Ann (1773). *See* Austin. L.

Vale, Elizabeth. S Summer 1739. He.

Vaill, George (1749). *See* Jay. Su.

Vale, Robert. T Oct 1729 *Forward*. E.

Valence, Thomas. S Mar 1756. Do.

Valentine, Mary (1750). *See* Oadway. M.

Vallett, Elizabeth. S Oct 1728. M.

Vallett, James, als Cut and Slash of St. Martin in Fields. SW Jun 1774. M.

Vallis, John. S Mar 1768. Ha.

Vallis, Stephen of Bermondsey, blacksmith. SQS Mar T Jun 1768 *Tryal*. Sy.

Vallony, John. R for Barbados or Jamaica May 1684. L.

Vallony, Robert. R for Barbados or Jamaica Dec 1683 & May 1684. L.

Valvin, Robert. S Apr T Jly 1770 *Scarsdale*. L.

Vancooler, John. S for assault at Bedwardine Lent 1764. Wo.

Vandelo, Sidley. R for Barbados Dec 1683. L.

Vanderancker, Elizabeth. S Aug T Oct 1726 *Forward* to Va. M.

Vanderhurst, John. S Oct T Dec 1724 *Rappahannock*. L.

Vanderson, Ann (1716). *See* Smith. M.

Vandervenvell, Jan Jonas. S Oct T Nov 1762 *Prince William*. M.

Van Gadwey, Jacob (1746). *See* Holloway. L.

Vannage, Elias. R for Barbados Jly 1668. L.

Vanstechelen, Ann. S s spoons Jan T Apr 1735 *Patapsco* LC Md Oct 1735. M.

Vanstone, Jonas. R 14 yrs Aug 1737. So.

Vantear, John. S Aug T Oct 1724 *Forward* LC Annapolis Jun 1725. L.

Vardell, Thomas. R for Barbados Jly 1674. L.

Vargess, Elizabeth (1747). *See* Bargess. La.

Varity. *See* Verity.

Varley, William. S for assault at Otley Lent 1766. Y.

Varley, William. S for coining at Halifax Lent 1770 & R during pleasure; Thomas Varley acquitted. Y.

Varnanan, Mary. TB Aug T Sep 1718 *Eagle* LC Charles Town Mar 1719. L.

Varndell, John. T Apr 1760 *Thetis*. Sy.

Varnell, Arthur. S Feb 1663 to House of Correction unless he agrees to be transported. M.

Varnell, Johanne. S Feb 1663 to House of Correction unless she agrees to be transported. M.

Varnham, Thomas. S s at Langley Marsh & R Lent T Apr 1770 *New Trial*. Bu.

Varnial, Mary. S Oct 1773. L.

Varnom, John. S s horse Lent R 14 yrs Summer 1737. No.
Varnum, Oliver. S Feb T Mar 1729 *Patapsco* LC Annapolis Dec 1729. L.
Varron, Thomas. S Sep 1754. L.
Vartry, Mary. S & T Oct 1732 *Caesar* to Va. M.
Vassell, Matthew. R for Barbados Sep 1669. M.
Vassey, William. S City Summer 1762. Nl.
Vasthold, Martin. S & T Sep 1766 *Justitia*. M.
Vater, Robert. Rebel T 1685.
Vater, William. S Apr 1754. So.
Vaters, Catherine (1740). *See* Rossiter. So.
Vaters, John (1740).*See* Rossiter. So.
Vatiere, Peter (1735). *See* Voteer. L.
Vauchlin, Francis (1723). *See* Wanklin. L.
Vaughan, Edward. S Jan-Jun T Jun 1728 *Elizabeth* LC Potomack Aug
     729. M.
Vaughan, Edward. S Dec 1747. L.
Vaughan, Elizabeth. R Feb 1675. M.
Vaughne, Florents. R for Barbados or Jamaica Mar 1688. M.
Vaughan, Florence of Braughing. R for Barbados or Jamaica Jun
     1699. Ht.
Vaughan, George. S Dec 1733 T Jan 1734 *Caesar* LC Va Jly 1734. M.
Vaughan, George. R & T May 1736 *Patapsco* to Md. M.
Vaughan, George (1740). *See* Downes. M.
Vaughan, George. S s at Newent Summer 1767. G.
Vaughan, Henry. R for Barbados Sep 1670. L.
Vaughan, Henry. T 14 yrs Apr 1765 *Ann*. K.
Vaughan, Hester. S s at St. Mary, Shrewsbury, Summer 1729. Sh.
Vaughan als Ward, Isaac. R for Barbados or Jamaica Feb 1687. M.
Vaughan, James. S Oct T Dec 1724 *Rappahannock*. L.
Vaughan, John. S & T Jan 1722 *Gilbert* LC Annapolis Jly 1722. M.
Vaughan, John. S & T Apr 1725 *Sukey* to Md LC Annapolis Sep
     1725. M.
Vaughan, John. S for burglary Lent 1739 R Lent 1740. Wo.
Vaughan, John. S Lent 1746. Nf.
Vaughan, John. S Lent 1755. Sh.
Vaughan, John (1767). *See* Jones. Sh.
Vaughan, John. S May-Jly 1773. M.
Vaughan, Philip. S Summer 1765 R 14 yrs Lent 1766. He.
Vaughan, Richard of Ellesmere. R for America Mar 1710. Sh.
Vaughan, Richard. S Lent 1731. Sh.
Vaughan, Richard. S s at Abbey Dore Summer 1760 T *Atlas* 1761 from
     Bristol. He.
Vaughan, Thomas. R 14 yrs s horse Aug 1720. So.
Vaughan, Thomas. S s horse Lent R 14 yrs Summer 1734. Wo.
Vaughan, Thomas. S s calfskins Summer 1743. O.
Vaughan, Thomas. S s handkerchief at St. Bride's Jly T Oct 1768
     Justitia. L.
Vaughan, William. S Summer 1760. Wa.
Vaughan, William. S Aug T Sep 1764 *Justitia*. L.
Vaughan, William. S 14 yrs receiving goods stolen at Berkeley Lent
     1769. G.

Veale, Daniel. S & T Jan 1722 *Gilbert* LC Annapolis Jly 1722. M.
Veal, Jane. S Mar 1742. Co.
Veale als Webb, Jane. S Jan T Feb 1744 *Neptune*. L.
Veal, John. S Summer 1756 R 14 yrs Summer 1757. Wo.
Veal, John. S Dec 1773. L.
Veale, Thomas. S Lent R 14 yrs Summer 1759. He.
Veares, Daniel of Warwick. R for America Jly 1678. Wa.
Veares, Joseph of Birmingham. R for America Jly 1682. Wa.
Veezey, Katherine. S Sep T Oct 1750 *Rachael*. M.
Veltgen, Peter. S for life Oct 1744-Jan 1745. M.
Venables, George. S s horse Summer 1739 R 14 yrs Lent 1740 (SP). Sh.
Venables, Jane. S Lent 1739. Ch.
Vender, Mary wife of Samuel, als Mary Stone. S & T Jan 1765 *Tryal*. M.
Vender, Thomas. S & T Jly 1772 *Tayloe*. M.
Venham, Philip. S Aug T Oct 1726 *Forward* to Va. M.
Venice, Thomas. S for highway robbery Lent R 14 yrs Summer T Oct
     1750 *Rachael*. Sx.
Vennell, Richard. R for life Mar TB to Va Apr 1767. Wi.
Venill, William. S Mar TB to Va Sep 1744. Wi.
Ven, Edward. Rebel T 1685.
Venn, Jane. T Apr 1769 *Tryal*. Sx.
Venn, Martha. SQS Jly TB Aug 1766. So.
Vennell, William. SQS Oct 1765 TB Apr 1766. So.
Venner, Isaac. SQS Sep 1774. M.
Venner, James. T Jan 1749 *Laura*. K.
Venner, John of Tiverton, husbandman. R for Barbados Apr 1668. De.
Venner als Paine, John. T Jan 1736 *Dorsetshire*. K.
Venner, Thomas. Rebel T 1685.
Ventham, Richard. R 14 yrs Mar 1743. Ha.
Ventham, Richard. S Mar 1754. Ha.
Venting, William. Rebel T 1685.
Ventland als Vinckland, Elizabeth. S & T Sep 1731 *Smith* LC Va
     1732. L.
Ventris, Benjamin. S Oct 1749. L.
Ventris, John. S May T Jun 1756 *Lyon*. L.
Venus, Elizabeth of St. Giles in Fields. S & T May 1736 *Patapsco*
     to Md. M.
Venus, John. S s naval stores Summer 1749. K.
Verbracken, Thomas. R for America Feb 1692. Le.
Verdon, Joseph. T Jun 1764 *Dolphin*. Sy.
Vere, Cecily. R Feb T for life Apr 1762 *Dolphin*. M.
Vere, Sarah. T Dec 1736 *Dorsetshire*. E.
Vergoe. *See* Virgo.
Varity, John (1726). *See* West. X.
Verity, John. S Sep 1754. L.
Verity, Robert. S Summer T Sep 1773. Wa.
Varity, William (1726). *See* West. Db.
Verkin, James. S Aug 1757 TB to Va 1758. De.
Vermin als Green, Charles. S Jly T Aug 1721 *Prince Royal* LC Va Nov
     1721. M.
Vernam als Vernon, Sarah. S Mar 1755. De.

Verncombe, Henry (1771). *See* Farncombe. So.

Vernell, George. R 14 yrs Mar 1773. Ha.

Vernall, Richard. S & T Sep 1755 *Tryal*. L.

Verney, William. R 14 yrs Mar 1773. De.

Vernham, Albert. S Feb T Mar 1727 *Rappahannock*. L.

Vernom, Ann wife of Thomas. S & T Sep 1731 *Smith* LC Va 1732. M.

Vernon, Elizabeth. T May 1737 *Forward*. Sy.

Vernon, Henry of Camberwell. SQS Apr 1774. Sy.

Vernon als Verrowne, John. R for Barbados Jly 1668. L.

Vernon, Sarah (1755). *See* Vernam.

Vernon, Thomas. S Mar TB to Va Apr 1769. Le.

Veroni, Joseph. S Apr 1775. M.

Verriner als Verrier, James of St. John's. SQS s lead & T Jan 1769 *Thornton*. Sy.

Verrowne, John (1668). *See* Vernon. L.

Verryard, William. Rebel T 1685.

Vert, Catherine. S & T Apr 1733 *Patapsco* LC Annapolis Nov 1733. L.

Vesper, Mary (1730). *See* Naylor, Ann. M.

Vevers als Bever, John. S Dec 1767 T Apr 1768 *Thornton*. L.

Veysey als Dawlen, Ann. TB to Va from QS 1749. De.

Vibault, Lancelot. S Jun-Dec 1738 T Jan 1739 *Dorsetshire* to Va. M.

Viccary, Hugh. S Mar 1744. De.

Viccary, John. S Mar 1740. So.

Vicary, Mary. S Aug T Oct 1724 *Forward* LC Annapolis Jun 1725. M.

Viccary, Nicholas. S Jly 1722. So.

Vicary, Philip. S Mar 1764. So.

Vice, Thomas of Newport Pagnell. S Lent 1763. Bu.

Vickers, John. S May-Jly 1773. M.

Vickars, Joseph. S City Summer 1750. Y.

Vickars, Robert. S Feb 1719. M.

Vickars, Robert. S Jun T Sep 1767 *Justitia*. L.

Viccars, Thomas. PT Jan R Mar 1685. M.

Vickers, Thomas. S Lent R 14 yrs Summer 1755. Li.

Vickers, William. S s books in Temple Sep T Oct 1768 *Justitia*. L.

Victuals, Elizabeth (1773). *See* Vittals. De.

Viepont, Thomas. SQS East Retford s oats Apr TB Aug 1738. Nt.

Vigen, George. R for Barbados May 1664. M.

Vidgeon, Thomas. S s sheep Summer 1749. K.

Vigures, James. S Apr-May T Jly 1771 *Scarsdale*. M.

Vigures, Mary. S Mar 1767 TB to Va. De.

Vildey, Edward. Rebel T 1685.

Vile, Christopher. S Aug 1754. De.

Vile, Edward. Rebel T 1685.

Vile, Thomas. Rebel T 1685.

Viles, Thomas. Rebel T 1685.

Vilett, Nicholas. S Jly TB to Va Sep 1744. Wi.

Villan, William. S Aug 1740 TB to Va. De.

Villis, Edward. S Mar 1752. So.

Vince, John. S Jun T Sep 1767 *Justitia*. M.

Vincent, Charles. R 14 yrs Aug 1754. Co.

Vincent, Edward of Stapleford. R for America Jly 1702. Ca.

Vincent, Hezekiah. T May 1751 *Tryal*. Sy.

Vincent, John. Rebel T 1685.

Vincent, John (1722, 1726 & 1727). *See* Williams. M.

Vincent, John. T Oct 1722 *Forward*. Sx.

Vincent, John. S Jan T Feb 1742 *Industry*. L.

Vincent, John. S Jly T Sep 1765 *Justitia*. M.

Vincent, John. T Dec 1770 *Justitia*.

Vincent, Joshua. R Jly 1686. M.

Vincent, Margaret wife of Thomas. S Jly 1752. Do.

Vincent, Nicholas. TB to Va from QS 1738. De.

Vincent, Peter. S Mar 1741. Co.

Vincent, Richard (1729). *See* Viner. Bu.

Vincent, Richard. S Mar 1737. Co.

Vincent, Samuel of St. Paul, Covent Garden. SW & T Jan 1767 *Tryal*. M.

Vincent, Sarah. S Mar 1766. Do.

Vinckland, Elizabeth (1731). *See* Venntland. L.

Vine, Edward. LC from *Forward* Annapolis Jun 1723. X.

Vine, James. T Sep 1767 *Justitia*. K.

Vine, Michael. S Sep T Oct 1720 *Gilbert*. L.

Vine, Rowland. S s horse Summer 1721 R 14 yrs Summer 1722. Ru.

Vine, Susanna. S Oct 1727-Jun 1728 T Jun 1728 *Elizabeth* LC Potomack Aug 1729. M.

Vinegar, Ann. S Lent 1754. Sy.

Viner, Jane. S Jan T Apr 1735 *Patapsco* LC Annapolis Oct 1735. M.

Viner als Vincent, Richard of Winchendon. S Summer T Oct 1729 *Forward*. Bu.

Viner, Thomas. PT Jly 1672. M.

Vines, Daniel. S Lent R 14 yrs Summer 1758. G.

Vines, John. S Mar 1753. Ha.

Vines, Mary. S May T Jun 1727 *Susanna* to Va. M.

Viney, Edward. S Summer 1748 T Jan 1749 *Laura*. K.

Viney, Thomas. S Summer 1748, found at large & S Lent 1749. K.

Vinicombe, Thomas. S Mar 1765. Co.

Vinicott, Joseph. Rebel T 1685.

Vining, Abraham. S Mar 1774. So.

Vining, Ambrose. Rebel T 1685.

Vintner, Henry of Assington. R for America Jly 1682. Su.

Vinyard, Abraham. S Jan-Feb T Apr 1753 *Thames*. M.

Vipond als Vipont, Isaac. R 14 yrs s mare Summer 1730. Du.

Virgine, Catherine. SQS May T Jly 1771 *Scarsdale*. M.

Virgo, Thomas. S s sheep Lent R 14 yrs Summer 1756. Bu.

Vergoe als Bergum, William. S for highway robbery Lent R 14 yrs Summer 1721. G.

Virtue, Thomas. SQS Jan TB Feb 1757. So.

Visage, George. S & T May 1736 *Patapsco*. L.

Visiter, Elizabeth wife of Firman. S s cloth at St. Peter Mancroft, Norwich, Summer 1767. Nf.

Vittals als Victuals, Elizabeth. S Aug 1773. De.

Vivian, William. S for Va Jly 1718. Co.

Vizard als Trull, John. S Lent TB May 1755. G.

Vizard, Nathaniel. S Apr T Sep 1737 *Pretty Patsy* to Md. M.

Vizard, Thomas. S Mar TB to Va Aug 1749. Wi.

Vogwell, George. TB to Va from QS 1771. De.

Voice, George. S for assisting escape from Hereford Gaol Summer 1769. He.

Vollard, Peter. R May TB Jun 1691. M.

Vosper, Richard. S Mar 1746. Co.

Vosse als Stephens, Jane. R for Barbados Sep 1677 & Jan 1679. L.

Vosse, Mary. R for Barbados or Jamaica for highway robbery Mar 1685. L.

Vosse, Morris (1685). *See* Furse.

Votier, Elizabeth (1727). *See* Huggins. L.

Votiere, Peter. S Feb T Apr 1735 *Patapsco* LC Annapolis Oct 1735. L.

Vowells, Mary. S & T Sep 1742 *Forward*. L.

Vowles, Michael. R 14 yrs Aug 1749. So.

Vye, Henry. S Aug T 14 yrs Oct 1726 *Forward*. L.

W

Wackett, Joseph. S & T Apr 1765 *Ann*. L.

Wadcase, Richard. S s gelding at West Wycombe & R 14 yrs Lent 1773. Bu.

Waddesley, John. S Dec 1754. L.

Waddilove, Mary. S for burning mansion house Summer 1714 R 14 yrs Summer 1721 T *Forward* Oct 1723. Y.

Waddingham, Edward. R for America Feb 1692. No.

Waddington, Alice. S & T Nov 1762 *Prince William*. L.

Waddington, John. R 14 yrs Summer 1721. Li.

Waddington, John. S Lent 1771. La.

Waddington, Ralph. R 14 yrs Summer 1758. Y.

Waddington, Richard of All Saints, Hertford. R for Barbados or Mar 1682. Ht.

Waddington, Robert. S Summer 1738. Y.

Waddington, Robert of Middleton, weaver. SQS for false pretences May 1770. La.

Wade als Dempier als Leviston als Nelson, Ann. S Dec 1762 T Mar 1763 *Neptune*. M.

Wade, Elinor. S & T Aug 1718 *Eagle* LC Charles Town Mar 1719. L.

Wade als Boucher, Elizabeth. S Aug T 14 yrs Sep 1727 *Forward* LC Rappahannock May 1728. L.

Wade, Elizabeth (1768). *See* Berry. La.

Wade, George (1727). *See* Ward.

Wade, George. S Summer 1744. Y.

Wade, Henry. S Aug T Sep 1725 *Forward* LC Annapolis Dec 1725. L.

Wade, Henry. S s sheep Summer 1752 R 14 yrs Lent 1753. Li.

Wade, John. R (Norfolk Circ) for America Jly 1663. X.

Wade, John. S Sep T Nov 1743 *George William*. M.

Wade, John (1747). *See* Ward. Do.

Wade, John. S Jan-Apr 1749. M.

Wade, John. S & T Nov 1762 *Prince William*. L.

Wade, Joseph (1756). *See* Williamson. Ch.

Wade, Joseph. S Apr T Jun 1768 *Tryal*. M.

Wade, Joseph. R Jan-Feb T 14 yrs Apr 1772 *Thornton*. M.

Wade als Taylor als Jackson, Margaret. R for America Aug 1715. M.

Wade, Margaret. S & T Sep 1764 *Justitia*. M.

Wade, Mary. S & T Aug 1718 *Eagle* LC Charles Town Mar 1719. L.

Wade, Michael of St. Olave, Southwark. SQS Jan T Apr 1770 *New Trial*. Sy.

Wade, Sarah wife of Solomon. S Feb-Apr 1746. M.

Wade, Sarah. S Dec 1772. M.

Wade, Sarah. S Jan-Feb 1774. M.

Wade, Thomasin. S Summer 1745. Sy.

Wade, William, aged 35, barber. S & T Oct 1720 *Gilbert* LC Md May 1721. M.

Wade als Williams, William. S Summer 1764. Mo.

Wadford, William. Rebel T 1685.

Wadham, Elizabeth. S Apr 1745. So.
Wadham, Richard. Rebel T 1685.
Wadhams, Richard. S s hen at Walsall Lent 1759. St.
Wadhams, William. S Mar TB to Va Apr 1771. Wi.
Wadley, Elizabeth of Romford. S Lent 1774. E.
Wadmen als Tue, Whitehill. R 14 yrs Aug 1739. So.
Wadsworth, James of Manchester. SQS Jly 1751. La.
Wadsworth, Thomas. S & T Apr 1733 *Patapsco* LC Annapolis Nov 1733. M.
Wadsworth, William. S Aug TB to Va Sep 1751. Le.
Wagg als Wagstaffe, Thomas of Doverdale. R for America Jly 1698. Wo.
Wagg, Thomas. S & T Oct 1730 *Forward* LC Potomack Jan 1731. M.
Wagger, Thomas. S Lent 1749. K.
Waggott, Thomas. Rebel T 1685.
Wagstaffe, Mary (1736). *See* Hanson. Db.
Wagstaffe, Thomas (1698). *See* Wagg. Wo.
Wagstaff, Thomas. S Oct T Nov 1728 *Forward* LC Rappahannock Jun 1729. M.
Wagstaff, William. S Aug T Sep 1727 *Forward* LC Rappahannock May 1728. L.
Waine. *See* Wayne.
Waines, Frances (1745). *See* Clarke. M.
Wainman als Swainman, Lawrence. T Oct 1726 *Forward*. Sy.
Wainscoate, George. S Sep T Nov 1743 *George William*. L.
Wainscott, Richard (1727). *See* Walley. M.
Wainwick, Thomas. S Apr-May T May 1744 *Justitia*. M.
Wainewright, Elizabeth of St. George, Southwark. R for Barbados or Jamaica Jly 1677. Sy.
Wainewright, George. S s sheep Lent R 14 yrs Summer 1754. Bd.
Wainwright, Esther. T Apr 1753 *Thames*. Sy.
Wainewright, Hester. R for Barbados Sep 1682. L.
Wainwright, John. S s at Condover Lent 1757. Sh.
Vainwright, John. SQS Apr T Jly 1772 *Tayloe*. M.
Wainwright, Thomas of Kings Cliffe. R for America Jly 1678. No.
Wainwright, William of Manchester, slater. SQS Oct 1766. La.
Waite, Andrew. R for Barbados or Jamaica Aug 1700. L.
Waite, Charles. SQS Jan TB Apr 1765. So.
Waight, Daniel. S Mar 1740. Ha.
Weight, Elizabeth. LC from *Forward* Annapolis Dec 1725. X.
Wayte als White, Gerrard. R for Barbados Aug 1664. L.
Waite, John. S Feb T Apr 1732 *Patapsco* LC Annapolis Oct 1732. L.
Waite, John. S s at Ducklington Lent 1736. O.
Waite, John. S s horse Summer 1739 R 14 yrs Lent 1740. Li.
Waite, John. S s cow Lent R 14 yrs Summer 1746. Y.
Wate, Jonathan (1673). *See* White. L.
Waite, Richard of St. George, Southwark. SQS Feb T May 1767 *Thornton*. Sy.
Waite, Robert of Long Hanborough. R for America Feb 1681. O.
Waite, Thomas. S Oct T Nov 1759 *Phoenix*. L.
Waite, Thomas. S s horse Summer 1767 R 14 yrs Summer 1768. Nl.
Wayte, Thomas. T 14 yrs Apr 1768 *Thornton*. Sy.

Waites, Samuel. S Apr 1756. So.

Waites, Thomas. S & R 14 yrs Aug 1767. Nl.

Whaits, Thomas. S s pigs at Weston Market Lent 1772. Su.

Wake, James. Rebel T 1685.

Wake als Demogg, William. R for Barbados or Jamaica Dec 1695 & Jan 1697. M.

Wakefield, James. S s at Cowley Summer 1723. G.

Wakefield, John. S Summer 1751 R 14 yrs Lent 1752. St.

Wakefield, Mary. S Dec 1727. M.

Wakefield, Richard of Tarrington. R for Barbados Mar 1663. He.

Wakefield, Samuel. T Nov 1741 *Sea Horse*. K.

Wakefield, Sarah. S Lent R 14 yrs Summer 1760 T *Atlas* from Bristol 1761. He.

Wakefield, Thomas. T Jun 1727 *Susanna*. K.

Wakefield, Thomas. R Summer 1773. Sx.

Wakeford, George of Dodington. R for Barbados or Jamaica Jun 1684. K.

Wakeham, Loveday. S Mar 1750. Co.

Wakeham, William. S Jly 1752. De.

Wakelyn, Daniel of Much Leighs. SQS Apr T Jun 1740 *Essex*. E.

Wakeling, Elizabeth. S Aug T Oct 1724 *Forward* LC Annapolis Jun 1725. M.

Wakeling, John of Camberwell. SQS & T 14 yrs Jan 1756 *Greyhound*. Sy.

Wakelin, John. S s sheep Lent R 14 yrs Summer 1757. Wa.

Wakeling, John, als Barnes, Thomas. S s asses at Hurley Lent 1770. Be.

Wakeling, John. T 14 yrs Dec 1771 *Justitia*. E.

Wakelinn, Robert of Chaddesley Corbett. R for America Feb 1690. Wo.

Wakelin, Thomas. S Sep T 14 yrs Oct 1722 *Forward* LC Annapolis Jun 1723. L.

Wakelings, Samuel. S Feb 1774. L.

Wakely, John. S Mar 1775. Ha.

Wakely, Sarah wife of Richard. S Jly 1758 TB to Va 1759. De.

Waker, Edward. SL & T Jan 1767 *Tryal*. Sy.

Wal....., John. PT Jan 1699. M.

Walbancke, John of Waltham Cross. R for Barbados or Jamaica Mar 1682. E.

Walbancke, John. PT Sep 1684 R Mar 1685. M.

Walbrook, Thomas. T Jun 1728 *Elizabeth*. K.

Walby, Elizabeth wife of William of Cheshunt. S Summer 1745. Ht.

Walcraft, Thomas, als Gardner, George. S s coat at St. Helen's Lent 1768. Be.

Walden, Anne (1722). *See* Merritt. M.

Waldon, Edward. S & T Apr 1769 *Tryal*. M.

Walden, James. S Lent 1773. E.

Walden, Susanna. SQS Feb T May 1767 *Thornton*. M.

Walden, William. S Jan-Feb T Apr 1753 *Thames*. M.

Walding als Rogers, John. R for highway robbery Lent 1772. Wa.

Waldron, Elizabeth. R 14 yrs Summer 1736. He.

Waldron, Elizabeth. S 14 yrs for receiving Jly 1753. Ha.

Waldrond, Grace. S Aug 1731 TB to Va. De.

Waldron, Joan (1748). *See* Pain. De.

Waldren, Lawrence. S Jly T Aug 1721 *Prince Royal* to Va. M.
Waldron, Mary. R for Barbados Dec 1667. M.
Wale. *See* Whale.
Wales, James. R May T for life Sep 1758 *Tryal* to Annapolis. M.
Walker, Alice. S Oct 1772. L.
Walker, Alice. S 14 yrs Jly 1774. L.
Walker, Andrew. Died on passage in *Rappahannock* 1726. X.
Walker, Anne. S Aug T Sep 1725 *Forward* LC Annapolis Dec 1725. M.
Walker, Ann. T Apr 1732 *Patapsco*. Sy.
Walker, Ann. S Dec 1733 T Jan 1734 *Caesar* LC Va Jly 1734. L.
Walker, Ann. S & T Sep 1767 *Justitia*. L.
Walker, Ann. S Lent T Apr 1772 *Thornton*. K.
Walker, Ann. S Dec 1775. M.
Walker, Atty als Hetty als Hester. S & T Dec 1740 *Vernon*. L.
Walker, Caleb. S Jly-Sep T Sep 1742 *Forward*. M.
Walker, Charles. S s oats & R 14 yrs Summer TB Aug 1758. Y.
Walker, Christopher. SQS Feb 1759. M.
Walker, Eleanor. S Jan T Feb 1733 *Smith* to Md or Va. M.
Walker, Eleanor (1769). *See* Morgan. M.
Walker, Elizabeth. S s horse Lent R 14 yrs Summer 1721 T *Forward* LC
    Annapolis Jun 1723. Be.
Walker, Elizabeth, aged 21, fair. S Jan T Feb 1723 *Jonathan* LC
    Annapolis Jly 1724. L.
Walker, Elizabeth. S Aug T Sep 1725 *Forward* LC Annapolis Dec
    1725. M.
Walker, Elizabeth (1735). *See* Jones. K.
Walker, Elizabeth. S s cloth at Evesham Lent 1745. Wo.
Walker, Elizabeth. S for murder of bastard child Lent R 14 yrs Summer
    1748. Wo.
Walker, Elizabeth (1749). See Oldham. Li.
Walker, Esther (1749). *See* Smith, Ann. La.
Walker, Francis. S & T Dec 1771 *Justitia*. M.
Walker, George. T Sep 1730 *Smith*. Ht.
Walker, George. S s handkerchief at St. Martin Ludgate May T Jun
    1768 *Tryal*. L.
Walker, George. S Summer T Oct 1770 *Rachael*. K.
Walker, George of Warrington. SQS Jan 1775. La.
Walker, George. S & R 14 yrs Lent 1775. Y.
Walker, Henry of Whitchurch. R for Barbados Jun 1692. Y.
Walker, Hugh. S & T Apr 1725 *Sukey* LC Annapolis Sep 1725. M.
Walker, Humphrey of Portsmouth. R for Barbados Feb 1683. Ha.
Walker, Isaac. S & T Dec 1752 *Greyhound*. M.
Walker, Isabell. S Lent 1731. Y.
Walker, Israel. S Feb T Mar 1758 *Dragon*. L.
Walker, James. S Norwich Summer 1764. Nf.
Walker, James. S s at St. Chad, Shrewsbury, Lent 1765. Sh.
Walker, James. SQS Feb T Apr 1768 *Thornton*. M.
Walker, James. S at Bristol Lent 1772. G.
Walker, John. S Jan 1627. M.
Walker, John of St. Olave, Southwark. R 10 yrs Lent 1655; to be
    transported by Thomas Vincent & Samuel Highland. Sy.

Walker, John. R for Barbados or Jamaica Mar 1685. M.

Walker, John of Lambourne. R for Barbados or Jamaica Jly 1712. E.

Walker, John. R s horse Jun 1730 (SP). Wo.

Walker, John. S Lent 1731. O.

Walker als Hatter, John. S Sep 1733 T Jan 1734 *Caesar* LC Va Jly 1734. M.

Walker, John. S May T Sep 1737 *Pretty Patsy* to Md. M.

Walker, John. S Dec 1737 T Jan 1738 *Dorsetshire*. L.

Walker, John. S s horse Summer 1738 R 14 yrs Lent 1739. No.

Walker, John. S Jly 1740. Ha.

Walker, John. S Jan-Apr 1748. M.

Walker, John. S s at Churchdown Summer TB Aug 1751. G.

Walker, John of St. Saviour, Southwark, tailor. SQS Jan T Apr 1753 *Thames*. Sy.

Walker, John. S Jun 1754. L.

Walker, John. T Jan 1756 *Greyhound*. K.

Walker, John. T Jun 1756 *Lyon*. K.

Walker als Frankland, John. S 14 yrs s linen yarn Lent 1763. La.

Walker, John. S Jun T Sep 1764 *Justitia*. M.

Walker, John. S Feb T Apr 1766 *Ann*. M.

Walker, John. S Oct 1766 T Jan 1767 *Tryal*. M.

Walker, John. S Sep T Dec 1767 *Neptune*. M.

Walker, John (1774). *See* Beeley. Y.

Walker, Joseph of Bitton. R for America Jly 1693. G.

Walker, Joseph. S May T Jun 1726 *Loyal Margaret* LC Annapolis Oct 1726. M.

Walker, Letitia. S Feb-Apr T May 1751 *Tryal*. M.

Walker, Mabell. S Jly T Dec 1735 *John* LC Annapolis Sep 1736. M.

Walker als Walters, Margaret. S & T Oct 1730 *Forward* LC Potomack Jan 1731. M.

Walker, Margaret. AT Lent 1737. Y.

Walker, Margaret. S Lent 1771. La.

Walker, Martha. S & T Jly 1771 *Scarsdale*. M.

Walker, Mary of Ashford Carbonell. R for America Jly 1686. Sh.

Walker, Mary. T Oct 1721 *William & John*. K.

Walker als Bouchier als Hitchman als Smith, Mary. S & T Jan 1722 *Gilbert* LC Annapolis Jly 1722. M.

Walker, Mary. LC from *Alexander* Annapolis Sep 1723. X.

Walker, Mary. S Feb T Mar 1729 *Patapsco* LC Annapolis Dec 1729. M.

Walker, Mary. S Mar 1740. So.

Walker als Johnson, Mary. S Jan-Apr 1748. M.

Walker als Sparrow, Mary. S Jun 1754. L.

Walker, Mary. S Lent R Summer 1759. Su.

Walker, Mary. S Feb 1773. L.

Walker, Meredith. S Lent R 14 yrs Summer TB Aug 1757. G.

Walker, Peter. S Apr T May 1752 *Lichfield*. L.

Walker, Philip of Bermondsey. R 10 yrs in plantations Feb 1656. Sy.

Walker, Priscilla. S May T Jun 1726 *Loyal Margaret* LC Md Oct 1726. M.

Walker, Richard. R for America Jly 1707. Wa.

Walker, Richard. T Sep 1730 *Smith*. K.

Walker, Richard. S May-Jly T Sep 1751 *Greyhound*. M.

Walker, Richard. S Sep-Oct T Dec 1752 *Greyhound*. M.

Walker, Richard. S for ripping lead from house Sep 1756. M.

Walker, Richard. S Lent 1763. K.

Walker als Weedon, Robert of Bermondsey. R for Barbados or Jamaica Jly 1674. Sy.

Walker, Robert of Denton. R for Barbados or Jamaica Mar 1694. La.

Walker, Robert. S & T Sep 1766 *Justitia*. M.

Walker, Robert. S Jan-Feb T 14 yrs Apr 177? *Thornton*. M.

Walker, Robert. R for life Dec 1773. M.

Walker, Samuel. S & T 14 yrs Dec 1734 *Caesar* LC Va Jly 1735. L.

Walker, Samuel. S Jan-May T Jun 1738 *Forward* to Md or Va. M.

Walker, Samuel of Gorton, weaver. SQS Apr 1769. La.

Walker, Sarah. S Oct T Nov 1762 *Prince William*. M.

Walker, Stephen, aged 35, fair. S Jan T Feb 1723 *Jonathan* LC Annapolis Jly 1724. L.

Walker, Thomas. PT Aug R Dec 1683. M.

Walker, Thomas. S Jly T Aug 1721 *Prince Royal* but died on passage. M.

Walker, Thomas (1741). *See* Watts. Nt.

Walker, Thomas. S Feb T Apr 1765 *Ann*. L.

Walker, Thomas. S Lent 1768. Bd.

Walker, Thomas (1771). *See* Watts. Nt.

Walker, Thomas. SQS Sep 1772. M.

Walker, Thomas. SQS Jan 1774. M.

Walker, Timothy. T 14 yrs Oct 1768 *Justitia*. E.

Walker, William. S s horse Summer 1720 R 14 yrs Summer 1721 T *Forward* LC Annapolis Jun 1723. Li.

Walker, William. S s horse Lent R 14 yrs Summer 1731. Db.

Walker, William (1749). See Oldham. Li.

Walker, William. S Apr T May 1750 *Lichfield*. L.

Walker, William. T Dec 1753 *Whiteing*. M.

Walker, William. S s at Yarm Summer TB Aug 1765. Y.

Walker, William. S s sheep & R 14 yrs Summer 1775. St.

Walker, William. R Jly 1775. Ha.

Walkey, Benjamin. S Jan-May T Jun 1738 *Forward* to Md or Va. M.

Walklin, Thomas. S May-Jly 1773. M.

Wall, Ann, spinster. S Jly T Sep 1757 *Thetis*. M.

Wall, Charles. S Oct 1772. L.

Wall, Charles. S Summer 1774. K.

Wall, Edward. S Summer 1757. Hu.

Wall, Francis. S for burglary Lent R Summer 1741 (SP). Wo.

Wall, George. S Oct T Dec 1769 *Justitia*. M.

Wall, George. S Apr 1774. M.

Wall, Jane. T May 1744 *Justitia*. Sy.

Wall, John. R Dec 1681 AT Jan 1682. M.

Wall, John. S s horse Lent R 14 yrs Summer 1722. St.

Wall, John. T Oct 1723 *Forward*. Sy.

Wall, John. TB Aug 1741. Db.

Wall, Luke. S Feb T Mar 1727 *Rappahannock* to Md. M.

Wall, Mary. S Aug T Sep 1725 *Forward* LC Annapolis Dec 1725. M.

Wall, Mary. S Sep T Oct 1744 *Susannah*. L.
Wall, Mary. S Summer 1747. Sy.
Wall, Mary. S Sep-Oct T Dec 1771 *Justitia*. M.
Wall, Patrick. R 14 yrs Mar 1750. Ha.
Wall, Richard. S s at Withington Summer 1735. He.
Wall, Richard. S s gelding at Leominster Lent 1749. He.
Wall, Thomas. T May 1737 *Forward*. Sy.
Wall, William. SQS Jly 1730. Db.
Wall, William. S for ripping lead from Magdalene College Lent 1746. O.
Wallace. *See* Wallis.
Walldeck, Joseph. R Jun T 14 yrs Dec 1769 *Justitia*. M.
Wallen. *See* Walling.
Waller, Edward. S Summer 1755 R 14 yrs Lent 1756. Hu.
Waller, Elizabeth. T Aug 1752 *Tryal*. Sy.
Waller, Elizabeth. S Feb T Apr 1770 *New Trial*. M.
Waller, Francis. R for Barbados or Jamaica Dec 1699 & Aug 1700. M.
Waller, Jane. S Jly 1750. L.
Waller, John. S May 1728 TB to New York with Samuel Waller of
    Stepney, mariner. L.
Waller, John. S Feb T for life Mar 1750 *Tryal*. L.
Waller, Mary (1723). *See* Jackson. M.
Waller, Mary (1742). *See* Scott. L.
Waller, Mary (1761). *See* Green. M.
Waller, Peter. S Mar 1756. Ha.
Waller, Thomas of Murston. R for Barbados or Jamaica Jly 1710. K.
Waller, William. T Apr 1770 *New Trial*. K.
Wallett, Charles. S s at Stapleton Summer 1728. Sh.
Wallexelson, Thomas. S & T Oct 1729 *Forward* LC Va Jun 1730. L.
Wally, Mary. S Jan T Feb 1719 *Worcester* LC Annapolis Jun 1719. L.
Walley als Wainscott, Richard. S Dec 1727. M.
Wallford, Lucas. S s clothing at Wellington Lent 1728. He.
Wallford, Mary of St. Martin in Fields, spinster. S s sheets Oct 1740 T
    Jan 1741 *Harpooner* to Rappahannock. M.
Walford, Thomas. S Jun T Sep 1767 *Justitia*. L.
Walford, William. S Mar TB to Va Apr 1768. Wi.
Wallgrove, Roger of St. Ann, Westminster. S s household goods Oct
    1740 T Jan 1741 *Harpooner* to Rappahannock. M.
Wallin, Ann. R for Barbados Jun 1671. L.
Wallen, John. S Aug 1720. So.
Wallin, John. S Jan T Mar 1764 *Tryal*. L.
Walling, Peter of Charlton Mackrell. R for Barbados Jly 1688. So.
Wallington, Ann. S Feb 1761. M.
Wallington, William. S s at Bicester Summer 1733 AT Summer 1736. O.
Wallis, Ann. S Summer 1756. Sy.
Wallis, Edward. R for America Feb 1700. Li.
Wallis, Eleanor. S Oct T Nov 1759 *Phoenix*. M.
Wallis, Francis. T Jan 1741 *Vernon*. E.
Wallis, George. S & T Apr 1765 *Ann*. L.
Wallace, George. S Dec 1766 T Jan 1767 *Tryal*. M.
Wallis als Palmer, Hannah. S & T Oct 1732 *Caesar* to Va. M.
Wallace, Hendry. S Mar 1762. De.

Wallis, Henry. S Sep T Dec 1763 *Neptune*. M.

Wallis, James. S Jun T 14 yrs Aug 1769 *Douglas*. L.

Wallis, Jane wife of John *(qv)*. SQS Jly 1768. La.

Wallis, John. R for Barbados Feb 1664 (SP). M.

Wallis, John. S Jly 1730. Wi.

Wallis, John. S for obstructing Customs officers Summer 1737. Nf.

Wallis, John, als Black Jack. S Apr-May T May 1741
Catherine & Elizabeth. M.

Wallis, John. S Jly 1741 TB to Md Apr 1742. Le.

Wallis, John. S & T Jan 1764 *Tryal*. M.

Wallis, John of Ormskirk. SQS Jly 1768. La.

Wallace, Lawrence. S & T Jly 1771 *Scarsdale*. L.

Wallis, Margaret. SQS Apr 1773. M.

Wallis, Peter. SQS Jan 1754. M.

Wallis, Richard (1738). *See* Ignell. Nf.

Wallis, Robert. R for Barbados Jun 1670. M.

Wallis, Robert. PT Jan 1675. M.

Wallis, Robert. S & T Jly 1772 *Tayloe*. M.

Wallis, Samuel. S & TB Apr 1742. G.

Wallis, Thomas of Marlborough, gent. R (Oxford Circ) for Barbados
Oct 1663. Wi.

Wallis, Thomas Jr. of Great Coggeshall. R for Barbados or Jamaica Jly
1710. E.

Wallis, Thomas. S Sep 1737. M.

Wallis, Thomas. S Sep T for life Oct 1750 *Rachael*. M.

Wallis, Thomas. S Mar 1763. Co.

Wallis, William als Husband. S Summer T Oct 1723 *Forward* from
London. Y.

Wallis, William. T Jly 1724 *Robert* LC Md Jun 1725. Sy.

Wallis, William. SQS Dec 1774. M.

Wallows, Hannah. S Lent 1742. St.

Walls, Dorothy wife of John. S Lent 1766. Wa.

Walls, Dorothy. S s at Monkwearmouth Summer 1772. Du.

Walls, Mary (1765). *See* Jones. Wa.

Wamsley, John. T Oct 1722 *Forward* LC Annapolis Jun 1723. K.

Walmsley, Philip. S Oct T Dec 1770 *Justitia*. M.

Walmsley als Lucas als Johnson, Sarah. S Jan T Feb 1733 *Smith*. M.

Walmsley, William (1729). *See* Boddy. Y.

Walpole, Edward. T Sep 1767 *Justitia*. Ht.

Walpole, John of Dartford. S Summer T Oct 1739
Duke of Cumberland. K.

Walpole, John. S Summer 1757 R for life Lent 1758. Nf.

Walpole, William. S s hogs Lent 1767. Nf.

Walsh, Edward. SQS for perjury Jly 1773. M.

Walsh, Mary wife of Richard of Manchester (but now a soldier). SQS
Aug 1762. La.

Walsh, Stephen. Rebel T 1685.

Walsham, Robert. T Apr 1742 *Bond*. Sy.

Walsingham, Benjamin. S s harness at Shottisham Lent 1775; Sarah
Walsingham, widow, acquitted. Su.

Walsingham, John. S s harness at Shottisham Lent 1775. Su.

Walsom, Isaac. S Oct 1724. L.
Walsom, Thomas. R 14 yrs Jly 1774. M.
Walter, Ann. S s at Hartlebury Lent 1752. Wo.
Walter, Elizabeth. T May 1737 *Forward*. Sx.
Walter, Hannah (1766). *See* Gregory. L.
Walter, James of Culmersdon. R for Barbados Mar 1686. So.
Walter, John. Rebel T 1685.
Walter, John. S & T Dec 1731 *Forward*. L.
Walter, John. S Summer 1748 T Jan 1749 *Laura*. K.
Walter, Mary (1725). *See* Gray. Sy.
Walter, Mary. S Mar TB Sep 1728. Wi.
Walter, Richard. S s wheat at Holmer Lent 1767. He.
Walter, Samuel, aged 27, dark, husbandman. S Feb T May 1720 *Gilbert* LC Annapolis May 1721. L.
Walter, Thomas. Rebel T 1685.
Walter als Wettie, Thomas. S Feb T Mar 1750 *Tryal*. M.
Walter, Thomas. T May 1751 *Tryal*. Sy.
Walter, William. Rebel T 1685.
Walters, Ann. R for Barbados or Jamaica May AT Jly 1697. M.
Walters, Edward. R 14 yrs Aug 1740 TB to Va. De.
Walters, Elizabeth. S Sep 1754. L.
Walters, Elizabeth. S & T Sep 1765 *Justitia*. M.
Walters, Isaac. R 14 yrs Jly 1724. De.
Walters, James. S Feb T Apr 1734 *Patapsco*. L.
Walters, John. S s horse Lent R 14 yrs Summer 1733; then given free pardon. St.
Walters, John. S May T Sep 1766 *Justitia*. M.
Walters, John. SQS May T Jly 1771 *Scarsdale*. M.
Walters, John. R Jly 1773. M.
Walters, Margaret (1730). *See* Walker. M.
Walters als Willson, Martha. R for Barbados or Jamaica Jan 1692. M.
Walters, Philip. S Feb T Mar 1730 *Patapsco* LC Annapolis Sep 1730. M.
Walters, Redfern. SQS & T Sep 1765 *Justitia*. M.
Walters, Richard. S Mar 1733. Co.
Walters, Thomas. R for Barbados Jly 1674. M.
Walterton, James. LC from *Sukey* Annapolis Sep 1725. X.
Walthew, Jane. S Oct 1751-Jan 1752. M.
Walton, Alice wife of James of Little Lever. SQS Aug 1765. La.
Walton, Anne. R for Jamaica Feb 1665. M.
Walton, Charles. S s cows Lent 1725 AT to Summer 1727. Y.
Walton, Edward. S Jan-Jun T Jun 1728 *Elizabeth* LC Potomack Aug 1729. M.
Walton, Elizabeth. R for Barbados or Jamaica May 1691. M.
Walton, Elizabeth (1735). *See* Tooley. M.
Walton, Esther (1749). *See* Smith, Ann. La.
Walton, George. S Lent 1755. Y.
Walton, Joseph. S for highway robbery Lent R 14 yrs Summer 1738. Ru.
Walton, Joseph. S May-Jly 1746. M.
Walton, Joseph of Blackburn. SQS Apr 1774. La.
Walton, Margaret. S & T Jan 1767 *Tryal*. L.
Walton, Mary. T Apr 1735 *Patapsco*. Sy.

Walton, Matthew. R Dec 1699 & Aug 1700. M.

Walton, Nicholas of Long Sutton. R for America Jly 1673. Li.

Walton, Roger. S & T 14 yrs Jan 1722 *Gilbert* LC Annapolis Jly 1722. M.

Walton, Samuel. R 14 yrs Summer 1753. Y.

Walton, Sara. S Apr T May 1718. L.

Walton, Susannah wife of Aaron. S Jly T Oct 1741 *Sea Horse* to Va. M.

Walton, Thomas of Wortley. R for Barbados Jly 1705. Y.

Walton, Thomas. S s boars at Alrewas Summer 1723. St.

Walton, Thomas. S & R 14 yrs Summer 1742. Bd.

Walton, Thomas. AT Lent 1766. Y.

Walton, William. S for false impersonation Jan 1627. M.

Wandless, Thomas. S City for ripping lead from building Summer 1773. Nl.

Wandon als Bannister, Richard. S Jun T Oct 1744 *Susannah*. M.

Wanklin or Vauchlin, Francis, aged 16, dark. S Jan T Feb 1723 *Jonathan* LC Annapolis Jly 1724. L.

Wanless als Newby, Elizabeth. S Dec 1749-Jan 1750 T Mar 1750 *Tryal*. M.

Wanless, Margaret. AT Summer 1764 & 1765. Du.

Wanne, Elizabeth. R for Barbados or Jamaica Dec 1693. L.

Wann, Richard. T Apr 1743 *Justitia*. K.

Wannop, James. SQS s plates at Whitehaven Summer 1764. Du.

Wapshott, James. SQS Apr 1774. M.

Wapshott, Jane. R for Barbados Jly 1674. L.

Warburton, Edye. S Apr T May 1718. L.

Warburton, John of Stone. R for Barbados Jly 1664. St.

Warburton als Lathom, Margaret. S Lent 1745. La.

Warburton, Mary. S s at Stanton Summer 1726. Sh.

Warburton, Thomas. S Lent R 14 yrs Summer 1767. St.

Warburton, William. S s tools at Upton upon Severn Lent 1765. Wo.

Warburton, William. S Aug 1772. So.

Warbey, Edward. T 14 yrs Dec 1758 *The Brothers*. Ht.

Warby, James. R Jly 1773. M.

Ward, Ann. R for Barbados Jun 1665. L.

Ward, Ann. S s satin Feb T Apr 1735 *Patapsco* LC Annapolis Oct 1735. M.

Ward, Ann. T Aug 1741 *Sally*. Sy.

Ward, Ann. S & T Sep 1757 *Thetis*. M.

Ward, Ann. S Jly 1760. M.

Ward, Ann. S Oct T Dec 1771 *Justitia*. L.

Ward, Bridget. PT Apr R Oct 1673. M.

Ward als Bullocke, Katherine. R Oct TB Nov 1662. L.

Ward, Catherine. S & T Oct 1722 *Forward*. L.

Ward, Catherine (1733). *See* Vert. L.

Ward, Catherine. S Nov T Dec 1752 *Greyhound*. L.

Ward, Celia. S & T Sep 1764 *Justitia*. L.

Ward, Christopher. S Feb-Apr T May 1751 *Tryal*. M.

Ward, Dorothy. SQS Jun T Aug 1755 *Tryal*. M.

Ward, Edmund. S Lent 1765. No.

Ward, Edward. R Lent 1755. Ht.

Ward, Edward. SWK 5 yrs as incorrigible rogue Apr 1763. K.

Ward, Edward. S Oct 1764 T 14 yrs Jan 1765 *Tryal*. M.
Ward als Butler, Elizabeth. S Jun-Dec 1738 T Jan 1739 *Dorsetshire* to Va. M.
Ward, Elizabeth. S Jan 1740. L.
Ward, Elizabeth. S Lent 1749. Sy.
Ward, Elizabeth. T Sep 1755 *Tryal*. M.
Ward als English, Elizabeth. S Jly 1756. M.
Ward, Elizabeth wife of Thomas. S Sep-Oct T Dec 1771 *Justitia*. M.
Ward, Esther. AT from QS Lent 1726 T *Loyal Margaret* LC Md Oct 1726. St.
Ward, Francis. S Summer 1755 R 14 yrs Lent T Jun 1756 *Lyon*. E.
Ward, Francis. S for highway robbery Lent R 14 yrs Summer 1765. Nt.
Ward, Francis. S s sheep at Clenchwarton Summer 1767 R 14 yrs Lent 1768. Nf.
Ward als Wade, George. S Summer 1727 AT to Summer 1728. Y.
Ward, George. S for assault & robbery Lent 1752. Bd.
Ward, George. S Summer 1764 R 14 yrs Lent 1765. He.
Ward, Henry of Nottingham. R for America Jly 1682. Nt.
Ward, Isaac (1687). *See* Vaughan. M.
Ward, James. S s fustian Summer 1749 R 14 yrs Lent 1750. La.
Ward, James. S Jan T Mar 1750 *Tryal*. L.
Ward, James. R for life Jly 1763. M.
Ward, James. S s sheep & R 14 yrs Lent 1771. Y.
Ward, Job. R 14 yrs Jly 1738. Ha.
Ward, John, aged 30. R for Barbados Feb 1664. L.
Ward, John. R for Jamaica Mar 1665. L.
Ward, John. R & TB for Barbados Oct 1667. L.
Ward, John. T Oct 1724 *Forward* LC Md Jun 1725. K.
Ward, John. S May T Jun 1727 *Susanna* to Va. M.
Ward, John. TB to Md Aug 1729. Db.
Ward, John. T Dec 1731 *Forward*. Sy.
Ward, John. S Mar TB to Md Apr 1741. Le.
Ward, John. S & TB Jly 1742. G.
Ward, John. S s horse at Aldridge Lent R 14 yrs Summer 1744. St.
Ward als Wade, John. R 14 yrs Aug 1747. Do.
Ward, John. S Apr 1748. L.
Ward, John. S Feb 1754. M.
Ward, John. S Lent 1755. Wo.
Ward, John. S s linen bag Lent TB May 1755. G.
Ward, John. S Lent T May 1755 *Rose*. E.
Ward, John. S Lent 1758. Le.
Ward, John. S s at Bitton Summer 1759. G.
Ward, John. S s at Leeds Lent 1767. Y.
Ward, John. S 14 yrs s linen yarn Summer 1768. Su.
Ward, John. S & T Jan 1769 *Thornton*. M.
Ward, John. S Nov T Dec 1770 *Justitia*. L.
Ward, John (1772). *See* Ward, William. M.
Ward, John. S Dec 1773. M.
Ward, John. S May-Jly 1774. M.
Ward, John Moor. S Lent 1768 R 14 yrs Summer 1770. G.
Ward als Manners, Joseph of Hagnaby. R for America Feb 1681. Li.

Ward, Joseph. S Mar 1730. De.
Ward, Joseph. S May T Nov 1743 *George William*. M.
Ward, Joseph. S Feb T Apr 1769 *Tryal*. M.
Ward, Joseph. S May T Jly 1771 *Scarsdale*. L.
Ward, Joseph of Greasley. SQS s fowl Jan 1775. Nt.
Ward, Luke. S Jly-Dec 1747. M.
Ward, Margaret. S Oct 1773. L.
Ward, Mary (1699). *See* Bignall. Sy.
Ward, Mary wife of John of Little Bookham. R for Barbados or Jamaica
   Jly 1702. Sy.
Ward, Mary (1726). *See* Boswell. M.
Ward, Mary. S Oct 1737 T Jan 1738 *Dorsetshire* to Va. M.
Ward, Mary, als Holmes, Hannah. S Feb T Apr 1759 *Thetis*. M.
Ward, Mary. S Lent TB Apr 1759. Db.
Ward, Mary. S Dec 1764 T Jan 1765 *Tryal*. M.
Ward, Mary wife of William. S s at St. Michael, Oxford, Summer
   1769. O.
Ward, Mary (1770). *See* Whitely. M.
Ward, Mathew. S Oct T Nov 1728 *Forward* LC Rappahannock Jun
   1729. M.
Ward, Michael. S & T Oct 1729 *Forward* LC Va Jun 1730. M.
Ward, Patrick. T Sep 1742 *Forward*. E.
Ward, Patrick. S Jan-Feb 1775. M.
Ward, Richard. S s horse Lent R 14 yrs Summer 1722. No.
Ward, Richard, aged 22, fair, husbandman. LC from *Jonathan* Md Jly
   1724. X.
Ward, Richard. S s ducks at Banbury Lent 1760. O.
Warde, Robert of Abbots Bickington. R for Barbados Jly 1672. De.
Ward, Robert. T Oct 1721 *William & John*. Ht.
Ward, Robert. S Jan-Apr 1749. M.
Ward, Robert of Croydon. SQS May T Jun 1764 *Dolphin*. Sy.
Ward, Samuel. S Mar TB to Va Apr 1751. Wi.
Ward, Samuel. S Lent 1757. Y.
Ward, Samuel. SQS Jly 1774. M.
Ward, Samuel. S Jly 1775. M.
Ward, Sara. S Aug T Sep 1718 *Eagle* LC Charles Town Mar
   1719. L.
Ward, Sara. S Sep T Oct 1719 *Susannah & Sarah* LC Annapolis Apr
   1720. L.
Ward, Sarah. R 14 yrs Jly 1755. Ha.
Ward, Thomas. R for Barbados Jun 1665. L.
Ward, Thomas. R for Barbados Dec 1670. M.
Ward als Wyatt, Thomas. R for Barbados or Jamaica Mar 1688. L.
Ward, Thomas. SQS Mar TB Aug 1720 to be shipped to Md from
   Liverpool. Db.
Ward, Thomas. S & T Dec 1731 *Forward* to Md or Va. M.
Ward, Thomas of Bexhill. S for armed smuggling Summer T Oct 1739
   Duke of Cumberland. Sx.
Ward, Thomas. T 14 yrs Sep 1767 *Justitia*. E.
Ward, Thomas. SW & T Apr 1770 *New Trial*. M.
Ward, Thomas. S Sep-Oct T 14 yrs Dec 1771 *Justitia*. M.

Ward als Parker, Thomas. S Jan-Feb T Apr 1772 *Thornton*. M.
Ward, Thomas. S Jan-Feb 1775. M.
Ward, William. R for Barbados Sep TB Oct 1669. L.
Ward, William of Thorne. R for Barbados Jly 1671. Y.
Ward, William of Plymouth. R for Barbados Dec 1686. De.
Ward, William of Barham. R for Barbados or Jamaica Jly 1705. K.
Ward, William. S Aug T Sep 1718 *Eagle* but died on passage. L.
Ward, William. S & T Oct 1722 *Forward* to Md. M.
Ward, William. S Jan T Feb 1726 *Supply* LC Annapolis May 1726. L.
Ward, William. S s horse Lent R 14 yrs Summer 1727 T *Elizabeth* LC
    Potomack Aug 1729. Be.
Ward, William. S Oct T Nov 1728 *Forward* LC Rappahannock Jun
    1729. M.
Ward, William. R 14 yrs Apr 1747. De.
Ward, William. S s ducks at Banbury Lent 1760. O.
Ward, William. S Apr 1763. M.
Ward, William. S Lent R 14 yrs Summer 1766. Wa.
Ward, William. T 14 yrs Jun 1768 *Tryal*. Sy.
Ward, William. S & T Jan 1769 *Thornton*. M.
Ward, William als John. S Jan-Feb T Apr 1772 *Thornton*. M.
Ward, William of Lancaster. SQS Jly 1772. La.
Ward, William. S Oct 1774. L.
Wardell. *See* Wardle.
Warden, Arthur. S Feb 1775. L.
Warden, Elizabeth. R Mar 1770. Ha.
Warden, James. S May T Aug 1769 *Douglas*. M.
Worden, John. S Mar 1751. De.
Wardin, John. S Feb T Apr 1769 *Tryal*. M.
Warden, Richard Morse. S Lent 1763. Sy.
Warden, Thomas. S s mare Lent R 14 yrs Summer 1725 but died on
    passage in *Sukey*. Hu.
Warden, William. S Feb-Apr 1746. M.
Warden, William. S Lent 1763. Wa.
Wardens, James. S Dec 1772. M.
Warder, Mark. S s horse & R 14 yrs Summer 1772. Be.
Warder, Willoughby. S Jly 1741. Ha.
Wardle als Wardell, Hannah. S Summer 1775. Y.
Wardell, Leonard. S Apr 1774. M.
Wardle als Wardell, Richard Sr. S Summer 1775. Y.
Wardle, William. R for America Jun 1684. Db.
Wardley, Francis. S 14 yrs May 1760. M.
Wardley, John. S s mare & R 14 yrs Lent 1770. Nt.
Wardlow, William. S s coat Feb T Apr 1735 *Patapsco* LC Md Oct
    1735. M.
Wardrill, Francis. S Lent 1764. Nt.
Ware, Agnes (1775). *See* Christie. M.
Ware, Edward. S Jan 1757. L.
Ware, James. S Aug 1742. So.
Ware, John. S Lent T Jun 1756 *Lyon*. K.
Ware, Robert. SQS May T Jun 1768 *Tryal*. M.
Wear, Samuel. T May 1751 *Tryal*. K.

Ware, Susanna. S & T Oct 1722 *Forward*. L.

Ware, Thomas. S Mar 1750 TB to Va. De.

Ware, William of Clerkenwell. R for America Aug 1713. M.

Ware, William. S Feb T Mar 1730 *Patapsco* LC Annapolis Sep 1730. L.

Wareham, William. S & R 14 yrs Lent 1764. Ch.

Warfield, John (1677). *See* Barfield. So.

Waring, Ann. T Apr 1742 *Bond*. Bu.

Waring, Ann. S Jly 1748. L.

Wareing, John. S for highway robbery Summer 1756 R 14 yrs Lent 1757. La.

Wareing, William of Cambridge. R for America Jly 1703. Ca.

Warman, Margaret. S s at East Hendred Lent 1728. Be.

Warman, Thomas. S & T Aug 1718 *Eagle* but died on passage. L.

Warminger, James. S & T Jan 1722 *Gilbert* LC Annapolis Jly 1722. L.

Worn, Edward. S & T Jly 1770 *Scarsdale*. M.

Warne, James. R 14 yrs Mar 1750. Co.

Warne als Trethewey, John. S Aug 1753. Co.

Warn, Richard. T Aug 1752 *Tryal*. E.

Warner, Daniel. S Oct T Nov 1728 *Forward* LC Rappahannock Jun 1729. L.

Warner, Daniel. S s wool at Benson Lent 1753. O.

Warner, Edmund (1773). *See* Mayhew. Be.

Warner, Edward. T Nov 1728 *Forward*. Bu.

Warner, Elizabeth. R Dec 1681 AT Jan 1682. M.

Warner, Elizabeth. S Aug T Sep 1725 *Forward* LC Annapolis Dec 1725. L.

Warner, Elizabeth. S Sep T Dec 1770 *Justitia*. M.

Warner, John. T 14 yrs Aug 1752 *Tryal*. K.

Warner, John. S & T Apr 1753 *Thames*. L.

Warner, John. S Feb 1761. M.

Warner, John. R 14 yrs Mar 1772. So.

Warner, Joseph of Leighton Buzzard. R for Barbados Mar 1679. Bd.

Warner, Joseph of Kedington. R for America Feb 1687. Su.

Warner, Michael of Streatham. SQS Oct 1754; found at large & S to hang Lent 1755. Sy.

Warner, Richard. R for Barbados Jun 1663. M.

Warner, Richard. S for life Dec 1746. L.

Warner, Simon. R from QS s horse Summer 1722. No.

Warner, Stephen. S Summer R for Barbados Aug 1663. E.

Warner, Thomas. S Dec 1753-Jan 1754. M.

Warner, Thomas. S Sep T Dec 1767 *Neptune*. L.

Warner, William. S for killing deer in enclosed park Summer 1730 R 14 yrs Lent TB to Va Apr 1731. Le.

Warner, William. S Apr 1737. M.

Warner, William. S Norwich Summer 1749. Nf.

Warner, William of Bermondsey. S Summer T Oct 1750 *Rachael*. Sy.

Warner, William. S Lent T Jun 1756 *Lyon*. E.

Warner, William. T 14 yrs Apr 1768 *Thornton*. Ht.

Warnum, John. R for Barbados Apr TB Oct 1669. M.

Warr, Ann. S Summer 1757 R 14 yrs Lent 1758. He.

War, Betty (1753). *See* Popple. Do.

Warr, Edith. S Aug 1753. Do.

Warr, Jeremiah. S Aug 1752. So.

Warr, John. S Aug 1775. So.

Warren, Alexander. S Oct T Nov 1725 *Rappahannock* LC Rappahannock Apr 1726. M.

Warren, Ann (1749 & 1750). *See* Wilson. M.

Warren, Ann. S Jan 1767. M.

Warren, Anthony. T Jan 1738 *Dorsetshire*. Sy.

Warren, Birtle. S Jan-Feb 1773. M.

Warren, Catherine wife of John. S Jan T Feb 1733 *Smith* to Md or Va. M.

Warrin, Catherine of Clerkenwell, spinster. S s shirts Sep 1740 T Jan 1741 *Harpooner* to Rappahannock. M.

Warren, Charles. TB to Va from QS 1765. De.

Warren, Francis. S Mar 1742. De.

Warren, George. Rebel T 1685.

Warren, George. S for burglary Lent R Summer 1741 (SP). Su.

Warren, Jacob. S Mar 1763. So.

Warren, James. T Apr 1769 *Tryal*. E.

Warren, Jane. S Lent R 14 yrs Summer 1734. G.

Warren, Jasper. S Jly-Oct 1740 T Jan 1741 *Harpooner* to Rappahannock. M.

Warren, John. Rebel T 1685.

Warren, John. S Jly 1725. Do.

Warren, John. T May 1736 *Patapsco*. Sy.

Warren, John. T Apr 1739 *Forward*. E.

Warren, John. R 14 yrs Jly 1752. De.

Warren, John of Buttsbury. SQS Jan 1754. E.

Warren, John. R 14 yrs Aug 1764. So.

Warren, John. S Jan-Feb 1774. M.

Warren, John. S s sheep & R 14 yrs Summer TB to Va Aug 1774. Le.

Warren, Joseph. Rebel T 1685.

Warren, Joseph. S Lent 1753. Ca.

Warren, Margaret. S Jly 1741. De.

Warren, Margaret. S Summer 1747. Sy.

Warren, Nicholas. Rebel T 1685.

Warren, Peter. T Jly 1724 *Robert* LC Md Jun 1725. Sy.

Warren, Robert. S Aug 1734. So.

Warren, Susanna. S Jan T Feb 1733 *Smith* to Md or Va. M.

Warren, Susanna of Great Oakley, chapwoman. SQS Jly 1749. E.

Warren, Thomas. TB to Va from QS 1743. De.

Warren, Thomas. SQS Sep T Dec 1771 *Justitia*. M.

Warren, William. Rebel T 1685.

Warren, William. S Mar 1741. Do.

Warren, William Jr. R Mar 1773. Ha.

Warriker, Abraham. S Summer 1755 R 14 yrs Summer 1756. E.

Warrecker, William. R & T for life Apr 1770 *New Trial*. M.

Warriner, Edmund. S s from warehouse Summer 1769 R 14 yrs Lent 1770. Wa.

Warrington, Elizabeth. S Feb T Mar 1764 *Tryal*. M.

Warrington, Mary. S Aug 1763. L.

Warrington, William. R for Barbados Jan 1693. M.
Warrington, William. S Sep-Oct 1774. M.
Warsdale, Francis. S & T Jly 1772 *Tayloe*. L.
Warsdail, George. S s horse Lent R 14 yrs Summer 1726. Li.
Warsup, Samuel. S s sheep Lent R 14 yrs Summer 1753. Nt.
Warsop, William. S Lent 1760. Nt.
Warsop, William. S Lent 1761. Nl.
Wartell, Francis. SQS Sep T Dec 1753 *Whiteing*. M.
Warwick, Christopher. S May-Jly 1773. M.
Warwick, Edward. S Oct T Nov 1728 *Forward* LC Rappahannock Jun
  1729. M.
Warwick, James. SQS Dec 1768 T Jan 1769 *Thornton*. M.
Warwick, Joseph (1737). *See* Plumsey, William. Ha.
Warwick, Richard. S Jan T 14 yrs Feb 1744 *Neptune* to Md. M.
Warwick, Richard. S Mar 1745. Ha.
Warwick, Thomas. S 14 yrs Jan 1726. M.
Warwick, Thomas. SQS Jly T Sep 1767 *Justitia*. M.
Warwick, William. S Mar 1751. Ha.
Wash, James. T Nov 1741 *Sea Horse*. E.
Washfield, James. S May T Jly 1723 *Alexander* LC Annapolis Sep
  1723. L.
Washford, Mary. T Oct 1738 *Genoa*. Sy.
Washington, Philip of Honiton. R for Barbados Jly 1695. De.
Washington, Richard. S & T 14 yrs Sep 1718 *Eagle*. L.
Waskett, Ann (1740). *See* Ingersole. L.
Waskett, Mary Jr. T Apr 1759 *Thetis*. E.
Waskett, William. T Apr 1759 *Thetis*. E.
Wass, George of Osbaldwick. SQS Thirsk s at Ampleforth Oct 1735 TB
  Aug 1736. Y.
Wast, Susannah. S Norwich Summer 1755. Nf.
Wastfield, John (1677). *See* Barfield. So.
Wateman, Edward. S Dec 1736. L.
Water, Thomas of Lower Kemeys. R for America Jly 1675. Mo.
Watercombe, Thomas of St. George, Southwark. R for Barbados or
  Jamaica Jly 1702. Sy.
Waterer als Waters, John Jr. T Apr 1735 *Patapsco*. Sy.
Waterfall, John of Derby. R for America Jly 1682. Db.
Waterfall, Peter of Derby. R for America Jly 1682. Db.
Waterhouse, Elizabeth. S Jly 1773. L.
Waterhouse, John. T Summer 1739. Y.
Waterhouse, Thomas. AT Lent T Oct 1723 *Forward* to Va from
  London. Y.
Wateridge, Nathaniel of Hursley. R for Barbados Feb 1665. Ha.
Waterland, Thomas of New Sarum. R for Barbados Sep 1665. Wi.
Waterman, John of Good Easter. SQS Oct 1737 T Jun 1738 *Forward*. E.
Waterman, Laurence of Stanwell. R for America Aug 1713. M.
Waterman, Michael. T Dec 1763 *Neptune*. K.
Waters, Abel (1766). *See* Jennings. K.
Waters als Robinson, Catherine. S & T Oct 1730 LC Potomack Jan
  1731. M.
Waters, Catherine. S May-Jly 1773. M.

Waters, Elizabeth. S Sep 1756. M.

Waters, Holden. T Apr 1735 *Patapsco*. K.

Waters als Bryant, James. R 14 yrs Aug 1721. So.

Waters, James. S Dec 1737 T Jan 1738 *Dorsetshire*. L.

Waters, James (1754). *See* Jarvis. Nf.

Waters, John. R for Barbados or Jamaica Dec 1698. M.

Waters, John (1735). *See* Waterer. Sy.

Waters, John. S Jly-Sep T Oct 1739 *Duke of Cumberland* to Va. M.

Waters, John. S May T Jun 1768 *Tryal*. M.

Waters, John. R & T 14 yrs Jly 1772 *Tayloe*. M.

Waters, Joseph. S Lent R 14 yrs Summer 1742. Wo.

Waters, Joseph. S Lent 1768. Bd.

Waters, Leonard of Limpsfield. SQS Jly T Sep 1765 *Justitia*. Sy.

Waters, Margaret (1729). *See* Mumford. M.

Waters, Martha. S & T Sep 1751 *Greyhound*. L.

Waters als Pynes als Gibbons, Mary. R for Barbados or Jamaica May
    AT Jly 1697. M.

Waters, Mary. S Sep T Oct 1744 *Susannah*. M.

Waters, Moses. S May T Aug 1769 *Douglas*. M.

Waters, Richard. S Lent R 14 yrs Summer 1747. Ht.

Waters, Sarah. S Feb T Mar 1764 *Tryal*. M.

Waters, Thomas. S Jan-May T Jun 1738 *Forward* to Md or Va. M.

Waters, Thomas. S Feb 1754. L.

Waters, Thomas. SQS Warminster Jly TB Aug 1754. Wi.

Waters, Thomas. S Apr 1763. L.

Waters, Thomas. S May-Jly 1774. M.

Waters, William. S Jan T Mar 1743 *Justitia*. L.

Waters, William. S Lent 1761. Su.

Waters, William. R Apr 1773. M.

Watkin, James. S & T Dec 1752 *Greyhound*. L.

Watkins, Ann wife of William. S Aug 1756. So.

Watkins, Benjamin. S Jan T Apr 1770 *New Trial*. M.

Watkins, Christian. S Sep 1740. L.

Watkins, Daniel of Stroud. S s brass pot Lent 1719. G.

Watkins, Elizabeth. S Jan-Jun T Jun 1728 *Elizabeth* LC Potomack Aug
    1729. L.

Watkins, Elizabeth. S Oct 1757 T Mar 1758 *Dragon*. M.

Watkins, Eustace (1731). *See* Watkins, Thurstus. L.

Watkins, George. S s at Llandogo Lent 1727. Mo.

Watkins, Griffith. S Aug T Oct 1724 *Forward* LC Annapolis Jun
    1725. M.

Watkins, Hannah. S Feb 1757. M.

Watkins, James. R for Barbados or Jamaica May 1684. L.

Watkins, James. S for assault at Rockfield Lent 1750. Mo.

Watkins, James. S Lent R 14 yrs Summer 1751. He.

Watkins, James. S s sheeting at Sonning Lent 1765. Be.

Watkins, Jane. S Jan T Feb 1719 *Worcester* LC Annapolis Jun 1719. L.

Watkins als Maddringham, Jane. S Oct 1744-Jan 1745. M.

Watkins, John. R for Barbados Mar 1681. M.

Watkins, John, aged 21, brown hair, carpenter. S Jan T Feb 1723
    Jonathan LC Annapolis Jly 1724. L.

Watkins, John. S s at Reading Lent 1725 T *Sukey* LC Md Sep 1725. Be.
Watkins, John. S s at Hill Summer 1729. G.
Watkins, John. S Jan T 14 yrs Apr 1741 *Speedwell*. L.
Watkins, John. S & T Sep 1765 *Justitia*. L.
Watkins, John. S s horse Lent R 14 yrs Summer 1767. He.
Watkins, John. S Dec 1774. M.
Watkins, John. S & R 14 yrs Summer 1775. Mo.
Watkins, Joseph. S & R 14 yrs Summer 1769. Mo.
Watkins als Ware, Margaret. S Jan T Apr 1759 *Thetis*. M.
Watkins, Marmaduke. S Apr T May 1752 *Lichfield*. L.
Watkins, Martha. S Jan T Feb 1765 *Tryal*. L.
Watkins, Mary. S Jly T Sep 1764 *Justitia*. M.
Watkins, Mary. S May T Sep 1766 *Justitia*. M.
Watkins, Philip, aged 21. R for Barbados Feb 1664. L.
Watkins, Richard. S Oct 1761 T Apr 1762 *Dolphin*. M.
Watkins, Richard. T Sep 1764 *Justitia*. Ht.
Watkins, Samuel. S Summer 1758 R 14 yrs Lent 1759. Wo.
Watkins, Thomas of Michaelchurch Escley. R for America Jly 1675. He.
Watkins, Thomas. S s lamb at Llanvihangelcrucorney Summer
    1752. Mo.
Watkins, Thomas (1753). *See* James. He.
Watkins, Thomas. SQS May 1754. M.
Watkins, Thomas. S s mare Lent R 14 yrs Summer 1764. O.
Watkins, Thomas. S s harness at Ribbesford Summer 1768. Wo.
Watkins, Thomas. S Jly 1773. Ha.
Watkins, Thurstus als Eustace. S & T Sep 1731 *Smith* LC Va 1732. L.
Watkins, Trevor. S s at Clifton Lent TB Aug 1727. G.
Watkins, Walter. S Lent R 14 yrs Summer 1760 T *Atlas* from Bristol
    1761. He.
Watkins, Walter. T 14 yrs Sep 1766 *Justitia*. E.
Watkins, William of Llangarren. R for America Jly 1688. He.
Watkins, William. S s at Dymock Lent R 14 yrs Summer TB Sep
    1736. G.
Watkins, William. S s at Berrow Lent 1752. Wo.
Watkins, William. S Jly T Sep 1765 *Justitia*. L.
Watkins, William. S Sep T Dec 1767 *Neptune*. L.
Watkins, William. SQS Feb T Apr 1770 *New Trial*. M.
Watkins, William. S s wheat at Prestbury Lent 1774. G.
Watkinson, Alice. SQS & T Sep 1766 *Justitia*. M.
Watkinson, Elizabeth. S Apr T May 1719. L.
Watkinson, James. S for obtaining goods by false pretences Feb 1773. L.
Watling, John. S s sacks Summer 1742. Nf.
Watling, John. S Jan-Feb T Apr 1753 *Thames*. M.
Watmore, James. S Sep 1740. L.
Watmore, James. R 14 yrs Jly 1758. Ha.
Watnall, John. S Lent R 14 yrs Summer 1732. Wa.
Wattson, Ann. S & T Dec 1734 *Caesar* LC Va Jly 1735. L.
Watson, Ann. S Jly 1746. L.
Watson, Ann of Bolton in the Moors, singlewoman. SQS Aug 1760. La.
Watson, Anthony. S Oct T Dec 1771 *Justitia*. L.

Watson, Arthur, aged 69, dark. S Jan T Feb 1723 *Jonathan* LC
Annapolis Jly 1724. M.
Watson, Christopher. T May 1767 *Thornton*. K.
Watson, Daniel. S Dec 1742 T Mar 1743 *Justitia*. L.
Watson, Edward of Hitchin. R for Barbados or Jamaica Feb 1683. Ht.
Watson, Elizabeth of St. Andrew, Holborn, spinster. S s tablecloth Apr
T May 1740 *Essex*. M.
Watson, Elizabeth. S Apr T Jun 1742 *Bladon* to Md. M.
Watson, Elizabeth. S Apr T May 1750 *Lichfield*. M.
Watson als Johnson, Esther. S & T Sep 1731 *Smith* LC Va 1732. M.
Watson, Frances. R for Barbados May 1676. L.
Watson, Francis. R for plantations Jan 1665. L.
Watson, Francis. S Jan-May T Jun 1738 *Forward* to Md or Va. M.
Watson, George. S May T Jly 1722 *Alexander* to Nevis or Jamaica. M.
Watson, George, als Clark, William. S Dec 1762. M.
Watson, George, als Simpson, William. R for life Jly 1763. M.
Watson, George (1766). *See* Harrison. Wa.
Watson, George. S Dec 1773. M.
Watson, Henry of Barrington.R for Barbados Aug 1671. Ca.
Watson, Henry Drake. S Sep-Oct 1774. M.
Watson, Isaac. R for Va Oct 1670 (SP). O.
Watson, Isabella. S Nov T Dec 1763 *Neptune*. L.
Watson, James. S Feb 1774. L.
Watson, James (1775). *See* Douglas. De.
Watson, James William. T Apr 1771 *Thornton*. M.
Watson, Jane. S Feb T Mar 1729 *Patapsco* but died on passage. M.
Watson, Jane. S Lent 1743. La.
Watson, Jane wife of Robert. S s handkerchief Summer 1747. Nl.
Watson, Jennett. S Summer 1732. Nl.
Watson, John of Bewcastle, blacksmith. R for Barbados Jun 1694. Cu.
Watson, John. R 14 yrs Summer 1735 TB Aug 1736. Y.
Watson als Williams, John. T Oct 1738 *Genoa*. Sx.
Watson, John. S Sep 1746. So.
Watson, John. SQS Coventry Mar AT Aug 1751. Wa.
Watson, John. S Lent R 14 yrs Summer 1751. Wa.
Watson, John. S Jly 1753. Ha.
Watson, John. S Dec 1753-Jan 1754. M.
Watson, John. S Jly-Sep 1754. M.
Watson, John. T Sep 1764 *Justitia*. E.
Watson, John of St. Martin in Fields. SW Oct 1766 T Jan 1767 *Tryal*. M.
Watson, John, als Davies, William. R & T for life Apr 1770 *New
Trial*. M.
Watson, Joseph. S Oct T Dec 1724 *Rappahannock* to Va. M.
Watson als Madera, Joshua. S Feb-Apr 1746. M.
Watson, Margaret. R for Barbados Oct 1673. M.
Watson, Mary. S & T Oct 1730 *Forward* LC Potomack Jan 1731. M.
Watson, Mary. S Feb T 14 yrs Mar 1731 *Patapsco* LC Annapolis Jun
1731. M.
Watson, Mary. S & T Apr 1733 *Patapsco* LC Annapolis Nov 1733. M.
Watson, Mary. S Jan-Apr 1748. M.
Watson, Nathaniel. R for America Jly 1702. Li.

Watson, Nicholas. SQS Jan 1751. M.
Watson, Rachael. S & T Oct 1732 *Caesar*. L.
Watson, Ralph. R for Barbados or Jamaica Jly 1685. M.
Watson, Richard. S & T Oct 1732 *Caesar* to Va. M.
Watson, Richard. S Jan T Feb 1733 *Smith* to Md or Va. M.
Watson, Richard. S Jly T for life Sep 1755 *Tryal*. L.
Watson, Richard. S Oct 1773. L.
Watson, Richard. S s cloth at St. Mary, Shrewsbury, Summer 1774. Sh.
Watson, Robert. T Oct 1723 *Forward* to Va from London. Y.
Watson, Robert. S Jan-Apr 1749. M.
Watson, Robert. S Apr T Jly 1770 *Scarsdale* but then stopped. M.
Watson, Sarah. S Apr T May 1718. M.
Watson, Sarah (1752). *See* Garner. Nf.
Wattson, Stephen. S for highway robbery Summer 1738 R 14 yrs Summer 1739. Y.
Watson, Thomas. R for Jamaica Aug 1661. M.
Watson, Thomas of Stowlangtoft. R for Barbados Jan 1665. Su.
Watson, Thomas (1723). *See* Watts. L.
Watson, Thomas. S & T Sep 1731 *Smith* LC Va 1732. M.
Watson, Thomas. S s cereals at Weeford Lent 1758. St.
Watson, Thomas. S Lent 1763. Sy.
Watson, Thomas. AT City Summer 1763. Nl.
Watson, Thomas. T 14 yrs Apr 1769 *Tryal*. E.
Watson, Thomas. S May-Jly 1773. M.
Watson, Thomas, als McKenzie, James. SQS Oct 1773. M.
Watson, William. T Oct 1723 *Forward* to Va from London. Y.
Watson, William. S May T Jun 1726 *Loyal Margaret* LC Md Oct 1726. M.
Watson, William. T Sep 1742 *Forward*. K.
Watson, William. S s Scotch linen Summer 1749. Nl.
Watson, William. S Jly 1753. Ha.
Watson, William, yeoman. S for highway robbery & R for life Summer 1762 AT Summer 1763. Du.
Watson, William. T Jun 1764 *Dolphin*. Sy.
Watt, William. T Sep 1767 *Justitia*. K.
Wattar, John. LC from *Elizabeth* Potomack Aug 1729. No.
Wattison, Joseph. LC from *Margaret* Md Aug 1719; sold to Richard Snowden. X.
Watton, James. S Sep 1754. L.
Watton, John. S s at Stoke Bliss Lent 1750. He.
Watton, Joseph (1774). *See* Wotton. Wa.
Watts, Anne. R for Barbados Jun 1665. L.
Watts, Ann. S Apr-May T Jly 1771 *Scarsdale*. M.
Watts, Charles. S Jan-Apr 1748. M.
Watts, David. S Mar 1741. Ha.
Watts, Edward. S Lent 1770. G.
Watts, Elizabeth. S Apr TB to Va Apr 1750. Wi.
Watts als King, George. S s at Chippenham Summer 1771. Ca.
Watts, Hannah. S Mar 1764. So.
Watts, Henry. S as pickpocket Lent R 14 yrs Summer 1728. Sh.
Watts, Henry. S s handkerchiefs at Bitton Lent TB Apr 1747. G.

Watts, Henry. S Mar 1765. Do.

Watts, Isaac. SQS Devizes Apr TB to Va May 1770. Wi.

Watts, James. SQS Warminster Jly TB to Va Oct 1740. Wi.

Watts, Jane. R for Barbados Feb 1673. L.

Watts, Jane. S & T Apr 1725 *Sukey* LC Annapolis Sep 1725. M.

Watts, Joan. S s saucepan Jun T Dec 1736 *Dorsetshire* to Va. M.

Watts, John. Rebel T 1685.

Watts, John of Besthorpe. R for Barbados or Jamaica Mar 1697. Nf.

Watts, John. T Jun 1764 *Dolphin*. K.

Watts, John. S Oct 1766 T Jan 1767 *Tryal*. M.

Watts, John. SQS & T Jly 1770 *Scarsdale*. Ht.

Watts, John (1775). *See* Meed. E.

Watts, Margaret. R Jun T 14 yrs Aug 1769 *Douglas*. M.

Watts, Mary. S & T Oct 1730 *Forward* but died on passage. M.

Watts, Mary. S Oct T Dec 1770 *Justitia*. M.

Watts, Samuel. S for highway robbery Summer 1719 R 14 yrs Lent 1721. G.

Watts, Samuel. S Aug 1767. So.

Watts als Watson, Thomas. S May T Jly 1723 *Alexander* LC Md Sep 1723. L.

Watts, Thomas, aged 25, fair, wigmaker. LC from *Jonathan* Md Jly 1724. X.

Watts als Mead, Thomas. T May 1741 *Miller*. K.

Watts als Walker, Thomas. S 14 yrs Jly T Aug 1741 *Betty* from Hull. Nt.

Watts, Thomas. S Lent R 14 yrs Summer 1755. Wa.

Watts, Thomas. S s skins at Holmer Summer 1761. He.

Watts, Thomas. S Feb 1775. L.

Watts, William. R & T Dec 1716 *Lewis* to Jamaica. L.

Watts, William. S Mar 1750. So.

Watts, William. R for life Sep 1756. M.

Watts, William. S Sep T Nov 1762 *Prince William*. M.

Waugh, Thomas. S 14 yrs s from bleaching ground at Anam Lent 1764. Y.

Wawby, Thomas. R for America Jly 1683. Li.

Wawn, John of Donington. R for America Feb 1713. Li.

Way, Edward. Rebel T 1685.

Way, George of Stowey. R for Barbados Feb 1701. So.

Way, George of Stowey. R for Barbados Jly 1715. So.

Way als Green, George. T Oct 1720 *Gilbert*. E.

Way, Richard. S s cheeses at Newbury Lent 1753. Be.

Waybank, Elizabeth wife of William. S & T Sep 1731 *Smith* LC Va 1732. M.

Wayland als Hickson, Ann. S Feb T Apr 1741 *Speedwell* or *Mediterranean*. M.

Wayland, Elizabeth. S & T Oct 1722 *Forward* LC Annapolis Jun 1723. L.

Wayland, John. S Lent 1751. Nf.

Weyman, Michael. LC from *Patapasco* Annapolis Dec 1729. X.

Wayman, Samuel. T Oct 1729 *Forward*. E.

Wheymark, Elizabeth. S Summer T Sep 1755 *Tryal*. Sy.

Waymark, Sarah of Beddington, spinster. SQS Apr T May 1750 *Lichfield*. Sy.

Wayne, John. S s horse Summer 1738 R 14 yrs Lent 1739. Le.
Waine, John. S Oct 1749. L.
Wain, John. S Summer 1751 R 14 yrs Lent 1752. Nt.
Waine, Richard. S s at Shipton Lent 1722. O.
Wain, Sarah. S for murder Lent 1721. St.
Wayne, William (1767). *See* Cane. M.
Wead. *See* Weed.
Weakland, Dorothy. S Mar 1765. Ha.
Weale, John. R Dec 1679 AT Feb 1680. M.
Weal, John. S Feb T Mar 1729 *Patapsco* LC Annapolis Dec 1729. M.
Weale, Nathaniel. Rebel T 1685.
Weales, Mariah (1725). *See* Wells, Mary. L.
Wear. *See* Ware.
Wearne, John. R 14 yrs Mar 1758. Co.
Weaver als Stephens, Charles of Corse. R for America Jly 1708. G.
Weaver, Elizabeth of St. John's. SQS Jan T Mar 1758 *Dragon*. Sy.
Weaver, Hannah. SQS Apr TB May 1757. So.
Weaver, John. R for Barbados or Jamaica Dec 1695 & Jan 1697. M.
Weaver, John of South Haysted. R for Barbados or Jamaica Jly 1715. E.
Weaver, John. S Dec 1757 T Mar 1758 *Dragon*. M.
Weaver, John. S s handkerchief at St. Peter, Hereford, Lent 1759. He.
Weaver, John. S s watch at Whitchurch Summer 1763. Sh.
Weaver, Mary wife of John of Kings Stanley. R for Barbados Jly
     1664. G.
Weaver, Mary. S Dec 1753-Jan 1754. M.
Weaver, Richard. R 14 yrs Aug 1757. So.
Weaver, Richard. S Jly T Sep 1766 *Justitia*. M.
Weaver, Samuel. Rebel T 1685.
Weaver, Stephen. S s pewter sign Sep T Dec 1736 *Dorsetshire* to Va. M.
Weaver, Thomas. S Lent R 14 yrs Summer 1738. He.
Weaver, Thomas. S Summer 1749. E.
Weaver, Thomas. S May-Jun T Jly 1753 *Tryal*. M.
Weaver, William of Hereford. R for America Feb 1690. He.
Weaver, William. S s sheep Lent R 14 yrs Summer 1769. Wo.
Weaver, William. S Sep-Oct T Dec 1771 *Justitia*. M.
Webb, Andrew. T Apr 1765 *Ann*. K.
Webb als Tooworth, Ann. S Sep T Oct 1744 *Susannah*. M.
Webb, Daniel. R 14 yrs Mar TB to Va Apr 1741. Wi.
Webb, Elizabeth (1686). *See* Hacker. M.
Webb, Henry. Rebel T 1685.
Webb, Henry. S Jan 1745. L.
Webb, Henry Sr. S 14 yrs for receiving fishing net from Richard
     Clements *(qv)* Summer 1758. Be.
Webb, James. Rebel T 1685.
Webb, James. SQS & TB Jan 1773. So.
Webb, James. R Jly 1773. M.
Webb, Jane. S May T Jun 1738 *Forward*. L.
Webb, Jane (1744). *See* Veale. L.
Webb, John of Jacobstowe. R for Barbados Jly 1684. Co.
Webb, John. Rebel T 1685.
Webb, John. R for Barbados or Jamaica Oct 1694. L.

Webb, John. S & T Dec 1731 *Forward* to Md or Va. M.

Webb, John. S s ham Apr T May 1740 *Essex* to Md or Va. M.

Webb, John. S Lent TB Apr 1742. G.

Webb, John. S Apr 1746. L.

Webb, John. S Dec 1746. L.

Webb, John. S s sheep Summer 1753 R 14 yrs Lent 1754. Ca.

Webb, John. T Dec 1753 *Whiteing*. K.

Webb, John. S s wheat at Sedgley Summer 1758. St.

Webb, John. S Aug T Sep 1764 *Justitia*. L.

Webb, John. S & T Sep 1766 *Justitia*. L.

Webb, John. S s mare Lent R 14 yrs Summer 1770. He.

Webb, John of Camberwell. SQS Apr T Jly 1772 *Orange Bay*. Sy.

Webb, Jonathan. SQS Jan 1765. Ha.

Webb, Joseph. R Jly T 14 yrs Oct 1768 *Justitia*. M.

Webb, Margaret wife of John. S Dec 1733 T Jan 1734 *Caesar* LC Va Jly 1734. M.

Webb, Mary. S Jan-Jun T Jun 1728 *Elizabeth* to Md or Va. M.

Webb, Mary. S Lent 1747. Nf.

Webb, Mary. SQS Lent TB Apr 1768. Db.

Webb, Nathaniel. S s at Westerleigh Lent 1737. G.

Webb, Nicholas. S Oct T Nov 1725 *Rappahannock* but died on passage. L.

Webb, Richard. R 14 yrs for Boston NE Jly 1718. Wi.

Webb, Richard. T Oct 1729 *Forward*. K.

Webb, Richard. SQS Jan 1732. So.

Webb, Richard. R 14 yrs Jly 1738. De.

Webb, Richard. S Sep 1754. L.

Webb, Richard. S Lent TB May 1755. G.

Webb, Samuel. S Dec 1757 T Mar 1758 *Dragon*. L.

Webb, Samuel. S Jan 1759. L.

Webb, Samuel. R 14 yrs for highway robbery Summer 1775. Nt.

Webb, Sarah. S Jan T Apr 1735 *Patapsco* LC Annapolis Oct 1735. M.

Webb, Sarah. S Aug TB to Va Sep 1742. Le.

Webb, Stephen. S s sheep Lent TB Apr 1740. G.

Webb, Thomas. S Mar 1734. Co.

Webb, Thomas. S Sep T Nov 1743 *George William*. M.

Webb, Thomas. S Oct 1766 T Jan 1767 *Tryal*. M.

Webb als Steele, Thomas. R Mar 1771. Ha.

Webb, Thomas. S Summer 1772. Wa.

Webb, Timothy. R 14 yrs for Va Jly 1719. So.

Webb, Walter. S for assault & theft at Bottisham Lent 1769. Ca.

Webb, William. R 14 yrs Mar 1736. Wi.

Webb, William. T May 1736 *Patapsco*. Sy.

Webb, William. S s horse Lent R 14 yrs Summer 1747. Wa.

Webb, William. S Jly-Sep 1754. M.

Webb, William. SQS Oct T Dec 1758 *The Brothers*. M.

Webb als Longweaver, William. SQS Jan TB Mar 1768. So.

Webb, William. S 14 yrs s linen from bleaching yard Lent 1775. Wa.

Webber, Betty. SQS Jly TB Aug 1761. So.

Webber, Katherine. R for Barbados Aug 1679. L.

Webber, Charity. S Aug 1757. So.

Webber, Elizabeth. S Mar 1774. So.
Webber, John. S Feb T May 1767 *Thornton*. M.
Webber, John. SQS Sep T Dec 1771 *Justitia*. M.
Webber, Josiah. R 14 yrs Aug 1740. So.
Webber, Mary. S Jan 1751. L.
Webber, Nathaniel. Rebel T 1685.
Webber, Nathaniel. S Lent 1767. Nf.
Webber, Richard. SQS & TB Jly 1757. So.
Webber, Richard. S s mare Lent R 14 yrs Summer 1767. Nf.
Webber, Robert. T 14 yrs Sep 1766 *Justitia*. K.
Webber, Robert. S Lent 1768. Su.
Webber, Ruth. R Mar AT Apr 1677. M.
Webber, Sarah. S Mar 1766. So.
Webber, Sarah. R Aug 1772. So.
Webber, Susannah wife of William. S Jly 1760 TB to Va 1761. De.
Webber, Thomas. S Jly 1733. Do.
Webber, Thomas. SQS Sep 1773. M.
Webber, William. S Jan-Apr 1749. M.
Webber als Thurston, William. S s at Brooke & R Lent 1769. Nf.
Webdell, Thomas. T Apr 1753 *Thames*. K.
Webley, Ann. S Dec 1746. L.
Webley, Benjamin. S s at Llangstone Lent 1738. Mo.
Webley, Henry. S Dec 1766 T Jan 1767 *Tryal*. M.
Webley, Percifall of Suckley. R for America Jun 1714. Wo.
Webley, Percival. S s at Hallow Lent 1726. Wo.
Webley, William. S s tankard at Tewkesbury Lent TB Mar 1747. G.
Weblin, Samuel. S May 1743. M.
Weblin, William of St. Clement Danes. S s coat Jly 1740 T Jan 1741
    Harpooner to Rappahannock. M.
Webster, Alison (1670). *See* Bell. M.
Webster, John. S Summer 1740. Y.
Webster, John of Liverpool, butcher. S s sheep at Walton on Hill
    Summer 1764 R 14 yrs Lent 1765. La.
Webster, John. S Summer 1772. Wa.
Webster, John Michael. SW & T Apr 1770 *New Trial*. M.
Webster, Jonathan. S Summer 1720 R 14 yrs Summer 1721 T Oct 1723
    Forward from London. Y.
Webster, Margaret. T Sep 1742 *Forward*. Sy.
Webster, Martha. T Apr 1741 *Speedwell* or *Mediterranean*. Sy.
Webster, Mary. S Lent 1763. Y.
Webster, Mary. S Apr-Jun T Jly 1772 *Tayloe*. M.
Webster, Sarah. S & T Jan 1739 *Dorsetshire*. L.
Webster, Thomas of Thetford. R for America Feb 1664. Nf.
Webster, Thomas of Peterborough. R for America Jly 1716. No.
Webster, Thomas. S Aug T Sep 1725 *Forward* LC Annapolis Dec
    725. L.
Webster, Thomas. S s sheep Lent R 14 yrs Summer 1749. Le.
Webster als Padge, Thomas. S Jly 1749. Le.
Webster, Thomas. S s goose Lent 1768. Nf.
Webster, William. S Lent 1734. Y.

Webster, William of Stepney. S s aprons Oct 1740 T Jan 1741 *Harpooner*. M.
Webster, William. T May 1752 *Lichfield*. Ht.
Webster, William. S s watch Summer 1773. Nl.
Wedgwood, John. S & T Oct 1722 *Forward* LC Annapolis Jun 1723. L.
Weech, John. Rebel T 1685.
Weech, John. S Apr 1728. So.
Weech, Rebecca. S & T Dec 1759 *Phoenix*. M.
Wead, James. S Lent 1768. Nt.
Weeden, Edward. S Jly T Oct 1741 *Sea Horse*. L.
Weedon, Isaac. S Apr T May 1720 *Honor* LC York River Jan 1721. L.
Weedon, James. S Feb-Apr T May 1755 *Rose*. M.
Weedon als Fletcher, Jane. S Apr T Oct 1719 *Susannah & Sarah* LC Annapolis Apr 1720. L.
Weedon, Robert (1674). *See* Walker. Sy.
Weedon, William. S s at Binfield Summer 1727. Be.
Weeds, Stephen. S Lent R 14 yrs Summer 1767. Nf.
Weekley, Roger. R for Barbados or Jamaica May 1684. M.
Weeks, Agnes. TB to Va from QS 1736. De.
Weekes, Christopher of Staplehurst. R for Barbados Apr 1668. K.
Weeks, Elizabeth. S Jly TB to Va Aug 1752. Wi.
Weeks, Francis. S & TB to Va Mar 1769. Wi.
Weeks, James. S & T Sep 1765 *Justitia*. M.
Weekes, John. R for Jamaica Feb 1665. M.
Weeks, John. R Aug 1747. De.
Weeks, John. R for life Mar 1767. Ha.
Weeks, Knight. SQS & T Dec 1752 *Greyhound*. M.
Weeks, Phillippa. S Mar 1730. De.
Weekes als Wicks, Richard of Beccles. R for America Feb 1688. Su.
Weeks, Samuel. TB to Va from QS 1736. De.
Weeks, Samuel. R 14 yrs Aug 1754. So.
Weeks, Susanna. T Nov 1759 *Phoenix*. K.
Weekes, Thomas of Barnstaple. R for Barbados Jly 1677. De.
Weeks, Thomas of Calne. R for Barbados Jly 1715. Wi.
Weene, John of Colemore. R for Barbados Feb 1683. Ha.
Weighill, James. S Lent T Oct 1723 *Forward* to Va from London. Y.
Weight. *See* Wait.
Were, George. S Apr 1728. So.
Welbeloved, John. SQS & T Jan 1765 *Tryal*. M.
Welbred, Mary (1774). *See* Wellbrand. M.
Welch. *See* Welsh.
Welchborne, Thomas. S Lent R 14 yrs Summer 1760. Bd.
Welchman, Samuel (1722). *See* Armstrong. M.
Wheeldon, Benjamin. TB May 1741. Db.
Welldon, George. S s sheep Oct 1768 T Jan 1769 *Thornton*. M.
Wheeldon, Elias. TB Aug 1733. Db.
Wheeldon, William. TB May 1741. Db.
Weldon, John. T Oct 1722 *Forward* LC Md Jun 1723. Sy.
Weldon, Robert Walker of St. Saviour, Southwark. SQS Feb 1772. Sy.
Wheeldon, William. S for highway robbery Summer 1739 R 14 yrs Lent 1740. Db.

Weldon, William. S s mare Lent R 14 yrs Summer 1765. Hu.
Welham, James (1774). *See* Fenn. K.
Wellum, Jane (1723). *See* Burk. M.
Wellam, Robert. S Oct-Dec 1750. M.
Wellham, Robert. S Lent 1768. Su.
Welland, Nicholas of Bridgewater. R for Barbados Jly 1715. So.
Welland, Richard of Witley. SQS Oct T Dec 1767 *Neptune*. Sy.
Wellard, Thomas. S Lent 1746. K.
Wellbrand als Welbred als Summers, Mary. S Dec 1774. M.
Weller, John of St. James, Westminster. S s coins Sep 1740 T Jan 1741
    Harpooner to Rappahannock. M.
Wellar, John. S Lent R 14 yrs Summer 1758. O.
Weller, Thomas (1663). *See* Peters. Sx.
Weller, William. T Oct 1722 *Forward*. K.
Welling, Elizabeth wife of John of Christchurch. S s clothing Jly-Oct
    1740 T Jan 1741 *Harpooner* to Rappahannock. M.
Welling, James. R for Barbados Dec 1668. M.
Welling, John. R for Barbados Sep 1682. L.
Welling, Richard. S & T Aug 1752 *Tryal*. L.
Welling, Thomas. S & T Sep 1755 *Tryal*. L.
Wellington, George. S s mare Lent R 14 yrs Summer 1758. Le & No.
Wellington, James. S s at Ross Lent 1759. He.
Wellington, Mary, aged 34. R for Barbados Feb 1664. M.
Wellins, John. S & T Sep 1765 *Justitia*. M.
Welman, Matthew. T Jan 1736 *Dorsetshire*. Sy.
Wellman, Richard. S Mar 1765. Ha.
Wells, Anne. S Apr T May 1720 *Honor* to York River Va. L.
Wells, Ann. S & T Sep 1731 *Smith* LC Va 1732. M.
Wells, Ann, als wife of Thomas Wilson of St. George. S s apron Oct-
    Dec 1739 T Jan 1740 *York*. M.
Wells, Ann. S Feb-Apr T May 1755 *Rose*. M.
Wells, Ann. S Norwich Lent TB Oct 1763. Nf.
Wells, Katherine. S s horse Summer 1720 R 14 yrs Summer 1721. Nt.
Wells als Davis, Catherine. S Jan T Mar 1758 *Dragon*. M.
Wells als Dudley, Charles. R for Barbados Feb 1672. M.
Wells, Charles. R Jly 1686. M.
Wells, Daniel. S 14 yrs Apr-Jun 1739. M.
Wells, Edmund. SWK Jan 1775. K.
Wells, Edward. S Jun-Dec 1738 T Jan 1739 *Dorsetshire* to Va. M.
Wells, Edward of St. Martin in Fields. SW Oct 1773. M.
Wells, Elizabeth wife of John of St. Saviour, Southwark. R for Barbados
    or Jamaica Jly 1704. Sy.
Wells, Elizabeth. S Jly T Aug 1721 *Prince Royal* LC Va Nov 1721. L.
Wells, Elizabeth Mary (1742). *See* Shamble. M.
Wells, George. Rebel T 1685.
Wells, George. S Lent 1758. Su.
Wells, Granby Thomas. S Apr-May T Jly 1771 *Scarsdale*. M.
Wells, Jacob. S s horse Lent R 14 yrs Summer 1750. Li.
Wells, James. T Apr 1742 *Bond*. K.
Wells, James. R 14 yrs Jly 1758. Ha.
Wells, Jeremiah. T Nov 1741 *Sea Horse*. Sx.

Wells, Jeremiah. S Apr-Jun T 14 yrs Jly 1772 *Tayloe*. M.

Wells, John. R for America Jly 1687. Nt.

Wells, John. T Oct 1729 *Forward*. E.

Wells als King, John. S Jun-Dec 1738 T Jan 1739 *Dorsetshire* to Va. M.

Wells, John. S 14 yrs Jan-Apr 1748. M.

Wells, John. S & T Mar 1763 *Neptune*. L.

Wells, John. S Summer 1774. Ht.

Wells, John. S s wheat at Polstead Lent 1775. Su.

Wells, Joseph. S Jly 1723. Wi.

Wells, Joseph. T Jun 1727 *Susanna*. K.

Wells, Joseph. T Jun 1738 *Forward*. Sy.

Wells, Joseph of Heston. R for highway robbery & T 14 yrs Feb 1740 *York*. M.

Wells, Joshua. S Feb T Apr 1766 *Ann*. M.

Wells, Mary. S Jan 1719. M.

Wells, Mary. T Oct 1721 *William & John*. Sy.

Wells or Weales, Mariah. S Aug T Sep 1725 *Forward* LC Md Dec 1725. L.

Wells, Nathaniel of Wiston. R for Barbados or Jamaica Jly 1704. Sx.

Wells, Paul William. S May T Jun 1768 *Tryal*. M.

Wells, Richard. R for Barbados Jun 1671. M.

Wells, Robert of Killingworth. R for America Jly 1678. Wa.

Wells, Samuel. T Apr 1739 *Forward*. Sy.

Wells, Sarah. S & T 14 yrs Oct 1720 *Gilbert* to Md. M.

Wells, Sarah. S May T 14 yrs Jly 1723 *Jonathan* LC Annapolis Sep 1723. L.

Wells, Thomas. PT Jun R Dec 1698. M.

Wells, Thomas. T Jan 1736 *Dorsetshire*. Sx.

Wells, Thomas. T May 1737 *Forward*. Sx.

Wells, Thomas. S s sheep Summer 1765 R 14 yrs Lent 1766. Nf.

Wells, Thomas. S Lent 1766. Bd.

Wells, Thomas of Egham. SQS Oct 1772. Sy.

Wells, Valentine of Rotherhithe. SQS Mar T Apr 1753 *Thames*. Sy.

Wells, William of Brixworth. R for America Jly 1673. No.

Wells, William. S Jan T Feb 1742 *Industry*. L.

Wells, William. S for smuggling Summer 1748 T Jan 1749 *Laura*. K.

Wells, William. S s pigs at Caversham Lent 1752. O.

Wells, William. S Jan 1757. L.

Wells, William. R 14 yrs Jly 1758. Ha.

Wells, William. S Lent 1774. E.

Wellum. *See* Wellam.

Welly, Peter. Rebel T 1685.

Welsby, Margaret of St. Sepulchre, widow. SQS for Jamaica Jan 1665 for attendance at unlawful religious assembly. M.

Welsh, Abraham. R for Barbados Jan 1693. M.

Welch, Alice. S Summer 1739. Wo.

Welch, Andrew. R & T 14 yrs Jly 1772 *Tayloe*. M.

Welsh, Ann. S Jly-Dec 1747. M.

Welch, Edmund. T Dec 1736 *Dorsetshire*. Sy.

Welch, Edward. S Feb T Mar 1731 *Patapsco* LC Annapolis Jun 1731. L.

Welch, Edward. S Feb T Apr 1772 *Thornton*. L.

Welsh, Eleanor. S Jun-Dec 1738 T Jan 1739 *Dorsetshire* to Va. M.
Welch als Robinson, Elizabeth. R Aug AT Oct 1700. M.
Welch, Elizabeth. S Sep-Oct T Dec 1771 *Justitia*. M.
Welsh, George. S s gowns & T May 1736 *Patapsco* to Md. M.
Welch, Hannah. S & T Jly 1771 *Scarsdale*. M.
Welch, Henry. SQS Sep T Oct 1768 *Justitia*. M.
Welch, Henry. S Dec 1774. M.
Welch, James. S Aug T 14 yrs Sep 1727 *Forward* LC Rappahannock
    May 1728. L.
Welch, James. S Dec 1755 T Jan 1756 *Greyhound*. L.
Welch, James. R 14 yrs Mar 1762. Ha.
Welch, James of St. John's. SQS & T Jan 1767 *Tryal*. Sy.
Welch, James. S s at Old Swinford Summer 1769. Wo.
Welch, James. SQS & T Jly 1771 *Scarsdale*. M.
Welch, James. S Dec 1774. L.
Welsh, John. S s sheep at Shefford Summer 1728. Be.
Welsh, John. S May T Jun 1738 *Forward*. L.
Welch, John. S for highway robbery Lent R 14 yrs Summer 1741
    (SP). Ca.
Welsh, John. S Jly-Dec 1747. M.
Welch, John. S Nov T Dec 1752 *Greyhound*. L.
Welch, John als Thomas. S Feb-Apr T 14 yrs May 1755 *Rose*. M.
Welch, John. T Apr 1766 *Ann*. M.
Welch, John. S Feb T Apr 1771 *Thornton*. L.
Welch, John of St. James, Westminster. SW Jly 1773. M.
Welsh, Joseph. S Jly 1741. De.
Welch, Joseph. S Lent R 14 yrs Summer T Oct 1750 *Rachael*. E.
Welch, Laurence. R for Barbados or Jamaica Dec 1689. L.
Welch, Lawrence. S Jan-Apr 1749. M.
Welch als Edwards, Martha. S Jun 1761. M.
Welch, Mary. S & T Oct 1732 *Caesar* to Va. M.
Welsh, Mary. S Dec 1742 T Mar 1743 *Justitia*. L.
Welch, Mary. R 14 yrs Jly 1756. Ha.
Welch, Mary wife of John. S Sep T Nov 1762 *Prince William*. M.
Welch, Mary. S Jly 1763. M.
Welch, Michael. S Jan-Feb T Apr 1771 *Thornton*. M.
Welch, Philip. S Dec 1772. M.
Welch, Richard of St. Ann, Westminster. S s salver Sep 1740. M.
Welch, Richard. S & T Apr 1762 *Dolphin*. L.
Welsh, Robert of Tonge. R for America Sep 1671. Sh.
Welsh als Shipmarsh, Robert of Hadlow. R for Barbados or Jamaica Jly
    1688 & 1691. K.
Welch, Robert. S Jan 1755. L.
Welch, Robert. S May T Jun 1764 *Dolphin*. M.
Welsh, Samuel. SQS Sep T Oct 1768 *Justitia*. M.
Welch, Susannah. S Sep-Oct 1773. M.
Welch, Thomas. R for America Feb 1700. Le.
Welsh, Thomas. S Mar 1739. Wi.
Welsh, Thomas. S Jan 1746. M.
Welsh, Thomas. S May-Jly 1748. M.
Welch, Thomas (1755). *See* Welsh, John. M.

Welch, Thomas. S Jly 1757. Ha.
Welch, Thomas. S Apr T Jly 1770 *Scarsdale*. L.
Welch, William. S Jan T Feb 1724 *Anne*. L.
Welch, William. T Apr 1733 *Patapsco* LC Md Nov 1733. Sy.
Welch, William. S Lent R 14 yrs Summer 1738. Wa.
Welch, William of Shoreditch. S s tobacco & T Dec 1740 *Vernon*. M.
Welthresher, Joseph. S Jly-Dec 1747. M.
Welton, Edward. S s horse Summer 1740 R 14 yrs Lent 1741 (SP). Nf.
Wenden, James. S Dec 1766 T Jan 1767 *Tryal*. M.
Wenlock, Edward of Cottesloe. R for America Jly 1675. O.
Wenn, John of Skipton. R for America Mar 1710. Y.
Wensley, Thomas. R 14 yrs Aug 1731. So.
Went, Elizabeth. S May T Nov 1759 *Phoenix*. M.
Went, James. R & T 14 yrs Feb 1740 *York*. L.
Wentland, Ann. S & T 14 yrs Oct 1732 *Caesar* to Va. M.
Wentworth, Ellzabeth. S Sep-Oct 1773. M.
Wentworth, James. S Jan T Mar 1750 *Tryal*. L.
Wentworth als Winckworth, Nathaniel of Husborne Tarrant. R for
    Barbados Mar 1694. Ha.
Were. *See* Weir.
Wessells, Francis. S s gelding Summer 1754 R 14 yrs Lent 1755. Nf.
West, Ann. S Aug T 14 yrs Sep 1718 *Eagle* LC Charles Town Mar
    1719. L.
West, Ann. S Oct T Dec 1771 *Justitia*. L.
West, Benjamin. T Apr 1733 *Patapsco*. K.
West, Benjamin. S 14 yrs for receiving Aug 1758. So.
West, Denima. S 14 yrs for receiving Aug 1758. So.
West, Henry of Beckington, husbandman. R for Barbados Feb 1673. So.
West, Henry. S Mar 1738. So.
West, Henry. R Apr 1773. M.
West, James. S & T Jan 1765 *Tryal*. M.
West, James. SQS Oct 1773 TB Jan 1774. So.
West, James. S s at Newport Pagnell Lent 1775. Bu.
West, Jarvis. S s seat of chair Apr T Dec 1735 *John* LC Annapolis Sep
    1736. M.
West als Hallett, John. R for Jamaica Jan 1663. M.
West, John. T May 1719 *Margaret* LC Md May 1720; sold to John
    Baldwin. Sy.
West, John. S s horse Summer 1725 R Summer 1726. Li.
West als Varity, John. S s horse Lent R Summer 1726. Db.
West, John. S Feb T Mar 1727 *Rappahannock* to Md. M.
West, John of Warminster, weaver. SQS Marlborough & TB to Va Oct
    1742. Wi.
West, John of Wormingford. SQS Jan 1754. E.
West, John. S s silver watch Lent 1755. He.
West, John. T 14 yrs Apr 1759 *Thetis*. Sx.
West, John. S Mar 1761. Ha.
West, John. S Jan T Mar 1763 *Neptune*. M.
West, John. R 14 yrs Jly 1763. M.
West, John. S Aug T Sep 1764 *Justitia*. L.
West, John. S Feb T Apr 1766 *Ann*. M.

West, John. SWK s vegetables in Chatham Jan T Apr 1768 *Thornton*. K.
West, John. S Jan-Feb T Apr 1772 *Thornton*. M.
West, John. S Apr 1774. L.
West, Joseph. S Jun 1747. L.
West, Joseph. S Mar 1753. Ha.
West, Joshua. S Feb 1752. L.
West, Luke. AT Lent & Summer 1765. Y.
West, Luke. S Jun T Jly 1772 *Tayloe*. L.
West, Martha of Bristol. R for Barbados Jun 1699. G.
West, Mary. R Feb 1675. M.
West, Mary. R 14 yrs Aug 1721. So.
West, Mary. S Jan-May T Jun 1738 *Forward* to Md or Va. M.
West, Mary. S Mar 1751. De.
West, Matthew. T Sep 1758 *Tryal*. Sy.
West, Richard. Rebel T 1685.
West, Richard. S Apr-May 1754. M.
West, Roger. S s mare Lent R 14 yrs Summer 1748 T Jan 1749
   Laura. Ht.
West, Samuel. R Dec 1716 T Jan 1717 *Queen Elizabeth*. L.
West, Sarah of Christchurch, spinster. SQS Jan T Apr 1762 *Neptune*. Sy.
West, Thomas. S Aug T 14 yrs Oct 1726 *Forward* to Va. M.
West, Thomas. S Feb T Jun 1738 *Forward* to Md or Va. M.
West, Thomas. SWK Jly T Oct 1768 *Justitia*. K.
West, William. R for Barbados Sep 1682. L.
West als Varity, William. TB to Md Jly 1726. Db.
West, William. S Feb T Mar 1727 *Rappahannock* to Md. M.
West, William. S & T Sep 1731 *Smith* LC Va 1732. M.
West, William. S for highway robbery Lent R 14 yrs Summer 1743. St.
West als Best, William. S for murder Summer 1746 R 14 yrs Lent
   1747. O.
West, William. S s at Wootton Lent 1766. Be.
West, William. S Apr-May T Jly 1771 *Scarsdale*. M.
Westbrooke, Samuel of Kirtlington. R for America Jly 1698. O.
Westbrook, William. S Oct T Dec 1771 *Justitia*. L.
Westcar, John. S Lent R 14 yrs Summer 1737. O.
Westcombe, Thomas. R 14 yrs Mar 1764. So.
Westcombe, William. S Aug 1734. So.
Westcott, James. S Aug 1729. De.
Westcutt, John. R for Barbados or Jamaica Dec 1699 & Aug 1700. L.
Westcoat, John. S Aug 1727. So.
Westcoate, Josias of Sidmouth. R for Barbados Jly 1688. De.
Westcoate, Peter. S Apr-May T Jly 1771 *Scarsdale*. M.
Westcott, Stephen. S Aug 1729. De.
Westcott, Thomas. S Mar 1743. De.
Westcote, Thomas. S Jly T Sep 1755 *Tryal*. L.
Westell, Patience. S Feb T Mar 1729 *Patapsco* LC Annapolis Dec
   1729. M.
Wester, Ursula. T Summer 1739. Y.
Westerman, Thomas. S Lent 1741. Y.
Westerne, John of Kenton. R for Barbados Jly 1715. De.
Western, John. R 14 yrs Mar 1764. De.

Westerne, Robert of St. Decumans. R for Barbados Jun 1687. So.
Westfield als Shaw, Elizabeth. S s at Ampney Crucis Summer 1775. G.
Westfield, Grace of Coventry, spinster. R for America Jly 1716. Wa.
Westfield, Richard. S Dec 1745. L.
Westgate, Edmund (1743). *See* Youngman. Nf.
Westgood, William. S Sep 1775. M.
Westhall, Henry. S May 1775. L.
Westlake, Jane. S Mar 1751. De.
Westlake, John. Rebel T 1685.
Westlake, Joseph. S for Va Jly 1718. De.
Westlake, Richard of Kings Brimpton. R for Barbados Jly 1693. So.
Westlake, William. R 14 yrs Mar 1759 TB to Va. De.
Westley, Samuel. S Lent 1763. E.
Westley, Thomas. S Lent 1737. Su.
Westley, William. S Lent R 14 yrs Summer 1746. O.
Westmore, Elizabeth. S Feb T Mar 1731 *Patapsco* LC Annapolis Jun 1731. L.
Weston, Abraham. S for highway robbery Summer 1759 R 14 yrs Lent 1760. Le.
Weston als Wilson, Ann. S Mar TB to Va Apr 1758. Wi.
Weston, Charles of Gloverstone. R for Barbados Jly 1677. Ch.
Weston, George. S Summer 1754. Sx.
Weston, George. T Sep 1758 *Tryal*. K.
Weston, James. S s wool at Bitton Summer 1759; wife Ann & George & Elizabeth Weston acquitted. G.
Weston, John. S Lent 1748. Sy.
Weston, John. S Sep-Dec 1755 T Jan 1756 *Greyhound*. M.
Weston, Joseph. S Aug 1755. So.
Weston, Margaret. R Dec 1765 T Jan 1766 *Tryal*. M.
Weston, Mary. S Summer 1754. Sy.
Weston, Thomas. S for assault at Goring Lent 1775. O.
Weston, William. S s with menaces at Tortworth Lent 1775. G.
Westwood, John. R for Jamaica Feb 1665. M.
Westwood, Richard. S s horse Summer 1746 R 14 yrs Lent 1747. La.
Westwood, William. T by special bond May 1755. L.
Weatherspun. *See* Witherspoon.
Wetherell, Francis. S Aug T Oct 1724 *Forward* LC Annapolis Jun 1725. M.
Weatherill, Francis. R 14 yrs Summer TB Sep 1759. Y.
Witherell, Gabriel of Penkridge. R for America Sep 1671. St.
Wetherell, George. S Summer 1722 T Oct 1723 *Forward* to Va from London. Y.
Weatherell, James (1744). *See* Wetherley. Du.
Wetherall, Jane wife of Thomas. S Jly 1763. M.
Wetherill, John. R for America Feb 1683. Li.
Wetherell, John. R Jly T Sep 1757 *Thetis*. M.
Wytherell, Joseph. Rebel T 1685.
Wetherell, Margaret. S Lent R 14 yrs Summer 1742. Li.
Witherell, Robert. S s at Lechlade Lent R 14 yrs Summer TB Oct 1735. G.
Wetherall, William. S Apr T May 1720 *Honor* but escaped in Spain. L.

Wetherill, William. S Jly T Aug 1721 *Prince Royal* LC Va Nov 1721. L.

Wetherford, Thomas. S Apr T May 1750 *Lichfield*. L.

Wheatherhead, Joseph. LC from *Dorsetshire* Va Sep 1736. X.

Wetherley als Weatherell, James. S s sheep Summer 1744 R 14 yrs Summer 1746. Du.

Weatherley, John. T Jan 1741 *Vernon*. Bu.

Wetman, William. S Lent R 14 yrs Summer 1741. Be.

Wettie, Thomas (1750). *See* Walter. M.

Wexham, Margaret, spinster, als wife of Nicholas. R for Barbados Oct TB Nov 1667. L.

Wey, Reuben. S s sheep Lent R 14 yrs Summer 1758. Le.

Weyman. *See* Wayman.

Wail, ——. AT Summer 1736. O.

Wale, Ann. T Apr 1732 *Patapsco*. Sy.

Wale, Edward. Rebel T 1685.

Wale, John. Rebel T 1685.

Whale, John. R 14 yrs Aug TB to Va Sep 1753. Wi.

Wale, Mary. S Sep-Oct T Dec 1753 *Whiteing*. M.

Wale als Isles, William of Cowley, yeoman. R for America Feb 1714. G.

Whale, William of Kensington. S s lead & T May 1736 *Patapsco* to Md. M.

Wale, William. S Apr 1773. M.

Whalebone, John. S Aug T Oct 1723 *Forward* to Va. M.

Wales, John. S Lent R 14 yrs Summer 1724 (SP). Nf.

Whales, Richard. S May 1719. M.

Whaley, Alexander. S s horse Lent R 14 yrs Summer 1736. Wa.

Whaley, George. S s pumps at Doncaster Summer 1764. Y.

Whaley, John. S Lent 1755. Y.

Whaley, William. S Nov T Dec 1753 *Whiteing*. L.

Whalock, James. S Sep-Oct 1749. M.

Whalon, Pevice. S Lent T Apr 1772 *Thornton*. K.

Wharley, John. T Jun 1740 *Essex*. E.

Wharton, Benjamin. T Oct 1724 *Forward* LC Md Jun 1725. Ht.

Wharton, Katherine. S Feb T Mar 1730 *Patapsco* LC Md Sep 1730. L.

Wharton, Cuthbert. S Jly T Aug 1721 *Prince Royal* LC Va Nov 1721. M.

Wharton, James. R for Va Aug 1622 (PC). Nf.

Wharton, James. T Sep 1764 *Justitia*. M.

Wharton als Jones, Jane. R for Barbados Jun 1665. L.

Wharton, John. S & T Apr 1733 *Patapsco* LC Annapolis Nov 1733. L.

Wharton, Robert of Aughton. S s horse & R Lent 1772. La.

Wharton, Sarah. S s clothing May T Jun 1738 *Forward*. L.

Wharton, Susannah. S Jan T Feb 1733 *Smith*. L.

Wharton, Thomas. S Sep-Oct T Dec 1771 *Justitia*. M.

Wharton als Thomas, William. R & T for life Jly 1770 *Scarsdale*. M.

Wharton, William. T 14 yrs Apr 1771 *Thornton*. K.

Whatman, William. T Jan 1741 *Vernon*. Sx.

Wheat, John. S for Va Jly 1718. Ha.

Wheatfield, George. T Sep 1764 *Justitia*. E.

Wheatland, Mary. S Nov T Dec 1763 *Neptune*. L.

Wheatley, Ann. S s at Yarm Summer 1765 TB Aug 1767. Y.

Wheatley, Elizabeth. S Sep-Dec 1746. M.

Wheatley, George. SQS Jly 1774. M.

Wheatley, Henry (1728). *See* Bartlett, Thomas. M.

Wheatley als Allison, Hester. S Jan-Jun T Jun 1728 *Elizabeth* LC Potomack Aug 1729. M.

Wheatley, John. S & T Dec 1734 *Caesar* LC Va Jly 1735. M.

Wheatly, John. S & T Feb 1744 *Neptune*. L.

Wheatley, Mary. S Feb R for Barbados Jun 1663. M.

Wheatley, Mary. T Sep 1757 *Thetis*. K.

Wheatley, Mary. S Apr T Jly 1770 *Scarsdale*. M.

Wheatley, Michael. R 14 yrs Summer 1730. Du.

Wheatley, Peter. S Feb 1656. M.

Wheatley, Richard. S to hang Lent 1774 for being at large after sentence of transportation. Nt.

Wheatley, Robert. R for Barbados or Jamaica May 1684. L.

Wheatley, Robert. S Lent R 14 yrs Summer 1739. No.

Wheatley, Thomas. S s sheep at Topcliffe Lent R 14 yrs Summer 1767. Y.

Wheatley, William. T Apr 1732 *Patapsco*. Ht.

Wheatley, William. S Jan T 14 yrs Apr 1741 *Speedwell*. L.

Wheelas, John (1745). *See* Wheelhouse. Y.

Wheeldon. *See* Weldon.

Wheeler, Ann, spinster, als wife of Samuel Beancott. S Feb 1730. M.

Wheeler, Ann wife of Richard. S Feb 1738. Ha.

Wheeler, Ann. SW & T Dec 1767 *Neptune*. M.

Wheeler, Charles. S Lent 1769. G.

Wheeler, Edward of Evesham. R for America Mar 1683. Wo.

Wheeler, Edward. S Feb T Mar 1731 *Patapsco* but died on passage. M.

Wheeler, Edward. S Summer 1758 R 14 yrs Lent 1759. O.

Wheeler, Henry of Rockhampton. R for America Mar 1701. G.

Wheeler, Henry. S Mar TB to Va Apr 1767. Wi.

Wheeler, James. S for highway robbery Summer 1730 R 14 yrs Lent 1731 (SP). Be.

Wheeler, James (1738). *See* Eyre. Wi.

Wheeler, James. T Apr 1760 *Thetis*. Sy.

Wheeler, Joan (1711). *See* Davis. De.

Wheeler, John. R for Barbados May AT Sep 1684. M.

Wheeler als Whidler, John of Winford. R for Barbados Mar 1686. So.

Wheeler, John. R for Barbados or Jamaica Dec 1699. L.

Wheeler, John. T Jan 1734 *Caesar*. Bu.

Wheeler, John. S s horse Lent R 14 yrs Summer 1736. Wa.

Wheeler, Lawrence. R 14 yrs Mar 1742. De.

Wheeler, Mary, servant at Bowl Yard by St. Giles. S s sword & T Dec 1734 *Caesar* LC Va Jly 1735. M.

Wheeler, Mary. S for burglary Lent R Summer 1741 (SP). Wo.

Wheeler, Mary. S 14 yrs Summer 1773. Sy.

Wheeler, Ralph. S Jun-Dec 1745. M.

Wheeler, Richard. R Dec 1679 AT Feb 1680. M.

Wheeler, Richard of St. Saviour, Southwark. SQS Oct T Dec 1767 *Neptune*. Sy.

Wheeler, Robert. S & T Oct 1730 *Forward* LC Potomack Jan 1731. M.

Wheeler, Robert. S & T Oct 1732 *Caesar*. L.

Wheeler, Roger Jr. of Potterne, blacksmith. R for Barbados Jly 1698. Wi.

Wheeler, Rose (1675). *See* Goodman. M.

Wheeler, Samuel. R Jly 1685. M.

Wheeler, Susanna. S & T Oct 1722 *Forward* to Md. M.

Wheeler, Susannah. S Sep T Nov 1743 *George William*. M.

Wheeler als Day, Thomas. R for Barbados Jan 1693. M.

Wheeler, Thomas. S Apr-May T Jly 1771 *Scarsdale*. M.

Wheeler als Eyres, William. SQS Jly TB to Md Oct 1737. So.

Wheeler, William. S s at Ripple Summer 1766. Wo.

Wheeler, William. R Summer 1773. Ht.

Wheeler, William. S Jan-Feb 1774. M.

Wheelhouse als Wheelas, John. S City Lent 1745. Y.

Wheelock, William Sr. S Lent 1769; Joseph Wheelock hanged, wife Sarah branded, son William hanged. Ch.

Wheldrake, John of Pocklington. R for Barbados Jly 1699. Y.

Whelpley, Robert (1768). *See* Whitely. Wi.

Whepson, William. T Jan 1741 *Vernon*. Ht.

Wherrett, John. R 14 yrs Mar 1774. Do.

Whetcomb, Sarah. S May T Jly 1723 *Alexander* to Md LC Annapolis Sep 1723. M.

Whetland, John. S Lent 1746. K.

Whetley, William. R 14 yrs Aug 1739. So.

Whetstone, John. S Lent R 14 yrs Summer 1752. Li.

Whetten als Jarrat, John. S s horse Summer 1745 R 14 yrs Lent 1746. Wa.

Whetter als Whitehorne als Whitehall, Stephen of Boxgrove. R for Barbados or Jamaica Feb 1684. Sx.

Wheymark. *See* Waymark.

Whiat. *See* Wyatt.

Whibby, Simon of Fordham. R for America Apr 1697. Su.

Whiddon, Henry. R 14 yrs Mar 1746. De.

Whiddon, John. S Mar 1730. De.

Whidler, John (1686). *See* Wheeler. So.

Whiffen, John. S Feb T Apr 1768 *Thornton*. M.

Whiffin, William. S s at Preston Lent 1746. La.

Whims, Thomas. SQS Feb T May 1767 *Thornton*. M.

Whipple, Frances (1683). *See* Marshall. L.

Whippy, Edward. S May T Oct 1719 *Susannah & Sarah* LC Md Apr 1720. L.

Whiskin, Richard. S s at Haverhill Summer 1757. Su.

Whiston, Jane. S Mar 1736. De.

Whiston, John. S for burglary Summer 1723 R 14 yrs Lent 1725. Sh.

Whitaker, Andrew of St. Saviour, Southwark. S Lent T Oct 1750 *Lichfield*. Sy.

Whitaker als Shepherd, Ann of Rossendall, spinster. SQS Apr 1774. La.

Whitaker, David. SQS Jun T Sep 1766 *Justitia*. M.

Whittaker, George of York. R for Barbados Jun 1692. Y.

Whitacre, Grace. SQS Jan TB Apr 1766. So.

Whittaker, James. S s jewelry at St. Dunstan in East Sep T Oct 1768 *Justitia*. L.

Whitaker, John. S Jan T Mar 1750 *Tryal*. L.

Whitaker, John. S Sep 1754. L.
Witaker als Slade, Mary. S May-Jun T Jly 1753 *Tryal*. M.
Whittaker, Mary Ann. SQS Dec 1766 T Jan 1767 *Tryal*. M.
Whitaker, Thomas. S Feb T Mar 1727 *Rappahannock*. L.
Whittaker, Thomas. S Oct T Nov 1728 *Forward* LC Rappahannock Jun
   1729. M.
Whitaker als Wyer, William. S Lent 1754. Su.
Whitall, Daniel. S s peas at Culmington Summer 1766. Sh.
Whitall, John. S May T Jly 1723 *Alexander* to Md. M.
Whytall, William. S s from Lady Gertrude Carey Dec 1765 T Jan 1766
   Tryal. M.
Whitby, Thomas. S s horse Lent R 14 yrs Summer 1757. Li.
Whitby, William. R 14 yrs Jly 1747. Ha.
Whitby, William. T Aug 1752 *Tryal*. M.
Whitchelo, William. T Jly 1722 *Alexander*. Bu.
Whitcher, Thomas. S for highway robbery & R 14 yrs Summer 1733. Be.
Whitcherley, Thomas. S s horse Lent 1723 R 14 yrs Summer 1724. Sh.
Whitcliff, Richard of Newington. SQS Apr T Sep 1751 *Greyhound*. Sy.
White, Alexander. S May-Jly T Sep 1751 *Greyhound*. M.
White, Ann. R Jly 1747. Ha.
White, Ann als Elener. S May-Jly 1748. M.
White, Ann. S Feb-Apr T May 1755 *Rose*. M.
White, Ann. S & T Jan 1767 *Tryal*. M.
White, Ann (1772). *See* Hicks. M.
White, Ann wife of John. R 14 yrs Aug 1773. So.
White, Benjamin. SL Jun 1754. Sy.
White als Whitwood, Katherine. R for Barbados or Jamaica Dec
   1689. L.
White als Blood, Catherine. S May T Jly 1723 *Alexander* LC Annapolis
   Sep 1723. M.
White, Catherine. S Jly T Sep 1764 *Justitia*. M.
White, Catherine Maria. S Jly 1734. M.
White, Charles. S & T Apr 1766 *Ann*. L.
White, Charles. SQS Sep 1773. M.
White, Christopher. S & T Apr 1766 *Ann*. M.
White, Daniel. S & R 14 yrs Lent TB Aug 1757. G.
White, Edward. S & T Apr 1733 *Patapsco* LC Annapolis Nov 1733. M.
White, Edward. S Lent 1749. E.
White, Edward. S Oct T Dec 1771 *Justitia*. L.
White, Eleanor (1736). *See* Higginson. M.
White als Smith, Elizabeth wife of John of Diss. R for America Jly
   1700. Nf.
White, Elizabeth. S & T Apr 1725 *Sukey* LC Annapolis Sep 1725. M.
White, Elizabeth. S Aug T 14 yrs Sep 1725 *Forward* LC Annapolis Dec
   1725. L.
White, Elizabeth. S Jun-Dec 1738 T Jan 1739 *Dorsetshire* to Va. M.
White, Elizabeth. T Jun 1740 *Essex*. Sy.
White als Wilkes, Elizabeth. S Oct 1744-Jan 1745. M.
White, Elizabeth. S Jun-Dec 1745. M.
White, Elizabeth. S Jly-Dec 1747. M.
White, Elizabeth. S Summer T Sep 1751 *Greyhound*. Sy.

White, Elizabeth. S Apr 1761. L.
White, Elizabeth. SQS Jly T Sep 1764 *Justitia*. M.
White, Elizabeth, als wife of Gervase Turner of Sheffield, cutler. SQS
Oct 1775. La.
White, Frances. S Aug T Oct 1741 *Sea Horse* to Va. M.
White, Gabriel. S Mar 1763 TB to Va. De.
White, George. R 14 yrs Lent 1721. Wo.
White, George. S May T Jun 1726 *Loyal Margaret* LC Annapolis Oct
1726. M.
White, George. S Summer 1737. Nf.
White, George of Stepney. S for highway robbery Jly T 14 yrs Dec 1740
Vernon. M.
White, George. S May T Jun 1756 *Lyon*. L.
White, George. S Nov T Dec 1763 *Neptune*. L.
White als Towser, George. T 14 yrs Sep 1766 *Justitia*. Ht.
White, George. T 14 yrs May 1767 *Thornton*. K.
White, George. S & T Jly 1771 *Scarsdale*. M.
White, Gerrard (1664). *See* Wayte. L.
White, Hannah. S Jan T Apr 1743 *Justitia*. M.
White, Hannah wife of Robert. S 14 yrs for receiving Lent 1768. O.
White, Hannibal. R Aug AT Oct 1700. M.
White, Henry. PT Jan 1685. M.
White, Henry. S Apr TB May 1719. L.
White, Henry. R 14 yrs Aug 1726. De.
White, Henry. R 14 yrs Aug 1731. So.
White, Henry. S & T Jan 1739 *Dorsetshire*. L.
White, Henry. T Apr 1743 *Justitia*. Sy.
White, Henry. S Apr 1745. L.
White, Henry. S & R 14 yrs Lent T May 1772. No.
White, James. S May T Jly 1722 *Alexander*. L.
White, James. S & T May 1736 *Patapsco* to Md. M.
White, James. S Feb T Apr 1741 *Speedwell* or *Mediterranean* to Md. M.
White, James. R 14 yrs Mar 1743. De.
White, James. R 14 yrs Jly 1745. Ha.
White, James. S Lent 1750. Y.
White als Haycock, James. S Lent 1766. Wa.
White, James (1768). *See* Griggs. L.
White, James. T 14 yrs Oct 1768 *Justitia*. Sx.
White, James. T 14 yrs Apr 1769 *Tryal*. K.
White, James. S s horse & R 14 yrs Summer 1770. La.
White, Jane, spinster, als wife of John. R for Barbados Jly 1663. L.
White, Jane. R Dec 1716 T Jan 1717 *Queen Elizabeth* to Jamaica. M.
White, Jane of St. Margaret, Westminster, spinster. S s gown & T May
1740 *Essex*. M.
White, Joan. R for Barbados Feb 1672. M.
White, John (1668). *See* Edmonds. Wi.
White, John (1674). *See* Williams. M.
White, John of Bagshot. R for Barbados or Jamaica Jly 1677. Sy.
White, John of Coventry. R for America Jly 1682. Wa.
White, John of Thetford. R for America Feb 1684. Nf.
White, John. Rebel T 1685.

White, John. R for America Aug 1715. M.

White, John. S Jly T 14 yrs Aug 1718 *Eagle* LC Charles Town Mar 1719. L.

White, John. S Apr T May 1720 *Honor* LC Port York Jan 1721. L.

White, John. S Jly T Aug 1721 *Prince Royal* LC Va Apr 1722. L.

White, John. S Jly T Aug 1721 *Prince Royal* but died on passage. L.

White, John. T Oct 1723 *Forward*. E.

White, John. S Aug T Sep 1725 *Forward* to Md. M.

White, John, als Reynolds, Arnold. S Feb 1730. L.

White, John. S & T Apr 1733 *Patapsco* LC Annapolis Nov 1733. L.

White, John. T Jan 1738 *Dorsetshire*. Sy.

White, John. S Lent 1738. Hu.

White, John. T Oct 1738 *Genoa*. Sx.

White, John. T Jun 1740 *Essex*. K.

White, John. S Aug T Oct 1741 *Sea Horse* to Va. M.

White, John. S Jan 1745. L.

White, John. R 14 yrs Summer 1748. Y.

White, John. S Feb T Mar 1750 *Tryal*. M.

White, John. S Summer 1751 R 14 yrs Lent T May 1752 *Lichfield*. K.

White als Young, John. R 14 yrs Summer 1753. Nl.

White, John (1754). *See* Cleave. So.

White, John. S Oct T Nov 1759 *Phoenix*. L.

White, John. S Jly 1763 TB to Va. De.

White, John (1764). *See* Pinchin. M.

White, John (1764). *See* Lee. Sy.

White, John of St. George, Southwark. SQS Jan T Mar 1764 *Tryal*. Sy.

White, John. S Jly T Oct 1768 *Justitia*. M.

White, John (1769). *See* Symes. De.

White, John. S Oct T Dec 1771 *Justitia*. L.

White, John. R Mar TB to Va Apr 1773. Wi.

White, John. S Jly 1774. Ha.

White, John. S Jan 1775. M.

White als Wate, Jonathan. R for Barbados Oct 1673. L.

White, Joseph. S Jan T Feb 1733 *Smith*. L.

White, Joseph. S Summer T Sep 1751 *Greyhound*. Sy.

White, Joseph. SQS Jly 1763. M.

White, Joseph. S & TB to Va Apr 1769. Wi.

White, Laurence (1686). *See* King. E.

White, Leonard. R Mar 1774. So.

White, Margaret. S Dec 1772. M.

White als Raven, Mary, widow aged 42. R for Barbados Feb & Aug 1664. L.

White, Mary (1677). *See* Toole. L.

White, Mary (1679). *See* Penryn.

White als Cass, Mary. S Jly T 14 yrs Aug 1718 *Eagle* LC Charles Town Mar 1719. L.

White als Fearn, Mary. T Oct 1723 *Forward*. K.

White, Mary. S Feb T Apr 1734 *Patapsco*. L.

White, Mary. S & T May 1736 *Patapsco*. L.

White, Mary. S Apr T Sep 1737 *Pretty Patsy* to Md. M.

White als Shays, Mary. S Jly-Sep T 14 yrs Sep 1742 *Forward*. M.

White, Mary. S May T Nov 1743 *George William*. M.
White als Brown, Mary. S City Summer 1743. Nl.
White, Mary. SQS & T Sep 1751 *Greyhound*. M.
White, Mary. S Oct 1751-Jan 1752. M.
White, Mary. S Jly T Nov 1759 *Phoenix*. M.
White als Scamp, Mary. S Lent 1765 for obtaining goods at Hanley
   Castle by falsely pretending to know where treasure was buried. Wo.
White, Mary. S & T Sep 1766 *Justitia*. M.
White, Mary. S Feb T May 1767 *Thornton*. L.
White, Mary. S Sep T Dec 1769 *Justitia*. M.
White, Matthias. T Jun 1740 *Essex*. K.
White, Michael. S Jan T Feb 1765 *Tryal*. L.
White, Nehemiah. S Mar 1748. Ha.
White, Orlando. T Dec 1734 *Caesar*. E.
White, Perry of Hampstead Marshall. R for America Feb 1684. Be.
White, Randall als William. S Lent T 14 yrs Apr 1772 *Thornton*. K.
White, Rebecca. S Jly T Aug 1721 *Prince Royal* LC Va Nov 1721. L.
White, Richard. S Jan T Feb 1719 *Worcester* LC Annapolis Jun 1719. L.
White, Richard. AT Lent T Oct 1723 *Forward* to Va from London. Y.
White, Richard. T Apr 1732 *Patapsco*. K.
White, Richard. S s hats May 1735 T Jan 1736 *Dorsetshire* LC Va Sep
   1736. M.
White, Richard. S Lent R 14 yrs Summer TB to Va Sep 1765. Le.
White, Robert. Rebel T 1685.
White, Robert. S s horse Lent 1724 R 14 yrs Lent 1729. Y.
White, Robert. R 14 yrs Jly TB to Va Oct 1742. Wi.
White, Robert. SQS Oct 1751. M.
White, Robert. S s at Great Tew Lent 1766. O.
White, Samuel. S Mar 1726. Do.
Wight, Samuel. S Aug 1727 T *Forward* LC Rappahannock May 1728. M.
White, Samuel. T Aug 1752 *Tryal*. Sy.
White, Sarah. S May T Jun 1727 *Susanna* to Va. M.
White, Sarah. S Lent 1763. E.
White, Sophia wife of John. S Feb T Apr 1739 *Forward* to Va. M.
White, Susanna. S Jun 1733 T Jan 1734 *Caesar* LC Va Jly 1734. M.
White, Susanna. T Sep 1757 *Thetis*. K.
White, Thomas of Great Horningheath. R for Barbados Mar 1679. Su.
White, Thomas. R for America Feb 1700. No.
White, Thomas of Newent. R for America Feb 1714. G.
White, Thomas. S City Lent 1733. Y.
White, Thomas. S & TB Aug 1740. G.
White, Thomas. T Apr 1742 *Bond*. E.
White, Thomas. S s sheep & R 14 yrs Summer 1746. Hu.
White, Thomas. S Lent R 14 yrs Summer TB Aug 1747. G.
White, Thomas. S May-Jly 1749. M.
White, Thomas. S Summer T Sep 1751 *Greyhound*. Sx.
White, Thomas. R 14 yrs Jly 1753. Ha.
White, Thomas. SQS Mar TB Apr 1755. Le.
White, Thomas. S Mar 1761. Ha.
White, Thomas. T for life Dec 1771 *Justitia*. Sy.
Wight, Thomas. S s clothing Summer 1773. Nl.

White, William (1664). *See* Farlow. Sy.

White, William of Benson. R for America Jly 1688. O.

White, William. S for Boston NE Jly 1718. Ha.

White, William. T Oct 1723 *Forward*. K.

White, William. TB to Va Nov 1725 T *Rappahannock* LC Rappahannock Apr 1726. Le.

White als Deacombe, William. S Mar 1728. Ha.

White, William. S & T Lent 1729. Y.

White, William. S Feb T Mar 1731 *Patapsco* LC Annapolis Jun 1731. M.

White, William. S & T Apr 1733 *Patapsco* LC Annapolis Nov 1733. M.

White, William. S & T Jan 1739 *Dorsetshire*. L.

White, William. S Mar 1749 TB to Va. De.

White, William. R 14 yrs Mar 1750. Co.

White, William. R 14 yrs Aug 1751. So.

White, William. S Apr T May 1755 *Rose*. L.

White, William. S for highway robbery Summer 1761 R 14 yrs Lent 1762. No.

White, William. T 14 yrs Nov 1762 *Prince William*. K.

White, William. S & T Apr 1766 *Ann*. L.

White, William. S Jly 1767. Ha.

White, William (1772). *See* White, Randall. K.

White als Jennings, William of North Mimms. S Lent T Apr 1772 *Thornton*. Ht.

Wight, William (1774). *See* Wright. Nl.

White als Rigglesworth, William. S Sep-Oct 1774. M.

White, William. S Oct 1774. L.

Whitebourn, John. S Oct T 14 yrs Dec 1724 *Rappahannock*.L.

Whitebread, Jane of Chesham, spinster. R for America Jly 1702. Bu.

Whitecake, John of Lexden or Marks Tey. R 14 yrs Lent T Apr 1772 *Thornton*. E.

Whitefoot, Edward. S for killing sheep Summer 1743 R 14 yrs Lent 1744. He.

Whitefoot, Thomas. S Apr 1773. M.

Whitehall, Stephen (1684). *See* Whetter. Sx.

Whitehand, William. R for Barbados Jun 1671. L.

Whitehart, Richard. R for Barbados Dec 1671. M.

Whitehead, Abraham. S Sep T Nov 1743 *George William*. L.

Whitehead, Charles. S Feb T Mar 1730 *Patapsco* LC Annapolis Sep 1730. L.

Whitehead, Daniel. S May 1715 T Dec 1716 *Lewis* to Jamaica. M.

Whitehead, Daniel. S as pickpocket Summer 1739 R 14 yrs Lent 1740. Wa.

Whitehead, Elizabeth. R for Barbados Mar 1677. L.

Whitehead, Elizabeth. S Feb T May 1736 *Patapsco* to Md. M.

Whitehead, Isaac of Chatterton, weaver. SQS Jly 1747. La.

Whitehead, John of Read. SQS May 1753. La.

Whitehead, John. S Jan-Feb 1773. M.

Whitehead, Joseph. S & R Summer 1761. Nl.

Whitehead, Joseph. S s sheep Lent R 14 yrs Summer 1761. Nt.

Whitehead, Mary. S Apr 1720. M.

Whitehead, Richard. S Jan T Feb 1742 *Industry*. L.

Whitehead, Rose. R for Barbados Dec 1668. M.

Whitehead, Thomas. S s gold watch Summer 1741 R 14 yrs Summer 1743. Du.

Whitehead, Timothy. S & T Apr 1733 *Patapsco* LC Annapolis Nov 1733. L.

Whitehead, William. R for Barbados Mar 1683. L.

Whitehead, William. S Aug T Sep 1764 *Justitia*. L.

Whitehorn, John. LC from *Alexander* Annapolis Sep 1723. X.

Whitehorne, Nicholas. S Jan T Feb 1724 *Anne* to Carolina. M.

Whitehorne, Stephen (1684). *See* Whetter. Sx.

Whitehouse, James. R 14 yrs Jly 1774. M.

Whitehouse, Jeremiah. S 14 yrs Apr-Jun 1739. M.

Whitehouse, John. S s nails at Tipton Lent 1769. St.

Whitehouse, Joseph. S & R Summer T Sep 1773. Wa.

Whitehouse, Joseph. SQS Dec 1774. M.

Whitehouse, Joseph. S s at Dudley Lent 1775. Wo.

Whitehouse, Samuel. S s at Wolverhampton Summer 1764. St.

Whitley, Ann. S & T Dec 1736 *Dorsetshire*. L.

Whietley, George of Fulmer. S Lent 1761. Bu.

Whitley, James of Manchester. SQS Oct 1774. La.

Whitley, Joseph. Died on passage in *Alexander* 1723. X.

Whitely als Ward, Mary. S Feb T Apr 1770 *New Trial*. M.

Whitely als Whelpley, Robert. R 14 yrs Mar TB to Va Oct 1768. Wi.

Whiteman, Ann. S & T Jan 1756 *Greyhound*. M.

Whiteman, Sarah. S Jly 1760. M.

Whitman, William. S for highway robbery & R Summer 1736. Su.

Whitemarsh, James. R Aug 1700. M.

Whitenail, Thomas of St. Andrew, Hertford, cordwainer. SQS Oct T Dec 1763 *Neptune*. Ht.

Whitenit, William of Birmingham. R for America Jly 1678. Wa.

Whiteoake, Thomas of Isle of Ely. R for Barbados or Jamaica Oct 1664. Ca.

Whiteside, Thomas, als Bradshaw, Henry. S s horse Summer 1752 R 14 yrs Lent 1753. La.

Whitesides, Henry. S Feb T Apr 1734 *Patapsco*. L.

Whiteway, William. R for Barbados or Jamaica Oct 1694. L.

Whitwood, Ann (1689). *See* Dye. M.

Whitwood, Katherine (1689). *See* White. L.

Whitewood, John. SWK Jan 1773. K.

Whitfield, Barthia. S Feb-Apr 1746. M.

Whitfield, Charles. S s mare & R Summer 1775. Wa.

Whitfield, Daniel. S s sacks Lent 1768. Ca.

Whitfield, Henry. S Apr-Jun T Jly 1772 *Tayloe*. M.

Whitfield, John of Waltham Cross. R for Barbados or Jamaica Feb 1686. E.

Whitfield, John. S Lent 1758. La.

Whitfield, Joshua. S s sheep Summer 1763 R 14 yrs Lent 1764. Li.

Whitfield, Joshua. S Oct 1765 T Jan 1766 *Tryal*. L.

Whitfield, Richard. S s from bleaching croft at Whorlton & R 14 yrs Lent TB Aug 1770. Y.

Whitfield, Thomas. R for Barbados May 1665. X.

Whitfield, Thomas. T Apr 1765 *Ann*. M.

Whithier, Arthur. S Mar 1752. De.

Whiteing als Turpin, Daniel. S s horse Lent R 14 yrs Summer 1749. Be.

Whiting, George. S Lent 1730 but dead by Summer 1730. Y.

Whiteing, James. S for highway robbery Summer 1728 (SP). Hu.

Whiteing, Mary. S Jun 1733 T Jan 1734 *Caesar* LC Va Jly 1734. M.

Whiting, Samuel. SQS Apr TB May 1756. So.

Whiteing, Thomas. R for Barbados Jun 1665. L.

Whiteing, Thomas. S s horse Lent 1725 R 14 yrs Lent 1729. Y.

Whiting, Thomas. T Oct 1738 *Genoa*. Ht.

Whiting, Thomas. S Sep T Dec 1763 *Neptune*. M.

Whitelock, John. AT City Summer 1758. Nl.

Whitlock, Robert of St. Martin, Norwich. S Summer 1731. *Nf.

Whitlock, William. TB to Va from QS 1729. De.

Whitlock, William. T Jan 1734 *Caesar*. E.

Whitlow, William. SW & T Jun 1768 *Tryal*. M.

Whitman. *See* Whiteman.

Whitmill, Ann of Farthinghoe. R for America Feb 1713. No.

Whitmill, Richard. S s horse Lent R 14 yrs Summer 1746. Wa.

Whitmore, Francis. S Nov T Dec 1753 *Whiteing*. L.

Whitmore, John (1770). *See* Palser. G.

Whitmore, Lydia. S Oct 1749. L.

Whitmore, Robert. S Lent R Summer 1739 (SP). St.

Whitmore, Thomas of Coton. R for America Jly 1678. Wa.

Whitmore, William. S Jan T Apr 1735 *Patapsco* LC Annapolis Oct 1735. M.

Whitmore, William. SQS Dec 1773. M.

Whitney als Dribray, Elizabeth of St. Clement Danes, spinster. S for robbery with violence & T May 1740 *Essex*. M.

Whitney, James (1752). *See* James, John. Y.

Whitney, John. S & T Dec 1770 *Justitia*. M.

Whitten, Mathew. S Jan R 14 yrs for Md or Va Feb 1719. L.

Whittenbury, Mary of Cottered, spinster, a Quaker. SQS 1664 R for plantations Jly 1665. Ht.

Whittimore, George (1763). *See* Morris. Wo.

Whittingham, John. S Lent 1748. Ch.

Whittingham, Joseph. S Jan T Jun 1738 *Forward* to Md or Va. M.

Whittingham, Samuel. S Aug 1727 T *Forward* LC Rappahannock May 1728. M.

Whittington, Edmund. S Dec 1727. L.

Whittle, Giles. Rebel T 1685.

Whittle, Samuel. S & T Aug 1718 *Eagle*. L.

Whittle, William. S Lent 1748. Ch.

Whittles, Austin. T Dec 1731 *Forward*. Sy.

Whittock, Joseph of Bristol. R for Barbados Feb 1700. G.

Whiton, Henry. S s calf Lent R 14 yrs Summer 1763. O.

Whitton, Henry. S s mare at Badingham & R Summer 1770. Su.

Whitton, John. S Feb T Mar 1731 *Patapsco* LC Annapolis Jun 1731. M.

Witton, John. S for killing sheep Summer 1757 R 14 yrs Summer TB Sep 1758. Nf.

Witton, Mary. AT from QS Summer 1729. St.

Whitton, Matthew. S & T Feb 1719 *Worcester* LC Annapolis Jun 1719. M.

Witton, William. S Lent T Jun 1756 *Lyon*. Sy.

Whitwell, John. PT Dec 1674 R Feb 1675. M.

Whitwell, William. S Feb-Apr T May 1755 *Rose*. M.

Whitwick, Edward. R for Barbados Mar 1681. M.

Whitwood. *See* Whitewood.

Whitworth, Alice. S Jan-Feb 1775. M.

Whitworth, Peter. S Summer 1740. Y.

Whood. *See* Wood.

Whorewood als Horrod, Sarah. S s silver spoon from New College Lent 1756. O.

Wick, Jane. S Lent R 14 yrs Summer 1742. Wo.

Wick, Matthew. S for forgery & R Summer 1773. Sh.

Wickenden, David. T Apr 1753 *Thames*. K.

Whicker, Benjamin. Rebel T 1685.

Whicker, John. Rebel T 1685.

Wicker, John. LC from *Gilbert* Annapolis Jly 1722. X.

Wicker, John. T Dec 1753 *Whiteing*. E.

Wickers, John. R for Barbados Jun 1671. M.

Wickett, Daniel. S Apr T 14 yrs May 1743 *Indian Queen* to Potomack. M.

Wickett, John. S Mar 1751. De.

Wickham, Catherine. S May-Jun T Aug 1752 *Tryal*. M.

Wickham, John. S Sep-Oct 1746. M.

Wickham, Joseph. Rebel T 1685.

Wickham, Matthew. SQS & T Sep 1764 *Justitia*. M.

Wickham, Thomas. T Jly 1723 *Alexander* LC Md Sep 1723. Sx.

Wicking, Richard. S Lent 1749. Nf.

Wicks, Charles. S Summer 1757. Nf.

Wicks, Edmund. S Lent 1738. Nf.

Wicks, Edward. S s from Exeter College Summer 1723 R 14 yrs Summer 1724 T *Forward* LC Annapolis Jun 1725. O.

Wicks, Henry. S s at St. Lawrence, Reading, Lent 1753. Be.

Wicks, John. S s mare Lent R 14 yrs Summer 1734. Be.

Wicks, John of Stratford at Bow. S & T Feb 1740 *York* to Md. M.

Wicks, Joseph. S for burglary Lent R for life Summer 1753 (SP). O.

Wicks, Mary. S Feb T Mar 1729 *Patapsco* LC Annapolis Dec 1729. L.

Wicks, Richard (1688). *See* Weekes. Su.

Wicks, Thomas. T Oct 1738 *Genoa*. Sx.

Wicks, William. S Lent 1774. G.

Wicksey, Roger. PT Sep 1684. M.

Widdowson, Richard of Bootle cum Lineaker. R for Barbados Jly 1683. La.

Widdup, Paul. R 14 yrs Summer 1753. Y.

Widerington. *See* Witherington.

Widgeon, Sarah. SQS Apr 1773. M.

Widgeon, William. S Apr 1745. L.

Widlake, Jabez Jr. S Mar 1749. So.

Wiechard, Anne. S Oct T Nov 1728 *Forward* LC Rappahannock Jun 1729. M.

Wiesenthall, Charles Frederick. T Sep 1757 *Thetis*. L.
Wiggan, Joseph. S & T Sep 1765 *Justitia*. L.
Wiggin, Lawrence. S Mar TB to Md Apr 1742. Le.
Wiggin, William. S Nov T Dec 1752 *Greyhound*. L.
Wiggington, John (1772). *See* East. M.
Wiggington, William. S Lent T May 1767 *Thornton*. Bu.
Wiggins, James. S s bacon at Brize Norton Lent 1775. O.
Wiggins, John. S & T Jly 1753 *Tryal*. L.
Wiggins, Mary. SQS Jun T Jly 1772 *Tayloe*. M.
Wiggins, Richard of Ragdale. R for America Jly 1678. Le.
Wiggins, Robert of St. Giles in Fields. S s shoes Apr T May 1740
    Essex. M.
Wiggins, Thomas. S Jan T 14 yrs Feb 1719 *Worcester* LC Annapolis Jun
    1719. L.
Wiggins, Thomas. T Jun 1740 *Essex*. Sy.
Wiggins, William. S s at Charlbury Lent 1727. O.
Wigginson, Peter. S & T Dec 1767 *Neptune*. M.
Wiggs, Francis. S Lent R 14 yrs Summer T Oct 1750 *Rachael*. Ht.
Wigham, William, als Greene, Thomas of High Crosby. R for Barbados
    Jly 1682. Cu.
Wight. *See* White.
Wigley, Elizabeth. R & T Dec 1716 *Lewis* to Jamaica. M.
Wigley, Elizabeth. R 14 yrs Dec 1774. M.
Wigley, John. S Mar 1748. Ha.
Wigmore, Catherine. SL & T Sep 1767 *Justitia*. Sy.
Wigmore, Catherine. S Jan-Feb 1775. M.
Wigmore, John. S Feb-Apr T Jun 1756 *Lyon*. M.
Wiggmore, Richard. S & T Oct 1732 *Caesar* to Va. M.
Wigmore, William. AT Winter 1667 & 1669. Bd.
Wignall, James. S Summer 1750. Hu.
Wignall, Thomas. S Jan-May T Jun 1738 *Forward* to Md or Va. M.
Wilbert, William. S Dec 1733 T Jan 1734 *Caesar* LC Va Jly 1734. L.
Wilbourne, John. S Feb-Apr T May 1755 *Rose*. M.
Wilburn, Sarah. S May T Jly 1722 *Alexander* LC Annapolis Sep 1723. M.
Wilcock, David. S Lent 1725 R 14 yrs Lent 1729. Y.
Wilcocks. *See* Wilcox.
Wilcockson, Thomas (1749). *See* Simpson, Charles. St.
Wilcox, Daniel. PT Sep 1691 R Jan 1692. M.
Wilcox, Edward. S s at Cardington Lent T Oct 1765. Bd.
Wilcox, Elizabeth. S Apr T May 1740 *Essex*. L.
Willcocks, Henry. R Mar 1772 TB to Va. De.
Wilcox, John. S Jly T Aug 1721 *Prince Royal* LC Va Nov 1721. M.
Wilcox, John. S s pewter at Old Swinford Summer 1765. Wo.
Wilcox, John. S for highway robbery Lent R for life Summer 1766. No.
Wilcocks als Hurred, John. TB to Va from QS 1767. De.
Wilcox, John. R Lent 1773. Sy.
Willcox, Margaret. S Feb T Apr 1732 *Patapsco* LC Annapolis Oct
    1732. L.
Wilcox, Mary. S Feb T Mar 1760 *Friendship*. M.
Wilcox, Peter. S Summer 1766. Wa.
Wilcocks, Philip. S Mar 1735. De.

Wilcox, Richard. Rebel T 1685.

Wilcocks, Robert. S Feb T Apr 1772 *Thornton*. L.

Wilcocks, Samuel. R for Barbados or Jamaica Jan 1692. M.

Wilcox, Thomas of St. Philip & Jacob. R for America Jly 1696. G.

Wilcox, Thomas. S & T Oct 1730 *Forward* LC Potomack Jan 1731. L.

Wilcox, Thomas. S Jan-Apr 1748. M.

Wilcox, Thomas. S s at Cound Lent 1756. Sh.

Wilcox als Cox, Thomas. S May T Sep 1765 *Justitia*. M.

Wilcocks, Walter. S Mar 1752. De.

Wyld, Abel. S & T Oct 1722 *Forward* LC Annapolis Jun 1723. M.

Wild, Abraham of Farnworth, weaver. SQS Jan 1766. La.

Wild, Edward. S Feb T Apr 1770 *New Trial*. M.

Wyld, Elizabeth. R for Barbados Sep TB Oct 1669. L.

Wild, Elizabeth (1732). *See* Taylor. M.

Wild, Francis. S Lent R 14 yrs Summer 1738. St.

Wild, Henry. T Aug 1720 *Owners Goodwill*. K.

Wild, Jane wife of Stephen. S Jan T Feb 1744 *Neptune* to Md. M.

Wild, John. S Oct T 14 yrs Dec 1724 *Rappahannock* to Va. M.

Wilde, John. S Jly TB to Va Sep 1756. Wi.

Wyld, John. S & T Dec 1771 *Justitia*. M.

Wild, John. S Feb 1774, found at large in Stepney & ordered to hang Sep 1775. M.

Wild, Joseph. R for life for counterfeiting Lent 1775. Sy.

Wild, Peter. S s at Beaconsfield Lent T Apr 1769 *Tryal*. Bu.

Wild, Robert. S s sheep Summer 1742 R 14 yrs Lent TB Apr 1743. Db.

Wild, Stephen (1756). *See* Cleeve, Edward. Ha.

Wild, Thomas. S Feb T Apr 1741 *Speedwell* or *Mediterranean* to Md. M.

Wild, Thomas. S & T May 1744 *Justitia*. L.

Wildblood, Thomas. R for America Jly 1687. Wa.

Wilder als Hawkins, Ann. S Sep T Oct 1744 *Susannah*. L.

Wilder, Sarah. T Mar 1758 *Dragon*. L.

Wilder, Thomas. R for life Feb 1738. Ha.

Wilder, William of Stoke next Guildford. SQS Jan 1754. Sy.

Wilder, William. S Jan T Mar 1758 *Dragon*. L.

Wildicke, Joseph. S Aug T Oct 1741 *Sea Horse* to Va. M.

Wilding, Henry. S s sheep at Bradwell Abbey & R 14 yrs Lent 1774. Bu.

Wilding, Jacob. S s hog at Swilland Lent 1769. Su.

Wilding, James. S s at Bromfield Summer 1764. Sh.

Wilding, John of Yalding. R for Barbados or Jamaica Jly 1704. K.

Wildman, John. S Apr T May 1767 *Thornton*. M.

Wildman als Woods, William. S s horse at Kilnwick & R Lent 1773. Y.

Wilds, Hannah. S Dec 1772. M.

Wildy, Joan. S s at Painswick Lent TB Mar 1738. G.

Wile, Thomas. S s sheep at Yardley Summer 1761 R 14 yrs Lent 1762. Wo.

Wiles, Charles. T Apr 1766 *Ann*. K.

Wiles, Henry. S Lent 1753. Su.

Wyles, William of Ash cum Ridley. R for Barbados or Jamaica Mar 1680. K.

Wiley, John. S s at Aldridge Summer 1759. St.

Whiley, John. SW & T Jly 1772 *Tayloe*. M.

Wilford, Anthony. S Summer 1769. Db.

Willford, David, aged 26, dark. S & T Oct 1720 *Giibert* LC Md May 1721. L.

Wilford, Eleanor. S Feb T May 1736 *Patapsco* to Md. M.

Wilford, Hannah. SW & T Apr 1768 *Thornton*. M.

Wilford, Joseph. R & T Sep 1766 *Justitia*. M.

Wilford, Rachel. S Apr T May 1743 *Indian Queen* to Potomack. M.

Wilkes. *See* Wilks.

Wilkeshire. *See* Wiltshire.

Wilkins, Francis. S s sheep Lent R 14 yrs Summer 1750. Bd.

Wilkins, Henry of Evesham. R for America Mar 1680. Wo.

Wilkins, Henry. S 14 yrs for receiving Lent 1772. O.

Wilkins als Philpott als Johnson als Awdrey, Jane. S Jan-Jun 1747. M.

Wilkins als Hiscock, John. R 14 yrs Mar 1744. So.

Wilkins, John. S Jly 1775. L.

Wilkins, Joseph. S Aug T Oct 1724 *Forward* LC Annapolis Jun 1725. M.

Wilkins, Martha (1736). *See* Hadley. M.

Wilkins, Mary. S & R for life Summer 1772. G.

Wilkins, Nicholas. S Feb T Mar 1730 *Patapsco* but died on passage. M.

Wilkins, Phebe. S Lent 1773. K.

Wilkins, Philis. S Jly TB to Va Sep 1738. Wi.

Wilkins, Richard of Woodchester. R for America Jly 1687. G.

Wilkins, Robert. Rebel T 1685.

Wilkins, Samuel. R 14 yrs Mar 1737. So.

Wilkins, Stephen. R 14 yrs Jly 1728. Ha.

Wilkins, Thomas. R 14 yrs Mar 1743. So.

Wilkins, Thomas. R for life Aug 1759. Co.

Wilkins, Thomas. T Jly 1770 *Scarsdale*. M.

Wilkins, Thomas of Reigate. R s sheep Lent T 14 yrs Apr 1772 *Thornton*. Sy.

Wilkins, Thomas. S Oct 1772. L.

Wilkins, William. R 14 yrs Mar 1743. So.

Wilkinson, Alice. S Jan T Feb 1724 *Anne* to Carolina. M.

Wilkinson, Benjamin of St. Saviour, Southwark. R for Barbados or Jamaica Mar 1682 & Feb 1683. Sy.

Wilkinson, Catherine of Little Bolton, singlewoman. SQS Jan 1768. La.

Wilkinson, Edward. S May-Jly 1750. M.

Wilkinson, Eleanor (1722). *See* Emmett. So.

Wilkinson, Elisha. S s ribbon at St. Mary, Huntingdon, Summer 1769. Hu.

Wilkinson, Eliza. S s at Penkridge Summer 1765. St.

Wilkinson, Elizabeth. R for Barbados Mar 1681. L.

Wilkinson, Elizabeth. TB Jly 1745. Db.

Wilkinson, Elizabeth of Bolton in the Moors, spinster. SQS Aug 1755. La.

Wilkinson, Elizabeth (1756). *See* Wright. M.

Wilkinson, Elizabeth. S Jly T Nov 1762 *Prince William*. M.

Wilkinson, Francis. S Aug T Sep 1764 *Justitia*. L.

Wilkinson, George. S & T Mar 1763 *Neptune*. L.

Wilkinson, George. S Jly T Sep 1765 *Justitia*. M.

Wilkinson, Henry. T Jly 1770 *Scarsdale*. Bu.

Wilkinson, James. S Sep-Oct T Dec 1771 *Justitia*. M.

Wilkinson, John. R & T Dec 1716 *Lewis* to Jamaica. M.

Wilkinson, John. LC from *Robert* Annapolis Jun 1725. X.

Wilkinson, John. S Jun-Dec 1738 T Jan 1739 *Dorsetshire* to Va. M.

Wilkinson, John. S Jan T Apr 1741 *Speedwell* or *Mediterranean* to Md. M.

Wilkinson, John. SQS Jly 1754. M.

Wilkinson, John, clerk. S 14 yrs Jly 1756 for performing illegal marriages. M.

Wilkinson, John. S Dec 1763 T Mar 1764 *Tryal*. M.

Wilkinson, John. S Oct 1766 T Jan 1767 *Tryal*. L.

Wilkinson, John. S Feb T May 1767 *Thornton*. M.

Wilkinson, Joseph. Died on passage in *Rappahannock* 1726. X.

Wilkinson, Joshua. S s sheep Lent R 14 yrs Summer 1746. Ht.

Wilkinson, Margaret. S Feb T Mar 1729 *Patapsco* LC Annapolis Dec 1729. L.

Wilkinson, Mary. S Jan-Jun 1747. M.

Wilkinson, Mary. S Summer 1751. Y.

Wilkinson, Mary. SQS & T Dec 1752 *Greyhound*. M.

Wilkinson, Mary (1756). *See* Wilson. M.

Wilkinson, Mary als Watkins. S Dec 1757 T Mar 1758 *Dragon*. M.

Wilkinson, Nicholas. S Summer 1758. We.

Wilkinson, Nicholas of Mearley, Clitherow. SQS Jan 1767. La.

Wilkinson, Richard. S Oct T Dec 1724 *Rappahannock* to Va. M.

Wilkinson, Richard. S Mar 1737. De.

Wilkinson, Robert (1736). *See* Wilson. L.

Wilkinson, Samuel. S & T Apr 1733 *Patapsco* LC Annapolis Nov 1733. L.

Wilkinson, Thomas. R for Barbados Jan 1665. M.

Wilkinson, Thomas of Chesham. R for America Mar 1698. Bu.

Wilkinson, Thomas of Plaistow. R for Barbados or Jamaica Jly 1702. E.

Wilkinson, Thomas. S Lent 1739 R 14 yrs Lent TB Sep 1740. Y.

Wilkinson, Thomas. R 14 yrs Summer 1764. Y.

Wilkinson, Thomas of Bermondsey. SQS Oct 1764 T Feb 1765 *Tryal*. Sy.

Wilkinson, William of Hoar Cross. R for Barbados Jly 1664. St.

Wilkinson, William of Aston by Budworth. R for Barbados Mar 1682. Ch.

Wilkinson, William. S & T Oct 1730 *Forward* LC Potomack Jan 1731. M.

Wilkinson, William. T Oct 1732 *Caesar*. Sy.

Wilkinson, William. S Aug T Sep 1764 *Justitia*. L.

Wilkinson, William. T May 1767 *Thornton*. Sy.

Wilkes als Bolton, Catherine. S Dec 1765 T Jan 1766 *Tryal*. L.

Wilkes, Charles. S Jun T 14 yrs Aug 1769 *Douglas*. M.

Wilks, Edward. S Oct T Nov 1725 *Rappahannock* but died on passage. M.

Wilkes, Edward. S Lent 1755; wife Elizabeth Wilkes als Ellis acquitted. Wo.

Wilkes, Elizabeth (1745). *See* White. M.

Wilks, Emanuel. T Oct 1726 *Forward*. E.

Wilkes, Francis. S s at Stone Summer 1722. St.

Wilks, Francis. S s horse Lent R 14 yrs Summer 1758. Li.

Wilks, Henry. T Oct 1726 *Forward*. E.

Wilkes, Isaac. S May 1763. M.

Wilkes, Joseph. S s at Dixton Summer 1768. Mo.

Wilkes als Boswell als Griffiths, Mary. S Dec 1750. L.

Wilkes als Wilson, Nathaniel. S s at Newbury Lent 1752. Be.

Wilks als Peisley, Thomas. S Aug T Sep 1725 *Forward* LC Md Dec 1725. M.

Wilks, Thomas. S Apr T 14 yrs Jun 1742 *Bladon*. L.

Wilkes, William. S Summer TB to Va Aug 1768. Le.

Wilkes, William. S 14 yrs s cloth from yard at Stow on Wold Lent 1773. G.

Wilkey, John. S Jan T Feb 1719 *Worcester* LC Annapolis Jun 1719. M.

Wilkson, Robert. LC from *Dorsetshire* Va Sep 1736. X.

Willard, Nicholas. T May 1751 *Tryal*. Sx.

Willers, Robert. S Summer 1761. E.

Willert, William. LC from *Forward* Annapolis Jun 1723. X.

Willesmore, Thomas. S Lent R for Barbados May 1664. E.

Willett, Ann. S Jan-Feb 1773. M.

Willett, Humphry. S Nov T Dec 1770 *Justitia*. L.

Willett, Jonas. S Mar 1736. Do.

Willetts, Samuel. S & TB Aug 1740. G.

Willey, Elizabeth. S Lent TB Oct 1748. Y.

Willy, Elizabeth. S Jan 1775. M.

Willey, John. Rebel T 1685.

Willey, John. S Summer 1732. Nl.

William, David of Abergavenny. R for America Feb 1673. Mo.

William, David. S s at Cwmyoy Lent 1749. Mo.

William, John. S & TB Mar 1737. G.

William, John. S s at Redwick Lent 1749. Mo.

William als Williams, Lewis. S & R for life Summer 1775 for plundering the *William* stranded at Sully, Glamorgan. He.

William, Morgan of Llangattock. R for America Mar 1701. Mo.

Williamhurst, Alice. SQS Apr T Jly 1772 *Tayloe*. M.

Williams, Abel. S Dec 1737 T Jan 1738 *Dorsetshire*. L.

Williams, Alice, spinster, als wife of Morgan. R Oct TB Nov 1662. L.

Williams als Steele, Alice of Westbury. R for America Jly 1678. G.

Williams, Alice. S Summer 1749. Sy.

Williams, Andrew. S Lent 1762. Su.

Williams, Anne wife of David of Bridgenorth. R for America Jly 1677. Sh.

Williams, Anne. S Oct T Nov 1728 *Forward* LC Rappahannock Jun 1729. M.

Williams, Ann of Whitechapel. S s linen & T Feb 1740 *York* to Md. M.

Williams als Morrice, Ann. S Oct 1741 T Feb 1742 *Industry*. L.

Williams, Ann, spinster. S s at St. Philip & Jacob Summer 1750. G.

Williams, Ann of Warrington, spinster. SQS Apr 1757. La.

Williams, Ann. S Dec 1761 T Apr 1762 *Dolphin*. M.

Williams, Ann. S s at St. Lawrence, Reading, Summer 1768. Be.

Williams, Ann. S s at Little Missenden & R Lent T Apr 1772 *Thornton*. Bu.

Williams, Barbara. R for Barbados or Jamaica Mar 1685. L.

Williams, Barbara. S Apr 1734. M.

Williams, Benjamin of Henbury. R for America Jly 1682. G.

Williams, Benjamin. S s at St. Nicholas, Hereford, Lent 1760. He.

Williams, Katherine. PT Aug 1678. M.

Williams, Katherine. S for murder of bastard child Lent R 14 yrs Summer 1750. Sh.

Williams, Catherine wife of Joseph. S Summer 1769. Wa.

Williams, Charles. R 10 yrs in plantations Oct 1662. M.

Williams, Charles. T Jly 1722 *Alexander.* Sy.

Williams, Charles. S Dec 1756. M.

Williams, Christopher. R May TB for Barbados Jun 1668. M.

Williams, Christopher. S s at Cannock Lent 1735. St.

Williams, Christian. S Feb T Mar 1730 *Patapsco* LC Annapolis Sep 1730. M.

Williams als Penprose, Daniel. S Jly 1725. Co.

Williams, Daniel. S s sheep & R 14 yrs Summer 1775. St.

Williams, David. PT Oct R Dec 1699. M.

Williams, David. S Jan T Apr 1762 *Dolphin.* L.

Williams, David. T Jun 1764 *Dolphin.* K.

Williams, David. S s silver cup at Oldcastle Lent 1766. Mo.

Williams, David. S s at Kilpeck Lent 1766. He.

Williams, David. SQS Feb T May 1767 *Thornton.* M.

Williams, David, als Delirio, Dio. S s harness at Abbey Dore Summer 1774. He.

Williams, Edward of Oswestry. R for Barbados Mar 1663. Sh.

Williams, Edward of Bermondsey. R for Barbados or Jamaica Jly 1702. Sy.

Williams, Edward. R 14 yrs for Va Aug 1718. L.

Williams, Edward. S Oct T Nov 1728 *Forward* LC Rappahannock Jun 1729. M.

Williams, Edward of Ryton. S s at Claverley Lent 1734. Sh.

Williams, Edward. S s animal skins Sep 1735. M.

Williams, Edward. S Mar TB to Va Apr 1740. Wi.

Williams, Edward. S Sep T Dec 1758 *The Brothers.* M.

Williams, Edward (1765). *See* Jones. M.

Williams, Edward. R Jly T Sep 1767 *Justitia.* L.

Williams, Edward. SQS Jly T Aug 1769 *Douglas.* M.

Williams, Edward (1772). *See* Thomas. X.

Williams, Edward. S & R 14 yrs Summer 1772 for being at large in Whittington while under sentence of transportation. Sh.

Williams, Eleanor. S Feb T Mar 1764 *Tryal.* M.

Williams, Eleanor. S & T Apr 1765 *Ann.* L.

Williams, Elizabeth. R Oct TB Nov 1662. L.

Williams, Elizabeth. R 10 yrs in plantations Oct 1662. M.

Williams, Elizabeth of Hungerford. R for Barbados Jly 1664. Be.

Williams, Elizabeth. R for Barbados Aug 1668. M.

Williams, Elizabeth. R for Barbados Jly 1674. M.

Williams, Elizabeth. R for Barbados Jly 1674. L.

Williams, Elizabeth. R for America Mar 1697. Le.

Williams, Elizabeth. S & T Oct 1722 *Forward.* L.

Williams, Elizabeth. S Jan T Feb 1724 *Anne* to Carolina. M.

Williams, Elizabeth. S Aug T Oct 1724 *Forward* LC Annapolis Jun 1725. M.
Williams, Elizabeth. LC from *Rappahannock* Rappahannock Apr 1726. X.
Williams, Elizabeth. S May T Dec 1734 *Caesar* LC Va Jly 1735. M.
Williams, Elizabeth. S Oct T Dec 1734 *Caesar* LC Va Jly 1735. M.
Williams, Elizabeth. S Jly T Dec 1736 *Dorsetshire* to Va. M.
Williams, Elizabeth. S Feb T Apr 1741 *Speedwell* or *Mediterranean*. M.
Williams, Elizabeth. S Feb-Apr 1746. M.
Williams, Elizabeth. S Sep-Dec 1746. M.
Williams, Elizabeth. SQS Sep T Oct 1750 *Rachael*. M.
Williams, Elizabeth. S Mar 1754. L.
Williams, Elizabeth. S Apr T May 1755 *Rose*. L.
Williams, Elizabeth. S Oct 1756. L.
Williams, Elizabeth. SQS Jan TB Feb 1757. So.
Williams, Elizabeth. S Feb 1761. L.
Williams, Elizabeth. T Sep 1765 *Justitia*. K.
Williams, Elizabeth. SQS & T Dec 1767 *Neptune*. M.
Williams, Elizabeth. S & T Jly 1772 *Tayloe*. M.
Williams, Elizabeth. S for false pretences Lent 1774. Sh.
Williams, Elizha. S May-Jly 1746. M.
Williams, Essex, als Essex, William. S Jan-Feb T Apr 1753 *Thames*. M.
Williams, Evan. S s at Chepstow Summer 1774. Mo.
Williams, Frances. R Dec 1716 T Jan 1717 *Queen Elizabeth* to Jamaica. M.
Williams, Frances of St. Margaret, Westminster. S & T May 1736 *Patapsco*. M.
Williams, Frances wife of Rice. S Apr T May 1767 *Thornton*. M.
Williams, Francis of Wellington. R for Barbados Feb 1669. So.
Williams, Francis. S Lent 1733 T *Patapsco* LC Annapolis Nov 1733. Be.
Williams, Francis. T Oct 1738 *Genoa*. K.
Williams, Francis. T Apr 1742 *Bond*. E.
Williams, George. S Oct 1661 to House of Correction unless he agrees to be transported. M.
Williams, George (1715). *See* Morgan. M.
Williams, George. T May 1719 *Margaret* LC Md May 1720; sold to Patrick Sympson. Sy.
Williams, George. S & T Dec 1734 *Caesar* but died on passage. L.
Williams, George. T Apr 1759 *Thetis*. Sy.
Williams, George. S Sep T Dec 1763 *Neptune*. M.
Williams, George. T Sep 1764 *Justitia*. K.
Williams, Grace. S & T May 1736 *Patapsco*. L.
Williams, Hannah. S Feb T May 1767 *Thornton*. M.
Williams, Henry of Welney. R for America Mar 1680. Nf.
Williams, Henry of Lambeth. SQS Jan T Apr 1765 *Ann*. Sy.
Williams, Henry. S Sep T Dec 1767 *Neptune*. M.
Williams, Henry. S Feb T Apr 1768 *Thornton*. M.
Williams, Hester. SQS Jan 1761. M.
Williams, Isabella. S Oct T 14 yrs Nov 1725 *Rappahannock* to Va. M.
Williams, James of Roche, tinner. R for Barbados Feb 1701. Co.
Williams, James. S Feb T Mar 1727 *Rappahannock* to Va. M.

Williams, James. S Lent 1738. He.
Williams, James. S s at Gloucester Summer 1739. G.
Williams, James. S Jly 1741. De.
Williams, James of Chipping Barnet. R Summer 1745. Ht.
Williams, James. S Oct 1751-Jan 1752. M.
Williams, James. T Dec 1758 *The Brothers*. K.
Williams, James, als Parrott, Thomas. S May T Nov 1762
Prince William. M.
Williams, James. S Summer T Sep 1770. Wa.
Williams, Jane. R for Barbados or Jamaica Jan 1692. L.
Williams, Jane of St. Saviour, Southwark, spinster. R for Barbados or
Jamaica Jun 1692. Sy.
Williams, Jane of Worcester, spinster. R for America Jly 1708. Wo.
Williams, Jane. S Aug 1734. De.
Williams, Jane. TB to Va from QS 1750. De.
Williams, Jane. S May-Jly T Sep 1751 *Greyhound*. M.
Williams, Jarratt. S & R 14 yrs Lent 1773. G.
Williams, Jervis. S s handkerchief at Caerleon Summer 1772. Mo.
Williams, John of Whittington. R for Barbados Jly 1664. St.
Williams, John of Madley. R for Barbados Feb 1671. He.
Williams als Matchett als White, John. R Jly 1674 & Feb 1675 AT Apr
1675. M.
Williams, John Sr. Rebel T 1685.
Williams, John Jr. Rebel T 1685.
Williams, John. R for Barbados or Jamaica Dec 1693. L.
Williams als Stephens, John of Camborne. R for Barbados Feb
1700. Co.
Williams, John of Shrewsbury. R (Western Circ) for America Jly
1710. Sh.
Williams, John (1718). *See* Jones. M.
Williams, John. S Jly T Sep 1718 *Eagle* LC Charles Town Mar 1719. L.
Williams, John of Arborfield. S s coat Summer 1718 R 14 yrs Lent 1721
T *Owners Goodwill* LC Annapolis Jly 1722. Be.
Williams, John (1719). *See* Jones. L.
Williams als Coose, John. T Oct 1720 *Gilbert*. Sy.
Williams, John. S for shoplifting Lent R 14 yrs Summer 1722. Wa.
Williams, John. S s at Panteg Lent 1723. Mo.
Williams, John. T Jly 1724 *Robert* LC Md Jun 1725. K.
Williams, John. S s at Gloucester Summer 1724. G.
Williams, John, aged 57, dark, grazier. LC from *Jonathan* Md Jly
1724. X.
Williams, John (2). S Oct T Dec 1724 *Rappahannock*. L.
Williams als Vincent, John. S 14 yrs Jan 1726 & Aug 1727. M.
Williams, John. S s at Newland Lent TB Aug 1727. G.
Williams, John. T Jun 1728 *Elizabeth* LC Va Aug 1729. Sy.
Williams, John. S as pickpocket Lent R Summer TB Sep 1730. Db.
Williams, John. S Summer 1730. Mo.
Williams, John. S & T Dec 1731 *Forward*. L.
Williams, John. S Summer 1733 R 14 yrs Lent 1734. He.
Williams, John. S Mar 1737. So.
Williams, John (1738). *See* Watson. Sx.

Williams, John. TB to Va from QS 1738. De.

Williams, John. S s at Clifton Lent 1738. G.

Williams, John. S Lent R 14 yrs Summer 1738. Sh.

Williams, John. S Apr-Jun 1739. M.

Williams, John. R 14 yrs Aug 1740 TB to Va. De.

Williams, John of St. Andrew, Holborn. S s hat Sep 1740 T Jan 1741 *Harpooner* to Rappahannock. M.

Williams, John. S for highway robbery Summer 1743 R 14 yrs Lent 1744. Y.

Williams, John. T May 1744 *Justitia*. Ht.

Williams, John. S Jly-Dec 1747. M.

Williams, John. S Summer 1748 R 14 yrs Lent 1749. Sy.

Williams, John. S Jan-Apr 1749. M.

Williams, John. S s at Shrewsbury Lent 1749. Sh.

Williams, John. S Lent R 14 yrs Summer TB Aug 1749. G.

Williams, John. S Oct 1749. L.

Williams, John of Rotherhithe. SQS Apr T May 1750 *Lichfield*. Sy.

Williams, John. S Sep T Oct 1750 *Rachael*. M.

Williams als Charles, John. S Apr 1751. So.

Williams, John. S Mar 1752. Ha.

Williams, John. S Lent R 14 yrs Summer TB Jly 1752. G.

Williams als Hopkins, John. R 14 yrs Aug 1753. De.

Williams, John. S Lent R 14 yrs Summer 1754. Ht.

Williams, John of Liverpool, mariner. S Summer 1754. La.

Williams, John. S & TB Sep 1755. G.

Williams, John. S Aug 1758. Co.

Williams, John. SQS Oct 1758 TB May 1759. So.

Williams, John. S & R 14 yrs Apr 1759. Fl.

Williams, John. S Sep T Nov 1759 *Phoenix*. M.

Williams, John. R 14 yrs Mar 1760. Ha.

Williams, John. S s at Upton Warren Lent R 14 yrs Summer 1761. Wo.

Williams, John. Apprehended Summer 1761 while "under a fit of lunacy" S s gelding at Lydney Lent R 14 yrs Summer 1762. G.

Williams, John. S Aug 1762 TB to Va. De.

Williams, John. S Lent 1763. Wa.

Williams, John. S Sep T Dec 1763 *Neptune*. M.

Williams, John. SWK Oct T Dec 1763 *Neptune*. K.

Williams, John, als King Kago. SQS Dec 1764 T Jan 1765 *Tryal*. M.

Williams, John. S s heifers Lent R 14 yrs Summer 1765. Mo.

Williams, John. S Summer 1765. Wa.

Williams, John. S s sheepskins at St. Swithin, Worcester, Lent 1766. Wo.

Williams, John. S for blackmail Jun T Sep 1767 *Justitia*. M.

Williams, John (1768). *See* Monk. M.

Williams, John. SW & T Apr 1768 *Thornton*. M.

Williams, John. S & T Dec 1769 *Justitia*. L.

Williams, John of Bristol. R for life Feb 1771 (SP). G.

Williams, John. S Lent 1773. Ht.

Williams, John. SQS Apr 1773. M.

Williams, John. S Mar 1774. Do.

Williams, John. R 14 yrs Aug 1774. De.

Williams, John. S s sheep & R 14 yrs Lent 1775. Wo.

Williams als Williamson, John. S for highway robbery & R 14 yrs Summer 1775. Sh.

Williams, John. S for highway robbery & R 14 yrs Summer 1775. St.

Williams, Joseph. S s bullock Lent 1742. Mo.

Williams, Joseph. S s at Awre Lent TB Mar 1752. G.

Williams, Joseph. S s at Teddington Lent 1765. Wo.

Williams, Judy. LC from *Loyal Margaret* Annapolis Oct 1726. X.

Williams, Lewis of Facknait. R for Barbados Jly 1683. Fl.

Williams, Lewis. R 14 yrs Oct 1772. M.

Williams, Lewis. S Sep-Oct 1774. M.

Williams, Lewis (1775). *See* William. He.

Williams, Margaret. S Sep T Oct 1719 *Susannah & Sarah* LC Md Apr 1720. L.

Williams, Margaret (1731). *See* Oxley. M.

Williams, Margaret. S Lent 1754. Sy.

Williams, Margery. S Lent 1731. Sh.

Williams, Martha. S Feb T Mar 1727 *Rappahannock*. L.

Williams, Mary. R for Barbados Jun 1663. M.

Williams, Mary of Whitchurch, spinster. R for America Jly 1673. Sh.

Williams, Mary (1682). *See* Harris. M.

Williams, Mary. R for Barbados or Jamaica Dec 1693. L.

Williams als Glass, Mary. R for Barbados or Jamaica May AT Jly 1697. M.

Williams, Mary. R for Barbados or Jamaica Aug 1700. L.

Williams, Mary. S Aug T Oct 1726 *Forward*. L.

Williams, Mary. S Aug T Oct 1726 *Forward* to Va. M.

Williams als Foster, Mary. S Feb T Mar 1730 *Patapsco* LC Md Sep 1730. M.

Williams, Mary. S Apr T Dec 1734 *Caesar* but died on passage. M.

Williams, Mary. S May T Jun 1738 *Forward*. L.

Williams, Mary. S for murder of bastard child Lent R Summer 1741 (SP). He.

Williams, Mary. S Summer 1741. Wo.

Williams, Mary. S Jly 1750. L.

Williams, Mary. S Sep-Oct T Dec 1752 *Greyhound*. M.

Williams als Jordan, Mary. S s gown at Castle Powderbatch Lent 1756. Sh.

Williams, Mary wife of John. S May T Sep 1757 *Thetis*. M.

Williams, Mary. S Oct 1757 T Mar 1758 *Dragon*. L.

Williams, Mary. S Jan 1759. L.

Williams, Mary. S s at St. Helen, Worcester, Summer 1760. Wo.

Williams, Mary (1764). *See* Tanner. M.

Williams, Mary. R Feb T for life Mar 1764 *Tryal*. M.

Williams, Mary of Bristol. R 14 yrs Nov 1765 (SP). G.

Williams, Mary. S & T Apr 1766 *Ann*. M.

Williams, Mary. SQS Apr TB May 1767. So.

Williams, Mary. T Apr 1771 *Thornton*. Sy.

Williams, Mary. S s at Whittington Lent 1772. Sh.

Williams, Mary. S May-Jly 1773. M.

Williams, Mary. S Lent 1775. Sy.

Williams, Michael. S Mar 1772 TB to Va. De.

Williams, Morgan. S s at Llangeview Lent 1763. Mo.
Williams, Peter. R for Barbados Mar 1683. M.
Williams, Peter. T Sep 1730 *Smith*. Ht.
Williams, Phila. T Oct 1722 *Forward*. E.
Williams, Philip. R for Barbados or Jamaica Oct 1690. L.
Williams, Philip. S Dec 1749-Jan 1750 T Mar 1750 *Tryal*. M.
Williams, Philip. S May-Jly 1750. M.
Williams, Pleasant of Bermondsey. SQS Mar T Jun 1768 *Tryal*. Sy.
Williams, Randolph. S Jly T Aug 1721 *Prince Royal* LC Va Nov
    1721. L.
Williams, Rebecca (1727). *See* Gardner. L.
Williams, Rebecca. S 14 yrs for receiving Lent 1769. Sh.
Williams, Rees. S s mare Lent R 14 yrs Summer 1769. He.
Williams, Richard. R for Barbados Aug 1670. M.
Williams, Richard of Chipping Wycombe. R for America Feb 1688. Bu.
Williams, Richard of Newbury. R for America Jun 1692. Be.
Williams, Richard. S Jan T Feb 1726 *Supply* LC Annapolis May
    1726. M.
Williams, Richard. S s clothing at Oswestry Lent 1729. Sh.
Williams, Richard. S Sep-Oct 1749. M.
Williams, Richard (1755). *See* Smith. Le.
Williams, Richard. S Aug 1757 TB to Va 1758. De.
Williams, Richard. S & T Sep 1757 *Thetis*. L.
Williams, Richard. S s veal at St. Mary, Shrewsbury, Lent 1765. Sh.
Williams, Richard (1766). *See* Harling. Wa.
Williams, Richard. R for life Mar 1768. Co.
Williams, Richard. S & R Lent 1773. Sh.
Williams, Robert of Swindon, husbandman. R for Barbados Jun
    1666. Wi.
Williams, Robert. R for Barbados Jun 1671. M.
Williams, Robert. R for Barbados Jly 1674. L.
Williams, Robert of Wellington. R for America Jly 1686. Sh.
Williams, Robert. S s chairpin of dray Jan T Apr 1735 *Patapsco* LC Md
    Oct 1735. L.
Williams, Robert. S s bullock Summer 1759 R 14 yrs Lent 1760. Nf.
Williams, Robert. S s at Loppington Summer 1761. Sh.
Williams, Robert. S May T Aug 1769 *Douglas*. M.
Williams, Robert. S for highway robbery & R 14 yrs Summer 1773. Be.
Williams, Roger. S Apr 1745. So.
Williams, Rotherick of Cirencester. R for America Jly 1683. G.
Williams, Samuel of Cam. R for America Feb 1684. G.
Williams, Samuel of St. Luke. S s stewpan Jly 1740 T Jan 1741
    Harpooner. M.
Williams, Samuel. S s spoons at St. Giles, Oxford, Lent 1762. O.
Williams, Sarah of Bristol. R for Barbados Jun 1699. G.
Williams als Newell, Sarah. S Aug 1727 T 14 yrs *Forward* LC
    Rappahannock May 1728. M.
Williams, Sarah. S Jan 1733. M.
Williams, Sarah. S Dec 1753-Jan 1754. M.
Williams, Sarah (1761). *See* Parsons. G.
Williams als Beauman, Sarah. SWK Jly T Dec 1770 *Justitia*. K.

Williams, Sarah (1774). *See* King. M.

Williams, Simon. R for Barbados Jun 1671. M.

Williams, Susanna. S Jan T Feb 1733 *Smith* to Md or Va. M.

Williams, Susannah. TB to Va from QS 1740. De.

Williams, Susan. T May 1744 *Justitia*. Sy.

Williams, Susanna. S Jan 1755. M.

Williams, Susanna. S Jan 1757. L.

Williams, Susanna. S & T Sep 1764 *Justitia*. L.

Williams, Susan. S & T Apr 1769 *Tryal*. M.

Williams, Thomas (1654). *See* Bennett. Sy.

Williams, Thomas. Rebel T 1685.

Williams als Floyd, Thomas. PT Apr R May 1691.M.

Williams, Thomas of Kidderminster. R for America Jly 1693. Wo.

Williams, Thomas of Shrewsbury. R (Western Circ) for America Jly 1700. Sh.

Williams, Thomas of East Malling. R for America Jly 1700. K.

Williams als Bell, Thomas of Bermondsey. R for Barbados or Jamaica Jly 1702. Sy.

Williams, Thomas. S Feb T May 1719 *Margaret*; sold to John Welch Md Aug 1719. L.

Williams, Thomas. S Lent 1721. Be.

Williams, Thomas, als Wood, George. R 14 yrs Lent 1721. G.

Williams, Thomas. S & T Oct 1722 *Forward* LC Annapolis Jun 1723. L.

Williams, Thomas, aged 21, fair. R Jan T 14 yrs Feb 1723 *Jonathan* LC Md Jly 1724. M.

Williams, Thomas. S Aug T Sep 1725 *Forward* LC Annapolis Dec 1725. L.

Williams, Thomas. S s horse Lent R 14 yrs Summer 1726. G.

Williams, Thomas. S s at Rumney Summer 1729. Mo.

Williams, Thomas. S Jly 1729. Ha.

Williams, Thomas. T Oct 1729 *Forward*. Sy.

Williams, Thomas (1730). *See* Woodward. G.

Williams, Thomas. S & T 14 yrs Oct 1730 *Forward* LC Potomack Jan 1731. M.

Williams, Thomas. S s horse Summer 1731 R Lent 1732 (SP). St.

Williams als Munday, Thomas. S Mar 1734. Do.

Williams, Thomas. T Dec 1734 *Caesar*. K.

Williams, Thomas. S s sheepskins at Cleobury Summer 1735. Sh.

Williams, Thomas. S Lent R 14 yrs Summer TB Jly 1743. G.

Williams, Thomas. S Jan T Feb 1744 *Neptune*. L.

Williams, Thomas. S Apr 1744. L.

Williams, Thomas. S Jly 1748. L.

Williams, Thomas. S Dec 1750. L.

Williams, Thomas. S Nov T Dec 1752 *Greyhound*. L.

Williams, Thomas. S for highway robbery Summer 1753 R 14 yrs Lent 1754. No.

Williams, Thomas. S Sep-Oct T Dec 1753 *Whiteing*. M.

Williams, Thomas. S Feb-Apr T Jun 1756 *Lyon*. M.

Williams, Thomas (1758). *See* Clarke. Wi.

Williams, Thomas. S s harness at Sedgley Lent 1764. St.

Williams, Thomas. S s at Newland Lent 1765. G.

Williams, Thomas. S Summer 1765. Cu.
Williams, Thomas. S Summer 1765 R 14 yrs Lent 1766. He.
Williams, Thomas. T Sep 1766 *Justitia*. M.
Williams, Thomas. S Feb T May 1767 *Thornton*. L.
Williams, Thomas. SQS Feb T May 1767 *Thornton*. M.
Williams, Thomas. S s mare Lent R 14 yrs Summer 1767. Sh.
Williams, Thomas. S & R Summer 1767. Ch.
Williams, Thomas. R 14 yrs Mar TB to Va Apr 1768. Wi.
Williams, Thomas. S Lent 1768. Bd.
Williams, Thomas. SQS Jly T Oct 1768 *Justitia*. M.
Williams, Thomas. S s at Llangover Lent 1772. Mo.
Williams, Thomas. S for rape at Alderley & R for life Summer 1772. G.
Williams, Thomas. S Oct 1772. L.
Williams, Thomas. SQS Apr 1773. M.
Williams, Thomas of St. Martin in Fields. SW Apr 1773. M.
Williams, Thomas. S 14 yrs for receiving Lent 1774. Ch.
Williams, Thomas, als Thomas, William. S s at Westbury on Trym Lent 1774. G.
Williams, Thomas. S & R 14 yrs Lent 1775. G.
Williams, Thomasin. S Jly 1752. De.
Williams, Tutor. S May T Jun 1726 *Loyal Margaret* to Va. M.
Williams, William. R for Barbados May 1665. X.
Williams, William (1668). *See* Phillips. Mo.
Williams, William of Ruan Minor. R for Barbados Jly 1681. Co.
Williams, William. Rebel T 1685.
Williams, William. R for Barbados or Jamaica Mar 1685. M.
Williams, William of Malmesbury. R for Barbados Jly 1688. Wi.
Williams, William (1700). *See* Smith. L.
Williams, William of Chipping Wycombe. R for America Jly 1702. Bu.
Williams, William of Eye. R for America Mar 1710. He.
Williams, William. R for America Aug 1715. M.
Williams, William of St. John, Worcester. S Summer 1718. Wo.
Williams, William, aged 16, fair. S Jly T Oct 1720 *Gilbert* LC Md May 1721. L.
Williams, William. S & T Jan 1722 *Gilbert* LC Annapolis Jly 1722. M.
Williams, William. TB Sep 1727. Nt.
Williams, William. S & T Dec 1731 *Forward* to Md or Va. M.
Williams als Morgan, William. S for highway robbery Summer 1738 R 14 yrs Lent TB Aug 1739. G.
Williams, William. S & TB Aug 1740. G.
Williams, William. S Jly-Dec 1747. M.
Williams, William. S s at St. Philip & Jacob Lent TB Mar 1748. G.
Williams, William als John. S s at St. Michael, Gloucester, Lent 1749. G.
Williams, William. S Jan T Mar 1750 *Tryal*. L.
Williams, William. S s horse Lent R 14 yrs Summer 1750. Li.
Williams, William, als Strong Will. S Aug 1750. Co.
Williams, William. S Jly 1752. Ha.
Williams, William of Manchester, shoemaker. SQS Feb 1756. La.
Williams, William. S 14 yrs Oct 1756. L.
Williams, William (1764). *See* Wade. Mo.

Williams, William. S s at Tidenham Lent 1764. G.

Williams, William. S s horse Lent R 14 yrs Summer 1764. He.

Williams, William. T 14 yrs Sep 1766 *Justitia*. K.

Williams, William of Christchurch. SQS & T Jan 1767 *Tryal*. Sy.

Williams, William. S s silver mug Lent 1768. He.

Williams, William. S & T Jly 1770 *Scarsdale*. L.

Williams, William. S Mar R Apr 1771. Fl.

Williams, William (1772). *See* Pritchard. He.

Williams, William. S Feb T Apr 1772 *Thornton*. L.

Williams, William. R Jly 1773. M.

Williams als McKenzie, William. R 14 yrs Dec 1773. M.

Williamson, Ann (1761). *See* Harrison. M.

Williamson, Anthony. S & T Sep 1764 *Justitia*. L.

Williamson, Catherine. T Summer 1739. Y.

Williamson, David. S s handkerchief at St. Mary Woolchurch Apr T Jun 1768 *Tryal*. L.

Williamson, Edward. S Dec 1745. L.

Williamson, Eleanor. S & T Apr 1766 *Ann*. M.

Williamson, Henry. S for returning from transportation & T Jan 1722 *Gilbert*. L.'

Williamson, James. TB to Md Mar T *Loyal Margaret* LC Annapolis Oct 1726. Db.

Williamson, James. S & T Oct 1730 *Forward* LC Potomack Jan 1731. M.

Williamson, James. S & T Dec 1734 *Caesar* LC Va Jly 1735. M.

Williamson, James. S s horse Summer 1744 R 14 yrs Summer 1746. Du.

Williamson, James. S Jan 1746. L.

Williamson, John of Bletchley. R for America May 1693. Bu.

Williamson, John. R from QS s horse Sep 1718. No.

Williamson, John. S Jun 1739. L.

Williamson, John. S Summer 1754. Sy.

Williamson, John (1755). *See* Hunn. Nf.

Williamson, John. S s at Monmouth Lent 1764. Mo.

Williamson, John (1775). *See* Williams. Sh.

Williamson, Joseph. R for America Aug 1715. M.

Williamson, Joseph. S Dec 1719. M.

Williamson als Wade, Joseph. S Summer 1756. Ch.

Williamson, Mary. S s from Lady Hamilton Oct 1768 T Jan 1769 *Thornton*. M.

Williamson, Robert. S Jly 1750. L.

Williamson, Sarah. S s cows Summer 1742 R 14 yrs Lent 1743. Li.

Williamson, Shadrack. S Lent T Jun 1764 *Dolphin*. Bu.

Williamson, Thomas. SQS Knaresborough Oct 1724 T *Supply* LC Md May 1726. Y.

Williamson, Thomas. S s silver tankard Lent AT Summer 1765. Y.

Williamson als Meakin, Thomas. TB Sep 1770. Db.

Williamson, William. T Jun 1738 *Forward*. Sx.

Williamson, William. S & T Sep 1755 *Tryal*. L.

Willicomb, William. S s pestle & mortar Jan T Apr 1735 *Patapsco* LC Md Oct 1735. M.

Willier, Elianor wife of Richard of Burford. R for Jamaica, Barbados or Bermuda Feb 1686. O.

Willing, John (1730). *See* James. De.

Willinger, Richard (1716). *See* Loes. Wa.

Willingham, John. S Lent 1768. Su.

Willington als Brown als Morgan, John. S s at St. Chad, Shrewsbury, Summer 1767. Sh.

Willington, Thomas. S Jly 1766. De.

Willington, William. S Sep 1718 T *Eagle* LC Charles Town Mar 1719. L.

Willins, Sarah. S Lent 1754. K.

Willis als Gillars, Anthony of Brammingham. R for Barbados Feb 1664. Bd.

Willis, Benjamin. S Apr T Jun 1768 *Tryal*. M.

Willis, Dulick. S Jly 1750. L.

Willis, Eleanor. S Aug 1736. De.

Willes, Elizabeth (1758). *See* Meadows. M.

Willes, Elizabeth. S Jan T 14 yrs Apr 1759 *Thetis*. M.

Willis, George. S s shirts at New Malton Lent 1766. Y.

Willis, Israel (1726). *See* Merrett. So.

Willis, Jacob. T Apr 1768 *Thornton*. Sy.

Willis, James. R 14 yrs Aug 1735. De.

Willis, James. S s horse Lent R 14 yrs Summer 1740. Bd.

Willis, James. S Jan T Apr 1759 *Thetis*. M.

Willis, Jane. SQS Sep T Dec 1769 *Justitia*. M.

Willis, John. Rebel T 1685.

Willis, John. S s sheep & R 14 yrs Summer 1746. Nf.

Willis, John. S Summer 1756. Bu.

Willis, John. SQS s brush Summer 1770. Du.

Willis, John. S s chickens at Polstead Lent 1775. Su.

Willis, John. S Lent 1775. Wa.

Willis, Leonard. S Mar TB to Va Apr 1762. Wi.

Willis, Lydia. S Jan 1757. L.

Willis, Mary (1747). *See* Page, Ann. M.

Willis, Richard. R 14 yrs Lent 1721. G.

Willis, Robert. Rebel T 1685.

Willis, Samuel. S Lent R 14 yrs Summer 1739 (SP). Be.

Willis, Sarah. S Oct 1751-Jan 1752. M.

Willis, Sarah of Stroud. S s pumps Lent TB Mar 1754. G.

Willis, Sarah (1761). *See* Parsons. G.

Willes, Theodore of East Ham. S Lent T Apr 1772 *Thornton*. E.

Willis, Thomas of Tangley. R for Barbados Jly 1683. Ha.

Willis, Thomas. S s gelding at Newnham & R 14 yrs Summer 1768. G.

Willis, William. R for Barbados Jly 1668. L.

Willis, William. S Oct 1743 T Jan 1744 *Neptune* to Md. M.

Willison, William. TB 14 yrs Oct 1719. L.

Willnose, John. S Summer 1765. Cu.

Willoughby, John. T Apr 1732 *Patapsco*. Sy.

Willoughby, Mary. S Jly T 14 yrs Aug 1718 *Eagle* LC Charles Town Mar 719. L.

Willoughby, Thomas. T May 1767 *Thornton*. M.

Willoughby, William. S s sheep Lent R 14 yrs Summer 1763. Li.

Wills, Benjamin. S Aug 1757. Co.

Wills, Ezechiel of Broadwindsor. R for Barbados JJy 1681. Do.

Wills, Hugh. R 14 yrs Aug 1734. So.

Wilse, John. S Jly 1756. Wi.

Wills, Joseph. S Mar 1733. De.

Wills, Joseph. S Feb T Apr 1741 *Speedwell* or *Mediterranean*. M.

Wills, Mary. R 14 yrs Aug 1734. De.

Wills, Richard. S Mar 1760. Co.

Wills, Richard. SQS Oct 1772 TB Jan 1773. So.

Wills als Cordin, Robert. S s horse Summer 1741 R 14 yrs Lent 1742. Le.

Wills, Samuel. S Lent 1760. No.

Wilse, Thomas of Tuffley. R for America Jly 1675. G.

Wills, Thomas. TB to Va from QS 1740. De.

Wills, Thomas. S Jly T Oct 1741 *Sea Horse* to Va. M.

Wills, Thomas. R 14 yrs Aug 1748. So.

Wills, William. Rebel T 1685.

Wills, William. S Lent 1775. Db.

Wilmer, Charles. R Feb 1675. M.

Wilmore, Elizabeth. S Jan T Apr 1741 *Speedwell* or *Mediterranean*. M.

Wilmore, John. S Summer 1755 R 14 yrs Lent 1756. Wo.

Wilmore, Joseph. T Aug 1720 *Owners Goodwill*. K.

Willmore, Sarah. R Oct 1694 AT Jan 1695. M.

Wilmore, Sarah (1750). *See* Hockingham. Ha.

Wilmot, Cuckold als Jacob (1768). *See* May, John. Do.

Willmott, Derry. S & T Dec 1734 *Caesar* but died on passage. L.

Wilmott, Edward (2). Rebels T 1685.

Wilmott, Elizabeth. S Mar 1729 TB to Va. De.

Wilmot, Elizabeth. S & T Mar 1763 *Neptune*. L.

Wilmot, Henry. S for highway robbery Summer 1767 R 14 yrs Lent TB Apr 1768. Db.

Wilmot, James. T Jan 1738 *Dorsetshire*. Sy.

Wilmott, John. S Mar 1726. Do.

Willmott, Jonas of Danbury. R for Barbados or Jamaica Mar 1694. E.

Wilmott, Stephen. S Apr T Sep 1737 *Pretty Patsy* to Md. M.

Wilmott, Thomas (1731). *See* Boston. L.

Willmott, Thomas. S & T Sep 1731 *Smith* LC Va 1732. M.

Wilmott, William. R for Barbados May 1676. M.

Wilmot, William. S s at Abberley Summer 1764. Wo.

Wilshire. *See* Wiltshire.

Wilson, Alexander. S for perjury Jun T 14 yrs Aug 1769 *Douglas*. L.

Wilson, Ann (1695). *See* Goddard. M.

Wilson, Anne. S Aug T Oct 1724 *Forward* LC Annapolis Jun 1725. M.

Wilson, Ann. S Feb T Mar 1731 *Patapsco* LC Annapolis Jun 1731. L.

Wilson, Ann. S Sep 1733. M.

Wilson, Ann. S May T Sep 1737 *Pretty Patsy* to Md. M.

Wilson, Ann (1739). *See* Wells. M.

Willson, Ann. TB Apr 1742. Db.

Wilson, Ann. S Apr T May 1743 *Indian Queen* to Potomack. M.

Wilson als Warren, Ann. SQS Dec 1749 T Mar 1750 *Tryal*. M.

Wilson, Ann (1758). *See* Weston. Wi.

Wilson, Ann wife of Andrew of Ulverstone. SQS Jan 1775. La.

Wilson, Benjamin. AT from QS Lent TB Apr 1766. Db.

Wilson, Benjamin of Camberwell. SQS Jly T Sep 1766 *Justitia*. Sy.

Wilson, Cecilia. S & T Jun 1742 *Bladon*. L.

Wilson, Charles. S s horse Summer 1753 R 14 yrs Lent 1754. No.

Wilson, Charles (1774). *See* Lockett. M.

Wilson, Christopher. S & R Summer 1734. Su.

Wilson, David. S Apr T May 1720 *Honor* LC York River Jan 1721. L.

Wilson als Jordan, David. R 14 yrs s horse Summer 1763. We.

Wilson, Edward. R for America Jly 1694. Li.

Wilson, Edward. S & T Apr 1753 *Thames*. L.

Wilson, Edward. S s mare Lent R 14 yrs Summer 1754. Li.

Wilson, Edward. S for forgery Lent 1756 R for life Lent TB Apr 1757. G.

Wilson, Edward als Joseph. S Jun 1761. M.

Wilson, Edward. S Lent 1767. La.

Wilson, Edward. S Sep-Oct 1773. M.

Wilson, Eleanor. S Lent 1753. Y.

Wilson als Dickson, Elizabeth of Royston. R for Barbados Apr
1668. Ht.

Wilson als Roycroft, Elizabeth. R for Barbados or Jamaica Jly 1686. L.

Wilson, Elizabeth. R for Barbados or Jamaica May 1691. L.

Wilson, Elizabeth of St. Saviour, Southwark. R for Barbados or Jamaica
Mar 1698. Sy.

Wilson, Elizabeth. R 14 yrs Summer 1741. Y.

Wilson, Elizabeth. S Apr T May 1767 *Thornton*. M.

Wilson, Elizabeth. R Lent 1773. E.

Wilson, Ezekiel. R for life Jly 1766. De.

Wilson, George of York Castle. R for Barbados Jly 1677. Y.

Wilson, George. SQS Apr 1719. Du.

Wilson, George. S Apr-May T May 1744 *Justitia*. M.

Wilson, George. S Jly T Sep 1767 *Justitia*. L.

Wilson, George. S Oct 1775. M.

Wilson, Gilbert. S Feb T May 1719 *Margaret*; sold to John Payburn Md
Sep 1719. L.

Wilson als Johnson, Hannah, als wife of William Scutt. S Jly T Oct
1741 *Sea Horse* to Va. M.

Wilson, Hannah. S Apr-May 1754. M.

Wilson, Henry. S s cow Summer 1734. Su.

Wilson, Henry. S Jly T Sep 1757 *Thetis*. L.

Wilson, Henry. S Mar 1760. Ha.

Wilson, Henry. S Summer 1774. Sy.

Wilson, James. R for Barbados Jly 1675. M.

Wilson, James. S Jan T Feb 1719 *Worcester* LC Annapolis Jun 1719. L.

Wilson, James. S Apr T May 1720 *Honor* but escaped in Vigo, Spain. L.

Willson, James. S & T Oct 1730 *Forward* LC Potomack Jan 1731. M.

Wilson als Horsley, James. S Summer 1733. Nl.

Wilson, James. S May T Sep 1737 *Pretty Patsy* to Md. M.

Wilson, James. S s mare Lent R 14 yrs Summer T Aug 1752 *Tryal*. Bu.

Wilson, James. T Sep 1754 *Justitia*. K.

Wilson, James of Barking. SQS Jan T May 1755 *Rose*. E.

Wilson, James. T Sep 1757 *Thetis*. Sy.

Wilson, James. R Apr 1773. M.

Wilson, Jane. S Mar 1721 T Mar 1723. Bu.

Wilson, Jane wife of Thomas. S s clothing at St. Sepulchre Feb T Apr 1768 *Thornton*. L.

Wilson, Jane of St. Martin in Fields, spinster. SW Apr T Jly 1772 *Tayloe*. M.

Wilson, Jasper. T May 1744 *Justitia*. E.

Wilson, Jeremiah. S Summer 1754. Ht.

Wilson als Cox, John. R for Barbados Mar 1677. L.

Wilson, John. Rebel T 1685.

Wilson, John of Chester. R for America Jly 1687. Ch.

Wilson, John. R for Barbados or Jamaica Oct 1690. M.

Wilson, John of York. R for Barbados Jun 1692. Y.

Willson, John of Elvetham. R for Barbados Feb 1698. Ha.

Wilson, John of Wandsworth. R for Barbados or Jamaica Jly 1712. Sy.

Wilson, John. R Summer 1721 T Oct 1723 *Forward* to Va from London. Y.

Wilson, John. S Aug T Oct 1724 *Forward* LC Annapolis Jun 1725. M.

Wilson als Smith, John. S May T Jun 1727 *Susanna*. L.

Wilson, John. S Dec 1727. M.

Wilson, John. S Lent 1729 R 14 yrs & T Summer 1733. Y.

Wilson als Thomson, John. S s horse Lent R 14 yrs Summer 1740. La.

Wilson, John. T Apr 1741 *Speedwell* or *Mediterranean*. Sy.

Wilson, John. S Sep T Nov 1743 *George William*. M.

Wilson, John. S Summer 1745 R 14 yrs Lent 1746. Be.

Wilson, John. S City Summer 1746. Nl.

Wilson, John. S Summer T Oct 1750 *Rachael*. Sy.

Wilson, John. S May-Jly T Sep 1755 *Tryal*. M.

Wilson, John. S Summer 1757. Y.

Wilson, John. S Mar 1760 TB to Va. De.

Wilson, John. S Feb T Mar 1764 *Tryal*. M.

Wilson, John. T Jun 1764 *Dolphin*. E.

Wilson, John. SQS Jly T Sep 1767 *Justitia*. M.

Wilson, John. S Jun T Aug 1769 *Douglas*. L.

Willson, John. S s at Leeds Lent 1770. Y.

Wilson, John. R Aug 1770 TB to Va 1771. De.

Wilson, John. S Apr-May T Jly 1771 *Scarsdale*. M.

Wilson, John of Goosnargh. SQS Jan 1772. La.

Wilson, John. S Apr 1773. M.

Wilson, John. S Summer 1773. Db.

Wilson, John. S Apr 1775. M.

Wilson, John, als Smith, Thomas, aged 31, 5'10" tall, silk weaver born at Newcastle upon Tyne. S & R Summer T Sep 1775 by *Rebecca* to Baltimore. Ru.

Wilson, Joseph. S Aug T Oct 1726 *Forward*. L.

Willson, Joseph. S s horse Summer 1740 R 14 yrs Lent 1741. Wa.

Wilson, Joseph. S Jan-Apr 1749. M.

Wilson, Joseph. S Summer 1749. La.

Wilson, Joseph. R 14 yrs Mar 1752. Ha.

Wilson, Joseph. R 14 yrs Summer 1757. Y.

Wilson, Joseph (1761). *See* Wilson, Edward. M.

Wilson, Joseph. S & T Jly 1770 *Scarsdale*. M.

Wilson, Joseph. S Oct 1773. L.

Wilson, Joseph. S Summer 1775. Y.

Wilson, Margaret. S Apr T May 1720 *Honor* LC York River Jan 1721. L.

Wilson, Margaret. S Jly T Aug 1721 *Prince Royal* LC Va Nov 1721. M.

Wilson, Margaret. S & T Jan 1722 *Gilbert* LC Annapolis Jly 1722. L.

Wilson, Margaret (1738). *See* Seagoe. M.

Wilson, Margaret. S as pickpocket Summer 1746 R 14 yrs Lent 1747. Li.

Wilson, Margaret. S Apr-May 1775. M.

Wilson, Maria wife of George. T Dec 1770 *Justitia*. Sy.

Wilson, Martha (1692). *See* Walters. M.

Wilson, Mary. R & T Dec 1716 *Lewis* to Jamaica. M.

Wilson, Mary. S & T Aug 1718 *Eagle* LC Charles Town Mar 1719. L.

Wilson, Mary. S Apr T May 1719 *Margaret*; sold to Patrick Sympson & William Black Md Sep 1719. L.

Wilson, Mary (1732). *See* Foster. Y.

Wilson, Mary. S s silver & gold Feb T Jun 1738 *Forward* to Md or Va. M.

Wilson, Mary. S Oct 1743 T Feb 1744 *Neptune* to Md. M.

Wilson, Mary. T May 1744 *Justitia*. E.

Wilson, Mary of Cromwell. SQS s cloth Jly 1752. Nt.

Wilson, Mary. S Sep 1754. L.

Wilson als Wilkinson, Mary. S Oct 1756. M.

Wilson, Mary. S Lent 1757. Y.

Wilson, Mary. SQS s gown Lent 1770. Du.

Wilson, Mary. S Apr-May T Jly 1771 *Scarsdale*. M.

Wilson, Mary. SQS Oct T Dec 1771 *Justitia*. M.

Wilson, Matthew. S Mar 1764. De.

Wilson, Nathaniel (1752). *See* Wilkes. Be.

Wilson, Owen. S & T Jan 1739 *Dorsetshire*. L.

Wilson, Peter, aged 21, dark. S & T Oct 1720 *Gilbert* LC Md May 1721. M.

Wilson, Richard of North Creake. R for Barbados Jan 1665. Nf.

Wilson, Richard. PT Jan 1675. M.

Wilson, Richard of Stourbridge. R for Jamaica, Barbados or Bermuda Feb 1686. Wo.

Wilson, Richard. S Jan T Apr 1734 *Patapsco* to Md. M.

Wilson, Richard. S Sep T Dec 1734 *Caesar* LC Va Jly 1735. M.

Wilson, Richard. S Summer 1735. Cu.

Wilson, Richard. S & T Jly 1772 *Tayloe*. M.

Wilson als Morley, Robert of Newcastle upon Tyne. R for Barbados Jly 1682. Nl.

Wilson, Robert. T Jan 1734 *Caesar* LC Va Jly 1734. Sy.

Wilson als Wilkinson, Robert. S & T Jan 1736 *Dorsetshire* LC Va Sep 1736. L.

Wilson, Robert. T Oct 1738 *Genoa*. Sy.

Wilson, Robert. S Sep 1740. L.

Wilson, Robert. S Feb-Apr 1746. M.

Wilson, Robert. S Lent R 14 yrs Summer 1748 T Jan 1749 *Laura*. Sy.

Wilson, Robert. S Jan-Apr 1749. M.

Wilson, Robert. S s gold coin Lent 1767. Ca.

Wilson, Samuel of Chalfont St. Peter. R for Barbados Aug 1671. Bu.

Wilson, Samuel. S s coach furniture at Leominster Summer 1722. He.

Wilson, Samuel. S Mar TB May 1724 T *Robert* LC Md Jun 1725. Nt.
Wilson, Samuel of Washington. S Summer 1772. Sx.
Wilson, Samuel. S Lent 1774. Wa.
Wilson, Sarah wife of Thomas of St. Andrew, Holborn. S s aprons Jly-Oct 1740 T Jan 1741 *Harpooner* to Rappahannock. M.
Wilson, Stephen. T Jun 1727 *Susanna*. Bu.
Wilson, Susan of Hollingbourne, spinster. R for Barbados or Jamaica Mar 1688. K.
Wilson, Tebay als Tebah. S Summer 1750. We.
Wilson, Thomas. S Aug TB to Va Sep 1727. Le.
Wilson, Thomas. S Feb T Mar 1731 *Patapsco* but died on passage. M.
Wilson, Thomas. S Sep 1733 T Jan 1734 *Caesar* LC Va Jly 1734. M.
Wilson, Thomas. S Lent 1735. Hu.
Wilson, Thomas. S City Summer 1740. Nl.
Wilson, Thomas. T Sep 1742 *Forward*. K.
Wilson, Thomas. S Summer 1745. Nl.
Wilson, Thomas. S City Lent 1750. Y.
Wilson, Thomas. S Jly 1750. L.
Willson, Thomas. S Summer T Sep 1755 *Tryal*. Ht.
Wilson, Thomas. T Apr 1765 *Ann*. L.
Wilson, Thomas. T 14 yrs Sep 1767 *Justitia*. K.
Wilson, Thomas of Putney. SQS for false pretences Mar T Apr 1768 *Thornton*. Sy.
Wilson, Thomas. S & T Jan 1769 *Thornton*. M.
Wilson, Thomas. S Lent 1774. Li.
Wilson, William. R for America Jly 1687. Db.
Wilson, William. PT Sep R Oct 1690. M.
Wilson, William. LC from *Susannah & Sarah* Annapolis Apr 1720. X.
Wilson, William. S Jan-Jun T Jun 1728 *Elizabeth* LC Potomack Aug 1729. L.
Wilson, William of York Castle. SQS Easingwold s at Newbrough Jan 1729. Y.
Wilson, William. S for forging deeds Lent R Summer 1733 (SP). He.
Wilson, William of Shoreditch. S s tankard Dec 1740 T Jan 1741 *Harpooner*. M.
Wilson, William. S & T Aug 1752 *Tryal*. L.
Wilson, William. S s sheep Lent R 14 yrs Summer 1754. Nt.
Wilson, William. S 14 yrs breaking & entering at Burton upon Ure TB Aug 1756. Y.
Wilson, William. S Feb T Apr 1759 *Thetis*. M.
Wilson, William. S 14 yrs for receiving Summer 1770 T *Lowther & Senhouse* LC Va May 1772. Nl.
Wilthy, George. S Lent 1736. Nf.
Wilton, James. S Dec 1766 T Jan 1767 *Tryal*. M.
Wilton, John. S s sheep Lent R 14 yrs Summer TB to Va Sep 1767. Le.
Wilton, Samuel. S Jan-Feb T Apr 1772 *Thornton*. M.
Wiltshire, David (1769). *See* Mills, Alexander. L.
Wiltshear, George. S s muslin Apr T Jun 1742 *Bladon*. L.
Wiltshire, Henry. S Mar 1752. Ha.
Wiltshire, Isaac. R 14 yrs Jly TB to Va Sep 1744. Wi.
Wiltshire, James. SQS Marlborough Oct 1772 TB to Va Apr 1773. Wi.

Wiltshire, John. T Jan 1736 *Dorsetshire*. Sx.

Wiltshire, John. SQS Jan TB to Md Feb 1743. So.

Wiltshire, John. S for highway robbery Lent R 14 yrs Summer 1755 T 1756. Bd.

Wiltshire, John. S Dec 1768 T Jan 1769 *Thornton*. M.

Wiltshire, Jonathan. S Mar TB to Va Apr 1767. Wi.

Willshire, Mary. S Oct T Nov 1728 *Forward* LC Rappahannock Jun 1729. M.

Wilshere, Sarah. R for Jamaica Aug 1661. L.

Wilshire, Thomas. S & T Oct 1722 *Forward* LC Annapolis Jun 1723. M.

Willshire, Thomas. S 14 yrs s linen from yard Summer 1749. Sy.

Wiltshire, William of Road, alehouse keeper. R for Barbados Jun 1703. So.

Wilkeshire, William. S Lent T May 1755 *Rose*. K.

Wiltshire, William. S Jly TB to Va Aug 1758. Wi.

Wiltshire, William. S Mar 1773. De.

Wimbleton, William. S Jly 1733. Ha.

Winch, Ellis. T May 1751 *Tryal*. K.

Winch, Isaac. T Apr 1769 *Tryal*. Ht.

Winch, John of St. Saviour, Southwark. SQS Jan T Apr 1765 *Ann*. Sy.

Winchelsea, Donbarty. SL & T Jan 1766 *Tryal*. Sy.

Winchester, Thomas. S Jly 1722. Wi.

Winchurch, John of Newington. SQS Jan 1751. Sy.

Winckles, James of Rugby. R for America Jly 1677, 1678 & 1679. Wa.

Wincks, Joseph. S Jan T Feb 1742 *Industry*. L.

Wynd, John. S Dec 1737 T Jan 1738 *Dorsetshire*. L.

Wind, Mary. S & T Aug 1752 *Tryal*. L.

Wynde, Samuel. S s at Ludlow Lent 1764. Sh.

Windeatt, Enoch. TB to Va from QS 1765. De.

Winder, George. R for Barbados or Jamaica Dec 1693. L.

Winder, John. SQS s wheat Easter 1765. Du.

Windham, John. S City for assisting escape of prisoners Summer 1744. Nl.

Windham, Sarah (1719). *See* Scott. M.

Windell, Elizabeth. S May-Jly T Sep 1755 *Tryal*. M.

Windle, Francis. S Lent R 14 yrs Summer 1764. La.

Windmill, Benjamin of Compton Dando. R for Barbados Jly 1693. So.

Windmill als Francklin, John. T Oct 1721 *William & John*. Ht.

Windon, Elizabeth. S Sep T Dec 1770 *Justitia*. M.

Windover, Mary. S Mar 1740. De.

Windows, William. S s at Ripple Lent 1747. Wo.

Windram, John. S Oct T 14 yrs Dec 1724 *Rappahannock*. L.

Windsor, Bacon. S Sep T Nov 1743 *George William*. M.

Windsor, Thomas. R Jly T Oct 1768 *Justitia*. M.

Windsor, William. S Apr T May 1750 *Lichfield*. L.

Windwright, Anne. R for Barbados Jly 1675. M.

Windy, John. T Jun 1728 *Elizabeth* LC Va Aug 1729. Sy.

Winepress, Catherine. S Sep-Oct 1748 T Jan 1749 *Laura*. M.

Winfield, Richard. S Apr T Dec 1735 *John* LC Annapolis Sep 1736. L.

Winfield, William. S & T Jan 1722 *Gilbert* LC Annapolis Jly 1722. L.

Winfield, William. S Feb T Mar 1764 *Tryal*. M.

Wing, Daniel. S & T Sep 1765 *Justitia*. L.

Wing, John. LC from *Elizabeth* Va Aug 1729. Sy.

Wing, Tabitha of Coventry, spinster. R for America Feb 1700. Wa.

Wingar, William. R (Home Circ) for Barbados Apr 1663. X.

Wingarden, William, aged 40 odd, attorney at law. LC from *Gilbert* Md May 1721. X.

Wingcot, Philip. SQS Apr T May 1752 *Lichfield*. M.

Wingfield, James. S s mare & R 14 yrs Lent 1746. Nf.

Wingfield, James. S s cloth Lent 1765. Nf.

Wingfield, Robert. S Jun 1621. M.

Wingrove, John. S Dec 1755 T Jan 1756 *Greyhound*. L.

Wingrove, John. R for life Summer 1773. Sy.

Wingrove, John. S Lent 1775. Sy.

Wingrove, Thomas. T Apr 1741 *Speedwell* or *Mediterranean*. Bu.

Winkett, James. S s silver watch Summer TB Aug 1740. G.

Winkworth, Hugh. S Mar 1747. Ha.

Winkworth, Jane. S Summer 1740. Be.

Winckworth, John. T May 1737 *Forward*. Sy.

Winckworth, Nathaniel (1694). *See* Wentworth.Ha.

Winckworth, Stephen. R 14 yrs Jly 1752. Ha.

Winn/Winne. *See* Wynn.

Winnell, Thomas of St. Saviour, Southwark. SQS Apr T Sep 1751 *Greyhound*. Sy.

Winnick, Elizabeth. S Jan-Jun T Jun 1728 *Elizabeth* LC Potomack Aug 1729. L.

Winnington, Nathan. S s iron bars Jly 1735 T Jan 1736 *Dorsetshire* LC Va Sep 1736. M.

Winnington, Robert. R 14 yrs Mar 1745 TB to Va. De.

Winsborough, Elizabeth. S Mar 1763 TB to Va. De.

Winslett, John. T Apr 1766 *Ann*. Sx.

Winslett, Samuel. T Apr 1766 *Ann*. Sx.

Winslow, George. R 14 yrs Mar TB to Va Apr 1741. Wi.

Winson, John. R Mar 1764. De.

Winson, William. R Summer 1728 (SP). Su.

Winstanley, Francis. SL Jun T for life Aug 1769 *Douglas*. Sy.

Winstanley, James. S & T Jan 1739 *Dorsetshire*. L.

Winstanley, Peter of Orrell. SQS Apr 1766. La.

Winstanley, Peter of Orrell. SQS May 1770. La.

Winston als Bradley, Richard. S s heifers at Burford Summer 1727. O.

Winston, Thomas. S & T Apr 1725 *Sukey* LC Annapolis Sep 1725. M.

Winter, Ambrose. Rebel T 1685.

Winter, Catherine. S Feb 1752. L.

Winter, James. S Apr 1748. L.

Winter, John (1751). *See* Bauskin. Wi.

Winter, John. S Summer 1758. Nf.

Winter, John. R Jly T Sep 1767 *Justitia*. L.

Winter, Margaret. T Sep 1758 *Tryal*. K.

Winter, Richard of Westminster. R Aug 1663 (PC). M.

Winter, Samuel. S Lent 1748. Sy.

Winter, Samuel. S Mar 1754. L.

Winter, Thomas. R for Barbados or Jamaica Jly 1687. M.

Winter, Thomas. S Aug T Oct 1724 *Forward* LC Annapolis Jun 1725. M.

Winter, Thomas. AT Summer 1734. He.

Winter, Thomas of St. Clement Danes. S s sheep & T Feb 1740 *York* to Md. M.

Winter, Thomas. S Lent 1756. Nf.

Winter, Thomas of Manchester. SQS Apr 1756. La.

Winter, Thomas. S Lent T Apr 1759 *Thetis*. Bu.

Winter, Thomas. SQS New Sarum Jan TB to Va Apr 1772. Wi.

Winter, William. S Mar 1736. De.

Winter, William of St. Luke. S s stewpan Jly 1740 T Jan 1741 *Harpooner*. M.

Winter, William. S Jly 1750. L.

Winter, William. S s hog at Oxenhall Lent 1764. G.

Winter, William. S s gelding at Beetley & R 14 yrs Summer 1775. Nf.

Winterbottom, Joseph. S Apr T May 1720 *Honor* to York River. L.

Winterbottom, Margaret. T Sep 1757 *Thetis*. K.

Winterbourne, Elizabeth. PT Aug 1676 R Mar 1677. M.

Winterburn, John. S s at Hutton Bushell Lent 1764. Y.

Winters, Edward. S & R 14 yrs Summer 1775. Wo.

Wintersale, Joseph. S s from Tetbury church Summer 1768. G.

Winthrop, Thomas of Lancaster. S s horse & R 14 yrs Summer 1768. La.

Wintle, Samuel of Westbury. R for America Jly 1693. G.

Winton, Peter of Mosston, tailor. SQS Jan 1741. La.

Wintour, William (1720). *See* Jewkes. St.

Winwood, Mary. S & T Oct 1730 *Forward* LC Potomack Jan 1731. M.

Winyard, William. S Feb T Mar 1731 *Patapsco* LC Annapolis Jun 1731. M.

Wisdom als Cambell, William. R for America Feb 1692. Li.

Wise, Abraham. R 14 yrs Jly 1758. Ha.

Wise, Edward. S Summer R for Barbados Aug 1664. K.

Wise, Edward. S Mar 1738. So.

Wise, Edward. R 14 yrs Jly 1744 TB to Va 1745. De.

Wise, Edward. S Feb T May 1767 *Thornton*. L.

Wise, Elizabeth. S Apr T May 1718 *Tryal* LC Charles Town Aug 1718. L.

Wise, John. Died on passage in *Gilbert* 1721. X.

Wise, John. S s horse Lent R 14 yrs Summer 1741 (SP). Be.

Wise, John. S Aug 1748. So.

Wise, John. S Mar 1765 TB to Va. De.

Wise, Peter. R Dec 1699. M.

Wise, Richard. R 14 yrs Aug 1726. De.

Wise, Sarah. S 14 yrs for receiving Feb 1758. Ha.

Wise, Stephen. T Jly 1723 *Alexander* LC Md Sep 1723. Sx.

Wise, Susanna. S Dec 1727. L.

Wise, Thomas. S May-Jly 1749. M.

Wise, Thomas. S Feb T Mar 1763 *Neptune*. M.

Wise, Thomas. R Jly T Sep 1767 *Justitia*. M.

Wisedale, Roger. S Jan T Feb 1719 *Worcester* to Md. L.

Wiseley, Thomas. S Oct 1761 T Apr 1762 *Dolphin*. M.

Wiseman, Elizabeth (1754). *See* Taylor. M.

Wiseman, Henry. S Jan T Feb 1719 *Worcester* LC Annapolis Jun
 1719. LM.
Wiseman, James. S Jan-Apr 1748. M.
Wiseman, John of Burton, blacksmith. R for Barbados Feb 1673. So.
Wiseman, John. PT Jly 1701. M.
Wiseman, Margaret. S Feb-Apr T May 1755 *Rose*. M.
Wiseman, Richard. Rebel T 1685.
Wiseman, Thomas. S s at Smallburgh Summer 1767. Nf.
Wish, Margaret. S Aug 1720. De.
Wisham, Robert. S s horse Lent R Summer 1683. Ha.
Wissen, John. T May 1752 *Lichfield*. E.
Witchell, Daniel. S Summer 1757 R 14 yrs Lent 1758. G.
Witchett, Elizabeth. SQS Sep T Dec 1770 *Justitia*. M.
Witchingham, Mary of St. Peter Mancroft, Norwich. S Summer
 1731. *Nf.
Withall, Thomas. R Summer 1773. Sy.
Withall, Thomas. S 14 yrs Jly 1774. L.
Witham, Henry. S Feb T Mar 1730 *Patapsco* LC Annapolis Sep 1730. M.
Witham, John, a Quaker. R for plantations Jly 1665 (PC). Ht.
Witham, John. S s sheep Lent R 14 yrs Summer 1750. Nt.
Wittam, John. S May T Sep 1765 *Justitia*. M.
Witham, Samuel. S for life Mar 1754. L.
Witherell. *See* Wetherall.
Witheridge, Isaac. TB to Va from QS 1743. De.
Witheridge, Joan. S Aug 1734. De.
Witheridge, John. S Mar 1743. De.
Witherington, Anne. R for Barbados Aug 1668. M.
Witherington, Elizabeth. S & T Dec 1758 *The Brothers*. L.
Witherington, Henry. S Jan-Jun 1747. M.
Witherington, Jane. S Jan T Mar 1758 *Dragon*. M.
Widerington, Oswald. S for highway robbery Lent R for life Summer
 1764. O.
Witherow, William. S Lent 1731. Hu.
Withers, John. T May 1737 *Forward*. Sy.
Withers, John. S Feb T Apr 1770 *New Trial*. L.
Withers, Nathaniel. R 14 yrs Mar 1774. So.
Withers, Rebecca. S Jly T Aug 1721 *Prince Royal* LC Va Nov 1721. M.
Withers, Sarah. S Oct-Dec 1739 T Jan 1740 *York* to Md. M.
Withers, Sarah. S s lambs Summer 1742 R 14 yrs Lent TB Mar 1743. G.
Withers, Sarah. SQS Oct T Dec 1758 *The Brothers*. M.
Withers, Thomas of Stratford Langthorne. R for Barbados or Jamaica
 Mar 1682 & Feb 1683. E.
Withers, Thomas (1744). *See* Wittas. La.
Weatherspun, Elizabeth (1757). *See* Avery. De.
Witherspoon, Robert. SQS Feb 1773. M.
Withey, Daniel. S Jan T Feb 1719 *Worcester* LC Annapolis Jun
 1719. LM.
Withey, Thomas. S Mar 1727. Wi.
Wythyman, John Jr. Rebel T 1685.
Withrington, Thomas. S Norwich Summer 1748. Nf.
Witt, James. S Dec 1753-Jan 1754. M.

Wittam. *See* Witham.

Wittas als Withers, Thomas of Aintree, chimney sweep. SQS Jan 1744. La.

Wittens, Sara (1697). *See* Wittings. M.

Wittensloe als Wittey, Elizabeth. S s at Knighton on Teme Lent 1764. Wo.

Wittingham, George (1763). *See* Morris. Wo.

Wittings als Wittens als Hodges, Sara, spinster. R for Barbados or Jamaica May 1697. M.

Wittings, Uriah. R Mar AT Jun 1677. M.

Witton. *See* Whitton.

Witts, Elizabeth. S (Western Circ) Dec 1766 AT Lent 1767. G.

Witts, Stephen. S s at Minchinhampton Lent TB Mar 1738. G.

Wittey, Elizabeth (1764). *See* Wittensloe. Wo.

Whyttie, Thomas. Rebel T 1685.

Witty, Thomas of Buxworth (Derbys). R for America Jly 1677. No.

Woadam. *See* Woodham.

Wockley, Margaret. S Jan-May T Jun 1738 *Forward* to Md or Va. M.

Woolfe, Barbara. R for Barbados or Jamaica Dec 1689. L.

Wolfe, Elizabeth. R for Barbados Dec 1681 & Sep 1682. L.

Woofe, James. S Lent R 14 yrs Summer 1757. Sh.

Wolfe, John. R for Barbados Mar 1677. L.

Wolfe, John. S Summer 1754. Ca.

Wolph, John. SQS New Sarum or Warminster & TB to Va Oct 1768. Wi.

Wolfe, Joseph of Esher. SQS Oct T 14 yrs Dec 1763 *Neptune*. Sy.

Wolfe, Saunders. S May T Sep 1765 *Justitia*. L.

Wolfe, Solomon (1774). *See* Solomon, Wolfe als Benjamin. Co.

Wolfington, Henry. S Feb T for life Mar 1750 *Tryal*. M.

Wolfrey, Lucy. R for Barbados Jly 1674. M.

Wolsey, George. S s mare & R Lent T May 1770. Wa.

Wonnell, James. S Jan T Feb 1719 *Worcester* LC Annapolis Jun 1719. LM.

Wood, Ann. T Oct 1732 *Caesar*. Sy.

Wood, Ann. R 14 yrs Mar 1743. De.

Wood, Ann. SQS Feb T Apr 1768 *Thornton*. M.

Wood, Benjamin. R (Home Circ) for Barbados Apr 1663. X.

Wood, Benjamin. S Jly T Oct 1741 *Sea Horse* to Va. M.

Wood, Brittania, als wife of Charles Woolstonecraft of Christ Church. S s silk Oct 1740 T Jan 1741 *Harpooner* to Rappahannock. M.

Wood, Catherine. S Sep T Nov 1743 *George William*. L.

Wood, Catherine. S s at Shrewsbury Summer 1746. Sh.

Wood, Charles of Mansfield Woodhouse. SQS s saddle Jly TB Aug 1771. Nt.

Wood, Daniel. S Feb T Mar 1731 *Patapsco* LC Annapolis Jun 1731. M.

Wood, Daniel. T Jun 1740 *Essex*. E.

Wood, Dorothy, spinster. S Lent R for Barbados Apr 1663. Sx.

Wood, Dorothy. S Jly-Sep T Sep 1742 *Forward*. M.

Wood, Eady. S Feb T Mar 1729 *Patapsco* LC Annapolis Dec 1729. L.

Wood, Edward of Whitechapel. R 10 yrs Lent 1655; to be transported by Thomas Vincent & Samuel Highland. Sy.

Wood, Edward. S Sep T Oct 1768 *Justitia*. M.

Wood, Elizabeth. R for Barbados Aug 1664. M.

Wood, Elizabeth. R for America Aug 1715. M.

Wood, Elizabeth. S & T Apr 1725 *Sukey* LC Annapolis Sep 1725. M.

Wood, Elizabeth wife of Francis. S Jly T Dec 1734 *Caesar* LC Va Jly 1735. M.

Wood, Elizabeth. S Sep T Oct 1739 *Duke of Cumberland*. L.

Wood als Johnson als Smith, Elizabeth. S Sep-Oct 1772. M.

Wood, Enoch. S s wheat at Compton Summer 1742. Be.

Wood, Francis. SQS Mar TB Aug 1720 to be shipped to Md from Liverpool. Db.

Wood, George. R for plantations Jan 1665. L.

Wood, George (1721). *See* Williams, Thomas. G.

Wood, George. T 14 yrs Apr 1770 *New Trial*. E.

Wood, Grace. T Apr 1725 *Sukey* LC Md Sep 1725. Sy.

Wood, Hannah. T Jan 1741 *Vernon*. Sx.

Whood, James. PT Jan 1675. M.

Wood, James. TB Nov 1736. Db.

Wood, James. S Jan 1740. L.

Wood, James. S Dec 1749-Jan 1750 T Mar 1750 *Tryal*. M.

Wood, James. S Mar 1752. De.

Wood, James. S Feb T Apr 1765 *Ann*. L.

Wood, James. R 14 yrs Lent 1766. Nt.

Wood, Jane. S Aug T Sep 1725 *Forward* LC Annapolis Dec 1725. M.

Wood, Jane. S Jan-Jun T Jun 1728 *Elizabeth* LC Potomack Aug 1729. L.

Wood, Jane. S Jan T 14 yrs Apr 1743 *Justitia*. M.

Wood, Jane. T Sep 1755 *Tryal*. M.

Wood, Joane. S & T 14 yrs Sep 1718 *Eagle* LC Charles Town Mar 1719. L.

Wood, John. R for Va Jan 1620. M.

Wood, John. S for Va Jly 1718. De.

Wood, John. S & T 14 yrs Aug 1718 *Eagle* LC Charles Town Mar 1719. L.

Wood, John. S Jly T Aug 1721 *Prince Royal* LC Va Nov 1721. L.

Wood, John. R 14 yrs Aug 1728 TB to Md. De.

Wood, John. S s tankard at St. Philip & Jacob Lent TB Mar 1737. G.

Wood, John. T May 1744 *Justitia*. E.

Wood, John. S & TB Mar 1747. G.

Wood, John. S s sheep Summer 1748 R 14 yrs Lent 1749. Li.

Wood, John. S Feb-Apr T Jun 1756 *Lyon*. M.

Wood, John. S Lent 1756. Y.

Wood, John. SQS Jly TB Aug 1758. So.

Wood, John. AT Lent & Summer 1765. Y.

Wood, John of Berkhampstead St. Peter. SQS Jan T Apr 1768 *Thornton*. Ht.

Wood, John. S City s at St. Sampson & R 14 yrs Summer 1768. Y.

Wood, John. T 14 yrs Dec 1771 *Justitia*. Sy.

Wood, John. S s horse & R 14 yrs Summer 1772. Li.

Wood, John. S Sep-Oct 1772. M.

Wood, John. S 14 yrs for receiving from Hannah Guy *(qv)* Summer 1774. Y.

Wood, John. S s at West Bromwich Summer 1774. St.

Wood, Jonathan of York. R for Barbados Jly 1671 & Feb 1673. Y.
Wood, Joseph. S s horse Lent R 14 yrs Summer 1737. Y.
Wood, Joseph (1765). *See* Newton. Ch.
Wood, Joseph. S Lent 1766. Nt.
Wood, Joseph. S Lent 1772. Wa.
Wood, Knightly. T Jan 1738 *Dorsetshire.* Sy.
Wood, Margaret. R for plantations Jan 1665. L.
Wood, Margaret. T Nov 1741 *Sea Horse.* Sx.
Wood, Margaret (1768). *See* Guildford. M.
Wood, Martha of Shoreditch. S s cloth Jan-May T Jun 1738 *Forward.* M.
Wood, Mary. R for Barbados or Jamaica May AT Jly 1697. M.
Wood, Mary (2). TB Oct 1719 T *Susannah & Sarah* LC Annapolis Apr 1720. L.
Wood, Mary. S & T May 1736 *Patapsco.* L.
Wood, Mary. S Jan 1740. L.
Wood, Mary wife of Richard. S Jly T Sep 1765 *Justitia.* M.
Wood, Mary. S Jan-Feb T 14 yrs Apr 1771 *Thornton.* M.
Wood, Mary. S Jan-Feb 1773. M.
Wood, Michael. S Jly 1773. L.
Wood, Obadiah. S for perjury Lent 1760; to be imprisoned 3 months before transportation. St.
Wood, Paul. S Sep 1754. L.
Wood, Peter. S Summer 1757 R 14 yrs Lent TB Apr 1758. Db.
Wood, Rebecca wife of William. SQS Coventry Mar 1766. Wa.
Wood, Richard (1698). *See* Hawkins. So.
Wood, Richard. S Jly T 14 yrs Aug 1718 *Eagle* LC Charles Town Mar 1719. M.
Wood, Richard. S & T Sep 1731 *Smith* LC Va 1732. L.
Wood, Richard. T May 1736 *Patapsco.* K.
Wood, Richard. R 14 yrs Mar 1754 TB to Va. De.
Wood als Batchelor, Robert. R for Jamaica Aug 1661. L.
Wood, Robert of Brasted. R for Barbados Apr 1668. K.
Wood, Robert. S Dec 1749-Jan 1750 T Mar 1750 *Tryal.* M.
Wood, Robert. S Lent 1761. No.
Wood, Samuel. S Summer 1735 R 14 yrs Summer 1736. Wa.
Wood, Samuel. S Jly-Sep T Sep 1742 *Forward.* M.
Wood als Janney, Samuel. S s horse Lent R 14 yrs Summer 1756. Nt.
Wood, Solomon. S Feb T Apr 1771 *Thornton.* L.
Wood, Susan of Lambeth. R for Barbados or Jamaica Jun 1699. Sy.
Wood, Susannah of Bristol. R 14 yrs Apr 1768 (SP). G.
Wood, Thomas. S Summer 1664 for attending conventicles. Ht.
Wood, Thomas of Worcester. R for America Mar 1680. Wo.
Wood, Thomas. R for America Mar 1687. Ru.
Wood, Thomas. R Dec 1699 & Aug 1700. M.
Wood, Thomas. R for America Feb 1700. Li.
Wood, Thomas of Durham. R for Barbados Jly 1701. Du.
Wood, Thomas. R 11 yrs Jly 1744 TB to Va 1745. De.
Wood, Thomas. TB Mar 1750. Db.
Wood, Thomas. S for perjury Lent 1760; to be imprisoned 3 months before transportation. St.
Wood, Thomas. S Sep T Dec 1763 *Neptune.* M.

Wood, Thomas of St. Saviour, Southwark. SQS Mar T Apr 1768 *Thornton*. Sy.
Wood, Thomas. T Apr 1771 *Thornton*. K.
Wood, Timothy. AT Summer 1756. Y.
Wood, Walter. S s at Tettenhall Lent 1739. St.
Wood, William of Castle. R for Barbados Jly 1683. La.
Wood, William. R for America Aug 1685. Wa.
Wood, William. T May 1719 *Margaret*. Sy.
Wood, William. S Feb T Mar 1729 *Patapsco* LC Annapolis Dec 1729. M.
Wood, William. T Sep 1730 *Smith*. Sy.
Wood, William. T May 1737 *Forward*. Sx.
Wood, William. S Summer 1738. Y.
Wood, William. R 14 yrs Summer TB Aug 1753. Y.
Wood, William. T Sep 1758 *Tryal*. Sy.
Wood, William. S Jan T Mar 1763 *Neptune*. M.
Wood, William. SEK & T Jan 1766 *Tryal*. K.
Wood, William. T 14 yrs Apr 1769 *Tryal*. Sy.
Woodamore, William. S Jan 1656 to House of Correction unless he agrees to be transported. M.
Woodar, Mary of St. Saviour, Southwark. R for Barbados or Jamaica Jly 1702. Sy.
Woodard, William. S as an "old convict" 1697. Ht.
Woodason, Richard. S Jly 1738. Ha.
Woodbegood als Robins, Mary. T Sep 1755 *Tryal*. M.
Woodburne, James of Dalton in Furness. SQS Jly 1755. La.
Woodbourne, William. T Dec 1736 *Dorsetshire*. E.
Woodbridge, Edward. S s sheep Lent R 14 yrs Summer 1765. O.
Woodcock, Diana. S Apr-May T May 1744 *Justitia*. M.
Woodcock, Edward. S s at Weobley Lent 1774. He.
Woodcock, James. S Lent R 14 yrs Summer 1742. St.
Woodcocke, John of Great Yarmouth. R for America Mar 1686. Nf.
Woodcock, John. S Lent R 14 yrs Summer 1734. Y.
Woodcocke, John. S May T Jun 1764 *Dolphin*. M.
Woodcocke, Nicholas Sr. R for America Jly 1683. No.
Woodcock, Robert. S Dec 1750. L.
Woodcock, Sarah. S Jun-Dec 1738 T 14 yrs Jan 1739 *Dorsetshire* to Va. M.
Woodcocke, Thomas of Church Hulme. R for Barbados Mar 1678. Ch.
Woodcock, William. Rebel T 1685.
Woodcock, William of Wells. R for Barbados Jun 1699. So.
Woodcock, William. S Jan T Apr 1743 *Justitia*. M.
Wooden, Elizabeth. T Nov 1741 *Sea Horse*. K.
Woodey, Thomas. S Jun T Sep 1758 *Tryal*. L.
Woodfield, Jane of St. George, Southwark, widow. SQS Feb T 14 yrs Apr 1771 *Thornton*. Sy.
Woodfield, John. T Oct 1722 *Forward* LC Md Jun 1723. Sy.
Woodfield, Maria of St. Saviour, Southwark. SQS Feb T Apr 1771 *Thornton*. Sy.
Woodfield, Thomas. R for Va Oct 1670. O.
Woodford, Charles. S Jan T Apr 1741 *Speedwell* or *Mediterranean*. M.
Woodford, Richard. R 14 yrs Aug 1740. De.

Woodford, Robert of St. Giles in Fields. S s shoes Apr T May 1740 *Essex*. M.

Woodger, James. S for highway robbery Lent R for life Summer 1758. Bd.

Woodhall, Edward. S s at Wolverhampton Lent 1773. St.

Woodham, George. SQS Oct 1773. M.

Woodham, Richard. S Apr T May 1718 *Tryal* LC Charles Town Aug 1718. LM.

Woadam, William. S Mar 1725. Wi.

Woodhouse, George. S Lent 1775. Li.

Woodhouse, John. Died on passage in *Rappahannock* 1726. Li.

Woodhouse, John. S s horse Summer 1729 R 14 yrs Summer TB Aug 1730. Nt.

Woodhouse, Mary. S Feb T Mar 1731 *Patapsco* LC Annapolis Jun 1731. M.

Woodhouse, Samuel. S Feb 1663 to House of Correction unless he agrees to be transported. M.

Woodhouse, Thomas. S s wool at Rodborough Lent TB Apr 1753. G.

Woodhouse, Thomas. S Dec 1761 T Apr 1762 *Dolphin*. M.

Wooding, John. S Lent R 14 yrs Summer 1749. Bu.

Woodin, John. S & T Apr 1766 *Ann*. M.

Woodin, Michael. S Summer 1737. Bd.

Woodington, Dorothy of St. Saviour, Southwark, spinster. SQS Oct 1751. Sy.

Woodland, Christopher. S Dec 1753-Jan 1754. M.

Woodland, Lydia. S Lent T Jun 1756 *Lyon*. E.

Woodland, Matthew. Rebel T 1685.

Woodland, Samuel. R 14 yrs Aug 1764. So.

Woodley, Benjamin. S Jan-Feb T Apr 1772 *Thornton*. M.

Woodley, John of Crediton, husbandman. R for Barbados Feb 1668. De.

Woodley, John. S Mar 1748. De.

Woodly, Mary. R 14 yrs Aug 1735. De.

Woodley, William. S Oct 1775. M.

Woodliffe, Nathaniel. S Norwich Summer 1748. Nf.

Woodman, Phillis. SQS & T Sep 1764 *Justitia*. M.

Woodman, Thomas. S Apr T May 1719 *Margaret*; sold to William Black Md Sep 1719. LM.

Woodman, William. T Jan 1741 *Vernon*. Sx.

Woodman, William. T Apr 1768 *Thornton*. K.

Woodmanson, Richard. R for Barbados Sep 1672. L.

Woodmason, Mary. R 14 yrs Aug 1750 TB to Va. De.

Woodnoth, William of Great Malvern. S s stockings Lent 1719. Wo.

Woodridge, William (1760). *See* Woolridge. Be.

Woodrow, Anthony. Rebel T 1685.

Woodrow, John. Rebel T 1685.

Woodrow, Matthew. S Aug 1740 TB to Va. De.

Woodruff, James. S s at St. Philip & Jacob Summer TB Aug 1742. G.

Woodruff, Thomas. S & TB Aug 1740. G.

Woods, Anthony. T Oct 1732 *Caesar*. Sx.

Woods, Caleb. R 14 yrs Jly 1740. Ha.

Woods, Edward. S 1 yrs Feb 1757. M.

Woods, George. S Mar 1763. Ha.

Woods, Martha. S Sep T Oct 1719 *Susannah & Sarah* LC Md Apr 1720. LM.

Woods, Robert. S s mare Summer 1759 R 14 yrs Lent 1760. Su.

Woods, Robert. S Lent 1761. Su.

Woods, Robert. S s rabbits at Eriswell Lent 1774. Su.

Woods, Stainsby. S Summer 1757. Hu.

Woods, Susanna. S Lent 1752. Su.

Woods, Thomas. SQS Marlborough Oct 1766 TB to Va Apr 1767. Wi.

Woods, Thomas. R 14 yrs Mar 1768. Ha.

Woods, William of Saham Toney. R for America Mar 1686. Nf.

Woods, William. S Summer 1736. Nf.

Woods, William (1773). *See* Wildman. Y.

Woodthey, John. R Jun T 14 yrs Aug 1769 *Douglas*. M.

Woodward, Alexander of Gravesend. R for Barbados or Jamaica Feb 1690. K.

Woodward, Ann. SQS Sep 1754. M.

Woodward, Catherine. S Jly T Dec 1735 *John* LC Annapolis Sep 1736. M.

Woodward, Christopher of Wotton Under Edge. R for America Jly 1686. G.

Woodward, Elizabeth als Franklin. S & T Sep 1731 *Smith* but died on passage. M.

Woodward, Elizabeth. S Jun T Nov 1743 *George William*. M.

Woodward, Elizabeth. R Summer 1756. Ht.

Woodward, Elizabeth. S Jly 1761. L.

Woodward, George. PT Oct R Dec 1716 T Jan 1717 *Queen Elizabeth* to Jamaica. M.

Woodward, Henry. S Mar 1721. So.

Woodward, James. S s horse Lent R 14 yrs Summer 1738. Wo.

Woodward, James. S Jan-Feb 1774. M.

Woodward, John. Rebel T 1685.

Woodward, John. S Feb T May 1719 *Margaret*; sold to Timothy Sullivan Md Aug 1719. L.

Woodward, John. T Apr 1722 *Sukey*. Sy.

Woodward, John. S Jly 1738. De.

Woodward, John. S Jan-Jun 1747. M.

Woodward, John. S Lent R 14 yrs Summer 1756. Wa.

Woodward, John. S s brass kettle at Avening Lent 1768. G.

Woodward, Mary. S & T Apr 1741 *Speedwell* or *Mediterranean*. M.

Woodward, Richard. S s heifer Summer 1739. St.

Woodward, Samuel. S & R Summer 1761. Nl.

Woodward, Samuel. S Lent R 14 yrs Summer 1761. Nt.

Woodward, Thomas. R for Barbados Aug 1664. M.

Woodward als Williams als Greenaway, Thomas. S s horse Lent R 14 yrs Summer 1730. G.

Woodward, Thomas of St. Andrew, Hertford. SQS Apr T Jun 1764 *Dolphin*. Ht.

Woodward, William of Brickenden. R for Barbados or Jamaica Mar 1698. Ht.

Woodward, William. R for life Summer 1766. Wa.

Woofe. *See* Wolfe.

Woolcock, John. S Apr 1747. Co.

Woolcock als Paul, John. S Mar 1749. Co.

Woolcock, Richard. S Apr 1747. Co.

Woolcott, George. S Aug 1771. So.

Woolcott, Samuel. R 14 yrs Mar 1764. De.

Wooldridge, William. S Jly T Oct 1768 *Justitia*. M.

Woolfenden, Roger of Bury, tailor. SQS Apr 1765. La.

Woolford, Henry. LC from *Susannah & Sarah* Annapolis Apr 1720. L. or M.

Woolford, Sarah. S Mar TB to Va Apr 1768. Wi.

Woolford, Thomas. SQS Marlborough Oct 1767 TB to Va Apr 1768. Wi.

Whoulfrey, John. R Mar 1773. Ha.

Woolhouse, Jonathan. S s tankard at Sheffield Lent 1767. Y.

Wollacott, John. S Mar 1734. De.

Woollam als Woolard, John. S & T Oct 1729 *Forward* but died on passage. M.

Woolham, John of Palsbury. R (Western Circ) for America Jly 1700. O.

Woollard, James. S Jan 1746. L.

Woolard, John (1729). *See* Woollam.

Woolard, Michael. S Lent 1756. Su.

Woollard, William, als Smith, John of Croydon. SQS for false pretences Oct 1768 T Jan 1769 *Thornton*. Sy.

Woollaway, William. R 14 yrs Aug 1773. De.

Woollen, Ann. S May T Sep 1757 *Thetis*. M.

Woolen, Sarah (1748). *See* Phillips. He.

Woolener, William. S Lent R Summer 1745. E.

Woollens, Isaac. R for Barbados or Jamaica Oct 1690. M.

Wooler, George. R for Jamaica Aug 1661. M.

Wooler, James. AT Lent 1766. Y.

Wooller, John. AT Summer 1765. Y.

Woollestone, Samuel, a Quaker. R for plantations Jly 1665 (PC). Ht.

Wolley, James. R 14 yrs Aug 1747. De.

Woolley, Joseph. TB Apr 1765. Db.

Woolley als Lawrence, Rebecca. S May-Jly 1746. M.

Woolley, Richard. S Feb T Sep 1737 *Pretty Patsy* to Md. M.

Woolley, Richard. S s at Enville Lent 1770. St.

Wooley, Richard. SQS Sep T Dec 1771 *Justitia*. M.

Woolley, Robert. T Apr 1769 *Tryal*. E.

Wooley, William. S Apr-May 1775. M.

Woolmer, John of St. Michael, Norwich. S Summer 1731. *Nf.

Woolner, William. S Oct-Dec 1754. M.

Woolridge, Roger. S Apr T May 1752 *Lichfield*. L.

Woolridge, William. Rebel T 1685.

Woolridge als Woodridge, William. S s breeches at Newbury Summer 1760. Be.

Wools, Richard. S & T Sep 1731 *Smith* to Va. M.

Woolls, William. S Sep T Dec 1767 *Neptune*. L.

Woolstonecraft, Brittania (1740). *See* Wood. M.

Woone, Benjamin. S Jly 1749. Co.

Woon, Stephen. R 14 yrs Jly 1749. Co.

Woore, John. S s fowls Lent 1754; Ann Woore acquitted. He.

Wootton als Hudson, Alice. S Sep-Oct 1775. M.

Wotton, Ann wife of John. S Aug 1774. De.

Wootton, James. SQS Warminster Jly TB to Va Sep 1774 & Apr 1775. Wi.

Wotton als Watton, Joseph. S Lent 1774. Wa.

Wootton, Margaret. S Summer T Sep 1770. Wa.

Wootton, Mary wife of Edward. R Mar AT Dec 1688. M.

Wootton, Mary. S & T 14 yrs Jan 1736 *Dorsetshire* LC Va Sep 1736. L.

Wotton, Michael. S Mar 1731 TB to Va. De.

Wooton, Paul. S s from Wraysbury church Lent T Apr 1771 *Thornton*. Bu.

Wootton, Richard. PT Jan R Mar 1677. M.

Wooten als Watton, Robert (1695). *See* Parkway. M.

Wotton, Thomas of Rotherhithe. SQS Oct T Dec 1769 *Justitia*. Sy.

Worster als Worcester, Andrew. S May T Sep 1758 *Tryal* to Md. M.

Worden. *See* Warden.

Wordly, William. S Mar 1759. Wi.

Worgan, William. S Oct 1743 T Feb 1744 *Neptune*. L.

Workman, Daniel. S Mar TB to Va Apr 1746. Wi.

Workman, Samuel. S s cloth at Minchinhampton Summer 1765. G.

Worledge, Samuel of Portsmouth. R for Barbados Jly 1678. Ha.

Worley, John. S s shoes Lent 1755. Be.

Worley, Thomas. S s sheep Summer 1753 R 14 yrs Lent 1754. Bu.

Wormelayton, Robert of Rusper. R for Barbados Apr 1668. Sy.

Wormer, William of Peterborough. R for America Jun 1684. No.

Worn. *See* Warne.

Wornell, George of Burbridge. R for Barbados Jly 1679. Wi.

Wornoll, John. T May 1751 *Tryal*. K.

Worrall, Charles. R Oct TB Nov 1662. L.

Worrall, Charles of Warrington, shoemaker. SQS Jan 1743. La.

Worrell, Frances. S Jan-Feb T Apr 1753 *Thames*. M.

Worrell, Francis. S Feb 1752. L.

Worrell, Francis. S Apr-May 1754. M.

Worrill, Henry. R & T Apr 1734 *Patapsco* to Md. M.

Worrall, John. Rebel T 1685.

Worral, Margaret Ann. S Oct T Dec 1767 *Neptune*. M.

Worrall als Dingley, Mark. S Mar 1771. Ha.

Whorrall, Mary. S s at Wellington Lent 1765. Sh.

Worrell, Sarah. R for Barbados or Jamaica Feb 1686. M.

Worrell, Thomas. LC from *Forward* Rappahannock May 1728. X.

Worral, Thomas. R 14 yrs Summer T Sep 1765 *Justitia*. Bu.

Worrill, William. R 14 yrs Lent 1761. Li.

Worsfold, Thomas of Abinger. SQS Jan 1773. Sy.

Worsley, Alice. S Lent 1755. Sh.

Worsley, William. S Jly 1721 T Mar 1723. Bu.

Worth, Andrew. TB to Va from QS 1772. De.

Worth, James of West Teignmouth. R for Barbados Jly 1677. De.

Worth als Bibey, Mary. S Dec 1773. M.

Worth, Michael (1736). *See* Newman. X.

Worth, Robert of Scotforth. SQS Jly 1746. La.

Worthing, Thomas. T Oct 1720 *Gilbert*. Sy.

Worthing, William (1764). *See* Worthington. He.

Worthington, John. S Lent R for Barbados May 1664. E.

Worthington, Thomas. S Mar 1751. De.

Worthington als Worthing, William. S 14 yrs for receiving Summer 1764. He.

Wostendale, John. S s horse Lent R Summer 1726. Db.

Wotenden, Ralph of Newcastle under Lyme. R for America Jly 1675.St.

Wotton. *See* Wootton.

Wray, Jacob. S Lent R 14 yrs Summer 1757. O.

Wray als Spink als Boyer, John. S s at Harwood & Ampleforth Lent TB Aug 1756. Y.

Wreathcocke, William. R & T May 1736 *Patapsco* to Md. M.

Wrecknorth, John. R for life Lent 1774. Sy.

Wrenn, Sarah. S Apr T May 1720 *Honor* to York River. L.

Wren, Susan. R for Barbados Feb 1664 (SP). M.

Wrenshaw, Elizabeth of Lancaster. R for Barbados Jly 1699. La.

Wrentmore, Henry. Rebel T 1685.

Wresle, John of York. R for America Mar 1710. Y.

Wrexham, Charles. R for America Jly 1694. Le.

Wride, John. R 14 yrs Apr 1754. So.

Wrigglesworth, Joseph. T Sep 1742 *Forward*. Ht.

Wrigglesworth, Samuel. AT Lent 1748. Y.

Wright, Abraham. S May-Jly 1750. M.

Wright, Abraham. S s cloth at Leeds Lent 1773. Y.

Wright, Alice wife of Peter of St. Thomas Apostle, Southwark. R for Barbados Jly 1679. Sy.

Wright, Anne (1725). *See* Price. M.

Wright, Ann. S s sheets Sep 1735 T Jan 1776 *Dorsetshire* but died on passage. M.

Wright, Ann. S Dec 1747. L.

Wright, Ann (1758). *See* Merritt. L.

Wright, Ann of Braintree, spinster. SQS Jan T Apr 1762 *Neptune*. E.

Wright, Ann wife of John. S & T Jly 1770 *Scarsdale*. L.

Wright, Benjamin. S & R 14 yrs Summer 1774. St.

Wright, Katherine, aged 19. R for Barbados Feb 1664. M.

Wright, Charles. S Dec 1766 T Jan 1767 *Tryal*. L.

Wright, Charles. S Apr T May 1767 *Thornton*. L.

Wright, Charles. S Mar 1774. Wi.

Wright, Charles. S s at Chester & R 14 yrs Summer 1775. Du.

Wright, David. S & T Jly 1770 *Scarsdale*. L.

Wright, Edward, aged 19, fair, watchmaker. S Sep T 14 yrs Oct 1720 *Gilbert* LC Md May 1721. L.

Wright, Edward. S Oct 1774. L.

Wright, Elizabeth. R for Barbados & TB Aug 1668. L.

Wright, Elizabeth. R Feb 1675. M.

Wright, Elizabeth. R for Barbados or Jamaica May AT Jly 1697. M.

Wright, Elizabeth (1718). *See* Storey. L.

Wright, Elizabeth (1722). *See* Brown. M.

Wright, Elizabeth. S Aug T Sep 1725 *Forward* LC Annapolis Dec 1725. M.

Wright, Elizabeth. S & T Dec 1734 *Caesar* LC Va Jly 1735. L.

Wright, Elizabeth als Wilkinson. S Feb-Apr T Jun 1756 *Lyon*. M.

Wright, Elizabeth. T Apr 1760 *Thetis*. Sy.

Wright, Elizabeth. S Aug 1763. L.

Wright, Frances (1676). *See* Russell. L.

Wright, Francis. S Feb T Mar 1730 *Patapsco* LC Annapolis Sep 1730. L.

Wright, George. S Apr T May 1751 *Tryal*. L.

Wright, George. S Sep 1756. M.

Wright, George. T Apr 1769 *Tryal*. E.

Wright, Giles. S s clothing at Arborfield Summer 1722 T *Forward* LC
Md Jun 1723. Be.

Wright, Gladduce. TB to Va from QS 1759. De.

Wright, Hannah. S for shoplifting Summer 1754 R 14 yrs Lent
1755. Wa.

Wright, Henry. S Aug 1763. L.

Wright, Huckvill of Reading. R for America Feb 1690. Be.

Wright, James. S Oct 1661 to House of Correction unless he agrees to
be transported. M.

Wright, James. S & T Mar 1763 *Neptune*. L.

Wright, James. S s at Kingswinford Lent 1764. St.

Wright, James. R 14 yrs Jly 1767. Ha.

Wright, James. S Feb T Apr 1768 *Thornton*. M.

Wright, James. S Oct 1774. L.

Wright, John of Marsh Gibbon. R for Barbados Feb 1664. Bu.

Wright als Greene, John. R for Barbados & TB Oct 1667. L.

Wright, John. R for Barbados Mar 1681. M.

Wright, John of Carlehouses. R for Barbados Jly 1684. Du.

Wright, John. R for America Jly 1687. No.

Wright, John of Egham. R for Barbados or Jamaica Jun 1692. Sy.

Wright, John. R 14 yrs for Carolina May 1719. L.

Wright, John. S Aug T Oct 1723 *Forward* to Va. M.

Wright, John. S Jan T Feb 1726 *Supply* LC Annapolis May 1726. M.

Wright, John. S Aug T Oct 1726 *Forward* to Va. M.

Wright, John. R Summer 1728.

Wright, John. S Jun 1733 T Jan 1734 *Caesar* LC Va Jly 1734. M.

Wright, John. S & T Jan 1736 *Dorsetshire* LC Va Sep 1736. L.

Wright, John (1739). *See* Jones, William. L.

Wright, John. S Apr-Jun 1739. M.

Wright, John. S Jly T Oct 1741 *Sea Horse*. L.

Wright, John. S Jly-Dec 1747. M.

Wright, John. S Summer 1750 T May 1751 *Tryal*. K.

Wright, John. S Nov T Dec 1752 *Greyhound*. L.

Wright, John. T Apr 1753 *Thames*. K.

Wright, John. S Summer 1753 R 14 yrs Lent 1754. Sx.

Wright, John. S Summer TB Sep 1757. Db.

Wright, John. S Oct T Nov 1759 *Phoenix*. M.

Wright, John. S Jly 1760. M.

Wright, John. S Lent R 14 yrs Summer 1765. Wo.

Wright, John (1766). *See* Everett. M.

Wright, John. S & T Jan 1766 *Tryal*. M.

Wright, John. S Oct 1766 T Jan 1767 *Tryal*. M.

Wright, John. SQS Jly T Aug 1769 *Douglas*. M.
Wright, John of St. Margaret, Westminster. SW Apr 1774. M.
Wright, Jonas. R for Barbados Jly 1663. L.
Wright, Joseph of Hillingdon. R for Barbados Aug 1679. M.
Wright, Joseph, als Broadway, Robert. S Lent 1724 R 14 yrs Lent 1725. Sh.
Wright, Joseph. LC from *Robert* Annapolis Jun 1725. X.
Wright, Joseph. S Feb T Mar 1730 *Patapsco* LC Annapolis Sep 1730. M.
Wright, Joseph. AT Summer 1755. Y.
Wright, Joseph. S s sheep Summer 1758 R 14 yrs Lent 1759. No.
Wright, Joseph. S Lent R 14 yrs Summer 1760. St.
Wright, Lucretia wife of John of Broxbourne. SQS Apr T Jun 1764 *Dolphin*. Ht.
Wright, Lydia. S & T Dec 1736 *Dorsetshire*. L.
Wright, Margaret of St. Olave, Southwark. R for Barbados Aug 1662. Sy.
Wright, Martha. S & T Oct 1732 *Caesar*. L.
Wright, Martha. S Summer TB Sep 1757. Db.
Wright, Martin. S & T May 1736 *Patapsco*. L.
Wright, Martin. S Jan-May T 14 yrs Jun 1738 *Forward* to Md or Va. M.
Wright, Martin. S Oct T Dec 1758 *The Brothers*. L.
Wright, Mary. S & T Sep 1718 *Eagle* but died on passage. L.
Wright, Mary. S Sep T 14 yrs Oct 1720 *Gilbert* but died on passage; sentenced with Edward Wright *(qv)*. L.
Wright, Mary. T Jly 1724 *Robert* LC Md Jun 1725. Sy.
Wright, Mary. S Dec 1733 T Jan 1734 *Caesar* LC Va Jly 1734. M.
Wright, Mary (1735). *See* Matthews. M.
Wright, Mary. S Feb-Apr 1746. M.
Wright als Brown, Mary. S & T Apr 1766 *Ann*. M.
Wright, Mary. S Summer 1766. La.
Wright, Mary. S Jly T Sep 1767 *Justitia*. M.
Wright, Mary. S Dec 1768 T 14 yrs Jan 1769 *Thornton*. L.
Wright, Misael. S for demanding money with menaces Lent R 14 yrs Summer 1758. Su.
Wright, Peter. S Apr T May 1750 *Lichfield*. M.
Wrighte, Philip. S s sheep Lent R 14 yrs Summer 1753. Wa.
Wright, Richard of Northwold. R for America Feb 1695. Nf.
Wright, Robert. S Lent 1735. Ca.
Wright, Richard. S s lead Lent 1745. Sy.
Wright, Richard of Fobbing, singleman. SQS Apr T May 1752 *Lichfield*. E.
Wright, Robert. S Lent 1762. Su.
Wright, Robert. S s mare at Salthouse & R Summer 1772. Nf.
Wright, Samuel of Rochford. R for Barbados or Jamaica Jly 1710. E.
Right, Samuel. T Aug 1721 *Owners Goodwill*. E.
Wright, Samuel. S Lent 1774. Sy.
Wright, Thomas (1700). *See* Jones. M.
Wright, Thomas. S Apr T 14 yrs May 1718 *Tryal* LC Charles Town Aug 1718. L.
Wright, Thomas. TB 14 yrs Oct 1719 T *Susannah & Sarah* LC Annapolis Apr 1720. L.
Wright, Thomas. TB to Md Oct 1721. Le.

Wright, Thomas. S Lent 1750. Su.
Wright, Thomas. S & T Sep 1751 *Greyhound*. M.
Wright, Thomas. S & T Aug 1752 *Tryal*. L.
Wright, Thomas. S Summer 1752. Y.
Wright, Thomas. T Dec 1753 *Whiteing*. K.
Wright, Thomas (1755). *See* Longden, John. Nf.
Wright, Thomas. S Lent 1756. Nf.
Wright, Thomas. S Lent 1756. Y.
Wright, Thomas of Trumpington. S Lent 1760. Ca.
Wright, Thomas. SQS May 1763. M.
Wright, Thomas. R 14 yrs Lent 1765. Ch.
Wright, Thomas. S Dec 1775. M.
Wright, Tobias. R for Barbados Sep 1669. M.
Wright, Tobias. R for life May 1699. M.
Wright, William. S Summer R for Barbados Aug 1665. Sy.
Wright, William of St. George, Southwark. R for Barbados Apr 1668. Sy.
Wright, William. R for Barbados Jun 1671. M.
Wright, William. PT Oct 1687. M.
Wright, William of Reading. R for America Feb 1690. Be.
Wright, William. PT Jun R Oct 1690. M.
Wright, William. PT Mar 1701. M.
Wright, William. T 14 yrs Dec 1758 *The Brothers*. E.
Wright, William. S Mar 1766. Ha.
Wright, William. S s at Kidlington Summer 1772. O.
Wright, William of Ashton with Mackerfield, collier. SQS Apr 1774. La.
Wright als Wight, William. S & R 14 yrs Jly 1774. Nl.
Wright, William. S Jan 1775. M.
Wright, William. R s sheep Summer 1775. Nt.
Wright, William. S s sheep & R Summer 1775. Db.
Riton, John. S City s sheep Lent 1743 R 14 yrs Lent 1744. Y.
Rigley, Richard. S s horse Lent R 14 yrs Summer TB Jly 1766. Db.
Writus, Thomas. S s sheep Lent R 14 yrs Summer 1768. St.
Wroth, Francis. R Oct 1694 AT Jan 1695. M.
Wroth, William. S Mar 1742. De.
Wyatt, Benjamin of Fisherton Anger. R for Barbados Jly 1698. Wi.
Wyat als Helligan, Katherine of St. Minver, spinster. R for Barbados Feb 1672. Co.
Wyatt als Newell, Elizabeth. S Oct 1744-Jan 1745. M.
Wyatt, Henry of Ottery, tanner. R for Barbados Mar 1686. De.
Wyatt, John. R Oct AT Dec 1688. M.
Wiatt, John. R for America Jly 1694. Wa.
Wyatt, John. S Feb T Mar 1731 *Patapsco* LC Annapolis Jun 1731. M.
Whiat, John. TB Aug 1733. Db.
Wyatt, John of Manchester. SQS Jan 1742. La.
Wyatt, John. S Apr 1773. L.
Wyatt, Martha. S Mar 1721. De.
Wyatt, Mary (1722). *See* Harris. M.
Wyatt, Richard of St. Endellion. R for Barbados Feb 1668. Co.
Wyatt, Richard. S Summer 1749 R 14 yrs Lent 1750. Wo.
Wyatt, Thomas (1688). *See* Ward. L.
Wyatt, Thomas. R 14 yrs Mar 1744. So.

Wyatt, Thomas. S Feb 1752. L.

Wyatt, William. S s cows at Hampstead Lent 1729. Be.

Wyatt, William. S Summer 1738 R 14 yrs Lent 1739. Wa.

Wyatt, William. S Jan 1751. L.

Wyborn, John. S Lent R Summer T Oct 1739 *Duke of Cumberland*. K.

Wye, Ann. S Sep-Oct 1772. M.

Wyre, Abraham. SQS Feb T Mar 1750. M.

Wyer, John. S Apr T Oct 1719 *Susannah & Sarah* LC Md Apr 1720. L.

Wyer, John. S s mare Lent R 14 yrs Summer T Sep 1755 *Tryal*. E.

Wyer, William (1754). *See* Whitaker. Su.

Wier, William. S Norwich for killing sheep Summer 1757 R 14 yrs Summer TB Sep 1758. Nf.

Wyers, Richard. S Jan T Feb 1724 *Anne*. L.

Wyke als Deacomb, Edward. R Dec 1698 AT Jan 1699. M.

Wikes, Francis. S Lent T Apr 1768 *Thornton*. Bu.

Wykes, Richard. S Sep T Dec 1767 *Neptune*. M.

Wyld. *See* Wild.

Wyles. *See* Wiles.

Wylett, Ann (1766). *See* Morley. M.

Wylie, John. S Dec 1733 T Jan 1734 *Caesar* LC Va Jly 1734. L.

Wyman, Michael. S Feb T Mar 1729 *Patapsco* to Md. M.

Wynd. *See* Wind.

Winn, Alice. S Apr T May 1743 *Indian Queen* to Potomack. M.

Winne, Anne als Mary. R Jan AT Feb 1679. M.

Wynne, Bacon. S Aug T Oct 1724 *Forward* LC Annapolis Jun 1725. M.

Wynn, Benjamin. R 14 yrs for murder Mar 1753. Co.

Wynn, Francis. S & T Jan 1722 *Gilbert* LC Annapolis Jly 1722. M.

Wynn, Henry (1725). *See* Jones, Thomas. Sh.

Wynne, James. S Lent R for Barbados May 1664. Sy.

Wynn, John. S Sep-Oct 1775. M.

Wynn, Mary of St. Martin in Fields. S s chamber pot Feb T May 1736 *Patapsco*. M.

Wynn als Fielder, Priscilla. R Mar AT Apr 1681. M.

Wynne, Richard. S Oct T 14 yrs Dec 1724 *Rappahannock* to Va. M.

Winn, Rosamund. R 14 yrs Summer 1753. Y.

Winn, Sampson. T Apr 1769 *Tryal*. K.

Winn, Thomas. S s horse Lent R 14 yrs Summer 1751. Li.

Wynne, William. S Apr T May 1720 *Honor* LC Port York Jan 1721. L.

Wynn, William. S Feb T Mar 1731 *Patapsco* LC Annapolis Jun 1731. M.

Wyrrall, Ann of Worcester, spinster. R for America Mar 1701. Wo.

Y

Yalden, John. S Mar 1775. Ha.

Yallopp, Robert of Bungay. R for Barbados Feb 1664. Su.

Yarde, Yard. R for Barbados Jly 1675. L.

Yardley, Elizabeth. S Sep T Oct 1750 *Rachael*. M.

Yardley, John. S Feb T Apr 1770 *New Trial*. M.

Yardley, Mary. S s butter Sep T Oct 1750 *Rachael*. M.

Yardley, Nathaniel. S Summer 1752. Su.

Yardley, Richard. S s sheep Lent R 14 yrs Summer 1754. No.

Yardsey, John of Glovers Stone. R for Barbados Feb 1679. Ch.

Yardsley, Robert of Glovers Stone. R for Barbados Jly 1677. Ch.

Yarlett, Thomas. S for murder of bastard child Lent R 14 yrs Summer 1725. St.

Yarmouth, Edward of Rotherhithe. SQS Apr T Sep 1751 *Greyhound*. Sy.

Yarmouth, John (1732). *See* Crotch. L.

Yarner, Benjamin. S s gelding & R 14 yrs Lent TB to Va Aug 1768. Le.

Yarpe, John. R for Barbados Jly 1674. M.

Yarrall, Matthew. R for Barbados Sep 1669. M.

Yarrington, Dorothy of Hanley Child. R for America Jly 1678. Wo.

Yarrington, Jasper. S s hops at All Saints, Worcester, Lent 1743. Wo.

Yarum, Thomas. S s sheep Lent R 14 yrs Summer 1753. Nf.

Yarwood, John. S Jan T Feb 1724 *Anne*. L.

Yate, James of Walmsley. SQS Oct 1753. La.

Yate, John. R for Barbados Feb 1664. L.

Yeate, John. S s horse Lent R 14 yrs Summer TB Jly 1742. G.

Yates, Alice of St. Saviour, Southwark. R for Barbados or Jamaica Mar 1688. Sy.

Yates, Alice wife of James of Salford. SQS Aug 1755. La.

Yates als Mills als Clarke, Anne. R for Barbados or Jamaica Oct 1688. L.

Yates, Ann. R for Barbados or Jamaica May 1691 for burning Newgate. L.

Yates, Charles (1720). *See* Thompson. K.

Yeates, Charles. S Summer 1746. K.

Yates, Elizabeth. T May 1737 *Forward*. Sy.

Yeates, Elizabeth. S & T Jan 1756 *Greyhound*. M.

Yeates, George (1765). *See* Gates. M.

Yates, John. S Lent 1721. Sh.

Yates, John. S s shirts at Hanwell Lent 1726. O.

Yates, John. T Jun 1727 *Susanna*. E.

Yates, John. R 14 yrs & TB to Va Oct 1768. Wi.

Yates als Ates, Joseph. S s spoons at St. Michael Cornhill Jly T Oct 1768 *Justitia*. L.

Yates, Mary, aged 24, dark. LC from *Gilbert* Annapolis May 1721. X.

Yeates, Mary. S Sep 1740. L.

Yates, Mary (1743). *See* Holmes. M.

Yates, Ralph of Egham. R for America Jly 1700. Sy.

Yates, Richard. R May AT Jly 1697. M.

Yates, Richard. T May 1737 *Forward*. Sy.

Yeates, Robert of St. George, Hanover Square. S s timber Jly 1740 T Jan 1741 *Harpooner*. M.

Yates, Samewell. T Apr 1739 *Forward*. E.

Yates, Sarah. SQS Jun T Sep 1758 *Tryal* to Annapolis. M.

Yates, Susannah. S Feb T Apr 1766 *Ann*. M.

Yates, Thomas. S Feb T Apr 1734 *Patapsco*. L.

Yates, Willdy. T Sep 1730 *Smith*. Sy.

Yates, William. S Oct T Nov 1728 *Forward* but died on passage. L.

Yates, William. T May 1737 *Forward*. Sy.

Yates, William of Manchester, weaver. SQS Jan 1750. La.

Yeates, William. S Dec 1754. L.

Yawdell, Mabel (1683). *See* Blathwaite. Cu.

Yaxley, Stephen. S Lent 1758. Nf.

Yaxley, William. S s mare & R Lent 1765. Nf.

Yearby, John. S Dec 1743 T Feb 1744 *Neptune*. M.

Yearwood als Haywood, Joseph. S & T Mar 1760 *Friendship*. L.

Yeast, William of Stretford. SQS Feb 1755. La.

Yeates. *See* Yates.

Yeavsley, Thomas of Teignmouth. R for Barbados Feb 1683. De.

Yellox, Thomas. S Jan-Jun T Jun 1728 *Elizabeth* LC Potomack Aug 1729. L.

Yelverton, Matthew of Peterborough. R for America Aug 1685. No.

Yemm, John. S s sheep Lent R 14 yrs Summer 1766. G.

Yeo, Elizabeth. S Mar 1730. So.

Yeo, George of Orchard. R for Barbados Jly 1698. So.

Yeo, John of Orchard Portman. R for Barbados Jly 1698. So.

Yeo, John. S Oct T Dec 1724 *Rappahannock*. L.

Yeo, Samuel. S Sep T Oct 1719 *Susannah & Sarah* LC Md Apr 1720. L.

Yeo, William of Rotherhithe. S Lent T May 1719 *Margaret* LC Md May 1720; sold to Richard Hampton. Sy.

Yeoman, John. T Aug 1752 *Tryal*. Ht.

Yeoman, John of Cropton. SQS Guisborough s wheat Jly TB Sep 1756. Y.

Yeoman, Joseph. SQS New Malton s at Lastingham Jan TB May 1772. Y.

Yeoman als Newman, Richard. S Apr T 14 yrs May 1718 *Tryal* LC Charles Town Aug 1718. L.

Yeoman, Samuel. S & R 14 yrs Lent T May 1736 *Patapsco*. Bu.

Youman, Susanna. S Feb 1761. L.

Yeomans als Booth, Margaret. S Jly T 14 yrs Aug 1721 *Prince Royal* LC Va Nov 1721. L.

Yeomans, Mary. S May T Jly 1722 *Alexander*. L.

Yeomans, Samuel. R for America Jly 1708. Le.

Yeomans, Thomas. S s saddle at Witney Summer 1752. O.

Yetts, John. TB to Va from QS 1740. De.

Yollard, Robert of South Brent, husbandman. R for Barbados Jly 1667 & Feb 1668. De.

York, John. T Sep 1767 *Justitia*. Sy.

Yorke, Richard. S Lent R for Barbados May 1664. E.

York, Richard. S s silver spoon at Hungerford Lent 1753. Be.
York, Samuel. S Mar TB to Va Apr 1765. Wi.
York, Sarah. S May T Jly 1722 *Alexander* to Nevis or Jamaica. M.
Yorke, William. R May T Jun 1691. M.
York, William. TB to Va from QS 1733. De.
York, William. S Lent 1757 but then ordered to serve in fleet. Su.
Yorkshire Hannah (1740). *See* Stewart, Hannah. M.
Yorkshire, Thomas. SQS Jun T Jly 1772 *Tayloe*. M.
Youins, Rachael of St. James, Westminster, spinster. S s shirts & T Dec
   1740 *Vernon*. M.
Youlton, John. R 14 yrs Mar 1768. Co.
Youman. *See* Yeoman.
Young, Adam. S City s at Spurriergate Lent AT Summer 1767. Y.
Young, Andrew. AT Summer 1765. Nl.
Young, Ann. S Oct T Dec 1771 *Justitia*. L.
Young, Bartholomew. R 14 yrs Summer 1729. Nl.
Young, Catherine. S & T Oct 1732 *Caesar* to Va. M.
Young, Daniel. TB Sep 1737. Db.
Young, Deborah. SQS Sep T Dec 1770 *Justitia*. M.
Young, Edward. S Jan 1745. L.
Young, Elizabeth. T Apr 1743 *Justitia*. K.
Young, Elizabeth. S Jly T Nov 1759 *Phoenix*. M.
Young, Elizabeth. S Apr-Jun T Jly 1772 *Tayloe*. M.
Young, Elizabeth. S for perjury Dec 1773. L.
Young, Frederick. S Jan T Feb 1765 *Tryal*. L.
Young, George. SW & T Apr 1770 *New Trial*. M.
Young, Henry. SQS Feb T Apr 1772 *Thornton*. M.
Young, Honor. S Summer 1759. Li.
Young, Hugh John. S & T Nov 1762 *Prince Williams*. L.
Young, James of Bristol. R for Barbados Feb 1701. G
Young, James. S Summer 1749. Sy.
Young, James. S Feb-Apr T for life May 1755 *Rose*. M.
Young, James. S Sep T Dec 1767 *Neptune*. L.
Young, James. SQS & T Dec 1769 *Justitia*. Ht.
Young, Jane. S Lent R 14 yrs Summer 1761. Sh.
Young, Jane wife of John. SQS Jan T Apr 1762 *Dolphin*. M.
Young, John of Farningham. R for Barbados Aug 1662. K.
Young, John. S Jan T Feb 1719 *Worcester* LC Annapolis Jun 1719. L.
Young, John. T Sep 1730 *Smith*. Sy.
Young, John. S Jly TB to Va Oct 1742. Wi.
Young, John. SQS at Peterborough Summer 1744. No.
Young, John (1749). *See* Low. L.
Young, John. S Apr TB to Va Apr 1750. Wi.
Young, John. S & T for life Sep 1751 *Greyhound*. M.
Young, John (1753). *See* White. Nl.
Young, John. S Summer 1759. Li.
Young, John. S s at Bransford Lent 1762. Wo.
Young, John (1764). *See* Lee. Sy.
Young als Smith, John. R Jan-Feb T 14 yrs Apr 1772 *Thornton*. M.
Young, John. S s sheep & R 14 yrs Summer 1775. Wo.

Young, John Eldridge of Hamsey. S Lent 1774. Sx.
Young, Margaret (1731). *See* Blackbourne. Sy.
Young, Martha. S Oct T Dec 1769 *Justitia*. M.
Younge, Mary. T Oct 1720 *Gilbert*. E.
Young, Mary. T 1721 *Gilbert* but died on passage. K.
Young, Mary. S Oct 1756. M.
Young, Matthew. S City s horse Summer 1736 R 14 yrs Summer 1737 Y.
Young, Matthew. AT Summer 1757. Y.
Young, Nathaniel. S May T Jun 1726 *Loyal Margaret* LC Md Oct 1726. M.
Young, Richard. Rebel T 1685.
Young, Richard. S & T Dec 1731 *Forward*. L.
Young, Robert. S Apr 1723. So.
Young, Robert. S Mar 1743. Do.
Young, Robert. R for life Mar 1767. Ha.
Young, Sarah. S s at Bucklebury Summer 1729. Be.
Young, Stephen. T Sep 1764 *Justitia*. K.
Young, Susanna. S Oct T Nov 1728 *Forward* LC Rappahannock Jun 1729. M.
Young, Thomas. S Feb T Mar 1731 *Patapsco* LC Annapolis Jun 1731. M.
Young, Thomas. S Mar 1744. Do.
Young, Thomas. AT City Summer 1761. Y.
Young, Thomas. SQS Marlborough & TB to Va Oct 1764. Wi.
Young, Thomas. S Feb T May 1767 *Thornton*. M.
Young, Timothy. S & T Dec 1731 *Forward*. L.
Young, William. S s gelding Summer 1725 R 14 yrs Lent 1727. Ca.
Younger, James. R 14 yrs Dec 1773. M.
Younger, Margaret. S s shirt at Cirencester Lent 1760. G.
Younger, Sarah. SQS May T Jly 1773 *Tayloe* to Va. M.
Younger, Thomas. S Apr-Jun T Jly 1772 *Tayloe*. M.
Younghusband, Mary. S Summer 1745. Cu.
Youngman als Westgate, Edmund. S s gelding Summer 1743 R 14 yrs Lent 1744. Nf.
Youngs, John. S Summer 1757 R 14 yrs Lent 1758. Nf.
Youngs, Richard. S s mare Summer 1750 R 14 yrs Lent 1751. Nf.
Youre. *See* Ewer.
Yowell, John. S Jan 1746. M.
Yure. *See* Ewer.

Z

Zacherby, Ann. LC from *Loyal Margaret* Annapolis Oct 1726. X.
Zane, Simon. S Mar 1758. So.
Zeanell, Phillip. S Oct T Dec 1724 *Rappahannock*. L.
Zell, Thomas. S Jan 1746. M.
Zouch, Elizabeth (1681). *See* Sparke. L.
Zouch, Miles. R for Barbados Aug 1670. M.
Zyne, William of Nettlecombe. R for Barbados Feb 1669. So.

PARDONS ON CONDITION OF TRANSPORTATION
(Patent Rolls: PRO series C66)

Year				Circuits			
	Newgate	Home	Western	Oxford	Norfolk	Northern & Chester	Midland
1655		2912/3					
1656	2912/7	2912/2					
1657							
1658							
1659							
1660							
1661	2986/1						
1662	3011/5	3011/44					
1663	3048/15	3049/16 3048/12		3048/8,16	3048/10		
1664	3049/14 3066/12,13 3071/3	3066/17	3066/21	3049/21 3066/23	3071/13,15 3066/10		
1665	3066/5 3074/10,99	3074/95	3074/94,100		3066/8	3066/6	
1666			3086/17	3086/3,16		3086/2	
1667	3088/4		3091/5				
1668	3101/6,19 3098/11 3102/3	3101/6,20,22	3098/2 3101/18	3101/11 3102/2			
1669	3107/41,47	3107/41,47	3107/45,48				
1670	(LRO copy)						
1671	3128/21	3128/17	3128/13 3137/12,25	3128/42	3128/9	3128/2,10	3128/39
1672	3137/2,17		3137/12,25		3137/6	3137/5	
1673	3145/2 3148/17		3145/6 3148/20	3148/5,19		3148/18	3148/4
1674	3167/1	3167/2					3167/3
1675	3170/38 3173/3	3173/23	3166/1	3174/17	3174/16	3173/22	
1676	(LRO copy)	3187/24	3178/15			3186/11	
1677	3188/6 3200/15	3200/17	3200/21	3200/24		3200/22,23	3200/25
1678	3204/7	3204/10	3206/20	3204/9		3204/5	3204/13
1679	3205/31 3208/8 3214/25	3214/13	3210/2 3214/10	3214/17	3210/3	3210/6 3214/7	3214/16
1680	(LRO copy)	3216/32 3218/16			3216/33		
1681	3222/17 3225/7		3223/4	3219/11 3223/1	3219/7		3219/6
1682	3229/4	3228/2 3235/36	3224/12	3229/1 3230/11	3228/14	3228/15 3229/2	3228/1,10
1683	3235/30 3236/12		3235/37 3239/27		3239/26	3239/25,30	3239/24
1684	3245/16	3245/13,18	3245/11,19	3245/14	3245/12	3245/15	3245/17
1685	3275/2 3276/12					3276/6	3276/1

Year		Newgate	Home	Western	Oxford	Norfolk	Northern & Chester	Midland
Year					*Circuits*			
1686		3282/10 3288/20	3282/7	3282/6 3288/21 3290/11	3282/14 3287/7	3282/5	3288/25	3288/28
1687		3291/11 3297/16	3296/1	3296/1	3291/14 3296/2	3291/9	3297/11	3297/23
1688		3301/1 3309/1	3302/6 3305/8	3302/9 3303/11 3305/14	3302/8 3305/11	3302/10 3303/12	3305/9	3305/13
1689		3332/5						
1690		3335/9 3338/4,12	3337/16	3334/21	3339/3		3334/15 3337/1	3340/6
1691		3345/2		3340/7	3345/5	3345/6	3345/3	
1692		3348/11	3353/12	3349/12	3353/16		3353/13	3349/15
1693		3356/11 3360/15		3365/7	3359/11 3365/5	3359/5 3365/6		3365/8
1694		3375/10,12	3369/20	3369/21	3375/2		3369/19 3371/12	3371/10
1695		3381/14		3380/9 3378/13		3380/13		
1696		3381/2	3380/15 3384/7		3384/6			
1697		3390/13		3393/19	3393/16	3391/3 3393/13	3393/20	3393/14
1698		3398/12	3403/11	3403/15	3403/8 3405/3	3403/9	3405/7	
1699		3411/16	3413/16	3412/16 3413/17	3413/13		3412/7 3413/8,14	
1700		3416/5	3416/7	3416/13 3417/27	3412/14	3416/8	3416/4	3412/13 3417/25
1701		3420/3		3419/29	3420/15		3419/14	
1702		3429/21	3429/33	3426/13	3429/31	3426/9		3426/10
1703				3440/9	3438/6	3440/2		
1704		3445/5	3444/17	3444/12				3444/10
1705		3452/4	3452/D8				3452/D7	
1706		3454/10						3456/8
1707			3461/17		3451/16			3460/5
1708				3465/7	3465/5			3465/6
1709		3468/4				3472/1		3469/7 3472/5
1710		3474/D2	3475/3	3472/2	3473/19		3478/2	
1711				3484/20	3482/8			3482/7
1712		3488/1	3488/2					
1713		3493/3			3486/9	3490/15		3486/10
1714				3494/9	3494/6 3497/11	3497/6		3497/14
1715		3512/27	3507/12	3508/21				
1716		3519/10		3516/4	3513/4			3510/5
1717				3520/4				

CONVICT SHIPS TO THE AMERICAN COLONIES 1716-1775

Sailing Date	Name of Ship	Master	Destination	Reference
Dec 1716	Lewis	Roger Laming	Jamaica	T53/25/224
Jan 1717	Queen Elizabeth		Jamaica	T53/25/225
May 1718	*Unknown*		Barbados & Antigua	
May 1718	Tryal		S. Carolina	
Aug 1718	Eagle	Robt. Staples	S. Carolina	T53/27/36
Feb 1719	Worcester	Edwin Tomkins	Maryland	T53/27/220
May 1719	Margaret	Wm. Greenwood	Maryland	T53/27/266
Oct 1719	Susannah & Sarah	Peter Wills	Maryland	T53/27/415
May 1720	Honor	Richd. Langley	Virginia	T53/28/157
Oct 1720	Gilbert	Darby Lux	Maryland	T53/28/331
Aug 1721	Prince Royal	Thos. Boyd	Virginia	T53/29/146
Aug 1721	Owners Goodwill	John Lux	Maryland	T53/29/147
Oct 1721	William & John	John Thompson	Maryland	T53/29/453
Jan 1722	Gilbert	Darby Lux	Maryland	T53/29/451
Feb 1722	Christabella	Amb. Griffin	Jamaica	
Jly 1722	Alexander	John Graham	Nevis	T53/29/531
Oct 1722	Forward	Dan. Russell	Maryland	T53/30/118
Feb 1723	Jonathan	Darby Lux	Maryland	T53/30/341
May 1723	Victory	Wm. Wharton	W. Indies	T53/30/339
Jly 1723	Alexander	John King	Maryland	T53/30/340
Oct 1723	Forward	Dan. Russell	Virginia	T53/30/453
Feb 1724	Anne	Thos. Wrangham	Carolina	T53/31/77
Jly 1724	Robert	John Vickers	Maryland	T53/31/255
Oct 1724	Forward	Dan. Russell	Maryland	T53/31/376
Dec 1724	Rappahannock Mcht.	John Jones	Virginia	T53/31/376
Apr 1725	Sukey	John Ellis	Maryland	T53/32/93
Sep 1725	Forward	Dan. Russell	Maryland	T53/32/219
Nov 1725	Rappahannock Mcht.	Chas. Whale	Virginia	T53/32/220
Feb 1726	Supply	John Rendell	Maryland	T53/32/385
Jun 1726	Loyal Margaret	John Wheaton	Maryland	T53/32/386
Oct 1726	Forward	Dan. Russell	Virginia	T53/33/294
Mar 1727	Rappahannock Mcht.	Chas. Whale	Maryland	T53/33/296
Jly 1727	Susanna	John Vickers	Virginia	T53/33/364
Sep 1727	Forward	Wm. Loney	Virginia	
Dec 1727	*Unknown*	Wm. Williams	*Unknown*	
May 1728	*Unknown*	Sam. Waller	New York	
Jun 1728	Elizabeth	Wm. Whithorne	Virginia	T53/34/154
Nov 1728	Forward	Wm. Loney	Virginia	T53/34/303
Mar 1729	Patapsco Merchant	Darby Lux	Maryland	T53/34/418
Nov 1729	Forward	Wm. Loney	Virginia	T53/35/43
Mar 1730	Patapsco Merchant	Darby Lux	Maryland	T53/35/174
Sep 1730	Smith	Wm. Loney	Virginia	T53/35/379
Nov 1730	Forward	Geo. Buckeridge	Virginia	T53/35/380
Mar 1731	Patapsco Merchant	Darby Lux	Maryland	T53/35/496
Apr 1731	Bennett	James Reed	Virginia	T53/35/498
Oct 1731	Smith	Wm. Loney	Virginia	T53/36/138
Dec 1731	Forward	Geo. Buckeridge	Virginia	T53/36/212

Sailing Date	Name of Ship	Master	Destination	Reference
Apr 1732	Patapsco Merchant	Darby Lux	Maryland	T53/36/306
Oct 1732	Caesar	Wm. Loney	Virginia	T53/36/424
Feb 1733	Smith	Geo. Buckeridge	Maryland or Va.	T53/37/10
Apr 1733	Patapsco Merchant	Darby Lux	Maryland	T53/37/11
Jan 1734	Caesar	Wm. Loney	Virginia	T53/37/212
Apr 1734	Patapsco Merchant	Darby Lux	Maryland	T53/37/304
Dec 1734	Caesar	Wm. Loney	Virginia	T53/37/446
Apr 1735	Patapsco Merchant	Darby Lux	Maryland	T53/38/80
Dec 1735	John	John Griffin	Maryland	T53/38/255
Feb 1736	Dorsetshire	Wm. Loney	Virginia	T53/38/256
May 1736	Patapsco Merchant	Francis Lux	Maryland	T53/38/337
Dec 1736	Dorsetshire	Wm. Loney	Virginia	T53/38/456
May 1737	Forward	John Magier	Virginia	T53/39/123
Sep 1737	Pretty Patsy	Francis Lux	Maryland	T53/39/121
Jan 1738	Dorsetshire	John Whiting	Virginia	T53/39/182
Jun 1738	Forward	John Magier	Virginia or Md.	T53/39/248
Oct 1738	Genoa	Darby Lux	Maryland	T53/39/409
Jan 1739	Dorsetshire	John Whiting	Virginia	T53/39/408
Apr 1739	Forward	Ben. Richardson	Virginia	T53/39/448
Jly 1739	*Unknown*	Adam Muir of Md	Maryland	Middlesex Bond
Oct 1739	Duke of Cumberland	Wm. Harding	Virginia	T53/40/45
Feb 1740	York	Ant. Bacon	Maryland	T53/40/170
Jun 1740	Essex	Amb. Cock	Maryland or Va.	T53/40/204
Jan 1741	Vernon	Henry Lee	Maryland	T53/40/289
Jan 1741	Harpooner	John Wilson	Virginia	T53/40/290
Apr 1741	Speedwell	Wm. Camplin	Maryland	T53/40/337
Apr 1741	Mediterranean	Geo. Harriot	Maryland	T53/40/338
May 1741	Catherine & Eliz.	Wm. Chapman	Maryland	T53/40/338
Aug 1741	Sally	Wm. Napier	Maryland	T53/40/415
Oct 1741	Sea Horse	John Rendell	Virginia	T53/40/414
Feb 1742	Industry	Chas. Barnard	Maryland	T53/40/484
Apr 1742	Bond	John Gardiner	Maryland	T53/40/485
Jun 1742	Bladon	Sam. Laurence	Maryland	T53/41/129
Sep 1742	Forward	John Sargent	America	T53/41/130
Apr 1743	Justitia	Barnet Bond	America	T53/41/227
Apr 1743	Bond	Matt. Johnson	America	T53/41/326
May 1743	Indian Queen	Edw. Maxwell	Maryland	T53/41/326
Nov 1743	George William	Jack Campbell	America	T53/41/327
Feb 1744	Neptune	James Knight	Maryland	T53/41/419
May 1744	Justitia	Jack Campbell	America	T53/41/462
Oct 1744	Savannah	James Dobbins	America	T53/42/64
May 1745	?Tryal	John Johnstoun	America	Middlesex Bond
Jly 1745	Italian Merchant	Alexander Reid	America	T53/42/220
Jan 1746	Plain Dealer	James Dobbins	America	T53/42/220
Apr 1746	Laura	William Gracie	America	T53/42/220
Sep 1746	Mary	John Johnstoun	America	T53/42/335
Jan 1747	George William	James Dobbins	America	T53/42/335
Jly 1747	Laura	William Gracie	America	T53/42/427
Jan 1748	St. George	James Dobbins	America	T53/42/519
Jan 1748	Laura	William Gracie	America	T1/330/55
Jun 1748	Lichfield	John Johnstoun	America	T53/43/101
Jly 1748	*Unknown*	John Ramsey	America	Middlesex Bond
Jan 1749	Laura	William Gracie	America	T53/43/190
May 1749	Lichfield	John Johnstoun	America	T53/43/273
Aug 1749	Thames	James Dobbins	America	T53/43/320
Nov 1749	Mary	Leonard Gerrard	America	T53/43/320

Sailing Date	Name of Ship	Master	Destination	Reference
Apr 1750	Tryal	John Johnstoun	America	T1/340/20
May 1750	Lichfield	William Gracie	America	T1/340/33
Oct 1750	Rachael	John Armstrong	America	T1/342/35
Jan 1751	Thames	James Dobbins	America	T53/44/63
May 1751	Tryal	John Johnstoun	America	T1/346/29
Sep 1751	Greyhound	William Gracie	America	T1/349/1
Feb 1752	Thames	James Dobbins	America	T53/44/243
May 1752	Lichfield	Leonard Gerrard	America	T1/348/8
Aug 1752	Tryal	John Johnstoun	America	T53/44/379
Dec 1752	Greyhound	William Gracie	America	T1/348/26
Apr 1753	Thames	James Dobbins	America	T1/351/17
Jly 1753	Tryal	John Johnstoun	America	T1/353/29
Dec 1753	Whiteing	Matt. Johnson	America	T1/358/1
Mar 1754	Thames	James Dobbins	America	T53/45/116
Jun 1754	Tryal	Isaac Johns	America	T53/45/116
Oct 1754	Ruby	Edward Ogle	America	T53/45/117
Feb 1755	Greyhound	Alex. Stewart	America	T53/45/117
May 1755	Rose	Thomas Slade	America	T1/361/39
Sep 1755	Tryal	Wm. McGachin	America	T1/361/67
Jan 1756	Greyhound	Alex. Stewart	America	T1/367/2
Jun 1756	Lyon	James Dyer	America	T1/365/98
Oct 1756	Barnard	Ph. Weatherall	America	T53/45/575
Mar 1757	Tryal	Alex. Scott	America	T53/46/110
Sep 1757	Thetis	James Edmonds	America	T1/378/64
Mar 1758	Dragon	Wm. McGachin	America	T1/387/17
Sep 1758	Tryal	Geo. Freebairn	America	T1/387/29
Dec 1758	The Brothers	Allan Boyd	America	T1/390/156
Feb 1759	?Dragon	Wm. McGachin	America	Middlesex Bond
Apr 1759	Thetis	Matt. Craymer	America	T1/391
Dec 1759	Phoenix	Dougal McDougal	America	T1/397/15
Mar 1760	Friendship	Dougal McDougal	America	T1/401
Apr 1760	Thetis	Matt. Craymer	America	T1/401
Oct 1760	Phoenix	Wm. McGachin	America	T53/47/56
Mar 1761	Neptune	Ben. Dawson	America	T53/47/56
Apr 1761	Dolphin	Dougal McDougal	America	T53/47/56
Oct 1761	Maryland	Alex. Ramsay	America	T53/47/57
Apr 1762	Dolphin	Matt. Craymer	Maryland	T1/418
Apr 1762	Neptune	Ben. Dawson	America	T1/418
Nov 1762	Prince William	Dougal McDougal	America	T1/418
Mar 1763	Neptune	Colin Somervell	America	T1/423
May 1763	Dolphin	Matt. Craymer	America	T53/48/57
Aug 1763	Beverly	Robt. Allan	America	T53/49/136
Dec 1763	Neptune	Colin Somervell	America	T1/423
Mar 1764	Tryal	Wm. McGachin	America	T1/429
Jun 1764	Dolphin	Dougal McDougal	America	T1/429
Sep 1764	Justitia	Colin Somervell	America	T1/429
Jan 1765	Tryal	John Errington	America	T1/437
Apr 1765	Ann	Chris. Reed	America	T1/437
Sep 1765	Justitia	Colin Somervell	America	T1/437
Jan 1766	Tryal	John Errington	America	T1/449
Apr 1766	Ann	Chris. Reed	America	T1/449

Sailing Date	Name of Ship	Master	Destination	Reference
Oct 1766	Justitia	Colin Somervell	America	T1/450
Jan 1767	Tryal	John Somervell	America	T53/50/93
May 1767	Thornton	Chris. Reed	America	T1/460/4
Sep 1767	Justitia	Colin Somervell	America	T1/456
Dec 1767	*Unknown*	John Gill	America	
Jan 1768	Neptune	James Arbuckle	America	T1/465
Apr 1768	Thornton	Chris. Reed	America	T1/465
Jun 1768	Tryal	Dougal McDougal	America	T1/465
Oct 1768	Justitia	Colin Somervell	America	T1/465
Feb 1769	Thornton	Chris. Reed	America	T1/470
May 1769	Tryal	Dougal McDougal	America	T53/51/132
Sep 1769	Douglas	Wm. Beckenridge	America	T1/470
Feb 1770	Justitia	Colin Somervell	America	T1/478
Apr 1770	New Trial	Dougal McDougal	Maryland	T1/478
Jly 1770	Scarsdale	Chris. Reed	America	T1/478
Dec 1770	Justitia	Colin Somervell	America	T1/483
May 1771	Thornton	Dougal McDougal	America	T1/483
Jly 1771	Scarsdale	Chris. Reed	America	T1/483
Jan 1772	Justitia	Neil Gillis	America	T1/483
Apr 1772	Thornton	John Kidd	America	T1/490
Jly 1772	Orange Bay	Neil Somerville	America	T1/490
Jly 1772	Tayloe	Dougal McDougal	America	T1/490
Jan 1773	*Unknown*	Finlay Gray	America	Middlesex Bond
Mar 1773	?Thornton	John Kidd	America	Middlesex Bond
May 1773	Hanover Planter	Wm. McColloch	America	Middlesex Bond
Jly 1773	?Tayloe	John Ogilvy	Virginia	Middlesex Bond
Jan 1774	*Unknown*	Finlay Gray	America	Middlesex Bond
Apr 1774	?Thornton	John Kidd	America	Middlesex Bond
Jly 1774	?Green Garland	John Ogilvy	America	Middlesex Bond
Jan 1775	*Unknown*	John Kidd	America	Middlesex Bond
Apr 1775	Thornton	Finlay Gray	America	Middlesex Bond
Jly 1775	Green Garland	John Ogilvy	America	Middlesex Bond
Oct 1775	*Unknown*	John Kidd	America	Middlesex Bond

APPENDIX III

LIST OF PRINCIPAL ASSIZE RECORDS USED

Home Circuit

    Gaol Delivery Rolls: ASSI 35.

Western Circuit

    Gaol Books: ASSI 23.
    Order Books: ASSI 24.
    Crown Minute Books: ASSI 21.

Oxford Circuit

    Gaol Delivery Rolls: ASSI 5.
    Crown Minute Books: ASSI 2.

Norfolk Circuit

    Gaol Delivery Rolls: ASSI 16.
    Gaol Books: ASSI 33/1, 34/17, 33/2-5.
    (also one volume now held by Gray's Inn Library as MS45).
    Indictment Rolls: ASSI 35.

Northern Circuit

    Crown Minute Books: ASSI 41.
    Gaol Books: ASSI 42.
    Indictment Rolls: ASSI 44.

Midland Circuit

The documents of this circuit prior to 1800 were destroyed and the names of those sentenced to transportation after 1718 have therefore been retrieved from alternative sources, principally:

    Sheriffs' Cravings: E 370.
    Domestic Papers: SP 35,36
    Criminal Papers: SP 44.

Palatinates

    Chester and Flint
        Rough Minute Book: CHES 35/24.
        Crown Minute Books: CHES 21/7.
        Session Rolls: CHES 24.

    Durham
        Crown Minute Books: DUR 15/1, 16/1.
        Assize Rolls: DUR 17.
        Assize Proceedings: DUR 19/3.

    Lancaster
        Minute Books and Pardons: PL 28/1-3.
        Assize Rolls: PL 25.
        Indictments: PL 26.

APPENDIX IV

SUMMARY BY COUNTY OF RECORDS USED

County	Circuit	Quarter Sessions Records Included?	Comments on Quarter Sessions Records
Bedfordshire	Norfolk	Yes	
Berkshire	Oxford	No	No separate records of transportation available
Buckinghamshire	Norfolk	Yes	
Cambridgeshire	Norfolk	Yes	
Cheshire	Chester	No	Quarter Sessions Order Books published on microfilm
Cornwall	Western	No	No separate records of transportation available
Cumberland	Northern	Yes	Abstracts not necessarily complete
Derbyshire	Midland	Yes	
Devonshire	Western	Yes	
Dorset	Western	Yes	
Durham	(Palatinate)	Yes	
Essex	Home	Yes	
Flint	(Palatinate)	No	
Gloucestershire	Oxford	Yes	
Hampshire	Western	Yes	
Herefordshire	Oxford	No	No separate records of transportation available
Hertfordshire	Home	Yes	
Huntingdonshire	Norfolk	No	
Kent	Home	Yes	
Lancashire	(Palatinate)	Yes	
Leicestershire	Midland	Yes	
Lincolnshire	Midland	No	No separate records of transportation available
London	(Old Bailey)	Yes	
Middlesex	(Old Bailey)	Yes	
Monmouthshire	Oxford	No	
Norfolk	Norfolk	Yes	
Northamptonshire	Midland	Yes	
Northumberland	Northern	Yes	
Nottinghamshire	Midland	Yes	
Oxfordshire	Oxford	No	No separate records of transportation available
Rutland	Midland	No	
Shropshire	Oxford	No	No references to transportation found in indexes
Somerset	Western	Yes	
Staffordshire	Oxford	No	No separate records of transportation available
Suffolk	Norfolk	No	No separate records of transportation available
Surrey	Home	Yes	
Sussex	Home	Yes	
Warwickshire	Midland	No	No references to transportation found in indexes
Westmorland	Northern	No	
Wiltshire	Western	Yes	
Worcestershire	Oxford	Yes	Abstracts not necessarily complete
Yorkshire	Northern	Yes	North Riding only

CPSIA information can be obtained at www.ICGtesting.com

264714BV00003B/69/P

9 780806 312217